Explains the different level
and the relationship among them.

OS Data Processing

with Review of OS/VS

HARRY CARROLL

Advisory Planner
IBM Systems Development Division
Poughkeepsie, New York

OS Data

Processing

WITH REVIEW OF OS/VS

A WILEY-INTERSCIENCE PUBLICATION

JOHN WILEY & SONS
NEW YORK · LONDON · SYDNEY · TORONTO

Library of Congress Cataloging in Publication Data:

Carroll, Harry, 1920–
    OS data processing with review of OS/VS.

    "A Wiley-Interscience publication."
    1. IBM 370 (Computer) I. Title.

QA76.8.I123C37   001.6'4'044   74-2047
ISBN 0-471-13600-X

Printed in the United States of America

10 9 8 7 6 5 4 3 2 1

To Emily

PREFACE

A modern data processing system exists on several levels. To learn data processing, we must know the nature of these levels and the relationships among them. Convinced that material for learning these relationships is not generally available, I decided to write this book.

My approach was to use the IBM System/360 to run an elementary program. Part of the computer system's response to a user's request (and to his program) is to provide documentation, and this gives us material which illustrates the relations among the system's levels. The key to the success of this method is the reader's understanding of what the applied source program is trying to do. This knowledge can be used to explain different systems, or to explain diverse functions within the same system.

The crucial understanding of the nature of individual levels can be reached by an explanation of their historical development into System/370 form.

In Chapter 1, OS Data Processing introduces the various levels. Knowing the outcome, we can cast earlier developments into the mold of the modern operating system. By doing so we perceive not just the solution but also the underlying problem; we learn not just System/370 but also data processing.

System/370 hardware and OS/360 software are discussed in Chapters 2 and 3, respectively. Chapters 4 and 5 introduce the structure of OS/360 and OS/VS. Chapters 6 through 9 deal in detail with the interaction among operating-system components.

Although learning an operating system through a sample program seems reasonable, many would wonder why one learns an operating system at all, since the higher level languages such as COBOL, FORTRAN and PL/I have effectively hidden much of the detail of the machine system.

To answer this, consider the following: on the same system two different COBOL programs give identical answers to the same problem. Program 1 uses twice as much system time as program 2. Programmer 2 knows the system (as distinct from the COBOL language) better than programmer 1.

Consider also the reverse: program 1 runs at two-thirds the speed of program 2 because it reads back and checks the information it writes to an output device. The slower program is more reliable. Knowing where to put the checking requires systems knowledge. The very knowledge that read after write exists implies familiarity with the operating system.

Moreover, intellectual curiosity beckons the user to explore beyond higher level languages. Having one's knowledge of data processing bounded by the procedure division of COBOL after, say, 10 years of coding, benefits neither the employee nor the concern.

Finally, there are those with an interest other than the direct use of data processing; those who plan it, develop it, market it, and order it—and others who will someday do so. Knowledge of what an operating system is and does is increasingly important to these people.

This tutorial volume complements IBM Systems Reference Library handbooks, which are primarily reference material. There is a great deal of detail in System/370, and some exposure to it is unavoidable. However, the sample program minimizes it. Knowing this program's intent, the user can quickly orient himself among active system components and understand the interactions that occur.

HARRY CARROLL

Poughkeepsie, New York
April 1974

CONTENTS

Appendix

ABBREVIATIONS

CCHHR   Cylinder cylinder head head record—a 5 byte address on a direct access storage device that is used in conjunction with a *Seek* channel command

CCW   Channel command word

CPU   Central processing unit

DAT   Dynamic address translation—circuitry in the cpu associated with relocation

DASD   Direct access storage device

DCB   Data control block—a control block that describes the characteristics of a data set and resides within the space occupied by a user's program

DEB   Data extent block—a control block that describes to OS the extents on direct access storage occupied by a user's data set

ECB   Event control block—a control block within space occupied by a user program where a Wait bit is set and posted

FIFO   First in first out—a means of enqueueing elements in a chain

GPR   General purpose registers—16 fixed point registers in the central processing unit

IOS   Input-output supervisor—the OS component that issues SIO in response to SVC O, EXCP and receives control when an input-output request completes

JCL   Job control language—the language in which the operating system is instructed

JES   Job entry system—a subsystem of OS/VS release 2 which accepts and releases work from the operating system

LIFO   Last in first out—a means of enqueueing elements of a chain

LR   Logical record—the object of a COBOL READ or WRITE

QEL   Queue element—the unit in a line awaiting the service of some system resource

QCB   Queue control block—the unit that represents a system resource to OS

RB   Request block—a control block that represents a load module to task management routines

TCB   Task control block—the user's job step request transformed into data operated on by task management routines—a QEL.

VTOC   Volume table of contents—a directory containing the names of the data sets of a volume

OS Data Processing

with Review of OS/VS

chapter 1

HISTORY OF DATA PROCESSING

1.1 INTRODUCTION

A data processing system is a set of resources responding to user job requests. A job request has steps; each job step request always specifies a program and the data and resources that program needs. A user creates a source program which may, in turn, specify either (1) a problem program, which processes data for a scientist or accountant, or (2) a system program, which has to do with the system itself, in support of all specified programs. In contrast, a resource request is input data to the system, dealing directly with its resources. In early systems handwritten instructions directed a machine operator to run a certain problem program on a certain machine at a certain time.

The system responds to a request with the activity of its resources directed by problem or system programs. The notion of a system as a set of resources evolved into the design philosophy of OS/360 and OS/VS. The evolution is enlightening.

The short history of mechanized data processing symbolizes the rate of technological advance in our society. Data processing time divides into manual, electric, and electronic ages.

The manual age is the prehistorical period. It left one major trace: manual procedures represent the ideal way of specifying a problem program to a system (e.g., C=A+B).

History begins with the commercial procedures of the electric age, where some of today's methods are visible. Most of today's technology awaited the electric age.

Certain patterns of data processing use have persisted across the three ages. The user concerned with results, not systems, was present at the beginning and is with us yet.

A second user, one directly requesting data processing services for the end user, is our primary concern. From here on the term "user" designates this prototype individual.* The user's functions have been in a continual state of flux. It is said of him, "His job didn't even exist 15 years ago." In the electric age the user wired plug boards called control panels. Today he is called programmer.

Finally, the individual most concerned with the operation of the physical system, the machine room operator, has remained. In the electric age the operator was

---

* Where it becomes necessary to distinguish between the two classes of users, the terms "end user" and "user requester" will be used.

part of the system. By combining functions, electronic technology eliminated many manual operations.

End use productivity justifies a data processing system. Its dimensions are of interest to us now as we survey the ages of data processing. They are performance, function, usability, and reliability and serviceability.

1.2 ELECTRIC AGE

Data processing history begins with the installation of electrical power around the turn of the century.

Using manual methods, the 1880 census took 7 years to complete; the published information was obsolete. For large-scale record keeping manual systems performed inadequately, lacked function, and were cumbersome to use.

Applying electricity to data processing tasks, Dr. Herman Hollerith of the Bureau of the Census invented the punched-card system and underwrote the electric age. Crucial was his realization that manual systems reused data repeatedly.

Punched-Card Systems

A mechanized system reuses data that has once entered the system; the importance thereof is readily demonstrated. Consider a parts wholesaler billing a customer. The billing department reuses item number for many different customers and name and address and customer number for the same customer many different times. Billing sends the invoice total it calculates, together with customer number, to the accounts receivable department for reuse in payment collection procedures. Only item quantity is used once.

In comparison, a manual system repeatedly reenters the same data into the system. Name and address, and customer number are entered by, say typing, for each invoice. Item number and quantity are typed anew for each line item thereof.

Reuse made punched-card systems efficient; the unit record, a group of related fields, made them practicable. Technology limited each machine of the day to one function. Each machine used the unit record as input and output for its function in a procedure that flowed through the system in steps. Say a billing procedure required six steps. Procedure analysts designed a unit record that contained all of the data for all of the steps. Data reuse was high; manual entry of new data was low; the system was efficient.

The unit record is a concept. Punched-card users viewed the unit record as data for the 80-column card or the 100-character print line. The separation of logical from physical records awaited electronic systems where the user works with simplified (logical) records, leaving physical detail to the system.

Punched-Card Machines

Sensing perforating machines with a card transport mechanism used the punched card as a data storage medium. The card material acted as an insulator. Each machine accepted or read, input data, processed the data into output information, and released the information from the system. Reading was performed as follows:

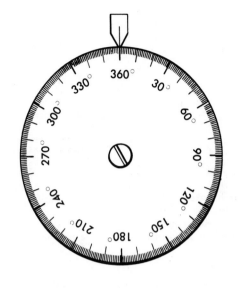

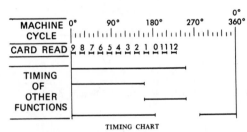

TIMING CHART

Figure 1.1 Representation of clock—punched-card .machine. From *Functional Wiring Principles,* IBM Reference Manual A-24-1007. (Top) Index timing disk—one revolution per machine cycle, shown in degrees.

A brush and a metallic roller formed an electrical circuit associated with an electromechanical clock synchronized with the position of a card. As they moved past read stations, card holes were sensed (Figs. 1.1 and 1.2).

Some machines punched their output using a dye-stripper to perforate the card at the proper position. An accounts receivable card was punched from a billing card, or a new billing card was reproduced from an old billing card. Other machines printed their output. Print wheels or movable type bars were selected and positioned from the punched holes.

In processing, data in a card, say item quantity and item price, were multiplied together, forming item amount. This item amount was then added to other item amounts, developing a grand total for the invoice. A punching calculator multiplied, divided, added and subtracted.

Machines processed card files as well as individual cards. A sorter arranged, say, a file of active item cards in customer number sequence. A collator, matching the customer number fields of (previously sorted) item and name and address cards, merged the two files for ultimate use by a printer. By wiring an empty plug board called a control panel, the user directed the collator's matching and merging.

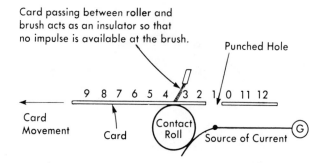

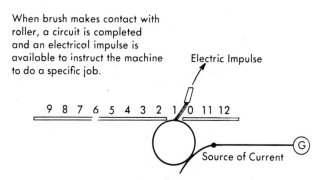

Figure 1.2 Brush reading numeral 1. From *Functional Wiring Principles,* IBM Reference Manual A-24-1007.

The wiring was the source program component of his request. In general, users wired one panel for each application for each machine.

Batch Processing

In larger installations, card file volumes ran in the tens of thousands and were of two types, master and transaction files, both sorted. In an inventory application, a transaction card was created for each part's shipment and each part's receipt. Transaction cards were matched-merged with item master cards and passed through a punching calculator, creating an updated master inventory card.

Efficiency of sorting, and collating, etc, dictated collecting transaction cards into a batch before processing them. Batch processing persists in today's systems. Master and transaction files persist, as well, despite technology that has gone far beyond the card. Files may reside on high-speed disks now, but in payroll the logic depicted in Figure 1.3 still applies; all transactions against George M. Eisele's Master records are processed before T. D. Forrest's transactions occupy system resources.

User Request

What follows describes a request submitted to a logical or idealized system. As shown in Figure 1.4, the system has three units: input–output (i–o) system, storage, and central processing unit (CPU). The i–o subsystem handles communication between storage and the outside environment. The cpu processes data from, and returns information to, storage.

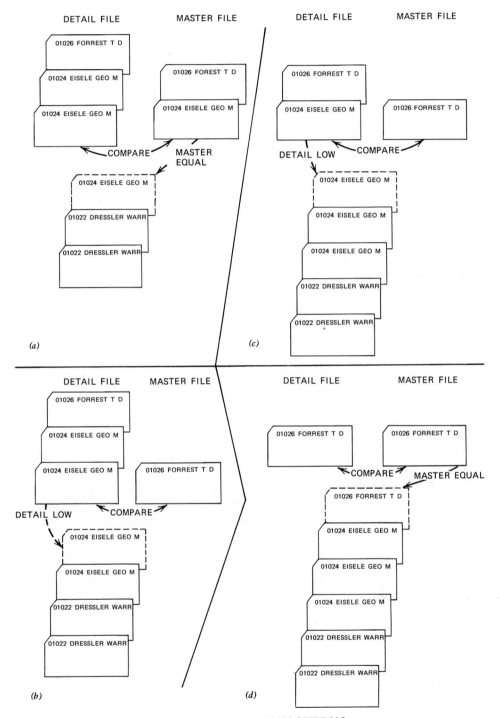

Figure 1.3 Merging master and detail decks on EMPLOYEE-NO.

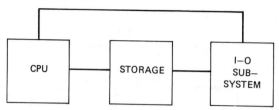

Figure 1.4 Data processing system.

Figure 1.5 depicts a COBOL source program request, SALARIES, directed to the idealized system. SALARIES contains English–like syntax.* The verbs READ, REWRITE, and DISPLAY direct data transmissions between the i–o unit and storage. The verbs IF, COMPUTE, and GO TO, direct CPU processing. The nouns READ-WEEKLY, READ-YTD, LIMIT-TEST, and LIMIT-CALC label the statements of the program. The program is thought of as, normally, executing statements in sequence (line 49 and 50). The labels enable the user to change the sequence by branching (see line 51).

The source program directs the system to perform the common Social Security calculation of a weekly earnings statement. Starting at line 44, a unit record from each of two files, EMPLOYEE-WEEKLY (detail) and EMPLOYEE-YTD (Master), is READ.

The employee number fields of the two records are compared (EMPLOYEE-NO-WEEKLY and EMPLOYEE-NO-YTD). If these fields are not identical, a new EMPLOYEE-YTD record is READ. If they are identical, SOCIAL-SEC-YTD is computed, and this field of EMPLOYEE-YTD is updated. Lines 60 through 62 specify a limit calculation for that pay period when the employee's FICA contribution has almost reached the legal maximum of 4.8% of his gross salary. This calculation is of the form $A_2 = A_1 + (B - A_1) * C$.

We use SALARIES to explain the intent of a sample application. In electric age systems, a series of machine steps would have been necessary had these functions actually been carried out. For example, the IF statement, lines 47 and 48 of Figure 1.5, would have been implemented as a merge step (see Fig. 1.6). The calculate step of Figure 1.6 would have carried out the COMPUTE statements of lines 54 and 55 as well as 60 and 61 of Figure 1.5.

The Operating System in the Electric Age

The source program SALARIES described an application; Figure 1.6 (see page 8) described the application's steps in the physical system; Table 1.1 (see page 9) interprets the steps in the light of the modern operating system.

The job request called USERJOB consists of steps (REPRODUCESTEP, CALCSTEP, etc.). The step name describes the step's function.

---

* COBOL (COmmon Business Oriented Language) is a programming language, similar to English, that is used for commercial data processing. It was developed by the Conference of Data Systems Languages (CODASYL). COBOL is an industry language and is not the property of any company or group of companies, or of any organization or group of organizations. The particular version of the COBOL language used herein predates the presently released ANS COBOL standard language; the language is that used as input by the OS/360 COBOL F compiler.

```
LEVEL 1JAN67                                    COBOL F

  1

00001            IDENTIFICATION DIVISION.
00002            PROGRAM-ID.
00003            'SALARIES'.
                           ⋮
00040            PROCEDURE DIVISION.
00041                OPEN I-C EMPLOYEE-YTD.
00042                OPEN INPUT EMPLOYEE-WEEKLY.
00043            READ-WEEKLY.
00044                READ EMPLOYEE-WEEKLY AT END GO TO READ-YTD.
00045            READ-YTD.
00046                READ EMPLOYEE-YTD AT END GO TO FINIS.
00047                IF EMPLOYEE-NO-YTD IS EQUAL TO EMPLOYEE-NO-WEEKLY
00048                                 GO TO LIMIT-TEST.
00049                REWRITE YTD-RECORD.
00050                DISPLAY YTD-RECORD.
00051                GO TO READ-YTD.
00052            LIMIT-TEST.
00053                IF SLIMIT - SOCIAL-SEC-YTD < GROSS-PAY GO TO LIMIT-CALC.
00054                COMPUTE SOCIAL-SEC-YTD
00055                      ROUNDED = SOCIAL-SEC-YTD + GROSS-PAY * .048.
00056                REWRITE YTD-RECORD.
00057                DISPLAY YTD-RECORD.
00058                GO TO READ-WEEKLY.
00059            LIMIT-CALC.
00060                COMPUTE SOCIAL-SEC-YTD
00061                      ROUNDED = SOCIAL-SEC-YTD +
00062                             (SLIMIT - SOCIAL-SEC-YTD) * .048.
00063                REWRITE YTD-RECORD.
00064                DISPLAY YTD-RECORD.
00065                GO TO READ-WEEKLY.
00066                CLOSE EMPLOYEE-YTD.
00067                CLOSE EMPLOYEE-WEEKLY.
00068            FINIS. ENTER LINKAGE.
00069                CALL 'DUMPIT'.
00070                ENTER COBOL.
00071                STOP RUN.
```

Figure 1.5 SALARIES—A source program request in the COBOL language.

In a job step request, the source program was a wired control panel. The request for system resources was a handwritten set of instructions to the machine room operator. The concerns of user and operator were separate. Through control panel wiring the user programmed counters in machines and dealt with data formats in cards. The operator mounted the prescribed control panel and card deck in the machine, oblivious to programs and formats.

Problem program activity, the punched-card machine's response to the user's step request, was to execute the source program specified by control panel wiring. Response to the system resource request component of, say, CALCSTEP was the operator's control panel and card deck activity, following which he pressed the calculator start button.

Unit record machines were dedicated to responding to only one job step at any one time. They recognized neither jobs nor job steps. These elements of systems response had their only existence in the minds of the user and machine room operator.

1.3 ELECTRONIC AGE

As its name implies, electronic data processing was based on vacuum tube technology. A vacuum tube switched on or off some 30,000 times faster than an electromechanical relay. In both electric and electronic systems, the elementary cycle time depends on switching time. Instructions being combinations of primitive machine cycles, reduced switching time increased system speed.

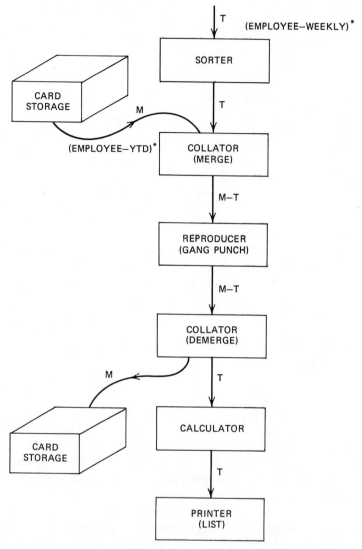

Figure 1.6 Six job steps of a job. Key: M, master card deck; T, transaction card deck; *, sequenced by sorting at a prior time.

At least as important as vacuum tube development was the definition of stored program systems. The major work on the subject was by John von Neumann, H. H. Goldstine, and A. W. Burks, a series of reports published in 1946.

The von Neumann machine consisted of the CPU, storage, and i–o units we have previously referred to as an idealized system. The CPU fetched instruction and data operands from the storage unit at high speed; the i–o unit transferred data and information between storage and the outside environment.

The systems of first, second, third, and fourth generation were "von Neumann machines." The stored program was the single most important advance in the history of systems technology.

Table 1.1 User Request and System Response in the Electric Age

User Request		System Response	
Name	Description	Name	Description
USERJOB	Job request	USERJOB	Job
COLLATESTEP	Job step 1 request	COLLATESTEP	Job step 1
	System resource specification (manual)		Allocate system resources (manual)
	Source program (wired control panel)		Problem program execution
	Data (card decks)		
REPRODUCESTEP	Job step 2 request	REPRODUCESTEP	Job step 2
	System resource specification (manual)		Allocate system resources (manual)
	Source program (wired control panel)		Problem program execution
	Data (card decks)		
.	.	.	.
.	.	.	.
.	.	.	.
CALCSTEP	Job step n request	CALCSTEP	Job step n
	System resource specification (manual)		Allocate system resources
	Source program (wired control panel)		Problem program execution
	Data (card decks)		

9

In addition to its switching and wired-program shortcomings, the punched-card system suffered from lack of storage. Data were stored in electromechanical devices that were bulky, expensive to produce, and slow. Storage sizes were measured in hundreds of characters, limiting the amount of information retainable in a job step. Card handling by the operator consumed inordinate amounts of job time.

First-Generation Systems

In first-generation systems, large storage required development. Vacuum tube circuits, practicable for CPUs, were impracticable for storage because of cost, bulk, and heat dissipation. Industry searched for a large-volume, compact, low-cost medium and found the magnetic core, announced with the IBM 704 in 1954. Although, like the CPU, main storage now switched in microseconds, its capacity remained a problem. Capacities of millions of characters were needed, capacities of tens of thousands of characters were feasible. Demand for a secondary storage mechanism was thus defined.

A major shortcoming of punched-card systems was that job executions required sequences of job steps; cards repeatedly reentered the system. In an electronic system with sufficient storage, the EMPLOYEE-WEEKLY transaction file, output of a sort step, could be retained within the system as input to CALCSTEP. The efficiency of consolidating function into a single step, coupled with the cost–performance constraint of main core storage, defined the requirement for mass secondary storage.

Fulfillment came through the magnetic tape with capacities in the tens of millions of characters. Although core storage outperformed tape storage, which was electromechanical, by some 10 to 1, tape enabled the consolidation of, say, sorting, collating, and calculating steps, substituting automatic processes for manual operator processes. SALARIES functions that took 45 minutes in a punched-card system required 1.5 minutes on a tape-in, tape-out IBM 705.

Demand quickly became defined as scientific (IBM 701–704) or commercial (IBM 702–705). Scientific systems performed much computation on little data; commercial systems performed little computation on much data. The 701–704 did parallel binary* arithmetic. A binary system requires data format conversion between main storage and the i–o subsystem. In addition, by automating decimal point control, floating-point arithmetic instructions relieved the user of considerable labor. The 702–705 did serial arithmetic, which, though less efficient than parallel computation, made data format conversion unnecessary.

Though scientific and commercial systems organized their computational registers and data flows differently, they adhered to the von Neumann design. The CPU fetched instructions from main storage sequentially. Transparent to the user, the processor kept track of its location in the stored program through an instruction counter, which normally located the next instruction and, in branching situations, underwent special loading operations.

Stored-program systems changed not only the user's functions but also his identity. Programmers directed the system through instructions punched in cards, not

* Radix one.

Table 1.2   Some Basic Characteristics of Symbolic Language Translators

Characteristic	Language Translator		
	Interpreter	Assembler	Compiler
Resident in main storage with translated program at execution time	Yes	No	No
Multiple object (output) instructions per input language statement	Yes	No	Yes

wires plugged in holes. Powerful function attracted scientists and accountants who had never wired control panels. For part-time users, especially, the system had to be easy to use. Symbolic programming, CPU instruction architecture, and relocatability made this happen. Emphasis on the stored program meant emphasis on the programmer. Systems executed thousands of instructions per second; humans had to keep them busy with programs.

Symbolic programming was a great aid to ease of use; we might remember ADD; we might not remember 06, the operation code the hardware recognizes. Three directions were taken: language compilers, assemblers, and interpreters. Table 1.2 compares their pertinent characterisitcs. Assemblers and compilers were the most widely accepted of these programs, setting a pattern that still persists—separate language translation and execution steps in a single job request. The leading first-generation compiler was FORTRAN (FORmula TRANslation)* The name described the function, translating mathematical expressions into CPU instructions (see Fig. 1.7, line 0008).

Natural to stored-program machines, program looping, illustrated by lines 7 and 8 of Figure 1.7, specifies that statement 100 is to execute 100 times. Looping required fewer explicit instructions from the programmer and less storage space for the program. User acceptance of the loop resulted in prompt hardware response by the manufacturer. The index register architecture in the IBM 704 provided a significant hardware assist to looping efficiency.

In carrying out the matrix multiply of Figure 1.7 without *automatic* indexing the 704 would have had to execute three extra instructions for the two million modifications of the variables B and C.

That the stored program was relocatable in main storage belongs in the first rank of its advantages over the wired program. In SALARIES, Figure 1.5, line 69, CALL 'DUMPIT', requests the system to dump main storage to an output device before STOP RUN executes. SALARIES and DUMPIT are independent source programs. SALARIES is being compiled now, say. DUMPIT was assembled then—yesterday. Their translations being independent, DUMPIT and SALARIES locations are independent. Whether SALARIES is 1 or 100 statements long, DUMPIT connects with it in the execution step.

* COBOL, used illustratively throughout this section, was not developed until the second generation.

```
                                        OS/360   FORTRAN H

         COMPILER OPTIONS - NAME=  MAIN,OPT=OO,LINECNT=50,SIZE=OOOOK,
                                SOURCE,EBCDIC,LIST,NODECK,LOAD,NOMAP,NOEDIT,NOID,NOXREF
ISN 0002              DIMENSION A(100,100),B(100,100),C(100,100)
ISN 0003              READ (1) B,C
ISN 0004              DO 100 I = 1,100
ISN 0005              DO 100 J = 1,100
ISN 0006              A(I,J) =0.
ISN 0007              DO 100 K=1,100
ISN 0008          100 A(I,J) = B(I,K) * C(K,J) + A(I,J)
ISN 0009              STOP
ISN 0010              END
```

Figure 1.7   A FORTRAN source program. (Excerpt from Appendix 8.)

In first-generation systems one consolidated card deck, the output of SALARIES and DUMPIT translations, was read in. As a prelude to the execution step, a loader program processed the two sets of locations so that the programs connected.

One system programmer writes a routine to do something many users need, dumping main storage, say, or translating decimal to binary. Reproduced into card decks, the routine becomes part of many programs invoked by statements like CALL 'DUMPIT'. Thus through program relocation, the system programmer's work became available to the problem programmer. The seeds of the operating system had been sown.

Finally, in performance, first-generation CPUS and main storage were electronic; i–o subsystems were electromechanical. Moreover, initial entry and final exit of data involved the slower classes of electromagnetic units, card readers and printers. To reduce degradation by electromechanical units, a separate peripheral system of card-to-tape and tape-to-card machines was devised for "off-line" operations (Fig. 1.8). Input–output to the "on-line" system was by magnetic tape. The idleness of CPUs caused by such source program logic as "George M. Eisele's payroll master record (EMPLOYEE-YTD) must not be updated until his transactions (EM-PLOYEE-WEEKLY) are READ" was held to a minimum because George M. Eisele's transactions were on tape.

The Operating System in First-Generation Systems

From this time on, source language program requests became input data to a language translation program, as in COBSTEP (Table 1.3). USERJOB problem activity would have included separate COBOL and execution job steps.*

COBOL output, a punched-card deck, would have reentered the system from the input reader along with user data during the execution step. Between job steps the services of the machine-room operator were required.

Systems resources were unshared, dedicated exclusively to the job step in execution. As in electric age systems, jobs and job steps that responded to corresponding steps of the user's job request had their only existence in the minds of the user and machine-room operator.

Second-Generation Systems

First-generation technology was but a prelude. Users innovated, new requirements emerged. Where the first generation was a revolution, the second generation was

---

* First-generation systems used FORTRAN.

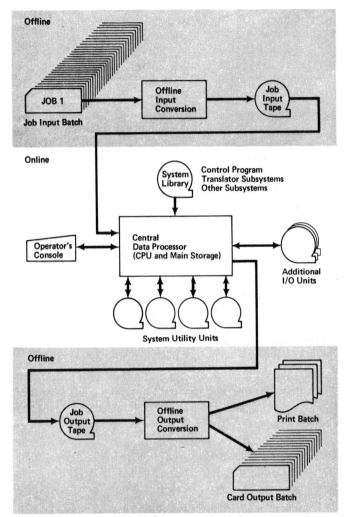

Figure 1.8 Peripheral operations. From *IBM System/360 Operating System, Introduction,* IBM Systems Reference Library Manual C-28-6534.

a consolidation and improvement. Technology continued to make previously impossible functions possible. There was a significant lowering of the cost of computing. Electronic data processing penetrated into areas of the economy where first-generation systems had been unable to go. The capability of the IBM 705 was now available to smaller and middle-sized businesses through the IBM 1400. The smallest 1400 brought integrated data processing to the business of modest size. The largest brought 705 levels of productivity to middle-sized establishments.

IBM second-generation 1400 and 7000 series systems are identified by standard modular system (SMS) transistor technology. In switching time, heat dissipation, and reliability the transistor outperformed the vacuum tube in CPU and i–o subsystem circuits. Magnetic core storage cycle times were speeded up. The IBM 704 CPU fetched a data operand from memory in 12 microseconds compared to

Table 1.3   User Request and System Response in First- and Second-Generation Systems

	User Request		System Response	
Name	Description		Name	Description
USERJOB	Job request		USERJOB	Job
COBSTEP	Job step request—Compile		COBSTEP	Job step—Compile
	System resource specification			Allocate system
	Data (SALARYS)[a]			resources
EXECSTEP	Job step request—Execute[a]		EXECSTEP	Job step—Execute
	System resource specification			Allocate system
	Data (SALARYL + EMPWKLY)[b]			resources

[a]Combined collate, reproduce, and calculate steps of electric age request.
[b]See glossary in Figure 3.12.

2 microseconds in the 7094. The average installed memory capacity of the latter was easily twice that of the former.

In the i–o subsystem, magnetic tape files presented a new development target. Consider inventory-transaction files updating inventory master files in volumes of 1000 and 100,000 tape records (Fig. 1.9); 99,000 records occupy system resources without productive purpose.

Job step consolidation remained a development target, in different form. Although first-generation systems consolidated functions within an application, demand for consolidation between applications still existed. Consider billing, inventory, and accounts receivable. A shipment must be billed to the customer, subtracted from inventory, and entered into accounts receivable. Inconsistent with sequential tape files, the need to update all affected files *during* a transaction defined the requirement for the magnetic disk.

Like tape, disk technology used magnetic hysteresis as an electronic switch. There the similarity ended. Disk files were organized in tracks located on multiple disks rotating together on a single unit; multiple units could be attached to a system. Individual disk locations were addressable (indirectly) through CPU instruc-

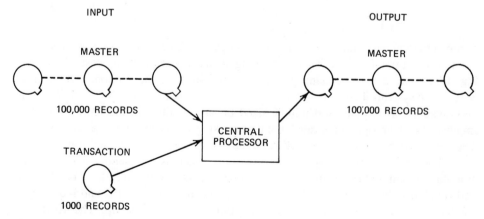

Figure 1.9 Update function in a data processing system.

tions. Tape locations were not. Without batching and sorting transaction file inputs, George M. Eisele's and T. D. Forrest's EMPLOYEE-YTD records were directly retrievable by EMPLOYEE-NO; two separately addressed spaces, main storage and disk, were now an established part of hardware system design.

Addressability enabled update-in-place processing on disk. On tape, a philosophy of EMPLOYEE-WEEKLY transaction-in and EMPLOYEE-YTD master-in, transmitted to a fresh copy of EMPLOYEE-YTD master-out, updated, was employed. Addressing locations and updating them in place resembled what main storage did. The disk became an adjunct of storage in which program libraries as well as data files were placed for rapid retrieval. That effective storage sizes were now tens of millions of bytes was of great consequence in the development of the modern operating system.

In addition to the magnetic disk, storage of the i–o subsystem took the form of the fixed-head magnetic drum. Disk versus drum represented a capacity versus performance trade.

State of the art in first generation dictated a strict READ/COMPUTE/RE-WRITE sequence in problem program executions (Fig. 1.6). Improvement over this lockstep procedure came through the buffered channel of the i–o subsystem, which came into its own in second-generation systems as a second intelligence.

Independent instruction streaming by CPU and i–o subsystem improved performance through electromagnetic/electronic overlap. Figure 1.10 illustrates the improvement in the execution of a single job step, SALARIES. The most profound effect of the buffered channel, impact on multiple job step operations, we defer to the discussion of third-generation systems and OS/360.

The Second-Generation Operating System

The operating system was largely a second-generation development (see Table 1.3). Multistep jobs and the problem programmer's need for the system programmer's work for the management of his data identified areas for improvement. Expanded, these functions later became job and data management in OS/360.

The USERJOB request in second-generation systems included a source program in compiler language, as before. As the system-dependent component of the job step request, the user submitted control cards, machine readable, in contrast to the handwritten instructions to the operator of the past. Problem program activity encompassed compile and execution response steps, as in first-generation systems. Response to the system-dependent component of USERJOB included locating and fetching into main storage the programs specified in the job step request. Inter-job-step activity, done by the operator in first-generation systems, was automated in the more advanced systems of the day.

General purpose utility functions, established through use as the province of the system, not the user, became common in the second generation. An operating system comprised of component programs communicating with each other and with user problem programs became a natural development goal. The usability of an operating system was now recognized as proportional to the amount of the system programmer's work at the disposal of the problem programmer.*

---

* The terms "problem program" and "application program," and "problem programmer" and "application programmer" are used interchangeably throughout this text.

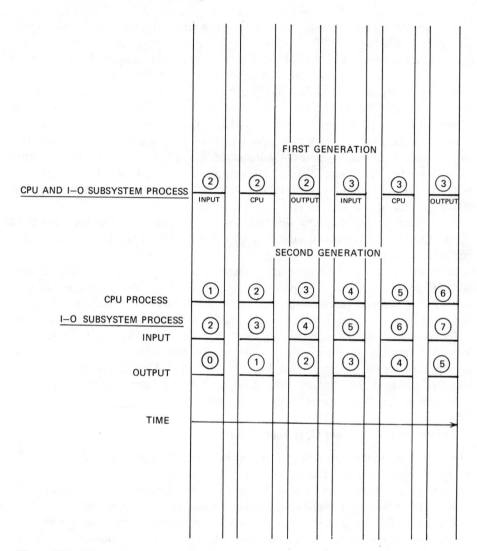

Figure 1.10 Schematic of systems productivity advance: first- and second-generation systems. ⓝ is record.

EXERCISES*

1.1 In Figure 1.5, line 47, EMPLOYEE-NO-WEEKLY is equal to EMPLOYEE-NO-YTD. Which line receives control?

1.2 EMPLOYEE-WEEKLY consists of a set of 100 properly edited cards; EMPLOYEE-YTD consists of a set of 1000 properly edited cards. According to SALARIES language, (a) how many year-to-date cards are read? (b) How many weekly cards are read?

1.3 Assume numbers of WEEKLY and YTD cards according to the following table:

EMPLOYEE-WEEKLY	100	0	0	2
EMPLOYEE-YTD	0	1000	0	2

* Answers to the questions at the end of this and subsequent chapters may be found on pages 201–206.

How many EMPLOYEE-WEEKLY and EMPLOYEE-YTD cards are READ in each of the above?

1.4 Using nested* IF statements, write SALARIES to handle all of the following situations (send error conditions to ERROR-PROC):

| EMPLOYEE-WEEKLY | 01050 | 01051 | blank | 01050 | xyzab | 01050 |
| EMPLOYEE-YTD | 01051 | 01050 | 01050 | blank | 01050 | 01050 |

* If condition statement 1 ELSE statement 2 . . . . See *IBM COBOL,* IBM Systems Reference Library Manual C28–6516 for further detail.

chapter 2

S/370 HARDWARE

2.1 SECOND-GENERATION PROBLEMS

The productivity afforded second-generation users increased the demand for technology. The broadened user base resulting from symbolic languages meant new applications installed and new requirements levied.

Although diminished by improved i–o subsystem technology, electronic/electromagnetic imbalance remained; reduced CPU and main storage cycle times presented a moving target for the i–o subsystem to overlap.

System proliferation persisted. Table 2.1 lists the many architectural families of IBM second-generation systems.

Supplying, maintaining, and constantly upgrading the hardware strained the manufacturers' resources; software requirements were as great.

Scientific computations might be the main justification of an IBM 7094 system, but use of the system by the commercial department of the installation was necessary as well. Furthermore, an IBM 7094 commercial user required a COBOL. Conversely, the commercially justified IBM 7074 or IBM 7080 system needed a FORTRAN. A scan of the literature showed 33 second-generation language translator implementations being distributed in January 1968, almost four years after System/360 announcement.

System/360 architecture addressed proliferation by including both serial decimal and floating-point (commercial and scientific) instructions. Hardware and software attacked imbalance. Electronic as well as electromechanical switching times were speeded up; the old ratio between these two persisted. Figure 2.1 exhibits some

Table 2.1   Families of IBM First- and Second-Generation IBM Systems

First Generation	Second Generation	Primary Application Area
IBM 704	IBM 7040–7044, 7090–7094–7094II	Scientific
IBM 705	IBM 7080	Commercial
	IBM 7070–7074	Commercial
	IBM 1401	Commercial
	IBM 1410–7010	Commercial
	IBM 1440	Commercial
	IBM 1460	Commercial
	IBM 1620–1710	Scientific

electronic component technologies involved. Adopting a multiprogramming design, OS/360 software increased efficiency by enabling independent resources to act simultaneously (Fig. 2.2).

A brief chronology of third-generation announcements of IBM large-scale systems will clarify what follows. In April 1964 IBM announced System/360, consisting of S/360 hardware and OS/360 software. OS/360 remained the operating system for System/370, announced in February 1970. In July 1972, a relocate system, System/370R, was announced. System/370R has two modes, basic control (OS/360 runs) or extended control (OS/VS runs). The discussion in this chapter applies to System/360, System/370, and System/370R, basic control mode. The terms "System/370," "S/370," and "OS/360" denote system, hardware, and software.

Figure 2.3 depicts System/370—S/370 hardware and OS/360 software. In Chapter 3, we encounter OS/360, manager of all System/370 resources. Our main concern now is hardware.

2.2 S/370

Figure 2.4 depicts the organization of S/370.

A primary data processing characteristic is intelligence: the ability of a unit to decode and execute a stream of instructions. Both the CPU and i–o subsystem possess this. Decoding more instructions and more sophisticated instructions, the CPU's intelligence is superior (see Table 2.2). OS/360 values intelligence more than any other resource attribute. The operating system allocates its intelligent resources only after less precious resources have been assigned.

Central Processing Unit

Architecture. The assembly language user deals with a unit's architecture. As shown in Figure 2.5, the CPU appears as a collection of registers and a control mechanism—its instructions apparent to the user, its operations transparent.

Sixteen general purpose registers (GPRs) serve as accumulators in binary arithmetic and logic instructions, and specify main storage addresses. Data and information pass between OS/360 problem and control programs through these registers. Four floating-point registers perform the arithmetic functions of earlier scientific systems (e.g., IBM 7094).

Finally, System/370 architecture defines a program status word, (PSW) (Fig. 2.6), which serves, among other things, as an instruction counter. Fixed locations in storage function with the PSW.

Central processing unit design is based on primitive cycles combined into instructions or operations.

Instructions. Instructions in storage contain data operand information. Normally the CPU fetches instructions in the sequence in which they reside, under control of the PSW instruction counter field, bits 40–63.

Instruction activity has two cycles, each comprised of multiple subcycles. In an instruction (I) cycle the CPU fetches the instruction from storage, activity 1; if a data operand resides in storage, calculates the address, activity 2; and fetches an operand, activity 3. Responding to the instruction's operation field, execution (E) cycle activity consists of operations on the fetched data.

Instruction streaming includes branching. During the I cycle the CPU decodes the operation field of the instruction, activity 1; calculates the next I fetch address, activity 2 (usually different from the current address); and, taking a second I cycle, fetches the next instruction, activity 3. Sequencing resumes from the branched-to area.

A decision to branch (normally) results from a test of the PSW's condition code field or as a result of address arithmetic and counting operations. A "Branch on Condition" instruction inspects this two-bit code reflecting the results of arithme-

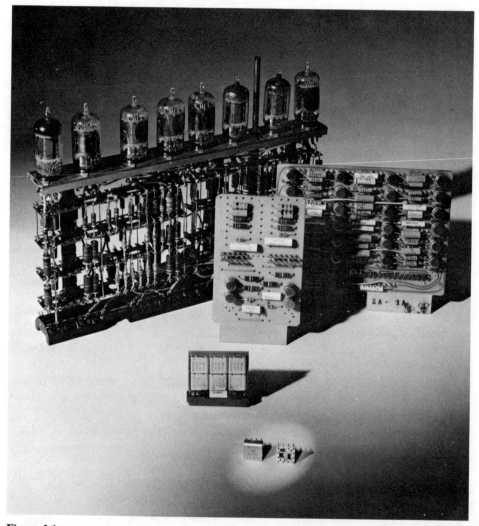

Figure 2.1

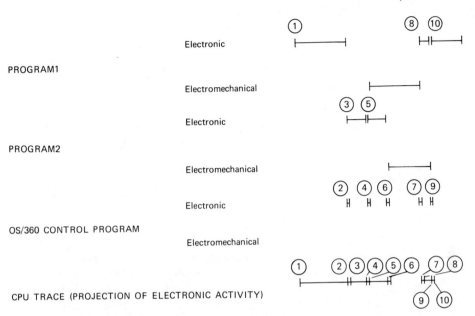

PROGRAM1

PROGRAM2

OS/360 CONTROL PROGRAM

CPU TRACE (PROJECTION OF ELECTRONIC ACTIVITY)

ACTIVITY DESCRIPTION

① Program1 executes CPU Instructions.
② Program1 requests i-o subsystem service, which the OS/360 control program schedules. Program1 must wait.
③ Program2 executes CPU instructions.
④ Program1 request becomes dispatchable.
⑤ Program2 resumes execution of CPU instructions.
⑥ Program2 requests i-o subsystem service, which the OS/360 control program schedules. Program2 must wait.
⑦ Program1 request completes. Program2 request thereby becomes dispatchable.
⑧ Program1 executes CPU instructions.
⑨ Program2 request completes.
⑩ Program1 resumes execution of CPU instructions.

Figure 2.2   Electronic/electromechanical overlap.

Figure 2.1   Highlights of component technology evolution at IBM, showing (in the background) a typical pluggable unit that utilized vacuum tubes and discrete axial lead components resistors and diodes). Some pluggable units were used extensively in the IBM 7000 series of data processing systems.

Standard modular system (SMS) technology is illustrated by the single and double printed-circuit cards (right of center), initially adopted in 1958 for the IBM 1400 series of computers. SMS technology employed discrete transistors (e.g., the TO-5s shown at the right edge of the large SMS card), plus axial lead resistors and diodes as shown.

SMS technology is commonly used in various IBM systems, along with solid logic technology (SLT), announced in April 1964 in conjunction with IBM System/360 computers. Six SLT modules are shown mounted on a printed-circuit card (center foreground), along with an encapsulated and an unencapsulated SLT module at the bottom of the photo.

Monolithic systems technology (MST), which evolved from SLT, utilizes much the same packaging scheme at the module level as SLT. MST is used in System/370. Monolithic memory technology used in System/370 also utilizes a circuit packaging similar to that shown at the bottom of the figure.

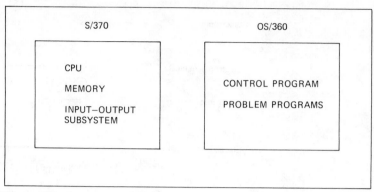

Figure 2.3   System/370 components.

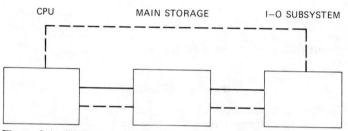

Figure 2.4   S/370 organization. The solid and broken lines indicate data and control flow, respectively.

tic, logical, and i–o instructions. "Branch on Index" or "Branch on Count" instructions perform loop control (see Fig. 2.7, location 1D6AC).

Five CPU instruction formats designate the origin and destination of data operands: RR, RX, RS, SI, and SS. Format R denotes a register. Formats S and X are storage addresses in which

$$S = \text{displacement} + c(\text{GPR}_{base})$$
$$X = S + c(\text{GPR}_{index})$$

Table 2.2   Instruction Types Decoded by S/370 Intelligent Resources

Central Processing Unit	Input-Output Subsystem
Problem:	Problem:
Arithmetic (three kinds)	Input–output
Logical	Branching
Character handling	Device control
Branching	
Supervisor call	
Privileged:	
Input–output addressing	
Dispatching and status switching	

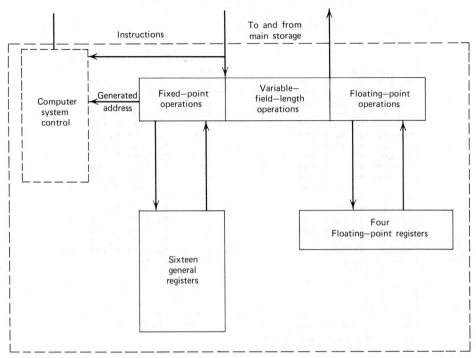

Figure 2.5 Organization of central processing units in S/370. From *IBM System/360 Principles of Operation*, IBM Systems Reference Library Manual GA-22-6821.

System Mask	Key	AMWP	Interruption Code

0   7 8   11 12   15 16   31

ILC	CC	Program Mask	Instruction Address

32 33 34 35 36   39 40   63

0-7	System mask	14	Wait state (W)
0	Channel 0 mask	15	Problem state (P)
1	Channel 1 mask	16-31	Interruption code
2	Channel 2 mask	32-33	Instruction Length code (ILC)
3	Channel 3 mask	34-35	Condition code (CC)
4	Channel 4 mask	36-39	Program mask
5	Channel 5 mask	36	Fixed-point overflow mask
6	Channel 6 mask	37	Decimal overflow mask
7	External mask	38	Exponent underflow mask
8-11	Protection key	39	Significance mask
12	ASCII(A)	40-63	Instruction address
13	Machine-check mask (M)		

Figure 2.6 Program status word format in S/370. From *IBM System/360 Principles of Operation*, IBM Systems Reference Library Manual GA-22-6821.

Displacement (D) is $0 \leq D \leq 4095$. The symbol I, immediate, denotes a byte included in the instruction as a data operand (Fig. 2.8).

Storage addressing. A storage address is specified by a base register and a displacement. Effective addresses in RX instructions are specified by an index register as well (Fig. 2.7, location 1D688).

Figure 2.9 illustrates base register use. USING, line 8, instructs assembler to establish GPR_3 as the base register. Lines 9, 10, 14, and 17 result. The Branch

Main Storage Locations	Actual (Instructions)		Symbolic (Instructions)
⋮	⋮		⋮
01D67E	18 65		LR 6, 5
01D680	5A 60 C 018		A 6, 24(0,12)
01D684	58 70 C 008		L 7, 8(0,12)
01D688	78 06 7 000		LE 0, 0(6, 7)
01D68C	7A 00 C 014		AE 0, 20(0,12)
01D690	58 60 C 010		L 6, 16(0,12)
01D694	70 06 7 000		STE 0, 0(6, 7)
01D698	58 00 D 054	100	L 0, 84(0,13)
01D69C	5A 00 D 068		A 0, 104(0,13)
01D6A0	50 00 D 068		ST 0, 104(0,13)
01D6A4	59 00 D 058		C 0, 88(0,13)
01D6A8	58 50 C 02C		L 5, 44(0,12)
01D6AC	07 D5		BCR 13, 5
01D6AE	58 00 D 054	100004	L 0, 84(0,13)
01D6B2	5A 00 D 064		A 0, 100(0,13)
01D6B6	50 00 D 064		ST 0, 100(0,13)
01D6BA	59 00 D 058		C 0, 88(0,13)
01D6BE	58 50 C 028		L 5, 40(0,12)
01D6C2	07 D5		BCR 13, 5
⋮	⋮		⋮

Figure 2.7 Excerpt from Appendix 8, matrix multiply. See Figure 2.8 for actual instruction formats.

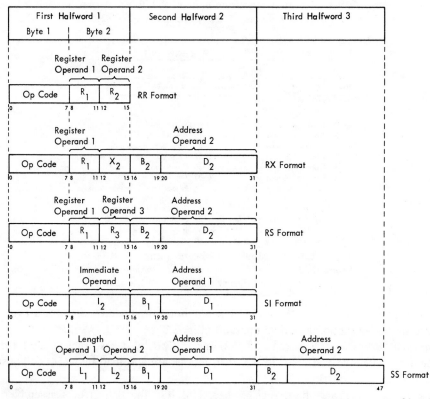

Figure 2.8 Actual S/370 instruction format. From *IBM System/360 Principles of Operation,* IBM Systems Reference Library Manual GA-22-6821.

```
  LOC   OBJECT CODE    ADDR1 ADDR2  STMT    SOURCE STATEMENT                                    ASM 0102 18.56 09/27/73
000000                              1 DUMPIT   CSECT
                                    2          SAVE   (14,12),,*
000000  47F0 F00C      0000C        3+         B      12(0,15)                  BRANCH AROUND ID        00860000
000004  06                          4+         DC     AL1(6)                                            00680000
000005  C4E4D407C9E3                5+         DC     CL6'DUMPIT'               IDENTIFIER              00900000
00000B  00
00000C  90EC D00C      0000C        6+         STM    14,12,12(13)              SAVE REGISTERS          01180000
000010  05B0                        7          BALR   3,0
                       00012        8          USING  *,3
000012  50D0 3026      00038        9          ST     13,SAVE+4
000016  41D0 3022      00034        10         LA     13,SAVE
                                    11         ABEND  256,DUMP
00001A                              12+        DS     0H                                               00080019
00001A  0700                        13+        CNOP   0,4                                              00860000
00001C  47F0 3012      00024        14+        B      *+8                BRANCH AROUND CONSTANT        00880019
000020  80                          15+        DC     AL1(128)                  DUMP/STEP CODE          00900000
000021  000100                      16+        DC     AL3(256)                  COMPLETION CODE         00920000
000024  5810 300E      00020        17+        L      1,*-4                     LOAD CODES INTO REG 1   00940000
000028  0A0D                        18+        SVC    13                        LINK TO ABEND ROUTINE   00960000
                                    19 RETURN  RETURN (14,12),T
00002A                              20+RETURN  DS     0H                                               00100000
00002A  98EC D00C      0000C        21+        LM     14,12,12(13)              RESTORE THE REGISTERS   00280000
00002E  92FF D00C      0000C        22+        MVI    12(13),X'FF'              SET RETURN INDICATION   00640000
000032  07FE                        23+        BR     14                        RETURN                  00800000
000034                              24 SAVE    DS     18F
                                    25         END
```

Figure 2.9   Assembly language program DUMPIT. (Excerpt from Appendix 1.)

and Link Register (BALR) of line 7 loads GPR$_3$ from storage at execution time, establishing the absolute address of the program illustrated.*

The OS/360 control program. Third-generation users demanded more than hardware. It was wasteful to have each installation writing, say, complex i–o subsystem management routines. The manufacturer provided a unified set of system routines, a control program, serving many users.

The design of S/370 hardware assumes a control program. The CPU's program status word includes privilege, protect key zero, and masking for control program use (Fig. 2.6). OS/360 monitoring and service demonstrate how control program designers availed themselves of these features.

A problem program is never more than one instruction from control program monitoring. On an occurrence in, say, some System/370 resource acting independently of the CPU, the hardware loads the PSW, automatically, from a predetermined storage location. Instantly setting the CPU to privileged, protect key zero, and masked state, loading is performed by a CPU operation, the interrupt—the control program is interrupted to. By virtue of protect key zero, the control program may store (for later retrieval) problem program$_1$'s GPRs in storage locations protected by program$_1$'s nonzero key. By virtue of masking, the control program executes undisturbed by i–o interrupts. Control program privilege includes addressing the PSW. Through an instruction, Load PSW (LPSW), the control program decides which program uses the CPU and how it uses it.

Each user knows only what his program does. By monitoring problem program execution, denying thereby privilege to problem programs, the PSW prohibits this

* The format of BALR (see Figs. 2.8 and 2.9, line 7) can be depicted as follows:

	S/370 RR Format of BALR	Assembly Language Source Format of BALR
OP CODE R1 R2		
05 | 3 | 0		BALR 3,0

General purpose register 3, designated by the user as R$_1$, is loaded from the instruction address field of the PSW, l(BALR+2), and R$_2$ is the branch address. BALR is often used where a main program CALLs a library routine.

```
00001              IDENTIFICATION DIVISION.
00002              PROGRAM-ID. 'A PLUS B3'.
                          ⋮
00013              PROCEDURE DIVISION.
00014              COMPUTE B = A + 3.
00015                   IF C IS GREATER THAN B  MOVE 1 TO TEST.
00016                   ENTER LINKAGE.
00017                   CALL 'DUMPIT'.
00018                   ENTER COBOL.
00019                   STOP RUN.
```

(a)

NO	VERB
14	COMPUTE

```
                    0001F4                           START    EQU    *
                    0001F4   F8 70 D 190 C 008                ZAP    190(8,13),008(1,12)
                    0001FA   FA 21 D 195 6 000                AP     195(3,13),000(2,6)
                    000200   F8 11 6 002 D 196                ZAP    002(2,6),196(2,13)
            15 IF   000206   F9 11 6 006 6 002                CP     006(2,6),002(2,6)
                    00020C   58 F0 C 004                      L      15,004(0,12)
                    000210   07 DF                            BCR    13,15
            15 MOVE 000212   D2 01 6 004 C 009                MVC    004(2,6),009(12)
```

(b)

NO	VERB
14	COMPUTE

```
                    0001EC                           START    EQU    *
                    0001EC   48 30 C 008                      LH     3,008(0,12)
                    0001F0   4A 30 6 000                      AH     3,000(0,6)
                    0001F4   40 30 6 002                      STH    3,002(0,6)
            15 IF   0001F8   48 30 6 006                      LH     3,006(0,6)
                    0001FC   49 30 6 002                      CH     3,002(0,6)
                    000200   58 F0 C 004                      L      15,004(0,12)
                    000204   07 DF                            BCR    13,15
            15 MOVE 000206   D2 01 6 004 C 00A                MVC    004(2,6),00A(12)
```

(c)

NO	VERB
14	COMPUTE

```
                    0001FA                           START    EQU    *
                    0001FA   F8 F0 D 060 C 010                ZAP    060(16,13),010(1,12)
                    000200   58 FC C 000                      L      15,000(0,12)
                    000204   05 EF                            BALR   14,15
                    000206   0000                             DC     X'0000'
                    000208   2B 22                            SDR    2,2
                    00020A   78 20 6 000                      LE     2,000(0,6)
                    00020E   2A 02                            ADR    0,2
                    000210   70 C0 6 004                      STE    0,004(0,6)
            15 IF   000214   78 20 6 00C                      LE     2,00C(0,6)
                    000218   79 20 6 004                      CE     2,004(0,6)
                    00021C   58 F0 C 008                      L      15,008(0,12)
                    000220   07 DF                            BCR    13,15
            15 MOVE 000222   F8 F0 D 060 C 011                ZAP    060(16,13),011(1,12)
                    000228   58 FC C 000                      L      15,000(0,12)
                    00022C   05 EF                            BALR   14,15
                    00022E   0000                             DC     X'0000'
                    000230   70 00 6 008                      STE    0,008(0,6)
```

(d)

Figure 2.10 (a) COBOL source (excerpt from Appendix 6). Note A and C entered as constants before line 13. (b) COBOL-produced object module listing from the COBOL source above—packed decimal. (c) COBOL-produced object module listing from the COBOL source above—binary. (d) COBOL-produced object module listing from the COBOL source above—floating point.

user's instructions from affecting that user's program.* Problem programs must request the privileged services they need by issuing an instruction, Supervisor Call, SVC.

The OS/360 problem program. The control program is interrupted to; problem programs are entered by execution of LPSW. Unprivileged† problem program instructions resemble the arithmetic, logical, and data-handling instructions of earlier systems. We illustrate problem instructions generated by COBOL in response to IF, COMPUTE, and MOVE source statements, identical inputs to three separate compilations. The instructions in Figures 2.10b–d, generated from Figure 2.10a, reflect the fact (not shown) that different data specification statements were inputs to each compilation.

---

* A problem program issuing a privileged instruction causes an interrupt.
† Unprivileged instructions may execute only when there is a one in PSW bit 15.

Figure 2.10*b* illustrates COBOL's translation of COMPUTE into packed-decimal arithmetic instructions of the SS format. Expansion of the MOVE statement exemplifies instructions for the handling of nonarithmetic data, commonly known as strings; notice the RX-format load preceding the RR-format branch. Figures 2.10*c* and 2.10*d* are binary and floating-point format analogs of the packed-decimal example.

Hardware and software oversee System/370 instruction executions. Before an instruction may become active, the CPU tests the authority, conferred by the PSW, of that program to execute that instrucion. These tests "steal" some of the elementary cycles of which an instruction is constructed and are carried out transparently to the user, who thinks of his program as follows:

.
.
.

```
PACK  198(8,13),020(8,7)
MP    199(7,13),07B(2,12)
```
.
.
.

not

.
.
.

```
test authority for PACK
PACK  198(8,13),020(8,7)
test authority for MP
MP    199(7,13),07B(2,12)
```
.
.
.

Should a problem program attempt to execute, say, a privileged instruction or, say, store into storage space protected, through OS/360 assignment, by another user's key, an interrupt is taken.

Storage

Instructions and data operands of the CPU and i–o subsystems reside in storage. Unintelligent, storage passively serves the intelligent resources that address it.

In A plus B, Figure 2.10*c*, A, a single precision floating-point word, is the contents of location 1B060 of Figure 2.11. System/370 architecture defines locations like 1B060 (divisible by 4) as word boundaries. Assume A to be offset by one byte to location 1B061. Now two data fetches plus alignment in the floating-point register are required.

System/370 architecture governs parallel (fixed and floating) operand handling. A problem program attempting to store A in 1B061 would cause a program interrupt. In SALARIES and A plus B, COBOL shields the user from the details.

Figure 2.12 depicts storage geometry. Storage keys protect areas within the boundaries shown.

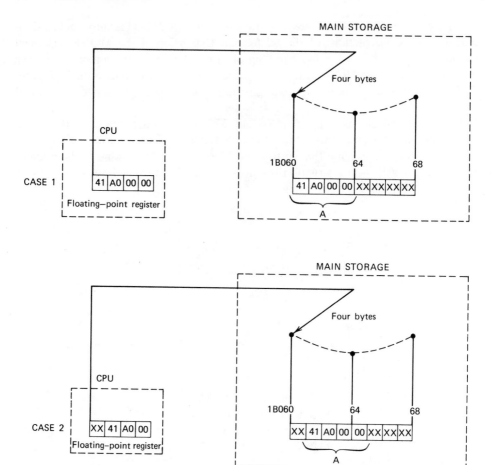

Figure 2.11   Boundary alignment schematic.

Storage protection is a hardware/software system of defending one user program's storage space from another's programs. The S/370 part is a PSW field, the key, and storage circuitry, the lock. Prior to execution of each store instruction, CPU operations matching key and lock test whether this user's store operand violates that user's space.

The OS/360 part acts at two times: loading the four-bit lock when the storage resource is first assigned to *this* program; and loading the four-bit key when *this* program is dispatched (by LPSW).

Table 2.3 depicts permanent locations of importance in CPU and i–o subsystem operations.

Central Processing Unit Operations with Storage

The interrupt. Control passes from problem to control program by interruption. In microseconds the current PSW is stored and a new PSW with a new instruction counter and new CPU status field is fetched.

This operation is aptly named; it interrupts an instruction's I cycle. In that sequence's stead, one of five constants (new PSWs), corresponding to one of five

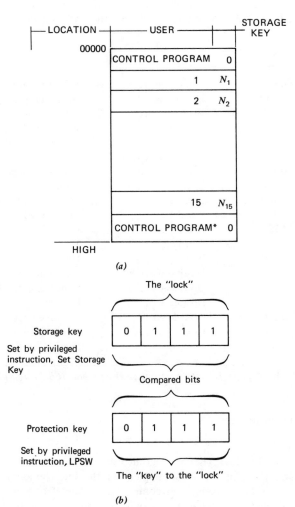

LOCATION — USER — STORAGE KEY

00000

CONTROL PROGRAM	0	
	1	N_1
	2	N_2
	15	N_{15}
CONTROL PROGRAM*	0	

HIGH

(a)

The "lock"

Storage key

| 0 | 1 | 1 | 1 |

Set by privileged instruction, Set Storage Key

Compared bits

Protection key

| 0 | 1 | 1 | 1 |

Set by privileged instruction, LPSW

The "key" to the "lock"

(b)

Figure 2.12 Schematics of (a) main storage and (b) storage and protection keys. In (a), the asterisk indicates reenterable routines.

types of interrupt, is fetched from a permanent location into the PSW. Next, fetch of the first control program instruction is directed by the instruction counter of the new PSW.

Control program processing is a frequent need. One hundred and ninety two devices requiring i–o supervision may be addressed on a single (multiplexor) channel of the i–o subsystem.

Example. Let us refer to Figures 2.6 and 2.13. Since multiprogramming means that the CPU and i–o subsystem may act at the same time, a problem state instruction may be executing when an i–o data transmission completes. Efficiency dictates the immediate dispatching of any request waiting for the lately idle i–o subsystem, on *this* instruction's completion. Our example illustrates the control and problem program activity involved. The state, instruction counter, and key fields of the PSW, and the contents of GPRs are of interest.

Table 2.3   Permanent Main Storage Assignments[a]

Address		Length	Purpose
0	0000 0000	Double word	Initial program loading PSW
8	0000 1000	Double word	Initial program loading CCW1[b]
16	0001 0000	Double word	Initial program loading CCW2
24	0001 1000	Double word	External old PSW
32	0010 0000	Double word	Supervisor call old PSW
40	0010 1000	Double word	Program old PSW
48	0011 0000	Double word	Machine check old PSW
56	0011 1000	Double word	Input–output old PSW
64	0100 0000	Double word	Channel status word
72	0100 1000	Word	Channel address word
76	0100 1100	Word	Unused
80	0101 0000	Word	Timer
84	0101 0100	Word	Unused
88	0101 1000	Double word	External new PSW
96	0110 0000	Double word	Supervisor call new PSW
104	0110 1000	Double word	Program new PSW
112	0111 0000	Double word	Machine check new PSW
120	0111 1000	Double word	Input–output new PSW
128	1000 0000		Diagnostic scan–out area[c]

[a]See IBM Systems Reference Library manual *IBM System/360 Principles of Operation*, GA-22-6821, p. 15.
[b]Channel command word.
[c]A maintenance area in storage.

Prior to activity 1, the SALARIES program executes with the PSW in the enabled (bits $0-7 = 1$) and problem states. Subsequent to the interruption at activity 1, the consequence of an i–o data transmission completion in behalf of program X, the CPU state has been switched from enabled to masked and from problem to supervisor. The masked CPU now streams the instructions of the OS/360 control program. Prior to activity 2, the old PSW is rescued from its fixed location so that it cannot be overwritten in the event of another i–o interrupt. The i–o supervisor notifies program X of the availability of its previously requested data, activity 3. Activity 4 occurs after issuance of the privileged instruction SIO (START i–o.) Activity 5 marks resumption of SALARIES processing at location 49786 (relative 4A6) after the control program issues the instruction Load Program Status Word.

Interrupt types. There are five types of S/370 interrupt: SVC, program, machine check, external, and the i–o interrupt we met in the preceding section.

The OS/360 response to a COBOL user's READ EMPLOYEE-YTD statement includes an SVC. A routine invoked by SVC 0, EXCP, schedules *this* request for the i–o subsystem resource into the control program. Depending on the resource's idle or busy state, the control program initiates the request immediately or enqueues it at the end of a waiting line of requests. Later, when the request completes, the i–o subsystem initiates an i–o interrupt.

An attempt by an OS/360 user to utilize a zoned decimal data operand in a packed-decimal instruction results in a program interruption.

Apparent | **OS/360 (Transparent) Control Program Stream**

COBOL Symbolic Listing				Interrupt Handler/Task Supervisor		Input–Output Supervisor (IOS)	
COBOL Source Statement	Main Storage Location (Abs.)	(Rel.)	Instruction	Main Storage Location	Instruction	Main Storage Location	Instruction
COMPUTE	49774	494	PACK 198(8,13),020(8,7)				
	4977A	49A	MP 199(7,13),07B(2,12)				
	.	.	.				
	.	.	.				
	49786	4A6	MP 190(8,13),07D(3,12)				
	.	.	.				
	.	.	.				

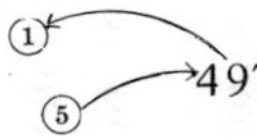

PSW Prior to Event

Event	State	Protect Key
① INTERRUPT SALARIES*	ENABLED/PROBLEM	10
② ROUTE TO IOS	MASKED/SUPERVISOR	0
③ POST I–O	MASKED/SUPERVISOR	0
④ START I–O		
④ RETURN TO SUPERVISOR	MASKED/SUPERVISOR	0
⑤ RETURN TO SALARIES	MASKED/SUPERVISOR	0

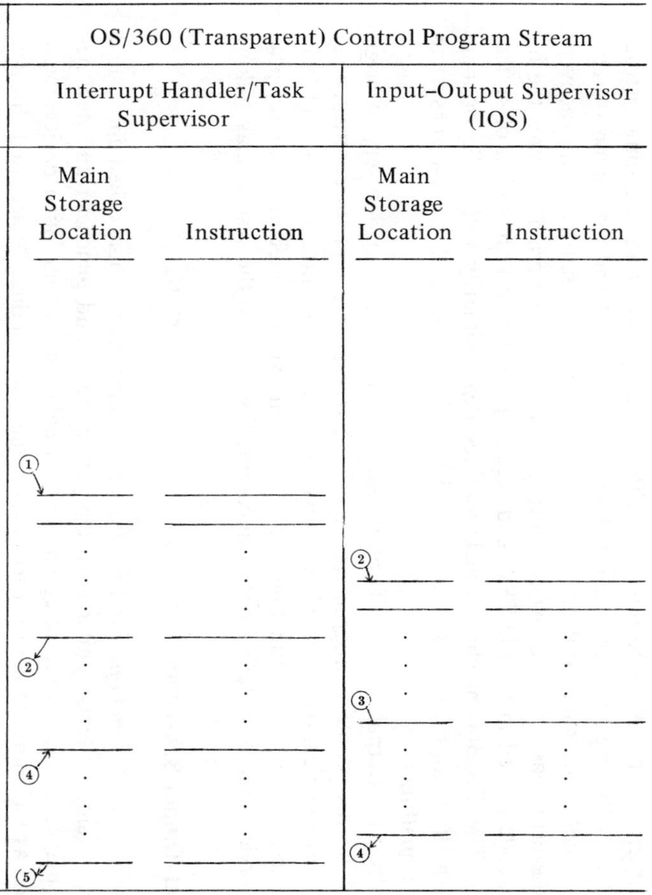

*Directed by c(location 120_{10}), see Table 2.3.

Figure 2.13 Input–Output interrupt. Abstracted from Appendix 1.

An S/370 malfunction detected during a CPU instruction results in a machine check interruption.* Prior to interrupt, CPU circuitry retries an offending instruction or corrects single bit errors on data or instructions fetched from main storage. If these actions are successful, the interrupt merely records that hardware recovery from the error has occurred. After interrupt, the control program analyzes the interrupt code passed in the old PSW and sees to recovery or termination of system activity. The OS/360 machine check routines deal primarily with CPU or main storage malfunctions; routines associated with i–o interrupts deal with i–o subsystem resource malfunctions.

Finally, an external interrupt is provided. A user's request for i–o service originated from his problem program (by SVC). External interrupt, in contrast, may aid the communications terminal user whose program is currently idle, yet who needs service. A terminal function key invokes an external interrupt. Control program service such as entering communications line data to the system may follow.

Input–Output Subsystem

Distribution of function. First-generation systems were often called integrated data processing systems: unit record devices (readers and punches) and new devices (magnetic tape) were integrated into a coherent system. Such devices were designed as i–o units. In contrast to storage, they were indirectly accessed through communications operations initiated by a special (i–o) class of CPU instructions.

With System/360 the i–o device became defined as a unit holding data transferable between the device and storage under program control. The unit in the i–o subsystem charged with the program control of a device is the channel. The user instructs the channel through *commands.*

Why a channel *program?* Why not just *Read,* say, the device. The answer lies with the mechanical nature of devices. Disks have heads that must first *Seek* the desired track, *Search* within the track for the desired data block, and then *Read* the data. *Seek, Search, Read* commands constitute a channel program.

Multiprogramming demands that CPU and i–o subsystem programs be executed simultaneously. A sequence of: CPU instructions, *Seek,* CPU instructions, *Search,* CPU instructions, *Read* is thus inconsistent with multiprogramming efficiency. Accordingly, channel instruction streaming or chaining, involving high-speed command fetch and decode, and high-speed data fetch/store communication with storage, was defined. Because of the different functions performed, differently defined CPU instructions and channel instructions, or commands, evolved.

Since much i–o subsystem function, such as contending with the CPU for storage access, has little to do with the diversity of devices, the need for an all-electronic, device-independent unit, the channel, is seen.

The varied characteristics of devices make diverse i–o subsystem functions necessary as well. Decoded commands streaming from the channel specify actions unique by device class. In data transmission, a disk, resembling a stack of spinning phonograph records, would hardly be expected to obey a *Read Backward* command, standard practice for a tape unit. Similarly, in control commands, space printer differs from move disk arm.

---

* The machine check activity described applies to S/370, and not S/360.

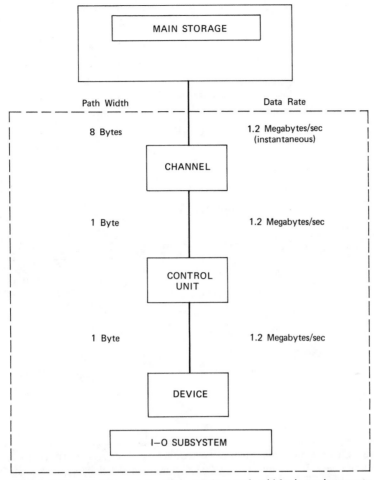

Figure 2.14 Maximum data rates and data path widths in various parts of the i–o subsytem in an IBM S/370 M 165.

In addition to uniqueness, high speed is implied. The IBM 2305 M 1 streams data to the channel at three megabytes per second.

An all-electronic, device-dependent component is needed; this is the S/370 control unit. Diversity, of course, is most present in the electronic/electromagnetic devices attached to S/370.

The i–o subsystem we have discussed is a logical construct, a component of an idealized von Neumann system. In S/370, multiple channels attach multiple control units; to each controller multiple devices attach.*

Figure 2.14 depicts a single channel-control unit-device complex of an S/370

---

* Input–output instruction operands, that is, SIO ⑲⑨, reflect this. The operand format is:

Digit	1	2	3
Unit	Channel	Control unit	Device
Address	1	9	2

CHANNEL COMMAND FORMAT

Command code	Data address
0 7	8 31

Flags	000	//////	Count
32 36	37 39	40 47	48 63

MAIN STORAGE

Location		Contents		
		Symbolic		Absolute
		OP	Command chain	
6F6A0	(buffer)	ROHR Fred A.*		
⋮		⋮		⋮
////////		OP	Command chain	////////
706B8		SEARCH	√	31 0706E3 40 000 05
706C0		TIC	X	08 0706B8 00 000 00
706C8		TIC	X	08 0706D0 00 000 00
706D0		READ COUNT	√	92 070763 60 000 06
706D8		READ DATA	X	86 06F6A0 00 000 00
⋮		⋮		⋮
70763		CCHHR		00 00 00 02 02

Figure 2.15 Channel program (indirectly specified by) READ EMPLOYEE-YTD. The asterisk indicates data. In the command, bit 33 causes command chaining, that is, the command code and data address of the next channel command word are used (√).

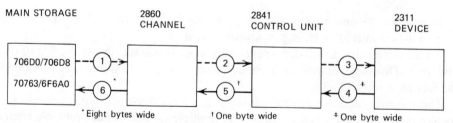

MAIN STORAGE	2860 CHANNEL	2841 CONTROL UNIT	2311 DEVICE

706D0/706D8 --①→ | | --②→ | | --③→
70763/6F6A0 ←⑥-- | | ←⑤-- | | ←④--

*Eight bytes wide   †One byte wide   ‡One byte wide

Figure 2.16 Activity diagram for the i–o subsystem. The solid and broken numbered lines indicate data and control flow, respectively.

M 165 configuration. Data path width and data rate decline in moving from main storage out. On input, in a local storage, the channel collects eight bytes before transmitting data to main storage. Buffering reduces storage contention between channel and CPU. Like data rate, intelligence declines in moving from main storage out. Control units and devices, incapable of instruction streaming, robotlike, obey channel commands.

Example 1—asynchronous service. We consider the asynchronous (to CPU instruction streaming) channel program in an S/370 M 165 2860 configuration. Figures 2.15 and 2.16 depict channel program and i–o subsystem interface activity.

In activity 1 of the latter figure, the channel fetches the contents of location 706D0, the *Read Count* command. After decoding, the channel sends the command's operation code, 92, to the 2841, control unit for the 2311 direct access storage device (DASD), activity 2. The 2841 requests the spinning 2311 unit to read five bytes of count* data, activity 3, and the device accommodates, activities 4, 5, and 6. The count data are transmitted to location 70763 under channel control.

From the symbolic contents of fig. 2.15, location 706D0, the on condition of the channel command chain bit specifies fetch of the next command. *Read Data. Read Data* results in operation code 86 being sent to the 2841 and 2311 (Fig. 2.16, activities 2 and 3), and, consequently, data are read into location 6F6A0, for the eventual use of an applications program. The chain flag is off. Accordingly the channel program ends after *Read Data*. Next a channel-invoked interrupt alerts the control program to that unit's idleness. The control program dispatches the next queued request for channel service.

Example 2—synchronous activity. The *Read* commands of Figure 2.15 executed asynchronously to CPU streaming. Prior to channel *Read* executions, channel activity was initiated by SIO execution (Fig. 2.17). Executions in the instruction (rather than the command) stream are called synchronous.

Prior to issuing SIO, the control program stores a channel address word (CAW) in permanent location 72. Activity 2 results in automatic channel fetch of the CAW, a pointer to the location of the first command to be fetched into the channel. Following command (CCW) fetch, activity 3, the channel signals the successful channel program initiation to the condition code of the PSW, activity 4. Asynchronous to CPU streaming, the channel program proceeds eventually to the *Read Count* and *Read Data* of Figure 2.15, while the CPU fetches the instruction following SIO in the control program stream.

Device classes. System/370 devices are differentiated by their usefulness to human beings. End-use devices used by humans—printers, card readers, punches, and the like—have relatively slow data rates. Circulating storage devices have data rates of hundreds of kilobytes per second. We met magnetic tape in earlier systems; although physically improved in third-generation systems, they remain the same in principle. On the other hand, third-generation DASDs are different—and important. They will be described in some detail.

Direct-Access Storage Devices. A large operating system is, necessarily, a general purpose one. For one thing, the system must accommodate both commercial and scientific users.

A general purpose system needs vast, rapidly accessible secondary data storage. FORTRAN and COBOL must be available (programs are data in secondary storage). Often each must be present in several varieties. For example, FORTRAN version 1 may compile rapidly and execute slowly, thus having a different clientele in the installation than some FORTRAN version 2 that does the opposite.

---

* The count includes a DASD control field that locates *this* data item. It is useful to control program remembrance in a sequential access situation.

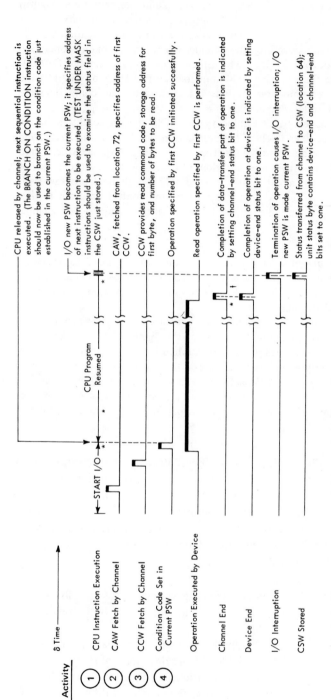

Figure 2.17 The SIO sequence in S/370. From *IBM System/360 Principles of Operation, IBM Systems Reference Library Manual* SA-22-6821.

Efficiency demands accessibility. The user demands immediate access to COBOL version 2; reaching COBOL by accessing and then rejecting FORTRAN version 1, FORTRAN version 2 and COBOL version 1, in the manner of magnetic tape, is unacceptable.

In a large secondary storage device, rapid access to and within a data set for program and problem data retrieval is a unique DASD virtue.* The CPU addressing of the i–o subsystem locates any device (i.e., SIO 192); a DASD addressing adjunct to CPU addressing (i.e., *Read Count* CCHHR) provides the rapid access within a great quantity of data required by OS.†

A DASD unit is a set of magnetic disks mechanically coupled to a rotating shaft. An access arm, or comb, includes read–write sensing heads, one head for each disk. Figure 2.18 depicts a disk surface divided into tracks. Tracks are subdivided into data blocks, the smallest addressable units.

DASD operation can be described as follows: After SIO 392, say, selects the unit, a control command, *Seek,* is fetched into the channel. Fetching and decoding of a five-byte DASD address in the control unit follow. Two bytes, CC, position the comb to a track; HH selects the disk on the vertical comb; R selects the data block on the track. The DASD data block, associated with a unique five-byte address on a disk, is divided into three subblocks: a count, a key, and a data subblock (Fig. 2.19).

The five-byte (CCHHR) location is used to both OPEN and READ, or access, the EMPLOYEE-YTD data set in Fig. 1.5 (excerpt from Appendix 1). OPEN, line 41 of Figure 1.5, executes but once.‡ In response, an SVC routine references a Volume Table of Contents (VTOC), DASD resident, containing the beginning location of the data blocks comprising EMPLOYEE-YTD (EMPYTD).§ With this CCHHR in hand, the executing program may access EMPLOYEE-YTD (see Fig. 2.20).

In Figure 1.5, in contrast to OPEN, READ, line 46, accesses EMPLOYEE-YTD repetitively. Each READ involves a *Seek* command with a CCHHR data operand. Transparent to the SALARIES user, OS/360 systems programs modify the beginning location provided by OPEN and generate the addresses of the sequential DASD blocks as operands for the *Seek*s.

Another mode of access is by a symbolic key, provided in addition to, but independently of, CCHHR. Whereas CCHHR selects the track and disk, the symbolic key selects the data block in the track. The *Search Key* channel command matches the symbolic key, provided by the user, against the contents of the key subblocks within the track—automatically—in the DASD control unit. Following location of the DASD block being sought, transmission command execution begins.

As we shall see in Chapter 9, symbolic accessing may proceed by *Searching* through index tracks that locate the actual data.

Symbolic accessing is of great importance because of ease of use and device independence advantages. Library program and problem data retrievals are both requested by this means.

---

* "Data set" is an OS/360 term for a grouped collection of data.

† 3330 DASD affords 800 megabytes on line.

‡ More properly, the verb OPEN specifies the generation of instructions by the language translator, which, at a later time, execute but once.

§ The connection between EMPYTD and EMPLOYEE-YTD is explained in Chapter 6.

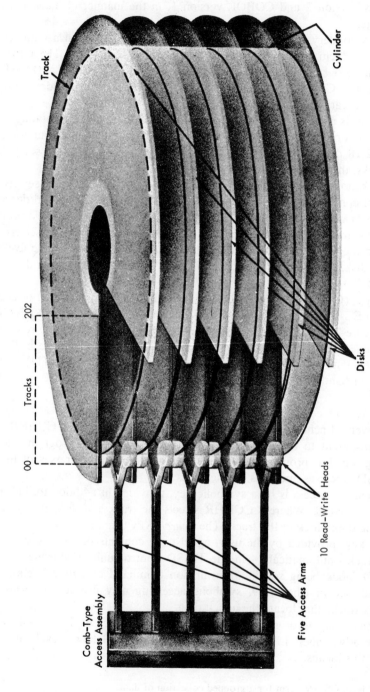

Figure 2.18 System/360 direct-access storage devices. From the IBM handbook *Introduction to IBM System/360 Direct Access Devices and Organization Methods*, C-20-1649.

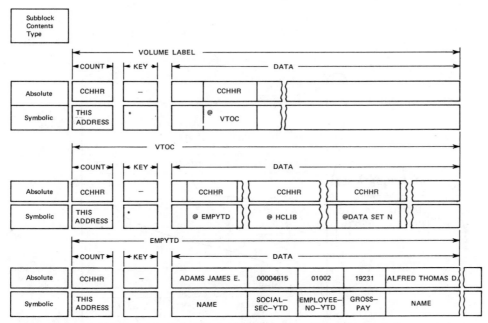

Figure 2.19 Subblocks of DASD organization. Key: C, cylinder; H, head; R, record; *, symbolic information; @ stands for "DASD address of."

Channel considerations. In our earlier discussion of channels we took no notice of type; there are three System/370 channel architectures. Two of these have design differences that center about the DASD *Search* command.

High-speed devices attach to a selector channel, say the IBM 2860. Lower speed devices attach to a byte multiplexor channel, say the IBM 2870. The difference between these two is their duration of dedication to an i–o device. Selector channels transmit blocks of data at high speed. In executing the command *Read Data,* a 2860 is dedicated until the byte count specified in the command is exhausted.

The byte multiplex channel is dedicated to the transmission of a single byte (byte mode) or some fixed but low number of bytes (burst mode) over the channel–outboard (control unit) interface. Multiplexing involves the channel's keeping track of each device's input–output separately. The channel collects the device's data until a sufficient quantity for transmission to main storage buffers is accumulated.

The IBM 2880 block multiplexor, like the 2860 selector channel, transmits data between i–o devices and main storage at high speed. The block multiplexor's ability to multiprogram in the channel is the main difference between the two designs. Figure 2.15 implies a selector dedicated to a channel program and hence idle for long periods because of the electronic/electromechanical cycle time imbalance between channel and device. Hence the block multiplexor design.

Block multiplexing has to do with disconnect command chaining involving two transparent channel operations, channel end and device end. Recognizing that it has finished with the data transmission path to the control unit, the channel generates channel end. Recognizing completion of an order (decoded from a command), a device or control unit generates device end.

INOUT DD DSNAME = EMPYTD

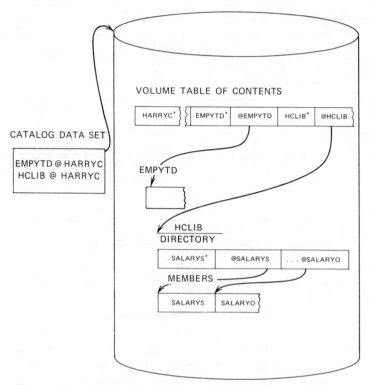

Figure 2.20 DASD unit schematic of various data set organizations. The asterisks indicate symbolic names, and the symbol @ stands for "DASD address of."

Suppose we have two channel programs:

Program 1	Program 2
Search	*Search*
Read	*Read*

The block multiplexor, disconnecting after the transmission activity of the *Search* of program 1—channel end—applies itself to fetching and decoding program$_2$'s *Search* command. Accordingly, while the device and control unit *Search* on behalf of program 1, the channel *Searches* on behalf of program 2.

The IBM 2305 fixed-head file and the 3330 direct-access storage facility, say, exploit block multiplexing through rotational position sensing (RPS). Their data lie within marked angular sectors accounted for by their control units. A block multiplexor might transmit data from several sectors on several units in the time it would take a selector channel to transmit a single block of data.

Only certain i–o devices are suited for block multiplexing, namely DASD and devices with electronic buffer storage in their control units, such as the IBM 3505/3525 card read punch.

We have yet to encounter S/370R—relocate hardware. Before we may do so an introduction to OS/360 software is in order. Relocate hardware and software will be introduced together in Chapter 5. By this sequence the relation between System/370R and System/370—the former being an extension of the latter—will be understood.

EXERCISES

2.1 Write the arithmetic S/370 instructions to perform C = A+B in assembly language for data operands of the following formats: (a) packed decimal, (b) short precision floating point, (c) fixed-point binary.

For the following exercises, refer to Figure 1.5 and Appendix 1:

2.2 Identify the S/370 instruction format types (RX, RR, SS, etc.,) that COBOL generates from source language statements IF, GO, and COMPUTE, statements 53 and 54 on page 212 of Appendix 1, respectively.

2.3 Identify the S/370 type of data operand represented by SOCIAL-SEC-YTD, GROSS-PAY, SLIMIT.

2.4 Can an S/370 CPU perform arithmetic instructions directly on SOCIAL-SEC-YTD? If not, which format instructions are involved in transforming it for computation?

2.5 Data operands intended for nonarithmetic-character-handling processes are commonly known as strings. Identify a SALARIES variable for which COBOL will generate string-handling instructions.

2.6 SALARYL, (see Appendix 1, p. 212) is interrupted between instructions generated from statements 49 and 50. Discuss the impact on processed EMPLOYEE-YTD information.

2.7 Identify SALARIES statements that direct the activities of S/370 CPU, i–o, and main storage.

2.8 The System/360 floating-point registers are optional on the IBM M 40.

(a) Given a version of SALARIES that specifies GROSS-PAY to be in floating-point format, what major consideration determines whether the source program will compile on an M 40 without the floating-point option?

(b) Assume SALARIES compiles on a given S/360 M 40 configuration; will it necessarily execute on the same physical system? On an S/360 M 75?

2.9 Given that the average 2311 disk SEEK time is milliseconds, consider the following channel command sequence in OS/360 and then comment:

Operation	Command Chain
Seek	√
Search Key	—

chapter 3

OS/360 SOFTWARE, THE
TOOLS OF OUR
INQUIRY

3.1 INTRODUCTION

In OS/360, the user relies on the system to do much of the programming work. This chapter, mainly using documentation produced by OS/360, introduces what the system does and what the application programmer does.

First we describe how problem and system programs communicate through CPU local storage, S/370 general purpose registers. Then we analyze the response of System/370 to a SALARIES READ request. Data management and the i–o supervisor, two levels of system programming, are introduced in the process. Later in the chapter we encounter list structures as preparation for understanding OS/360 design.

Although ultimately we address both the problem and system components of the user's request, our concern now is with the former.

3.2 USER REQUEST—TRANSLATION

Our sample request consists of three job steps: language translation, link-edit, and execute.

A system program, COBOL, translates source program input into object module output. A second system program, link-edit, translates an object module into a load module. In the execution step, the instructions of the load module are streamed, transforming the user's input problem data. The complete prototype user job request is included as Appendix 1.

COBOL Language

The first step request includes SALARIES, as input to an OS/360 COBOL language translator (Fig. 3.1). The now familiar statements of lines 40 through 71 appear in the PROCEDURE DIVISION, one of the four basic divisions of the COBOL language. PROCEDURE DIVISION statements specify actions, one verb per statement.

A DATA DIVISION defines PROCEDURE DIVISION nouns. Definition of

1

```
00001              IDENTIFICATION DIVISION.
00002              PROGRAM-ID.
00003              'SALARIES S/Q/U'.
00004              ENVIRONMENT DIVISION.
00005              CONFIGURATION SECTION.
00006              SOURCE-COMPUTER. IBM-360 I65.
00007              OBJECT-COMPUTER. IBM-360 I65.
00008              INPUT-OUTPUT SECTION.
00009              FILE-CONTROL.
00010                  SELECT EMPLOYEE-YTD
00011                      ASSIGN TO 'INOUT' DIRECT-ACCESS 2311.
00012                  SELECT EMPLOYEE-WEEKLY ASSIGN TO 'SYSIN' UNIT-RECORD.
00013              DATA DIVISION.
00014              FILE SECTION.
00015              FD  EMPLOYEE-YTD
00016                  LABEL RECORDS ARE STANDARD
00017                  RECORDING MODE IS F
00018                  BLOCK CONTAINS 10 RECORDS
00019                  RECORD CONTAINS 120 CHARACTERS
00020                  DATA RECORD IS YTD-RECORD.
00021              01  YTD-RECORD.
00022                  02 NAME PICTURE A(32).
00023                  02 SOCIAL-SEC-YTD PICTURE 9(6)V99.
00024                  02 EMPLOYEE-NO-YTD PICTURE 9(5).
00025                  02 CNTROL PICTURE X(1).
00026                  02 GROSS-PAY PICTURE 9(6)V99.
00027                  02 FILLER PICTURE X(66).
00028              FD  EMPLOYEE-WEEKLY
00029                  LABEL RECORDS ARE OMITTED
00030                  RECORDING MODE IS F
00031                  BLOCK CONTAINS 10 RECORDS
00032                  RECORD CONTAINS 80 CHARACTERS
00033                  DATA RECORD IS WEEKLY-RECORD.
00034              01  WEEKLY-RECORD.
00035                  02 EMPLOYEE-NO-WEEKLY PICTURE 9(5).
00036                  02 NAME PICTURE X(32).
00037                  02 FILLER PICTURE X(43).
00038              WORKING-STORAGE SECTION.
00039              77  SLIMIT PICTURE 9(6)V99 COMPUTATIONAL-3 VALUE IS 374.40.
00040              PROCEDURE DIVISION.
00041                  OPEN I-O EMPLOYEE-YTD.
00042                  OPEN INPUT EMPLOYEE-WEEKLY.
00043              READ-WEEKLY.
00044                  READ EMPLOYEE-WEEKLY AT END GO TO READ-YTD.
00045              READ-YTD.
00046                  READ EMPLOYEE-YTD AT END GO TO FINIS.
00047                  IF EMPLOYEE-NO-YTD IS EQUAL TO EMPLOYEE-NO-WEEKLY
00048                                               GO TO LIMIT-TEST.
00049                  REWRITE YTD-RECORD.
00050                  DISPLAY YTD-RECORD.
00051                  GO TO READ-YTD.
00052              LIMIT-TEST.
00053                  IF SLIMIT - SOCIAL-SEC-YTD < GROSS-PAY GO TO LIMIT-CALC.
00054                  COMPUTE SOCIAL-SEC-YTD
00055                      ROUNDED = SOCIAL-SEC-YTD + GROSS-PAY * .048.
00056                  REWRITE YTD-RECORD.
00057                  DISPLAY YTD-RECORD.
00058                  GO TO READ-WEEKLY.
00059              LIMIT-CALC.
00060                  COMPUTE SOCIAL-SEC-YTD
00061                      ROUNDED = SOCIAL-SEC-YTD +
00062                                      (SLIMIT - SOCIAL-SEC-YTD) * .048.
00063                  REWRITE YTD-RECORD.
00064                  DISPLAY YTD-RECORD.
00065                  GO TO READ-WEEKLY.
00066                  CLOSE EMPLOYEE-YTD.
00067                  CLOSE EMPLOYEE-WEEKLY.
00068              FINIS. ENTER LINKAGE.
00069                  CALL 'DUMPIT'.
00070                  ENTER COBOL.
00071                  STOP RUN.
```

Figure 3.1 SALARIES, source program input. (Excerpt from Appendix 1.)

Table 3.1   COBOL Language System Independence—Identical Data Card
Information as It Exists in the Memory of Different Systems

System	Main Storage Address					Comments
	1	2	3	4	5	
IBM 7080	3	0	4	6	+	Six data bits per character
S/370	03	04	6+	?	?	Eight data bits per character, packed-decimal format

the noun SOCIAL-SEC-YTD specifies the type of CPU instructions to compile; depending on its DATA DIVISION context, COMPUTE, line 54, directs the generation of fixed-point, floating-point, or packed-decimal arithmetic instructions.

PROCEDURE DIVISION statements and DATA DIVISION noun definitions highlight the machine independence of the COBOL language. As shown in Table 3.1, no language distinction is made between that SOCIAL-SEC-YTD data appearing in S/370 and IBM 7080 main storage.

In the IDENTIFICATION DIVISION the user names his program, SALARIES.

Finally, an ENVIRONMENT DIVISION groups the machine dependencies of the source programs. Converting a source program from one system to another affects these entries most.

The COBOL language represents a logical system. In lines 54 and 55 of Figure 3.1, the user adds SOCIAL-SEC-YTD to GROSS PAY * .048. He does not PACK, MP, PACK (see Fig. 3.2).

COBOL Program

This system program expands its input, a source program in the COBOL language, into its output, an object module.

COBOL also prints out user debugging aids. These include a listing of input source statements, a symbolic object module listing, a storage map, and a glossary.

SALARIES prefixes a line number to each statement, as shown in Figure 3.2.

The symbolic object module listing is in S/370 symbolic assembly format. From Figure 3.2, line 53, we see: 46A, the instruction's relative location;* F2 . . . , the generated machine instruction; and PACK. . . , the symbolic representation of the generated instruction. The compiler assigns relative locations from zero, counting up.

The glossary displays how COBOL has interpreted definitions in the DATA DIVISION (Fig. 3.3).

The storage map contains locations essential to a program executing in the OS/360 multiprogramming environment. In SALARIES these are unreferenced; COBOL, providing a software level of transparency, generates them gratis.

Figure 3.3 depicts COBOL general purpose register assignments, useful in locating source program nouns in execution-time dumps. Nouns are addressed by dis-

* See Appendix 12, Hexidecimal Tables.

```
            1

            00001              IDENTIFICATION DIVISION.
            00002              PROGRAM-ID.
            00003              'SALARIES S/O/U'.
                                      :
            00049                     REWRITE YTD-RECORD.
(a)         00050                     DISPLAY YTD-RECORD.
            00051                     GO TO READ-YTD.
            00052              LIMIT-TEST.
            00053                     IF SLIMIT - SOCIAL-SEC-YTD < GROSS-PAY GO TO LIMIT-CALC.
            00054                     COMPUTE SOCIAL-SEC-YTD
            00055                          ROUNDED = SOCIAL-SEC-YTD + GROSS-PAY * .048.
            00056                     REWRITE YTD-RECORD.
```

```
   49    REWRITE   000444                   GN=04    EQU  *
                   000444  58 10 C 054                L    1,054(0,12)            DCB=1
                   000448  58 F0 1 030                L    15,030(0,1)
                   00044C  45 E0 F 004                BAL  14,004(0,15)
   50    DISPLAY   000450                   GN=05    EQU  *
                   00045C  58 F0 C 000                L    15,000(0,12)           V(IHCFDISP)
                   000454  C5 1F                      BALR 1,15
                   000456  00C1                       DC   X'0001'
                   000458  C0                         DC   X'00'
                   000459  000078                     DC   X'000078'
                   00045C  0D0001C4                   DC   X'0D0001C4'            BLI=1
                   000460  C000                       DC   X'0000'
                   000462  FFFF                       DC   X'FFFF'
   51    GO        000464  58 10 C 00C                L    1,00C(0,12)            PN=02
                   000468  07 F1                      BCR  15,1
   52    *LIMIT-TEST
                   00046A                   PN=03    EQU  *
   53    IF        00046A  F2 77 D 198 7 020          PACK 198(8,13),020(8,7)     TS=09      DNM=1-168
                   000470  F8 74 D 190 6 000          ZAP  190(8,13),000(5,6)     TS=01      DNM=1-391
                   00047E  FB 44 D 193 D 198          SP   193(5,13),198(5,13)    TS=04      TS=012
                   00047C  F2 77 D 198 7 02E          PACK 198(8,13),02E(8,7)     TS=09      DNM=1-230
                   000482  F9 44 D 193 D 198          CP   193(5,13),198(5,13)    TS=04      TS=012
                   000488  58 F0 C 030                L    15,030(0,12)           GN=06
                   00048C  07 AF                      BCR  10,15
   53    GO        00048E  58 10 C 014                L    1,014(0,12)            PN=04
                   000492  07 F1                      BCR  15,1
   54    COMPUTE   000494                   GN=06    EQU  *
                   000494  F2 77 D 198 7 02E          PACK 198(8,13),02E(8,7)     TS=09      DNM=1-230
                   00049A  FC 61 D 199 C 07B          MP   199(7,13),07B(2,12)    TS=010     LIT+27
                   0004A0  F2 77 D 190 7 020          PACK 190(8,13),020(8,7)     TS=C1      DNM=1-168
                   0004A6  FC 72 D 190 C 07D          MP   190(8,13),07D(3,12)    TS=C1      LIT+29
                   0004AC  FA 65 D 199 D 192          AP   199(7,13),192(6,13)    TS=C10     TS=03
                   0004B2  F9 70 D 198 C 07F          CP   198(8,13),07F(1,12)    TS=09      LIT+31
                   0004B8  58 F0 C 044                L    15,044(0,12)           GN=011
                   0004BC  07 4F                      BCR  4,15
                   0004BE  FA 61 D 199 C 080          AP   199(7,13),080(2,12)    TS=010     LIT+32
                   0004C4  58 F0 C 048                L    15,048(0,12)           GN=012
                   0004C8  C7 FF                      BCR  15,15
                   0004CA                   GN=011   EQU  *
                   0004CA  FB 61 D 199 C 080          SP   199(7,13),080(2,12)    TS=C10     LIT+32
                   0004D0                   GN=012   EQU  *
                   0004D0  F1 75 D 198 D 198          MVC  198(8,13),198(6,13)    TS=C9      TS=C9
                   0004D6  F3 74 7 020 D 198          UNPK 020(8,7),198(5,13)     DNM=1-168  TS=012
                   0004DC  96 F0 7 027                OI   027(7),X'F0'           DNM=1-168+7
   56    REWRITE   0004E0  58 10 C 054                L    1,054(0,12)            DCB=1
                   0004E4  58 F0 1 030                L    15,030(0,1)
                   0004E8  45 E0 F 004                BAL  14,004(0,15)
```

(b)

Figure 3.2 SALARIES source statements (a), which COBOL translates to object module instructions (b). (Excerpt from Appendix 1).

INTRNL NAME	LVL	SOURCE NAME	BASE	DISPL	INTRNL NAME	DEFINITION	USAGE	R	O	Q
DNM=1-109	FD	EMPLOYEE-YTD	DCB=01		DNM=1-109		QSAM			
DNM=1-133	01	YTD-RECORD	BLI=1	000	DNM=1-133	CS 0CL120	GRCUP			
DNM=1-155	02	NAME	BLI=1	000	DNM=1-155	DS 32C	DISP			
DNM=1-168	02	SOCIAL-SEC-YTD	BLI=1	020	DNM=1-168	DS 8C	DISP-NM			
DNM=1-191	02	EMPLOYEE-NO-YTD	BLI=1	028	DNM=1-191	DS 5C	DISP-NM			
DNM=1-215	02	CNTROL	BLI=1	02D	DNM=1-215	DS 1C	DISP			
DNM=1-230	02	GROSS-PAY	BLI=1	02E	DNM=1-230	DS 8C	DISP-NM			
DNM=1-248	02	FILLER	BLI=1	036	DNM=1-248	DS 66C	DISP			
DNM=1-263	FD	EMPLOYEE-WEEKLY	DCB=02		DNM=1-263		QSAM			
DNM=1-290	01	WEEKLY-RECORD	BLI=2	000	DNM=1-290	CS 0CL80	GROUP			
DNM=1-315	02	EMPLOYEE-NO-WEEKLY	BLI=2	000	DNM=1-315	DS 5C	DISP-NM			
DNM=1-342	02	NAME	BLI=2	005	DNM=1-342	DS 32C	DISP			
DNM=1-358	02	FILLER	BLI=2	025	DNM=1-358	DS 43C	DISP			
DNM=1-391	77	SLIMIT	BLI=3	000	DNM=1-391	DS 5P	COMP-3			

```
REGISTER ASSIGNMENT
   REG 6   BLI=3
   REG 7   BLI=1
   REG 8   BLI=2
```

Figure 3.3 COBOL-produced glossary and general purpose register assignment. (Excerpt from Appendix 1.)

placements to the locations in general purpose base registers. In Figure 3.2, we find SOCIAL-SEC-YTD in the object module at location 20(8,7).* At execution time, register 7 contains 6FAD8 and SOCIAL-SEC-YTD resides in location 6FAF8.

Figure 3.2 demonstrates that COBOL directly generates instructions to handle data, perform arithmetic, and control sequencing. In contrast, COBOL expands DISPLAY by setting up a Branch And Link to a subroutine. Link-edit, the second step of our request, combines the generated object module with the subroutine IHDFDISP.

3.3 USER REQUEST—LINK-EDIT

Like building blocks, OS/360 object and load modules are combined into executable load modules by the link-edit system program.

Each module contains two dictionaries.† The first includes addresses that might change when *this* module is combined with another; the second retains source program symbols, which, like DUMPIT, are cross-referenced between combined modules. Link-edit processes these dictionaries.

Figure 3.4 demonstrates load module relocatability, essential in a multiprogramming operating system. The execution step loader, as well as link-edit, processes the relocation dictionary. Figure 3.5 depicts link-edited combinations specifiable by the user.

In our example, link-edit accepts object module input, SALARYO, and provides output, SALARYL, to a load module library. In addition to its main function, linking, link-edit produces a storage map and a cross-reference listing of its handiwork. From the cross-reference, SALARYO locations remain referenced to zero (Fig. 3.6).

---

* The SS instruction address format of displacement (length, base register).

† Source module libraries are retained in System/370 in symbolic form exactly as they appear in the input card deck.

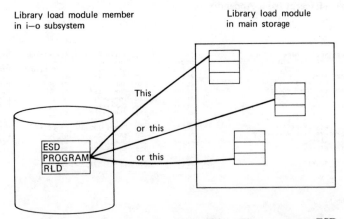

Figure 3.4 Library program relocatability. The acronyms ESD and RLD stand for external symbol dictionary and relocation dictionary, respectively.

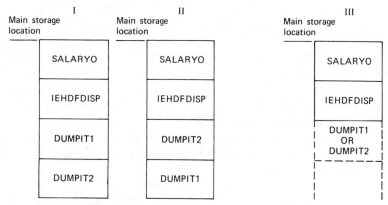

I	II	III
Main storage location	Main storage location	Main storage location
SALARYO	SALARYO	SALARYO
IEHDFDISP	IEHDFDISP	IEHDFDISP
DUMPIT1	DUMPIT2	DUMPIT1 OR DUMPIT2
DUMPIT2	DUMPIT1	

Figure 3.5 Various possible SALARYL main storage configurations. In configuration III, DUMPIT1 and DUMPIT2 time share the same space in an overlay structure.

CROSS REFERENCE TABLE

```
CONTROL SECTION                       ENTRY

    NAME    ORIGIN  LENGTH            NAME   LOCATION   NAME   LOCATION   NAME   LOCATION   NAME   LOCATION
$PRIVATE      00     68E
 DUMPIT      690      7C
 IHDFDISP*   710     60A


 LOCATION  REFERS TO SYMBOL  IN CONTROL SECTION          LOCATION  REFERS TO SYMBOL  IN CONTROL SECTION
   2F8          IHDFDISP       IHDFDISP                    2FC          DUMPIT           DUMPIT

ENTRY ADDRESS        00
TOTAL LENGTH         D20

****RUN       DOES NOT EXIST BUT HAS BEEN ADDED TO DATA SET
```

Figure 3.6 Link-edit map and cross-reference. (Except from Appendix 1).

```
                LEVEL 1JAN67                                         COBOL F


                    1


                   00001            IDENTIFICATION DIVISION.
                   00002            PROGRAM-ID.
                   00003            'SALARIES S/O/U'.
                                        :
                                        :
                   00057                DISPLAY YTD-RECORD.
                   00058                GO TO READ-WEEKLY.
                   00059         LIMIT-CALC.
                   00060                COMPUTE SOCIAL-SEC-YTD
    (a)            00061                    ROUNDED = SOCIAL-SEC-YTD +
                   00062                           (SLIMIT - SOCIAL-SEC-YTD) * .048.
                   00063                REWRITE YTD-RECORD.
                   00064                DISPLAY YTD-RECORD.
                   00065                GO TO READ-WEEKLY.
                   00066                CLOSE EMPLOYEE-YTD.
                   00067                CLOSE EMPLOYEE-WEEKLY.
                   00068         FINIS. ENTER LINKAGE.
                   00069                CALL 'DUMPIT'.
                   00070                ENTER COBOL.
                   00071                STOP RUN.


           68    *FINIS
                              000620                    PN=05    EQU   *
           68    ENTER
    (b)    69    CALL        000620  58 FC C 004                 L     15,004(0,12)      V(DUMPIT )
                              000624  05 EF                       BALR  14,15
           70    ENTER
           71    STOP        000626  58 DC D 004                 L     13,004(0,13)
                              00062A  98 EC D 00C                 LM    14,12,00C(13)
```

Figure 3.7 SALARIES statements (a), which COBOL translates to object module instructions (b). (Excerpt from Appendix 1).

SALARIES invokes link-edit explicitly through CALL and implicitly.

In response to CALL, link-edit retrieves DUMPIT from a user library and then combines DUMPIT and SALARYO into SALARYL. In Figure 3.7, SALARIES, lines 68 through 70 and object module locations 620 through 624 illustrate the source statements and generated instructions for link-editing SALARYL.

In response to DISPLAY, line 57 of Figure 3.7, link-edit invokes a routine from the language translator's private library. Such IBM-supplied programs display data, convert from decimal to binary, and the like.

Tables 3.2, 3.3, and 3.4 follow an object module resulting from SALARIES through link-edit into the first execution time activity, the loading of the combined load module SALARYL into storage.

Table 3.2   Situation after Translation Step. The Arrow Indicates Contents to be Modified in Subsequent Step(s).

Object Module SALARYO

S/370 Address		Contents		
Relative	Symbolic	Absolute	Symbolic	*Comments*
000	INIT1	07 00	BCR 0,0	Start
.	.	.	.	
.	.	.	.	
.	.	.	.	
2F8	PGT	00 00 0 000	–	Table
.	.	.	.	
.	.	.	.	
620	–	58 FO C 000	L 15,004(0,12)	⎱ Link
624	–	05 EF	BALR 14,15	⎰
.	.	.	.	
.	.	.	.	
68C	–	–	–	End

Load Module IHDFDISPLAY from COBOL Language Translator Library

000	ENTRY	–	–	Start
.	.	.	.	
.	.	.	.	
60A	END	–	–	End

Object Module DUMPIT from User-Written Library

000	ENTRY	–	–	Start
.	.	.	.	
.	.	.	.	
034	END	–	–	End

Table 3.3   Situation after Link-Edit Step. The Symbol / Designates a Location; The Arrow Indicates Contents Modified During This Step.

Load Module SALARYL

S/370 Address		Contents		
Relative	Symbolic	Absolute	Symbolic	*Comments*
000	INITI	07 00	BCR 0,0	Start of SALA-RYL load module
.	.	.	.	
.	.	.	.	
2F8	PGT	00 00 0 710	l(IHDFDISPLAY)	Table
.	.	.	.	
.	.	.	.	
.	.	.	.	
620	–	58 FO 0 000	L 15,000(0,12)	Link
624	–	05 IF	BALR 1, 15	
.	.	.	.	
.	.	.	.	
.	.	.	.	
68E	–	–	–	End of SALARYO (modified)
690	ENTRY	–	–	Start of DUMPIT
.	.	.	.	
.	.	.	.	
6C4	END	–	–	End of DUMPIT
710	ENTRY	–	–	Start of IEHDISPLAY
.	.	.	.	
.	.	.	.	
D1A	END	–	–	End of IEH-DISPLAY End of SALARYL

Having created a load module, link-edit inserts it into a library. Link-edit inserts supervisory and problem state routines into SYS1.SVCLIB and SYS1.LINKLIB respectively.* A user may specify a load module to be shareable among multiple programs in execution. During library insertion, link-edit marks the module accordingly.

* The name SYS1. infers that the volume and S/370 unit of residence of the library data set (e.g., 191) are known to the control program through its catalog data set, SYS1.CATLG. SVC service load modules reside on SVCLIB; LINKLIB members include FORTRAN, COBOL, and PL/I, job and data management routines, and user problem load modules.

Table 3.4 Situation after Execution Step Loading into S/370 Memory. The Symbol *l* Designates An S/370 Location; The Arrow Indicates Contents Modified During Execution Step Loading into S/370 Memory. Note: After Loading, S/370 CPU Control is Passed to INIT1. Subsequently Register 12 is Initialized to Location of PGT.

Load Module SALARYL

S/370 Address		Contents		
Absolute	Symbolic	Absolute	Symbolic	*Comments*
492E0	INIT1	07 00	BCR 0,0	Start of SALA-RYL load module
495D8	PGT	00 499 F0	*l*(IHDFDISPLAY)	Table
49900	–	58 F0 C 004	L 15,004(0,12)	Link
49904	–	05 EF	BALR 14,15	
4996E	–	–	–	End of SALARYO (modified)
49970	ENTRY	–	–	DUMPIT
499EC	END	–	–	
499F0	ENTRY	–	–	IEHDISPLAY
49FFA	END	–	–	

3.4 USER REQUEST—EXECUTION

Translated and link-edited, SALARYL is relocated and loaded into storage in the execution step.

An OS/360 dump program documents SALARYL execution. Dump may be invoked by a user, through A bend, SVC 13, or by the OS/360 supervisor in program or hardware error circumstances.

Dump displays storage at the time of the dump program's invocation. SALARYL, Figure 3.11*a*, and SALARYO, Figure 3.11*b*, demonstrate relocation during execution time loading. In the dump printout the format is hexidecimal to the left and byte to the right. In the beginning of the dump critical control program information from storage appears. A snapshot of SALARYL begins in location 492E0. Preceding SALARYL the contents of CPU registers are displayed.

In addition to main storage dumps, OS/360 provides auxiliary storage dumps, such as the DASD unit dump of Appendix 9.

```
41    OPEN      00037A                   START  EQU  *
                00037A  58 1C C 054              L    1,054(0,12)           DCB=1
                00037E  50 10 D 1D0              ST   1,1D0(0,13)           PRM=1
                000382  92 84 D 1D0              MVI  1D0(13),X'84'         PRM=1
                000386  41 10 D 1D0              LA   1,1D0(0,13)           PRM=1
                00038A  0A 13                    SVC  19
                00038C  58 1C C 054              L    1,054(0,12)           DCB=1
                000390  58 2C C 03C              L    2,03C(0,12)           GN=09
                000394  91 10 1 030              TM   030(1),X'10'
                000398  C7 12                    BCR  1,2
                00039A  D2 1A D 1A0 C 06C        MVC  1A0(27,13),06C(12)    TS2=1      LIT+0
                0003A0  D2 07 D 1BB 1 028        MVC  1BB(8,13),028(1)      TS2=28
                0003A6  41 10 D 1A0              LA   1,1A0(0,13)           TS2=1
                0003AA  0A 23                    SVC  35
                0003AC                   GN=09  EQU  *
42    OPEN      0003AC  58 1C C 058              L    1,058(0,12)           DCB=2
                0003B0  50 10 D 1D0              ST   1,1D0(0,13)           PRM=1
                0003B4  92 80 D 1D0              MVI  1D0(13),X'80'         PRM=1
                0003B8  41 10 D 1D0              LA   1,1D0(0,13)           PRM=1
                0003BC  0A 13                    SVC  19
                0003BE  58 1C C 058              L    1,058(0,12)           DCB=2
                0003C2  58 20 C 040              L    2,040(0,12)           GN=010
                0003C6  91 10 1 030              TM   030(1),X'10'
                0003CA  07 12                    BCR  1,2
                0003CC  D2 1A D 1A0 C 06C        MVC  1A0(27,13),06C(12)    TS2=1      LIT+0
                0003D2  D2 07 D 1BB 1 028        MVC  1BB(8,13),028(1)      TS2=28
                0003D8  41 10 D 1A0              LA   1,1A0(0,13)           TS2=1
                0003DC  0A 23                    SVC  35
                0003DE                   GN=010 EQU  *
43    *READ-WEEKLY
                0003DE                   PN=01  EQU  *
44    READ      0003DE  58 1C C 058              L    1,058(0,12)           DCB=2
                0003E2  D2 02 1 021 C 01D        MVC  021(3,1),01D(12)                 GN=01+1
                0003E8  58 F0 1 030              L    15,030(0,1)
                0003EC  05 EF                    BALR 14,15
                0003EE  50 1C D 1C8              ST   1,1C8(0,13)           BLI=2
                0003F2  58 8C D 1C8              L    8,1C8(0,13)           BLI=2
                0003F6  58 1C C 00C              L    1,00C(0,12)           PN=02
                0003FA  07 F1                    BCR  15,1
```

$$\vdots$$

```
REGS AT ENTRY TO ABEND

    FLTR 0-6    D46E3B8C5370170F    0000000020000000         0000000000000000    0001DC0800000088

    REGS 0-7    00000218    80000100    000496BE    70049982    330492E0    50049938    000493F0    0006FAD8
    REGS 8-15   00070618    00049960    000492E0    000492E0    000495D8    000499A4    70049906    00049970

LOAD MODULE   SALARYL

0492E0  070090EC D00C185D 05F0989F F00607FF    00049960 000492E0 000492E0 000495D8    *.........0..0..............Q*
049300  000493F8 0004965A 00049912 96121034    07FEFFFF FFFFD9D7 C4F04040 40400207    *....8...............RPD0   K.*
049320  00000000 14000000 00000001 00008082    00210E29 0206F698 00004000 00000001    *...............6... .....*
049340  46049700 90000000 00544848 C001CF8C    1606EC60 0006EDC8 10000001 00490480    *................H........*
049360  30037040 00070668 0006FB50 0006FAD8    00000078 00000001 00000000 0007E3C0    *.... ...........Q.......T.*
049380  00000000 98481000 00000000 2D000000    005A000A 000B0B8A 00281C7E 020705C0    *.................=...=...*
0493A0  00504000 00000001 4604960C 90000000    00684800 C001D82C 1207E8E0 0007E800    *. ..............Q...Y...Y.*
0493C0  08000001 10010050 00005000 00070568    00070668 00070618 00000050 00000001    *.........................*
0493E0  00000000 0007E3C0 00000000 B23258F0    00003744 0FF0805A 18445850 00070780    *......T.......0....0......*
049400  00084160 70049906 00049970 00000218    00049900 0004968E 5001DC7C 330492E0    *.........Q.......=...Q...*
049420  50049938 000493F0 0006FAD8 00070618    00049960 000492E0 000492E0 000495D8    *..0..Q..............Q*
049440  2000004B 4780B21C 95F92000 0004965A    00000A8E E3C46009 00000078 C4000000    *........9......YTD.R...D..*
049460  00000000 00000000 00000000 00000000    00400024 00E6C5C5 D2D3E860 D9C5C3D6    *............WEEKLY.RECO*
049480  D9C40000 00000000 00000000 00000000    00000040 C3E340D5 E4D4C2C5 D9400A23    *RD.............CT NUMBER ..*
0494A0  4510A368 0A062AD0 00062ACC 00210000    C9C5C6C1 C3E3D840 40D9C5D7 D3E840D7    *...........IEFACTQ REPLY P*
0494C0  D9D601C5 C3E340D5 E404C2C5 D9100A23    41108546 41000001 A011B811 5010B546    *RJECT NUMBER.............*
0494E0  18184120 B54A47F0 B2B8E5818 00000000    00000000 000497DE 0004968E 01000000    *..........0.......*
049500  900497CC 000499F0 00000001 000497E0    000496BE 5001DC7C 330492E0 50049938    *..........0........*
049520  000493F0 0006FAD8 00049960 0004968E    000492E0 000492E0 000495D8 000497E0    *...0...Q...H...........Q...*
049540  000499F0 00000001 8F0704B0 0004968E    00010000 000497DE 00000000 00000000    *...0.............*
049560  00000000 00000000 00000000 00000000    00000000 00000000 00000000 8A000603    *...................*
049580  00000108 02080002 00000000 4200000C    00000000 0004800C 30080080 00200108    *...................*
0495A0  02080002 A80D0000 00000000 00000000    00000000 00000000 00000000 0006FAD8    *...................Q*
0495C0  00070618 000493F0 80049388 00000000    00000000 00000000 000499F0 00049970    *...0............0...0...*
0495E0  000496BE 000496E2 0004974A 000497E6    000496BE 000496DC 00049700 00049706    *........S.....W.........*
049600  00049724 00049730 00049774 000497CC    0004984A 0004968C 0004968E 000497AA    *...................*
049620  000497B0 00049828 0004982E 00049320    00049388 330492E0 00230000 C9C5D8F9    *...................IEQ9*
049640  F9F9C940 D5D640C4 C440C3C1 D9C440C6    D6D94040 8C01000C 500C5810 C0545010    *991 NO DD CARD FOR ..........*
049660  D1D09284 D1D04110 D1D00A13 5810C054    5820C03C 91101030 0712D21A D1A0C060    *J...J...J.............K.J..*
049680  D20701BB 10284110 D1A00A23 5810C058    5010D1D0 9280D1D0 4110D1D0 0A135810    *K.J...J.........J..J..J...*
0496A0  C0585820 C0409110 10300712 D21AD1A0    C060D207 D1BB1028 4110D1A0 A235810    *......K.J..K.J....J...*
0496C0  C058D202 1021C01D 58F01030 05EF5010    D1C85880 D1C85810 C00C07F1 5810C00C    *...K....0....JH.JH.......1*
0496E0  07F15810 C0540202 1021C021 58F01030    05EF5010 D1C45870 D1C45810 C02407F1    *.1....K....0.....JD..JD....1*
```

Figure 3.11 SALARYO (a), and SALARYL (b) loaded in the execution step. The arrow indicates Start. (Excerpt from Appendix 1.)

```
                              EXTERNAL SYMBOL DICTIONARY                                    PAGE    1

SYMBUL   TYPE  ID    ADDR  LENGTH LDID                                        ASM 0102 18.56 09/27/73

DUMPIT    SD  0001 000000 00007C
    LOC   OBJECT CODE    ADDR1 ADDR2  STMT    SOURCE STATEMENT                 ASM 0102 18.56 09/27/73

   000000                               1 DUMPIT    CSECT
                                        2            SAVE    (14,12),,*
   000000 47F0 F00C      0000C          3+           B       12(0,15)          BRANCH AROUND ID        00860000
   000004 06                            4+           DC      AL1(6)                                    00880000
   000005 C4E4D4D7C9E3                  5+           DC      CL6*DUMPIT*       IDENTIFIER              00900000
   000008 00
   00000C 90EC D00C      0000C          6+           STM     14,12,12(13)      SAVE REGISTERS          01180000
   000010 053C                          7            BALR    3,0
                         00012          8            USING   *,3
   000012 500C 3026      00038          9            ST      13,SAVE+4
   000016 41D0 3022      00034         10            LA      13,SAVE
   00001A                              11            ABEND   256,DUMP
   00001A 0700                         12+           DS      0H                                        06080019
   00001C 47F0 3012      00024         13+           CNOP    0,4                                       00860000
   000020 8C                           14+           B       *+8                BRANCH AROUND CONSTANT  00880019
   000021 000100                       15+           DC      AL1(128)                                  00900000
   000024 5810 300E      0002C         16+           DC      AL3(256)           DUMP/STEP CODE          00920000
   000028 0A0D                         17+           L       1,*-4              COMPLETION CODE         00940000
                                       18+           SVC     13                 LOAD CODES INTO REG 1   
   00002A                              19 RETURN     RETURN  (14,12),T          LINK TO ABEND ROUTINE   00960000
   00002A 98EC D00C      0000C         20+RETURN     DS      0H
   00002E 92FF D00C      0000C         21+           LM      14,12,12(13)       RESTORE THE REGISTERS   00100000
   000032 07FE                         22+           MVI     12(13),X*FF*       SET RETURN INDICATION   00260000
   000034                              23+           BR      14                 RETURN                  00640000
                                       24 SAVE       DS      18F                                        00800000
                                       25            END

SYMBOL    LEN    VALUE   DEFN    REFERENCES                                    ASM 0102 18.56 09/27/73

DUMPIT   00001 00000000 00001
RETURN   00002 0000002A 00020
SAVE     00004 00000034 00024  00009 00010
```

Figure 3.12 Assembler output. (Excerpt from Appendix 1.)

3.5 ASSEMBLY LANGUAGE

We frequently use COBOL to invoke OS/360 functions. An OS/360 assembly language translator could assume this role, at some loss of the clarity of the user's intent. Assembler, like the COBOL of our prototype, may be the first of three steps of a language translation request. In contrast to COBOL, assembly language source programs are essentially system dependent.

In addition to an object module, the assembler produces a secondary output, printed listings. These include listings of the dictionaries used by link-edit; a cross-reference glossary; and a symbolic module listing (Fig. 3.12). As in first- and second-generation implementations, the OS/360 assembler normally creates one instruction for each input source language instruction, statements 7 and 9. Abend, statement 11, expands into an instruction sequence with the character "+" appended to the symbolic operation field.

Abend, an assembler macro, resembles a COBOL verb; one macro expands into multiple instructions. Indeed, READ, COMPUTE, and WRITE of SALARIES are macros in the coherent framework of the COBOL language. For now, we acknowledge the assembly macro's existence and alert ourselves to distinguish between these and identical COBOL verbs.*

3.6 PROTOTYPE REQUEST EXAMPLE

We turn to SALARYL in execution. In SALARIES, COBOL translates OPEN EMPLOYEE-YTD into Open, SVC 19; SVC 19 is an initialization routine. By

---

* The publication *OS/360 Supervisor Macros* IBM Systems Reference Library Manual C28-6647, is a detailed exposition of IBM–provided macros processed by the assembly language translator. In addition to these system-defined macros, the user may define and expand his own independent set using assembler facilities.

CDE

```
01F330  ATR1 0B  NCDE 000000  ROC-RB 0001E170  NM RUN       USE 01  EPA 0492D8  ATR2 20
01E5B0  ATR1 31  NCDE 01F330  ROC-RB 00000000  NM IGC0A05A  USE 02  EPA 06F980  ATR2 28
020380  ATR1 88  NCDE 020380  ROC-RB 00000000  NM IGG019CD  USE 07  EPA 07E480  ATR2 20
020290  ATR1 88  NCDE 0202C0  ROC-RB 00000000  NM IGG019BA  USE 07  EPA 07DE80  ATR2 20
020250  ATR1 88  NCDE 020290  ROC-RB 00000000  NM IGG019BB  USE 07  EPA 07E118  ATR2 20


01F170  ATR1 0B  NCDE 000000  ROC-RB 0001E170  NM RUN       USE 01  EPA 0492E0  ATR2 20
01E518  ATR1 31  NCDE 01D6C0  ROC-RB 00000000  NM IGC0A05A  USE 02  EPA 06E180  ATR2 28
020380  ATR1 88  NCDE 020380  ROC-RB 00000000  NM IGG019CD  USE 07  EPA 07E480  ATR2 20
020290  ATR1 88  NCDE 0202C0  ROC-RB 00000000  NM IGG019BA  USE 07  EPA 07DE80  ATR2 20
020250  ATR1 88  NCDE 020290  ROC-RB 00000000  NM IGG019BB  USE 07  EPA 07E118  ATR2 20
020380  ATR1 88  NCDE 020380  ROC-RB 00000000  NM IGG019CD  USE 08  EPA 07E480  ATR2 20
020220  ATR1 B0  NCDE 020250  ROC-RB 00000000  NM IGG019AI  USE 04  EPA 07E098  ATR2 20
020380  ATR1 B0  NCDE 0203E0  ROC-RB 00000000  NM IGG019AR  USE 04  EPA 07E690  ATR2 20
020320  ATR1 B0  NCDE 020350  ROC-RB 00000000  NM IGG019CH  USE 03  EPA 07E350  ATR2 20
020480  ATR1 B0  NCDE 020480  ROC-RB 00000000  NM IGG019AA  USE 03  EPA 07E8E0  ATR2 20
0203E0  ATR1 B0  NCDE 020420  ROC-RB 00000000  NM IGG019AQ  USE 03  EPA 07E800  ATR2 20
020350  ATR1 B0  NCDE 020380  ROC-RB 00000000  NM IGG019CC  USE 04  EPA 07E3C0  ATR2 20
0202F0  ATR1 B0  NCDE 020320  ROC-RB 00000000  NM IGG019CI  USE 04  EPA 07E268  ATR2 20
01D6C0  ATR1 30  NCDE 01D6D8  ROC-RB 00000000  NM IGG019C3  USE 01  EPA 06EA20  ATR2 20
01D6D8  ATR1 30  NCDE 01D948  ROC-RB 00000000  NM IGG019CG  USE 01  EPA 06EB68  ATR2 20
01D948  ATR1 30  NCDE 01D8E0  ROC-RB 00000000  NM IGG019AE  USE 01  EPA 06EC60  ATR2 20
01D8E0  ATR1 30  NCDE 01DF30  ROC-RB 00000000  NM IGG019AW  USE 01  EPA 070820  ATR2 20
01DF30  ATR1 30  NCDE 01F170  ROC-RB 00000000  NM IGG019AF  USE 01  EPA 06EDC8  ATR2 20
```

Figure 3.13 Data management load modules loaded by Open. Top: before Open; bottom: after Open. (Excerpt from Appendix 1.)

providing DASD addresses it enables SALARYL to access (READ/WRITE) EMPLOYEE-YTD repetitively. It obtains the system programs and the storage buffers to READ and WRITE EMPLOYEE-YTD records. It initializes the data control block (DCB), a communications area in SALARYL's storage space.

Figure 3.11a depicts the object module instructions resulting from OPEN SALARY-FILE. Open connects SALARYL to system load modules, the access methods of data management, charged with creating channel programs. Figure 3.13 compares the S/370 memory map before and after Open's execution. The two contents directory entries (CDEs) (before and after), containing names of storage-resident programs, differ by the names of access method load modules.

Activity Diagram, READ of Logical Record 20

SALARYL executes with EMPLOYEE-YTD OPENed. The access methods serve the translated READ statement. In Figure 3.14, line 46, assume that SALARYL has processed the first 19 logical input records (LRs) and is about to process LR 20 by READing EMPLOYEE-YTD for the twentieth time.

Figures 3.15a–c express the control and data situation when LR 20 is READ, or presented to SALARYL. In Figure 3.15a, in activity 1, SALARYL places the storage location of the EMPLOYEE-YTD data control block into general purpose register 1 and then passes control to data management Get, activity 2. Get places the location of EMPLOYEE-YTD LR 20 into general purpose register 1, activity 3, and returns control to SALARYL, activity 4.

The DCB describes a data set to Open and data management routines.* Data management, using displacements to the DCB base address, accesses that block's fields. Table 3.5 depicts SALARYL's storage geometry.

Figure 3.15b illustrates what the data management program, Get, sees on receiving control. Cognizant of input buffer locations in storage, data management

---

* Many data management load modules are reentrant, which by definition prohibits them from storing data into their own main storage space. Each multiprogramming load module provides in its DCB a convenient area for such data.

```
LEVEL 1JAN67                                          COBOL F


     00001              IDENTIFICATION DIVISION.
     00002              PROGRAM-ID.
     00003              'SALARIES S/O/U'.
                              ⋮

     00040              PROCEDURE DIVISION.
     00041                  OPEN I-O EMPLOYEE-YTD.
     00042                  OPEN INPUT EMPLOYEE-WEEKLY.
     00043              READ-WEEKLY.
     00044                  READ EMPLOYEE-WEEKLY AT END GO TO READ-YTD.
(a)  00045              READ-YTD.
     00046                  READ EMPLOYEE-YTD AT END GO TO FINIS.
     00047                  IF EMPLOYEE-NO-YTD IS EQUAL TO EMPLOYEE-NO-WEEKLY
     00048                                              GO TO LIMIT-TEST.
     00049                  REWRITE YTD-RECORD.
     00050                  DISPLAY YTD-RECORD.
     00051                  GO TO READ-YTD.
     00052              LIMIT-TEST.
     00053                  IF SLIMIT - SOCIAL-SEC-YTD < GROSS-PAY GO TO LIMIT-CALC.
     00054                  COMPUTE SOCIAL-SEC-YTD
```

```
     43     *READ-WEEKLY
            0003DE                      PN=01      EQU    *
     44     READ   0003DE  58 1C C 058             L      1,058(0,12)           DCB=2
            0003E2  D2 C2 1 021 C 01D              MVC    021(3,1),01D(12)                  GN=01+1
            0003E8  58 F0 1 030                    L      15,030(0,1)
            0003EC  05 EF                          BALR   14,15
            0003EE  50 10 D 1C8                    ST     1,1C8(0,13)           BLI=2
            0003F2  58 8C D 1C8                    L      8,1C8(0,13)           BLI=2
            0003F6  58 1C C 00C                    L      1,00C(0,12)           PN=02
            0003FA  07 F1                          BCR    15,1
     44     GO     0003FC                 GN=01     EQU    *
            0003FC  58 10 C 00C                    L      1,00C(0,12)           PN=02
            000400  07 F1                          BCR    15,1
     45     *READ-YTD
            000402                      PN=02      EQU    *
(b)  46     READ   000402  58 1C C 054             L      1,054(0,12)           DCB=1
            000406  D2 02 1 021 C 021              MVC    021(3,1),021(12)                  GN=02+1
            00040C  58 F0 1 030                    L      15,030(0,1)
            000410  05 EF                          BALR   14,15
            000412  50 10 D 1C4                    ST     1,1C4(0,13)           BLI=1
            000416  58 70 D 1C4                    L      7,1C4(0,13)           BLI=1
            00041A  58 10 C 024                    L      1,024(0,12)           GN=03
            00041E  07 F1                          BCR    15,1
     46     GO     000420                 GN=02     EQU    *
            000420  58 1C C 018                    L      1,018(0,12)           PN=05
            000424  07 F1                          BCR    15,1
     47     IF     000426                 GN=03     EQU    *
            000426  F2 74 D 190 7 028              PACK   190(8,13),028(5,7)    TS=01         DNM=1-191
            00042C  F2 74 D 198 8 000              PACK   198(8,13),000(5,8)    TS=09         DNM=1-315
            000432  F9 22 D 195 D 19D              CP     195(3,13),19D(3,13)·  TS=06         TS=014
            00043B  58 F0 C 028                    L      15,028(0,12)          GN=04
            00043C  07 7F                          BCR    7,15
     48     GO     00043E                          L      1,010(0,12)           PN=03
            00043E  58 1C C 010
            000442  07 F1                          BCR    15,1
```

Figure 3.14 SALARIES READ source statements (a) and translated object module instructions (b). (Excerpt from Appendix 1.)

has previously passed logical records 11 through 19 to SALARYL without recourse to i–o devices.*

In Figure 3.15a, a load instruction passes the data control block location to data management, activity 1. The load at 40C places the location of Get, obtained from the EMPLOYEE-YTD DCB, into general purpose register 15, preceding BALR, activity 2.

From the symbolic listing, general purpose registers 6, 7, and 8 contain COBOL noun locations. Register 12 points to the program global table (PGT) locating the SALARYL DCB and other information of the OS/360 environment.

General purpose register 13 points to system-dependent information such as register contents saved within SALARYL on that module's interruption. Such information causes a load module to be a nonreusable System/370 resource.

* The OS/360 access method that deblocks logical records in physical data blocks and presents them to a problem program is called the queued sequential access method (QSAM). Accessing records directly from an input or output buffer area is known as locate mode or record i–o.

Executing programs access vital fields using known displacements to table origins held in base registers.

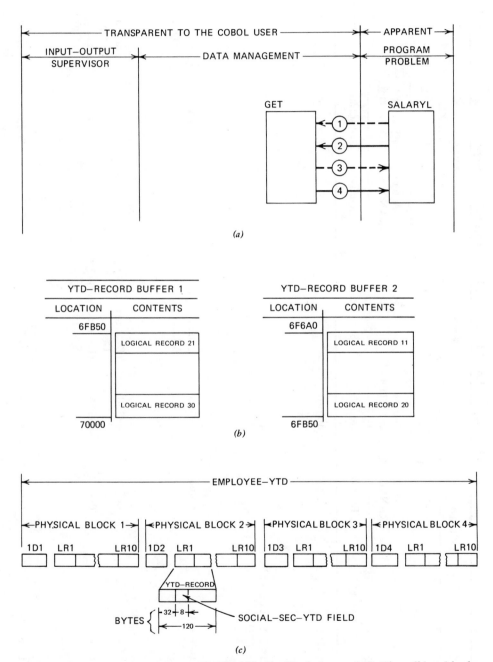

Figure 3.15 (a) Event diagram, COBOL READ of logical record 20. The solid and broken lines indicate control and data flow, respectively. (b) Input buffer schematic for READ of logical records 11 through 20. (c) EMPLOYEE-YTD as it physically exists on external device. (See Appendix 1.)

Table 3.5 SALARYL Storage Map During Selected Steps.

	S/370 Address			Contents		Comments[c]
	Step			Step		
	After TRANSLATE	During EXECUTE[a]		After TRANSLATE	During EXECUTE	
Symbolic[b]	Relative	Absolute	Symbolic	Relative	Absolute	
INIT1	00000	492E0	—	—	070090EC	Start load module, S/370 register 11
DCB EMPLOYEE-YTD	00040	49320			00000	
DCB + 32_{10}	00060	49340	l(End of Data Address)	—	49700	Location, l, furnished by Open
DCB + 48_{10}	00070	49350	l(Data management Get)	—	6EC60	Location, l, furnished by Open
DCB + 52_{10}	00074	49354	l(Data management Synch)	—	6EDC8	Location, l, furnished by Open
DCB + 68_{10}	00084	49364	l(IOB)[c]	—	70668	l Via data management Get

DCB + 72_{10}	00088	49368	l(End of buffer	—	6FB50	l Via data management Get
DCB + 76_{10}	0008C	4936C	l(Current logical record	—	6FAD8	l Via data management Get
DCB + 92_{10}	0009C	4937C	l(Data management EOB	—	7E3C0	Location, l, furnished by Open, end of DCB
PGT	002F8	495D8	—	—	499F0	Pointed to by register 12
.	.	.	.	.	.	
PGT + 52_{10}	00034C	4962C	@ DCB EMPLOYEE-YTD	00040	49320	
.	.	.	.	.	.	
Last half-word SALARYL	X	49FFC	—	X	45C0	

[a] After Open.
[b] N_{10} is base 10.
[c] Input–Output Buffer contains location of channel program.

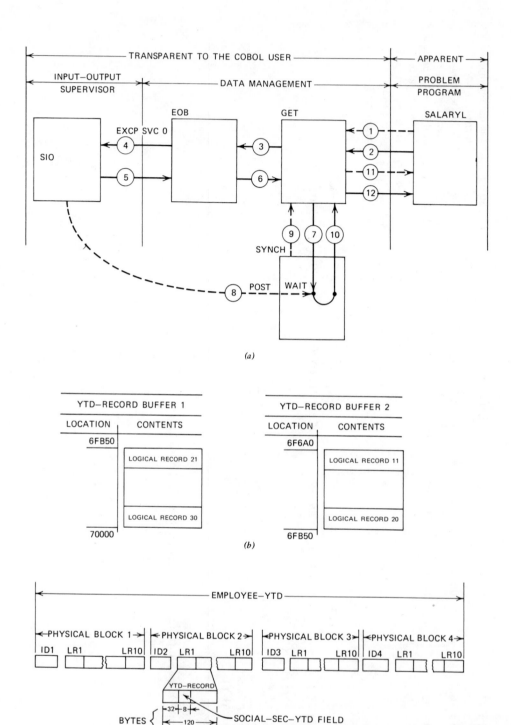

Figure 3.16 (a) Event diagram, COBOL READ of logical record 21. The solid and broken lines indicate control and data flow, respectively. (b) Input buffer schematic for READ of logical records 21 through 30. (c) EMPLOYEE-YTD on external device. (See Appendix 1.)

Activity Diagram, READ of Logical Record 21

We refer to Figure 3.14, relative location 402. In this situation we must distinguish among data management components. The SALARYL–data management interface remains as in the twentieth READ.

From Figure 3.16 we see that SALARYL passes the location of the DCB EM-PLOYEE-YTD, via general purpose register 1, activity 1, and then branches to data management Get, activity 2. Get processing, determining that the records of buffer 2 have been exhausted, passes CPU control to the data management component, End of Block (EOB), activity 3. End of Block unconditionally issues SVC 0, Execute Channel Program (EXCP), activity 4, interrupting the CPU's present execution and invoking the OS/360 control program. By EXCP, End of Block requests the filling of input buffer 2 from the i–o device on which EMPLOYEE-YTD resides. Input–output supervisor (IOS) routines respond to EXCP by scheduling the i–o request; when i–o device, control unit, and channel become available, Start Input Output (SIO) is issued. Independent of CPU activity, channel commands direct the filling of input buffer 2 with LRs 31 through 40. After IOS schedules the i–o request, it passes control to Synchronize, activities 5, 6, and 7. Synchronize tests whether buffer 1 is filled with block 3 as a result of the eleventh READ request.

If buffer 1 is filled, Synchronize passes the location of LR 21 to Get, activity 10, which, in turn, passes it to SALARYL via general purpose register 1, activity 11. Get returns control to SALARYL, activity 12.

If buffer 1 is not filled, Synchronize issues SVC 1, Wait, causing the control program to suspend Synchronize, and, hence, SALARIES READ execution. Later, IOS Posts, SVC 2, completion of the awaited event. After having resumed Synchronize Returns; SALARYL, becoming active, executes the instructions generated from COMPUTE. Tables 3.6 and 3.7 depict additional detail of input buffer availability.

Table 3.6 Execution Time Activity in Input Buffers.

Description, COBOL Source Time		YTD-RECORD Physical Block Number Contained in		Data Mgmt Pointer is to	Logical Records
Before	After	Buffer 1	Buffer 2	Buffer Number	READ
OPEN	START OF EXECUTION	Does not exist		—	—
1ST READ	OPEN	1	—	—	—
11TH READ	1ST READ	1	2	1	1–10
21ST READ	11TH READ	3	2	2	11–20
31ST READ	21ST READ	3	4	1	21–30
41ST READ	31ST READ	—	4	2	31–40
CLOSE	41ST READ	—	—	—	—
STOP RUN	CLOSE	Does not exist		—	—

Table 3.7   Absolute Values Representing Pointer to the Current Logical Record: Returned by Data Management to SALARYL via General Purpose Register 1 Subsequent to READ

Buffer Displacement	Absolute	Logical Record No.
000	6F6A0	11
078	6F718	12
0F0	6F790	13
168	6F808	14
1E0	6F880	15
258	6F8F8	16
2D0	6F970	17
348	6F9E8	18
3C0	6FA60	19
438	6FAD8	20

Activity Diagram, READ of Logical Record 1

We refer again to Figure 3.14. In addition to retrieving data management routines and providing i–o buffers, Open fills input buffer 1 with LRs 1 through 10 and provides an initial end of block condition by storing information in the EMPLOYEE-YTD DCB. Table 3.8 describes the activity shown in Figure 3.17a.

Table 3.8   Description of Activity Diagram for READ of First Logical Record.

Activity No.	Type	Description
1	Data	After first READ, SALARYL passes L(EMPLOYEE-YTD), a DCB, to Get
2	Control	SALARYL branches to Get
3	Control	Get, on finding an End of Block condition in the DCB, branches to the EOB routine
4	Control	By issuing EXCP, SVC 0, EOB passes control to IOS
5–7	Control	After scheduling the EOB i–o request, CPU control returns to Synchronize via Get
8 and 10	Data	If Synchronize finds buffer 1 filled, it passes the buffer location in general purpose register 1, via Get, to SALARYL;
9 and 11	Control	it relinquishes control, via Get, to SALARYL

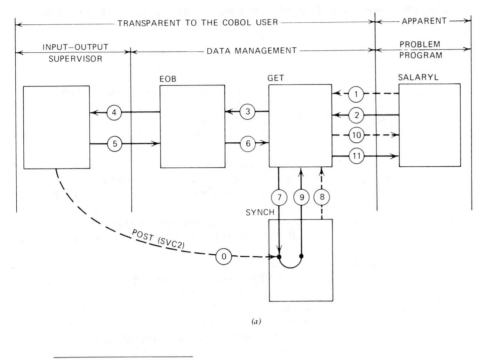

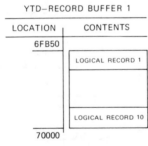

(b)

Figure 3.17 Diagram of events immediately after first SALARYL READ. The solid and broken numbered lines indicate control and data flow, respectively. (*b*) Input buffer situation after Open and prior to READ of logical record 1.

Activity Diagram, READ of Last Logical Record

Our reference figure is again Figure 3.14. Because of the anticipatory buffering QSAM Open provides, it is necessary to analyze the READing at two different times, the READ of LR 31 and the READ of LR 40. Table 3.9 describes the activity shown in Figure 3.18.

3.7 CONSIDERATIONS

Data Management Usability

Depending on which logical record or physical block is accessed, data management issues (or does not issue) EXCP for buffer filling and initiates end of block and end of extent activity. Oblivious to whether he directs access to the first or the

Table 3.9 Description of Activity Diagram for READ of Last Logical Record.

Activity No.	Type	Description
1	Data	After the 31ST READ, SALARYL passes L(EMPLOYEE-YTD), a DCB, to Get
2	Control	SALARYL branches to Get
3	Control	Get, on finding an end of block condition in the DCB, branches to the EOB routine
4	Control	By issuing EXCP, SVC 0, the EOB passes control to IOS
5	Data	Recognizing end of extent of the input data set, IOS omits the scheduling of the EOB i-o request but issues Post, SVC 2.
6–8	Control	Control is passed to Synchronize via Get
9 and 11	Data	@(LR 31) is passed to SALARYL in general purpose register 1
10 and 12	Control	Control is returned to SALARYL for all-electronic processing of LRS 31–40. On the 41st READ, data management, recognizing an end of block and end of extent, returns control not to the SALARIES COMPUTE but to the SALARIES FINIS statement. End of Data Address (EODAD), a field in the EMPLOYEE-YTD DCB is used to effect this transfer.

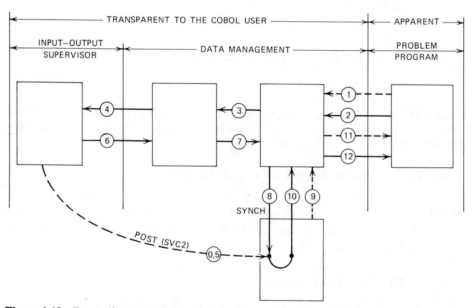

Figure 3.18 Event diagram, READ of logical record 31. The solid broken numbered lines indicate control and data flow, respectively.

*n*th logical record in the file, the COBOL user writes READ EMPLOYEE-YTD. A logical data processing system is a greatly simplified system.

Execution Step Decisions

Open and the data control block enable binding decisions about data sets to be deferred until the execution job step, for not until Open time are channel programs applied to load modules. A large installation moves a data set from IBM 2311 to 2314, say. An access method routine changes. Rerunning hundreds of compilations and link-edits may be avoided; the job control language of the execution step reflects the data set's change of residence.

Deferral applies to storage buffer allocation as well. Only on the explicit demand OPEN EMPLOYEE-YTD is the space reserved; until then the space remains allocable for other use.

Finally, after REWRITing YTD-RECORD, data management might either proceed or read from the device back into storage for validation. According to what he prefers, performance or reliability, in his execution step request, the user specifies which option the system uses in Opening the DCB.

Table 3.10   Glossary of Names.

	Job Management		Task Management
	Function		
Name	Card Deck Input (SYSIN)	OS/360 Job Queue (SYS1. JOBQUE)	Name
USERJOB	User job request	OS/360 Job	
COBSTEP	User job step request	OS/360 Job step	COBTASK, COBTCB, COBRB
LESTEP	User job step request	OS/360 Job step	LETASK, LETCB, LERB
EXECSTEP	User job step request	OS/360 Job step	EXECTASK, EXECTCB, SALRB

User Library Load Module Members of SYS1.LINKLIB

Name	Description
COBOLL	OS/360 COBOL language translator
LINKEDITL	OS/360 link-editor
SALARYL	Output of LINKEDITL

Data Set Names

OS/360 (physical)	User (logical)
EMPYTD	EMPLOYEE-YTD
EMPWEEKLY	EMPLOYEE-WEEKLY

Names

System/370 names are frequently confusing. An OS/360 request is made in two different languages, source language and job control language (JCL). This text reflects the separation of source language and system-dependent names.* In SALARIES, EMPLOYEE-YTD designates a data set. In JCL, EMPYTD designates the same data set. In COBOL, SALARIES designates a program. In JCL, SALARYS, SALARYO, or SALARYL is used for a source, object, or load module library member (see Table 3.10).

In different source languages there are ambiguities among names. COBOL processes READ, WRITE, and OPEN. Assembler processes Read, Write, and Open. We intend the typography to supply the context. Moreover, Open represents both an assembler macro and the supervisory state load module invoked by SVC 19. "Open, SVC 19" designates the load module. Finally, S/370 channels *Read, Write, Seek,* and *Search.*

Our subsequent examples use labels unincluded in OS/360. For instance, COBTASK is undefined for the OS/360 task attached in response to COBSTEP specification. Also, in our discussions we include such labels as ". . . specified in the user job step request for compilation [COBSTEP]. . . ." Let us agree that the meaning of the word in brackets is "as exemplified by COBSTEP."

3.8   LIST PROCESSING

In multiprogramming, an unknown number of users make requests of a limited number of resources. A request waits in a list structure, or queue, until a resource becomes available. The OS control program manipulates its data, the queue, in performing list processing. The base/displacement architecture causes the process to be efficient.

A Queue Element (QEL) represents a request. A Queue Control Block (QCB) represents a resource. In list processing, some control program supervisor *enqueues* the request initially, *dispatches* it when its resource becomes available, and *dequeues* it when the request is satisfied. In OS, enqueueing is associated with the scheduling of resources and the attaching of tasks.

A line of QELs queues on a QCB (Fig. 3.19). The QCB points to the location of an active dispatched queue element, which points to the next element, and so on, down to the last QEL in the chain, where the fixed pointer field contains

---

* Not strictly adhered to up to the present point for expository reasons.

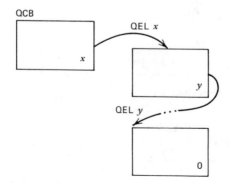

Figure 3.19   List structure.

zero. There are several procedures for enqueueing and dispatching based on arrival and departure of the request. Some we shall meet later are the "first in, first out" (FIFO) and "last in, first out" (LIFO) methods of serializing requests.

The QEL often contains "do something" space, data for its resource supervisor's use. In general, OS/360 associates one supervisor with one resource. Task management processes the Task Control Block (TCB), a QEL queued on a QCB that represents the CPU; job management processes jobs, a system of QELs. Contents supervisor's QELs represent OS/360 programs in storage.

System/370 resources are immediately usable, called reentrant; one-time usable; or serially reusable (self-initializing).

An example of a one-time-usable resource is a program that modifies itself during its execution and does not perform self-initialization. The program's execution in behalf of *this* request destroys its value to any other request. A reentrant program, on the other hand, is unmodified.

OS queues only on serially reusable resources, which, by design, may serve only one request at a time. So the control program may keep matters straight, each request has an OS status recorded in an Event Control Block (ECB), shown in Figure 3.20. An activity resulting in change of a request's status is an event. An OS supervisory state program implements this change. When some i–o completion event, say, occurs, the supervisor issues Post, SVC 2, with an ECB operand. As a result SALARYL, waiting, say, READs an EMPLOYEE-YTD logical record. After posting the ECB the resource supervisor detaches the lately active QEL and advances the rest of the waiting line. That data management furnishes an ECB is transparent to the SALARIES user.

The ECB and queue structure of OS software working with S/370 hardware architecture implement "waiting without stopping," the heart of System/370 resource sharing.

3.9   OS OBJECTIVES AND DIMENSIONS

We are about to learn more detail of how System/370 does things. Before we do we pause for a word on why System/370 does things and what things it does.

The objective of System/370 is to respond to user requests so as to provide increased productivity to the installation. The objective of OS/360 is to optimize use of System/370 resources. Objective 1 depends on the success of objective 2.

| Bit | 0 | 1 | 2 | 31 |

W	P	Completion code

		State	
Time		W	P
1	ECB creation and before reuse	0	0
2	After Wait SVC	1	0
3	After Post SVC	0	1

Figure 3.20   Event control block schematic. Key: W, Wait bit; P, Post bit.

Productivity is the classical economics ratio, output/input. Depending on the application, the ratio may be bills produced per hour/cost of the billing procedure or checked out COBOL statements per day/cost of producing the statements. Some ratio of value/cost justifies a system. Simulating a missile's behavior is more efficient than shooting it off. In firms doing business mid complex regulations and rising costs, an added margin of productivity may amount to survival.

System/370 is a general purpose system serving the applications programmer and system programmer alike. Primarily it provides usability to the former, performance to the latter, and function and reliability for both. Moreover, it does this on different models; a program that runs on S/370 M 135 runs on the larger S/370 M 165.

The high-speed main and auxiliary storage components of System/370 offer great improvement over the performance of second-generation systems. Nevertheless, the real advance is in systems technology, multiprogramming. Problem programs 1 . . . *n* and system programs 1 . . . *n* share electronic and electromagnetic resources whose activity is overlapped. The sight of an operator stacking multiple job decks in the input reader is commonplace today.

The kinds of requests it responds to for its various users determine a system's functional capability. By pressing a key on a terminal, an end user may request the system to take a square root. By submitting a SALARIES statement, a COBOL user may request the system to READ. On another level, in the READ-YTD paragraph in Figure 3.21, lines 45 to 50 update EMPLOYEE-YTD with data from EMPLOYEE-WEEKLY, Figures 3.22*a* and *b*. Although two different DASD organizations of EMPYTD appear in Figure 3.22, the identical statements specify the updating in both cases.

In organization 2, update is by indices associated with the symbolic key EMPLOYEE-NO-YTD. Because of these indices, the user may request the functions of *update* and communications terminal (teletype) *inquiry,* in contrast to the *up-*

```
00001          IDENTIFICATION DIVISION.
00002          PROGRAM-ID.
00003          'SALARIES'.
                    ⋮
00040          PROCEDURE DIVISION.
00041              OPEN I-C EMPLOYEE-YTD.
00042              OPEN INPUT EMPLOYEE-WEEKLY.
00043          READ-WEEKLY.
00044              READ EMPLOYEE-WEEKLY AT END GC TO READ-YTC.
00045          READ-YTD.
00046              READ EMPLCYEE-YTD AT END GO TC FINIS.
00047              IF EMPLOYEE-NC-YTD IS EQUAL TO EMPLOYEE-NO-WEEKLY
00048                              GC TO LIMIT-TEST.
00049              REWRITE YTD-RECORD.
00050              DISPLAY YTD-RECORD.
00051              GO TO READ-YTD.
00052          LIMIT-TEST.
00053              IF SLIMIT - SOCIAL-SEC-YTD < GROSS-PAY GC TO LIMIT-CALC.
00054              COMPUTE SOCIAL-SEC-YTD
00055                      ROUNDED = SOCIAL-SEC-YTD + GRCSS-PAY * .048.
00056              REWRITE YTD-RECORD.
00057              DISPLAY YTD-RECORD.
00058              GO TO READ-WEEKLY.
00059          LIMIT-CALC.
00060              COMPUTE SOCIAL-SEC-YTD
00061                      RCUNDED = SOCIAL-SEC-YTD +
00062                              (SLIMIT - SOCIAL-SEC-YTD) * .048.
00063              REWRITE YTD-RECORD.
00064              DISPLAY YTD-RECORD.
00065              GO TO REAC-WEEKLY.
00066              CLOSE EMPLOYEE-YTD.
00067              CLOSE EMPLCYEE-WEEKLY.
00068          FINIS. ENTER LINKAGE.
00069              CALL 'DUMPIT'.
00070              ENTER COBOL.
00071              STOP RUN.
```

Figure 3.21 SALARIES PROCEDURE DIVISION for sequential update of the two physical organizations shown in Figure 3.22.

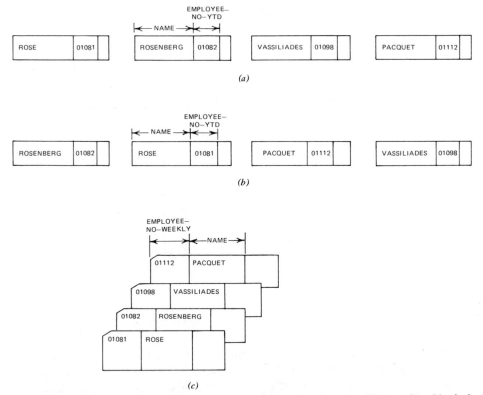

Figure 3.22 (a) Physical organization 1 of EMPYTD data set, simplified. (b) Physical organization 2 of EMPYTD data set, simplified. (c) Organization of EMPWEEKLY data set used to access EMPYTD.

date only capability of organization 1. With organization 2, the user may ask, "What is George M. Eisele's SOCIAL-SEC-YTD amount?" Any volume of such questions is meaningless using organization 1; George M. Eisele's record may be buried in the 1200th foot of a sequential tape.

In regard to usability, Table 3.11 exhibits that the user conceives of logical System/370, a von Neumann system.

Oblivious to SIO, word boundaries, and general purpose registers, the user specifies READ, MOVE, and COMPUTE.

In regard to reliability, let us look at Figure 3.23, which depicts SALARYL reading EMPYTD. The picture is incomplete. The activities that occur in an error situation are missing.

SALARYL *Reads* through a channel that may transmit billions of characters in a day's operation. With a channel error rate of, say, one part in one billion,

Table 3.11

Function	Subsystem
READ EMPLOYEE-YTD	Input–Output
MOVE EMPLOYEE-NO-WEEKLY	Main storage
COMPUTE SOCIAL-SEC-YTD	Central processing unit

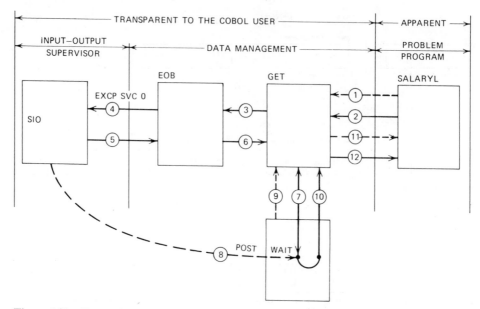

Figure 3.23 Event diagram, SALARYL twenty-first READ. The solid and broken numbered lines indicate control and data flow, respectively. (See also Fig. 3.21.)

several errors might occur in an eight-hour shift. Through circuitry, S/370 detects i–o errors and indicates these to OS retry programs; 100 retries is an OS standard. Through retry, an intermittent error, caused by, say, dust on a DASD track, will often clear. Whether SALARYL successfully reads on the first or fiftieth try is transparent to the user.

Figure 3.24 depicts a common method of handling errors on an exception basis after the 100th try. Recall the discussion of interrupt types in Section 2.2 that covered CPU retry.

Now, knowing the intent of System/370 and having the tools to analyze its structure, we shift from the user's point of view of the system to the system's view of that subelement in a data structure, the user's program.

```
00001          IDENTIFICATION DIVISION.
00002          PROGRAM-ID.
00003          'SALARIES S/Q/U'.
                         ⋮
00034          01  WEEKLY-RECORD.
00035              02 EMPLOYEE-NO-WEEKLY PICTURE 9(5).
00036              02 NAME PICTURE X(32).
00037              02 FILLER PICTURE X(43).
00038          WORKING-STORAGE SECTION.
00039          77  SLIMIT PICTURE 9(6)V99 COMPUTATIONAL-3 VALUE IS 374.4C.
00040          PROCEDURE DIVISION.
00041          DECLARATIVES.
00042          ERR-SECTION.
00043              USE AFTER STANDARD ERROR ON EMPLOYEE-YTD.
00044              ENTER LINKAGE.
00045              CALL 'CHECKIT'.
00046              ENTER COBOL.
00047          END DECLARATIVES.
00048              OPEN I-O EMPLOYEE-YTD.
00049              OPEN INPUT EMPLOYEE-WEEKLY.
00050          READ-WEEKLY.
00051              READ EMPLOYEE-WEEKLY AT END GO TO READ-YTD.
00052          READ-YTD.
00053              READ EMPLOYEE-YTD AT END GO TO FINIS.
00054              IF EMPLOYEE-NO-YTD IS EQUAL TO EMPLOYEE-NO-WEEKLY
00055                          GO TO LIMIT-TEST.
00056              REWRITE YTD-RECORD.
00057              DISPLAY YTD-RECORD.
                         ⋮
```

Figure 3.24 SALARIES with error procedure.

EXERCISES

3.1 Write COBOL PROCEDURE DIVISION statements to perform C = A + B, READing in A and B.

3.2 Referring to the COBOL Glossary, Appendix 1, page 211, write C = A + B specifying A as COMPUTATIONAL and B and C as COMPUTATIONAL-1.

3.3 Write A plus B3 in floating point to produce printed output.

3.4 Fill in the following table:

	Input Data to		
Name	COBOLL	LNKEDITL	SALARYL
SALARIES			
SALARYS			
SALARYO			
SALARYL			
EMPLOYEE-YTD			
EMPYTD			

3.5 Compare OPEN, Open, and Open, SVC 19.

3.6 Write SALARIES to perform READ-YTD five times.

3.7 The logic of a problem program is frequently expressible as follows:

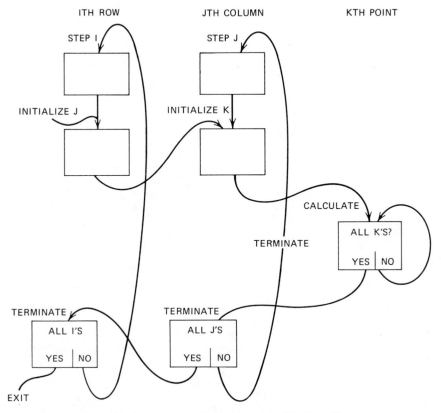

Express the logic of matrix multiply of Figure 1.8 in the above form.

3.8   Comment on the use of the word "COMPUTE" in following COBOL program:

.
.
.

$$\text{COMPUTE. COMPUTE } A = B + 1.$$

.
.
.

3.9   Comment on the use of the word "READ" in following FORTRAN program:

.
.
.

```
READ (1)  B,C
READ = READ + 1
```

.
.
.

3.10   Discuss initialization of the following serially reusable resources: (a) unit record machine, (b) turret lathe, (c) first-generation cpu.

3.11   Is initialization generally a system-dependent function?

3.12   Give an example of a nonreusable resource.

chapter 4

OS/360 TASK
MANAGEMENT

4.1 INTRODUCTION

We now encounter the routines of the OS/360 control program that supervise requests for the resources of System/370. We emphasize tasks, requests for the CPU, and their supervisor, task management. Although an OS/360 user submits job step requests to System/370, it is user tasks, altered forms of the original requests, that the supervisory routines of the OS control program recognize. How the user's tasks relate to his job step requests lays the foundation for what follows.

The user decides which job step requests make up his job request. His unit of work is the *job step request*.

A job request and its step requests are transformed by job management routines into a job and its steps. Job management also transforms job steps into tasks, the form recognized by task management. Job management's unit of work is the *job step*.

The OS/360 supervisor operates on data structures, resident in storage belonging to the supervisor, and representing physical parts of System/370. The task, a structure, represents a user's job step request, translated, to task management. Task management's unit of work is the *task*.

Our discussion of task management in OS/360 is concerned primarily with the version known as multiprogramming with a variable number of tasks (MVT). We discuss OS/360 task management in versions other than MVT toward the end of the chapter, in Section 4.8. (We discuss task management in OS/VS, to which OS/360 task management is a prerequisite, in Chapter 6.) Finally, we discuss the input–output supervisor (IOS) illustrating its close relation to task management and setting these two supervisors forth as prototypes of all OS/360 supervisors.

4.2 THE OS/360 TASK

Figure 4.1 depicts the introduction, activity, and release to and from OS/360 of a job request, USERJOB. OS/360 transforms USERJOB request steps into the USERJOB steps COBSTEP, LESTEP, and EXECSTEP.

USERJOB steps are data used in establishing three tasks, COBTASK, LETASK, and EXECTASK. An OS/360 user task is established for each job step of USERJOB.

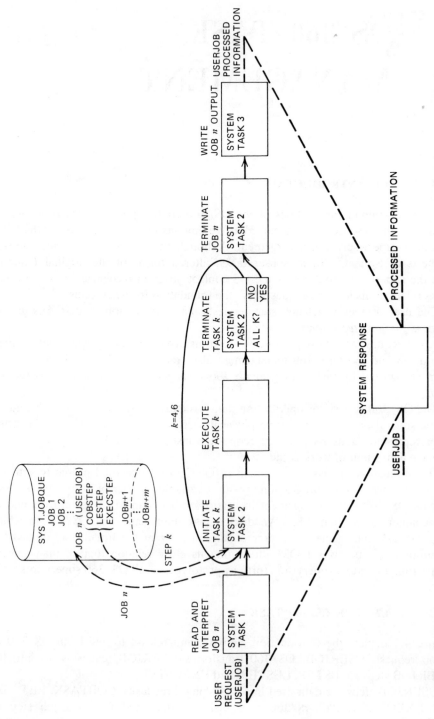

Figure 4.1 Flow of USERJOB through System/370. The solid and broken lines indicate control and data flow, respectively.

Jobs, job steps, and tasks are born, are active, and are erased during System/370 response to the user's job request. Job steps and tasks are i–o to different systems programs. EXECSTEP is input to job management. Task management programs create dispatch, and redispatch EXECTASK.

Control program and tasks are as lessor and lessee. The control program owns System/370 resources. A task is a mechanism for accounting for resources. Through job and task structures, OS/360 accounts for whether resources are on loan to tasks, allocated, or whether they are free and allocable.

4.3 SYSTEM/370 RESOURCES

These are hardware resources and OS/360 data sets and load modules.

The CPU and channel–control unit–device complexes are major hardware resources. In addition, space is controlled in two categories, main storage and direct-access device (Fig. 4.2). EXECTASK owns DASD unit 192 and EMPYTD's space thereon. Shareable with the contemporaries of EXECTASK, both resources are controlled through a Data Extent Block (DEB). EXECTASK data sets, EMPWKLY and EMPYTD, are also controlled through DEBs.

Locations 49000 to 71000 belong to EXECTASK exclusively. Allocations from this extent, the MVT region, are accounted for through subdivisions of the space, or subpools.

A request block (RB) in the EXECTASK structure requests task management to allocate the CPU for SALARYL streaming.

4.4 THE TASK STRUCTURE

Figure 4.3, depicts additional detail of EXECTASK resource control.

We see the Task Control Block (TCB) queue. The TCB is a request element, or QEL, queued on a Queue Control Block (QCB) located in a control program table called the Communications Vector Table. This QCB represents the CPU to the ready tasks of the system.

The QCB at EXECTCB + 0, 1CB30, points to the request block queue for EXECTASK. This LIFO queue helps task management's interrupt control: the control program stores the old program status word in SALRB space when SALARYL is transparently interrupted. EXECTASK, hence SALARYL, is redispatched when the task supervisor issues the instruction Load Program Status word, specifying as operand the address of the old program status word within SALRB space.

At EXECTCB + 8, 1D1F4 points to the first member of the DEB chain representing the SALARYL Opened data sets. EMPYTDDEB, 1CF8C, contains the limits of the EMPYTD DASD extent.

The DEB pointer to the Unit Control Block (UCB) associated with device address 192 exhibits the connection between data set and device made at Open time. The DEB also contains the address of the data set DCB.

The contents of EXECTCB + 18, 1F4C0, points to a subpool queue element (SPQE) locating the EXECTASK storage allocations. The DEB and SPQE differ from elements queued on a serially reusable resource. The DEB and SPQE are

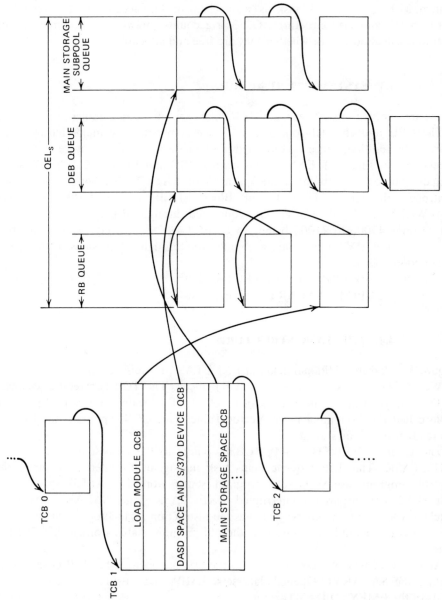

Figure 4.2 Schematic of queue elements representing requests for some major resources. (See Appendix 1 dump).

74

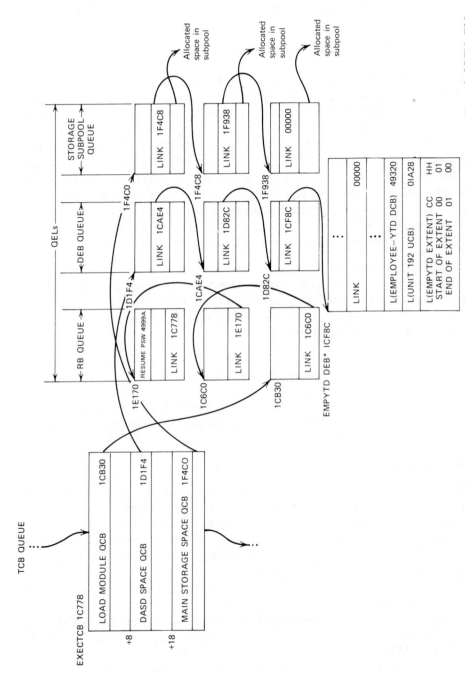

Figure 4.3 The structure of EXECTCB. The asterisk indicates DEB created in response to the execution of OPEN EMPLOYEE-YTD. L (item) refers to main storage location. (See Appendix 1.)

75

members of a chain of control blocks. The Closing of EMPYTD during the execution of SALARYL would mean the immediate detachment of EMPYTDDEB regardless of whether it had been the first or last element scheduled into its chain.

4.5 THE TASK IN OPERATION

On the scheduling of EXECTCB into the TCB queue, EXECTASK becomes active. It may sponsor requests that enter the resource queues of the operating system.

While active, EXECTCB is switched back and forth between ready and wait queues of TCBs qualified for, or disqualified from, requesting CPU services. EXECTASK may disqualify itself by executing Wait, SVC 1, shortly after it has requested some service, say EXCP.* An operand of Wait designates some event that must complete before the instructions following the SVC may be streamed.

The awaited event causes a CPU interruption. A resource supervisor, i–o supervisor in this case, may notify task management to remove EXECTCB from the waiting queue and enter it at the tail end of the (FIFO) ready queue.

The multiprogramming design of OS/360 centers around the following:

1. Tasks sponsor requests for system resources.
2. These requests, which may become members of queues resident in main storage, remain intact between episodes of their processing by the CPU.
3. Supervisory processing executes so rapidly that significant resource capacity remains for productive problem streaming.

4.6 RESOURCE ALLOCATION TIME

Allocation is static or dynamic. Static allocation is the scheduling of a request into the task structure. Dynamic allocation is the dispatching of a request in a list maintained by a resource supervisor.

Static Allocation

Referring to Figure 4.4, we see that the channel–control unit–DASD unit, 192, and its space, as well as the data set name EMPYTD, are statically allocated. As a consequence of these three levels of control, job management may assign unit 192 and its space, as well as the EMPYTD data set, to multiple tasks of its creation and assign EMPYTD to more than one unit. Later, during EXECTASK activity, dynamic allocations will be made accordingly.

Figure 4.5 depicts the storage region allocated to EXECTASK by the initiator. Space within the region is dynamically allocated.

Finally, the initiator allocates SALARYL. Before allocation, SALARYL is a load module member of a DASD library. Subsequent to task creation, SALARYL is an EXECTASK resource.

Static allocation concludes when the "S" resources of Figure 4.4 have been assigned to the incipient user task. The initiator, issuing Attach, SVC 42, activates EXECTASK.

---

* Wait, SVC 1, is a software wait, distinct from hardware wait (1 in PSW bit 14) set by the control program when all tasks wait.

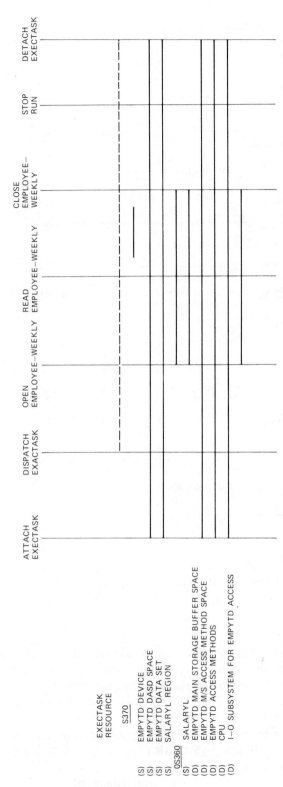

Figure 4.4 Schematic of time of allocation of selected EXECTASK resources. The letters S and D indicate static and dynamic allocation, respectively.

77

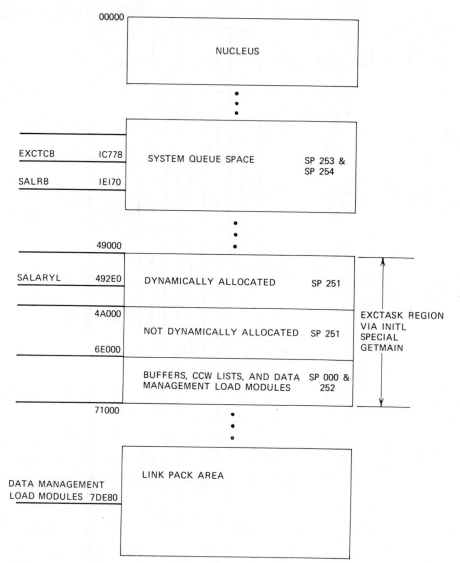

Figure 4.5 EXECTASK Main storage. (See Appendix 1.)

Dynamic Allocation

EXECTASK is ready when EXECTCB is scheduled into the TCB ready queue. EXECTASK is dispatched when, after EXECTCB has advanced to the head of tasks of the highest priority in the ready queue, task management has allocated the available CPU to it. The EXECTASK load modules may then execute and so initiate requests for other resources.

DASD space for an output data set statically allocated to EXECTASK involves dynamic allocation as well. During SALARYL execution, if the initial space proves insufficient, additional space may be requested.

Channel–device complex 192 will have been dynamically allocated when READ EMPLOYEE-YTD results in i–o transmission. When an EMPYTD data block has been transmitted to storage, IOS Posts, SVC 2, this event, and then removes EX-ECTASK's request for 192 from its records.

Getmain, issued by the initiator, allocates main storage from 49000_{16} to 71000_{16} ($256K_{10}$ bytes) the EXECTASK region (see Appendix 1). To use any piece of this region, the EXECTASK load modules must directly, or indirectly through a system's program, request that piece's dynamic allocation by issuing an additional Getmain.*

It is necessary that region space be allocated in different ways. The EXECTASK region may house, say, systems program *a* executing under protect key *a*. SALARYL, executing with, say, key *b*, could contaminate program *a* by storing into it, thus violating an assumption underlying System/370 design—the control program is errorless. Accordingly, some space in the EXECTASK region may be protected under key zero, not the user's key; SALARYL cannot store into such space. Additional control is provided through a system of storage subpools. Subpool 252 is allocated for key zero programs; 251 space houses SALARYL, protected by a user key.

As Figure 4.5 indicates, EXECTASK storage allocations may lie outside its region as well. System queue space for control blocks [SALRB] and space in the link pack area, residence of reentrant systems modules, may be requested.

EXECTASK's eligibility to request dynamic allocations normally concludes when SALARYL executes Return, resulting in the deletion of EXECTCB.

4.7 EXAMPLES OF DYNAMIC PROGRAM MANAGEMENT

Problem programs invoke the services of control program modules in storage and SYS1.SVCLIB, and problem state modules in SYS1.LINKLIB and user private libraries, through dynamic allocation.† Our four examples illustrate the allocation, during EXECSTEP, of a problem state program, DUMPITL. Each example illustrates DUMPITL being entered on a different level into an EXECTASK structure. In each case CALLITL, which, like DUMPITL, is a load module resource of EXECTASK, invokes DUMPITL by SVC. In each case, task management modifies the EXECTASK structure. In the example of Attach, SVC 42, a new subtask structure is created. We analyze the schematics of these structures, abstracted from execution step dumps (see Appendices 2 through 5).

Link, SVC 6

It is frequently impracticable to anticipate and link-edit together all of the programs required during a load module's execution; it may waste storage as well. OS/360 load modules are designed as building blocks. They may Link to, or be Linked by, other library modules, dynamically, during EXECSTEP, as they may Call, or be Called by, other library modules, statically, during LESTEP. Because task management Links programs, transfer of CPU control from the module in the problem state to one in the supervisor state, or the reverse, is possible.

In our example an assembly language program, CALLIT, includes a Link macro,

---

* There is more than one type of Getmain SVC.
† Often called dynamic program management.

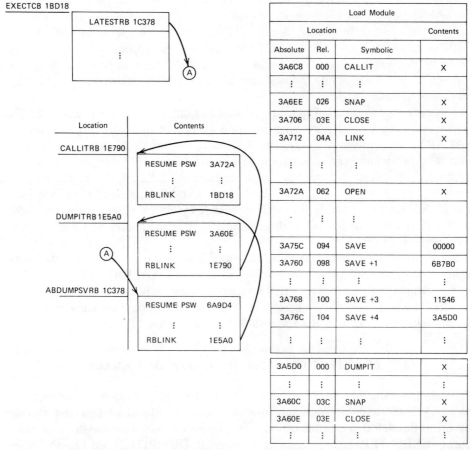

EXECTCB 1BD18

Load Module			
Location			Contents
Absolute	Rel.	Symbolic	
3A6C8	000	CALLIT	X
⋮	⋮	⋮	
3A6EE	026	SNAP	X
3A706	03E	CLOSE	X
3A712	04A	LINK	X
⋮	⋮	⋮	
3A72A	062	OPEN	X
.	⋮	⋮	
3A75C	094	SAVE	00000
3A760	098	SAVE +1	6B7B0
⋮	⋮	⋮	⋮
3A768	100	SAVE +3	11546
3A76C	104	SAVE +4	3A5D0
⋮	⋮	⋮	⋮
3A5D0	000	DUMPIT	X
⋮	⋮	⋮	⋮
3A60C	03C	SNAP	X
3A60E	03E	CLOSE	X
⋮	⋮	⋮	⋮

Figure 4.6 Schematic of request block queue at the time of DUMPIT Snap after CALLIT Link. The crosses (×) indicate instructions not depicted. Note: Contents of SAVE + 1 = SAVE area of load module relinquishing control; SAVE + 3 = Exit address; SAVE + 4 = entry point of linked-to module. (See Appendix 2.)

which, expanded, includes Link, SVC 6. DUMPIT, the linked-to program, contains a Snap macro.

Figure 4.6 depicts EXECTASK following Snap; Abdump, SVC 51, appears in the Snap expansion. In the figure, Abdump is the active load module of EX-ECTASK. The supervisor request block (SVRB) representing Abdump demonstrates that supervisory as well as problem state programs are involved with the request block queue.*

The DUMPITRB resume program status word field contains the address of Snap plus 2. Task management uses this address to Return control to DUMPITL after Abdump conclusion. Abdump Returns through Exit, SVC 3, which modifies the LATESTRB contents of EXECTCB from 1C378 to 1E5A0 and deletes ABDUMPSVRB from the request block queue. The program status word address field, 3A72A, indicates that CALLITL execution resumes at Open. CAL-

---

* See Appendix 11 for a discussion of type I, II, III, and IV SVCs.

LITRBLINK specifies the location of EXECTCB, which at the time of CALLITL Return (again via Exit, SVC 3) denotes end of task to task management.

Symbolic operands called SAVE appear in CALLITL space beginning at 3A75C. The general purpose registers of CALLITL were saved in this area immediately after the Link SVC interruption. Register 13 is the means of communication between CALLITL and the supervisory state routines that store these registers (see Appendix 2, p. 222, statements 1 through 10).

Finally, our discussions have dealt with traces of the EXECTASK structure at particular times, during Abdump, DUMPITL, and CALLITL instruction streaming. Those times when supervisory state service programs execute merit mention as well.

Figure 4.7 depicts the EXECTASK structure during SVC 6 service; task management schedules an SVRB into the request block queue. Subsequently, when

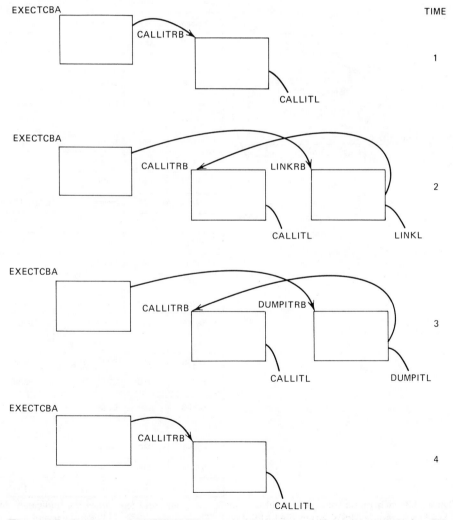

Figure 4.7 Structure of EXECTASK request block queue before (1) and during (2) CALLIT's Linking to DUMPIT; also, structure during execution (3) and after return from (4) DUMPIT.

Exit, SVC 3, service is rendered, the EXECTASK structure will again be affected. The exact structure depends on whether the executing SVC program is of type I, II, III, or IV.

Load, SVC 8

Often a library load module that is dynamically allocated must be entered repetitively.

Branch entry, used by Load, avoids the overhead of supervisor-assisted Linking. Branching, unlike Linking, implies that the transferred to routine is of the same state and has the same storage protect key as the invoking program.

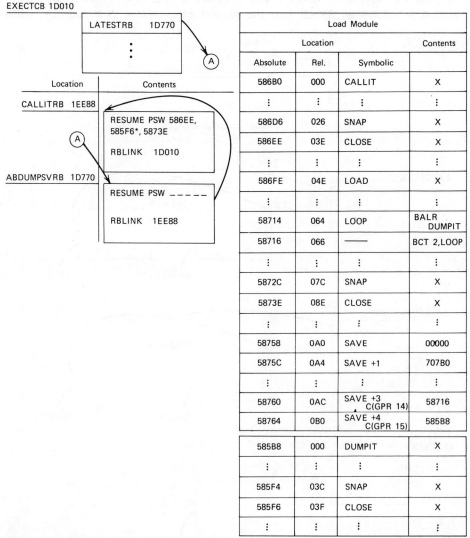

Figure 4.8 Schematic of request block queue at four selected times as indicated by CALLITRB resume PSW after CALLIT Load. The crosses (×) indicate instructions not depicted. The asterisk indicates that the address appears twice. (See Appendix 3.)

Referring to Figure 4.8, location 04E, Load fetches DUMPITL into storage and passes the module's address to CALLITL via general purpose register 0. CALLITL may later use this address in a BALR instruction. DUMPITL remains in storage until CALLITL invokes Return for itself at the end of EXECTASK. In contrast to Link no DUMPITRB is created; CALLITRB contains the resume program status word, which during ABDUMP execution points to a resume location, 585F6, within DUMPITL space.

OS/360 Open, SVC 19, Loads data management modules providing SALARYL access to EMPYTD.

XCTL, SVC 7

XCTL, SVC 7, is used when no Return to the XCTLed-from load module [CALLITL] is intended. The request block chain prior to XCTL appears in Fig. 4.9. After XCTL, CALLITRB contains the resume program status word for DUMPITL (see Fig. 4.10). DUMPITL overlays CALLITL in storage. Supervisor assistance is required to preserve the integrity of the high save area, c (SAVE + 1), in order to effect normal Return from DUMPITL.

Attach, SVC 42

Attach, like the other dynamic program management SVCs, fetches a library load module into storage. Unlike the others, it establishes a new task. Figures 4.11 and 4.12 illustrate the task structure prior and subsequent to Attach.

Attach creates a new TCB at location 1E910 from which DUMPITRB and ABDUMPSVRB are chained. DUMPITL is interrupted by execution of Abdump, SVC 51, in the Snap expansion. From DUMPITRB, Return is to 3F5D2. CALLITL, Waiting, will resume by Opening the Snap data set at 3F720 after

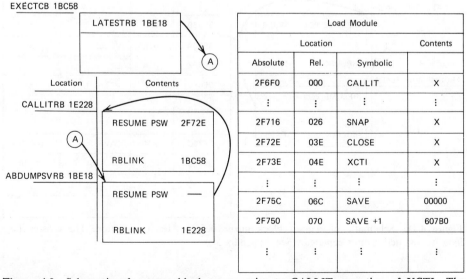

Figure 4.9 Schematic of request block queue prior to CALLIT execution of XCTL. The crosses ($\times$) indicate instructions not depicted. (See Appendix 4.)

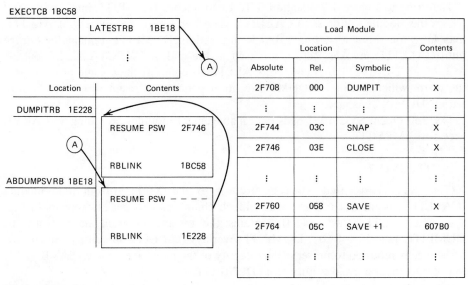

Figure 4.10 Schematic of request block queue after CALLIT execution of XCTL (DUMPIT overlays CALLIT). The crosses (×) indicate instructions not depicted. (See Appendix 4.)

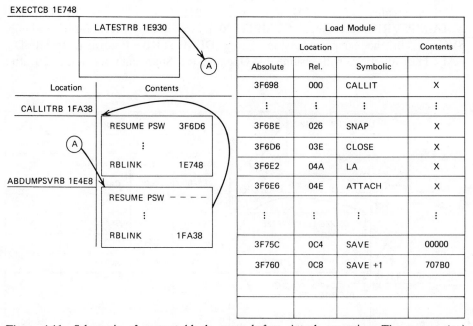

Figure 4.11 Schematic of request block queue before Attach execution. The crosses (×) indicate instructions not depicted. (See Appendix 5.)

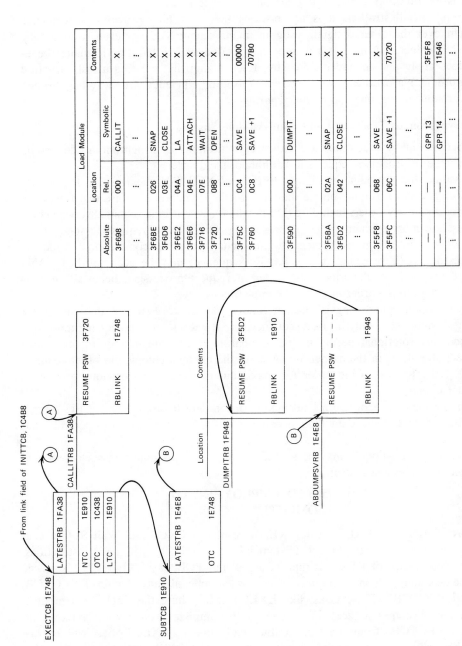

Figure 4.12 Task structure after Attach and during first execution of Snap. The crosses (×) indicate instructions not depicted. (See Appendix 5.)

DUMPITL Exits. Exit, a supervisor-assisted Return to EXECTASK, removes the subtask from the operating system.

DUMPITL may issue Link or Attach a second subtask whose load modules may issue still other dynamic program management SVCs.

From our illustrations it is not obvious that Attaching provides performance benefit over the other dynamic program management SVCs or even over a static LESTEP-effected, Call. Yet it is important to understand that a performance benefit does apply and to understand why. Recognizing that creating a task structure is unproductive overhead, we seek some offsetting efficiency. Our way lies through asynchronous processing and module sharing.

Asynchronous Processing and Load-Module Sharing

A load module's executions are either asynchronous or synchronous, depending on whether it processes requests in variable or fixed order.

Assume that a module had issued to IOS n EXCP SVC requests, R_1, R_2, . . . , R_n, for access to a multivolume data set. In the asynchronous case the processing may occur in any order, including that in which asynchronous channel service completes, the most efficient order of processing. Given three requests, issued in R_1, R_2, R_3 sequence, to access three 3330 units, channel service completion and request processing, both provided in R_3, R_2, R_1 sequence, may be accomplished within one device rotational period. The order of request processing, being variable, is free to adapt to the order of channel completion events.

Synchronous processing is another matter. Since processing of the same three requests may occur only in fixed sequence, say R_1, R_2, R_3, the processing that overlapped one rotational period in the asynchronous case might require three such periods, for if, as in the asynchronous case, the channel completion order requires an R_3, R_2, R_1 processing order for maximum efficiency, synchronous processing cannot comply.

In sharing, we recognize a load module to be data in storage until CPU activity is directed to it. The data then become a set of instructions and operands that are streamed.

A single load module may be shared among tasks. Assume that such a module reflects the source specifications,

$$\begin{cases} \text{READ EMPLOYEE-YTD} \\ \text{COMPUTE} \end{cases}$$

where, during say, EXECTASK$_3$, READ results in EXCP and Wait SVC executions in sequence, and COMPUTE expands to a series of arithmetic instructions. The consequence of READ is that an associated TCB, say EXECTCB$_3$, is placed in the task management wait queue, which, we assume, already contains EXECTCB$_1$ and EXECTCB$_2$. These tasks, like EXECTASK$_3$, share the single load module.

It now becomes a race; the first event to complete results in the removal of, say, EXECTCB$_3$ from the wait to the ready queue. EXECTASK$_3$ will be dispatched, and its load module resource will execute COMPUTE ahead of the other two tasks. The order in which requests may be issued and processed is independent—asynchronous processing.

PL/I Example. Our source program is written in PL/I because of its multitasking language. We refer to Figures 4.13 and 4.14.

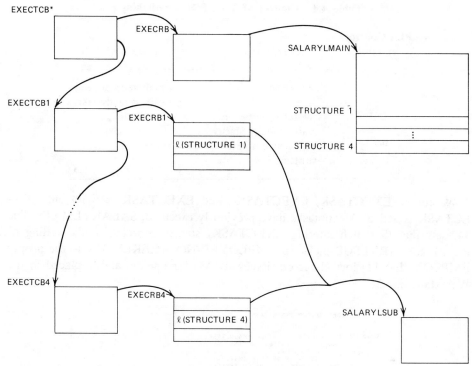

EXECTCB*

EXECRB

SALARYLMAIN

EXECTCB1

EXECRB1

STRUCTURE 1

ℓ (STRUCTURE 1)

STRUCTURE 4

EXECTCB4

EXECRB4

ℓ (STRUCTURE 4)

SALARYLSUB

Figure 4.13 Structure of a shared load module. The asterisk indicates that the TCB Wait queue is shown; the symbol *l* denotes "location of."

The application follows: punched-card inquiries in EMPLOYEE-WEEKLY are made of an indexed sequential data set, EMPLOYEE-YTD.* EMPLOYEE-YTD resides on several DASD units. The objective is to overlap electronic CPU-storage processes with electromechanical card reader and DASD processes.

A mother task [EXECTASK] attaches $i = 4$ daughter tasks [EXECTASK$_1$, EXECTASK$_2$, . . . , EXECTASK$_4$]. [A single reentrant load module, SALARYLSUB, is dynamically allocated among the daughter tasks. SALARYLSUB is independent of i; subtask particularity is in the EXECTASK$_i$ structure, not in SALARYLSUB. The TCBs of EXECTASK and its progency are elements in the TCB queue. Before reallocating the CPU, task management initializes EXECTASK or EXECTASK$_i$ by restoring its general purpose registers as they were when control was previously relinquished.

SALARYLSUB of EXECTASK$_i$ uses the storage space of SALARYLMAIN of EXECTASK; SALARYLMAIN READs EMPWEEKLY, and SALARYLSUB READs and REWRITEs EMPYTD. To update EMPYTD, SALARYLSUB must obtain a key, EMPLOYEE-NO-WEEKLY, from EXECTASK-owned storage space.

We now analyze our PL/I example. We begin with the CALL statement, line 18 in Figure 4.14. Under DO loop control, SALARYMAIN attaches $I = 4$ subtasks, EXECTASK$_i$, into OS/360 and then enters LOOP at statement 20. From within LOOP, statements 20 to 37, SALARYLMAIN READs EMPLOYEE-WEEKLY and controls the switching of EXECTCB between the wait and ready queues. Controls are applied to task status switching as shown in Table 4.1.

* For indexed sequential details see Chapter 8.

Table 4.1   Control of Task Status Switching

PL/I Control Variable	EXECTASK	EXECTASK$_i$
PS	Sets switch	Is switched between wait or ready status
DSP	Is switched between wait or ready status	Sets switch
PC	Identifies completed subtask, i	Sets switch

We follow EXECTASK, EXECTASK$_1$, and EXECTASK$_2$ activity only. EX-ECTASK is active. All subtasks have previously executed. SALARYLMAIN, line 34, sets the PS switch altering EXECTASK$_1$ status according to the setting of PC(1). SALARYLSUB picks up EMPLOYEE-NO-WEEKLY, key to the proper EMPLOYEE-YTD logical record, issues READ for update, and is placed in the Wait state, line 56.

```
         MAIN: PROC(PARM) OPTIONS(MAIN,TASK);

1        SALARIESMAIN: PROC(PARM) OPTIONS(MAIN,TASK);
2                 DCL PARM CHAR(16) VARYING,
                      DSP EVENT,
                      DSPCNT FIXED BIN INIT(0),
                      1 STRUCTURE(IM) CONTROLLED,
                      2 (PS,PC,PE) EVENT,
                      2 ID2 FIXED BIN,
                      2 TRMSW BIT(1) ALIGNED,
                      2 INBUF,
                      3 EMPLOYEE_NO_WEEKLY PICTURE '(5)9',
                      3 NAME CHAR(32),
                      3 FILLER CHAR(43),
                      TEMPBUF LIKE INBUF BASED(P),
             SEE  INFILE FILE INPUT RECORD,
             LEGEND MASTER FILE UPDATE KEYED DIRECT EXCLUSIVE
                      ENVIRONMENT(INDEXED);
3                 ON ENDFILE(INFILE) GO TO LAST;
         /* PICK UP PARAMETER IM, NUMBER OF PROCESS TASKS */
5                 IM=PARM;
         /* ALLOCATE AND INITIALIZE VARIABLES, OPEN FILES */
6                 ALLOCATE STRUCTURE;
7                 TRMSW='0'B;
8                 COMPLETION(DSP)='1';            /* PERMIT INITIAL DISPATCH */
9                 DO I=1 TO IM;
10                    ID2(I)=I;
11                    END;
12                OPEN FILE(INFILE),FILE(MASTER);
13                PUT LIST('   TIME   EVENT   CNT TSK        RECORD')SKIP;
         /* ATTACH PROCESS TASKS */
14                DO I=1 TO IM;
15                    COMPLETION(PS (I))='0';     /* DON'T LET IT START */
16                    COMPLETION(PC(I))='1';      /* MAKE IT AVAILABLE */
17                    PUT LIST(TIME||' CALL PROCESS')SKIP;
18                    CALL PROCESS(STRUCTURE(I)) EVENT(PE(I));
19                    END;
         /* WAIT FOR A PROCESS TO COMPLETE */
20       LOOP: WAIT(DSP);
21                COMPLETION(DSP)='0'B;
22                DSPCNT=DSPCNT+1;
23                PUT EDIT(TIME||' DSP      ',DSPCNT)(A,F(4))SKIP;
         /* FIND THE AVAILABLE PROCESS TASK */
24                DO I=1 TO IM;
25                    IF COMPLETION(PE(I)) THEN CALL IHEDUMP;   /* ERROR */
27                    IF COMPLETION(PC(I)) THEN DO;
29                        COMPLETION(PC(I))='0';   /* MAKE PROCESS TASK UNAVAILABLE */
         /* READ TRANSACTION INTO PROCESS TASK BUFFER */
30                        READ FILE(INFILE) SET(P);
31                        INBUF(I)=TEMPBUF;
32                        RDCNT=RDCNT+1;
33                        PUT EDIT(TIME||' READIN ',RDCNT,STRING(TEMPBUF))
                              (A,F(4),X(5),A)SKIP;
34                        COMPLETION(PS(I))='1';   /* START PROCESS TASK */
35                        END;
36                    END;
37                GO TO LOOP;
38       LAST: PUT LIST(TIME||' EOF ')SKIP;
         /* TERMINATE ALL PROCESS TASKS */
```

Figure 4.14   PL/I example. Read all references INFILE = EMPLOYEE-WEEKLY; MASTER = EMPLOYEE-YTD.

```
                 MAIN: PROC(PARM) OPTIONS(MAIN,TASK);

39                          DO I=1 TO IM;
40                             TRMSW(I)='1';
41                             COMPLETION(PS(I))='1';       /* START PROCESS TASK */
42                             WAIT(PE(I));     /* WAIT FOR IT TO COMPLETE */
43                             END;
44                          PUT LIST(TIME||' EOJ')SKIP;
45                          RETURN;


                   /* PROCESS TASK */
46                 SALARIESSUB: PROC(STRUCTURE);
47                          DCL 1 STRUCTURE,
                              2 (PS,PC,PE) EVENT,
                              2 ID2 FIXED BIN,
                              2 TRMSW BIT(1) ALIGNED,
                              2 INBUF,
                                3 EMPLOYEE_NO_WEEKLY PICTURE '(5)9',
                                3 NAME CHAR(32),
                                3 FILLER CHAR(43),
                              PROCNT FIXED BIN INIT(0),
                              1 INOUT,
                              2 NAME CHAR(32),
                              2 SOCIAL_SEC_YTD PICTURE '(6)9V99',
                              2 EMPLOYEE_NO_YTD PICTURE '(5)9',
                              2 CNTROL CHAR(1),
                              2 GROSS_PAY PICTURE '(6)9V99',
                              2 FILLER CHAR(66);
48                          ON ERROR COMPLETION(DSP)='1'B;
50                 LOOP: WAIT(PS);     /* START SWITCH */
51                          COMPLETION(PS)='0'B;
52                          PROCNT=PROCNT+1;
53                          IF TRMSW THEN RETURN;     /* TERMINATE SWITCH */
55                          PUT EDIT(TIME||' PROCESS',PROCNT,ID2,STRING(INBUF))
                                 (A,F (4),F(4),X(1),A)SKIP;
                   /* DEVELOP KEY HERE */
56                          READ FILE(MASTER) INTO(INOUT) KEY(EMPLOYEE_NO_WEEKLY);
57                          PUT EDIT(TIME||' RDMSTR ',PROCNT,ID2,STRING(INOUT))(R(FMT))SKIP;
58                   FMT:FORMAT(A,F (4),F(4),X(1),A(94));
                   /* UPDATE MASTER RECORD HERE */
59                          REWRITE FILE(MASTER) FROM(INOUT) KEY(EMPLOYEE_NO_WEEKLY);
60                          PUT EDIT(TIME||' REWRITE',PROCNT,ID2,STRING(INOUT))(R(FMT))SKIP;
61                          COMPLETION(PC),COMPLETION(DSP)='1'B;
62                          GO TO LOOP;
63                          END;
64                          END;
```

Figure 4.14—continued

Assume all subtasks, EXECTASK$_i$, now Wait. A previous READ, issued by SALARYLSUB under, say, EXECTASK$_2$ control completes. EXECTASK$_2$ is dispatched. SALARYLSUB, an EXECTASK$_2$ resource, executes statement 57, where the PL/I i–o statement PUT causes it to be placed in the Wait state again. When READ of EXECTASK$_1$ completes, that task again receives dynamic allocation of the CPU and SALARYLSUB executes line 57 where EXECTASK$_1$ is returned to the Wait state.

At length, SALARYLSUB proceeds to line 61, where the PC event variable is set to "1," notifying EXECTASK of the completion of, say, EXECTASK$_2$. SALARYLSUB then loops back to line 50, where event variable PS is set to "0"; consequently EXECTCB$_2$ is placed in the task management wait queue.

From the PL/I DCL (abbreviation of DECLARE) of line 2, INBUF is specified as BASEd.* This enables multiple unit record images to exist in EXECTASK-owned space, allowing multiple EXECTASK$_i$ generations to obtain EMPLOYEE-NO-WEEKLY for EMPLOYEE-YTD accessing at electronic, rather than card-reading, speed.

Our example illustrates transaction processing. In practice the inquiries would likely come to the system by telephone lines. EXECTASK$_i$ processing would be more comprehensive than shown. An inquiry might be: print out the retirement benefits for employees with between 20 and 25 years of service in order of length of service. Such a response requires a sort.

* DECLARE is the PL/I analogue of COBOL's DATA DIVISION.

4.8   OTHER VERSIONS OF OS/360

There are three versions of OS/360: multiprogramming with a variable number of tasks, (MVT), multiprogramming with a fixed number of tasks (MFT), and the primary control program (PCP).

Each version has a unique dispatching structure. In contrast to MVT, MFT tasks are established prior to *this* work period on the basis of storage partitions designated by the installation.* Where in MVT EXECSTEP results in the creation of EXECTCB, in MFT it results in the creation of SALRB and its chaining off of, say, PARTITION1TCB. Where in MVT, after SALARYL Returns, EXECTCB is erased from the annals of the operating system, in MFT PARTITION1TCB remains to control the steps of USERJOBs 1 . . . *n*.

In MFT, SYSIN Reader and SYSOUT Writer load modules execute under, say, PARTITION2TCB and PARTITION3TCB control in task structures similar to that of SALARYL.† With its fixed task structure, MFT would be unable to dispatch the several tasks of our PL/I example.

The dispatching structure of PCP resembles that of MFT where storage consists of a single partition. Consequently EXECSTEP consists of READERRB, SALRB, and WRITERRB being scheduled into the PARTITIONTASK structure one after another.

4.9   INPUT–OUTPUT SUPERVISOR

EXCP, issued by a data management program, say, results in interrupt to input–output supervisor (IOS) routines. After scheduling a request element on a serially reusable resource, IOS returns control to the data management program, which may make a second request, Wait, SVC 1. This SVC specifies that EXECTASK, say, must suspend execution until the i–o request completes.

A resource, lately busy, having become available, the i–o subsystem interrupts CPU processing. Entered at a second (different from EXCP) point, IOS dequeues the lately satisfied request and advances its successors in the FIFO waiting line. When EXECTASK's request arrives at the head of the line, IOS dispatches it. Following i–o completion, IOS dequeues this request, satisfying EXECTASK's Wait.

The i–o request queue resembles the TCB queue—both are FIFO. The i–o resource enqueued on is the logical S/370 channel. Multiple logical channels may transmit data simultaneously. The IOS is of a multiprocessing, as well as a multiprogramming, character.

Hardware architecture aids interrupt handling by the software. In the decision diamond of Figure 4.15, unmasking enables the CPU to accept interrupts pending in the i–o subsystem. In addition to channel mask bits, the architecture includes a fixed order of channel interruption and a Test Channel CPU instruction. For more than one device–control unit complex per channel, interrupts are stacked, priority down to the device applies. One interrupt per channel is made known to IOS at

---

* In MFT, tasks can also be established *during this* work period under the control of the operator.

† See Chapter 7.

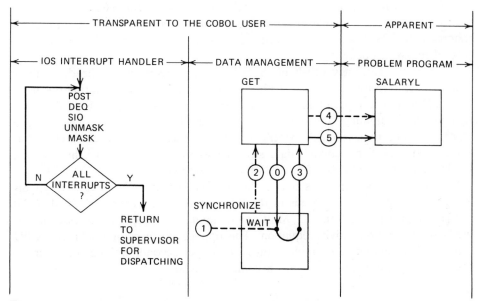

Figure 4.15 IOS asynchronous Posting of EXECTASK of the event of EMPYTD buffer filling: EXECTASK is dispatched at Synchronize. Note: Post includes event 1. (See Appendix 1.)

one time. As Figure 4.15 depicts, when IOS has handled all interrupts, it relinquishes CPU control. Should IOS's posting have readied a high priority task, the dispatcher's instruction, Load Program Status Word, returns the CPU to problem streaming.

The IOS optimizes resource utilization. An independently acting i–o resource signals its availability by interruption; the IOS quickly dispatches work to it.

4.10 SUMMARY

In Chapter 1, a data processing system was described as a set of resources that responds to user requests. Thereafter we saw that this design concept may be made productive actually through the simultaneous activity of the independent resources of the system.

In hardware, the channel resource streams commands in parallel with CPU instruction sequencing. In software, OS/360 load modules may be reentrant, shared.

A task views System/370 as a serially reusable resource on which it is scheduled.

The system is initialized for EXECTASK when that task's instructions and data operands are in storage. Through static allocation, job management initializes System/370 before the system's first use by a task. Task management initializes System/370 before each reuse by a task, a two-stage process.

After static allocation, EXECTCB is scheduled into task management's ready queue. After having been dispatched, EXECTASK requests dynamic allocation by issuing, say, EXCP. Recognizing that its System/370 has become unready, EXECTASK signals task management to schedule EXECTCB into the Wait queue. At length, an event results in the reinitialization of System/370, and EXECTCB is scheduled into task management's ready queue. When the TCB arrives at the head of its line, task management performs the second stage of initialization; it restores CPU, PSW, and general purpose registers as they were when EXECTCB entered the Wait queue.

What of the efficiency of all of this? Queue processing is overhead, a minus; simultaneous resource activity is a plus. In performance, after factoring out hardware differences, comparing second-generation uniprogramming with third-generation multiprogramming, the advantage lies with third generation. The cause is higher resource utilization. A system with highly used CPU and channels is balanced, hence efficient; enough data stream into storage across the channels that hardware waits (1 in bit 14 of the PSW) seldom occur.

System/370 productivity is above that of first- or second-generation systems. The ratio of cpu internal speeds in the three generations (IBM 704:7094:S/370 M168) approximates 1:6:72. Multiprogramming has become an essential ingredient of the productivity equation. The opportunity cost of an M 168 CPU, capable of executing three million instructions per second, waiting too often for events of, say, 30 milliseconds, has become expensive.

EXERCISES

4.1 In Appendix 1, DUMPIT, relative locations 10 and 11 (lines 7 and 8), establish addressability. Why are no instructions generated from USING? Explain the BALR function. At what step time is (a) USING processed; (b) BALR executed?

4.2 In Appendix 2, what base register does CALLIT use? What are its contents during CALLITL execution?

4.3 In general, a non-reusable executing load module contains S/370 general purpose register save areas within its own main storage space. How many save areas does SALARYL contain (Appendix 1, p. 218)?

4.4 A save area is system dependent. Discuss the COBOL user's relation to the specification of the save area of SALARYL.

4.5 Does the executing load module resulting from the matrix multiplication program in Fig. 1.8 have a save area?

4.6 During data management Get processing an S/370 malfunction occurs. Where would the general purpose register status at the time of the fault be saved? From Appendix 1, what would R15 contain? (Note: Get is load module IGGO19AA—see the contents directory entry.)

4.7 What system program inserts the V type address constant DUMPIT (Appendix 1)?

4.8 From Appendix 1 locate the SALARYL save area: (a) in the COBOL memory map; (b) in the dump.

4.9 (a) From the dump save area (Appendix 1), when DUMPITL returns control to SALARYL, at what location will SALARYL execution resume? (b) What is the DUMPITL branch-to location? (c) DUMPITL issues SNAP at relative location 26, resulting in SVC 51. Would you expect to see DUMPITL's general purpose registers saved subsequent to SVC 51 execution? Are they? (Hint: see the indicative portion of the dump.)

4.10 Is SALARYL reentrant, reusable or non-reusable?

4.11 The FORTRAN programmer who writes matrix multiply includes instructions to CALL DUMPIT in a simple program management structure. How many save areas will the resultant load module contain? In the branch from matrix multiply to DUMPITL, what role does the OS/360 supervisor play

4.12 CALLITL Calls DUMPITL. DUMPITL, in turn, Calls DUMPITL1. Should DUMPITL have its own save area?

4.13 The DUMPITL Snap macro expands to include SVC 51 service (Abdump). From Appendix 1, p. 216, identify the DUMPITL general purpose register contents at the time of Snap.

4.14 CALLITL Links to DUMPITL (Fig. 5.6). How many save areas are involved? Does the CPU change state during the Linking process? Assuming that DUMPITL is a DASD-resident library member, are any SVC other than Link, SVC 6, involved?

4.15 CALLITL Links to DUMPITL. DUMPITL in turn Links to DUMPITL1. Draw the request block structure of EXECTASK during the existence of DUMPITL1.

4.16 Comment—if LINK is inappropriate substitute a different system macro in the following:

Location	Instruction	Comment
LINK	LINK	
	BCT 10, LINK	C (GPR 10) = 5

4.17 (a) From Figure 5.6, to what point does CPU control Return after Link to DUMPITL? (b) Notice that this point is not in CALLITL space. What routine provides this Return location? (c) Give a possible reason for the supervisor-assisted Return process.

4.18 CALLITL Links to DUMPITL. Show the EXECTASK request block queue during (a) Link service (implies Link is a type II SVC—see Appendix 11), (b) DUMPITL execution, (c) Return from DUMPITL (implies Exit is a type I SVC—see Appendix 11), (d) after Return and during CALLITL execution.

4.19 From Figure 5.7, to what point in CALLITL does control Return after the BALR to DUMPITL at relative location 064

4.20 In Figures 5.8 and 5.9, DUMPITL overlaps CALLITL in main storage. A new entry point results. What save area location(s) is affected?

4.21 CALLITL issues Attach for DUMPITL. DUMPITL in turn Links to DUMPITL1. (a) Indicate the structure processed by task management. (b) CALLITL Opens EMPYTD for i–o. Can DUMPITL access EMPYTD? (c) To which task is the i–o resource involved statically allocated?

4.22 Assemble CALLITL to Read a logical record (BSAM) by modifying the source program of Appendix 5.

4.23 (a) In Figure 5.12, how many copies of SALARIESSUB exist in main storage simultaneously? (b) Can SALARIESSUB in its turn issue a PL/I language CALL to a second level of subprogram?

4.24 From the dump of Appendix 1 depict EXECSTEP main storage geometry (see Fig. 5.5).

4.25 From the dump of Appendix 1 identify the routines resident in the link pack area. See the Contents Directory Entry format in the IBM Systems Reference Library Manual *OS/360 System Control Blocks,* C-28-6628.

4.26 In Chapter 2, control program service and supervision were described as being provided by routines in S/370 supervisor state. Discuss each of these program types in relation to dynamic resource allocation. Is dynamic resource allocation part of a service? Does it occur in conjunction with task supervision?

4.27 Random accesses to data blocks of a data set are sorted into queues, each of which is associated with a subtask, device queue 1 with subtask 1, and so on. The initial condition is that all subtasks have a queue of outstanding requests. Subtask process sequence is as follows: start—issue i–o request; end—process completed i–o request. The main task controls the activation of subtasks.

(a) Using the pattern below as a guide, draw a bar chart depicting each i–o activity as being of eight times the duration of each CPU process (either start or end).

(b) As a second exercise, construct a simple program management structure to accomplish the same function as (a) and comment on the relative efficiency between these two.

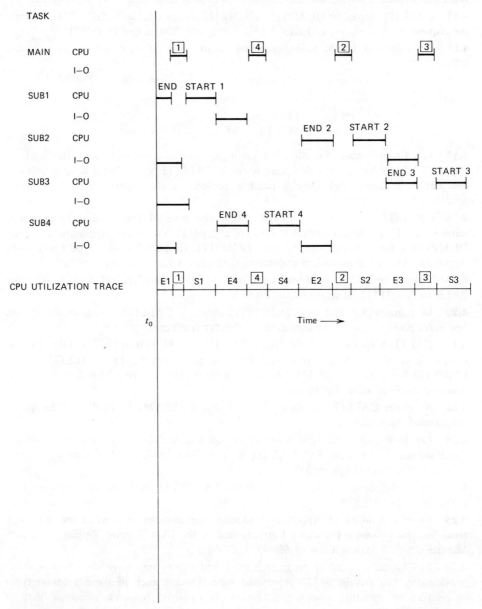

Figure 4.16 Pattern for Dynamic Program Management for Exercise 4.27 (a). Numbers in boxes denote sub-task for which main task streams instructions.

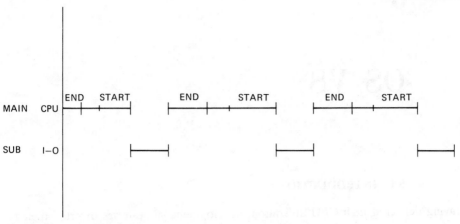

Figure 4.17   Pattern for Simple Program Management for Exercise 4.27 (b).

4.28   Using EXCP logic, construct a CCW list to violate the DEB extent limits of EMPYTD (refer to Appendix 1).

4.29   Consider REWRITE-YTD RECORD, Appendix 1. The EMPYTD data set shares its DASD residence with various other data sets. (a) In REWRITEing, can the user disturb another data set? (b) What did the SALARIES user state to protect others? (c) Where is the protection provided?

4.30   An S/370 operator depresses the attention key of a 1052 for terminal service. What kind of interrupt results?

chapter **5**

OS/VS

5.1 INTRODUCTION

Having delivered high CPU utilization, development laboratories diverted their resources to communications teleprocessing, with a new emphasis—improved response time. System/370R resulted.

Often the high utilization of System/370 was achieved through an initiation strategy. $EXECSTEP_a$ of $USERJOB_1$, which frequently Waited for i–o, was initiated with $EXECSTEP_b$ of $USERJOB_2$, which seldom Waited. Job control language specified $EXECSTEP_a$ to be of the higher dispatching priority; during execution its i–o activity overlapped the CPU activity of $EXECSTEP_b$.

OS/VS systems achieve high utilization through more multiprogramming than OS/360 offered. In circumstances where OS/360 may not have initiated job steps because of limited main storage, OS/VS often initiates the steps because of its greater storage capacity.

Unlike OS/360, primarily a batch operating system, OS/VS, primarily a teleprocessing operating system, is driven by unpredictable activities. An inquiry from a communications terminal, "What is George M. Eisele's year-to-date Social Security amount?" occurs at an unpredictable time. The OS/VS2 release 2 operating system is particularly sensitive to the activities resulting from such an inquiry, for instance, retrieving the amount from DASD, where the time of the i–o completion is unpredictable.

The amount of time it takes for the system to respond to a terminal is crucial. A secretary will wait seconds, she may wait minutes, but she will not wait hours for a response.

In software, OS/VS2 has two implementations: a single (16 megabyte) virtual storage system, release 1, and a multiple (16 megabyte) virtual storage system, release 2.* As to hardware, where S/370 operated with a program status word in the basic control mode, S/370R, augmenting the program status word with 16 transparent control registers, operates in extended control mode. Because we deal wih two relocate systems and refer back to a nonrelocate system, Table 5.1 is included to keep matters straight.

Release 2 is of multiprocessing as well as of virtual storage design. Simultaneously active CPUs bring new problems. In the discussion of multiprocessing in Section 5.7, we encounter the lock, which guarantees the integrity of serially reusable resources.

---

* The terms "release 1" and "release 2" will be used hereafter.

Table 5.1

System[a]	Hardware[a]	Software
System/370R	S/370R	OS/VS2 (release 1)
		OS/VS2 (release 2)
System/370	S/370	OS/360
System/360	S/360	OS/360

[a]R indicates a relocate system.

In Chapter 4, we saw a control program as a set of routines using data structures as i–o; in OS/VS2 this holds. Since OS/VS systems are extensions to OS/360, similarities between the two systems exist. JCL written for OS/360 may specify EXECSTEP's resource requirements to OS/VS. OS/360 load modules, unchanged, run on OS/VS.

Release 2, in addition to differing from OS/360 in its management of storage (as all OS/VS systems do), has a different data structure as well. Before we discuss how and why, we turn to prerequisite topics: virtual storage, paging, relocation, and release 1.

5.2 VIRTUAL STORAGE

System/370 users contemplated large storage—and with good reason. With it many diverse job steps could be initiated together; also, programmers were freed from writing large program segments that overlayed one another in storage.

In System/370, the term "16 megabytes of storage" meant 16 megabytes of main storage. A large System/370 typically had a storage of 2 megabytes; 16-megabyte storage was unfeasible.

There was more to large storage than the vague yearnings of users; S/370 CPUs could handle (effective) addresses of up to 24 bits. Using this address space, OS/VS can simulate 16 megabytes of storage, using an inexpensive mix of some real storage and much DASD to do so. A CPU's address space available to the user through operating system supervision is called virtual storage.

The schematic of System/370R virtual storage resembles that of System/370 main storage (Fig. 5.1). A systems area starts at address zero and includes a control program nucleus. A dynamic area is the residence of user jobs and systems tasks. High virtual storage includes a link pack area. That no great homogeneous extent of locations is accessed by the CPU is transparent. Virtual storage appears to the user as System/370 main storage did; his dumps reflect this.

5.3 PAGING

Large storage at economical cost was one target for OS/VS advance. More efficient management of what main storage did exist was another. Consider an OS/360 system with 250 kilobytes of storage available to its users. Figure 5.2 depicts job steps A, B, and C of USERJOBs 1, 2, and 3 as initiated; job steps D and E of USERJOBs 4 and 5, say, await initiation. Coexistence of tasks D and E with tasks

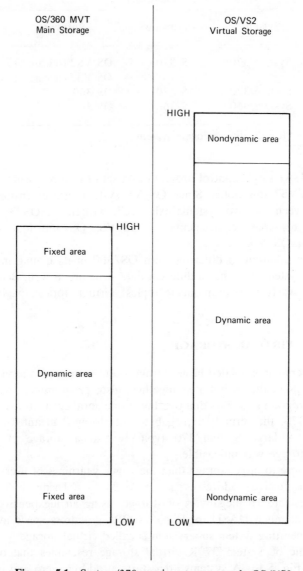

Figure 5.1 System/370 main storage and OS/VS2 virtual storage. The ends of storage with low and high address are indicated. From the IBM handbook *IBM Systems, OS/VS2 Planning Guide,* GC-28-0600.

A, B, and C is impossible. This problem, caused by the variable length of load modules, is called storage fragmentation. OS/VS2 reduces fragmentation by transforming load modules into fixed-sized blocks, of 4096 bytes each, called pages. Pages are transmitted between fixed-size extents in real storage (the System/370R name for main storage) frames and external page storage slots, under the control of a paging supervisor.

Two distinct OS/VS2 components transfer data between real storage and DASD. One is apparent; one is transparent. The VS IOS responds to READ-EM-

User main storage (kilobytes)

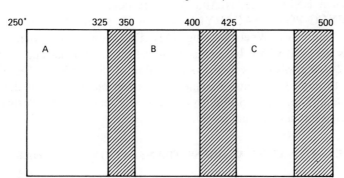

Figure 5.2 Schematic of storage occupancy by job steps A, B, and C. Job steps D and E (50 kilobytes each) await initiation. The shaded areas indicate unoccupied storage. The asterisk indicates a 256-kilobyte-design point control program nucleus (rounded to 250 kilobytes).

PLOYEE-YTD. The VS paging supervisor responds to a paging interrupt, unpredictably active during CPU streaming.

5.4 FUNCTIONS OF A PAGING SUPERVISOR

A virtual operating system causes a limited amount of real storage to appear as a vast amount of virtual storage. Its paging supervisor processes page faults and steals, swaps, and initializes pages.

The S/370R CPUs translate virtual to real storage addresses automatically. Fault processing occurs when a program references an address in a page not in real storage. In EXECTASK, SALARYL instructions and data operands may be automatically translated by the CPU for, say, 2000 instruction fetches and executions—until SALARYL refers to a missing page. An S/370R program interrupt results. Then OS/VS2 locates and obtains the absent page, which may be on DASD, in real storage but not allocated to EXECTASK, or enroute between real storage and DASD.

Stealing, unlike page fault processing, is invoked by the control program. OS/VS2 steals infrequently referenced pages from tasks, thereby maintaining a reserve of allocable frames.* The stolen pages are transmitted to external page storage on DASD. Later the victimized tasks may suffer page faults.

Like stealing, swapping is supervisory. In communications processing we say that a task's pages have been swapped out. We mean that the control program, initializing the dispatching of task A, has swapped the pages of task B from real to external page storage. The pages of task A are then swapped in from external to real page storage. Later, before task B may resume, its pages must be swapped back in.

The supervisor initializes load modules for paging and loads the page and segment tables used in dynamic address translation.

---

* The control program periodically tests a reference bit in the real storage key to determine if a page has been lately referenced.

Before its initialization in OS/VS, SALARYL is a library member, as it was in OS/360. When EXECTASK is Attached in response to EXECSTEP job control language [EXEC PGM=SALARYL], SALARYL addresses are relocated to virtual storage addresses. When fetching SALARYL into real storage, the OS/VS loader loads the SALARYL base registers to reflect the module's position in virtual storage. The loader also sees to the initialization of the EXECTASK segment and page tables to point to the task's frame locations in real storage. If during loading the paging supervisor steals SALARYL pages, slot locations in external page storage are entered into an external page table.

5.5   DYNAMIC ADDRESS TRANSLATION (DAT) HARDWARE

Relocation uses the extended-control mode of S/370R; 16 control registers are defined. These registers, augmenting the S/370R program status word, are addressable by privileged instructions and are used in transparent operations. In extended control, some fields that in basic control were in the program status word are stored in control registers. In dynamic address translation, control register 1 plays a particularly important role.

After being loaded into virtual storage, the SALARYL addresses are in the base register (B), index register (X), and displacement (D) format of System/370. For each instruction execution a 24-bit effective address, $E = c(B) + c(X) + D$ (for RX format, say), is calculated. A second set of S/370R instruction time operations translates the virtual address E to a real address (Fig. 5.3). The 12 high-order bits of E, translated by CPU circuitry, specify a page within a segment; the 12 low-order bits, untranslated, locate an operand in a page down to the byte. Translation locates a page in real or external page storage. Translation operations use segment and page frame tables in real storage.* The segment and page frame fields of the virtual address are offsets to the table origins.

Figure 5.4 depicts a translation. At activity 1, the segment offset, added to the origin of the segment table, previously loaded into control register 1, locates the page frame table origin. This origin address, added to the page frame offset, locates the real page frame address, which, combined with the 12 low-order bytes of virtual address, forms the 24-bit real storage address. Pure hardware translation occurs only when a referenced page is in real storage. Other situations involve OS/VS.

Stimulated by a program interrupt, the OS paging supervisor locates a page in external storage. A page translation exception occurs when the invalid bit in the page frame table entry for a virtual address has been set on (after the page has

---

* Sometimes after being accessed, these are in CPU local storage.

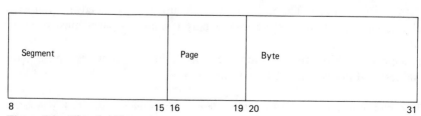

Segment	Page	Byte
8 15	16 19	20 31

Figure 5.3   Virtual address.

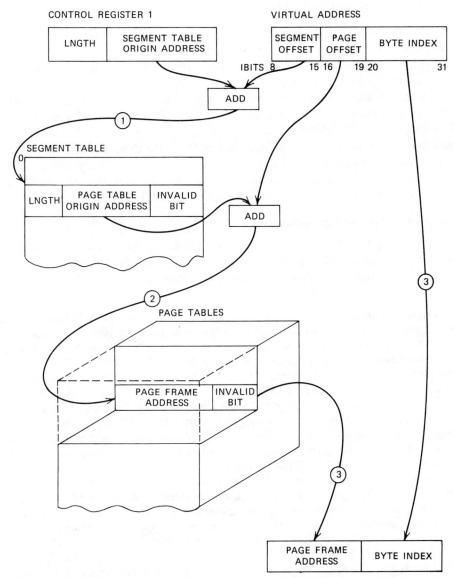

Figure 5.4 Dynamic address translation—table look-up operation.

been, say, swapped or stolen). The page on auxiliary storage is accessed through an external page table with arguments resembling those of the page frame table and entries that locate a page in external storage.*

A segment table exception occurs when the invalid bit in a segment table entry is set on. In release 1, USERJOB$_1$ is allocated, say, virtual storage segment 1, and USERJOB$_2$ is allocated segment 2. If USERJOB$_1$ references an address in the space of USERJOB$_2$, a segment table exception occurs.

_____

* In using a telephone book the person's name is the argument and the telephone number is the entry.

5.6   OS/VS2 RELEASE 1

Figure 5.1 depicts OS/VS2 virtual storage as divided into a low and a high systems area that is not pageable and a dynamic area that is. The segment table resides in the high area; the page and external page tables reside in the dynamic area, along with individual user regions.

Resource managers account for storage. The virtual storage manager (VSM) maintains a structure of PQEs and DQEs, thereby controlling static and dynamic allocations of virtual storage. The real storage manager (RSM) initializes and maintains page frame and external page slot tables in the dynamic area, supporting dynamic address translation and the paging functions. The auxiliary storage manager (ASM) retrieves pages by translating logical page addresses, the entries of the external page table, into physical addresses (CCHHR).

Components of the Paging Supervisor

Fault processing requiring a page-in and stealing requiring a page-out then a page-in illustrate that part of this supervisor executes under ordinary OS task control and that part is non-task-controlled. The supervisor's resource managers appear in both components.

Example—Fault Processing. SALARYL references an address in, say, page A, with no real storage frame currently assigned. A program interrupt occurs, activity 1 in Figure 5.5. Through an extension, the program first level interrupt handler passes control to the real storage manager, activities 2 and 3. Using the SALARYL virtual page address, the real storage manager looks up the address of page A in the external page table; it also tests if EXECTASK, say, has issued and the virtual storage manager has processed Getmain for this page.* If so, it allocates a page frame from an available inventory and Returns, activity 4. A program control block (PCB) is scheduled into a page i–o initiation work queue, activity 5. After Return from this scheduler, activity 6, the paging supervisor, having recognized that the page fault cannot be processed in microseconds, places EXECTASK in RB/Wait.

Control passes to the task-controlled component via the regular OS dispatcher, activities 8 and 9. The page i–o initiation queue is interrogated for work, activity 10. All page-in and page-out requests in this queue are sorted (slot sorting, see p. 105) for efficient transmission to the paging device and are then scheduled into a page i–o active work queue for IOS scheduling. Paging supervisor Returns, activities 11 and 12, and, say, TCB$_x$ is dispatched. Later, during the execution of say, EXECTASK$_x$, the transmission of page A to a frame in real storage completes. The consequent i–o interrupt invokes the page i–o activity routine, resulting in EXECTASK being posted ready, activities 13 through 19.

Example—Stealing. The task-controlled supervisor has a set of queue manager routines controlled by a master routine, page task queue scanner. Each queue manager receives CPU control in the order of its priority relative to that of other queue managers. Elements are moved from queue to queue by a routine, Move PCB, which detaches requests from queue A, say, and schedules them as requests for the next function to be performed. Each queue may have work, be empty, or be suppressed. Our example, stealing, fills in some details of task-controlled paging supervision omitted in our page fault example.

---

* If the outcome of this test is no, the program interrupt was caused by, say, an addressing exception as in OS/MVT; as a consequence, EXECTASK (usually) will be terminated.

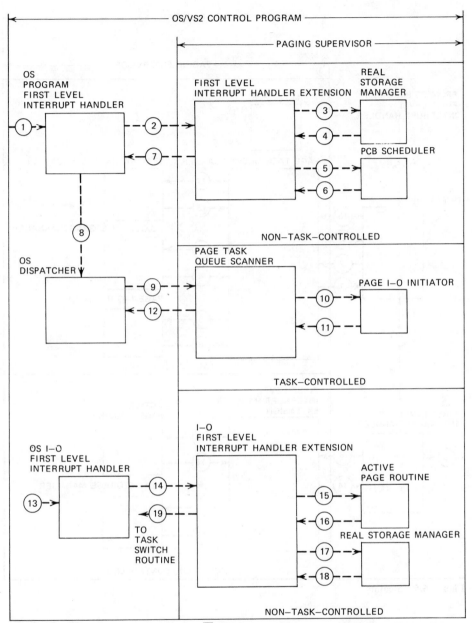

Figure 5.5 Page fault. Note that the page task queue scanner is represented by the highest priority TCB in the system.

On allocation of a frame for, say, page A, the real storage manager, recognizing that its allocable-fame inventory has fallen below some predetermined limit, steals frames from active tasks.

For pages to be stolen, the paging supervisor allocates external page storage, initializes page-out requests to IOS, and Returns (Fig. 5.6).

Initially pages D . . . G have been selected for page-out and PCBs D . . . C have been scheduled into the auxiliary storage manager queue before the paging supervisor, executing under the highest priority TCB in the system, is entered.

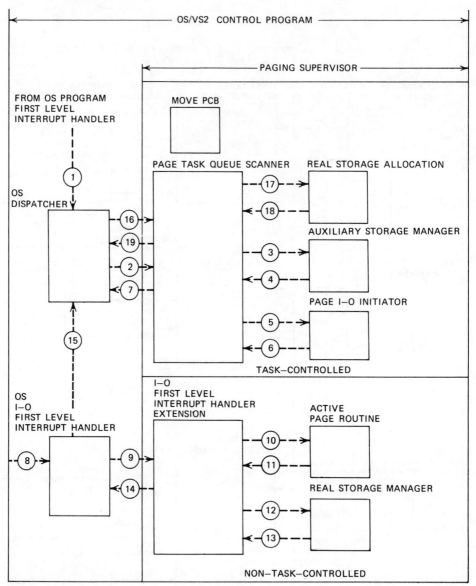

Figure 5.6   Stealing.

After the auxiliary storage manager allocates external page slots, PCBs D . . . G are moved to the page i–o initiator queue for sorting, activities 5 and 6, and are then moved into the active page i–o queue for scheduling by IOS, after which the page supervisor Returns, activities 6 and 7, and the task controlled component is placed in RB/Wait. $EXECTCB_y$, say, is dispatched. $EXECTASK_y$ takes a page fault resulting in the scheduling of PCB_y into the real storage allocation queue, which thereupon is suppressed (no more allocable frames). $EXECTASK_y$ is placed in RB/Wait. $EXECTASK_z$ is dispatched.

Subsequent to activities 8 through 11 the real storage manager, advised that page-out of pages D through G has completed, updates its inventory of available frames, activities 12 and 13; suppression of the real storage allocation queue is removed, and Return to the dispatcher is effected, activities 14 and 15. The task-controlled component is entered, activity 16. Real storage allocation supervisor, the highest ready routine, dispatches all of its requests for frames, activity 17. Control is Returned to the dispatcher, activities 18 and 19, which activates the highest priority ready task.

Consideration. Performance governs whether task- or nontask-controlled routines are entered. In stealing, page-out is under task control. Where pages are unchanged, page-out is unnecessary, a backup copy resides in external page storage. The supervisor reclaims such pages at high speed, under nontask control.

Task-controlled supervision executes under the highest priority TCB in the system. Task switching to this supervisor occurs at high speed, avoiding the usual decision processing of the TCB queue, which is time consuming.

The work queues controlled by the task-controlled supervisor page-out not only the programs and data but also the page tables and external page tables of EXECTASK.

Slot Sorting

Virtual storage is partially DASD. Slot sorting chains channel programs of the independent requests of the page i–o queue, accessing thereby the most auxiliary storage (DASD) slots in the fewest device rotations. An external page table entry contains a group number and a slot number; the group number designates, say, a cylinder of 3330 movable-head file or an entire 2305 fixed-head file; there is no mechanical head motion within a group. Groups have slots, relative external page locations within groups.

A 3330 group has 57 slots (57 4096 byte pages fit on a 3330 cylinder). The number of groups and slots is device dependent, which concerns the operating system, not the user—paging is transparent.

We illustrate the slot-sorting routines of page i–o initiator manipulating channel programs.

A number of paging channel programs, created at the beginning of *this* work period, exist. Dequeuing its paging requests, page i–o initiator schedules inactive channel programs into the slot queues, illustrated as columns in Table 5.1. Channel programs are command chained together: the first program manipulates the page for slot 1 of the group, the second for slot 2 of the group, and so on, until the supply of available channel programs is exhausted. The PCBs corresponding to these channel programs (one PCB per program) are then moved to the page i–o

Table 5.1 Slot Queue Schematic for a Paging Device Group—Five Slots per Track

Track	Slot				
	1	2	3	4	5
A	A_1	A_2	A_3	A_4	A_5
B	B_1	B_2	B_3	B_4	B_5
C	C_1	C_2	C_3	C_4	C_5

activity work queue by Move PCB. When a channel–control unit–device complex becomes available, EXCP is issued.

The last command of every fourth program is conditioned to cause a form of i–o interrupt (PCI see Chapter 9), whereupon an OS interrupt handler extension adds available channel programs (channel programs for the pages of slots A_1, A_2, and A_3 in our example) to the back end of the series as A_5, B_1, and B_2. Thus, the channel program chain for Table 5.1 is represented by PCBs A_1, A_2, A_3, A_4, A_5, B_1 . . . , C_5 in the five slot queues.

Channel programs accessing slots are chained according to an algorithm. In our example, should slot queues 2 and 5 be empty, only slot A_1 would be accessed.

Channel Address Translation

In SALARYL EMPYTD is read into a real buffer as a result of the channel command RD . . . XXXXX; XXXXX is a virtual address. Unlike the CPU, the channel has no dynamic address translation mechanism but relies on IOS. Our examples illustrate this support.

Activity diagram—READ of logical record 20. Initially, SALARYL has Opened EMPYTD; what follows in OS/VS2 resembles OS/360. In addition, VS2 fixes a frame in real storage for SALARYL buffers. (A fixed page may not be swapped or stolen.) Figure 3.15 depicts SALARYL's reading of the twentieth logical record of EMPYTD. Virtual locations of logical records are passed to SALARYL in general purpose register 1, activity 3.

Acitvity diagram—READ of logical record 21. Let us refer to Figure 3.16. There data management Get is the target of the SALARYL branch, activity 2, after the location of the DCB EMPLOYEE-YTD is passed to data management via general purpose register 1, activity 1. Get, determining that this request represents an end-of-block condition for buffer 2, passes control to EOB, activity 3, which issues EXCP, activity 4; IOS translates the virtual addresses of the channel program to the real addresses, allocated by the real storage manager, of buffer 2.

OS/VS2 Considerations

The OS/360 type II, III, and IV SVC load modules, normally enabled, at times executed disabled for i–o interrupt. In OS/VS2 such SVCs pose a problem—it has to do with paging.

A program interrupt, unaffected by masking in the program status word (disablement) stimulates page fault processing. In OS/360, the intent of (periodically) disabling during SVC execution was to protect some serially reusable resource. In release 1, if, during disablement, an SVC routine suffers a page fault, resulting in, say, EXECTASK$_1$ being placed in RB/Wait, EXECTASK$_2$ might get control. EXECTASK$_2$ may call on the identical SVC—the serially reusable resource and hence the system's integrity are exposed.

Release 1 uses a lock controlled by the supervisor to overcome this problem.* Before, say, SVC$_n$, which takes disabled page faults, may serve SALARYL, EXECTASK$_1$ must obtain a lock. If SVC$_n$ takes a page fault and EXECTASK$_1$ is placed in RB/Wait and if, say, EXECTASK$_2$ is switched to, before the latter may issue SVC$_n$ it must attempt to obtain the lock. It may not—only one task at a

---

* See also the discussion of multiprocessing in Section 5.7.

time holds a lock. Instead, EXECTASK$_2$ is placed in TCB/RB Wait. Control goes to, say, EXECTASK$_3$. EXECTASK$_1$ only, uses the serially reusable resource until the lock is released.

5.7   OS/VS2 RELEASE 2

Introduction

Fetching from 16 megabytes rather than, say, 1 megabyte of storage, release 1 runs more batch tasks and supports more terminals than OS/360 MVT. Supporting multiple 16-megabyte storages, release 2 increases the number of tasks and terminals again. Each terminal user may have his own 16 megabytes of virtual storage.

There is one segment table for each virtual storage. After, say EXECTASK$_2$ of USERJOB$_2$ receives control following the RB/Wait of EXECTASK$_1$ of USERJOB$_1$, the control program initializes control register 1 with the segment table origin of the address space of EXECTASK$_2$.

Virtual storage divides into a low and high systems area and a pageable dynamic area. The high area subdivides into a pageable common area and a nonpageable systems area. Through page table entries that are identical for each address space each such space addresses common.

In release 1, we described a paging supervisor; in release 2, we describe individual resource managers. The virtual storage manager, through a structure of PQEs and DQEs, maintains static and dynamic control of virtual allocations. The real storage manager maintains page frame and external slot tables. The auxiliary storage manager translates logical page identifiers, passed by the real storage manager, into DASD addresses. Finally, we introduce the virtual block processor (VBP), the access method of paging.

Where release 1 adapted the MVT work structure release 2 alters it. Switching to and from address spaces, overhead, must be efficient—communications tasks residing in individual address spaces require a system sensitive to unpredictable activity; also, for performance and reliability, multiprocessing configurations may be installed. Two new elements, the address space and the service module, in addition to the task, are dispatched according to the priority scheme shown in Table 5.2.

Request elements within each priority are chained FIFO within priority for that class.

Table 5.2

Priority	Request Element—Representing	Description
1	Service Request Block, SRB—service module	System-wide, controlled through a Service Priority List
2	Address Space Control Block, ASCB—address space	One per space
3	Service Request Block, SRB—service module	Within one user's address space, controlled through a Service Priority List
4	Task Control Block, TCB—task	Within one user's address space

Example 1. We refer to Figure 5.7. The execution of EXECTASK₁ interrupted by the i–o completion of EXECTASK₃ introduces the new structure: we assume one CPU.

Issued by EXECTASK₁, EXCP₁ executes enabled, activity 1 in Figure 5.7a; an i–o interrupt for EXECTASK₃ occurs, activity 2. The control program schedules SRB₃ₓ a request for IOS completion service, activity 3. The newly idle channel is reactivated with previously scheduled work for, say, EXECTASK₂.

After EXCP₁ Returns, activity 4, SRB₃ₓ is dispatched, and EXECTASK₃ is thereby made ready, activities 5 and 6. Whether EXECTASK₁ or EXECTASK₃ is dispatched next depends on their relative priorities.

Considerations. After activity 2, the origin of the segment table for address space 1 is in control register 1, yet the control program schedules work for address space 3; no switch of address spaces is involved since such spaces have areas addressed in common (through identical entries in their several segment tables). Service modules reside in common areas of virtual storage.

In OS MVT, EXCP, a type I SVC, executed masked against i–o interruptions. OS/360 would have been insensitive to activity 2.

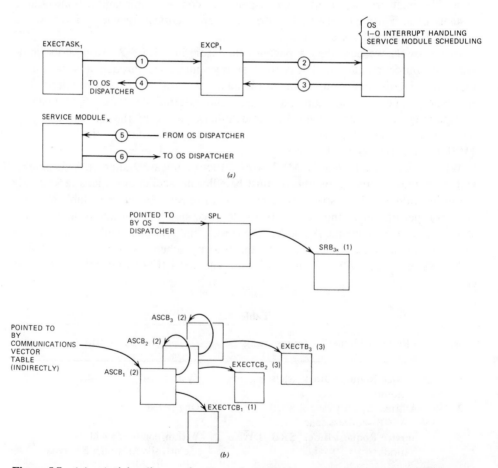

Figure 5.7 (*a*) Activity diagram for Example 1. Service module 3 executes under the control of SRB₃. (*b*) Dispatching structure for Example 1. The numerals in parentheses indicate dispatching priority.

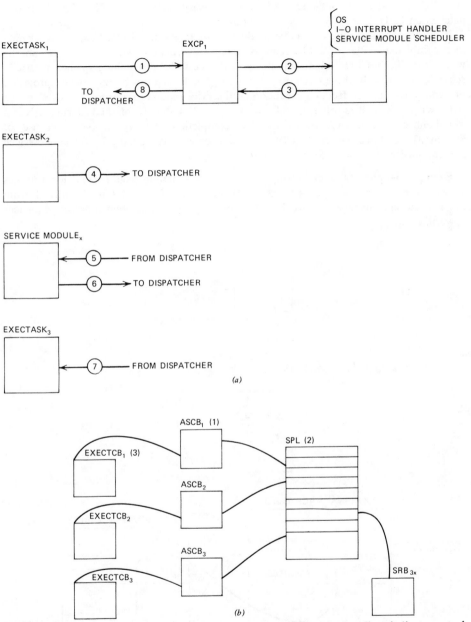

Figure 5.8   (*a*)   Activity diagram for Example 2. The solid and broken lines indicate control by CPU 1 and CPU 2, respectively.   (*b*)   Dispatching structure for Example 2. The numerals in parentheses indicate dispatching priority.

Example 2. The activity diagram is shown in Figure 5.8*a* and the dispatching structure, in Figure 5.8*b*. We assume two CPUs. EXECTASK$_1$ and EXECTASK$_2$ are active on CPUs 1 and 2 respectively; EXECTASK$_3$ Waits.

EXECTASK$_1$ issues EXCP$_1$, activity 1. Input–output interrupt for EXECTASK$_3$ occurs, and SRB$_{3x}$ is scheduled, activity 2. Control Returns to EXCP$_1$, activity 3. Now EXECTASK$_2$ Returns, activity 4, and service module$_x$ under SRB$_{3x}$ control, is dispatched

110   OS/VS

on CPU 2, activity 5, making EXECTASK₃ ready, activity 6. EXECTASK₃ is dispatched on CPU 2, activity 7; EXCP₁ continues.

If during the streaming of service moduleₓ, EXCP₁ Returned to EXECTASK₁, which then completed, CPU 1 would stream dispatcher instructions while the service module was active. Both CPUs might simultaneously access the dispatching queue, a serially reusable resource. In these circumstances, CPU 1 is locked out by the control program, prevented from any instruction execution until service moduleₓ Returns.

Given the activities of Fig. 5.8, in OS MVT CPU 1, masked during EXCP₁, would have been insensitive to the i–o completion, activity 2. Nor, because of System/370 architecture, could CPU 2, idle after activity 4, have sensed and serviced this completion.

Example 3—page fault processing. Control passes among page supervision routines in set patterns. In fault processing, the sequence in Figure 5.9 is downward from the real storage manager, whereas in Posting page i–o completion, control sequences upward.

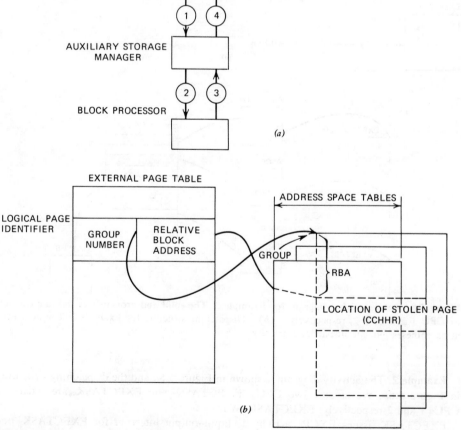

Figure 5.9 (*a*) Activity diagram, stolen-page retrieval, release 2. (*b*) ASM tables, release 2.

In our example, as an initial condition, EXECTASK has taken a page fault. An interrupt to RSM through program first level interrupt handler has occurred. These two components of the control program have tested whether the cause of the interrupt was a program check or a page fault; the status of the Getmain bit in the page table entry has indicated which. If this bit was on, the operand address of the last instruction decoded was legitimate at the time of the test; the page was as yet unfetched, or it was swapped or stolen. If in the external page table entry there was an external slot address, the page was stolen or swapped out; if there was a zero, the page was not fetched into real storage. Our example follows the retrieval of a stolen page.

The real storage manager passes a logical page identifier (LPID) to the auxiliary storage manager, activity 1 in Figure 5.9a. From the logical group number the auxiliary storage manager locates the origin of an address space table. Using the relative block address as an offset to this table origin, the auxiliary storage manager locates the stolen page, and then passes control to the block processor, activity 2, which builds a channel program and issues EXCP. On i–o completion, first IOS, and then the block processor, auxiliary storage manager, and real storage manager are posted in that order; EXECTASK becomes dispatchable.

Initialization of Pages

In OS/360 MVT, INITL invokes Attach, SVC 42, which issues Getmain for storage space for SALARYL; program fetch relocates SALARYL addresses to conform to this space and requests IOS to bring the module from DASD to storage.

In release 2, initiation brings SALARYL into virtual storage. INITL invokes Attach, which issues Getmain for SALARYL virtual storage. Fetch function includes formatting SALARYL into page-size blocks, relocating the load module's relative addresses to virtual addresses, and invoking RSM to make page table entries for SALARYL pages. Finally, the block processor requests IOS to schedule transmission of the formatted pages into real storage. Prior to transmission, IOS issues a Pagefix macro for the frame being loaded. At the time of i–o completion, IOS issues Pagefree. SALARYL pages in real storage, other than the one being transmitted, are subject to stealing.

Virtual Input–Output (VIO)

Using virtual storage buffers, VIO routines access data sets. During SALARYL execution, EMPYTD, a VIO data set, is moved into virtual storage from direct-access storage in sections (a 3330 track-full of pages might be a section). EXECTASK page table and external page table entries are updated to account for the slot and frame locations of sections of EMPYTD in virtual storage; such sections are called VIO windows.

A track of 3330 is some 13,000 bytes, or three pages of storage. Three pages transmitted into real storage from a track implies that some 120 EMPYTD logical records of, say, 100 bytes are accessed without any electromechanical activity.

Example. Our SALARIES example is the reading of the twenty-first logical record of EMPYTD. In Figure 5.10, the virtual block processor (VBP) is the target of the SALARYL branch, activity 2 after the location of the DCB EMPLOYEE-YTD has been passed to VBP via general purpose register 1, activity 1. The VBP determines that SALARYL's request is for logical record 21, well within the current page of the virtual access method (VIO) window in real storage. The VBP Returns, activity 4, after passing the virtual address of logical record 21 to SALARYL, via general purpose register 1, activity 3.

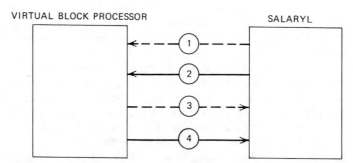

Figure 5.10   Activity diagram—virtual block processor.

Consideration. VIO is used with conventional OS/360 access methods for temporary data sets. In the preceding example, EMPYTD is a sequential access method (SAM) temporary data set. On the first access (READ EMPLOYEE-YTD) a window intercept routine was entered. Window intercept interpreted the SAM program so that from then on EMPYTD would be accessed directly by the VBP.

Multiprocessing

Like MVT and release 1, release 2 protects serially reusable resources, denying simultaneous access to, say, the dispatching queue by CPU 1 and CPU 2.

In release 2, serialization remains the primary means of protection. Each system program specifies that the control program is to serialize its request for a reusable resource. Often in MVT and release 1, the control program could mask the CPU from i–o interruption and thus comply; in release 2, it may not. CPU 2 is independent of the mask of CPU 1. Release 2 uses a lock.

A control program routine serving EXECTASK, in CPU 1 requires a lock for the dispatching queue. If CPU 2 is not accessing this queue, CPU 1 may proceed, the control program stores the identification of CPU 1, a lockword, in a reserved storage location—CPU 1 holds the lock. If CPU 2 already holds the lock, CPU 1 is placed in a spin loop (see Fig. 5.11).

Global (spin) and local locks control access to global and local resources.* Locking a local serially reusable resource resembles MVT enqueuing. Usually, denied some local lock, CPU 1 may stream instructions; denied some global lock, it may not.

Global locks are held disabled against i–o interrupt. A routine holding this lock may not take page faults.

In release 2, the user requests service by SVC. In contrast to OS MVT and release 1, control program routines normally branch to other control program routines only occasionally using SVC. Abend, SVC 13, results when a routine holding a lock issues SVC. The control program grants a lock to a routine presuming that certain conditions apply while the lock is held. Being privileged, SVC routines may change these conditions, exposing resource integrity.

Release 2 uses multiple locks. Figure 5.12 depicts the locking hierarchy, the sequence in which locks must be unconditionally requested. A system routine may

---

* Local locks are locks for resources known to only one memory.

CPU1
INSTRUCTION SEQUENCE

INSTRUCTION
PATH LEGEND

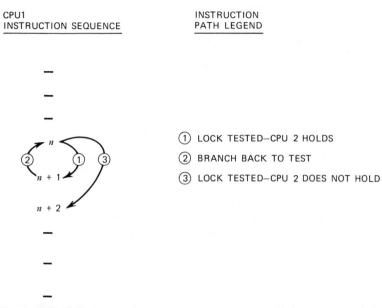

① LOCK TESTED—CPU 2 HOLDS

② BRANCH BACK TO TEST

③ LOCK TESTED—CPU 2 DOES NOT HOLD

Figure 5.11 Spin loop.

not request the dispatching queue (highest priority) lock and then ask for a lower priority lock. In Table 5.3, the hierarchy rule is violated. At time 8, $EXECTASK_1$ Waits on resource 4 of $EXECTASK_2$ while $EXECTASK_2$ Waits on resource 2 of $EXECTASK_1$. Given that these are global resources, both CPUs would spin; the system would be inoperative.

In multiprocessing, serialization, at bottom, depends on CPU instructions. When CPUs 1 and 2 both request the same lock at the same time, S/370R architecture breaks the tie.

DISPATCHER
↑
IOS CHANNEL AVAILABILITY TABLE
↑
IOS UNIT CONTROL BLOCK
↑
IOS LOGICAL CHANNEL QUEUE
↑
AUXILIARY STORAGE MANAGER
↑
SPACE ALLOCATION
↑
SYSTEM RESOURCE MANAGER
↑
CROSS-MEMORY SERVICES
↑
LOCAL MEMORY

Figure 5.12 Locking hierarchy. Arrows indicate order in which locks must be obtained.

Table 5.3 Error Scenario—LCKWDS Are Requested/Held by Control Program Routines on Behalf of the Indicated Tasks

Time	EXECTASK$_1$		EXECTASK$_2$	
	Requested	Held	Requested	Held
1	1,2	–	–	–
2	–	1,2	–	–
3	–	1,2	3,4	–
4	–	1,2	–	3,4
5	4	1,2	–	3,4
6	WAIT ON 4		–	3,4
7	WAIT ON 4		2	3,4
8[a]	WAIT ON 4		WAIT ON 2	

[a]Interlock situation.

The release 2 control program uses the instruction Compare and Swap (CS) in servicing a lock request. While executing in CPU 1, this instruction defends the lockword from CPU 2 access. A synchronization between two Compare and Swap instructions results—CPU 1 obtains the lock—serialization.

Managing the System

Job control language (JCL) specifies performance objectives and identifies a job with a previously defined performance group. Release 2 management routines, after considering the heavy or light workload with which the job is multiprogrammed, assist the installation in fulfilling the objectives.

Prior to the current work period a system programmer defines a group number for each type of job step request the installation will run. Through JCL the user specifies a performance group number by which the system classifies his request into a group. Through group numbers the installation exercises control over resource allocation by the system.

In addition, user JCL specifies a performance objective and its duration. The release 2 attempts to reconcile the performance objectives of the system's users.

Figure 5.13 depicts performance objectives and their duration, by performance group, for three jobs. Multiprogrammed with a very heavy workload, a job in performance group 1 asks for and receives 20 units of service. Multiprogrammed with a heavy workload, the same job asks for and receives 35 units of service.

A unit of service, U, is defined as

$$U = a \times (\text{cpu}) + b \times (\text{i–o}) + c \times (\text{frames})$$

where cpu is one set of 10K instructions, i–o is one EXCP, a frame is one real storage frame for 1 second, and a, b, and c are weighting factors. The six quantities are stored in SYS1.PARMLIB prior to, say, work period m.

Workload manager routines determine the quantity of service each job gets; resource manager routines measure the effects on a resource of swapping an address space.

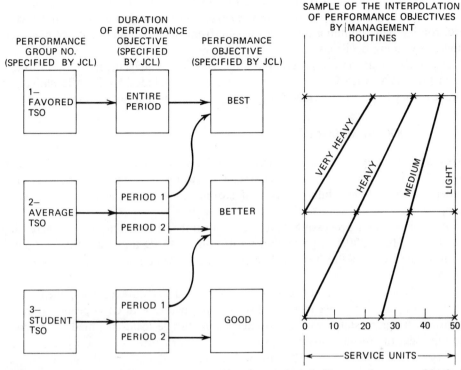

Figure 5.13 Specification to the manager. The crosses (×) indicate performance objectives specified by job control language.

Among resource management routines, a real storage occupancy algorithm attempts to keep the number of allocated real pages near some target value. A program replenishment algorithm attempts to steal pages unlikely to be referenced in the near future if swapping fails to free up pages or if all ASCBs are nonswappable.

Table 5.4 lists other individual optimization attempts. As we might expect, an overall optimization is attempted as well in the form of CPU i–o overlap.

Table 5.4   Individual Routines of Resource Management and Their Function

Name	Function
Input–output load balancing	Device allocation decision-making
Automatic Priority Grouping	Reordering of the dispatching queue based on USER-JOB's expected execution time to Wait (users who release the CPU quickly are given highest priority)
Enqueue–dequeue	Inhibits swap-out of user's queued-on resources in demand by systems tasks
Real page shortage prevention	Swaps out users when critical page shortages occur
Auxiliary page and system queue area prevention	Avoids the creation of new memories and performs selective swap-outs when shortages occur

Release 2 management routines have four logical parts: a routine that communicates with the control program; the workload and resource managers; and a control routine that, summing quantities passed from workload and resource manager, makes swapping decisions.

An authorized control program routine enters a management routine through a macro, SYSEVENT, the expansion of which includes SVC. Alternatively a branch entry has been provided for system components that hold a lock.

5.8 SUMMARY

System/370 component and system technologies continue to pace each other. Within two decades, access to a character in storage has improved by some five orders of magnitude while the cost of storing a byte has declined in the same proportion.

All eras of data processing have taken advantage of memory's ever increasing availability. In S/370R in particular, transforming DASD to storage that is directly addressable by the CPU has accelerated systems productivity by any measure one chooses.

With System/360 the concept of hardware and software as components of a unified systems design became a reality. The hardware, with CPU general purpose registers, program status word, and fixed main storage locations, made it practical to represent the resources of the system as a data structure managed by the operating system. Similarly S/370R hardware, dynamic address translation, causes an OS/VS 2 software design, virtual storage, to be feasible. When, in addition, System/370R multiprocessing is considered, the productivity gain is clear. The enhanced system supports communications and control applications that, because of demanding response time and reliability constraints, were unapproachable before.

chapter 6

THE JOB CONTROL LANGUAGE OF JOB MANAGEMENT

6.1 INTRODUCTION

The processing of USERJOB begins with the introduction of the job request into OS; it ends with the release of the job from OS. OS converts card images, a job request, into internal tables, a job.

A job request includes system-dependent statements in job control language (JCL), input data to a language translator. Job control language statements define the job and its steps to the operating system.

The next two chapters discuss JCL and job processing in OS/360 and OS/VS releases 1 and 2, generally. Let us agree that the terms "SYSIN reader" and "SYSOUT writer" are generic, denoting OS functions. The particular SYSIN reader of OS/360 and release 1 will be called reader-interpreter, or READERL, or the job management reader. A similar pattern applies for writers.

6.2 JOB AND STEP DEFINITION

The unit of request to OS is the job step request. Like predecessor systems, System/370 requires users to identify the program and data sets of a job step (Table 6.1). The JCL card format is

```
Card
Column    12 . . . . 80
          //fields
```

Job control language defines a name, operation, operand, and comments field for each statement. In a JCL card each field is separated from its neighbor by a space.

The name field, a label, enables one statement to reference another. USERJOB and EXECSTEP are labels (see Fig. 6.1). The operation type identifies a job, step, or data set request to job-processing routines; each type has a set of operands for the user to choose from.

Operands are of positional or keyword type—they depend on the position of

Table 6.1 Schematic of Request User Provides and Response of System/370

User Request		System/370 Response			
		Via Job Management		Via Task Management	
Name	Description	Name	Description	Name	Description
USERJOB	Job request	USERJOB	Job		
COBSTEP	Job step 1 request for system resources; data (SALARYS) is provided	COBSTEP	Job step 1 Allocate static resources including COBOLL and SALARYS	COBTASK	Allocate/deallocate dynamic System/370 resources
LESTEP	Job step 2 request for system resources; data is provided	LESTEP	Job step 2 Allocate static resources including LINKEDTL	LETASK	Allocate/deallocate dynamic System/370 resources
EXECSTEP	Job step 3 request for systems resources; data (EMPWKLY) is provided	EXECSTEP	Job step 3 Allocate static resources including SALARYL and EMPWKLY	EXECTASK	Allocate/deallocate dynamic System/370 resources

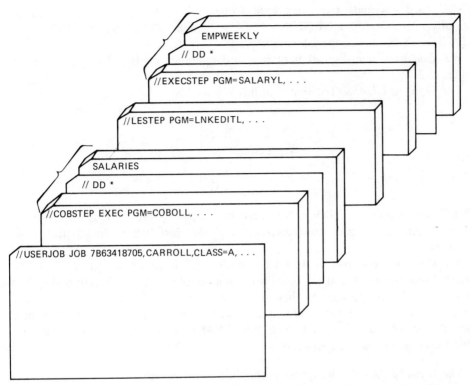

Figure 6.1 User request deck. The symbol // on the card denotes job control language.

the operand in the statement or they are defined by a particular word, spelled exactly, recognizable to job management routines.

In the operand form, KEYWORD = parameter, the user selects one of the following:

$$
\left\{
\begin{array}{c}
\text{parameter } 1 \\
\cdot \\
\cdot \\
\cdot \\
\text{parameter } n
\end{array}
\right\}
$$

In Figure 6.1, the job card requests that *this* job be named and established in OS. The EXEC cards request in this case that three named job steps be established.* The number of data definition (DD) cards that trail an EXEC card depends on the data set requirements of a step.

Job Card Operands

Every OS job requires a job name [USERJOB]. The system controls USERJOB, a data structure, through its name. OS holds USERJOB in a queue or the operator cancels USERJOB—not SALARIES. JOB card operands have job-wide scope;

* The user knows a job request and its steps by the same names that the system knows jobs and job steps by [USERJOB, EXECSTEP].

EXEC card operands have step-wide scope. Where these two conflict, as in //USERJOB JOB . . . REGION = 160K . . . and //EXECSTEP EXEC . . . REGION = 80K . . . , the job card prevails.

We shall base our discussion of job card operands on the example shown in Figure 6.2.

The keyword CLASS. The syntax of this keyword is

$$CLASS = \begin{Bmatrix} A \\ \cdot \\ \cdot \\ \cdot \\ O \end{Bmatrix}$$

CLASS = A stipulates USERJOB's entry into input queue A (Fig. 6.3). Each CLASS parameter has attributes enabling the installation to control task coexistence.

"CLASS = A" jobs run in 160 kilobytes if "A" is so attributed at SYSGEN time.* Input queue "C" might contain i–o bound jobs. OS/360 initiators dequeue by class or classes specified by their user, the operator. To run "A" and "C" jobs concurrently, the operator might attach two initiators, one to dequeue A and then B-type jobs, another for C-type jobs. CLASS = B jobs will be dequeued only after the A queue, has been drained.

The keyword PRTY. The syntax in this case is as follows:

$$PRTY = \begin{Bmatrix} 13 \\ \cdot \\ \cdot \\ \cdot \\ O \end{Bmatrix}$$

USERJOB$_1$ of CLASS = A, PRTY = 8 . . . , will be initiated from input queue A ahead of USERJOB$_2$ with PRTY = 7. Initiation priority is converted by OS into dispatching priority.

Using PRTY, step execution times may be controlled. At SYSGEN time, OS associates a parameter, say 7, with the time-slicing attribute; steps of PRTY = 7 jobs share the CPU for a predetermined amount of time.

The keyword TYPRUN. Like PRTY and CLASS, TYPRUN deals with initiation from the input queues. Designated by TYPRUN = HOLD, USERJOB may be initiated only after the operator RELEASEs the job from the console keyboard.

HOLDing a job defers initiation and hence device allocation. The volume on which EMPYTD resides may be in a cabinet drawer when USERJOB is read in; dequeuing USERJOB means that INITL, its space, its devices, USERJOB devices, and all jobs behind USERJOB might await the minutes of the retrieval and mounting of the missing volume on, say, unit 192. In remote job entry, where the input device allocated to the SYSIN reader is distant from the system site, HOLD becomes particularly important (see Section 7.11).

* See Chapter 9.

//USERJOB JOB 7B63418705,CARROLL,CLASS=A,PRTY=8,TYPRUN=HOLD,MSGLEVEL=1,NOTIFY=HC,COND=(12,GT)

Figure 6.2 Job statement.

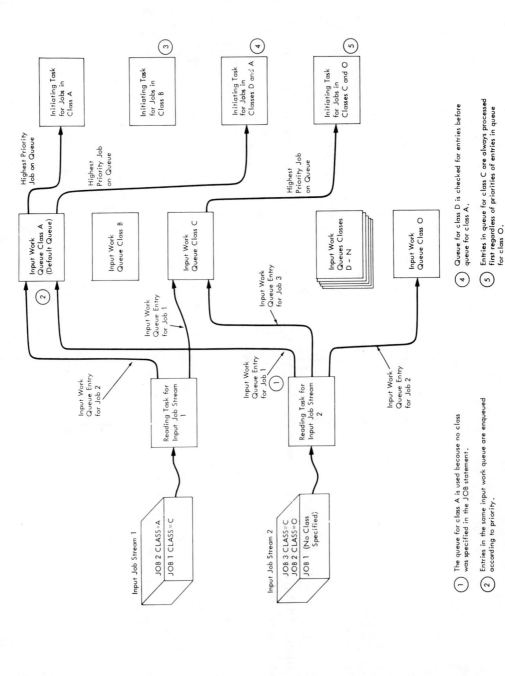

Figure 6.3 Example of processing of input work queues. From the IBM handbook *IBM System/360 Operating System MVT Control Program Logic Summary*, Y-28-6658.

122

The keyword MSGCLASS. The syntax in this case is MSGCLASS = classname, where the classname parameter options are

$$\begin{Bmatrix} A \\ \cdot \\ \cdot \\ \cdot \\ Z \\ 0 \\ \cdot \\ \cdot \\ \cdot \\ 9 \end{Bmatrix}$$

Each option is associated with one of 36 output queues. By choosing a classname parameter, the user specifies the DASD queue into which system program [INITL] messages are written.

Each SYSOUT writer may be associated with a unit record device and a classname. An operator types START WTR.A,00E,A at a system console. Writer A transfers A queue (output) messages to the print device, 00E.

In Figure 6.2, the JOB statement omits MSGCLASS, and consequently OS assigns SYSOUT message output to a default class, A.* Where SYSOUT=A is specified in COBSTEP, LESTEP, and EXECSTEP, the SYSOUT writer dequeues all USERJOB output from the same waiting line. The unified presentation of Appendix 1 exemplifies this situation.

The keyword MSGLEVEL. The syntax for this keyword is

$$\text{MSGLEVEL} = \begin{Bmatrix} 0 \\ 1 \\ 0 \end{Bmatrix}, \begin{Bmatrix} 1 \\ 2 \end{Bmatrix}$$

This keyword specifies the level of detail to be provided by the SYSOUT writer in system program messages. In USERJOB, from MSGLEVEL = 1 the level of job control language detail of Appendix 1 appears. The absence of the second parameter (in Figure 6.2) signals job-processing routines to assume a default case 1. A detailed message pattern such as that of Appendix 1 might result.

The keyword NOTIFY. This keyword, whose syntax is NOTIFY = HC, may be used where USERJOB is submitted from a remote terminal under the time-sharing feature of OS/360. The operating system will NOTIFY the user of USERJOB completion by writing a message directly to the terminal.

The keyword COND. The syntax is COND = (code, operator), . . . , where the code ranges from 0 to 4095. The code is compared with a return code that may be issued by a problem program during a job step. The operator designates the comparison type from the following:

GT—greater than
GE—greater than or equal to
EQ—equal to

---

* The choice of default class is installation dependent.

```
//USERJOB JOB
            .                .
            .                .
            .                .
//COBSTEP EXEC PGM=COBOLL,PARM='BUF=13000,MAP,LIST',REGION=120K...
//        DD        .
                    .
                    .
```

Figure 6.4

LT—less than
LE—less than or equal to
NE—not equal to

Up to eight different return code tests are specifiable.

In USERJOB, if COND = (12,GT) is punched and COBOLL, based on its having detected serious source program errors, issues a return code of 16, LESTEP and EXECSTEP never execute; the job is terminated after COBSTEP.

Other JOB operands are connected with job processing (see Chapter 7). Through TIME, a user specifies the maximum time a job may use the CPU; the RD and RESTART keywords are associated with Checkpoint-Restart; ROLL is associated with the operating system's roll-out roll-in facility. All could have been added to the JOB statement in Figure 6.2.

The EXEC Card

Many keyword operands of JOB statements may appear in EXEC statements—for example, COND,PRTY (specified in the EXEC statement as DPRTY), RD, REGION, ROLL, and TIME. Our discussion is based on the example shown in Figure 6.4.

The keyword PGM. The syntax is PGM = parameter, where the user chooses one of the following:

$$\left\{ \begin{array}{l} \text{program name} \\ \text{*.stepname.ddname} \\ \text{*.stepname.procstepname.ddname} \end{array} \right\}$$

Figure 6.4 depicts an EXEC card with stepname COBSTEP; the program name COBOLL is the chosen parameter.

Choosing * causes a job-processing routine to refer back to the stepname to identify the member load module intended. The choice between the two forms of the asterisked parameter depends on whether the step is part of the input stream, as in Figure 6.4, or of a cataloged procedure (see Chapter 7).

The keyword PARM. The syntax is as follows: PARM = value. The operating system passes value to a systems program. In Figure 6.4, from PARM='BUF= 13000,MAP,LIST . . . , OS passes COBOLL the amount of storage buffer space to use and the amount of documentation to provide. The listing and storage map (Appendix 1, pp. 210 and 211) result from the latter.

6.3 DATA SET REQUEST—THE DD CARD

The DD mechanism addresses (static) device allocation, associating a unit address with a data set name specified in a DD card [392,EMPYTD], Figure 6.5.

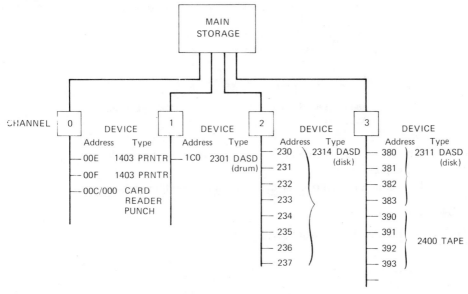

Figure 6.5 Four-channel S/370 configuration.

Why is allocation necessary? A physical configuration runs USERJOB. On his DD card, let the user demand that HARRYC be mounted on unit 392, as in first-generation systems.

The difficulty is that job control language is created before EXECSTEP executes. When *this* job, say USERJOB20, is initiated, USERJOB19 may own unit 392 exclusively. The demand of USERJOB20 delays its initiation.

When allocating for the steps of USERJOB20, the initiator knows what devices are assignable; to the user creating DD statements the situation at EXECSTEP time is impossible to foresee. Consequently user request and system response must meet on common ground. For this encounter OS adopted the symbolic device name, wherein the system selects allocation candidates from the devices of a class. At sysgen time a connection between device names and unit addresses is established in the operating system (Table 6.2). How at the time of EXECSTEP initiation

Table 6.2   System Generation Time Association of S/370 Addresses with Generic Names for the High-Speed Units of Figure 6.5

	Permissible Data Set Organization		
	Partitioned or Direct	Sequential	
GROUP NAME	SYSDA	SYSSEQ	TAPE
DEVICE ADDRESS	1C0 230–237 380–383	236,237 382,383 392,393	390–393

```
//INOUT DD DSNAME=EMPYTD,DISP=(OLD,KEEP),VOLUME=SER=HARRYC,UNIT=2311
                    ⋮
PROGRAM-ID.
'SALARIES S/C/U'.
ENVIRONMENT DIVISION.
           ⋮
FILE-CONTROL.
    SELECT EMPLOYEE-YTD
        ASSIGN TO 'INOUT' DIRECT-ACCESS 2311.
```

Figure 6.6 Sample DD statement. (Excerpt from Appendix 1.)

INITL uses the depicted tabular information as input to its allocation processing becomes our next concern.

The discussion that follows is based on the example shown in Figure 6.6.

The Keyword UNIT

The syntax for this keyword is UNIT = parameter(s).

$$UNIT = \begin{Bmatrix} \text{device type} \\ \text{unit address} \\ \text{group name} \\ . \\ . \\ . \end{Bmatrix}$$

Figure 6.6 illustrates the job control language for an existing sequential data set to be updated.

Using the device type "2311" as input, INITL allocates EMPYTD to one of the unit addresses, 390 to 393. After allocation, INITL may write a console message directing the operator to mount HARRYC on unit 39X (see keyword VOLUME).

Other options of the keyword UNIT. The keyword UNIT has other options in addition to those listed in Figure 6.6.

In UNIT = 392, demand allocation lightens the initiator's processing load. It delays initiation if the device is already committed.

In UNIT = SYSDA, the group name specifies a new data set. SYSDA suggests itself for a data set intended to endure for the life of EXECSTEP or, at most, for that of USERJOB. By electing SYSDA, the user grants INITL permission to select from its currently available DASD space [2311 or 2314 or 2301]. For a new data set a SPACE parameter must be specified. For old data sets the systems programmer, by specifying device type [2311], lessens what INITL does to locate a volume.

UNIT=SYSSEQ resembles SYSDA broadened to allow the allocation of tape devices. INITL logic goes like this: if my DASDs are allocated, I shall assign a tape unit on channel 3.

Some other parameters of UNIT. In the statement

//INOUT DD DSNAME = EMPYTD, . . . ,UNIT = (2311,3,DEFER)

the second parameter, 3, specifies that EMPYTD resides on three physical units. DEFER stipulates that the three units of EMPYTD should be allocated, but that operator mount messages should be withheld until the data set is Opened. If SALARYL Opens EMPYTD well into EXECSTEP, the presumption is that the three units may be useful to other tasks in the meantime.

To allocate the initiator needs more than UNIT parameters. Does EMPYTD already exist? What should the system do with the data set when USERJOB completes? On what volume does EMPYTD reside?

The user expresses data set status and location by the DISP and VOLUME keywords of the DD statement.

The Keyword DISP

The Syntax is as follows:

$$DISP = \begin{Bmatrix} OLD \\ NEW \\ SHR \\ MOD \end{Bmatrix} \begin{Bmatrix} ,KEEP \\ ,DELETE \\ ,PASS \\ ,CATLG \\ ,UNCATLG \end{Bmatrix}$$

For DISP = (OLD), we return to Figure 6.6. The input data set EMPYTD was created previously. It occupies a DASD extent; it has descriptive information in its label on DASD, so the //INOUT specification must be reconciled with an earlier specification currently represented in the EMPYTD label.

Other options of DISP follow:

DISP = (NEW): EMPYTD will be created during EXECSTEP. INITL will allocate a fresh extent on HARRYC.

DISP = (MOD): OLD EMPYTD will be added to.

DISP = (SHR): INITL will allocate EMPYTD as shareable with other tasks. The default, omission of SHR, results in exclusive ownership of EMPYTD by EXECTASK.

DISP = (,KEEP) specifies that after the termination of EXECSTEP the EMPYTD label will remain in the Volume Table of Contents (VTOC) of HARRYC; the data set remains available for future retrieval.

DISP = (,PASS): EMPYTD will remain available to subsequent steps of USERJOB. In OS/360, after the final step, the job management terminator will delete EMPYTD if it was created in USERJOB or keep it if it existed before.

DISP = (,DELETE): the terminator will delete EMPYTD's label from the VTOC.

DISP = (,CATLG): a system data set, SYS1.CATLG, will receive an entry that includes EMPYTD, HARRYC, and 2311, derived from //INOUT. Through SYS1.CATLG conditioning, future job control language may invoke allocation of EMPYTD through DSNAME.

DISP = (,UNCATLG): the terminator will delete the EMPYTD entry in SYS1.CATLG.

The Keyword VOLUME

VOLUME denotes some medium of secondary storage that can be mounted and dismounted from a device. A unique label identifies a volume to the operating system.

VOLUME = SER = HARRYC and its parameters identify the residence of the EMPYTD data set to INITL (see Fig. 6.6). With the automatic volume recognition feature generated into the operating system, the operator may mount HARRYC prior to EXECSTEP time on a 2311 device, say 392. INITL will locate this unit by matching the volume-resident label with the DD card parameter HARRYC. Should HARRYC yet be unmounted, INITL will allocate a unit from addresses 390–393 and issue a mount message to the operator. INITL allocates in a prescribed order (low address first).

The Keyword DSNAME

The last keyword of Figure 6.6 that we discuss is DSNAME. Often applications and system programmers are different individuals. The author of SALARIES need never know of EMPYTD, nor of its UNIT, VOLUME, or DISP. The systems programmer need never know the name EMPLOYEE-YTD. By means of a link, the ddname, the data control block becomes a communication area where the work of these two, hopefully, meets. COBOLL initially constructs the data control block from the user's statements in the SALARIES ENVIRONMENT DIVISION.

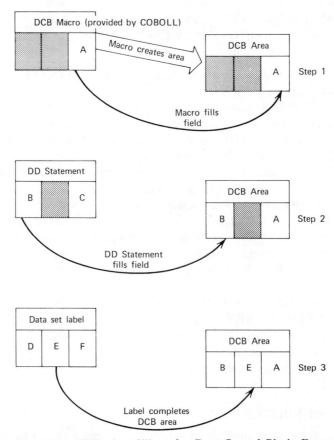

Figure 6.7   OPEN-time filling of a Data Control Block. From *Concepts and Facilities,* IBM Systems Reference Library Manual GC-28-6535.

As Figure 6.7 depicts, data derived from INOUT, after processing by INITL, are merged with data in the EMPYTD label into the data control block.

Consideration

Beyond our purpose, understanding OS, some job control language topics and options have gone undiscussed. For those interested in running jobs, *IBM Job Control Reference Manual,* GC-6704, is a handbook of job control language syntax.

We turn now to job processing, the system's response to the job control language request.

chapter 7

JOB PROCESSING BY
JOB MANAGEMENT

7.1 INTRODUCTION

Job processing routines transform the requests originally expressed by the various users in the installation in job control language.

Often a few system programmers write job control language statements for many application programmers, setting forth which steps constitute a job (step selectability) and modes of running or rerunning jobs (checkpoint/restart). Application programmers frequently use cataloged procedures to avail themselves of job control language created by system programmers.

As users of system tasks, operators introduce, hold, or cancel jobs.

Finally, the installation manager uses the systems management facilities of job processing.

We describe OS/360 job processing then, toward the end of the chapter, OS/VS release 2 job processing.

7.2 STEP SELECTABILITY

Figures 7.1 through 7.4 illustrate four job requests for SALARYL execution, each with a different amount of job control language detail.

Figure 7.1, depicts a four-step assemble, compile, link-edit, execute procedure, useful where the source statement input to a language translator has not been checked out. USERJOB requests initiation from the B input queue. A 160-kilobyte region for the system and application programs of all four steps is requested. Allocation messages of the level of detail of Appendix 1, page 209, are specified.

Each of the four job steps ends with a DD statement with an * in the operand field, meaning that data cards follows in the SYSIN stream as input to the library member named as processor [SALARYL] for that step.

In three of the four steps a load module member of the system library, SYS1.LINKLIB, is automatically requested by use of PGM=membername. EXECSTEP is the exception, invoking SALARYL from a temporary library, &GODATE, into which LNKEDITL has placed it.

In COBSTEP, COBOLL places its object module output in a temporary data set, &LADSET, later used as input to LNKEDITL. A second input to link editor, an assembled object module, is stored in the temporary data set, &GODATA. The

```
//USERJOB JOB MSGLEVEL=1,CLASS=B,REGION=160K
//ASMSTEP EXEC PGM=ASMBLRL
//SYSLIB DD DSNAME=SYS1.MACLIB,DISP=SHR
//SYSUT1 DD UNIT=SYSDA,SPACE=(400,(400,50))
//SYSUT2 DD UNIT=SYSDA,SPACE=(400,(400,50))
//SYSUT3 DD UNIT=SYSDA,SPACE=(400,(400,50))
//SYSPRINT DD SYSOUT=A
//SYSUDUMP DD SYSOUT=A
//SYSPUNCH DD DSNAME=&GODATA,UNIT=SYSDA,SPACE=(80,(200,50)),
//               DISP=(NEW,PASS)
//SYSIN DD *
     (data cards)
//COBSTEP EXEC PGM=COBOLL,PARM='BUF=13000,SIZE=120000,MAP,LIST'
//SYSPRINT DD SYSOUT=A
//SYSUT1 DD UNIT=SYSDA,SPACE=(TRK, (100,10))
//SYSUT2 DD UNIT=SYSDA,SPACE=(TRK, (100,10))
//SYSUT3 DD UNIT-SYSDA,SPACE=TRK, (100,10))
//SYSUT4 DD UNIT=SYSDA,SPACE=(TRK, (100,10))
//SYSLIN DD DSNAME=&LADSET,DISP=(NEW,PASS),UNIT=SYSDA,
//               SPACE=(80,(200,50))
//SYSIN DD *
     (data cards)
//LESTEP EXEC PGM=LNKEDITL,PARM='XREF,LIST'
//SYSABEND DD SYSOUT=A
//SYSLIB DD DSNAME=SYS1.COBLIB,DISP=SHR
//SYSPRINT DD SYSOUT=A
//SYSLMOD DD DSNAME=&GODATE(SALARYL),DISP=(NEW,PASS),UNIT=SYSDA,
//               SPACE=(1024,(50,20,1))
//SYSLIN         DD DSNAME=&LADSET,DISP=(OLD,DELETE)
//               DD DDNAME=DAIN
//SYSUT1 DD UNIT=(SYSDA,SEP=(SYSLIN,SYSLMOD)),SPACE=(1024,(50,20))
//MYLIB DD DSNAME=&GODATA,DISP=(OLD,DELETE)
//DAIN DD *
  INCLUDE MYLIB (data card)
/*             (denotes end of data cards)
//EXECSTEP EXEC PGM=*.LESTEP.SYSLMOD
//SYSABEND DD SYSOUT=A
//SYSOUT DD SYSOUT=A,DCB=(LRECL=121,BLKSIZE=121)
//INOUT DD DSNAME=EMPYTD,DISP=(OLD,KEEP),VOLUME=SER=HARRYC,UNIT=2311
//SYSIN DD *
     (data cards)
```

Figure 7.1   Four-step assemble, compile, link, and execute procedure. In this figure, * LESTEP.SYSLMOD refers back to SALARYL.

DD operand DDNAME=DAIN points to a LNKEDITL data card, INCLUDE, establishing &GODATA as this secondary input through the MYLIB DD statement.

The UNIT=parameter, SEP, instructs INITL to allocate the LNKEDITL i–o data sets on separate units.

UNIT=SYSDA appears in temporary data set situations.

EXECSTEP includes a DCB keyword, directing that the two parameters exhibited be inserted into that communications area at Open time. Consequently 121-byte logical records from EMPYTD will be taken from the "A" output queue and transmitted to a print device.

Figure 7.2 illustrates a three-step compile, link, execute request, useful where

```
//USERJOB JOB 7B3358101,MSGLEVEL=1
//JOBLIB DD DSNAME=HCLIB,VOLUME=SER=HARRYC,UNIT=2311,DISP=(OLD,KEEP)
//COBSTEP EXEC PGM=COBOLL,PARM='BUF=13000,SIZE=120000,MAP,LIST'
//SYSIN DD DSNAME=HCLIB(SALARYS),VOLUME=SER=HARRYC,UNIT=2311,
//               DISP=(OLD,KEEP)
//SYSPRINT DD SYSOUT=A
//SYSUT1 DD UNIT=SYSDA,SPACE=(TRK,(100,10))
//SYSUT2 DD UNIT=SYSDA,SPACE=(TRK,(100,10))
//SYSUT3 DD UNIT=SYSDA,SPACE=(TRK,(100,10))
//SYSUT4 DD UNIT=SYSDA,SPACE=(TRK,(100,10))
//SYSLIN DD DSNAME=&LADSET,DISP=(NEW,PASS),UNIT=SYSDA,
//               SPACE=(80,(200,50))
//LESTEP EXEC PGM=LNKEDITL,PARM='XREF,LIST'
//SYSABEND DD SYSOUT=A
//SYSLIB DD DSNAME=SYS1.COBLIB,DISP=SHR
//SYSPRINT DD SYSOUT=A
//SYSLMOD DD DSNAME=&GODATE(SALARYL),DISP=(NEW,PASS),UNIT=SYSDA,
//               SPACE=(1024,(50,20,1))
//SYSLIN         DD DSNAME=&LADSET,DISP=(OLD,DELETE)
//               DD DDNAME=DAIN
//SYSUT1 DD UNIT=(SYSDA,SEP=(SYSLIN,SYSLMOD)),SPACE=(1024,(50,20))
//MYLIB DD DSNAME=HCLIB2(DUMPITO),DISP=(OLD,KEEP)
//DAIN DD *
  INCLUDE MYLIB (data card)
/*                  (denotes end of data cards)
//EXECSTEP EXEC PGM=*.LESTEP.SYSLMOD
//SYSABEND DD SYSOUT=A
//SYSOUT DD SYSOUT=A,DCB=(LRECL=121,BLKSIZE=121)
//INOUT DD DSNAME=EMPYTD,DISP=(OLD,KEEP),VOLUME=SER=HARRYC,UNIT=2311
//SYSIN DD *
    (data cards)
```

Figure 7.2   Three-step compile, link, and execute procedure. In this figure, *.LESTEP. SYSLMOD refers back to SALARYL.

source statements have not been checked out. This version of USERJOB deals with three types of libraries, data sets containing programs. SYS1.LINKLIB, a system library, contains COBOLL. HCLIB, a private library contains SALARYS, the SALARIES source statements COBOLL uses as input. HCLIB2, a second private library contains DUMPITO, assembled prior to this running of USERJOB and link-edited into SALARYL. Temporary libraries are &LADSET into which COBOLL places SALARYO, its compiled output, and &GODATE in which LNKEDITL places its output, SALARYL.

Figure 7.3 is a two-step link and execute request, useful where the source language inputs to the assembler and compiler have been previously checked out. In this request, JOBLIB specifies HCLIB, a library data set consisting of object modules. The primary input data set to LNKEDITL is defined to be SALARYO, a member of HCLIB. Link-edit secondary input, also in HCLIB, is the assembled object module DUMPITO, defined to LNKEDITL through the DDNAME= DAIN, DD *, INCLUDE mechanism.

Figure 7.4 depicts a one-step job request, useful in a production situation where source statements are checked out and the object modules of a load module are as desired for this run. Constant recompilation and re-link-editing of checked-out

```
//USERJOB JOB 7B63358101,MSGLEVEL=1
//JOBLIB DD DSNAME=HCLIB,VOLUME=SER=HARRYC,UNIT=2311,DISP=(OLD,KEEP)
//LESTEP EXEC PGM=LNKEDITL,PARM='XREF,LIST'
//SYSABEND DD SYSOUT=A
//SYSLIB DD DSNAME=SYS1.COBLIB,DISP=SHR
//SYSPRINT DD SYSOUT=A
//SYSLIN DD DSNAME=HCLIB(SALARYO),VOLUME=SER=HARRYC,UNIT=2311,
//            DISP=(OLD,KEEP)
//            DD DDNAME=DAIN
//MYLIB DD DSNAME=HCLIB(DUMPITO),DISP=(OLD,KEEP)
//SYSLMOD DD DSNAME=&GODATE(SALARYC),DISP=(NEW,PASS),UNIT=SYSDA,
//            SPACE=(1024,(50,20,1))
//SYSUT1 DD UNIT=(SYSDA,SEP=(SYSLIN,SYSLMOD)),SPACE=(1024,(50,20))
//DAIN DD *
  INCLUDE MYLIB (data card)
/*
//EXECSTEP EXEC PGM=*.LESTEP.SYSLMOD
//SYSABEND DD SYSOUT=A
//SYSOUT DD SYSOUT=A,DCB=(LRECL=121,BLKSIZE=121)
//INOUT DD DSNAME=EMPYTD,DISP=(OLD,KEEP),VOLUME=SER=HARRYC,UNIT=2311
//SYSIN DD *
     (data cards)
```

Figure 7.3 Two-step link and execute procedure.

```
//USERJOB JOB 7B63358101,MSGLEVEL=1
//JOBLIB DD DSNAME=HCLID,VOLUME=SER=HARRYC,UNIT=2311,DISP=(OLD,KEEP)
//GO EXEC PGM=SALARYL
//SYSABEND DD SYSOUT=A
//SYSOUT DD SYSOUT=A,DCB=(LRECL=121,BLKSIZE=121)
//INOUT DD DSNAME=EMPYTD,DISP=(OLD,KEEP),VOLUME=SER=HARRYC,UNIT=2311
//SYSIN DD *
     (data cards)
01002 ADAMS JAMES E.
        .
        .
        .
/*
```

Figure 7.4 One-step execute only procedure. Here EMPWEEKLY is equivalent to DD *, which denotes the SYSIN data set.

source statements, even with the most efficient translator and editor, are, at best, less than optimum procedures.

The JOBLIB statement defines HCLID, a private (usually portable) load module library that, in conjunction with PGM = parameter, directs that HCLID is to be scanned before SYS1.LINKLIB in the search for SALARYL.

7.3 CATALOGED PROCEDURES

The job control language labeled USERPROC in Figure 7.5 depicts minimum user-specified detail and thus maximum usability. Job-processing routines use the name PROCED to access job control language, previously stored as a member of a catalogued system library, SYS1.PROCLIB. The name PROCED may access any type of job request, two-step, three-step, four-step, and so on.

```
//USERJOB JOB MSGLEVEL=1,CLASS=B,REGION=160K
//USERPROC EXEC PROCED
//EXECSTEP.SYSIN DD *
                  (data cards)
```

Figure 7.5 Cataloged procedure.

System programmers enter sets of job control language into SYS1.PROCLIB for recurring user requests. Application programmers retrieve the proper procedure by name, PROCED, in the first EXEC card.

7.4 COMPILE TIME FEATURES

Processing options within COBSTEP may be exercised. Using the COBOL verb COPY, the author of SALARIES may incorporate prewritten DATA DIVISION entries from a DASD library with his PROCEDURE DIVISION statements. Thus the system programmer's work becomes available to the applications programmer within the COBOL language. The system programmer wrestles with the complexities of optimizing i–o; the application programmer issues a COPY of the prewritten data specification.

Similarly the COBOL verb INCLUDE enables the applications programmer to avail himself of prewritten library procedures to incorporate with his PROCEDURE DIVISION statements.

7.5 CHECKPOINT/RESTART

This feature is used with long-running programs caused to terminate before completion. The cause may be a hardware malfunction or an operator action to free resources needed in a higher priority job request. Two load modules of task management, CHECKL and RESTARTL, implement this feature.

SALARIES directs CHECKL invocation by statements in the ENVIRONMENT DIVISION, specifying checkpoints at strategic junctures in SALARYL execution (Fig. 7.6, RERUN). At each checkpoint CHECKL writes a snapshot of EXECTASK current storage, general purpose registers, current psw, etc., to a data set intended as input to RESTARTL in the event the latter load module is later called on. Figure 7.6 depicts three cases of checkpoint invocation by SALARYL.

The checkpoint routine CHECKL advises the operator of the status of the checkpoints taken by displaying information messages on the console. When a checkpoint has successfully completed, the following message appears at the console:

IHJ004I jobname (ddname,unit,volser)
CHKPT checkid

where IHJ004I signifies the OS load module issuing the message, in this case CHECKL, and checkid is the identification name of the checkpoint (C0000003).

SALARYL may be restarted immediately after checkpointing (automatic restart) or some time later (deferred restart). The OS restart routine RESTARTL

```
//CHECKPT    DD DSNAME=CHECK1,                          X
//           VOLUME=SER=HARRYCT,                         X
//           UNIT=2400,DISP=(NEW,KEEP),                  X
//           LABEL=(,NL)
                    .

PROGRAM-ID.
'SALARIES'.
                    .
                    .

ENVIRONMENT DIVISION
                    .
                    .

    RERUN ON 'CHECKPT' EVERY 500 RECORDS
        OF EMPLOYEE-YTD.
```

(a)

```
//CHEK      DD DSNAME=CHECK2,                            X
//          VOLUME=(PRIVATE,RETAIN,SER=HARRYC,           X
//          UNIT=2314,DISP=(NEW,KEEP),                   X
//          SPACE=(TRK,300)
                    .

PROGRAM-ID.
'SALARIES'.
                    .
                    .

ENVIRONMENT DIVISION
                    .
                    .

    RERUN ON 'CHEK' EVERY 200 RECORDS OF
        EMPLOYEE-YTD.
    RERUN ON 'CHEK' EVERY 300 RECORDS OF
        EMPLOYEE-WEEKLY.
```

(b)

```
//CHEKPT    DD DSNAME=CHECK3,                            X
//          VOLUME=SER=HARRYCT,                          X
//          UNIT=2400,DISP=(MOD,KEEP),                   X
//          LABEL=(,NL)
                    .

PROGRAM-ID.
'SALARIES'.
                    .
                    .

ENVIRONMENT DIVISION
                    .
                    .

    RERUN ON 'CHEKPT' EVERY 100 RECORDS
        EMPLOYEE-YTD.
```

(c)

Figure 7.6 Procedures for writing (a) single-checkpoint records using tape, (b) single-checkpoint records using disk, and (c) multiple contiguous checkpoint records on tape. Note that in procedure b, more than one data set may share one ddname. From the IBM Systems Reference Library manual *IBM System/360 Operating System—COBOL (F) Programmer's Guide,* GC-28-6380, p. 92.

retrieves the information recorded by CHECKL, restores the contents of storage and registers, repositions tape and direct-access devices, and gives control to SALARYL.

The RD parameter of user job control language determines whether the restart mode is to be automatic or deferred. An RD parameter may appear in either the JOB or EXEC statement of the program being checkpointed. For automatic restart RD = R is coded. This type of restart occurs only at the latest checkpoint taken. In addition to the RD parameter, automatic restart requires authorization from the operator. System/370 displays the following message on the operator's console to request authorization:

xxIEF225D SHOULD jobname.stepname.procstep RESTART checkid

The operator will reply in the following form:

REPLY xx,'{|YES|NO|HOLD|}'

where YES authorizes restart, NO prevents restart, and HOLD delays restart until the operator issues a RELEASE command.

Unlike automatic restart, deferred restart involves reentering the job into System/370. Unlike automatic mode too, deferred restart may occur at any checkpoint, rather than the latest one taken. Necessary to the delayed process is inclusion of the RESTART parameter on the JOB card and, if restart is to occur at a particular checkpoint within a job step, a SYSCHK DD statement to identify the checkpoint data set (see Fig. 7.7).

```
        //jobname   JOB   ,MSGLEVEL=1,                          X
        //                RESTART=(request,[checkid])
 (A)    //SYSCHK    DD    DSNAME=data-set-name,                 X
        //                DISP=OLD,UNIT=deviceno,               X
        //                DCB=(,RECFM=U,BLKSIZE=nnnn),          X
        //                VOLUME=SER=volser


        //USERJOB   JOB   ,MSGLEVEL=1,                          X
        //                 RESTART=(EXECSTEP,C0000003)
        //SYSCHK    DD    DSNAME=CHEKPT,                        X
        //                DISP=OLD,UNIT=2400,                   X
        //                VOLUME=SER=HARRYC                     X
 (B)    //                DCB=(,RECFM=U,                        X
        //                BLKSIZE=3625)
        //EXECSTEP  EXEC PGM=SALARYL
                  .
                  .
                  .
```

DD statements similar to original deck

Figure 7.7 Restart job control language: (A) format; (B) example, MSGLEVEL = 1 is required in MVT. RESTART = (request, [checkid]) identifies the checkpoint at which restart is to occur. "Checkid" identifies the checkpoint where restart is to occur. From the IBM Systems Reference Library manual *IBM System/360 Operating System—COBOL (F) Programmer's Guide*, GC-28-6380, p. 94.

7.6   ROLL-OUT AND ROLL-IN

This is an OS performance feature specified in either the JOB or EXEC statement as $ROLL = (x,y)$, where x and y are of the form

$$\begin{Bmatrix} YES \\ NO \end{Bmatrix}$$

In a specification of //USERJOB JOB . . . ROLL = (YES,YES), RE-GION = 160K. . ., the first parameter signals the operating system that, in any of its steps, USERJOB may call on the system to provide more than 160 kilobytes. The second parameter signifies that USERJOB may itself be rolled out of storage by the demand of a higher priority job.

Roll-out means that a task temporarily donates its storage to a task of higher priority. On completion of the recipient task's execution, the donation is released; the lower priority task, rolled back in, again becomes dispatchable.

7.7   CHAINED SCHEDULING

Figure 7.8 depicts the operation of chained scheduling, which uses the program-controlled interrupt (PCI) invoked by the S/370 channel. Chained scheduling is specifiable in the DD card.

Consider two storage buffers prior to transmission of the second EMPYTD DASD block. Initially, at time, 1', data management routines invoked by SALARYL have finished processing the data block, in buffer 1; the channel program has sequenced to the command, *Read Data* (for block 2), which has the command chain, and PCI flags on. Program-controlled interrupt occurs on the channel's decoding of the *Read Data* operation field. In the ensuing interrupt processing the control program inspects buffer 1 to determine if space is available for EMPYTD block 3. Since it is, the channel executes *Tic RD,* a branching operation, directing command streaming to location *RD*.

At *RD,* time 2', a PCI is again taken. The question now becomes, have the data in buffer 2, EMPYTD block 2, been processed? If not, the control program ends the channel program by changing *Tic* to *Nop*.

Given a sequential data organization, the increase in device utilization afforded by synchronization of the instruction and command streams may be substantial indeed.

Like chained scheduling, other productivity features of OS are specifiable by the DCB keyword of the DD statement using the OPTCD parameter. For example, the reliability feature, read after write is coded

//INOUT DD . . . DCB = (OPTCD = W) . . .

Write verification ensures that output information is actually recorded, on say DASD, using control program (transparent) reread service to see to it.

For further detail on the use of job control language, the IBM Systems Reference Library manual *Job Control Language User's Guide,* GC-28-6703, is recommended.

7.8   SYSIN AND SYSOUT

Much data processing use is predictable, and predictability is often the basis for efficient system response. First- and second-generation systems committed input

Activity Diagram

Time	Buffer 1 Block No. in	Buffer 1 Status of	Buffer 2 Block No. in	Buffer 2 Status of	Location	Operation	Operand	Flags	Comment
1′	1	Available for Filling	—	Available for Filling	RD	Read Data / Tic	RD	PCI, CC	Block 2 / Block 3
2′	1	Unavailable for Filling	2	Active	RD	Read Data / Nop	RD	PCI, CC	Block 3 / Block 4

Channel Program

IOS — Problem Program

Nop→Tic ①—— INTERRUPT ②—→ RETURN TO PROBLEM PROGRAM

Nop OK ①—— INTERRUPT ②—→ RETURN TO PROBLEM PROGRAM

Figure 7.8 Chained-scheduling schematic. Here "block" represents the **EMPYTD** data sub block and CC stands for command chain.

card decks to tape, offline; the tape data then became high-speed input to the system, on line.

OS overlaps electromagnetic and electronic processes, on line. Systems tasks—readers, writers, and initiators—preside over the entrance and exit of the work of the system. Among system data sets allocated to these tasks are the multijob SYSIN and SYSOUT data sets.

An OS/360 SYSIN data set exists on a device elected by the operator [IBM 2540 card reader]. This data set is allocated to the reader-interpreter. READERL of READERTASK Opens and accesses SYSIN.* An output data set of the reader-interpreter is SYS1.SYSJOBQE within which jobs and job steps reside. The reverse (to SYSIN) procedure applies in job management's release of work. WRITERL uses the SYS1.SYSJOBQE data set as input and SYSOUT as an output data set. Multiple reader and writer tasks, sharing resources with multiple user job step executions, are the form to which the first-generation peripheral system has evolved in System/370.

7.9 SYSTEMS MANAGEMENT FACILITIES

The installation manager has different requirements than the individual programmer. The programmer's concern is the development and maintenance of SALARIES for, say, the payroll department. The manager's concern is not with *this* job but with *all* jobs as they apply to the costs and values of installation productivity.

Consider System/370 cost control. With n jobs simultaneously extant, the assignment of job costs, based on each job's resource usage, defines the functional requirement for the routines of systems management facilities (SMF).

These routines solve the following: The USERJOB JOB card specifies 160 kilobytes of storage while the job has the requirements of Table 7.1. Given that OS (via EXEC job control language) permits storage specification, in job step requests, USERJOB is wasting space.

The responsibility for correcting the (admittedly extreme) situation rests with

---

* In the COBSTEP job control language of Figure 7.1, SYSIN appears as a ddname. The ambiguity between the reader-interpreter's and language translator's use of the name is a frequent source of confusion. In these discussions SYSIN identifies the data set resident in the physical reader. The ddname could have been "codfish." The SYSOUT data set is likewise used by systems tasks (terminator and output writer) and problem programs. By SYSOUT the output writer data set is intended.

Table 7.1

Step	Main Storage Size (kilobytes)		Step Execution Time (min)
	Specified	Used	
COBSTEP	160	160	3
LESTEP	160	44	2
EXECSTEP	160	3	300

the manager. Desire to rapidly develop and maintain his program dominates the individual programmer. His tendency to wastefulness, as real as it is lamentable, when multiplied by the wastefulness of 100 others, can be expensive, as well.

Information about the jobs in an installation is available to the manager through two basic functions systems management facilities provide, data collection and user exits.

Systems management facilities collect data by recording, at user option, each job's CPU, storage, and i–o utilization. Programs written at the installation and stored in SYS1.LINKLIB use these data. At the beginning of each work period, in an OS initialization process, IPL (see Chapter 9) links OS to these library members. Whenever a systems program reaches a user exit, it branches to an installation program that either controls or analyzes job processing each time it executes. For example, during SYSIN processing of USERJOB, the reader exits to a user's routine for each job control language statement interpreted. This routine may verify or modify selected fields or reject any job not in accord with installation standards.

In addition to the analysis of storage utilization (Table 7.1), DASD space and volume use, and the number of lines a job prints may be reported. The activity of systems management facilities is not specified in job control language. USERJOB suffers systems management activity, along with other jobs run during the work session. Specification occurs earlier at system generation time.

7.10 OS/360 JOB MANAGEMENT

Components

The problem state programs of job management execute within the OS/360 task structure and access (system) data sets through data management. Like the OS/360 control program, they operate with protect key zero. Each of these system tasks provides service to many user jobs (Fig. 7.9).

Job management has reading, initiating, and writing tasks, and a master scheduler task. Responding to START commands from the operator's console, a master scheduler attaches system tasks into the operating system.

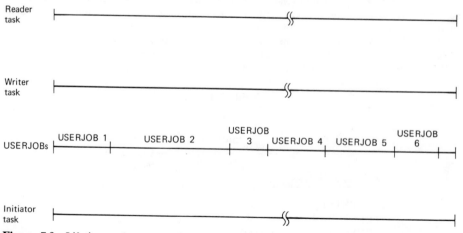

Figure 7.9 Lifetimes of some typical USERJOBs and reader, writer, and initiator system tasks compared.

Reading task. This task accepts the independent requests of the input job stream data set, SYSIN, and builds the control blocks and tables, the jobs and job steps on which initiating task(s) operate. Reading tasks also store problem data in the input stream.

The primary routine of a reading task—the interpreter control routine—reads the input stream, builds blocks and tables in its region, and invokes a queue manager routine to write these into a priority queue on the SYS1.SYSJOBQE data set. The information enqueued particular to USERJOB, a work queue entry, consists of DASD blocks chained together by location within SYS1.SYSJOBQE.

Fifteen input work queues, one for each job class specifiable in the JOB statement, are stored FIFO within priority. An initiator seeking a new job to process dequeues an entry.

The major control blocks and tables in a work queue entry are the following:

1. Job control table (JCT), built from the JOB statement containing job and job step attributes.

2. Step control table (SCT), built from the EXEC statement, containing job step attributes.

3. Step i–o table (SIOT), built for each DD statement, containing information needed to assign devices to a data set.

4. Job file control block (JFCB), built for each DD statement containing data set attributes. Open, SVC 19, completes the JFCB.

Figure 7.10 shows the flow of information between the control statements and these blocks and tables.

An operator issues a STOP READER command, or an end of data condition on the associated reader device terminates a reading task.

Initiating task. An initiating task has two parts: the initiating of user tasks into OS/360 from job step data and the performing of termination processing when tasks are complete.

The initiation of a task consists of the following:

1. Acquiring a region of main storage.
2. Locating input data sets of the executing load module.
3. Allocating i–o devices for the task.
4. Reserving auxiliary storage for data sets created during the task.
5. Issuing Attach (SVC 42) and creating the task.

An initiator routine invokes a queue manager routine to dequeue the first entry on an input work queue, the highest priority job yet to be initiated.

When an initiating task is assigned to more than one job class, the order in which the queues were specified in the operator's START command determines the order in which the queues are checked.

Once a job has been assigned to an initiating task, initiation, execution, and termination of its steps are performed sequentially under the control of that task. A multijobbing type of multiprogramming obtains when several initiating tasks concurrently process the work queue entries of SYS1.SYSJOBQE.

In multijobbing, one data set may be required for two or more coexisting jobs. Before initiating the first step of a job, the initiator invokes the SVC routine ENQ/DEQ to determine if a data set for this job is in use by another job and

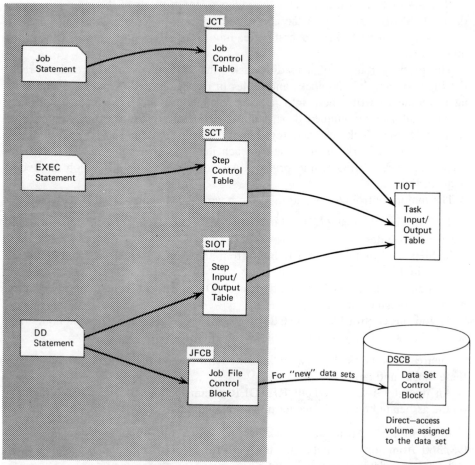

Figure 7.10 Relationship of the work queue blocks of the initiating task to the work queue blocks of the reading task. The shaded and unshaded areas represent blocks created by the reading and initiating tasks, respectively. From the IBM handbook *IBM System/360 Operating System MVT Control Program Logic,* Y-28-6658.

cannot be shared. Multiple use is allowed only when all users have specified that the data set can be shared. If a data set for any job step is unavailable, initiation of the first step is suspended pending availability.

Acquiring a region. After reading the SCT, an initiator routine in the link pack area, releasing the current region, requests a new region meeting the requirement of the job step or the initiating task—whichever is larger. If contiguous storage in the dynamic area or space in the supervisor queue area for tables and queues is unavailable, the initiating task is put in RB/Wait. Following region allocation, a device allocation routine is loaded into the region.

Locating input data sets. The allocation routine determines which volumes contain input data sets from either the DD operand DISP=OLD or, where the VOLUME parameter is absent, by searching SYS1.CATALOG. (A catalog management SVC routine is invoked to perform this search.) With OLD volumes determined, allocation begins.

Assigning i–o devices. The allocation routine determines if a job step's devices are available. If they are, they are assigned to the step; if not, a message is issued. Failing to make the required devices available, the operator may have the initiating task put in RB/Wait, or he may cancel the job.

After assigning devices, the allocation routine builds a task i–o table (TIOT). It contains the work queue and system [*l*(UCB)] information necessary to Open, SVC 19, EMPYTD. The TIOT is in the system queue area of storage (see Appendix 1, p. 217).

Reserving auxiliary storage space. For DASD output data sets, device allocation requests the service of a space management routine, DADSM. When assigning space, DADSM partially builds a Data Set Control Block (DSCB) for the output data set that will occupy the space. The DSCB, or label, contains the name and data set characteristics obtained from the JFCB. It also contains the track addresses assigned. Construction of a DSCB for an output data set completes when the associated Data Control Block is Opened.

If space on a volume is unavailable, DADSM returns control to allocation, which issues an operator message. The operator makes a new volume available, cancels the job, or signifies that the initiating task is to be put in RB/Wait.

Attaching a task for the job step. Finally, the initiator issues Attach, SVC 42, which builds a job step TCB [EXECTCB]. With step initiation complete, the initiating task is placed in RB/Wait until the step is to be terminated.

Terminating a job step. When a job step completes, the OS/360 supervisor loads the termination routine into the step's region. This routine disposes of data sets created or used and releases i–o devices assigned, during the step. The initiator issues Detach, SVC 62, removing the job step TCB from the system.

After terminating the last step of a job, the initiator deletes the input work queue entry for the job from the SYS1.SYSJOBQE data set and invokes a queue manager to make entries in output work queues for use by a SYSOUT writer. Thirty-six output work queues reside in SYS1.SYSJOBQE indicating SYSOUT data sets and system messages to be written. During step termination the initiator builds a Data Set Block (DSB) for each SYSOUT data set created during execution of the problem programs of that step. Systems Message Blocks (SMBs) are created for system messages as they are generated.

A job step is terminated either when it is complete, when a specified time interval expires, when an error prevents any more processing, or when the job is cancelled.

Writing task. A writing task controls output of all system messages and SYSOUT data sets in a specified class (or classes) from the direct-access volume on which they were initially placed. In Figure 7.1, //SYSOUT is the ddname of the data set written by SALARYL and associated with YTD-RECORD. In the same DD statement the operand SYSOUT=A designates the A queue in which the DSBs that control this data set reside.

Writer routines indicate to queue manager routines which message class is to be written. The queue manager passes queue entries to the writer. After all messages and data sets of an entry and associated with an individual job are written, the writer requests the next entry.

When all entries in all classes associated with this writing task have been processed, the task is placed in RB/Wait. A writing task is again made ready when an output work queue entry is placed in one of the queues associated with it.

SYS1.SYSJOBQE

This data set contains the 15 input and 36 output queues processed by the system readers, writers, and initiators. In SYSJOBQE processing, a queue manager supervises a data structure of 51 queues. Each of 51 queue control records (QCRs), doubly enqueued on, acts as queue control block.

In figure 7.11, prioritized queues of logical track header (LTH) elements request the services of system tasks. Second, a queue of event control blocks, acting as queue elements, indirectly represent the requests of system tasks for work.

Figure 7.12 depicts an input queue of requests. The serial nature of such a queue is illustrated in the following way: Assume that the reader-interpreter is enqueuing a work queue entry, z, for user 1, while the initiator is dequeuing an entry, y, for user 2. The enqueuing seeks to establish the user job pointers as z, y, x, o. The dequeue seeks to set them to x, o. The result of these two tasks simultaneously accessing the queue is unpredictable, an intolerable situation in operating system design.

The inference is clear; the serially reusable QCR resource must be exclusively available to one systems task at a time until that task is finished with it. For example, a dequeuing request issued by an initiator seeking to process USERJOB tables results in an event control block being created and enqueued. If the QCR is currently busy, the initiator task is placed in RB/Wait.

Consideration. The patterns of job processing, like the specifications of job control language, have a variety of options too numerous for detailed exposition here.

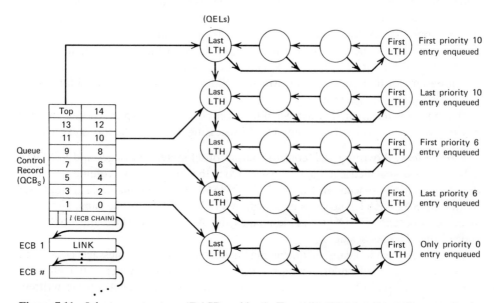

Figure 7.11 Job queue structure (DASD resident). From the IBM handbook *Program Logic, MVT JOB MANAGEMENT*, Y-28-6660.

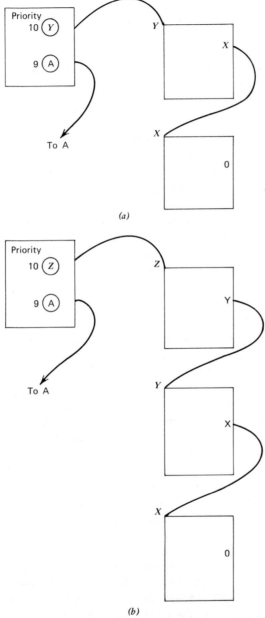

Figure 7.12 Multiple-priority LIFO queue structure:
(*a*) before USERJOB processing; (*b*) after enqueuing
of "request element z."

An IBM Systems Reference Library Manual, *JCL Users Guide,* GC-6703, contains further detail for those with interest or the need.

7.11   RELEASE 2 JOB PROCESSING

In release 2, the job entry subsystem (JES) has replaced OS/360 job management.* JES2 is a successor to, and a superset of, the OS/360 routines HASP, described in this section.

The Problem

Among other things, the OS/360 SYSIN reader writes card images to DASD.† Compared to these write times and the reader's process times, physical card reading is slow. SYSIN readers, and SYSOUT writers as well, frequently Wait upon card or printer i–o. The amount of productive use of the CPU by other tasks during, say, READERL's RB/Waits depends on the multitasking environment. For example, some SYSOUT writer might not be switched to at, say, time 1 for, needing SYS1.SYSJOBQE, the writer might Wait until, say, INITL or Open, SVC 19, relinquishes that serially reusable resource. In addition, when RDRTASK is redispatched later, it often has to reposition a disk arm before writing card images to SYS1.SYSJOBQE.

The HASP Solution

A set of routines coresident with OS/360, HASP solved the card/printer i–o and the disk-repositioning problems. In addition to making disk i–o appear like card or printer i–o to OS/360 readers or writers, HASP integrated SYSIN/SYSOUT functions.

Prior to the processing of USERJOB, HASP read the SYSIN stream(s) into track-size buffers. Operating at top speed, reading devices fed cards and filled storage buffers continuously. After a buffer became full, HASP issued EXCP. IOS unloaded the buffer onto DASD.

HASP intercepted all EXCPs for unit record i–o issued during the lifetimes of OS jobs. In USERJOB, the READERL request for the twenty-fifth card image resulted in 80 characters being moved electronically from a HASP buffer into READERTASK storage. HASP issued the EXCPs that kept these buffers filled from DASD.

Similarly, HASP intercepted the EXCPs of SYSOUT writers, and enabled the printer to run at high speed, by unloading 132 byte lines from a track-size buffer.

By integrating SYSIN and SYSOUT functions, HASP transferred card/print line images between storage and DASD efficiently. HASP owned the DASD unit that held these images, knew where the images were, and got control when an OS/360 system routine read or wrote them. EXCPs issued by HASP caused the arm to "creep" across the disk surface using 15-millisecond Seeks rather than randomly "sweep" across the surface using 50-millisecond Seeks.

---

* The term "OS/360" is used for OS and release 1.

† The job control language listed in Appendix 1 is written in card image form by the SYSIN Reader.

The efficiency of HASP carried over to remote job entry. HASP commonly ran mixed local and remote job entry work under OS/MFT. In addition, it often supported important functions before OS/360 job management did. An instance of this was HASP support for multiple consoles, permitting tape units to be installed, say, one story above the computer site.

System/370 Attach Support Processor (ASP)

An ASP installation may include multiple data processing systems. In, say, a four-CPU configuration, ASP, performing local and remote SYSIN/SYSOUT processing, runs in a support system. OS/360 job, task, and data management run in main systems. A request for unit record i–o, issued from a main system, comes to ASP, which, using the channel-to-channel feature of the IBM 2860 channel, transfers a card image or print line to or from that main system's storage.*

The ASP checks volume mounting prior to job processing, effective in remote job entry. When USERJOB is read in from a remote card reader, volume HARRYC say, is unavailable at the system site. The ASP HOLDS USERJOB in its input queue until the reel is located, transported, and mounted. Meanwhile, the system does other work.

Job Entry System

Although HASP and ASP demonstrated the advantages of a separate job entry system under OS, they duplicated functions of the operating system with resulting inefficiencies. In addition, these adjunct systems failed to address the frequent serialization on SYS1.SYSJOBQE by OS job management routines and Open and Close.

In release 2, JES not only incorporates the advantages of HASP and ASP but also addresses their unsolved problems. In release 2's definition, on input, job entry ends when job control language card images have been converted to internal text and tables. Where the card images of EXECSTEP are JES units of work, the step's text and tables are the units of work of an initiator defined apart from the subsystem (JES). Standard conventions enable operating system and subsystem to call on one another readily.

In batch processing, a reader, internal to the subsystem, stores EXECSTEP JCL card images until an initiator becomes available to schedule resources for address space 1, say. Only then does the subsystem present the operating system with the EXECSTEP text and tables. Thus the OS/360 reader-interpreter function has been redefined. The subsystem converts the card images of EXECSTEP to internal text and tables just prior to the step's activity. Where many steps coexist, great quantities of DASD space are saved.

More important than space saving, the new design breaks the job queue bottleneck, for text and tables are stored into each user's virtual storage in a scheduler work area. The placement of the EXECSTEP job queue entries into a private virtual storage eliminates Waiting by INITL on a job queue being accessed by, say, WRITERL.

Conversational teleprocessing and the processing of the commands of the ma-

---

* The channel-to-channel feature causes one system to appear as an i–o device to another system.

chine operator imply different paths through job entry than that followed by a batch job. Rather than being entered through the SYSIN reader, as in batch, job control language for such job steps, stored in advance in SYS1.PROCLIB, must be converted by the JES and passed as text and tables to the initiator.

In being redefined as a general purpose operating system resource, the initiator may be called on during, say, EXECSTEP to allocate resources to an interactive job step created from a terminal. Similarly resources may be deallocated during, say, EXECTASK activity. SYSOUT might be CLOSED and spooled out by JES while SALARYL continues to execute.

In the new definition, JES is designed as an independent subsystem by virtue of its having its own Communications Vector Table (CVT). Other subsystems may be so defined.

Job entry subsystem 2. This subsystem performs functions formerly performed by HASP and job management, including the following:

1. Reading local and remote SYSIN job control language and data.
2. Scheduling jobs into OS.
3. Starting and stopping initiators.
4. Writing SYSOUT.

New features include the following:

1. Integration of the checkpoint/restart facility; JES2 maintains a system job journal to support system restart, automatic step restart, and checkpoint restart.
2. Immediate detection of job control language syntax errors before job processing has begun.
3. Dynamic allocation and deallocation of output data sets.
4. A facility to request SYSOUT printing and routing options by data set as well as by job.

Job entry subsystem 3. JES3 serves from one to four release 2 uniprocessors or multiprocessors, or any combination of both. Release 2 S/370Rs must have at least one million bytes of real storage. The functions of JES3 are generally compatible with ASP version 3.

A major advantage of JES3 is improved system availability; it is designed to minimize the potentially disruptive effect of failures in both hardware and software. For hardware failures, unaffected units continue activity. Software components are individually restartable. Therefore control malfunctions and transient hardware faults can be localized.

When JES3 manages a complex, one CPU, the global system, controls job scheduling and device allocation for the complex. The other processors are called local systems. A local system can function as a global system when a global failure occurs.

Normally the switch from local to global system is made without logically disrupting jobs on the local processors.

Additional JES3 availability features are the following:

1. Failing local processors can be restarted without disrupting other processors.
2. The global system can be warm started (from input work queues) without disrupting work on local processors.

3. Error exits are defined to allow continued system operation when failures can be confined to subfunctions.

Other JES3 features include

1. Automatic scheduling of work to multiple processors.
2. Scheduling of peripheral devices.
3. Mounting and verifying private volumes before a job is scheduled.
4. Time-sharing support for all systems.
5. Checkpoint/restart support for all systems.
6. Systems management facilities support for all systems.

JES3 supports a variety of system configurations. For example, it can connect up to four release 2 systems and share DASD and tape devices among systems. In a JES3 complex, all release 2 processors share a set of direct-access volumes containing SYSIN/SYSOUT data.

JES3 can attach ASP version 3 main processor CPUs to a global CPU.

JES3 uses system consoles, one per CPU, and device and global consoles. The same physical console can be a device and global console. The global system advises the device console operator of the condition of the devices he controls. Typically he receives requests to mount and dismount forms, trains, carriage tapes, and tape and disk volumes. The operator of the global console controls the entire complex; he has access to the centralized job source, all local systems, and all devices.

EXERCISES

7.1   In Appendix 1 identify which step produced each page of printed output.

7.2   Create SALARYS as a library source module number.

7.3   Use SALARYS as input in a two step compile and link job and store as a load module member SALARYL.

7.4   Use SALARYS as input to the COBOL language translator and compile library member SALARYO.

7.5   Compile SALARIES COPYing the EMPLOYEE-YTD specification.

7.6   Assume SALARIES has been checked out. Write the job control language to optimize the performance of running it in an execution environment.

7.7   Write the job control language to demand that SALARYL be put on unit 191.

7.8   Place the job control language for USERJOB into SYS1.PROCLIB and use it to compile link and execute SALARIES.

7.9   Using the COBOL word DISPLAY direct SALARYL to provide output to a SYSOUT device.

7.10   Assume that EMPYTD has been copied from 2311 to 2314. Identify the USERJOB EXECSTEP job control language of Appendix 1 affected.

7.11   SALARIES includes SALARYL and EMPYTD as data operands—comment.

7.12   USERJOB job control language includes //INOUT DD DSNAME=EM-PLOYEE-YTD . . . Comment.

7.13   USERJOB job control language includes //SYSIN DD *
Ordinarily the user enters data to System/360 by the above means, implying the use of DASD as an intermediate storage device. Can the user enter data from a card reader, avoiding DASD residence? Specify how this could be done.

7.14 In Monday's USERJOB execution EMPYTD was accessed via channel 2. In Tuesday's execution EMPYTD was accessed via channel 1. From EXECSTEP, Appendix 1, would changing channels in this manner require a change in EXECSTEP job control language?

7.15 OS/360 system residence is moved from unit address 191 to 291. Does SALARYS, SALARYO, or SALARYL have to change?

7.16 Write USERJOB—store the job control language in SYS1.PROCLIB and run it.

7.17 SALARYO CALLs DUMPITL. DUMPITL OPENs EMPLOYEE-YTD. Write a DD statement that includes DSNAME=EMPYTD and indicate its placement in USERJOB.

7.18 EXECTASK load module resource SALARYL CALLs DUMPITL. DUMPITL Attaches DUMPITL1 as an EXECTASK1 resource. RUMPITL1 Opens EMPYTD. To which task does EMPYTD belong? Generalize with respect to statically allocated resources.

7.19 A system programmer planning an installation's work deals with the following specifications (time in minutes):

	Program	
Step	A	B
Compiler	2	5
Link-editor	1	1
Execution	15	4

For each program comment on (a) job step selection in a production environment; (b) step selection in a development environment.

7.20 An installation has S/370 M 145 and M 155 systems installed. A malfunction develops in the M 155 toward the end of a busy work period during EXECSTEP processing. Briefly comment on the problems of transferring the work to the M 145. Discuss partially processed data sets such as EMPYTD, SYSIN, SYSOUT. Identify system-dependent configuration considerations.

7.21 Job management routines perform static allocation (scheduling) in OS/360. Is it possible to design an operating system such that dynamic scheduling could occur? Consider function and performance trade-offs. Include discussion of the graphics and teleprocessing-devices resources of such a system. Would you approach priority resource scheduling such as i–o devices first, main storage last?

7.22 USERJOB requests the use of which serially reusable resource?

7.23 COBTCB, representing COBTASK, output of the job management initiator, is a request for which serially reusable resource?

7.24 In MVT, can a chain of requests queue on more than one resource? Give an example of where this situation occurs within job management.

7.25 EXECSTEP is associated with the initialization of what? EXECTASK is associated with the initialization of what?

7.26 What if any consideration must the COBOL user give to the utilization of the serially reusable resource, System/370.

7.27 Compare the initialization of an electric age system with that of System/370.

chapter 8

DATA MANAGEMENT

8.1 INTRODUCTION

The most important thing to learn about a user's view of his data is how he perceives of his master files as being organized and accessed. These concepts determine the types of transactions his application program may handle and the types of statements he writes to handle them. The user's load modules access data through OS systems programs, IOS and data management.

Consisting of supervisory state routines resident in storage, IOS schedules, dispatches, and detaches i–o requests for *all* OS executing programs.

Shared only by *some* OS programs, data management routines generate channel commands to access data in sequential, indexed sequential, or direct organization. When SALARYL* OPENs EMPLOYEE-YTD, Open, SVC 19, Loads, SVC 8, the access methods. Henceforth, whenever SALARYL* READs EMPLOYEE YTD, data management deblocks logical records, provides error recovery, and protects the data set from unauthorized access by another's program. Data management routines invoke IOS service issuing EXCP, SVC 0.

OS/360 access methods operate under OS/VS releases 1 and 2. The release 2 access method, VSAM, is described toward the end of this chapter.

8.2 DATA SETS

To manipulate data, OS requires related records grouped and named, and information describing the data.†

In EXECSTEP, the initiator locates and Open initializes access to a data set through the DSNAME EMPYTD (see Fig. 2.20, p. 40).

Descriptive information is supplied when EMPYTD is created; when SALARIES is compiled (COBSTEP); and when EMPYTD is Opened, SVC 19.

Data sets are physical or logical according to the user's view of physical or logical System/370.

As shown in Table 8.1, physical data sets are either library data sets [SYS1.LINKLIB], or i–o data sets of executing load modules [EMPYTD]. Job control language deals with physical data sets. The EXEC statement specifies members of library data sets. The DD statement usually specifies i–o data sets.

---

* Directed by SALARIES statements.

† Names are an OS/360 resource. Two separate jobs may refer to the same name [EMPYTD] within OS. OS enqueues requests by the jobs on the resource.

Table 8.1   Examples of OS/360 Data Set Types and Names

Library Data Sets or Load Modules		I-O DATA SETS	
Physical	Logical	Physical	Logical
COBOLL	–	SALARYS	–
SALARYL	SALARIES	EMPYTD	EMPLOYEE-YTD

```
00001        IDENTIFICATION DIVISION.
00002        PROGRAM-ID.
00003        'SALARIES'.
                     ⋮
00040        PROCEDURE DIVISION.
00041            OPEN I-O EMPLOYEE-YTD.
00042            OPEN INPUT EMPLOYEE-WEEKLY.
00043        READ-WEEKLY.
00044            READ EMPLOYEE-WEEKLY AT END GO TO READ-YTD.
00045        READ-YTD.
00046            READ EMPLOYEE-YTD AT END GO TO FINIS.
00047            IF EMPLOYEE-NO-YTD IS EQUAL TO EMPLOYEE-NO-WEEKLY
00048                                       GO TO LIMIT-TEST.
00049            REWRITE YTD-RECORD.
00050            DISPLAY YTD-RECORD.
00051            GO TO READ-YTD.
00052        LIMIT-TEST.
00053            IF SLIMIT - SOCIAL-SEC-YTD < GROSS-PAY GO TO LIMIT-CALC.
00054            COMPUTE SOCIAL-SEC-YTD
00055                   ROUNDED = SOCIAL-SEC-YTD + GROSS-PAY * .048.
00056            REWRITE YTD-RECORD.
00057            DISPLAY YTD-RECORD.
00058            GO TO READ-WEEKLY.
00059        LIMIT-CALC.
00060            COMPUTE SOCIAL-SEC-YTD
00061                   ROUNDED = SOCIAL-SEC-YTD +
00062                            (SLIMIT - SOCIAL-SEC-YTD) * .048.
00063            REWRITE YTD-RECORD.
00064            DISPLAY YTD-RECORD.
00065            GO TO READ-WEEKLY.
00066            CLOSE EMPLOYEE-YTD.
00067            CLOSE EMPLOYEE-WEEKLY.
00068        FINIS. ENTER LINKAGE.
00069            CALL 'DUMPIT'.
00070            ENTER COBOL.
00071            STOP RUN.
```

Figure 8.1   SALARIES source statements. (Excerpt from Appendix 1.)

The applications user deals with logical data sets. In COBOL, they are the objects of READ/WRITE and CALL verbs (Fig. 8.1).

8.3   SEQUENTIAL ACCESSING OF DATA SETS

Sequential accessing of data sets was used prior to S/370 in magnetic tape, card readers, and so on. Sorted data were stored and then later retrieved in key sequence. Because of the labor of conversion, sequential access lasted in third-generation systems. From the second generation on, however, the pressure to convert to a random mode was strong. Direct retrieval of a logical record, avoiding thereby a scan of all preceding (and unwanted) data blocks, had a performance advantage. Productivity, as well as tradition, caused the retention of sequential access. A utility's billing data set has information on millions of customers.

Experience has proved it efficient to break the data into sections and process a section, customer names beginning with A through C, say, on a comparable working day of each month, a naturally sequential process.

In general, the human mind appreciates an orderly process; we sequence, we alphabetize, we rank.

In performance, the choice between sequential and random data processing depends on the application. A sequential data set must be sorted necessitating two job steps on input, sort and execution. Moreover, a low ratio of transaction to master record volumes indicates inefficient execution—many inactive master records are bypassed (see Fig. 8.2). A high transaction-to-master ratio indicates efficiency.

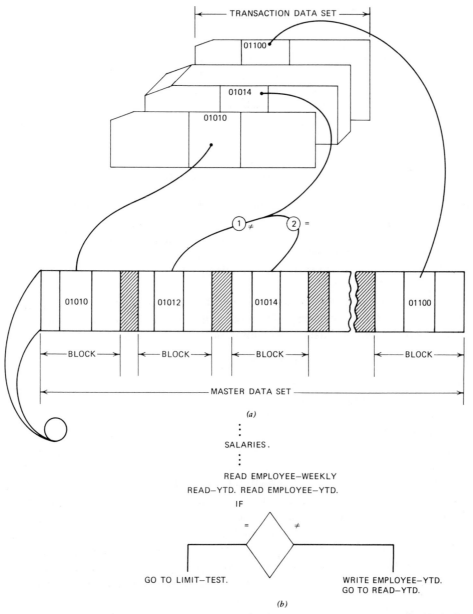

Figure 8.2 (*a*) Physical tape sequential transaction processing. (*b*) SALARIES logic. The shaded areas indicate tape gaps. (See Appendix 1.)

8.4 RANDOM ACCESSING OF DATA SETS

An automotive parts distributor maintaining an inventory of 25,000 items wants to instantaneously record each transaction affecting each item. By receiving out of stock notifications immediately, he orders replacement parts as soon as possible.

In sequential accessing, he batches his orders, sorts them into part number sequence, then processes the sorted data set against the entire master inventory data set at the end of each day.

In random accessing, he processes each transaction as it occurs. Each part's master data subblock is located by a key, is read, updated, and then stored back in the space from which it came.

Random accessing makes inquiring into or updating a file feasible. A terminal user, keying an inquiry, demands response in seconds. It is impracticable to pass 2400 feet of tape to find a master part data subblock for each of, say, 50 simultaneous inquiries. In addition, tape technology requires that a new copy of the entire master data set be created for each update.

In OS the same data set may be used for both sequential and random accessing (ISAM and VSAM).

8.5 DATA MANAGEMENT ACCESS METHODS

Much complexity is transparent to the COBOL PROCEDURE DIVISION user who conceives of accessing a neatly organized logical data set. It is in physical data set organizations and their accessing by data management's access methods that complexity lies. We distinguish OS data sets by how the records they contain are stored. We distinguish OS access methods by how they present records to application programs.

We approach the access methods through their logical data set representations, through SALARIES language, and through the interaction of their component routines with the physical data set organization.

The OS Sequential Access Method (SAM), Sequential Processing*

Figure 8.3a depicts EMPLOYEE-YTD, a logical data set; sorted records are sequenced by a key field. Figure 8.1 depicts SALARIES, the language that accesses EMPLOYEE-YTD. Beginning with the READ-WEEKLY paragraph, line 44, SALARIES READs an EMPLOYEE-WEEKLY and EMPLOYEE-YTD transaction and master record, and matches them, line 48. Lines 46 to 50 demonstrate that EMPLOYEE-YTD is READ from start to finish.

Figure 8.3b depicts . . . DSNAME=EMPYTD . . . with DASD subblocks within blocks, blocks within tracks, and tracks within cylinders. In the SALARIES PROCEDURE DIVISION, blocks, tracks, and cylinders are unreferenced by the user—these concern IOS and data management.

In sequential organization, mapping physical records into logical records is straightforward; SAM access methods provide good performance. Accordingly the OS/360 control program accesses many of its data sets through SAM. For exam-

---

* By SAM, the OS queued mode of access and the queued sequential access method (QSAM) are implied.

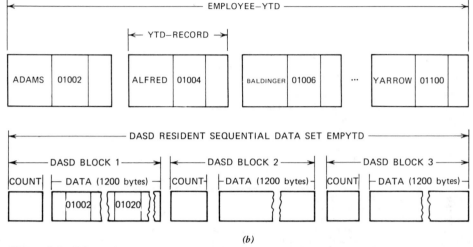

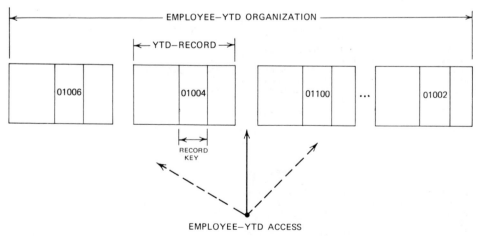

Figure 8.3 Schematic of (*a*) logical sequential data set EMPLOYEE-YTD and (*b*) DASD-resident sequential data set EMPYTD. Each data subblock contains 10 physical 120-byte records.

ple, job management retrieves the COBOL language translator (EXEC PGM = COBOLL) from SYS1.LINKLIB by use of the partitioned access method (PAM), which, in turn, uses SAM.

The OS Indexed Sequential Access Method (ISAM)*

Indexed sequential, a DASD access method, is used for both sequential and random processing.

ISAM—random processing. Figure 8.4 is a schematic of EMPLOYEE-YTD, an ISAM data set, processed randomly. To the user EMPLOYEE-YTD appears

* The OS queued index sequential access method (QISAM) is implied.

Figure 8.4 Schematic of organization of, and access to, indexed sequential (random-mode) data set.

```
00001          IDENTIFICATION DIVISION.
00002          PROGRAM-ID. 'SALARIES S/M/I/BU'.
00003          ENVIRONMENT DIVISION.
00004          CONFIGURATION SECTION.
00005          SOURCE-COMPUTER. IBM-360 165.
0C006          OBJECT-COMPUTER. IBM-360 165.
00007          INPUT-OUTPUT SECTION.
0C008          FILE-CONTROL.
00009              SELECT EMPLOYEE-YTD ASSIGN TO 'INOUT' DIRECT-ACCESS 2311
00010                  ORGANIZATION IS INDEXED
00011              ACCESS IS RANDOM
00012              SYMBOLIC KEY IS NUMBER-S
00013                  RECORD KEY IS EMPLOYEE-NO-YTD.
00014              SELECT EMPLOYEE-WEEKLY ASSIGN TO 'SYSIN' UNIT-RECORD.
00015          DATA DIVISION.
00C16          FILE SECTION.
00017          FD  EMPLOYEE-YTD
00018              LABEL RECORDS ARE STANDARD
00019              RECORDING MODE IS F
00020              BLOCK CONTAINS 10 RECORDS
00021              RECORD CONTAINS 120 CHARACTERS
00022              DATA RECORD IS YTD-RECORD.
00023          01  YTD-RECORD.
00024              02 NAME PICTURE A(32).
00025              02 SOCIAL-SEC-YTD PICTURE 9(6)V99.
00026              C2 EMPLOYEE-NO-YTD PICTURE 9(5).
00027              C2 CNTROL PICTURE X(1).
00028              02 GROSS-PAY PICTURE 9(6)V99.
00029              02 FILLER PICTURE X(66).
00030          FD  EMPLOYEE-WEEKLY
00031              LABEL RECORDS ARE OMITTED
0CC32              RECORDING MODE IS F
00033              BLOCK CONTAINS 1 RECORDS
00034              RECORD CONTAINS 80 CHARACTERS
00035              DATA RECORD IS WEEKLY-RECORD.
00036          01  WEEKLY-RECORD.
00037              02 EMPLOYEE-NO-WEEKLY PICTURE 9(5).
0CC38              02 NAME PICTURE X(32).
00039              C2 FILLER PICTURE X(43).
00040          WORKING-STORAGE SECTION.
00041          77  NUMBER-S PICTURE 9(5).
00042          77  SLIMIT PICTURE 9(6)V99 COMPUTATIONAL-3 VALUE IS 374.40.
00043          PROCEDURE DIVISION.
00044              OPEN I-O EMPLOYEE-YTD.
00045              OPEN INPUT EMPLOYEE-WEEKLY.
0CC46          READ-WEEKLY.
00047              READ EMPLOYEE-WEEKLY AT END GO TO FINIS.
00048              MOVE EMPLOYEE-NO-WEEKLY TO NUMBER-S.
00049          READ-YTD.
00050              READ EMPLOYEE-YTD.
0CC51          LIMIT-TEST.
00052              IF SLIMIT - SOCIAL-SEC-YTD < GROSS-PAY GO TO LIMIT-CALC.
00053              COMPUTE SOCIAL-SEC-YTD
00054                  ROUNDED = SOCIAL-SEC-YTD + GROSS-PAY * .048.
0CC55              REWRITE YTD-RECORD.
00056              GO TO READ-WEEKLY.
00057          LIMIT-CALC.
00058              COMPUTE SOCIAL-SEC-YTD
00059                  ROUNDED = SOCIAL-SEC-YTD +
0CC60                                  (SLIMIT - SOCIAL-SEC-YTD) * .048.
0CC61              REWRITE YTD-RECORD.
00062              GO TO READ-WEEKLY.
00063              CLOSE EMPLOYEE-YTD.
00064              CLOSE EMPLOYEE-WEEKLY.
00065          FINIS. ENTER LINKAGE.
00066              CALL 'DUMPIT'.
0CC67              ENTER COBOL.
0CC68              STOP RUN.
```

Figure 8.5 SALARIES—indexed sequential organization, random access. (Excerpt from Appendix 5.)

unsorted. Each logical record has an embedded key, RECORD KEY. In Figure 8.5, SALARIES accesses a logical record in EMPLOYEE-YTD by providing a search argument, SYMBOLIC KEY, which ISAM, in presenting SALARYL with the desired logical record, matches against RECORD KEY.* Line 12 defines NUMBER-S as the SYMBOLIC KEY; line 13 defines EMPLOYEE-NO-YTD as the RECORD KEY. EMPLOYEE-YTD and EMPLOYEE-WEEKLY definitions begin at lines 17 and 30.

Based on the READ-WEEKLY paragraph, line 46, ISAM retrieves the DASD block with matching RECORD KEY, transfers it to storage, and presents the desired YTD-RECORD to SALARYL. In retrieving, ISAM uses six keys: three in a track index area and three in a data area within the EMPYTD organization (see Table 8.2 and Fig. 8.6).

Using SYMBOLIC KEY as a search argument in the track index area (of the index area), ISAM locates the data area track, then a DASD block in the data area, and then a logical record.

After an equal or low compare, SYMBOLIC KEY versus c(key subblock), locates the desired index block, ISAM extracts the data track location from the corresponding data subblock. After using this CCHH as a Seek operand, ISAM *Searches* (on key) in the data track until it locates the block it needs.† Transferring this block to storage, the access method deblocks the proper logical record for presentation to SALARYL.

ISAM—sequential mode. Unaware of track index and data area, the user of SALARIES accessing EMPLOYEE-YTD in the sequential mode conceives of a SAM logical data set. In being identical, the PROCEDURE DIVISION statements of Figures 8.1 and 8.7 demonstrate that whether the access method is ISAM or SAM the language of the SALARIES user is the same. The ISAM and SAM channel programs passed to IOS by EOB (of data management) differ greatly, however.

File activity, updates and deletions. Inevitably a master data set will have additions and deletions. Figure 8.8 depicts a data area track with two blocks containing

---

* In scanning a telephone directory the name in the user's mind is the search argument. The name in the book is a table argument.

† A *Search,* like all commands of its kind, is performed in the DASD control unit.

Table 8.2   Description of ISAM Physical Keys by DASD Subblock and Area

	Area	
DASD Subblock	Track Index	Data
COUNT	CCHHR of this block	CCHHR of this block
KEY	Highest key on data area track	Highest key in this DASD block
DATA	CCHH location of data area track	RECORD KEY

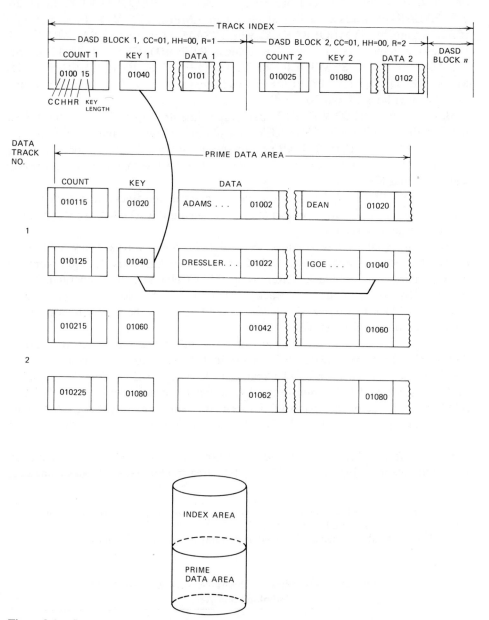

Figure 8.6 ISAM track index and prime data area subblocks and blocks.

20 logical records. With the additions of Figure 8.9, records with RECORD KEY 1071–1080, unable to fit within block 2, are stored in an overflow area associated with cylinder 1, track 2. If required, an overflow chain, located by a separate track index entry, is set up for each prime data area track. In Figure 8.8, each overflow record points to its predecessor. In creating a data set users commonly reserve space for expansion through dummy records consisting only of a key.

In Figure 8.8, had block 1 contained logical records 1062–1080 and block 2

```
00001               IDENTIFICATION DIVISION.
00002               PROGRAM-ID.
00003               'SALARIES S/QI/U'.
00004               ENVIRONMENT DIVISION.
00005               CONFIGURATION SECTION.
00006               SOURCE-COMPUTER. IBM-360 165.
00007               OBJECT-COMPUTER. IBM-360 165.
00008               INPUT-OUTPUT SECTION.
00009               FILE-CONTROL.
00010                   SELECT EMPLOYEE-YTD ASSIGN TO 'INOUT' DIRECT-ACCESS 2311
00011                       ORGANIZATION IS INDEXED
00012                       RECORD KEY IS EMPLOYEE-NO-YTD.
00013                   SELECT EMPLOYEE-WEEKLY ASSIGN TO 'SYSIN' UNIT-RECORD.
00014               DATA DIVISION.
00015               FILE SECTION.
00016               FD  EMPLOYEE-YTD
00017                   LABEL RECORDS ARE STANDARD
00018                   RECORDING MODE IS F
00019                   BLOCK CONTAINS 10 RECORDS
00020                   RECORD CONTAINS 120 CHARACTERS
00021                   DATA RECORD IS YTD-RECORD.
00022               01  YTD-RECORD.
00023                   C2 NAME PICTURE A(32).
00024                   C2 SOCIAL-SEC-YTD PICTURE 9(6)V99.
00025                   02 EMPLOYEE-NO-YTD PICTURE 9(5).
00026                   C2 CNTROL PICTURE X(1).
00027                   02 GROSS-PAY PICTURE 9(6)V99.
00028                   02 FILLER PICTURE X(66).
00029               FD  EMPLOYEE-WEEKLY
00030                   LABEL RECORDS ARE OMITTED
00031                   RECORDING MODE IS F
00032                   BLOCK CONTAINS 1 RECORDS
00033                   RECORD CONTAINS 80 CHARACTERS
00034                   DATA RECORD IS WEEKLY-RECORD.
00035               01  WEEKLY-RECORD.
00036                   C2 EMPLOYEE-NO-WEEKLY PICTURE 9(5).
00037                   02 NAME PICTURE X(32).
00038                   02 FILLER PICTURE X(43).
00039               WORKING-STORAGE SECTION.
00040               77  SLIMIT PICTURE 9(6)V99 COMPUTATIONAL-3 VALUE IS 374.40.
00041               PROCEDURE DIVISION.
00042                   OPEN I-O EMPLOYEE-YTD.
00043                   OPEN INPUT EMPLOYEE-WEEKLY.
00044               READ-WEEKLY.
00045                   READ EMPLOYEE-WEEKLY AT END GO TO READ-YTD.
00046               READ-YTD.
00047                   READ EMPLOYEE-YTD AT END GO TO FINIS.
00048                   IF EMPLOYEE-NO-YTD IS EQUAL TO EMPLOYEE-NO-WEEKLY
00049                                       GO TO LIMIT-TEST.
00050                   REWRITE YTD-RECORD.
00051                   GO TO READ-YTD.
00052               LIMIT-TEST.
00053                   IF SLIMIT - SOCIAL-SEC-YTD < GROSS-PAY GO TO LIMIT-CALC.
00054                   COMPUTE SOCIAL-SEC-YTD
00055                            ROUNDED = SOCIAL-SEC-YTD + GROSS-PAY * .048.
00056                   REWRITE YTD-RECORD.
00057                   GO TO READ-WEEKLY.
00058               LIMIT-CALC.
00059                   COMPUTE SOCIAL-SEC-YTD
00060                            ROUNDED = SOCIAL-SEC-YTD +
00061                                      (SLIMIT - SOCIAL-SEC-YTD) * .048.
00062                   REWRITE YTD-RECORD.
00063                   GO TO READ-WEEKLY.
00064                   CLOSE EMPLOYEE-YTD.
00065                   CLOSE EMPLOYEE-WEEKLY.
00066               FINIS. ENTER LINKAGE.
00067                   CALL 'DUMPIT'.
00068                   ENTER COBOL.
00069                   STOP RUN.
```

Figure 8.7 SALARIES—indexed sequential organization, sequential access. (Excerpt from Appendix 4.)

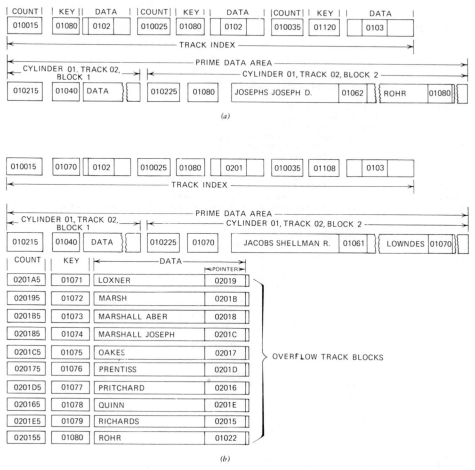

Figure 8.8 (*a*) Newly created ISAM data set. (*b*) ISAM EMPYTD after additions. Note: C is represented as an eight-bit byte; CC and HH are translated from Appendix 9.

Before			After	
Contents of DASD Block 2 Newly Created ISAM EMPYTD			Contents of DASD Block 2 After Additions to ISAM EMPYTD	
Key Subblock	RECORD-KEY	Additions to EMPYTD	Key Subblock	RECORD-KEY
01080	01062	01061	01070*	01061
	01064	01063		01062
	01066	01065		01063
	01068	01067		01064
	01070	01069		01065
	01072	01071		01066
	01074	01073		01067
	01076	01075		01068
	01078	01077		01069
	01080	01079		01070

*01071–01080 TO OVERFLOW AREA

Figure 8.9 Block 2 before and after update (see also Appendix 9, p. 225).

been reserved, records bumped from block 1 would have filled block 2 before overflow occurred.

Considerations. That with use EMPYTD with DISP = NEW becomes distributed into prime and overflow tracks, so that READ accesses an overflow
rather than a prime track, is invisible to the COBOL user. When EMPYTD becomes so dispersed, performance is degraded. A utility routine (see Chapter 9)
restores the data set to prime tracks only.

Figure 8.8 depicts a track index with two blocks per (prime data) track. Since
there are approximately 3000 bytes on a 2311 track and since the two index blocks
consist of approximately 100 bytes, the ratio of data bytes to index track bytes
is on the order of 30:1. Indices above the track index (cylinder index) eliminate
large data transmission operations through the lower level indices.

The OS Basic Direct Access Method (BDAM)

A method of random processing for DASD, BDAM is organized with data blocks
of one logical record. Unlike queued access methods, basic routines do no
deblocking.

SALARIES illustrates two modes of BDAM organization: relative track and
relative record.

*Relative track.** Our discussion is based on the example shown in Figure 8.10.
To the SALARIES programmer EMPLOYEE-YTD logical records appear unsorted in logical tracks (see Fig. 8.11).

The records of EMPLOYEE-YTD are randomly accessed through the unsorted
data set EMPLOYEE-WEEKLY. SYMBOLIC KEY, a search argument, locates
a logical record after ACTUAL KEY locates a relative track in EMPYTD. SYM-
BOLIC KEY and ACTUAL KEY, defined on lines 14 and 15 of Figure 8.10,
are presented to BDAM in the READ-WEEKLY paragraph beginning on line 53.
EMPLOYEE-NOM-WEEKLY is a function of EMPLOYEE-NO-WEEKLY;
given man number in the transaction data set, lines 57 to 60 provide ACTUAL
KEY.

Lines 57 to 60 exhibit that 11 tracks contain the EMPYTD data set. If 1000
tracks were required, the COBOL literal 1000 instead of 11 would have been used.

For each READ and REWRITE, BDAM uses ACTUAL KEY to derive the
CCHH of a channel command's *Seek* operand and then issues EXCP. In a subsequent asynchronous *Search,* the DASD control unit matches SYMBOLIC KEY
against the contents of each key subblock until it gets a hit; in the command chaining that follows the data subblock is *Read* into storage.

Relative record. To the SALARIES user the logical records of EMPLOYEE-
YTD appear in relative sequence, 1–1000, say (Fig. 8.12). EMPLOYEE-
WEEKLY transactions are READ in random sequence. SYMBOLIC KEY is used
as a search argument in retrieving the master lr to be updated. In Figure 8.13,
SYMBOLIC KEY, a binary key, defined on line 11 and derived (from EM-
PLOYEE-NO-WEEKLY) on line 46, is presented to BDAM on line 47.

---

* A data set is contained in, say, 11 tracks; a relative track is, say, the fifth physical
track.

```
00001          IDENTIFICATION DIVISION.
00002          PROGRAM-ID.
00003          'SALARIES D/U'.
00004          ENVIRONMENT DIVISION.
00005          CONFIGURATION SECTION.
00006          SOURCE-COMPUTER. IBM-360 165.
00007          OBJECT-COMPUTER. IBM-360 165.
00008          INPUT-OUTPUT SECTION.
00009          FILE-CONTROL.
00010              SELECT EMPLOYEE-YTD
00011                   ASSIGN TO 'INOUT' DIRECT-ACCESS 2311
00012              ORGANIZATION IS DIRECT
00013              ACCESS IS RANDOM
00014              SYMBOLIC KEY IS NUMBER-S
00015              ACTUAL KEY IS EMPLOYEE-NOM-WEEKLY.
00016              SELECT EMPLOYEE-WEEKLY ASSIGN TO 'SYSIN' UNIT-RECORD.
00017          DATA DIVISION.
00018          FILE SECTION.
00019          FD  EMPLOYEE-YTD
00020              LABEL RECORDS ARE STANDARD
00021              RECORDING MODE IS F
00022              RECORD CONTAINS 120 CHARACTERS
00023              DATA RECORD IS YTD-RECORD.
00024          01  YTD-RECORD.
00025              02 NAME PICTURE A(32).
00026              02 SOCIAL-SEC-YTD PICTURE 9(6)V99.
00027              02 EMPLOYEE-NO-YTD PICTURE 9(5).
00028              02 CNTROL PICTURE X(1).
00029              02 GROSS-PAY PICTURE 9(6)V99.
00030              02 FILLER PICTURE X(66).
00031          FD  EMPLOYEE-WEEKLY
00032              LABEL RECORDS ARE OMITTED
00033              RECORDING MODE IS F
00034              BLOCK CONTAINS 1 RECORDS
00035              RECORD CONTAINS 80 CHARACTERS
00036              DATA RECORD IS WEEKLY-RECORD.
00037          01  WEEKLY-RECORD.
00038              02 EMPLOYEE-NO-WEEKLY PICTURE 9(5).
00039              02 NAME PICTURE X(32).
00040              02 FILLER PICTURE X(43).
00041          WORKING-STORAGE SECTION.
00042          77  SLIMIT PICTURE 9(6)V99 COMPUTATIONAL-3 VALUE IS 374.40.
00043          77  NUMBER-S PICTURE 9(5).
00044          77  HELD PICTURE 9(5).
00045          77  EMPLOYEE-NOM-WEEKLY PICTURE S9(5) USAGE COMPUTATIONAL.
00046          77  SAVE PICTURE S9(5) USAGE COMPUTATIONAL.
00047          77  QUOT PICTURE S9(5) USAGE COMPUTATIONAL.
00048          77  PROD PICTURE S9(5) USAGE COMPUTATIONAL.
00049          77  KEEP PICTURE S9(5) USAGE COMPUTATIONAL.
00050          PROCEDURE DIVISION.
00051          OPEN I-O EMPLOYEE-YTD
00052          OPEN INPUT EMPLOYEE-WEEKLY.
00053          READ-WEEKLY.
00054              READ EMPLOYEE-WEEKLY AT END GO TO FINIS.
00055              MOVE EMPLOYEE-NO-WEEKLY TO NUMBER-S.
00056              MOVE EMPLOYEE-NO-WEEKLY TO HELD.
00057              MOVE EMPLOYEE-NO-WEEKLY TO SAVE.
00058              DIVIDE 11 INTO SAVE GIVING QUOT.
00059              MULTIPLY QUOT BY 11 GIVING PROD.
00060              SUBTRACT PROD FROM SAVE GIVING EMPLOYEE-NOM-WEEKLY.
00061              MOVE EMPLOYEE-NOM-WEEKLY TO KEEP.
00062          READ-YTD.
00063              READ EMPLOYEE-YTD.
00064              MOVE HELD TO NUMBER-S.
00065              MOVE KEEP TO EMPLOYEE-NOM-WEEKLY.
00066          LIMIT-TEST.
00067              IF SLIMIT - SOCIAL-SEC-YTD < GROSS-PAY GO TO LIMIT-CALC.
00068              COMPUTE SOCIAL-SEC-YTD
00069                   ROUNDED = SOCIAL-SEC-YTD + GROSS-PAY * .048.
00070              REWRITE YTD-RECORD.
00071              GO TO READ-WEEKLY.
00072          LIMIT-CALC.
00073              COMPUTE SOCIAL-SEC-YTD
00074                   ROUNDED = SOCIAL-SEC-YTD +
00075                              (SLIMIT - SOCIAL-SEC-YTD) * .048.
00076              REWRITE YTD-RECORD.
00077              GO TO READ-WEEKLY.
00078              CLOSE EMPLOYEE-YTD.
00079              CLOSE EMPLOYEE-WEEKLY.
00080          FINIS. ENTER LINKAGE.
00081              CALL 'DUMPIT'.
00082              ENTER COBOL.
00083              STOP RUN.
```

Figure 8.10 SALARIES—basic direct organization, relative track. (Excerpt from Appendix 6.)

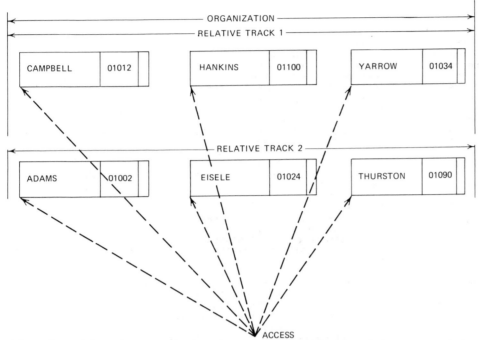

Figure 8.11 Schematic of organization of, and access to, EMPLOYEE-YTD, BDAM relative track mode.

Responding to READ, BDAM uses NUMBER-S to calculate CCHH, which it stores as the operand of a channel *Seek* command. BDAM then issues EXCP. On locating the proper track, the control unit *Searches,* matching NUMBER-S against c(key subblock) until it gets a hit; command chaining follows and the data subblock is *Read.* SALARYL resumes with the instructions generated from the LIMIT-TEST paragraph.

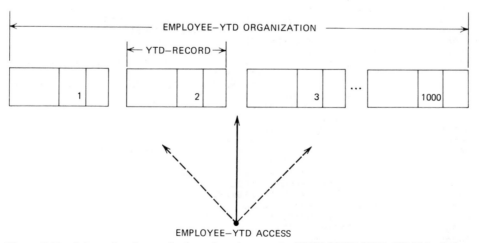

Figure 8.12 Schematic of organization of, and access to EMPLOYEE-YTD, BDAM relative record mode.

1

```
00001          IDENTIFICATION DIVISION.
00002          PROGRAM-ID. 'SALARYOCR'.
00003          ENVIRONMENT DIVISION.
00004          CONFIGURATION SECTION.
00005          SOURCE-COMPUTER. IBM-360 I65.
00006          OBJECT-COMPUTER. IBM-360 I65.
00007          INPUT-OUTPUT SECTION.
00008          FILE-CONTROL.
00009              SELECT EMPLOYEE-YTD ASSIGN TO 'INOUT' DIRECT-ACCESS 2311
00010              ACCESS IS RANDOM
00011              SYMBOLIC KEY IS NUMBER-S
00012                  ORGANIZATION IS RELATIVE.
00013              SELECT EMPLOYEE-WEEKLY ASSIGN TO 'SYSIN' UNIT-RECORD.
00014          DATA DIVISION.
00015          FILE SECTION.
00016          FD  EMPLOYEE-YTD
00017              RECORD CONTAINS 120 CHARACTERS
00018              RECORDING MODE IS F
00019              LABEL RECORDS ARE STANDARD
00020              DATA RECORD IS YTD-RECORD.
00021          01  YTD-RECORD.
00022              02 NAME PICTURE A(32).
00023              02 SOCIAL-SEC-YTD PICTURE 9(6)V99.
00024              02 EMPLOYEE-NO-YTD PICTURE 9(5).
00025              02 CNTROL PICTURE X(1).
00026              02 GROSS-PAY PICTURE 9(6)V99.
00027              02 FILLER PICTURE X(66).
00028          FD  EMPLOYEE-WEEKLY
00029              BLOCK CONTAINS 1 RECORDS
00030              RECORD CONTAINS 80 CHARACTERS
00031              RECORDING MODE IS F
00032              LABEL RECORDS ARE OMITTED
00033              DATA RECORD IS WEEKLY-RECORD.
00034          01  WEEKLY-RECORD.
00035              02 EMPLOYEE-NO-WEEKLY PICTURE 9(5).
00036              02 NAME PICTURE X(32).
00037              02 FILLER PICTURE X(43).
00038          WORKING-STORAGE SECTION.
00039          77  SLIMIT PICTURE 9(6)V99 COMPUTATIONAL-3 VALUE IS 374.40.
00040          77  NUMBER-S PICTURE S9(8) USAGE IS COMPUTATIONAL.
00041          PROCEDURE DIVISION.
00042              OPEN I-O EMPLOYEE-YTD.
00043              OPEN INPUT EMPLOYEE-WEEKLY.
00044          READ-WEEKLY.
00045              READ EMPLOYEE-WEEKLY AT END GO TO FINIS.
00046              COMPUTE NUMBER-S = (EMPLOYEE-NO-WEEKLY - 1001)
00047              READ EMPLOYEE-YTD.
00048          LIMIT-TEST.
00049              IF SLIMIT - SOCIAL-SEC-YTD < GROSS-PAY GO TO LIMIT-CALC.
00050              COMPUTE SOCIAL-SEC-YTD
00051                      ROUNDED = SOCIAL-SEC-YTD + GROSS-PAY * .048.
00052              REWRITE YTD-RECORD.
00053              GO TO READ-WEEKLY.
00054          LIMIT-CALC.
00055              COMPUTE SOCIAL-SEC-YTD
00056                      ROUNDED = SOCIAL-SEC-YTD +
00057                                  (SLIMIT - SOCIAL-SEC-YTD) * .048
00058              REWRITE YTD-RECORD.
00059              GO TO  READ-WEEKLY.
00060              CLOSE EMPLOYEE-YTD.
00061              CLOSE EMPLOYEE-WEEKLY.
00062          FINIS. ENTER LINKAGE.
00063              CALL 'DUMPIT'.
00064              ENTER COBOL.
00065              STOP RUN.
```

Figure 8.13 SALARIES—basic direct organization, relative record. (Excerpt from Appendix 7.)

164

**Table 8.3   Schematic of Read-Process
and Write-Process Overlap
of Figure 8.14**

	Time	
Activity	1	2
READ	LR_{m+1}	—
PROCESS	LR_m	LR_{m+1}
WRITE	—	LR_m

The OS Basic Partitioned Access Method (BPAM)

In response to the statement, EXEC PGM = COBOLL, job management retrieves the language translator from a library data set. An assembly language user may do the same. The initiator and the user program rely on BPAM.

To the user COBOLL appears as an unblocked SAM data set.

Our example illustrates the reading, updating, and writing of the blocks of COBOLL with overlap.

In Figure 8.14, from the Open macro to FINISH, the source program resembles a COBOL PROCEDURE DIVISION; both specify processing of previously defined data operands (see also Table 8.3). Beginning at READRECD, two Read macros specify that two logical records, lr_m and lr_{m+1}, are to be read in. After Checking that lr_m is completely (and correctly) in storage, UPDATE is Called; lr_m is updated while lr_{m+1} is being Read. Next lr_{m+1} is Checked before its updating at R3UPDATE and a Write for lr_m is issued. Then lr_{m+1} is Written, and both lr_m and lr_{m+1} are Checked (for correct output transmission). The loop is closed with a branch back to READRECD.

In BPAM, the user specifies Check for each i–o transmission macro; between Read (2) . . . Check (2) (or Write (2) . . . Check (2)) no Read (2) or Write (2) may intervene. OS must Check the correctness of *this* transmission.

The first macro in the program, DCB, defines the Data Control Block. Immediately thereafter the two Read macros define the Data Event Control Blocks, the locations that are Checked.*

BPAM processes physically partitioned data sets [HCLIB] where a directory contains the name and beginning locations of members [COBOLL]. Open's processing causes HCLIB's directory to be invisible in the assembly source program.

The OS Virtual Storage Access Method (VSAM) ˙

The OS/VS access method for direct access devices supersedes and is a superset of the OS/360 DASD access methods.

To the VSAM user EMPLOYEE-YTD appears much as it did in OS/360 SAM, ISAM, and DAM. He accesses master records sequentially, at high performance; sequentially or randomly from a single data set; or randomly by providing a relative key.

* MF = L specifies a Read to be of defining, rather than executing, form.

```
- - - - - - - - - - - - - - - - - - - - - - - - - - - - - - - - - - - - - - - - - - - - - - - - - - - - - - - - - - - -
//PDSDD        DD          DSNAME=HCLIB(COBOLL),DISP=OLD,- - -
- - - - - - - - - - - - - - - - - - - - - - - - - - - - - - - - - - - - - - - - - - - - - - - - - - - - - - - - - - - -
UPDATDCB       DCB         DSORG=PS,DDNAME=PDSDD,MACRF=(R,W),NCP=2,
                           EODAD=FINISH
               READ        DECBA,SF,UPDATDCB,AREAA,MF=L      Define DECBA
               READ        DECBB,SF,UPDATDCB,AREAB,MF=L      Define DECBB
AREAA          DS          - - -                            Define buffers
AREAB          DS          - - -
               . . .
               OPEN        (UPDATDCB,UPDAT)      Open for update
               LA          2,DECBA               Load DECB addresses
               LA          3,DECBB
READRECD       READ        (2),SF,MF=E           Read a record
NEXTRECD       READ        (3),SF,MF=E           Read the next record
               CHECK       (2)                   Check previous read operation
               (If update is required, branch to R2UPDATE)
               LR          4,3                   If no update is required, switch
               LR          3,2                      DECB addresses in registers 2
               LR          2,4                      and 3 and loop
               B           NEXTRECD
* In the following statements, "R2" and "R3" refer to the records
* that were read using the DECBs whose addresses are in registers
* 2 and 3, respectively. Either register may point to either
* DECBA or DECBB.
R2UPDATE       CALL        UPDATE,((2))          Call routine to update R2
               CHECK       (3)                   Check read for next record (R3)
               WRITE       (2),SF,MF=E           Write updated R2
               (If R3 requires an update, branch to R3UPDATE)
               CHECK       (2)                   If R3 requires no update, check
               B           READRECD                 write for R2 and loop
R3UPDATE       CALL        UPDATE,((3))          Call routine to update R3
               WRITE       (3),SF,MF=E           Write updated R3
               CHECK       (2)                   Check write for R2
               CHECK       (3)                   Check write for R3
               B           READRECD              Loop
FINISH         CLOSE       (UPDATDCB)            End-of-data exit routine
```

Figure 8.14 Updating a member of a partitioned data set. To overlap i–o and CPU activity, one can start several read or write operations before checking the first for completion. One cannot overlap read and write operations, however, as operations of one type must be checked for completion before operations of the other type are started or resumed. Note that each concurrent read or write operation requires a separate channel program and also a separate DECB. If a single DECB were used for successive read operations, only the last record read could be updated. In the example shown here, overlap is achieved by having a read or write request outstanding which each record is being processed. Note the use of execute- and list-form macro instructions, identified by the operands MF = E and MF = L, (see *IBM System/360 Operating System Supervisor and Data Management Services and Macros,* IBM Systems Reference Library manual GC-28-6647. From *IBM System/360 Operating System Data Management Services,* IBM Systems Reference Library Manual GC-26-3746.

Table 8.4   Logical Resemblances—OS/VS and OS/360 Access Methods

VSAM Access Method	OS/360 Access Method and Mode
For key-sequenced organization:	
Keyed sequential	ISAM, sequential (Fig. 8.3*A*)
Keyed direct	ISAM, random (Fig. 8.4)
Addressed sequential	SAM (Fig. 8.3*B*)
Addressed direct[a]	DAM, relative record (Fig. 8.12)
For entry-sequenced organization:	
Addressed sequential	SAM (Fig. 8.3*B*)
Addressed direct[a]	DAM, relative record (Fig. 8.12)

[a]User presents relative *byte* address.

Respecting additional function, VSAM processes multiple keys. A buyer, wanting to know what styles are selling, wants to know about sizes and colors as well.

VSAM includes a key-sequenced organization, distinguished by the presence of an index, from an entry-sequenced data set organization. Like ISAM, VSAM accesses key-sequenced data records in either keyed direct (random), or keyed sequential mode (see Table 8.4).*

Accessing in key-sequenced organization. In ISAM SALARIES, for ACCESS IS RANDOM, the user provides a SYMBOLIC KEY; in ACCESS IS SEQUENTIAL, the SYMBOLIC KEY is absent—ISAM knows to provide the next logical record in key sequence. VSAM keyed direct and keyed sequential access modes differ as their ISAM counterparts differ.

Keyed direct retrieval locates a data record after searching through an index hierarchy. An index entry includes the highest key in the next lower level (Fig. 8.15).

Starting at the top of the hierarchy, VSAM matches a symbolic key against index set key entries until it gets a hit. It then extracts a sequence set location entry.

* VSAM data records are analogous to OS/360 logical records.

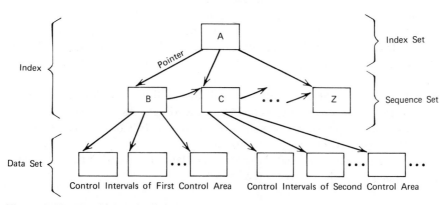

Figure 8.15   The highest-level index record (A) controls the entire next level (records B through Z); each sequence-set index record controls a control area.

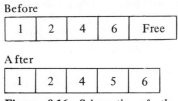

Figure 8.16 Schematic of the insertion of data record 5 in a control interval.

VSAM next matches symbolic key against sequence set key entries. Getting a hit, it extracts a control interval location. A control interval search follows. When c(key subblock) equal or greater than symbolic key is found, the search ends. VSAM (physically) transfers *this* control interval into virtual storage.

Consisting of data records and their description, the control interval is the unit of data VSAM transfers between virtual and auxiliary storage. It is a logical unit. Physically a control interval may span, say, multiple tracks or cylinders. Using a catalog, VSAM maps control intervals into the data blocks it accesses. When SALARYL READs EMPLOYEE-YTD, VSAM either presents a data record from a control interval already in virtual storage or issues EXCP for the next control interval. The EMPTYD DASD unit, virtual buffer size, and data record size influence the VSAM choice.

Key entries in VSAM indices are compressed; for example, in 01100 01101 01110 01111 10000, only the underlined bits would appear in, say, sequence set key entries. Indices are assignable to virtual storage. Key compression means that more indices reside in real storage at a given time.

A set of VSAM utilities, access method services, distribute available free space among control intervals and extend data set space. New record insertions occupy the free space; special overflow areas are absent in VSAM (Fig. 8.16).

In keyed sequential access, VSAM omits searching through the index set. Remembering that it has lately processed control interval m, VSAM locates control interval $m + 1$ by searching the sequence set only.

The addressed direct and addressed sequential modes of access ignore the index in transferring control intervals into virtual storage.

In addressed direct an application program presents VSAM with a relative byte address (RBA) of the data record to be deblocked and presented.* Since, for inserts and deletions, VSAM moves data records within control intervals, the user must maintain each record's RBA by providing a routine to record changes during processing.

In addressed direct, initially a data set is loaded with blanks. A routine randomly associates an RBA with a data record's embedded key. As a result, later, records will be distributed uniformly throughout the data set. In storing a record initially, a routine (in SALARYL, say) converts a key field to an RBA that VSAM uses as a key to retrieve a preformatted record (of blanks). SALARYL, using this key (RBA), updates and then rewrites the record.

---

* Defined as the data record's displacement in bytes counting from the beginning of the logical data set.

Table 8.5 Some Access Method Service Functions

Command	Function
DEFINE	DASD data space both initial allocations and extensions:
	Number of data records[a] (VSAM calculates control interval size)
	Percentage of free space in control intervals[a]
	Number of tracks or cylinders[a]
	Minimum virtual storage space for i–o buffers
	Data sets and, where applicable, their indices (for key-sequenced data sets, space may be allocated on volumes according to ranges of key values)
	Password authorization (to access a data set)
ALTER	Catalog entry modification
REPRO	Data set conversion and reorganization

	Input data organization	Output information organization
EXPORT ⎫ IMPORT ⎭	Indexed sequential, OS/360	Sequential, VSAM
	OS/VS EMPYTD ⟵——————————⟶ DOS/VS EMPYTD	
VERIFY	Access method services investigate if a VSAM data set has been properly closed.	

[a]Mutually exclusive.

Table 8.6 Some OS/360 ISAM AND OS/VSAM Characteristics Compared[a]

Index Structure. Both a VSAM key-sequenced data set and an indexed sequential data set have an index that consists of levels, with a higher level controlling a lower level. In ISAM, either all or none of the index records of a higher level are kept in virtual storage. VSAM keeps individual index records in virtual storage, the number depending on the amount of buffer space the user provides. It optimizes the use of the space by keeping those records it judges to be most useful at a particular time.

Relation of Index to Data. The relation of a VSAM index to the auxiliary-storage space whose records it controls differs from ISAM with respect to overflow areas for record insertion. VSAM, unlike ISAM does not distinguish between primary and overflow areas.

Deleting Records. With ISAM, the user marks records he wants to delete, either for the user to erase subsequently or for ISAM to drop should they be moved into the overflow area; VSAM automatically reclaims the space in a key-sequenced data set and combines it with any existing free space in the affected control interval. Because of its use of distributed free space for insertions and deletions, VSAM requires less data-set reorganization than ISAM does.

Defining and Loading a Data Set. The user defines all VSAM data sets in a catalog and allocates space for them by way of Access Method Services rather than by way of JCL. He can load records into a data set with his own processing program or with Access Method Services at one time or in stages.

[a]See IBM Publication GC26-3799; *OS/VS Virtual Storage Access Method (VSAM) Planning Guide.*

Table 8.7   VSAM Functions Not Included in ISAM[a]

VSAM has functions that Go Beyond ISAM.

Skip Sequential Access. Processing a key-sequenced data set sequentially, skipping records automatically in VSAM direct access.

Multiple-request Processing. Processing by concurrent sequential or direct access or both, without closing and reopening a data set.

Addressed Sequential Access. Retrieval and storage of records by relative byte address.

Direct Retrieval by Generic Key. With VSAM a user may retrieve with both a full key and a generic key (leading key bits) search argument.

Automatic Secondary Allocation of Auxiliary Storage Space.

Automatic Data-set Reorganization. VSAM partially reorganizes a key-sequenced data set by splitting a control area when it has no more free control invervals in that area and an interval is needed to insert a record.

[a]See IBM Publication GC26-3799, *OS/VS Virtual Storage Access Method (VSAM) Planning Guide.*

The control interval is used in all VSAM organization and access modes. Containing data descriptions, it enables fixed- and variable-length data records to be accessed in all modes. Being logical, it facilitates conversion from, say, DASD unit 1 to DASD unit 2. READ EMPLOYEE-YTD now accesses, say one track of unit 1 versus $\frac{1}{2}$ track of unit 2 as before. SALARYL created with unit 1 in mind executes unchanged.

In creating EMPYTD using VSAM commands the user specifies, say, the amount of DASD space to be allocated to access method services. Using this input, the service routines derive and catalog the information VSAM uses during EXECSTEP.

Table 8.5 lists some access method service functions.

Table 8.6 compares certain OS/360 ISAM and OS/VS access method characteristics, and Table 8.7 lists VSAM functions not included in ISAM.

EXERCISES

8.1 SALARIES1 of EXECTASK1 executes in MVT region 1, SALARIES2 of EXECTASK2 in region 2. SALARIES1 Waits in data management Synchronize. Describe the dynamic CPU allocation activity.

8.2 Punch up and compile (a) QSAM SALARIES, (b) QISAM SALARIES, (c) BDAM relative track SALARIES, (d) BDAM relative record SALARIES.

8.3 Use SALCR (see appendix 7) to create EMPTYD and run QSAM SALARIES.

8.4 Use utilities to create EMPYTD for Exercises 8.2b, 8.2c, and 8.2d, modifying the SALARIES DATA DIVISION as necessary (reference IBM Systems Reference Library Manual C28-6586).

8.5 In Exercise 8.2b cause EMPYTD to spill into the overflow area and run SALARYL.

8.6 Considering the proportions of question 5.26, discuss random-mode QISAM SALARIES processing in a simple as compared to a dynamic program management structure.

8.7 Compile, link, and execute SALARIES so as to dump main storage with EMPLOYEE-YTD OPENed for random-mode processing. Using the channel program found in the dump and the following table of DASD execution times, draw a bar graph depicting a comparison of SALARYL in simple versus dynamic program management mode.

Seek	3750
Search	600
Read 1200 BYTES	200
Read 5 BYTES	1

8.8 Use the COBOL OCCURS DEPENDING clause to create EMPYTD in variable-length record format. READ EMPLOYEE-YTD and DISPLAY it.

8.9 EMPYTD is reorganized from SAM to ISAM. Discuss the impact on SALARYS, SALARYO, and SALARYL.

8.10 In Exercise 8.9, what new function is now available to the user?

8.11 Three EMPYTD buffers are allocated to EXECTASK for SALARYL processing.

(a)	*(b)*	*(c)*
Awaiting Process	In Process	Processed

Using EXCP logic, construct a channel command list that interrupts the CPU to determine buffer availability before issuing a CCW, *RD,* for the next sequential DASD block. (Hint: use PCI flag, *TIC, No-Op.*)

8.12 Refers to Appendix 1, REWRITE YTD-RECORD statement 21. The statement directs i–o subsystem activity implying a CCW *Write* operation. (a) How does the user know that his EMPYTD data subblocks are correctly written to DASD? (b) Can he direct protection for himself, as through specification of Read after Write control program service? (c) What operating system productivity dimensions are affected by his specifications?

8.13 Trace the EMPYTD overflow chain for cylinder 17 track 2, locating the CCHHR for each record that overflowed (see Appendix 9, pp. 262–264.

chapter 9

TELEPROCESSING

9.1 INTRODUCTION

System/370 teleprocessing and batch data handling programs, both OS components, differ in major respects.

In batch processing, when SALARYL reads EMPTYD, a DASD data block enters storage. In teleprocessing, the question, "What is George M. Eisele's present Social Security amount," keyed into the system from a remote terminal, enters storage at an unpredictable time. Yet to the teleprocessing applications programmer, analogous to the batch case, the inquiry appears to be stored when a module [SALARYL] reads a message data set. System programs, the teleprocessing access methods, make this appear so.

To the operating system teleprocessing and batch devices are as different as the data they contain. Often there are more teleprocessing terminals than there are, say, tape units. Were terminals, like tape drives, activated by SIO unit address, the number of addresses in most teleprocessing installations would challenge the capacity of System/370 i–o address space. Also, where disk drives execute with data processing systems exclusively, terminals [teletypes] execute in networks that may or may not be controlled by computers, and hence teleprocessing data processing systems must conform to terminal convention and design.

9.2 TELEPROCESSING APPLICATIONS

Data Collection

In the simplest mode of teleprocessing operation, batch data collection, data are transferred to storage after a terminal operator dials System/370 or after the system dials an unattended terminal—autocall.

In autocall, at the close of business, an outlying office places operating data in a card reader. At night, using lines that carry voice traffic during business hours, the computer calls the terminal, collects data, and hangs up.

Data coming to the central system intermittently rather than in batches require a different means of communication—it would be impractical to dial each time data were ready. Instead, a group of terminals share a permanently connected, or multipoint, line. This private line is owned or leased from a common carrier (a company providing communications services). Since only one terminal can use the line at any one time, occasionally a terminal must wait.

Two common types of control of multipoint lines are (1) contention, where terminals vie for the line and an interlocking mechanism resolves "ties," and (2) polling, where a control mechanism invites each terminal in turn to send what data it has.

We approach intermittent data collection operations through polling, where, because they are numerous, terminals must be indirectly addressed by the system. In System/360 polling, communications *lines*, in being addressed by the CPU resemble batch i–o devices. In System/370 polling, communications *devices* [3705] resemble batch devices. First we describe the 360 system that uses 27XX communications multiplexors.

In Figure 9.1, an i–o interrupt, caused by completion of a teleprocessing data transmission, brings CPU control to IOS, activities 1 and 2, and, ultimately, to a teleprocessing appendage within IOS, activity 3, which, issuing SIO 0XX, initiates the asynchronous activity, polling.

Figure 9.2 depicts what follows SIO 0XX. The channel fetches the first command, *Write* activity 1. The operand 0XX refers to one section of a 2703, say, controlling a single communications line. To this section the channel [2870] passes the *Write* command field, activity 2. The command's data operand locates for the channel the message the 2703 writes from storage to the terminal in activity 3; the message contains a symbol, say, *abc*, recognized by one particular terminal as its address.

That terminal may signify that it has a message (the user has pressed a bid key, say) by generating a second symbol, ⓨ —"yes"—which it sends back to the 2703. The 2703 interpreting from ⓨ that input data follow, stores bits in a status byte and terminates its write activity. After the channel interprets the status byte, the channel program chains to the next command in sequence, *Read,* activities 4 and 5; after the message text from the terminal is read into storage, the channel program disconnects. The process repeats for each terminal that shares a line.

Alternatively a terminal with no message may generate the symbol ⓝ —"no"— when polled or, if the power is off, fail to generate a line control character for use by the 2703. In either case, the 2703 stores bits in the status byte, causing the channel program to end without chaining to a *Read* command.

Considerations. Although to a terminal System/370 and System/360 polling appear identical, they are different. Where the System/360 SIO addresses a section of a 27XX associated with a single line, the System/370 SIO addresses an entire 37XX.

Through an internal program a 3705, say, may poll all the terminals that share a multipoint line and then initiate an i–o interrupt. As its name, multiplexor, implies, the 3705 polls multiple lines simultaneously, initiating an interrupt when polling on any one line completes.

In addition to controlling terminals, multiplexors check, and may correct, erroneous data transmissions. Also, multiplexors, performing code conversion, may change a five-bit character transmitted from a teletype, say, to the eight-bit byte of an S/370 storage location.

Communications lines have disciplines, synchronous [bisynchronous] and asynchronous [start–stop]. In the synchronous type, line control bits mark the beginning and end of an entire message. In the asynchronous type, control bits mark the beginning and end of each character. In general, terminals with low data rates attach to asynchronous lines.

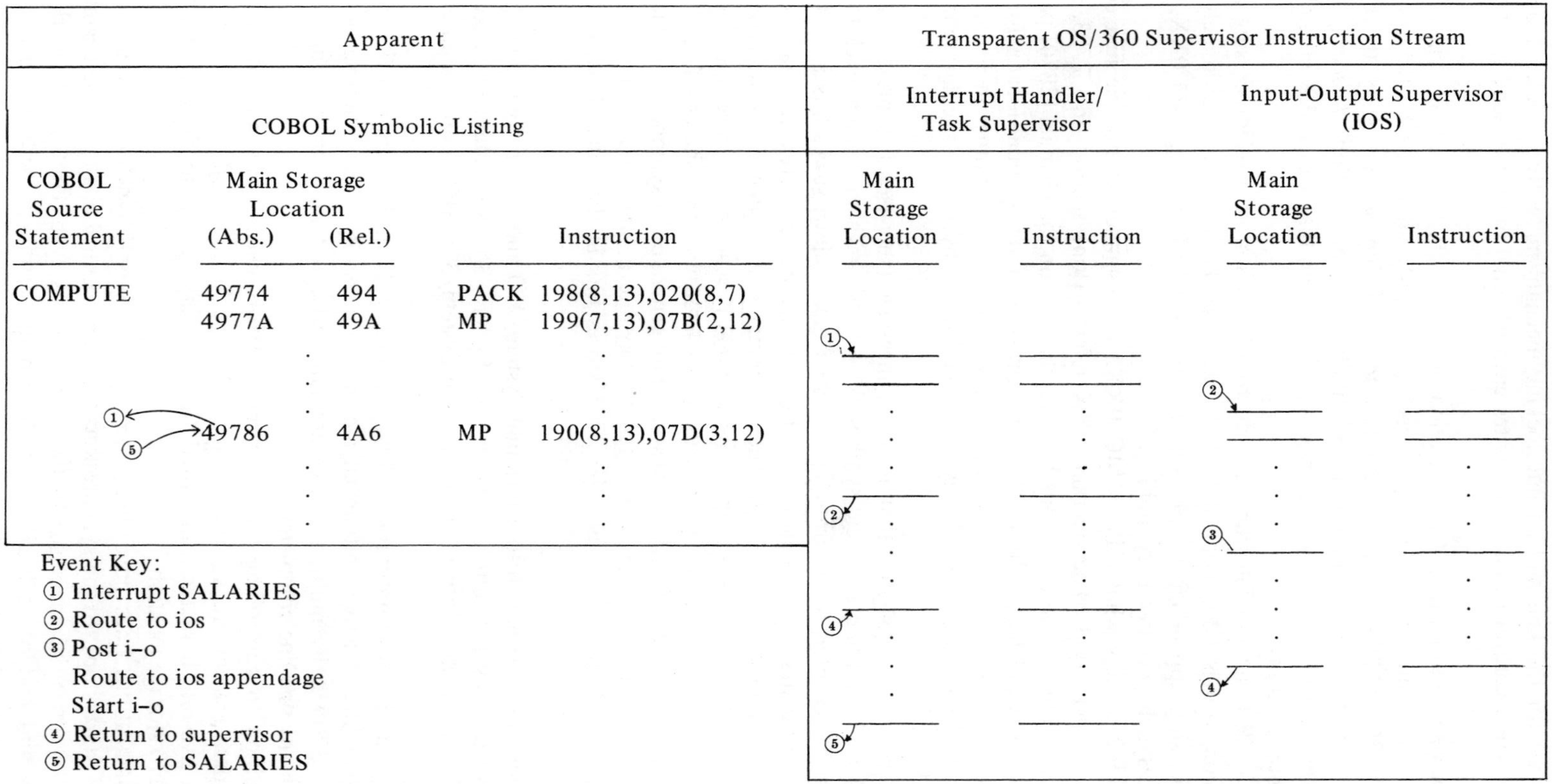

Figure 9.1 Input–output interrupt. Note: activity 1, interrupt SALARIES is directed by (location 120_{10}), see Table 2.3.

Apparent

COBOL Symbolic Listing

Transparent OS/360 Supervisor Instruction Stream

Interrupt Handler/Task Supervisor

Input-Output Supervisor (IOS)

COBOL Source Statement	Main Storage Location (Abs.)	(Rel.)	Instruction
COMPUTE	49774	494	PACK 198(8,13),020(8,7)
	4977A	49A	MP 199(7,13),07B(2,12)
	49786	4A6	MP 190(8,13),07D(3,12)

Interrupt Handler/Task Supervisor: Main Storage Location — Instruction

Input-Output Supervisor (IOS): Main Storage Location — Instruction

Event Key:
① Interrupt SALARIES
② Route to ios
③ Post i–o
    Route to ios appendage
    Start i–o
④ Return to supervisor
⑤ Return to SALARIES

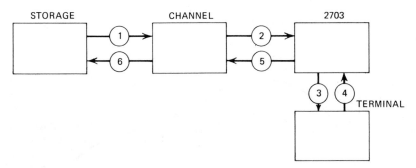

Figure 9.2   Activity diagram for the data flow of polling.

Message Switching

Message switching is one of several S/370 applications programs that process TP data collected in storage. A terminal may send to one or more receiving terminals by noting in the beginning of the message, the header, one or more symbolic addresses of the terminals to which the remainder of the message, the text, is to be sent. The message-switching program analyzes the header, converts symbolic destinations to actual locations, addresses the receiving terminal, and transmits the message. If an addressed terminal is busy, the program enqueues the message on DASD until the terminal becomes available and then sends it. Message switching is often called store and forward switching.

Inquiry

An inquiry comes to System/370 from a terminal; the system, responding, processes data from a DASD and then replies to the terminal. As distinguished from message switching, inquiry analyzes the complete message text, not just the header.

We use inquiry to describe three levels of usability aids supplied by IBM, routines included in the libraries of OS releases or shipped as licensed applications programs.

Basic teleprocessing access methods, BTAM and VTAM, aid the OS/360 and OS/VS programmer who deals directly with physical IOS.

Queued access methods, QTAM and TCAM queue to DASD input that awaits processing and output that awaits transmission.

Finally, CICS and IMS Data Base/Data Communications (DB/DC) system programs enable terminal applications programs to be written in higher level languages. We proceed by way of a QTAM example before turning to DB/DC.

A terminal user might inquire, "What is George M. Eisele's current SOCIAL-SEC-YTD?" The inquiry is processed by SALARYL, which accesses EMPYTD (Fig. 9.3).

Prior to the inquiry, two separate jobs, USERJOB1 and USERJOB2, containing CTRLSTEP and PROCSTEP, respectively, job steps for control and processing of messages, enter the system in the local job stream. CTRLTASK and PROCTASK, Attached by the initiator, reside in storage throughout the teleprocessing session. Input to CONTROLL of CTRLTASK is the message data from the remote terminals of the i–o subsystem. CONTROLL transforms message input into output message queues.

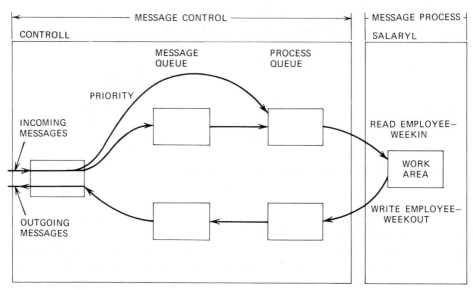

Figure 9.3 Data flow—inquiry.

PROCTASK owns SALARYL, adapted for inquiry. SALARYL updates EMPYTD (ISAM), based on EMPWEEKIN, from the CONTROLL message queue.

The SALARYL message output is input to CTRLTASK load modules which transmit processed information to remote terminals.

In System/370, 37XX multiplexors incorporate control functions (polling and code conversion) performed by teleprocessing access method routines in System/360 with 27XX.

9.3 DATA BASE/DATA COMMUNICATIONS

Of the system programs that aid application programmers, data base programs (CICS and IMS) offer the most function. In addition to serving as access methods for large teleprocessing networks, they enable users to interact with data sets shared by different departments, the installation's data base. In a data base system data once captured is reused again and again. A description of a rental car application demonstrates the value and use of a data base system.

We begin with a toll-free call made in Sacramento. A customer requests a Plymouth Fury without air conditioning to be driven for three days in St. Louis, two days hence. The customer reads an identifying number from a credit card he carries with the rental company to a reservations clerk located in San Francisco. The clerk, querying a data base at the System/370 site in Chicago, determines the makes and models available in St. Louis. Satisfied the request can be honored, the clerk confirms to the customer and then initiates the storing of the reservation in the data base.

Printing on a rental agent's terminal in St. Louis the next day, the system lists from the data base all reservations made for that rental counter for the next three days. Knowing he has a Plymouth Fury in maintainance for minor repairs, the St. Louis counter supervisor alters a maintenance schedule, thereby making a vehicle available for tomorrow for the Sacramento customer. A rental agent uses the customer's credit card number, obtained from the reservations list, to initiate the advance preparation of he customer's rental agreement from the data base.

Because of a change of plan, the customer checks the car in five days later at Springfield, Mo., rather than three days later at the St. Louis airport as he had originally stipulated.

At check in, the rental agent in Springfield, using a cut form feed in his terminal, positions the rental agreement surrendered by the customer. The agent keys the customer's number and the car's current mileage into the system. System/370 responds by retrieving the mileage and rates applied at checkout time from the data base, computing the billable amount and printing it on the form; the system completes the transaction.

What of the two days between St. Louis and Springfield? The Fury, a $4000 asset, was missing. How was the rental company's management notified?

A motor vehicle history data set on DASD, scanned for unusual activities, reveals the discrepancy. The system transmits a report notifying regional management in Kansas City of the exceptional situation. If the case is chronic, the report may go to national headquarters in Boston as well.

Each of the personnel identified above—the reservations clerk, the rental agents and their supervisors, the regional manager, the national manager—if authorized, may inquire into and update the data base in the interest of their several responsibilities. The system might process a hundred transaction types as it controls tens of thousands of vehicles.

All of this is multiprogrammed with other activities that go with a data base system. Data sets must be maintained—executed rental agreements, when purged from DASD, may become input to accounts receivable procedures. At the same time new programs must be developed, and statistics on cars, rental counters, and reservations centers must be kept.

Installing and maintaining a data base system can be complex and expensive. For this reason IBM provides CICS and IMS, routines that significantly lessen the labor and expense of installing data bases in organizations whose primary business is other than data processing.

Customer Information Control System (CICS)

We have described a data base/data communications system as a national communications system with a central store of information. Through CICS we observe the design of such a system.

A CICS user queries a master data set from a terminal. An applications program, originally written in a combination of COBOL and CICS macro language, processes the inquiry. Operating under OS control, CICS manages the execution of the applications load module.

Since the original source program contained CICS macros of the Get and Put type, language unacceptable to COBOLL, a modified language translation procedure replaces the OS translation job step with which we are familiar. A CICS translation occurs in three steps. A preprocessor transforms the mixture of COBOL and CICS source language to assembly language. An assembler translates its input to COBOL language, from which COBOLL produces an object module.

The CICS executes in an OS region. Initially, a CICS job step enters the input stream. From the step the operating system establishes a task. CICS load modules run under the control of that task.

Its internal structure distinguishes CICS from most other OS load modules. A CICS task management program attaches, dispatches, and detaches internal CICS tasks. Using OS SVCs, this routine controls multitasking in the CICS region. Single copies of application programs in storage may be shared by multiple CICS tasks. Such programs must be written to be serially reusable between each entry to and exit from CICS—an executing program temporarily loses control on execution of a CICS macro expansion. For each such execution the application programmer must initialize and restore any instructions or data altered during CICS streaming. The serially reusable part of an application program is executed under the control of only one task at a time.

CICS includes program management as well as task management functions. CICS macro instructions specify levels of program control enabling loading, linking, and transferring control without return to subprograms.

Application load modules are stored in a CICS library in relocatable format and are accessed through CICS program fetch/data management facilities. The relocatable library is a standard partitioned data set prepared by the OS linkage editor. Users may include other private libraries in this library.

CICS intercepts program interrupts caused by an application program. By terminating the internal CICS task causing the program check, the data base program prevents OS from terminating the entire CICS task. The remaining tasks in the region continue undisturbed.

CICS terminal management provides for communication between terminals and application programs. The user selects only the CICS load modules pertaining to terminals on his system. Each module contains the linkage to an access method. BTAM is used for most terminal data management.

To read data from terminals, the user specifies the terminals' characteristics and desired polling intervals. (A polling interval is the period between successive attempts to read from a terminal or group of terminals.) When a read completes, CICS converts the data (if necessary) to the Extended Binary Coded Decimal Interchange Code (EBCDIC). When a task must process a message, a task origination macro is issued by a CICS terminal management program. When data are to be transmitted to a terminal, application programs execute CICS Write macro expansions. Translation of output from EBCDIC to the appropriate terminal code may be performed.

Finally, CICS provides file management, a combination of a file control program, logic dependent on each access method described to the system, and a file control table. The file control program uses OS ISAM and BDAM. User data set descriptions are used to generate the file control table.

When the file control program retrieves a record, if the user has so specified, the program will present a logical segment (as distinct from an OS logical record) to the applications program.

Segment handling, a powerful data base function, is a major feature of the other widely installed data base system, IMS; its description is deferred to the next section.

Information Management System (IMS)

Like CICS, IMS executes as a system within OS. Where CICS design emphasizes terminal handling, IMS features comprehensive handling of the shared data base.

A hierarchical organization of segmented data sets distinguishes IMS from CICS. We use the terms "parent" and "children" to describe IMS segments and logical hierarchy. An IMS program typically would request the names (twin children) of employees with the skill machinist (parent).

Figure 9.4 portrays a physical data base record of a data base, EMP-PERS. The logical data base structure of EMP-PERS is depicted in Figure 9.5. In our first example, the personnel department requests the name and employee number of all employees with over 10 years of machinist experience. Responding, PERSNLL scans the EMP-PERS data base.

From Figure 9.6 we see that, at activity 1, PERSNLL directs IMS to locate, then retrieve the first segment, George M. Eisele, with the requisite experience. At activity 2, PERSNLL loops back and repeats the procedure. Subsequent to activity 1, PERSNLL, executing the CALL linking it to IMS and the hierarchical direct access method (HIDAM) passes the access method the keys that guide the retrieval.

As in ISAM, HIDAM uses MACH as an argument to search a track index. Getting a hit, HIDAM extracts the data subblock contents, locating the CCHH of a root segment containing the location of the DASD blocks of Figure 9.4.

Unlike in ISAM, in HIDAM the track index and the data areas are in separate data sets thus avoiding the necessity, as in ISAM, of maintaining an overflow data area with its concomitance—periodic reconstruction of the entire file.

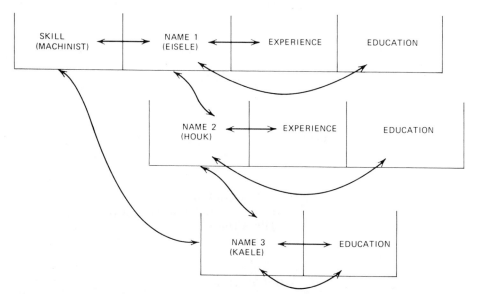

Figure 9.4 Hierarchical direct data base record. From *Information Management System/360, Version 2, General Information Manual,* IBM Program Products Manual GH-20-0765.

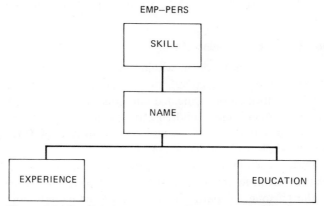

EMP–PERS

Figure 9.5 Logical data structure. From *Information Management System/360, Version 2, General Information Manual,*
IBM Program Products Manual GH-20-0765.

A data base segment consists of two parts: a header describing the data and
containing pointers to related data items, and the data itself. Our next examples
are based on Figures 9.7 and 9.8, schematics illustrating that segment headers
and their pointers enable two physical data bases to appear as one logical data
base.

An end user wishing to know George M. Eisele's present Social Security amount
inquires into System/370 through a 3270 alphanumeric display remote from the

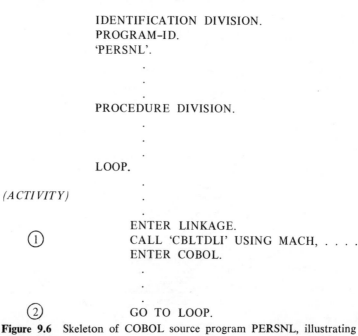

```
              IDENTIFICATION DIVISION.
              PROGRAM–ID.
              'PERSNL'.
                     .
                     .
                     .
              PROCEDURE DIVISION.
                     .
                     .
                     .
       LOOP.          .
(ACTIVITY)            .
                     .
                      ENTER LINKAGE.
   ①                  CALL 'CBLTDLI' USING MACH, . . . .
                      ENTER COBOL.
                     .
                     .
                     .
   ②                  GO TO LOOP.
```

Figure 9.6 Skeleton of COBOL source program PERSNL, illustrating
CALL to IMS.

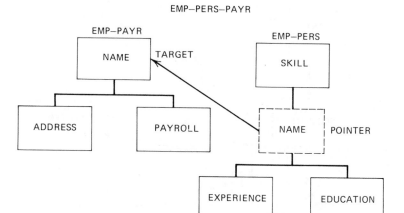

Figure 9.7 Structure—two physical data bases. From *Information Management System/360, Version 2, General Information Manual*, IBM Program Products Manual GH-20-0765.

system site. After an initialization procedure, the following prompting sequence might appear on the face of the cathode ray tube.

(Supplied by System/370)	(Keyed in by the user)
Name	Eisele, George M.
Job title	Machinist
Field	Social Security amount

Acting on the information entered through the keyboard, PAYRLL presents the skill, the name, and the field to HIDAM which retrieves the requisite information from EMP-PERS-PAYR for PAYRLL and then Returns to that load module.

For a query "Which machinists and carpenters have Social Security amounts > than $150?" PAYRLL accesses EMP-PERS-PAYR through the skill segment. The sequence Eisele, Houk, and Kaele, carpenters and machinists all, might emerge. The segments of Igoe, a materials clerk, would not be processed.

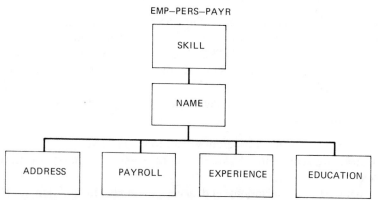

Figure 9.8 Structure—one logical data base. *Information Management System/360, Version 2, General Information Manual*, IBM Program Products Manual GH-20-0765.

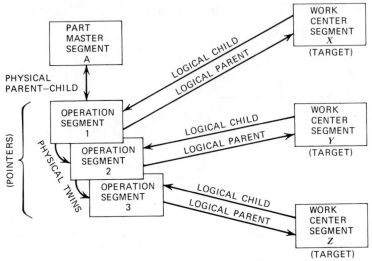

Figure 9.9 Relationships of a data base in the manufacturing industry. Assume that part master A has operations 1, 2, and 3 performed in its fabrication at work centers X, Y, and Z, respectively. The operation segment under other part masters, where the operation is performed at work center Y, would be the logical twin of the operation segment 2 under part master A. By following the logical child relationship from work center segment Y to operation segment 2 and then following the logical twin relationship to related operation segments, the question of all parts affected by operations at a particular work center can be answered. From *Information Management System/360, Version 2, General Information Manual*, IBM Program Products Manual GH-20-0765.

Finance, utilities, medicine, and other industries use shared data bases. In manufacturing, the complementary questions "What operations are performed in fabricating *this* part—and at what work centers are these performed?" and "What operations are performed at a particular work center—and what parts are affected by these operations?" form an inverse pair. From Figure 9.9 we see that in answering the first question HIDAM would use part number as the key. In answering the second it would use work center.

Consideration. In addition to providing the function of data set sharing, IMS improves the usability of System/370 by affording device and data independence. In an installation converting its DASD from 2314 to 3330, load modules using IMS are unaffected by the change. Similarly revision of segment formats leave load modules unaffected.

To provide independence, three definitions are required prior to the use of a data base by a program:

1. The segments to which a program wishes to be sensitive.

2. The structure represented by one or more segments from one or more physical records.

3. The data base organizations and access methods. In addition to HIDAM, IMS supports other hierarchical access methods. HISAM retrieves segments from a prime data area within the HISAM data set. Among access methods without in-

dices are hierarchical direct (an algorithm locates the data) and hierarchical sequential.

In addition to COBOL, IMS supports PL/I and assembler source programs. In all three, the segment serves as the logical unit of data.

Teleprocessing networks extending from coast to coast have become almost commonplace. Also, development of large-scale integration of component circuitry has been achieved. Storage and logic units that once occupied cubic yards occupy cubic inches. Consequently a requirement has been identified: apply large-scale integration to teleprocessing networks. Since mass-produced compact logic packages are economical, put logic at the terminal and thus reduce communications traffic. In remote locations, store the questions that prompt the rental agent to enter the information the central system needs. It would lower communications costs: less traffic, less cost. It would free the central system for more productive work; and, often, it would enable terminals to function when communications lines failed.

Distributed intelligence brings visions of computer networks of varying degrees of intelligence solving problems that relate to today's problems as those of today relate to those run on the IBM 602A.

9.4   TIME SHARING OPTION (TSO)

The Data Base/Data Communications systems process inquiries and updates of the end user at a terminal. This user appears to hold a conversation with System/370. Similarly, TSO, a subsystem under OS/360, causes the appearance of a conversation between user and system. Although the discussion of TSO that follows emphasizes a program development application, this option of OS is used for simple DB/DC operations as well.

In a batch environment, a user submits USERJOB, a card deck. In SALARIES, he has omitted, say, the hyphen in EMPLOYEE-YTD. A COBOLL diagnostic message results. Hours elapse from commission to redemption of this data processing sin. The process involves transporting the deck to the S/370 site; waiting for a batch of jobs to be collected for the input stream; Read-in to the system; USERJOB processing (compile, link, edit-execute steps); SYSOUT printing; bursting SYSOUT pages into job groups; transporting USERJOB from the site to the user, who, at last, acts on COBOLL's message.

In TSO, the user, at a remote terminal, keys in a job step request; responding to the terminal printer, the system requests what further information it needs.

He may be one among many, but each terminal user feels the system to be his own, an illusion created by substituting System/370 milliseconds for the hours of manual batch processes.

Implementation

Running in a foreground region, TSO is multiprogrammed with batch jobs running in a background region. A terminal user may request execution of a job in the background region. In TSO background processing, SALARYL, EMPYTD, and EMPWEEKLY reside on devices at the System/370. At the keyboard the user enters system-dependent input for USERJOB; job control language previously stored in SYS1.PROCLIB is accessed; COBSTEP, COBTASK, and COBRB are established. Batch processing proceeds.

In OS/360 at any one time, the foreground region contains one task, representing the request of one user. System/370 resources are shared by swapping user programs in this region. A time sharing task occupies the region for a time slice (milliseconds) at the end of which USERTASK$_1$ is swapped from the region to a DASD "swapping device." USERTASK$_2$ is then swapped in.

On an IBM 2305 M 2, which has a data rate of 1.5 megabytes per second, a swap-out/swap-in of, say, 60,000 bytes requires

$$80 \text{ milliseconds} = \frac{2 \times 60 \times 10^3}{1.5 \times 10^6}$$

A terminal session begins when a user keys in his identity, initiating a conversational log-on procedure. The system matching the identity against prestored authorization to use the system prints a go-ahead. The user submits simplified job control language. The system establishes a TSO job, say USERJOBT.

TSO job scheduling uses job management. In OS/360, for example, a time sharing scheduling subtask is Attached in the foreground region. The TSO scheduling module within this subtask structure XCTL's to the reader-interpreter, which in turn XCTL's to the initiator.

Before an OS/360 batch user submits a job he ordains its steps. In contrast, TSO foreground processing responds to unpredictable sequences of user terminal commands*. In OS/360, a TSO EDIT command, used in creating the data set SALARYS, stimulates creation by the subsystem of EDTSTEP1 and EDTTASK1. The substructure of EDTTCB1 includes EDTRB, controller of EDTL, a load module called from the TSO library to do the command processing work.

EDTTASK1 may be ready, active, or waiting. In Figure 9.10, while the DISPLAY statement, line 430, is being keyed in, EDTTASK1, Waiting, is not swapped in.

Performing analogous functions to the TSO adjunct to OS/360, the manager of the system in release 2 impacts the dispatching structure more fundamentally.

Address space control blocks (ASCB) 1 through 10 represent time sharing users 1 through 10, say, ASCBs 11 through 15 represent batch users 11 through 30 or, say, users 11 through 50: the manager decides.

Example. The TSO user enters, compiles, and tests SALARIES from his terminal.†

Using the TSO EDIT command, he enters operands that name the data set (HCLIB) containing the source module (SALARYS) and identify SALARYS as old and modifiable or new. The TSO COBOL command invokes COBOLL to process SALARIES source statements.

We turn to our illustration, Figure 9.10. The user keys in commands to first compile and then execute an inquiry form of SALARIES.‡ The LOGON command identifies user, CARROLL, who keys in a password, HC. TSO uses HC to authorize CARROLL to use the system and to access a cataloged procedure, the job control language for USERJOBT.

---

* To be distinguished from S/370 channel commands.

† ANS standard COBOL supports the functions herein described. The OS principles illustrated through COBOL F apply.

‡ In our description the name SALARIES is used to refer to the various forms SALARYS, SALARYO, and SALARYL that we have used throughout. For consistency's sake we shall include the library member name along with the COBOL name as follows: SALARIES (SALARYL) according to the form of SALARIES under discussion.

```
1  LOGON  CARROLL/HC
2  edit salaries. cobol new
3  INPUT

   00010     IDENTIFICATION  DIVISION.
   00020     PROGRAM-IC.  'SALARIES  S/M/I/BU'.
   00030     ENVIRONMENT  DIVISION.
   00040     CONFIGURATION  SECTION.
   00050     SOURCE-COMPUTER.  IBM-360  165.
   00060     OBJECT-COMPUTER.  IBM-360  165.
   00070     INPUT-OUTPUT  SECTION.
   00080     FILE-CONTROL.
   00090        SELECT  EMPLOYEE-YTD  ASSIGN  TO  'INPUT'  DIRECT-ACCESS
   00100           2311  ORGANIZATION  IS  INDEXED.
   00110        ACCESS  IS  RANDOM.
   00120        SYMBOLIC  KEY  IS  NUMBER-S.
   00130           RECORD  KEY  IS  EMPLOYEE-NO-YTD.
   00140     DATA  DIVISION.
   00150     FILE  SECTION.
   00160     FD    EMPLOYEE-YTD.
   00170           LABEL  RECORDS  ARE  STANDARD.
   00180           RECORDING  MODE  IS  F.
   00190           BLOCK  CONTAINS  10  RECORDS.
   00200           RECORD  CONTAINS  120  CHARACTERS.
   00210           DATA  RECORD  IS  YTD-RECORD.
   00220     01    YTD-RECORD.
   00230           02 NAME PICTURE A(32).
   00240           02 SOCIAL-SEC-YTD PICTURE 9(6)V99.
   00250           02 EMPLOYEE-NO-YTD PICTURE 9(5).
   00260           02 CNTROL PICTURE X(1).
   00270           02 GROSS-PAY PICTURE 9(6)V99.
   00280           02 FILLER PICTURE X(65).
   00290     WORKING-STORAGE  SECTION.
   00300     77 NUMBER-S PICTURE 9(5).
   00310     77 SLIMIT PICTURE 9(6)V99 COMPUTATIONAL-3 VALUE IS 374.40.
   00320     PROCEDURE  DIVISION.
   00330        OPEN  I-O  EMPLOYEE-YTD.
   00340        OPEN  INPUT  EMPLOYEE-WEEKLY.
   00350     READ-WEEKLY.
   00360        ACCEPT  NUMBER-S.
   00370     READ-YTD.
   00380        READ  EMPLOYEE-YTD.
   00390     LIMIT-TEST.
   00400        IF SLIMIT - SOCIAL-SEC-YTD ) GROSS-PAY GO TO LIMIT-CALC.
   00410        COMPUTE  SOCIAL-SEC-YTD
   00420           ROUNDED = SOCIAL-SEC-YTD + GROSS-PAY * .048.
   00430        DISPLAY  YTD-RECORD.
   00440        GO  TO  READ-WEEKLY.
   00450     LIMIT-CALC.
   00460        COMPUTE  SOCIAL-SEC-YTD
```

Figure 9.10

```
    00470          ROUNDED = SOCIAL-SEC-YTD +
    00480                         (SLIMIT - SOCIAL-SEC-YTD) * .048.
    00490      DISPLAY YTD-RECORD.
    00500      GO TO READ-WEEKLY.
    00510      CLOSE EMPLOYEE-YTD.
    00520      CLOSE EMPLOYEE-WEEKLY.
    00530  FINIS. ENTER LINKAGE.
    00540      CALL 'COMPIL'.
    00550      ENTER COBOL.
    00560      STOP RUN.
 4  00570
 5  EDIT
 6  save
 7  end
 8  READY

 9  cobol salaries print source xref dmap pmap
10  SOURCE SCANNED
11  READY

12  allocate data set(*) file(sysin)
    READY

13  allocate data set(*) file(inout)
    READY

14  loadgo salaries coblib
15  01024

16  01024 EISELE GEORGE M.    30.40      126.92
    READY

17  link salaries load(commands(salaries)) coblib
    READY

18  salaries
    01032

    01032 GEORGE WESLEY T.  48.46      201.92
    READY
```
Figure 9.10—continued.

As activity 2, the user enters an edit command to create a new data set, SALARIES (SALARYS). In input mode, EDIT invites the user to enter statements and then types out line number 00010, activity 3. The user submits SALARIES lines. After each line he strikes the carriage RETURN key, and EDITL types the succeeding line number. At activity 4 the user, by striking the RETURN key only, requests a transfer to the *edit* mode of EDIT processing.

The user keys in save and creates the new data set, SALARIES, activity 6. End commands termination of EDITL, activity 7. The cobol command at activity 9 invokes the compiler to process SALARIES. At activities 12 and 13, the user assigns SYSIN and SYSOUT data sets to the terminal. The LOADGO command at activity 14 calls on the OS/360 loader to locate the object program, (SALARYO), link-edit it with

COBLIB members, and pass control to it.* The coblib operand specifies that the standard COBOL library is to be used to resolve external references. At activity 15, the user enters an EMPLOYEE-NO-WEEKLY logical record in order to test SAL-ARIES. Using SYMBOLIC-KEY, SALARIES (SALARYL) locates the corrresponding logical record in EMPLOYEE-YTD and DISPLAYs it, activity 16. At activity 17, the user invokes link-edit to create a load module, SALARIES (SALARYL), and add it to his command library, a partitioned data set chained to the system command library. From this point on, by keying in the name salaries as a command, the user invokes the load module, activity 18.

Considerations. Prior to TSO, application programmers wrote source language, system programmers wrote job control language. With TSO, the system-dependent PGM= and PROC operand of the EXEC card gave way to edit, test, and salaries commands; the command became the unit of request. Thus functions formerly performed by the system programmer are now performed by the terminal user of logical System/370.

---

* Functionally the loader resembles link-edit. However, the loader link-edits *and* loads modules for execution in one job step.

chapter 10

MISCELLANEOUS TOPICS

10.1 INTRODUCTION

The topic initialization brings to our understanding a fuller notion of OS time. The initialization of the operating system by the system generation program (SYSGEN), then by initial program load (IPL) and the nucleus initialization program (NIP) are briefly explained. The three system programs define the resources job and task management later allocate. OS utilities, which, in addition to initializing data sets, help users maintain them, are discussed next. Other operating systems, DOS and VMS, are then treated. Our miscellaneous topics conclude with a brief word on the social aspect of data processing.

10.2 SYSTEM GENERATION

OS comes as a library of source, object, and load modules, shipped from a central location by IBM—the same for each installation. Intended for current use, OS releases are mailed as magnetic tape reels and copied to DASD at the site.*

The nth release contains the systems programs of the $n - $ 1st release plus additions and improvements. A problem program that ran on the $n - $ 1st release will run on the nth release. IBM mails releases periodically, and each supersedes its predecessor.

At the site, the user, editing the general release to conform to his S/370 configuration, his operating system, and his hardware and software features, generates his system.

The user constructs his operating system of required, alternative or optional modules (Fig. 10.1). Any system requires part of task management and one of alternative job schedulers. System programs in problem state, [COBOLL, LINKEDITL] and most data management routines are optional. Such OS features as the resident LINKLIB directory and type III and IV SVCs are optional as well. We designate SYSGEN output as the generated operating system. The SYSGEN program running under the current operating system creates the generated system in two stages.

In stage 1, SYSGEN transforms its input, macros specifying the user's gener-

---

* Part of one 3330 will contain OS.

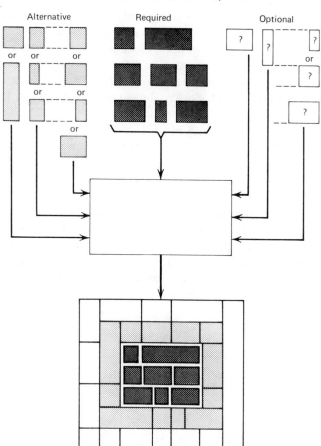

Figure 10.1 Constructing /360. From *IBM System/360 Operating System, Introduction,* IBM Systems Reference Library Manual GC-28-6534.

ated system, into its output, a job stream of job control language and assembler source statements. The assembler expands and translates the user's macros.

In stage 2, the stage 1 output becomes the input job stream. Library modules of the new release are additional input. If these are source modules, the assembler translates them into object modules. If they are object and load modules, the linkage editor combines those selected for the libraries of the generated control program.

Utility programs construct and initialize new libraries on the system's residence DASD device. After stage 2, the generated OS is ready for use.*

10.3 WORK PERIOD LOADING

To be operational, OS must be loaded into storage by a system program, initial program load (IPL). The OS nucleus is impermanent. In, say, magnetic core

* A new OS user is supplied with a so-called generating system.

storage, power off implies that the nucleus is lost. At the beginning of each work period the nucleus must be reloaded from SYS1.NUCLEUS, a library data set.

IPL may modify the generated operating system. The user may specify QSAM Get, say, to be resident in main storage for the next work period only.

At the start of IPL, OS consists of library load modules on DASD. The operator initiates storage loading, setting the unit address of the system residence device into console switches and pressing the console load button. Circuitry generates a program status word and two channel command words in storage. Data transfers follow.

IPL ends up in the lower addresses of storage (Fig. 10.2).

The IPL load module next loads some of the OS control program nucleus into storage after having relocated itself to avoid being overwritten. In addition, IPL loads the nucleus initialization program (NIP), to which it passes control (Fig. 10.3).

NIP establishes the installation's version of the operating system from choices expressed at system generation time. The following describes another NIP function. During the prior work period, a system programmer requested, say, SALARYL to be placed in SYS1.LINKLIB; this may mean that a new DASD extent had to be added for this new member. NIP applies the new extent information to a SYS1.LINKLIB DEB, resident in storage throughout the work period.

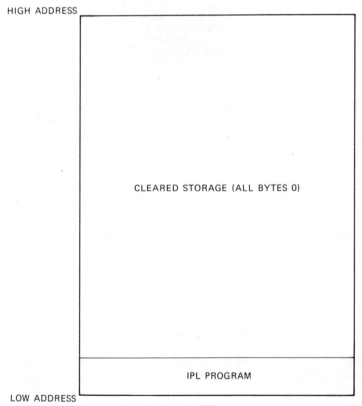

HIGH ADDRESS

CLEARED STORAGE (ALL BYTES 0)

IPL PROGRAM

LOW ADDRESS

Figure 10.2 Storage after clearing by IPL.

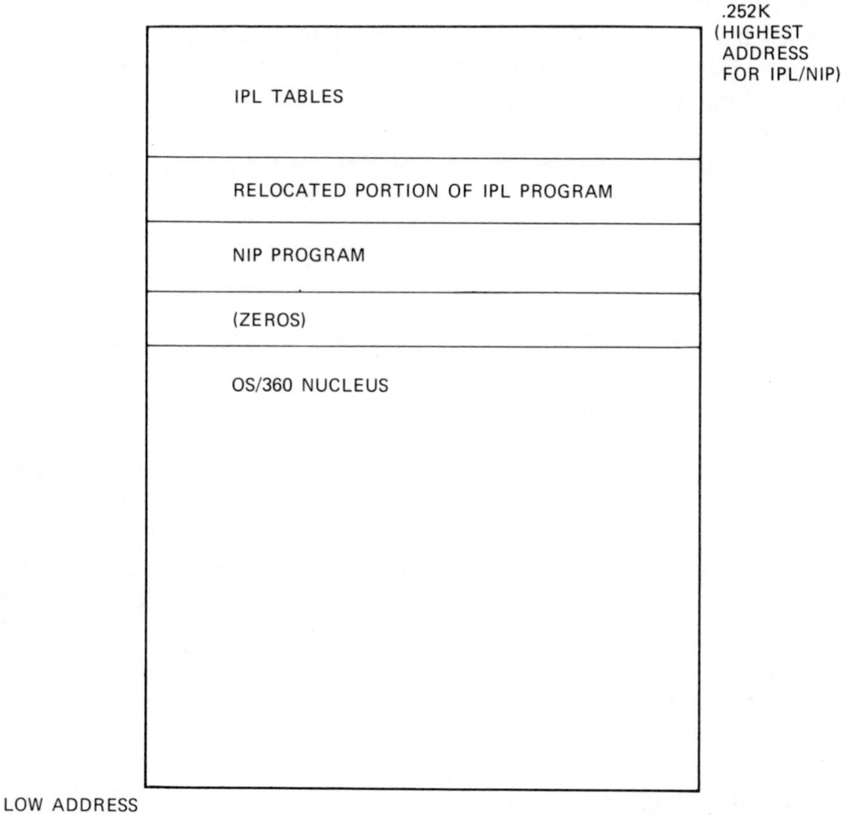

```
                                                        .252K
                                                        (HIGHEST
                                                        ADDRESS
                                                        FOR IPL/NIP)
          IPL TABLES


          RELOCATED PORTION OF IPL PROGRAM

          NIP PROGRAM

          (ZEROS)

          OS/360 NUCLEUS
```

LOW ADDRESS

Figure 10.3 Layout of main storage after loading the first sections of the nucleus.

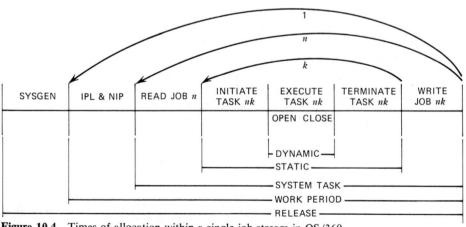

Figure 10.4 Times of allocation within a single job stream in OS/360.

Figure 10.4 depicts OS times. After IPL and NIP, System/370 becomes operational when the operator has started system programs such as an OS/360 reader and initiator. During the work period he starts additional systems tasks as needed. At the end of the work period, the SYSOUT writer drains the output work queues before shutdown.

Power off destroys the resident nucleus. Startup for the next work period begins with IPL.

10.4   UTILITIES

In SALARIES, data set creation and maintenance (originally recording a NEW data set, and adding and deleting records to and from an OLD data set, EMPYTD) was not included in our illustrations. Generally, OS utility load modules include these capabilities.

As shown in Table 10.1, there are three classes of utilities: system, data set, and independent. A user needing control information (i.e., how much space remains on volume HARRYC) uses the system utility IEHLIST and prints the VTOC. Requiring a printout of EMPYTD, say, he uses the data set utility IEHPTPCH. If an additional volume for HARRYC is needed, he uses the independent utility DASDI to format the tracks of the disk. Standard job control language invokes the first two utility types (Fig. 10.5). Further details may be found in *IBM System/360 Operating System Utilities,* IBM Systems Reference Library Manual C28-6586.

System Utility Programs

These programs are used to maintain system control data. The user controls the operation of a system utility program through job control and utility control statements. The general functions of these programs are listed in Table 10.2.

Table 10.1   System/370 Utility Types

Utility	Level (Example)	Dependent on OS?
System	System (VTOC)	Yes
Data set	Data set or record (EMPYTD)	Yes
Independent	System (format DASD track)	No

```
//USERJOB JOB 7863418735,MSGLEVEL=1,CLASS=A,CARROLL
//STEPP EXEC PGM=IEHLIST
//SYSPRINT DD SYSOUT=A
//DD2 DD UNIT=2311,VOLUME=SER=HARRYC,DISP=OLD
//SYSIN DD *
  LISTVTOC DUMP,VOL=2311=HARRYC
/*
```
Figure 10.5 Job control language specifying execution of an OS utility.

Table 10.2 Functions of System Utility Programs

Program	Function
IEHPROGM	Building and maintaining system control data
IEHMOVE	Moving or copying data collections
IEHLIST	Listing system control data
IEHUCSLD	Placing character sets into printer control units
IEHINITT	Writing standard labels onto magnetic tape volumes
IEHIOSUP	Updating entries in the supervisor cell library
IFCEREP0	Editing and listing error environment records
IFCDIP00	Reinitializing the system data set SYS1.LOGREC

Table 10.3 Functions of Data Set Utility Programs

Program	Function
IEBCOPY	Copying or merging partitioned data sets
IEBGENER	Copying records from sequential data sets or converting data sets from sequential to partitioned organization
IEBCOMPR	Comparing records in sequential or partitioned data sets
IEBPTPCH	Printing or punching records in sequential or partitioned data sets
IEBUPDTE and IEBUPDAT	Updating symbolic libraries
IEBISAM	Placing source data from indexed sequential data sets into sequential data sets suitable for subsequent reconstruction.

The Data Set Utility Programs

These programs are used to reorganize, change, or compare data at the data set level and/or at the record level. The user controls the operation of a data set utility program through job control and utility control statements. The general functions of these programs are listed in Table 10.3.

The Independent Utility Programs

The independent utility programs operate outside the job, task, and data management structure. The System/370 under which these programs run need not even contain OS.

These programs are used to prepare direct-access devices for system use and to ensure that any permanent hardware errors incurred on a direct-access device (i.e., defective tracks) do not seriously degrade the performance of that device. The user controls the operation of an independent utility program through utility control statements. Since the programs are independent of the operating system, job control statements are not required. The general functions of these programs are listed in Table 10.4.

Table 10.4   Functions of Independent Utility Programs

Program	Function
IBCDASDI	Initializing and assigning alternate tracks to direct-access volumes
IBCDMPRS	Dumping and restoring the data contents of direct-access volumes
IBCRCVRP	Recovering usable data from defective tracks, assigning alternate tracks, and merging replacement data with the recovered data onto the alternate tracks

10.5   OTHER SYSTEM/370 OPERATING SYSTEMS

DOS/360

Disk Operating System/360 (DOS/360), like OS/360, is a System/370 operating system. DOS/VS is the System/370R operating system. Designed for smaller systems, DOS is widely installed today.*

In managing S/370 hardware, DOS/360 and OS/360 have much in common. Controlling systems of disparate power, they have major differences as well. Like OS, DOS supports multiprogramming using task, data, and job management components. On the other hand, OS automates more function and defers the binding of decisions into programs more than DOS does.

Task management. DOS/360 load modules execute in main storage partitions fixed at system generation time and modifiable either at IPL time or during a work period. Job management routines may use a large background partition to allocate resources for the smaller foreground partitions where jobs reside.

DOS/360 processes SALARIES in a compile, link-edit, and execute procedure. In transforming SALARYO to SALARYL, link-edit generates the absolute addresses of the DOS partition where SALARYL will reside during execution. Data management modules, in OS loaded by Open, are link-edited into SALARYO to form SALARYL in DOS. LESTEP binding is less flexible than OS EXECSTEP binding. A change in a data management module in a DOS release, say, means a re-link-edit; SALARYL in OS would be unimpacted.

Job management. DOS job steps resemble their OS counterparts. Nevertheless, in DOS, the DD card and the Open-time DCB merge are absent. In the ENVIRONMENT DIVISION, SALARIES ASSIGNS EMPLOYEE–YTD to 2311;† in DOS, data set and device are bound during COBSTEP. OS defers binding until

* There are several other System/360 operating systems, namely, Basic Operating System (BOS) and Basic Programming System (BPS), which are primarily card systems, and Tape Operating System (TOS), primarily for a tape configuration. These systems are less sophisticated than those discussed in this section. They are uniprogramming systems built around a sequential scheduler design.

† In the OS/360 ENVIRONMENT DIVISION, statements similar to those in DOS appear in SALARIES; OS/360 may override these statements with the DSNAME and unit parameters of the DD card.

EXECSTEP. In DOS, moving EMPYTD from 2311 to 2314 necessitates SAL-ARYL's recompilation.

In DOS, SYSIN and SYSOUT (unit record) devices operate directly with a partition. Thus READing or WRITEing EMPLOYEE-WEEKLY means reading or writing unit record devices.

Larger DOS installations SELECT DASD or tape for SYSIN or SYSOUT, performing the card-to-tape and tape-to-printer operations thus required as separate jobs. Alternatively POWER, a DOS i–o subsystem similar to OS/360 HASP, reads cards or writes lines to or from DASD. At a cost of storage space (for residence and buffers) POWER improves SALARYL efficiency and System/370 performance. In data management, DOS provides SAM, ISAM, DAM, and PAM capability similar to that found in OS/360. The interface between DOS physical IOS and logical IOS is the familiar S/370 SVC 0, and EXCP.

DOS/VS

Using less storage than OS/360, DOS/360 provided less function. Availing a smaller user of large virtual storage at economical cost in DOS/VS meant installation of applications hitherto unfeasible.

DOS/VS uses S/370R dynamic address translation hardware and DOS/VS supervision of segment, page, and external page tables.* A single virtual storage of up to 16 megabytes divides into 64-kilobyte segments subdivided into 32 two-kilobyte pages.

At the beginning of a job step, (pageable) job management routines are loaded into a virtual partition. Using the job control statements of EXECSTEP, say, the system routines attach the step as a unit of work for task management. Unlike DOS/360 load modules, DOS/VS load modules contain dictionaries and consequently can be loaded into any suitable virtual storage partition at execution time. Load modules can be paged out during loading.

As in OS/VS, the DOS/VS paging supervisor consists of virtual, real, and auxiliary storage managers. In data management, DOS/VS supports VSAM in addition to the access methods supported by DOS/360.

VM/370

After having been installed for several years, an operating system represents a considerable investment in programs. The expense of rewriting hundreds of DOS/360 routines for OS/VS might well cause an installation to postpone conversion. In other cases, some applications program for, say, the insurance industry may be exclusive to DOS/360, yet an insurance company requires OS function. Conversion may be impracticable, even impossible.

VM/370, a System/370R operating system, addresses the problem by simulating virtual machines, say, System/370 or System/370R. VM/370 comprises CP, a control program, and application programs. To CP, other System/370 and System/370R operating systems are application programs. CP, which is privileged, supervises, say, OS/360 and DOS/360. An insurance company using VM/370 to convert from DOS/360 to OS/VS2 can multiprogram them.

---

* S/370R used in extended control mode.

Table 10.5   Description of Interface Activity Diagram Shown in Figure 10.6

Activity No.	Type	Description
1	Data	SALARYL passes location of EMPLOYEE-YTD, a DCB, via general purpose register 1
2	Control	SALARYL executes branch
3	Control	Get finds end of block in buffer 2, executes branch
4	Control	EOB executes EXCP, SVC 0
5	Control	CP recognizes interrupt as EXCP type, executes LPSN
6–12	Control and data	Input–output supervisor schedules SALARYL's request and returns control; assume channel 2 busy

VM/370 handles interrupts. In problem state, attempting to execute SIO (privileged), OS/360 causes an interrupt.

Interface activity diagram, READ of twenty-first EMPYTD logical record. To understand the relation between CP and OS/360, let us refer to Appendix 1, page 212, Table 10.5, and Figure 10.6.

Subsequent to activity 12 in Figure 10.6, channel end for, say, channel 2 causes an i–o interrupt to CP, which immediately passes control to IOS. The IOS Posts the lately completed request and then attempts to dispatch the latest SALARIES request by issuing SIO. A program interrupt passes control to CP, which initiates the SALARIES request after translating the channel program's virtual addresses

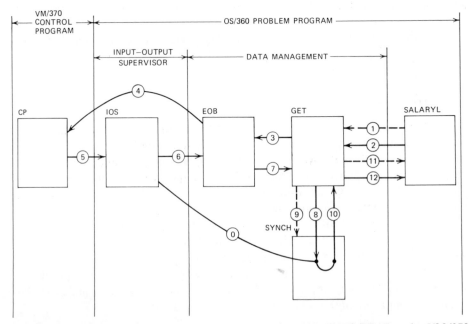

Figure 10.6   Interface activity diagram for the twenty-first SALARIES READ under VM/370. The solid and broken numbered lines indicate control and data flow, respectively.

to real addresses and fixing a real storage buffer page to receive the data transmission.

10.6   THE SOCIAL SIDE

The Author

We have spoken at length of the operating system and its properties primarily as exemplified by OS. Little has been said of the human being who conceives and develops such a system.

Operating system design is a creative process, fine minds engage in it. Much enthusiasm is present during the process, as anyone present during the heated debates leading to OS development will testify. It would be excessive to compare the creation of an operating system to the creation of a fine work of art. The art is tangible. An operating system is visible only by its effect. Although lesser on the scale of nobility of creative enterprise than fine art, it certainly entails many of the joys and satisfactions of the creative process. Because of this attractiveness, operating system design will, doubtless, be the object of superlative creative and intellectual energies for many years to come.

The Fifth Dimension

A long list of reasons supports that the present high growth rate of data processing technology will continue in the future. We likely deal with a momentous appreciation in technology; it is one thing to deal with exponential growth on a small base. Exponential growth on a sizable technological base has enormous consequences.

In today's world the social consequences of the technological pace are of great concern. How will the technology be used?

It is well to remind ourselves that in all ages and generations systems have cleared memory prior to executing applications programs. What follows a human mind directs for human purposes. A neutral system responds to a man's request; a man who has the sense of good and evil activates system service for a good or an evil purpose. Consider some applications:

Chemical simulations
Weather
War gaming
Electrical power system network analysis
Nuclear fuel management
Inventory control
Employee productivity

Incorporating the unifying thread of productivity, the list is long and honorable. Consider applications either missing from the list or, as yet, substantially undeveloped:

Population effects
Resource depletion
Pollution
Mass transit
Consumer affairs

Data processing is applicable to the latter problems. Their inclusion within the achievement set requires human resolve translated into action. We know many of the technological ingredients necessary. We have good and increasing confidence in data processing technology's part of the solution.

Which problems are we really determined to solve? First we must agree on a list of candidates. Next comes the setting of priorities for the resources at hand. Our problems are here and exploding, and it is necessary that we apply the technology to their solution, or they will outrun our very ability to survive. Technology *could* keep abreast of our very considerable physical problems present and to come. Will it be allowed to?

10.7   AND WHAT ABOUT YOU?

It is amazing how much information you can get out of OS about itself by executing a compile–link–execute procedure concluding with an Abend dump. You do not even have to keypunch the cards. Give SALARIES, Appendix 1, to the key punch operator.*

Once you have your request deck back in hand, the rest is simple. Walk into the machine room. Ask the machine room operator for the job control language for a compile–link–go cataloged procedure. Have him fix up your deck by adding the job control language cards to SALARIES. Give the deck to the operator. He will put the deck in the reader and press the start button. You will have put OS to work teaching you OS.

10.8   SUMMING UP

Since World War II, switching speeds and memory capacities have increased hundreds of thousands of times. Data processing history is largely a recounting of how systems productivity has kept pace.

By the 1950s unit record systems were accepted where large volumes of logic or calculation were necessary to the control of an enterprise. Electronic systems, in succeeding unit record systems in larger enterprises, capitalized on the logic and memory developments of the early 1950s not only in fetch speed but also in the power of the instructions they fetched. The IBM 704 used a parallel adder and a shift register to process and hold data during cycles transparent to a user who specified, say, "+" in FORTRAN. And high speed meant to the power of System/370's string handling instructions serving FORTRAN, COBOL, and PL/I language translations what it had meant to the floating-point instructions serving execution step programs in first generation systems. In System/370R, the high-speed table look-ups of page frame and segment tables extend the process into the fourth generation.

Nor was the relation between high-speed componentry and productivity restricted to the CPU; the data and address registers and internal storages of buffered channels and device control units amply attest to this. The efficiencies of OS data management and IOS arose in no small measure from these developments.

In fourth-generation systems, communications is the new systems theme. Today a hierarchy of shared data, queried and updated from outlying locations, involves

---

* Note that a program to create EMPLOYEE-YTD in SAM has been included, Appendix 7.

a network—general purpose computers at the center, intelligent controllers and terminals at the periphery—made feasible by the diminished size and high speed afforded by large-scale integration.

What caused productivity to follow technology was the potential embedded in the inspired insight of John von Neumann's stored-program system. Advance after advance of component and system technology, building on this remarkable framework, broadened the use and value of data processing.

In the first generation, CPU index registers, main storage traps (forerunner to the interrupt), symbolic programming, and program relocation come to mind. In the second generation, there were buffered channels. In the third generation, resource control, with its hardware/software concomitants of structure and state were identified. In the fourth generation, there was relocate. All are predicated on the stored-program concept. All are enhancements to the system of i–o, storage, and processor enunciated by von Neumann over 25 years ago.

ANSWERS

CHAPTER 1

1.1   Line 52.

1.2   (a) 100; (b) 1,000.

1.3

Case No.	EMPLOYEE-WEEKLY	EMPLOYEE-YTD
1	1	—
2	—	1000
3	—	—
4	2	2

1.4   If EMPLOYEE-NO-YTD=EMPLOYEE-NO-WEEKLY, GO TO LIMIT-TEST; ELSE IF EMPLOYEE-NO-WEEKLY > EMPLOYEE-NO-YTD OR EMPLOYEE-NO-YTD > 99999, GO TO ERROR-PROC.

CHAPTER 2

2.1   As in Figure 2.10.

2.2

SALARIES Statement No.	Object Module Instruction Format	Location
53 IF	SS	46A–482
	RX	488
	RR	48C
53 GO	RX	48E
	RR	492
54 COMPUTE	SS	494–4B2,4BE,4CA, 4D0,4D6
	RX	4B8,4C4
	RR	4BC,4C8
	SI	4DC

2.3   SOCIAL-SEC-YTD, zoned decimal; GROSS-PAY, zoned decimal; SLIMIT, packed decimal.

2.4   No; SS format instructions, (PACK).

2.5   NAME.

2.6   There is no impact. The interruption is transparent to SALARIES. The integrity of all of its storage areas is guaranteed.

2.7   COMPUTE; READ; MOVE.

2.8   (a) Whether or not the COBOL language translator uses floating-point instructions. (b) No. If the M 40 does not have the floating-point option and the translated program includes such instructions, this program will not execute. The program will execute on on the M 75 since floating point is standard on that model.

2.9 Such a command sequence is poor practice. Where OS/360 data management routines generate channel commands this sequence would be avoided since it ties up electronic resources for a significant period of electro-mechanical activity.

CHAPTER 3

3.4 The table should be filled in as follows:

Name	Input Data to			OS Program Fetch
	COBOLL	LINKEDITL	SALARYL	
SALARIES	✓			
SALARYS	✓			
SALARYO		✓		
SALARYL				✓
EMPLOYEE-YTD	✓			
EMPYTD			✓	

3.5 OPEN is source program input to the COBOL language translator. Open is source program input to the assembly language translator. Open, SVC 19, is an IBM-supplied library program which executes in response to an interrupt. This program executes with the CPU in supervisory state. It resides on DASD in SYS1.SVCLIB.

3.7

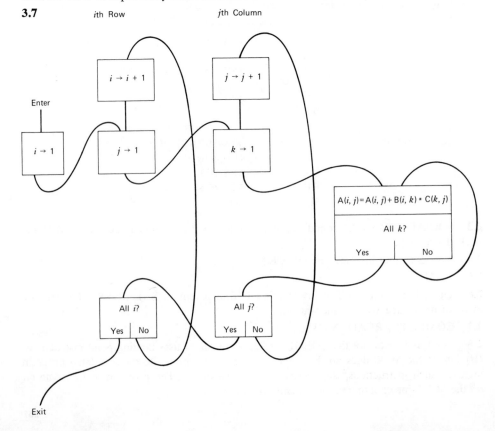

3.8   The COMPUTE statement is invalid. COMPUTE is a COBOL reserved word, a verb, not usable as a variable paragraph name.

3.9   In this FORTRAN program, READ may serve the double purpose (verb and noun) depicted. FORTRAN does not have reserved words.

3.10   (a) Unit record machine: insert card deck and control panel for each job step. (b) Turret lathe: set up tool, etc., for each job step. (c) First generation data processing system: insert card decks and control panels, clear memory for each job step.

3.11   Invariably.

3.12   In data processing, the executing load module, SALARYL, is non-reusable.

CHAPTER 4

4.1   No execution time activity occurs as a result of the specification of USING, which is input to the assembly language translator only. BALR is used to load a general purpose register as base register 3 at step execution time.

4.2   Base register 3; from Appendix 2, p. 224, 3A6DA.

4.3   From Appendix 1, p. 218, two.

4.4   The COBOL language translator provides a save area, transparently to the user.

4.5   Yes; this save area is transparently provided by the FORTRAN language translator.

4.6   In the save area of the program for which Get service was Loaded, at Open time.

4.7   LNKEDITL: this address is modified by Program Fetch during the loading of the program in the execution step.

4.8   (a) Relative location 118; (b) absolute location 493F8.

4.9   (a) 49906; (b) 49970; (c) see SVRB at location 1C6C0.

4.10   Non-reusable.

4.11   Two; None.

4.12   Yes. Should DUMPITL1 be transparently interrupted, its registers would overlay the record of DUMPITL registers in the latter's save area.

4.13   See the SVRB at location 1C6C0.

4.14   Two save areas: one for CALLITL and one for DUMPITL. Yes: Link, SVC 6, service is provided in supervisor state. Yes: Getmain for main storage space for DUMPITL, also EXCP.

4.15

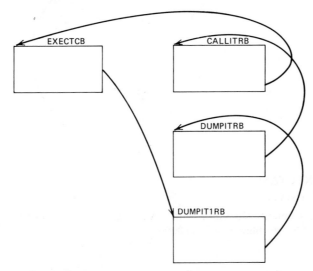

4.16 The link entails too much supervisor overhead processing to be efficient for the purpose depicted. Load, SVC 8, would be more appropriate.

4.17 (a) 11546; (b) Link; (c) To remove DUMPITRB from the RB queue.

4.18

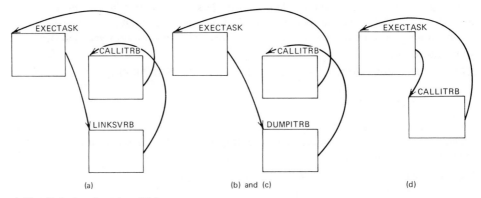

(a)   (b) and (c)   (d)

4.19 Relative location 066.

4.20 The save area locations in CALLITL space, and those in DUMPITL space and the high save area, 607B0.

4.21 (a) The structure processed by task management is as follows:

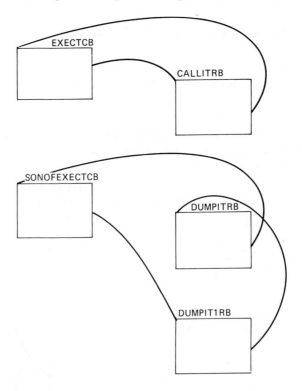

(b) Yes. (c) EXECTASK.

4.23 (a) One. (b) Yes.

4.25 From the Contents Directory Entry, Appendix 1, p. 216, all routines residing in locations with addresses higher than 71000.

4.26 Dynamic allocation may occur in both a service and a supervision situation. For example, EXCP, SVC 0, is a request for service which includes dynamic allocation of the channel–control unit–device complex. An example of supervision that implies dynamic resource allocation is an abnormal end to a load module's execution, involving access to a library member such as SYSABEND, which, among other things, sees to the detaching of the errant task from the operating system.

4.29 (a) No. (b) Nothing. (c) In data management a file mask is automatically set on the user's behalf.

4.30 An external interrupt.

CHAPTER 7

7.1 //EXEC PGM=COBOLL et al. . . . READERL. IEF 236I et al. . . . INITL within COBSTEP. IEF 285I et al. . . . TERML within COBSTEP. SALARIES. MEMORY MAP, etc., pp. 4–12. . . COBOLL within COBSTEP. //EXEC PGM=LINKEDTL et al. . . . READERL. IEF 236I et al. . . . INITL within LESTEP. IEF 285I et al. . . . TERML within LESTEP. IEW0000, CROSS REFERENCE TABLE, etc. . . . LINKEDTL within LESTEP. //EXECSTEP EXEC PGM= *.LESTEP.SYSLMOD et al. . . . READERL. IEF 236I et al. . . . INITL within EXECSTEP. ppl 15–19 load modules within EXECSTEP. IEF 285I et al. . . . TERML within EXECSTEP.

7.10 //EXECSTEP DD DSNAME=EMPYTD. . . . UNIT-2314.

7.11 These operands are legal in COBOL source programs. The fact that they are identical with job control language operands is of no consequence.

7.12 More than eight letters in EMPLOYEE-YTD is illegal job control language. The fact that this operand is a SALARIES variable is of no consequence. Job control language and COBOL are independently defined.

7.13 Yes, by using // DD DSNAME=EMPWEEKLY instead of // DD * (SYSIN).

7.14 No changes to SALARIES are necessary in this situation. EXECSTEP demands UNIT=2311, not UNIT=29X, which latter specification would have necessitated a change.

7.15 No.

7.17 It is placed in EXECSTEP, which requests the scheduling for the load module SALARYL, which is composed of SALARYO + DUMPITL.

7.18 EXECTASK. Statically allocated resources belong to the job step task.

7.19 In production, a single-step job // DD DSNAME SALARYL. . . would be the preferred approach. In development, a three-step compile, link-edit, execute job would be preferable.

7.20 A major consideration is the checkpointing of the partially processed EMPYTD data set. Given that checkpointing had been invoked with restart on the M 145, a complete rerun of USERJOB would be unnecessary. The SYSIN and SYSOUT (DASD) queues would be transferred to the M 145 and processed from there.

In regard to system configuration, in general, the M 155 is said to be upward compatible with the M 145. It must be ensured that the M 145 has the main storage capacity, the devices that are demand allocated, and the addresses correctly system generated into its operating system, to conform to unit specifications that run on the M 155.

7.21 Such a design envisions a load module CALLITL executing under EXECTASK sponsorship Attaching EXECTASK1; EXECTASK1 resources are allocated without benefit of INITL services prior to its Attachment.

In interactive systems, users characteristically request service from communications terminals generally remote from the computer site. The user issues commands by means of terminal function keys. Each command results in the scheduling that establishes a task. Hence more tasks exist in an interactive than in a batch system. In such an environment, a design based on scheduling the maximum number of resources a task might need under any operating condition is not as acceptable as it is in a primarily batch-oriented system.

7.22 System/370.

7.23 The S/370 CPU.

7.24 An input queue may await the services of more than one initiator resource.

7.25 User request; system response.

7.26 None.

7.27 The electric age system was initialized manually; the machine room operator inserted a deck in the hopper, and a control panel, and pressed the start button. System/370 initialization is an automatic procedure accomplished by the control program through event processing.

CHAPTER 8

8.1 When data management Synchronize issues Wait, EXECTASK1 is put in that state. Task management thereupon moves EXECTCB1 from the head of the ready queue to the Wait queue. If EXECTASK2 is at the head of the ready queue at this time, task management makes it the active task and SALARY2 streams instructions.

8.6 SALARYL is a multitasking, dynamic program management structure accesses the random records of EMPYTD in parallel by subtask in opposition to the serial access implied by simple program management. (Since COBOL does not support multitasking, the discussion is theoretical, although comparison may be made to the PL/I multitasking example discussed at the end of Chapter 5).

8.9 The SALARIES PROCEDURE DIVISION is unaffected in scan mode; however new JCL would have to be written. For ISAM, random mode, a new source program would have to be written.

8.10 Inquiry.

8.12 (a) He is dependent on OS i–o error routine service, which provides protection over the channel but does not, however, guarantee that the information was written correctly on the i–o device. (b) Yes. (c) Reliability and performance.

appendix 1

SALARIES MACHINE LISTING

In this appendix we present an actual System/370 machine listing for a four-step USERJOB. The following table of contents will help the reader identify the various components of this listing:

Note: A number of main storage dumps are included within these appendices. For details concerning dumps, see *IBM System/360 Operating System—Programmer's Guide to Debugging*, IBM System Reference Library Manual GC28–6670.

```
UU      UU   SSSSSSSSSS    EEEEEEEEEEEE   RRRRRRRRRR    JJJJJJJJJJ   000000000000   BBBBBBBBBB
UU      UU   SSSSSSSSSSSS  EEEEEEEEEEEE   RRRRRRRRRRR   JJJJJJJJJ    00000 0000000  BBB BBBBBBBBB
UU      UU   SS        SS  EE             RR       RR        JJ      00        00   BB        BB
UU      UU   SS            EE             RR       RR        JJ      00        00   BB        BB
UU      UU   SSS           EE             RR       RR        JJ      00        00   BB        BB
UU      UU   SSSSSSSSS     EEEEEEE        RRRRRRRRRRRR       JJ      00        00   BBBBBBBBBB
UU      UU   SSSSSSSSS     EEEEEEE        RRRRRRRRRR         JJ      00        00   BBBBBBBBBB
UU      UU         SSS     EE             RR    RR           JJ      00        00   BB        BB
UU      UU         SS      EE             RR    RR      JJ   JJ      00        00   BB        BB
UU      UU   SS    EE      EE             RR     RR     JJ   JJ      00        00   BB        BB
UUUULUUUUUU  SSSSSSSSSSS   EEEEEEEEEEEE   RR      RR    JJJJJJJJ     000000000000   BBBBBBBBBBBB
 UUULUUUUUU  SSSSSSSSSS    EEEEEEEEEEEE   RR       RR   JJJJJ        000000000000   BBBBBBBBBB
```

```
                    AAAAAAAAAA
                    AAAAAAAAAAAA
                    AA        AA
                    AA        AA
                    AA        AA
                    AAAAAAAAAAAA
                    AAAAAAAAAAAA
                    AA        AA
                    AA        AA
                    AA        AA
                    AA        AA
                    AA        AA
```

```
     //USERJOB JOB MSGLEVEL=1,CLASS=B,REGION=160K
     //ASMSTEP EXEC PGM=ASMBLRL
     //SYSLIB  DD   DSNAME=SYS1.MACLIB,DISP=SHR
     //SYSUT1  DD   UNIT=SYSDA,SPACE=(400,(400,50))
     //SYSUT2  DD   UNIT=SYSDA,SPACE=(400,(400,50))
     //SYSUT3  DD   UNIT=SYSDA,SPACE=(400,(400,50))
(a)  //SYSPRINT DD  SYSOUT=A
     //SYSUDUMP DD  SYSOUT=A
     //SYSPUNCH DD  DSNAME=&GODATA,UNIT=SYSDA,SPACE=(80,(200,50)),    X
     //           DISP=(NEW,PASS)
     //SYSIN DD  *
     IEF236I ALLOC. FOR USERJOB  ASM1
     IEF237I 337  ALLOCATED TO SYSLIB
     IEF237I 190  ALLOCATED TO SYSUT1
```

```
                                          EXTERNAL SYMBOL DICTIONARY

     SYMBOL   TYPE ID  ADDR  LENGTH LD ID
(b)

     DUMPIT    SD  01 000000 00007C


        LOC  OBJECT CODE    ADDR1 ADDR2 STMT   SOURCE STATEMENT

        C00000                           1 DUMPIT  CSECT
                                         2         SAVE  (14,12),,*
        C00000 47F0 F00C         0000C   3+        B     12(0,15) BRANCH AROUND ID
        C00004 06                        4+        DC    AL1(6)
        C00005 C4E4D4D7C9E3             5+        DC    CL6'DUMPIT' IDENTIFIER
        C0000B 00
        C0000C 90EC D00C         0000C   6+        STM   14,12,12(13) SAVE REGISTERS
        C00010 0530                      7         BALR  3,0
        C00012                           8         USING *,3
        C00012 50D0 3026         00038   9         ST    13,SAVE+4
        C00016 41D0 3022         00034  10         LA    13,SAVE
(c)                                     11         ABEND 256,DUMP
        C0001A                          12+        DS    0H
        C0001A 0700                     13+        CNOP  0,4
        C0001C 47F0 3012         00024  14+        B     *+8 BRANCH AROUND CONSTANT
        C00020 80                       15+        DC    AL1(128) DUMP/STEP CODE
        C00021 000100                   16+        DC    AL3(256) COMPLETION CODE
        C00024 5810 300E         00020  17+        L     1,*-4 LOAD CODES INTO REG 1
        C00028 0A0D                     18+        SVC   13 LINK TO ABEND ROUTINE
                                        19 RETURN  RETURN (14,12),T
        C0002A                          20+RETURN  DS    0H
        C0002A 98EC D00C         0000C  21+        LM    14,12,12(13) RESTORE THE REGISTERS
        C0002E 92FF D00C   0000C        22+        MVI   12(13),X'FF' SET RETURN INDICATION
        C00032 07FE                     23+        BR    14 RETURN
        C00034                          24 SAVE    DS    18F
                                        25         END


     SYMBOL   LEN  VALUE  DEFN    REFERENCES

(d)  DUMPIT   00001 000000 00001
     RETURN   00002 00002A 00020
     SAVE     00004 000034 00024    0009  0010
```

```
   //COBSTEP EXEC PGM=COBOLL,PARM='BUF=13000,SIZE=120000,MAP,LIST'
   //SYSPRINT DD SYSOUT=A
   //SYSUT1 DD UNIT=SYSDA,SPACE=(TRK,(100,10))
   //SYSUT2 DD UNIT=SYSDA,SPACE=(TRK,(100,10))
   //SYSUT3 DD UNIT=SYSDA,SPACE=(TRK,(100,10))
   //SYSUT4 DD UNIT=SYSDA,SPACE=(TRK,(100,10))
   //SYSLIN DD DSNAME=&LADSET,DISP=(NEW,PASS),UNIT=SYSDA,            X
   //           SPACE=(80,(200,50))
   //SYSIN DD *
   IEF236I ALLOC. FOR A170P108
   IEF237I 335    ALLOCATED TO SYSPRINT
   IEF237I 191    ALLOCATED TO SYSUT1
(a) IEF237I 193    ALLOCATED TO SYSUT2
   IEF237I 191    ALLOCATED TO SYSUT3
   IEF237I 192    ALLOCATED TO SYSUT4
   IEF237I 193    ALLOCATED TO SYSLIN
   IEF237I 333    ALLOCATED TO SYSIN


   IEF285I    SYS70170.T104054.SV000.A170P108.R0000007    SYSOUT
   IEF285I    VOL SER NOS= SPLIT3.
   IEF285I    SYS70170.T104054.RV000.A170P108.R0000008    DELETED
   IEF285I    VOL SER NOS= X8313 .
   IEF285I    SYS70170.T104054.RV000.A170P108.R0000009    DELETED
   IEF285I    VOL SER NOS= 231100.
   IEF285I    SYS70170.T104054.RV000.A170P108.R0000010    DELETED
   IEF285I    VOL SER NOS= X8313 .
(b) IEF285I    SYS70170.T104054.RV000.A170P108.R0000011    DELETED
   IEF285I    VOL SER NOS= HARRYC.
   IEF285I    SYS70170.T104054.RV000.A170P108.LADSET      PASSED
   IEF285I    VOL SER NOS= 231100.
   IEF285I    SYS70170.T104054.RV000.A170P108.S0000012    SYSIN
   IEF285I    VOL SER NOS= SPLIT5.
   IEF285I    SYS70170.T104054.RV000.A170P108.S0000012    DELETED
   IEF285I    VOL SER NOS= SPLIT5.
   IEF373I STEP /        / START 70170.1050
   IEF374I STEP /        / STOP  70170.1052 CPU  00MIN 02.78SEC MAIN 124K LCS   OK
   A170P108              STEP TIME=   00.04    MINUTES
```

1

```
C0001          IDENTIFICATION DIVISION.
C0002          PROGRAM-ID.
C0003          'SALARIES S/Q/U'.
C0004          ENVIRONMENT DIVISION.
00005          CONFIGURATION SECTION.
00006          SOURCE-COMPUTER. IBM-360 I65.
C0007          OBJECT-COMPUTER. IBM-360 I65.
C0008          INPUT-OUTPUT SECTION.
C0009          FILE-CONTROL.
C0010              SELECT EMPLOYEE-YTD
C0011                      ASSIGN TO 'INOUT' DIRECT-ACCESS 2311.
C0012              SELECT EMPLOYEE-WEEKLY ASSIGN TO 'SYSIN' UNIT-RECORD.
C0013          DATA DIVISION.
C0014          FILE SECTION.
00015          FD  EMPLOYEE-YTD
C0016              LABEL RECORDS ARE STANDARD
00017              RECORDING MODE IS F
00018              BLOCK CONTAINS 10 RECORDS
C0019              RECORD CONTAINS 120 CHARACTERS
C0020              DATA RECORD IS YTD-RECORD.
C0021          01  YTD-RECORD.
C0022              02 NAME PICTURE A(32).
C0023              02 SOCIAL-SEC-YTD PICTURE 9(6)V99.
C0024              02 EMPLOYEE-NO-YTD PICTURE 9(5).
C0025              02 CNTROL PICTURE X(1).
C0026              02 GROSS-PAY PICTURE 9(6)V99.
C0027              02 FILLER PICTURE X(66).
C0028          FD  EMPLOYEE-WEEKLY
C0029              LABEL RECORDS ARE OMITTED
C0030              RECORDING MODE IS F
C0031              BLOCK CONTAINS 1 RECORDS
C0032              RECORD CONTAINS 80 CHARACTERS
C0033              DATA RECORD IS WEEKLY-RECORD.
C0034          01  WEEKLY-RECORD.
C0035              02 EMPLOYEE-NO-WEEKLY PICTURE 9(5).
C0036              02 NAME PICTURE X(32).
C0037              02 FILLER PICTURE X(43).
C0038          WORKING-STORAGE SECTION.
C0039          77  SLIMIT PICTURE 9(6)V99 COMPUTATIONAL-3 VALUE IS 374.40.
C0040          PROCEDURE DIVISION.
C0041              OPEN I-O EMPLOYEE-YTD.
C0042              OPEN INPUT EMPLOYEE-WEEKLY.
C0043          READ-WEEKLY.
C0044              READ EMPLOYEE-WEEKLY AT END GO TO READ-YTD.
C0045          READ-YTD.
C0046              READ EMPLOYEE-YTD AT END GO TO FINIS.
C0047              IF EMPLOYEE-NO-YTD IS EQUAL TO EMPLOYEE-NO-WEEKLY
00048                                      GO TO LIMIT-TEST.
C0049              REWRITE YTD-RECORD.
C0050              DISPLAY YTD-RECORD.
C0051              GO TO READ-YTD.
C0052          LIMIT-TEST.
00053              IF SLIMIT - SOCIAL-SEC-YTD < GROSS-PAY GO TO LIMIT-CALC.
C0054              COMPUTE SOCIAL-SEC-YTD
C0055                      ROUNDED = SOCIAL-SEC-YTD + GROSS-PAY * .048.
C0056              REWRITE YTD-RECORD.
00057              DISPLAY YTD-RECORD.
C0058              GO TO READ-WEEKLY.
C0059          LIMIT-CALC.
C0060              COMPUTE SOCIAL-SEC-YTD
C0061                      ROUNDED = SOCIAL-SEC-YTD +
C0062                                  (SLIMIT - SOCIAL-SEC-YTD) * .048.
C0063              REWRITE YTD-RECORD.
C0064              DISPLAY YTD-RECORD.
C0065              GO TO READ-WEEKLY.
C0066              CLOSE EMPLOYEE-YTD.
C0067              CLOSE EMPLOYEE-WEEKLY.
C0068          FINIS. ENTER LINKAGE.
C0069              CALL 'DUMPIT'.
C0070              ENTER COBOL.
C0071              STOP RUN.
```

INTRNL NAME	LVL	SOURCE NAME	BASE	DISPL	INTRNL NAME	DEFINITION	USAGE	R O Q
DNM=1-109	FD	EMPLOYEE-YTD	DCB=01		DNM=1-109			
DNM=1-133	01	YTD-RECORD	BLI=1	000	DNM=1-133	DS 0CL120	QSAM	
DNM=1-155	02	NAME	BLI=1	000	DNM=1-155	DS 32C	GROUP	
DNM=1-168	02	SOCIAL-SEC-YTD	BLI=1	020	DNM=1-168	DS 8C	DISP	
DNM=1-191	02	EMPLOYEE-NO-YTD	BLI=1	028	DNM=1-191	DS 5C	DISP-NM	
DNM=1-215	02	CNTROL	BLI=1	02D	DNM=1-215	DS 1C	DISP-NM	
DNM=1-230	02	GROSS-PAY	BLI=1	02E	DNM=1-230	DS 8C	DISP	
DNM=1-248	02	FILLER	BLI=1	036	DNM=1-248	DS 66C	DISP-NM	
DNM=1-263	FD	EMPLOYEE-WEEKLY	DCB=02		DNM=1-263		DISP	
DNM=1-290	01	WEEKLY-RECORD	BLI=2	000	DNM=1-290	DS 0CL80	QSAM	
DNM=1-315	02	EMPLOYEE-NO-WEEKLY	BLI=2	000	DNM=1-315	DS 5C	GROUP	
DNM=1-342	02	NAME	BLI=2	005	DNM=1-342	DS 32C	DISP-NM	
DNM=1-358	02	FILLER	BLI=2	025	DNM=1-358	DS 43C	DISP	
							DISP	
DNM=1-391	77	SLIMIT	BLI=3	000	DNM=1-391	DS 5P	COMP-3	

```
                       MEMORY MAP

            TGT                          00118

         SAVE AREA                       00118
         SWITCH CELL                     00160
         TALLY CELL                      00164
         UNUSED                          00168
         ENTRY-SAVE                      00170
         UNUSED                          00174
         WORKING CELLS                   00178
         OVERFLOW CELLS                  002A8
         TEMPORARY STORAGE CELLS         002A8
         TEMPORARY STORAGE-2 CELLS       002B8
         VLC-O CELLS                     002DC
         SBL-O CELLS                     002DC
         BLS CELLS                       002DC
         BLL CELLS                       002DC
         VLC-I CELLS                     002DC
         SBL-I CELLS                     002DC
         BL-I CELLS                      002DC
         SUBADR-I CELLS                  002E8
         ONCTL-I CELLS                   002E8
         PFMCTL-I CELLS                  002E8
         PFMSAV-I CELLS                  002F8
         VN-I CELLS                      002E8
         DECBADR-I CELLS                 002E8
         SAVE AREA =2                    002E8
         SAVE AREA =3                    002E8
         XSASW-I CELLS                   002E8
         XSA-I CELLS                     002E8
         PARAM CELLS                     002E8
         RPTSAV AREA                     002F0
         CHECKPOINT SAVE CELLS           002F0
         RPI CELLS                       002F0

LITERAL POOL (HEX)

00358 (LIT+0)     00230000  C9C5D8F9  F9F9C940  D5D640C4  C440C3C1  D9C44CC6
00370 (LIT+24)    D6D94004  8C01000C  500C

            PGT                          002F8

         OVERFLOW CELLS                  002F8
         VIRTUAL CELLS                   002F8
         PROCEDURE NAME CELLS            00300
         GENERATED NAME CELLS            00314
         DCB ADDRESS CELLS               0034C
         VNI CELLS                       00354
         LITERALS                        00358
         DISPLAY LITERALS                0037A
```

```
REGISTER ASSIGNMENT
   REG 6    BLI=3
   REG 7    BLI=1
   REG 8    BLI=7

41    OPEN      00037A                           START   EQU   *
                00037A   58 10 C 054                      L     1,C54(0,12)              DCB=1
                00037F   50 10 D 1D0                       ST    1,1D0(0,13)              PRM=1
                000382   92 84 D 1D0                       MVI   1D0(13),X'84'            PRM=1
                000386   41 10 D 1D0                       LA    1,1D0(0,13)              PRM=1
                00038A   0A 13                             SVC   19
                00038C   58 10 C 054                       L     1,C54(0,12)              DCB=1
                000390   58 20 C 03C                       L     2,03C(0,12)              GN=09
                000394   91 10 1 030                       TM    C30(1),X'10'
                000398   07 12                             BCR   1,2
                00039A   D2 1A D 1A0 C 060                 MVC   1A0(27,13),060(12)       TS2=1      LIT+0
                0003A0   D2 07 D 1BB 1 028                 MVC   1BB(8,13),028(1)         TS2=28
                0003A6   41 10 D 1A0                       LA    1,1A0(0,13)              TS2=1
                0003AA   0A 23                             SVC   35
                0003AC                          GN=C9   EQU   *
42    OPEN      0003AC   58 10 C 058                       L     1,C58(0,12)              DCB=2
                0003B0   50 10 D 1D0                       ST    1,1D0(0,13)              PRM=1
                0003B4   92 80 D 1D0                       MVI   1D0(13),X'80'            PRM=1
                0003B8   41 10 D 1D0                       LA    1,1D0(0,13)              PRM=1
                0003BC   0A 13                             SVC   19
                0003BF   58 10 C 058                       L     1,C58(0,12)              DCB=2
                0003C2   58 20 C 040                       L     2,040(0,12)              CN=010
                0003C6   91 10 1 030                       TM    C30(1),X'10'
                0003CA   07 12                             BCR   1,2
                0003CC   D2 1A D 1A0 C 060                 MVC   1A0(27,13),060(12)       TS2=1      LIT+0
                0003D2   D2 07 D 1BB 1 028                 MVC   1BB(8,13),C28(1)         TS2=28
                0003D8   41 10 D 1A0                       LA    1,1A0(0,13)              TS2=1
                0003DC   0A 23                             SVC   35
                0003DE                          GN=010  EQU   *
43    *READ-WEEKLY
                0003DE                          PN=01   EQU   *
44    READ      0003DE   58 10 C 058                       L     1,058(0,12)              DCB=2
                0003E2   D2 02 1 021 C 01D                 MVC   C21(3,1),01D(12)                    GN=01+1
                0003E8   58 F0 1 030                       L     15,030(0,1)
                0003EC   05 EF                             BALR  14,15
                0003EE   50 10 D 1C8                       ST    1,1C8(0,13)              BLI=2
                0003F2   58 80 D 1C8                       L     8,1C8(0,13)              BLI=2
                0003F6   58 10 C 00C                       L     1,00C(0,12)              PN=02
                0003FA   07 F1                             BCR   15,1
44    GO        0003FC                          GN=01   EQU   *
                0003FC   58 10 C 00C                       L     1,00C(0,12)              PN=02
                000400   07 F1                             BCR   15,1
45    *READ-YTD
                000402                          PN=02   EQU   *
46    READ      000402   58 10 C 054                       L     1,C54(0,12)              DCB=1
                000406   D2 02 1 021 C 021                 MVC   C21(3,1),021(12)                    GN=02+1
                00040C   58 F0 1 030                       L     15,030(0,1)
                000410   05 EF                             BALR  14,15
                000412   50 10 D 1C4                       ST    1,1C4(0,13)              BLI=1
                000416   58 70 D 1C4                       L     7,1C4(0,13)              BLI=1
                00041A   58 10 C 024                       L     1,C24(0,12)              GN=03
                00041F   07 F1                             BCR   15,1
46    GO        000420                          GN=02   EQU   *
                000420   58 10 C 018                       L     1,018(0,12)              PN=05
                000424   07 F1                             BCR   15,1
47    IF        000426                          GN=03   EQU   *
                000426   F2 74 D 190 7 028                 PACK  190(8,13),028(5,7)       TS=01      DNM=1-191
                00042C   F2 74 D 198 8 000                 PACK  198(8,13),000(5,8)       TS=09      DNM=1-315
                000432   F9 22 D 195 D 19D                 CP    195(3,13),19D(3,13)      TS=06      TS=014
                000438   58 F0 C 028                       L     15,028(0,12)             GN=04
                00043C   07 7F                             BCR   7,15
48    GO        00043E   58 10 C 010                       L     1,010(0,12)              PN=03
                000442   07 F1                             BCR   15,1
49    REWRITE   000444                          GN=04   EQU   *
                000444   58 10 C 054                       L     1,C54(0,12)              DCB=1
                000448   58 F0 1 030                       L     15,030(0,1)
                00044C   45 E0 F 004                       BAL   14,004(0,15)
50    DISPLAY   000450                          GN=05   EQU   *
                000450   58 F0 C 000                       L     15,000(0,12)             V(IHOFDISP)
                000454   05 1F                             BALR  1,15
                000456   0001                             DC    X'0001'
                000458   00                               DC    X'00'
                000459   000078                           DC    X'000078'
                00045C   0D0001C4                         DC    X'0D0001C4'              BLI=1
                000460   0000                             DC    X'0000'
                000462   FFFF                             DC    X'FFFF'
51    GO        000464   58 10 C 00C                       L     1,00C(0,12)              PN=02
                000468   07 F1                             BCR   15,1
52    *LIMIT-TEST
                00046A                          PN=03   EQU   *
53    IF        00046A   F2 77 D 198 C 020                 PACK  198(8,13),C20(8,7)       TS=09      DNM=1-168
                000470   F8 74 D 190 6 000                 ZAP   190(8,13),000(5,6)       TS=01      DNM=1-391
                000476   FB 44 D 193 D 198                 SP    193(5,13),198(5,13)      TS=04      TS=012
                00047C   F2 77 D 198 7 02E                 PACK  198(8,13),02E(8,7)       TS=09      DNM=1-230
                000482   F9 44 D 193 D 198                 CP    193(5,13),198(5,13)      TS=04      TS=012
                000488   58 F0 C 030                       L     15,030(0,12)             GN=06
                00048C   07 AF                             BCR   10,15
53    GO        00048E   58 10 C 014                       L     1,014(0,12)              PN=04
                000492   07 F1                             BCR   15,1
54    COMPUTE   000494                          GN=06   EQU   *
                000494   F2 77 D 198 7 02E                 PACK  198(8,13),C2E(8,7)       TS=09      DNM=1-230
                00049A   FC 61 D 199 C 078                 MP    199(7,13),078(2,12)      TS=010     LIT+27
                0004A0   F2 77 D 190 7 020                 PACK  190(8,13),020(8,7)       TS=01      DNM=1-168
                0004A6   FC 72 D 190 C 07D                 MP    190(8,13),07D(3,12)      TS=01      LIT+29
                0004AC   FA 65 D 199 D 192                 AP    199(7,13),192(6,13)      TS=010     TS=03
                0004B2   F9 70 D 198 C 07F                 CP    198(8,13),07F(1,12)      TS=09      LIT+31
```

```
          0004BB  58 F0 C 044              L     15,044(0,12)           GN=011
          0004BC  07 4F                    BCR   4,15
          0004BF  FA 61 D 199 C 080        AP    199(7,13),C80(2,12)    TS=010      LIT+32
          0004C4  58 F0 C 048              L     15,048(0,12)           GN=012
          0004C8  07 FF                    BCR   15,15
          0004CA                   GN=011  FQU   *
          0004CA  FB 61 D 199 C 080        SP    199(7,13),C80(2,12)    TS=010      LIT+32
          0004D0                   GN=012  EQU   *
          0004D0  F1 75 D 198 D 198        MVC   198(8,13),198(6,13)    TS=09       TS=09
          0004D6  F3 74 7 020 D 198        UNPK  C20(8,7),198(5,13)     DNM=1-168   TS=012
          0004DC  96 F0 7 027              OI    C27(7),X'F0'           DNM=1-168+7
56  REWRITE   0004E0  58 10 C 054          L     1,C54(0,12)            DCB=1
          0004E4  58 F0 0 030              L     15,030(0,1)
          0004E8  45 E0 F 004              BAL   14,004(0,15)
57  DISPLAY   0004EC                GN=07  FQU   *
          0004EC  58 F0 C 000              L     15,000(0,12)           V(IHDFDISP)
          0004F0  05 1F                    BALR  1,15
          0004F2  0001                     DC    X'0001'
          0004F4  00                       DC    X'00'
          0004F5  000078                   DC    X'000078'
          0004F8  000001C4                 DC    X'000001C4'           RLI=1
          0004FC  0000                     DC    X'0000'
          0004FE  FFFF                     DC    X'FFFF'
58  GO        000500  58 10 C 008          L     1,008(0,12)            PN=01
          000504  07 F1                    BCR   15,1
59  *LIMIT-CALC
          000506                   PN=C4  EQU   *
60  COMPUTE   000506  F2 77 D 198 7 020    PACK  198(8,13),C20(8,7)     TS=09       DNM=1-168
          00050C  F8 74 D 190 6 000        ZAP   190(8,13),000(5,6)     TS=01       DNM=1-391
          000512  FB 44 D 193 D 198        SP    193(5,13),198(5,13)    TS=04       TS=012
          000518  FC 61 D 191 C 07B        MP    191(7,13),07B(2,12)    TS=02       LIT+27
          00051E  F2 77 D 198 7 020        PACK  198(8,13),C20(8,7)     TS=09       DNM=1-168
          000524  FC 72 D 198 C 07D        MP    198(8,13),C7D(3,12)    TS=09       LIT+29
          00052A  FA 65 D 191 D 19A        AP    191(7,13),19A(6,13)    TS=02       TS=011
          000530  F9 70 D 190 C 07F        CP    190(8,13),C7F(1,12)    TS=01       LIT+31
          000536  58 F0 C 04C              L     15,04C(0,12)           GN=013
          00053A  07 4F                    BCR   4,15
          00053C  FA 61 D 191 C 080        AP    191(7,13),080(2,12)    TS=02       LIT+32
          000542  58 F0 C 050              L     15,050(0,12)           GN=014
          000546  07 FF                    BCR   15,15
          000548                   GN=013  FQU   *
          000548  FB 61 D 191 C 080        SP    191(7,13),080(2,12)    TS=02       LIT+32
          00054E                   GN=014  FQU   *
          00054E  F1 75 D 190 D 190        MVC   190(8,13),190(6,13)    TS=01       TS=01
          000554  F3 74 7 020 D 193        UNPK  C20(8,7),193(5,13)     DNM=1-168   TS=04
          00055A  96 F0 7 027              OI    C27(7),X'F0'           DNM=1-168+7
63  REWRITE   00055E  58 10 C 054          L     1,C54(0,12)            DCB=1
          000562  58 F0 0 030              L     15,030(0,1)
          000566  45 E0 F 004              BAL   14,004(0,15)
64  DISPLAY   00056A                GN=C8  EQU   *
          00056A  58 F0 C 000              L     15,000(0,12)           V(IHDFDISP)
          00056F  05 1F                    PALR  1,15
          000570  0001                     DC    X'C001'
          000572  00                       DC    X'00'
          000573  000078                   DC    X'000078'
          000576  0D0001C4                 DC    X'CD0001C4'           RLI=1
          00057A  0000                     DC    X'0000'
          00057C  FFFF                     DC    X'FFFF'
65  GO        00057E  58 10 C 008          L     1,008(0,12)            PN=01
          000582  07 F1                    BCR   15,1
66  CLOSF     000584  58 10 C 054          L     1,054(0,12)            DCB=1
          000588  58 20 1 02C              L     2,02C(0,1)
          00058C  91 0F 2 00C              TM    CCC(2),X'0F'
          000590  05 50                    BALR  5,0
          000592  47 E0 5 010              RC    14,010(0,5)
          000596  58 20 1 04C              L     2,C4C(0,1)
          00059A  4B 20 1 052              SH    2,052(0,1)
          00059E  50 20 1 04C              ST    2,C4C(0,1)
          0005A2  58 10 C 054              L     1,054(0,12)            DCB=1
          0005A6  50 10 D 1D0              ST    1,1D0(0,13)            PRM=1
          0005AA  92 90 D 1D0              MVI   1D0(13),X'90'          PRM=1
          0005AE  41 10 D 1D0              LA    1,1D0(0,13)            PRM=1
          0005B2  0A 14                    SVC   20
          0005B4  58 20 C 054              L     2,054(0,12)            DCB=1
          0005B8  58 10 2 014              L     1,C14(0,2)
          0005BC  96 01 2 017              OI    C17(2),X'01'
          0005C0  48 40 1 004              LH    4,C04(0,1)
          0005C4  4C 40 1 006              MH    4,006(0,1)
          0005C8  41 00 4 008              LA    C,008(0,4)
          0005CC  41 10 1 000              LA    1,C00(0,1)
          0005D0  0A 0A                    SVC   10
67  CLOSE     0005D2  58 10 C 058          L     1,C58(0,12)            DCB=2
          0005D6  58 20 1 02C              L     2,C2C(0,1)
          0005DA  91 0F 2 00C              TM    CCC(2),X'0F'
          0005DE  05 50                    BALR  5,0
          0005E0  47 E0 5 010              RC    14,010(0,5)
          0005E4  58 20 1 04C              L     2,C4C(0,1)
          0005E8  4B 20 1 052              SH    2,C52(0,1)
          0005EC  50 20 1 04C              ST    2,04C(0,1)
          0005F0  58 10 C 058              L     1,C58(0,12)            DCB=2
          0005F4  50 10 D 1D0              ST    1,1D0(0,13)            PRM=1
          0005F8  92 90 D 1D0              MVI   1D0(13),X'90'          PRM=1
          0005FC  41 10 D 1D0              LA    1,1D0(0,13)            PRM=1
          000600  0A 14                    SVC   20
          000602  58 20 C 058              L     2,C58(0,12)            DCB=2
          000606  58 10 2 014              L     1,014(0,2)
          00060A  96 01 2 017              OI    C17(2),X'01'
          00060E  48 40 1 004              LH    4,C04(0,1)
          000612  4C 40 1 006              MH    4,006(0,1)
          000616  41 00 4 008              LA    C,008(0,4)
          00061A  41 10 1 000              LA    1,C00(0,1)
          00061F  0A 0A                    SVC   10
```

```
68      *FINIS
                000620                          PN=05    EQU    *
68      ENTER
69      CALL    000620  58 F0 C 004            L      15,004(0,12)       V(DUMPIT  )
                000624  05 EF                  BALR   14,15
70      ENTER
71      STOP    000626  58 D0 D 004            L      13,004(0,13)
                00062A  98 EC D 00C            LM     14,12,00C(13)
                00062E  1B FF                  SR     15,15
                000630  07 FE                  BCR    15,14
                000632  50 D0 5 008    INIT2   ST     13,008(0,5)
                000636  50 50 D 004            ST     5,004(0,13)
                00063A  50 E0 D 054            ST     14,054(0,13)
                00063E  91 20 D 048            TM     C48(13),X'20'      SWT+0
                000642  07 19                  BCR    1,9
                000644  96 20 D 048            OI     C48(13),X'20'      SWT+0
                000648  41 60 0 004            LA     6,C04(0,0)
                00064C  41 10 C 008            LA     1,008(0,12)        PN=01
                000650  41 70 C 060            LA     7,C60(0,12)        LIT+0
                000654  06 70                  BCTR   7,0
                000656  05 50                  BALR   5,0
                000658  58 40 1 000            L      4,C00(0,1)
                00065C  1E 4B                  ALR    4,11
                00065E  50 40 1 000            ST     4,000(0,1)
                000662  87 16 5 000            BXLE   1,6,000(5)
                000666  41 80 D 1C4            LA     8,1C4(0,13)        BLI=1
                00066A  41 70 0 003            LA     7,003(0,0)
                00066E  05 10                  BALR   1,0
                000670  58 00 8 000            L      C,C00(0,8)
                000674  1E 0B                  ALR    C,11
                000676  50 00 8 000            ST     C,C00(0,8)
                00067A  41 80 8 004            LA     8,004(0,8)
                00067E  06 71                  BCTR   7,1
                000680  58 60 D 1CC    INIT3   L      6,1CC(0,13)        BLI=3
                000684  58 70 D 1C4            L      7,1C4(0,13)        BLI=1
                000688  58 80 D 1C8            L      8,1C8(0,13)        BLI=2
                00068C  07 FE                  BCR    15,14
                000000  07 00          INIT1   BCR    C,C
                000002  90 EC D 00C            STM    14,12,00C(13)
                000006  18 5D                  LR     5,13
                000008  05 F0                  BALR   15,0
                00000A  98 9F F 006            LM     9,15,006(15)
                00000E  07 FF                  BCR    15,15
                000010  00000680               ADCON  L4(INIT3)
                000014  00000000               ADCON  L4(FXITR)
                000018  00000000               ADCON  L4(INIT1)
                00001C  000002F8               ADCON  L4(PGT)
                000020  00000118               ADCON  L4(TGT)
                000024  0000037A               ADCON  L4(START)
                000028  00000632               ADCON  L4(INIT2)
                00002C  96 12 1 034            OI     034(1),X'12'
                000030  07 FE                  BCR    15,14
                000032  FFFFFFFF               DC     X'FFFFFFFF'
                000036  D9D7C4F040404040       DC     X'D9D7C4F040404040'
```

```
       //LESTEP EXEC PGM=LNKEDITL,PARM='XREF,LIST'
       //SYSABEND DD SYSOUT=A
       //SYSLIB DD DSNAME=SYS1.COBLIB,DISP=SHR
       //SYSPRINT DD SYSOUT=A
       //SYSLMOD DD DSNAME=&GODATE(RUN),DISP=(NEW,PASS),UNIT=SYSDA,        x
       //            SPACE=(1024,(50,20,1))
       //SYSLIN      DD DSNAME=&LADSET,DISP=(OLD,DELETE)
       //            DD DDNAME=DAIN
       //SYSUT1 DD UNIT=(SYSDA,SEP=(SYSLIN,SYSLMOD)),SPACE=(1024,(50,20))
   (a) //MYLIB DD DSNAME=&GODATA,DISP=(OLD,DELETF)
       //DAIN DD *
       IEF236I ALLOC. FOR USERJOB LESTEP
       IEF237I 337    ALLOCATED TO SYSABEND
       IEF237I 337    ALLOCATED TO SYSLIB
       IEF237I 332    ALLOCATED TO SYSPRINT
       IEF237I 190    ALLOCATED TO SYSLMOD
       IEF237I 193    ALLOCATED TO SYSLIN
       IEF237I 334    ALLOCATED TO
       IEF237I 192    ALLOCATED TO SYSUT1
       IEF237I 190    ALLOCATED TO MYLIB


       F88-LEVEL LINKAGE EDITOR OPTIONS SPECIFIED XREF,LIST
                 VARIABLE OPTIONS USED - SIZE=(92160,8192)          DEFAULT OPTION(S) USED
       IEW0000    INCLUDE MYLIB


                                   CROSS REFERENCE TABLE


       CONTROL SECTION                ENTRY

           NAME    ORIGIN  LENGTH         NAME   LOCATION   NAME   LOCATION   NAME   LOCATION   NAME   LOCATION
   (b) $PRIVATE     00     68E
       DUMPIT       690     7C
       IHOFDISP*    710    60A


       LOCATION  REFERS TO SYMBOL   IN CONTROL SECTION          LOCATION  REFERS TO SYMBOL   IN CONTROL SECTION

         2F8          IHOFDISP        IHOFDISP                    2FC          DUMPIT          DUMPIT

       ENTRY ADDRESS       00
       TOTAL LENGTH       D20

       ****RUN      DOES NOT EXIST BUT HAS BEEN ADDED TO DATA SET



       IEF285I    SYS70170.T104054.SV000.A170P108.R0000013      DELETED
       IEF285I    VOL SER NOS= CLR001.
       IEF285I    SYS1.COBLIB                                    KEPT
       IEF285I    VOL SER NOS= CLR001.
       IEF285I    SYS70170.T104054.SV000.A170P108.R0000014      SYSOUT
       IEF285I    VOL SER NOS= SPLIT6.
       IEF285I    SYS70170.T104054.RV000.A170P108.GODATE        PASSED
       IEF285I    VOL SER NOS= XB331 .
       IEF285I    SYS70170.T104054.RV000.A170P108.LADSET        DELETED
       IEF285I    VOL SER NOS= 231100.
       IEF285I    SYS70170.T104054.RV000.A170P108.S0000016      SYSIN
       IEF285I    VOL SER NOS= SPLIT4.
       IEF285I    SYS70170.T104054.RV000.A170P108.S0000016      DELETED
       IEF285I    VOL SER NOS= SPLIT4.
       IEF285I    SYS70170.T104054.RV000.A170P108.R0000015      DELETED
       IEF285I    VOL SER NOS= HARRYC.
       IEF285I    SYS70170.T104054.RV000.A170P108.GODATA        DELETED
       IEF285I    VOL SER NOS= XB331 .
       IEF373I STEP /LKED    / START 70170.1052
       IEF374I STEP /LKED    / STOP  70170.1053 CPU  00MIN 00.66SEC MAIN 112K LCS    OK
       USERJOB LESTEP          STEP TIME=      00.01     MINUTES
       //EXECSTEP EXEC PGM=*.LESTEP.SYSLMOD
       //SYSABEND DD SYSOUT=A
       //SYSOUT DD SYSOUT=A,DCB=(LRECL=121,BLKSIZE=121)
       //INOUT DD DSNAME=EMPYTD,DISP=(OLD,KEEP),VOLUME=SER=HARRYC,UNIT=2311
       //SYSIN DD *
       IEF236I ALLOC. FOR A170P108 GO
       IEF237I 190    ALLOCATED TO PGM=*.DD
       IEF237I 337    ALLOCATED TO SYSABEND
       IEF237I 333    ALLOCATED TO SYSOUT
       IEF237I 192    ALLOCATED TO INOUT
       IEF237I 335    ALLOCATED TO SYSIN
```

```
JOB A170P108        STEP GU              TIME 105341    DATE 70170

COMPLETION CODE       USER = 0256

PSW AT ENTRY TO ABEND   FFF5000D 7004999A

TCB  01C778  RBP  0001C830  PIE  00000000   DEB 0001D1F4  TIO 0001D4F8  CMP  80000100  TRN 00000000
             MSS  0201F4C0  PK-FLG F0850409  FLG 0001181B  LLS 0001E730  JLB  00000000  JPQ 0001E518
             FSA  01070780  TCB  00000000   TME 00000000  JST 0001C778  NTC  00000000  DTC 0001E188
             LTC  00000000  IQE  00000000   ECB 0001DC70  STA 00000000  D-PQE 0001F918 SQS 0001BD08
             NSTAE 00000000 TCT  0001D138   USER 00000000


ACTIVE RBS

PRB  01E170  RESV  00000000  APSW  00000000  WC-SZ-STAB 00040082  FL-CDE 0001F170  PSW FFF5000D 7004999A
             Q/TTR 00000000  WT-LNK 0001C778

SVRB 01C6C0  TAB-LN 001803C8  APSW  F2F0F1C3  WC-SZ-STAB 0012D002  TQN   00000000  PSW 00040033 50006866
             Q/TTR 00004D11  WT-LNK 0001E170
             RG 0-7   00000218  80000100  000496BE  70049982  330492E0  50049938  000493F0  0006FAD8
             RG 8-15  00070618  00049960  000492E0  000495D8  000499A4  70049906  00049970
             EXTSA    000029BE  00070FA0  2000FFFF  00070DF8  FF030000  0001C73C  0001C744  E2E8E2C9
                      C5C1F0F1  C9C5C178  C1C2C5D5  C4000901


SVRB 01C830  TAB-LN 00480360  APSW  F1F0F5C1  WC-SZ-STAB 0012D002  TQN   00000000  PSW FF040001 4007E13C
             Q/TTR 00004F13  WT-LNK 0001C6C0
             RG 0-7   00000000  0001C720  80006860  000089F4  0001C778  0001C6C0  0001F170  00000000
             RG 8-15  0001C778  400067D2  0001C778  00070FA0  300D528   0001C744  40007BDA  00000000
             EXTSA    00510700  000018A1  901ED00C  05801841  58300010  5833000C  41000020  45108012
                      0A0A5820  401C1861  D71F6000  60005850


LOAD LIST

             NE 0001F4E0  RSP-CDE 0201E518     NE 0001F538  RSP-CDE 01020380     NE 0001F540  RSP-CDE 01020290
             NE 0001D7E8  RSP-CDE 01020250     NE 0001DCD0  RSP-CDE 01020380     NE 0001E4E0  RSP-CDE 01020220
             NE 0001D7F0  RSP-CDE 010203B0     NE 0001D7F8  RSP-CDE 01020320     NE 0001DAB0  RSP-CDE 01020480
             NE 0001E268  RSP-CDE 010203E0     NE 0001E2E0  RSP-CDE 02020350     NE 0001E538  RSP-CDE 020202F0
             NE 0001E5B0  RSP-CDE 0101D6C0     NE 0001E720  RSP-CDE 0101D6D8     NE 0001E898  RSP-CDE 01010948
             NE 0001F1A0  RSP-CDE 0101DBE0     NE 00000000  RSP-CDE 0101DF30

CDE

  01F170    ATR1 0B   NCDE 000000   ROC-RB 0001E170   NM RUN        USE 01   EPA 0492E0   ATR2 20   XL/MJ 01F160
  01E518    ATR1 31   NCDE 01D6C0   ROC-RB 00000000   NM IGG0A05A   USE 02   EPA 06E180   ATR2 28   XL/MJ 01F4D0
  020380    ATR1 B8   NCDE 020380   ROC-RB 00000000   NM IGG019CD   USE 08   EPA 07DE80   ATR2 20   XL/MJ 020370
  020290    ATR1 B8   NCDE 0202C0   ROC-RB 00000000   NM IGG019BA   USE 07   EPA 07E480   ATR2 20   XL/MJ 020280
  020250    ATR1 B8   NCDE 020290   ROC-RB 00000000   NM IGG019BB   USE 08   EPA 07E118   ATR2 20   XL/MJ 020240
  020380    ATR1 B8   NCDE 0203B0   ROC-RB 00000000   NM IGG019CD   USE 08   EPA 07E480   ATR2 20   XL/MJ 020370
  020220    ATR1 B0   NCDE 020250   ROC-RB 00000000   NM IGG019A1   USE 04   EPA 07E098   ATR2 20   XL/MJ 020210
  0203B0    ATR1 B0   NCDE 0203E0   ROC-RB 00000000   NM IGG019AR   USE 04   EPA 07E690   ATR2 20   XL/MJ 0203A0
  020320    ATR1 B0   NCDE 020350   ROC-RB 00000000   NM IGG019CH   USE 03   EPA 07E350   ATR2 20   XL/MJ 020310
  020480    ATR1 B0   NCDE 020480   ROC-RB 00000000   NM IGG019AA   USE 03   EPA 07E8E0   ATR2 20   XL/MJ 020470
  0203E0    ATR1 B0   NCDE 020420   ROC-RB 00000000   NM IGG019AQ   USE 03   EPA 07E800   ATR2 20   XL/MJ 0203D0
  020350    ATR1 B0   NCDE 020380   ROC-RB 00000000   NM IGG019CC   USE 04   EPA 07E3C0   ATR2 20   XL/MJ 020340
  0202F0    ATR1 B0   NCDE 020320   ROC-RB 00000000   NM IGG019CI   USE 04   EPA 07E268   ATR2 20   XL/MJ 0202E0
  01D6C0    ATR1 30   NCDE 01D6D8   ROC-RB 00000000   NM IGG019C3   USE 01   EPA 06EA20   ATR2 20   XL/MJ 01D5F0
  01D6D8    ATR1 30   NCDE 010948   ROC-RB 00000000   NM IGG019CG   USE 01   EPA 06E868   ATR2 20   XL/MJ 01D788
  01D948    ATR1 30   NCDE 01DBE0   ROC-RB 00000000   NM IGG019AE   USE 01   EPA 06EC60   ATR2 20   XL/MJ 01D9F0
  01DBE0    ATR1 30   NCDE 01DF30   ROC-RB 00000000   NM IGG019AW   USE 01   EPA 070820   ATR2 20   XL/MJ 01DBD0
  01DF30    ATR1 30   NCDE 01F170   ROC-RB 00000000   NM IGG019AF   USE 01   EPA 06EDC8   ATR2 20   XL/MJ 01DCC0

XL                                       LN         ADR         LN        ADR         LN        ADR

  01F160    SZ 00000010   NO 00000001   80000020   000492E0
  01F400    SZ 00000010   NO 00000001   80000680   0006E180
  020370    SZ 00000010   NO 00000001   80000210   0007E480
  020280    SZ 00000010   NO 00000001   80000180   0007DE80
  020240    SZ 00000010   NO 00000001   80000058   0007E118
  020370    SZ 00000010   NO 00000001   80000210   0007E480
  020210    SZ 00000010   NO 00000001   80000080   0007E098
  0203A0    SZ 00000010   NO 00000001   80000090   0007E690
  020310    SZ 00000010   NO 00000001   80000070   0007E350
  020470    SZ 00000010   NO 00000001   80000068   0007E8E0
  0203D0    SZ 00000010   NO 00000001   80000078   0007E800
  020340    SZ 00000010   NO 00000001   800000C0   0007E3C0
  0202E0    SZ 00000010   NO 00000001   800000E8   0007E268
  01D5F0    SZ 00000010   NO 00000001   80000148   0006EA20
  01D788    SZ 00000010   NO 00000001   800000F8   0006E868
  01D9F0    SZ 00000010   NO 00000001   80000168   0006EC60
  01DBD0    SZ 00000010   NO 00000001   800000C0   00070820
  01DCC0    SZ 00000010   NO 00000001   80000238   0006EDC8


DEB

  01D1C0                                              0000109E 0000109E 0000109E 0000109E  *.....................*
  01D1E0   0000109E 00000000 01000016 00002BE0        0E000000 0001C778 0401CAE4 88000000  *.............G.....U..*
  01D200   8F000000 01000000 18000000 FF070FA0        0401D100 10002284 000000AF 00000083  *..............J.......*
  01D220   00130064 00010001 C2C2C2C1 C3C40000        00000000 00000000 00000000 A01307FC  *........BBBACD........*


DEB

  01CAC0   0000109E 0000109E 0000109E 0000109E        0000109E 00000000 00000210 00019EE0  *.......G...Q.........*
  01CAE0   0E000000 0301C778 0401D82C 88000000        0F000000 01000000 18000000 FF070480  *.......G..............*
  01C800   0401CAC0 18002184 0000006E 00130073        00120064 00010001 C1D9C1C9 C3C40000  *..................ARAICD..*
  01C820   00000000 00000000 00000000 F0000000                                             *............0......0205A......*
```

```
DEB

01D800                    0007E350 0000109E    0000109E 0007E268 0000109E 00000000    *...........T............S.........*
01D820    00000213 00010AE0 0E000000 0501C778    0401CF8C F8000000 00000000 01FFFFFF    *...............G......8...........*
01D840    18000000 FF049388 0401D808 58002204    0000005A 000A005A 000A0001 00010001    *.......................Q..........*
01D860    C1D8C1C1 C3C8C3C9 C3C30000 00000000    00000000 C001C9FC                       *AQAACHCICC..............I.........*


DEB

01CF60                    00070820 0006E868    0000109E 0007E268 0006EA20 00000000    *...........~.............S.........*
01CF80    05000003 00010AE0 0E000000 0701C778    04000000 68000000 04003000 01FFFFFF    *...............G..................*
01CFA0    18000000 FF049320 0401CF68 18001A28    00000000 00010001 0000000A 00010001    *..................................*
01CFC0    C1C6C1E6 C1C5C3C7 C3F3C3C9 C3C30000    00000000 00000024                       *AFAWAECGC3CICC...........X....    *


TIOT   JOB  A170P108    STEP GO
       DD              14040100   PGM=*.DD      009A0800      800019A8
       DD              14040100   SYSABEND      00990A00      80002284
       DD              14040100   SYSOUT        0098D000      80002184
       DD              14040100   INOUT         009A1400      80001A28
       DD              14040100   SYSIN         0098D400      80002204


MSS              ************ SPQE ************    **************** DQE ****************    ******* FQE ********
                 FLGS   NSPQE   SPID    DQE       BLK      FQE      LN       NDQE          NFQE          LN

     01F4C0      00    01F4C8   251    01F090    00049000 00049000 00001000 00000000       00000000      000002E0
     01F4C8      80    01F938   000    01F670
     01F670      60    000000   000    01F6A8    00070000 00070000 00000800 0001E100       00000000      000002A0
                                                 0006F000 0006F000 00001000 00000000       00000000      00000698
     01F938      40    000000   252    01F7F8    00070800 000708E0 00000800 0001D8F8       00070800      00000060
                                                                                           00000000      00000020
                                                 0006E800 0006E800 00000800 0001F3C8       00000000      00000220
                                                 0006E000 0006E000 00000800 00000000       00000000      00000180


D-PQE  0001F918    FIRST 0001E2E8    LAST 0001E2E8
PQE  01E2E8    FFB 0004A000    LFB 0004A000    NPQ 00000000    PPQ 00000000
               TCB 0001E188    RSI 00028000    RAD 00049000    FLG 0000

FBQE 04A000    NFB 0001E2E8    PFB 0001E2E8    SZ 00024000


QCB TRACE

MAJ 01F1A8   NMAJ 0001E500   PMAJ 00012048   FMIN 0001F188   NM  SYSDSN

MIN 01F188   FQEL 0001F6B8   PMIN 0001F1A8   NMIN 0001DEA0   NM FF  DATK

             NQEL 00000000   PQEL 0001F188   TCB  0001E188   SVRB 0001C798

MIN 01DEA0   FQEL 0001F688   PMIN 0001F188   NMIN 0001DD30   NM FF  SYS1.COBLIB

             NQEL 00000000   PQEL 8001DEA0   TCB  0001E188   SVRB 0001C798

MIN 01DD30   FQEL 0001E588   PMIN 0001DEA0   NMIN 00000000   NM FF  SYS1.MACLIB

             NQEL 00000000   PQEL 8001DD30   TCB  0001E188   SVRB 0001C798

MAJ 01E500   NMAJ 00000000   PMAJ 0001F1A8   FMIN 0001E4E8   NM  SYSIEA01

MIN 01E4E8   FQEL 0001E540   PMIN 0001E500   NMIN 00000000   NM F0  IEA

             NQEL 00000000   PQEL 0001E4E8   TCB  0001C778   SVRB 0001C570
```

```
SAVE AREA TRACE

RUN     WAS ENTERED VIA LINK

SA   070780  WD1 00000000   HSA 00000000   LSA 000493F8   RET 000104AE   EPA 010492E0   R0  FFFFFF2E
             R1  000707F8    R2  0001DC68    R3  5001DC7C    R4  0001DFA0    R5  0001E1B8    R6  0001D4F0
             R7  0001F070    R8  0001DC50    R9  00000000    R10 00000090    R11 00000000    R12 6007EC9A

RUN     WAS ENTERED VIA CALL        AT EP DUMPIT

SA   0493F8  WD1 18445850   HSA 00070780   LSA 00084160   RET 70049906   EPA 00049970   R0  00000218
             R1  00049900    R2  0004968E    R3  5001DC7C    R4  330492E0    R5  50049938    R6  000493F0
             R7  0006FAD8    R8  00070618    R9  00049960    R10 000492E0    R11 000492E0    R12 000495D8
```

(a)

```
INTERRUPT AT 04999A


PROCEEDING BACK VIA REG 13

SA   0499A4  WD1 D20784A4   HSA 000493F8   LSA 000CD203   RET C0248492   EPA D201C02A   R0  84CD58F0
             R1  00000000    R2  07000000    R3  0000000C    R4  07FE5820    R5  100C1881    R6  41100001
             R7  0A0B5000    R8  84DA5010    R9  85021818    R10 58302000    R11 88300008    R12 1B0345A0

RUN     WAS ENTERED VIA CALL        AT EP DUMPIT

SA   0493F8  WD1 18445850   HSA 00070780   LSA 00084160   RET 70049906   EPA 00049970   R0  00000218
             R1  00049900    R2  0004968E    R3  5001DC7C    R4  330492E0    R5  50049938    R6  000493F0
             R7  0006FAD8    R8  00070618    R9  00049960    R10 000492E0    R11 000492E0    R12 000495D8
```

```
NUCLEUS

000000   00000000 00000000 00000000 00000000     000089F4 00000000 FF060080 80000000   *....................4..............*
000020   FF040001 4000E914 FFF50004 C0059DE4     0000FF00 00000000 FE040336 90000F76   *..... .Z..5......U..............*
000040   000702F0 50000000 00001388 000089F4     02720545 0000CF0C 00040000 0000A200   *...0...............4..N.........*
000060   00040000 0000A798 00040000 0000A2E4     00000000 00003F48 00040000 0000A282   *..........U...................*
000080   0000D8D0 00000000 00000000 00000000     00000000 00000000 00000000 00000000   *...............................*
0000A0   00000000 00000000 00000000 00000000     00000000 00000000 00000000 00000000   *...............................*
         LINES 0000C0-000140 SAME AS ABOVE
```

(b)

⋮

```
REGS AT ENTRY TO ABEND

    FLTR 0-6     D46E3B8C5370170F     0000000020000000          0000000000000000     0001DC0800000088

    REGS 0-7     00000218   80000100   0004968E   70049982      330492E0   50049938   000493F0   0006FAD8
    REGS 8-15    00070618   00049960   000492E0   000492E0      000495D8   000499A4   70049906   00049970
```

(c)

```
LOAD MODULE   SALARYL

0492E0   070090EC D00C185D 05F0989F F00607FF     00049960 000492E0 000492E0 000495D8   *.........0..0...............Q*
049300   000493F8 0004965A 00049912 96121034     07FEFFFF FFFFD9D7 C4F04040 40400207   *....8...............RPD0   K.*
049320   00000000 14000000 00000001 00008082     00210E29 0206F698 00004000 00000001   *................6....... ...*
049340   46049700 90000000 00544848 C001CF8C     1606EC60 0006EDC8 10000001 00490480   *.......................H.........*
049360   30037040 00070668 0006FB50 0006FAD8     00000078 00000001 00000000 0007E3C0   *...  .........Q.............T.*
049380   00000000 98481000 00000000 20000000     005A000A 0000B08A 00281C7E 020705C0   *................................*
0493A0   00504000 00000001 460496DC 90000000     00684800 C001D82C 1207E8E0 0007E800   *..  ..............Q...Y...Y.*
```

```
0493C0   08000001 10010050 00005000 00070568     00070668 00070618 00000050 00000001     *................................*
0493E0   00000000 0007E3C0 00000000 B23258F0     00003744 0FF0805A 18445850 00070780     *......T.........O.......O........*
049400   00084160 70049906 00049970 00000218     00049900 000496BE 5001DC7C 330492E0     *................................*
049420   50049938 000493F0 0006FAD8 00070618     00049960 000492E0 000492E0 000495D8     *........O...Q................Q*.*
049440   20000048 4780B21C 95F92000 0004965A     00000AE8 E3C46009 00000078 C4000000     *.......9........YTD.R....D...*
049460   00000000 00000000 00090000 00000000     00400024 0DE6C5C5 D2D3E860 D9C5C3D6     *.............WEEKLY.RECO*
049480   D9C40000 00000000 00000000 00000000     00000040 C3E34DD5 E4D4C2C5 D94004A23     *RD..............CT NUMBER ..*
0494A0   4510B368 0A062AD0 00062ACC 00210000     C9C5C6C1 C3E3D840 4009C5D7 D3E840D7     *................IEFACTQ REPLY P*
0494C0   09D6D1C5 C3E34DD5 E4D4C2C5 D9100A23     41108546 41000001 0A011811 50108546     *ROJECT NUMBER...............*
0494E0   18184120 85444 7F0 82BE5818 00000000     00000000 000497DE 0004968E 01000000     *................................*
049500   900497CC 000499F0 00000001 000497E0     000496BE 5001DC7C 330492E0 50049938     *................................*
049520   000493F0 0006FAD8 000705C8 00049960     000492E0 000492E0 000495D8 000497E0     *.....O...Q...H...........Q...*
049540   000499F0 00000001 8F070480 0004968E     00010000 000497DE 00000000 00000000     *...O...........................*
049560   00000000 00000000 00000000 00000000     00000000 00000000 00000000 8A000603     *................................*
049580   00000108 02080002 00000000 4200000C     00000000 0004800C 300B0080 00200108     *................................*
0495A0   02080002 A80D0000 00000000 00000000     00000000 00000000 00000000 0006FAD8     *................................Q*
0495C0   00070618 000493F0 80049388 00000000     00000000 00000000 000499F0 00049970     *...O...........O....*
0495E0   000496BE 000496E2 0004974A 000497E6     00049900 000496DC 00049700 00049706     *......S......W..................*
049600   00049724 00049730 00049774 000497CC     0004984A 0004968C 0004968E 00049 7AA     *................................*
049620   00049780 00049828 0004982E 00049320     00049388 330492E0 00230000 C9C5D8F9     *................................IEQ9*
049640   F9F9C940 D5D640C4 C440C3C1 D9C440C6     D6D94004 8C01000C 500C5810 C0545010     *991 NO DO CARD FOR ........*
049660   D1D09284 D1D04110 D1D00A13 5810C054     5820C03C 91101030 0712D21A D1A0C060     *..J...J...........K.J...*
049680   D207D1BB 10284110 D1A00A23 5810C058     50100D1D 9280D1D0 4110D1D0 0A135810     *K.J...................J...J.*
0496A0   C0585820 C0409110 10300712 D21AD1A0     C060D207 D1B81028 4110D1A0 0A235810     *.....K.J..K.J.......J...*
0496C0   C058D202 1021C01D 58F01030 05EF5010     D1C85880 D1C85810 C00C07F1 5810C00C     *..K....O...JH..JH....1....*
0496E0   07F15810 C054D202 1021C021 58F01030     05EF5010 D1C45870 D1C45810 C02407F1     *.1...K....O....JD..JD....1*
049700   5810C018 07F1F274 D1907028 F274D198     8000F922 D19DD19D 58F0C028 077F5810     *.....12.J...2.J...9.J.O....*
049720   C01007F1 5810C054 58F01030 45E0F004     58F0C000 051F0001 00000078 0D0001C4     *...1.......O...O.............D*
049740   0000FFFF 5810C00C 07F1F277 D1987020     F874D190 6000F B44 D193D198 F277D198     *............12.J..8.J.....J.J.2.J.*
049760   702EF944 D193D19B 58F0C030 07AF5810     C01407F1 F277D198 702EFC61 0199C07B     *..9.J.J...O......12.J....J...*
049780   F277D190 7020FC72 D190C07D FA65D199     D192F970 D198C07F 58F0C044 074FFA61     *2.J..........r....9.J.O....*
0497A0   0199C080 58F0C048 07FFF861 0199C080     F1750198 D198F374 7020D198 96F07027     *J......O....8.J........J.9.O.*
0497C0   5810C054 58F01030 45E0F004 58F0C000     051F0001 00000078 0D0001C4 0000FFFF     *.....O...O....D....*
0497E0   5810C008 07F1F277 01987020 F874D190     6000FB44 D193D198 FC61D191 C07BF277     *.....12.J..8.........J.J.2.*
049800   D1987020 FC72D198 C07DFA65 D191D19A     F9700190 C07F58F0 C04C074F FA61D191     *.J.........O.L...J.*
049820   C08058F0 C05007FF FB61D191 C080F175     01900190 F3747020 D19396F0 70275810     *...O.P...J.....3...O....*
049840   C05458F0 103045E0 F00458F0 C000051F     00010000 00780D00 01C40000 FFFF5810     *...O....O...O...D....*
049860   C00807F1 5810C054 5820102C 910F200C     055047E0 50105820 104C4820 10525020     *...1........J...........*
049880   104C5810 C0545010 D1D09290 D1D04110     D1D00A14 5820C054 58102014 96012017     *.....J...J...J.........*
0498A0   48401004 4C401006 41004008 41101000     0A0A5810 C0585820 102C910F 200C0550     *.....................P*
0498C0   47E05010 5820104C 4B201052 5020104C     5810C058 5010D1D0 92900D10 4110D1D0     *.....L...L....J........J*
0498E0   0A145820 C0585810 20149601 20174840     10044C40 10064100 40084110 10000A0A     *................*
049900   58F0C004 05EF5800 0004 98EC D00C1BFF     07FE50D0 50085050 00000450E0 D0549120     *.O..............*
049920   D0480719 9620D048 41600004 4110C008     4170C060 06700550 58401000 1E485040     *.O..............*
049940   10008716 50004180 D1C44170 00030510     58008000 1E085000 80004180 80040671     *.........JD.......P.....*
049960   5860D1CC 5870D1C4 5880D1C8 07FE50F0     47F0F00C 06C4E4D4 D7C9E300 90ECD00C     *.J..JD..JH..O..J..JD..JH...O.00..DUMPIT.....*
049980   053050D0 30264100 30220700 47F03012     80000100 5810300E 0A0D98EC D00C92FF     *.......0.....................*
0499A0   D00C07FE D207B4A4 000493F8 000CD203     C0248492 D201C02A 84CD58F0 00000000     *....K....8..K....K....O....*
0499C0   07000000 0000D00C 07FE5820 100C1881     41100001 0A0B5000 84DA5010 85021818     *................*
0499E0   58302000 88300008 180345A0 8292D209     90ECD108 D201D158 10004580 F1DA4700     *...........K..J.K.J...1...*
049A00   000447F0 F01E416D 007C5870 F5C09400     D1049180 10004111 00024710 F3EE9400     *...O...|...5..J.........3...*
049A20   D1059540 10004770 F0781BEE 43E10001     1AE141EE 00039101 10014710 F0524 1EE     *.J........O..............O...*
049A40   000150ED 01149140 D0484780 F1D41855     43510001 41410002 18750670 4450F1A4     *........IM...........1.*
049A60   9601D104 47F0F01C D200D060 10049640     D0604380 00604480 F5D84441 00069110     *..J..01.K.........5Q......*
049A80   10004710 F09A5844 00004A41 0008910F     10004740 F3309120 10004710 F0C4D203     *....O..........  3....DK.*
```

```
(a)  06F680                                               00000000 00020480  *0       ....  ......0............
     06F6A0  D9D6C8D9 40C6D9C5 C440C14B 40404040  40404040 40404040 40404040 40404040  *ROHR FRED A.
     06F6C0  F0F0F0F0 F4F9F4F6 F0F1F0F8 F0404040  40F1F2F8 F8F54040 40404040 40404040  *0000494601080    12885
     06F6E0  40404040 40404040 40404040 40404040  40404040 40404040 40404040 40404040  *
     06F700  40404040 40404040 40404040 40404040  40404040 40404040 D9D6E2C5 D5C2C5D9  *                            ROSENBER
     06F720  C740D9D6 C2C5D9E3 40D44B40 40404040  40404040 40404040 F0F0F0F0 F5F0F2F2  *G ROBERT M.                 00005022
                                        .
                                        :
     06FF80  40404040 40404040 D8F4C9D5 D540D7C1  E3D9C9C3 D240E34B 40404040 40404040  *        QUINN PATRICK T.
     06FFA0  40404040 40404040 F0F0F0F0 F5F6F1F4  F0F1F0F7 F8404040 40F1F4F6 F1F54040  *        0000561401078    14615
     06FFC0  40404040 40404040 40404040 40404040  40404040 40404040 40404040 40404040  *
              LINE 06FFE0 SAME AS ABOVE


     SP 000

(b)  0702A0  410702A0 48000650 00000000 7F01BD58  000702F0 0C000000 400702D0 00070FA0  *.....................0.... .......
     0702C0  00000000 00000000 00000000 82000F02  310702C8 40000005 080702D0 00000660  *.....................  ..........

     SP 252

     070940  06500000 007D0000 40F0F6C5 C6F2F040  4040F9F1 F4F0F2F0 F3C440F4 F7C5F0F8  *........ 06EF20   91402030 47E08
     070960  F0F9F640 F1F8F0F3 F1F8F1F2 40F4F1F1  F1F0F0F0 F0404040 40F0C1F3 F7F4F7C6  *096 18031812 41110000    0A3747F


     LOAD MODULE  IGG019CD

(c)  07E480  909AD040 9120203C 4710F15C 58A0200C  5810202C 48673006 9101203C 4780F024  *..... .......1.........0.
     07E4A0  4860205A 12664740 F07A1844 4340A007  18044340 20041804 91882024 47E0F048  *. .....0....00.........0.
     07E4C0  91403000 4710F04E 1F0647F0 F06A5893  00184199 00004899 000E1299 4740F07A  *.  .....0....00.........0.
     07E4E0  19694740 F0681896 1E094900 201247C0  F17E4900 A00447C0 F08C4810 F08A4100  *.... 0.........1.....0...0..
     07E500  00808900 00181610 0A002000 41202005  42730004 183F184E 185B186C 187D58F0  *........................0
     07E520  001058F0 F02005EF 58903208 1E091880  58F00010 58F0F01C 05EF12FF 478030C8  *...00........00....00.....H
     07E540  96202037 47F03122 95002000 47703122  91041008 47E03122 18991BAA 18BB1BCC  *.....0..................
     07E560  43920000 89900004 43A91029 4389102D  43C20006 19C44740 3100198C 47803122  *..........B.......
     07E580  1808188A 58902007 43A09003 18A846A0  311289A0 00101E0A 58F00010 58F0F01C  *.....3............0....00.
     07E5A0  05FF18F3 41900005 18295880 20305830  204458A0 200C18D7 18774373 000418B5  *....3.........P........
     07E5C0  18C618E4 48673006 9101203C 4780F154  4860205A 9120203C 4780F170 9620203C  *.F.U.........1........1...
     07E5E0  96013014 5843000C 92404000 47F0F200  58A0200C D2012012 A0049200 200C1846  *........ .02....K........
     07E600  4850A00A 1C443E40 00094340 A0061E54  43402004 1F544840 20121845 40402012  *.........................
     07E620  02073028 20051844 4340200C 41440001  42402000 91403000 4710F1C4 4243002F  *K.............1D...
     07E640  47F0F1F8 43402040 18531A54 43402041  89400003 1A540204 50002008 4B50F20C  *.018. ......K.....2.
     07E660  91802034 4780F1EC 40605000 1B444340  20101864 40650008 41430008 18140A00  *.....1. .......
     07E680  989AD040 07FE0000 00010000 00020700                                       *.... .............


     END OF DUMP
(d)
     ADAMS JAMES E.             0000738401002    19231
     ALFRED THOMAS D.           0000590601004    15385
```

```
COMPLETION CODE - SYSTEM=000  USER=0256
IEF285I   SYS70170.T104054.RV000.USERJOB  .GODATE        PASSED
IEF285I     VOL SER NOS= XB331 .
IEF285I   SYS70170.T104054.SV000.USERJOB  .R0000017      SYSOUT
IEF285I     VOL SER NOS= CLR001.
IEF285I   SYS70170.T104054.SV000.USERJOB  .R0000018      SYSOUT
IEF285I     VOL SER NOS= SPLIT5.
IEF285I   EMPYTD                                         KEPT
IEF285I     VOL SER NOS= HARRYC.
IEF285I   SYS70170.T104054.RV000.USERJOB  .S0000019      SYSIN
IEF285I     VOL SER NOS= SPLIT3.
IEF285I   SYS70170.T104054.RV000.USERJOB  .S0000019      DELETED
IEF285I     VOL SER NOS= SPLIT3.
IEF373I STEP /GO      / START 70170.1053
IEF374I STEP /GO      / STOP  70170.1054 CPU  00MIN 04.27SEC MAIN  52K LCS    OK
USERJOB     GO       STEP TIME=    00.07      MINUTES
IEF285I   SYS70170.T104054.RV000.USERJOB  .GODATE        DELETED
IEF285I     VOL SER NOS= XB331 .
IEF375I JOB /USERJOB / START 70170.1050
IEF376I JOB /USERJOB / STOP  70170.1054 CPU  00MIN 10.25SEC
USERJOB  /7863358101 / 10.90 / 10.90 / 00.17  / 70.170
```

LINK MACHINE LISTING

The following table of contents will help the reader identify the various components of this machine listing:

```
   LOC   OBJECT CODE      ADDR1 ADDR2  STMT   SOURCE STATEMENT

000000                                    1 CALLIT CSECT
                                          2        SAVE   (14,12),,*
000000  47F0 F00C            0000C        3+       B      12(0,15) BRANCH AROUND ID
000004  06                                4+       DC     AL1(6)
000005  C3C1D3D3C9E3                      5+       DC     CL6'CALLIT' IDENTIFIER
00000B  00
00000C  90EC D00C            0000C        6+       STM    14,12,12(13) SAVE REGISTERS
000010  0530                              7        BALR   3,0
000012                                    8        USING  *,3
000012  5000 3086            00098        9        ST     13,SAVE+4
000016  41D0 3082            00094       10        LA     13,SAVE
                                         11        OPEN   (SNAP,(OUTPUT))
00001A  0700                             12+       CNOP   0,4
00001C  4510 3012           00024        13+       BAL    1,*+8 LOAD REG1 W/LIST ADDR.
000020  8F                               14+       DC     AL1(143) OPTION BYTE
000021  00000C                           15+       DC     AL3(SNAP) DCB ADDRESS
000024  0A13                             16+       SVC    19 ISSUE OPEN SVC
                                         17 NTEST  SNAP   DCB=SNAP,ID=56,SDATA=ALL,PDATA=ALL
000026  0700                             18+       CNOP   0,4
000028  4510 302A           0003C        19+NTEST  BAL    1,IHB0003 BRANCH AROUND PARAM LIST
00002C  38                               20+       DC     AL1(56) ID NUMBER
00002D  00                               21+       DC     AL1(0)
00002E  BB                               22+       DC     AL1(187) OPTION FLAGS
00002F  BE                               23+       DC     AL1(190) OPTION FLAGS
000030  0000000C                         24+       DC     A(SNAP) DCB ADDRESS
000034  00000000                         25+       DC     A(0) TCB ADDRESS
000038  00000000                         26+       DC     A(0) ADDRESS OF SNAP-SHOT LIST
00003C                                   27+IHB0003 DS    0H
00003C  0A33                             28+       SVC    51
                                         29        CLOSE  (SNAP)
00003E  0700                             30+       CNOP   0,4
000040  4510 3036           00048        31+       BAL    1,*+8 BRANCH AROUND LIST
000044  80                               32+       DC     AL1(128) OPTION BYTE
000045  00000C                           33+       DC     AL3(SNAP) DCB ADDRESS
000048  0A14                             34+       SVC    20 ISSUE CLOSE SVC
                                         35        LINK   EP=DUMSLM
00004A  0700                             36+       CNOP   0,4
00004C  45F0 304F           00060        37+       BAL    15,*+20 LOAD SUP.PARAMLIST ADR
000050  00000058                         38+       DC     A(*+8) ADDR OF EP PARAMETER
000054  00000000                         39+       DC     A(0) DCB ADDRESS PARAMETER        LC0A
000058  C4E4D4E2D3D44040                 40+       DC     CL9'DUMSLM' EP PARAMETER
000060  0A06                             41+       SVC    6 ISSUE LINK SVC
                                         42        OPEN   (SNAP,(OUTPUT))
000062  0700                             43+       CNOP   0,4
000064  4510 305A           0006C        44+       BAL    1,*+8 LOAD REG1 W/LIST ADDR.
000068  8F                               45+       DC     AL1(143) OPTION BYTE
000069  00000C                           46+       DC     AL3(SNAP) DCB ADDRESS
00006C  0A13                             47+       SVC    19 ISSUE OPEN SVC
                                         48        SNAP   DCB=SNAP,ID=56,SDATA=ALL,PDATA=ALL
00006E  0700                             49+       CNOP   0,4
000070  4510 3072           000B4        50+       BAL    1,IHB0008 BRANCH AROUND PARAM LIST
000074  38                               51+       DC     AL1(56) ID NUMBER
000075  00                               52+       DC     AL1(0)
000076  BB                               53+       DC     AL1(187) OPTION FLAGS
000077  BE                               54+       DC     AL1(190) OPTION FLAGS
000078  0000000C                         55+       DC     A(SNAP) DCB ADDRESS
00007C  00000000                         56+       DC     A(0) TCB ADDRESS
000080  00000000                         57+       DC     A(0) ADDRESS OF SNAP-SHOT LIST
000084                                   58+IHB0008 DS    0H
000084  0A33                             59+       SVC    51
000086  58D0 3086           00098        60 FINIS  L      13,SAVE+4
                                         61 FINIS  RETURN (14,12),T
00008A                                   62+FINIS  DS     0H
00008A  98EC D00C           0000C        63+       LM     14,12,12(13) RESTORE THE REGISTERS
00008E  92FF D000      0000C             64+       MVI    12(13),X'FF' SET RETURN INDICATION
000092  07FE                             65+       BR     14 RETURN
000094                                   66 SAVE   DS     18F
000094                                   67 SNAP   DCB    DSORG=PS,RECFM=VBA,MACRF=W,BLKSIZE=1632,LRECL=125,    X
                                                          DDNAME=SNAPT

                                         69+*                           DATA CONTROL BLOCK
                                         70+*
0000DC                                   71+       ORG    *-0 TO ELIMINATE UNUSED SPACE
0000DC                                   72+SNAP   DS     OF ORIGIN ON WORD BOUNDRY
0000DC                                   73+       ORG    *+0 TO ORIGIN GENERATION

                                         75+*                           DIRECT ACCESS DEVICE INTERFACE

0000DC  0000000000000000                 77+       DC     BL16'0' FDAD,DVTBL
0000EC  00000000                         78+       DC     A(0) KEYLE,DEVT,TRBAL

                                         80+*                           COMMON ACCESS METHOD INTERFACE

0000F0  00                               82+       DC     AL1(0) BUFNO
0000F1  000001                           83+       DC     AL3(1) BUFCB
0000F4  0000                             84+       DC     AL2(0) BUFL
0000F6  4000                             85+       DC     BL2'0100000000000000' DSORG
0000F8  00000001                         86+       DC     A(1) IOBAD

                                         88+*                           FOUNDATION EXTENSION

0000FC  00                               90+       DC     BL1'00000000' BFTEK,BFALN,HIARCHY
0000FD  000001                           91+       DC     AL3(1) EODAD
000100  54                               92+       DC     BL1'01010100' RECFM
000101  000000                           93+       DC     AL3(0) EXLST
```

```
                                    95+*                                   FOUNDATION BLOCK

000104 F2D5C1D7E3404040            97+        DC      CL8'SNAPT' DDNAME
00010C 02                          98+        DC      BL1'00000010' OFLGS
00010D 00                          99+        DC      BL1'00000000' IFLG
00010E 0020                       100+        DC      BL2'0000000000100000' MACR

                                   102+*                                 BSAM-BPAM-QSAM INTERFACE

000110 00                         104+        DC      BL1'00000000' RER1
000111 000001                     105+        DC      AL3(1) CHECK, GERR, PERR
000114 00000001                   106+        DC      A(1) SYNAD
000118 0000                       107+        DC      H'0' CIND1, CIND2
00011A 0660                       108+        DC      AL2(1632) BLKSIZE
00011C 00000000                   109+        DC      F'0' WCPO, WCPL, OFFSR, OFFSW
000120 00000001                   110+        DC      A(1) IOBA
000124 00                         111+        DC      AL1(0) NCP
000125 000001                     112+        DC      AL3(1) EOBR, EOBAD

                                   114+*                                 BSAM-BPAM INTERFACE

000128 00000001                   116+        DC      A(1) EOBW
00012C 0000                       117+        DC      H'0' DIRCT
00012E 007D                       118+        DC      AL2(125) LRECL
000130 00000001                   119+        DC      A(1) CNTRL, NOTE, POINT
                                   120        END
```

```
JOB A293P462        STEP HCGO        TIME 180652   DATE 69293   ID = 056                                      PAGE 0001

PSW AT ENTRY TO SNAP    FFE50033 4003A706

TCB  01BD18   RBP  0001C378   PIE    00000000   DEB  0001C7FC   TIO 0001D918   CMP  00000000   TRN 00000000
              MSS  0201F998   PK-FLG F0010000   FLG  00001B18   LLS 0001EEC0   JLB  0001E6E8   JPQ 0001E5EA
              FSA  01068780   TCB    00000000   TME  00000000   JST 0001BD18   NTC  00000000   NTC 0001CC10
              LTC  00000000   IQE    00000000   ECB  0001D818   STA 00000000   D-PQE 0001FF30  SQS 00018800
              NSTAE 00000000  TCT    0001C048   USER 00000000


ACTIVE RBS

PRB  01F790   RESV 00000000   APSW   00000000   WC-SZ-STAB 00040082   FL-CDE 0001EEC8   PSW FFE50033 4003A706
              Q/TTR 00000000  WT-LNK 0001BD18

SVRB 01C378   TAB-LN 00380360 APSW   F1F0F5C1   WC-SZ-STAB 00120002   TQN    00000000   PSW FF040007 00007200
              Q/TTR 00005113  WT-LNK 0001E790
              RG 0-7  00000030  8003A6F4  0001DB10  4003A6DA  0001CA88  0001CC10  0001D910  0001E2DA
              RG 8-15 0001DAF8  00000000  00000074  00000000  6007EC9A  0003A75C  00011546  00000000
              EXTSA   FF040000  0001C3F4  0003A6F8  E2E8F2C9  C5C1F0F1  00000000  00000000  00000000
                      0012C002  00000000  00000000  00000000


LOAD LIST

     NE 0001EF28   RSP-CDE 0101E5EA      NE 0001F240   RSP-CDE 01020BB0      NE 0001F920   RSP-CDE 01020A90
     NE 00000000   RSP-CDE 01020A50


CDE

     01FFCB   ATR1 0B   NCDE 000000   ROC-RB 0001E790   NM RUN      USE 01   EPA 03A6C8   ATR2 20   XL/MJ 01FF00
     01F5EA   ATR1 31   NCDE 01FFCB   ROC-RB 00000000   NM IGC0A05A USE 01   EPA 06A980   ATR2 28   XL/MJ 01E910
     020BB0   ATR1 BB   NCDE 020BB0   ROC-RB 00000000   NM IGG019CD USE 07   EPA 07E488   ATR2 20   XL/MJ 020B70
     020A90   ATR1 BB   NCDE 020AC0   ROC-RB 00000000   NM IGG019BA USE 06   EPA 07DEA0   ATR2 20   XL/MJ 020A80
     020A50   ATR1 BB   NCDE 020A90   ROC-RB 00000000   NM IGG019BB USE 06   EPA 07E120   ATR2 20   XL/MJ 020A40


XL                                               LN         ADR       LN       ADR       LN       ADR

     01FF00   SZ 00000010   NO 00000001   8000013B  0003A6C8
     01F910   SZ 00000010   NO 00000001   80000680  0006A980
     020B70   SZ 00000010   NO 00000001   80000210  0007E488
     020A80   SZ 00000010   NO 00000001   80000180  0007DE80
     020A40   SZ 00000010   NO 00000001   80000058  0007E120


DEB

01C7C0                                                             00000BF0 00000BF0   *.........................O...O*
01C7E0   00000BF0 00000BF0 00000BF0 00000000   0000020F 00002BE0 0F000000 0301BD18   *....O...O...O...................*
01C800   04000000 88000000 0F000000 01000000   18000000 EF03A7A4 0401C7D8 18002ACC   *..........................GQ....*
01C820   00000065 000F006A 000E0064 00010001   C2C2C2C1 C3C40000 00000000 00000000   *...................BBBACD......*
01C840   00000000 00000000                                                           *...........R8........O...O...O*


TIOT   JOB  A293P462    STEP HCGO
       DD        14140100   JOBLIB      0068E400   80002230
       DD        14040100   PGM=*.DD    0068D000   800022B0
       DD        14040100   SYSABEND    0068BC00   80002B0C
       DD        14040100   SNAPT       0068BE00   80002ACC


MSS           ************ SPQE ************      *************** DQE ***************      ******* FQE ********
              FLGS  NSPQE   SPID   DQE       BLK       FQE       LN       NDQE       NFQE       LN

     01F998   00    01FF70  251    01EC98    0003A000 0003A000 00000800 00000000      00000000   000006C8
     01FF70   80    020F88  000    01EEBA
     01FFBB   60    000000  000    01F228    0006B000 0006B000 00000800 00000000      00000000   00000710
     020F88   40    000000  252    01FF08    0006B800 0006B800 00000800 0001E720      00000000   00000198
                                             0006A800 0006A800 00000800 0001E598      00000000   000001B0
                                             00069800 00069800 00001000 00000000      00000000   00000380

D-PQE 0001FF30   FIRST 0001E880   LAST 0001E880
PQE  01E880   FFB 0003A800   LFB 0003A800   NPQ 00000000   PPQ 00000000
              TCB 0001CC10   RST 00032000   RAD 0003A000   FLG 0000

FBQE 03A800   NFB 0001E880   PFB 0001E880   SZ 0002F000


QCB TRACE

MAJ 01D7F0   NMAJ 0001E5A8   PMAJ 000130DA   FMIN 0001D378   NM  SYSDSN

MIN 01ED98   FQEL 0001FF40   PMIN 0001D338   NMIN 0001F7B8   NM FF  SYS1.MACLIB

             NQEL 00000000   PQEL 8001ED98   TCB  0001CC10   SVRB 0001BE3A

MIN 01F7BB   FQEL 0001F658   PMIN 0001FD98   NMIN 00000000   NM FF  DUMR

             NQEL 00000000   PQEL 0001F7BB   TCB  0001CC10   SVRB 0001BE38

MAJ 01E5A8   NMAJ 00000000   PMAJ 0001D7E0   FMIN 0001DF10   NM  SYSIEA01

MIN 01DF10   FQEL 0001E6D0   PMIN 0001E5A8   NMIN 00000000   NM FQ  0003A7A4

             NQEL 00000000   PQEL 0001DF10   TCB  00018D18   SVRB 0001BAD0
```

```
SAVE AREA TRACE

RUN      WAS ENTERED VIA LINK       AT EP CALLIT

SA   06B7B0  WD1 00000000  HSA 00000000  LSA 00000000  RET 00011546  EPA 0103A6C8  R0  FFFFFF2F
             R1  0006B7F8  R2  00010B10  R3  5001DB24  R4  0001CA88  R5  0001CC10  R6  00010910
             R7  0001E2D8  R8  00010AF8  R9  00000000  R10 00000074  R11 00000000  R12 6007EC9A

INTERRUPT AT 03A706

PROCEEDING BACK VIA REG 13

SA   03A75C  WD1 00000000  HSA 0006B7B0  LSA 00000000  RET 00000000  EPA 00000000  R0  00000000
             R1  00000000  R2  00000000  R3  00000000  R4  00000000  R5  00000000  R6  00000000
             R7  00000000  R8  00000000  R9  00000000  R10 00000000  R11 00000000  R12 00000000

RUN      WAS ENTERED VIA LINK       AT EP CALLIT

SA   06B7B0  WD1 00000000  HSA 00000000  LSA 00000000  RET 00011546  EPA 0103A6C8  R0  FFFFFF2F
             R1  0006B7F8  R2  00010B10  R3  5001DB24  R4  0001CA88  R5  0001CC10  R6  00010910
             R7  0001E2D8  R8  00010AF8  R9  00000000  R10 00000074  R11 00000000  R12 6007EC9A

REGS AT ENTRY TO SNAP

     FLTR 0-6     00674100F080C191      C1F2F9F3D7F4F6F2      0000000000000000      006A100000000000

     REGS 0-7     00000030  8003A6F4  00010B10  4003A6DA      0001CA88  0001CC10  00010910  0001E2D8
     REGS 8-15    00010AF8  00000000  00000074  00000000      6007EC9A  0003A75C  00011546  00000000

LOAD MODULE   SALARYL

03A6C0               47F0F00C 06C3C1D3   D3C9E300 90ECD00C 05305DD0 308641D0   *.........00..CALLIT.........*
03A6E0  30820700 45103012 8F03A7A4 0A130700   4510302A 3800BBBE 0003A7A4 00000000   *...........................*
03A700  00000000 0A330700 45103036 8003A7A4   0A140700 45F0304E 0003A720 00000000   *......................0.....*
03A720  C4E404E2 D3D04040 0A060700 4510305A   8F03A7A4 0A130700 45103072 3800BBBE   *DUMSL  .....................*
03A740  0003A7A4 00000000 00000000 0A335800   308698EC D00C92FF D00C07FE 00000000   *...........................*
03A760  0006B7B0 00000000 00000000 00000000   00000000 00000000 00000000 00000000   *...........................*
03A780  00000000 00000000 00000000 00000000   00000000 00000000 00000000 00000000   *...........................*
03A7A0  00000000 00000100 2D000000 00690000   020082FA 0080E70 00000001 00004000   *...........................*
03A7C0  00000001 04000001 54000000 00540020   0001C7FC 9207DE80 0007E120 08000001   *.....................G.....*
03A7E0  00000660 30040048 41068710 0107F488   0007E488 0000007D 00000001 00000000   *..............U...U........*
```

```
JOB A293P462        STEP HCGO         TIME 180707   DATE 69293   ID = 056                        PAGE 0001

PSW AT ENTRY TO SNAP   FFE50033 4003A60F

TCB  01BD18  RBP  0001C378   PIE   00000000   DEB  0001C4C4   TIO 0001D918   CMP  00000000   TRN 00000000
             MSS  0201F998   PK-FLG E0010000   FLG  0001B1B   LLS 0001EFC0   JLB  0001E6E8   JPQ 0001DF10
             FSA  010687B0   TCB   00000000   TME  00000000   JST 0001BD18   NTC  00000000   OTC 0001CC10
             LTC  00000000   IQE   00000000   ECB  0001DB1B   STA 00000000   D-PQE 0001FF30  SQS 0001B800
             NSTAE 00000000  TCT   0001C048   USER 00000000


ACTIVE RBS

PRB  01F790  RESV  00000000   APSW  00000000   WC-SZ-STAB 00040082   FL-CDE 0001EEC8   PSW FFE50006 4003A72A
             Q/TTR 00000000   WT-LNK 0001BD18

PRB  01F5A0  RESV  00000000   APSW  00000000   WC-SZ-STAB 00040002   FL-CDE 0001E5E8   PSW FFE50033 4003A60E
             Q/TTR 00000000   WT-LNK 0001F790

SVRB 01C378  TAB-LN 00180360  APSW  F1F0F5C1   WC-SZ-STAB 0012D002   TQN  00000000   PSW FF04000F E006A9D4
             Q/TTR 00005113   WT-LNK 0001E5A0
             RG 0-7   00000030   8003A5FC   0001DR10   4003A5E2   0001CABB   0001CC10   0001D910   0001E2D8
             RG 8-15  0001DAF8   00000000   00000074   00000000   6007EC9A   0003A628   00011546   00000000
             EXTSA    FF040000   0001C3F4   0003A600   E2E8E2C9   C5C1F0F1   00000000   00000000   00000000
                      0012C002   00000000   00000000   00000000


LOAD LIST

        NE 0001FF28   RSP-CDE 0101DF10        NE 0001F240   RSP-CDE 01020B80        NE 0001F920   RSP-CDE 01020A90
        NE 00000000   RSP-CDE 01020A50


CDE

        01EFC8        ATR1 0B   NCDE 000000   ROC-RB 0001E790   NM RUN       USE 01   EPA 03A6CB   ATR2 20   XL/MJ 01EF00
        01F5E8        ATR1 0B   NCDE 01EFC8   ROC-RB 0001E5A0   NM DUMSLM    USE 01   EPA 03A5D0   ATR2 20   XL/MJ 01E910
        010F10        ATR1 31   NCDE 01E5E8   ROC-RB 00000000   NM IGC0A05A  USE 01   EPA 06A9R0   ATR2 28   XL/MJ 01F720
        020B80        ATR1 BB   NCDE 020B80   ROC-RB 00000000   NM IGG019CD  USE 07   EPA 07E488   ATR2 20   XL/MJ 020B70
        020A90        ATR1 BB   NCDE 020AC0   ROC-RB 00000000   NM IGG019BA  USE 06   EPA 07DER0   ATR2 20   XL/MJ 020A80
        020A50        ATR1 BB   NCDE 020A90   ROC-RB 00000000   NM IGG019BB  USE 06   EPA 07E120   ATR2 20   XL/MJ 020A40


XL

                                              LN         ADR          LN        ADR         LN        ADR
        01FF00   SZ 00000010   NO 00000001   80000138   0003A6C8
        01F910   SZ 00000010   NO 00000001   800000F8   0303A5D0
        01F720   SZ 00000010   NO 00000001   80000680   0006A9R0
        020B70   SZ 00000010   NO 00000001   80000210   0007E4B8
        020A80   SZ 00000010   NO 00000001   80000180   0007DER0
        020A40   SZ 00000010   NO 00000001   80000058   0007E120


DEB (SNAPT)

01C4A0   00000BF0 00000BF0 00000BF0 00000BF0   00000BF0 00000000 0000020F 00002BE0   *...O...O...O...O............*
01C4C0   0F000000 0301B018 04000000 A8000000   0F000000 01000000 1R000000 EF03A670   *............................*
01C4E0   0401C4A0 18002ACC 00000065 000F006A   000E0064 00010001 C2C2C2C1 C3C40000   *..D.....................BBBACD..*
01C500   00000000 00000000 00000000 00000000                                        *................F....A293P385*


TIOT   JOB A293P462   STEP HCGO
        DD        14140100   JOBLIB      00682400   80002230
        DD        14040100   PGM=*.DD    006A1D00   80002280
        DD        14040100   SYSABEND    00683C00   80002ROC
        DD        140401R0   SNAPT       00683F00   80002ACC


MSS              ************ SPQE ************     ************** DQE ************      ******* FQE *******
                 FLGS  NSPQE    SPID    DQE         BLK       FQE       LN      NDQE      NFQE          LN
        01F998   00    01FF70   251     01EC98      0003A000  0003A000  00000800 00000000  00000000      00005D0
        01FF70   80    020F88   000     01EBR8      00000000  00000000  00000000 00000000  00000000
        01FFR8   60    000000   000     01F228      0068B000  0068B000  00000800 00000000  00000000      0000710
        020EBR   40    000000   252     01FF08      0006A800  0006A800  00000800 0001F600  00000000      000019R
                                                    0006A800  0006A800  00000800 0001C988  00000000      0000180
                                                    00069800  00069800  00001000 00000000  00000000      00003R0

D-PQE  0001FF30   FIRST 0001F880   LAST 0001EB80
PQE  01F880   FFR 0003A800   LFB 0003A800   NPQ 00000000   PPQ 00000000
              TCR 0001CC10   RSI 00032000   RAD 0003A000   FLG 0000

FRQE 03A800   NFR 0001F880   PFR 0001F880   SZ 0002F000


QCB TRACE

MAJ 01D7F0   NMAJ 0001D848   PMAJ 0001D0D8   FMIN 0001D378   NM  SYSDSN

MIN 01FD98   FQEL 0001FF40   PMIN 0001D338   NMIN 0001F7BB   NM FF  SYS1.MACLIB

             NQEL 00000000   PQEL 8001ED98   TCB  0001CC10   SVRB 0001BE3A

MIN 01F7BB   FQEL 0001F658   PMIN 0001FD98   NMIN 00000000   NM FF  DUMR

             NQEL 00000000   PQEL 0001F7B8   TCB  0001CC10   SVRB 0001BE38

MAJ 01D848   NMAJ 00000000   PMAJ 0001D7F0   FMIN 0001CDC8   NM  SYSIEA01

MIN 01CDC8   FQEL 0001CDB8   PMIN 0001D848   NMIN 00000000   NM EO  0003A670

             NQEL 00000000   PQEL 0001CDC8   TCB  0001BD18   SVRB 0001BBE8
```

```
SAVE AREA TRACE

RUN      WAS ENTERED VIA LINK        AT EP CALLIT

SA    06B7B0   WD1 00000000   HSA 00000000   LSA 00000000   RET 00011546   EPA 0103A6C8   R0  FFFFFF2E
               R1  0006B7F8    R2  00010B10   R3  50010B24   R4  0001CA88   R5  0001CC10   R6  00010910
               R7  0001E2D8    R8  0001DAF8   R9  00000000   R10 00000074   R11 00000000   R12 6007EC9A


INTERRUPT AT 03A60F


PROCEEDING BACK VIA REG 13

SA    03A628   WD1 00000000   HSA 0003A75C   LSA 00000000   RET 00000000   EPA 00000000   R0  00000000
               R1  00000000    R2  00000000   R3  00000000   R4  00000000   R5  00000000   R6  00000000
               R7  00000000    R8  00000000   R9  00000000   R10 00000000   R11 00000000   R12 00000000

DUMSLM   WAS ENTERED VIA LINK        AT EP DUMPIT

SA    03A75C   WD1 00000000   HSA 0006B7B0   LSA 00000000   RET 00011546   EPA 0103A5D0   R0  00000030
               R1  0006BFC8    R2  0001DB10   R3  4003A6DA   R4  0001CA88   R5  0001CC10   R6  00010910
               R7  0001E2D8    R8  0001DAF8   R9  00000000   R10 00000074   R11 00000000   R12 6007EC9A


REGS AT ENTRY TO SNAP

     FLTR 0-6      00674100E080C191      C1F2F9F3D7F4F6F2            0000000000000000      006A1D0000000000

     REGS 0-7      00000030   8003A5FC   00010B10   4003A5E2      0001CA88   0001CC10   00010910   0001E2D8
     REGS 8-15     0001DAF8   00000000   00000074   00000000      6007EC9A   0003A628   00011546   00000000

LOAD MODULE   RUN

03A6C0                   47F0F00C 06C3C1D3   D3C9E300 90ECD00C 05305000 30A641D0   *.........00..CALLIT...........*
```

228   Appendix 2

```
JOB A293P462      STEP HCGO           TIME 180730   DATE 69293    ID = 056                    PAGE 0001

PSW AT ENTRY TO SNAP    FFE50033 4003A74E

TCB  01BD18  RBP   0001C480  PIE   00000000  DEB  0001C7CC  TIO 0001D918'  CMP  00000000  TRN 00000000
             MSS   0201F998  PK-FLG E0010000  FLG  0001B1B  LLS 0001EEC0   JLB  0001E6EB  JPQ 0001E5EB
             FSA   0106B7B0  TCB   00000000  TME  00000000  JST 0001BD18   NTC  00000000  OTC 0001CC10
             LTC   00000000  IQE   00000000  ECB  0001DB18  STA 00000000   D-PQE 0001FF30  SQS 0001B800
             NSTAE 00000000  TCT   0001C048  USER 00000000


ACTIVE RBS

PRB  01E790  RESV  00000000  APSW  00000000  WC-SZ-STAB 00040082  FL-CDE 0001EECB  PSW FFF50033 4003A74F
             Q/TTR 00000000  WT-LNK 0001BD18

SVRB 01C4B0  TAB-LN 00380360  APSW  F1F0F5C1  WC-SZ-STAB 0012D002  TQN  00000000     PSW FF040007 00007200
             Q/TTR 00005113  WT-LNK 0001F790
             RG 0-7  00000030  8003A73C  0001DB10  4003A6DA  0001CABB  0001CC10  0001D910  0001F2DB
             RG 8-15 0001DAFB  00000000  00000074  00000000  6007EC9A  0003A75C  4003A72A  00000030
             EXTSA   FF040000  0001C4EC  0003A740  E2E8E2C9  C5C1F0F1  10002ACC  00000058  0000305B
                     00130014  00010001  C2C2C2C1  C3C40000


LOAD LIST

       NE 0001FF28  RSP-CDE 0101E5FB      NE 0001F240  RSP-CDE 01020B80      NF 0001F920  RSP-CDE 01020A90
       NE 00000000  RSP-CDE 01020A50

CDE

       01FEC8   ATR1 08   NCDE 000000   ROC-RB 0001E790   NM RUN      USE 01   EPA 03A6C8   ATR2 20   XL/MJ 01FF00
       01E5FB   ATR1 31   NCDE 01EEC8   ROC-RB 00000000   NM IGG0A05A  USE 01   EPA 06A980   ATR2 28   XL/MJ 01E910
       020AB0   ATR1 BB   NCDE 020BB0   ROC-RB 00000000   NM IGG019CD  USE 07   EPA 07E488   ATR2 20   XL/MJ 020B70
       020A90   ATR1 BB   NCDE 020AC0   ROC-RB 00000000   NM IGG019BA  USE 06   EPA 07DF80   ATR2 20   XL/MJ 020A80
       020A50   ATR1 BB   NCDE 020A90   ROC-RB 00000000   NM IGG019BB  USE 06   EPA 07E120   ATR2 20   XL/MJ 020A40

XL                                              LN          ADR         LN        ADR        LN        ADR

       01FF00   SZ 00000010   NO 00000001   80000138  0303A6C8
       01F910   SZ 00000010   NO 00000001   80000680  0006A980
       020B70   SZ 00000010   NO 00000001   80000210  0007E48B
       020A80   SZ 00000010   NO 00000001   80000180  0007DE80
       020A40   SZ 00000010   NO 00000001   B0000058  0007E120


DEB

01C7A0                 00000BF0 00000BF0       00000BF0 00000BF0 00000BF0 00000000      *............0...0...0...0....*
01C7C0   0000020E 00002BE0 14000000 0301BD18   04000000 AB000000 0F000000 04000000      *..................0.........*
01C7E0   1B000000 FF03A7A4 0401C7A8 1B002ACC   00000065 000F006A 000E0064 1B002ACC      *...............G............*
01C800   00000057 00000057 00130014 1B002ACC   00000058 00000058 00130014 1B002ACC      *............................*
01C820   00000059 00000059 00130014 00010001   C2C2C2C1 C3C40000 00000000 00000000      *................BBBACD......*
01C840   00000000 00000000                                                              *..........BB.......0...0...0*


TIOT  JOB  A293P462   STEP HCGO
       DD    14140100  JOBLIB   006B2400  80002230
       DD    14040100  PGM=*.DD  006B1D00  80002280
       DD    14040100  SYSABEND  006B3C00  80002B0C
       DD    14040180  SNAPT     006B3E00  80002ACC


MSS       *********** SPQE ***********      *********** DQE ***********       ****** FQE ******
           FLGS   NSPQE    SPID    DQE       BLK       FQF       LN      NDQE      NFQE      LN

       01F998   00   01FF70   251   01EC98   0003A000 0003A000 00000800 00000000    00000000   000006C8
       01FF70   B0   020F88   000   01EBB8
       01EBB8   60   000000   000   01F22B   0006B000 0006B000 00000800 00000000    00000000   00000710
       020EBB   40   000000   252   01FF08   0006B800 0006B800 00000800 0001E720    00000000   00000198
                                             00064800 00064800 00000800 0001E59B    00000000   00000180
                                             00069800 00069800 00001000 00000000    00000000   00000380

D-PQE 0001FF30   FIRST 0001F8B0   LAST 0001F8B0
PQE  01F8B0   FFR 0003AB00   LFR 0003AB00   NPQ 00000000   PPQ 00000000
              TCB 0001CC10   RSI 00032000   RAD 0003A000   FLG 0000

FBQE 03AB00   NFR 0001F8B0   PFR 0001F8B0   SZ 0002F000


QCB TRACE

MAJ 01D7F0   NMAJ 0001E5A8   PMAJ 00013008   FMIN 0001D378   NM SYSDSN

MIN 01ED98   FQEL 0001FF40   PMIN 0001D338   NMIN 0001F7B8   NM FF  SYS1.MACLIB

             NQFL 00000000   PQFL 8001ED98   TCB  0001CC10   SVRB 0001BF38

MIN 01F7B8   FQFL 0001F658   PMIN 0001FD98   NMIN 00000000   NM FF  DUMP

             NQFL 00000000   PQEL 0001F7B8   TCB  0001CC10   SVRB 0001BF38

MAJ 01E5A8   NMAJ 00000000   PMAJ 0001D7F0   FMIN 0001DF10   NM SYSIEA01

MIN 01DF10   FQFL 0001E6D0   PMIN 0001E5A8   NMIN 00000000   NM FQ  0003A7A4

             NQFL 00000000   PQFL 0001DF10   TCB  0001BD18   SVRB 0001BBEB
```

```
SAVE AREA TRACE

RUN       WAS ENTERED VIA LINK        AT FP CALLIT

SA   06B780   WD1 00000000    HSA 00000000    LSA 00000000    RET 00011546    EPA 0103A6C8    R0  FFFFFF2E
              R1  0006B7E8     R2  0001DB10     R3  5001DB24     R4  0001CA88     R5  0001CC10     R6  0001D910
              R7  0001E2D8     R8  0001DAF8     R9  00000000     R10 00000074     R11 00000000     R12 6007EC9A


INTERRUPT AT 03A74E

PROCEEDING BACK VIA REG 13

SA   03A75C   WD1 00000000    HSA 0006B780    LSA 00000000    RET FF011546    EPA 0103A5D0    R0  00000030
              R1  0006BFC8     R2  0001DB10     R3  4003A6DA     R4  0001CA88     R5  0001CC10     R6  0001D910
              R7  0001E2D8     R8  0001DAF8     R9  00000000     R10 00000074     R11 00000000     R12 6007EC9A

RUN       WAS ENTERED VIA LINK        AT FP CALLIT

SA   06B780   WD1 00000000    HSA 00000000    LSA 00000000    RET 00011546    EPA 0103A6C8    R0  FFFFFF2E
              R1  0006B7E8     R2  0001DB10     R3  5001DB24     R4  0001CA88     R5  0001CC10     R6  0001D910
              R7  0001E2D8     R8  0001DAF8     R9  00000000     R10 00000074     R11 00000000     R12 6007EC9A

REGS AT ENTRY TO SNAP

   FLTR 0-6      00674100F080C191      C1F2F9F3D7F4F6F2           0000000000000000      006A1D0000000000

   REGS 0-7      00000030   8003A73C   0001DB10   4003A6DA       0001CA88   0001CC10   0001D910   0001E2D8
   REGS 8-15     0001DAF8   00000000   00000074   00000000       6007EC9A   0003A75C   4003A72A   00000000

LOAD MODULE   RUN

03A6C0                  47F0F00C 06C3C1D3    D3C9F3D0 90ECD00C 05305DD0 30864100   *.........00..CALLIT...........*
03A6E0   30B20700 45103012 8F03A7A4 0A130700    4510302A 3800B8BF 0003A7A4 00000000   *.............................*
03A700   00000000 0A330700 45103036 8003A7A4    0A140700 45F0304F 0003A720 00000000   *....................0........*
03A720   C4F4D4F2 03D44040 0A060700 4510305A    8F03A7A4 0A130700 45103072 3800B8BF   *DUMSLM  .....................*
03A740   0003A7A4 00000000 00000000 0A335BD0    308698FC D00C92FF D00C07FE 00000000   *.............................*
03A760   0006B780 00000000 FF011546 0103A5D0    00000030 0006BFC8 0001DB10 4003A6DA   *....................H.... ...*
```

appendix 3

LOAD MACHINE
LISTING

The following table of contents will help the reader identify the various components of this listing:

```
LOC   OBJECT CODE    ADDR1 ADDR2  STMT    SOURCE STATEMENT

000000                                    1 CALLIT CSECT
                                          2        SAVE  (14,12),,*
000000 47F0 F00C       0000C          3+        B     12(0,15) BRANCH AROUND ID
000004 06                             4+        DC    AL1(6)
000005 C3C1D3D3C9E3                   5+        DC    CL6'CALLIT' IDENTIFIER
00000B 00
00000C 90EC D00C       0000C          6+        STM   14,12,12(13) SAVE REGISTERS
000010 0530                           7         BALR  3,0
000012                                8         USING *,3
000012 50D0 309A       000AC          9         ST    13,SAVE+4
000016 41D0 3096       000A8          10        LA    13,SAVE
                                      11        OPEN  (SNAP,(OUTPUT))
00001A 0700                           12+       CNOP  0,4
00001C 4510 3012       00024          13+       BAL   1,*+8 LOAD REG1 W/LIST ADDR.
000020 8F                             14+       DC    AL1(143) OPTION BYTE
000021 0000F0                         15+       DC    AL3(SNAP) DCB ADDRESS
000024 0A13                           16+       SVC   19 ISSUE OPEN SVC
                                      17        SNAP  DCB=SNAP,ID=56,SDATA=ALL,PDATA=ALL
000026 0700                           18+       CNOP  0,4
000028 4510 302A       0003C          19+       BAL   1,IHB0003 BRANCH AROUND PARAM LIST
00002C 38                             20+       DC    AL1(56) ID NUMBER
00002D 00                             21+       DC    AL1(0)
00002E BB                             22+       DC    AL1(187) OPTION FLAGS
00002F BE                             23+       DC    AL1(190) OPTION FLAGS
000030 000000F0                       24+       DC    A(SNAP) DCB ADDRESS
000034 00000000                       25+       DC    A(0) TCB ADDRESS
000038 00000000                       26+       DC    A(0) ADDRESS OF SNAP-SHOT LIST
00003C                                27+IHB0003 DS   0H
00003C 0A33                           28+       SVC   51
                                      29        CLOSE (SNAP)
00003E 0700                           30+       CNOP  0,4
000040 4510 3036       00048          31+       BAL   1,*+8 BRANCH AROUND LIST
000044 80                             32+       DC    AL1(128) OPTION BYTE
000045 0000F0                         33+       DC    AL3(SNAP) DCB ADDRESS
000048 0A14                           34+       SVC   20 ISSUE CLOSE SVC
00004A 5820 3136       00148          35        L     2,COUNTER
                                      36        LOAD  EP=DUMSLM
00004E 4100 3044       00056          37+       LA    0,*+8 LOAD PARAMETER INTO REGISTER ZERO
000052 47F0 304C       0005E          38+       B     *+12 BRANCH AROUND CONSTANT(S)
000056 C4E4D4E2D3D44040               39+       DC    CL8'DUMSLM' ENTRY POINT NAME
00005E 1B11                           40+       SR    1,1 SHOW NO DCB PRESENT
000060 0A08                           41+       SVC   8 ISSUE LOAD SVC
000062 18F0                           42        LR    15,0
000064 05EF                           43 LOOP   BALR  14,15
000066 4620 3052       00064          44        BCT   2,LOOP
                                      45        OPEN  (SNAP,(OUTPUT))
00006A 0700                           46+       CNOP  0,4
00006C 4510 3062       00074          47+       BAL   1,*+8 LOAD REG1 W/LIST ADDR.
000070 8F                             48+       DC    AL1(143) OPTION BYTE
000071 0000F0                         49+       DC    AL3(SNAP) DCB ADDRESS
000074 0A13                           50+       SVC   19 ISSUE OPEN SVC
                                      51        SNAP  DCB=SNAP,ID=56,SDATA=ALL,PDATA=ALL
000076 0700                           52+       CNOP  0,4
000078 4510 307A       0008C          53+       BAL   1,IHB0007 BRANCH AROUND PARAM LIST
00007C 38                             54+       DC    AL1(56) ID NUMBER
```

PSW AT ENTRY TO SNAP   FFE50033 400586EF

```
TCB  010010  RBP   00010770  PIE   00000000   DEB  0001D9AC  TIO  0001DA88  CMP  00000000  TRN  00000000
             MSS   0201FBCB  PK-FLG F0010000   FLG  00001B1B  LLS  0001F000  JLB  0001E918  JPQ  0001FE50
             FSA   010707B0  TCB   00000000    TME  00000000  JST  0001D010  NTC  00000000  OTC  0001DB28
             LTC   00000000  IQE   00000000    ECB  0001EC58  STA  00000000  D-PQE 0001FDCB  SQS  0001C6C0
             NSTAE 00000000  TCT   0001CFB0    USER 00000000
```

ACTIVE RBS

```
PRB  01FF88  RESV  00000000  APSW  00000000   WC-SZ-STAB 00040082  FL-CDE 0001FA58  PSW FFE50033 400586EF
             Q/TTR 00000000  WT-LNK 0001D010

SVRB 01D770  TAB-LN 00080360  APSW  F1F0F5C1  WC-SZ-STAB 0012D002  TQN  00000000  PSW FF040007 000065FB
             Q/TTR 00005113  WT-LNK 0001EE88
             RG 0-7   00000030  8005860C  0001EC50  400586C2  0001D548  0001DB28  0001DA80  0001E5B0
             RG 8-15  0001FC3B  00000000  00000074  00000000  6007EC9A  0005B758  00011546  00000000
             EXTSA    FF040000  0001D7DC  000586E0  E2F8E2C9  C5C1F0F1  00000000  C9C5C6E2  C4F0F6F5
                      0A079827  901F000C  05801841  58300010
```

LOAD LIST

```
        NE 0001F070  RSP-CDE 0101EE50      NE 0001F150  RSP-CDE 01020B80      NE 0001FAA0  RSP-CDE 01020A90
        NE 00000000  RSP-CDE 01020A50
```

CDE

```
   01FA58  ATR1 0B  NCDE 000000  ROC-RB 0001FEB8  NM RUN       USE 01  EPA 0586B0  ATR2 20  XL/MJ 01FBF0
   01FF50  ATR1 31  NCDE 01FA58  ROC-RB 00000000  NM IGC0A05A  USE 01  EPA 06F980  ATR2 28  XL/MJ 01F060
   020B80  ATR1 80  NCDE 020B80  ROC-RB 00000000  NM IGG019CD  USE 07  EPA 07E488  ATR2 20  XL/MJ 020B70
   020A90  ATR1 80  NCDE 020AC0  ROC-RB 00000000  NM IGG019BA  USE 07  EPA 07DE80  ATR2 20  XL/MJ 020A80
   020A50  ATR1 88  NCDE 020A90  ROC-RB 00000000  NM IGG019BB  USE 07  EPA 07E120  ATR2 20  XL/MJ 020A40
```

XL

```
                                            LN         ADR       LN       ADR       LN       ADR
   01FBF0  S7 00000010  NO 00000001  80000150  000586B0
   01F060  S7 00000010  NO 00000001  800006B0  0006F980
   020B70  S7 00000010  NO 00000001  80000210  0007E488
   020AB0  S7 00000010  NO 00000001  80000180  0007DE80
   020A40  S7 00000010  NO 00000001  80000058  0007E120
```

DEB

```
01D9B0                00000BF0 00000BF0   00000BF0 00000BF0 00000BF0 00000000   *............0....0....0....0.....*
01D9A0  00000216 00002BF0 0F000000 0301D010   04000000 88000000 0F000000 01000000   *................................*
01D9C0  18000000 FF05B7A0 0401D988 1800280C   00000094 00040099 00030064 00010001   *................R...............*
01D9F0  C2C2C2C1 C3C40000 00000000 00000000   00000000 10000802                      *BBBACD..................S......*
```

```
TIOT   JOB A294P014    STEP HCGO
       DD        14140100  JOBLIB    00150800  80002230
       DD        14040100  PGM=*.DD  00150100  80002270
       DD        14040100  SYSABEND  00143500  R0002B0C
       DD        14040100  SNAPT     00143700  80002B0C
```

MSS

```
           ************ SPQE ************     *************** DQE ***************    ******* FQE ********
           FLGS  NSPQE    SPID     DQE         BLK      FQF      LN       NDQE        NFQF       LN

   01FBCB  00    01FDB0   251      01F158      00058000 00058000 00000800 00000000   00000000   000006B0
   01FDB0  R0    01FDCB   000      01DF98      00000000 00000000 00000000 00000000   00000000   00000710
   01DF98  60    000000   000      01FA70      00070000 00070000 00000800 0001F03B   00000000   00000198
   01FDCB  40    000000   252      01F928      00070B00 00070B00 00000800 0001FF3B   00000000   00000180
                                               0006F800 0006F800 00030800 0001FF3B   00000000   00000180
                                               0006EB00 0006EB00 00001000 00000000   00000000   00000380
```

SAVE AREA TRACE

RUN   WAS ENTERED VIA LINK   AT EP CALLIT

```
SA  070780  WD1 00000000  HSA 00000000  LSA 00000000  RET 00011546  EPA 010586B0  R0  FFFFFF2F
            R1  000707FB  R2  0001EC50  R3  5001EC64  R4  0001D548   R5  0001DB28   R6  0001DA80
            R7  0001E5B0  R8  0001EC38  R9  00000000  R10 00000074   R11 00000000   R12 6007EC9A
```

INTERRUPT AT 0586FF

PROCEEDING BACK VIA REG 13

```
SA  05B758  WD1 00003800  HSA 000707B0  LSA 00040000  RET 01010100  EPA 00000004  R0  002C70B2
            R1  27F1001B  R2  07121108  R3  00000003  R4  020D1C03   R5  00113200   R6  00003C00
            R7  00480800  R8  00000000  R9  00010000  R10 00000002   R11 00177040   R12 0A0R0012
```

RUN   WAS ENTERED VIA LINK   AT EP CALLIT

```
SA  070780  WD1 00000000  HSA 00000000  LSA 00000000  RET 00011546  EPA 010586B0  R0  FFFFFF2F
            R1  000707FB  R2  0001EC50  R3  5001EC64  R4  0001D548   R5  0001DB28   R6  0001DA80
            R7  0001E5B0  R8  0001EC38  R9  00000000  R10 00000074   R11 00000000   R12 6007EC9A
```

REGS AT ENTRY TO SNAP

```
   FLTR 0-6    0000021600001BE2   0E0000000601D750        04000000C8000000   1700000001FFFFFF

   REGS 0-7   00000030  R005A5F4  00000001  400585CA        00010548  0001DB28  0001DA80  0001E5B0
   REGS 8-15  0001FC3B  00000000  00000074  00000000        6007EC9A  00058610  40058716  00000000
```

LOAD MODULE   RUN

```
05A6A0                                         47F0F00C 06C3C1D3 D3C9E300 90ECD00C   *..U...U..........00..CALLIT.....*
0586C0  05305000 309A4100 30960700 45103012   RF05A7A0 0A130700 45103024 3R008BBF   *.U.............................*
0586F0  000587A0 00000000 00000000 0A330700   45103036 800587A0 0A145820 31364100   *...............................*
058700  304447F0 304CC4F4 04F2D3D4 40401R11   0A0818F0 05FF4620 30520700 45103062   *....0..DUMSLM .....0............*
058720  RF05R7A0 0A130700 4510307A 3800BBBF   000587A0 00000000 00000000 0A330700   *...............................*
058740  45103086 800587A0 0A145RD0 309A9RFC   D00C92FF D00C07FE 00003800 00070780   *...............................*
058760  00040000 40058716 000585R8 000585R8   00000001 00000001 400586C2 0001D548   *......................R..N.*
058780  0001DB28 0001DA80 0001F5R0 0001FC3R   00000000 00000074 00000000 6007EC9A   *...Q..........V.................*
0587A0  00000100 20000000 0097000C 0400B2FA   002800E4 00000001 00004000 00000001   *...................U........*
0587C0  04000001 54000000 F2D5C1D7 F3404040   02000020 00000001 0R000001 00000660   *.........SNAPT .................*
0587F0  00000000 00000000 00000000 00000001   0000007D 00000001 00000002 32323232   *...............................*
```

```
JOB A294P014        STEP HCGO          TIME 091309   DATE 69294    ID = 056                              PAGE 0001

PSW AT ENTRY TO SNAP   FFF50033 400585F6

TCB  01D010   RRP  0001D770   PIE  00000000   DEB  0001CF9C   TIO  0001DA88   CMP  00000000   TRN  00000000
              MSS  0201FBCR   PK-FLG F0010000  FLG  00001B1R   LLS  0001ED40   JLB  0001E91R   JPQ  0001EA30
              FSA  01D707B0   TCB  00000000    TME  00000000   JST  0001D010   NTC  00000000   OTC  0001D828
              LTC  00000000   IQF  00000000    ECB  0001EC58   STA  00000000   D-PQF 0001FDC8  SQS  0001C6C0
              NSTAE 00000000  TCT  0001CFR0    USER 00000000

ACTIVE RBS

PRB  01FFB8   RFSV 00000000   APSW 00000000    WC-SZ-STAB 00040082   FL-CDE 0001FA58    PSW FFE50033 400585F6
              Q/TTR 00000000  WT-LNK 0001D010

SVRB 01D770   TAB-LN 00280360  APSW F1F0F5C1   WC-SZ-STAB 0012D002   TQN 00000000       PSW FF040007 00006E88
              Q/TTR 00005113   WT-LNK 0001FF88
              RG 0-7   00000030    800585F4    00000002    400585CA    0001D548    0001DA28    0001DA80    0001F5B0
              RG 8-15  0001EC38    00000000    00000074    00000000    6007EC9A    00058610    40058716    00000000
              EXTSA    FF040000    0001D70C    000585F8    E2E8E2C9    C5C1F0F1    00000000    C9C5C6E2    C4F0F6F5
                       0A079R27    901ED00C    05R01841    58300010

LOAD LIST

          NF 0001EDC0   RSP-CDE 0101EA30      NE 0001EF58   RSP-CDE 01020B80      NE 0001F070   RSP-CDE 01020A90
          NF 0001FRA0   RSP-CDE 01020A50      NE 00000000   RSP-CDE 0101E3F8

CDE

      01FA5R    ATR1 0B    NCDE 000000    ROC-RB 0001EE88   NM RUN      USE 01   EPA 0586R0   ATR2 20   XL/MJ 01FBF0
      01FA30    ATR1 31    NCDE 01E3FR    ROC-RB 00000000   NM IGC0A05A USE 01   EPA 06F9R0   ATR2 28   XL/MJ 01DFBR
      020B80    ATR1 R0    NCDE 020BR0    ROC-RB 00000000   NM IGG019CD USE 07   EPA 07E4RR   ATR2 20   XL/MJ 020B70
      020A90    ATR1 R0    NCDE 020AC0    ROC-RB 00000000   NM IGG019RA USE 07   EPA 07DE80   ATR2 20   XL/MJ 020AR0
      020A50    ATR1 RR    NCDE 020A90    ROC-RB 00000000   NM IGG019RR USE 07   EPA 07E120   ATR2 20   XL/MJ 020A40
      01F3F8    ATR1 03    NCDE 01FA5R    ROC-RB 00000000   NM DUMSLM   USE 01   EPA 0585R8   ATR2 20   XL/MJ 01DFER

XL                                                    LN         ADR        LN        ADR        LN        ADR

      01FBF0    S7 00000010   N0 00000001   80000150   000586R0
      01DFB8    S7 00000010   N0 00000001   80000680   0006F9R0
      020B70    S7 00000010   N0 00000001   80000210   0007E4R8
      020AR0    S7 00000010   N0 00000001   80000180   0007DF80
      020A40    S7 00000010   N0 00000001   R000005R   0007E120
      01DFF8    S7 00000010   N0 00000001   R00000F8   0005858R

DEB

01CF60                                                     00000BF0 00000BF0      *...................0...0*
01CF80    00000BF0 00000BF0 00000BF0 00000000   00000216 00002BE0 0F000000 0301D010   *..0...0...0.............*
01CFA0    04000000 A8000000 0F000000 01000000   1R000000 FF05R658 0401CF78 18002B0C   *.......................*
01CFC0    00000094 00040099 00030064 00010001   C2C2C2C1 C3C40000 00000000 00000000   *............BBBACD......*
01CFE0    00000000 00000BF0                                                            *........0..R....0....S......P.*

TIOT  JOB A294P014    STEP-HCGO
      DD         14140100    JOBLIB        00150800    R0002230
      DD         14040100    PGM=*.DD      00150100    R0002270
      DD         14040100    SYSABEND      00143500    R0002B0C
      DD         14040180    SNAPT         00143700    R0002B0C

MSS               ************ SPQE ************      *********** DQE ***********       ******* FQF ********
            FLGS  NSPQE      SPID    DQE          BLK      FQE      LN     NDQE        NFQE        LN
      01FRCR   00    01FDR0   251    01F158    00058000 0005R000 00000800 00000000   00000000   000005R8
      01FDR0   R0    01FDC8   000    01DF9R    00070000 00070000 00000800 00000000   00000000   00000710
      01DF9R   60    000000   000    01FA70    00070800 00070800 00000800 0001DFAR   00000000   00000198
      01FDCR   40    000000   252    01F92R    0006FR00 0006F800 00000800 0001DF18   00000000   00000180
                                               0006ER00 0006E800 00001000 00000000   00000000   000003R0

SAVE AREA TRACE

RUN        WAS ENTERED VIA LINK       AT EP CALLIT

SA  0707R0   WD1 00000000   HSA 00000000   LSA 00000000   RET 00011546   EPA 0105R6R0   R0  FFFFFF2F
             R1  000707F8   R2  0001FC50   R3  5001EC64   R4  0001D54R   R5  0001D828   R6  0001DA80
             R7  0001F5R0   RR  0001EC38   R9  00000000   R10 00000074   R11 00000000   R12 6007EC9A

INTERRUPT AT 0585F6

PROCEEDING BACK VIA REG 13

SA  058610   WD1 00000000   HSA 0005875R   LSA 00000000   RET 00000000   EPA 00000000   R0  00000000
             R1  00000000   R2  00000000   R3  00000000   R4  00000000   R5  00000000   R6  00000000
             R7  00000000   RR  00000000   R9  00000000   R10 00000000   R11 00000000   R12 00000000

SA  05875R   WD1 00003800   HSA 000707R0   LSA 00040000   RET 40058716   EPA 00058588   R0  0005R5RR
             R1  00000001   R2  00000002   R3  400586C2   R4  0001D54R   R5  0001D828   R6  0001DA80
             R7  0001E5R0   RR  0001EC38   R9  00000000   R10 00000074   R11 00000000   R12 6007EC9A

REGS AT ENTRY TO SNAP

      FLTR 0-6     0000021600001RE2    0F0000000601D750         04000000C8000000         1700000001FFFFFF

      REGS 0-7     00000030    800587?C    00000000    400586C2    0001D548    0001D828    0001DA80    0001E5R0
      REGS 8-15    0001FC38    00000000    00000074    00000000    6007EC9A    0005875R    40058716    00000000

LOAD MODULE  RUN

0586A0                                                   47F0F00C 06C3C1D3 D3C9E300 90ECD00C   *.............00..CALLIT.....*
0586C0    053050D0 309A41D0 30960700 45103012   RF05R7A0 0A130700 4510302A 3800BRRE   *........................*
0586E0    0005R7A0 00000000 00000000 0A330700   45103036 800587A0 0A145820 31364100   *........................*
058700    30444TF0 304CC4F4 D4F2D3D4 40401R11   0A081RF0 05EF4620 30520700 45103062   *....0..DUMSLM ......0........*
058720    8F05R7A0 0A130700 4510307A 3R00BRRF   0005R7A0 00000000 00000000 0A330700   *........................*
058740    45103086 800587A0 0A145800 309A9REC   D00C92FF D00C07FE 00003800 000707B0   *........................*
058760    00040000 FF058716 00058588 00058588   00000001 00000001 400586C2 00010548   *.............B..N.*
058780    0001D82R 0001DA80 0001E5R0 0001EC3R   00000000 00000074 00000000 6007EC9A   *..0.....V.......*
0587A0    00CF0300 2D090000 00890006 070082FA   00280E70 00000000 00004000 00000001   *...................*
0587C0    04000001 54000000 00540020 0001C634   92070E80 0007E120 0R000001 00000660   *.............F......*
0587E0    3004004R 41070710 0107E4R8 0007F4RR   0000007D 00000001 00000002 32323232   *...........U...U.......*
```

233

PSW AT ENTRY TO SNAP   FFE50033 400585F6

```
TCB   01D010   RBP   0001D770   PIE   00000000   DEB   0001CA24   TIO  0001DA88   CMP  00000000   TRN 00000000
               MSS   0201FBCB   PK-FLG F0010000   FLG   00001B18   LLS  0001F070   JLB  0001E918   JPQ 0001EA30
               FSA   01070780   TCB   00000000   TME   00000000   JST  0001D010   NTC  00000000   OTC 0001D828
               LTC   00000000   IOE   00000000   ECB   0001EC58   STA  00000000   D-PQE 0001FDC8   SQS 0001C6B8
               NSTAE 00000000   TCT   0001CE80   USER  00000000
```

ACTIVE RBS

```
PRB   01FF88   RESV  00000000   APSW  00000000   WC-SZ-STAB 00040082   FL-CDE 0001FA58   PSW FFE50033 400585F6
               Q/TTR 00000000   WT-LNK 0001D010

SVRB  01D770   TAB-LN 00680360   APSW  F1F0F5C1   WC-SZ-STAB 0012D002   TQN   00000000   PSW FF040007 00007EA8
               Q/TTR 00005113   WT-LNK 0001EEB8
               RG 0-7  00000030   800585F4   00000001   400585CA   00010548   0001D828   0001DA80   0001E5B0
               RG 8-15 0001EC38   00000000   00000074   00000000   6007EC9A   00058610   40058716   00000000
               EXTSA   FF040000   0001D7DC   000585F8   E2E8F2C9   C5C1F0F1   00000000   C9C5C6E2   C4F0F6F5
                       0A079827   901ED00C   05801841   58300010
```

LOAD LIST

```
         NE 0001F150   RSP-CDE 0101EA30         NE 0001FBD0   RSP-CDE 01020B80         NE 0001FD78   RSP-CDE 01020A90
         NE 0001FBA0   RSP-CDE 01020A50         NE 00000000   RSP-CDE 0101E3F8
```

CDE

```
         01FA58       ATR1 0B   NCDE 000000   ROC-RB 0001EEB8   NM RUN       USE 01   EPA 0586B0   ATR2 20   XL/MJ 01FBF0
         01EA30       ATR1 31   NCDE 01E3FR   ROC-RB 00000000   NM IGC0A05A  USE 01   EPA 06F980   ATR2 28   XL/MJ 01FF58
         020B80       ATR1 B0   NCDE 020B80   ROC-RB 00000000   NM IGG019CD  USE 07   EPA 07E488   ATR2 20   XL/MJ 020B70
         020A90       ATR1 B0   NCDE 020AC0   ROC-RB 00000000   NM IGG0198A  USE 07   EPA 07DEA0   ATR2 20   XL/MJ 020AA0
         020A50       ATR1 B8   NCDE 020A90   ROC-RB 00000000   NM IGG019BB  USE 07   EPA 07E120   ATR2 20   XL/MJ 020A40
         01E3FA       ATR1 03   NCDE 01FA58   ROC-RB 00000000   NM DUMSLM    USE 01   EPA 0585B8   ATR2 20   XL/MJ 01DFER
```

XL

```
                                                        LN         ADR        LN        ADR        LN        ADR
         01FBF0   SZ 00000010   NO 00000001   80000150   000586B0
         01FF58   SZ 00000010   NO 00000001   80000680   0006F980
         020B70   SZ 00000010   NO 00000001   80000210   0007E488
         020AB0   SZ 00000010   NO 00000001   800001B0   0007DEA0
         020A40   SZ 00000010   NO 00000001   80000058   0007F120
         01DFEB   SZ 00000010   NO 00000001   800000F8   000585B8
```

DEB

```
01CA00   00000BF0 00000BF0 00000BF0 000000BF0   00000BF0 00000000 00000216 00002BF0   *...0...0....0...0...0..........*
01CA20   12000000 0301D010 04000000 AB000000   0F000000 03000000 1B000000 FF058658   *...............................*
01CA40   0401CA00 18002B0C 00000094 00040099   00030064 18002B0C 0000007E 000F007F   *...............................*
01CA60   000F0014 18002B0C 00000057 00000057   00130014 00010001 C2C2C2C1 C3C40000   *.....................BBBACD..*
01CA80   00000000 00000000 00000000 00000000                                          *..............................K.*
```

```
TIOT   JOB  A294P014   STEP HCGO
         DD            14140100      JOBLIB      00150800   80002230
         DD            14040100      PGM=*.DD    00150100   80002270
         DD            14040100      SYSABEND    00143500   80002B0C
         DD            14040180      SNAPT       00143700   80002B0C
```

MSS

```
              ************ SPQE ************          *************** DQE ****************        ******* FQE ********
              FLGS   NSPQE   SPID   DQE        BLK        FQE        LN        NDQE        NFQF        LN
         01FBCB   00   01FDB0   251   01F158   00058000 00058000 00000800 00000000      00000000      000005B8
         01FDB0   80   01FDC8   000   01DF98   00000000                                                00000710
         01DF98   60   000000   000   01FA70   00070000 00070000 00000800 00000000      00000000      00000710
         01FDC8   40   000000   252   01F928   00070800 00070800 00003800 0001F378      00000000      00000198
                                              0006F800 0006F800 00000800 0001E2D8      00000000      000001B0
                                              0006E800 0006F800 00001000 00000000      00000000      000003B0
```

SAVE AREA TRACE

RUN   WAS ENTERED VIA LINK   AT EP CALLIT

```
SA   070780   WD1 00000000   HSA 00000000   LSA 00000000   RET 00011546   EPA 010586B0   R0  FFFFFF2F
              R1  000707F8   R2  0001EC50   R3  5001EC64   R4  00010548   R5  0001D828   R6  0001DA80
              R7  0001E5B0   R8  0001EC38   R9  00000000   R10 00000074   R11 00000000   R12 6007FC9A
```

INTERRUPT AT 0585F6

PROCEEDING BACK VIA REG 13

```
SA   058610   WD1 00000000   HSA 00058758   LSA 00000000   RET 00000000   EPA 00000000   R0  00000000
              R1  00000000   R2  00000000   R3  00000000   R4  00000000   R5  00000000   R6  00000000
              R7  00000000   R8  00000000   R9  00000000   R10 00000000   R11 00000000   R12 00000000

SA   058758   WD1 00003800   HSA 00070780   LSA 00040000   RET 40058716   EPA 00058588   R0  00058588
              R1  00000001   R2  00000001   R3  400586C2   R4  00010548   R5  0001D828   R6  0001DA80
              R7  0001E5B0   R8  0001EC38   R9  00000000   R10 00000074   R11 00000000   R12 6007EC9A
```

REGS AT ENTRY TO SNAP

```
         FLTR 0-6        0000021600001BF2   0F00000006010750                04000000C8000000      1700000001FFFFFF

         REGS 0-7   00000030   800586DC   0001EC50   400586C2            0001D548   00010828   0001DA80   0001E5B0
         REGS 8-15  0001EC38   00000000   00000074   00000000            6007EC9A   00058758   00011546   00000000
```

LOAD MODULE RUN

```
0586A0
0586C0   05305000 309A4100 30960700 45103012   47F0F00C 06C3C1D3 D3C9F300 90ECD00C   *................0.00..CALLIT.....*
0586E0   000587A0 00000000 00000000 0A330700   8F0587A0 0A130700 4510302A 38008BBE   *................................*
058700   304447F0 304CC4E4 D4E2D3D4 40401B11   45103036 800587A0 0A145820 31364100   *...0...DUMSLM..........0.........*
058720   8F0587A0 0A130700 4510307A 3800BBBE   000587A0 00000000 00000000 0A330700   *................................*
058740   45103086 800587A0 0A145800 309A9AEC   D00C92FF D00C07FE 00003800 000707B0   *................................*
058760   00040000 01010100 00000004 002C7082   27E10018 0712110R 00000003 020D1C03   *................................*
058780   00113200 00003C00 00480800 00000000   00010000 00000002 00177000 0A080012   *................................*
0587A0   00000100 20000000 00970007 0300B2FA   00280769 00000001 00004000 00000001   *................................*
0587C0   04000001 54000000 00540020 0001D9AC   9207DE80 0007E120 0B000001 00000660   *...........................R.....*
0587E0   30040048 41070710 0107F488 0007F488   0000007D 00000001 00000002 32323232   *........U...U.............*
```

PSW AT ENTRY TO SNAP   FFE50033 4005873E

```
TCB  010010   RBP  0001D9F0   PIE  00000000   DEB 0001C874  TIO 0001DA8B  CMP  00000000  TRN 00000000
              MSS  0201FBCB   PK-FLG E001000   FLG 0001D81B  LLS 0001F070  JLB  0001E918  JPQ 0001EA30
              FSA  010707B0   TCB  00000000    TME 00000000  JST 0001D010  NTC  00000000  DTC 0001D82B
              LTC  00000000   IQE  00000000    ECB 0001EC58  STA 00000000  D-PQF 0001F0C8  SQS 0001C700
              NSTAE 00000000  TCT  0001CE80    USER 00000000
```

ACTIVE RBS

```
PRB  01FFB8   RESV  00000000   APSW  00000000   WC-SZ-STAB 00040082   FL-CDE 0001FA58   PSW FFE50033 4005873E
              Q/TTR 00000000   WT-LNK 0001D010
```

```
SVRB 01D9F0   TAB-LN 00480360  APSW  F1F0F5C1   WC-SZ-STAB 0012D002   TQN  00000000   PSW FF040007 0000771B
              Q/TTR 00005113   WT-LNK 0001EF8B
              RG 0-7   00000030   8005872C   00000000   400586C2   0001D548   0001D82B   0001DA80   0001F580
              RG 8-15  0001EC3B   00000000   00000074   00000000   6007EC9A   00058758   40058716   00000000
              EXTSA    FF040000   0001DA5C   00058730   E2E8E2C9   C5C1F0F1   00000000   00000000   00000000
                       00000000   00000000   10000050   00000000
```

LOAD LIST

```
NE 0001F150  RSP-CDE 0101EA30   NE 0001FBD0  RSP-CDE 01020B80   NE 0001FD78  RSP-CDE 01020A90
NE 0001FBA0  RSP-CDE 01020A50   NE 00000000  RSP-CDE 0101E3FB
```

CDE

```
01FA58   ATR1 0B  NCDE 000000   ROC-RB 0001EE8B   NM RUN      USE 01  EPA 0586B0  ATR2 20  XL/MJ 01F8F0
01EA30   ATR1 31  NCDE 01E3F8   ROC-RB 00000000   NM IGC0A05A  USE 01  EPA 06F980  ATR2 2B  XL/MJ 01EF5B
020B80   ATR1 B0  NCDE 020B80   ROC-RB 00000000   NM IGG019CD  USE 07  EPA 07E488  ATR2 20  XL/MJ 020B70
020A90   ATR1 B0  NCDE 020AC0   ROC-RB 00000000   NM IGG019AA  USE 07  EPA 07E0B0  ATR2 20  XL/MJ 020A80
020A50   ATR1 BB  NCDE 020A90   ROC-RB 00000000   NM IGG019BB  USE 07  EPA 07E120  ATR2 20  XL/MJ 020A40
01E3F8   ATR1 03  NCDE 01FA58   ROC-RB 00000000   NM DUMSLM   USE 01  EPA 05A5BB  ATR2 20  XL/MJ 01DFEB
```

XL

```
                                              LN          ADR          LN        ADR        LN        ADR
01F8F0   S7 00000010   NO 00000001   80000150   000586B0
01FF58   S7 00000010   NO 00000001   80000680   0006F980
020B70   S7 00000010   NO 00000001   80000210   0007E488
020A80   S7 00000010   NO 00000001   80000180   0007DE80
020A40   S7 00000010   NO 00000001   8000005A   0007E120
01DFEB   S7 00000010   NO 00000001   800000F8   000585AB
```

DEB

```
01C840                                      00000BF0 00000BF0 00000BF0 00000BF0  *................0...0...0...0...0*
01C860   00000BF0 00000000 00000216 00002BF0  1A000000 03010D10 04000000 AB000000  *...0.............................*
01C880   0F000000 07000000 18000000 FF058700A  0401C850 18002B0C 00000094 00040099  *.....................H...........*
01C8A0   00030064 18002B0C 0000007E 000F007F  000F0014 18002B0C 00000057 00000057  *.................................*
01C8C0   00130014 18002B0C 00000058 00000058  00130014 18002B0C 00000059 00000059  *.................................*
01C8E0   00130014 18002B0C 00000084 000F0085  000E0014 18002B0C 00000085 000F0086  *.................................*
01C900   000E0014 00010001 C2C2C2C1 C3C40000  00000000 00000000 00000000 00000BF0  *........BBBACD..................0*
```

```
TIOT   JOB  A294P014   STEP HCGO
       DD   14140100   JOBLIB   00150A00  80002230
       DD   14040100   PGM=*.DD  00150100  80002270
       DD   14040100   SYSABEND  00143500  80002B0C
       DD   14040180   SNAPT    00143700  80002B0C
```

```
MSS         ************ SPQE ************    *************** DQE ***************    ******* FQE ********
            FLGS  NSPQE    SPID    DQE         BLK      FQE      LN       NDQE        NFQE       LN
01FBCB   00  01FDB0   251   01F158    00058000 0005A000 00000800 00000000   00000000 000005BB
01FDB0   80  01F0C8   000   01DF98    00070000 00070000 00000800 00000000   00000000 00000710
01DF98   60  000000   000   01FA70    00070B00 00070B00 00000800 0001E378   00000000 00000198
01F0C8   40  000000   252   01F928    0006F800 0006F800 00000800 0001F2D8   00000000 000001B0
                                       0006E800 0006FB00 00010000 00000000   00000000 000003B0
```

SAVE AREA TRACE

RUN   WAS ENTERED VIA LINK   AT EP CALLIT

```
SA  0707B0   WD1 00000000  HSA 00000000  LSA 00000000  RET 00011546  EPA 010586B0  R0 FFFFFF2F
             R1 000707F8  R2 0001FC50  R3 5001EC64  R4 0001D548  R5 0001D828  R6 0001DA80
             R7 0001F5A0  R8 0001EC38  R9 00000000  R10 00000074  R11 00000000  R12 6007EC9A
```

INTERRUPT AT 05873E

PROCEEDING BACK VIA REG 13

```
SA  058758   WD1 00003A00  HSA 000707B0  LSA 00040000  RET FF058716  EPA 000585B8  R0 000585BB
             R1 00000001  R2 00000001  R3 400586C2  R4 0001D548  R5 0001D82B  R6 0001DA80
             R7 0001E580  R8 0001EC38  R9 00000000  R10 00000074  R11 00000000  R12 6007EC9A
```

RUN   WAS ENTERED VIA LINK   AT EP CALLIT

```
SA  0707B0   WD1 00000000  HSA 00000000  LSA 00000000  RET 00011546  EPA 010586B0  R0 FFFFFF2F
             R1 000707F8  R2 0001FC50  R3 5001EC64  R4 0001D548  R5 0001D828  R6 0001DA80
             R7 0001F5A0  R8 0001EC38  R9 00000000  R10 00000074  R11 00000000  R12 6007EC9A
```

REGS AT ENTRY TO SNAP

```
FLTR 0-6    0000021600001BF2   0E00000006010750           04000000C8000000        1700000001FFFFFF
REGS 0-7    00000030   A00585E4   00000002   400585CA      0001D548   0001D828   0001DA80   0001E5B0
REGS 8-15   0001FC38   00000000   00000074   00000000      6007EC9A   00058610   4005A716   00000000
```

LOAD MODULE   RUN

```
05A6A0                                         47F0F00C 06C3C1D3 D3C9E300 90ECD00C  *..U...U.......00..CALLIT.....*
05A6C0   05305000 309A41D0 30960700 45103012  8F058A7A0 0A130700 4510302A 3800BBBE  *.................................*
05A6E0   000587A0 00000000 00000000 0A330700  45103036 8005A7A0 0A145A20 31364100  *.................................*
05A700   30444F70 304CC4E4 D4E2D3D4 0401B11L  0A0818F0 05EF4620 30520700 45103062  *....0..DUMSLM .....0.............*
05A720   8F05A7A0 0A130700 4510307A 3800BBBF  000587A0 00000000 00000000 0A330700  *.................................*
05A740   45103086 8005B7A0 0A1458D0 309A98EC  D00C92FF D00C07FE 00003800 000707B0  *.................................*
05A760   00040000 4005A716 000585BB 000585BB  00000001 00000002 400586C2 0001D548  *.............B..N.*
05A780   0001D828 0001DA80 0001E5B0 0001EC38  00000000 00000074 00000000 6007EC9A  *..0.....V........*
05A7A0   00000100 2D000000 0097000C 0A00B2FA  0002D0E4 00000001 00004000 00000001  *.......U.....U....*
05A7C0   04000001 54000000 E2D5C1D7 E3404040  02000020 00000001 0A000001 00000660  *........SNAPT   .................*
05A7E0   00000000 00000000 00000000 00000001  0000007D 00000001 00000002 32323232  *.................................*
```

appendix 4

XCTL MACHINE
LISTING

The following table will help the reader identify the various components of this machine listing:

```
 LOC  OBJECT CODE    ADDR1 ADDR2  STMT   SOURCE STATEMENT                                    F30SEP69  10/21/69

000000                                  1 CALLIT CSECT
                                        2        SAVE  (14,12),,*
000000 47F0 F00C        0000C           3+       B     12(0,15) BRANCH AROUND ID
000004 06                               4+       DC    AL1(6)
000005 C3C1D3D3C9E3                     5+       DC    CL6'CALLIT' IDENTIFIER
00000B 00
00000C 90EC D00C        0000C           6+       STM   14,12,12(13) SAVE REGISTERS
000010 0530                             7        BALR  3,0
000012                                  8        USING *,3
000012 5000 305E        00070           9        ST    13,SAVE+4
000016 41D0 305A        0006C          10        LA    13,SAVE
                                       11        OPEN  (SNAP,(OUTPUT))
00001A 0700                            12+       CNOP  0,4
00001C 4510 3012        00024          13+       BAL   1,*+8 LOAD REG1 W/LIST ADDR.
000020 8F                              14+       DC    AL1(143) OPTION BYTE
000021 0000B4                          15+       DC    AL3(SNAP) DCB ADDRESS
000024 0A13                            16+       SVC   19 ISSUE OPEN SVC
                                       17 SNAP    DCB=SNAP,ID=56,SDATA=ALL,PDATA=ALL
000026 0700                            18+       CNOP  0,4
000028 4510 302A        0003C          19+       BAL   1,IHB0003 BRANCH AROUND PARAM LIST
00002C 38                              20+       DC    AL1(56) ID NUMBER
00002D 00                              21+       DC    AL1(0)
00002E BB                              22+       DC    AL1(187) OPTION FLAGS
00002F BE                              23+       DC    AL1(190) OPTION FLAGS
000030 000000B4                        24+       DC    A(SNAP) DCB ADDRESS
000034 00000000                        25+       DC    A(0) TCB ADDRESS
000038 00000000                        26+       DC    A(0) ADDRESS OF SNAP-SHOT LIST
00003C                                 27+IHB0003 DS    0H
00003C 0A33                            28+       SVC   51
                                       29        CLOSE (SNAP)
00003E 0700                            30+       CNOP  0,4
000040 4510 3036        00048          31+       BAL   1,*+8 BRANCH AROUND LIST
000044 80                              32+       DC    AL1(128) OPTION BYTE
000045 0000B4                          33+       DC    AL3(SNAP) DCB ADDRESS
000048 0A14                            34+       SVC   20 ISSUE CLOSE SVC
00004A 58D0 305E        00070          35        L     13,SAVE+4
                                       36        XCTL  (2,12),EP=DUMSLM
00004E 0700                            37+       CNOP  0,4
000050 45F0 3052        00064          38+       BAL   15,*+20 LOAD SUP.PARAMLIST ADR
000054 0000005C                        39+       DC    A(*+8) ADDR OF EP PARAMETER
000058 00000000                        40+       DC    A(0) DCB ADDRESS PARAMETER        LC0A
00005C C4F4D4E2D3D44040                41+       DC    CL8'DUMSLM' EP PARAMETER
000064 98AC D01C        0001C          42+       LM    2,12,28(13) RESTORE REGISTERS
000068 0A07                            43+       SVC   7 ISSUE XCTL SVC
00006C                                 44 SAVE    DS    18F
                                       45 SNAP    DCB   DSORG=PS,RECFM=VBA,MACRF=W,BLKSIZE=1632,LRECL=125,    X
                                                        DDNAME=SNAPT

                                       47+*                   DATA CONTROL BLOCK
                                       48+*
0000B4                                 49+       ORG   *-0 TO ELIMINATE UNUSED SPACE
0000B4                                 50+SNAP    DS    0F ORIGIN ON WORD BOUNDRY
0000B4                                 51+       ORG   *+0 TO ORIGIN GENERATION
```

```
JOB A294P039        STEP HCGO           TIME 100541   DATE 69294   ID = C56                           PAGE 0001

PSW AT ENTRY TO SNAP    FFD50033 4002F72E

TCB  01BC58  RBP   0001BE18   PIE   00000000   DEB  001C124   TIO 0001C178   CMP   00000030   TRN 00000000
             MSS   0201F06B   PK-FLG 00010000  FLG  0001B1B   LLS 0001F1CB   JLB   0001CCR0   JPQ 0001F1F0
             FSA   010607B0   TCB   00000000   TME  00000000  JST 0001BC58   NTC   00000000   OTC 00010250
             LTC   00000000   IQE   00000000   ECB  0001D4B0   STA 00000000   D-PQE 0001F0B8   SQS 001D9A0
             NSTAE 00000000   TCT   0001D6B0   USER 00000000

ACTIVE RBS

PRB  01F22B  RESV  00000000   APSW  00000000   WC-SZ-STAB 00040082   FL-CDE 0001EF40   PSW FFD50033 4002F72E
             Q/TTR 00000000   WT-LNK 0001BC58

SVRB 01BE18  TAB-LN 00480360  APSW  F1F0F5C1   WC-SZ-STAB 00120002   TQN  00000000   PSW FF040007 00007718
             Q/TTR 00005113   WT-LNK 0001F22B
             RG 0-7  00000030   8002F71C   0001D4A8   4002F702   0001D0CB   00010250   0001C170   0001DC8B
             RG 8-15 0001D490   00000000   00000074   00000000   6007FC9A   0002F75C   00011546   00000002
             FXTSA   FF040000   0001BEB4   0002F720   E2E8F2C9   C5C1F0F1   0000CB10   00009B3C   00075100
                     80002B0C   00075344   B007B024   0007AF66

LOAD LIST

             NE 0001EBC0   RSP-CDE 0101F1F0      NE 0001ED40   RSP-CDE 01020BB0      NE 0001ED98   RSP-CDE 01020A9C
             NE 00000000   RSP-CDE 01020A50

CDE

    01FF40   ATR1 0B   NCDE 000000   ROC-RB 0001E228   NM RUN       USE 01   EPA 02F6F0   ATR2 20   XL/MJ 01E4D0
    01F1F0   ATR1 31   NCDE 01FF40   ROC-RB 00000000   NM IGC0A05A  USE 01   EPA 05F9B0   ATR2 2B   XL/MJ 01F1F0
    020BB0   ATR1 BB   NCDE 020BB0   ROC-RB 00000000   NM IGG019CD  USE 0A   EPA 07E4RB   ATR2 20   XL/MJ 020B70
    020A90   ATR1 BB   NCDE 020AC0   ROC-RB 00000000   NM IGG019BA  USE 0B   EPA 07DFB0   ATR2 20   XL/MJ 020AB0
    020A50   ATR1 BB   NCDE 020A90   ROC-RB 00000000   NM IGG019BB  USE 0B   EPA 07E120   ATR2 20   XL/MJ 020A40

XL                                          LN         ADR       LN       ADR       LN        ADR

    01F4D0   SZ 00000010  NO 00000001   80000110   0002F6F0
    01F1F0   SZ 00000010  NO 00000001   80000680   0005F9B0
    020B70   SZ 00000010  NO 00000001   80000210   0007E4RB
    020AB0   SZ 00000010  NO 00000001   800001B0   0007DE80
    020A40   SZ 00000010  NO 00000001   80000058   0007E120

DEB

01C100   00000BF0 00000BF0 00000BF0 00000BF0   00000BF0 00000000 00000215 00002BF0   *...0...0...0...0...0...........*
01C120   0F000000 0301BC58 04000000 8R000000   0F000000 01000000 1B000000 DF02F7A4   *.....................7.*
01C140   0401C100 1R002B0C 0000007F 000F00B3   000F0064 00010001 C2C2C2C1 C3C40000   *..A..............BBBACD..*
01C160   00000000 00000000 00000000 D9E4D540   *.............RUN ..A.....A294P039*

TIOT   JOB  A294P039   STEP HCGO
       DD       14140100   JOBLIB    001D2F00   B0002230
       DD       14040100   PGM=*.DD  001D2B00   B00022B0
       DD       14040100   SYSABEND  001D1900   B0002B0C
       DD       14040100   SNAPT     001D1B00   80002B0C

MSS          *********** SPQE ***********        ************** DQE ***************        ******* FQE *******
             FLGS  NSPQE     SPID     DQE        BLK      FQE       LN        NDQE         NFQE          LN

    01F06B   00    01F070    251      01F328     0002F000 0002F000 00000800 00000000      00000000      000006F0
    01F070   R0    01FFCB    000      01F038     00000000 00000000 00000000 00000000      00000000      00000710
    01F038   60    000000    000      01FBA0     00060000 00060000 00000800 0001F1D0      00000000      00000198
    01FFCB   40    000000    252      01FBC8     00060800 00060800 00000800 0001DFA8      00000000      00000180
                                                 0005FB00 0005FB00 00000800 0001DFAB      00000000      00000180
                                                 0005FB00 0005FB00 00001000 00000000      00000000      00000380

SAVE AREA TRACE

RUN      WAS ENTERED VIA LINK       AT EP CALLIT

SA   0607B0   WD1 00000000   HSA 00000000   LSA 00000000   RET 00011546   EPA 0102F6F0   R0  FFFFFF2F
              R1  000607FB   R2  0001D4A8   R3  5001D4BC   R4  0001D0CB   R5  00010250   R6  0001C170
              R7  0001DC8B   R8  00010490   R9  00000000   R10 00000074   R11 00000000   R12 6007FC9A

INTERRUPT AT 02F72E

PROCEEDING BACK VIA REG 13

SA   02F75C   WD1 58100010   HSA 000607B0   LSA 58110000   RET 1B155510   EPA C0244740   P0  A1025810
              R1  C0245B50   R2  A16A4450   R3  A15A4040   R4  800C9R0F   R5  60048A58   R6  0004C230
              R7  00000048   R8  0001CF18   R9  00010044   R10 0001043B   R11 0001CE18   R12 0001CDB8

RUN      WAS ENTERED VIA LINK       AT EP CALLIT

SA   0607B0   WD1 00000000   HSA 00000000   LSA 00000000   RET 00011546   EPA 0102F6F0   R0  FFFFFF2E
              R1  000607FB   R2  0001D4A8   R3  5001D4BC   R4  0001D0CB   R5  00010250   R6  0001C170
              R7  0001DC8B   R8  00010490   R9  00000000   R10 00000074   R11 00000000   R12 6007FC9A
```

```
JOB A294P039      STEP HCGO        TIME 100609   DATE 69294   ID = 056                        PAGE 0001

PSW AT ENTRY TO SNAP    FFD50033 4002F746

TCB  01BC58   RBP   0001BFF0   PIE   00000000   DEB  0001C0AC   TIO 0001C178   CMP   00000000   TRN 00000000
              MSS   0201F068   PK-FLG 00010000   FLG  00001B1B   LLS 0001F078   JLB   0001CCB0   JPQ 0001E1F0
              FSA   010607B0   TCB   00000000   TME  00000000   JST 0001BC58   NTC   00000000   OTC 0001D250
              LTC   00000000   IQE   00000000   ECB  0001D4B0   STA 00000000   D-PQE 0001F0B8   SQS 0001BA30
              NSTAE 00000000   TCT   0001D6B0   USER 00000000

ACTIVE RBS

PRB  01F228   RESV  00000000   APSW  00000000   WC-SZ-STAB 00040082   FL-CDE 0001EF40   PSW FFD50033 4002F746
              Q/TTR 00000000   WT-LNK 0001BC58

SVRB 01BFE0   TAB-LN 00680360   APSW  F1F0F5C1   WC-SZ-STAB 00120002   TQN   00000000   PSW FF040007 00007EAB
              Q/TTR 00005113   WT-LNK 0001E22B
              RG 0-7   00000030   8002F734   0001D4A8   4002F71A   0001D0C8   0001D250   0001C170   0001DC88
              RG 8-15  0001D490   00000000   00000074   00000000   6007EC9A   0002F760   00011546   00000000
              EXTSA    FF040000   0001C05C   0002F73A   F2E8E2C9   C5C1F0F1   00400000   00000000   00000000
                       0012C002   00000000   00000000   00000000

LOAD LIST

              NE 0001FF38   RSP-CDE 0101E1F0       NE 0001FD70   RSP-CDE 01020B80       NE 0001FD88   RSP-CDE 01020A90
              NE 00000000   RSP-CDE 01020A50

CDE

     01FF40   ATR1 0B   NCDE 000000   ROC-RB 0001E22B   NM DUMSLM    USE 01   EPA 02F70B   ATR2 20   XL/MJ 01FF40
     01F1F0   ATR1 31   NCDE 01FF40   ROC-RB 00000000   NM IGC0A05A  USE 01   EPA 05F980   ATR2 28   XL/MJ 01E32B
     020B80   ATR1 B8   NCDE 020B80   ROC-RB 00000000   NM IGG019CD  USE 0A   EPA 07E4BB   ATR2 20   XL/MJ 020B70
     020A90   ATR1 B8   NCDE 020AC0   ROC-RB 00000000   NM IGG019BA  USE 0A   EPA 07DEA0   ATR2 20   XL/MJ 020A80
     020A50   ATR1 B8   NCDE 020A90   ROC-RB 00000000   NM IGG019BB  USE 0A   EPA 07F120   ATR2 20   XL/MJ 020A40

XL
                                              LN         ADR         LN         ADR         LN         ADR
     01FF40   SZ 00000010   NO 00000001   800000FB   0302F70B
     01E32B   SZ 00000010   NO 00000001   80000680   0005F980
     020B70   SZ 00000010   NO 00000001   80000210   0007E4BB
     020A80   SZ 00000010   NO 00000001   800001B0   0007DEA0
     020A40   SZ 00000010   NO 00000001   8000005B   0007E120

DEB
01C0A0                    00000BF0 00000BF0    00000BF0 00300BF0 00200BF0 00000000   *.............0...0...0...0...0....*
01C0A0   00000215 00002BF0 0F000000 0301BC58   04000000 A8000000 0F000000 01000000   *.................................*
01C0C0   1B000000 DF02F7AB 0401C088 1B00280C   0000007E 000F00B3 000F0064 00010001   *.......7.........................*
01C0E0   C2C2C2C1 C3C40000 00000000 00000000   00000000 00000000                     *BBBACD...........................*

TIOT   JOB A294P039    STEP HCGO
       DD   14140100   JOBLIB   001D2F00   B0002230
       DD   14040100   PGM=*.DD 001D2B00   B00022B0
       DD   14040100   SYSABEND 001D1900   B0002B0C
       DD   14040180   SNAPT    001D1B00   B0002B0C

MSS            ************ SPQE ************    *************** DQE ***************    ******* FQE ********
               FLGS  NSPQE   SPID   DQE           BLK      FQE      LN       NDQE        NFQE        LN

     01F068   00   01F070   251   01EDD0      0002F000 0002F000 00000800 00000000     00000000    0000070B
     01F070   80   01FFCB   000   01FD3B      00000000 00060000 00000800 00000000     00000000    00000710
     01FD3B   60   000000   000   01FBA0      00060800 00060800 00000800 0001F1C0     00000000    0000019B
     01FFCB   40   000000   252   01FBC8      0005F800 0005F800 00000800 0001DFA0     00000000    000001B0
                                              0005E800 0005E800 00001000 00000000     00000000    0000038B

SAVE AREA TRACE

DUMSLM   WAS ENTERED VIA LINK        AT EP DUMPIT

SA   0607B0   WD1 00000000   HSA 00000000   LSA 00000000   RET 00011546   EPA 0102F70B   R0  FFD50040
              R1  00060FC8   R2  0001D4A8   R3  5001D4BC   R4  0001D0CB   R5  00010250   R6  0001C170
              R7  0001DC8B   R8  0001D490   R9  00000000   R10 00000074   R11 00000000   R12 6007EC9A

INTERRUPT AT 02F746

PROCEEDING BACK VIA REG 13

SA   02F760   WD1 00000000   HSA 000607B0   LSA 00000000   RET 00000000   EPA 00000000   R0  00000000
              R1  00000000   R2  00000000   R3  00000000   R4  00000000   R5  00000000   R6  00000000
              R7  00000000   R8  00000000   R9  00000000   R10 00000000   R11 00000000   R12 00000000

DUMSLM   WAS ENTERED VIA LINK        AT EP DUMPIT

SA   0607B0   WD1 00000000   HSA 00000000   LSA 00000000   RET 00011546   EPA 0102F70B   R0  FFD50040
              R1  00060FC8   R2  0001D4A8   R3  5001D4BC   R4  0001D0CB   R5  00010250   R6  0001C170
              R7  0001DC8B   R8  0001D490   R9  00000000   R10 00000074   R11 00000000   R12 6007EC9A

REGS AT ENTRY TO SNAP

     FLTR 0-6   0401016C50002270      000000BA000000BA         0009000A00000000      0000000000000000

     REGS 0-7   00000030   8002F734   0001D4A8   4002F71A      0001D0CB   0001D250   0001C170   0001DC88
     REGS 8-15  0001D490   00000000   00000074   00000000      6007EC9A   0002F760   00011546   00000000

LOAD MODULE   DUMSLM

02F700                    47F0F00C 06C4E4D4   D7C9E300 90ECD00C 053050D0 304A41D0   *.........00..DUMPIT..............*
02F720   30460700 45103012 AF02F7AB 0A130700   4510302A 38008BBF 0002F7AB 00000000   *..........7...........7..........*
02F740   00000000 0A330700 45103036 8002F7AB   0A145800 304A98EC D00C92FF D00C07FE   *..............7..................*
02F760   00000000 000607B0 00000000 00000000   00000000 00000000 00000000 00000000   *.................................*
02F780   00000000 00000000 00000000 00000000   00000000 00000000 00000000 00000000   *.................................*
02F7A0   00000000 00000000 00480200 20020000   00580013 010082FA 002B1577 00000001   *.................................*
02F7C0   00004000 00000001 04000001 54000000   00540020 0001C5BC 9207DE80 0007F120   *..................E..............*
02F7E0   0B000001 00000660 30040048 41060710   0107E4BB 0007E48B 0000007D 00000001   *..................U...U..........*
```

ATTACH MACHINE LISTING

The following table will help the reader identify the components of this machine listing:

```
 LOC   OBJECT CODE     ADDR1 ADDR2  STMT    SOURCE STATEMENT

000000                                  1 DUMPIT   CSECT
                                        2          SAVE   (14,12),,*
000000 47F0 F00C          0000C         3+         B      12(0,15) BRANCH AROUND ID
000004 06                               4+         DC     AL1(6)
000005 C4E4D407C9E3                     5+         DC     CL6'DUMPIT' IDENTIFIER
00000B 00
00000C 90EC D00C          0000C         6+         STM    14,12,12(13) SAVE REGISTERS
000010 0530                             7          BALR   3,0
000012                                  8          USING  *,3
000012 5040 30F6          0010A         9          ST     4,LECB
000016 5000 305A          0006C        10          ST     13,SAVE+4
00001A 41D0 3056          0006B        11          LA     13,SAVE
                                       12          OPEN   (SNAP1,(OUTPUT))
00001E 0700                            13+         CNOP   0,4
000020 4510 3016          0002B        14+         BAL    1,*+8 LOAD REG1 W/LIST ADDR.
000024 8F                              15+         DC     AL1(143) OPTION BYTE
000025 0000B0                          16+         DC     AL3(SNAP1) DCB ADDRESS
000028 0A13                            17+         SVC    19 ISSUE OPEN SVC
00002A                                 18          SNAP   DCB=SNAP1,ID=56,SDATA=ALL,PDATA=ALL
00002A 0700                            19+         CNOP   0,4
00002C 4510 302F          00040        20+         BAL    1,IHB0003 BRANCH AROUND PARAM LIST
000030 38                              21+         DC     AL1(56) ID NUMBER
000031 00                              22+         DC     AL1(0)
000032 BB                              23+         DC     AL1(187) OPTION FLAGS
000033 BF                              24+         DC     AL1(190) OPTION FLAGS
000034 000000B0                        25+         DC     A(SNAP1) DCB ADDRESS
000038 00000000                        26+         DC     A(0) TCB ADDRESS
00003C 00000000                        27+         DC     A(0) ADDRESS OF SNAP-SHOT LIST
000040                                 28+IHB0003  DS     0H
000040 0A33                            29+         SVC    51
                                       30          CLOSE  (SNAP1)
000042 0700                            31+         CNOP   0,4
000044 4510 303A          0004C        32+         BAL    1,*+8 BRANCH AROUND LIST
000048 80                              33+         DC     AL1(128) OPTION BYTE
000049 0000B0                          34+         DC     AL3(SNAP1) DCB ADDRESS
00004C 0A14                            35+         SVC    20 ISSUE CLOSE SVC
00004F 5840 30F6          0010A        36          L      4,LECB
                                       37          POST   (4)
000052 1814                            38+         LR     1,4 LOAD PARAMETER REG 1
000054 1B00                            39+         SR     0,0 SET CODE VALUE OF 0
000056 0A02                            40+         SVC    2 ISSUE POST SVC
000058 58D0 305A          0006C        41          L      13,SAVE+4
                                       42 FINIS    RETURN (14,12),T
00005C                                 43+FINIS    DS     0H
00005C 98EC D00C          0000C        44+         LM     14,12,12(13) RESTORE THE REGISTERS
000060 92FF D00C          0000C        45+         MVI    12(13),X'FF' SET RETURN INDICATION
000064 07FE                            46+         BR     14 RETURN
000068                                 47 SAVE     DS     18F
                                       48 SNAP1    DCB    DSORG=PS,RECFM=VBA,MACRF=W,BLKSIZE=1632,LRECL=125,       X
                                                          DDNAME=SNAPT

                                       50+**                   DATA CONTROL BLOCK
                                       51+**
0000B0                                 52+         ORG    *-0 TO ELIMINATE UNUSED SPACE
0000B0                                 53+SNAP1    DS     OF ORIGIN ON WORD BOUNDRY
0000B0                                 54+         ORG    *+0 TO ORIGIN GENERATION

                                       56+**                   DIRECT ACCESS DEVICE INTERFACE

0000B0 0000000000000000                58+         DC     BL16'0' FDAD,DVTBL
0000C0 00000000                        59+         DC     A(0) KEYLE,DEVT,TRBAL

                                       61+**                   COMMON ACCESS METHOD INTERFACE

0000C4 00                              63+         DC     AL1(0) BUFNO
0000C5 000001                          64+         DC     AL3(1) BUFCB
0000C8 0000                            65+         DC     AL2(0) BUFL
0000CA 4000                            66+         DC     BL2'0100000000000000' DSORG
0000CC 00000001                        67+         DC     A(1) IOBAD

                                       69+**                   FOUNDATION EXTENSION

0000D0 00                              71+         DC     BL1'00000000' BFTEK,BFALN,HIARCHY
0000D1 000001                          72+         DC     AL3(1) EODAD
0000D4 54                              73+         DC     BL1'01010100' RECFM
0000D5 000000                          74+         DC     AL3(0) EXLST

                                       76+**                   FOUNDATION BLOCK

0000D8 E2D5C1D7E3404040                78+         DC     CL8'SNAPT' DDNAME
0000E0 02                              79+         DC     BL1'00000010' OFLGS
0000E1 00                              80+         DC     BL1'00000000' IFLG
0000E2 0020                            81+         DC     BL2'0000000000100000' MACR

                                       83+**                   BSAM-BPAM-QSAM INTERFACE

0000E4 00                              85+         DC     BL1'00000000' RER1
0000E5 000001                          86+         DC     AL3(1) CHECK,GERR,PERR
0000E8 00000001                        87+         DC     A(1) SYNAD
0000EC 0000                            88+         DC     H'0' CIND1, CIND2
0000EE 0660                            89+         DC     AL2(1632) BLKSIZE
0000F0 00000000                        90+         DC     F'0' WCPO, WCPL, OFFSR, OFFSW
0000F4 00000001                        91+         DC     A(1) IOBA
0000F8 00                              92+         DC     AL1(0) NCP
0000F9 000001                          93+         DC     AL3(1) EOBR, EOBAD

                                       95+**                   BSAM-BPAM INTERFACE

0000FC 00000001                        97+         DC     A(1) EOBW
000100 0000                            98+         DC     H'0' DIRCT
000102 007D                            99+         DC     AL2(125) LRECL
000104 00000001                       100+         DC     A(1) CNTRL, NOTE, POINT
                                      101 LECB     DC     1F
      *** ERROR ***
                                      102          END
```

```
LOC   OBJECT CODE      ADDR1 ADDR2  STMT  SOURCE STATEMENT

000000                                1 CALLIT CSECT
                                      2        SAVE  (14,12),,*
000000 47F0 F00C        0000C         3+       B     12(0,15) BRANCH AROUND ID
000004 06                             4+       DC    AL1(6)
000005 C3C1D3D3C9E3                   5+       DC    CL6'CALLIT' IDENTIFIER
00000B 00
00000C 90EC D00C        0000C         6+       STM   14,12,12(13) SAVE REGISTERS
000010 05B0                           7        BALR  3,0
000012                                8        USING *,3
000012 50D0 3036        00048         9        ST    13,SAVE+4
000016 41D0 3082        0009C        10        LA    13,SAVE
                                     11        OPEN  (SNAP,(OUTPUT))
00001A 0700                          12+       CNOP  0,4
00001C 4510 3012        00024        13+       BAL   1,*+8 LOAD REG1 W/LIST ADDR.
000020 8F                            14+       DC    AL1(143) OPTION BYTE
000021 00010C                        15+       DC    AL3(SNAP) DCB ADDRESS
000024 0A13                          16+       SVC   19 ISSUE OPEN SVC
                                     17        SNAP  DCB=SNAP,ID=54,SDATA=ALL,PDATA=ALL
000026 0700                          18+       CNOP  0,4
000028 4510 302A        0003C        19+       BAL   1,IHB0003 BRANCH AROUND PARAM LIST
00002C 38                            20+       DC    AL1(56) ID NUMBER
00002D 00                            21+       DC    AL1(0)
00002E 8B                            22+       DC    AL1(187) OPTION FLAGS
00002F 8F                            23+       DC    AL1(192) OPTION FLAGS
000030 00010C                        24+       DC    A(SNAP) DCB ADDRESS
000034 00000000                      25+       DC    A(0) TCB ADDRESS
000038 00000000                      26+       DC    A(0) ADDRESS OF SNAP-SHOT LIST
00003C                           27+IHB0003    DS    CH
00003C 0A33                          28+       SVC   51
                                     29        CLOSE (SNAP)
00003E 0700                          30+       CNOP  0,4
000040 4510 3036        00048        31+       BAL   1,*+8 BRANCH AROUND LIST
000044 80                            32+       DC    AL1(128) OPTION BYTE
000045 00010C                        33+       DC    AL3(SNAP) DCB ADDRESS
000048 0A14                          34+       SVC   20 ISSUE CLOSE SVC
00004A 4140 3152        00164        35        LA    4,SYNCH
                                     36        ATTACH EP=DUMMLM,ECB=SYNCH
00004E 41F0 3046        00058        37+       LA    15,IHB0005 LOAD 15 WITH LIST ADDR
000052 47F0 F024        00024        38+       B     36(0,15)
000058                          39+IHB0005     DS    0F SUP. PARAM. LIST
000058 00000074                      40+       DC    A(*+28) ADDRESS OF SYMB NAME         LCS1
00005C 00                            41+       DC    AL1(0) NO HIARCHY
00005D 00000C                        42+       DC    AL3(0) DCB ADDRESS                   LCS1
000060 00000164                      43+       DC    A(SYNCH) ECB ADDRESS
000064 00000000                      44+       DC    A(0) GSPV VALUE OR GSPL ADR
000068 00000000                      45+       DC    A(0) SHSPL OR SHSPV
00006C 02                            46+       DC    AL1(2) SET ROLLOUT BITS  RORT
00006D 000000                        47+       DC    AL3(0) ETXR ROUT. ADDRESS   RORT
000070 0000                          48+       DC    AL2(0) DPMOD VALUE
000072 00                            49+       DC    AL1(0) LPMOD VALUE
000073 00                            50+       DC    AL1(0)
000074 C4E4D4E4D3D44040              51+       DC    CL8'DUMMLM' EP SYMBOL
00007C 0A2A                          52+       SVC   42 ISSUE ATTACH SVC
                                     53        WAIT  ,ECB=SYNCH
00007E 4110 3152        00164        54+       LA    1,SYNCH LOAD PARAMETER REG 1
000082 4100 0001        00001        55+       LA    0,1(0,0) COUNT OMITTED,1 USED
000086 0A01                          56+       SVC   1 LINK TO WAIT ROUTINE
                                     57        OPEN  (SNAP,(OUTPUT))
000088                               58+       CNOP  0,4
000088 4510 307F        00090        59+       BAL   1,*+8 LOAD REG1 W/LIST ADDR.
00008C 8F                            60+       DC    AL1(143) OPTION BYTE
00008D 00010C                        61+       DC    AL3(SNAP) DCB ADDRESS
000090 0A13                          62+       SVC   19 ISSUE OPEN SVC
                                     63        SNAP  DCB=SNAP,ID=56,SDATA=ALL,PDATA=ALL
000092 0700                          64+       CNOP  0,4
000094 4510 3096        000A8        65+       BAL   1,IHB0009 BRANCH AROUND PARAM LIST
000098 38                            66+       DC    AL1(56) ID NUMBER
000099 00                            67+       DC    AL1(0)
00009A 8B                            68+       DC    AL1(187) OPTION FLAGS
00009B 8F                            69+       DC    AL1(192) OPTION FLAGS
00009C 00010C                        70+       DC    A(SNAP) DCB ADDRESS
0000A0 00000000                      71+       DC    A(0) TCB ADDRESS
0000A4 00000000                      72+       DC    A(0) ADDRESS OF SNAP-SHOT LIST
0000A8                           73+IHB0009    DS    CH
0000A8 0A33                          74+       SVC   51
                                     75        CLOSE (SNAP)
0000AA 0700                          76+       CNOP  0,4
0000AC 4510 30A2        000B4        77+       BAL   1,*+8 BRANCH AROUND LIST
0000B0 80                            78+       DC    AL1(128) OPTION BYTE
0000B1 00010C                        79+       DC    AL3(SNAP) DCB ADDRESS
0000B4 0A14                          80+       SVC   20 ISSUE CLOSE SVC
0000B6 58D0 3086        000C8        81        L     13,SAVE+4
                                     82 FINIS  RETURN (14,12),T
0000BA                           83+FINIS      DS    0H
0000BA 98EC D00C        0000C        84+       LM    14,12,12(13) RESTORE THE REGISTERS
0000BE 92FF D00C        0000C        85+       MVI   12(13),X'FF' SET RETURN INDICATION
0000C2 07FE                          86+       BR    14 RETURN
0000C4                            87 SAVE      DS    18F
                                     88 SNAP   DCB   DSORG=PS,RECFM=VBA,MACRF=W,BLKSIZE=1632,LRECL=125,    X
                                                     DDNAME=SNAP

                                     90+*                      DATA CONTROL BLOCK
                                     91+*
00010C                               92+       ORG   *-0 TO ELIMINATE UNUSED SPACE
00010C                            93+SNAP      DS    0F ORIGIN ON WORD BOUNDRY
00010C                               94+       ORG   *+0 TO ORIGIN GENERATION

                                     96+*                 DIRECT ACCESS DEVICE INTERFACE

00010C 0000000000000000              98+       DC    BL16'0' FDAD,DVTBL
00011C 00000000                      99+       DC    A(0) KEYLE,DEVT,TRBAL
```

```
JOB A296P034          STEP HCGO          TIME 102023   DATE 69296   ID = 056                          PAGE 0001

PSW AT ENTRY TO SNAP    FFE50033 4003F6D6

TCB  01F748  RBP   0001F930   PIE   00000000   DEB  0001FA7C  TIO 0001F9CB   CMP  00000000   TRN 00000000
             MSS   0201FBD0   PK-FLG F0010000   FLG  0000181B  LLS 0001FA60   JLB  0001F9CB   JPQ 0001F968
             FSA   010707B0   TCB   00000000    TME  00000000  JST 0001E748   NTC  00000000   NTC 0001C4B8
             LTC   00000000   IQE   00000000    ECB  0001F248   STA 00000000   D-PQE 0001FEF8  SQS 0001F430
             NSTAE 00000000   TCT   0001C650    USER 00000000


ACTIVE RBS

PRB  01FA38  RESV  00000000   APSW  00000000    WC-SZ-STAB 00040082    FL-CDE 0001FC40   PSW FFE50033 4003F6D6
             Q/TTR 00000000   WT-LNK 0001F748

SVRB 01F930  TAB-LN 00280360  APSW  F1F0F5C1    WC-SZ-STAB 00120002    TQN    00000000   PSW FF040007 00006F88
             Q/TTR 00005113    WT-LNK 0001FA38
             RG 0-7   00000030   8003F6C4   0001F240   4003F6AA   0001C210   0001C4B8   0001F9C0   0001CFC0
             RG 8-15  0001F228   00000000   00000074   00000000   6007FC94   0003F75C   00011546   00000000
             EXTSA    FF040000   0001F99C   0003F6C8   F2F6F2C9   C5C1F0F1   00000000   0001F8D0   00000090
                      0012C002   00000000   00000000   00000000


LOAD LIST

        NE 0001FA68   RSP-CDE 0101F968      NE 0001FAA0   RSP-CDE 01020BB0      NE 0001FBC8   RSP-CDE 01020A90
        NE 00000000   RSP-CDE 01020A50


CDE

    01FC40     ATR1 0B   NCDE 000000   ROC-RB 0001FA38   NM RUN        USE 01   EPA 03F698   ATR2 20   XL/MJ 01FC30
    01F968     ATR1 31   NCDE 01FC40   ROC-RB 00000000   NM IGC0A05A   USE 01   EPA 06F980   ATR2 28   XL/MJ 01F958
    020BB0     ATR1 B0   NCDE 020BB0   ROC-RB 00000000   NM IGG019CD   USE 07   EPA 07F488   ATR2 20   XL/MJ 020B70
    020A90     ATR1 B0   NCDE 020AC0   ROC-RB 00000000   NM IGG019RA   USE 07   EPA 07DFB0   ATR2 20   XL/MJ 020AB0
    020A50     ATR1 B0   NCDE 020A90   ROC-RB 00000000   NM IGG019BB   USE 07   EPA 07E120   ATR2 20   XL/MJ 020A40


XL                                           LN        ADR        LN        ADR        LN        ADR

    01FC30     SZ 00000010   NO 00000001    8000016B   0003F698
    01F958     SZ 00000010   NO 00000001    8000006B0  006F980
    020B70     SZ 00000010   NO 00000001    80000210   0007F488
    020AB0     SZ 00000010   NO 00000001    80000180   0007DEB0
    020A40     SZ 00000010   NO 00000001    8000005B   0007F120


DEB

01FA40                                                         00000BF0 C0000BF0  *.........................0....0*
01FA60   00000BF0 00000BF0 00000BF2 00000000   00000219 00002BF0 0F000000 0301F748  *....0....0....0..........7.......X.*
01FA80   04000000 88000000 0F000000 01000000   1B000000 FF03F7A4 0401FA58 18002B0C  *..............7.........*
01FAA0   00000067 000A006C 00090064 00010001   C2C2C2C1 C3C40000 00000000 00000000  *..............BBBACD........*
01FAC0   00000000 58300010                                                          *.................INIT    B      *


TIOT   JOB A296P034   STEP HCGO
       DD        14140101   JOBLIB     000C2400   80022230
       DD        14040101   PGM=*.DD   000C1000   80022230
       DD        14040100   SYSABEND   000C0E00   80002A0C
       DD        14040100   SNAPT      000C1000   80002B0C


MSS            ************ SPQE ************    ************* DQE *************    ******* FQE ********
               FLGS  NSPQE    SPID    DQE        BLK       FQE       LN      NDQE   NFQE       LN

    01FBD0     00    01FFF0   251     01FB08     0003F000  0003F000  00000800  00000000   00000000   00000698
    01FFF0     80    01FFF8   000     01F900     00000000                                  00000000   00000710
    01F900     60    000000   000     01FCC8     00070000  00070000  00000800  0001F948   00000000   00000198
    01FFF8     40    000000   252     01FFC8     0007D800  0006F800  00000800  0001FB40   00000000   00000180
                                                 0006B800  0006F800  00001000  00000000   00000000   00000380


D-PQE 0001FEF8   FIRST 0001FB38   LAST 0001FB38
PQE  01FB38   FFB 0003F800   LFB 0003F800   NPQ 00000000   PPQ 00000000
              TCB 0001C4B8   RSI 00032000   RAD 0003F000   FLG 0000

FBQE 03F800   NFB 0001FB38   PFB 0001FB38   SZ 0002F000


QCB TRACE

MAJ 01FACB   NMAJ 0001F878   PMAJ 000130D8   FMIN 0001D4F0   NM  SYSDSN

MIN 01D4F0   FQFL 0001FF08   PMIN 0001FACB   NMIN 0001F6D8   NM FF  SYS1.MACLIB

             NQFL 00000000   PQEL 8001D4F0   TCB  0001C4B8   SVRB 0001C400

MIN 01F6D8   FQFL 0001F768   PMIN 0001D4F0   NMIN 00000000   NM FF  DUMT

             NQFL 00000000   PQFL 0001F6D8   TCB  0001C4B8   SVRB 0001C400

MAJ 01F878   NMAJ 00000000   PMAJ 0001FACB   FMIN 0001FB60   NM  SYSIFA01

MIN 01FB60   FQFL 0001F908   PMIN 0001F878   NMIN 00000000   NM EQ  0003F7A4

             NQFL 00000000   PQFL 0001FB60   TCB  0001F748   SVRB 0001F3A0
```

```
SAVE AREA TRACE

RUN     WAS ENTERED VIA LINK         AT EP CALLIT

SA   070780   WD1 00000000   HSA 00000000   LSA 00000000   RET 00011546   EPA 0103F698   R0  FFFFFF2F
              R1  000707E8   R2  0001F240   R3  5001F254   R4  0001C210   R5  0001C4B8   R6  0001E9C0
              R7  0001CFC0   R8  0001F228   R9  00000000   R10 00000074   R11 00000000   R12 6007FC9A


INTERRUPT AT 03F606


PROCEEDING BACK VIA REG 13

SA   03F75C   WD1 C3E3D9E3   HSA 00070780   LSA C2404040   RET 40404040   EPA 404040C8   R0  C1E240C9
              R1  D5E5C1D3   R2  C9C440D1   R3  D6C240D5   R4  F404C2C5   R5  D9404040   R6  40400A23
              R7  4510B1EB   R8  0B062BB0   R9  00062B7C   R10 001F0000   R11 C9C5C6C1   R12 C3E3D840

RUN     WAS ENTERED VIA LINK         AT EP CALLIT

SA   070780   WD1 00000000   HSA 00000000   LSA 00000000   RET 00011546   EPA 0103F698   R0  FFFFFF2F
              R1  000707E8   R2  0001F240   R3  5001F254   R4  0001C210   R5  0001C4B8   R6  0001E9C0
              R7  0001CFC0   R8  0001F228   R9  00000000   R10 00000074   R11 00000000   R12 6007FC9A


020FC0   0007F790 4007BC04 00000000 00077A94    0007B6C8 4007BA06 00002B0C 0007B70C   *..7...............H.........*
020FE0   00002ACC 0007B6C8 00000026 00000001    00000026 0007B6E4 0001DBE0 00020078   *.......H.............4......*


REGS AT ENTRY TO SNAP

    FLTR 0-6    CB253B8CC69296F    0000000020000000         000000000000000C0    0001C64B000000BB

    REGS 0-7    00000030   B003F6C4   0001F240   4003F6AA      0001C210   0001C4B8   0001E9C0   0001CFC0
    REGS 8-15   0001F228   00000000   00000074   00000000      6007FC9A   0003F75C   00011546   00000000

LOAD MODULE  RUN

03F680                                                      47F0F00C 06C3C1D3   *.....0...............00..CAL*
03F6A0   D3C9E300 90EC000C 05305000 30B64100    30B20700 45103012 8F03F7A4 0A130700   *LIT...............7.....*
03F6C0   45103024 3800BBBE 0003F7A4 00000000    00000000 0A330700 45103036 8003F7A4   *..........7.........7.*
03F6E0   0A144140 315241F0 304647F0 F024B535    0003F70C 00000000 0003F7FC 00000000   *... ...0...00....7.......7.....*
03F700   00000000 02000000 00000000 C4E4D4F4    03044040 0A244110 31524100 00010A01   *............DUMULM .........*
03F720   4510307F 8F03F7A4 0A130700 45103096    3800BBBE 0003F7A4 00000000 00000000   *......7.............7.......*
03F740   0A330700 45103042 8003F7A4 0A145800    30B69BEC D00C92FF D00C07EE C3E3D9E3   *..........7..............CTRT*
03F760   00070780 C2404040 40404040 40404000    C1E240C9 D5E5C1D3 C9C440D1 D6C24005   *....B     HAS INVALID JOB N*
03F780   F404C2C5 D9404040 40400A23 4510B1EB    0B062BB0 00062B7C 001F0000 C9C5C6C1   *UMBER    .....Y.......IEFA*
03F7A0   C3E3D840 00000100 20000000 006A0000    0300B2FA 00280769 00000001 00004000   *CTQ ................. .*
03F7C0   00000001 04000001 54000000 00540020    0001EA7C 92070FB0 0007F120 0B000001   *................1.........*
03F7E0   00000660 30040048 41070710 0107F4B8    0007F4B8 0000007D 00000001 00000000   *...............U...U..........*
```

```
JOB A296P034        STEP HCGO              TIME 102037   DATE 69296    ID = 056                      PAGE 0001

PSW AT ENTRY TO SNAP   FFE50033 4003F5D2

TCB  01F910  RBP  0001F4E8   PIE  00000000   DEB  0001F4D4   TIO 0001E9C8   CMP  00000000   TRN 00000000
             MSS  0001FBC8   PK-FLG F0010000  FLG  0001A1B   LLS 0001F90F   JLB  0001F9CR   JPQ 00000000
             FSA  01070720   TCB  00000000    TME  00000000  JST 0001E748   NTC  00000000   DTC 0001E748
             LTC  00000000   IOE  00000000    FCB  0003F7EC   STA 00002200   D-PQF 0001FFF8  SQS 0001E3A0
             NSTAE 00000000  TCT  0001C650    USER 00000000

ACTIVE RBS

PRB  01F948  RESV  00000000   APSW  00000000   WC-SZ-STAB 00040082   FL-CDE 0001F968   PSW FFE50033 4003F5D2
             Q/TTR 00000000   WT-LNK 0001F910

SVRB 01F4E8  TAB-LN 00380360  APSW  F1E0F5C1   WC-SZ-STAB 0012D002   TQN 00000000   PSW FF040007 00007200
             Q/TTR 00005113   WT-LNK 0001F948
             RG 0-7  00000030  8003F5C0  0001F240  4003F5A2  0003F7EC  0001C4B8  0001E9C0  0001CFE0
             RG 8-15 0001F228  00000000  00000074  00000000  6007EC9A  0003F5FB  00011546  00000000
             EXTSA   FF040000  0001F554  0003F5C4  F2E8F2C9  C5C1E0F1  0006F980  0006F980  0101E748
                     0001F930  8001FFF8  82040000  7F01F56C

LOAD LIST

      NE 0001F910  RSP-CDE 0101FB78      NE 0001FA30  RSP-CDE 01020B80      NE 0001FAA0  RSP-CDE 01020A90
      NE 00000000  RSP-CDE 01020A50

CDE

      01F968  ATR1 08  NCDE 01FC40  RDC-RB 0001F948  NM DUMULM   USE 01  EPA 03F590  ATR2 20  XL/MJ 01FA60
      01FB78  ATR1 31  NCDE 01F968  RDC-RB 00000000  NM IGC0A05A USE 01  EPA 06F980  ATR2 28  XL/MJ 01FB68
      020B80  ATR1 80  NCDE 020BB0  RDC-RB 00000000  NM IGG019CD USE 07  EPA 07E488  ATR2 20  XL/MJ 020B70
      020A90  ATR1 80  NCDE 020AC0  RDC-RB 00000000  NM IGG019BA USE 07  EPA 07DER0  ATR2 20  XL/MJ 020A80
      020A50  ATR1 80  NCDE 020A90  RDC-RB 00000000  NM IGG019BB USE 07  EPA 07E120  ATR2 20  XL/MJ 020A40

XL                                          LN        ADR       LN        ADR       LN        ADR

      01FA60  SZ 00000010  NO 00000001  8000010R  0003F590
      01FB68  SZ 00000010  NO 00000001  80000680  0006F980
      020B70  SZ 00000010  NO 00000001  80000210  0007E488
      020A80  SZ 00000010  NO 00000001  80000180  0007DER0
      020A40  SZ 00000010  NO 00000001  80000058  0007E120

DEB

01F6A0                                  00000BE0 00000BE0 00000BE0 00000BE0  *.............YY.........0....0....0....0*
01F6C0  00000BE0 00000000 00000219 00002BE0  0F000000 3301F910 04000000 AB000000  *....0................................7.......*
01F6E0  0F000000 01000000 1B000000 FF03F640  0401F6B0 18002B0C 00000067 000A006C  *...........................6...W.............*
01F700  00090064 00010001 C2C2C2C1 C3C40000  00000000 00000000 00000000 0000000R  *..........BBBACD.....................*

TIOT  JOB A296P034   STEP HCGO
      DD       14140101   JOBLIB    000C2400  80002230
      DD       14040101   PGM=*.DD  000C1D00  80002230
      DD       14040100   SYSABEND  000C0F00  80002A0C
      DD       14040180   SNAPT     000C1000  80002B0C

MSS     ************ SPQF ************      *************** DQF ***************      ******* FQF *******
        FLGS NSPQF   SPID    DQF         BLK        FQF       LN      NDQF          NFQF       LN

      01FBC8  C0  000000   000   01F900
      01F900  60  000000   000   01FCC8  00070000 00070000 00002800 00000000   00000000  000006C8

D-PQF 0001FFF8  FIRST 0001FB38  LAST 0001FB38
PQF  01FB38  FFB 0003F800  LFB 0003F800  NPQ 00000000  PPQ 00000000
             TCB 0001C4B8  RSI 00032000  RAD 0003F000  FLG 0000

FBQF 03F800  NFB 0001FB38  PFB 0001FB38  SZ 0002F000

DCB TRACE

MAJ 01FAC8  NMAJ 0001F600  PMAJ 000130D8  FMIN 000104E0  NM SYSDSN

MIN 0104E0  FQFI 0001FF08  PMIN 0001FAC8  NMIN 0001F608  NM FF SYS1.MACLIB

            NQFI 00000000  PQFL 800104E0  TCB 0001C4B8  SVRB 0001C400

MIN 01F6D8  FQFL 0001F768  PMIN 000104E0  NMIN 00000000  NM FF DUMT

            NQFI 00000000  PQFL 0001F6D8  TCB 0001C4B8  SVRB 0001C400

MAJ 01F600  NMAJ 00000000  PMAJ 0001FAC8  FMIN 0001F5A8  NM SYSTEA01

MIN 01F5A8  FQFI 0001F640  PMIN 0001F600  NMIN 00000000  NM EO 0003F640

            NQFL 00000000  PQFL 0001F5A8  TCB 0001F910  SVRB 0001DE70
```

```
SAVE AREA TRACE

DUMULM   WAS ENTERED VIA LINK       AT EP DUMPIT

SA   070720   WD1 00000000   HSA 00000000   LSA 00000000   RET 00011546   EPA 0103F590   R0  00000030
              R1  00070FC8    R2  0001F240    R3  4003F6AA    R4  0003F7FC    R5  0001C4B8    R6  0001F9C0
              R7  0001CFC0    R8  0001F228    R9  00000000    R10 00000074    R11 00000000    R12 6007FC9A

INTERRUPT AT 03F502

PROCEEDING BACK VIA REG 13

SA   03F5E8   WD1 00000000   HSA 00070720   LSA 00000000   RET 00000000   EPA 00000000   R0  00000000
              R1  00000000    R2  00000000    R3  00000000    R4  00000000    R5  00000000    R6  00000000
              R7  00000000    R8  00000000    R9  00000000    R10 00000000    R11 00000000    R12 00000000

DUMULM   WAS ENTERED VIA LINK       AT EP DUMPIT

SA   070720   WD1 00000000   HSA 00000000   LSA 00000000   RET 00011546   EPA 0103F590   R0  00000030
              R1  00070FC8    R2  0001F240    R3  4003F6AA    R4  0003F7FC    R5  0001C4B8    R6  0001F9C0
              R7  0001CFC0    R8  0001F228    R9  00000000    R10 00000074    R11 00000000    R12 6007FC9A


     FLTR 0-6        00000000000007E0      0001F96000000000           000000000070E70     000000000000000

     REGS 0-7        00000030   8003F5C0   0001F240   4003F5A2        0003F7FC   0001C4B8   0001F9C0   0001CFC0
     REGS 8-15       0001F228   00000000   00000074   00000000        6007EC9A   0003F5E8   00011546   00000000

LOAD MODULE   DUMULM

03F580                                                     47F0F00C 06C4E4D4 D7C9E300 90ECD00C   *...W.............00..DUMPIT.....*
03F5A0     05305040 30F65000 30544100 30560700            45103016 8F03F640 0A130700 4510302E   *... .6.............6 .........*
03F5C0     3800B8BE 0003F640 00000000 00000000            0A330700 4510303A 8003F640 0A145840   *......6 ................6 ... *
03F5E0     30F61814 18000A02 58D0305A 98FCD00C            92FFD00C 07FE0000 00000000 00070720   *.6..............................*
03F600     00000000 00000000 00000000 00000000            00000000 00000000 00000000 00000000   *................................*
       LINE 03F620 SAME AS ABOVE
03F640     00440500 20020000 006F0002 0300B2FA            00280769 00000001 00004000 00000001   *...............................*
03F660     04000001 54000000 00540020 0001F6C4            92070E80 0037F120 08000001 00000660   *.............WD................*
03F680     30040948 410706C8 0107E488 0007E488            0000007D 00000001                     *........H..U...U...........7..CAL*
```

```
JOB A296P034          STEP HCGO          TIME 102056   DATE 69296                                    PAGE 0001

COMPLETION CODE       SYSTEM = 103

PSW AT ENTRY TO ABEND   FF040000 40009036

TCB  01F74R  RBP   0001F45R  PIE   00000000  DEB  0001F624  TIO  0001F9CR  CMP  82103000  TRN  00000000
             MSS   0201FRD0  PK-FLG F0850409  FLG  00001R1B  LLS  0001FA60  JLB  0001F9CR  JPQ  0001F96R
             FSA   010707R0  TCR   00000000   TMF  00000000  JST  0001F74R  NTC  00000000  DTC  0001C4RR
             LTC   0001F910  IQE   00000000   ECR  0001F24R  STA  00000000  D-PQF 0001FFFR  SQS  0001DERR
             NSTAE 00000000  TCT   0001C650   USER 00000000


ACTIVE RBS

PRB  01FA3R  RESV  00000000  APSW  00000000  WC-SZ-STAB 00040082  FL-CDE 0001FC40  PSW FFF50013 4003F72A
             Q/TTR 00000000  WT-LNK 0001F74R

SVRB 01F4FR  RESV  00000000  APSW  7007R596  WC-SZ-STAB 0112C002  FL-CDE 00000000  PSW FF040000 40008036
             Q/TTR 00000000  WT-LNK 0001FA3R
             RG 0-7   00000001  8003F724  0001F240  4003F6AA  0003F7FC  0001C4RR  0001F9C0  0001CFF0
             RG R-15  0001F229  00000000  00000074  00000000  6227FC9A  0003F75C  20011546  6200FC22
             EXTSA    0A091REF  0A03F554  0003F5C4  F2FRF2C9  C5C1F0F1  0006F9R0  0006F9R0  0101F74R
                      0001F930  8001FFFR  82040000  7F01F56C

SVRB 01FA3R  TAB-LN 002R03CR  APSW  F2F0F1C3  WC-SZ-STAB 0012D002  TQN  00000000  PSW 00040033 5000721F
             Q/TTR 00004F11  WT-LNK 0001F4FR
             RG 0-7   00000001  00070F24  RF03F7A4  52078402  00070E10  8003F724  00070FF0  8003F724
             RG R-15  00070500  0001F9CR  5000DF26  0000RC60  00000006  00002001  0001FA1C  6300FC22
             EXTSA    000029RF  00070088  2000FFFF  00070RE0  FF030000  0001FAR4  0001FARC  E2FRE2C9
                      C5C1F0F1  C9C5C14R  C1C2C5D5  C4300010

SVRB 01F45R  TAB-LN 00580360  APSW  F1F0F5C1  WC-SZ-STAB 0012D002  TQN  00000000  PSW FF040001 4007F144
             Q/TTR 00005113  WT-LNK 0001FA3R
             RG 0-7   00000000  0001FA98  R0006F18  02008C60  0001F74R  0001FA3R  0001FC40  00000000
             RG R-15  0001F74R  40006FRA  0001F74R  00070088  0001FA0C  0001FARC  40008292  03000000
             EXTSA    00530700  0006FC40  00000000  00070800  00070R00  0006F9R0  0006F9R0  0101F910
                      0001F4FR  0001FRCR  82044040  40404040


LOAD LIST

     NE 0001FA68  RSP-CDE 0201F96R     NE 0001FAA0  RSP-CDE 01020BR0     NE 0001FRCR  RSP-CDE 01020A90
     NE 00000000  RSP-CDE 01020A50


CDE

     01FC40    ATR1 OR   NCDE 000000   RQC-RB 0001FA3R  NM RUN       USE 01  EPA 03F69R  ATR2 20  XL/MJ 01FC30
     01F96R    ATR1 31   NCDE 01FC40   RQC-RB 00000000  NM IGCOA05A  USE 02  EPA 06F9R0  ATR2 28  XL/MJ 01F95R
     020RR0    ATR1 R0   NCDE 020RR0   RQC-RB 00000000  NM IGG019CD  USE 07  EPA 07F4RR  ATR2 20  XL/MJ 020R70
     020A90    ATR1 R0   NCDE 020AC0   RQC-RB 00000000  NM IGG019RA  USE 07  EPA 07DER0  ATR2 20  XL/MJ 020AR0
     020A50    ATR1 R0   NCDE 020A90   RQC-RB 00000000  NM IGG019RR  USE 07  EPA 07E120  ATR2 20  XL/MJ 020A40


XL                                     LN         ADR         LN        ADR         LN       ADR

     01FC30    SZ 00000010   NO 00000001  R000016R   0003F69R
     01F95R    SZ 00000010   NO 00000001  R0000680   0306F9R0
     020R70    SZ 00000010   NO 00000001  R0000210   0307F4RR
     020AR0    SZ 00000010   NO 00000001  R00001R0   00070F80
     020A40    SZ 00000010   NO 00000001  R000005R   0007E120


DEB

01F6A0                                           00000RF0 00000RF0 00000RF0 00000RF0  *..........YY........0...0....0....0*
01F6C0    00000RF0 00000000 02000A05 00002RF0   0F000000 0001F74R 04000030 R8000000  *....0...............X..........*
01FAF0    RF000000 01000000 1R000000 FF070088   0401F6R0 1000240C 00000023 00000007  *................W...........*
01F700    00130064 00010001 C2C2C2C1 C3C40000   00000000 00000000 00000000 C3C40008  *........RRRACD...........CD..*


TIOT  JOB A296P034   STEP HCGO
      DD          14140101    JOBLIR      000C2400   R0002230
      DD          14040101    PGM=*.DD    000C1000   R0002230
      DD          14040100    SYSABEND    000C0F00   R0002A0C
      DD          14040180    SNAPT       000C1000   R0002R0C


MSS            ************ SPQF ***********   ************** DQF **************   ******* FQF ********
               FLGS  NSPQE   SPID   DQE       BLK    FQE    LN   NDQE             NFQE        LN

     01FRD0    00   01FFF0   251   01FR0R    0003F000 0003F0C0 00000800 00000000    00000000    00000698
     01FFF0    80   01FFFR   000   01F900    00000000 00000000 00000000 00000000    00000000    00000698
     01F900    60   000000   000   01FCCR    00070000 00070000 00000800 00000000    00000000    000006CR
     01FFFR    40   000000   252   01FEC8    00070R00 00070R00 00000800 0001F94R    00000000    000005RR
                                             0006F8R0 0006F8R0 00000R00 0001F740    00000000    00000180
                                             0006F000 0006F000 00000800 00000000    00000000    000001A0


D-PQF  0001FFFR   FIRST 0001FR3R   LAST 0001FR3R
PQF  01FR3R   FFR 0003FR00   LFR 0003FR00   NPQ 00000000   PPQ 00000000
              TCR 0001C4RR   RSI 0003200    RAD 0003F000   FLG 0000

FRQF 03FR00   NFR 0001FR3R   PFR 0001FR3R   SZ 0002FR00
```

```
QCB TRACE

MAJ 01FACR    NMAJ 0001F87R    PMAJ 0001300R    FMIN 0001D4F0    NM  SYSDSN

MIN 01D4F0    FQEL 0001FF0R    PMIN 0001FACR    NMIN 0001F6DR    NM FF  SYS1.MACLIB

              NQEL 00000000    PQEL 800104F0    TCB  0001C4RR    SVRB 0001C400

MIN 01F6DR    FQEL 0001F76R    PMIN 0001D4F0    NMIN 00000000    NM FF  DUMT

              NQEL 00000000    PQEL 0001F60R    TCB  0001C4RR    SVRB 0001C400

MAJ 01F87R    NMAJ 00000000    PMAJ 0001FACR    FMIN 0001F860    NM  SYSIFA01

MIN 01F860    FQEL 0001F90R    PMIN 0001F87R    NMIN 00000000    NM FO  IFA

SAVE AREA TRACE

RUN     WAS ENTERED VIA LINK

SA    070780   WD1 00000000   HSA 00000000   LSA 00000000   RET 00011546   EPA 0103F698   R0  FFFFFF2F
               R1  000707FR   R2  0001F240   R3  5001F254   R4  0001C210   R5  0001C4RR   R6  0001F9C0
               R7  0001CFC0   R8  0001F228   R9  00000000   R10 00000074   R11 00000000   R12 6007FC9A

INTERRUPT AT 03F72A

PROCEEDING BACK VIA REG 13

SA    03F75C   WD1 C3F309F3   HSA 000707R0   LSA C2404040   RET 40404040   EPA 404040CR   R0  C1E240C9
               R1  D5F5C1D3   R2  C9C440D1   R3  D6C240D5   R4  F404C2C5   R5  D9404040   R6  40400A23
               R7  451081ER   R8  0R062BR0   R9  00062R7C   R10 001F0000   R11 C9C5C6C1   R12 C3F3D840

RUN     WAS ENTERED VIA LINK

SA    070780   WD1 00000000   HSA 00000000   LSA 00000000   RET 00011546   EPA 0103F698   R0  FFFFFF2F
               R1  000707FR   R2  0001F240   R3  5001F254   R4  0001C210   R5  0001C4RR   R6  0001F9C0
               R7  0001CFC0   R8  0001F228   R9  00000000   R10 00000074   R11 00000000   R12 6007FC9A

REGS AT ENTRY TO ABEND

      FLTR 0-6       C8253R8RCC69296F       0000000020000000       0000000000000000       0001C64800000R8R

      REGS 0-7     00000001   00070F24   8F03F7A4   5007R402   0007DF10   8003F724   000700ED   8003F724
      REGS 8-15    00070F00   0001F9CR   50000F26   0000RC60   00000006   00000001   0001FA1C   6000EC22

LOAD MODULE   RUN

03F680
03F6A0    D3C9F300 90FC000C 05305000 30R641D0         0003F7EC 06C3C1D3    *................7..CAL*
03F6C0    45103R02A 3R00R8RF 0003F7A4 00000000    00000000 0A330700 45103036 R003F7A4    *LIT.............7...........7.*
03F6E0    0A144140 31524100 304647F0 F024R535    0003F70C 00000000 0003F7EC 00000000    *.....0...00....7.......7...*
03F700    00000000 02000000 00000000 C4F4D4F4    D3044040 0A2A4110 31524100 C0010A01    *...........DUMUM M ........*
03F720    45103D7F 8F03F7A4 0A130700 45103096    3R00R8RF 0003F7A4 00000000 00000000    *.......7.............7.......*
03F740    0A330700 45103DA2 R003F7A4 0A145R00    30R698FC 000C92FF 000C07FF C3F309F3    *...........7...............CTRT*
03F760    000707R0 C2404040 40404040 404040C8    C1F240C9 D5F5C1D3 C9C440D1 D6C240D5    *....R      HAS INVALID JOB N*
03F780    F404C2C5 D9404040 40400A23 451081EB    08062RR0 00062B7C 001F0000 C9C5C6C1    *UMBER    ....Y............IEFA*
03F7A0    C3F3D840 00000100 2D000000 006A0012    0400R2FA 002R00E9 00000001 00004000    *CTO ........Z........*
03F7C0    00000001 04000001 54000000 00540020    00070F10 03000020 00000201 0R000001    *..............................*
03F7E0    00000660 00000000 00000000 00000000    00000001 0020007D 00000001 40000000    *.............................*
```

FLOAT MACHINE LISTING

LEVEL 1JAN67   COBOL F

   1

```
00001          IDENTIFICATION DIVISION.
00002          PROGRAM-ID. 'A PLUS 83'.
00003          ENVIRONMENT DIVISION.
00004          CONFIGURATION SECTION.
00005          SOURCE-COMPUTER. IBM-360 I65.
00006          OBJECT-COMPUTER. IBM-360 I65.
00007          DATA DIVISION.
00008          WORKING-STORAGE SECTION.
00009          77  A VALUE IS +.10E+02 USAGE IS COMPUTATIONAL-1.
00010          77  B             USAGE. IS COMPUTATIONAL-1.
00011          77  TEST          USAGE IS COMPUTATIONAL-1.
00012          77  C VALUE IS +.20E+02 USAGE IS COMPUTATIONAL-1.
00013          PROCEDURE DIVISION.
00014          COMPUTE B = A + 3.
00015              IF C IS GREATER THAN B  MOVE 1 TO TEST.
00016              ENTER LINKAGE.
00017              CALL 'DUMPIT'.
00018              ENTER COBOL.
00019              STOP RUN.
```

INTRNL NAME	LVL	SOURCE NAME	BASE	DISPL	INTRNL NAME	DEFINITION	USAGE	R	Q
DNM=1-030	77	A	BLI=1	000	DNM=1-030	DS 1F	COMP-1		
DNM=1-040	77	B	BLI=1	004	DNM=1-040	DS 1F	COMP-1		
DNM=1-050	77	TEST	BLI=1	008	DNM=1-050	DS 1F	COMP-1		
DNM=1-063	77	C	BLI=1	00C	DNM=1-063	DS 1F	COMP-1		

```
14   COMPUTE    0001FA                      START   EQU   *
                0001FA  F8 F0 D 060 C 010            ZAP   060(16,13),010(1,12)                    LIT+0
                000200  58 F0 C 000                  L     15,000(0,12)          V(IHDFIDIF)
                000204  05 EF                        BALR  14,15
                000206  0000                         DC    X'0000'
                000208  2B 22                        SDR   2,2
                00020A  78 20 6 000                  LE    2,000(0,6)            DNM=1-30
                00020E  2A 02                        ADR   0,2
                000210  70 00 6 004                  STE   0,004(0,6)            DNM=1-40
14   IF         000214  78 20 6 00C                  LE    2,00C(0,6)            DNM=1-40
                000218  79 20 6 004                  CE    2,004(0,6)            DNM=1-40
                00021C  58 F0 C 008                  L     15,008(0,12)          GN=01
                000220  07 DF                        BCR   13,15
15   MOVE       000222  F8 F0 D 060 C 011            ZAP   060(16,13),011(1,12)                    LIT+1
                000228  58 FC C 000                  L     15,000(0,12)          V(IHDFIDIF)
                00022C  05 EF                        BALR  14,15
                00022E  0000                         DC    X'0000'
                000230  70 00 6 008                  STE   0,008(0,6)            DNM=1-50
16   ENTER
```

appendix 7

SALARIES CREATE
MACHINE LISTING

1

```
00001          IDENTIFICATION DIVISION.
00002          PROGRAM-ID. 'SALARIES2'.
00003          ENVIRONMENT DIVISION.
00004          CONFIGURATION SECTION.
00005          SOURCE-COMPUTER. IBM-360 I65.
00006          OBJECT-COMPUTER. IBM-360 I65.
00007          INPUT-OUTPUT SECTION.
00008          FILE-CONTROL.
00009              SELECT CARD-FILE ASSIGN TO 'SYSIN' UNIT-RECORD.
00010              SELECT SALARY-FILE ASSIGN TO 'OUTPUT' DIRECT-ACCESS 2311.
00011          DATA DIVISION.
00012          FILE SECTION.
00013          FD  SALARY-FILE
00014              LABEL RECORDS ARE STANDARD
00015              RECORDING MODE IS F
00016              BLOCK CONTAINS 10 RECORDS
00017              RECORD CONTAINS 120 CHARACTERS
00018              DATA RECORD IS SALARY-RECORD.
00019          01  SALARY-RECORD.
00020              02 FILLER PICTURE X(120).
00021          FD  CARD-FILE
00022              LABEL RECORDS ARE OMITTED
00023              RECORDING MODE IS F
00024              DATA RECORDS ARE CARD-REC.
00025          01  CARD-REC.
00026              02 NUMBER PICTURE X(5).
00027              02 NAME PICTURE A(32).
00028              02 SOC-SEC-CUMULATIVE PICTURE IS 9(6)V99.
00029              02 CNTROL PICTURE X(1) VALUE IS SPACE.
00030              02 GROSS-PAY PICTURE IS 9(6)V99.
00031              02 FILLER PICTURE X(26).
00032          WORKING-STORAGE SECTION.
00033          77  COUNT    PICTURE 9(4) USAGE IS COMPUTATIONAL-3.
00034          01  OUTAREA.
00035              02 N PICTURE A(32) VALUE IS SPACES.
00036              02 S-S-C PICTURE IS 9(6)V99.
00037              02 NUM PICTURE X(5).
00038              02 C PICTURE X(1).
00039              02 G-P PICTURE 9(6)V99.
00040              02 FILLER PICTURE A(66) VALUE IS SPACES.
00041          PROCEDURE DIVISION.
00042          START. OPEN OUTPUT SALARY-FILE.
00043              OPEN INPUT CARD-FILE.
00044          READIT.
00045              READ CARD-FILE AT END GO TO FINIS.
00046              MOVE NAME TO N.
00047              MOVE SOC-SEC-CUMULATIVE TO S-S-C.
00048              MOVE NUMBER TO NUM.
00049              MOVE CNTROL TO C.
00050              MOVE GROSS-PAY TO G-P.
00051              WRITE SALARY-RECORD FROM OUTAREA.
00052              GO TO READIT.
00053          FINIS. ENTER LINKAGE.
00054              CALL 'DUMPIT'.
00055              ENTER COBOL.
00056              CLOSE SALARY-FILE.
00057              STOP RUN.
```

MATRIX MULTIPLY

This appendix presents the FORTRAN source statements and the FORTRAN-produced symbolic listing of the object module from matrix multiply (see Figure 1.7).

```
                                   OS/360   FORTRAN H

          COMPILER OPTIONS - NAME=  MAIN,OPT=00,LINECNT=50,SIZE=0000K,
                            SOURCE,EBCDIC,LIST,NODECK,LOAD,NOMAP,NOEDIT,NOID,NOXREF
ISN 0002           DIMENSION A(100,100),B(100,100),C(100,100)
ISN 0003           READ (1) B,C
ISN 0004           DO 100 I = 1,100
ISN 0005           DO 100 J = 1,100
ISN 0006           A(I,J) =0.
ISN 0007           DO 100 K=1,100
ISN 0008           A(I,J) = B(I,K) * C(K,J) + A(I,J)
ISN 0009       100 CONTINUE
ISN 0010           STOP
ISN 0011           END
```

```
ADCONS FOR EXTERNAL REFERENCES
              01D564  00000000              DC    XL4'00000000'            IBCOM#
              01D598  58 F0 C 00C   100000  L     15, 12( 0,12)            IBCOM#
              01D59C  45 E0 F 014           BAL   14, 20( 0,15)
              01D5A0  00000001              DC    XL4'00000001'            1
              01D5A4  45 E0 F 020           BAL   14, 32( 0,15)
              01D5A8  00009CD4              DC    XL4'00009CD4'            B
              01D5AC  04702710              DC    XL4'04702710'
              01D5B0  45 E0 F 020           BAL   14, 32( 0,15)
              01D5B4  00013914              DC    XL4'00013914'            C
              01D5B8  04702710              DC    XL4'04702710'
              01D5BC  45 E0 F 024           BAL   14, 36( 0,15)
              01D5C0  41 00 0 001           LA    0,  1( 0, 0)            1
              01D5C4  50 0C D 060           ST    0, 96( 0,13)            I
              01D5C8  41 00 0 001   100001  LA    0,  1( 0, 0)            1
              01D5CC  50 0C D 064           ST    0, 100( 0,13)           J
              01D5D0  58 0C D 060   100002  L     0, 96( 0,13)            I
              01D5D4  89 00 0 002           SLL   0,  2( 0, 0)
              01D5D8  50 00 C 010           ST    0, 16( 0,12)            .S00
              01D5DC  41 50 0 190           LA    5, 400( 0, 0)           190
              01D5E0  5C 40 D 064           M     4, 100( 0,13)           J
              01D5E4  18 65                 LR    6, 5
              01D5E6  5A 60 C 010           A     6, 16( 0,12)            .S00
              01D5EA  78 00 D 050           LE    0, 80( 0,13)            O
              01D5EE  58 7C C C08           L     7,  8( 0,12)
              01D5F2  70 06 7 000           STE   0,  0( 6, 7)            A
              01D5F6  41 00 0 001           LA    0,  1( 0, 0)            1
              01D5FA  50 00 D C68           ST    0, 104( 0,13)           K
              01D5FE  58 00 D 060   100003  L     0, 96( 0,13)            I
              01D602  89 00 0 002           SLL   0,  2( 0, 0)
              01D606  50 00 C 010           ST    0, 16( 0,12)            .S00
              01D60A  41 50 0 190           LA    5, 400( 0, 0)           190
              01D60F  5C 40 D 064           M     4, 100( 0,13)           J
              01D612  5A 50 C 010           A     5, 16( 0,12)            .S00
              01D616  50 50 C 010           ST    5, 16( 0,12)            .S00
              01D61A  58 00 D 060           L     0, 96( 0,13)            I
              01D61E  89 00 0 002           SLL   0,  2( 0, 0)
              01D622  50 00 C 014           ST    0, 20( 0,12)            .S01
              01D626  41 50 0 190           LA    5, 400( 0, 0)           190
              01D62A  5C 40 D C68           M     4, 104( 0,13)           K
              01D62E  18 65                 LR    6, 5
              01D630  5A 6C C 014           A     6, 20( 0,12)            .S01
              01D634  58 7C C 000           L     7,  0( 0,12)
              01D638  78 06 7 000           LE    0,  0( 6, 7)            B
              01D63C  70 00 C 014           STE   0, 20( 0,12)            .S01
              01D640  58 00 D C68           L     0, 104( 0,13)           K
              01D644  89 00 0 002           SLL   0,  2( 0, 0)
              01D648  50 0C C C18           ST    0, 24( 0,12)            .S02
              01D64C  41 50 0 190           LA    5, 400( 0, 0)           190
              01D650  5C 40 D 064           M     4, 100( 0,13)           J
              01D654  18 65                 LR    6, 5
              01D656  5A 6C C 018           A     6, 24( 0,12)            .S02
              01D65A  58 70 C 004           L     7,  4( 0,12)
              01D65E  78 06 7 000           LE    0,  0( 6, 7)            C
              01D662  7C 00 C 014           ME    0, 20( 0,12)            .S01
              01D666  70 0C C 014           STE   0, 20( 0,12)            .S01
              01D66A  58 00 D 060           L     0, 96( 0,13)            I
              01D66E  89 00 0 002           SLL   0,  2( 0, 0)
              01D672  50 00 C 018           ST    0, 24( 0,12)            .S02
              01D676  41 50 0 190           LA    5, 400( 0, 0)           190
              01D67A  5C 40 D 064           M     4, 100( 0,13)           J
              01D67E  18 65                 LR    6, 5
              01D680  5A 60 C 018           A     6, 24( 0,12)            .S02
              01D684  58 7C C 008           L     7,  8( 0,12)
              01D688  78 06 7 000           LE    0,  0( 6, 7)            A
              01D68C  7A 00 C 014           AE    0, 20( 0,12)            .S01
              01D690  58 6C C 010           L     6, 16( 0,12)            A
              01D694  70 06 7 000           STE   0,  0( 6, 7)            A
              01D698  58 00 D 054   100     L     0, 84( 0,13)            I
              01D69C  5A 00 D 068           A     0, 104( 0,13)           K
              01D6A0  50 00 D 068           ST    0, 104( 0,13)           K
              01D6A4  59 00 D 058           C     0, 88( 0,13)            64
              01D6A8  58 50 C 02C           L     5, 44( 0,12)
              01D6AC  07 D5                 BCR   13, 5
              01D6AE  58 0C D 054   100004  L     0, 84( 0,13)            I
              01D6B2  5A 00 D 064           A     0, 100( 0,13)           J
              01D6B6  50 00 D 064           ST    0, 100( 0,13)           J
              01D6BA  59 00 D 058           C     0, 88( 0,13)            64
              01D6BE  58 50 C 028           L     5, 40( 0,12)            <
              01D6C2  07 D5                 BCR   13, 5                   <
              01D6C4  58 00 D 054   100005  L     0, 84( 0,13)            I
              01D6C8  5A 0C D 060           A     0, 96( 0,13)            I
              01D6CC  50 0C D 060           ST    0, 96( 0,13)            I
              01D6D0  59 00 D 058           C     0, 88( 0,13)            64
              01D6D4  58 50 C 024           L     5, 36( 0,12)            H
              01D6D8  07 D5                 BCR   13, 5                   H
              01D6DA  58 F0 C 00C   100006  L     15, 12( 0,12)           IBCOM#
              01D6DE  45 E0 F 034           BAL   14, 52( 0,15)
              01D6E2  05                    DC    XL1'05'
              01D6E3  40                    DC    XL1'40'
              01D6E4  40                    DC    XL1'40'
              01D6E5  40                    DC    XL1'40'
              01D6E6  40                    DC    XL1'40'
              01D6E7  F0                    DC    XL1'F0'
ADDRESS OF EPILOGUE
              01D6E8  58 F0 C 00C           L     15, 12( 0,12)
              01D6EC  45 E0 F 034           BAL   14, 52( 0,15)           IBCOM#
              01D6F0  0540                  DC    XL2'0540'
              01D6F2  404040F0              DC    XL4'404040F0'
```

```
ADDRESS OF PROLOGUE
               01D6F8  58 C0 3 048        L     12,   72( 0, 3)
               01D6FC  58 F0 C 00C        L     15,   12( 0,12)
               01D700  45 F0 F 040        BAL   14,   64( 0,15)          IBCOM#
               01D704  18 D3              LR    13,  3
               01D706  58 F0 C 020        L     15,   32( 0,12)
               01D70A  07 FF              BCR   15,15
ADCON FOR PROLOGUE
               000020  0001D6F8           DC    XL4'0001D6F8'
ADCON FOR SAVE AREA
               000024  00000028           DC    XL4'00000028'
ADCON FOR EPILOGUE
               000028  0001D6E8           DC    XL4'0001D6E8'
ADCON FOR REG 12
               000070  0001D558           DC    XL4'0001D558'
TEMPORARIES AND PHASE 20 CONSTANTS
               01D568  00000000           DC    XL4'00000000'
               01D56C  00000000           DC    XL4'00000000'
               01D570  00000000           DC    XL4'00000000'
               01D574  00000000           DC    XL4'00000000'
ADCONS FOR B BLOCK LABELS
               01D578  0001D598           DC    XL4'0001D598'
               01D57C  0001D5C8           DC    XL4'0001D5C8'
               01D580  0001D5D0           DC    XL4'0001D5D0'
               01D584  0001D5FE           DC    XL4'0001D5FE'
               01D588  0001D698           DC    XL4'0001D698'
               01D58C  0001D6AE           DC    XL4'0001D6AE'
               01D590  0001D6C4           DC    XL4'0001D6C4'
               01D594  0001D6DA           DC    XL4'0001D6DA'
```

QISAM EMPYTD
MACHINE LISTING

The following table of contents will help the reader identify the components of the QISAM machine listing:

```
   04/19/69                    SYSTEM SUPPORT UTILITIES --- IEHDASDR  17.0                    PAGE 001

   DUMP FROMDD=DUMPFROM,TODD=SYSPRINT,BEGIN=00600000,END=00600009

**** TRACK  00600000       R0 DATA  0000000000000000

       COUNT  00600000010500A

   000000    F0F1F0F0 F0010000 00600000 16081B                                   *01000.....................*

       COUNT  00600000020500A

   000000    F0F1F0F0 F0010000 00600000 FF1007                                   *01000......  ...............*

       COUNT  00600000030500A

   000000    F0F1F0F4 F0010000 00600001 00001B                                   *01040.....................*

       COUNT  00600000040500A

   000000    F0F1F0F4 F0010000 00600001 FF1007                                   *01040......  ..............*

       COUNT  00600000050500A

(a) 000000    F0F1F0F8 F0010000 00600002 00001B                                   *01080.....................*

       COUNT  00600000060500A

   000000    F0F1F0F8 F0010000 00600002 FF1007                                   *01080......  ..............*

       COUNT  00600000070500A

   000000    F0F1F1F2 F0010000 00600003 00001B                                   *01120.....................*

       COUNT  00600000080500A

   000000    F0F1F1F2 F0010000 00600003 FF1007                                   *01120......  ..............*

       COUNT  00600000090500A

   000000    FFFFFFFF FF000000 00000000 003007                                   *      .....................*

   000000    FFFFFFFF FF000000 00000000 002007                                   *      .....................*

       COUNT  006000001605048O

   000000    F0F1F0F0 F0FFFFFF FFFF4040 40404040    40404040 40404040 40404040 40404040  *01000                      *
   000020    40404040 40404040 40404040 40F0F0F9    F8F24040 40404040 40404040 40404040  *             00982        *
   000040    40404040 40404040 40404040 40404040    40404040 40404040 40404040 40404040  *                          *
   000060    40404040 40404040 40404040 40404040    40404040 40404040 40404040 40FFFFFF  *                          *
   000080    FFFF4040 40404040 40404040 40404040    40404040 40404040 40404040 40404040  *                          *
(b) 0000A0    40404040 40F0F0F9 F8F44040 4C404040    40404040 40404040 40404040 40404040  *       00984               *
                                                        :
   000420    40404040 40404040 40404040 40404040    40404040 40404040 40404040 40FFFFFF  *                          *
   000440    FFFF4040 40404040 40404040 40404040    40404040 40404040 40404040 40404040  *                          *
   000460    40404040 40F0F1F0 F0F04040 40404040    40404040 40404040 40404040 40404040  *       01000              *
   000480    40404040 40404040 40404040 40404040    40404040 40404040 40404040 40404040  *                          *
   000480    40404040 40404040 40404040 40404040    40404040 40404040 40404040 40404040  *                ..........*
   0004A0    40404040 40404040 40404040 40404040    40404040 40                          *                ..........*
```

```
**** TRACK  00600001    RO DATA  0000000000000000

    COUNT  0060000101050480

    000000   F0F1F0F2 F0C1C4C1 D4F240D1 C1D4C5E2    40C54B40 40404040 40404040 40404040  *01020ADAMS JAMES E.              *
    000020   40404040 40F0F0F0 F1F4F2F6 F8F0F1F0    F0F24040 40404040 40404040 40404040  *    0001426801002              *
    000040   40404040 40404040 40404040 40404040    40404040 40404040 40404040 40404040  *                                *
    000060   40404040 40404040 40404040 40404040    40404040 40404040 40404040 40C1D3C6  *                             ALF*
```
(a)
        ⋮
```
    000420   4C4C4040 40404040 40404040 40404040    40404040 40404040 40404040 40C4C5C1  *                             DEA*
    000440   D540F4D3 D4C5D940 C14B4040 40404040    40404040 40404040 40404040 40F0F0F0  *N ULMER A.                   000*
    000460   F1F4F2F6 F8F0F1F0 F2F04040 40404040    40404040 40404040 40404040 40404040  *1426801020                   *
    000480   40404040 40404040 40404040 40404040    40404040 40404040 40404040 40404040  *                             *
    0004A0   40404040 40404040 40404040 40404040    40404040 40                          *..........*

    COUNT  0060000102050480

    000000   F0F1F0F4 F0C4D9C5 E2E2D3C5 D940E6C1    D9D9C5D5 40E64B40 40404040 40404040  *01040DRESSLER WARREN W.          *
    000020   40404040 40F0F0F0 F1F4F2F6 F8F0F1F0    F2F24040 40404040 40404040 40404040  *    0001426801022              *
    000040   40404040 40404040 40404040 40404040    40404040 40404040 40404040 40404040  *                                *
    000060   40404040 40404040 40404040 40404040    40404040 40404040 40404040 40C5C9E2  *                             EIS*
```
(b)
        ⋮
```
    000420   40404040 40404040 40404040 40404040    40404040 40404040 40404040 40C9C7D6  *                             IGO*
    000440   C540E3C8 F4D9F2E3 D6D540D4 4B404040    40404040 40404040 40404040 40F0F0F0  *E THURSTON M.                000*
    000460   F1F4F2F6 F8F0F1F0 F4F04040 40404040    40404040 40404040 40404040 40404040  *1426801040                   *
    000480   40404040 40404040 40404040 40404040    40404040 40404040 40404040 40404040  *                             *
    0004A0   40404040 40404040 40404040 40404040    40404040 40                          *..........*

**** TRACK  00600002    RO DATA  0000000000000000

    COUNT  0060000201050480

    000000   F0F1F0F6 F0FFFFFF FFFF4040 40404040    40404040 40404040 40404040 40404040  *01060                            *
    000020   40404040 40404040 40404040 40F0F1F0    F4F24040 40404040 40404040 40404040  *                   01042          *
    000040   40404040 40404040 40404040 40404040    40404040 40404040 40404040 40404040  *                                *
    000060   40404040 40404040 40404040 40404040    40404040 40404040 40404040 40FFFFFF  *                                *
    000080   FFFF4040 40404040 40404040 40404040    40404040 40404040 40404040 40404040  *                                *
```
(c)
        ⋮
```
    000420   40404040 40404040 40404040 40404040    40404040 40404040 40404040 40FFFFFF  *                                *
    000440   FFFF4040 40404040 40404040 40404040    40404040 40404040 40404040 40404040  *                                *
    000460   40404040 40F0F1F0 F6F04040 40404040    40404040 40404040 40404040 40404040  *           01060                 *
    000480   40404040 40404040 40404040 40404040    40404040 40404040 40404040 40404040  *                                *
    0004A0   40404040 40404040 40404040 40404040    40404040 40                          *..........*

    COUNT  0060000202050480

    000000   F0F1F0F8 F0D1D6E2 C5D7C8E2 40D1D6F2    C5D7C840 C44B4040 40404040 40404040  *01080JOSEPHS JOSEPH D.           *
    000020   40404040 40F0F0F0 F1F4F2F6 F8F0F1F0    F6F24040 40404040 40404040 40404040  *    0001426801062              *
    000040   40404040 40404040 40404040 40404040    40404040 40404040 40404040 40404040  *                                *
    000060   40404040 40404040 40404040 40404040    40404040 40404040 40404040 40D2C1C5  *                             KAE*
```
        ⋮
```
    000420   40404040 40404040 40404040 40404040    40404040 40404040 40404040 40D9D6C8  *                             ROH*
    000440   D940C6D9 C5C440C1 4B404040 40404040    40404040 40404040 40404040 40F0F0F0  *R FRED A.                    000*
    000460   F1F4F2F6 F8F0F1F0 F8F04040 40404040    40404040 40404040 40404040 40404040  *1426801080                   *
    000480   40404040 40404040 40404040 40404040    40404040 40404040 40404040 40404040  *                             *
    0004A0   4C4C4040 40404040 40404040 40404040    40404040 40                          *..........*

**** TRACK  00600003    RO DATA  0000000000000000

    COUNT  0060000301050480

    000000   F0F1F1F0 F0D9D6E2 C5D5C2C5 D9C740D9    D6C2C5D9 E340D44B 40404040 40404040  *0110ROSENBERG ROBERT M.          *
    000020   40404040 40F0F0F0 F1F4F2F6 F8F0F1F0    F8F24040 40404040 40404040 40404040  *    0001426801082              *
    000040   40404040 40404040 40404040 40404040    40404040 40404040 40404040 40404040  *                                *
    000060   40404040 40404040 40404040 4C404040    40404040 4C404040 40404040 40D9D6E2  *                             ROS*
```
        ⋮
```
    000420   4C4C4040 40404040 40404040 40404040    40404040 40404040 40404040 40E8C1D9  *                             YAR*
    000440   D9D6F640 C8C1D9D6 D3C440D6 4B404040    40404040 40404040 40404040 40F0F0F0  *ROW HAROLD O.                000*
    000460   F1F4F2F6 F8F0F1F1 F0F04040 40404040    40404040 40404040 40404040 40404040  *1426801100                   *
    000480   40404040 40404040 40404040 40404040    40404040 40404040 40404040 40404040  *                             *
    0004A0   40404040 40404040 40404040 40404040    40404040 40                          *..........*

    COUNT  0060000302050480

    000000   F0F1F1F2 F0FFFFFF FFFF4040 40404040    40404040 40404040 40404040 40404040  *01120                            *
    000020   40404040 40404040 40404040 40F0F1F1    F0F24040 40404040 40404040 40404040  *                   01102          *
    000040   40404040 40404040 40404040 40404040    40404040 40404040 40404040 40404040  *                                *
```
        ⋮
```
    000420   40404040 40404040 40404040 4C404040    40404040 40404040 40404040 40FFFFFF  *                                *
    000440   FFFF4040 40404040 40404040 40404040    40404040 40404040 40404040 40404040  *                                *
    000460   40404040 40F0F1F1 F2F04040 40404040    40404040 40404040 40404040 40404040  *           01120                 *
    000480   40404040 40404040 40404040 40404040    40404040 40404040 40404040 40404040  *                                *
    0004A0   40404040 40404040 40404040 40404040    40404040 40                          *..........*

**** TRACK  00600004    RO DATA  0000000000000000

    COUNT  0060000401000000
```
        ⋮
```
**** TRACK  00600009    RO DATA  0000000000000000
```

```
           **** TRACK  0016 0009      R 0 D A T A   0000000000000000
                COUNT  0016 000901 05 000A
(a)  000000    F0F1 F1F2  F001 0000  0015 0000  16 01 0B                                    *01120.................*
                COUNT  0016 000902 05 000A
     000000    FFFFFFFF  FF000000  00000000  002107                                         *.....................*


           **** TRACK  00170000       RO DATA  00000000000000000

                COUNT  0017000000105000A

     C00000    F0F1F0F0  FC010000  00170000  160818                                         *01000................*

                COUNT  0017000000205000A

     CC0000    F0F1F0F0  F0010000  00170000  FF1CC7                                         *01000................*

                COUNT  0017000003050CCA

     CC0000    F0F1F0F2  F0C10000  00170001  00001B                                         *0102C................*

                COUNT  0017000004050CCA

     C00000    F0F1F0F4  F0010000  00180000  0B18C7                                         *01040................*

                COUNT  0017000C05050CCA

(b)  C00000    F0F1F0F7  F0C10000  00170002  00001B                                         *0107C................*

                COUNT  0017000006050CCA

     C00000    F0F1F0F8  F0C10000  00180001  0A18C7                                         *01C80................*

                COUNT  0017000007050000A

     C00000    F0F1F1F0  F8010000  00170003  00001B                                         *011C8................*

                COUNT  0017000008050CCA

     C00000    F0F1F1F2  F0010000  00180001  0F18C7                                         *01120................*

                COUNT  0017000009050CCA

     C00000    FFFFFFFF  FF000000  00C00000  0030C7                                         *....................*


                COUNT  0017000015050CCA

     C00000    FFFFFFFF  FF000000  00000000  0020C7                                         *....................*

                CCUNT  0017000016050480

     C00000    F0F1F0F0  F0FFFFFF  FFFF4040  40404040   4C4C4040 40404C40 40404C40 40404040  *01000.....          *
     C00020    404C4040 40404040 40404040 40F0F0F9   F8F24040 40404040 40404C40 40404040  *               00982 *
     CC0040    404C4040 40404040 40404040 40404040   404C4040 40404040 40404C40 40404040  *                     *
     CC0060    40404040 40404040 40404040 40404040   404C4040 40404C40 40404C40 40FFFFFF  *                  ...*

                                              ⋮

     C00420    40404040 40404040 40404040 40404040   404C4040 40404040 40404040 40FFFFFF  *                  ...*
     C00440    FFFF4040 40404040 40404040 40404040   4C4C4040 40404040 40404C40 40404040  *..                   *
     C00460    40404040 40F0F1F0 F0F04040 40404040   404C4040 40404040 40404040 40404040  *       01000         *
     C00480    40404040 40404040 40404040 40404040   4C4C4040 40404040 40404C40 40404040  *                     *
     C00480    40404040 40404040 40404040 40404040   40404040 40404040 40404C40 40404040  *                     *
     C004A0    4C404040 40404040 40404040 40404040   4C4C4040 40                           *            .........*

           **** TRACK  00170001       RO DATA  0000000000000C0000

                COUNT  0017000101050480

     C00000    F0F1F0F1  F0C1C1D9  D6D540C4  C1F5C9C4   4CC34840 40404040 404C4C40 40404040  *01010AARON DAVID C.  *
     C00020    40404040 40404040 40404040 40F0F1F0   F0F16340 4040F1F8 F5F1F200 00000000  *         001001   18512....*
     C00040    00000000 00000000 07C00000 0C000000   0CCC3000 C000C0C0 000C0C00 00000000  *............         *
     C00060    00900000 00900000 00C00000 0C00C000   0CCC0000 C003C0CC 00000000 00C1C4C1  *..................ADA*
     C00080    D4E240D1 C1D4C5E2 40C54840 40404040   40404040 40404040 40404040 40F0F0F0  *MS JAMES E.       000*
     C000A0    F0F6F4F6 F1F0F1F0 F0F24040 4040F1F9   F2F3F140 40404040 40404C40 40404040  *0646101002   19231   *
     C000C0    40404040 40404040 40404040 40404040   4C4C4040 40404040 40404040 40404040  *                     *
     C000E0    4C404040 40404040 404C4040 40404040   40404040 40C1C4C4 C1D4E240 C8C1D9E5  *            ADDAMS HARV*
     C00100    C5E84CC3 4B404040 40404040 40404040   4C4C4C40 40404C40 40404040 F0F0F1F0  *EY C.             0C10*
     C00120    F0F34040 4040F1F6 F6F3F040 40404040   40404040 40404040 40404040 40404040  *03   16630           *
     C00140    40404040 40404040 40404040 40404040   4C4C4040 40404040 40404040 40404040  *                     *
     C00160    40404040 4040404C 40404040 40C1D3C6   D9C5C440 E3C8C6D4 C1E240C4 4B404040  *            ALFRED THOMAS D. *
     C00180    40404040 40404040 404C4040 40F0F0F0   F0F5F1F6 F8F0F1F0 F0F44040 4040F1F5  *            0000516801004   15*
     C001A0    F3F8F540 4C404040 40404040 40404040   4C4C4040 40404040 40404040 40404040  *385                  *
     C001C0    40404040 40404040 40404040 40404040   40404040 40404040 40404040 40404040  *                     *
     C001E0    40404040 40C1D3D3 C5D540C4 E4C1D5C5   40C94840 40404040 40404040 40434040  *     ALLEN DUANE R.   *
     C00200    40404040 40404040 40404040 F0F0F1F0   FCF54040 4040F1F5 F7F1F840 40404040  *         001005   15718   *
     C00220    404C4040 40404040 40404040 40404040   40404040 40404040 40404040 40404040  *                     *
     C00240    40404040 40404040 40404040 40404040   4C4C4040 40404040 40404040 40CC2C1  *                   BA*
     C00260    D3C4C9D5 C7C5D940 C5C4C7C1 D940C44B   40404040 40404040 40404040 40F0F0F0  *LDINGER EDGAR M.    000*
     C00280    F0F3F7F6 F6F0F1F0 F0F66040 4040F1F3   FCF7F740 40404040 40404C40 40404040  *0376601006   13077   *
     C002A0    40404040 40404040 40404040 40404040   4C4C4040 40404C40 40404040 40404040  *                     *
     C002C0    40404040 40404040 40404040 40404040   4C4C4040 40C2C1C1 D3C5D940 C5D3E6D6  *           BAALER ELWO*
     C002E0    D6C440D3 4B404040 40404040 40404040   4C4C4040 40404040 40404040 F0F0F1F0  *OD L.             0010*
     C00300    F0F74040 4040F1F4 F8F6F240 40404040   4C4C4040 40404040 40404C40 40404040  *07   14862           *
     C00320    40404040 40404040 40404040 40404040   4C4C4040 40404040 40404C40 40404040  *                     *
     C00340    40404040 40404040 40404040 40C2C1D2   C5D540C3 C8C1D9D3 C5E24CE3 4B404040  *           BAKER CHARLES T.  *
     C00360    40404040 40404040 404C4040 40F0F0F0   F0F4F6F5 F3F0F1F0 F0F84C40 4040F1F3  *            0000465301008   13*
     000380    F8F4F640 40404040 40404040 40404040   4C4C4040 40404040 40404C40 40404040  *846                  *
     C003A0    40404040 40404040 40404040 40404040   40404040 40404040 40404040 40404040  *                     *
     C003C0    4C4C4040 40C2C1D2 D2C5D540 C8C5D5D9   E840C34B 40404040 40404040 40404040  *   BAKKEN HENRY C.   *
     C003E0    40404040 40404040 40404040 F0F0F1F0   FCF54040 4040F1F1 F8F6F040 40404040  *         001009   11860   *
     C00400    40404040 40404040 40404040 40404040   4C4C4040 40404040 40404C40 40404040  *                     *
     C00420    40404040 40404040 40404040 40404040   4C4C4040 40404040 40404040 43C2C1D5  *                   BAN*
     CC0440    D5C5D940 D9D6C2C5 D9E340C3 4B404040   40404040 40404040 40404040 40F0F0F0  *NER ROBERT C.      000*
     C00460    F0F7F7F5 F4F0F1F0 F1F04040 4040F2F3   F0F7F740 40404040 40404C40 40404040  *0775401010   23077   *
     C00480    40404040 40404040 40404040 40404040   4C4C4040 40404C40 40404C40 40404040  *                     *
     C004A0    40404040 40404040 40404040 40404040   4C4C4040 40                           *            .........*
```

258

```
      COUNT   C0170001C20504B0

CC0000   F0F1F0F2 F0C3C1D3 C4E6C5D3 D340C1C1   C3D2F2D6 C5404040 40404C40 40404040   *01020CALDWELL JACKSON         *
CC0020   40404040 40404040 40404040 F0F0F1F0   F1F14040 4040F1F7 F5F2F240 40404040   *          001011    17522     *
CC0040   4C4C4040 40404040 40404040 40404040   40404040 40404C40 40404C40 40404040   *                              *
CC0060   40404040 40404040 40404040 40404040   40404040 40404040 40404040 40C3C1D4   *                           CAM*
CC0080   C2D7C2C5 D3D340C5 E4C7C5D5 C540C94B   4C4C4040 40404040 40404C40 40F0F0F0   *BPBELL EUGENE R.           COO*
CC00A0   F0F2F9F0 F7F0F1F0 F1F24040 40404CF8   F6F5F440 40404C4C 40404040 40404040   *0290701012      8654          *
CC00C0   40404040 40404040 40404040 40404040   4C4C4040 40404040 40404040 40404040   *                              *
CC00E0   40404040 40404040 40404040 40404040   4C4C4040 40C3C1D9 C2C5D9D9 E840E6C9   *                    CARBERRY WI*
CC0100   D3D3C9C1 D440F34B 40404040 40404040   4C4C404C 40404040 40404040 F0F0F1F0   *LLIAM T.                  0010*
CC0120   F1F34040 4040F1F4 F1F2F040 40404040   40404040 40404040 40404040 404C4040   *13    14120                   *
CC0140   40404040 40404040 40404040 40404040   4C4C4040 40404C40 40404040 40404040   *                              *
CC0160   40404040 40404040 40404040 40C3C1D9   D9D6D3D3 40D7C8C9 D3D3C9D7 40E64840   *                    CARROLL PHILLIP W. *
C00180   43404040 40404040 40404040 40F0F0F0   FCF4F0F7 F2F0F1F0 F1F44040 4040F1F2   *              0000407201014      12*
CC01A0   F1F1F540 40404040 40404040 40404040   4C4C4040 40404040 404C4040 40404040   *115                           *
CC01C0   40404040 40404040 40404040 40404040   4C4C4040 40404040 40404040 40404040   *                              *
CC01E0   40404040 40C3C1D9 E3C5D940 C1D3D3C5   D54CD94B 40404040 40404C40 40404040   *    CARTER ALLEN R.           *
CC0200   40404040 40404040 40404040 F0F0F1F0   F1F54040 4040F1F1 F8F5F64C 40404040   *                  001015   11856 *
CC0220   4C4C4040 40404040 40404040 40404040   4C4C4040 40404040 40404040 40404040   *                              *
CC0240   40404040 40404040 40404C40 40C3C1D9   4C4C4040 40404C40 40404040 40F0F0F0   *                           CAR*
CC0260   E3C8C5E6 40E6C9D3 D3C9C1D4 40E34840   4C4C4040 40404040 40404040 40F0F0F0   *THEW WILLIAM T.            COO*
CC0280   F0F5F6F8 F6F0F1F0 F1F64040 404CF1F6   F9F2F340 40404C40 40404C40 40404040   *0568601016    16923           *
CC02A0   4C4C4040 40404040 40404040 40404040   40404040 40404040 40404C40 40404040   *                              *
CC02C0   40404040 40404040 40404040 40404040   4C4C4040 40C3C1E2 E2C5D340 C3C8C1D9   *                    CASSEL CHAR*
CC02E0   D3C5E240 C34B4040 40404040 40404040   4C4C4040 40404C40 40404040 F0F0F1F0   *LES C.                    0C10*
CC0300   F1F74040 4040F1F6 F2F0F440 40404040   4C4C4040 40404040 40404C40 40404040   *17    16204                   *
CC0320   40404040 40404040 40404040 40404040   4C4C4040 40404C40 40404C40 40404040   *                              *
CC0340   40404040 40404040 40404040 40C3C1E2   E2C9C4E8 40C3C8C1 D9D3C5E2 40C54840   *                    CASSIDY CHARLES E. *
CC0360   40404040 40404040 40404040 40F0F0F0   FCF4F9F7 F6FCF1F0 F1F84040 4040F1F4   *              0000497601018      14*
CC0380   F8F0F840 40404040 40404040 40404040   4C4C4040 40404040 40404C4C 40404040   *808                           *
C003A0   40404040 40404040 40404040 40404040   4C4C4040 40404040 40404040 40404040   *                              *
C003C0   40404040 40C3C1E3 E3D6D540 C6D9C5C4   40E34840 40404040 40404040 40404040   *    CATTON FRED T.            *
C003E0   40404040 40404040 40404040 F0F0F1F0   F1F54040 4040F1F2 F3F8F640 40404040   *                  001019   12386 *
C00400   4C4C4040 40404040 40404040 40404040   4C4C4040 40404040 40404040 40404040   *                              *
CC0420   40404040 40404040 40404C40 40404040   4C4C4040 40404040 40404C40 40C4C5C1   *                           CEA*
CC0440   D540E4D3 D4C5D940 C14B4040 40404040   4C4C4040 40404040 40404040 40F0F0F0   *N ULMER A.                 COO*
CC0460   F0F5F3F6 F3F0F1F0 F2F04040 40404CF5   F9F6F240 40404C40 40404040 40404040   *0536301020    15962           *
CC0480   4C4C4040 40404040 40404040 40404040   4C4C4040 40404C40 40404C40 40404040   *                              *
CC0480   40404040 40404040 40404040 40404040   4C4C4040 40404040 40404C40 40404040   *                              *
C004A0   404C4040 40404040 40404040 40404040   4C4C4040 40                           *                  ..........*

**** TRACK  C0170002     RO DATA  0000C00000000C00C

      COUNT   C0170002C10504B0

C00000   FCF1F0F6 F0FFFFFF FFFF4040 40404040   4C4C4040 40404C40 40404040 40404040   *01060.....                    *
CC0020   40404040 40404040 40404040 40F0F1F0   F4F24040 40404C40 40404040 40404040   *                   01042      *
CC0040   40404040 40404040 40404040 40404040   4C4C4040 40404040 40404040 40404040   *                              *
CC0060   40404040 40404040 40404040 40404040   4C4C4040 40404040 40404C40 40FFFFFF   *                           ...*
                                        ⋮
C00420   40404040 40404040 40404040 40404040   4C4C4040 40404C40 40404040 40FFFFFF   *                           ...*
CC0440   FFFF4040 40404040 40404040 40404040   4C4C4040 40404C40 40404040 40404040   *..                            *
CC0460   40404040 40F0F1F0 F6F04040 40404040   4C4C4040 40404040 40404040 40404040   *     01060                    *
C00480   40404040 40404040 40404040 40404040   4C4C4040 40404040 40404C40 40404040   *                              *
CC004A0  40404040 40404040 40404040 40404040   4C4C4040 40                           *                  ..........*
```

```
     COUNT  0017000202050480

C00000   F0F1F0F7 F001C1C3 D6C2E240 E2C8C5D3   D3C4C1D5 40094B40 40404C40 40404040   *01070JACOBS SHELLMAN R.          *
C00020   404C4040 40404040 40404040 F0F0F1F0   F6F14040 4040F1F8 F6F3F240 40404040   *          001061    18632       *
C00040   404C4040 40404040 40404040 40404040   4C4C4040 40404C40 40404040 40404040   *                                *
C00060   40404040 40404040 40404040 40404040   40404040 40404C40 40404040 40D1D6E2   *                             JOS*
C00080   C5D7C8F2 40D1D6E2 C5D7C840 C44B4040   404C4040 40404C40 40404040 43404040   *EPHS JOSEPH D.                   *
C000A0   40F4F2F9 F2F0F1F0 F6F24040 4040F1F7   F8F8F540 40404C40 40404040 40404040   * 429201062    17885             *
C000C0   404C4040 40404040 40404040 40404040   404C4040 40404040 40404040 40404040   *                                *
C000E0   40404040 40404040 40404040 40404040   4C4C4040 40D2C1C3 D206E6E2 D2C940D7   *                      KACKOWSKI P*
C00100   C5E3C5D9 40E34R40 40404040 40404040   404C4040 40404C40 40404040 F0F0F1F0   *ETER T.                    0C10*
C00120   F6F34040 4040F1F7 F4F5F640 40404040   404C4040 40404C40 40404040 43404040   *63   17456                      *
C00140   40404040 40404040 40404040 40404040   404C4040 40404C40 40404040 40404040   *                                *
C00160   40404040 40404040 40404040 40D2C1C5   D3C540E3 C8C5C6C4 D6D9C540 E34R4040   *            KAELE THEODORE T.    *
C00180   40404040 40404040 40404040 40404040   40F4F1F5 F4F0F1F0 F6F44040 4040F1F7   *            415401064       17*
C001A0   F3F0C840 40404040 40404040 40404040   404C4040 40404C40 40404040 40404040   *308                             *
C001C0   40404040 40404040 40404040 404C4040   404C4040 40404C40 40404040 40404040   *                                *
C001E0   40404040 40D2C5C9 C7C8D3C5 E840E6C9   D3D3C9C1 D4404040 404C4040 40404040   *      KEIGHLEY WILLIAM           *
C00200   40404040 40404040 40404040 F0F0F1F0   F6F54040 4040F2F3 F2F1F040 40404040   *            001065    23210      *
C00220   40404040 40404040 40404040 40404040   404C4040 40404C40 40404040 40404040   *                                *
C00240   40404040 40404040 40404040 40D2C5D3   4C404040 40404040 40404040 40404040   *                      KEL*
C00260   D3E840E3 C8D6D4C1 E240D44B 40404040   404C4040 40404040 40404040 40404040   *LY THOMAS M.                    *
C00280   40F2F5F3 F8F0F1F0 F6F64040 4040F1F0   F5F7F740 40404040 40404040 40404040   * 253801066    10577             *
C002A0   40404040 40404040 40404040 40404040   40404040 40404040 40404040 40404040   *                                *
C002C0   40404040 40404040 40404040 43404040   404C4040 40D2C5D4 E2D6D540 C1D9E3C8   *                      KEMSON ARTH*
C002E0   40C74R40 40404040 40404040 4040F2F1   40404040 40404C40 40404040 F0F0F1F0   * G.                        0C10*
C00300   F6F74040 4040F2F1 F4F1F440 40404040   404C4040 40404040 40404C40 40404040   *67   21414                      *
C00320   40404040 40404040 40404040 40404040   404C4040 40404040 40404C40 40404040   *                                *
C00340   40404040 40404040 40404040 40D2D9F4   C5C7C5D9 40C8C1C5 E240C84B 40404040   *            KRUEGER HANS H.      *
C00360   40F3F1F3 F8F0F1F0 F6F8404 0 4040F1F3   40F3F1F3 F8F0F1F0 F6F8404 0 4040F1F3   *            313801068      13*
C00380   F0F7F740 40404040 40404040 40404040   404C4040 40404040 40404C40 40404040   *077                             *
C003A0   40404040 40404040 40404040 40404040   404C4040 40404040 40404C40 40404040   *                                *
C003C0   40404040 40D3C1D9 E2C5D540 C6D9C1D5   C3C9E240 E74B4C40 40404040 40404040   *      LARSEN FRANCIS X.          *
C003E0   40404040 40404040 40404040 F0F0F1F0   F6F94040 4040F1F8 F8F5F64C 40404040   *            001069    18856      *
C00400   40404040 40404040 40404040 40404040   404C4040 40404040 40404040 40404040   *                                *
C00420   40404040 40404040 40404040 40D3D6E6   40404040 40404040 40404040 40404040   *                      LOW*
C00440   D5C4C5E2 40C3D6D9 D3C9E2F2 40C44R40   404C4040 40404040 40404040 40404040   *NDES CORLISS D.                 *
C00460   40F3F5F5 F4F0F1F0 F7F04040 4040F1F4   F8F0F840 40404040 4040404C 40404040   * 355401070    14808             *
C00480   40404040 40404040 40404040 40404040   404C4040 40404C40 40404040 40404040   *                                *
C00480   40404040 40404040 40404040 40404040   404C4040 40404C40 40404040 40404040   *                                *
C004A0   40404040 40404040 40404040 40404040   404C4040 40                           *                       ..........*

**** TRACK  C0170003   RO DATA  00000C00000C0CCC

     COUNT  0017000301050480

C00000   F0F1F0F9 F0D9D6E2 C540C6D9 C5C4C5D9   C9C3D240 E54B4040 40404C40 40404040   *01090ROSE FREDERICK V.           *
C00020   40404040 40404040 40404040 F0F0F1F0   F8F14040 4040F1F6 F5F3F240 40404040   *          001081    16532       *
C00040   40404040 40404040 40404040 40404040   404C4040 40404C40 40404040 40404040   *                                *
C00060   40404040 40404040 40404040 40D9D6E2   40404040 40404C40 40404040 40D9D6E2   *                             FOS*
C00080   C5D5C2C5 D9C74D09 D6C2C5D9 E340D44B   404C4040 40404040 40404040 40404040   *ENBERG ROBERT M.                *
C000A0   40F3F1F3 F8F0F1F0 F8F24040 4040F1F3   F0F7F740 40404040 40404C40 40404040   * 313801082    13077             *
C000C0   40404040 40404040 40404040 40404040   404C4040 40404040 40404C40 40404040   *                                *
C000E0   40404040 40404040 40404040 40D9D6E2   C5D5C2C5 D9C740E4   40404040 40404040   *                      ROSENBERG U*
C00100   D3D9C9C3 C840C44R 40404040 40404040   4C4C4040 40404C40 40404040 F0F0F1F0   *LRICH D.                    0010*
C00120   F8F34040 4040F1F4 F7F8F840 40404040   404C4040 40404040 40404040 40404040   *83   14788                      *
C00140   40404040 40404040 40404040 40D9D6E2   C5D5C2C5 D9D9E840 C4C1E5C9 C440C44R   *            ROSENBERRY DAVID D.*
C00160   40404040 40404040 40404040 40404040   40F2F2F6 F2F0F1F0 F8F44040 40404040   *            226201084      9*
C00180   F4F2F340 40404040 40404040 40404040   404C4040 40404040 40404040 40404040   *423                             *
C001A0   40404040 40404040 40404040 40404040   404C4040 40404040 40404040 40404040   *                                *
C001C0   40404040 40D9D6E2 C5D5D2D9 C1D5E3E9   40C3C5E6 C9E3E340 D34B4040 40404040   *      ROSENKRANTZ LEWITT L.      *
```

```
C00200    404C4040 40404040 40404040 F0F0F1F0    F8F54040 4040F1F6 F5F3F240 40404040    *                001085     16532         *
C00220    404C4040 40404040 40404040 4J404040    4C4C4040 40404040 40404040 40404040    *                                            *
C00240    4C4C4040 40404040 40404040 40404040    40404040 40404C40 40404C40 40D9D6E2    *                                        ROS*
C00260    F240E3C8 C5D6C4D6 D9C540D1 4B404040    40404040 40404040 40404040 40404040    *S THEODORE J.                               *
C00280    40F2F4F4 F6F0F1F0 F8F64040 4040F1F0    F1F9F240 40404040 40404040 40404040    * 244601086     10192                        *
C002A0    40404040 40404040 40404040 40404040    40404040 40404040 40404040 40404040    *                                            *
C002C0    40404040 40404040 40404040 40404040    4C4C4040 40E3C1D9 D9C1D5E3 40D2D9C9    *             TARRANT KRI*
C002E0    E2E3C5D5 40D94840 40404040 40404040    4C4C4040 40404040 40404C40 F0F0F1F0    *STEN R.                              0C1O*
C00300    F8F74040 4040F1F7 F7F5F240 40404040    4C4C4040 40404040 40404040 40404040    *87   17752                                  *
C00320    40404040 40404040 40404040 40404040    40404040 40404040 40404C40 40404040    *                                            *
C00340    40404040 40404040 40404040 40E3C1F3    E4D440D9 D6C2C5D9 E340D44B 40404040    *             TATUM ROBERT M.               *
C00360    40404040 40404040 40404040 40404040    40F2F5F3 F8F0F1F0 F8F84040 4040F1F0    *             253801088               10*
C00380    F5F7F740 40404040 40404040 40404040    4C4C4040 40C4C040 40404040 40404040    *577                                         *
C003A0    40404040 40404040 40404040 40404040    D3C440C8 48404040 40404040 40404040    *             TAWNEY HAROLD H.               *
C003C0    40404040 40E3C1E6 D5C5E840 C8C1D9D6    F8F94040 4040F1F8 F6F2F240 40404040    *             001089     18622               *
C003E0    40404040 40404040 40404040 F0F0F1F0    4C4C4040 40404040 40404040 40404040    *                                            *
C00400    40404040 40404040 40404040 40404040    40404040 40404040 40404040 40E3C8E4    *                                        THU*
C00420    40404040 40404040 40404040 40404040    4C4C4040 40404040 40404040 40404040    *                                            *
C00440    D9F2E3D6 D540E3C8 D6D4C1F2 40E34840    F9F2F340 4C4C4C40 40404040 40404040    *RSTON THOMAS T.                             *
C00460    40F2F8F6 F2F0F1F0 F9F04040 4040F1F1    4C4C4040 40404040 40404040 40404040    * 286201090     11923                        *
C00480    4C4C4040 40404040 40404040 40404040    4C4C4040 40                            *                            ..........*

        COUNT  C017000 3C20504RC
```

```
CC0000    F0F1F1F0 F8E3C9C5 C6C5D5E3 C8C1C3C5    D94007C1 E4D340C7 4B404C40 40404040    *011C8TIEFENTHALER PAUL G.                   *
C00020    404C4040 40404040 40404040 F0F0F1F0    F9F14040 4040F1F9 F5F2F240 40404040    *                001091     19522            *
C00040    40404040 40404040 40404040 40404040    4C4C4040 40404C40 40404040 40404040    *                                            *
C00060    40404040 40404040 40404040 40404040    4C4C4040 40404040 40404C40 40E3C9C6    *                                        TIF*
C00080    C6C5D5C2 F4D9C740 C4D6D5C1 D3C440E2    48404040 40404040 40404040 40404040    *FENBURG DONALD S.                           *
C000A0    40F3F5F0 F8F0F1F0 F9F24040 4040F1F4    F6F1F540 40404040 40404040 40404040    * 350801092     14615                        *
C000C0    40404040 40404040 40404040 40404040    4C4C4040 40404040 40404040 40404040    *                                            *
C000E0    40404040 40404040 40404040 40404040    4C4C4040 40E3C9C1 E2D240C1 D3C6D9C5    *             TRASK ALFRE*
C00100    C440C14B 40404040 40404040 40404040    4C4C4040 40404040 40F5F5F3 F8FCF1F0    *D A.                             5538C10*
C00120    F9F44040 4040F2F3 F0F7F740 40404040    4C4C4040 40404040 40404040 40404040    *94   23077                                  *
C00140    40404040 40404040 40404040 40404040    4C4C4040 40404040 40404040 40404040    *                                            *
C00160    40404040 40404040 40404040 40E4D3D9    C9C3C840 C4C1E5C9 C440D44B 40404040    *             ULRICH DAVID M.               *
C00180    40404040 40404040 40404040 4J404040    40F3F9F2 F3F0F1F0 F9F64040 4040F1F6    *             392301096               16*
C001A0    F3F4F640 40404040 40404040 40404040    4C4C4040 40404040 40404040 40404040    *346                                         *
C001C0    404C4040 40404040 40404040 40404040    4C4C4040 40404040 40404040 40404040    *                                            *
C001E0    40404040 40E5C1E2 E2C9D3C9 C1C4C5E2    4CD6D4C1 D940C44B 40404040 40404040    *             VASSILIADES OMAR D.            *
C00200    404C4040 40404040 40F3F0F0 F0F1F0F0    F9F84040 4040F1F2 F5F0FC40 40404040    *             300001098     12500            *
C00220    40404040 40404040 40404040 4J404040    4C4C4040 40404040 40404040 40404040    *                                            *
C00240    40404040 40404040 40404040 4J404040    4C4C4040 40404040 40404C40 40E8C1D9    *                                        YAR*
C00260    D9D6E640 C8C1D9D6 D3C440D6 4B404040    4C4C4040 40404040 40404040 40404040    *ROW HAROLD O.                               *
C00280    40F3F3F6 F9F0F1F1 F0F04040 4040F1F4    F0F3F840 40404040 40404040 40404040    * 336901100     14038                        *
C002A0    4C4C4040 40404040 40404040 40404040    4C4C4040 40404040 40404040 40404040    *                                            *
C002C0    40404040 40404040 40404040 40404040    4C4C4040 40FFFFFF FFFF4040 40404040    *                                      .....  *
C002E0    40404040 40404040 40404040 40404040    40404040 40404040 40404040 40F0F1F1    *                                        C11*
C00300    F0F24040 40404040 40404040 40404040    4C4C4040 40404040 40404040 40FFFFFF    *02                                      ...*
C00420    4C4C4040 40404040 40404040 40404040    4C4C4040 40404040 40404040 40FFFFFF    *                                        ...*
C00440    FFFF4040 40404040 40404040 40404040    4C4C4040 40404040 40404040 40404040    *..                                          *
C00460    40404040 40F0F1F1 F0F84040 40404040    4C4C4040 40404040 40404040 40404040    *             01108                          *
C00480    40404040 40404040 40404040 40404040    40404040 40404040 40404040 40404040    *                                            *
C00480    40404040 40404040 40404040 40404040    4C4C4040 40404040 40404040 40404040    *                                            *
C004A0    40404040 40404040 40404040 40404040    40404040 40                            *                            ..........*
```

```
**** TRACK  00170004     RO DATA  0000CC000000000C

     COUNT  0017000401000000
```

```
   03/25/71                    SYSTEM SUPPORT UTILITIES --- IEHDASDR  19.0                    PAGE 015

**** TRACK  00180000      R0 DATA  00000000000C0000

      COUNT  0018000001050082
                          †
C00000    F0F1F0F4 F0C10000 00170001 FF10C7C9   C7D6C540 E3C8E4D9 E2E3D6D5 40D44B40   *01040.........IGOE THURSTON M. *
C00020    40404040 40404040 40404040 40404040   404040F3 F3F2F3F0 F1F0F4F0 404C4040   *            332301040        *
CC0040    F1F3F8F4 F6404040 40404040 40404040   4C4C4040 40404040 40404040 40404040   *13846                        *
C00060    40404040 40404040 40404040 40404C40   4C4C4040 40404040 40404040 40404040   *                             *
C00080    40404040 404040                                                             *         ....................*

      COUNT  0018000002050082
                          †
C00000    F0F1F0F3 F8010000 00181801 04181BC8   D6E40240 C3D3C1D9 D240E348 40404040   *01038.........HOUK CLARK T.   *
C00020    4C4C4040 40404040 40404040 40404040   404040F3 F2F7F7F0 F1F0F3F8 40404040   *            327701038        *
C00040    F1F3F6F5 F4404040 404C4040 40404040   4C4C4040 40404040 40404040 40404040   *13654                        *
C00060    40404040 40404040 40404040 40404040   4C4C4040 40404040 40404040 40404040   *                             *
C00080    40404040 404040                                                             *         ....................*

      COUNT  00180000C3050082
                          †
C00000    FCF1F0F3 F6010000 00180001 03181BC8   C1D3D34C C6D9C5C4 C5D9C9C3 D240C44B   *01036.........HALL FREDERICK D.*
C00020    40404040 40404040 40404040 40404040   404040F3 F9F6F9F0 F1F0F3F6 40404040   *            396901036        *
C00040    F1F6F5F3 F8404040 40404040 40404040   4C4C4040 40404040 40404040 40404040   *16538                        *
C00060    40404040 40404040 40404040 40404040   4C4C4040 40404040 40404040 40404040   *                             *
CC0080    404C4040 404040                                                             *         ....................*

      COUNT  0018000004050082
                          †
CC0000    F0F1F0F3 F4C10000 00180001 02181BC8   C1D502C9 D5E24CF3 C8D6D4C1 E240D64B   *01034.........HANKINS THOMAS O.*
C00020    40404040 40404040 40404040 40404040   404040F3 F4F6F2F0 F1F0F3F4 40404040   *            346201034        *
C00040    F1F4F4F2 F3404040 40404040 40404040   4C4C4040 40404040 40404C40 40404040   *14423                        *
C00060    40404040 40404040 40404040 40404040   4C4C4040 40404040 40404040 40404040   *                             *
C00080    40404040 404040                                                             *         ....................*

      COUNT  C0180000C5050082
                          †
CC0000    F0F1F0F3 F2010000 00180001 01181BC7   C5D6D9C7 C540E6C5 E2D3C5E8 40E34B40   *01032.........GEORGE WESLEY T. *
C00020    4C4C4040 40404040 40404040 40404040   404040F4 F8F4F6F0 F1F0F3F2 43404040   *            484601032        *
CC0040    F2F0F1F9 F2404040 40404040 40404040   4C4C4040 40404040 40404C40 40404040   *20192                        *
C00060    4C4C4040 40404040 40404040 40404040   40404040 40404040 40404C40 40404040   *                             *
C00080    40404040 404040                                                             *         ....................*

      COUNT  0018000C06050082
                          †
CC0000    FCF1F0F3 F0010000 00180000 10181BC6   C9D9C5D4 C1D54001 D6E2C5D7 C840D34B   *01030.........FIREMAN JOSEPH L.*
C00020    404C4040 40404040 40404040 40404040   404040F4 F8F4F6F0 F1F0F3F0 40404040   *            484601030        *
000040    F2F0F1F9 F2404040 40404040 40404040   4C4C4040 40404040 40404040 43404040   *20192                        *
C00060    404C4040 40404040 40404040 40404040   4C4C4040 40404040 40404040 40404040   *                             *
C00080    404C4040 404040                                                             *         ....................*

      COUNT  0018000007050082
                          †
C00000    F0F1F0F2 F8C10000 00180000 0F181BC6   C9D9C5D5 E9C94003 C5D6D7D6 D3C440D9   *01028.........FIRENZI LEOPOLD R*
C00020    4B404040 40404040 40404040 40404040   404040F3 F3F2F3F0 F1F0F2F8 40404040   *.           332301028        *
C00040    F1F3F8F4 F6404040 40404040 404C4040   4C4C4040 40404040 40404040 40404040   *13846                        *
C00060    404C4040 40404040 40404040 40404040   4C4C4040 40404040 40404C40 40404040   *                             *
CC0080    404C4040 404040                                                             *         ....................*

      COUNT  0018000008050082
                          †
C00000    F0F1F0F2 F6010030 00180000 0E181BC6   D6D9D9C5 E2F34CE3 E4C3D2C5 D940C44B   *01026.........FORREST TUCKER D.*
C00020    40404040 40404040 40404040 40404040   404040F3 F0F4F6F0 F1F0F2F6 40404040   *            304601026        *
CC0040    F1F2F6F9 F2404040 40404040 40404040   4C4C4040 40404040 40404C40 40404040   *12692                        *
C00060    40404040 404040C40 40404040 40404C40   4C4C4040 40404C4C 4C4C4C40 40404040   *                             *
C00080    404C4040 404040                                                             *         ....................*

      COUNT  00180000C9050082
                          †
C00000    F0F1F0F2 F4C10000 00180000 0D181BC5   C9F2C5D3 C540C7C5 D6D9C7C5 40D44B40   *01024.........EISELE GEORGE M. *
C00020    4C4C4040 40404040 40404040 40404040   404040F3 F0F4F6F0 F1F0F2F4 40404040   *            304601024        *
C00040    F1F2F6F9 F2404040 40404040 40404040   40404040 40404040 40404040 40404040   *12692                        *
C00060    40404040 40404040 40404040 40404040   4C4C4040 40404040 40404040 40404040   *                             *
C00080    4C4C4040 404040                                                             *         ....................*

      COUNT  00180000CA050082
                          †
C00000    F0F1F0F2 F2C10000 00180000 0C181BC4   D9C5E2E2 C3C5C940 E6C1D9D9 C5D540E6   *01022.........DRESSLER WARREN W*
C00020    4B404040 40404040 40404040 404040F0   FCFCFCF4 F2FCFCF0 F1F0F2F2 40404040   *.           0000420001022    *
C00040    F1F2F5F0 F0404040 40404040 40404040   4C4C4040 40404040 40404C40 40404040   *12500                        *
C00060    40404040 40404040 40404040 40404040   4C4C4040 40404040 40404C40 40404040   *                             *
C00080    404C4040 404040                                                             *         ....................*

      COUNT  00180000C8050082
                          †
C00000    FCF1F0F2 F1010000 00180000 0A181BC4   C1E6E2D6 D540C1D9 E3C8E4D9 40D014B40   *01021.........DAWSON ARTHUR J. *
C00020    40404040 40404040 40404040 40404040   4C4C4040 4040FCF0 F1F0F2F1 40404040   *            001021           *
C00040    F1F3F1F6 F8404040 40404040 40404040   4C4C4040 40404040 404C4C40 40404040   *13168                        *
C00060    40404040 40404040 40404040 40404040   4C4C4040 40404040 404C4C40 40404040   *                             *
C00080    404C4040 404040                                                             *         ....................*

      COUNT  C0180000CC050082
                          †
C00000    F0F1F0F2 F3010000 00180000 09181BC5   C2C5D9D3 C540C9E5 C1D54C40 40404040   *01023.........EBERLE IVAN      *
C00020    4C4C4040 40404040 40404040 40404040   4C4C40F0 F1F0F2F3 43404040 40404040   *            001023           *
C00040    F1F1F9F1 F2404040 40404040 40404040   4C4C4040 40404040 404C4C40 40404040   *11912                        *
000060    4C404040 40404040 40404040 40404040   4C4C4040 40404040 40404C40 40404040   *                             *
C00080    40404040 404040                                                             *         ....................*
```

```
        COUNT   C0180000CD050082
                        ↑
C00000   F0F1F0F2 F5010000 00180000 08181BC6    C1E4E2E3 40D6C9C5 E2E3C5E2 40404040   *01025.........FAUST ORESTES    *
C00020   4C4C4040 40404040 40404040 40404040    4C404040 4040F0F0 F1F0F2F5 40404040   *              001025          *
C00040   F1F2F5F5 F2404040 40404040 40404040    404C4040 404C4040 40404C40 43404040   *12552                          *
C00060   404C4040 40404040 40404040 40404040    4C4C4040 40404040 40404C40 40404040   *                               *
C00080   40404040 404040                                                              *    ......................    *

        COUNT   001800000F050082
                        ↑
C00000   F0F1F0F2 F7C10000 00180000 07181BC6    C9C30240 E3C8C6D4 C1E240E3 40404040   *01027.........FICK THOMAS T    *
C00020   404C4040 40404040 40404040 40404040    4C404040 4040FCF0 F1F0F2F7 40404040   *              001027           *
C00040   F1F1F6F9 F8404340 40404043 40404040    4C4C4040 40404040 40404C40 43404040   *11698                          *
C00060   404C4040 40404040 40404040 40404040    4C4C4040 40404040 40404C40 40404040   *                               *
C00080   4C404040 404040                                                              *    ......................    *

        COUNT   C01800000F050082
                        ↑
C00000   F0F1F0F2 F9C10000 00180000 06181BC6    C9D9C2C5 D940C1D3 D3C5D540 D94B4040   *01029.........FIRBER ALLEN R.  *
C00020   4C404040 40404040 40404040 40404040    404C4040 4040FCF0 F1F0F2F9 40404040   *              001029           *
C00040   F1F7F8F2 F5404040 40404040 40404040    4C4C4040 40404040 40404C40 40404040   *17825                          *
C00060   40404040 40404040 40404040 40404040    4C4C4040 40404040 40404C40 40404040   *                               *
CC0080   40404040 404040                                                              *    ......................    *

        COUNT   0018000010050082
                        ↑
C00000   F0F1F0F3 F1C10000 00180000 05181BC7    C1D9F2D6 C540E2C8 C5D9D4C1 D540C34B   *01031.........GARSON SHERMAN C.*
C00020   40404040 40404340 40404040 40404040    4C4C4040 4040F0F0 F1F0F3F1 43404040   *              001031           *
C00040   F1F4F5F6 F2404040 40404040 40404040    4C4C4040 40404040 40404C40 40404040   *14562                          *
C00060   40404040 40404040 40404040 40404040    4C4C4040 40404040 40404C40 40404040   *                               *
C00080   40404040 404040                                                              *    ......................    *

**** TRACK  00180001      RO DATA  00J00CC0000000CC0

        COUNT   0018000101050082
                        ↑
C00000   F0F1F0F3 F3C10030 00180000 04181BC8    C1D4D4D6 D5C440E6 C9D3D3C9 C1D44040   *01033.........HAMMCND WILLIAM  *
C00020   40404040 40404040 40404040 40404040    40404040 4040FCF0 F1F0F3F3 40404040   *              001033           *
C00040   F1F6F3F2 F4404340 40404040 43404040    4C4C4040 40404C40 40404C40 40404340   *16324                          *
C00060   4C4C4040 40404040 40404040 40404040    4C4C4040 40404040 40404040 40404040   *                               *
C00080   40404040 404040                                                              *    ......................    *

        COUNT   C018000102050082
                        ↑
C00000   FCF1F0F3 F5010000 00180000 03181BC8    C1D5D3C5 E840C5C4 F6C1D9C4 40404040   *01035.........HANLEY EDWARD    *
C00020   4C404040 40404040 40404040 40404040    4C4C4040 4040F0F0 F1F0F3F5 40404040   *              001035           *
C00040   F1F7F4F5 F6404040 40404040 40404040    40404040 40404040 40404C40 40404040   *17456                          *
000060   40404040 40404040 4040C040 40404040    4C4C4040 40404040 40404C40 40404040   *                               *
C00080   40404040 404040                                                              *    ......................    *

        COUNT   0018000103050082
                        ↑
C00000   F0F1F0F3 F7C10000 00180000 02181BC8    D6E4C2C5 C9C9C3C8 40C4C1E5 C9C440D6   *01037.........HOUBERICH DAVIC D*
C00020   4B4C4040 40404043 40404040 40404040    40404040 4040FCF0 F1F0F3F7 40404040   *.             001037           *
C00040   F1F6F6F3 F2404040 40404040 40404040    4C4C4040 40404C40 40404C40 40404040   *16632                          *
C00060   40404040 40404040 40404040 40404040    4C4C4040 40404040 40404040 40404040   *                               *
C00080   40404040 404040                                                              *    ......................    *

        COUNT   0018000104050082
                        ↑
C00000   F0F1F0F3 F9C10000 00180000 01181BC9    C6C6C9D5 40E3C8C5 D6C4D6D9 C5404040   *01039.......IFFIN THEODORE    *
C00020   40404040 40404040 40404040 40404040    404C4040 4040FCF0 F1F0F3F9 40404040   *              001039           *
C00040   F2F1F0F3 F0404040 40404040 40404040    4C4C4040 40404040 40404C40 40404040   *21030                          *
C00060   40404040 40404040 40404040 40404040    4C4C4040 40404040 40404C40 40404040   *                               *
C00080   404C4040 404040                                                              *    ......................    *

        COUNT   0018000105050082
                        ↑
C00000   FCF1F0F8 F0C10000 00170002 FF1007D9    D6C8D940 C6D9C5C4 40C14B40 40404040   *01080.........ROHR FRED A.     *
C00020   40404040 40404040 40404040 40404040    404C40F3 F0F9F2F0 F1F0F8F0 40404040   *            309201080          *
C00040   F1F2F5F8 F5404040 40404040 40404040    4C4C4040 40404C40 40404C40 40404040   *12885                          *
000060   40404040 40404040 40404040 40404040    4C4C4040 40404040 40404C40 40404040   *                               *
C00080   40404040 404040                                                              *    ......................    *

        COUNT   0018000106050082
                        ↑
C00000   F0F1F0F7 F8C10000 00180001 0E181BD8    E4C9D5D5 40D7C1E3 D9C9C3D2 40E34B40   *01078.......QUINN PATRICK T. *
C00020   40404040 40404040 40404040 40404040    4C4C40F3 F5F0F8F0 F1F0F7F8 40404040   *            350801078          *
C00040   F1F4F6F1 F5404C40 40404040 40404040    4C4C4040 40404040 40404040 40404040   *14615                          *
C00060   40404040 40404040 40404040 40404040    4C4C4040 40404040 40404C40 40404040   *                               *
000080   40404040 404040                                                              *    ......................    *

        COUNT   C018000107050082
                        ↑
C00000   F0F1F0F7 F6C10000 00180001 0D181BD7    D9C505E3 C9E2E240 C7D3C5D5 D540C44B   *01076.........PRENTISS GLENN D.*
C00020   40404040 40404040 40404040 40404040    4C4C4040 40F3F1F0 F1F0F7F6 40404040   *            503101076          *
C00040   F2F0F9F6 F2404040 40404040 40404040    4C4C4040 40404040 40404C40 40404040   *20962                          *
C00060   404C4040 40404040 40404040 40404040    4C4C4040 40404040 40404C40 40404040   *                               *
C00080   404C4040 404040                                                              *    ......................    *

        COUNT   0018000108050082
                        ↑
C00000   FCF1F0F7 F4C10000 00180001 0C181BD4    C1D9E2C8 C1D3C340 D1D6E2C5 D7C840D1   *01074.........MARSHALL JOSEPH J*
C00020   484C4040 40404040 40404040 40404040    404C40F5 F5F8F5F0 F1F0F7F4 40404040   *.           558501074          *
C00040   F2F3F2F6 F9404040 40404040 40404040    4C404040 40404040 40404C40 40404040   *23269                          *
C00060   40404040 40404040 40404040 40404040    4C4C4040 40404040 40404C40 40404040   *                               *
C00080   4C404040 404040                                                              *    ......................    *
```

```
        COUNT   C0180001C9050082
                             †
CC0000  FCF1F0F7  F2C10000  00180001  08181B04      C1D9E2C8  40F5C5D9  D5D60540  E34B4040     *01072.........MARSH VERNON T.  *
C00020  404C4040  40404040  40404040  40404040      4C4040F3  F3F4F6F0  F1F0F7F2  40404040     *             334601072       *
000040  F1F3F9F4  F2404040  40404040  40404040      404C4040  40404040  40404C40  40404040     *13942                         *
C00060  404C4040  40404040  40404040  40404040      4C4C4040  40404C40  40404040  40404040     *                              *
C00080  4C4C4040  404040                                                                       *          ...................*

        COUNT   C0180001CA050082
                             †
C00000  FCF1F0F7  F1C10000  00180001  09181B03      D6E7D5C5  D940C1C5  D9D9E840  D94B4040     *01071.........LOXNER JERRY R.  *
C00020  4C4C4040  40404040  40404040  40404040      4C4C4040  40404C40  F1F0F7F1  40404040     *             001071          *
C00040  F1F7F4F4  F5404040  404C4040  40404040      4C4C4040  40404040  40404040  40404040     *17445                         *
C00060  434C4040  40404040  40404040  40404040      4C4C4040  40404C40  40404040  404340O40     *                              *
C00080  4C4C4040  404040                                                                       *          ...................*

        COUNT   0018000108050082
                             †
C00000  F0F1F0F7  F3C10000  00180001  08181B04      C1D9E2C8  C1D3C340  C1C2C5D9  40C64B40     *01073.........MARSHALL ABER F. *
C00020  40404040  40404040  40404040  40404040      40404F0F0  F1F0F7F3  40404040     *             001073          *
C00040  F1F3F1F2  E8404040  40404040  40404040      4C4C4040  40404040  40404040  40304040     *13128                         *
C00060  40404040  40404040  40404040  40404040      4C4C4040  40404040  40404040  40404040     *                              *
C00080  40404040  404040                                                                       *          ...................*

        COUNT   00180001CD050082
                             †
C00000  F0F1F0F7  F5C10000  00180001  07181B06      C1C2C5E2  40C3C1C9  D340C34B  40404040     *01075.........OAKES CARL C.   *
C00020  404C4040  40404040  40404040  40404040      4C4C4040  40404CF0  F1F0F7F5  40404040     *             001075          *
C00040  F1F3F1F2  F2404040  40404040  40404040      4C4C4040  40404040  404C4040  40404040     *13122                         *
C00060  40404040  40404040  40404040  40404040      4C4C4040  40404040  40404040  40404040     *                              *
C00080  404C4040  404040                                                                       *          ...................*

        COUNT   00180001CD050082
                             †
C00000  FCF1F0F7  F7C10000  00180001  06181B07      D9C9E3C3  C8C1D9C4  40D9C9C3  C8C1D9C4     *01077.........PRITCHARD RICHARD*
C00020  40C44840  40404040  40404040  40404040      4C4C4040  40404CF0  F1F0F7F7  43404040     * D.         001077          *
C00040  F1F6F8F6  F6404040  40404040  40404040      4C4C4040  40404040  40404040  40404040     *16866                         *
C00060  40404040  40404040  40404040  40404040      4C4C4040  40404040  40404040  40404040     *                              *
C00080  4C4C4040  404040                                                                       *          ...................*

        COUNT   00180001D0050082
                             †
C00000  FCF1F0F7  F9C10000  00180001  05181B09      C9C3C8C1  D9C4E240  C5D3D4C5  D940D94B     *01079.........RICHARDS ELMER R.*
C00020  40404040  40404040  40404040  40404040      4C4C4040  40404CF0  F1F0F7F9  40404040     *             001079          *
C00040  F1F5F4F4  F2404040  40404040  40404040      4C4C404C  4C404C40  40404040  40404040     *15442                         *
C00060  F3404040  40404040  40404040  40404040      4C4C4040  40404040  40404040  40304040     *                              *
C00080  40404040  404040                                                                       *          ...................*

        COUNT   00180001CF050082
                             †
CC0000  F0F1F1F2  F0C10030  00170003  FF1007FF      FFFFFFFF  40404040  40404C4C  40404040     *0112C.....................    *
C00020  40404040  40404040  40404040  40404040      4C4C4040  40404CF0  F1F1F2F0  40404040     *                     01120   *
C00040  40404040  40404040  40404040  40404040      4C4C4040  40404C40  404C4040  40404040     *                              *
C00060  40404040  40404040  40404040  40404040      4C4C4040  40404C40  40404040  40304040     *                              *
C00080  40404040  404040                                                                       *          ...................*

        COUNT   0018000110000000


**** TRACK   00180002     R0 DATA  000CCC0000000000

        COUNT   00180002C0100065D

C00000  065D0000  00700000  40F0F0F8  C5F0FC40      4C4CF0F0  F0F0C6C6  C3F8C4FC  F0F0F0F5     *........ 008E00   0000FFC8 00C05*
000020  C1F8F640  F0F0F0F0  F0F0F0F0  40F0F0F0      F0F0F0F0  F0404040  40F0F0F0F0  F0F0F0F0     *A86 00000000 00000000   0000000*
000040  F040F0F0  F0F0F0F0  F0F0F0F0  F0F0F0F8      C4C3F040  F0F0F0F0  40404040  40404040     *0 0CC00C00 00008DC0 00000000  .*
000060  4B4B4B48  4B4B4B4B  4B4B4B4B  4B4B4B4B      4B4B4B4B  4B4B4B4B  4B4B4B4B  4B4B4B4B     *0 0CC00C00 00008DC0 00000000  .*
0C0080  5C007D00  040F0F0  F8C5F2F0  40404040      F0F0F0F0  F0F0F040  F0F0FCFCF0  F0FCFCF0     *..... 008E20  00000000 00000000*
0000A0  40F0F0F0  F0F0F0F0  F04CFCF0  F0F0F0F0      FCF04040  4040F0F5  C6F0F9F1  F8F040F1     *0 0CC00C00 00008DC0 00000000  .*
0C0OC0  F0F0F0F0  F7F7F240  F1F8F6C1  F5F8C1F0      40F0F0F1  F0F5F8C1  C1404040  5C4B4B48     *0000772 186A58A0 001058AA  ....*
0O0OE0  4B4B4B4B  4B4B4B4B  4B4B4B4B  4B4BFO4B      F5F0F6F0  4B0C1F0F4  F8F5F8F6  F04CF0F0     *........0.........o..........*
000100  000040F0  F0F8C5F4  40404040  40F0F0F5      F5C5F6F0  C1F0F0F0  4B4B4B40  4B4B4B4B     *.. 008E40  00585060 A0485860 00*
000120  F5F0F8C1  F6F040F0  F0F0F1F1  F3F6F640      404040F5  C5F6F0C1  F0F0F040  F1F3F6F6     *508A60 00011366   5E60A000 1366*
000140  F5C5F6F1  40F0F0F0  C3F4F7F3  F0F2E140      F2C5F1C2  F6F64040  405C4B48  4B4B4B4B     *5F61 000C4730 F02E1866  .......*
000160  4B4B4B4B  4B4B4B4B  4B4BF04B  4B4B4B48      4B4BF0F0  7D0CC00040                       *........0.........o..........*
000180  F0F0F8C5  F6F04040  40F0F5F0  F1F0F0C0      C340F9F8  F4F5F1F0  F0F440F5  F0F4F5F0     *008E60  5061000C 98451004 50450*
0001A0  F0F0F440  F5F0F4F5  F0F0F0F8  40404040      F9F6F8F0  F1F0F0F0  F0404040  F5F5F0F0     *004 50540008   96801000 5550A06*
0001C0  F040F4F7  F6F0C6F0  F5F240F4  F1C6F0C6      F0F6F840  40405C4B  4B4B4B48  4B4B4B4B     *0 4760F052 41F0F068  ........*
0001E0  4B4B4B4B  4B4B4B4B  4B4B4B4B  4B4B4B4B      4B4B4B4B  5C007D0000  40FCF0F8                *0 4760F052 41F0F068  ........*
000200  C5F8FC40  4C40F4F7  C6F0C6F1  F0C540F5      F8C1F0C1  F0F4F840  F0F7C6F2  F1F8F8C1     *E80  47F0F10E 58A0A048 07F2188A*
000220  40F5F8F3  F0F0F0F1  40404040  40F5F8C1      F3F0F040  F5F8A30  F5F0F8F0  F4F8F040     * 58300010   58A30058 5080A048 0*
000240  F5C6F0F5  F8F6F040  F0F0F5F0  F1F2F6F6      40404040  4BF0F14B  4B4B4B4B  4BF24B4B     *5F05860 00501266  ..01......2..*
000260  4B4B4B4B  4B4B4B4B  4B4B4B4B  4BF04B4B      4B4BF0F0  4040F0F0  0040FCF0  4CF0F0F8     *........0.........o..... 008EA0*
000280  40404040  F7C1F0C6  F0F6F840  F5F8F3F0      F0F0F0F1  F040F5F8  C1F3F0F0  F5F8F0F0     *    47A0F068 58300010 58A30058 58*
0C02A0  F1F0C1F0  F0C34040  404C5F5F8  F6F7F1F0      4C404040  5C4040F0  F0F0F840  F5F8F4F0     **10A00C  98671004 50670004 5076*
0C02C0  F0F0F0F8  40F5F8F4  F0F1F0F0  F0404040      5C4B4B40  40F0F8C5  C340404040  40404040     * 0008 58401000  ...0....... 008EC0*
0002E0  4B4B4B4B  4B4B4B4B  4B4B4B4B  4B4B4B40      F0F0F4F7  F9F0C6F0  F6C540F9  F1F0F1F1     *........0....... 008EC0*
0C0300  F4F1F4F0  40404040  40F9F1F0  F3F1F0F0      40F9F1F0  F3F1F0F0  40F9F1F0  F3F1F0F0     *41404000 91031000 4790F06E 91011*
000320  F0F0F0C0  40404040  F7C6F3F0  F1C1C140      40404040  4BF0F04B  4B4B4B4B  4BF9F0C1     *000    47C0F1AA 186F5010 AC6C90A*
0C0340  C340C1F0  F5F0F1C2  F0F0F040  405C4B40      404B4B4B  4B4B4B4B  4BF04B4B  4B4B4B4B     *C A0501B00  ..  .........0...*
000360  F1494B4B  4B4B4B4B  4B4B4B4B  4B4B5C0C      7D000000  0F08C5  C5F04040  40F4F1F1     *1.........0..... 008EE0  411*
0003R0  F0F1F0F6  F040F5F8  C6F0FCF2  C2F240F4      F5C5C6F0  F0F0F040  F1F8F658  A040404040     *01060 58F0F2B2 45EF0004 18F658A0*
0003A0  40404040  F0F0F0F1  F5F8C1C1  40F0F0F5      40404040  40404040  40404040  40404040     *    000105AA 00585810 A06C9RAC A*
0003C0  F0F5F0F4  F7C6F040  40405C4B  4B4B4B4B      F0F2F4B4  4B4B4B4B  F6F4B4B48  4B4B4B4B     *05047F0   ......02......6.....*
0003E0  4B4B4B4B  4B4B4B4B  4B4BFC5C  0C7C0000      40F0F0F8  C6F0F040  40404C6F1  F0C1F5F8     *..........0..... 008F00  F10A58*
```

EMPWEEKLY MACHINE LISTING

```
01002ADAMS JAMES F.
01004ALFRED THOMAS D.
01008BAKER CHARLES T.
01010BANNER ROBERT C.
01012CAMBPBELL EUGENE R.
01014CARROIL PHILIP W.
01018CASSIDY CHARLES E.
01020DEAN ULMER A.
01022DRESSLER WARREN W.
01024EISELE GEORGE M.
01026FORRFST TUCKER D.
01028FIRENZI LEOPOLD R.
01030FIREMAN JOSEPH L.
01032GEORGE WESLEY T.
01034HANKINS THOMAS O.
01036HALL FREDERICK D.
01038HOUK CLARK T.
01040IGOE THURSTON M.
01062JOSEPHS JOSEPH D.
01064KAELE THEODORE F.
01068KRUEGER HANS H.
01070LOWNDES CORLISS D.
01072MARSH VERNON T.
01074MARSHALL JOSEPH J.
01076PRENTISS GLENN D.
01078QUINN PATRICK T.
01080ROHR FRED A.
01032ROSENBERG ROBERT M.
01084ROSENBERRY DAVID D.
01086ROSS THEODORE J.
01088TATUM ROBERT M.
01090THURSTON THOMAS F.
01092TIFFENBURG DONALD S.
01094TRASK ALFRED A.
01096ULRICH DAVID M.
01098VASSILIADES OMAR D.
01100YARROW HAROLD O.
```

appendix 11

CHARACTERISTICS OF SVC ROUTINES

All SVC routines operate in the supervisor state.

Location of the Routine

An SVC rountine can be either in main storage at all times as part of the resident control program or on a direct-access device as part of the SVC library. Type I and II routines are part of the resident control program, and types III and IV are in the SVC library.

Size of the Routine

SVC routines of type I, II, and IV are not limited in size. However, a type IV SVC routine must be divided into load modules of 1024 bytes or less. The size of a type III SVC routine must not exceed 1024 bytes.

Design of the Routine

Type I SVC routines must be reenterable or serially reusable. All other types must be reenterable.

Interruption of the Routine

When the SVC routine receives control, the CPU is masked for all maskable interruptions but the machine check interruption. All type I SVC routines must execute in this masked state. If one wants to allow interruptions to occur during the execution of a type II, III, or IV SVC routine, one must change the appropriate masks. If a type II, III, or IV SVC routine is expected to run for an extended period of time, it is recommended that interruptions be allowed to be processed where possible.

HEXADECIMAL TABLES

The following tables aid in converting hexadecimal values to decimal values, or the reverse.

Direct Conversion Table

This table provides direct conversion of decimal and hexadecimal numbers in these ranges:

HEXADECIMAL	DECIMAL
000 to FFF	0000 to 4095

For numbers outside the range of the table, add the following values to the table figures:

HEXADECIMAL	DECIMAL
1000	4096
2000	8192
3000	12288
4000	16384
5000	20480
6000	24576
7000	28672
8000	32768
9000	36864
A000	40960
B000	45056
C000	49152
D000	53248
E000	57344
F000	61440

	0	1	2	3	4	5	6	7	8	9	A	B	C	D	E	F
00_	0000	0001	0002	0003	0004	0005	0006	0007	0008	0009	0010	0011	0012	0013	0014	0015
01_	0016	0017	0018	0019	0020	0021	0022	0023	0024	0025	0026	0027	0028	0029	0030	0031
02_	0032	0033	0034	0035	0036	0037	0038	0039	0040	0041	0042	0043	0044	0045	0046	0047
03_	0048	0049	0050	0051	0052	0053	0054	0055	0056	0057	0058	0059	0060	0061	0062	0063
04_	0064	0065	0066	0067	0068	0069	0070	0071	0072	0073	0074	0075	0076	0077	0078	0079
05_	0080	0081	0082	0083	0084	0085	0086	0087	0088	0089	0090	0091	0092	0093	0094	0095
06_	0096	0097	0098	0099	0100	0101	0102	0103	0104	0105	0106	0107	0108	0109	0110	0111
07_	0112	0113	0114	0115	0116	0117	0118	0119	0120	0121	0122	0123	0124	0125	0126	0127
08_	0128	0129	0130	0131	0132	0133	0134	0135	0136	0137	0138	0139	0140	0141	0142	0143
09_	0144	0145	0146	0147	0148	0149	0150	0151	0152	0153	0154	0155	0156	0157	0158	0159
0A_	0160	0161	0162	0163	0164	0165	0166	0167	0168	0169	0170	0171	0172	0173	0174	0175
0B_	0176	0177	0178	0179	0180	0181	0182	0183	0184	0185	0186	0187	0188	0189	0190	0191
0C_	0192	0193	0194	0195	0196	0197	0198	0199	0200	0201	0202	0203	0204	0205	0206	0207
0D_	0208	0209	0210	0211	0212	0213	0214	0215	0216	0217	0218	0219	0220	0221	0222	0223
0E_	0224	0225	0226	0227	0228	0229	0230	0231	0232	0233	0234	0235	0236	0237	0238	0239
0F_	0240	0241	0242	0243	0244	0245	0246	0247	0248	0249	0250	0251	0252	0253	0254	0255
10_	0256	0257	0258	0259	0260	0261	0262	0263	0264	0265	0266	0267	0268	0269	0270	0271
11_	0272	0273	0274	0275	0276	0277	0278	0279	0280	0281	0282	0283	0284	0285	0286	0287
12_	0288	0289	0290	0291	0292	0293	0294	0295	0296	0297	0298	0299	0300	0301	0302	0303
13_	0304	0305	0306	0307	0308	0309	0310	0311	0312	0313	0314	0315	0316	0317	0318	0319
14_	0320	0321	0322	0323	0324	0325	0326	0327	0328	0329	0330	0331	0332	0333	0334	0335
15_	0336	0337	0338	0339	0340	0341	0342	0343	0344	0345	0346	0347	0348	0349	0350	0351
16_	0352	0353	0354	0355	0356	0357	0358	0359	0360	0361	0362	0363	0364	0365	0366	0367
17_	0368	0369	0370	0371	0372	0373	0374	0375	0376	0377	0378	0379	0380	0381	0382	0383
18_	0384	0385	0386	0387	0388	0389	0390	0391	0392	0393	0394	0395	0396	0397	0398	0399
19_	0400	0401	0402	0403	0404	0405	0406	0407	0408	0409	0410	0411	0412	0413	0414	0415
1A_	0416	0417	0418	0419	0420	0421	0422	0423	0424	0425	0426	0427	0428	0429	0430	0431
1B_	0432	0433	0434	0435	0436	0437	0438	0439	0440	0441	0442	0443	0444	0445	0446	0447
1C_	0448	0449	0450	0451	0452	0453	0454	0455	0456	0457	0458	0459	0460	0461	0462	0463
1D_	0464	0465	0466	0467	0468	0469	0470	0471	0472	0473	0474	0475	0476	0477	0478	0479
1E_	0480	0481	0482	0483	0484	0485	0486	0487	0488	0489	0490	0491	0492	0493	0494	0495
1F_	0496	0497	0498	0499	0500	0501	0502	0503	0504	0505	0506	0507	0508	0509	0510	0511

	0	1	2	3	4	5	6	7	8	9	A	B	C	D	E	F
20_	0512	0513	0514	0515	0516	0517	0518	0519	0520	0521	0522	0523	0524	0525	0526	0527
21_	0528	0529	0530	0531	0532	0533	0534	0535	0536	0537	0538	0539	0540	0541	0542	0543
22_	0544	0545	0546	0547	0548	0549	0550	0551	0552	0553	0554	0555	0556	0557	0558	0559
23_	0560	0561	0562	0563	0564	0565	0566	0567	0568	0569	0570	0571	0572	0573	0574	0575
24_	0576	0577	0578	0579	0580	0581	0582	0583	0584	0585	0586	0587	0588	0589	0590	0591
25_	0592	0593	0594	0595	0596	0597	0598	0599	0600	0601	0602	0603	0604	0605	0606	0607
26_	0608	0609	0610	0611	0612	0613	0614	0615	0616	0617	0618	0619	0620	0621	0622	0623
27_	0624	0625	0626	0627	0628	0629	0630	0631	0632	0633	0634	0635	0636	0637	0638	0639
28_	0640	0641	0642	0643	0644	0645	0646	0647	0648	0649	0650	0651	0652	0653	0654	0655
29_	0656	0657	0658	0659	0660	0661	0662	0663	0664	0665	0666	0667	0668	0669	0670	0671
2A_	0672	0673	0674	0675	0676	0677	0678	0679	0680	0681	0682	0683	0684	0685	0686	0687
2B_	0688	0689	0690	0691	0692	0693	0694	0695	0696	0697	0698	0699	0700	0701	0702	0703
2C_	0704	0705	0706	0707	0708	0709	0710	0711	0712	0713	0714	0715	0716	0717	0718	0719
2D_	0720	0721	0722	0723	0724	0725	0726	0727	0728	0729	0730	0731	0732	0733	0734	0735
2E_	0736	0737	0738	0739	0740	0741	0742	0743	0744	0745	0746	0747	0748	0749	0750	0751
2F_	0752	0753	0754	0755	0756	0757	0758	0759	0760	0761	0762	0763	0764	0765	0766	0767
30_	0768	0769	0770	0771	0772	0773	0774	0775	0776	0777	0778	0779	0780	0781	0782	0783
31_	0784	0785	0786	0787	0788	0789	0790	0791	0792	0793	0794	0795	0796	0797	0798	0799
32_	0800	0801	0802	0803	0804	0805	0806	0807	0808	0809	0810	0811	0812	0813	0814	0815
33_	0816	0817	0818	0819	0820	0821	0822	0823	0824	0825	0826	0827	0828	0829	0830	0831
34_	0832	0833	0834	0835	0836	0837	0838	0839	0840	0841	0842	0843	0844	0845	0846	0847
35_	0848	0849	0850	0851	0852	0853	0854	0855	0856	0857	0858	0859	0860	0861	0862	0863
36_	0864	0865	0866	0867	0868	0869	0870	0871	0872	0873	0874	0875	0876	0877	0878	0879
37_	0880	0881	0882	0883	0884	0885	0886	0887	0888	0889	0890	0891	0892	0893	0894	0895
38_	0896	0897	0898	0899	0900	0901	0902	0903	0904	0905	0906	0907	0908	0909	0910	0911
39_	0912	0913	0914	0915	0916	0917	0918	0919	0920	0921	0922	0923	0924	0925	0926	0927
3A_	0928	0929	0930	0931	0932	0933	0934	0935	0936	0937	0938	0939	0940	0941	0942	0943
3B_	0944	0945	0946	0947	0948	0949	0950	0951	0952	0953	0954	0955	0956	0957	0958	0959
3C_	0960	0961	0962	0963	0964	0965	0966	0967	0968	0969	0970	0971	0972	0973	0974	0975
3D_	0976	0977	0978	0979	0980	0981	0982	0983	0984	0985	0986	0987	0988	0989	0990	0991
3E_	0992	0993	0994	0995	0996	0997	0998	0999	1000	1001	1002	1003	1004	1005	1006	1007
3F_	1008	1009	1010	1011	1012	1013	1014	1015	1016	1017	1018	1019	1020	1021	1022	1023

	0	1	2	3	4	5	6	7	8	9	A	B	C	D	E	F
40_	1024	1025	1026	1027	1028	1029	1030	1031	1032	1033	1034	1035	1036	1037	1038	1039
41_	1040	1041	1042	1043	1044	1045	1046	1047	1048	1049	1050	1051	1052	1053	1054	1055
42_	1056	1057	1058	1059	1060	1061	1062	1063	1064	1065	1066	1067	1068	1069	1070	1071
43_	1072	1073	1074	1075	1076	1077	1078	1079	1080	1081	1082	1083	1084	1085	1086	1087
44_	1088	1089	1090	1091	1092	1093	1094	1095	1096	1097	1098	1099	1100	1101	1102	1103
45_	1104	1105	1106	1107	1108	1109	1110	1111	1112	1113	1114	1115	1116	1117	1118	1119
46_	1120	1121	1122	1123	1124	1125	1126	1127	1128	1129	1130	1131	1132	1133	1134	1135
47_	1136	1137	1138	1139	1140	1141	1142	1143	1144	1145	1146	1147	1148	1149	1150	1151
48_	1152	1153	1154	1155	1156	1157	1158	1159	1160	1161	1162	1163	1164	1165	1166	1167
49_	1168	1169	1170	1171	1172	1173	1174	1175	1176	1177	1178	1179	1180	1181	1182	1183
4A_	1184	1185	1186	1187	1188	1189	1190	1191	1192	1193	1194	1195	1196	1197	1198	1199
4B_	1200	1201	1202	1203	1204	1205	1206	1207	1208	1209	1210	1211	1212	1213	1214	1215
4C_	1216	1217	1218	1219	1220	1221	1222	1223	1224	1225	1226	1227	1228	1229	1230	1231
4D_	1232	1233	1234	1235	1236	1237	1238	1239	1240	1241	1242	1243	1244	1245	1246	1247
4E_	1248	1249	1250	1251	1252	1253	1254	1255	1256	1257	1258	1259	1260	1261	1262	1263
4F_	1264	1265	1266	1267	1268	1269	1270	1271	1272	1273	1274	1275	1276	1277	1278	1279
50_	1280	1281	1282	1283	1284	1285	1286	1287	1288	1289	1290	1291	1292	1293	1294	1295
51_	1296	1297	1298	1299	1300	1301	1302	1303	1304	1305	1306	1307	1308	1309	1310	1311
52_	1312	1313	1314	1315	1316	1317	1318	1319	1320	1321	1322	1323	1324	1325	1326	1327
53_	1328	1329	1330	1331	1332	1333	1334	1335	1336	1337	1338	1339	1340	1341	1342	1343
54_	1344	1345	1346	1347	1348	1349	1350	1351	1352	1353	1354	1355	1356	1357	1358	1359
55_	1360	1361	1362	1363	1364	1365	1366	1367	1368	1369	1370	1371	1372	1373	1374	1375
56_	1376	1377	1378	1379	1380	1381	1382	1383	1384	1385	1386	1387	1388	1389	1390	1391
57_	1392	1393	1394	1395	1396	1397	1398	1399	1400	1401	1402	1403	1404	1405	1406	1407
58_	1408	1409	1410	1411	1412	1413	1414	1415	1416	1417	1418	1419	1420	1421	1422	1423
59_	1424	1425	1426	1427	1428	1429	1430	1431	1432	1433	1434	1435	1436	1437	1438	1439
5A_	1440	1441	1442	1443	1444	1445	1446	1447	1448	1449	1450	1451	1452	1453	1454	1455
5B_	1456	1457	1458	1459	1460	1461	1462	1463	1464	1465	1466	1467	1468	1469	1470	1471
5C_	1472	1473	1474	1475	1476	1477	1478	1479	1480	1481	1482	1483	1484	1485	1486	1487
5D_	1488	1489	1490	1491	1492	1493	1494	1495	1496	1497	1498	1499	1500	1501	1502	1503
5E_	1504	1505	1506	1507	1508	1509	1510	1511	1512	1513	1514	1515	1516	1517	1518	1519
5F_	1520	1521	1522	1523	1524	1525	1526	1527	1528	1529	1530	1531	1532	1533	1534	1535

	0	1	2	3	4	5	6	7	8	9	A	B	C	D	E	F
60_	1536	1537	1538	1539	1540	1541	1542	1543	1544	1545	1546	1547	1548	1549	1550	1551
61_	1552	1553	1554	1555	1556	1557	1558	1559	1560	1561	1562	1563	1564	1565	1566	1567
62_	1568	1569	1570	1571	1572	1573	1574	1575	1576	1577	1578	1579	1580	1581	1582	1583
63_	1584	1585	1586	1587	1588	1589	1590	1591	1592	1593	1594	1595	1596	1597	1598	1599
64_	1600	1601	1602	1603	1604	1605	1606	1607	1608	1609	1610	1611	1612	1613	1614	1615
65_	1616	1617	1618	1619	1620	1621	1622	1623	1624	1625	1626	1627	1628	1629	1630	1631
66_	1632	1633	1634	1635	1636	1637	1638	1639	1640	1641	1642	1643	1644	1645	1646	1647
67_	1648	1649	1650	1651	1652	1653	1654	1655	1656	1657	1658	1659	1660	1661	1662	1663
68_	1664	1665	1666	1667	1668	1669	1670	1671	1672	1673	1674	1675	1676	1677	1678	1679
69_	1680	1681	1682	1683	1684	1685	1686	1687	1688	1689	1690	1691	1692	1693	1694	1695
6A_	1696	1697	1698	1699	1700	1701	1702	1703	1704	1705	1706	1707	1708	1709	1710	1711
6B_	1712	1713	1714	1715	1716	1717	1718	1719	1720	1721	1722	1723	1724	1725	1726	1727
6C_	1728	1729	1730	1731	1732	1733	1734	1735	1736	1737	1738	1739	1740	1741	1742	1743
6D_	1744	1745	1746	1747	1748	1749	1750	1751	1752	1753	1754	1755	1756	1757	1758	1759
6E_	1760	1761	1762	1763	1764	1765	1766	1767	1768	1769	1770	1771	1772	1773	1774	1775
6F_	1776	1777	1778	1779	1780	1781	1782	1783	1784	1785	1786	1787	1788	1789	1790	1791
70_	1792	1793	1794	1795	1796	1797	1798	1799	1800	1801	1802	1803	1804	1805	1806	1807
71_	1808	1809	1810	1811	1812	1813	1814	1815	1816	1817	1818	1819	1820	1821	1822	1823
72_	1824	1825	1826	1827	1828	1829	1830	1831	1832	1833	1834	1835	1836	1837	1838	1839
73_	1840	1841	1842	1843	1844	1845	1846	1847	1848	1849	1850	1851	1852	1853	1854	1855
74_	1856	1857	1858	1859	1860	1861	1862	1863	1864	1865	1866	1867	1868	1869	1870	1871
75_	1872	1873	1874	1875	1876	1877	1878	1879	1880	1881	1882	1883	1884	1885	1886	1887
76_	1888	1889	1890	1891	1892	1893	1894	1895	1896	1897	1898	1899	1900	1901	1902	1903
77_	1904	1905	1906	1907	1908	1909	1910	1911	1912	1913	1914	1915	1916	1917	1918	1919
78_	1920	1921	1922	1923	1924	1925	1926	1927	1928	1929	1930	1931	1932	1933	1934	1935
79_	1936	1937	1938	1939	1940	1941	1942	1943	1944	1945	1946	1947	1948	1949	1950	1951
7A_	1952	1953	1954	1955	1956	1957	1958	1959	1960	1961	1962	1963	1964	1965	1966	1967
7B_	1968	1969	1970	1971	1972	1973	1974	1975	1976	1977	1978	1979	1980	1981	1982	1983
7C_	1984	1985	1986	1987	1988	1989	1990	1991	1992	1993	1994	1995	1996	1997	1998	1999
7D_	2000	2001	2002	2003	2004	2005	2006	2007	2008	2009	2010	2011	2012	2013	2014	2015
7E_	2016	2017	2018	2019	2020	2021	2022	2023	2024	2025	2026	2027	2028	2029	2030	2031
7F_	2032	2033	2034	2035	2036	2037	2038	2039	2040	2041	2042	2043	2044	2045	2046	2047

	0	1	2	3	4	5	6	7	8	9	A	B	C	D	E	F
80_	2048	2049	2050	2051	2052	2053	2054	2055	2056	2057	2058	2059	2060	2061	2062	2063
81_	2064	2065	2066	2067	2068	2069	2070	2071	2072	2073	2074	2075	2076	2077	2078	2079
82_	2080	2081	2082	2083	2084	2085	2086	2087	2088	2089	2090	2091	2092	2093	2094	2095
83_	2096	2097	2098	2099	2100	2101	2102	2103	2104	2105	2106	2107	2108	2109	2110	2111
84_	2112	2113	2114	2115	2116	2117	2118	2119	2120	2121	2122	2123	2124	2125	2126	2127
85_	2128	2129	2130	2131	2132	2133	2134	2135	2136	2137	2138	2139	2140	2141	2142	2143
86_	2144	2145	2146	2147	2148	2149	2150	2151	2152	2153	2154	2155	2156	2157	2158	2159
87_	2160	2161	2162	2163	2164	2165	2166	2167	2168	2169	2170	2171	2172	2173	2174	2175
88_	2176	2177	2178	2179	2180	2181	2182	2183	2184	2185	2186	2187	2188	2189	2190	2191
89_	2192	2193	2194	2195	2196	2197	2198	2199	2200	2201	2202	2203	2204	2205	2206	2207
8A_	2208	2209	2210	2211	2212	2213	2214	2215	2216	2217	2218	2219	2220	2221	2222	2223
8B_	2224	2225	2226	2227	2228	2229	2230	2231	2232	2233	2234	2235	2236	2237	2238	2239
8C_	2240	2241	2242	2243	2244	2245	2246	2247	2248	2249	2250	2251	2252	2253	2254	2255
8D_	2256	2257	2258	2259	2260	2261	2262	2263	2264	2265	2266	2267	2268	2269	2270	2271
8E_	2272	2273	2274	2275	2276	2277	2278	2279	2280	2281	2282	2283	2284	2285	2286	2287
8F_	2288	2289	2290	2291	2292	2293	2294	2295	2296	2297	2298	2299	2300	2301	2302	2303
90_	2304	2305	2306	2307	2308	2309	2310	2311	2312	2313	2314	2315	2316	2317	2318	2319
91_	2320	2321	2322	2323	2324	2325	2326	2327	2328	2329	2330	2331	2332	2333	2334	2335
92_	2336	2337	2338	2339	2340	2341	2342	2343	2344	2345	2346	2347	2348	2349	2350	2351
93_	2352	2353	2354	2355	2356	2357	2358	2359	2360	2361	2362	2363	2364	2365	2366	2367
94_	2368	2369	2370	2371	2372	2373	2374	2375	2376	2377	2378	2379	2380	2381	2382	2383
95_	2384	2385	2386	2387	2388	2389	2390	2391	2392	2393	2394	2395	2396	2397	2398	2399
96_	2400	2401	2402	2403	2404	2405	2406	2407	2408	2409	2410	2411	2412	2413	2414	2415
97_	2416	2417	2418	2419	2420	2421	2422	2423	2424	2425	2426	2427	2428	2429	2430	2431
98_	2432	2433	2434	2435	2436	2437	2438	2439	2440	2441	2442	2443	2444	2445	2446	2447
99_	2448	2449	2450	2451	2452	2453	2454	2455	2456	2457	2458	2459	2460	2461	2462	2463
9A_	2464	2465	2466	2467	2468	2469	2470	2471	2472	2473	2474	2475	2476	2477	2478	2479
9B_	2480	2481	2482	2483	2484	2485	2486	2487	2488	2489	2490	2491	2492	2493	2494	2495
9C_	2496	2497	2498	2499	2500	2501	2502	2503	2504	2505	2506	2507	2508	2509	2510	2511
9D_	2512	2513	2514	2515	2516	2517	2518	2519	2520	2521	2522	2523	2524	2525	2526	2527
9E_	2528	2529	2530	2531	2532	2533	2534	2535	2536	2537	2538	2539	2540	2541	2542	2543
9F_	2544	2545	2546	2547	2548	2549	2550	2551	2552	2553	2554	2555	2556	2557	2558	2559

	0	1	2	3	4	5	6	7	8	9	A	B	C	D	E	F
A0_	2560	2561	2562	2563	2564	2565	2566	2567	2568	2569	2570	2571	2572	2573	2574	2575
A1_	2576	2577	2578	2579	2580	2581	2582	2583	2584	2585	2586	2587	2588	2589	2590	2591
A2_	2592	2593	2594	2595	2596	2597	2598	2599	2600	2601	2602	2603	2604	2605	2606	2607
A3_	2608	2609	2610	2611	2612	2613	2614	2615	2616	2617	2618	2619	2620	2621	2622	2623
A4_	2624	2625	2626	2627	2628	2629	2630	2631	2632	2633	2634	2635	2636	2637	2638	2639
A5_	2640	2641	2642	2643	2644	2645	2646	2647	2648	2649	2650	2651	2652	2653	2654	2655
A6_	2656	2657	2658	2659	2660	2661	2662	2663	2664	2665	2666	2667	2668	2669	2670	2671
A7_	2672	2673	2674	2675	2676	2677	2678	2679	2680	2681	2682	2683	2684	2685	2686	2687
A8_	2688	2689	2690	2691	2692	2693	2694	2695	2696	2697	2698	2699	2700	2701	2702	2703
A9_	2704	2705	2706	2707	2708	2709	2710	2711	2712	2713	2714	2715	2716	2717	2718	2719
AA_	2720	2721	2722	2723	2724	2725	2726	2727	2728	2729	2730	2731	2732	2733	2734	2735
AB_	2736	2737	2738	2739	2740	2741	2742	2743	2744	2745	2746	2747	2748	2749	2750	2751
AC_	2752	2753	2754	2755	2756	2757	2758	2759	2760	2761	2762	2763	2764	2765	2766	2767
AD_	2768	2769	2770	2771	2772	2773	2774	2775	2776	2777	2778	2779	2780	2781	2782	2783
AE_	2784	2785	2786	2787	2788	2789	2790	2791	2792	2793	2794	2795	2796	2797	2798	2799
AF_	2800	2801	2802	2803	2804	2805	2806	2807	2808	2809	2810	2811	2812	2813	2814	2815
B0_	2816	2817	2818	2819	2820	2821	2822	2823	2824	2825	2826	2827	2828	2829	2830	2831
B1_	2832	2833	2834	2835	2836	2837	2838	2839	2840	2841	2842	2843	2844	2845	2846	2847
B2_	2848	2849	2850	2851	2852	2853	2854	2855	2856	2857	2858	2859	2860	2861	2862	2863
B3_	2864	2865	2866	2867	2868	2869	2870	2871	2872	2873	2874	2875	2876	2877	2878	2879
B4_	2880	2881	2882	2883	2884	2885	2886	2887	2888	2889	2890	2891	2892	2893	2894	2895
B5_	2896	2897	2898	2899	2900	2901	2902	2903	2904	2905	2906	2907	2908	2909	2910	2911
B6_	2912	2913	2914	2915	2916	2917	2918	2919	2920	2921	2922	2923	2924	2925	2926	2927
B7_	2928	2929	2930	2931	2932	2933	2934	2935	2936	2937	2938	2939	2940	2941	2942	2943
B8_	2944	2945	2946	2947	2948	2949	2950	2951	2952	2953	2954	2955	2956	2957	2958	2959
B9_	2960	2961	2962	2963	2964	2965	2966	2967	2968	2969	2970	2971	2972	2973	2974	2975
BA_	2976	2977	2978	2979	2980	2981	2982	2983	2984	2985	2986	2987	2988	2989	2990	2991
BB.	2992	2993	2994	2995	2996	2997	2998	2999	3000	3001	3002	3003	3004	3005	3006	3007
BC_	3008	3009	3010	3011	3012	3013	3014	3015	3016	3017	3018	3019	3020	3021	3022	3023
BD.	3024	3025	3026	3027	3028	3029	3030	3031	3032	3033	3034	3035	3036	3037	3038	3039
BE_	3040	3041	3042	3043	3044	3045	3046	3047	3048	3049	3050	3051	3052	3053	3054	3055
BF.	3056	3057	3058	3059	3060	3061	3062	3063	3064	3065	3066	3067	3068	3069	3070	3071

	0	1	2	3	4	5	6	7	8	9	A	B	C	D	E	F
C0_	3072	3073	3074	3075	3076	3077	3078	3079	3080	3081	3082	3083	3084	3085	3086	3087
C1_	3088	3089	3090	3091	3092	3093	3094	3095	3096	3097	3098	3099	3100	3101	3102	3103
C2_	3104	3105	3106	3107	3108	3109	3110	3111	3112	3113	3114	3115	3116	3117	3118	3119
C3_	3120	3121	3122	3123	3124	3125	3126	3127	3128	3129	3130	3131	3132	3133	3134	3135
C4_	3136	3137	3138	3139	3140	3141	3142	3143	3144	3145	3146	3147	3148	3149	3150	3151
C5_	3152	3153	3154	3155	3156	3157	3158	3159	3160	3161	3162	3163	3164	3165	3166	3167
C6_	3168	3169	3170	3171	3172	3173	3174	3175	3176	3177	3178	3179	3180	3181	3182	3183
C7_	3184	3185	3186	3187	3188	3189	3190	3191	3192	3193	3194	3195	3196	3197	3198	3199
C8_	3200	3201	3202	3203	3204	3205	3206	3207	3208	3209	3210	3211	3212	3213	3214	3215
C9_	3216	3217	3218	3219	3220	3221	3222	3223	3224	3225	3226	3227	3228	3229	3230	3231
CA_	3232	3233	3234	3235	3236	3237	3238	3239	3240	3241	3242	3243	3244	3245	3246	3247
CB_	3248	3249	3250	3251	3252	3253	3254	3255	3256	3257	3258	3259	3260	3261	3262	3263
CC_	3264	3265	3266	3267	3268	3269	3270	3271	3272	3273	3274	3275	3276	3277	3278	3279
CD	3280	3281	3282	3283	3284	3285	3286	3287	3288	3289	3290	3291	3292	3293	3294	3295
CE_	3296	3297	3298	3299	3300	3301	3302	3303	3304	3305	3306	3307	3308	3309	3310	3311
CF_	3312	3313	3314	3315	3316	3317	3318	3319	3320	3321	3322	3323	3324	3325	3326	3327
D0_	3328	3329	3330	3331	3332	3333	3334	3335	3336	3337	3338	3339	3340	3341	3342	3343
D1	3344	3345	3346	3347	3348	3349	3350	3351	3352	3353	3354	3355	3356	3357	3358	3359
D2_	3360	3361	3362	3363	3364	3365	3366	3367	3368	3369	3370	3371	3372	3373	3374	3375
D3_	3376	3377	3378	3379	3380	3381	3382	3383	3384	3385	3386	3387	3388	3389	3390	3391
D4_	3392	3393	3394	3395	3396	3397	3398	3399	3400	3401	3402	3403	3404	3405	3406	3407
D5_	3408	3409	3410	3411	3412	3413	3414	3415	3416	3417	3418	3419	3420	3421	3422	3423
D6_	3424	3425	3426	3427	3428	3429	3430	3431	3432	3433	3434	3435	3436	3437	3438	3439
D7_	3440	3441	3442	3443	3444	3445	3446	3447	3448	3449	3450	3451	3452	3453	3454	3455
D8_	3456	3457	3458	3459	3460	3461	3462	3463	3464	3465	3466	3467	3468	3469	3470	3471
D9_	3472	3473	3474	3475	3476	3477	3478	3479	3480	3481	3482	3483	3484	3485	3486	3487
DA_	3488	3489	3490	3491	3492	3493	3494	3495	3496	3497	3498	3499	3500	3501	3502	3503
DB_	3504	3505	3506	3507	3508	3509	3510	3511	3512	3513	3514	3515	3516	3517	3518	3519
DC_	3520	3521	3522	3523	3524	3525	3526	3527	3528	3529	3530	3531	3532	3533	3534	3535
DD_	3536	3537	3538	3539	3540	3541	3542	3543	3544	3545	3546	3547	3548	3549	3550	3551
DE_	3552	3553	3554	3555	3556	3557	3558	3559	3560	3561	3562	3563	3564	3565	3566	3567
DF.	3568	3569	3570	3571	3572	3573	3574	3575	3576	3577	3578	3579	3580	3581	3582	3583

	0	1	2	3	4	5	6	7	8	9	A	B	C	D	E	F
E0_	3584	3585	3586	3587	3583	3589	3590	3591	3592	3593	3594	3595	3596	3597	3598	3599
E1_	3600	3601	3602	3603	3604	3605	3606	3607	3608	3609	3610	3611	3612	3613	3614	3615
E2_	3616	3617	3618	3619	3620	3621	3622	3623	3624	3625	3626	3627	3628	3629	3630	3631
E3_	3632	3633	3634	3635	3636	3637	3638	3639	3640	3641	3642	3643	3644	3645	3646	3647
E4_	3648	3649	3650	3651	3652	3653	3654	3655	3656	3657	3658	3659	3660	3661	3662	3663
E5_	3664	3665	3666	3667	3668	3669	3670	3671	3672	3673	3674	3675	3676	3677	3678	3679
E6_	3680	3681	3682	3683	3684	3685	3686	3687	3688	3689	3690	3691	3692	3693	3694	3695
E7_	3696	3697	3698	3699	3700	3701	3702	3703	3704	3705	3706	3707	3708	3709	3710	3711
E8_	3712	3713	3714	3715	3716	3717	3718	3719	3720	3721	3722	3723	3724	3725	3726	3727
E9_	3728	3729	3730	3731	3732	3733	3734	3735	3736	3737	3738	3739	3740	3741	3742	3743
EA_	3744	3745	3746	3747	3748	3749	3750	3751	3752	3753	3754	3755	3756	3757	3758	3759
EB_	3760	3761	3762	3763	3764	3765	3766	3767	3768	3769	3770	3771	3772	3773	3774	3775
EC_	3776	3777	3778	3779	3780	3781	3782	3783	3784	3785	3786	3787	3788	3789	3790	3791
ED_	3792	3793	3794	3795	3796	3797	3798	3799	3800	3801	3802	3803	3804	3805	3806	3807
EE_	3808	3809	3810	3811	3812	3813	3814	3815	3816	3817	3818	3819	3820	3821	3822	3823
EF_	3824	3825	3826	3827	3828	3829	3830	3831	3832	3833	3834	3835	3836	3837	3838	3839
F0_	3840	3841	3842	3843	3844	3845	3846	3847	3848	3849	3850	3851	3852	3853	3854	3855
F1_	3856	3857	3858	3859	3860	3861	3862	3863	3864	3865	3866	3867	3868	3869	3870	3871
F2_	3872	3873	3874	3875	3876	3877	3878	3879	3880	3881	3882	3883	3884	3885	3886	3887
F3_	3888	3889	3890	3891	3892	3893	3894	3895	3896	3897	3898	3899	3900	3901	3902	3903
F4_	3904	3905	3906	3907	3908	3909	3910	3911	3912	3913	3914	3915	3916	3917	3918	3919
F5_	3920	3921	3922	3923	3924	3925	3926	3927	3928	3929	3930	3931	3932	3933	3934	3935
F6_	3936	3937	3938	3939	3940	3941	3942	3943	3944	3945	3946	3947	3948	3949	3950	3951
F7_	3952	3953	3954	3955	3956	3957	3958	3959	3960	3961	3962	3963	3964	3965	3966	3967
F8_	3968	3969	3970	3971	3972	3973	3974	3975	3976	3977	3978	3979	3980	3981	3982	3983
F9_	3984	3985	3986	3987	3988	3989	3990	3991	3992	3993	3994	3995	3996	3997	3998	3999
FA_	4000	4001	4002	4003	4004	4005	4006	4007	4008	4009	4010	4011	4012	4013	4014	4015
FB_	4016	4017	4018	4019	4020	4021	4022	4023	4024	4025	4026	4027	4028	4029	4030	4031
FC_	4032	4033	4034	4035	4036	4037	4038	4039	4040	4041	4042	4043	4044	4045	4046	4047
FD_	4048	4049	4050	4051	4052	4053	4054	4055	4056	4057	4058	4059	4060	4061	4062	4063
FE_	4064	4065	4066	4067	4068	4069	4070	4071	4072	4073	4074	4075	4076	4077	4078	4079
FF_	4080	4081	4082	4083	4084	4085	4086	4087	4088	4089	4090	4091	4092	4093	4094	4095

Hexadecimal Addition and Subtraction Table

Example: 6 + 2 = 8, 8 − 2 = 6, and 8 − 6 = 2

	1	2	3	4	5	6	7	8	9	A	B	C	D	E	F
1	02	03	04	05	06	07	08	09	0A	0B	0C	0D	0E	0F	10
2	03	04	05	06	07	08	09	0A	0B	0C	0D	0E	0F	10	11
3	04	05	06	07	08	09	0A	0B	0C	0D	0E	0F	10	11	12
4	05	06	07	08	09	0A	0B	0C	0D	0E	0F	10	11	12	13
5	06	07	08	09	0A	0B	0C	0D	0E	0F	10	11	12	13	14
6	07	08	09	0A	0B	0C	0D	0E	0F	10	11	12	13	14	15
7	08	09	0A	0B	0C	0D	0E	0F	10	11	12	13	14	15	16
8	09	0A	0B	0C	0D	0E	0F	10	11	12	13	14	15	16	17
9	0A	0B	0C	0D	0E	0F	10	11	12	13	14	15	16	17	18
A	0B	0C	0D	0E	0F	10	11	12	13	14	15	16	17	18	19
B	0C	0D	0E	0F	10	11	12	13	14	15	16	17	18	19	1A
C	0D	0E	0F	10	11	12	13	14	15	16	17	18	19	1A	1B
D	0E	0F	10	11	12	13	14	15	16	17	18	19	1A	1B	1C
E	0F	10	11	12	13	14	15	16	17	18	19	1A	1B	1C	1D
F	10	11	12	13	14	15	16	17	18	19	1A	1B	1C	1D	1E

Hexadecimal Multiplication Table

Example: 2 × 4 = 08, F × 2 = 1E

	1	2	3	4	5	6	7	8	9	A	B	C	D	E	F
1	01	02	03	04	05	06	07	08	09	0A	0B	0C	0D	0E	0F
2	02	04	06	08	0A	0C	0E	10	12	14	16	18	1A	1C	1E
3	03	06	09	0C	0F	12	15	18	1B	1E	21	24	27	2A	2D
4	04	08	0C	10	14	18	1C	20	24	28	2C	30	34	38	3C
5	05	0A	0F	14	19	1E	23	28	2D	32	37	3C	41	46	4B
6	06	0C	12	18	1E	24	2A	30	36	3C	42	48	4E	54	5A
7	07	0E	15	1C	23	2A	31	38	3F	46	4D	54	5B	62	69
8	08	10	18	20	28	30	38	40	48	50	58	60	68	70	78
9	09	12	1B	24	2D	36	3F	48	51	5A	63	6C	75	7E	87
A	0A	14	1E	28	32	3C	46	50	5A	64	6E	78	82	8C	96
B	0B	16	21	2C	37	42	4D	58	63	6E	79	84	8F	9A	A5
C	0C	18	24	30	3C	48	54	60	6C	78	84	90	9C	A8	B4
D	0D	1A	27	34	41	4E	5B	68	75	82	8F	9C	A9	B6	C3
E	0E	1C	2A	38	46	54	62	70	7E	8C	9A	A8	B6	C4	D2
F	0F	1E	2D	3C	4B	5A	69	78	87	96	A5	B4	C3	D2	E1

Hexadecimal and Decimal Integer Conversion Table

HALFWORD								HALFWORD							
BYTE				BYTE				BYTE				BYTE			
BITS: 0123		4567		0123		4567		0123		4567		0123		4567	
Hex	Decimal	Hex	Decimal	Hex	Decimal	Hex	Decimal	Hex	Decimal	Hex	Decimal	Hex	Decimal	Hex	Decimal
0	0	0	0	0	0	0	0	0	0	0	0	0	0	0	0
1	268,435,456	1	16,777,216	1	1,048,576	1	65,536	1	4,096	1	256	1	16	1	1
2	536,870,912	2	33,554,432	2	2,097,152	2	131,072	2	8,192	2	512	2	32	2	2
3	805,306,368	3	50,331,648	3	3,145,728	3	196,608	3	12,288	3	768	3	48	3	3
4	1,073,741,824	4	67,108,864	4	4,194,304	4	262,144	4	16,384	4	1,024	4	64	4	4
5	1,342,177,280	5	83,886,080	5	5,242,880	5	327,680	5	20,480	5	1,280	5	80	5	5
6	1,610,612,736	6	100,663,296	6	6,291,456	6	393,216	6	24,576	6	1,536	6	96	6	6
7	1,879,048,192	7	117,440,512	7	7,340,032	7	458,752	7	28,672	7	1,792	7	112	7	7
8	2,147,483,648	8	134,217,728	8	8,388,608	8	524,288	8	32,768	8	2,048	8	128	8	8
9	2,415,919,104	9	150,994,944	9	9,437,184	9	589,824	9	36,864	9	2,304	9	144	9	9
A	2,684,354,560	A	167,772,160	A	10,485,760	A	655,360	A	40,960	A	2,560	A	160	A	10
B	2,952,790,016	B	184,549,376	B	11,534,336	B	720,896	B	45,056	B	2,816	B	176	B	11
C	3,221,225,472	C	201,326,592	C	12,582,912	C	786,432	C	49,152	C	3,072	C	192	C	12
D	3,489,660,928	D	218,103,808	D	13,631,488	D	851,968	D	53,248	D	3,328	D	208	D	13
E	3,758,096,384	E	234,881,024	E	14,680,064	E	917,504	E	57,344	E	3,584	E	224	E	14
F	4,026,531,840	F	251,658,240	F	15,728,640	F	983,040	F	61,440	F	3,840	F	240	F	15
8		7		6		5		4		3		2		1	

TO CONVERT HEXADECIMAL TO DECIMAL

1. Locate the column of decimal numbers corresponding to the left-most digit or letter of the hexadecimal; select from this column and record the number that corresponds to the position of the hexadecimal digit or letter.
2. Repeat step 1 for the next (second from the left) position.
3. Repeat step 1 for the units (third from the left) position.
4. Add the numbers selected from the table to form the decimal number.

EXAMPLE

Conversion of
Hexadecimal Value D34

1. D   3328
2. 3   48
3. 4   4
4. Decimal   3380

TO CONVERT DECIMAL TO HEXADECIMAL

1. (a) Select from the table the highest decimal number that is equal to or less than the number to be converted.
   (b) Record the hexadecimal of the column containing the selected number.
   (c) Subtract the selected decimal from the number to be converted.
2. Using the remainder from step 1(c) repeat all of step 1 to develop the second position of the hexadecimal (and a remainder).
3. Using the remainder from step 2 repeat all of step 1 to develop the units position of the hexadecimal.
4. Combine terms to form the hexadecimal number.

EXAMPLE

Conversion of
Decimal Value   3380

1. D $\frac{-3328}{52}$
2. 3 $\frac{-48}{4}$
3. 4   -4
4. Hexadecimal   D34

To convert integer numbers greater than the capacity of table, use the techniques below:

HEXADECIMAL TO DECIMAL

Successive cumulative multiplication from left to right, adding units position.

Example: $D34_{16} = 3380_{10}$

$$
\begin{aligned}
D &= 13 \\
&\underline{\times 16} \\
&208 \\
3 &= \underline{+ 3} \\
&211 \\
&\underline{\times 16} \\
&3376 \\
4 &= \underline{+4} \\
&3380
\end{aligned}
$$

DECIMAL TO HEXADECIMAL

Divide and collect the remainder in reverse order.

Example: $3380_{10} = X_{16}$

16 |3380   remainder
16 |211   → 4
16 |13   → 3
   → D

$3380_{10} = D34_{16}$

POWERS OF 16 TABLE

Example: $268,435,456_{10} = (2.68435456 \times 10^8)_{10} = 1000\ 0000_{16} = (10^7)_{16}$

16^n	n
1	0
16	1
256	2
4 096	3
65 536	4
1 048 576	5
16 777 216	6
268 435 456	7
4 294 967 296	8
68 719 476 736	9
1 099 511 627 776	10 = A
17 592 186 044 416	11 = B
281 474 976 710 656	12 = C
4 503 599 627 370 496	13 = D
72 057 594 037 927 936	14 = E
1 152 921 504 606 846 976	15 = F

Decimal Values

INDEX

READER

EDITED BY JESSICA HEMMINGS

BERG

London · New York

English edition

First published in 2012 by

Berg

Editorial offices:
50 Bedford Square, London WC1B 3DP, UK
175 Fifth Avenue, New York, NY 10010, USA

Berg is an imprint of Bloomsbury Publishing Plc.

Library of Congress Cataloging-in-Publication Data

A catalogue record for this book is available from the Library of Congress.

British Library Cataloguing-in-Publication Data

A catalogue record for this book is available from the British Library.

ISBN 978 1 84788 635 4 (Cloth)
978 1 84788 634 7 (Paper)

Typeset by Apex CoVantage, LLC, Madison, WI, USA

Printed in the UK by the MPG Books Group

www.bergpublishers.com

CONTENTS

LIST OF ILLUSTRATIONS

Cover image: *Html Patchwork*, facilitated by Ele Carpenter, 2007–2009. Mixed fabrics. 240 × 250 cm. Supported by Access Space and Arts Council England. http://www.open-source-embroidery.org.uk/patchwork.htm

The Html Patchwork was stitched in workshops at: Access Space, Sheffield; Isis Arts and Glue Gallery, Newcastle upon Tyne; Banff New Media Institute, Alberta, Canada; and individuals across the UK and internationally from: Australia, New Zealand and Ireland. With thanks to: Art through Textiles; The Patchwork Garden; Stannington Patchwork Group; Stocksbridge Knit n Chat; Totley Quilters; Fine Fabrics, Hillsbrough; Sheffield Fabric Warehouse; the Crucible Theatre costume department, Sheffield.

The patchworkers included: Astrid Abels, Hoda Adura, Sameera Ahmad, Sharon Bailey, Jon Ball, Julie Ballands, Diane Barry, Brian Batista, Stuart Bowditch, David Bouchard, Jane Brettle, Daisy Butler, David Butler, Steve Capps, Ele Carpenter, Ruth Catlow, Ina Charnley, Veronique Chance, Cam Christiansen, Clymene Christoforo, Iain Clarke, Keith Clarkson, Aleesa Cohene, Sarain Cuthand, Tony Dawson, Brian Degger, Anna Dumitriu, Lindsay Duncanson, Anne Eade, Stella Eleftheriades, Linda English, Rayna Fahey, Verina Gfader, Abi Gibbens, Mark Gibbens, Fran Gill, Geneviève Godin, Beryl Graham, Tricia Grindrod, Alison Harries, Jake Harries, Scott Hawkins, Nicola Hilton, Dougald Hine, Alex Hodby, Mike Howe, Ben Jones, Elizabeth Kane, John Keenan, Tony Kemplen, Susan Kennard, Anne-Marie Kilfeather, Joyce Kirk, Mara Livingston-McPhail, Richard Long, Harriet Lowe, Kari McQueen, Lindsay MacDonald, Sophie Malouin, Di McDonald, Jill M., Ilana Mitchell, Billy Moffatt, Caitlin O'Donovan, Keith o'Faoláin, Jo Owen, Tali Padnan, Emily Paige, Trevor Pitt, Marisa Plumb, Sarah Powell, Jim Prevett, Julian Priest, Jing Qian, Topsy Qur'et, Edith Raynor, Kate Readman, Norma Reaney, Catherine Roberts, Damien Robinson, Shelia Robinson, Beth Rowson, Clare Ruddock, Céline Seman, Cherry Sham, Kim Sheppard, Addison Smith, Ann Smith, Dominic Smith, Sneha Solanki, James Starkey, Cecilia Stenbom, Alison Stockwell, Kim Suleman, Kurt Sullivan, Reka Tackas, Kate Vale, James Wallbank, Lisa Wallbank, Hannah York, Mary, Fran, Kari, Shona, Rose, Christa, Albert, Shelia, Stella, Sue, Di, Pat, Doreen, Kathleen, Janet, Margie, Rusty, Miss Gunst, Burnt Out, Louise, Ellie, Sophie, Kiturah, Charlotte, Tia, Katie, Alisha, Lauren.

NOTES ON CONTRIBUTORS

Textile designer, weaver, writer and printmaker **Anni Albers** (1899–1994) was born in Germany. In 1922 she arrived at the Bauhaus School, then based in Weimar, Germany, and studied weaving. In 1933 she moved with her husband, the artist Joseph Albers, to the United States to contribute to the recently established Black Mountain College in North Carolina. The couple remained in the United States for the rest of their lives. Albers's weavings are characterized by an unassuming simplicity, often exploring materials unusual for the time within simple woven structures. Her writings on design and weaving provide a rare glimpse of design thinking and teaching of the time.

Elissa Auther is associate professor of contemporary art at the University of Colorado, Colorado Springs. She is the author of *String, Felt, Thread: The Hierarchy of Art and Craft in American Art* (Minnesota, 2010) and the coeditor of *West of Center: Art and the Counterculture Experiment, 1965–1977* (Minnesota, 2012). Auther is the codirector of Feminism & Co.: Art, Sex, Politics at the Museum of Contemporary Art, Denver.

Pennina Barnett writes about contemporary visual culture. She is currently writing a book (Berg Publishers, UK) that explores cloth as a multidimensional metaphor for ideas of subjectivity, materiality, process and language. She is a founding editor of the international peer reviewed journal *Textile: The Journal of Cloth and Culture* (also Berg Publishers). Her earlier work includes curatorial projects: "Craft Matters," "The Subversive Stitch," "Under Construction," and "Textures of Memory: The Poetics of Cloth," which toured the UK. From 1989–2011 Barnett was senior lecturer in the Department of Art, Goldsmiths, University of London, where she taught Critical Studies. She is currently a visiting tutor at the Royal College of Art, London.

Susan S. Bean curates South Asian and Korean art at the Peabody Essex Museum. She has written on the importance of cloth in India's freedom movement, on the American textile trade with India, including "Bengal Goods for America, the Nineteenth Century," in *Textiles from India: The Global Trade* (Rosemary Crill, ed., 2006) and "Bandanna: On the Indian Origins of an All-American Textile," in *Textiles in Early New England: Design, Production, and Consumption* (Peter Benes, ed., 1999), and with Diana Myers, on Bhutanese textiles, *From the Land of the Thunder Dragon: Textile Arts of Bhutan* (1994, reprinted 2008).

Philip Beesley is a professor at the University of Waterloo Architecture program and practices architecture and digital media art. Beesley's experimental projects focus on immersive digitally fabricated lightweight geotextile structures. The most recent generations of this work feature interactive kinetic systems that use dense arrays of microprocessors, sensors, and actuator systems combined with primitive chemical metabolisms. These environments pursue near-living qualities and distributed emotional consciousness. His projects include Canada's entry to the 2010 Venice Architecture Biennale. Publications include eight books and *WIRED*, *Casa Vogue*, and *Architectural Digest* features.

Maxine Bristow is a reader in fine art and MA Fine Art Programme Leader at the University of Chester. She trained in textiles and her research practice focuses on the tension between the formal and semantic conventions of the medium and the negotiation of these conventions within contemporary post-medium fine art context. Bristow has exhibited nationally and internationally and her work is part of the collections of the Crafts Council, Whitworth Art Gallery, and Nottingham Castle Museum & Art Gallery. She was selected for the Jerwood Textiles Prize in 2002, and in 2008 was one of the nominated artists for the Northern Arts Prize. She is currently engaged in a practice-as-research Ph.D., which investigates the potency of textile through pragmatics of attachment and detachment.

Julia Bryan-Wilson is associate professor of modern and contemporary art at the University of California, Berkeley. She is the author of *Art Workers: Radical Practice in the Vietnam War Era* (University of California Press, 2009), as well as numerous articles on artists such as Ida Applebroog, Anne Wilson, Sharon Hayes, Yoko Ono, and Francesca Woodman. Her current research project examines the politics of handmaking since 1970.

The Italian author and journalist **Italo Calvino** (1923–1985) was born in Cuba and is celebrated as one of the most widely translated postwar Italian authors. He studied literature at the University of Turin before working on the editorial staff of the publishing house Einaudi, where he was first known for his work editing Italian folktales. His deceptively simple fiction often draws on his strong political views, told through a unique and distinct fictional voice.

Ele Carpenter is a curator, artist, writer and lecturer on the MFA Curating at Goldsmiths College, University of London. As curator of the Open Source Embroidery project, she is currently facilitating the "Embroidered Digital Commons," a distributed embroidery exploring collective work and ownership, 2008–2014.

Judith Clark is an exhibition-maker based in London. She is a reader in the field of fashion and museology at the London College of Fashion, University of the Arts where she teaches on the MA Fashion Curation. Clark lectures widely on issues of dress display and is an associate lecturer at IUAV, Venice. She studied architecture at the Architectural Association Graduate School, London, and the Bartlett School of Architecture, University College London, and is currently involved with a number of projects that explore the emerging field of fashion curation.

Arthur C. Danto is Johnsonian Professor Emeritus Philosophy at Columbia University, where he has worked since 1951. He is the author of numerous books, including *Nietzsche as Philosopher*, *Mysticism and Morality*, *The Transfiguration of the Commonplace*, *Narration and Knowledge*, *Connections to the World: The Basic Concepts of Philosophy*, *Encounters and Reflections: Art in the*

Historical Present, a collection of art criticism that won the National Book Critics Circle Prize for Criticism (1990) and *Embodied Meanings: Critical Essays and Aesthetic Meditations*. He has served as vice-president and president of the American Philosophical Association, as well as president of the American Society for Aesthetics.

Isak Dinesen (1885–1962) is the pseudonym of the Danish author Baroness Karen von Blixen-Finecke. Blixen's well-known writings include *Out of Africa* and *Babette's Feast*, both adapted into acclaimed films, and her collection of short stories, *Seven Gothic Tales*. Blixen lived from 1914–1931 in Kenya, an experience that forms the basis of *Out of Africa*.

The French philosopher **Gilles Deleuze** (1925–1995) studied at the Sorbonne between 1944–1948. His first book, *Empiricism and Subjectivity*, was published in 1953 followed by the publication of his doctorial thesis *Différence et répétition* in 1968, which had a significant impact on the tenants underpinning the discipline of philosophy. He met Félix Guattari in the early 1970s and cowrote with him a number of influential texts including *Capitalism and Schizophrenia*, published in two volumes as *Anti-Oedipus* (1972) and *A Thousand Plateaus* (1980).

Rebecca Earley is a designer and researcher, known for both her printed textiles and her practice-led research into sustainable textile design strategies. She has worked at the University of the Arts London since graduating from the MA Fashion at Central St. Martins in 1994, while also creating textiles under her label B. Earley. Her textiles research has sought to develop strategies to reduce the environmental impact of textile production, consumption and disposal. She is currently the acting director of the Textile Futures Research Centre (TFRC) and a reader at the Textiles Environment Design (TED) project at Chelsea.

American novelist **James Fennimore Cooper** (1789–1851) was born in New Jersey. His romanticized depiction of American Indians in the four novels that make up *The Leatherstocking Tales*, which include his most well known book *The Last of the Mohicans*, has informed the imaginations of numerous readers. Cooper attended Yale for several years before being asked to leave, it is believed after a series of campus pranks. The fact that his writing continues to be enjoyed today is testament to its remarkable longevity.

Sabrina Gschwandtner is an artist who works with photographic and textile media. She has exhibited her work internationally, at institutions including the Victoria and Albert Museum, London; the Museum of Arts and Design, New York; Contemporary Arts Museum Houston, and the Smithsonian American Art Museum. She is the author of *KnitKnit: Profiles and Projects from Knitting's New Wave* (2007), and has lectured extensively on the revival of handcraft in popular culture.

French philosopher and psychotherapist **Félix Guattari** (1930–1992) trained with the psychoanalyst Jacques Lacan and worked at the experimental La Borde clinic. He founded a number of organizations during his lifetime, including, early in his career, the Association of Institutional Psychotherapy, and later the fr:CEFRI (Centre for the Study and Research of Institutional Formation). Guattari's final collaboration with Gilles Deleuze, *What is Philosophy?*, was published in 1991 and posthumous publications include a 1996 collection of essays *Soft Subversions*.

At the time of writing the article included in the *Reader*, **Anne Hamlyn** was a writer and lecturer in Visual Culture and Textiles at Goldsmiths College, London. She gained her Ph.D. from the London Consortium (a collaboration between the Architectural Association, Birkbeck College, University of London, the Institute of Contemporary Arts, Science Museum and TATE) in 2003. Since 2004 she has run her own wardrobe consultancy business. She is currently working on a research project on the subject of personal image and fashion that has grown out of her experience as a stylist.

Catherine Harper is dean of Arts and Digital Industries at University of East London. A Northern Irish weaver and visual artist by origin, her work is held in numerous public collections including those of the Irish Ministry for Arts, Culture and the Gaeltacht, Belfast City Council and Derry's Women's Centre. She now writes on textiles, bodies, gendered and subjective narratives, is the UK editor of *Textile: The Journal of Cloth and Culture* (Berg) and editorial board member of *The International Journal of Fashion Design, Technology and Education* (Taylor & Francis). Her 2007 book *Intersex* (Berg, 2007) is followed by *Textiles: Primary and Critical Sources* (Berg, 2012). *Fabrics of Desire* will be published in 2013 (Berg).

The American author **Nathaniel Hawthorne** (1804–1864) was born in Massachusetts and, after graduation from Bowdoin College, turned to his attention to writing. Early works include the short stories "My Kinsman, Major Molineux," "Roger Malvin's Burial," and "Young Goodman Brown." His most famous work, *The Scarlett Letter* (included as an excerpt in the *Reader*), was completed in 1850 and enjoyed considerable success. Further novels include *The House of Seven Gables*, *The Blithedale Romance*, and *The Marble Faun*. He died in New Hampshire and *The Dolliver Romance*, along with a number of other works, were published posthumously.

Robyn Healy is an associate professor, program director of fashion and higher degree research in the School of Architecture + Design at RMIT University, Melbourne, Australia. She has extensive experience curating public collections of fashion and textiles, with former roles as senior curator of fashion and textiles at the National Gallery of Victoria, Melbourne and curator of International fashion at the National Gallery of Australia in Canberra. Exhibitions she has curated include "Gianni Versace: The retrospective 1982–1997" at the National Gallery of Victoria (2000), "Housemix: Highlights of the International Fashion and Textiles Collection" also held at the National Gallery of Victoria (2003), "Noble Rot: An Alternate View of Fashion" at the National Trust of Australia, Melbourne (2006), "Nomadic Archive" at Craft Victoria, Melbourne (2008), and "The Endless Garment: The New Craft of Machine Knitting" at the RMIT Gallery, Melbourne (2010).

June Hill is a freelance curator and writer. She is closely associated with Bankfield Museum, Halifax where she curated the textile collection (1989–2005). She has subsequently collaborated on projects with Manchester Metropolitan University, the University for the Creative Arts, the University of Huddersfield, and Ruthin Craft Centre. Much of her work focuses on the relationship between, and contextualization of, historic textiles and contemporary practice. She is also interested in the role and place of process. Ongoing research into UK textile collections has been published in *Embroidery* since January 2006. She is a contributor to the *Dictionary of World Dress* (Berg, 2010) and the author of monographs on Diana Springall (A&C Black,

2011) and Beryl Dean (2011). Recent ventures include: "The Sleeping Bag Project: Hidden Voices" (2011–12) and exhibitions on the work of Jilly Edwards (2011) and Michael Brennand-Wood (2012).

Pamela Johnson is a novelist, poet, and associate tutor on the MA in Creative & Life Writing at Goldsmiths, University of London. She is former editor of the British Crafts Council's magazine *Crafts*, and has worked as an independent critic and curator, writing on the meanings of cloth in visual art. Publications include *Michael Brennand-Wood: You Are Here* (1999) and *Ideas in the Making: Practice in Theory* (1998). Touring exhibitions include: "Surfacing" (2003–2005), a critical assessment of the work of Polly Binns; "Bodyscape: Caroline Broadhead" (1999, with Pennina Barnett), and "Textures of Memory: The Poetics of Cloth" (1999–2000). Johnson is currently working on her fourth novel and edits the website *Words Unlimited*; http://www.wordsunlimited.typepad.com/.

Suzanne Lee is a designer working at the forefront of biological materials with a vision to grow future eco products from living organisms. Her BioCouture Research Project is focused on harnessing bacteria to produce direct-formed cellulose. Her original inspiration to "grow clothing" has extended to explore diverse applications for these compostable materials. BioCouture has received worldwide attention and is featured in many design books and journals. Suzanne is author of *Fashioning the Future: Tomorrow's Wardrobe* (Thames & Hudson). She lectures and exhibits internationally and is a 2012 Senior TED Fellow.

Sarat Maharaj was born and educated in South Africa during the Apartheid years. From 1980–2005 he was professor of History & Theory of Art at Goldsmiths, London and is professor of Visual Art & Knowledge Systems, Lund University & the Malmo Art Academies, Sweden. He was the first Rudolf Arnheim Professor, Humboldt University, Berlin (2001–02) and Research Fellow at the Jan Van Eyck Akademie, Maastricht (1999–2001). Research interests include publications on a vast range of topics from Marcel Duchamp, James Joyce, and Richard Hamilton as well as tackling themes such as "Visual Art as Knowledge Production & Non-Knowledge"; "Textiles, Cultural Translation and Difference"; and the convergence of image, sound, movement and consciousness studies.

Matilda McQuaid is deputy curatorial director and head of textiles at the Smithsonian's Cooper-Hewitt, National Design Museum. She organizes exhibitions and publications relating to textiles as well as contemporary architecture and design, and oversees one of the premier textile collections in the world. Major shows include "Color Moves: Art and Fashion by Sonia Delaunay" and "Extreme Textiles: Designing for High Performance." Her interests extend to writing and scholarship, and she is an author and editor of art, architecture, and design publications.

Melanie Miller is a lecturer, maker, writer, and curator. Issues of gender stereotyping, globalization and branding are explored in Miller's practice. She has worked at Manchester Metropolitan University for twenty years, teaching on the BA (Hons) Embroidery program, and the MA Textiles program. Melanie's area of specialism is machine embroidery: she completed her Ph.D. on this subject in 1997 and has cocurated exhibitions around this theme, notably "Mechanical Drawing—The Schiffli Project" with June Hill in 2007.

Victoria Mitchell is a senior lecturer in Fine Art at Norwich University College of the Arts, formerly course leader of MA Textile Culture (2001–2010). Her work interrogates relationships between critical and material forms of textile as, for instance, coinvestigator of "Beyond the Basket" (Art & Humanities Research Council 2009–2012) and in published texts such as "Drawing Threads from Sight to Site" (2006), and "A Marketplace in Miniature: Norwich Pattern Books as Cultural Agency" (2008). She is the book reviews editor of *Textile: The Journal of Cloth and Culture* and an editor of *Craft Research*.

Clio Padovani's work as an artist and researcher developed from her background as a tapestry weaver. Her practice includes representing textile metaphors and methodologies through video, most recently seen in *Quilts, 1700–2010* at the Victoria & Albert Museum, and writing on the interdisciplinary context of textiles. Between 1995 and 2009 she was senior lecturer in textiles at the Winchester School of Art, followed by a post as lead UK investigator on an EU-funded Culture Programme, EurotexID, 2008–2010. Current research focuses on ethical textile business models. She is currently the faculty education coordinator at Business and Law, University of Southampton.

Rozsika Parker (1945–2010) was a feminist, art historian, psychotherapist, and writer. In 1972 she joined the feminist magazine *Spare Rib* and for several years contributed and commissioned arts content. In 1973 she formed the feminist art history collective with Griselda Pollock. *Old Mistresses: Women, Art and Ideology* (1981), was one result of the collaboration, followed by *Framing Feminism: Art and the Women's Movement 1970–1985* (1987). In 1984, Parker published *The Subversive Stitch: Embroidery and the Making of the Feminine* (reissued in 2010) a key text in the development of critical dialogue about textiles.

The American writer **Charlotte Perkins Gilman** (1860–1935) was a lecturer, feminist, and social reformer. She penned numerous works of fiction and nonfiction during her life, many focusing on the role of women in society. Gilman attended the Rhode Island School of Design and in 1884 married Charles Walter Stetson. The couple had one child. Gilman moved to California after treatment for what may today be diagnosed as postpartum depression, separating from her husband and daughter. Her 1898 book *Women and Economics: A Study of the Economic Relation Between Men and Women as a Factor in Social Relations* enjoyed critical acclaim. Alongside further books she published *The Forerunner* (1909–1916), a monthly journal.

Sadie Plant is an author and philosopher. She earned her Ph.D. from the University of Manchester in 1989 and founded the Cybernetic Culture Research Unit at the University of Warwick. Her acclaimed book *Zeroes + Ones: Digital Women + The New Technoculture* was published in 1997 and her articles have appeared in the *Financial Times*, *Wired*, *Blueprint*, and *Dazed and Confused*.

Sue Prichard is curator of contemporary textiles at the Victoria & Albert Museum, London. She has curated a number of displays including "Textiles in Context: 40th Anniversary of the 62 Group"; "Recent Acquisitions 1992–2002: A Decade of Collecting Textiles"; "Concealed-Discovered-Revealed: New Work by Sue Lawty" and "Penelope's Thread: Contemporary Tapestry from the Permanent Collection." Prichard was the lead curator on the V&A's major exhibition "Quilts 1700–2010" and editor of *Quilts 1700–2010: Hidden Histories, Untold Stories*. She has a broad interest in domesticity and domestic production.

Kirsty Robertson is an assistant professor of Contemporary Art and Museum Studies at the University of Western Ontario. Her research focuses on activism, visual culture, and changing economies. She has published widely on the topic and is currently finishing her book *Tear Gas Epiphanies: New Economies of Protest, Vision, and Culture in Canada*. More recently, she has turned her attention to the study of wearable technologies, immersive environments, and the potential overlap(s) between textiles and technologies. She considers these issues within the framework of globalization, activism, and burgeoning "creative economies." Her coedited volume *Imagining Resistance: Visual Culture and Activism in Canada*, was released in 2011.

Yinka Shonibare, MBE was born in London and moved to Lagos, Nigeria at the age of three. He returned to London to study Fine Art first at Byam Shaw College of Art (now Central Saint Martins College of Art and Design) and then at Goldsmiths College, where he received his MFA, graduating as part of the "Young British Artists" generation. Shonibare was a Turner prize nominee in 2004 and awarded the decoration of Member of the "Most Excellent Order of the British Empire," an accolade he has added to his professional name. In addition to numerous exhibitions, in 2010 "Nelson's Ship in a Bottle" became his first public art commission on the Fourth Plinth in Trafalgar Square.

Elaine Showalter is an American literary critic associated with the school of feminist criticism coined gynocritics. She completed her Ph.D. at the University of California, Davis in 1970 and is Emeritus Professor of English at Princeton University, past president of the Modern Language Association and was formerly on the advisory board of the English Subject Centre. Showalter retired from Princeton in 2003 and is a freelance journalist and media commentator.

Gayatri Chakravorty Spivak's writing covers the fields of feminism, marxism, deconstruction and globalization. She completed her Ph.D. in Comparative Literature at Cornell University in 1967 and is a founding member of the Institute for Comparative Literature and Society at Columbia University. Her extensive list of publications include such significant articles as "Subaltern Studies: Deconstructing Historiography" (1985), "Three Women's Texts and a Critique of Imperialism" (1985), "Can the Subaltern Speak?" (1988), "The Politics of Translation" (1992), "Moving Devi" (1999), "Righting Wrongs" (2003), "Ethics and Politics in Tagore, Coetzee, and Certain Scenes of Teaching" (2004), "Translating into English" (2005), and "Rethinking Comparativism" (2010). She is self-described as an activist in rural education, ecological social movements, and a feminist.

Jenni Sorkin is assistant professor of Contemporary Art History and Critical Theory at the University of Houston. She is currently completing a book manuscript, titled *Live Form: Craft as Participation*, which examines the confluence of gender, artistic labor, and the history of postwar ceramics from 1945 to 1975. Her writing has appeared in the *New Art Examiner*, *Art Journal*, *Art Monthly*, *NU: The Nordic Art Review*, *Frieze*, *The Journal of Modern Craft*, *Modern Painters*, and *Third Text*. In 2010, she co-organized "Blind Spots/Puntos Ciegos: Feminisms, Cinema, and Performance," for the eighth edition of SITAC, the International Symposium of

Contemporary Art Theory, held in Mexico City. She holds a Ph.D. in the History of Art from Yale University. From 2010–2011, she was a postdoctoral fellow at the Getty Research Institute in Los Angeles.

Peter Stallybrass is Walter H. and Leonore C. Annenberg Professor in the Humanities and professor of English and of Comparative Literature and Literary Theory at the University of Pennsylvania. His memorial lecture "Worn Worlds: Clothes, Mourning, and the Life of Things" grew into the book *Renaissance Clothing and the Materials of Memory* (Cambridge University Press) written with Ann Rosalind Jones which won the James Russell Lowell prize by the Modern Language Association in 2001. In 2007, he was elected to the American Philosophical Society.

Lou Taylor is the professor of Dress and Textile History at the University of Brighton. She is author of *Mourning Dress: A Costume and Social History* (1983, reprinted by Routledge 2010), *The Study of Dress History* (2002) and *Establishing Dress History* (Manchester University Press, 2004).

Anna Von Mertens is an artist whose work is at the intersection of craft, science, and conceptual art. She was the recipient of a 2010 United States Artists Simon Fellowship and a 2007 Louis Comfort Tiffany Foundation Biennial Award. Her work has been exhibited at the Berkeley Art Museum; Museum of Art, Rhode Island School of Design; The Fleming Museum, Burlington, Vermont; Sun Valley Center for the Arts, Ketchum, Idaho; Yerba Buena Center for the Arts, San Francisco; Ballroom Marfa, Marfa, Texas and as part of the 2012 deCordova Biennial.

Alice Walker is a poet, short story writer, novelist, essayist, anthologist, teacher, editor, publisher, womanist, and activist. She graduated from Sarah Lawrence College in 1965. Her first novel, *The Third Life of Grange Copeland*, was published in 1970, followed by *Meridian* in 1976. She was awarded the Pulitzer Prize for Fiction for her 1983 novel *The Color Purple*, made into a film by Steven Spielberg in 1985. Her collections of short stories include *You Can't Keep a Good Woman Down* (1981); *Alice Walker: The Complete Stories* (1994); and *The Way Forward Is with a Broken Heart* (2000). She is also author of a number of works of nonfiction, including her celebrated essay "In Search of Our Mothers' Gardens" (1983).

Elizabeth Wayland Barber is Professor Emerita of Archaeology and Linguistics at Occidental College in Los Angeles. She received her Ph.D. from Yale University in 1968. Her research and publications focus on various aspects of anthropology and language. In addition to her book *Women's Work: The First 20,000 Years* (Norton, 1994) (included in this *Reader*) her publications include *Archaeological Decipherment* (Princeton, 1974), *Prehistoric Textiles* (Princeton, 1991), *The Mummies of Urumchi* (Norton, 1999), and *When They Severed Earth from Sky: How the Human Mind Shapes Myth* (Princeton, 2005).

Paul Whittaker is associate dean of the Faculty of Business and Law, University of Southampton, and has exhibited and published nationally and internationally. His research interests focus on promoting innovation through the reconsideration of established practices by way of unconventional means, and experimentation and speculation regarding temporality and time in the creative process. He is currently principle investigator in Plustex, a European Union funded

INTERREG project to explore the knowledge economy of textile design and its relation to the European creative industries.

Jane Wildgoose is an artist, writer, broadcaster, and NESTA Fellow who trained in textile design and was, for many years, a costume designer. She is keeper of her own collection, the Wildgoose Memorial Library, and works to commission with collections, archives and museums in the UK and United States. Recent commissions include the site-specific solo installation "Promiscuous Assemblage, Friendship, & the Order of Things" at the Yale Center for British Art (2009). Wildgoose is currently a Ph.D. candidate at Kingston University where she teaches contemporary creative practice on the Museum & Galleries Studies MA course in the School of Art & Design History.

Diana Wood Conroy is an artist and writer with degrees in archaeology and art. An archaeological approach informs her critical writing on textiles and tapestry as seen in her book *The Fabric of the Ancient Theatre: Excavation Journals from Cyprus* (Moufflon Publishing, Nicosia, 2007). She is an honorary professorial fellow, Faculty of Creative Arts, at the University of Wollongong, Australia.

Catherine de Zegher is currently the joint artistic director of the Biennale of Sydney, Australia (2012). De Zegher was the director of exhibitions and publications at the Art Gallery of Ontario in Toronto, where she was part of the transformation team overseeing the reinstallation of the renovated museum building by Frank Gehry (2007–2009). Previous to this position, she was the executive director of the Drawing Center in New York (1999–2006). Before de Zegher took up her work in North America, she was the cofounder and director of the Kanaal Art Foundation in Kortrijk, Belgium (1988–1998). Author and editor of numerous books, she is now preparing an anthology of her collected essays on the work of contemporary women artists. One of her most recent publications is the October Book *Women Artists at the Millennium* coedited with Carol Armstrong (MIT Press).

INTRODUCTION

It is fair to say that this *Textile Reader* is as concerned with *how* we write about textiles as it is interested in *what* we write about textiles. Contributors range from artists and designers to fiction authors and historians. The familiar essay format sits beside interviews, lists, short stories (some a paragraph in length), artist's statements, and blogs. The content contained within these genres is eclectic with the intention that familiar thinking is placed alongside more contentious approaches. While the range of styles and content included makes it impossible for all the material to be of equal interest to every reader, it is my hope that this book makes clear the diversity of voices and styles that are contributing to the emerging academic discipline of textile scholarship.

A number of individuals have generously contributed knowledge and resources to this project. A residency at the College of Fine Arts, University of New South Wales, Australia, in 2008, supported by Liz Williamson, allowed precious thinking space to begin this project. Vital time and resources to finish the project were provided by Alan Murray, head of the School of Design at Edinburgh College of Art. Glenn Adamson, Rebecca Earley, Sabrina Gschwandtner, Alice Kettle, David Littler, Angela Maddock, Victoria Mitchell, Nisha Obano, Sharon Peoples, and Carol Tulloch deserve particular thanks, among many others whose suggestions have confirmed that the writing collected here tackles only the tip of the iceberg. Finally, Sara Barnes has shown remarkable tenacity in the rather torturous task of helping to clear copyright on the material included.

Early in the project, I made the editorial decision to include only one example of writing from each contributor. In some cases, the choice was difficult to make, but my intention throughout has been to capture diversity in both genre and content. Where possible each text is reprinted in its entirety and the format preserved as closely as reasonable to the original publication. This means a range of styles are present: footnotes, endnotes, no notes! For the same reason, British and American spelling is preserved as found in the original.

The majority of the texts included in this *Reader* have been written in the past two decades, and a number of contributors make reference to the undervalued identity of textiles during this time. While there is no doubt that this has been the case, I hope that the range of thinking gathered here may begin to allow textile scholarship to move beyond a position of decrying the "undervalued" ground. Textiles not only inhabit all aspects of our lives today but also have much to teach us.

Dr. Jessica Hemmings
Edinburgh College of Art

PART I

TOUCH

PART INTRODUCTION

Anyone who loves textiles touches them. It is an instinct and a response that can prove embarrassingly inappropriate in unprepared company. "May I touch?" or "Would you mind if I felt . . . ?" are often spoken as belated formalities. In sympathetic company a sleeve or cuff is offered. While tugging at a friend's new dress is one thing, in settings such as a gallery or lecture hall touch is often forbidden or, at the very least, is absent from the conversation. When we are unable to understand cloth through touch, significant qualities often unique to the textile can be misunderstood.

The writing collected in this section uses a range of strategies to tackle the subject of touch. Examples vary from the dense theoretical application of ideas to the playful, seemingly innocent tactics of fiction, which teach and entertain in the same gesture. Common throughout is the observation that within the hierarchy of the senses, touch has long struggled for respect. Learning through seeing (and this includes reading) is somehow felt to be a superior or more legitimate way of knowing the world. This prejudice has done textiles, and the crafts in general, a long-standing disservice. But as the writing here reveals, it is also a hierarchy that is being reconsidered. In this section, the voices of academics, artists, and a fiction author observe—but also challenge—the undervalued place touch inhabits in our understanding of textiles.

A conference paper by Victoria Mitchell opens the *Reader* and considers the relationship between writing about textiles and making textiles. Mitchell recalls E. B. White's children's story *Charlotte's Web* and uses the seemingly innocent construction of words within the spider's web to begin a broader debate about what the construction of text and the construction of textiles share, as well as moments when the two differ. While touch is central to our understanding of textiles, writing and reading about textiles tend to be considered, in an academic context, to make a greater contribution to our understanding of cloth. "Reading" the textile, rather than "feeling" the textile, means the textile is judged against a value system that does not always respond to its strengths.

For Anne Hamlyn, touch is understood through the theoretical framework of psychoanalysis. Hamlyn "proposes that the sensory connection that we all (both male and female) have to cloth cannot be adequately expressed in language." This presents a curious predicament for critical writing about the textile and here is resolved through the use of psychoanalytic theory to expose the thinking embedded in examples such as the sculptures of Cathy de Monchaux. Compared to these first two academic papers, Catherine Harper's writing is experimental in style and questions the critical tone of textile dialogue. Her catalog essay about the Japanese textile company Nuno adopts a hybrid voice that is part confessional, part critical but also fictional to evoke the feeling of textiles experienced against the skin. Opening with the cityscape of Tokyo, Harper acknowledges the shift in meaning that occurs across cultures, questioning whether she is "lost in translation" (a reference to Sophia Coppola's popular 2003 film), but also suggests that touch and its connection to fetish are a way of experiencing the textile that may not always be culturally specific. Harper's writing is deft in its integration of critical texts from thinkers ranging from Roland Barthes to Walter Benjamin, but it embeds such references in a format that reads as a part-fiction journal entry.

Karen Blixen, writing under the pen name Isak Dinesen, offers us a further example of the knowing ways that fiction can contribute to our critical thinking about the textile. Dinesen uses the short story to suggest the intimate place the textile occupies, literally recording the experience of touch that consummates marriage, while also toying with the idea that the story can be at its most creative when details are left to the imagination. Dinesen essentially writes a short story about the telling of stories, beginning with the storyteller, an "old coffee-brown, black-veiled who made her living by telling stories" she had told "for two hundred years." But she also casts the textile as a storyteller, here intended to record the private events of the wedding night for public proof of the bride's virginity. Multiple explanations of the one unstained sheet in the royal family's collection remain unspoken, confirming Dinesen's paradoxical message that "where the story-teller is loyal, eternally and unswervingly loyal to the story, there, in the end, silence will speak."

June Hill's lecture "Sense and Sensibility" shows the place touch occupies in our understanding of projects as varied as the Hiroshima Peace Park, the documentary film *Into Great Silence*, and the work of textile artists Rozanne Hawksley and Jeanette Appleton. Hill considers the role of the curator in relation to our understanding of material culture and "argues for the value of listening (to objects as well as to people), of poetic understandings, and of integrity of process" (personal communication, March 2011). Touch here refers not only to physical contact with a surface but also to the ways in which we are touched, and moved, by our world. Finally, a conference paper by Maxine Bristow reflects on the artist's own practice and considers how touch fights for relevance in the broader system of fine art values that underpin her practice. Bristow's writing returns to the tension between touch and language that opened this section and observes, "it is the silent, but, undoubtedly, potent nature of this embedded/embodied material language which has resonances with my own practice." Importantly, this final text of the section offers us an example of critical writing used to inform the making of the author's practice.

1

TEXTILES, TEXT AND TECHNE

Victoria Mitchell

Editor's introduction: Victoria Mitchell's essay "Textiles, Text and Techne" opens this *Reader* because of its attention to the act of writing. Mitchell has written extensively about textiles and here provides us with a map of writing about textiles in relation to textile making. The etymological links between *text*, *textile*, and *techne* (Greek for craftsmanship or making with intention), as well as the distinct differences in the these ways of working, are acknowledged. This leads to Mitchell's reminder that the one thing the written word can never do is to physically touch, in the most literal sense, the textiles that are of central concern to all the writing in this *Reader*. "The privileging of words and the ocularcentrism of western culture can mask some of the sensibilities conveyed through textile practice," Mitchell observes. An attention to the needs of the textile is crucial to our understanding of not only textiles but also the value system that has relegated touch to its current undervalued position.

Mitchell is a senior lecturer at the Norwich University College of the Arts, England. This essay was first written for the conference Obscure Objects of Desire: Reviewing the Crafts in the Twentieth Century in 1997 and published in the conference proceedings edited by Tanya Harrod.

In E.B. White's story for children, *Charlotte's Web*, the spider Charlotte weaves the word 'SOME PIG' into her web.[1] The farmer Mr. Zuckerman and his workman Lurvy are taken aback at the sight of 'the writing on the web' and Mr. Zuckerman immediately informs his wife: ' "Edith," he said, trying to keep his voice steady, "I think you had best be told that we have a very unusual pig." ' He explains how the words were woven right into the web and were ' "actually part of the web . . . There can be no mistake about it. A miracle has happened and a sign occurred here on earth, right on our farm, and we have no ordinary pig". ' ' "Well," said Mrs Zuckerman, "it seems to me you're a little off. It seems to me we have no ordinary *spider*." '

Source: Victoria Mitchell, "Textiles, Text and Techne," in Tanya Harrod and Helen Clifford (eds.), *Obscure Objects of Desire: Reviewing the Crafts in the Twentieth Century* (London: Crafts Council, 1997) pp. 324–332. Reproduced with permission. With the permission of the author, some minor corrections or edits have been made in the version of the text published here.

Despite Mrs Zuckerman's observation, it is not Charlotte's skill which becomes the centre of attention. Charlotte's ability to transform the instinctual web into a slogan of support for her friend the pig Wilbur achieves the desired result and Wilbur is spared from a chopping-board death. She uses her ingenious skill to promote the specialness of the pig; going beyond her instinctual skills as a maker of orb webs for the purpose of mating and capturing prey, it might be said that the web is transformed from one kind of snare (for tricking flies) to another (tricking the reader).

The fact that the words are 'actually part of the web', and are therefore impressive on that account, reinforces the 'miracle' of their effect which causes the message to be divorced from the skill which produced it. Peter Dormer spoke of the making which begins with the production of the raw material, as 'below the line'—that which is hidden from sight and which the consumer takes for granted.[2] In the case of the spider this might be the secretion of silk from the abdominal glands, drawn out by spinnarets, or the highly developed muscular sense which enables it to detect changes in tension in the thread.[3] In *Charlotte's Web* these aspects are secondary to the function of the signifying power of words.

Charlotte's Web is of course a fiction. Spiders make webs throughout their lives but they don't get better at making them. Whilst their ability to send and receive signals through vibration is subtle and complex, this ability is understood in terms of the mechanics of the nervous system; it therefore falls short of the kind of language experience typically associated with the written word. The linguist D. McNeil says that: 'We tend to consider "linguistic" what we can write down, and "non-linguistic" everything else, but this division is a cultural artefact, an arbitrary limitation derived from historical evolution.'[4]

In this paper I consider transitions and boundaries between text, textiles and *techne*, many of which are implicit in E.B. White's fictional example. Text, textiles and *techne* are etymologically

linked, reflecting an intimacy and a complexity for thought in its association with making. Etymological links are not, however, the only form in which evidence of such association is manifest, and indeed the manner in which words are formed, in their differences and similarities, is often supple, subtle and cunningly playful in a way which can mask or even contradict those cognitive functions which are directly evidenced in the actions of making through materials.

Relationships between text, textiles and *techne* are of critical interest not only for what they may reveal about textiles and language; there are implications in their association which may be relevant to an understanding of what it means to create forms through materials. Such implications may require a refiguring and disrupting of the boundaries which divide instinct from cognition and nature from culture. The effect of such disrupting might be to create an enhanced significance for those practices which, sometimes with derogatory overtones, are referred to as 'craft'.

I begin by considering the senses as a basis of a phylogenetic and ontogenetic *conjunction* between language and textile. I will then suggest an historical, cultural context for their *separation*. Examples are drawn from the writings of Anni Albers and Edward Johnson to illustrate ways in which these associations and disassociations have affected the making of textiles and the perception of craft within the twentieth century. Finally I will consider the theorising of textiles from a contemporary perspective. I will argue that the privileging of words and the ocularcentrism of western culture can mask some of the sensibilities conveyed through textile practice, and that making sense through the tactility of textiles has implications for perception in a wider sense. In particular, the formative relationship between words and textiles alerts us to what I would like to call the textility of both thought and matter, a neologism which may be formative in minimising the separateness of the spheres within which text, textiles and *techne* might otherwise operate. The textility of making suggests a practice which informs thought; unlike an architectonic framework for cognition, it provides evidence of a more supple fabrication.

Language and textile formation share pliability as well as an inherent capacity to form structural relations between components. In both there is a suggestion of the drawing forth of minute physical sensation, fibre or particle into a form which is versatile and adaptable. The etymological and metaphorical use of words gives indications of some common associations, thus, according to Cecilia Vicuña: 'In the Andes the language itself, Quechua, is a chord of twisted straw, two people making love, different fibres united',[5] and in Hungarian, the word for fibres is the same as that for vocal chords. The word 'language' derives in Latin and in Sanskrit from that which makes it, namely the tongue, and on a spinning wheel the point at which the yarn emerges fully formed is called the orifice. Text and textile share common association through the Latin *texere*, to weave. These fragile references suggest for textiles a kind of speaking and for language a form of making.

Making and speaking, beginning with gesture and utterance, are both primarily tactile and sensory, of the body. Through the senses, touch and utterance share common origins in the neural system and in the pattern of synaptic, electrochemical connections between neurons. It is the fibrous form of the neuron which is said to provide 'the key to its role in the nervous system', and the synapse, both morphological and physiological in origin, which creates continuity and articulates differences between nerve cells. From each neuron, the dendrites which snake and twist as an extension of the cell body act as antennae, receiving impulses through the large surface area of their arborised endings.[6] Recent neuroscientific reconstructions of individual neurons are described by Peter Coveney and Roger Highfield as 'neural architectures',[7] but the intricacy of these architectures is of a fibrous form for which the metaphor of textiles might be more appropriate. In the fibrous tissue of the sensory body both the gestures of action and the utterance of speech are finely connected.

The complicated organisation of the nervous system confirms the views of psychologists of perception such as J.J. Gibson that the senses are perceptual systems and are integral to the formation of cognition.[8] Studies of gesture in the formation of language have also drawn on neurological evidence to support the link between oral and manual gestures and cognition. Language is an articulatory gesture of movement and feeling rooted in the body through neural activity:

> language, whether planned or produced, is always realized in some physical medium. At the level of planning, this medium is neural; at the level of utterance, it is articulatory (gestural). There is no translation from mental to physical; there is only motor activity brought about by neural activity.[9]

Of the various forms in which the senses are said to operate, the sense of sight has been, historically, the most privileged, whilst touch, with its implication of earth and base matter, has been less well served. Both philosophy and science have constructed a privileged role for sight as a cognitive organ, indeed Aristotle considered sight to be noble precisely because of the immateriality of its knowing, and hence its apparent approximation to the intellect.[10] In his book *The Eyes of the Skin*, the Finnish architect and theorist Juhani Pallasmaa tries to redress this onesidedness, by arguing that 'all the senses, including vision, can be regarded as senses of touch'.[11] This argument is necessary because, he suggests, sight has become a privileged social sense, whereas touch is now considered an archaic sensory remnant 'with a merely private function'.[12] He suggests that this is not the case for traditional cultures in which haptic and muscular senses of the body guide construction 'in the same way that a bird shapes its nest by movements of its body'.[13] The spinner and historian Patricia Baines reflects this polarising of the senses when she says that: 'it is difficult to describe in words and still pictures something which is a continuous movement, a rhythm and co-ordination between hands, foot and fibre, and which also sharpens the sense of feel.'[14]

It is clear that textiles are *not* words and the differences between them benefit the conceptual apparatus of thought at the expense of its sensory equivalent. Thus when an activity is *labelled* as textiles it ceases to be a substance and becomes instead a 'material of thought', and as such enters into the internal logic of a system which tends to privilege the autonomy of the mind. The word becomes surrogate for the substance. Despite the evocative power of the word, its potential to embody a presence through memory and association, there is a gap between word and thing which grows apace as verbal becomes written and written becomes printed, as the context of the thing itself recedes from view.

Historically, the development of writing coincides with a shift away from the locus of making. According to the structuralist Jean-Pierre Vernant, for example, a distinction was made, at the birth of the city state in Greece, between the private domain of the family and the public polis of the citizen, a category which excluded artisans, women and slaves.[15] Vernant suggests that the development of writing occurs in the exclusive public domain of the polis. Those who did not enter the polis, who did not write, who did not engage in the activities of the public space of the agora, were thereby marginalised both visibly and verbally. In the context of the polis, the deliberate and conscious construction of reflection was informed by the *Logos*, the authority of the word as instrument of exchange of ideas.

A similar shift, away from the sensibility that arises through making, occurs with the advent of technology. With the advent of technological progress, Baudrillard suggests that the integrity of objects no longer is contingent upon individual needs which can be satisfied by artisanal production but upon a system which is technological and economic and which coheres around

signifiers (notably words) which have the ability to select and direct the functioning of needs.[16] Thus exchange value, located in the signifying power of 'some pig' comes to predominate over the use value of the web. Charlotte's words, the *Logos* of the Greek citizen and the signifiers of exchange value reflect the privileged status of language as associated with notions of authority, truth and thought.

The yielding, domestic, female, decorative and material associations for textiles have in general determined their absence from this cultural hegemony, but it is an absence which may also be or have been an expression of resistance. In writings by textile practitioners in the twentieth century (until recently there are noticeably few), there is evidence of a desire to resist too great an involvement with words as the material of thought because it might hinder the articulation of meaning through the handling of materials. This resistance is repeatedly conveyed in the writings of Anni Albers, whose book *On Designing* (published in 1959 but based on writings from the late Thirties onwards) is one of the most substantial, analytic and wide-ranging in interpretation to have emerged from a textile practitioner in the modern period.

In her writing there is a tone of resistance to words as instruments of thought and, paradoxically, a note of discouragement to would-be maker-writers. Making through materials is justified as almost a superior kind of thought. She says: 'The inarticulateness of the artistic person is interpreted easily as a lack of intelligence while it is rather an intelligence expressing itself in other means than words.'[17] It is as if, by resisting one branch of intelligence, another will present itself through receptivity to the materials, thus: 'Resistance is one of the factors necessary to make us realise the characteristics of our medium and make us question our work procedure.'[18]

Albers distances herself from the subjective, and from the belief that knowledge gained through intellectual skills can benefit the maker. She says, for example, that 'with expanding knowledge goes limitation in range', that 'information means in-tellectualisation . . . onesidedness, incomplete-ness', and that 'layer after layer of civilised life seems to have veiled our directness of seeing' whereas the '*direct* experience of a medium' is seen as preferable. It is therefore 'better that the ma-terial speaks than that we speak ourselves'.[19] This denial of the self and of emotional introspection conveys a canonically Modern sensibility towards function and away from the obfuscating potential of art, or the privileging of the ego. For Albers, 'crafts become problematic when they are hybrids of art and usefulness',[20] and thus by 'losing our-selves in the task we . . . would arrive at a result that is not individualistically limited.'[21]

In her practice, Albers was both a weaver who believed in the primacy of what she called 'the most real thing that there is', namely material, but also a graphic designer, particularly at the end of her life.[22] Weaving, writing and drawing share a common denominator through the practice of *graphein*, the graphic, a practice which demon-strates a formative trait for both text and textiles. A number of her woven pieces are given titles and forms which suggest writing or graphic signs. She wanted, she said, 'to let the threads be articulate again'. Pieces such as *Ancient Writing* (1936), *Memo* (1958), *Jotting* (1959), *Haiku* (1961) and *Code* (1962), suggest that she was exploring and rediscovering a graphic potential in both text and textiles, a coincidence conveyed through a re-sponse to the material.[23] Her deep regard for an-cient Peruvian textiles, which predate the written word, reinforced this. Speaking of their double, triple and quadruple weaves she comments: 'if a highly intelligent people with no written lan-guage, no graph paper, and no pencils could man-age such invention, we should be able—easily I hope—to repeat these structures.'[24]

Despite her concern for material processes, much of her work was designed for contempla-tion rather than practical use, to be touched with the eyes rather than the hand. Also, Albers increas-ingly gave titles to her works from the late Thir-ties onwards, again suggesting a relinquishing of the tactile as the agent of formation. The naming and visual contemplation of textiles mark a shift in perception from the physical to the mental, a shift which grows apace through the develop-ment and proliferation of exhibition and publi-cation contexts for textile and other crafts. As a consequence, physical responses of use and touch cease to operate as primary entry points of under-standing. Like words and pictures in books, exhi-bitions tend to marginalise the technical, artisanal aspects of practice, and they do not, in general, allow the involvement of touch. In a review of the 1954 Arts and Crafts Exhibition Society exhi-bition, Peter Collingwood drew attention to the problem of textiles as objects of contemplation, suggesting that they suffered by not being felt: 'because a piece of cloth is only half-experienced unless it is handled, the visitors find it impossible to keep their hands off.'[25]

It may be said that words are substitutes for use. For Albers the articulation of threads as a for-mation from within and through interaction with the material gives way to a reading in which the threads are represented by the words which are used to describe them.

The typographer Edward Johnson, a maker for whom articulacy through words is formed through a combination of making *and* reading, analysed some of the problems posed by the dis-tancing of tactile involvement in the exhibition of crafts in an address given to members of the Arts and Crafts Exhibition Society in 1933:

> There is something necessarily artificial about a formal Exhibition. The objects are *posed* in a gallery to be *looked at*, and the Percipient—i.e., the 'Public'—can only use *one* of his five senses in appreciating them. On his own family goods and chattels all five senses confer in daily judge-ment. *Here* he must be content with Sight alone.
>
> But even the sense of sight is restricted to viewing *motionless material effects* often little more than one-sided views. The Exhibits can-not by action demonstrate their fitness for use. We may not touch, still less handle or try the

use of Things meant to be daily used and handled. An exhibition is, in fact, apt to be a kind of *lying in state*—of Talent at rest.[26]

It is in this gap, between use and sight, that words can function as a form of closure, as a mediation which can effect a partial recovery of that which has been lost. Rather than considering words as a further loss to sensory embodiment of meaning, Johnson's proposed solution is to encourage *makers* to 'write *critical and explanatory* . . . labels to accompany their work'. Even though, he suggests, the work itself is a 'sort of special language' and 'the thing he makes not only speaks for him, but also speaks for itself', through engagement in writing: 'we can give a partial *translation of our Works into Words* which will assist understanding.' He appeals to the poet in the maker and suggests that 'We are . . . *Makers* of word arrangements by which we exchange ideas'.

Whilst the main purpose of Johnson's address concerned the maker's written interpretation, he also went further in suggesting that exhibitions might show evidence and explanations of materials and processes. Johnson's overall aim is not only 'to help people to see what they are looking at', but also to assist the understanding of the maker, and to enable makers to communicate through words with one another. In other words, writing becomes a form of making—making words—*and* an aspect of seeing. The sense of touch functions vicariously through a combination of indirect agents. Writing establishes the involvement of the viewer in forming a relationship between seeing and making, potentially guiding the viewer away from the flatness of a static object to the activity and ideas which it embodies.

Both Albers and Johnson are, in interconnected ways, entering into a system which coheres around signifiers which select and direct the viewer's response to the work. Seen from a contemporary perspective, the exhibition may be encountered not as a space within which objects are contemplated from a physical distance through the immateriality of the eye but as a medium of making or an intertextuality of signs in which the viewer's response is formative. Nevertheless, the tactility of making, touching and using remain as secondary and are silenced.

Within recent literary and critical theory there is evidence of a desire to make sense of the gap between words and things. In this, metaphors referring to textiles have been formative and transformative. Thus Michel Foucault uses the metaphor of interweaving to describe the relationship between things and words, and Roland Barthes uses the analogy of braid to illustrate the multiplicity of intersecting codes that constitute what he calls textuality: 'each thread, each code, is a voice; these braided—or braiding—voices form the writing', and the feminist Gayatri Chakravorty Spivak speaks enticingly of the fraying of the edges of the language-textile as seen from the perspective of translation between one language and another.[27]

In transferring, perhaps appropriating, the articulacy of threads from material to textual practice, the metaphorical ambiguity of textile terminology has unleashed previously undisclosed meanings for textiles as well as for critical theory. In recent years textile practitioners have begun to participate in ambiguous verbal play, for example speaking of the 'language of textiles' and suggesting that textiles are a form of writing or speaking. Textiles as metaphor have assumed in recent writing the agency of a sensory idea, a material of thought, so that it becomes possible to speak of textile thought and tactile literacy. The haptic and the conceptual have moved closer together through the agency of textile experience as expressed through metaphor and through words. Such writing and the making to which it refers have become manifest at a time of critical appraisal and disruption of the primacy of language and its privileged relationship to thought and power, and it is significant that textiles, which the contemporary artist Pierrette Bloch suggests is a 'dark other side to writing', has entered into and contributed to the disruption of that primacy.[28]

Textile practice remains, however, rooted in material, and for textile practice which identifies with craft the role of making and of handling materials is only partly served by textile-theory word-play. In the catalogue of a recent textile art exhibition, *TextileArt*, curated by makers, Judith Duffey Harding asks: 'Can a practice that grows out of making, that thinks with its hands by making, evolve its own theory, in a way that doesn't intimidate or constrain the makers by imposing it?'[29]

Perhaps, in response to this, it may be helpful to return to the formation of the word textile, and reconsider its origin within the practice of making. Within literary criticism the etymological link between text and textile, from the Latin *texere*, to weave, has been central in developing notions of textuality and intertextuality. The etymology that links text and textile can, however, be traced further back, to Greek and Sanskrit associations which emphasise the activity of making and forming. The Sanskrit words *takman* meaning 'child' and *taksh*, to make, and the Indo-European root *tek-* used of men, meaning to beget, and of women, to bring forth, have all been linked to the Latin *texere*. In these, the sense of physical formation is emphatic. Through *tek-* the formation of *techne* further demonstrates the association of skill and through the Latin *texere* the sense of joining or fitting together reinforces the association of textiles with materials and away from the metaphorical associations illustrated by reference to text.

The notion of textuality, with its associated reference to textiles, evades, I suggest, these earlier traditions of making, joining and putting together, of bodies and buildings. Textiles, whilst they lend themselves to associations of text, also mediate between the fibrous body and the fabric of architecture. They articulate subtle physical sensations between substance and surface, and are most closely known to us through their relationship to the skin and to the sense of touch, a sense which is actively encountered through the making of textiles by hand. In addition to the analogy

with the textuality of language and the intertextuality of signs, textile practice may also acknowledge this contiguity with the physical forms of bodies and of things, a kind of textility operating through and in-between forms in space. As suggested here by Pallasmaa, the architectonic may give way to the tactile:

> With the loss of tactility and measures and details crafted for the human body—and particularly for the hand—architectural structures become flat, sharp edged, immaterial and unreal. The detachment of construction from the realities of matter and craft further turns architecture into stage sets for the eyes into a scenography devoid of the authenticity of matter and construction.[30]

In her reappraisal of the myth of Arachne and Athena, Nancy K. Miller reminds the reader of Virginia Woolf's awareness of the fragility but tenaciousness of fiction's relationship to the real:

> Fiction is like a spider's web, attached ever so lightly perhaps, but still attached to life at all four corners . . . When the web is pulled askew . . . one remembers that these webs are not spun in mid-air by incorporeal creatures, but are the work of suffering human beings, and are attached to grossly material things, like health and money and the houses we live in.[31]

We realise of course that it was a good thing Charlotte could write words in her web: it saved Wilbur's life. Within contemporary textiles it is also true that issues of gender and class, for example, have been voiced and heard through textiles. The subtle nuance and fragile pliability of textiles as embodied metaphor have contributed actively to the disruption of the authority of language, and have been abundant in intonations of sensory experience, thus serving to enable senses other than sight to achieve an enhanced status. Nevertheless, the manipulation of textiles has implications for meanings which come about directly, if not instinctively, through making, and these are often least well served in a culture of sign consumption. The spider's web has recently been the subject of tensile structure research with reference to use in architecture, as if, at last, Mrs Zuckerman's voice is heard.[32]

NOTES

1. E.B. White, *Charlotte's Web*, Hamish Hamilton, London, 1952; Puffin Books, London, 1963, p.78.

2. Peter Dormer, *The Meanings of Modern Design*, Thames & Hudson, London, 1970. p.15ff. Peter Dormer highlights the way in which engineering is often hidden and divorced from style. I am extending his notion of engineering in this instance (with reference to the production of spider silk), to suggest that 'natural' processes might be hidden from cultural products in a similar way. Dormer suggests that the hidden only comes to be questioned when the product (in this case the signifying power of words) fails in some way.

3. Theodore H. Savory, *The Spider's Web*, Frederick Warne & Co. Ltd., London and New York, 1952.

4. D. McNeill, 'So you think gestures are non-verbal', *Psychological Review* 92, 1985, p.351. Cited by David F. Armstrong, William C. Stokoe, Sherman E. Wilcox, *Gesture and the Nature of Language*, Cambridge University Press, Cambridge, 1995, pp.7–8.

5. Cecilia Vicuña and Rosa Acala, *Palabra e Hilo/ Word & Thread*, Morning Star Publications, Royal Botanic Gardens, Edinburgh, University Press, 1996.

6. Alan Peters, Sanford L. Paley, Henry de F. Webster, *The Fine Structure of the Nervous System*, 3rd edition, Oxford University Press, Oxford 1991.

7. Peter Coveney, Roger Highfield, *Frontiers of Complexity*, Faber & Faber, London, 1995, p.290 (illustrated). From a conversation between the neurophysiologist Colin Blakemore in 1994 and Coveney and Highfield, Blakemore is quoted as saying, 'The interesting parts of the brain are driven by the senses, right through to language, which surely evolved from sensory categorisation' (p.283).

8. J.J. Gibson, *The Senses Considered as Perceptual Systems*, Houghton Mifflin, Boston, 1966.

9. Armstrong, Stokoe and Wilcox, *op cit.*, p.33.

10. On this subject, a clear overview in Martin Jay, *Downcast Eyes: The denigration of vision in twentieth-century French thought*, University of California Press, Berkeley and Los Angeles, 1994.

11. Juhani Pallasmaa, *The Eyes of the Skin: Architecture and the Senses*, Academy Editions, 1996, p.29.

12. *Ibid.*, p.7.

13. *Ibid.*, p.16.

14. Patricia Baines, *Spinning Wheels, Spinners and Spinning*, Oxford University Press, Oxford 1976, p.13.

15. Jean-Pierre Vernant, *Myth and Thought Among the Greeks*. First published in French in 1965, in English by Routledge & Kegan Paul, London, 1983, pp.256 and 324. The four essays of Part Four, 'Work and Technological Thought', provide an excellent analysis of the way in which artisans were ostracised from the thought-forming *polis*.

16. Jean Baudrillard, *Selected Writings*, edited and introduced by Mark Poster, Polity Press, Cambridge, 1988, pp.14–15.

17. Anni Albers, *On Designing*, Pelango Press, New Haven, 1959, p.32.

18. *Ibid.*, p.33.

19. *Ibid.*, pp.5,6, 45.

20. *Ibid.*, p.15.

21. *Ibid.*, p.26.

22. *Ibid.*, p.50.

23. These works are reproduced in *The Woven and Graphic Art of Anni Albers*, Smithsonian Institution Press, Washington D.C., 1985.

24. Anni Albers, *On Weaving*, Wesleyan University Press, Middletown, Conn., p.50.

25. Peter Collingwood, 'Arts and Crafts Exhibition', *Quarterly Journal of the Guilds of Weavers, Spinners and Dyers*, no.14, June 1955, p.451.

26. Edward Johnson, *Four Papers*, The Arts and Crafts Exhibition Society, 1935, pp.5–8.

27. Michel Foucault, *The Order of Things*, Tavistock Publications, 1970; Routledge, 1989, p.160. Roland Barthes, *S/Z*, Hill and Wang, New York, p.160. Gayatri Chakravorty Spivak, 'The Politics of Translation', in Michèle Barrett & Anne Phillips, eds., *Destabilizing Theory*, Polity Press, Cambridge, 1992, pp.178, 181.

28. Pierrette Bloch, *Textile and Contemporary Art*, 16e Biennale Internationale de Lausanne, Benteli, Lausanne, 1996.

29. Judith Duffey Harding, 'Textile Thinking, Continuity and Craft', *Art Textiles*, Bury St Edmunds Art Gallery, 1996, p.13.

30. *Ibid.*, p.20.

31. Virginia Woolf, *A Room of One's Own*, pp.43–4, cited by Nancy K. Miller, *Subject to Change*, Columbia University Press, New York, 1988, p.83.

32. Lorraine Lin, 'Studying spider webs: a new approach to structures', *The Arup Journal*, Jan.1994, p.23.

FREUD, FABRIC, FETISH

Anne Hamlyn

Editor's introduction: Anne Hamlyn's thinking strategy for the textile draws on a range of theoretical approaches, from film and psychoanalytic theory to Sigmund Freud's notorious writing that likens weaving to a compensation strategy for women. (Freud proposed that all women must work toward the "concealment of genital deficiency," which the act of weaving handily provides.) Here, Hamlyn addresses the real physical stuff at the center of fetish: the textile. She observes, "Fabric is a substance, . . . across whose surface the modes of Marxist commodity fetishism and psychoanalysis may and do cross." Touch, in all its varied guises, is central to this conversation. This writing appeared in the first issue of the academic journal *Textile: The Journal of Cloth and Culture* in 2003 and has subsequently been referenced by a number of the contributors included in the *Reader*.

Hamlyn trained as a sculptor and has a PhD in visual culture from Birkbeck College, University of London. She is the owner of Dress Me, a wardrobe consultancy business based in London.

The film theorist Christian Metz reminds us that "A fetish is always material: in so far as one can make up for it by the power of the symbolic alone one is precisely no longer a fetishist."[1] I run the risk of exploiting a rather obvious pun on the word "material" here but, in this context, the etymological coincidence is not without significance. Without attempting to be exhaustive, this article will tie together some of the cultural discourses around the fetish and, at the same time, bring this excessively over-invested theoretical terrain back to the "matter at hand," that is to say *fabric*. This may go some way towards resolving the politically (with a small "p") uncomfortable associations between women and fetishism and cloth. I am not the first writer to have considered the fetish and textiles from the point of view of gender; however, the connection between them seems as yet unresolved. I will, therefore, return to Sigmund Freud's original definitions of sexual fetishism as one way of considering afresh the cultural significance of the textile.

THE THEORETICAL FETISHIST

In one of Sigmund Freud's earliest discussions of fetishism, a paper given to the Vienna Psychoanalytic Society in 1909, he described the case history of a male clothes fetishist for whom "all interest in women [was] displaced onto clothes"

Source: Anne Hamlyn, "Freud, Fabric, Fetish," *Textile* 1, no. 1 (2003) pp. 9–27. Reproduced with permission.

and whose symptoms during analysis included the "conspicuous [. . .] adjust[ing of] the creases of his trousers."[2] He was, according to Freud, "physically impotent, and despite his numerous affairs, had never successfully completed coitus."[3] The analyst describes how:

> Once, for example, he awaited a rendezvous with the lady who was his sweetheart: but his feelings of love immediately vanished when she appeared in poor clothes which had been thrown on hurriedly. It also turned out that his sudden fallings-out during later love affairs always originated in the fact that he objected to a piece of her clothing.[4]

While it may (or may not) be surprising that a man should be so thoroughly invested in such a superficial matter as women's clothing, what is the more remarkable about Freud's characterization of the fetishist is the man's less private idiosyncrasies:

> In this patient something similar to what took place in the erotic domain occurred in the intellectual domain: he turned his interest away from things onto words which are, so to speak, the clothes of ideas; this accounts for his interest in philosophy.[5]

In this case history a very useful parallel is being set up between a pathological and seemingly bizarre relation to cloth (or rather its derivations) and a relatively normal and acceptable (if not always comprehensible) passion for critical analysis. Freud's patient is a theorist!

At the start of this discussion Freud's case history leads one to question how one form of passion—the passion for critical analysis—can comprehend the other—the passion for surfaces? It is often assumed, in cultural theory in general, that one cannot be both seduced by the tactile play of surfaces of the kind that fabric sets up and critically incisive at the same time. In critical/academic circles, it seems, you either occupy the world of knowledge and insight, commanding

language and representation, both of which are grounded in the psychic register that Lacan calls the *Symbolic*, or you are fated to remain embedded in the seductive world of the sensual, distracted by surfaces and illusions, a narcissistic mode of experience that Lacan associates with the *Imaginary*.

I will go on to describe how fabric subversively occupies either or both of the two seemingly incompatible fields of "interest" laid out by Freud in his case history of the male clothes fetishist: that of (Imaginary) seduction by the surface issue of women's clothes and the (Symbolic) distance of the theorizing process. These two modes of response to the world (we might, for simplicity's sake, call them *touching* and *naming*) can be set up in critical relation to each other and this form of criticality is something that I will be staging here. I would like to suggest that much theory has conspicuously failed to address the relationship between these two positions because doing so might disclose some nasty "little secrets." As I will go on to suggest, the *secret* at issue here is the perpetually unresolved "problem" (as Freud had put it) of the female body and its desires.

With the help of visual examples from fine art and cinema, I will argue that the one process, naming, *can* comprehend the other, touching, but only once considered from the, so-called, feminine point of view. I do not, however, wish to proscribe who (male or female) may take on that point of view at any one time, but I will suggest that women, in their seeming social, sexual, and economic "intimacy" with fabric-as-fetish, *may*, if they choose, occupy that ambiguous position for critical ends. Hence, my discussions will emphasize that, for the fetishist, the woman's body is only *half hidden* and, as such, there is always the potential space for its own desires to make themselves felt. For the surface (the material attire in which the clothes fetishist so heartily invests) is also the ground for the expression of the woman's *own* psychic investments. This is something that the fetishist (any fetishist) necessarily fails to register. Here Freud's analysand falls in line with the traditional point of view of theory. That is to say, *his* objections to his lady friend's "attire" may appear loud and urgent but *her* objections to being told in what acceptable guise she should appear may be just as pressing.

FABRIC AS IT UNDOES ITSELF

Fabric acts to conceal and cover objects and persons while, at the same time, disclosing them—hinting at their presence. Man Ray's photograph *The Riddle* or *The Enigma of Isadore Ducasse* (1920) illustrates fabric's constitutional ambiguity: a vaguely recognizable object, or group of objects, is enveloped in a rough textile and tied up with a rope. The objects may be commonplace but the wrapping gives them a certain mystery, vitality, and seductiveness. Fabric is malleable. It lends itself to wrapping, draping, and swathing. It restricts direct access to the naked object, but it also has the ability to suggest, enhance, and draw attention to what it covers over and adorns.

Like a sumptuous textile, cinema has been seen as a seductive, fetishized and fetishizing, surface that both is, and is not, what it represents or enfolds. Christian Metz's application of the idea of fetishism to cinema is useful for textiles because it raises three closely related discourses, all of which are appropriate to fabric: those of desire, of gender, and of the surface. Metz's suggestion was that cinema conceals and discloses the absence of its referent and this emptiness, or lack, in the medium is fetishistically suspended by the absorbing nature of the surface images and the narratives they construct. Throughout its history popular cinema has tended to be perceived by its critics as rendering its consumer/audience passive, feminized, even mute in the face of its sensory immediacy.[6] The audience is seen as incapable of critical judgment because, we might say, they cannot *theorize* their object adequately. Such interpretations set up a distinct hierarchy of value in which truth, authenticity and knowledge (social, economic, moral etc.) are seen as structures that are hidden by the surface, and the

surface is further seen as something potentially (if not always) compromised and compromising.

In considering another discourse in which the discursive relationship between surface and depth, façade and structure has been of crucial importance—that of post-modernist architecture—Mark Wigley comments on how the seduction of surfaces:

> [. . .] is set up in opposition to theory: the theorist is the one who is able to resist seduction. The rejection of surface effects, like the whole tradition of such rejections around which the Western tradition of theory has organized itself, is tacitly understood as the control of sexual desire.[7]

The fetish is "tacitly" understood as something compulsive, an unthinking and self-indulgent erotic and/or atavistic foible associated with the unmastered body and the so-called primitive.[8] In film criticism, a film viewer who is passive and seduced by the technology or material elements of the projection is generally figured "in the feminine." The theorist, critic or avant-garde director on the other hand, the one who detaches him/herself from such surfaces, attacking what David Harvey calls the "malleability of appearances" and activating language to penetrate their hidden depths (or expose a lack thereof) is more often described as masculine: authoritative and phallic.[9] I would like to suggest that the refusal of seduction bares an unmistakable resemblance to the rejection of textiles as a significant art practice by those in positions of power and authority on the basis of its associations with the decorative and, of course, with femininity.[10]

A TWOFOLD FETISHISM

I will give an example of the interpretative dilemma that such epistemologies create by setting out a scene from Martin Scorsese's sumptuous adaptation of Edith Wharton's novel *The Age of Innocence* (1993) and allowing my further analyses to develop from it.[11]

Escaping from heavy snowfall on a busy city street the couple step into a covered carriage. He wears a caped overcoat and she is bustled and corseted in a fur-trimmed overdress. The interior of the carriage has walls of thick padded silk that force the pair into unaccustomed proximity. For a moment they sit awkwardly. After a pause he pronounces uncertainly, "Each time I see you you happen to me all over again." She smiles, abashed but gratified. "Yes I know, for me too," she places her gloved hand affectionately on top of his. He contemplates her hand momentarily and then, removing his own larger and coarser leather glove, turns it upwards to reveal the several bright pearl buttons that join the soft suede at the wrist. He slowly unfastens them to expose her pale skin. Prising apart the two halves of the opening he lifts the underside of her wrist to his lips. She watches him intently and then, overwhelmed, embraces him. The horses whinny as the carriage jerks forward and pulls away.

The meaning and effect of the scene described relies not so much on action nor even on dialogue, but on the use of fabric and furnishings to encourage a form of sensuous voyeurism in the audience: nonverbal (optical, oral, tactile) elements of the *mise en scène* combine to put across a feeling of stolen intimacy and heightened emotion. It does not take training in psychoanalytic terminology and techniques for this textile language to be understood and enjoyed. In the compressed and quilted space of the carriage, beneath the overcoats and corsetry, the limits of social and sexual decorum are being severely tested. In the scene described, and in *The Age of Innocence* as a whole, the material *stuff*—mounds of it—that is piled over the desiring bodies of the actor/protagonists evokes a fierce repression: desire is hemmed in and "stitched up" by overbearing external pressure, restrained, enfolded, and *bound* in its excessive material environment. It is by virtue of the weight of fabric that the emotional charge of the unbuttoning of the glove stands out so powerfully.

The glove is a classic figure for the fetish and the focal point of all the fetishisms expressed

in the sequence. Here, as in the original novel, Madame Olenska's dainty garment is figured poignantly as something of exaggerated preciousness: it is for Newland "as if he had kissed a relic."[12] It is, therefore, not the desired object that he lifts to his lips but something else, something *like it*, something that *stands in close contact with it*, something nearly but, crucially, not quite *it* but that is nonetheless an object of extraordinary power and reverence. We see, here, how the fetish treads a tightrope as the focus of desire for it encloses, but at the same time discloses, the presence of the *real* object of curiosity and desire. However, if the object of immediate attention comes too close to that "other" object the fetishism fails and desire is suddenly unbound. It is as if the fetishized surface (here the fabric of the glove) undoes itself and that undoing unleashes a potentially dangerous overspill of free-wheeling desire. Desire needs to be bound to something in order to be potentially satisfied, in other words, in order for there to be pleasure. *Too much* pleasure can itself be destabilizing and, in psychoanalytic terms, desire unbound *is anxiety*.

It is, therefore, interesting to speculate as to who shows the greater amount of fetishism, the protagonists *in the scene* or the viewer (myself) indulging in the upholstery of the romance. Both fabric and cinema (and in particular the cinema of historical romance) are products that have, culturally speaking, a highly gendered orientation to their consumers. Costume dramas are seen as the penchant of women and, I confess, there is a delicious form of pleasure to be derived from Bonnet Dramas and Bodice Rippers—a somewhat guilty pleasure given my own claims to a critical intellectualism.[13] Such is my seduction that, as I describe it, the scene smacks of romantic *cliché*; however, when seen within the film narrative this is a moment of intense erotic *frisson*. For strategic purposes, I will not attempt to disentangle myself from the tactile immediacy of the scenario. To be seduced by the sequence (as the countess gives herself up, *momentarily*, to Newland's advances) seems, *on the surface*, to have little potential as a critical act. Nonetheless, such criticality *can* be affected from his seduced position if the surfaces at issue are analyzed not as something that conceals some more legitimate structure of meaning but as *the* malleable ground across which highly contentious gender politics is being enacted. Hence, what I *will* attempt to do with this strategic self-feminizing is to draw something critical out of an *apparently* compromising and self-indulgent captivation with the glamour of surfaces. In order to do so I will (perhaps paradoxically) return to Freud's theory of fetishism.

THE FREUDIAN FETISH

Freud's well-known psychoanalytic rendering of the onset of fetishism in the child acknowledges the significance of the textile and textile-associated items in its generation. This is because of their natural proximity to the primary object of the child's desire. They are the man-made surfaces that envelop the idealized maternal body. Fabric occupies the interstices between the needy flesh of the infant and the nurturing flesh on which it depends and, as the child develops, such textile coverings naturally inspire curiosity as to what lies beneath their folds and stays.

What lies beneath—the "reality" that fabric brushes up against—is female genital difference. It is the refusal to recognize that difference that, for Freud, lies at the root of fetishism. The first moment of encounter with gender *as difference* is traumatic for the child because, he can only encompass *similarity* in his narcissistic purview. It is significant that in Freud's analysis the traumatized child is assumed to be male. In his reading of fetishism the little girl's relation to the maternal body is more problematic because she is *already similar*. She cannot, therefore, be traumatized in the same way by the sight of the female body. However, for Freud both the male and the female child perceive the lack in the female body as "genital deficiency" and invent an infantile "theory" for its absence—*castration*.[14]

According to Freud, in so-called normal sexual development, the male child will accept the "fact"

of castration, relinquish his desire for the phallic mother and, finally, identify with the father. He will thereby leave the narcissistic dyad of mother and child and enter into the triangular Oedipal relation. The Oedipal triad is the microcosm of the social and, for Lacan, the Symbolic realm. The entry into the Symbolic is, therefore, the beginning of adult sexual development. It was Freud's understanding that this "adult" form of sexuality was both genital and heterosexual. However, for the fetishist, the process is halted abruptly because the maternal figure is *still phallic*. The male child has provided the castrated woman with a new or "substitute phallus." He does not, therefore, have to relinquish his former belief that his mother is like him. The fetishist does not jettison his primary narcissism in order to enter the socio/sexual realm of adult (hetero)sexuality because he never fully separates himself from the maternal space.

As Freud describes in his well-known 1927 essay "Fetishism," the fetish is a "compromise formation" that allows the fetishist to believe the evidence of his eyes, on one level, but that also defends him from the wounding potential of what he sees by maintaining the earlier belief alongside the new one. Freud likens this to "the stopping of memory in traumatic amnesia."[15] In other words the fetishist goes back to the moment just before, or the moment after, the traumatic encounter and fills in the absence artificially with a reassuring image—an image that will later become the basis for the fetish object. The objects that the child perceives in that traumatic moment "the foot or shoe" or "pieces of underclothing," are often chosen because they "crystallize [. . .] the last moment in which the woman could still be regarded as phallic."[16] Without the presence of the fetish that knowledge would induce an intolerable anxiety.

It is this space of interplay between the fabric and the flesh of the woman's body, the space of potential revelation, that becomes the fetishized ground of male desires. Edith Wharton's novel presents to the reader the interaction between the woman and fabric under the scrutiny of a desiring and thoroughly fetishizing male gaze:

[. . .] Madame Olenska sat half reclined, her head propped on a hand and her wide sleeve leaving the arm bare to the elbow.

It was usual for ladies who received in the evening to wear what were called 'simple dinner dresses'; a close-fitting armour of whale-boned silk, slightly open at the neck, with lace ruffles filling in the crack, and tight sleeves with a flounce uncovering just enough wrist to show an Etruscan gold bracelet or a velvet band. But Madame Olenska, heedless of tradition, was attired in a long robe of red velvet bordered about the chin and down the front with glossy black fur. Archer remembered, on his last visit to Paris seeing a portrait by a new painter, Carolus Duran, whose pictures were the sensation of the Salon, in which the lady wore one of these bold sheath-like robes with her chin nestling in fur. There was something perverse and provocative in the notion of fur worn in the evening in a heated drawing room, and in the combination of a muffled throat and bare arms; but the effect was undeniably pleasing.[17]

In the passage we see a displacement of desire onto a detail of the woman's body—the phallic form of the hand and forearm, and the head and neck, framed by the fall of red velvet and fur. The description might be mistaken as having come from Sacher-Masoch's infamous erotic novel *Venus in Furs* but for the fact that this flagrantly erotic visual appraisal is couched in a description of received social/sartorial etiquette.[18] The narrator's message to the reader is that Newland does not know what is happening to him or at least he *prefers not to know*. We might suggest that he fails to *theorize* or name his fetishism because he is so willfully seduced by the distracting nature of the fabric that encloses his desired "object." It is this process of relinquishing reality in favor of its idealized alternative that Freud describes as *disavowal*. In Octave Mannoni's well-known maxim of the fetishist "I know very well but just the same": on an unconscious level the fetishist *knows* the reality of the situation but his own surrogate reality, the tactile textile surface, is an infinitely preferable alternative.[19]

Freud describes fetishism as a perversion. In fact, in psychoanalysis in general, the process of disavowal, of which it is the symptom, becomes the model form of all other sexual perversions. But for Freud it is only in *men* that one encounters fetishism as a perversion.[20] According to Freud the female child has nothing to fear because she is *already castrated. She has nothing to protect.* For Freud (perceived) genital deficiency that is disavowed by the female child is internalized by her and played out on and through her own body—as Lacan writes "It is the woman herself who assumes the role of the fetish."[21] Thus women, in an unresolved encounter with genital difference, become hysterics. The male child, on the other hand, is not so passive. His fetishism is a kind of skewed technology in which he invents a surrogate phallus that he *reaches out for* whenever the issue of gender difference becomes too pressing, that is to say, whenever he runs up against the thorny problem of sex.

Unlike the woman the male fetishist is able, through the mechanism of the fetish, to project the castrating threat away from his body. The woman (any woman) is compromised by her "nearness" to the fetish. The film theorist Mary Anne Doane writes that, in the Lacanian derivation of the Freudian fetish, "women are deprived of the distance required by language." They, therefore, remain trapped in the Imaginary, captivated in and by their self-image.[22] Nonetheless, according to Lacan and Granoff the fetishist shares something with the woman's entrapment for he is still, on one level, locked in the imaginary or dyadic maternal relation and hence, like the woman, cannot symbolize adequately. He also remains enraptured and seduced by the lure of the image. Lacan and Granoff refer specifically to the mirror image that Lacan had described in his analysis of the "mirror stage" of infantile development.[23] What the description implies is that the woman shares the fetishist's captivation with the image but her investment is doubly compromised because *she is the image.* Women are unable to disembody the fetish because they are "denied the symbolic code."[24] Such possession requires a certain distance—a distance that, according to Lacan, can only be provided by the successful (i.e. masculine) resolution of the castration complex. For Lacan "femininity is closeness, nearness, 'wrapped in its own contiguity'."[25]

This wrapping has obvious ramifications for textiles. In linguistic terms it could be said that the fetishism of fabric is metonymic rather than metaphoric. Textile objects are chosen for their contiguity, that is to say, their nearness to the maternal body rather than because they stand in symbolically for the missing phallus—in the manner of a bottle or a big toe.[26] On the other hand, women's bodies can be *appropriated* by another and used to symbolize the phallus with the aid of fabric in the form of corsets, stilettos and rubber cat-suits. This is the kind of appropriation that is seen in the work of the artist Alan Jones. Laura Mulvey in the excellently titled "Fears, Fantasies and the Male Unconscious or 'You Don't Know what is Happening, Do You, Mr. Jones?'" has drawn attention to the fact that, as an exploration of fetishism, Jones's work says very little about actual women and their desires and rather more about the artist's own anxieties concerning castration and the female body that figures it.[27]

In Jones's works the woman's body is presented as all surface transformed with the help of fabrics into a surrogate phallus. This phallusization is often quite literal and even comic. In *Bare Me* (1972), as Mulvey describes, "[t]he phallic woman, rigid and pointing upwards, holding her breasts erect with her hands, is standing in high heels on a tray-like board balanced on two spheres."[28] A more perfect graphic rendition of the woman as an erect penis would be difficult to achieve. Such an image serves to insure the fetishist against the loss that the woman's body might otherwise signify. The fabric in this and other such images by Jones is tight: leather, rubber or a diaphanous textile (more like cling-film than chiffon). This fabric functions like armor to lift and restrict the spread and fall of female flesh. It follows every curve of the body but, crucially, never actually exposes the "offending" mark of genital difference. Jones re-articulates the female body in phallic terms to the extent that one is not certain whether there is any flesh at all beneath the accumulated surfaces. What we seem to end up with is a strange form of female anatomy constructed entirely out of fabric. Jones's women are not unlike a series of articulated rubber dolls.

WOMEN CONSUMING TEXTILES

This problem of women's ambiguous relation both to fetishism and textiles is evident in one of Freud's most infamously misogynous passages from the paper "Femininity" (1933). From such a description it may be seen how in the Freudian canon women's intimate and complex relations to fabric are not seen as fetishistic but a form of "natural" intimacy:

Shame, which is considered to be a feminine characteristic par excellence but is far more a matter of convention than might be supposed, has as its purpose, we believe, concealment of genital deficiency. We are not forgetting that at a later time shame takes on other functions. It seems that women have made few contributions to the discoveries and inventions in the history of civilization, there is however one technique which they may have invented—that of plaiting and weaving. If that is so, we should be tempted to guess at the unconscious motive for the achievement. Nature herself would seem to have given the model which this achievement imitates by causing the growth at maturity of the pubic hair that conceals the genitals. The step that remained to be taken lay in making the threads adhere to one another, while on the body they stick into the skin and are only matted together.[29]

There is further evidence for such a contention that women's relation to fabric is natural and men's perverse in Freud's remarks on the fetish to the Vienna Psychoanalytic society. In commenting on the case history of the philosophizing clothes fetishist, Freud makes this curious but significant aside concerning women and here the relationship is formed through consumption as opposed to production:

> In the world of everyday experience, we can observe that half of humanity must be classed among the clothes fetishists. All women, that is, are clothes fetishists. Dress plays a puzzling role in them. It is a question again of the repression of the same drive [the drive to look] this time however in passive form of allowing oneself to be seen, which is repressed by clothes, and on account of which clothes are raised to a fetish. Only now do we understand why women behave defencelessly against the demands of fashion. For them clothes take the place of parts of the body, and to wear the same clothes means only to be able to show what the others can show, means only that one can find in her everything that one can expect from women, an assurance which the woman can give only in this form.[30]

What is it then that "one can expect from women?" For Freud, the man fetishizes sexually, and women produce textiles to assist the process of concealment and revelation. However, when it comes to a universal language of economic exchange it is women who are seen as the fetishists intoxicated by voluptuous surface effects of the commodity. But theirs is not a perverse action; their fetishism is merely a product of their drive to veil genital deficiency and thereby to make themselves attractive to men. This is the ultimate "assurance" that the fetishism of clothes is believed to provide. Consequently, shopping is as "natural" to the modern woman as the weaving of genital hair was to her primitive counterpart! Their/our intoxication with shopping functions

because it allows them (or so they believe) to perform the fetish for men. Within this psycho/economic regime their/our own value as objects of exchange is, for Freud, established.

A sort of mirroring is taking place here, a two-way fetishism via the textile with castration on the one side and industrial manufacture on the other. Both of these are, in different ways, realities that are subject to disavowal.[31] Thus, we may say that both men and women's relationship with fabric is informed by *both the unconscious and capitalist exchange*. In fact the boundaries between psyche and economics are blurred when it comes to fabric. Fabric is the ground of some of our earliest subject/object relations but it is also a commodity in the marketplace. This is something that any trip to Mothercare will indicate. One might even say that fabric is a substance, the most significant substance, across whose surface the modes of Marxist commodity fetishism and psychoanalysis may and do cross.[32] And it is, by and large, through the actions of women that such an overcrossing takes place.[33]

The artist Sylvie Fleury turns shopping into an artistic action. She chooses only the most exclusive and most highly prized shops in which to gather the material for her work. She collects her purchases from such places as Chanel, Gucci, and Hermès and then lays them out in the gallery, often still in their brightly colored bags, as if she had just returned from a massive shopping spree. But her luxurious purchases are, like the sexual fetish, never actually used for the purposes for which they were designed. They and the experience of interacting with them, are obsessively preserved, never degraded by everyday use. *Wild Pair* of 1994 shows a fantastically rococo interior, empty except for an elegant *chaise longue* and perhaps fifty pairs of shoes scattered haphazardly over a Chinese rug. In the catalog of the 1995 exhibition *Fetishism: Visualising Power and Desire*, Roger Malbert describes this "careless scattering of things [as] unashamedly extravagant [and] insouciant. It hints at decadence, the intoxication of trying on new clothes, of undressing and dressing, each time to delight in a new sensation, to be *sheathed, caressed, transfigured*."[34] But, here, as in other works, this exquisite pleasure is played out to excess.

In the 1992 video *Twinkle* a fixed camera shows a view of Fleury's feet as, again and again, she tries on a daunting variety of elaborate shoes. She appears to be engaged in an endless and frustrating attempt to find the perfect pair so that she can go out and leave the surveying camera behind. But as Malbert points out her indecision "translates into strip tease" so that it achieves no other ends than those of pleasuring the viewer and thus the perpetually staring camera becomes an act of fetishistic voyeurism.[35]

However it may appear, Fleury makes no claims to being engaged in feminist critique, rather the contrary: "I read all the women's magazines—or at least I try to. For me that's a full-time job and it inspires my work. And this is the answer to those women who think they cannot afford to do a thing like that."[36] In other words, the art gallery and the larger market system in which it plays its part allows her to indulge her consumer fetishism as a "full time job." Fleury, here, plays out the ultimate goal of every artist, as Freud had put it: fame, wealth, and the love of women, but in strategically *feminine* terms: fame, wealth, and the *love of shopping.*

Fleury's work is highly problematic in its approach to the issue of criticality. It seems on the one hand to be too heavily invested in commodity surfaces. It is too *near* to its fetishized object. Hers is a hermetically sealed cycle of gratification through acquisition and artistic representation which, in turn, stimulates *more acquisition* and sustains the constant constructive "work" of femininity as it is presented by the media. A fetishism for clothes, that Freud so easily and dismissively compares to the more theorizable perversion of his analysand, seems to be re-articulated by Fleury as an excessive self-pleasuring that effectively turns the tables on any viewer too quick to pass judgement. In the face of these images that same gallery viewer might find him/herself more than a

little seduced—compromised by their fetishisms. The foibles of Western women suddenly to appear to be something singularly disconcerting. All this seems to indicate that a potential for criticality can be salvaged from within the enmeshed space of seductive surfaces because what we witness in Fleury's work is the fetish as it oscillates—*as it undoes itself.* Here the constant processes of consumer fetishism with pleasure as their ends always also suggest the impending return to a state of anxiety.

EITHER/OR

In his earliest discussion of the subject Freud acknowledges that "a certain degree of fetishism is habitually present in normal love, especially in those stages of it in which the normal sexual aim seems unattainable or its fulfilment prevented." Freud connects this "normal" fetishism directly to textiles in a quote from Goethe:[37]

> Get me a kerchief from her breast,
> A Garter that her knee has pressed[38]

Here, a certain kind of fetishism serves to mediate between the lover and another person. Presumably this is the form of fetishism to which Freud's French contemporary, the psychiatrist G. G. de Clérambault was thinking of as his point of comparison when he spoke of women's relation to fabric as inherently selfish. Unlike the situation in "normal love" (and presumably, as in the above, the orientation of such love is from the male position) their fetishism does not serve to mediate between persons. Women's love of fabric and all its derivations is, thus, seen as narcissistic—and implicitly antisocial.[39]

Now, we all (men and women) feel the caress, the insistent draw of fabric more or less emphatically at different moments and this experience—this pleasure—is, as Clérambault suggests, inherently a "selfish" one. Freud, having established the grounds or "normal" fetishism, goes on to say that:

This situation only becomes pathological when the longing for the fetish passes beyond the point of being merely a necessary condition attached to the sexual object and actually takes the place of the normal aim, and, further, when the fetish becomes detached from a particular individual and becomes the sole sexual object.[40]

Hence, it may be said that if, in the case of pathological fetishism, the relationship to the body of another person is entirely replaced by the fetish, then, when it comes to textiles, distinctions between the normal and the pathological are thoroughly confused. It may also be possible to contend that all such interactions with fabric tend towards the pathological and further that this is precisely because our "normal" relation to fabric is articulated in terms of commodification. When it comes to fabric our fetishism is *perversely feminine*. By virtue of this perversity we can begin to see how fetishism, as a process of dealing with sexual difference, disrupts all neatly gendered categorizations.

It is interesting that, despite the fact that psychoanalytic film theory most often follows a Freudian/Lacanian analytic axis, the gendered dichotomy of male—active and perverse versus woman—passive and hysteric, has already been somewhat disrupted. In his review of "The Fetish in the Theory and History of the Cinema" Michael Vernet points out that Metz defines fetishism:

[. . .] not as a perversion but as a psychical process characterized by the fetishist's struggle between belief and knowledge, by the drive to restore a disparaged belief (we could also say, to repair or restore a wounded body, since that is how the fetishist perceives the female body), and also by the refusal of the fetishist to recognize sexual difference. What is interesting here is the hesitation, the position of uncertainty in the fetishist (whether a man or woman): between the sexes; between self and other—projecting onto oneself that which is believed to have been seen in the other; between belief and knowledge; and finally between symbolic distinctions, since the fetishist manifests a perversion of the symbolic in so far as it must challenge difference.[41] [emphasis is my own]

Now such a definition of fetishism is useful because it transforms the fetish from something that is gender exclusive, the object of men alone, into the object of a potentially universal, and none too private, pathology.

The challenge to difference that fetishism stages is powerfully articulated in the work of Cathy de Monchaux. The early work *Erase* (1989) is an object of half-phallic half-labial form produced by the bolting together of velvet, denim, and metal joints. While it uses a recognizably fetishistic language of materials, the form as whole is highly problematic as an erotic fetish object. That is because it singularly fails to erase the problem of gender difference but, rather, plays it out theatrically by flagrantly conflating male and female genital signifiers. Another work, *Scarring the Wound* (1993), threads together layers and layers of brass rib-like (or, perhaps, phallic) forms and folds of red velvet to produce an elaborate arabesque that builds up around a small heart-shaped hole. It looks like a strange form of ornamented trophy reminiscent of the rosettes given to small girls at gymkhanas. The attempt to suture the wound is a lost cause because the piling on of surfaces merely expands and enlarges the primary absence. What de Monchaux's works suggest is that fetishism touches all of us, male and female, because sex is a perpetually destabilizing force poised like a man trap to trip us up. This threat lurks in all de Monchaux's beautifully worked surfaces.

Certain of Jordan Baseman's works play out the problem of gender and anxieties about difference in alternative ways. *Closer to the Heart* (1994) is made up of a young boy's uniform shirt hung on a wire coat hanger. Emanating from the woven surface of one sleeve is a long fall of dark hair, each strand threaded delicately into the cloth at the

Figure 2.1. Cathy de Monchaux, *Scarring the Wound*, 1993. Copyright courtesy of the artist.

shoulder. The long hair confuses gendered signifiers and transforms the crisp and neatly tailored textile object so that it appears as if it were under an attack from within. But there is no "within." The shirt is empty, marked by a reminder of an absent body. The knowledge that hair and nails continue to grow after death makes us uncannily aware of the insistence of the body and its workings which can only be temporarily tailored and contained. Like de Monchaux's works, these objects give us a sense of the gendered self in a state of extreme vulnerability.

In Basemen's work this vulnerability is linked to a specific moment in the development of the male child when he begins to be taught how to take on the masculine attributes and modes of behavior that are perceived to be socially acceptable. The hair appears like a form of hysterical symptom, the surface signs of a frantically and chaotically desiring body. The fabric is here singularly lacking in the phallic prowess seen in Alan Jones's work from the 1960s and 1970s. The threads of hair that hang from the shoulder of the shirt are more closely reminiscent of Freud's description of primitive women's supposed "shame" at their own genital deficiency. These artists' interaction with fabric work its fetishistic potential excessively and in the process tip the scales of gender and skew its accepted signs in ways that suggest a powerful critique of the social/sexual status quo.

The fetishist's disavowal, his insistence on maintaining a narcissistic belief, always has the potential to set up a scrambling in the symbolic. Fabric is able to signify "something" without that something ever being fully spoken. The fetish is silent and its secret never submits to the social/sexual order of things. It insists on playing upon us with its overt tactility. Thus fabric can be seen as a mode of experience that does not depend on the Symbolic because it is, in the most beguiling of ways, antisocial, a selfish and self-pleasuring seduction of and by the surface. Its significance is established only insofar as that symbolic order and the difference on which it depends is resisted. Such resistance is liable to repression: in the Symbolic realm we are not *supposed* to indulge in the stuff of surfaces, to be what Sacher-Masoch calls "super-sensualists," or, at least, *not too often*. The surface is a potentially dangerous ground but the fetishist's indulgence puts paid to the idea that the *firm* structure of truth and the *malleable* surface of appearance are separate and irreconcilable entities. In doing so he/she allows for the free play of desire that is in itself a critical force to be reckoned with.

NOTES

1. Christian Metz, *Psychoanalysis and Cinema: The Imaginary Signifier*, ed. Stephen Heath and

Colin McCabe (London: Macmillan, 1982), p. 75.

2. Sigmund Freud (1909) quoted from "Freud and Fetishism: Previously Unpublished Minutes of the Vienna Psychoanalytic Society," ed. and trans. Louis Rose, in *Psychoanalytic Quarterly* LVII, 1988, p. 154.

3. Ibid.

4. Ibid.

5. Ibid.

6. For a comprehensive discussion of fetishism in relation to cinema and feminism see Laura Mulvey, "Some thoughts on Theories of Fetishism in the Context of Contemporary Culture," in October, no. 65, Summer 1993, pp. 3–20 and *Fetishism and Curiosity* (Bloomington, Indianapolis IN and London: Indiana University Press and the British Film Institute, 1996).

7. Mark Wigley, "Theoretical Slippage: The Architecture of Fetish," *Fetish, Princeton Architectural Journal* 14, 1992, p. 98.

8. For the history of the term fetish in its relation to colonialism see William Pietz, "The Problem of the Fetish," *Res* 9, 1985, "The Problem of the Fetish, II, The Origins of the Fetish," *Res* 13, Spring 1987, and "The Problem of the Fetish, IIIa, Bosman's Guinea and the Enlightenment Theory," *Res* 16, 1988. There is, unfortunately, no space to develop this connection here, although this historical aspect of the fetish may also be argued as having some considerable relevance to cloth and culture.

9. David Harvey, The Condition of Postmodernity (Oxford: Basil Blackwell, 1989), p. 7, quoted by Wigley, *Fetish, Princeton Architectural Journal* 14, 1992, p. 98.

10. Wigley, in fact, attacks such a position as projecting an illusion of authority and possession and further suggests that "[t]he phallic pretension of this desire to penetrate the other organizes all the discourses that identify fetishism only in order to reject it [. . .]" as something

dangerous or, rather, dangerously alluring. Wigley, ibid.

11. *The Age of Innocence* (Columbia Pictures, 1993), dr. Martin Scorsese. It is remarkable to what extent its revelations sit in opposition to the overtly phallic codes and action of the movies for which the director is better known.

12. Edith Wharton, *The Age of Innocence* (London: Penguin, 1974), p. 239.

13. It must be said that the actress, Michelle Pfeiffer, is as divinely seductive in a corset as she is in her famously fetishistic cat-suit.

14. The male child comes to believe that the idealized phallic mother has been punished by the removal of her penis and, furthermore, that he is also threatened with this fate. The female child, conversely, comes to believe that she is inadequate and can only compensate for her narcissistic wound by appropriating the *paternal* phallus. Hence, the theorizing process results in the onset of the "castration complex" in boys and "penis envy" in girls.

15. Sigmund Freud, "Fetishism" (1927), *Penguin Freud Library, Vol. 7. On Sexuality*, p. 354.

16. Ibid., pp. 354–5.

17. Edith Wharton, *The Age of Innocence* (London: Penguin, 1974), p. 90.

18. Leopold Sacher-Masoch, "Venus in Furs" in *Masochism* (New York: Zone Books, 1989), pp. 143–273.

19. Octave Mannoni, "L'Illusion comique ou le théâtre du point de vue de l'imaginaire" in *Clefs pour l'imaginaire ou l'autre scène* (Paris: Edition du Seuil, 1969), p. 180, quoted here from Christian Metz, *Psychoanalysis and Cinema: The Imaginary Signifier* (London: Macmillan, 1982), p. 71.

20. Freud and many of his followers assume that women *do not fetishize* or certainly not in the same manner. This distinction between men and women has been the grounds of heated debate in both psychoanalysis and feminist theory. See in particular Lorraine Gam-

man and Merja Makinen, *Female Fetishism: A New Look* (London: Lawrence & Wishart, 1994) for a comprehensive discussion of the debates in terms of cultural studies. See also Marjorie Garber, "Fetish Envy" in *October*, no. 54, Fall 1990. Emily Apter, *Feminizing the Fetish: Psychoanalysis and Narrative Obsession in Turn-of-the-Century France* (Ithaca, NY and London: Cornell University Press, 1991) and from the point of view of psychoanalysis, George Zavitzianos, "The Perversion of Fetishism in Women" in *Psychoanalytic Quarterly* LI, 1982.

21. Lacan quoted by Gamman and Makinen, *Female Fetishism: A New Look* (London: Lawrence & Wishart, 1994) p. 102. See also *Feminine Sexuality: Jacques Lacan and the École Freudienne*, eds Juliette Mitchel and Jacqueline Rose (London: Macmillan, 1982).

22. Gamman and Makinen, ibid., pp. 102–3

23. See Jacques Lacan. "The Mirror Stage as Formative of the Function of the *I* as Revealed in Psychoanalytic Experience" in *Écrits*, trans. Alan Sheriden (London and New York: Routledge, 1989), pp. 1–8.

24. Gamman and Makinen, *Female Fetishism: A New Look* (London: Lawrence & Wishart, 1994), p. 103.

25. Mary-Anne Doane, "Masquerade Reconsidered: Further Thoughts on the Female Spectator," *Discourse* 11, Fall/Winter 1988–1989, pp. 44–5, here quoted in Gamman and Makinen, ibid.

26. See George Bataille, "The Big Toe," in *Visions of Excess: Selected Writings 1927–1939*, ed. Alan Stoekl (Minneapolis, MN: University of Minnesota Press, 1985), pp. 20–3.

27. Laura Mulvey, "Fears, Fantasies and the Male Unconscious or 'You Don't Know what is Happening, Do You, Mr. Jones?'" in *Visual and Other Pleasures* (London: Macmillan, 1989), pp. 6–13.

28. Ibid., p. 12.

29. Sigmund Freud, "Femininity" (1933) quoted in *Psychoanalysis and Gender: An Introductory Reader*, ed. Rosalind Minsky (London: Routledge, 1996), p. 232.

30. Sigmund Freud (1909) quoted from "Freud and Fetishism: Previously Unpublished Minutes of the Vienna Psychoanalytic Society," *Psychoanalysis Quarterly* LVII, 1988, pp. 155–6.

31. For the differences and similarities between the Freudian and Marxian versions of the fetish see Laura Mulvey, "Some Thoughts on Theories of Fetishism in the Context of Contemporary Culture," in *October*, no. 65, Summer 1993, pp. 3–20.

32. For Karl Marx on the "Commodity Fetish" see "The Fetishism of The Commodity and its Secret" in *Capital*, vol. 1.

33. Although it must be pointed out that many men do actually *like* to buy clothes. Would Freud have considered this "perverse?"

34. Roger Malbert, in *Fetishism: Visualising Power and Desire* (London: The South Bank Centre, 1995) p. 91.

35. Ibid., p. 92.

36. Ibid.

37. Sigmund Freud, "Three Essays on Sexuality" (1927), *Penguin Freud Library, Vol. 7, On Sexuality*, p. 66.

38. Goethe, *Faust*, Part 1, Scene 7, quoted in Sigmund Freud, ibid., p. 66.

39. See Papetti, de, Freminville *et al.* (eds) *La passion des étoffes ches un neuro-psychiatre G. G. de Clérambault* (Paris: Solin, 1981). For a discussion in English of de Clérambault and his ideas see Joan Copjec, "The Sartorial Superego," *October*, no. 50, Fall 1989, pp. 57–95.

40. Ibid., pp. 66–7.

41. Marc Vernet, "The Fetish in the Theory and History of the Cinema," in *Endless Night: Cinema and Psychoanalysis, Parallel Histories*, ed. Janet Bergstrom, (Berkeley, CA, London and Los Angeles, CA: University of California Press, 1999), p. 91.

MEDITATION ON TRANSLATION AND SEDUCTION

Catherine Harper

Editor's introduction: Catherine Harper is dean of the School of Arts and Digital Industries, University of East London, London, United Kingdom. This text was first written for the exhibition catalog edited by Lesley Millar of the University for the Creative Arts to accompany the exhibition *2121: The Textile Vision of Reiko Sudo and Nuno*, which opened at the James Hockey Gallery in Farnham, England, on October 21, 2005, the year of Nuno's twenty-first anniversary, before touring. The illustrated catalog, printed in English and Japanese, includes an extensive interview with Reiko Sudo and Lesley Millar, recorded in Tokyo in 2005, and an essay by Laurel Reuter, director of the North Dakota Museum of Art, as well as writing by Keiko Kawashima and the editor. Harper's text sets itself apart by combining fiction with fact to create a hybrid, delivered to us in first person, that muses on the urban landscape of Tokyo, the meaning of several fabric names, and the slippery boundaries of sexual interest. What results is an evocative piece of writing that vividly brings the author's knowledge of Nuno's complex fabrics to life through touch. Visit http://www.2121vision. com for further information.

Midnight. The Peak Lounge, Park Hyatt, Tokyo.

Fifty *washi* paper lanterns.

An anonymous slow-tinkling piano.

Smooth saki in a tiny glass.

Tokyo spreads out to left and right, in vast and awesome twinkling-throbbing glory. Somewhere out there, karaoke is in full swing, geisha listen to boasting businessmen, and grown-up schoolgirls play potent power games . . .

I stand right up to the glass and touch the city with my fingertips. It ripples and pulses under my touch.

Am I lost in translation?

I put on Reiko Sudo's 'Otter Skin' and dive off into this night . . .

Otter Skin. Glinting, waterlogged, damp and loaded. Dense black, crow black, almost scaly. Affective, unsettling, brooding. Reiko Sudo's fabric holds its breath, merges into my skin and waits.

Can a textile, a piece of cloth, a woven substrate, be this potent?

Barthes writes of the 'destination' of a text as the place of its (provisional) unity, and identifies that place as lying within its reader.[1] That is, he articulates the moment of translation when the complexity of creation is in some way captured

Source: Catherine Harper, "Meditation on Translation and Seduction," in Lesley Millar (ed.), *21:21–The Textile Vision of Reiko Sudo and Nuno* (Canterbury: University for the Creative Arts, 2005) pp. 33–37. Reproduced with permission.

(albeit temporarily) by the reader (viewer) as a means to permit his/her subjective expression of (a) meaning. In this text, I will argue that Reiko Sudo's fabrics are such texts, for they allow this reader to peel them off and put them on for her own imaginative flight . . .

My translation may not be yours: translation is a tricky business.[2]

Lees-Maffei and Sandino quite rightly make a claim for the "machinations, seduction and jealousies of a ménage à trois" between Design, Craft and Art.[3] My interest in their work lies in the proposal of that territory as unstable, shifting, contingent, ultimately dangerous. It seems to me that Reiko Sudo's fabrics are potentially 'danger invested', sexually-charged, highly seductive. I believe, moreover, that she consciously mobilises the act of seduction to reveal the unspoken (unspeakable), the unauthorised (authoritatively), the uncensored (without censure) in her liaisons with cloth . . .

My seduction may not be yours: seduction is a tricky business.[4]

The pelt of the otter, and indeed that of the seal, presented to us by Reiko Sudo acts as a metaphor

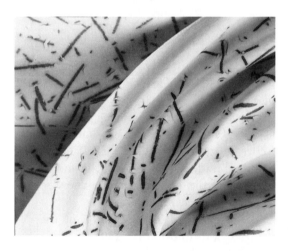

Figure 3.1. Reiko Sudo, *Scrapyard*, 1994. 100% rayon, 44 in. wide. Rusted iron plates, barbed wire, and nails are sandwiched between two layers of rayon cloth, topped with an electric blanket, and left to "sleep" for two days. After the scrap iron is removed, the rusted pattern remains fixed on the fabric.

for a translation and re-translation between Nature and Culture which seems to resonate throughout my understandings of the dichotomies of contemporary Japan. The conceptual or material coexistence of complementary states is, for example, offered as an essentially Japanese aesthetic by Curators McCarty and McQuaid in their framing of 'Structure and Surface: Contemporary Japanese Textiles' at the Museum of Modern Art, New York (1998).[5] I'm generally wary of essentialisms—there's a danger of reduction or misrepresentation—and, in cultural terms, that can lead quickly to exoticism of the worst kind. I am conscious of not wishing to either reduce the cultural identification of Reiko Sudo's fabric to either an exotic commodity or to code it with a 'them' and 'us' hierarchy.[6] As Greg Kwok Keung Leong notes in his articulations of 'centred' (traditional) and 'de-centred' (radical) cultural identity there is always a key "tension between the cultural identities we construct for ourselves . . . and [those] others construct for us".[7] That being said, Barthes' appeal to subjectivity in analysis is liberating in how one might then read or activate the text in the textiles.

I propose that Reiko Sudo, too, is highly conscious of the potential for exciting and even provocative narrative associations in her mobilisations of the rich textile and cultural traditions of Japan and her location of those within a highly contemporary methodology and materiality. The convergence of mechanical, technological and industrial techniques with labour-intensive handwork, plus the authoritative use of traditional and innovative materials, indicates a certain trend in Japanese textiles which arguably captures some form of essential currency[8], and Reiko Sudo knowingly activates these essences while not allowing herself to be subsumed by them . . .

Seal and otter slip effortlessly between land and sea, solid and fluid, dry and wet. Their graceful translation from one domain or way of being to another is mesmerisingly easy. Both 'Otter Skin' and 'Seal Skin' appear simple: the former dark, matt, brooding, the latter a bright, shiny dense weave in celebratory red . . . But it is their potential for narrative, proposed through their title, and then further invited through the simplicity of their surfaces that permits Barthes' textual proposition to be useful here. Both these fabrics beg to be mobilised by a viewer/reader: both resonate with a desire to be held, caressed, placed around the shoulders, swaddled over the body. My being aches to be sheathed like a seal, my body yearns for the elegant stream-lined form of the otter. I desire translation.

Interestingly, my reaction to many of Reiko Sudo's fabrics is somatic, that is my body literally speaks to this affective fabric. This is a different kind of desire for tactility to that of the hand (with its direct connection to the head). Rather the organ that is my skin (with its direct haptic connection to the heart) responds across its area to the fabric plane . . . nerves, pores, papillae reach out to Reiko Sudo's fabrics for contact, all over contact . . .

Declan McGonagle, then Director of the Museum of Modern Art, Dublin told me of a Quaker notion of "that which speaks to one's condition"[9], and my strong sense in Reiko Sudo's most abstract work is of a visceral interiority, an animal or primal reactivity transcendent of mere material, process or technique, oblique to the conceptual, and sideways on to the triangulation of design, craft or art. It echoes in such fabrics as 'Yak', Jellyfish' or 'Moth-Eaten', and activates discourses related to the notion of "fabric as envelope, as a second skin".[10] These fabrics speak to my condition as I

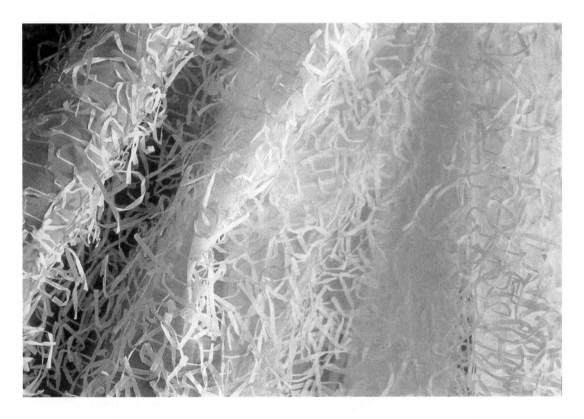

Figure 3.2. Reiko Sudo, *Patched Paper*, 1997. 57% mino washi paper/43% polyester, 44 in. wide. Long strips of *washi* paper ("slit yarn") are woven with polyester, leaving long loops, or "floats." The floats are first cut by machine, then by hand, to create the shaggy texture of this fabric.

look out over night-time Tokyo in all its animal breathing pelt-like beauty . . .

My condition may not be yours: you know the rest . . .

Undoubtedly, Reiko Sudo designs and orchestrates the making of fabrics that are sublime and extraordinary. Fabrics of enormous diversity and sophistication are her hallmark, each combining high-tech and low-tech production methods and a range of materials from the 'natural' (silk, wool, linen, banana fibre) to those that are synthetic, industrial, banal or unexpected (stainless steel, rubber, scrap fabric, laminate film, copper, oxidised metal). Reiko Sudo breaks convention in her processes as well as her materials: she characteristically interrupts the manufacture of woven fabric to manually insert feathers, she deliberately creates random rust marks on virgin cloth by scattering nails on its surface, she plies threads with incompatible shrinkages allowing applied heat to then buckle the woven results, she bonds metallic films to traditionally 'valuable' silk fabric. Reiko Sudo is a sophisticated 'avant-garde designer-craftsperson', challenging without difficulty the norms of materiality, process and technique. It's quite appropriate, for example, that Reiko Sudo played a key role in 'the space between' conference in Perth in 2004, where her habitation of the blurred territory between artisanal craft, high-end design, industrial manufacturing, and artistic creative intervention celebrated a new hybridity, a contemporary interdisciplinarity and a modern expressive synthesis in textiles.

Many of Reiko Sudo's fabrics are quite simply very beautiful, but it is those that promise a more intricate and insistent narrative that particularly interest me. Those that are the product of an abusive, even perverse, approach to the fabric substrate are especially evocative. The Nuno book 'BoroBoro', with its offer of 'Cruel and Unusual Treatment of Fabric'[11] offers a clue to a sub-text both apparent and significant to this reader . . . Sexual power games—neither essentially or exclusively Japanese, but nevertheless useful for the purposes of this text—offer abusive practices, humiliation, simulated pain, 'real tears', and vocal evidencing of 'cruel and unusual treatment'. Interestingly, the foreword to 'Boro-Boro' states "Mistreatment is not an end in itself (we are not textile sadists)".[12] In this collection, though, fabrics have been "roasted over burners, dissolved with acid, boiled and stewed, ripped with blades and pulled apart".[13] Other works involve baking, rubbing, moulding, weathering . . .

The text itself asks "what ever did these innocent fabrics do to deserve this rough handling?", and the list of fabric treatments reads like an inquisitor's 'to do' list . . .

I'm back at the glass, looking out over midnight Tokyo, a pelt of human culture stretching to the midnight sky. Under that pelt, countless acts of sexual cruelty, of rough trade, of sublime and seductive terror are enacted as an essential (nightly) part of human existence . . . Remember that 'Otter Skin', via Barthes, permitted me to be a witness to that night-time landscape . . .

If Reiko Sudo already is an active participant in Lees-Maffei and Sandino's ménage à trois, then it is only a short leap of narrative faith to consider the investment of sexual, seductive, sadistic energy in certain key textile pieces. Reiko Sudo is tantalising, however, in the odd tensions she constructs between textile fabric and textile title: 'Ginseng' is subtitled as "homage to the penetrating power of vegetable life"[14], and reads as a sophisticated creamy cloth, with softly decadent fringing of felted wool. It's delicious and delectable. Read the descriptor of method, however, and think again:

The process itself literally 'damages' normal woollen weaves . . . we resorted to prolonged soaking in alternating baths of hot and cold water before pounding our wool on the 'torture rack'.[15]

It is the making explicit, as a creative act, of the method of marking the textile skin that signals

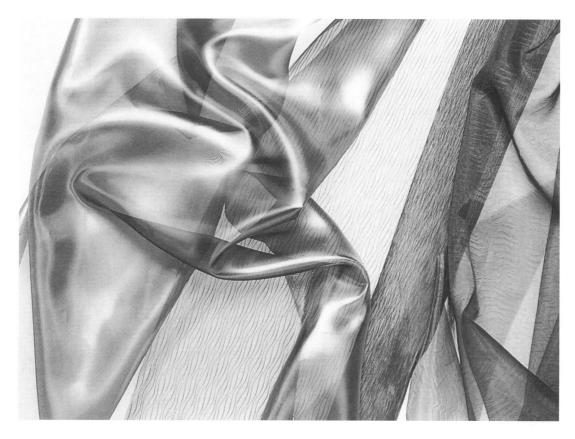

Figure 3.3. Reiko Sudo, *New Spattering Gloss*, 1990. 100% polyester, 44 in. wide. In a process akin to that used in the automotive industry to create chrome bumpers, a polyester base is "spatter-plated" with powdered metals.

some perverse delight in the hard hand labour of the work (even when ultimately it is mechanised labour that reproduces the textile). In her 'Scrapyard (Nail)', rusty nails are allowed to imprint their marks onto dampened virgin rayon in a counter-intuitive act of textile offence. In 'Spanish Moss' the weave structure is quite literally 'undone'. In 'Cracked Quilt', chemicals etch their traces into the flesh of a rayon and wool double-fabric. And so on . . .

Always remember, my sadism may not be yours . . . sadism being a tricky business . . .

What I find unsettling, and I believe this is a deliberate and most clever strategy on the part of Reiko Sudo, is the juxtapositioning of heightened and evocative language with tender fabric and matter-of-fact explanation. It's as though she wants to remain elusive, not one thing or the other.

In these creative power games, Reiko Sudo is ultimately dominant over the material, process and meanings held within her fabric, and most significantly her refusal to allow labelling keeps her dominance over us the reader/viewer.

I can speculate all I like, pull on and peel off the metaphoric layers of her designer-art-craft textiles, but I remain not her, and therefore outside the knowledge that is Reiko Sudo.

Can a textile, a piece of cloth, a woven substrate, be this potent?

Always . . .

NOTES

1. R. Barthes 'Image-Music-Text': p147, pub. Fontana 1977.
2. W. Benjamin 'Task of the Translator' in H. Arendt ed. Illuminations: p75. pub. Fontana Press 1992.
3. G. Lees-Maffei and L. Sandino 'Dangerous Liaisons: Relationships between Design, Craft and Art' in Journal of Design History pp207–219. Vol.17, No.3, 2004.
4. W. Benjamin 'Task of the Translator' in H. Arendt ed. Illuminations: p75. pub. Fontana Press 1992.
5. C. McCarty and M. McQuaid 'Structure and Surface: Contemporary Japanese Textiles: Museum of Modern Art, New York', pub. Museum of Modern Art 1998.
6. Diana Fuss 'Essentially Speaking: Feminism, Nature and Difference' pub. Routledge 1989.
7. G. Kwok Keung Leong Re-Constructing Chinese in 'Reinventing Textiles Vol.2: Gender and Identity' ed. Jeffries p91. pub. Telos Art Publishing 2001.
8. S.E. Braddock and M. O'Mahony 'Techno textiles: revolutionary fabrics for fashion and design' pub. Thames and Hudson 1998.
9. C. Harper Interview with Declan McGonagle in 'A Beginning Derry' pub. Orchard Gallery 1991.
10. G. Kwok Keung Leong Re-Constructing Chinese in 'Reinventing Textiles Vol.2: Gender and Identity' ed. Jeffries pp29–37. pub. Telos Art Publishing.
11. NunoNuno Books 'BoroBoro': p14. pub. Nuno Corporation 1997.
12. NunoNuno Books 'BoroBoro': p15. pub. Nuno Corporation 1997.
13. NunoNuno Books 'BoroBoro': p15. pub. Nuno Corporation 1997.
14. NunoNuno Books 'BoroBoro': p27. pub. Nuno Corporation 1997.
15. NunoNuno Books 'BoroBoro': p24. pub. Nuno Corporation 1997.

THE BLANK PAGE

Isak Dinesen

Editor's introduction: The Danish author Karen Blixen, writing under the pen name Isak Dinesen, is best known for her novel *Out of Africa*, published in 1937 and made into a film starring Robert Redford and Meryl Streep in 1985. In Dinesen's short story "The Blank Page," published in 1957, the textile and the act of storytelling are taken as one and the same. The story is structured as a tale within a tale that leaves the unspoken and untold—the blank page—as a creative route through narration. Dinesen sets her tale around the work of a Carmelite order of nuns in Portugal that grow flax and make the linen used by the royal family. Carmelite nuns take a vow of silence, and Dinesen's decision to make her illiterate narrator an expert of the oral tradition of storytelling suggests a loyalty to the adaptable, dynamic, and ever-shifting nature of the spoken word. Here, the textile acts as loyal record keeper of an unexplained conclusion. The story's subject matter is an intensely private moment made public, but like the blank page of an unwritten story, the narrative offers us multiple beguiling conclusions.

By the ancient city gate sat an old coffee-brown, black-veiled who made her living by telling stories.

She said:

'You want a tale, sweet lady and gentleman? Indeed I have told many tales, one more than a thousand, since that time when I first let young men tell me, myself, tales of a red rose, two smooth lily buds, and four silky, supple, deadly entwining snakes. It was my mother's mother, the black-eyed dancer, the often-embraced, who in the end—wrinkled like a winter apple and crouching beneath the mercy of the veil—took upon herself to teach me the art of story-telling. Her own mother's mother had taught it to her, and both were better story-tellers than I am. But that, by now, is of no consequence, since to the people they and I have become one, and I am most highly honoured because I have told stories for two hundred years.'

Now if she is well paid and in good spirits, she will go on.

'With my grandmother,' she said, 'I went through a hard school. "Be loyal to the story," the old hag would say to me. "Be eternally and unswervingly loyal to the story." "Why must I be that, Grandmother?" I asked her. "Am I to furnish you with reasons, baggage?" she cried. "And you mean to be a story-teller! Why, you are to become a story-teller, and I shall give you my reasons!

Source: Isak Dinesen (Karen Blixen), *Last Tales* (London: Random House, 1957). Reproduced by permission of Random House, Inc, and Penguin Books Ltd.

Hear then: Where the story-teller is loyal, eternally and unswervingly loyal to the story, there, in the end, silence will speak. Where the story has been betrayed, silence is but emptiness. But we, the faithful, when we have spoken our last word, will hear the voice of silence. Whether a small snotty lass understands it or not."

'Who then,' she continues, 'tells a finer tale than any of us? Silence does. And where does one read a deeper tale than upon the most perfectly printed page of the most precious book? Upon the blank page. When a royal and gallant pen, in the moment of its highest inspiration, has written down its tale with the rarest ink of all— where, then, may one read a still deeper, sweeter, merrier and more cruel tale than that? Upon the blank page.'

The old beldame for a while says nothing, only giggles a little and munches with her toothless mouth.

'We,' she says at last, 'the old women who tell stories, we know the story of the blank page. But we are somewhat averse to telling it, for it might well, among the uninitiated, weaken our own credit. All the same, I am going to make an exception with you, my sweet and pretty lady and gentleman of the generous hearts. I shall tell it to you.'

High up in the blue mountains of Portugal there stands an old convent for sisters of the Carmelite order, which is an illustrious and austere order. In ancient times the convent was rich, the sisters were all noble ladies, and miracles took place there. But during the centuries highborn ladies grew less keen on fasting and prayer, the great dowries flowed scantily into the treasury of the convent, and today the few portionless and humble sisters live in but one wing of the vast crumbling structure, which looks as if it longed to become one with the grey rock itself. Yet they are still a blithe and active sisterhood. They take much pleasure in their holy meditations, and will busy themselves joyfully with that one particular task which did once, long, long ago, obtain for

the convent a unique and strange privilege: they grow the finest flax and manufacture the most exquisite linen of Portugal.

The long field below the convent is ploughed with gentle-eyed, milk-white bullocks, and the seed is skilfully sown out by labour-hardened virginal hands with mould under the nails. At the time when the flax field flowers, the whole valley becomes air-blue, the very colour of the apron which the blessed virgin put on to go out and collect eggs within St Anne's poultry yard, the moment before the Archangel Gabriel in mighty wing-strokes lowered himself on to the threshold of the house, and while high, high up a dove, neck-feathers raised and wings vibrating, stood like a small clear silver star in the sky. During this month the villagers many miles round raise their eyes to the flax field and ask one another: 'Has the convent been lifted into heaven? Or have our good little sisters succeeded in pulling down heaven to them?'

Later in due course the flax is pulled, scutched and hackled; thereafter the delicate thread is spun, and the linen woven, and at the very end the fabric is laid out on the grass to bleach, and is watered time after time, until one may believe that snow has fallen round the convent walls. All this work is gone through with precision and piety and with such sprinklings and litanies as are the secret of the convent. For these reasons the linen, baled high on the backs of small grey donkeys and sent out through the convent gate, downwards and ever downwards to the towns, is as flower-white, smooth and dainty as was my own little foot when, fourteen years old, I had washed it in the brook to go to a dance in the village.

Diligence, dear Master and Mistress, is a good thing, and religion is a good thing, but the very first germ of a story will come from some mystical place outside the story itself. Thus does the linen of the Convento Velho draw its true virtue from the fact that the very first linseed was brought home from the Holy Land itself by a crusader.

In the Bible, people who can read may learn about the lands of Lecha and Maresha, where flax is grown. I myself cannot read, and have never seen this book of which so much is spoken. But my grandmother's grandmother as a little girl was the pet of an old Jewish rabbi, and the learning she received from him has been kept and passed on in our family. So you will read, in the book of Joshua, of how Achsah the daughter of Caleb lighted from her ass and cried unto her father: 'Give me a blessing! For thou hast now given me land; give me also the blessing of springs of water!' And he gave her the upper springs and the nether springs. And in the fields of Lecha and Maresha lived, later on, the families of them that wrought the finest linen of all. Our Portuguese crusader, whose own ancestors had once been great linen weavers of Tomar, as he rode through these same fields was struck by the quality of the flax, and so tied a bag of seeds to the pommel of his saddle.

From this circumstance originated the first privilege of the convent, which was to procure bridal sheets for all the young princesses of the royal house.

I will inform you, dear lady and gentleman, that in the country of Portugal in very old and noble families a venerable custom has been observed. On the morning after the wedding of a daughter of the house, and before the morning gift had yet been handed over, the Chamberlain or High Steward from a balcony of the palace would hang out the sheet of the night and would solemnly proclaim: *Virginem eam tenemus*—'We declare her to have been a virgin.' Such a sheet was never afterwards washed or again lain on.

This time-honoured custom was nowhere more strictly upheld than within the royal house itself, and it has there subsisted till within living memory.

Now for many hundred years the convent in the mountains, in appreciation of the excellent quality of the linen delivered, has held its second high privilege: that of receiving back that central piece of the snow-white sheet which bore witness to the honour of a royal bride.

In the tall main wing of the convent, which overlooks an immense landscape of hills and valleys, there is a long gallery with a black-and-white marble floor. On the walls of the gallery, side by side, hangs a long row of heavy, gilt frames, each of them adorned with a coroneted plate of pure gold, on which is engraved the name of a princes: Donna Christina, Donna Ines, Donna Jacintha Lenora, Donna Maria. And each of these frames encloses a square cut from a royal wedding sheet.

Within the faded markings of the canvases people of some imagination and sensibility may read all the signs of the zodiac: the Scales, the Scorpion, the Lion, the Twins. Or they may there find pictures from their own world of ideas: a rose, a heart, a sword—or even a heart pierced through with a sword.

In days of old it would occur that a long, stately, richly coloured procession wound its way through the stone-grey mountain scenery, upwards to the convent. Princesses of Portugal, who were now queens or queen dowagers of foreign countries, Archduchesses, or Electresses, with their splendid retinue, proceeded here on a pilgrimage which was by nature both sacred and secretly gay. From the flax field upwards the road rises steeply; the royal-lady would have to descend from her coach to be carried this last bit of the way in a palanquin presented to the convent for the very same purpose.

Later on, up to our own day, it has come to pass—as it comes to pass when a sheet of paper is being burnt, that after all other sparks have run along the edge and died away, one last clear little spark will appear and hurry along after them—that a very old highborn spinster undertakes the journey to Convento Velho. She has once, a long long time ago, been playmate, friend and maid-of-honour to a young princess of Portugal. As she makes her way to the convent she looks round to see the view widen to all sides. Within the building a sister conducts her to the gallery and to the plate bearing the name of the princess she has once served, and there takes leave of her, aware of her wish to be alone.

Slowly, slowly a row of recollections passes through the small, venerable, skull-like head under its mantilla of black lace, and it nods to them in amicable recognition. The loyal friend and confidante looks back upon the young bride's elevated married life with the elected royal consort. She takes stock of happy events and disappointments—coronations and jubilees, court intrigues and wars, the birth of heirs to the throne, the alliances of younger generations of princes and princesses, the rise or decline of dynasties. The old lady will remember how once, from the markings on the canvas, omens were drawn; now she will be able to compare the fulfilment to the omen, sighing a little and smiling a little. Each separate canvas with its coroneted name-plate has a story to tell, and each has been set up in loyalty to the story.

But in the midst of the long row there hangs a canvas which differs from the others. The frame of it is as fine and as heavy as any, and as proudly as any carries the golden plate with the royal crown. But on this one plate no name is inscribed, and the linen within the frame is snow-white from corner to corner, a blank page.

I beg of you, you good people who want to hear stories told: look at this page, and recognize the wisdom of my grandmother and of all old story-telling women!

For with what eternal and unswerving loyalty has not this canvas been inserted in the row! The story-tellers themselves before it draw their veils over their faces and are dumb. Because the royal papa and mama who once ordered this canvas to be framed and hung up, had they not had the tradition of loyalty in their blood, might have left it out.

It is in front of this piece of pure white linen that the old princesses of Portugal—worldly wise, dutiful, long-suffering queens, wives and mothers—and their noble old playmates, bridesmaids and maids-of-honour have most often stood still.

It is in front of the blank page that old and young nuns, with the Mother Abbess herself, sink into deepest thought.

SENSE AND SENSIBILITY

June Hill

Editor's introduction: June Hill is a curator and writer. From 1994 to 2005 she worked as museums manager for Bankfield Museum, West Yorkshire, England, and she has managed, curated, and coordinated a number of international textile projects over the past decade. The lecture printed here was first presented at the conference Memory and Touch: An Exploration of Textural Communication, organized by Lesley Millar and the University for the Creative Arts and held at the Royal Institute of British Architects on May 7, 2008. Hill's lecture covers a breadth of material, drawing on a range of references, from the documentary film *Into Great Silence*, directed by Philip Gröning, to the Peace Park at Hiroshima, Japan, to the textile artists Rozanne Hawksley and Jeanette Appleton. At the center of all these examples is an attention to the curator's response to an object's context; the power of "gifting" as equal to, if not greater in importance than, the gift; and the varied ways in which we understand and experience touch.

In an interview in *The Guardian* in 2001, Liv Ullman described the storyline of a short film she had made in the 1990s:

"An old man is lying in a double bed by himself. He wakes up all alone, has a bath, goes into the kitchen, makes a picnic basket, puts his hat on, looks in the mirror and leaves. He walks through the streets and he's old and little and nobody notices him because he's just . . . old. He goes to the hospital, walks through the corridor, and no one notices. He enters the room, and then finally he smiles because she's there. His wife has lost her mind. He gives her the soup he has made for her, waters the flowers,

kisses her, and leaves. No-one sees him leave. He walks back through the streets unnoticed. But we know that he is a carrier of love."

"This," Liv Ullman said, "is the sort of film I want to make." And this is the subject of the presentation I want to give.

Sense and Sensibility is a short, allusive study of the intangible aspects of touch: of touch defined as the ability to rouse tender or painful feelings within an individual human being. It may be an arousal of affectiveness within ourselves or one caused within another person. We will be looking at instances of both, and also examining the relationship between the two—how feelings are

Source: Unpublished lecture presented at the conference "Memory and Touch" organised by the University College for the Creative Arts and held at The Royal Institute for British Architects on May 7, 2008. Reproduced with permission.

conveyed, understood or intuited between and amongst people. In particular, we will be examining the role of materiality as a means of expressing such feelings. Not, as an alternative to verbal or written language, but as something that is integral to the process of feeling itself. Of feelings or ideas that can somehow only be expressed in some palpable form. Or perhaps not so much expressed as validated: of love proven through the making and sharing of soup, the watering of flowers, an unreciprocated kiss and a giving of self that is unnoticed and unacknowledged. This is an examination of the exterior expression of interiority; of the desire to make tangible the intangible and express the seemingly inexpressible.

So where do we begin? Well, let us begin at the beginning, with an object: something physical and material that has proven itself to be capable of both expressing and eliciting a very particular feeling. Let us begin with the paper cranes of Hiroshima.

One of the most affecting aspects of a visit to the Peace Park at Hiroshima, is the sight of what appears to be hundreds of multicoloured garlands carefully placed within the Peace Memorial Park. Look closer, and it becomes evident that these garlands are actually thousands upon thousands of hand-folded, paper cranes; strung together with precisely one hundred on each string. On any given day, these garlands form paper rainbows across the site. They are an installation of hope, of colour and life, at a point that marks the epicentre of the blast of an Atomic bomb; a blast so powerful that glass and metal melted and human beings were vaporised or turned into shadows.

And hope is what these paper cranes have come to represent. Not hope as in the form of rainbows, but the hope of peace, of no more Atomic bombs.

But can this be? Can a folded paper crane be a harbinger of hope or, knowing the story of Hiroshima, the significance of this place, is this but emotional projection on the individuals' part? We wish for hope, we wish for peace, so that is what we see.

How can we distinguish between projection and reality; between that which we might impose on an object and that which might proceed from it; that which we might imagine it to be, and the essence of what it is?

Let us imagine ourselves as museum curators: people whose professional lives are rooted in seeking to document and understand material culture. What would a curator look for to establish the truth of an object? How would they define its significance? How would they identify an object as one belonging to the field of hope?

Authenticity, significance and context—the curator's three-fold cry. We believe in the primacy of the real thing and we seek documentary evidence that the object is that which it is claimed to be. We want to know the story of an object, and the evident truth of that story. We want objects that have a significance that extends beyond themselves, yet are themselves significant: a concrete particularity that has generic relevance. Something that is individual, yet contingent.

So, whither the paper crane? What is its story? In what way can it be said to authentically represent hope?

We know the story of the paper crane. It is the story of a very particular individual; of a young girl born in Hiroshima who at the age of 11 became ill with leukaemia, having been exposed to the radiation of the Atom bomb nine years earlier, when she was but two years of age. We know this young girl as Sadako Sasaki. We know too, for we have been told this, that determined to live, Sadako set out to fold 1,000 paper cranes: her personal enactment of a traditional belief that anyone who did so would be made well.

It was 1954; paper was expensive and Sadako was in hospital, so she garnered the material she needed from wheresoever she could find it: the discarded paper wrappings of medicines; gift paper from get-well presents, printed advertisements. Day after day, Sadako made paper cranes; the other patients joined her in making them. As she continued to fold paper cranes, they gradually became smaller in size. By the time Sadako reached her target of 1,000, the paper cranes were so small she used a needle to shape their folds; intently folding one crane after another 'as if it were a prayer'. The number, we are told, wasn't important anymore—what mattered now was the act of folding into each crane her desire to live.

Sadako Sasaki made 1,300 paper cranes. She died—just eight months after the diagnosis was made.

So, we have the paper cranes, but where is the hope? There was no healing; her parents were understandably heartbroken. "Why didn't the 1,000 cranes sing? Why didn't they fly?" wrote her mother.[1]

The hope was not for Sadako, not for her getting well and living. Yet, almost since the time of her death, people have begun to associate this act of folding paper cranes as an expression of hope; of a desire for life against the odds; for friendship and peace. So, we have today, people, children from many different countries; unfamiliar with the art of origami, who will yet persist in the folding of paper cranes as a means of expressing their hopes and desires.

So where does the hope lie? Perhaps, it rests not so much in Sadako's paper cranes as in her story. Perhaps ours is primarily an empathetic response to the person, not the object: for would we not need hearts of stone to remain unmoved by a personal story of such poignancy. And here we can return to our imaginative role as curators. Where would the curator locate the hope? In the association between the two: in the place where the story becomes manifest within the object and the object is embedded within the story. For do we not know that, "In a sense, it is the story itself that is the object, insofar as it is not the item itself that is distinctive, but the associated history to which it is attached."[2]

So, whither again, our paper crane? Does its significance rest purely within its story? Would we have responded to it as an emblem of hope if we were ignorant of that history? Is the paper crane an expression of hope, a symbol, a cipher; an object that points us to something else—in this case a person's life to which we respond empathetically? Or could that same paper crane in any way be said to *be* hope, to be its embodiment; for hope to be somehow immanent within the object itself, or within its making?

To answer this question, perhaps we need to look not at the object entire—the paper crane itself—but rather at its making, and at the effect its story has on those who continue to make paper cranes.

And so we turn to Lewis Hyde: a man who has assured as that "we are only alive to the degree that we can let ourselves be moved", and that, "whatever we treat as living, begins to take on life".[3] What would he tell us of the paper crane? He would say that the significance lies within the giving, and he would point us to Marcel Mauss[4], who first mooted the idea that the giving of something imbues it with some essence of the giver and, in so doing, bestows an indelible power. Then he would go on to say that, even though a gift may seem innocent, anything given—even a greeting—demands a return.[5]

This is of interest to us, for Sadako's urge to make 1,000 paper cranes was a direct response to the gift of another 1,000 paper cranes; a gift sent to the hospital by the people of Nagoya. It was an act of kindness that was intended to encourage. It was a gift that caused Sadako to entrust her life to the making of her paper cranes: folding into each one that desire to live. This is the act, repeated time after time, that now motivates others to offer their own paper cranes to the Peace Park, where every string is acknowledged and becomes part of the city of Hiroshima's campaign for peace.

So, perhaps this is where hope lies: in the return that is demanded by the very making of the paper crane; in the hopes and feelings that are invested within the repeated act of their folding; in their giving as heartfelt desires made manifest; in their ability to touch and the capacity of touch to cause change.

Now, we move on in our investigation, but we take Lewis Hyde with us. We pause and hear him utter the words "a gift that has power to change us awakens a part of the soul", and we know that he is referring to something more than mere physical exchange. He is pointing us to the place where the being becomes; to that corporeal place where we give our very selves; the place where our interiorities find expression in, and through, material realities.

And so we turn to creative practice and to the role of practitioners: those individuals who are involved in the very genesis of material entities. Individuals whose daily labours focus on the making real of interiorities; those whose work lies in the place described by James Turrell "as the point where the imaginative feeling and outside feeling meet, where it becomes difficult to differentiate between seeing from the inside and seeing from the outside."

How is this meeting of the inward and outward expressed; how does it find form and how is it understood by those who are entirely other? How can that which is interior be validated externally? How do we know what it is, and that what it is, is true?

Process, outcome and response. We look at the making and at that which has been made. And we begin with the maker, one maker in particular: the artist, Rozanne Hawksley. These are her words:

"My work varies in scale from small hand-held pieces to large installations. I use any and all materials but only those that, at the time of working, answer the need to externalise a particular response or group of responses. I seldom start a piece knowing exactly of what it is to be made, other than the initial feel or essence of mind and material. I offer up continuously and the piece grows towards an often unforeseen conclusion. But the feeling, a kind of dread and excitement, has to exist and be kept going, until that conclusion happens and is recognised."

Note the words and of what they speak: openness; a sense of listening and looking; responsiveness to something that is felt but not always known; a process of discernment; an authenticity of materials and of making. And a letting go, an offering up: a loss of self at the very moment that the self is expressed.

Hawksley's work addresses the most visceral experiences of life: love and loss; suffering and war; isolation, poverty, power and its abuse. Her range is immense: each piece taking the form it appears to demand. The ideas are intensely felt and intensely executed. References are explicit and implicit. They combine that which is revealed and that which is withheld. Materials and images are intuitively selected for their innate sense of rightness; for that of which they speak—an empty glove, a lily, the drape of sheer chiffon cut on the bias, bleached bones, a photograph. These are deeply evocative works. They are individual expressions of contingent realities. They are tangible recollections of that which has been experienced, and of that which continues to be felt. For those who have endured the tenderings of life, the empathy with these works is all too real. They have said: "Thank you for expressing that of which we cannot speak ourselves".

They speak as those who know the truth of these works: those who see and hear their silent testimony—who absorb their unseen details; those who know because they understand the authenticity of feeling that is present within every fibre of their being. They are people who know the truth of these works because they have lived them.

It is as if "the making and the meaning are inextricably bound together". These are the words, not of Rozanne Hawksley, although they could as yet be. Rather, they are the words of another maker: Jeanette Appleton—someone whose concerns, while less overtly emotive, remain as deeply felt.

Appleton is an artist whose work explores the relationship of people to land, through cloth. Her particular interest is nomadism: a form of living where these three elements are most closely intertwined; where each inhabits and responds to the other. There is within nomadism, we could say, a mutuality of touch that is expressed within the hinterlands. How is this reflected within Appleton's work? We let her speak for herself. The following is the substance of a recent conversation with the artist. The image shown is a short,

Figure 5.1. Rozanne Hawksley, *Caiaphus*, 2007. The death of nature and its beauty. Bone, bird's foot, cloth, ribbon, glove, gold thread, and jewels, 11 x 10 x 2.5 cm.

unedited research video taken by Appleton in the moment of travel.

I ask the question: "Tell me, what is it that interests you in nomadism; how has this influenced you and how is this interest expressed within your work?"

This is her response: "Nomadism is a social structure that moves and works with nature; has

Figure 5.2. Rozanne Hawksley, *He always wanted to be a soldier I, All his life he wanted to be a soldier II*, 2006. One of three works inspired by Victorian and Edwardian regimental pin cushions, which were traditionally heart shaped. Cloth, medal ribbon, bird skeleton, spent bullet cases, and wood frame, 8.5 x 8.5 x 2 cm.

minimal possessions, is resourceful and is protected by a felted cloth—the yurt—that is made and used on the nomad's site. All this is of particular interest to me and has greatly influenced my working practice.

It encouraged me to follow a basic, partly nomadic lifestyle myself. This gave me the time and funds to produce artwork. I specialise in felting—a nomadic process. Felt can be made in stages and on any site, with the minimum of equipment. This means I can travel and experience different cultures. It inspires work on the move, as I journey through different landscapes.

The context of felt within nomadic cultures means that ideas of travel and protection are embedded in the work. Colours and shapes evolve within the design, because of the immediacy of the spatial experiences involved in the very process of moving and making. Travel itself is influential: journeys and international projects inform my research, expose me to the unknown and give me time to pursue ideas of how I can express this within my work."

Here, ideas and feelings are formed and expressed almost conjointly. Appleton's work is as much about life as it is about practice—the making and meaning simultaneously coming together in both. It is a totality of awareness and engagement. Appleton brings her whole self with openness to that moment of making and it is to the integrity of that process that she, and we, respond.

It is an approach Lewis Hyde would liken to a 'labour of gratitude': that is "something dictated by the course of life rather than by society, something that is often urgent but that nonetheless has its own interior rhythm, something bound up with feeling, more interior than work."

I want to end this session by not talking, but rather by looking at, and I hope experiencing, one final example of this aspect of touch. It is a short clip from Paul Gröning's film *Into Great Silence*: a documentary that portrays a year in the daily lives of the monks at a Carthusian monastery, set high up in a remote corner of the French Alps. Theirs is an austere life, lived in almost total silence, yet one lived in joy and, what Gröning describes as, a complete absence of fear. Materialism is renounced, but materiality is central to the living of their lives. For, it is through repetitive acts of being and doing—in silence—that these individuals make manifest the very essence of their lives. This is a place where materiality, experienced through time in silence, becomes a focus for complete engagement in the interior realities that are found within the concrete particularity of the specific and unrepeatable moment. The film is 162 minutes long. There are few spoken words and no formal commentary. It is for each individual to discern the import of that which they are experiencing.

Into Great Silence has been described as "an object in time" and as "a film that becomes a monastery rather than depicts one". Watching the film is to enter into this process of being and becoming; a process of engagement in time and of being open to being touched.

It is a process likened to making, best described by Cartier Bresson, that most affecting of photographers, who said of his craft:

"[It] is for me a spontaneous impulse coming from an ever attentive eye which captures the moment and its eternity.

I enjoy shooting a picture and being present, being in the moment and saying yes. Like the last words of James Joyce's Ulysses.

Yes, yes, YES.

And there's no maybe: it's an instant, it's a moment; an enjoyment, an affirmation."[6]

NOTES

1. Fujiko Sasaki's letter can be seen at http://www.sadako.org/sadakomotherletter.htm
2. 'Memorial Museums' Paul Williams (Assistant Professor in Museum Studies, New York University) 2008 p33
3. 'The Gift', Lewis Hyde, (Canongate) 2006, p. 21 and 26.
4. 'Essai sur le don' Marcel Mauss (1923)
5. David Lan, *The Guardian Review*, 16.2.08
6. Henri Cartier-Bresson Scrapbook Photographs, National Media Museum, Bradford 2008

6

CONTINUITY OF TOUCH—TEXTILE AS SILENT WITNESS

Maxine Bristow

Editor's introduction: Maxine Bristow is an artist and reader at the University of Chester, England. Her practice over the past decade is epitomized by an excruciating attention to the details of textile production. Work is often created in unassuming series that ask us to reconsider points of contact with the concrete world around us. In an expanded version of her original conference paper, presented in 2007 at the Repeat Repeat conference held at the University of Chester, Bristow determines that the focus of her practice at the time lies in what she refers to as "the ubiquitous, undifferentiated textile objects of the built environment" that are overlooked by many. In her writing, she explores the hierarchical treatment of the senses and a tendency to sideline touch as a way of knowing. Textiles, she writes, have the ability to operate as a "silent witness" and communicate through a thoroughly articulate material language of their own. To know this, you have to touch textiles, even when it looks like you shouldn't.

As a practitioner, conferences or symposia provide the opportunity both for research and for reflection; an occasion—like the more customary event of the exhibition—to temporarily formalise ideas. As well as providing a catalyst for research, the rigour of shaping and reshaping thoughts through the process of writing provides a useful framework for reflection and a means by which to try to make sense of practice and to understand the implications of actions. However, it is the to-ing and fro-ing—between the shaping of ideas through the process of writing and the shaping of ideas through the process of making— that is key. Crucial in this reciprocal relationship is the acknowledgement that it is indeed a process and that ideas are always provisional, formalised

only momentarily, albeit formalised and rehearsed within the public domain.

The occasion for which the following text was written, was an interdisciplinary conference entitled 'Repeat Repeat' held at the University of Chester in April 2007. The original paper provided an opportunity to reflect on some new pieces of work in relation to general research around the themes of material culture and touch; and in particular reference to the theme of the conference, to consider the way that textile material in both its raw state as cloth, and as the 'cooked' textile object of material culture acts as a silent witness to the repetitive routine of our daily lives. Reflections on the way that the repetitive routines instigated through textile mediate *between the self and the world also prompted reflection on the way that the repetitive gestures and actions involved in the making of work can similarly be seen as an agency of subject-object and object-subject transference.*

Within the traditional hierarchy of the senses and corresponding privileging of sight, visuality has tended to be the prevailing paradigm with subsequent and far reaching consequences for the development of western culture. Playing a significant role in philosophy, underpinning scientific reason, and as the foundation of empirical knowledge, the visual is inextricably bound up with notions of objective truth, seemingly providing the necessary reliable evidence through which we come to know ourselves and the world. Reaching an apogee in Clement Greenberg's tenet of opticality and the idea that modernist art should be apprehended through 'eyesight alone', it has been fundamental to the theory and history of visual culture and instrumental in the drive towards modernist aesthetic autonomy.[1]

Within this text, however, I would like to shift the focus from visuality and the realm of visual culture to consider the significance of the material dimension. I would like to propose, that the embodied testimony of material culture, is as David Howes suggests, 'the most fundamental domain of cultural expression, the medium through which all the values and practices of society are enacted'.[2] As such, I believe it can provide us with insights that are compelling and difficult to refute. These insights into the relationship between subjects and objects enabled by material culture can, in turn, provide a useful critical framework for practices such as my own where there is an interest in notions of objecthood and the abstract potency of textile.

It is my intention, therefore, to investigate the significance of the material dimension by providing some broad insights into the field of material culture and the way that objects bear witness and provide us with convincing testimony, 'not because they are evident and physically constrain or enable but often precisely because we do not see them'.[3] Operating on the threshold of the functional and symbolic and as the vehicles against which we stage the routines of our everyday lives, they are written into the structure of society like a language, yet it is a language that is essentially non-discursive.

Crucial to the operation of this non-discursive mode of communication is the sensory modality of touch. The historical relegation of touch in the hierarchy of the senses is challenged, and I consider what might be described as a sensual revolution within the arts, humanities, and social sciences, suggesting that the immediacy and continuity of touch in the reciprocal relationship between subject and object makes it a particularly potent vehicle for both cultural and artistic expression.

What has prompted the research are some new pieces of work (which take the form of ambiguous upholstered structures) conceived in relation to the proportions to the body where the point of bodily contact—at which the surface of the body meets the surface world—has been densely stitched.

This new work is a development of an earlier body of work[4] which explored our engagement with space, and in particular those aspects of the built environment such as light-switches, handles, and handrails, with which we have an actual physical though, often, unconscious bodily relationship and which instigate routinely repeated patterns of behaviour.

Positioned at points of transition, these often unnoticed aspects of our built environment invisibly mark boundaries between different realms of space: between inside and outside, public and private. Conceived as a free-standing form, the handrail becomes an actual physical barrier yet one that is clearly provisional, framing, dividing, or alternately denying or allowing access to space.

Fundamental to this earlier body of work and indeed to more recent practice is the particular role that textile plays in mediating between the body and the built environment—the way that textile as skin or membrane provides on the one hand a very real, tangible point of contact and material boundary and on the other hand a more ambiguous metaphorical boundary between self and 'not self'—and also of course, what is crucial to this relationship, the importance of tactility and continuity of touch.

Whereas the earlier work was largely concerned with gestures of the hand and localised touch, the new work is concerned with less focused touch, touch that is not limited to static contact between fingertips and surface but dispersed throughout the body like its corresponding organ of skin. The stimuli for this new work are the simple, anonymous, non-descript, mass-produced, upholstered pads and panels that constitute the non-spaces of our built environment. The padded surfaces found on the bus, tube and train or the upholstered panels of corporate furniture are characterised by their very lack of outstanding, individual or unusual features. Yet, as textile objects with which we have daily physical contact, they provide the stage against which the repetitive routines of our every-day lives are enacted, silently soaking up the clamour of activity in their dense, absorbent, and unyielding surfaces.

Reflections on the new work have instigated several lines of enquiry, but as already indicated the essential focus of the research has been materiality and material culture. Material culture, however, is itself a very broad interdisciplinary (and some say undisciplined) field which simultaneously intersects and transcends a range of other disciplines. It is, as Judy Attfield suggests in *Wild Things: The Material Culture of Everyday Life* 'a contradictory project, because although its main focus is on the material object it is not really about things in themselves, but how people make sense of the world through physical objects, what psychoanalytic theory calls 'object relations' in the explanation of identity formation, what sociology invokes as the physical manifestation of culture, and anthropology refers to as the objectification of social relations'.[5]

However, material culture, as the name would imply, centres 'on the idea that materiality is an integral dimension of culture', and that 'the study of the material dimension is as fundamental to understanding culture as is a focus on language'.[6] As Christopher Tilley suggests in the opening chapter of the *Handbook of Material Culture*, a recently published comprehensive volume dedicated to the field,

> Things are meaningful and significant not only because they are necessary to sustain life and society, to reproduce or transform social relations and mediate differential interests and values, but because they provide essential tools for thought. Material forms are essential vehicles for the (conscious or unconscious) self-realisation of the identities of individuals and groups because they provide a fundamental non-discursive mode of communication.[7]

In a further chapter in which Tilley discusses material culture's central concept of objectification he states:

> Material forms as objectifications of social relations and gendered identities, often 'talk' silently about . . . relationships in ways impossible in speech or formal discourses . . . the artefact through its "silent" speech and "written" presence, speaks what cannot be spoken, writes what cannot be written, and articulates that which remains conceptually separated in social practice. Material forms complement what can be communicated in language rather than duplicating or reflecting what can be said in words in a material form. If material culture simply reified in a material medium that which could be communicated in words it would be quite redundant. The non-verbal materiality of the medium is thus of central importance.[8]

So it is the silent, but, undoubtedly, potent nature of this embedded/embodied material language which has resonances with my own practice.

Again as already indicated, crucial to the idea of the material object as a non-discursive language is the suppressed modality of touch, a sense that is implicit in textile. 'Paradoxically it is the immediacy of touch that makes it a potent vehicle of expression but in its resistance to representation and "polymorphous diversity" impossible to pin down and unnameable to discourse'.[9] In its immediacy it is similar to material culture and the landscape of the everyday in which it operates and of which Henri Lefebvre writes '(it) is the most universal and the most unique condition, the most social and the most individuated, the most obvious and the best hidden'.[10] Historically ranked in relation to their degree of immediacy, of the five senses, taste and touch, in direct contact with the world, were deemed to be lowest. Whereas sight distances and objectifies and is characterised by a shift away from tangible sensory experience towards an abstracted system of visual representation, touch, by implication remains subjective and limited, and is subsequently equated with a lack of conceptual sophistication.

The past few years, however, have seen something of a sensual revolution in the humanities and social sciences with a considerable number of recent publications aiming, as David Howes suggests in *The Empire of the Senses: The Sensual Culture Reader*, to overturn 'linguistic and textual modes of interpretation and placing sensory experience at the forefront of cultural analysis'.[11]

Philosophy, visual culture, and architecture have, similarly, seen challenges to the hegemony of vision and a resurgence of interest in sensory values, practices and processes. The postmodern revival of interest in the Baroque's very conscious address to the senses has provided a useful point of reference for thinking through the concerns of my own work, as has the classic text of architectural theory *The Eyes of the Skin* by Juhani Pallasmaa, which has recently been republished as a revised and extended edition.

In *Quoting Caravaggio: Contemporary Art, Preposterous History*, Mieke Bal investigates how the Baroque resurfaces in the work of a number of contemporary artists and discusses the implications of this in terms of how we conceive of both history and culture in the present. Bal puts forward the idea that 'the current interest in the Baroque acts out what is itself a baroque vision, a vision that can be characterised as a vacillation between the subject and object of that vision and which changes the status of the both'.[12]

In *The Eyes of the Skin*, Pallasmaa discusses the importance of hapticity and unfocused peripheral vision to the experience of architecture and, indeed, as 'the very essence of lived experience', suggesting that while focused vision pushes us out of the space making us mere spectators, unconscious peripheral perception transforms retinal gestalt into spatial and bodily experiences.[13] As with the ideas that are informing my new work, it is this capacity of objects to remain anonymous and peripheral to our vision yet determinant of our behaviour that is of particular interest.

The relationship between optical visuality and haptic visuality also finds a context in contemporary painting which explores the sensuous materiality of paint and foregrounds the method of its own manufacture. In a chapter in *Unframed Practices and Politics of Women's Contemporary Painting* edited by Rosemary Betterton (which interestingly in the context of textile practice is entitled 'Threads'), Rosa Lee identifies in her own work and that of the other painters whom she discusses, 'characteristics that exceed the purely visual and relate to somatic senses of touch, rhythm and gesture'.[14] In considering this work, Lee makes reference to the critic, Laura Marks' book *The Skin of the Film* and her description of haptic visuality as 'the metaphorical caressing of the surface of an object'.[15] These notions of haptic visuality and the acknowledgement of a greater interaction of tactile, visual, and symbolic registers clearly provide useful critical frameworks for work such as my own that employs textile materials and processes.

However, to return to the silent witness that is the subject of this reflection; how do textile objects bear witness and what is the nature of their evidence?

In her article 'On Stuff and Nonsense: the Complexity of Cloth'[16] Claire Pajackowsa provides some insights into 'the complex and multidisciplinary significance of textiles in culture' suggesting that this complexity derives from the fact that 'textiles are culturally situated on the threshold between the functional and the symbolic'.

In terms of their functional dimension, like a second skin, the absorbent and ephemeral surfaces of textiles literally provide material evidence, bearing witness to the continual and repetitive contact with the body, accumulating a patina of use and revealing the wear and tear of routine activity. Caught within the supple striated surface of warp and weft or soft cut pile are the invisible yet incontestable indexical traces of the physical correspondences between subject and object. Maybe I have watched too much CSI but I can only imagine the complexity of the narratives that the upholstered panels of our transport system would yield if subjected to forensic investigation. What is interesting, however, in relation to the hard wearing moquette fabric that has been used within our transport systems since the age of Victorian railways, is the fact that it was designed specifically to disrupt or mask the presence of dirt or stains and thereby doesn't give of such evidence too readily.

In terms of their symbolic dimension, the significance of textiles in the formation of identity and subject relations has been well documented. 'Because clothes make direct contact with the body, and domestic furnishings define the personal spaces inhabited by the body, the material which forms a large part of the stuff of which they are made—cloth—is proposed as one of the most intimate of thing-types that materialises the connection between the body and the outer world'.[17] Like the skin to which it is often equated, cloth as a mediating tissue or membrane, or what Michael Serre calls a '*milieu*',[18] is often seen as an ambiguous boundary and it is this ambiguity that produces the complex relationship between subject and object. In *The Skin Ego*[19] the French theorist and psychoanalyst, Didier Anzieu notably explores relations between the experience of the skin and the formation and sustaining of the ego, identifying its nine functions as: supporting,

containing, shielding, individuating, connecting, sexualising, recharging, signifying, assaulting/destroying.[20] From Winnicott's baby's blanket as the exemplary metaphor of subject individuation to the role that dress plays in simultaneously revealing and concealing our personal and collective identities, textile performs a fundamental role in negotiating the changing relationship between our inner selves and the world that we inhabit.

But as Steven Connor suggests in *The Book of Skin*, 'It is not only individual psychological life but also cultural life that is lived at the level of, and through the intercession of, the skin, and its many actual and imaginary doublings and multiplications'.[21] As one of the largest categories of material culture, textile plays a fundamental role in structuring social rules and interactions. As essential accoutrement of cultural practice it performs both a material and symbolic role as it bears witness to the rituals and rites of passage that accompany us through our passage from birth to death, materialising and expressing otherwise immaterial or abstract entities.[22]

However, in terms of my own work, my interest is not in the textile objects that are loaded with subjective significance but in the ubiquitous, undifferentiated textile objects of the built environment which, like the mass produced upholstered pads and panels that constitute the non-spaces of our transport system and public institutions, are characterised by their uniformity and anonymity.

The significance of these objects does not noticeably reside in their form nor is there an overt subjective process of identification, instead the objects remain dormant and in a permanent state of potential only to be activated through the process of repetition. It is the social practices that are enacted in relation to these objects that unlock their meaning and in this respect these anonymous objects of the built environment are similar to other objects in the domain of material culture in that their meaning is inscribed by narratives of use. Examining our contemporary need for engagement with our environment and sense of belonging, Neil Leach discusses the role of performativity and the way that a visceral process of identification comes through repetitive routines and the 'accumulative iteration of certain practices'.

> Through the repetition of (bodily) rituals . . . spaces are 're-membered' . . . The space becomes a space of projection, as memories of previous experiences are 'projected' onto its material form. At the same time, the body becomes the site of introjection, as a recording surface registering those previous spatial experiences.[23]

The unconscious patterns of behaviour instigated through repetitive action and routine are echoed in my own work through its repetitive processes, particularly recently, through the techniques of needlepoint and darning. As with the previous handrail and barrier pieces, within the new work the temporal is collapsed into the spatial as both the imagined corporeal habits awakened by the form of the work and the laborious processes and the physical and mental drama of the work's production become concentrated and embodied in the intensely stitched surfaces. In an absurd reversal, the hardwearing, industrially-produced surfaces of the non-spaces of our environment have been replaced by handmade counterparts which materialise the point of bodily contact and transform the efficiency of the mass-produced cloth into something far more susceptible to the vagaries of use.

Similar to the human-centred design of the upholstered pads and panels of our built environment that have informed the new work, the back-rest forms and body-facing pad of *Surface to Surface Correspondence ref: 962/398* (2007) and *Surface to Surface Correspondence ref: 8000/8892* (2007), have a regular geometric uniformity and detached presence that belies their underlying ergonomic principles. Lacking the obvious bodily contours of traditional soft furnishings these upholstered forms, like the upholstered pads of gym equipment, are nonetheless designed in particular

relationship to the standardised average dimensions of the body providing invisible support, subtly manipulating, improving 'fit', and silently negotiating its physical engagement with the external world.

It is this interplay of formal autonomy and functional context and the tension between a seeming objective detachment and a quiet embodied presence that is a central concern of my practice.

The somatic sensuality of cloth and the imaginary subjective narratives that surround the busy objects of material culture are constrained and silenced in my work as it strategically reflects the autonomous and authoritative formality of a modernist aesthetic. Together with the sensuality of the materials and the laborious processes of production that are hidden behind the work's coolly detached façade (employing material strategies of geometric form, the grid, and repetitive non-relational composition), what we are presented with is the suppressed embodied subject. However such is the material and symbolic potency of textile that any protocols of reduction only serve to amplify and concentrate the message and any attempt at disinterestedness or formal autonomy is continually disrupted by the work's ambiguous sense of objecthood and countered by the tactility of the textile materials and processes employed in its production. The expressive potential of the work is not communicated outwardly through an overt sensuality or explicit references, but is deeply embedded and embodied, articulated through the awakening of corporeal practices, nuance of gesture, slow repetitive rhythms, and a dense accumulation of subtly modulated surfaces that silently speak of the process of their making.

In common with other objects of material culture, I would suggest that it is this embodied non-verbal materiality of the medium that makes textile a particularly potent vehicle of cultural and artistic expression. Placed in direct proximity to the body, implicated in the practices, rhythms, and routines of our everyday experience, and

Figure 6.1. Maxine Bristow, *Surface to Surface Correspondence ref: 962/398* (detail), 2007. Bellana Cotton 3256 (count 20), embroidery cotton, wadding, timber, powder-coated steel fabrication, 1.17 x 1.19 x 12 cm. Photographer: Rob Meighen.

continuously and invisibly negotiating the relationship between self and other, it provides us with what may be a silent yet undoubtedly powerfully convincing testimony.

NOTES

1. See Martin Jay, *Downcast Eyes, The Denigration of Vision in Twentieth Century French Thought*, University of California Press: Berkeley, Los Angeles, 1994, for what Jay calls a 'synoptic survey' of 'ocularcentric discourse'.

2. David Howes, *Sensual Relations: Engaging the Senses in Culture and Social Theory*, Ann Arbor, MI: University of Michigan Press, 2003, p.xi.

3. Daniel Miller, *Materiality (Politics, History, and Culture)*, Duke University Press: Durham and London, 2005, p.5.

4. See artist journals at *Through the Surface: Collaborating Textile Artists from Britain and Japan* http://www.throughthesurface.com, and accompanying catalogue essay: 'Material Trace—Marking Time and Defining Space' in *Through the Surface: Collaborating Textile Artists from Britain and Japan*, The Surrey Institute of Art and Design, 2004, p.58–59.

5. Judy Attfield, *Wild Things, The Material Culture of Everyday Life*. Berg: Oxford, New York, 2000, p.1.

6. Chris Tilley, Webb Keane, Susan Kuchler, Mike Rowlands, and Patricia Spyer (Eds), 'Introduction' in *Handbook of Material Culture*, London, Thousand Oaks, New Delhi: Sage Publications, p.1.

7. Christopher Tilley, 'Part I, Theoretical Perspectives' in *Handbook of Material Culture*, Chris

Tilley, Webb Keane, Susanne Kuechler, Mike Rowlands, and Patricia Spyer (Eds). London, Thousand Oaks, New Delhi: Sage Publications, p.7.

8. Christopher Tilley, 'Objectification' in *Handbook of Material Culture*, Chris Tilley, Webb Keane, Susanne Kuechler, Mike Rowlands, and Patricia Spyer (Eds). London, Thousand Oaks, New Delhi: Sage Publications, p.62.

9. David Howes, (Ed), 'Historicising Perception' in *Empire of the Senses, The Sensual Culture Reader*. Oxford, New York: Berg, 2004, p.56.

10. Henri Lefebvre, 1987, *The Everyday and Everydayness* p. 7–11. Yale French Studies, Volume 73, Fall, cited in Judy Attfield, *Wild Things: The Material Culture of Everyday Life*. Oxford, New York: Berg, 2000, p.9.

11. See David Howes, 'Introduction' in *Empire of the Senses: The Sensual Culture Reader*. Oxford, New York: Berg, 2005, p.56. Other publications by David Howes include: Howes, D. (2003), *Sensual Relations, Engaging the Senses in Culture and Social Theory*, Ann Arbor, MI: University of Michigan Press; Howes, D. ed., *The Varieties of Sensory Experience: A Sourcebook in the Anthropology of the Senses*, Toronto: University of Toronto Press, 1991. Berg publishing have also produced the 'Sensory Formations' series of 'readers' in the senses which in addition to Howes's general reader *Empire of the Senses* include: Bull, M., and Black, L., eds., (2003) *The Auditory Culture Reader*; Classen, C. ed., (2005) *The Book of Touch*; Korsmever, C. ed., (2005) *The Taste Culture Reader: Experiencing Food and Drink*; Drobnick, J. ed. (2006) *The Smell Culture Reader*.

12. Mieke Bal, *Quoting Caravaggio: Contemporary Art, Preposterous History*, University of California Press: Berkley, Los Angeles, 2001.

13. Juhani Pallasmaa, *The Eyes of the Skin: Architecture and the Senses*. John Wiley & Sons Ltd, 2005, p.13.

14. Rosemary Betterton (Ed.), *Unframed Practices and Politics of Women's Contemporary Painting*. London, New York: I.B. Tauris & Co Ltd, 2004, p.6.

15. Rosa Lee 'Threads' in *Unframed Practices and Politics of Women's Contemporary Painting*, Rosemary Betterton (Ed.). London, New York: I.B. Tauris & Co Ltd, 2004, p.126.

16. Claire Pajackowsa, 'On Stuff and Nonsense: the Complexity of Cloth' in *Textile: The Journal of Cloth & Culture*, Volume 3, Issue 3, Fall 2005, p.223.

17. Attfield, op. cit., p.124.

18. See Steven Connor, *The Book of Skin*, London: Reaktion Books Ltd, 2004, p.26.

19. Didier Anzieu, *The Skin Ego*, Trans Chris Turner. New Haven: Yale University Press, 1989.

20. See also Steven Connor, *A Skin that Walks*, http://www.bbk.ac.uk/English/skc/skinalks/

21. Steven Connor, *The Book of Skin*, op. cit., p. 48.

22. For a useful study on the tactile and tangible components of memory and how we use objects to give continuity to and meaning to human experience, see Marius Kwint, Christpher Breward, and Jeremy Aynsley (Eds) *Material Memories Design and Evocations*. Oxford, New York: Berg, 1999.

23. Neil Leach, *Camouflage*. Cambridge, Massachsetts: MIT Press, 2006. p. 182.

FURTHER READING: TOUCH

Constance Classen (ed.), *The Book of Touch* (Oxford: Berg, 2005).

Steven Connor, *The Book of Skin* (London: Reaktion, 2004).

Mary Douglas, *Purity and Danger* (London and New York: Routledge and Kegan Paul, 1966).

Jens Hauser (ed.), *Sk-Interfaces: Exploring Borders—Creating Membranes in Art, Technology and Society* (Liverpool: Fact and Liverpool University Press, 2008).

Janis Jefferies (ed.), *Reinventing Textiles: Gender and Identity*, vol. 2 (Winchester: Telos Art Publishing, 2001).

Ewa Kuryluk, "Cloth," in *Veronica and Her Cloth: History, Symbolism and Structure of a "True" Image* (Oxford: Blackwell, 1991) pp. 179–198.

Claire Pajaczkowska, "On Stuff and Nonsense: The Complexity of Cloth," *Textile: The Journal of Cloth and Culture* 3, no. 3 (2005) pp. 220–249.

Juhani Pallasmaa, *The Eyes of the Skin: Architecture and the Senses* (Chichester: John Wiley & Sons, 2005).

Peter Stallybrass, "Marx's Coat," in *Border Fetishisms: Material Objects in Unstable Places*, ed. Patricia Spyer (London and New York: Routledge, 1998), pp. 183–207.

Junichiro Tanizaki, *In Praise of Shadows* (Sedgwick: Leete's Island Books, 1977).

Cathryn Vasseleu, *Textures of Light: Vision and Touch in Irigaray, Levinas and Merleau-Ponty* (London and New York: Routledge, 1998).

PART II

MEMORY

PART INTRODUCTION

Textiles remember. This is not something that we necessarily ask of them, nor is it something we can divert them from doing. They do it regardless. And the memory of the textile is unremittingly democratic: moments of joy and tragedy are recorded on the surface and embedded into the structure of cloth, without permission and often without intention. Textiles remember, in part, because they are hostage to their own fragility. Unlike that of metal or stone, the life span of the textile is not dissimilar to that of our own bodies: newness gradually replaced by wear and tear until worn out.

The writing in this section dwells on the capacity of the textile to act as a record keeper of events that pass near its surface. The first four texts in this section are intimate in their focus. Each uses the stain as a starting point for discussions that reach out far beyond the literal marking of cloth. Jenni Sorkin begins her essay with a discussion of benign textile stains that then suggests far more troubling memories, drawing the reader into the burdened role the textile can occupy as witness to violence. Sorkin's essay was first published in an academic journal. Nonetheless, her writing style challenges academic conventions and creates an engaging and emotionally seductive piece of writing that strikes a balance between the creative and the critical. Here the textile acts as an entry point into a discussion of staining that extends far beyond the material qualities of cloth.

Jane Wildgoose considers two ways of thinking about the textile stain—the rational and the poetic—before considering the work of textile artist Shelly Goldsmith. Here, too, attention is given to information that may initially feel peripheral to the textile but that in fact informs a range of critical disciplines (such as forensic science) that consider the textile on very different terms and for very different reasons than the values of the artist or designer. Peter Stallybrass writes of his personal experience of the death of a friend. His moving text explores the grieving process and the bittersweet textile memory contained in the clothes of loved ones no longer with us. Because the textile is a constant record keeper, it provides us with often-unexpected, even forgotten, memories. Stallybrass refers not only to the size and shape of a garment bearing the imprint of the wearer's body but also to the textile's ability to absorb scent. Our sense of smell often acts as a profound evocation of memory, and the textile's ability to carry scent serves as yet another, often-unsolicited keeper of memory.

From the intimate, we then shift scale to the institutional with essays from the perspective of the museum and history. Decisions around the conservation of cloth—and the memories it contains—for the museum conservator and curator are addressed. Sue Prichard's essay considers the curator's responsibility to collect and preserve material that is "held in trust for the nation, so that those who come after us can make sense of the past and try to understand the people, customs, and value systems related to the material held in our institutions." The museum, in Prichard's case the Victoria and Albert in London, is—among other things—a giant storehouse of material for future generations. Prichard considers the role digital technologies may play in our future understanding of material culture within the museum context. In contrast, Robyn Healy challenges the typical stance of conservation within the museum and writes of her desire to "invoke the poetics of decay" that questions the institutional motivations for conservation and "symbolically challenges the authority of the museum itself."

Throughout this section the textile provides a source of information about the past. The material memory, particularly in the case of stains and scents, is often accurate in its recollection. What remains more dubious are the interpretations applied to these material memories—from the factual requirements of a crime scene to editing of the museum collection—that often betray the interpreter's alternative agendas. The final writing in this section skips over the need for interpretation of the textile and allows, quite literally, the textile to speak. The early nineteenth-century American author James Fenimore Cooper's humorous *Autobiography of a Pocket Handkerchief* is an early example of object narration. The story is a thinly disguised attack on American social values during Cooper's time as well as a critique of the harsh divisions in wealth and opportunity existing in France. The story is communicated via the main character—one uncommonly articulate handkerchief. Over the course of the narrative, the handkerchief muses on the many identities and occupations it has endured and enjoyed during the changing fortunes of its life. We often refer to the "language" of textiles and of what materials communicate. Cooper brushes metaphors aside and turns the textile into the central character and storyteller of his short novel, using its inhuman identity as a shield for his criticisms of class and economics.

STAIN: ON CLOTH, STIGMA, AND SHAME

Jenni Sorkin

Editor's introduction: Jenni Sorkin is a critic and historian. She completed her PhD in the history of art from Yale University in 2010; her topic was American women potters in the 1950s. She was a postdoctoral fellow at the Getty Center in Los Angeles, California, in the United States in 2011 and is an assistant professor of critical theory, design and media at the University of Houston in the United States. In this piece of writing, first published in the academic journal *Third Text* in 2000, Sorkin rejects the tired structures that are so often used to communicate academic research. In place of the conventional essay format that establishes defined intentions at the outset and leads the reader from point to point, Sorkin slips from innocent to difficult material without warning. Her strategy intentionally catches the reader off guard. Equal gravitas is given to all her references, which range from legal cases to song lyrics. Here, the textile's ability to remember is part of a serious conversation about violence and the role of cloth as a record keeper of the violated body.

As if we could ever leave anything behind.

Pierre Joris

Cloth holds the sometimes unbearable gift of memory. And its memory is exacting: it does not forget even the benign scars of accident: red wine on a white tablecloth, water on a silk blouse, dark patches beneath arms on a humid summer day.

The ritual and expectancy of stain[1] is such that we allow for it. We designate special cloth for its usage, from birth onward: rags, bibs, diapers, wipes. Sponges. Washcloths, tablecloths, dish cloths, aprons, rubber gloves, placemats. Doormats. Sportswear: shorts, t-shirts, sports bras, leotards. Sweats: sweatbands, sweatpants, sweatshirts. Footwear: galoshes, rain boots, mud boots, snow boots, shitkickers, Gortex. Chamois, oil cloths, tarp. Q-tips, make-up applicators, cotton balls, Band-Aids, bandages, gauze. Certain underwear for certain days of the month. The convenience and abundance of paper cloth: paper towels, paper napkins, pads and tampons, toilet paper, tissue. Handkerchiefs. Stain is daily, stain is common, stain is mundane.

Stain is a negation of an area of fabric: It destroys the continuity of the cloth, supplanting the original colour and texture of a portion of the

Source: Jenni Sorkin, "Stain: On Cloth, Stigma, and Shame," *Third Text* 14, no. 53 (2001) pp. 77–80. Reproduced with permission.

garment or textile. A true stain is permanent, forever altering the way a garment looks and therefore, is regarded.

Stains are nearly impossible to hide: The eye is drawn immediately to the damaged area. They differ in temperament, fabric to fabric. Pale, greasy, blotchy, crinkly, glossy, dark. Stains are not uniform. Like experiences, they are uneven, and irreproducible.

Stains mark the wearer: To be stained is to be dirty,[2] messy, poor, and/or careless. It infers a variety of judgements: One does not care for his or her clothing. One does not care about his or her presentation. One is unprofessional. One is obviously a slob. Many people feel embarrassment and/or scorn for the wearer of the stain. They hardly ever feel empathetic, preferring not to identify with the sloppy individual.

The wearer of the stain. What is the fabric of the wearer?

Stains are a record of what has been near, on, or is of the body.[3] Their ugliness, their offensiveness, is in their immediacy. Fresh, stains are the sores of a fabric, raw wounds that map an event. Aged, they are scars of retrospection. They function as both remainder and reminder of what has come to pass: both evidence and memory.

Nan Goldin's 1983 photograph *Brian After Coming* is an example of this kind of chronicle. Preceded by *My hand on Brian's dick* (1983), the photographic subject, Brian, lies next to marks of wetness, the spots a deeper shade of blue than the rest of the sheet. Who is the actual subject? Naked and sprawled across the bed, Brian is not alone. Who is witness to this intimacy? Who is responsible for its culmination? Here, the stain confirms Goldin's presence. She has, through the previous photograph, confirmed her participation. The sex act is not just one of self-pleasuring. Goldin inhabits the frame as much, if not more, than Brian. The stain is hers. Thus, the photographic record of this particular ejaculation acts as both validation and snapshot, laced with desire and self-witnessing.

Within the brevity of occurrence, stain taints *now* with *then*. A stain, thus, denotes the passage of time. If an ice cream cone drips down the front of a child's shirt, and he continues eating, the ice cream becomes a physical manifestation of a moment moments ago. Hence, stains result in an always present-past for the wearer of the damage.

Stains elicit shame: Nosebleeds, vomiting, bedwetting, incontinence. Wiping one's nose on one's sleeve. Wet dreams. Laughing so hard one begins to urinate. These are all examples of the staining one inflicts upon oneself—the self-stain. The self-stain renders the body uncontrollable: both capable and culpable of transmission, transgression and impurity, exceeding the acceptable, surpassing the boundaries of the skin. In her 1966 book *Purity and Danger*, Mary Douglas wrote, 'The mistake is to treat bodily margins in isolation from all other margins.'[4] This isolation, one of social taboo, is the source of the stigmatised stain. The action by which staining occurs is falsely tolerated, and in actuality, elicits fear and disgust. Thus the embarrassment, discomfort, and humiliation of the self-stain can be excruciating, especially when the staining occurs publicly, or becomes public. In the 1990s, no garment was more ill-famed than White House intern Monica Lewinsky's navy blue dress, marked with Bill Clinton's semen. But what of the other stain? That which is not self-originated, that which is incurred by outside action or force. Not from my own behaviour, or of my own body. That which I did not will, choose, nor want. That which is inflicted by another. That which is forced. Stain becomes, then, both an enactment and vestige of degradation, violence and coercion.

To stain another is to mark. To be marked is dark.

This darkness is constant foreboding and permanent grief. It constitutes, in its despair, a fixed sense of imperilled or impoverished destiny. Consistent and overwhelming spaces of terror specific to one's own experience interfere with living, violating the logic and assurance of reality. Memory asserts itself, rupturing and defying presence, perpetually confounding time and place, inserting, in the words of Ernst Bloch, 'this blind spot in the soul, this darkness of the lived moment'.[5]

If I am marked, I am discernible.[6] If I am discernible, I am different. If I am different, I am separate. I use discernment according to Georges Didi-Huberman's breakdown: in sifting, there is selection or deliberation. In seeing, there is visibility. In deciding, there is judgement. Huberman's signification is applicable to male assaults on women in rural Bangladesh. Over a three-year period, from 1996–1998, there were over 400 reported cases of acid attacks on women's faces and hands. Using corrosive battery acid, men have burned, blinded, and permanently disfigured women. The attacks are deliberate: most women know their attackers in the capacity of acquaintances whom have made unwanted sexual advances. The aftermath of the ordeal is one of visibility: a burned woman is considered objectionable and thus, flawed. Rural Bangladeshi women are often dependent on marriage for social and financial security. The accompanying physical marking and disfigurement ensures an unmarried status. According to Mary Douglas, differentiation is the basis for all defilement.[7] The sense of defilement or stigma that rape, incest, and all other forms of sexual violence retain in all parts of the world,[8] remains as both the individual injury and collective damage inflicted again and again upon women, before, during and after the crime. Stigma perpetuates the idea of self-stain, directing the blame at the survivor and not the perpetrator. Let it be noted that in botany, the word stigma is used to describe the part of the pistil which is the receptacle for pollen in impregnation; that is, the female region of the plant. Stigma is continually socialised as a female condition.

Sustain: the continuance and maintenance of stain. Su- is a prefix that comes from sub-: less than, not quite, lower than, secondary. A medium long considered inferior, needlework is the means by which Anne Wilson, in *Grafts #1* (1993), exaggerates and embellishes stains, holes and worn areas of table linen with human hair, re-enforcing the repellent portions of the cloth through the careful enunciation of its flaws. The title, *Grafts*, hints at medicine, referring to living tissue transplanted to an area of the body in need of adhesion and growth. An addition or extension of life, a graft forces an injury to adapt before it can heal. Wilson's abject renderings prolong the life of the wound, magnifying and permanently altering the cloth, committing it to a state of irrevocable loss.

Stains are intrusions within a garment: Rape, incest and all other forms of sexual violence toward women are intrusive:[9] not only a disruption of normality and consistency within the life cloth, but destructive as well, discolouring all future living. If, according to Salman Rushdie, 'Repression is a seamless garment,'[10] then staining is the silent event that binds the wearer.

Stigma functions as both a form of reproach and silencing: It is the censure and condemnation of the victim rather than her perpetrator, that minimises the consequences of the violation and furthermore, relegates the rape to an inferior status than that of her attacker.

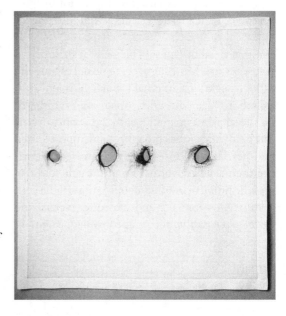

Figure 7.1. Anne Wilson, *Grafts #1*, 1993. Hair, thread, cloth 104 × 99 × 6 cm (41 × 39 × 2.5 in).

Stigma observes the dialectics of transference: In assigning culpability, the assertion of blame and subsequent burden of fault is thrust upon the survivor, essentially viewing the sadism of the perpetrator as the survivor's own masochism: that she desired the abuse, deserved the abuse, or 'asked for it'.[11]

Stigma protects the male perpetrator: In cultures socially and sexually oppressive toward women, the stigma is a natural extension of male tyranny, re-enforcing women's errant status. The preservation and maintenance of this dichotomy is a disavowal of male accountability. Evocative and ironic, Joseph Beuys' 1979 sculpture of a knife blade wrapped in gauze, titled *When you cut your finger, bandage the knife*[12] is a visual metaphor of this phenomenon of defence, cover, and sheltering. The knife, as is the penis, is the weapon of forced entry, removed from and sheltered against the damage it has incurred.

Stain is dangerous. The ownership of human residue affirms its occurrence. Cloth provides an exact topography of this marking, but the psychic implications are far graver. This essay seeks to integrate and negotiate an avowed space for the possession of sexual trauma. Stain is still disdained.

Women are almost always blamed for their perpetrator's crime. Most survivors of sexual assault and rape struggle with internal feelings of shame, humiliation, rage, and grief, which are exacerbated by the social stigma of rape: that the woman herself is at fault, or has brought shame upon herself and her family. This collective blame invalidates the trauma a survivor has been through, and creates the problem of undesirability, that is, the condemnation, avoidance and subsequent sexual and social ostracisation of the raped woman or girl.

NOTES

1. Stain (n.):

    1. a discoloration produced by foreign matter having penetrated into a material

    2. a patch of colour different from that of the basic colour, as on the body of an animal
    3. a cause of reproach; stigma
    4. to bring reproach or dishonour upon; blemish

    (Webster's New College Dictionary)

2. 'No child will play with her because she is "dirty", Ngoepe 32, said of her daughter [age 6], who was raped repeatedly by Ngoepe's boyfriend and, more recently, by her own 12-year-old son.' (Chicago Tribune, 'A Plague of Rape.' [South Africa] June 1, 1999, section 1, p 1, 14.)

3. 'Torn or bloody clothing suggests a forceful struggle and supports an inference of non-consent. Clothing stained with blood or semen may identify the defendant as the perpetrator. Clothing bearing traces of semen can be introduced to show penetration or intercourse.'
    Legal Framework for Admissibility of Clothing at a Rape Trial, People v Pride, 833 para 2d, 643, 670–71, California, 1992, as quoted by Alinor Sterling in 'Undressing the Victim: The Intersection of Evidentiary and Semiotic Meanings of Women's Clothing in Rape Trials,' *Yale Journal of Law and Feminism*, 1995.

4. Mary Douglas, *Purity and Danger*, Routledge, London, 1993, p 121.

5. Ernst Bloch, *The Spirit of Utopia*, Translated Anothony A. Nassar, Meridian, Stanford, CA, 2000, p 198.

6. 'A *discernment*, a word whose root cernere, contains the three signifying vectors, 'sifting', 'seeing', and deciding . . .' Georges Didi-Huberman, 'The Index of the Absent Wound (A Monograph on a Stain).' *October* no 29, summer 1984.

7. Mary Douglas, *Purity and Danger*, Routledge, London, 1993, p 160.

8. The following quotes attest to this worldwide phenomenon:

'The stigma of rape is so heavy that even victims' families tell the victims to shut up.' Chicago Tribune, 'A Plague of Rape.' [South Africa] June 1, 1999, section 1, p 1, 14.

'The stigma of rape often prevents victims from identifying themselves or telling what happened. 'It's certainly taboo,' a UN official said of the rape stigma. 'Many of the women said they were afraid of how their husbands would react if they knew.'

Chicago Tribune, 'Women from Kosovo village tell of a 3-day ordeal of rape by Serb police.' April 28, 1999, section 1, p 9.

9. 'Intrusion reflect the indelible imprint of the traumatic moment.' Judith Lewis Herman, *Trauma and Recovery*, HarperCollins, New York, 1992, p 35.
10. *Shame*, Penguin, London, 1983, Ibid, p 1.
11. 'Was she asking for it? Was she asking nice? She was asking for it. Did she ask you twice?' —Hole, 'Asking for it,' *Live Through This*, Geffen Records Inc, Los Angeles, CA, 1994.
12. Elaine Scarry, *The Body in Pain*, Oxford University Press, Oxford, 1985, p 16.

8

CONSIDERING THE EVIDENCE

Jane Wildgoose

Editor's introduction: Jane Wildgoose is an artist and writer and is keeper of the Wildgoose Memorial Library in London. The essay reprinted here was commissioned to accompany the Wellcome Trust–funded exhibition and conference *Indelible: Every Contact Leaves a Trace*, held at the Fabrica Gallery in Brighton, England, from April 12 to May 18, 2008. The event brought together a textile artist, forensic scientist, filmmaker, and forensic psychiatrist. At one pole, Wildgoose places Marcel Proust's intuitive approach to the analysis of memory; at the other, Edmond Locard's rational logic that became the foundation of forensic science as we know it today. Wildgoose touches on these differing positions in her discussion of the work that the textile artist, Shelly Goldsmith, developed for the exhibition in dialogue with the forensic scientist, Alison Fendley. The textile, perhaps unsurprisingly, occupies the territory between these two perspectives—inviting analysis from both.

The microscopic debris that covers our clothing and bodies are the mute witnesses, sure and faithful, of all our movements and all our encounters.

Edmond Locard (1877–1966)[1]

Locard's principle—that material interchange occurs wherever there is human activity, the traces of which offer clues to movements and encounters—was given practical formulation in France during World War I. Developing techniques to determine locations where soldiers and prisoners had been, through close examination of stains on their uniforms, Locard went on to devote his long career to the advancement of scientific methods for establishing evidence in criminal proceedings.

Meanwhile, in Paris, another great work of investigation was under way. Writing from bed, in his cork-lined apartment, Marcel Proust (1871–1922) was devoting his career to a single-minded process of examination: documenting, editing, and re-editing, the shifting experience of his own recollection.

Locard's and Proust's names have become synonymous with processes for reconstruction of past events and experiences. We now take for granted the routine collection and analysis of microscopic evidence in criminal investigations. We also expect that the authority of resulting testimony in court will be dependent upon the scientific

Source: Jane Wildgoose, "Considering the Evidence," 2008. Essay commissioned to accompany "Indelible: Every Contact Leaves a Trace," an exhibition and conference at Fabrica Gallery, Brighton, funded by the Wellcome Trust. © Jane Wildgoose 2008. Reproduced with permission.

witness's ability to remain emotionally detached from any narrative emerging from the evidence. Conversely, Proust's revelatory moment—still commonly cited when the mechanisms and effects of memory and recollection are discussed—was formulated through his commitment to painstaking examination of his own subjectivity. His description of the way in which the taste of a madeleine dipped in tea (the sensory experience of which flooded his memory with vivid recollections of childhood experience) retains authority to this day. Recent scientific research indicates that the senses of taste and smell connect directly to the hippocampus, "the part of the brain that modulates learning and memory"—the centre of long-term memory—adding empirical weight to Proustian (intuitive and subjective) understanding of the processes of recollection[2].

Carol Hayman's film installation, *No One Escapes*, reveals that Locard's principle concerning material traces is applicable to the subjective realm. For survivors, and the families of both victims and offenders, violent crimes leave indelible subjective effects. But it does not end there: profound emotional traces, left by acts of violence and abuse, extend to those who work with offenders, survivors and victims; they also reach into wider society. With news "breaking", daily, on a 24-hour basis—a phenomenon unknown either to Locard, or Proust—it sometimes seems hard to get through a day without encountering reports of at least one crime of the worst and most violent type. While Locardian, empirical principles of scientific detection prove invaluable in the conviction of violent criminals, how may Proustian principles of experience and recollection prove relevant to an understanding of traumatic experience?

The *Indelible* conference offers an opportunity to examine this question, bringing together textile artist Shelly Goldsmith, forensic scientist Alison Fendley, filmmaker Carol Hayman, forensic psychiatrist Anna Motz, and myself, Jane Wildgoose, in the chair—an artist and writer fascinated by the many different narratives that may attach to remains of all kinds.

Shelly Goldsmith's new work explores ways in which emotional experiences might seem to become "attached" to—or even integrated with—garments. Her work will, I expect, hold particular resonance for anyone who has had the task of disposing of clothes belonging to someone they are close to, after they have died. In this situation,

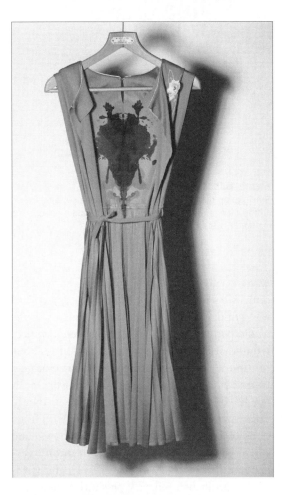

Figure 8.1. Shelly Goldsmith, *Cocktail Dress: Erupted*, 2010. Archival pigment print on Hahnemuhle photo paper, 120 x 88 cm. Photograph of a reclaimed dress sublimation-printed on the inside with symmetrical layers of flooded color, influenced by Rorschach ink blot tests (which are commonly used in forensic assessment of psychological health).

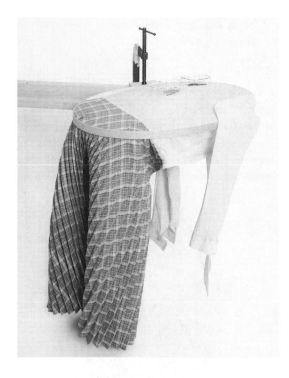

Figure 8.2. Shelly Goldsmith, *Outbursts 1 & 2*, 2010. Sublimation print on reclaimed garment, hand stitching on cotton tape, and dressmaking pins, embroidery hoop, and clamp, 85 x 80 x 44 cm.

material can prompt vivid emotion and recollection in a Proustian way. Goldsmith says: "As I was working with the reclaimed garments in my studio perfumes and bodily smells were revealed, I found it rather spooky and provocative." She continues: "thinking specifically about clothing, I think [. . .] we are unable to live our life without leaving a part of ourselves behind in them." This experience may well be connected with functions of empathy and intuition, but how—and where—may we give serious consideration to experience that is largely unquantifiable, and virtually unqualifiable, today? Goldsmith explains: "I see it as my role, in this project, to imagine this to magnify, and develop perceived narratives."[3]

Interestingly, all the forensic psychiatrists working with people convicted of acts of extreme violence and abuse, interviewed in Carol Hayman's film installation, *No One Escapes*, describe how the *inability* to empathise is a defining condition in the mental state of those who commit murder, who torture, and abuse. In other words, when they act in ways we prefer to consider "inhuman".

Hayman's interviews with relatives of victims and survivors, as well as professionals closely connected with some of the most notoriously violent offenders in this country, provide a spectrum of insights—deriving from personal experience—into ways in which society at large fails to recognise or understand contributory factors in the lives of the most violent members of our community. Their testimony also raises questions about how this wider lack of understanding may in itself be a contributing factor in patterns of violence that occur from generation to generation.

Set within the bleakest of emotional landscapes, some of the interviews in Hayman's work nonetheless reveal an extraordinary vision of redemption. Marian Partington, sister of one of the Fred and Rosemary Wests' victims, describes the processes through which she ultimately came to empathise with the history of abuse she believed Rosemary West herself had suffered, that may have contributed to her developing into a sadistic and predatory murderer. Partington explains how this insight in turn led to the opportunity for her to embark upon a process in which she might come to some kind of constructive terms with her sister's horrific death. In order to achieve this, Partington says she had to find a way of "connecting with the humanity of those who have caused suffering."

Anne-Marie West—a victim who suffered unimaginably at the Wests' hands as a child—who succeeded in running away, went on to give evidence against her father and stepmother leading to their conviction, and to pick up the pieces of her life with very little support from society—expresses a heartfelt wish to become a counselor for other victims of abuse and loss, to whom she could, genuinely, say: "I know how you feel".

Informed by her work with violent women offenders, forensic psychiatrist Anna Motz argues that countertransference (in which the professional detachment of psychiatric professionals is intruded upon by pressing emotional responses to the patient) may be used to constructive effect[4]. She argues that when she is able to examine her own (often profoundly negative) subjective responses and analyse them within their professional context, she becomes better equipped to act as an agent in helping the patient to articulate experiences and states of mind so painful and dangerous to them that they can otherwise only be communicated through profoundly destructive behaviour.

However, as forensic scientist Alison Fendley explains, the testimony that *she* provides as a witness—of the kind that can lead to the conviction of rapists and murderers—would be fundamentally undermined if she allowed herself to be drawn into speculation beyond the scientific parameters of the material evidence with which she works. But, as she also acknowledges, once she has gathered the evidence and is confident the findings have been properly tested, it is only human to feel a desire to present them to the jury in a way that will encourage empathy with the scientifically drawn conclusions[5].

This conference offers an independent forum in which the contributors will discuss, from their own perspectives, relationships between objective and subjective responses in their work. The event also offers opportunities for speakers to share experience and thoughts with one another, and in dialogue with the audience. Together with the *Indelible* exhibition, both Locardian and Proustian principles for reconstructing events and remembering may be compared, considered and, it is anticipated, inform one another.

NOTES

1. Edmond Locard, quoted in 'Fractured Patterns: Microscopical Investigation of Real Physical Evidence', Richard E. Bisbing, *The American Journal of Police Science*, Volume 1, 1930, p276, http://www.modernmicroscopy.com/main.asp?article=11—referenced 23.3.2008.
2. Jonah Lehrer, *Proust Was a Neuroscientist*, Houghton Mifflin, [New York] 2007, p80.
3. Shelly Goldsmith, email to author, 25.3.2008.
4. *The Psychology of Female Violence: crimes against the body* (second edition), Anna Motz, Routledge, 2008.
5. Alison Fendley in conversation with author, London, 7.3.2008.

WORN WORLDS: CLOTHES, MOURNING AND THE LIFE OF THINGS

Peter Stallybrass

Editor's introduction: Peter Stallybrass is the director of the History of Material Texts at the University of Pennsylvania in the United States. The text, reprinted here, was initially written as a memorial lecture in memory of the author's friend, Allon White. In remembering White, Stallybrass writes of his personal grief and the role of cloth as a mediating layer in the experience of loss. Drawing on poetry and fiction that tackles the uneasy subject of how to negotiate the emotional minefield of the garments the dead leave behind, Stallybrass observes the daunting accuracy of the textile's ability to remember size, shape and traces of the body that can make the clothes of the departed unbearably intimate. The lecture grew into a book-length collaboration with Ann Rosalind Jones entitled *Renaissance Clothing and the Materials of Memory*, published by Cambridge University Press and awarded the James Russell Lowell prize by the Modern Language Association in 2001. As Stallybrass so eloquently observes of the textile: "It endures, but is mortal."

For the past two years I have been writing about clothes. In fact, I've been doing so without even knowing it. I had no inkling that I was writing about clothes other than as a by-product of my interest in sexuality, colonialism, and the history of the nation-state. Then something happened which changed my sense of what I was doing. I was giving a paper on the concept of the individual when I was quite literally overcome. I could not read, and an embarrassing silence ensued. I cried. I had a close friend sitting next to me, and he simply took the paper from me and read on.

Later, when I tried to understand what had happened, I realized that for the first time since his death, Allon White had returned to me. Allon and I were friends; we had shared a house; we had

written a book together. After his death from leukemia in 1986, his widow, Jen, and I had both, in our different ways, tried to invoke Allon, but with remarkably little success. For others, there were active memories, active griefs. For me, there was simply a hole, an absence, and something like anger at my own inability to grieve. What memories I had seemed sentimental and unreal—quite incommensurable with the strident, loving articulacy that was Allon's. The one thing that had seemed real to me was the series of long conversations I had with Jen about what to do with Allon's remains: with the hat that still stood on the bookshelf in his study, a hat that he had bought to conceal the baldness that had arrived long before the physical humiliations of chemotherapy; with

Source: Peter Stallybrass, "Worn Worlds: Clothes, Mourning and the Life of Things," *The Yale Review* 81, no. 2 (1993) pp. 35–50. Copyright © 1993 Peter Stallybrass. Reproduced with permission from Blackwell Publishing, Ltd.

his glasses that had been beside the bed and still looked at you. For Jen, the question was whether and how to reorder the house, what to do with Allon's books and with all the ways in which he had occupied space. Perhaps, she thought, the only way to resolve this problem was to move, leaving the house once and for all. But in the meantime, she gave away some of his books and some of his clothes.

Allon and I had always exchanged clothes, having for two years shared a house, in which we were communal in just about everything except our filth—that alone, paradoxically, seemed irremediably individual, the object of the other's disgust. When Allon died, Jen gave me his American baseball jackets, which seemed appropriate enough, since I had by that time moved permanently to the United States. But she also gave me the jacket of Allon's which I had most coveted. He had picked it up in a secondhand shop down from Brighton station, and its mystery was, and is, simple enough to describe. It is made of a rather shiny black cotton-and-polyester weave, and on the outside it's still in good shape. But inside, much of the lining has been cut out and the rest is in tatters, as if several angry cats had been at work with their claws. Inside, the only remnant of former glory is the label: "Made Expressly for Turndorf's by Di Rossi, Hand Sewn." I've often wondered if it was the "Di Rossi" that attracted Allon, as he adored the Italian look from his childhood, but most likely it was just the fit of the jacket.

Anyway, this was the jacket which I was wearing when I read my paper on the individual, a paper which was in many ways an attempt to invoke Allon. But at no time in the writing of it was my invocation answered. Like the paper, Allon was dead. And then, as I began to read, I was inhabited by his presence, taken over. If I wore the jacket, Allon wore me. He was there in the wrinkles of the elbows, wrinkles which in the technical jargon of sewing are called "memory"; he was there in the stains at the very bottom of the jacket; he was there in the smell of the armpits. Above all, he was there in the smell.

So I began to think about clothes. I read about clothes, I talked to friends about clothes. The magic of cloth, I came to believe, is that it receives us: receives our smells, our sweat, our shape even. And our parents, our friends, our lovers die, the clothes in their closets still hang there, holding their gestures, both reassuring and terrifying, touching the living with the dead. But for me, more reassuring than terrifying, although I have felt both emotions. For I have always wanted to be touched by the dead; I have wanted them to haunt me; I have hoped that they will rise up and inhabit me. And they do literally inhabit us through the "habits" which they bequeath. I put on Allon's jacket. However worn, it has outlived its wearers and, I hope, will outlive me. In thinking of clothes as passing fashions, we repeat less than a half-truth. Bodies come and go; the clothes which have received those bodies survive. They circulate through secondhand shops, through rummage sales, through the Salvation Army; or they are transmitted from parent to child, from sister to sister, from brother to brother, from sister to brother, from lover to lover, from friend to friend.

Clothes receive the human imprint. Jewelry lasts longer, and can also move us. But even though it has a history, it resists the history of our bodies. Enduring, it rebukes our mortality, which it imitates only in the occasional scratch. On the other hand, food, which, like jewelry, is a gift which joins us to each other, rapidly *becomes* us and disappears. Like food, cloth can be shaped by our touch; like jewelry, it endures beyond immediate moment of consumption. It endures, but it is mortal. As Lear says disgustedly of his own hand, "It smells of mortality." It is a smell which I love.

It is the smell which attaches a child to its comforter. A piece of cloth, a teddy bear, whatever. Cloth that can be put in the mouth, chewed upon, anything but washed. Cloth that bears the teeth marks, the grime, the bodily presence of the child. Cloth that decays: the teddy bear's arm falls off, the edge of the cloth frays. Cloth that endures and comforts. Cloth that, as any child knows, is *specific*. Once, when I was looking after Anna, a friend's child, I attempted to "replace" her lost comforter with a piece of cloth that looked exactly like it. She, of course, knew immediately that it was a fraud, and I still remember her look of distrust and disgust at my betrayal. The comforter, however much it stands in for absences and loss, remains irrevocably itself even as it is transformed by touch and lips and teeth.

As I thought about cloth, I rethought my own work on early modern England. To think about cloth, about clothes, was to think about memory, but also about power and possession. I began to see the extent to which Renaissance England was a cloth society. By this I mean not only that its industrial base was cloth, and in particular the manufacture of wool, but also that cloth was the staple currency, far more so than gold or money. To be a member of an aristocratic household, to be a member of a guild, was to wear livery. It was to be paid above all in cloth. And when a guild member was set free, he—or, more rarely, she—was said to be "clothed."

Let me clarify what I mean by a cloth society. In its most extreme form, it is a society in which values and exchange alike take the form of cloth. When the Incas incorporated new areas into their kingdom, the new citizens "were granted (clothes to wear . . . which among them is highly valued." But the gift was not, of course, disinterested. This "gift" of textile was, as John Murra puts it, "a coercive and yet symbolic reiteration of the peasant's obligations to the state, of his or her conquered status." In exchange for this supposed gift, peasants were obliged by law "to weave cloth for crown and church needs." To the surprise of the European invaders, while some state warehouses contained food, weapons, and tools, there were "a large number holding wool and cotton, cloth and garments." Similarly, in the court of Emperor Akbar, there was "a special department for receiving the shawls and dresses (*khelats*) given as tributes or pledges by different notables and regions." As Bernard Cohn has argued, "the gift of dress was the essential act of homage and rule within the Mughal system of kingship, effecting the incorporation of the subject into the ruler's body."

In a cloth society, then, cloth is both a currency and a means of incorporation. As it changes hands, it binds people in networks of obligation. The particular power of cloth to effect these networks is closely associated with two almost contradictory aspects of its materiality: its ability to be permeated and transformed by maker and wearer alike; its ability to endure over time. Cloth thus tends to be powerfully associated with memory. Or, to put it more strongly, cloth *is* a kind of memory. When a person is absent or dies, cloth can absorb his or her absent presence. The poet and textile artist Nina Payne writes of sorting through her husband's clothes after his death:

> Everything to be saved was stored in an upstairs closet, jackets and trousers that Eric or Adam might eventually use, sweaters, ties, three shirts made of soft-checkered cotton, blue-grey, brick red and yellow ochre. I saw that the grey one had been worn once after ironing, then replaced on its hanger to be worn again. If I pressed my head into the clothes, I could smell him.

"I could smell him." Dead, he still hangs there in the closet, in the shape of his body impressed upon the cloth, in a frayed cuff, in a smell.

What is most astonishing to me about insights like Nina Payne's is that, in societies like ours—that is to say, in modern economies—they are so rare. I think this is because, for all our talk of the "materialism" of modern life, attention to material is precisely what is absent. Surrounded by an extraordinary abundance of materials, their value is to be endlessly devalued and replaced. Marx, for all his brilliant insight into the workings of capitalism, was mistaken in appropriating the concept of fetishism from nineteenth-century anthropology and applying it to commodities. He was, of course, right in insisting that the commodity is a "magical" (that is, mystified) form, in which the labor processes which give it its value have been effaced. But in applying the term *fetish* to the commodity, he in turn erased the true magic by which other tribes (and, who knows, perhaps even we ourselves) inhabit and are inhabited by what they touch and love. To put it another way: for us, to love things is something of an embarrassment. Things are, after all, mere things. And to accumulate things is not to give them life. It is because things are *not* fetishized that they remain lifeless.

In a cloth economy, though, things take on a life of their own. That is to say, one is paid not in the "neutral" currency of money but in material which is richly absorbent of symbolic meaning, and in which memories and social relations are literally embodied. In a capitalist economy—an economy of new cloth, new clothes—the life of textiles takes on a ghostly existence, emerging to prominence, or even to consciousness, only at moments of crisis. Yet such moments of crisis occur again and again as the trace elements of material life. Vladimir Nabokov, for instance, in his last novel, *Look at the Harlequins!*, describes how Vadim, after the death of his wife Iris, feels the need to banish those objects of hers which would overpower him:

A curious form of self-preservation moves us to get rid, instantly, irrevocably, of all that belonged to the loved one we lost. Otherwise, the things she touched every day and kept in their proper context by the act of handling them start to become bloated with an awful mad life of their own. Her dresses now wear their own selves, her books leaf through their own pages. We suffocate in the tightening circle of those monsters that are misplaced and misshapen because she is not there to tend them. And even the bravest among us cannot meet the gaze of her mirror.

How to get rid of them is another problem. I could not drown them like kittens; in fact, I could not drown a kitten, let alone her brush or bag. Nor could I watch a stranger collect them, take them away, come back for more. Therefore,

I simply abandoned the flat, telling the maid to dispose in any manner she chose of all those unwanted things. Unwanted! At the moment of parting they appeared quite normal and harmless; I would even say they looked taken aback.

Here, Nabokov captures the terror of the material trace. For Vadim, the life of these objects is bloated, monstrous, as if they themselves have usurped the place of their wearer. The dresses "now wear their own selves." But even as Vadim exterminates the monsters, they take on a new life: not just "normal and harmless" but "taken aback"—taken aback, perhaps, at his inability to take them back.

At such moments of crisis, these trivial matters, the matter of matter, seem to loom disproportionately large. What are we to do with the clothes of the dead? This question is addressed by Philip Roth in his autobiography, *Patrimony*. There he describes how, after his mother died, his father "disappeared into the bedroom and started emptying her bureau drawers and sorting through the clothes in her closet. I was still at the door with my brother, welcoming the mourners who'd followed us back from the cemetery." Roth, disturbed by his father's refusal to perform the usual social functions, pursues him into the bedroom:

The bed was already strewn with dresses, coats, skirts, and blouses pulled from the closet, and [my father] was now busily chucking things from a corner of [my mother's] lowest bureau drawer into a plastic garbage bag. . . . "What good is this stuff anymore? It's no good to me hanging here. This stuff can go to Jewish relief—it's in mint condition."

Like Vadim, Roth's father wants to erase the trace because the trace seems empty, a reminder of all that has been lost. The clothes are only, and merely, themselves, with a specific material value. For Roth, there is something almost heroic in this repudiation: his father, he writes, "was now an old man living alone and . . . symbolic relics were no substitute for the real companion of fifty-five years. It seemed to me that it was not out of fear of her things and their ghostlike power that he wanted to rid the apartment of them without delay—to bury *them* now, too—but because he refused to sidestep the most brutal of all facts."

Similarly, Laurence Lerner writes in a poem called "Residue" of his father getting rid of his mother's clothes after her death:

My mother dying left a wardrobeful,

A world half-worn, half-new:

Old-fashioned underclothes; a row of shoes,

Soles upward, staring; tangles of rings,

Impatient opals, bargain bangles, pearls;

And, flowered or jazzy, rayon, cotton, tulle,

A hundred dresses, waiting.

Left with that ragged past,

My poor truncated father sold the lot.

What could he do? The dealer shrugged, and said

"Take it or leave it—up to you." He took

And lost the fiver at the races.

The empty wardrobe stared at him for years.

There is an important sense in which the clothes *are* the pain that the father feels. The dresses hang there, "waiting," they endure, but only as a residue that re-creates "absence, darkness, death; things which are not." Yet even when they are gone, turned into instantly disposable cash, the wardrobe re-creates the ghostly presence of the dresses that are no longer there. There is, indeed, a close connection between the magic of lost clothes and the fact that ghosts often step out of closets and wardrobes to appall us, haunt us, perhaps even console us.

Yet there is nothing *given* about this radical separation, this discarding of cloth, this relegation of it to the merely symbolic. And I want to try to attend to the different ways in which clothing figures in, and figures, the ruptures of our lives. Let me return now to the three shirts which Nina Payne preserved after her husband's death, and which she stored away for future use. "The checkered shirts," she writes, "reappeared two years later":

Jessie and Emily started putting them on over turtlenecks, tucking in the shirttails, rolling up the bottom of the sleeve, the way a woman will wear a man's garment and expand, playfully, upon the shape of their difference. My daughters made outfits out of a scattered assortment of clothing in which their father's shirts became an emblem and a sign. Eric was working nights at a restaurant that year following his graduation from highschool. His schedule made it possible for him to avoid everyone in the family most of the time but we generally ate supper together on Sunday evenings. Once, when we were sitting round the table, he told the girls how ridiculous it was for them to be wearing shirts that were much too big for them. He said that he himself planned to wear the shirts and he didn't want them all worn out before he could fit into them. His sisters responded indignantly. The argument gathered undertow. I heard anger, accusation, and an exasperation bordering on despair. Under ordinary circumstances, I might have been called upon to give an opinion but no one dared ask for one. The phone rang. Adam got up to clear his plate and we all scattered for cover.

The shirts continued to be worn. When he left home, Eric took the grey one with him. The next time I saw it, I recognized the fatal pink of red dye that has seeped into a load of wash. For a moment, I felt as though everything would lose its original color, bleach out, disintegrate. But Eric smiled at my stricken look. "The same thing happened to my underwear in sixth grade, do you remember?" and he opened the door to the cellar to bring up more wood.

The title of Philip Roth's autobiography is, we may recall, *Patrimony*, and that title takes on a peculiar and powerful resonance in Payne's writing. In Roth's account, the mother's clothes are given away, but the father's legacy remains to be inherited (and dislocated) by the son. But Nina Payne preserves the clothes which become the site of grief and struggle between her sons and daughters. Or rather, between the elder son, Eric, who wants to put on the father's patrimony for himself, and the daughters, Jessie and Emily; the younger son, Adam, is the uncomfortable witness (he "got up to clear his plate"). Yet Eric, it seems, fails in his attempt to take the grief and the power of loss and of persistence to himself, since "the shirts continued to be worn." And when he leaves, taking only one of them with him, the wornness by which presence is transmitted will be transformed into the wornness of the worn-out Eric, who didn't want the shirts "all worn out before he could fit into them," discolors the gray shirt he takes with "the fatal pink of red dye." "For a moment, I felt as though everything would lose its original color, bleach out, disintegrate," Nina Payne writes. Eric's response is to reiterate the persistence of loss: his father's shirt is transformed, as his own underpants had been earlier. The shirt persists, joining parent to child, yet changing as it is reshaped by its new wearer.

The gendering of cloth, and of attitudes to it, has itself been materially inscribed through social relations: outside the capitalist marketplace, where the male weaver and the male tailor became increasingly the norm, it has been women who were both materially and ideologically associated with the making, repairing, and cleaning of clothes. It is difficult fully to recapture the density and complex transformation of this relation between women of different classes and cloth. But throughout most of early modem Europe and the Americas, the social life of women was profoundly connected to the social life of cloth. In fifteenth-century Florence, for instance, young girls were taken on as servants for five to ten years, and their contracts stipulated that they would be given clothes and food, and, at the termination of their contract, a dowry. In the second half of the fifteenth century, the dowry was usually of eighty *lire*, a dowry that was nearly always paid not in money but in clothes and bed linen.

Men, of course, were also paid in livery, but they were rarely so consistently involved from early childhood in the production of cloth. As late as the nineteenth century in the United States, most young women were expected to have made twelve quilts for their dower chests before they were ready to marry, and the thirteenth was called the "bridal quilt." But if stitching was, for women, compulsory labor, it was also, as Elaine Showalter has argued, a means of producing counter-memories. A New England mill worker, herself professionally engaged in the production of cloth, recorded her own life in the quilt she made. She writes in *The Lowell Offering* in 1845:

> How many passages of my life seem to be epitomized in this patchwork quilt. Here . . . are remnants of that bright copperplate cushion that graced my mother's chair . . . Here is a piece of the first dress I ever saw, cut with what were called "mutton-leg" sleeves. It was my sister's, . . . and here is a fragment of the first gown that was ever cut for me with a bodice waist. . . . Here is a fragment of the first dress which baby brother wore when he left off long clothes. . . . Here is a piece of the first dress which was ever earned by my own exertions! What a feeling of exultation, of self-dependence, of *self-reliance*, was created by this effort.

The quilt thus bears the marks of conflicting social structures: the materials of family-arity; the materials of self-dependence and wage labor.

And the quilt itself takes on a complex social life of its own. "Annette," its maker (probably Harriet Farley or Rebecca Thompson), after becoming a mill worker, gives the quilt to her sister for her marriage, thus returning it from the sphere "of self-dependence, of *self-reliance*" to the sphere of marriage. It is beneath this quilt that her sister dies, coughing up her medications, so that when the quilt is returned to Annette, there are "dark stains at the top of it." The quilt is made up of pieces of cloth that bear the traces of her history; and, in its use, the quilt comes to bear the traces of others, of her sister, of death.

Elaine Hedges notes how widespread in the nineteenth-century United States was the transmission of fabrics which "bound together members of dispersed families." In 1850, Hannah Shaw writes to her daughter Margaret: "I have been looking for something to send you, but I could not find anything that I could send in a letter bitt [sic] a piece of my new dress." Other dress scraps are sent from mother to daughter, from sister to sister: "Here is a piece of my gingham Lydia made me"; "a piece of my dress of delanes"; "a piece of my bonnet trimmed with green plaid ribbon"; and "some pieces of my new dresses for patch work." Hannall writes to Margaret that her daughter Rebecca "will now peace [sic] up your grandmother's dresses in quilts," after the grandmother had died. "Piecing" as "peacing": pieces that make peace between the living and the dead. A network of cloth can trace the connections of love across the boundaries of absence, of death, because cloth is able to carry the absent body, memory, genealogy, as well as literal material value.

But it is striking that, as cloth loses its economic value, it tends to lose its symbolic value. There seems, for instance, to be a connection between the ability to sell or pawn second-hand clothes and the careful transmission of clothes through wills. In the Renaissance, the pawnbroking accounts of Italy and England clearly show that clothes were by far the commonest pledge, followed by tools. As late as the 1950s, in the film *Some Like It Hot*, the jobless musicians played by Tony Curtis and Jack Lemmon begin by pawning their overcoats, even though it is the middle of a bitter Chicago winter. Once that money is gone, Curtis tries to persuade Lemmon to pawn their bass and saxophone, but Lemmon protests that those instruments are their livelihood. Clothes first, tools second.

A pawnbroker will only accept pledges for which there is a market. One can only pawn clothes if they're worth something. In Renaissance England, a single livery for the court dwarf, Ippolyta the Tartarian, cost more than the highest salary for a court lady. And when Philip Henslowe bought plays by writers like Shakespeare he usually paid about £6 for a play, whereas he paid £20 10s. 6d. for a single "black velvet cloak with sleeves embroidered all with silver and gold." A single jerkin bought for the earl of Leicester cost more than Shakespeare's grand house in Stratford. The sheer value of textiles until the manufacture of cheap cottons explains the extraordinary care with which they were itemized in early modern wills.

At one level, and particularly among the aristocracy, the leaving of clothes was an assertion of the power of the giver and the dependency of the recipient. Such is the chilling implication of the earl of Dorset's bequest of his wife's own clothes to her in 1624: "Item I doe give & bequeath to my deerlye beloved wife all her wearing apparel and such rings and jewels as were hers on her marriage and the rocke rubye ring which I have given her." His own apparel was divided by the earl among his servants.

The will of Dorset's wife, Anne Clifford, on the other hand, is far more detailed and moving in its association of apparel with memory: she leaves to her grandchildren "the remainder of the two rich armors which were my noble father's, to remaine to them and their posterity (if they soe please) as a remembrance of him." And to her "deare daughter," she leaves "my bracelett of little pomander beads, sett in gold and enamelling, containing fifty-seven beads in number, which usually I ware under my stomacher; which bracelett is above an hundred yeares old, and was given by Philip the Second, King of Spaine, to Mary, Queene of England [and by her] to my greate grandmother, Anne, Countesse of Bedford: and also two little pieces of my father and mother, sett in a tablett of gold, and enamelled with blew; and all those seaven or eight old truncks and all that is within them, being for the most part old things that were my deare and blessed mother's, which truncks commonly stand in my owne chamber or the next unto it." Here, the transmission of goods is a transmission of wealth, of genealogy, of royal connections, but also of memory and of the love of mother for daughter.

It was not only aristocrats who bequeathed their clothing and other possessions with such care. A master's typical legacy to his apprentice was the gift of clothes. Thus Augustine Phillips, an actor and sharer in the King's Men, made bequests in 1605 not only to fellow sharers like Henry Condell and William Shakespeare but also to the boy actor who had trained under him:

Item, I give to Samuel Gilborne, my late apprentice, the sum of forty shillings, and my mouse-colored velvet hose, and a white taffeta doublet, and black taffeta suit, my purple cloak, sword, and dagger, and my bass viol.

The clothes are preserved; they remain. It is the bodies which inhabit them that change.

What are the implications we can draw out from these wills bequeathing clothing? First, clothes have a life of their own: they both are material presences and they encode other material and immaterial presences. In the transfer of clothes, identities are transferred from a mother to a daughter, from an aristocrat to an actor, from a master to an apprentice. Such transfers are often staged by the Renaissance theater in scenes where a servant dresses as his or her master, a lover dresses in the borrowed garments of another lover, a skull inhabits the clothes which have survived it. In *Twelfth Night*, brother is transformed into sister and sister into brother through the costume identified as Cesario/Sebastian. Here we move closer to today's narrower meaning of *transvestism*, one that connotes cross-gendering. But what I want to emphasize is the extent to which the Renaissance theater, and the culture more generally, was fixated upon clothes in and of themselves.

It is only, I believe, in a Cartesian and post-Cartesian paradigm that the life of matter is relegated to the trashcan of the "merely"—the bad fetish which the adult will leave behind as a childish thing so as to pursue the life of the mind. As if consciousness and memory were about minds rather than things, or the real could only reside in the purity of ideas rather than in the permeated impurity of the material. It is about that permeated impurity which Pablo Neruda writes so movingly in *Passions and Impressions*:

It is worth one's while, at certain hours of the day or night, to scrutinize useful objects in repose: wheels that have rolled across long, dusty distances with their enormous load of crops or ore, charcoal sacks, barrels, baskets, the hafts and handles of carpenters' tools . . . Worn surfaces, the wear inflicted by human hands, the sometimes tragic, always pathetic, emanations from these objects give reality a magnetism that should not be scorned.

[Our] nebulous impurity can be perceived in them: the affinity for groups, the use and obsolescence of materials, the mark of a hand or a foot, the constancy of the human presence that permeates every surface.

This is the poetry we are seeking.

In *Landscape for a Good Woman*, an account of her working-class childhood, Carolyn Steedman writes about these permeated surfaces with pain and anger, as well as with love. Pain and anger, because in the erasure of the material is embodied the erasure of her mother's life and her own from the significances of history. "It was with the image of a New Look coat that, in 1950, I made my first attempt to understand and symbolize the content of my mother's desire." But the New Look coat was precisely what Carolyn Steedman's mother could not afford. Her face was pressed against a store window through which she saw, but could not grasp, what she desired:

[My mother] knew where we stood in relation to this world of privilege and possession, had shown me the place long before, in the bare front bedroom where the health visitor spoke haughtily to her. Many women have stood thus, at the window, looking out, their children watching their exclusion: "I remember as it were but yesterday:' wrote Samuel Bamford in 1849, "after one of her visits to the dwelling of that 'fine lady' " (his mother's sister, who had gone up in the world):

> she divested herself of her wet bonnet, her soaked shoes, and changed her dripping outer garments and stood leaning with her elbow on the window sill, her hand upon her cheek, her eyes looking upon vacancy and the tears trickling over her fingers.

What we learned now, in the early 1960s, through the magazines and the anecdotes she brought home, was how the goods of that world might be appropriated, with the cut and fall of a skirt, a good winter coat, with leather shoes, a certain voice; but above all with clothes, the best boundary between you and a cold world.

As Carolyn Steedman puts it, her mother

> wanted things. Politics and cultural criticism can only find trivial the content of her desires, and the world certainly took no notice of them. It is one of the purposes of this book to admit her desire for the things of the earth to political reality and psychological validity.

Clothes, then, are a form of memory, but they are also the stepping-stones upon which one walks away from an unbearable present—the present of childhood, for instance, when one is made over by one's parents. I remember Jen White telling me of a pair of shoes her parents bought her for school: sensible, practical shoes; shoes you wouldn't want to be caught dead in. It is difficult to take seriously enough the agony of such moments: the rage, the anguish, the despair. An all-too-visible identity is there on your feet, mocking you, humiliating you. For you have been made up, made over by another, put into the livery of abject dependency. And it is the ecstasy of release from such livery which Annette so finely captures in her memories of "the first dress which was ever earned by my own exertions." "A feeling of exultation," she calls it.

Many of us sense that feeling most powerfully through its negation. When Sasha Jansen goes to Paris in Jean Rhys's *Good Morning, Midnight* she thinks: "My dress extinguishes me. And then this damned fur coat slung on top of everything else—the last idiocy, the last incongruity." And later, working in a fashionable Parisian dress shop, she fantasizes buying the dress that will set all to rights: "It is a black dress with wide sleeves embroidered in vivid colours—red, green, blue, purple. It is my dress. If I had been wearing it I should never have stammered or been stupid . . . I start . . . longing for it, madly, furiously. If I could get it everything would be different." Sasha never gets the dress.

Allon White died at home, wearing his pajamas, in exactly the posture in which Lucas, the protagonist of the novel he wrote many years before, did. "Lucas was on his left side with his knees drawn up tight and his hands pushed down between his thighs. A blanket was pulled up over his shoulder." A blanket: as Carolyn Steedman puts it, "the best boundary between you and a cold world." But it is hard for us to live with the dead, not knowing what to do with their clothes, in which they still hang, inhabiting their closets and dressers; not knowing how to clothe *them*. Florence Reeve, a Mormon, died on 10 February 1887. Alice Isso writes: "I went to assist in laying her out. On the 11th we made her clothes. We worked all day, then packed her in ice. On the 12th, in the evening we dressed and repacked her." What will *we* do? How will we dress the dead? Not at all? In their most disposable clothes? In their best finery?

When Philip Roth's father died, his brother, searching a dresser, found "a shallow box containing two neatly folded prayer shawls. These he hadn't parted with":

When the mortician, at the house, asked us to pick out a suit for him, I said to my brother, "A suit? He's not going to the office. No, no suit—it's senseless." He should be buried in a shroud, I said, thinking that was how his parents had been buried and how Jews were traditionally buried. But as I said it I wondered if a shroud was any less senseless—he wasn't Orthodox and his sons weren't religious at all—and if it wasn't pretentiously literary and a little hysterically sanctimonious as well . . . But as nobody opposed me and as I hadn't the audacity to say, "Bury him naked," we used the shroud of our ancestors to clothe his corpse.

Then, one night some six weeks later, at around 4:00 A.M. he came in a hooded white shroud to reproach me. He said, "I should have been dressed in a suit. You did the wrong thing." I awakened screaming. All that peered out from the shroud was the displeasure in his dead face. And his only words were a rebuke: I had dressed him for eternity in the wrong clothes.

In the wrong clothes.

A necessary feature of transmission, if it is to take place at all, is that it can go astray: the letter does not arrive, the wrong person inherits, the legacy is an unwanted burden. Yet even in the wildest of transmissions, something always does arrive at its destination. For the last two years or so, my mother and father have increasingly been thinking and talking about the pieces of furniture they treasure, about what will happen to them when they die, about who will want them. Who will take in the desk of my mother's mother? Who will care for it? Who will have the portrait of my father playing the recorder with his brother? At first, I found such questions tiresome. To a good post-Cartesian, it all seemed rather grossly material. But, of course, I was wrong, and they were right. For the question is: who will remember my grandmother, who will give her a place? What space, and whom, will my father inhabit? I know this because I cannot recall Allon White as an idea, but only as the habits through which I inhabit him, through which he inhabits and wears me. I know Allon through the smell of his jacket.

10

COLLECTING THE CONTEMPORARY: "LOVE WILL DECIDE WHAT IS KEPT AND SCIENCE WILL DECIDE HOW IT IS KEPT"

Sue Prichard

Editor's introduction: Museums act as memory banks of the past, which is why Sue Prichard's forward-looking essay on the future of textile collecting is included here. In this essay, written in 2003, Prichard notes the ineffectiveness of many of the traditional categories of collection and definition when applied to contemporary textile art. While the slippery definition of textile art is often celebrated by artists, Prichard works through a number of acquisition examples to explain the challenge institutions, such as the Victoria and Albert Museum, London, face when taking recent textile work into their permanent collections. In looking to the future, she observes the importance virtual archives will have in our understanding of textiles—an observation perhaps slower in its realization than we may have imagined nearly a decade ago.

Eva Hesse once famously said "Life doesn't last, art doesn't last, it doesn't matter."[2] But for museum curators like myself, our role is to preserve and conserve the past, and indeed the present, for future generations. We are, for the most part, publicly funded custodians of diverse and sometimes bizarre collections of material culture, both historic and contemporary. Our remit is to ensure that these collections are held in trust for the nation, so that those who come after us can make sense of the past and try to understand the people, customs, and value systems related to the material held in our institutions. We are accountable for what we collect, and have to justify our acquisitions, both to our colleagues and to the public. This may be relatively easy when dealing with the acquisition of a unique 4,000-year-old terracotta

relief of a Babylonian goddess, but more problematic when you are responsible for acquiring examples of credit cards, both come under the collecting policy of the British Museum; and virtually impossible if you are collecting moist towelettes—such a collection does indeed exist. Wearable technology, nanotechnology, smart, intelligent, and e-textiles are all buzzwords generating much interest both for academic research and commercial industries seeking opportunities for development. Given the plethora of modern design and production, what criteria do we, as curators, use when collecting the contemporary? This raises a series of further questions. When does "the contemporary" start, and how can we ensure that what was once considered relevant and significant does not rapidly become trite

Source: Sue Prichard, "Collecting the Contemporary: 'Love will Decide What Is Kept and Science Will Decide How It Is Kept,'" *Textile* 3, no. 2 (2005) pp. 150–165. Reproduced with permission.

and meaningless? Does "contemporary" necessarily imply cutting-edge multimedia and digital processes? Is the exploration and exploitation of a traditional medium within the context of contemporary cultural discourse less significant than new technology? Does new technology drive or assist in the creative process? Should we cease physically collecting at all and concentrate on "virtual acquisitions?" How do we reconcile traditional museology, with its narrow parameters and genre hierarchy, with twenty-first century artistic practice?

HOW SHOULD MUSEUMS CLASSIFY WORK?

Classification and categorization is at the heart of what museums do; as early as 1565 the "cabinet of curiosity" was already being systematically reordered to make sense of the physical world. Objects were arranged according to their material base and these arrangements were replicated in the creation of specific museum collections and departments (Furniture and Woodwork, Textiles and Dress, Prints, Drawings and Paintings); as our knowledge of the known world expanded, collections were further divided into geographical areas (Indian, Far Eastern). However, in the twenty-first century, artistic practice and new technology is deliberately challenging the traditional categories by which we define our collections. This challenge is exacerbated by the blurring of physical and cultural boundaries that cut across traditional departmental structures and loyalties. Curators therefore need to "think out of the box" and take an active role to ensure that national collections are as representative as possible. The recognition that much contemporary artistic practice does not fit neatly into established material- and technique-based categories has resulted in the establishment of contemporary sections within some museums whose role it is to actively break down those traditional barriers that mitigate against an effective contemporary collecting policy. Whilst this change may have offered the

potential for new ways of working on an organizational level, we still have to address the fundamental issues raised by the expanded context in which some artists choose to work.

Contemporary textile practice is acquiring its own intellectually rigorous language and methodologies. As curators we need to have an understanding of these, be capable of appropriate critical analysis, and able to communicate ideas clearly and accessibly to our public. This may sound straightforward but, for many, the term "textiles" only has resonance if it refers to traditional materials and techniques. The following example raises a number of issues regarding the categorization of contemporary textiles, as well as demonstrating the ways in which many engaged in the making of contemporary textiles explore and question its meaning and histories. In 2004, the Department of Furniture, Textiles and Fashion at the Victoria and Albert Museum (V&A) acquired a work by Caroline Bartlett called "Bodies of Knowledge Volume 5: Arbiters of Taste" (T.154-2004 . . .),[3] a complex arrangement of a 1934 encyclopedia, printed silk crepeline, pins and embroidery hoops. First exhibited in *Textiles in Context*, the fortieth anniversary exhibition of the 62 Group of Textile Artists,[4] "Bodies of Knowledge" explored the relationship between "text" and "textiles," making reference to the V&A as an "encyclopaedia of treasures." The artist elucidates this analogy thus: "like encyclopaedias, content and presentation reflect governing ideologies and hierarchies of taste, demonstrating the way in which society and perception change over time."[5] Bartlett is an experienced textile designer and printer who exhibits internationally, drawing inspiration from architectural elements, myths, legends, and elements of various cultures around the world. She is interested in the ways in which textile processes play a role in our concepts of organization, structure, and community. Contextual framework is of primary importance to her work, as evidenced by her public commissions, and in this she shares some of the aesthetic resonance often implicit in the work of artists such as Cornelia Parker (whose flattened brass-band installation "Breathless" can be seen in the V&A's British Galleries). Bartlett is also interested in language and the written word as systems of knowledge central to the Western view of the world that give exclusive access to those able to decode it. In 1999/2000 she participated in a touring exhibition, *The Artist's Journey*, which explored the ways in which artists refer to, and are influenced by, cultural and historical artifacts and information. The brief was to produce new work through researching the lives of Frederic, Lord Leighton, the Victorian painter and sculptor (1830–96) and Sir Richard Burton, explorer and Orientalist (1821–90), examining their travels, houses, personal experiences, collections, and their role in Victorian society. Bartlett created "On the Shelves of Memory,"

which referenced systems of collecting and preserving, ideas of presence and absence, and the selective process of representing an individual to the public. The work contained 492 archival labels, each bearing detailed information of individual items sold by the auctioneers, Christie's, in 1896, which were suspended in front of fragments of objects cast from fabric, and organized as though in a museum display.

So how should we categorize Bartlett's work—textiles, textile art, art installation, text? Which V&A collection should acquire her work: Furniture, Textiles and Fashion; Word and Image; Sculpture? This issue was raised recently at an open discussion to launch *Inside Out: Commissions for the City, for the Country*, an exhibition organized in 2004 by Contemporary Applied Art,

Figure 10.1. Caroline Bartlett, *Bodies of Knowledge, Volume 5: Arbiters of Taste*, 2002. Materials: 1934 encyclopedia, embroidery hoops, silk crepeline, wadding, pins. Techniques: Silk screen print, stitch. Size: 34 x 84 x 5 cm. Photographer: Michael Wickes.

in London. Sharon Elphick, who has rejected the limitations of the commercial design studio to create dynamic photographic montages of the urban landscape, was asked whether she still considered herself to be a textile designer. Her response—"I don't care what you call me, I just want someone to collect my work"—may be pragmatic, but for museum curators, working within the limitations of current museological practice, it is not so simple.

CULTURAL CONVERGENCE

The process of cross-discipline artistic practice may challenge traditional collection boundaries, but is further complicated by the process of cross-cultural fertilization or cultural intermingling. Cultural difference has now given way to cultural convergence, tearing down fixed boundaries: territorial, cultural, and creative; it is now no longer viable to define an artist by their country of origin. The following example illustrates this point. In 2004, the Department of Furniture, Textiles and Fashion was approached by the Far Eastern Department of the V&A with a donation of a bamboo-dyed silk quilted hammock (T.1–2004) and quilted cushion (T.2–2004), made from nylon. The artist, Yoshiko Jinzenji, lives in Kyoto but since 1989 has based her studio in Bali. She began quilting in the 1970s, after discovering quilts made by North America's Mennonite and Amish communities. She also takes inspiration from the Indonesian "selendang," a traditional shawl, dyed with natural tropical dyes. Jinzenji combines antique fabrics collected from around the world with innovative synthetics, such as the black metallic cloth created by Junichi Arai.

Jinzenji is a superb natural dyer and often makes quilts from fabric or fiber she colors herself, including very subtle and rich bamboo-dyed silk. In the field of natural dyes, white is a tremendously difficult technical and creative feat, and Jinzenji experimented with all the plants, roots, and trees around her studio before finally hitting upon the idea of trying bamboo.

Initially she believed she had failed, as the fabric emerged from the boiled bamboo solution a dull, light brown. But it was transformed into shimmering white only when hung in the direct Bali sunlight. The dye is equally successful when applied to nylon filament, creating a flesh-colored tone. Jinzenji likens the bamboo-dyed white to the fusuma and shji sliding doors used to separate Japanese-style rooms, as well as the tradition of sumi ink drawing and calligraphy, and even the white sand of Zen gardens. When interviewed, she said that "a hammock always seems to me like the height of luxury, and particularly so when made with white quilted silk."[6] Strangely perhaps, it is not designed to hold body weight, though Jinzenji suggests it could be used in a child's room to hold a collection of stuffed animals or cushions, or at Christmas time, as a unique way of displaying gift-wrapped presents.

In choosing to use innovative synthetics at times, and at others to weave and dye her own fabric, Jinzenji has set a new aesthetic standard as a quilt-maker and maker of cloth. Her experiments with traditions and techniques reflect and challenge the concepts of globalization, ethnicity, and the blurring of cultural boundaries and influences, whilst highlighting her concern with the loss of traditional skills and individuality through increasing mass production of high-quality goods. Her choice of the Far Eastern Department through which to offer her donation was logical and based on geography; however, her use of a traditional Western technique placed her within the collecting policy of the Department of Furniture, Textiles and Fashion.

Another interesting example of cross-cultural collaboration is the British design duo Bentley and Spens' partnership with the Japanese company, Kawashima Textile Manufacturers. Originally Kawashima approached the Far Eastern Department of the V&A with the donation of their 2002 Yukata Collection (T.11–14-2004 . . .), but was referred to the Department of Furniture, Textiles and Fashion because the designers were British. Kim Bentley and Sally Spens design and produce one-off hand-stencilled and painted interior furnishings and screen-printed fabric. Their brightly colored, bold designs, combining traditional fabric painting and printing with increasingly exotic patterns, appealed to the Japanese love of tradition and modernism. In 2002, the designers collaborated with Kawashima to produce a range of textiles and garments for the Japanese market. In the latter half of the 1980s, the Yukata (Summer-kimono) began to make a comeback as casual summer wear amongst young Japanese women. Traditional versions were indigo and white, and, whilst today there are no restrictions on the use of color, the Yukata has not witnessed any great variation in the basic design. The overwhelming majority employ some sort of traditional pattern such as a flower design or water pattern, with the odd ice-cream cone or goldfish. The range of fabrics created by Bentley and Spens for the Japanese market has taken the traditional roots of the Yukata and embodied it with a chic and playful image, in a way that is not entirely different from Western clothing. In 2003, Bentley and Spens produced a second collection, refining their designs, simplifying pattern and motif in line with the demands of Yukata production.

Cultures only survive through self-transformation, and museum collections must reflect these transformations in order to preserve their vitality. By challenging the *status quo* of traditional demarcations, curators are able to develop new insights into their collections. Making connections between the historic and the contemporary is just as important as focusing on new developments, but we must also be wary of the ways in which we represent artists and makers in our collections—as attempts to articulate cultural identity can create as many problems as they solve. Traditionally, museums have disseminated a narrative or world view through the relationships they create between the objects they put on display. This narrative is further validated by the way in which these objects are interpreted for public consumption. In the nineteenth century, the rules of engagement with non-Western art were based on the values enshrined and safeguarded by the custodians of ethnographic collections: an object was valued because of its "purity," its ability to remain uncontaminated by the excesses of a decadent Europe. Today, globalization and innovation in communications technology has accelerated the pace of change; geographic and cultural boundaries constantly clash, combine, disintegrate, and reform. Cultural appropriation is now no longer the preserve of the West, as the example of Yoshiko Jinzenji illustrates. The concept of "the other" in contemporary society is constantly being challenged, and identities no longer presuppose continuous cultural traditions. In *Second Generation Sikhs*[7] Amrit Kaur Singh describes the cultural heritage that informs her own and her twin sister's artistic practice, citing "a number of perspectives that related not only to how we see ourselves but also to how other people have come to perceive us—as Indians, Sikhs, twins *and* artists" (Amrit's italics). Artists may indeed create works of art that are imbedded in the cultural context from which they have emerged, drawing on motifs found in indigenous cultures, reinventing them to create new works of art, but we need to continually challenge the contexts in which they will be seen and received.

Shirazeh Houshiary, nominated for the Turner Prize in 1994, was born in Iran and studied at Chelsea School of Art. She works with a range of materials and techniques, including drawing and print-making. The acquisition of a suite of etchings by the British Museum in 1995 was the result of a successful collaboration between the Department of Prints and Drawings, and what was then the Department of Oriental Antiquities. Houshiary's work is rooted in the mysticism of Islamic culture, but the choice of the Sir John Addis Islamic Gallery in which to display the suite created some tension between the museum and the artist. It was clear that Houshiary felt that her work would be better placed in the neutral environment of a prints and drawings gallery, rather than within the cultural context of a gallery devoted to the work of Islamic artists.[8] The British Museum has addressed the issue of cross-cultural and cross-discipline contemporary artistic practice by the creation of their electronic tour "Collecting the Modern World." The site is organized geographically, "reflecting the places of origin of the artists/producers, the regions to which they owe their primary cultural allegiance, or those where they have chosen to make their careers."[9] As curators, we need to exploit new technology to help us redefine our changing world, and to create new opportunities for learning.

HOW CAN COLLECTIONS MAKE EFFECTIVE USE OF ELECTRONIC MEDIA?

A museum should and must amount to more than just an accumulation of material, it should also function as a knowledge base and provide inspiration. Online learning can help us in our quest to make cultural connections, both within our own collections and with collections regionally, nationally, and internationally. New technology can also help us to provide increased public access to objects not on display, providing a "gateway" to information and expertise concerning our collections. The Constance Howard Resource and Research Centre in Textiles (CHRRCT), at Goldsmiths, University of London, combines a rich and diverse textile collection with an archive containing slides, teaching notes, and individual interviews with artists, providing a comprehensive account of the pioneering history of textiles at the college. A new project to put records from the slide collection and material archive online will facilitate access to both the material collection and the CHRRCT itself.

In 2003/4, over four million visits were made to the V&A's website, including the On-Line Museum. This surpassed the numbers physically visiting South Kensington, proving just how successful a tool the Web is for reaching audiences. Web-based projects can also help us to collect, document, and interpret those aspects of contemporary art and design practice based on the

transitory. The V&A's hugely successful "Fashion in Motion" series showcases established and emerging talent in a series of catwalk shows; by videoing the collections and interviewing the designers, we not only capture the philosophy behind the design process, but also "acquire" the event. In 1999, the Contemporary Team at the V&A was formed with the specific remit not to acquire objects, but rather to present the very best of contemporary art and design in a series of exhibitions, events, site-specific installations, and performances. Specifically targeted at a young and style conscious audience, it also brings contemporary art and design to audiences that might not otherwise experience it through reminiscence projects and "Days of Record," a series of events cataloguing applied and decorative arts in relation to the body. Past "Days of Record" have included Tattoo, April 2000; Nails, Weaves and Naturals, focusing on the hairstyles and nail art of Black British and Afro-Caribbean communities, May 2001; and the Notting Hill Carnival, August 2003. Given our limited storage resources, virtual collecting also offers real benefits in terms of ensuring that the developments in textile art and the overlap with fine art, soft sculpture, and fashion are represented in collections for the future, and are not bound by rigid collecting policies or conservation issues. Complex or large-scale installations, such as Helen Storey's "Primitive Streak" (ICA, London, 1997); "Textural Space: Contemporary Japanese Textile Art" (Whitworth Art Gallery, Manchester, 2001); or Do-Ho Suh's enormous diaphanous silk and nylon "interiors" (Serpentine Gallery, London 2002), could be successfully "acquired" and "displayed" with minimum resources.

New developments in the field of haptic technology point to even greater access to our collections, via a tactile interface that allows visitors to touch, stroke, and handle the objects they see on a computer screen. The days of the "Do Not Touch" signs are truly numbered, as individuals are able to feel and manipulate the texture of fabric and clothing, and artists are given new insights into collections. Haptic technology has already created a virtual exhibition at the British Library. "Turning the Pages" is an interactive program that allows visitors to virtually turn the pages of historic manuscripts in a realistic way, whilst keeping the original safely under glass. In April 2004, over 3,000 visitors a day viewed the selected volumes, including the Lindisfarne Gospels.[10] In February 2004, the UK Engineering and Science Research Council put out a call for proposals to establish a new research network centered around haptic technologies, interactive textiles, and haptic visuality. If successful, the network—comprising artists, engineers, computer scientists, museologists, and psychologists—would seek to examine the role of technology and touch within the area of interactive textiles from several different perspectives.

Whilst there is no doubt that new developments in technology can benefit curators and collections, are we in danger of replacing what was once defined as the fetishization of the object, with the fetishization of new technology? As the "temple-like architecture" of museums is deconstructed and remodeled, curators increasingly find themselves worshiping at the altar of the computer, driven by the need to create even more exciting ways in which to entice the public into cyberspace—the one area where funding is readily available. In "Collecting the Contemporary,"[11] Gil Saunders (2003) argues for the "primacy of the object over the digital surrogate," identifying that what makes a museum unique is its collection of objects. We need to use new technology to enhance our collection of objects, rather than replace them, and to be active in developing the methodology for using the web as a vehicle for collecting the contemporary, creating strict selection criteria that can be applied over predetermined periods of time. This will ensure that a representative set of objects can be documented for museum collections that truly reflects successful developments in the area of rapidly evolving technologies.

COLLECTING THE EPHEMERAL

In the UK, museum curators are bound by the ethical guidelines prepared by their professional body, the Museums Association, which state that we cannot ethically collect items for which the museum cannot provide long-term care and access. These guidelines provide flexible advice, but the basic principles still emphasize the long-term preservation and conservation of objects for the future. However, much contemporary art made and collected in the 1960s and 1970s, for example, when artists increasingly experimented with new materials and processes, has turned out to be very fragile. Many of the works in the Eva Hesse retrospective exhibition held at Tate Modern, London, in 2003 are now so fragile that they will never be displayed again. Whilst we may successfully argue that the Web provides the solution to such problematic conservation and collection management issues, we are still in the business of collecting material objects and face the technical and ethical challenge of how to preserve ephemeral or unstable artworks. Many contemporary artists, like Hesse, are prepared to accept the risk that the materials they deliberately choose to use will deteriorate rapidly, taking a similar view to that of Tracey Emin: "If I wanted it to last, I would make it from something else."[12] As curators we need to accept the physical limitations of each work of art, working closely not only with colleagues in our conservation departments, but with artist/makers to document and record processes.

Marielle Baylis created "Bed of Roses," a knitted wool and latex floor piece, for her final degree show in 2002 and exhibited at Decorex, the annual interior-design trade fair, held the same year. Inspired by her love of nature and her interest in domestic interiors, "Bed of Roses" was originally designed as a product for the bathroom; however, the artist was also aware of its potential as an artwork. Baylis is very fond of knitted textiles within the home and seeks to push the boundaries of how these are traditionally perceived, creating quirky and imaginative knitted toparies and hedges. "Bed of Roses" was offered to the V&A, where it was examined by the polymer scientist in the Science Conservation Department. Analysis of the materials involved revealed that the latex would degrade reasonably fast (possibly within ten years) and would become quite sticky and yellow. The conclusion of the report suggested that this degradation could cause damage to neighboring objects or cause storage problems. The solution to the problem was resolved by the Department of Furniture, Textiles and Fashion in consultation with the artist, agreeing to accept a small sample of the work, which could be easily stored and which could be used for display, study, and research purposes.

MERGING TECHNOLOGY WITH TRADITIONAL TECHNIQUES

The revival of interest in traditional techniques among young artists and designers challenges the perception that contemporary collecting is focused only on the acquisition of technologically advanced fabrics or new media. In reality, many artists use technology to assist, rather than drive, the creative process. Debbie Stack, a textile designer, who specializes in computer embroidery, believes the contemporary component provided by technology gives an additional creative edge to her work—it is the "accidents that happen during the production process that deliver the most rewarding results."[13] Gemma Burgess, who was selected as one of the young Graduate Designers of Texprint 2002, also marries traditional techniques with computer technologies, and in 2004 the V&A acquired a sample of her work for the textile collection (T.3-2004). Texprint is a nonprofit-making registered charity whose aim is to identify, select, and launch the most innovative textile design graduates of British colleges to the international textile industry. Burgess was also selected to show at New Designers 2002, her work featured in international textiles magazines, and her designs selected by both fashion

and interior-design buyers. At the time of writing she is continuing her studies at the Royal College of Art in London, and is interested in exploring new relationships and arrangements for overlaying pattern, translating paperwork onto fabric, and experimenting with different processes—screen-printing, devoré, the use of digital technology, and the diverse special effects that are possible using techniques like flocking, bonding, and embossing. She is fascinated by what happens when these techniques are combined, and by the diverse tactile qualities that can be produced.

Similarly, Kirsty McDougall is interested in bringing both craft and commercial/industrial techniques to a different audience, which she has done through her participation in the knitting circle "Cast Off." Cast Off is a knitting club for girls and boys, women and men, which promotes handicrafts as a fashionable and constructive pastime. The club meets in nightclubs, bars, cafés, shops, festivals, and on public transport, and aims to incorporate an element of youth culture in traditional craft. McDougall exhibited at Texprint 2002 along with Gemma Burgess, and won the prize for weaving. But McDougall is not bound by traditional structural weaving, as is evident in her use of words such as "jumbled" and "vandalised" to describe her experimentations, and she also works in the medium of embroidery and print, exploring the boundaries between textiles and fashion. She takes her influence from areas as diverse as traditionally woven tweeds, dogtooths, and flock wallpaper found in English pubs, which she recontextualizes and redefines in a witty and subversive way. In 2004, the V&A acquired a rag-rug sample (T.4-2004), which illustrates McDougall's experimentation with technique, in which she weaves rather than hooks the fabric. It illustrates her interest in recycling, for she often uses charity-shop bargains and found objects, rich sensual fabrics with lurid market-stall finds—a fusion of country casuals and the television character Pat Butcher from the UK soap opera *EastEnders*. Her interest in recycling moves beyond the objects themselves, exploring the recycling of patterns and ideas, pop art and disposable imagery. When interviewed, she explained "weaving is the physical manifestation of my ideas, fabric the messenger."[13] At the Texprint prizes held in Paris in 2002, Ronald Wesibrod of the Swiss Company Weisbrod-Zuerrer AG, who presented the awards, observed that the European textile industry could not continue to exist without maintaining a high standard of innovation and creativity, and that this was only possible if companies could constantly recruit new talent.

COLLECTING WEARABLE TECHNOLOGY AND SMART FABRICS

So what of wearable technology and smart fabrics—do they have a place in our collections? Again, a series of questions is raised. Should we be collecting cameras that can be worn as jewelry, or shawls with flexible communication screens made of glass-fiber fabric? Which collection should acquire biomedical clothing for personal healthcare—fashion, science or medicine? How innovative and cutting edge can a designer be without understanding the technical aspects of the materials at their disposal? A one-day symposium called "When is the Future" was hosted by the Crafts Council in October 2003 to discuss the complicated relationship between woven-textile designers and industry. It focused on the need for different disciplines to collaborate together to create a product that is not only scientifically innovative, but is well designed and, indeed, commercial. At the symposium Philippa Wagner, Senior Design Consultant at Philips Design, made it clear that the challenge for their product team—which includes fashion and textile designers working alongside electronic and software engineers—was to integrate electronics into fashionable clothes that people wanted to wear. In a similar vein, DuPont and Courtaulds are researching and producing innovative textiles, such as conductive fibers, which can be embroidered. The message was clear: new technology only becomes really interesting when it features

a synergy between design, research, development, art, and science.

The V&A continues to collect the best of textile design with new technologies. The collection has particularly fine examples from the Nuno Corporation, a Japanese company that uses traditional fibers and techniques, as well as the most sophisticated synthetics and technology. Nuno was founded in 1984, and is Japanese for "fabric." The company is well known internationally for its ability to create exciting new fibers and weaves, drawing on traditional Japanese aesthetics and creative processes, and combining these with dynamic technological processes. Industrial by-products ordinarily discarded, such as packing material and splatter plating used by the Japanese car industry, have all inspired Nuno designers. "Jellyfish" (T.122-1998 . . .) is made from an industrial vinyl polychloride fabric, developed primarily for seat covers in the motor vehicle manufacturing industry, and has a preset 50% heat-shrinkage ratio. To create "Jellyfish," Nuno has layered and partially affixed the fabric onto a polyester organdy using a special adhesive, screen-printed in a checkerboard pattern. The fabric is subjected to flash heat-treatment that causes the organdy to shrivel where adhered. Being a thermoplastic fabric, it retains the resulting crinkles even after the vinyl polychloride is peeled away. Another piece, "Pack Ice" (T.121-1998), is created from strapping tape, a common material made of flat rayon. It is very easy to tear horizontally but more difficult to tear vertically. In "Pack Ice" the rayon threads are tightly woven into large squares on a background of silk organdies. These squares are connected by unwoven rayon threads that float between the layers of the background material, suggesting spume among icebergs. Nuno is well known for its innovation, yet despite the focus on new technology, the company also continues to foster a new generation of weavers who employ traditional techniques and natural fibers, demonstrating their belief in the coexistence of contemporary and traditional technologies and techniques.

In 2001 the V&A acquired "Wandering Lines Red" (T.486-2001 . . .), a length of handwoven silk, nylon, and polyester monofilament that becomes phosphorescent under light. It was made by Sophie Roet, one of a small group of contemporary designers/weavers producing light-sensitive textiles. Roet says that she has "always been interested in breaking the normal rules of weave structure—creating movement within straight warp and weft thread"[14] and working with phosphorescent yarns in order to charge the textiles with glowing light. In 2000, Roet collaborated with C5 Interglas, via HITEC LOTEC, a lottery-funded organization encouraging joint working projects between industry (HITEC), and designer/craftworkers (LOTEC) to create aluminum-bonded textiles for fashion. C5 Interglas produces highly technical textiles for commercial vehicles, sports equipment, the aircraft industry, and for space flight. One of the processes they offer is bonding glass-fiber textiles to aluminum sheeting for high-quality metal building insulation facings. Roet was interested in exploring the sculptural quality produced by combining delicate, fragile textiles and the metallic bonding process that could hold its shape without assistance "to crumble a silk organza textile (so that) it remains in its tightly crumpled state."[15] In January 2002, the V&A featured Roet's "The Aluminium Bonded Red Dress" in the front entrance display of the museum, showing what we believe to be part of the most imaginative and innovative range of technologically aware textiles produced to date in the twenty-first century.

More recently, in 2004, the V&A's *Brilliant* exhibition provided a unique opportunity to acquire a range of new lighting forms made from various materials, technologies, and visual effects. Although acquisitions were distributed throughout the museum's collections according to "traditional" material type, so that "The Ingo Maurer LED Bench and Bulb" were proposed for the glass gallery, while two specific cases of textile artists using light were proposed for the Contemporary Textile Collection, the exhibition nevertheless provided a base from which to "cherry-pick" the very best of contemporary lighting design. The Contemporary Textile Collection finally acquired "Digital Dawn" (T.155-2004), an electroluminescent and silk blind designed by Rachel Wingfield, which functions as a traditional window blind that grows in luminosity in response to its surroundings. Manufactured by Elumin8, electroluminescent technology involves applying electricity to copper dipped in zinc sulfate ink, which then emits light. This is applied using a silk-screen process to an indium/tin-oxide splattered substrate. This substrate is flexible and can be fabricated into complex shapes. Eluminescent systems have been used primarily for outdoor media-related installations (most notably the launch of the *Love Actually* DVD, where a giant red heart adorned the sides of London buses and glowed on and off as the vehicles traveled through the city). However, "Digital Dawn" moves beyond the novelty value of the technology, engaging with the problems associated with sufferers of seasonal affective disorder (SAD), by providing a constant and responsive source of light. The tension between technology and the natural world is further explored by Wingfield's choice of pattern—organic plant forms that "grow" and evolve on the blind's surface, digitally emulating the process of photosynthesis—proving that functionality and aesthetics do not have to be mutually exclusive. "Digital Dawn" was first launched at 100% Design, where Wingfield, under the design tag "loop," was shortlisted for best newcomer 2003.

FINAL THOUGHTS

So what of the future? The V&A holds one of the most important textile collections in the world. From its foundation in the middle of the nineteenth century, the museum has always sought to include the very best of contemporary textile art and manufacture in its collections, and this policy continues to be vigorously pursued. In 2003, a new display "Recent Acquisitions 1992–2002: A Decade of Collecting Textiles" illustrated the eclectic range of contemporary objects in the collection, juxtaposing a variety of materials and textiles, and showing examples of new developments in textile design and production. The display space was deliberately chosen in close proximity to the textile study collection, to illustrate the strong tradition of textile design and production, whilst embracing and exploring the opportunities offered by new materials and technology. A commitment to making a contemporary collection that has meaning for us today will not only form a bridge between the historic collection and the present, but will also ensure the legacy of a dynamic collection for the future. Imposing limits on our contemporary collection will limit our potential to interest our audience. Realistically, the acquisition of some categories of objects, particularly those associated with new technology, are constrained by high costs and have subsequent storage and conservation issues. However, rather than limiting our collecting policies, I believe the issues involved in collecting the contemporary create new and exciting opportunities for curators to collaborate and work together. Far from replacing the hand, new technology is helping the creative process branch out in new directions, and as curators we need to learn from artists and makers. Harnessing new technology will help to build our collections, make them more accessible, and contribute to contemporary artistic discourse. Collections do not necessarily have to be all in one place, and virtual collecting offers us the ability to collect both small-scale experimental work and large-scale installations. As curators, we have yet to resolve many of the issues involved in building a contemporary collection, but I believe passionately that our role is to support both innovation and experimentation, and to continue to safeguard our collections, physical and virtual. The future, after all, is in our hands.

NOTES

1. David Hockey, quoted verbally at a Crafts Council Curator's Day "Working with the Ephemeral," October 22, 2001 by Mary Brookes, Senior Lecturer, Textile Conservation, University of Southampton, UK.

2. Quoted in *Tate Modern Introduction to Eva Hesse*, November 13 2002–March 9 2003.

3. All objects acquired by the V&A are assigned a museum number. The prefix indicates the collection that originally acquires the object— "T" indicates that it has been acquired by the Textiles and Fashion section. The number is the unique, sequential number assigned independently within each collection. Numbers start at "1" at the beginning of each calendar year—154 indicates that "Bodies of Knowledge" was the 154th object to be acquired. The year indicates the year of acquisition of an object by a collection.

4. *Textiles in Context* at the V&A, September 5 2002–January 5 2003.

5. Artist's exhibition submission statement, August 2002.

6. Interviewed by the author, August 26 2003.

7. *Second Generation Sikhs*, broadcast August 1 2004, transcript www.bbc.uk/religion/pro.

8. Francis Carey, "Elective Affinities: Collecting Contemporary Culture in the British Musem," p. 4. Paper given at Collecting Now, joint seminar between The British Museum and Kingston University, March 8 2003.

9. www.thebritishmuseum.ac.uk.

10. www.bl.uk/collections/treasures/digitisation.

11. This statement was quoted verbally at a Crafts Council Curator's Day "Working with the Ephemeral," October 22 2001 by Mary Brookes, Senior Lecturer, Textile Conservation, University of Southampton, UK.

12. Debbie Stack interviewed in *Marmalade: The Creative Spread* 2004(2): 36.

13. Interviewed by the author, March 2003.

14. Artist's acquisition statement, 2001.

15. Artist's exhibition statement, January 2002.

REFERENCE

Saunders, Gil. 2003. "Collecting the Contemporary." *Art Libraries Journal* 28(4): 5–11.

11

THE PARODY OF THE MOTLEY CADAVER: DISPLAYING THE FUNERAL OF FASHION

Robyn Healy

Editor's introduction: The mortality of cloth—the fact that the textile has a life span—is something of a conundrum for the curators and conservators tasked with protecting and prolonging the life of cloth. Here, Robyn Healy, associate professor at RMIT University in Melbourne, Australia, takes our typical desire to preserve and extend this life and turns it upside down. In place of preservation, she proposes a "poetics of decay . . . to question the politics of appearance and the experience of fashion." In place of the pristine and collectable, the memory of cloth and the traces of use and damage this inevitably entails are offered up as a far more engaging record of our material culture. Through questioning the condition of the textile deemed worthy of exhibition, collection, and display, Healy brings the value system underlying the museum collection itself into doubt: "The continuing breakdown creates a disorder that cannot be contained—one that symbolically challenges the authority of the museum itself."

THE NATURE OF FASHION

For fashion was never anything other than the parody of the motley cadaver, provocation of death through the woman, and bitter colloquy with decay whispered between shrill bursts of mechanical laughter. That is fashion. And that is why she changes so quickly; she titillates death and is already something different, something new, as he casts about to crush her . . . (Benjamin, 2004)

Benjamin's caustic depiction of fashion[1] opens this discourse, to consider the physical nature of things, the idea of renewal, the object of desire, absence and presence; addressing the radical changes and irreversible transformations that occur in the inevitable funeral of fashion. Referencing the satirical work of Leopardi, Benjamin brings forth sisters Fashion and Death, mythically related through their mother Decay. In the original dialogue their similarities are clearly laid out, the sisters are united through their family trait of destruction and their innate ability to change the world (Leopardi, 1983). In this potent yet rather outrageous association, fashion plays forever with death, her continuing attraction presenting the 'new' and 'the very latest' stylish offerings relying on her ephemeral nature and ensuing speedy

Source: Robyn Healy, "The Parody of the Motley Cadaver: Displaying the Funeral of Fashion," *Design Journal* 11, no. 3 (2008) pp. 255–268. Reproduced with permission.

death. The seduction of fashion's original appeal is rapidly disfigured into a decayed and rotting corpse.

This paper considers the ephemeral, fugitive nature of fashion in the context of documenting and presenting the history of design. Garments breaking down physically defy their original functions of wearability, an ideal image of attractiveness, overt display, commodity value and representation of the latest style. Attempting to reconsider the philosophical, political, aesthetic and commercial values placed on fashion and investigate how these readings impact on the placement of fashion in the museum, this paper gives pause for reflection about the experience of clothing when it is no longer 'fashionable' or pristine.[2]

EXHIBITING FASHION IN PUBLIC INSTITUTIONS

The act of collecting, selecting, preserving and in turn displaying fashion, within the context of a public collection, provides a form of immortality for the 'dated'. Extending the ephemeral, confronts the issues about the very nature of fashion, the design ideas that relate to a time and place. However, if fashion exhibitions can only offer a random sampling of the best condition garments unfortunately the most used and perhaps the most successful are then discarded due to a lack of newness. These examples are then destined to languish in storage, awaiting conservation, or perhaps remain in permanent incarceration, and are therefore totally dismissed, never seen. In calling forth these absent histories, it is my intention to invite an alternate view, a transgression to invoke the poetics of decay, the vicissitudes of transformation, the remnants of destruction into the display spaces of a public museum, to question the politics of appearance and the experience of fashion.

Over the past decade the fashion exhibition has become a major cultural phenomenon.

Popularity generated through a mixture of slick marketing, extensive conservation, styling and theatrical and multimedia effects, producing an extraordinary experience, well-attended exhibitions making substantial revenue for museums worldwide.[3] Here the missing pieces are described or replaced, petticoats are remade, clothes are padded and preened, accessories are assembled and, to further create a sense of completeness, garments are dressed on mannequins. However, the gloss and a constructed or imposed newness placed on objects to look good in an exhibition understandably bestows on these garments a seductive veneer and eventually provides a bland offering where everything starts to look the same. The expectation of the museum experience to resurrect fashion is articulated through the continual reliance and identification with a body, to animate the garment and perhaps recall a living memory. The cabinet of curiosities 'a storehouse of knowledge' that formed the basic model for the Museum, where a range of exotic objects were collected in a purpose-built cabinet, rarely included clothing. Instead early references to accumulations of fashion are listed in household inventories, assets that were named and housed in the Wardrobe (Roche, 1994). However the clothing display vernacular is based around the glass showcase and mannequin form, rather than the storage chest, thereby appropriating devices deriving from a retail experience— the world of trade fairs, the dressmaking atelier and the department store. Interestingly the waxworks exhibition provided an influential model, establishing a tableaux format, and defining fashion as an essential temporal mechanism. The waxworks spectacle democratized celebrity culture, introducing effigies based upon the accurate likeness of dignitaries and famous people. These figures were appropriately dressed in sophisticated replica clothing and accoutrements, or in many cases original historical pieces were procured to offer a potent degree of authenticity, and consequently invite a popular experience of time and place (Pilbeam, 2003).[4]

As fashion acts as 'an expression of the times', 'measuring the essence of its time', 'capturing the spirit' and perhaps in this most simplistic form, museum collections provide a sequential timeline by decade or century. However, the adoption of mannequins for the display of clothes and accessories introduces a supplementary element that can be disturbing or inappropriate. Some museums resist the temptation to dress-up mannequins with make-up and wigs in an attempt to evoke another era and, as a result, select the simple 'headless' and 'limbless' tailor's form to fill in the costume void. The use of mannequins introduces a further debate about clothing and the relationship to the body and the methods employed to simulate this representation.

EPHEMERAL

Following a Derridean approach, this paper studies the transformational possibilities offered by proposing a parallel exhibition dialogue and witness experience, which examines the detritus and the absent body. This approach would perhaps create a path leading away from the traditional vista of the museum spectacle or the department store gaze. Within this context the deterioration of a garment is read outside the conservation parameters. The radical and irreversible changes that occur through decay propose a framework to consider design and the culture of dress. The continuing breakdown creates a disorder that cannot be contained—one that symbolically challenges the authority of the museum itself.

Standard museological practice selects and parades only the best, curators abiding to strict collection briefs and ethical guidelines.[5] Works in the best condition are preferred, pieces that have survived ravages of time, whims in fashionable taste, are periodically exhibited in a place where the endless process of decay is retarded, where time on display is restricted and lights are turned down low. Yet, even in this environment, the ageing process and the act of disintegration continues, which destroys the original appearance; the ideal new image, the aura of attractiveness progressively fades, dies and morphs into something else. In a museum, condition reports document this progress through a language of vulnerability and loss, with descriptions of shattered silk, degraded fibres, disfiguring stains and insect attacks. When discussing museum collections and the ephemeral nature and vulnerability of the actual fashion objects, it is necessary to address the perhaps obvious questions of selection and survival—'What is preserved and what can be preserved' (Roche, 1994) and the rather random and incomplete selection of items that have survived (Blau, 1999). The sampling of clothes that have somehow survived and are selected for a museum provide only a hint of dressing complexities, the fashionable layering of these confections or their arrangement, with the common occurrence of various pieces missing. Unfortunately the most used, the most loved, are worn out, sometimes discarded, lost forever, leaving only the remains.

> For clothes are so much part of our living, moving selves that, frozen on display in the mausoleums of culture, they hint at something only half understood, sinister, threatening; the atrophy of the body, and the evanescence of life . . . Clothes without a wearer, whether on a second-hand stall, in a glass case, or merely a lover's garments strewn on the floor, can affect us unpleasantly, as if a snake had shed its skin. (Wilson 1985)

Clothing can cause apprehension, which is not experienced through the viewing of other artefacts. In the context of a museum the absent body provides quite different readings from fashionable dress observed worn on the streets, marketed in the media, merchandised in a shop, or hung in a private wardrobe. In a public setting like an exhibition where wearing is no longer the rationale, and clothes are no longer a dressed composition, we are left with something else, an abstraction, an object haunted, and the threat of transformation. Consequently this state of 'absented presence' is where we examine the meaning of what is not represented, the conditions of representation itself (Heidegger, 2004).

CLOTHING METAPHORS

Fashion's incremental and inevitable decay, the concomitant changing aesthetics of appearance brought on by time and use, is something that is charged with potent symbolism. Throughout history clothing is metaphorically appropriated, Lehmann (2000) noted throughout the 19th-century clothing represented 'beauty, open or repressed sexuality, social aspiration, or moral deviation'. Wilson (2004) identifies fashion's 'magical dimension', the extraordinary element that ignites the imagination, the irrational and the extreme elements that inspired the Surrealists to translate clothing in a metaphoric way. While clothing representing an allegory for humanity is drawn from the characteristics associated with masquerade or camouflage, such as the implication of a deception, a covering up, the secretive, the veil and multiple layers of meaning (Hollander, 1993). Another source for poetic inspiration is distilled from the clothing industry itself, drawing from the economic and social structures including the circulation of new clothes to the second hand clothing trade and the collection of rags, imparting a poignant imagery that documents a trail running from luxury to 'abject misery' (Roche, 1994). The rag picker is discussed by Benjamin (1989), to epitomise the motif of the down trodden yet picturesque scavenger, who wandered the streets seeking out materials for recycling and revival, picking through the cultural detritus left behind by capitalist societies. Marx employed the clothing metaphor in his theory of commodity fetishism and the hieroglyph of value. The story of the linen seller and the coat wearer illustrates the veneration which industrial society has towards the product, over the alienation of the worker who laboured over its production (Roche, 1994).

Of particular interest from this genre is the satirical novel *Sartor Resartus* (*The Tailor Patched*) (Carlyle, 1948), which is cleverly structured around the history and vernacular of clothing cultures, suggesting that the fabric of life is reflected through this construct. In the character of the make-believe Professor Teufelsdrockh (Professor Devil's Dust),[6] Carlyle proposes a philosophy of clothing, 'the grand Tissue of all Tissues, the only Real Tissue'. Bossche (1991) suggests that Carlyle's clothing metaphor 'represents the fundamental historicity of cultural institutions and the inevitability of periodic revolution. Since nothing can prevent the processes of decay that destroy old clothing. *Sartor's* persuasive organic imagery suggests that revolution and historical change are natural, noncataclysmic processes.' Playfully, throughout the novel Carlyle[7] refers to the occurrence of clothing *sans* a wearer; in these departures he observes the fetish value and status symbols of particular costume types and engages in the notion of reverence and idolatry. He claims: 'That reverence which cannot act without obstruction and perversion when the clothes are full, may have full course when they are empty' (Carlyle, 1948).

As a result of these observations Professor Teufeldrockh categorizes this displacement from the body, crafting a clothing nomenclature released from the burden of humanity, now a void or a receptacle of memory, subsequently christening these vessels with titles like 'an ornament', 'an architectural idea', 'shells', 'the outer husks of bodies', 'cast clothes', 'past witnesses', 'instruments of Woe and Joy', 'the hollow cloth garment', 'empty clothes' or 'ghosts of life' (Carlyle, 1948):

What still dignity dwells in a suit of Cast Clothes! How meekly it bears its honours! No haughty looks, no scornful gesture: silent and serene, it fronts the world; neither demanding worship or afraid to miss it. The Hat still carries the physiognomy of its Head: but the vanity and the stupidity, and goosespeech which was the sign of these two, are gone. The Coat-arm is stretched out, but not to strike; the Breeches, in modest simplicity, depend at ease, and now at last have a graceful flow; the Waistcoat hides no evil passion, no riotous desire; hunger or thirst now dwells not in it. (Carlyle, 1948)

Carlyle's descriptions allude to a state of redundancy where the empty state of the clothes implies dereliction.

DECAY AESTHETICS

The potency of ruins, the aesthetics of decay and their study and reflection, is an intrinsic part of Western cultural tradition stemming from antiquity (Roth *et al.,* 1997; Woodward, 2001). Buildings devastated by human interventions or lack of intervention, or the degrading forces of nature over time, elicit an emotional charge generated by a nostalgic longing for that which is lost, a sense of abandonment and a blurring and redefinition of visual boundaries describing beauty and value. To Western sensibilities ruins reveal the susceptibility and impermanency of civilization. In contrast to this view the Japanese aesthetic concepts of *wabi* and *sabi,* which also draw on the vestiges that time produces, conceive time as a cycle of natural flux: the beauty found in the patina of the worn, the surfaces of the decaying or the absence in the imperfect are admired (Crowley and Crowley, 2001).

The ephemeral nature of fashion is intrinsically related to its fugitive construction—as soon as it is made it starts to disintegrate, to age, to change colour. Surfaces distort and perhaps break down. Eventually everything falls apart!

The reaction and response to the breakdown of fashion can range from keeping items from view,

discarding, or conservation. Garments breaking down physically defy their original functions of wearability and overt display. In its place these objects can convey the abject and the picturesque concurrently through the act of transformation and disfigurement. Studying language and the application of particular terms used to articulate ideal or unfavourable personal attributes, shows that these are intrinsically linked to condition. The term *respectable*, for instance, is connected to dressing in a proper way. Clothes well maintained and tidy are a reflection of the body within. The fashion vernacular aligns negative associations with a change in condition, an altered condition or a less than perfect one. Phrases 'dressed in rags' or 'in tatters'[8] are maligned states, in which clothing and its deteriorating condition is linked, historically, to the morals of man. The word *stain* brings into play the most extreme cultural standards (Douglas, 1980) relating not only to hygiene but purity, moral and social order. Historically fine clothing is a marker of social status and morality. A stain is provocative in the way it disturbs, the way it mars a surface. Dirt has long been viewed as an enemy. It threatens appearances and the status of respectability. It causes work, and effort through the duty of care. Freud has suggested in regards to this obsession with eradication of dirt that 'we are not surprised in setting up the use of soap as an actual yardstick for civilization' (Gay, 1995). Fashion's dark secret is the continual struggle with and demands for an ideal image; looking good, maintaining the best condition through cleaning and storage—prolonging an aesthetic of beauty that demands the control and continuance of pristine fashion surfaces. A garment's condition is impregnated with responsibility and value. Donations to a museum collection, for example, are often generated through the moral obligations experienced by the family who feel overwhelmed by the duty of care placed upon them and the threat of neglect, consequently gifting an item in anticipation that the institution will return it to its former glory. The Miss Havisham scenario introducing the withered and yellowed wedding dress co-ordinating successfully with the occupant is a ghastly reminder of the fate of old clothes.

HAUNTING DEVICE

However, the concept of clothing as a haunting device (Jones and Stallybrass, 2000) serves to represent the previous wearers even though they have long departed and reveal the 'spirits of the past' (Derrida, 1994). The 'cast-off clothing', 'empty dress', 'ghosts of life' are no longer connected to the living but bear their marks. The interior of a garment is a privileged surface, which offers an aspect of familiarity known only to the maker, the cleaner and the wearer and perhaps the curator. It is the most intimate surface of clothing, touching the body. It is a façade that conceals and reveals the mysteries of construction and knowledge of the lining, guards the maker's label, protects the visible stitching trails, the repair secrets and alterations and shrouds the stains and signs of wear. The interior has the intimacy and breath of the wearer upon it. A garment inside out or outside in can reveal how a shape is formed, why fabric falls in a particular way. Its complexity can be quite astounding, contrasting a modest aesthetic rendered through humble materials and colours drained by wear and washing, that often contradict the impressive exterior.

By contrast, museum condition reports document a garment or accessory within the criteria of degradation, damage, previous repairs, alteration, soiling (surface) and staining (penetrating) with degrees of severity from minor to major, good, fair or bad. There are listed activities to stabilise these conditions, proposals to make the work strong again, revive it, to restore its appearance. Yet these maligned states also mark out other activities or events, histories that recall past textile technologies, the essence of fragility and record the way a garment wears. Naturally there are many signs; traces of a former use are left behind, which imbue the garment with the presence of the wearer: staining caused by splashed champagne, tea or rain; mud engrained on hems; jam dribbled on a child's dress turns black with age, while smoke eventually rots through a 19th-century skirt. Coloured dyes morph into bizarre hues exacerbated by heat, damp or strange chemical breakdowns. Black follows a faded journey, white withers, spots and yellows. Rubber perishes and gelatine sequins dissolve. Skirt trains trap mud from the streets, keeping it away from the finer materials. Inside delicate 19th-century silk bodices rubber sweat pads protect the fashionable garment from bodily fluids and the horror of underarm discolouration. The darned, patched, recycled, dyed and worn document the cycle of clothing culture as garments are revived, clobbered and translated over again to renew. The second-hand, the third-hand and so it goes on . . .

Inevitably the care and maintenance of clothes is critical to achieving standards of appearance, longevity of material assets and sustaining the 'new' look. This is certainly no simple undertaking. Historically it involved complex, time-consuming processes; cleaning, mending, plus putting clothes correctly away, in and out of storage (Walkley and Foster, 1978). Contemporary care labels list stoically the fibre content and recommended cleaning and preening methods, while wardrobe and storage specialists offer efficient systems for packing clothing away or discarding unwanted items.

CONTEMPORARY DESIGN AND REFERENCING THE WORN-OUT

A garment's shifting surface and construction can create extraordinary compositions from the formulation of shredded silk surfaces to the patterning formed by ironmould. Fashion designers have responded to the process of ageing and the transformation of fashion as an aesthetic device but also one that can be appropriated to charge an item with political and social meaning by unsettling the status quo. In response to the fetishist desire for new clothes and the status of appearance for instance, Malcolm McLaren and Vivienne Westwood in the late 1970s concocted an anti-establishment aesthetic based around the irregular and the worn out, selling t-shirts and trousers that were soiled, ripped and decorated with worthless objects or out-of-date trims. The 'destroy' shirt is perhaps the most recognized example of this genre, best remembered as the uniform of the notorious Sid Vicious in the punk music group the Sex Pistols. Contemporary designers continue to exploit the aesthetics of decay. For example Rei Kawakubo of Comme des Garçons, Hussein Chalayan, John Galliano, Martin Margiela and Jun Takahashi, seeking the patina and palette of the worn and the discarded. Evans (2003) has observed that 'rather than simply configuring images of dereliction, these designers introduce the idea of narrative and history into their clothes'.

Perhaps the most interesting response to the organic and ephemeral is from Martin Margiela.[9] Working with a microbiologist he created a museum installation where clothes modelled from recycled 'old' clothes were sprayed with various types of mould spores, and placed in conditions to encourage their growth. Consequently the garments were installed outdoors and continued to evolve throughout the course of the exhibition—resulting in the creation of 'living' garments.

ARTEFACT EXPERIENCE

Warhol's interventions in the museum environment offered a controversial stance against conventional institutional policies relating to display and conservation through his preference to present things to 'look as they are'. His personal collection displayed in the *Folk and Funk* exhibition[10] documented an eccentric preference for accumulating artefacts that revealed signs of use, misadventure, or even a fabrication fault (Ostrow, 1969). In the exhibition *Raid the Icebox 1*,[11] his

predictably unconventional approach and sometimes overtly subversive choices confronted the practice of the expert and museum professional (Bright, 2001). By selecting entire collections of objects, including their storage vessels, acknowledged fakes, multiples of the same object, items of varying condition and 'value', Warhol proposed another trajectory for museum artefacts to be observed. Forging a narrative outside the usual hype surrounding classification and labelling, where significance is oversimplified by referencing bland descriptive terms like masterpiece, priceless, rare and treasures, Warhol's curatorship instead placed emphasis on the evidence of experience (Bright, 2001).

When reconsidering the scope of public dress collections in regards to content, access and approach, it is perhaps pertinent to consider what is missing? Maynard (1994) has argued that everyday dress is not well represented and that collections contain a predominance of the more expensive, high fashion garments. My argument in this paper is not simply about institutional collection policies but to further investigate how the collections are presented, prepared and consequently perceived. For instance in current practice the acquisition rationale aligns with condition, 'value' aesthetics, which favours identifying garments which consequently reveal the minimum signs of wear or ageing or can respond well to remedial work within a restricted financial and time regime. This established doctrine of best condition, is further articulated and reinforced through consistent use of mannequin display, which relies on clothing in a premium state. A strategy, which further emulates the shopping environment, and the window display of a new product, in contrast to Warhol's museum philosophy, where an object was recognized for its worn patina or irregular characteristics.

CONCLUSION

My purpose by placing fashion in the museum outside of the body is to negate the demands of appearance that the body commands, which potentially positions 'past' 'old' fashion in an anti-fashion role, where clothing can age and the traces of experience are exposed. Why not view garments splayed on the floor, lying in a drawer, inside out, or positioned in a dishevelled state? In my alternate narrative the well-preserved exquisitely crafted are juxtaposed with items that are darned, patched, recycled or worn out. In this scenario possibly the consideration of fashion's funeral proposes a pathway to present metamorphosis? My subversive methodology attempts to further examine the guidelines and protocols underlying the museum experience, to re-imagine the conventional vision of historic fashion, from the choice of artefacts, exhibition design and their display. In this dialogue it is my purpose to broaden the presentation of fashion cultures, explore notions relating to image and reality, the seen and the unseen.

My intention outlined in this paper is to set the modishness of fashion against the ephemerality and wear-and-tear of the clothes themselves and provide a crucial intervention in the usual expectations and presentations of fashion and museology itself.

'Clothing is a worn world: a world of social relations put upon the wearer's body . . . clothing reminds' (Jones and Stallybrass, 2000).

NOTES

1. The incomplete study by Walter Benjamin on the subject of the Paris arcades. See Lehmann for a detailed discussion concerning Benjamin's writing about fashion.

2. The research for this paper is based on a curatorial project developed for the National Trust of Victoria (Australia) entitled *Noble Rot: An Alternate History of Fashion* displayed at Como Historic House and Garden, Melbourne Australia from 16 February to 7 May 2006.

3. For example, *Chanel* staged at the Metropolitan Museum of Art, New York, from 5–7 May 2005, drew crowds of 463,603, listed as thirteenth in *The Art Newspaper*'s annual ranking of the world's top exhibition attendance figures. Chanel sponsored the exhibition.

4. The first waxworks exhibition is recorded in 1756.

5. ICOM (International Council of Museums, 2006) 'sets minimum standards of professional practice and performance of museums and staff.' Available at: http//icom.museum/ethics.html. Costume guidelines formulated by the Costume committee offer basic standards of care, and display ethics that are adopted by museums worldwide. The intention of the document, which was last updated in 1998, is to assist curators and museum management dealing with fragile costumes.

6. Devil's dust was produced by the woollen manufacturers when they converted old clothing rags into cloth called shoddy. The process created clouds of dust, which consequently caused a major health problem, an aftermath of the Industrial Revolution. Carter suggests that a possibility for the origin of this insidious name is found in Engels, F., *The Condition of the Working Class in England 1844* (London: 1892).

7. For an intensive study of Carlyle's work in the context of Dress studies refer to Keenan and Carter.

8. Tatters, refers to torn and ragged clothing. A tatterdemalion was a ragged child, person dressed in old clothes, in use from 1608.

9. Martin Margiela: 9/4/1615 Museum Boijmans Van Beuningen, Rotterdam 6 June–17 August 1997. For details of the exhibition and a critique of Margiela's work, see Caroline Evans, 'The Golden Dustman: A Critical Evaluation of the Work of Martin Margiela: Exhibition (9/4/1615)', *Fashion Theory*, 2(1), pp. 73–94.

10. *Andy Warhol's Folk and Funk* exhibition staged at the Museum of American Folk Art, 20 September–19 November 1977.

11. *Raid the Icebox 1* staged at the Museum of Art of the Rhode Island School of Design in 1969, selected by Andy Warhol from basement storage. The exhibition included the holdings of the entire shoe collection, housed in the original museum storage vessel. All shoes were displayed *in situ* with no special preparation and visitors were invited to open the door of the cabinet and peer inside. Warhol insisted that full cataloguing details were researched and published for all exhibits, making no distinction between entries for the rubber galoshes or the Cézanne painting, ignoring traditional hierarchies of artistic practice.

REFERENCES

Bennett, T. (1995). *The Birth of the Museum*. London: Routledge.

Benjamin, W. (1989). *Charles Baudelaire: a Lyric Poet in the Era of High Capitalism*. Translated by H. Zohn. London, New York: Verso.

Benjamin, W. (2004). *The Arcades Project* [Das Passagen-Werk]. Translated by H. Eiland and K. McLaughlin. Cambridge: Belknap Press of Harvard University Press.

Blau, H. (1999). *Nothing in Itself: Complexions of Fashion*. Bloomington, IN: Indiana University Press.

Bossche, C. R. V. (1991). *Carlyle and the Search for Authority*. Columbus, OH: Ohio University Press. Available at: http://www.ohiostatepress.org [accessed 27 December 2006].

Brant, S. and Cullman, E. (1977). *Andy Warhol's Folk and Funk* [exhibition catalogue]. New York: Museum of American Folk Art.

Bright, D. (2001). 'Shopping the leftovers: Warhol's collecting strategies in Raid the Icebox 1'. *Art History*, 24(2), 278–291.

Carter, M. (2003). *Fashion Classics from Carlyle to Barthes*. Oxford: Berg.

Carlyle, T. (1948). *Sartor Resartus on Heroes Hero Worship*. London: J.M. Dent & Sons. (First published 1836.)

Crowley, J. and Crowley, S. (2001). *Wabi Sabi Style*. Layton: Gibbs Smith.

Derrida, J. (1994). *Specters of Marx: the State of the Debt, the Work of Mourning, and the New International*. Translated by P. Kamuf. New York and London: Routledge.

Douglas, M. (1980). *Purity and Danger: An Analysis of the Concepts of Pollution and Taboo*. London: Routledge & Kegan Paul.

Evans, C. (2003). *Fashion at the Edge: Spectacle, Modernity and Deathliness*. New Haven and London: Yale University Press.

Gay, P. (ed.) (1995). *The Freud Reader*. London: Vintage.

Hollander, A. (1993). *Seeing through Clothes*. Berkeley: University of California Press.

International Council of Museums (ICOM) (2006). *ICOM Code of Ethics for Museums, 2006*. Available at: http//icom.museum/ethics.html.

Jones, R. and Stallybrass, P. (2000). *Renaissance Clothing and the Materials of Memory*. Cambridge: Press Syndicate of the University of Cambridge.

Keenan, W. J. F. (2001). 'Sartor Resartus restored: a Carlylean perspective on dress studies'. In Keenan, W. J. F. (ed.), *Dressed to Impress: Looking the Part*. New York: Berg, pp. 1–49.

Krell, D. (ed.) (2004). *Martin Heidegger Basic Writings: From Being and Time (1927) to The Task of Thinking (1964)*. London and New York: Routledge.

Lehmann, U. (2000). *Tigersprung: Fashion in Modernity*. Cambridge: Massachusetts Institute of Technology.

Leopardi, G. (1983). *The Moral Essays* [Operette Morali]. Translated by P. Creagh. New York: Columbia University Press.

Maynard, M. (1994). *Fashioned from Penury: Dress as Cultural Practice in Colonial Australia*. Cambridge: Cambridge University Press.

Menkes, S. (2000). 'Museum shows win over public but can cause conflicts: designers are playing to the galleries'. *International Herald Tribune*, 12 July.

Ostrow, S. E. (1969). *Raid the Icebox 1 with Andy Warhol* [exhibition catalogue]. Providence, RI: Museum of Art Rhode Island School of Design.

Pilbeam, P. (2003). *Madame Tussaud and the History of Waxworks*. London: Hambeldon & London.

Roche, D. (1994). *The Culture of Clothing: Dress and Fashion in the Ancien Régime*. Translated by J. Birrell. Cambridge: Cambridge University Press.

Roth, M. S., Lyons, C. and Merewether, C. (eds) (1997). *Irresistible Decay: Ruins Reclaimed*. Los Angeles: The Getty Research Institute.

Stewart, S. (1993). *On Longing Narratives of the Miniature, the Gigantic, the Souvenir, the Collection*. Durham, NC: Duke University Press.

Walkley, C. and Foster, V. (1978). *Crinolines and Crimping Irons*. London: Peter Owen.

Wilson, E. (1985). *Adorned in Dreams: Fashion and Modernity*. London: Virago Press.

Wilson, E. (2004). 'Magic fashion'. *Fashion Theory*, 8(4), 375–386.

Woodward, C. (2001). *In Ruins*. London: Chatto & Windus.

12

AUTOBIOGRAPHY OF A POCKET HANDKERCHIEF

James Fenimore Cooper

Editor's introduction: The author James Fenimore Cooper is perhaps most famous for the film adaptation of his novel *The Last of the Mohicans*. The American was born in 1789 and died in 1851, publishing numerous novels during his lifetime. A portion of his short novel *Autobiography of a Pocket Handkerchief* is printed here. The story was first published in a magazine, and subsequently slightly different versions were released. The idea of an object acting as a narrator is now a familiar literary strategy, but when Cooper wrote the story the notion of an embroidered handkerchief acting as lead narrator was unfamiliar, and some consider him the first author to adopt the point of view of an object. The strategy provides us with a real—if humorous—example of the textile literally remembering the course of its life. Cleverness aside, the technique also provided the author with a thinly veiled cover for his criticism of the values of France and America at the time.

2

It is scarcely necessary to dwell on the scenes that occurred between the time I first sprang from the earth and that in which I was 'pulled.' The latter was a melancholy day for me, however, arriving prematurely as regarded my vegetable state, since it was early determined that I was to be spun into threads of unusual fineness. I will only say, here, that my youth was a period of innocent pleasures, during which my chief delight was to exhibit my simple but beautiful flowers, in honor of the hand that gave them birth.

At the proper season, the whole field was laid low, when a scene of hurry and confusion succeeded, to which I find it exceedingly painful to turn in memory. The 'rotting' was the most humiliating part of the process that followed, though, in our case, this was done in clear running water, and the 'crackling' the most uncomfortable.[1] Happily, we were spared the anguish that ordinarily accompanies breaking on the wheel, though we could not be said to have entirely escaped from all its parade. Innocence was our shield, and while we endured some of the disgrace that attaches to mere forms, we had that consolation of which no cruelty or device can deprive the unoffending. Our sorrows were not heightened by the consciousness of undeserving.

There is a period, which occurred between the time of being 'hatchelled'[2] and that of being 'woven,' that it exceeds my powers to delineate.

Source: London: Hesperus Press Limited 2006 (first published 1843).

All around me seemed to be in a state of inextricable confusion, out of which order finally appeared in the shape of a piece of cambric, of a quality that brought the workmen far and near to visit it. We were a single family of only twelve, in this rare fabric, among which I remember that I occupied the seventh place in the order of arrangement, and of course in the order of seniority also. When properly folded, and bestowed in a comfortable covering, our time passed pleasantly enough, being removed from all disagreeable sights and smells, and lodged in a place of great security, and indeed of honor, men seldom failing to bestow this attention on their valuables.

It is out of my power to say precisely how long we remained in this passive state in the hands of the manufacturer. It was some weeks, however, if not months; during which our chief communications were on the chances of our future fortunes. Some of our number were ambitious, and would hear to nothing but the probability, nay, the certainty, of our being purchased, as soon as our arrival in Paris should be made known, by the king, in person, and presented to the dauphine, then the first lady in France. The virtues of the Duchesse d'Angoulême[3] were properly appreciated by some of us, while I discovered that others entertained for her any feelings but those of veneration and respect. This diversity of opinion, on a subject of which one would think none of us very well qualified to be judges, was owing to a circumstance of such everyday occurrence as almost to supersede the necessity of telling it, though the narrative would be rendered more complete by an explanation.

It happened, while we lay in the bleaching grounds,[4] that one half of the piece extended into a part of the field that came under the management of a *legitimist*, while the other invaded the dominions of a *liberal*.[5] Neither of these persons had any concern with us, we being under the special superintendence of the head workman, but it was impossible, altogether impossible, to escape the consequences of our *locales*. While the *legitimist* read nothing but the *Moniteur*, the *liberal*

read nothing but *Le Temps*, a journal then recently established, in the supposed interests of human freedom. Each of these individuals got a paper at a certain hour, which he read with as much manner as he could command, and with singular perseverance as related to the difficulties to be overcome, to a clientele of bleachers, who reasoned as he reasoned, swore by his oaths, and finally arrived at all his conclusions. The liberals had the best of it as to numbers, and possibly as to wit, the *Moniteur* possessing all the dullness of official dignity under all the dynasties and ministries that have governed France since its establishment. My business, however, is with the effect produced on the pocket handkerchiefs, and not with that produced on the laborers. The two extremes were regular *côtés gauches* and *côtés droits*.[6] In other words, all at the right end of the piece became devoted Bourbonists, devoutly believing that princes, who were daily mentioned with so much reverence and respect, could be nothing else but perfect; while the opposite extreme were disposed to think that nothing good could come of Nazareth.[7] In this way, four of our number became decided politicians, not only entertaining a sovereign contempt for the sides they respectively opposed, but beginning to feel sensations approaching to hatred for each other.

The reader will readily understand that these feelings lessened toward the center of the piece, acquiring most intensity at the extremes. I may be said, myself, to have belonged to the *centre gauche*,[8] that being my accidental position in the fabric, when it was a natural consequence to obtain sentiments of this shade. It will be seen, in the end, how prominent were these early impressions, and how far it is worth while for mere pocket handkerchiefs to throw away their time, and permit their feelings to become excited concerning interests that they are certainly not destined to control, and about which, under the most favorable circumstances, they seldom obtain other than very questionable information.

. . .

4

From this time, the charming Adrienne frequently visited the bleaching grounds, always accompanied by her grandmother. The presence of Georges was an excuse, but to watch the improvement in our appearance was the reason. Never before had Adrienne seen a fabric as beautiful as our own, and, as I afterwards discovered, she was laying by a few francs with the intention of purchasing the piece, and of working and ornamenting the handkerchiefs, in order to present them to her benefactress, the dauphine. Madame de la Rocheaimard was pleased with this project; it was becoming in a de la Rocheaimard, and they soon began to speak of it openly in their visits. Fifteen or twenty napoleons[9] might do it, and the remains of the recovered trousseau would still produce that sum. It is probable this intention would have been carried out, but for a severe illness that attacked the dear girl, during which her life was even despaired of. I had the happiness of hearing of her gradual recovery, however, before we commenced our journey, though no more was said of the purchase. Perhaps it was as well as it was; for, by this time, such a feeling existed in our extreme *côté gauche*, that it may be questioned if the handkerchiefs of that end of the piece would have behaved themselves in the wardrobe of the dauphine with the discretion and prudence that are expected from every thing around the person of a princess of her exalted rank and excellent character. It is true, none of us understood the questions at issue, but that only made the matter worse; the violence of all dissensions being very generally in proportion to the ignorance and consequent confidence of the disputants.

I could not but remember Adrienne, as the *commissionaire* laid us down before the eyes of the wife of the head of the firm, in the rue de ———. We were carefully examined, and pronounced '*parfaits*;'[10] still it was not in the sweet tones, and with the sweeter smiles of the polished and gentle girl we had left in Picardie. There was a sentiment in *her* admiration that touched all

our hearts, even to the most exaggerated republican among us, for she seemed to go deeper in her examination of merits than the mere texture and price. She saw her offering in our beauty, the benevolence of the dauphine in our softness, her own gratitude in our exquisite fineness, and princely munificence in our delicacy. In a word, she could enter into the sentiment of a pocket handkerchief. Alas! how different was the estimation in which we were held by Desirée and her employers. With them, it was purely a question of francs, and we had not been in the *magasin* five minutes, when there was a lively dispute whether we were to be put at a certain number of napoleons, or one napoleon more. A good deal was said about Mme la Duchesse, and I found that it was expected that a certain lady of that rank, one who had enjoyed the extraordinary luck of retaining her fortune, being of an old and historical family, and who was at the head of fashion in the *faubourg*,[11] would become the purchaser. At all events, it was determined no one should see us until this lady returned to town, she being at the moment at Rosny, with Madame,[12] whence she was expected to accompany that princess to Dieppe, to come back to her hotel, in the rue de Bourbon, about the last of October. Here, then, were we doomed to three months of total seclusion in the heart of the gayest capital of Europe. It was useless to repine, and we determined among ourselves to exercise patience in the best manner we could.

Accordingly, we were safely deposited in a particular drawer, along with a few other favorite *articles*, which, like our family, were reserved for the eyes of certain distinguished but absent customers. These *specialités* in trade are of frequent occurrence in Paris, and form a pleasant bond of union between the buyer and seller, which gives a particular zest to this sort of commerce, and not unfrequently a particular value to goods. To see that which no one else has seen, and to own that which no one else can own, are equally agreeable, and delightfully exclusive. All minds that do not possess the natural sources of exclusion, are fond of creating them by means of a subordinate and more artificial character.

On the whole, I think we enjoyed our new situation, rather than otherwise. The drawer was never opened, it is true, but that next it was in constant use, and certain crevices beneath the counter enabled us to see a little, and to hear more, of what passed in the *magasin*. We were in a part of the shop most frequented by ladies, and we overheard a few tête-à-têtes that were not without amusement. These generally related to *cancans*.[13] Paris is a town in which *cancans* do not usually flourish, their proper theater being provincial and trading places, beyond a question; still there are *cancans* at Paris; for all sorts of persons frequent that center of civilization. The only difference is, that in the social pictures offered by what are called cities, the *cancans* are in the strongest light, and in the most conspicuous of the grouping, whereas in Paris they are kept in shadow, and in the background. Still there are *cancans* at Paris; and *cancans* we overheard, and precisely in the manner I have related. Did pretty ladies remember that pocket handkerchiefs have ears, they might possibly have more reserve in the indulgence of this extraordinary propensity.

We had been near a month in the drawer, when I recognized a female voice near us, that I had often heard of late, speaking in a confident and decided tone, and making allusions that showed she belonged to the court. I presume her position there was not of the most exalted kind, yet it was sufficiently so to qualify her, in her own estimation, to talk politics. '*Les ordonnances*'[14] were in her mouth constantly, and it was easy to perceive that she attached the greatest importance to these ordinances, whatever they were, and fancied a political millennium was near. The shop was frequented less than usual that day; the next it was worse still, in the way of business, and the clerks began to talk loud, also, about *les ordonnances*. The following morning neither windows nor doors were opened, and we passed a gloomy time of uncertainty and conjecture. There were ominous sounds in the streets. Some of us thought we heard the roar of distant artillery. At length the master and mistress appeared by themselves in the shop; money and papers were secured, and the female was just retiring to an inner room, when she suddenly came back to the counter, opened our drawer, seized us with no very reverent hands, and, the next thing we knew, the whole twelve of us were thrust into a trunk upstairs, and buried in Egyptian darkness. From that moment all traces of what was occurring in the streets of Paris were lost to us. After all, it is not so very disagreeable to be only a pocket handkerchief in a revolution.

Our imprisonment lasted until the following December. As our feelings had become excited on the questions of the day, as well as those of other irrational beings around us, we might have passed a most uncomfortable time in the trunk, but for one circumstance. So great had been the hurry of our mistress in thus shutting us up, that we had been crammed in in a way to leave it impossible to say which was the *côté droit*, and which the *côté gauche*. Thus completely deranged as parties, we took to discussing philosophical matters in general, an occupation well adapted to a situation that required so great an exercise of discretion.

One day, when we least expected so great a change, our mistress came in person, searched several chests, trunks and drawers, and finally discovered us where she had laid us, with her own hands, near four months before. It seems that, in her hurry and fright, she had actually forgotten in what nook we had been concealed. We were smoothed with care, our political order reestablished, and then we were taken below and restored to the dignity of the select circle in the drawer already mentioned. This was like removing to a fashionable square, or living in a *beau quartier*[15] of a capital. It was even better than removing from East Broadway into bona fide, real, unequaled, league-long, eighty feet wide, Broadway!

We now had an opportunity of learning some of the great events that had recently occurred in France, and which still troubled Europe. The Bourbons were again dethroned, as it was termed, and another Bourbon seated in their place. It would seem *il y a Bourbon et Bourbon*.[16] The result has since shown that 'what is bred in the bone will break out in the flesh.' Commerce was at a standstill; our master passed half his time under arms, as a national guard, in order to keep the revolutionists from revolutionizing the revolution. The great families had laid aside their liveries; some of them their coaches; most of them their arms. Pocket handkerchiefs of *our* caliber would be thought decidedly aristocratic; and aristocracy in Paris, just at that moment, was almost in as bad odor as it is in America, where it ranks as an eighth deadly sin, though no one seems to know precisely what it means. In the latter country, an honest development of democracy is certain to be stigmatized as tainted with this crime. No governor would dare to pardon it.

The groans over the state of trade were loud and deep among those who lived by its innocent arts. Still, the holidays were near, and hope revived. If revolutionized Paris would not buy as the *jour de l'an*[17] approached, Paris must have a new dynasty. The police foresaw this, and it ceased to agitate, in order to bring the republicans into discredit; men must eat, and trade was permitted to revive a little. Alas! how little do they who vote, know *why* they vote, or they who dye their hands in the blood of their kind, why the deed has been done!

The duchesse had not returned to Paris, neither had she emigrated. Like most of the high nobility, who rightly enough believed that primogeniture and birth were of the last importance to *them*, she preferred to show her distaste for the present order of things, by which the youngest prince of a numerous family had been put upon the throne of the oldest, by remaining at her château. All expectations of selling us to *her* were abandoned, and we were thrown fairly into the market, on the great principle of liberty and equality. This was as became a republican reign.

Our prospects were varied daily. The dauphine, Madame, and all the de Rochefoucaulds, de la Tremouilles, de Grammonts, de Rohans, de Crillons, &c. &c., were out of the question. The royal family were in England, the Orleans branch excepted, and the high nobility were very generally on their 'high ropes,' or, *à bouder*.[18] As for the bankers, their reign had not yet fairly commenced. Previously to July, 1830, this estimable class of citizens had not dared to indulge their native tastes for extravagance and parade, the grave dignity and high breeding of a very ancient but impoverished nobility holding them in some restraint; and, then, *their* fortunes were still uncertain; the funds were not firm, and even the honorable and worthy Jacques Lafitte,[19] a man to ennoble any calling, was shaking in credit. Had we been brought into the market a twelvemonth later, there is no question that we should have been caught up within a week, by the wife or daughter of some of the operatives at the Bourse.[20]

As it was, however, we enjoyed ample leisure for observation and thought. Again and again were we shown to those who, it was thought, could not fail to yield to our beauty, but no one would purchase. All appeared to eschew aristocracy, even in their pocket handkerchiefs. The day the fleurs de lys were cut out of the medallions of the treasury, and the king laid down his arms, I thought our mistress would have had the hysterics on our account. Little did she understand human nature, for the nouveaux riches, who are as certain to succeed an old and displaced class of superiors, as hungry flies to follow flies with full bellies, would have been much more apt to run into extravagance and folly, than persons always accustomed to money, and who did not depend on its exhibition for their importance. A day of deliverance, notwithstanding, was at hand, which to me seemed like the bridal of a girl dying to rush into the dissipations of society.

5

The holidays were over, without there being any material revival of trade, when my deliverance unexpectedly occurred. It was in February, and I do believe our mistress had abandoned the expectation of disposing of us that season, when I heard a gentle voice speaking near the counter, one day, in tones that struck me as familiar. It was a female, of course, and her inquiries were about a piece of cambric handkerchiefs, which she said had been sent to this shop from a manufactory in Picardie. There was nothing of the customary alertness in the manner of our mistress, and, to my surprise, she even showed the customer one or two pieces of much inferior quality, before we were produced. The moment I got into the light, however, I recognized the beautifully turned form and sweet face of Adrienne de la Rocheaimard. The poor girl was paler and thinner than when I had last seen her, doubtless, I thought, the effects of her late illness; but I could not conceal from myself the unpleasant fact that she was much less expensively clad. I say less expensively clad, though the expression is scarcely just, for I had never seen her in attire that could properly be called expensive at all; and, yet, the term mean would be equally inapplicable to her present appearance. It might be better to say that, relieved by a faultless, even a fastidious neatness and grace, there was an air of severe, perhaps of pinched economy in her present attire. This it was that had prevented our mistress from showing her fabrics as fine as we, on the first demand. Still I thought there was a slight flush on the cheek of the poor girl, and a faint smile on her features, as she instantly recognized us for old acquaintances. For one, I own I was delighted at finding her soft fingers again brushing over my own exquisite surface, feeling as if one had been expressly designed for the other. Then Adrienne hesitated; she appeared desirous of speaking, and yet abashed. Her color went and came, until a deep rosy blush settled on each cheek, and her tongue found utterance.

'Would it suit you, madame,' she asked, as if dreading a repulse, 'to part with one of these?'

'Your pardon, mademoiselle; handkerchiefs of this quality are seldom sold singly.'

'I feared as much—and yet I have occasion for only *one*. It is to be worked—if it—'

The words came slowly, and they were spoken with difficulty. At that last uttered, the sound of the sweet girl's voice died entirely away. I fear it was the dullness of trade, rather than any considerations of benevolence, that induced our mistress to depart from her rule.

'The price of each handkerchief is five and twenty francs, mademoiselle—' she had offered the day before to sell us to the wife of one of the richest *agents de change*[21] in Paris, at a napoleon a piece—'the price is five and twenty francs, if you take the dozen, but as you appear to wish only *one*, rather than not oblige you, it may be had for eight and twenty.'

There was a strange mixture of sorrow and delight in the countenance of Adrienne; but she did not hesitate, and, attracted by the odor of the eau de cologne, she instantly pointed me out as the handkerchief she selected. Our mistress passed her scissors between me and my neighbor of the *côté gauche*, and then she seemed instantly to regret her own precipitation. Before making the final separation from the piece, she delivered herself of her doubts.

'It is worth another franc, mademoiselle,' she said, 'to cut a handkerchief from the *center* of the piece.'

The pain of Adrienne was now too manifest for concealment. That she ardently desired the handkerchief was beyond dispute, and yet there existed some evident obstacle to her wishes.

'I fear I have not so much money with me, madame,' she said, pale as death, for all sense of shame was lost in intense apprehension. Still her trembling hands did their duty, and her purse was produced. A gold napoleon promised well, but it had no fellow. Seven more francs appeared in single pieces. Then two ten-sous[22] were produced; after which nothing remained but copper. The purse was emptied, and the reticule rummaged, the whole amounting to just twenty-eight francs seven sous.

'I have no more, madame,' said Adrienne, in a faint voice.

The woman, who had been trained in the school of suspicion, looked intently at the other, for an instant, and then she swept the money into her drawer, content with having extorted from this poor girl more than she would have dared to ask of the wife of the *agent de change.* Adrienne took me up and glided from the shop, as if she feared her dear bought prize would yet be torn from her. I confess my own delight was so great that I did not fully appreciate, at the time, all the hardship of the case. It was enough to be liberated, to get into the fresh air, to be about to fulfill my proper destiny. I was tired of that sort of vegetation in which I neither grew, nor was watered by tears; nor could I see those stars on which I so much doted, and from which I had learned a wisdom so profound. The politics, too, were rendering our family unpleasant; the *côté droit* was becoming supercilious—it had always been illogical; while the *côté gauche* was just beginning to discover that it had made a revolution for other people. Then it was happiness itself to be with Adrienne, and when I felt the dear girl pressing me to her heart, by an act of volition of which pocket handkerchiefs are little suspected, I threw up a fold of my gossamer-like texture, as if the air wafted me, and brushed the first tear of happiness from her eye that she had shed in months.

The reader may be certain that my imagination was all alive to conjecture the circumstances that had brought Adrienne de la Rocheaimard to Paris, and why she had been so assiduous in searching me out, in particular. Could it be that the grateful girl still intended to make her offering to the Duchesse d'Angoulême? Ah! no—that princess was in exile; while her sister was forming weak plots on behalf of her son, which a double treachery was about to defeat. I have already hinted that pocket handkerchiefs do not receive and communicate ideas, by means of the organs in use among human beings. They possess a clairvoyance that is always available under favorable circumstances. In their case the mesmeritic trance may be said to be ever in existence, while in the performance of their proper functions. It is only while crowded into bales, or thrust into drawers for the vulgar purposes of trade, that this instinct is dormant, a beneficent nature scorning to exercise her benevolence for any but legitimate objects. I now

mean legitimacy as connected with cause and effect, and nothing political or dynastic.

. . .

When Adrienne laid me on the frame where I was to be ornamented by her own pretty hands, she regarded me with a look of delight, nay, even of affection, that I shall never forget. As yet she felt none of the malign consequences of the self-denial she was about to exert. If not blooming, her cheeks still retained some of their native color, and her eye, thoughtful and even sad, was not yet anxious and sunken. She was she felt the importance of keeping her in ignorance of her own value. By paying the franc, it might give her assistant premature notions of her own importance; but, by bringing her down to fifteen sous, humility could be inculcated, and the chance of keeping her doubled. This, which would have defeated a bargain with any common *couturière*,[23] succeeded perfectly with Adrienne. She received her fifteen sous with humble thankfulness, in constant apprehension of losing even that miserable pittance. Nor would her employer consent to let her work by the piece, at which the dear child might have earned at least thirty sous, for she discovered that she had to deal with a person of conscience, and that in no mode could as much be possibly extracted from the assistant, as by confiding to her own honor. At nine each day she was to breakfast; at a quarter past nine, precisely, to commence work for her employer; at one, she had a remission of half an hour; and at six, she became her own mistress.

'I put confidence in you, mademoiselle,' said the *marchande de mode,* 'and leave you to yourself entirely. You will bring home the work as it is finished, and your money will be always ready. Should your grandmother occupy more of your time than common, on any occasion, you can make it up of yourself, by working a little earlier, or a little later; or, once in a while, you can throw in a day, to make up for lost time. You would not do as well at piecework, and I wish to deal generously by you. When certain things are wanted in a hurry, you will not mind working an hour or two beyond time, and I will always find lights with the greatest pleasure. Permit me to advise you to take the intermissions as much as possible for your attentions to your grandmother, who must be attended to properly. *Si*—the care of our parents is one of our most solemn duties! *Adieu, mademoiselle; au revoir!'*

. . .

'Who is your *boss*, pocket handkerchief?' demanded the shirt, a perfect stranger to me, by the way, for I had never seen him before the accidents of the washtub brought us in collision; 'who is your boss, pocket handkerchief, I say?—you are so very fine, I should like to know something of your history.'

From all I had heard and read, I was satisfied my neighbor was a Yankee shirt, both from his curiosity and from his abrupt manner of asking questions; still I was at a loss to know the meaning of the word *boss*, my clairvoyance being totally at fault. It belongs to no language known to the savans[24] or academicians.

'I am not certain, sir,' I answered, 'that I understand your meaning. What is a *boss*?'

'Oh! that's only a republican word for "master." Now, Judge Latitat is *my* boss, and a very good one he is, with the exception of his sitting so late at night at his infernal circuits, by the light of miserable tallow candles. But all the judges are alike for that, keeping a poor shirt up sometimes until midnight, listening to cursed dull lawyers, and prosy, caviling witnesses.'

'I beg you to recollect, sir, that I am a female pocket handkerchief, and persons of your sex are bound to use temperate and proper language in the presence of ladies.'

'Yes, I see you are feminine, by your ornaments—still, you might tell a fellow who is your boss?'

'I belong, at present, to Colonel Silky, if that is what you mean; but I presume some fair lady will soon do me the honor of transferring me to her own wardrobe. No doubt my future employer—is not that the word?—will be one of the most beautiful and distinguished ladies of New York.'

'No question of that, as money makes both beauty and distinction in this part of the world, and it's not a dollar that will buy you. *Colonel Silky?* I don't remember the name—which of *our* editors is he?'

'I don't think he is an editor at all. At least, I never heard he was employed about any publication, and, to own the truth, he does not appear to me to be particularly qualified for such a duty, either by native capacity, or, its substitute, education.'

'Oh! that makes no great difference—half the corps is exactly in the same predicament. I'fegs![25] if we waited for colonels, or editors either, in this country, until we got such as were qualified, we should get no news, and be altogether without politics, and the militia would soon be in an awful state.'

'This is very extraordinary! So you do not wait, but take them as they come. And what state is your militia actually in?'

'Awful! It is what my boss, the judge, sometimes calls a "statu quo." '

'And the newspapers—and the news—and the politics?'

'Why, they are *not* in "statu quo"—but in a *"semper eadem"*[26]—I beg pardon, do you understand Latin?'

'No, sir—ladies do not often study the dead languages.'

'If they did they would soon bring 'em to life! *"Semper eadem"* is Latin for "worse and worse." The militia is drilling into a "statu quo," and the press is enlightening mankind with a *"semper eadem."* '

After properly thanking my neighbor for these useful explanations, we naturally fell into discourse about matters and things in general, the weather in America being uniformly too fine to admit of discussion.

'Pray, sir,' said I, trembling lest my *boss* might be a colonel of the editorial corps, after all—'pray, sir,' said I, 'is it expected in this country that the wardrobe should entertain the political sentiments of its boss?'

'I rather think not, unless it might be in high party times; or, in the case of editors, and such extreme patriots. I have several relatives that belong to the corps, and they all tell me that while their bosses very frequently change their coats, they are by no means so particular about changing their shirts. But you are of foreign birth, ma'am, I should think by your dress and appearance?'

'Yes, sir, I came quite recently from France; though, my employer being American, I suppose I am entitled to the rights of citizenship. Are you European, also?'

'No, ma'am; I am native and to the "*manor* born," as the modern Shakespeare has it.[27] Is Louis Philippe likely to maintain the throne, in France?'

'That is not so certain, sir, by what I learn, as that the throne is likely to maintain Louis Philippe. To own the truth to you, I am a Carlist,[28] as all genteel articles are, and I enter but little into the subject of Louis Philippe's reign.'

This remark made me melancholy, by reviving the recollection of Adrienne, and the conversation ceased. An hour or two later, I was removed from the line, properly ironed, and returned to my boss. The same day I was placed in a shop in Broadway, belonging to a firm of which I now understood the colonel was a sleeping partner. A suitable entry was made against me, in a private memorandum book, which, as I once had an opportunity of seeing it, I will give here.

Super-extraordinary Pocket handkerchief, French cambric, trimmed and worked, in account with Bobbinet & Gull.
DR.
To money paid first cost, francs 100, at 5.25—$19.04
To interest on same for—00.00
To portion of passage money—00.04

To porterage—00.00 1/4
To washing and making up—00.25
(*Mem.*—See if a deduction cannot be made from this charge.)
CR.
By cash, for allowing Miss Thimble to copy pattern—not to be worked until our article is sold—$1.00
By cash for sale, &c.—

Thus the account stood the day I was first offered to the admiration of the fair of New York. Mr. Bobbinet, however, was in no hurry to exhibit me, having several articles of less beauty, that he was anxious to get off first. For my part, I was as desirous of being produced, as ever a young lady was to come out; and then my companions in the drawer were not of the most agreeable character. We were all pocket handkerchiefs, together, and all of French birth. Of the whole party, I was the only one that had been worked by a real lady, and consequently my education was manifestly superior to those of my companions. *They* could scarcely be called comme il faut, at all; though, to own the truth, I am afraid there is *tant soit peu de*[29] vulgarity about all *worked* pocket handkerchiefs. I remember that, one day, when Mme de la Rocheaimard and Adrienne were discussing the expediency of buying our whole piece, with a view of offering us to their benefactress, the former, who had a fine tact in matters of this sort, expressed a doubt whether the dauphine would be pleased with such an offering.

'Her Royal Highness, like all cultivated minds, looks for fitness in her ornaments and tastes. What fitness is there, *ma chère*,[30] in converting an article of real use, and which should not be paraded to one's associates, into an article of senseless luxury? I know there are two doctrines on this important point—'

But, as I shall have occasion, soon, to go into the whole philosophy of this matter, when I come to relate the manner of my next purchase, I will not stop here to relate all that Mme de la Rocheaimard said. It is sufficient that she, a woman of tact in such matters at least, had strong doubts concerning the *taste* and propriety of using worked pocket handkerchiefs, at all.

My principal objection to my companions in the drawer was their incessant senseless repinings about France, and their abuse of the country in which they were to pass their lives. I could see enough in America to find fault with, through the cracks of the drawer, and if an American, I might have indulged a little in the same way myself, for I am not one of those who think fault-finding belongs properly to the stranger, and not to the native. It is the proper office of the latter, as it is his duty to amend these faults, the traveler being bound in justice to look at the good as well as the evil. But, according to my companions, there was *nothing* good in America—the climate, the people, the food, the morals, the laws, the dress, the manners, and the tastes, were all infinitely worse than those they had been accustomed to. Even the physical proportions of the population were condemned, without mercy. I confess I was surprised at hearing the *size* of the Americans sneered at by *pocket handkerchiefs*, as I remember to have read that the *noses* of the New Yorkers, in particular, were materially larger than common. When the supercilious and vapid point out faults, they ever run into contradictions and folly; it is only under the lash of the discerning and the experienced that we betray by our writhings the power of the blow we receive.

9

I might have been a fortnight in the shop, when I heard a voice as gentle and ladylike as that of Adrienne, inquiring for pocket handkerchiefs. My heart fairly beat for joy; for, to own the truth, I was getting to be wearied to death with the garrulous folly of my companions. They had so much of the *couturières* about them! not one of the whole party ever having been a regular employee in genteel life. Their *niaiseries*[31] were endless, and there was just as much of the low-bred anticipation as to their future purchases, as one

sees at the balls of the *Champs Elysées* on the subject of partners. The word 'pocket handkerchief,' and that so sweetly pronounced, drew open our drawer, as it might be, instinctively. Two or three dozen of us, all of exquisite fineness, were laid upon the counter, myself and two or three more of the better class being kept a little in the background, as a skillful general holds his best troops in reserve.

The customers were sisters; that was visible at a glance. Both were pretty, almost beautiful—and there was an air of simplicity about their dress, a quiet and unobtrusive dignity in their manners, which at once announced them to be real ladies. Even the tones of their voices were polished, a circumstance that I think one is a little apt to notice in New York. I discovered, in the course of the conversation, that they were the daughters of a gentleman of very large estate, and belonged to the true elite of the country. The manner in which the clerks received them, indeed, proclaimed this; for, though their other claims might not have so promptly extracted this homage, their known wealth would.

Mr. Bobbinet attended these customers in person. Practiced in all that portion of human knowledge that appertains to a salesman, he let the sweet girls select two or three dozen handkerchiefs of great beauty, but totally without ornament, and even pay for them, before he said a word on the subject of the claims of his reserved corps. When he thought the proper moment had arrived, however, one of the least decorated of our party was offered to the consideration of the young ladies. The sisters were named Anne and Maria, and I could see by the pleasure that beamed in the soft blue eyes of the former that she was quite enchanted with the beauty of the *article* laid before her so unexpectedly. I believe it is in *female* 'human nature' to admire every thing that is graceful and handsome, and especially when it takes the form of needlework. The sweet girls praised handkerchief after handkerchief, until I was laid before them, when their pleasure extracted exclamations of delight. All was done so quietly, however, and in so ladylike a manner, that the attention of no person in the shop was drawn to them by this natural indulgence of surprise. Still I observed that neither of the young lades inquired the *prices*, these being considerations that had no influence on the intrinsic value, in their eyes; while the circumstance caused my heart to sink within me, as it clearly proved they did not intend to purchase, and I longed to become the property of the gentle, serene-eyed Anne. After thanking Mr. Bobbinet for the trouble he had taken, they ordered their purchases sent home, and were about to quit the shop.

'Can't I persuade you to take *this?*' demanded Bobbinet, as they were turning away. 'There is not its equal in America. Indeed, one of the house, our Colonel Silky, who has just returned from Paris, says it was worked expressly for the dauphine, who was prevented from getting it by the late revolution.'

'It *is* a pity so much lace and such exquisite work should be put on a pocket handkerchief,' said Anne, almost involuntarily. 'I fear if they were on something more suitable, I might buy them.'

A smile, a slight blush, and curtsy, concluded the interview; and the young ladies hastily left the shop. Mr. Bobbinet was disappointed, as, indeed, was Col. Silky, who was present, *en amateur*;[32] but the matter could not be helped, as these were customers who acted and thought for themselves, and all the oily persuasion of shop-eloquence could not influence them.

'It is quite surprising, colonel,' observed Mr. Bobbinet, when his customers were properly out of hearing, 'that *these* young ladies should let such an article slip through their fingers. Their father is one of the richest men we have; and yet they never even asked the price.'

'I fancy it was not so much the *price* that held 'em back,' observed the colonel, in his elegant way, 'as something else. There are a sort of customers that don't buy promiscuously; they do every thing by rule. They don't believe that a nightcap is intended for a bed-quilt.'

Bobbinet & Co. did not exactly understand his more sophisticated partner; but before he had time to ask an explanation, the appearance of another customer caused his face to brighten, and changed the current of his thoughts. The person who now entered was an exceedingly brilliant looking girl of twenty, dressed in the height of fashion, and extremely well, though a severe critic might have thought she was *over* dressed for the streets; still she had alighted from a carriage. Her face was decidedly handsome, and her person exquisitely proportioned. As a whole, I had scarcely ever seen a young creature that could lay claim to more of the loveliness of her sex. Both the young ladies who had just left us were pleasing and pretty; and to own the truth, there was an air of modest refinement about them, that was not so apparent in this new visitor; but the dazzling appearance of the latter, at first, blinded me to her faults, and I saw nothing but her perfection. The interest manifested by the master—I beg his pardon, the boss of the store—and the agitation among the clerks, very plainly proved that much was expected from the visit of this young lady, who was addressed, with a certain air of shop-familiarity, as Miss Halfacre—a familiarity that showed she was an habitué of the place, and considered a good customer.

Luckily for the views of Bobbinet & Co., we were all still lying on the counter. This is deemed a fortunate circumstance in the contingencies of this species of trade, since it enables the dealer to offer his uncalled-for wares in the least suspicious and most natural manner. It was fortunate, also, that I lay at the bottom of the little pile—a climax being quite as essential in sustaining an extortionate price, as in terminating with due effect, a poem, a tragedy, or a romance.

'Good morning, Miss Halfacre,' said Mr. Bobbinet, bowing and smiling; if his face had been half as honest as it professed to be, it would have *grinned*. 'I am glad you have come in at this moment, as we are about to put on sale some of the rarest articles, in the way of pocket handkerchiefs, that have ever come to this market. The Misses Burton have just seen them, and *they* pronounce them the most beautiful articles of the sort they have ever seen; and I believe they have been over half the world.'

'And did they take any, Mr. Bobbinet? The Miss Burtons are thought to have taste.'

'They have not exactly *purchased*, but I believe each of them has a particular article in her eye. Here is one, ma'am, that is rather prettier than any you have yet seen in New York. The price is *sixty* dollars.'

The word *sixty* was emphasized in a way to show the importance that was attached to *price*— that being a test of more than common importance with the present customer. I sighed when I remembered that poor Adrienne had received but about ten dollars for *me*—an article worth so much more than that there exhibited.

'It is really very pretty, Mr. Bobbinet, very pretty, but Miss Monson bought one not quite as pretty, at Lace's; and *she* paid *sixty-five*, if I am not mistaken.'

'I dare say; we have them at much higher prices. I showed you *this* only that you might see that *our sixties* are as handsome as *Mr. Lace's* sixty-*fives*. What do you think of *this*?'

'That *is* a jewel! What *is* the price, Mr. Bobbinet?'

'Why, we will let *you* have it for seventy; though I do think it ought to bring five more.'

'Surely you do not abate on pocket handkerchiefs! One doesn't like to have such a thing *too* low.'

'Ah, I may as well come to the point at once with such a customer as yourself, Miss Halfacre; here is the article on which I pride myself. *That* article never *was* equaled in this market, and never *will* be.'

I cannot repeat half the exclamations of delight that escaped the fair Eudosia, when I first burst on her entranced eye. She turned me over and over, examined me with palpitating bosom, and once I thought she was about to kiss me; then, in a trembling voice, she demanded the price.

'One hundred dollars, ma'am;' answered Bobbinet, solemnly. 'Not a cent more, on my honor.'

'No, surely!' exclaimed Eudosia, with delight instead of alarm. 'Not a *hundred*!'

'*One hundred*, Miss Eudosia, to the last cent; then we scarcely make a living profit.'

'Why, Mr. Bobbinet, this is the highest-priced handkerchief that was ever sold in New York.' This was said with a sort of rapture, the fair creature feeling all the advantage of having so good an opportunity of purchasing so dear an *article*.

'In America, ma'am. It is the highest-priced handkerchief, by twenty dollars, that ever crossed the Atlantic. The celebrated Miss Jewel's, of Boston, only cost seventy-nine.'

'Only! Oh, Mr. Bobbinet, I *must* have it. It is a perfect treasure!'

'Shall I send it, Miss Eudosia; or don't you like to trust it out of your sight?'

'Not yet, sir. To own the truth, I have not so much money. I only came out to buy a few trifles, and brought but fifty dollars with me; and Pa insists on having no bills. I never knew anybody as particular as Pa; but I will go instantly home and show him the importance of this purchase. You will not let the handkerchief be seen for *one* hour— only *one* hour—and then you shall hear from me.'

To this Bobbinet assented. The young lady tripped into her carriage, and was instantly whirled from the door. In precisely forty-three minutes, a maid entered, half out of breath, and laid a note on the counter. The latter contained Mr. Halfacre's check for one hundred dollars, and a request from the fair Eudosia that I might be delivered to her messenger. Every thing was done as she had desired, and, in five minutes, I was going up Broadway as fast as Honor O'Flagherty's (for such was the name of the messenger) little dumpy legs could carry me.

10

Mr. Henry Halfacre was a speculator in townlots—a profession that was, just then, in high repute in the city of New York. For farms, and all the more vulgar aspects of real estate, he had a sovereign contempt; but offer him a bit of land that could be measured by feet and inches, and he was your man. Mr. Halfacre inherited nothing, but he was a man of what are called energy and enterprise. In other words, he had a spirit for running in debt, and never shrunk from jeoparding property that, in truth, belonged to his creditors. The very morning that his eldest child, Eudosia, made her valuable acquisition, in my person, Henry Halfacre, Esq., was the owner of several hundred lots on the island of Manhattan; of 123 in the city of Brooklyn; of nearly as many in Williamsburg; of large undivided interests in Milwaukie, Chicago, Rock River, Moonville, and other similar places; besides owning a considerable part of a place called Coney Island. In a word, the landed estate of Henry Halfacre, Esq., 'inventoried,' as he expressed it, just 2,612,000 dollars; a handsome sum, it must be confessed, for a man who, when he began his beneficent and energetic career in this branch of business, was just 23,417 dollars worse than nothing. It is true, that there was some drawback on all this prosperity, Mr. Halfacre's bonds, notes, mortgages, and other liabilities making a sum total that amounted to the odd 600,000 dollars; this still left him, however, a handsome paper balance of two millions.

Notwithstanding the amount of his 'bills payable,' Mr. Halfacre considered himself a very prudent man: first, because he insisted on having no book debts; second, because he always took another man's paper for a larger amount than he had given of his own, for any specific lot or lots; thirdly, and lastly, because he was careful to 'extend himself,' at the risk of other persons. There is no question, had all his lots been sold as he had inventoried them; had his debts been paid; and had he not spent his money a little faster than it was bona fide made, that Henry Halfacre, Esq. would have been a very rich man. As he managed, however, by means of getting portions of the paper he received discounted, to maintain a fine figure account in the bank, and to pay all current demands, he began to be known as the *rich* Mr. Halfacre. But one of his children, the fair Eudosia,

was out;[33] and as she had some distance to make in the better society of the town, ere she could pass for aristocratic, it was wisely determined that a golden bridge should be thrown across the dividing chasm. A hundred-dollar pocket handkerchief, it was hoped, would serve for the keystone, and then all the ends of life would be attained. As to a husband, a pretty girl like Eudosia, and the daughter of a man of 'four figure' lots, might get one any day.

Honor O'Flagherty was both short-legged and short-breathed. She felt the full importance of her mission; and having an extensive acquaintance among the other Milesians of the town, and of her class, she stopped no less than eleven times to communicate the magnitude of Miss Dosie's purchase. To two particular favorites she actually showed me, under solemn promise of secrecy; and to four others she promised a peep some day, after her *bossee* had fairly worn me. In this manner my arrival was circulated prematurely in certain coteries, the pretty mouths and fine voices that spoke of my marvels being quite unconscious that they were circulating news that had reached their ears via Honor O'Flagherty, Biddy Noon, and Kathleen Brady.

Mr. Halfacre occupied a very genteel residence in Broadway, where he and his enjoyed the full benefit of all the dust, noise, and commotion of that great thoroughfare. This house had been purchased and mortgaged, generally simultaneous operations with this great operator, as soon as he had 'inventoried' half a million. It was a sort of patent of nobility to live in Broadway; and the acquisition of such a residence was like the purchase of a marquiseta in Italy. When Eudosia was fairly in possession of a hundred-dollar pocket handkerchief, the great seal might be said to be attached to the document that was to elevate the Halfacres throughout all future time.

Now the beautiful Eudosia—for beautiful, and even lovely, this glorious-looking creature was, in spite of a very badly modulated voice, certain inroads upon the fitness of things in the way of expression, and a want of a knowledge of the finesse of fine life—now the beautiful Eudosia had an intimate friend named Clara Caverly, who was as unlike her as possible, in character, education, habits, and appearance; and yet who was firmly her friend. The attachment was one of childhood and accident—the two girls having been neighbors and school-fellows until they had got to like each other, after the manner in which young people form such friendships, to wear away under the friction of the world, and the pressure of time. Mr. Caverly was a lawyer of good practice, fair reputation, and respectable family. His wife happened to be a lady from her cradle, and the daughter had experienced the advantage of as great a blessing. Still Mr. Caverly was what the world of New York, in 1832, called poor; that is to say, he had no known bank-stock, did not own a lot on the island, was director of neither bank nor insurance company, and lived in a modest two-story house, in White Street. It is true his practice supported his family, and enabled him to invest in bonds and mortgages two or three thousand a year; and he owned the fee of some fifteen or eighteen farms in Orange County, which were falling in from three-lives leases, and which had been in his family ever since the seventeenth century. But, at a period of prosperity like that which prevailed in 1832, 3, 4, 5, and 6, the hereditary dollar was not worth more than twelve and a half cents, as compared with the 'inventoried' dollar. As there is something, after all, in a historical name, and the Caverlys still had the best of it, in the way of society, Eudosia was permitted to continue the visits in White Street, even after her own family were in full possession in Broadway, and Henry Halfacre, Esq., had got to be enumerated among the Manhattan nabobs. Clara Caverly was in Broadway when Honor O'Flagherty arrived with me, out of breath, in consequence of the shortness of her legs, and the necessity of making up for lost time.

'There, Miss Dosie,' cried the exulting house-maid, for such was Honor's domestic rank, though preferred to so honorable and confidential a

mission—'There, Miss Dosie, there it is, and it's a jewel.'

'What has Honor brought you *now?*' asked Clara Caverly in her quiet way, for she saw by the brilliant eyes and flushed cheeks of her friend that it was something the other would have pleasure in conversing about. 'You make so many purchases, dear Eudosia, that I should think you would weary of them.'

'What, weary of beautiful dresses? Never, Clara, never! That might do for White Street, but in Broadway one is never tired of such things—see,' laying me out at full length in her lap, 'this is a pocket handkerchief—I wish your opinion of it.'

Clara examined me very closely, and, in spite of something like a frown, and an expression of dissatisfaction that gathered about her pretty face—for Clara was pretty, too—I could detect some of the latent feelings of the sex, as she gazed at my exquisite lace, perfect ornamental work, and unequaled fineness. Still, her education and habits triumphed, and she would not commend what she regarded as ingenuity misspent, and tasteless, because senseless, luxury.

'This handkerchief cost *one hundred dollars,* Clara,' said Eudosia, deliberately and with emphasis, imitating, as near as possible, the tone of Bobbinet & Co.

'Is it possible, Eudosia! What a sum to pay for so useless a thing!'

'Useless! Do you call a pocket handkerchief useless?'

'Quite so, when it is made in a way to render it out of the question to put it to the uses for which it was designed. I should as soon think of trimming gumshoes with satin, as to trim a handkerchief in that style.'

'Style? Yes, I flatter myself it *is* style to have a handkerchief that cost a hundred dollars. Why, Clara Caverly, the highest priced thing of this sort that was ever before sold in New York only came to seventy-nine dollars. Mine is superior to all, by twenty-one dollars!'

Clara Caverly sighed. It was not with regret, or envy, or any unworthy feeling, however; it was a fair, honest, moral sigh, that had its birth in the thought of how much good a hundred dollars might have done, properly applied. It was under the influence of this feeling, too, that she said, somewhat inopportunely it must be confessed, though quite innocently—

'Well, Eudosia, I am glad you can afford such a luxury, at all events. Now is a good time to get your subscription to the Widows' and Orphans' Society. Mrs. Thoughtful has desired me to ask for it half a dozen times; I dare say it has escaped you that you are quite a twelvemonth in arrear.'

'*Now* a good time to ask for three dollars! What, just when I've paid a hundred dollars for a pocket handkerchief? That was not said with your usual good sense, my dear. People must be *made* of money to pay out so much at one time.'

'When may I tell Mrs. Thoughtful, then, that you will send it to her?'

'I am sure that is more than I can say. Pa will be in no hurry to give me more money soon, and I want, at this moment, near a hundred dollars' worth of articles of dress to make a decent appearance. The Society can be in no such hurry for its subscriptions; they must amount to a good deal.'

'Not if never paid. Shall I lend you the money—my mother gave me ten dollars this morning, to make a few purchases, which I can very well do without until you can pay me.'

'*Do*, dear girl—you are always one of the best creatures in the world. How much is it? three dollars I believe.'

'Six, if you pay the past and present year. I will pay Mrs. Thoughtful before I go home. But, dear Eudosia, I wish you had not bought that foolish pocket handkerchief.'

'Foolish! Do you call a handkerchief with such lace, and all this magnificent work on it, and which cost a *hundred dollars*, foolish? Is it foolish to have money, or to be thought rich?'

'Certainly not the first, though it may be better not to be thought rich. I wish to see you always dressed with propriety, for you do credit to your dress; but this handkerchief is out of place.'

'Out of place! Now; hear me, Clara, though it is to be a great secret. What do you think Pa is worth?'

'Bless me, these are things I never think of. I do not even know how much my own father is worth. Mother tells me how much I may spend, and I can want to learn no more.'

'Well, Mr. Murray dined with Pa last week, and they sat over their wine until near ten. I overheard them talking, and got into this room to listen, for I thought I should get something new. At first they said nothing but "lots—lots—uptown—downtown—twenty-five feet front—dollar, dollar, dollar." La! child, you never heard such stuff in your life!'

'One gets used to these things, notwithstanding,' observed Clara, drily.

'Yes, one *does* hear a great deal of it. I shall be glad when the gentlemen learn to talk of something else. But the best is to come. At last, Pa asked Mr. Murray if he had inventoried lately.'

'Did he?'

'*Yes,* he did. Of course you know what that means?'

'It means to *fill*, as they call it, does it not?'

'So I thought at first, but it means no such thing. It means to count up, and set down how much one is worth. Mr. Murray said he did *that* every month, and of course he knew very well what *he* was worth. I forget how much it was, for I didn't care, you know George Murray is not as old as I am, and so I listened to what Pa had inventoried. Now, how much do you guess?'

'Really, my dear, I haven't the least idea,' answered Clara, slightly gaping—'a thousand dollars, perhaps.'

'A thousand dollars! What, for a gentleman who keeps his coach—lives in Broadway—dresses his daughter as I dress, and gives her hundred-dollar handkerchiefs. Two hundred million, my dear; two hundred million!'

Eudosia had interpolated the word 'hundred' quite innocently, for, as usually happens with those to whom money is new, her imagination ran ahead of her arithmetic. 'Yes,' she added, 'two hundred millions; besides sixty millions of odd money!'

'That sounds like a great deal,' observed Clara quietly; for, besides caring very little for these millions, she had not a profound respect for her friend's accuracy on such subjects.

'It is a great deal. Ma says there are not ten richer men than Pa in the state. Now, does not this alter the matter about the pocket handkerchief? It would be mean in me not to have a hundred-dollar handkerchief, when I could get one.'

'It may alter the matter as to the extravagance; but it does not alter it as to the fitness. Of what *use* is a pocket handkerchief like this? A pocket handkerchief is made for *use*, my dear, not for show.'

'You would not have a young lady use her pocket handkerchief like a snuffy old nurse, Clara?'

'I would have her use it like a young lady, and in no other way. But it always strikes me as a proof of ignorance and a want of refinement when the uses of things are confounded. A pocket handkerchief, at the best, is but a menial appliance, and it is bad taste to make it an object of attraction. *Fine*, it may be, for that conveys an idea of delicacy in its owner; but ornamented beyond reason, never. Look what a tawdry and vulgar thing an embroidered slipper is on a woman's foot.'

'Yes, I grant you that, but everybody cannot have hundred-dollar handkerchiefs, though they may have embroidered slippers. I shall wear my purchase at Miss Trotter's ball tonight.'

To this Clara made no objection, though she still looked disapprobation of her purchase. Now the lovely Eudosia had not a bad heart; she had only received a bad education. Her parents had given her a smattering of the usual accomplishments, but here her superior instruction ended. Unable to discriminate themselves, for the want of this very education, they had been obliged to trust their daughter to the care of mercenaries, who fancied their duties discharged when they

had taught their pupil to repeat like a parrot. All she acquired had been for effect, and not for the purpose of everyday use; in which her instruction and her pocket handkerchief might be said to be of a piece.

11

And here I will digress a moment to make a single remark on a subject of which popular feeling, in America, under the influence of popular habits, is apt to take an ex parte view. Accomplishments are derided as useless, in comparison with what is considered household virtues. The accomplishment of a cook is to make good dishes, of a seamstress to sew well, and of a lady to possess refined tastes, a cultivated mind, and agreeable and intellectual habits. The real *virtues* of all are the same, though subject to laws peculiar to their station; but it is a very different thing when we come to the mere accomplishments. To deride all the refined attainments of human skill denotes ignorance of the means of human happiness, nor is it any evidence of acquaintance with the intricate machinery of social greatness and a lofty civilization. These gradations in attainments are inseparable from civilized society, and if the skill of the ingenious and laborious is indispensable to a solid foundation, without the tastes and habits of the refined and cultivated, it never can be graceful or pleasing.

Eudosia had some indistinct glimmerings of this fact, though it was not often that she came to sound and discriminating decisions even in matters less complicated. In the present instance she saw this truth only by halves, and that, too, in its most commonplace aspect, as will appear by the remark she made on the occasion.

'Then, Clara, as to the *price* I have paid for this handkerchief,' she said, 'you ought to remember what the laws of political economy lay down on such subjects. I suppose your Pa makes you study political economy, my dear?'

'Indeed he does not. I hardly know what it means.'

'Well, that is singular; for Pa says, in this age of the world, it is the only way to be rich. No it is by means of a trade in lots, and political economy, generally, that he has succeeded so wonderfully; for, to own the truth to you, Clara, Pa hasn't always been rich.'

'No?' answered Clara, with a half-suppressed smile, she knowing the fact already perfectly well.

'Oh, no—far from it—but we don't speak of this publicly, it being a sort of disgrace in New York, you know, not to be thought worth at least half a million. I dare say your Pa is worth as much as that?'

'I have not the least idea he is worth a fourth of it, though I do not pretend to know. To me half a million of dollars seems a great deal of money, and I know my father considers himself poor— poor, at least, for one of his station. But what were you about to say of political economy? I am curious to hear how *that* can have any thing to do with your handkerchief.'

'Why, my dear, in this manner. You know a distribution of labor is the source of all civilization—that trade is an exchange of equivalents—that custom houses fetter these equivalents—that nothing that is fettered is free—'

'My dear Eudosia, what *is* your tongue running on?'

'You will not deny, Clara, that any thing that is fettered is not free? And that freedom is the greatest blessing of this happy country; and that trade ought to be as free as any thing else?'

All this was gibberish to Clara Caverly, who understood the phrases, notwithstanding, quite as well as the friend who was using them. Political economy is especially a science of terms; and free trade, as a branch of it is called, is just the portion of it which is indebted to them the most. But Clara had not patience to hear any more of the unintelligible jargon which has got possession of the world today, much as Mr. Pitt's celebrated sinking fund scheme for paying off the national debt of Great Britain did,[34] half a century since, and under very much the same influences; and she

desired her friend to come at once to the point, as connected with the pocket handkerchief.

'Well, then,' resumed Eudosia, 'it is connected in this way. The luxuries of the rich give employment to the poor, and cause money to circulate. Now this handkerchief of mine, no doubt, has given employment to some poor French girl for four or five months, and, of course, food and raiment. She has earned, no doubt, fifty of the hundred dollars I have paid. Then the custom house—ah, Clara, if it were not for that vile custom house, I might have had the handkerchief for at least five-and-twenty dollars lower—!'

'In which case you would have prized it five-and-twenty times less,' answered Clara, smiling archly.

'*That* is true; yes, free trade, after all, does *not* apply to pocket handkerchiefs.'

'And yet,' interrupted Clara, laughing, 'if one can believe what one reads, it applies to hackney coaches, ferry boats, doctors, lawyers, and even the clergy. My father says it is—'

'What? I am curious to know, Clara, what as plain speaking a man as Mr. Caverly calls it.'

'He is plain speaking enough to call it a— *humbug*,' said the daughter, endeavoring to mouth the word in a theatrical manner. 'But, as Othello says, the handkerchief.'[35]

'Oh! Fifty dollars go to the poor girl who does the work, twenty-five more to the odious custom house, some fifteen to rent, fuel, lights, and ten, perhaps, to Mr. Bobbinet, as profits. Now all this is very good, and very useful to society, as you must own.'

Alas, poor Adrienne! Thou didst not receive for me as many francs as this fair calculation gave thee dollars; and richer wouldst thou have been, and, oh, how much happier, hadst thou kept the money paid for me, sold the lace even at a loss, and spared thyself so many, many hours of painful and anxious toil! But it is thus with human calculations: the propositions seem plausible, and the reasoning fair, while stern truth lies behind all to level the pride of understanding, and prove the fallacy of the wisdom of men. The reader may wish to see how closely Eudosia's account of profit and loss came to the fact, and I shall, consequently, make up the statement from the private books of the firm that had the honor of once owning me, viz.:

Super-extraordinary Pocket handkerchief, &c., in account with Bobbinet & Co.

DR.

To money paid, first cost, francs 100, at 5.25—$19.04

To interest on same for ninety days, at 7 percent—00.33

To portion of passage money—00.04

To porterage—00.00 1/4

To washing and making up—00.25

$19.66 1/4

CR.

By cash paid by Miss Thimble—$1.00

By cash paid for article—100.00

By washerwoman's deduction—00.05

101.05

By profit—$81.39?

NOTES

1. 'Rotting' (or 'retting') is the process of soaking flax in water, to soften it in preparation for weaving. Its fibers are then separated out by beating, which is probably what Cooper means by 'crackling'.

2. Combed, the final stage of preparing the flax for weaving.

3. Marie Thérèse d'Angoulême (1778–1851), the only daughter of Louis XVI.

4. Open spaces where new linen is stretched out on the ground to whiten in the sun.

5. *Legitimist*: a royalist who supported the claims of the representative of the senior line of the house of Bourbon to be the legitimate king of France. Leftist *liberals* argued for reform.

6. 'Left side' liberals and 'right side' *legitimists* (French).

7. "Nazareth! Can anything good come from there?"' (John 1:46)

8. Center left (French).

9. Gold coin minted in the reign of Napoleon I, equal to twenty francs.

10. Prefect (French).

11. Neighborhood (French).

12. The Duchesse d'Angoulême (see note 3).

13. Gossip (French).

14. Four decrees establishing absolute rule, issued by King Charles X on 25th July 1830, which touched off the July Revolution.

15. Good area (French).

16. There are Bourbons and there are Bourbons (French).

17. New Year's Day (French).

18. Sulking, silent (French).

19. French banker and politician (1767–1844).

20. Stock exchange (French).

21. Stockbrokers (French).

22. Small coin (five centimes); twenty sous are equal to one franc.

23. Seamstress (French).

24. Learned people.

25. An archaic exclamation derived from 'In faith'.

26. Always the same (Latin). The shirt is presumably being ironic.

27. 'To the manner born', from *Hamlet*, 1.4.14ff, frequently misquoted as 'to the manor born'.

28. Supporter of King Charles X.

29. Ever so little of (French).

30. My dear (French).

31. Stupid or inane remarks (French).

32. As a connoisseur (French).

33. 'Was out'—had been presented to society.

34. In 1786 William Pitt the Younger (1759–1806) introduced a sinking fund to underpin national finances.

35. 'Fetch me the handkerchief', from Shakespeare's *Othello*, 1.4.98.

FURTHER READING: MEMORY

Jean Baggott, *The Girl on the Wall: One Life's Rich Tapestry* (London: Icon Books, 2009).

Pennina Barnett, "Making, Materiality and Memory," in *The Body Politic: The Role of the Body and Contemporary Craft*, ed. Julian Stair (London: Crafts Council, 2000) pp. 141–148.

bell hooks, "Aesthetic Inheritances: History Worked by Hand," in *Yearning: Race, Gender and Cultural Politics* (Boston: South End Press, 1990) pp. 115–122.

Floss M. Jay, "Knitting Gloves," in *LIP from Southern African Women*, ed. Susan Brown, Isabel Hofmeyer, and Susan Rosenberg (Johannesburg: Raven Press, 1983) pp. 32–36.

Ann Rosalind Jones and Peter Stallybrass, *Renaissance Clothing and the Materials of Memory* (Cambridge: Cambridge Studies in Renaissance Literature and Culture, 2000).

Haruki Murakami, "Tony Takitani," in *Blind Willow, Sleeping Woman* (London: Vintage Books, 2007). Also, Jun Ichikawa (film director), *Tony Takitani* (Culver City, CA: Strand Releasing, 2004).

Justine Picardie, *My Mother's Wedding Dress: The Fabric of Our Lives* (London: Picador, 2005).

Ruth Scheuing, "Penelope and the Unraveling of History," in *New Feminist Art Criticism*, ed. Katy Deepwell (Manchester: Manchester University Press, 1995) pp. 188–195.

Otto von Busch, "Textile Punctum," available at http://www.kulturservern.se/wronsov/selfpassage/textilePunctum/textPunctum.pdf.

PART III

STRUCTURE

PART INTRODUCTION

Textiles have particular structures. Woven, knitted, and felted cloth all present specific types of construction, from the warp and weft of weaving, to the single looped thread of knitting, to the fulling of loose fibers to create felt. These structures gain further complexity when fabric is made into quilts or embellished with embroidery. Textile structures provide poetic inspiration for thinking about and making a raft of networks—at times on a scale that far exceeds the typical textile. But the structural importance of cloth extends beyond the mechanics of its making. The textile structure is also compared to the structure of language by a number of contributions in this section. Both are based on small components (words and fibers) that are combined to make more complex wholes (sentences, paragraphs, and cloth).

Italo Calvino opens this section with his description of two fictional cities. One maps the social, political, and trade relations of the city through a code of colored thread. The other literally hangs like a net in space. In Calvino's two stories, thread acts first as the material strength of a community and then as the map of the relations that make a community possible. Both make use of the incongruous fragility of thread to suggest the physical and social impermanence of the ways we live. The architect Philip Beesley creates environments in which architecture makes use of textile structures and, with the aid of sensors, becomes responsive to our presence. In the early piece of writing included here, he writes of several experimental projects with students that created geotextiles. Of interest is not only the scale of textiles that Beesley constructed with his students but also the structure of the writing that documents his work. Patched together from pieces of journal entries and critical reflections, the structure of this writing is as inspired by the textile as the material "stuff" that is made. Catherine de Zegher writes about the work of Cecilia Vicuña and discusses the textile as a way to map (precarious) spaces and make poetry. Here, too, the textile is both a physical structure existing in space and a way of working with language. De Zegher writes of Vicuña's work: "the line—as a cord and as a single row of words in a poem—is a trail of communication."

Elaine Showalter focuses on yet another textile structure, the quilt, and considers it in relation to time and the development of women's literature. Showalter observes that the quilt's structure can be seen as a creative template taken up by early fiction written by women in America. "Piecing," she writes, "is the art form which best reflects the fragmentation of women's time, the dailiness and repetitiveness of women's work." Showalter sees a connection between the construction of the quilt— how its making fit the demands of women's time—and the "dominant genre of American women's writing . . . the short story, the short narrative piece."

Paul Whittaker and Clio Padovani take yet a different textile structure, the loop of knitting, and use it as a way of exploring psychoanalytic ideas and reflecting on the meaning of contemporary knitting practice. In their writing, the pair aim "to establish what might be at stake in an extended classification of the practice of the knotting and looping of thread." Here the structure of the loop is understood both literally, as physically evident in the photography of Margi Geerlinks and the sculptures of the late Louise Bourgeois, and symbolically, as present in the psychoanalytic theories of Jacques Lacan. Following Whittaker and Padovani's text is a short excerpt from the writing of Gilles Deleuze and Félix Guattari, whose influence can be felt throughout this *Reader*. Deleuze and Guattari use the structure of woven and felted cloth to communicate their theoretical ideas about smooth and striated space. The textile is one of numerous examples explored in their discussion of smooth and striated space, but their text is of interest here because the textile offers an articulate structure for the exploration of dense theoretical thinking. Again we are shown how textiles can—in many differing ways—communicate thinking that extends far beyond the physical reality of cloth.

Pennina Barnett takes up the thinking of another of Deleuze's influential writings, this time on the fold, to speak of an alternative way of theorizing textile practice that rejects the binary structure of ideas and instead calls for a "soft logic" of textile thought. Barnett's essay was originally written for an exhibition catalog, and its poetic tone evokes the rhythms of textile making. She suggests an alternative system of values to the rigid structuring of analysis (often borrowed by textile writers from other disciplines) and proposes the importance of touch and of thinking via the structure of the fold "in a continuous present." Judith Clark also writes outside the conventional structures of academic writing. Writing about space and the curation of fashion, Clark uses the functional format of the list. Her writing style captures the variable speed and focus of the thinking process, which often gives us ideas in a seemingly random sequence and at an unpredictable, uncontrollable pace. Rather than edit, tidy, and conform, Clark allows us insight into this raw phase where ideas are often, ironically, at their most dynamic—before the red pen has squeezed original intentions into tidy paragraphs and footnotes.

13

INVISIBLE CITIES

Italo Calvino

Editor's introduction: Cuban-born Italian writer Italo Calvino's novel *Invisible Cities* was published in 1972. Calvino uses the explorer Marco Polo as a central narrative voice in the novel, which travels through a number of imagined sites. In the section "Trading Cities" Calvino describes a "woven" urban landscape, one where colored threads map and mark networks of communication in much the same way that our virtual connections chart our web-based communication patterns today. But Calvino's city of Ersilia is essentially nomadic, moving on and leaving only a network of threads behind. The inhabitants' ambitions feel prescient—an endless quest for a system that is both "more complex and at the same time more regular than the other." In "Thin Cities" Calvino imagines another woven landscape, this time suspended precariously as a net providing "passage and . . . support." This inverted world is not considered foolhardy; instead, it is described as a setting acutely aware of a finite existence, while—it is suggested—the rest of us live on in ignorance of the inevitability that this is in fact a shared reality.

TRADING CITIES

In Ersilia, to establish the relationships that sustain the city's life, the inhabitants stretch strings from the corners of the houses, white or black or gray or black-and-white according to whether they mark a relationship of blood, of trade, authority, agency. When the strings become so numerous that you can no longer pass among them, the inhabitants leave: the houses are dismantled; only the strings and their supports remain.

From a mountainside, camping with their household goods, Ersilia's refugees look at the labyrinth of taut strings and poles that rise in the plain. That is the city of Ersilia still, and they are nothing.

They rebuild Ersilia elsewhere. They weave a similar pattern of strings which they would like to be more complex and at the same time more regular than the other. Then they abandon it and take themselves and their houses still farther away.

Thus, when traveling in the territory of Ersilia, you come upon the ruins of the abandoned cities, without the walls which do not last, without the bones of the dead which the wind rolls away: spider-webs of intricate relationships seeking a form.

THIN CITIES

If you choose to believe me, good. Now I will tell how Octavia, the spider-web city, is made. There is a precipice between two steep mountains: the city is over the void, bound to the two crests with ropes and chains and catwalks. You walk on the little wooden ties, careful not to set your foot in the open spaces, or you cling to the hempen strands. Below there is nothing for hundreds and hundreds of feet: a few clouds glide past; farther down you can glimpse the chasm's bed.

This is the foundation of the city: a net which serves as passage and as support. All the rest, instead of rising up, is hung below: rope ladders, hammocks, houses made like sacks, clothes hangers, terraces like gondolas, skins of water, gas jets, spits, baskets on strings, dumb-waiters, showers, trapezes and rings for children's games, cable cars, chandeliers, pots with trailing plants.

Suspended over the abyss, the life of Octavia's inhabitants is less uncertain than in other cities. They know the net will last only so long.

14

REFLEXIVE TEXTILE

Philip Beesley

Editor's introduction: Canadian Philip Beesley is a Toronto-based architect and professor at the School of Architecture, University of Waterloo. In 2010 he represented Canada at the Venice Architecture Biennale with *Hylozoic Ground*—"an immersive, interactive environment that moves and breathes around its viewers." *Hylozoism* refers to the ancient belief that all matter has life. Beesley's responsive, semi-living architecture uses "next-generation artificial intelligence, synthetic biology, and interactive technology to create an environment that is nearly alive."[a] His writing on geotextiles reprinted here was first published in *Surface Design Journal* in 1999 and earned an Award of Merit in the 1998 Surface Design Association Critical Writing Competition. Beesley's scale of reference for what a textile might be goes far beyond the confines of the body, or even the home, which we commonly regard as textile territory. In the student projects he discusses, the textile operates as a version of the landscape. The narrative he provides uses an explanatory voice "interwoven" (quite literally) with poetic diary entries, punctuated by visual documentation of the projects.

And the curtain of the temple was torn . . .[1]

This article explores hybrid textiles involving large-scale net fabrics that dress the ground, following and emphasizing topography.

The projects were produced by the author in collaboration with a number of visual artists including Warren Seelig of Philadelphia and Rockport, Maine, Seattle sculptor Katherine Gray, students of Haystack Mountain School for Crafts, DalTech School of Architecture, and the University of Waterloo Faculty of Architecture.

The discussion explores a particular approach to critique in contemporary textile art. Qualities of the work are explored using analogies to textiles in clothing and including a number of personal journal entries alluding to the projects. This pursuit leads to questions about our own bodies, and our sense of domain. The fabrics described here have immersive and reflexive qualities. *Reflex* is a response that suggests the textile being touched touches back. *Immersion* goes beyond the familiar sense of being clothed and surrounded by a fabric. Here the term implies animated space expanding and dissolving boundaries. In these fabrics boundaries of our selves—body and psyche—are questioned.

Source: Philip Beesley, "Reflexive Textile," *Surface Design Journal* (Spring 1999) pp. 4–10. Reproduced with permission.
a. Canadian Pavillion, Venice Biennale 2010, Hylozoic Ground, http://www.hylozoicground.com/intro/intro03.html.

The "hand" of fabric—the particular interaction of nap, bias and weave that combines to give every fabric a specific quality of movement and interaction when it is handled—is often referred to in descriptive reviews of textile art. We know that handling textile has a particular link to human emotion. There are poignant implications in the way textile flexes and moves with us. When we grieve, we grasp and caress and tear cloth.

This textile "hand" is a reference for the projects here in several ways. The first example shown concentrates on flexible draping that pronounces and extends the shape of the land. The next project attempts a porous, ephemeral space that opens boundaries. Other examples tend toward an intimate prosthetic relationship in which living functions are implied in the fabric. Here the hand is active, flexing and recoiling.

The projects *Haystack Veil, Erratics Net, Synthetic Earth* and *Palatine Burial*[2] attempt special qualities:

Haystack Veil is a landscape of cut saplings, thirty thousand twigs cut and bundled into a "knit" veil floating over a moss and lichen covered cliff alongside the Atlantic Ocean. *Haystack Veil* bears on the land following primordial topography, a cloak over the earth.

Erratics Net is a complex interlinked wire fabric mounted on a glacier-scoured terrain in Nova Scotia. Layers of new strata floating just above the surface of the land are developed within the foam-like filigree of this textile installation.

Synthetic Earth is a composite material involving a mass of sealed glass vessels holding digestive fluids covered by a densely layered net. The elements in this covering material are designed with springing barbed details encouraging accretive massing and clumping, a slow process of ingestion. A lurking, carnivorous quality results.

Palatine Burial is a grotto of densely massed barbed wire shards with individual links configured to grasp and puncture adjacent surfaces. Like the links used in *Synthetic Earth*, these details are ambivalent. They act as a reef supporting new growth, while at the same time their acute physical nature repels.

Scoured granite. solid. On the surface, giving: a thick sponge of lichen and moss crust softening every step. I moved to the bare mass below. At first hunched like before, still cradled on the memory of permanently floating city floors, every sidewalk hollow. But the ground here was different: not a tremor. Stone—not broken, not strained, not sailing up into vibrating light nor folded inflections trembling nor resonating with a hundred thousand voices of neighborhood. Silent.

My legs changed.

I stood on the ground.[3]

Haystack Veil was constructed on the glacier-formed shorecliffs flanking Haystack Mountain School of Crafts in Maine. A quarter-acre in size, the fabric is a triaxial lattice structure made from a network of repeating sapling tripods carrying long bundled twig fibers. The fibers form a continuous meshwork floating about sixteen inches above the ground. The firmly planted feet of each tripod stand toe to toe and brace each other.

This resilient anchoring makes the fabric behave like a second skin for the ground. The floating layer rolls and creases, following the earth. It spreads, wrapping over minor log falls and bridging over gullies, stretching over the dense mass of lichens and mosses at ground level while at the same time throwing into high relief the penetrations of tree trunks, groundfall branches and boulders breaking through the fabric. By filtering out the detail of the tangled forest floor, the primordial terrain of the glaciated bedrock underfoot is pronounced, telegraphing its hidden forms into the new hovering surface.

Figure 14.1. Philip Beesley with warren seeling and textile students, *Haystack Veil*, 1997. Partial view, Maine.

A curious sense results. On the surface, the aura of the work is of cottage industry, a hive of workers constructing an intimate cloak for the ground. At the same time an archaic presence prevails revealing deep land beneath. The result is a surface tension, a resilient meniscus.[4]

Just below my hand stirring the ocean surface, they flickered—sparks, sputtering and extinguishing, rising and sinking. A wild thicket of pulsing light close to my hand, in waves following my waving, dispersing clusters like stars. Opening into trails, carried by tiny swirling currents away from fingertips. Trails leading away from the swarm, into the dark of the water: yet out there, too, a quiet refrain of slow murmuring flashes. If my hand grew still, the phosphorescence would grow quieter, though a halo of intermittent pulses remained

around my hand—the sheer warmth of touch was enough to excite them. And, even deeper, one flash—then silence. But again, ten feet out; forty feet . . . Not touchable, but continually flexing in response to my touch. Dissolving; alive.

Erratics Net is a hovering, elusive filigree extending a glacier-scoured granite terrain on a Nova Scotia shore. A scattered field of enormous rounded boulders lies on the bedrock surface, the residue of the last ice age. The ground here is bare save for fragile patches of mosses and grasses clinging to hollows above the reach of the high ocean tides. The atmosphere is in constant flux, alternately bathed in thick humid washes of fog and stripped by gales rolling in from North Atlantic currents.

A special soil reinforcing mesh was developed for this shore. The mesh has two states. The first

Figure 14.2. Philip Beesley with Dal Tech architecture students, *Erratics Net*, 1998. First stage of installation, Nova Scotia.

is a widespread net anchoring into the rock surface. This artificial reef encourages turf growth by means of myriad hooked clips catching windblown plant matter, holding and amassing a matted matrix serving as synthetic soil. In this state, the textile is organized in a pillowed form of alternating peaks and valleys, presenting barbs outward, catching new material, and inward for anchoring beneath. These anchors hold the net just above the bare rock, making a shallow film of still, sheltered air allowing delicate growth to emerge. The net is made with wire joints clamped by sliding flexible tubes that lock each link to its neighbor making a tough, resilient structure.

The second state responds to extended times of deep fog where the air stills and the ground is soaked in vapor. Responding to this state the net can expand into multiple layers, each outward facing peak formed within a matrix layer, in turn serving as the foot for an inward facing valley of the next layer. A foam-like cellular lattice results, a filigree extending throughout the thickened atmosphere. The natural growth encouraged by this armature is froth-like, filling space with infinitesimal mass. The material is marked by regular intervals, momentarily thickening and making a porous stratified border, then opening again. A striated penumbra emerges, an aura floating outward from the land. Like plankton phosphorescing in the ocean, *Erratics Net* offers dissociated space, an absorption into ether.

A skin of bull's blood. The ground was dry before she poured it. Past crimson and past rubedo, black-red. The earthen kitchen floor was the center, not like the clean porcelain inside or

Figure 14.3. Phillip Beesley with Dal Tech architecture students, *Erratics Net,* 1998. Ground level view, Nova Scotia.

the planks at the front. The hearth in the back like forever, a floor with a burnished crust of red. Each fall, refreshing. Seeping into the crazed labyrinth of surface cracks, settling under to soften for a moment, then rubbing furiously and setting into gleaming skin covering the deep ground.[5]

Synthetic Earth, the collaborative installation with glass artist Katherine Gray, contains a mound of stacked wax-sealed glass vessels holding dark fluids. Each vessel bears a long collar with a holster of crimped wire joint details. These junctions form roots for fronds of intertwining twisted wire links that slide and lock together making a helical geometry of ropy strands. Each link contains outflung arms detailed with hooked barbs, acting like burrs grasping and tangling with neighboring links. A dense mass of these strands make a tangled shroud engulfing the glasswork contents of bile and blood. These contents are partly natural, from human donations, and partly synthetic, from fermented soy and salt solutions. Like feltwork, the fabric amasses complexes of individual fibers. The network tends to assemble itself by sticking to adjacent surfaces. The grasping details of the wire strands anchored to each vessel pull inward, implying that the fluids within the glasswork were ingested from without, giving a lurking, predatory presence. In spite of this outwardly aggressive posture, the interior of this material is intimate, acutely in need of its thick covering fabric. In this way the fabric is like flesh.

Swaddling: a wide band, brought down the shins, tucked under the heels then over to clamp the beginning of the shroud. Spiraling

Figure 14.4. Philip Beesley with Caroline Munk, *Erratics Net,* 1998. Detail of second stage, Nova Scotia.

up the long thin body, three full turns until the shoulders, a long serpentine edge from above to below. Bound, a coiling sheath. Turning at the shoulders, hooding up over the crown of the tiny skull, caressing the edge of exposed temples, falling behind ears and hinge of jaw. Loosening at the throat, a fibula brooch shaped like a smooth egg holding the gathered linen. A wide smooth throat falling deep within the opening in the cloth. Eyes wider than pools receiving everything, offering to every guilt-filled gaze of the throng: for you.

A vessel shaped by clean hands, cut into the soft tufa stone beneath the gate. Barely stone: warm hued, remembering its flow from the Alban crater. Stone like bread, honey colored, shot through with shattered bits: exploded magma in iridescent bits, fused basalt shards, chalked travertines crushed and folded and worried through and through the volcanic mud. The depression cut and shaped down and out, rhythmic scorings by iron making a deep depressed circle like a world. Lined with layers of finest softest clay siftings like young skin.

Within this bed the child is laid. With him, the beaker and the bowl. The ointments are poured: frankincense, myrrh. Above is fitted the cypress threshold. My body is safe.[6]

Like *Synthetic Earth*, *Palatine Burial* is a fabric "soil," a spreading geotextile reinforcing the soil and fostering new growth. *Palatine Burial* responded to a recent excavation in Rome in which traces were found of a baby that was sacrificed and buried beneath the ancient fortifications of the city. The project involved construction of a textile cover used for reburial of the archeological

Figure 14.5. Philip Beesley with Katherine Gray, *Synthetic Earth,* 1996. Installation view, Ontario.

site. The sacrifice was for propitiation, protecting the boundary of the city. Making sacred. A mundus, a little world offered instead of the world around. Beneath the wall at the edge of the city, a pit was dug into the volcanic mudstone tufa, fitted to the clay dolium vessel enclosing the tiny body. Sifted linings filled in the spaces closing the void between the vessel and the stone. Tiny fragments of the burial remained: a brooch; a tooth. Laid bare. What material could be adequate for covering there?

Each link of the fabric net received special details. Inside was an anatomy of transparent vessels cushioned by sprung tenons and terminated by serrated hollow needles to puncture and drain. Toward the outside, angled crampons, bent back for springing and grasping, were set up with hair-trigger antennae. Around, there was a spread of open joints with outflung guides to catch and link with neighbors.

Each of these protozoan links was thin and meager, but by linking and clumping together they made mass and thickness. At first a bare lattice-work controlled by the geometry of its elements then increasingly formless and growing darker as it ingested decomposing matter. Thicker and fertile, enveloping the wire implants and making a complete turf. This cover was finally dense, redolent with growth. And within that vital new earth, a convulsion glimmered—a poise telegraphing through from the sprung armature deep within.

IMPLICATION:

The physical nets constructed in these projects are a class of geotextiles, structural materials developed to reinforce and sustain natural landscapes. Engineering fabric materials used for reinforcement of large-scale civic works are a common technology involved in shaping modern landscapes. The nets use physical detailing encouraging self-assembly, invoking pursuit of artificial life. These projects can be understood as an extension of an ordinary industrial practice.

At the same time, the projects tend to question boundaries of psyche. Their large-scale field structures offer immersion, an expansion rendering our physical bodies porous and offering wide-flung dispersal of identity. This might remind us of a long mystic tradition. A recent example from modern European culture could be the mid-century writing of Georges Bataille, pursuing ecstatic *alterity: . . . I stood up, and I was completely taken . . . Only my legs—which kept me standing upright, connected what I had become to the floor—kept a link to what I had been: the rest was an inflamed gushing forth, overpowering, even free of its own convulsion. A character of dance and of decomposing agility. . . situated this flame "outside of me" And as everything mingles in a dance, so there was nothing which didn't go them to become consumed. I was thrown into this hearth, nothing remained of me but this hearth . . .*[7] In this passage Bataille finds dark space, a spiritual encounter experienced as annihilation of identity. This work shares common interests with early strains of psychoanalysis. In a passage presented to a surrealist circle in 1937, Bataille's associate Roger Caillois studied insect behavior as an analogy for a psychopathy of dissociated identity—specifically, the assimilation of insects into space through mimicry:

> To these dispossessed souls, space seems to be a devouring force. Space pursues them, encircles them, digests them in a gigantic phagocytosis[8] . . . It ends by replacing them. Then the body separates itself from thought, the individual breaks the boundary of his skin and occupies the other side of his sense. He tries to look at himself from any point whatever in space . . . And he invents spaces of which he is 'the convulsive possession'. . . . [T]his attraction by space, as elementary and mechanical as are tropisms, and by the effect of which life seems to lose ground, blurring in its retreat the frontier between the organism and the milieu and expanding to the same degree the limits within which, according to Pythagoras, we are allowed to know, as we should, that nature is everywhere the same.[9]

The "tropisms" that Caillois speaks of are primeval turning movements of living things, turning toward the light, turning toward nourishment. But in our turn towards dissociation there is a risk that life might "lose ground." Anxiety is latent in this pursuit. At the same time that subtle dimensions of anima are revealed, loss of ordinary identity seems inevitable.

This general context suggests that the projects illustrated here are romantic, sharing the same quest as intrepid spiritualists of the late nineteenth and early twentieth century. The purpose of these works is to open boundaries allowing nascent dimensions to emerge. The artificial nature of the pursuit lends poignancy, for while anima is treated in these works as a sacred quality it is also rendered as product of geometry and material synthesis. Artificial, alive.

Then Jacob rent his cloths . . .[10]

NOTES

1. Matthew 27:51, NRSV
2. *Haystack Veil*, Haystack Mountain School of Crafts, Maine 1997, collaboration with Warren Seelig and students: Judith Botzan, Sophie Hammond-Hagman, Emily Harris, Mi-kyoung Lee, Dale McDowell, Kelli Phariss, Stephanie Ross, Michele Rubin, Kristine Woods. *Erratics Net*, Peggy's Cove, Nova Scotia, 1998, with Caroline Munk of the University of

Waterloo Faculty of Architecture and DalTech Faculty of Architecture students: Kelly Chow, Chris Ferguson, Nicola Grigg, Sandra Lee, Beth Lewis, Sunil Sarwal, Vicco Yip, Thomas Wright. *Palatine Burial*, Rome, 1996, under auspices of Prix de Rome in Architecture (Canada) *Synthetic Earth*, collaboration with Katherine Gray, Glass Architecture exhibition, Canadian Clay and Crafts Gallery, Kitchener, 1996/Design Exchange, Toronto 1997

3. Author's journal entry, Haystack Mountain School of Crafts, August 1997

4. The gently bulging meniscus shape signals attraction and repulsion. It can relate to surface tension in drops of liquid, or tidal gravity in oceans.

5. South African domestic ritual maintaining kitchen hearth with bull's blood, related by Caroline Munk, Toronto, 1998.

6. Author's journal entry, Palatine, Rome, 1996, documenting propitiatory sacrifice at Porticus Margataria site identified as Porte Mugonia, c. 700 BCE

7. IV. "Ecstasy," *Inner Experience*, Georges Bataille, trans. Leslie Anne Boldt, New York, 1988 [1943]

8. Some antibiotic cells consume intruders by phagocytosis, surrounding, engulfing and digesting them.

9. "Mimicry and Legendary Psychasthenia," Roger Caillois, trans. John Shepley, in *October: the First Decade*, Cambridge, 1987 [1937].

10. Genesis 37:24, NRSV

15

OUVRAGE: KNOT A NOT, NOTES AS KNOTS

Catherine de Zegher

Editor's introduction: Catherine de Zegher is a curator and writer. In 1997 she edited *The Precarious: The Art and Poetry of Cecilia Vicuña*, which includes the essay reprinted here. De Zegher's discussion of Chilean artist and poet Cecilia Vicuña's experimental practice likens the structure of the textile to the structure of language. Vicuña's temporary, ephemeral installations have been created since 1966 in what she describes as an effort at "hearing an ancient silence waiting to be heard."[a] These fleeting explorations of space often make use of textile materials and adopt expanded, temporary textile structures. The studies de Zegher observes here are all provisional and defined to a large extent by the political instability of the artist's homeland.

Cecilia Vicuña is also a political activist. Catherine de Zegher is joint artistic director, with Gerald McMaster, of the 18th Biennale of Sydney in 2012.

Crisscrossing the Antivero river a single white thread joins rocks and stones under and over the clear water. In this remote place, high up in the Chilean Andes, Cecilia Vicuña—an artist and a poet—is tracing the fragrance of the *ñipa* leaves and tying one verdant side of the river to the other with cord. Flexible, straight, and light, the line that she draws is a visible act. When suddenly two boys come up the river, jumping from stone to stone, they watch her carefully dropping lines inside the water. Without saying a word they slowly approach closer and closer in the prints of her hands. While Vicuña is securing the yarn as into a warp—the loom of the Antivero: the river is the warp, the crossing threads are the weft—their curiosity turns into interest.

Sitting on a rock they observe her gestures/signs and finally ask her what it is. When she returns them the question, the boys reply that they do not know, but that they would like very much to get the string. With a laugh Vicuña grants their request and immediately they start to untie all the rocks and plants, gradually dissolving the spatialized drawing or geometric pattern of woven lines into the current.

A DRAWN GAME

To the boys the line is a valuable length of cord used with or without a rod for catching fish. To Vicuña, the line—as a cord and as a single row of words in a poem—is a trail of communication,

Source: Catherine de Zegher, "*Ouvrage*: Knot a Not, Notes as Knots" from *The Precarious: The Art and Poetry of Cecilia Vicuña*. © 1997 by Catherine de Zegher and reprinted with permission from Wesleyan University Press.
a. Cecilia Vicuña, About Cecilia Vicuña, http://www.ceciliavicuna.org/en_about.htm.

and the gift is the completion of the circle, in which the process of forming through disappearance is taken up again in the flow of events. Perhaps to some the line is a contour of an overtly romantic and idealistic story about "nomad space," because it blurs the borderline between the "real" and the "imaginary," between art and life—the object consumed in the act; because it circumscribes and "protects" the mountain water as a source of life before contamination; because it alludes to joy, play and ramble; because it refers to the whole meaning in the action—even more, to the perpetual motion of "doing" and "undoing" in weaving as in language; and because it recovers in a distant past our sensory memory of a children's game at school: "cat's cradle."

Played by two or more persons, cat's cradle is a game of making geometrical string figures, looped over the fingers and stretched between the two hands. The figures change as the string is passed from one person to another. Of the games people play string figures enjoy the reputation of having been the most widespread form of amusement in the world. Over two-thousand individual patterns have been recorded worldwide since 1888, when anthropologist Franz Boas first described a pair of Eskimo string figures.[1] "The popularity of string figures derived from the novelty of being able to construct highly complex designs instantaneously in a reproducible fashion using readily available materials such as plant fibers, leather thongs, or even plaited human hair."[2] Moreover, hundreds of individual patterns can be generated from the same loop of string. Unfortunately, string figures disappeared rapidly in regions heavily influenced by European culture. Often missionaries discouraged the making of string figures because of their frequent association with pagan myths or depiction of sexual acts.[3]

As if speaking and listening to each other with the fingers alternately restricted and free, the players seek not only to take over the string, but also to recast the pattern without losing the thread. Drawing patterns of construction/dissolution, cat's cradle is a play of beginnings, an interplay between the new and the customary without which a beginning cannot take place: an "intertext." Similarly, in Vicuña's work *Antivero* (1981), the two rocky banks of the river can be considered two hands, where the intertwined thread seems to function as the cradle and the communication, as the "nest" and the "text." Etymologically "nest" derives from "net,"[4] an open-meshed fabric of cord, hair, or twine used for protecting, confining or carrying. A meshwork relates to a framework of interwoven flexible sticks and twigs used to make walls, fences, and roofs in which to rear the young. To give birth and to protect the lineage, women needed to weave nests into wattle-and-daub shelters.

A POINT BETWEEN LINES

Although we can no longer recapture details of prehistoric women's lives, it seems that weaving has always been associated with caring: child care and food preparation. In *Note on the Division of Labor by Sex* Judith Brown states that whether or not the community relies upon women as the chief providers of a given type of labor depends upon "the compatibility of this pursuit with the demands of child care."[5] This is particularly the case for the crafts of spinning, weaving, and sewing: "repetitive, easy to pick up at any point, reasonably child-safe, and easily done at home."[6] Still, Brown notes "that this particular division of labor revolves around *reliance*, not around *ability*, within a community in which specialization was desirable." Being perishable, the textiles themselves at best only provide fragmentary evidence about women's lives, but materials and metaphors of weaving do inform, since they permeate both: childbearing and food. "Weaving (resulting in cloth) and parturition[7] (resulting in babies) both display women's generative capability. Tzutujil Maya use anatomical terms for loom parts (i.e., head, bottom, ribs, heart, umbilical cord), indicating that weaving is considered equivalent to giving birth. Midwives in Santiago Atitlàn bind a pregnant woman's belly with the long hair ribbons that Atiteco women wind around their heads. These mimetically regulate the uterus's snake-like coils to correctly position the baby for delivery. In Chenalho, fine *huipiles*[8] are thrown into the nearby lake when women dream that the Virgin Mary needs this nourishment."[9] According to Vicuña, caring and weaving fuse in naming: to care, to carry, to bear children, to bear a name.[10]

In South America the name *Quechua* synthesizes well this relation between text, textile, and the notion of survival in collaboration. The word designates a member of a group of Inca tribes and also the language of these tribes, still spoken among 4,000,000 Indians of Peru, Ecuador, Bolivia, and Argentina. Etymologically *Quechua* not only means the twine of two (or more) strands twisted together, but also the interlacement of two persons copulating. Significantly, in the Andes the more meanings (double, triple . . .) a word has, the higher its value in the hierarchy of words: it belongs then to the *Hatunsimi*,[11] which means "important language." Vicuña points out that language is inherited from the dead and yet again and again it is "recovered"—meaning to regain control, to repossess, to create again, or to conceal again—by the living. So words are simultaneously old and new. Their universe is "version"—in the sense of transformation—and version indicates passage, direction, action, movement.

Still, in a recent thread piece, *La bodega negra* (Barn Yarn, 1994), which was made in an old barn in the region of Vicuña's childhood near San Fernando (Chile), it is clear that the "directional" remains an important issue of her work. When the artist catches the intense sunrays inside the dilapidated barn piercing the roofholes and producing starlike points on the stone walls, earthen floor, plough share, harrow, sacks, crops, and fodder, once again dispersal and inversion take place. Dazzled when entering the barn, the viewer experiences the exterior brightness of the day turning into the interior obscurity of the night. As blind spots the constellations are cast down to earth. On her arm Vicuña is seizing a (circular)

Figure 15.1. Cecilia Vicuña, *River Weeping*, El Espinalillo, Chile, 1989. Photograph by César Paternosto.

point, another one, and another, and one more: the Southern Cross. She has fastened across the space, from stones in the wall to stones on the floor, threads that, as the extension of her body, momentarily hold the suspending light. In the desire to map, this microcosmos provides protection and offers "abstracted points of identification with the human body."[12] As Henri Michaux writes in *Beginnings*: "Hands off in the distance, still farther off, as far away as possible, stiff, outspread fingers, at the self's outer limits, fingers . . . Surface without mass, a simple thread encompassing a void-being, a bodiless body."[13] Later in the evening, inversely, when the sun is setting and the angle of light is changing, the stars in the barn disappear in the twilight to reappear in the night sky. "Space is now time ceaselessly metamorphosed through action."[14]

Besides the use of roof holes by the French Revolutionary architect Etienne-Louis Boullée in his domed Cenotaph dedicated to Newton, another more recent example comes to mind in the *Sun Tunnels* of Nancy Holt. During the early seventies Nancy Holt concentrated on urban or landscape spaces as seen through holes in tunnels, pipes, and other devices that made the viewer consider both outside and inside, perceptual and physiological sensations.[15] The difference is that the tubular conduits were perforated on purpose as well as oriented in a very specific area by the artist. If land art claims to be concerned with nature as the incontestable provider of ideas and with light as the constitutive element in art and architecture, Vicuña's work introduces a different way of marking, one that addresses nature and (agri)culture in a dialogic way. *La bodega negra* is responding to a sign, it is not imposing a mark. Being a "nonsite" piece, it is not about appearance, but about disappearance.

ODDS AND ENDS

Considering the linguistic relation of text, textile, and architecture, it seems appropriate to introduce the French word *ouvrage* to describe Vicuña's art practice as an open-ended work, an ongoing practice with links to writing, weaving, and constructing. Since January 1966, when Cecilia Vicuña made her first outdoor piece *Con-cón* on the beach at the junction of two waters, the Aconcagua River and the Pacific Ocean in Chile, she has examined transience and has named her work "*precario.*" "Precarious is what is obtained by prayer. Uncertain, exposed to hazards, insecure. From the Latin *precarius*, from *precis*, prayer."[16] "Prayer" understood not as a request, but as a response, is a dialogue or a speech that addresses what is (physically) "there" as well as what is "not there," the place as well as the "no place," the site as well as the "non-site." Prayer is dialogue as a

form of transition from what is to what could be. "Sacrifice" is an act-made-sacred and transcendent by the awareness that this act is not only physical but retains another dimension and thus has a double meaning, is ambiguous. Vicuña quotes from a Vedic text: "the first sacrifice is 'seeing,' because the act of seeing is a response." The root of the word *respond* is "to dedicate again," to receive something and to donate it back. More or less about the same time, Lygia Clark was writing: "Art is not bourgeois mystification. What has changed is the form of communicating the proposition. It's you who now give expression to my thoughts, to draw from them whatever vital experience you want . . . This feeling of totality captured within the act should be encountered with joy, in order to learn how to live on the ground of precariousness. This feeling of the precarious must be absorbed for one to discover in the immanence of the act the meaning of existence."[17]

Born of contemplation and made of refuse, Vicuña's earth works are an answer to the land and the sun, to the lost feathers and accumulated objects. Many times she has used a stick to comb the beach into lines, circles, and spirals. Gathering flotsam and jetsam, she recognizes the inherent value of discarded materials that are lying down, and stands them up. Her desire to order things is a kind of response to their language: garbage/language, in the sense that garbage has a signifying potention and impulse that give new tension to the signifier. But whatever order she has created,[18] the wind scatters it, and long waves rolling up onto the sand—also called beachcombers—erase her work *Con-cón* at high tide. Thus, since the mid-1960s Vicuña has been producing *precarios*, which consist of small, multicolored assemblages of found materials such as fragments of driftwood, feathers, stones, lumps of shredded plastic, herbs, thin sticks, electric wire, shells, bones, and thread. Each piece is composed in such a way that every material holds another in balance. And, although not featuring any symmetry, each whole structure stands up in a fragile state of suspended equilibrium. Vicuña says of her *basuritas*: " 'We are made of throwaways and we will be thrown away,' say the objects. Twice precarious they come from prayer and predict their own destruction. Precarious in history they will leave no trace. The history of art written in the North includes nothing of the South. Thus they speak in prayer, precariously."

Read in comparison with the land art of Nancy Holt or Richard Long, Cecilia Vicuña's earth works differ not only in their relationship to the environment and the body, but also in their diffusion of knowledge. In contradistinction to Vicuña's perception, these artists have staged a landscape for the viewer to colonize in order to aggrandize the self and to summon awe for the sublime Other, as a reason for obliterating it.[19] "In Richard Long's work the body is absent, though implied there is in fact a disembodied consciousness, a romantic primitivist fantasy of virgin nature projected no matter where in the world by an observing eye enjoying a sovereign isolation: residues of the colonial mind-set."[20] Again, in the case of Vicuña, the earth work is not about appearance, but about disappearance. And in Chile the *desaparecidos* (the disappeared ones) of the Junta during the seventies have a body.[21] For this reason Vicuña drew, on her first return from exile to Chile, the work *Tunquen* (1981) on the sand with colors of pigment featuring the encounter of sun and bone, life and death.[22]

BY NAME

From 1966 to 1972 Cecilia Vicuña often practiced her work in the streets of Santiago de Chile, where she created various unannounced performances and events. In 1971 she had her first solo exhibition at the National Museum of Fine Arts in Santiago with the work *Otoño* (Autumn), for which she filled the main room with autumn leaves three feet deep. In 1972 she traveled to London with a fellowship for postgraduate study at the Slade School of Fine Arts; in 1973 she had an exhibition at the Institute of Contemporary Art. When the military coup occurred in 1973

and President Allende died, Vicuña decided not to return to her country and remained in exile in Great Britain. She became a political activist and founded, together with Guy Brett, David Medalla, and John Dugger, the organization Artists for Democracy to oppose the military dictatorship in Chile. The ideas formulated by Artists for Democracy were linked to Vicuña's first revolutionary group action in 1967: the formation of the Tribu No (the No Tribe), which issued manifestos and staged public interventions. Having read the creationist manifestos of Huidobro, the futurists, and the surrealists, she believed that the only contribution of the inhabitants of the Southern Hemisphere in the second part of the twentieth century was to say "no," as proclaimed in the "No-manifesto," which circulated as a manuscript from hand to hand (Santiago de Chile, 1967). The "No-manifesto" was attended with actions such as installing the Banco de Ideas (for Allende), putting the question of "what is poetry to you?" over the telephone, circulating "circular" letters, composing a dictionary of *piropos e insultos* (sexist words and insults) and an *enclocepedia del asco* (encyclopedia of disgust). At the same time the art, poetry, and music of Violeta Parra have greatly influenced Vicuña's ideas. Violeta Parra (1917–67) was a Chilean peasant woman, whose research on the weaving, oral poetry, and music of Chile, as well as her own work, formed the foundations of the movement called La Nueva Cancion Chilena. Political and contemporary in its focus, it retained at the same time the ancient mestizo rhythms of traditional music and electrified all of South America.

Confronted with a sense of loss and isolation, Cecilia Vicuña left London in 1975 and returned to South America. She went to Bogota, where for several months she continued to make banners and sets for revolutionary theater companies such as Teatro La Candelaria. She lectured throughout Colombia about the "Chilean Struggle for Liberation," made a film at a bus stop near a *fabrica de santitos*, and made a living reading succesfully her own "erotic" poetry. During this period, Vicuña stunned people with her performance of a spilled glass of milk, *Vaso de leche* (Glass of Milk, 1979). When it was estimated that every year 1,920 children in Bogota died from drinking contaminated milk produced in Colombia, and the government neither prosecuted the distributors nor took any action to stop the "milk crime," Vicuña decided to announce and perform the spilling of a glass of milk in front of a government building under a blue sky. She attached a short cord around the glass of milk, pulled it over, and thus "the poem was written on the pavement." About this performance Leon Golub once said that it was the most efficacious political work: inversely proportional to its small size and precarious content, the act had a powerful and complex impact.

In Vicuña's artistic practice, and particularly as it relates to political protest, the investigation of language and the politics of definition are always at stake, because for her "naming" is the most political act of all. *Arte precario* is the name she gives to her independent voice within the Southern Hemisphere, challenging her colonized position. Her art *is* Andean, it is not *about* Andean art. It belongs to this urban mestizo culture and not to the Western purist version of it appropriating "the little lama." Her work concerns *la batalla de los significados* (the battle of the signifieds). According to Vicuña, submission and poverty begin with the acceptance of definitions that others create for you. When one general designation of "indian"—at first a mistaken definition by the *conquistadores*—covered the othering of all tribes, the massacre of the native populations of the Americas was made possible. Recognition needs a name, one's own name.

NOTES AS SNOT

Small objects, much like Vicuña's *precarios*, consisting of branches and cords, as well as string figures, have appeared in many cultures as depictions of the natural environment, the material culture (tools, food, clothing sources, food gathering, and other daily activities), interpersonal relationships, legends . . .[23] Oftentimes chants and stories were recited as a string figure was displayed. Kathleen Haddon suggests that string figures merely served as a ready means of illustration for the objects or beings portrayed in the accompanying legend. The illustration was readily prepared in the absence of drawing materials, was highly reproducible, and was not dependent on the maker's artistic ability.[24] Being a sort of cultural archive, a repository for beliefs and observations deemed worthy of preserving, the objects and the stories attached to them served not only to locate people with reference to the constellation of celestial objects but also within a kinship system. Claude Lévi-Strauss states that "like phonemes, kinship terms are elements of meaning; like phonemes, they acquire meaning only if they are integrated into systems. 'Kinship systems', like 'phonemic systems', are built by the mind on the level of unconscious thought."[25]

Key elements in Vicuña's work are: *star* and *stone*, *warp* and *word*, which she defines as points of exact observation (i.e., a tall stone—for example a menhir—in a vast area indicates a fixed place from which to observe the earth and the sky; a constellation indicates a reference in the universe; etc.) constructed within models outside the self such as: constellations, weavings, and language. Moreover, although these "structured sets" or models are permanent and account for various aspects of empirical social reality, they possess an inner movement (i.e., the celestial course, the weaving grid, the alphabet), and thus call forth responses from the viewer/reader. A warp is many threads, a word is many sounds, many ideas.[26] The strangeness or otherness of the self occurs as soon as it is constructed, that is, as soon as it is symbolized; thus these structures, simultaneously constitutive and alien, are vehicles to define the self—and are thus a means of empowerment.

Any act of symbolization is both a loss and a formation of the self and its reality and should therefore remain a coming-into-language, a continuous process of defining, open to shifts in its mapping. Star, stone, warp, word: each of these points gives rise to inner movement and ambiguity and should be used only as a reference for movement within the unlimited. Motion avoids the petrifying effect implicit in the fixed gaze. Everything in Vicuña's work is about connecting, weaving, studying the relations of lines to points and references. However, once these points and references are fixed, "immovability within movement is created and along with it the Illusion of Order and Time." Cecilia Vicuña writes in May 1973:

> In thinking of the form for which I am looking I can't help but find other forms for things outside my paintings, for any search must associate and connect with the search for a social way. If not, it is a castrated search, an apolitical occupation good for nothing, or good to help maintain the present structures which have been established for the benefit of the few and the destruction of the rest. But now these structures must be established taking into consideration facts other than profit or power. It will be possible to simplify these facts to these three categories: the way in and out of air, of food, of semen in the body.[27]

In this sense Vicuña proclaims "laws" as necessary, but movable and directional, written for the benefit of what goes in and out of the body: breath, snot, semen, urine, excrement, babies.

STAR, STONE, STOMACH

Vicuña's working field consists of the exploration of the symbolic function of weaving and language, stressing the fundamental place of textiles in the Andean system of knowledge. Affirming a basic congruence among the realms of writing, agriculture and weaving, the opening lines of the Popol Vuh (the Quiché Maya's ancient sacred text) have two possible translations: "This is the beginning of the Ancient Word, here in this place called Quiché. Here we shall inscribe, we shall implant the Ancient Word"; or "Here we shall design, we shall brocade the Ancient Word."[28] This multivocal translation suggests that the Maya recognize these three realms as diverse yet congruent paths of knowledge. The concept of intertextuality, linking the arts of music, weaving, oratory, architecture, and agriculture, gives insight into the permeability of the boundaries between different domains of knowledge.[29] If it seems, as Claude Lévi-Strauss writes, that the unconscious activity of the mind consists in imposing forms upon content, and if these forms are fundamentally the same for all minds—ancient and modern, primitive and civilized (as the study of the symbolic function, expressed in language, so strikingly indicates)—then a single structural scheme exists behind the chaos of rules and customs and operates in different spatial and temporal contexts.[30] Grasping in word and thread—*palabra e hilo*—the unconscious structure underlying each social institution, Cecilia Vicuña offers a principle of interpretation accurate for other institutions or systems of representation. I return to the issue of this rather totalizing thought and address the problem of it further on.

Most valued and respected products in Andean culture are textiles,[31] which construct and carry or, rather, *are* meaning and identification. Technically, a woven fabric consists of two elements with different functions: the fixed vertical threads (warp) and the mobile horizontal threads (weft or woof), which intersect the fixed threads perpendicularly and pass above them. Stake and thread, warp and woof have been analyzed in basketry and weaving as figures of "supple solids."[32] Determined by the loom (the frame of the warp), the textile can be infinite in length but not in width, where it is closed by a back and forth motion. Warp-patterned weaving, characteristic of all remaining Andean weaving today, was slow to be recognized as having value for studies of gender, social identity, economic networks, and modernization. As a strong indicator of cultural patterns—what the Maya of Mexico and Guatemala call *costumbre*—textile has communicative,

Figure 15.2. Cecilia Vicuña, *Antivero*, Chile, 1981. Photograph by César Paternosto.

but also poetic, economic, ritual, and political power. Weaving is meaning in multiple ways.

WORD AND THREAD

Compared to the privileged status given to painting, sculpture, and architecture, textile arts have been virtually ignored. Following the Bauhaus, the distinction and interrelationship of design and art were greatly elaborated in the work of Anni Albers. She overcame "two fallacious premises: that designing and making art are conflicting occupations; and that work in the fiber medium is categorically craft and not art."[33] Exploring the randomness of a discarded string in *Knot II* (1947), Albers said that, "although it is small, each thread seems charged with uninterrupted energy: the underlying units twine and intertwine with nonstop vitality, as if to say that they exist singly but also as part of something greater."[34] Working with material "is a listening for the dictation of the material and a taking in of the laws of harmony. It is for this reason that we can find certitude in the belief that we are taking part in an eternal order." Albers also came to appreciate the challenge of the discipline of weaving. Unlike painting, which allowed limitless freedom, the inherent properties of textiles (its tactile qualities, material combinations, and so forth) and the specific laws of their production (the grid) provided a framework that Albers found stimulating rather than restrictive.[35]

In the late 1920s and 1930s, Anni Albers introduced cellophane and other synthetics, as well as plastic and metallic threads that added luster and color to her weavings but were also light reflective and dust and water repellent. Taking these materials further than anyone else at that time, as Mary Jane Jacobs argues, Albers also revived long-forgotten methods, particularly those used in Peruvian textiles, which she studied and collected. The ancient Peruvians employed almost all known hand methods and their work constitutes perhaps the richest body of textile art by any culture in the world. Albers praised the Peruvians' adventurous use of threads and commented on their "surprising and ingenious ways of varying in inventiveness from piece to piece."[36] Mostly overlooked by the artworld, Andean textile arts also eloquently express transmutation of culture, women's concerns with indigenous and nonindigenous traditions, and intercultural exchanges. Cecilia Vicuña, using thread and cloth as her main medium, proposes weaving as a form of participation issuing from popular culture, but she has always perceived and understood weaving as an alternative discourse and a dynamic model of resistance (as do most indigenous Latin American women). Janet Catherine Berlo points out "that all of the cultural cross-currents and overlaps in textile art of Latin America are not, however, simply a 'making do'. They are not merely a passive, defensive response to five centuries of colonialism." In "Beyond Bricolage" she argues that "the improvisations and appropriations in women's textiles are deliberate and sometimes culturally subversive." Although world-famous as tourist items, their fabrics are signs of renewal, of new forms and topical themes, coming directly from the people. Although both women and textiles are crucial to the study of postcolonial representation, Western biases have until recently viewed women's textiles as 'sub-Primitive' art.

Using examples from two groups, the Kuna and the Maya, Janet Catherine Berlo shows that:

. . . cloth makes manifest deeply held cultural values that may otherwise be imperceptible. In fact, it may be women's very crucial job to translate these ephemeral values into material objects. In a number of Amerindian societies, men's arts are oral while women's are, literally, material: men speak, women make cloth. Hierarchical codes within our own word-obsessed culture dictate that the public, the verbal, is the area of status, autonomy, importance. But this is not so clear within the indigenous systems. The most clear-cut dichotomy between the expressive roles of men and those of women occurs among the Kuna Indians of Panama.[37] Two types of communal gatherings, or *congresos*, are a vital part of Kuna life. At secular gatherings men gain status and prestige through public displays of their verbal fluency. Only the most eloquent men rise to positions as village chiefs who conduct sacred gatherings attended by both men and women. In this forum, chiefs display their consummate verbal skills through chanted dialogues that cover sacred history, politics, and a host of traditions. The Kuna sacred gathering encapsulates the aesthetic ideals of the Kuna universe: the chiefs, arrayed at the center of the gathering house, engage in verbal discourse. They are surrounded by rows of women, dressed in their finest garments, who work on textiles while the chiefs chant. Around the outside of the circle, sit the rest of the men.[38]

Mary W. Helms observes that "by long and arduous hours of *mola*[39] production, by the display created by *mola* wearing, and perhaps in the symbolism contained in *mola* designs, they assist the community in the furtherance of these ends by creating a form of 'silent oratory' that publicly expresses, with form and vibrant color, the same views of the 'world-as-event' and the same concepts of group cohesion and morality as are proclaimed by the spoken oratory of the men."[40] There is some evidence that a similar pattern of men's verbal and women's visual modes of expression occurs among the highland Maya. Male members of the native religious hierarchy use a style of speech in which repetition, metaphor, and patterns of parallel syntax are common. The fine nuances, repetitions, and rhythmic yet asymmetrical color and design patterns characteristic of Maya women's backstrap-loomed textiles serve in the female arena as the equivalent of Maya men's complex verbal play.[41] In her performances, Vicuña speaks while she weaves, and weaves while she sings.

MISTRESSES OF THE NEEDLE[42]

It seems that even in an excluding patriarchal culture, spaces of intervention exist where suppressed voices not only articulate their experiences and self-defined positions, but where they also express their participation in culture as active agents of transformation. The techniques of weaving allow a mobility of doing and undoing within the accumulative medium of textiles (adding brocade, embroidery, trim, and appliqué), thus increasing the meaning, power, value, and visual display. Women in Latin America transform alien objects, influences, materials, and ideas in purposeful collages, as they adopt multivocal aesthetics to indigenous culture. From this point of view textiles can be read as active texts that play out the ongoing intercultural dialogue of self-determination and cultural hegemony, as well as the dialogue of exchange between conservatism and innovation, continuity and transmutation.[43] In the material realm, Latin American women confront otherness—whether as a result of remoteness of time (colonialism) or remoteness of space (first world)—by creating a vision of indigenous culture that balances both and at the same time demonstrates its durability through the strength and vitality of their fabric. "This is a subversive act for it co-opts the hegemonic tradition that views the third world as a dumping ground for its products."[44]

Considering the work of Cecilia Vicuña, it becomes clear how actively she participates in defining culture and the social fabric of language by disrupting the grammar imposed by figures of authority and by recovering the texture of communication. Vicuña's strategies of purposeful improvisation, thoughtful linguistics, and accumulation allow her to express a multilevelled and referential body of meanings and to display this in numerous spheres of action. During the sixties, when she daily rode buses in the capital of Santiago, she decided to wear a different woven invention as a multicolored glove over her hand every day. For weeks she manufactured many types of sometimes funny gloves in all colors and forms. As an operator of signs, she wanted these handfuls of threads to function as a surprise, new—"as art"—each time she took the bus and raised her hand to reach for a hand grip. Her use of the body as a material for performance art inscribed itself in the city and its human movements. For both the artist and the "person in society" a liberating force was implicated in the awakening of each of one's gestures. Turning the familiar material (a glove) and daily gesture (reaching for the handgrip) into a question mark, she exposed the passengers' quiescent habits and tried to intensify the desire and capacity to reformulate models of signification.

Vicuña's bus performance, *El guante* (The Glove), was prompted by the necessity to restructure the language of creativity, so that the artwork could remain a means of opposing authority (be it military or multinational) and its concepts of meaning. Art here was a tool to retain independence and to nourish resistance. On the one hand, her action seems to relate to the earlier dissatisfaction of rebellious young poets, writers, and painters in South America—such as Violeta Parra, Jorge Luis Borges, Xul Solar, and the manifesto-issuing *vanguardistas*[45]—with the prevailing norm of Spanish literary language as a system of repressive and deadening constraints. For them, "a model of a perpetually reinvented language, constantly shifting to accommodate new concepts and information, was close at hand—again, in the streets of Buenos Aires, where Argentines daily enriched the staid speech of Castille with Italianisms, fragments of German and English, and their own surprising coinages."[46] On the other hand, Vicuña's glove performance seems to retrace an ancient Mapuche practice in Chile, where an old myth tells that the Mapuche women learned how to weave from observing spiders at work and from contemplating their cobwebs (both nests and traps). When a baby girl is born, mothers walk out to catch a spider and let it walk on the baby's hand: the movements of the spider will stick to her hands, and the spider will teach her.

EL MIRAR CRUZADO[47]

More recently, in 1994, two outdoor works in Chile reframe Vicuña's concern with crossing the boundaries that separate the individual and the collective, the private and the public, the local and the global, the "smooth" and the "striated," the "nomad space" and the "sedentary space."[48] For *Hilo en el cerro* (Thread in the Ridge) at Cerro Santa Lucia in the public park, the trysting place of lovers and others in the center of Santiago, she wove with a ball of red yarn spun in the house of a Mapuche woman. Was she using the thread in order to find her way out of the labyrinthine garden, or to enweb the little mountain? Does the red string indicate the solution of a problem or does it entail a question? Her *12 Hilos en un corral* (The Corral Grid) was made in the corral of a farm in the mountains near San Fernando. The corral is a trapezoidal space created by stone walls (*una pirka*) for the mestizo purpose of domesticating horses. Always falling apart, the *pirka* is periodically repaired with new stones, which are added to the ancient ones in an ongoing process. Inside the irregular corral, Vicuña's woven striation was suspended in midair at wall height. Emphasizing the

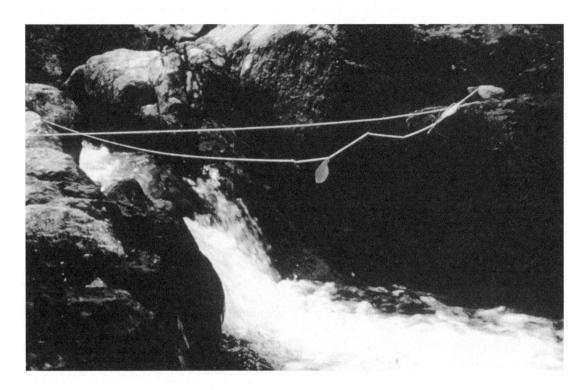

Figure 15.3. Cecilia Vicuña, *Puente de Hilo, Antivero*, Chile, 1994. Photograph by Catherine de Zegher.

spatial "imperfection" of the corral, the weaving is an open work for the viewer to enter, by sliding one's head in to look at it. Essential in both weavings is the crossing of threads, the crossing of straightened lines at right angles, the intercrossing of opposed forces, the intertexture. Vicuña's art exists at the *crux*, where fertility sprouts and change or transformation happens through the encounter. However, while the former weaving consists of her usual unrolled woolen lines revealing an optional trajectory between trees and flowers, local linkages between parts, and multiple orientation or constant change in direction, the latter weaving represents a most regular grid structure.

In principle, a fabric has a certain number of characteristics that define it as a striated space. However, it seems that this conventional view of weaving should be suspended so as to observe some specific processes. For example, felt is a supple, solid material that has an altogether different effect; it is "an antifabric." Since it involves no separation of threads, no intertwining, but is only an entanglement of fibers obtained by fulling, it constitutes a smooth space.[49] Like paper, felt uses a matrix without entering it. But, according to Gilles Deleuze and Félix Guattari, striated space is not simply opposed to or different from smooth space. Although there is a distinction between the two, in fact they only exist in mixture and in passages from one to another. In this sense, and conversely to one's expectation about the striated nature of fabric, most of Vicuña's weavings seem to belong to smooth space, where variation and development of form are continuous and unlimited, where the lines go in all directions, where "the stop follows from the trajectory." To quote Deleuze and Guattari: "Smooth space is directional rather than dimensional or metric. Smooth space is filled by events or haecceities, far more than by formed and perceived things. It is a space of affects, more than one of properties. It is *haptic*[50] rather than optical perception. Whereas in the striated forms organize a matter, in the smooth materials signal forces and serve as

symptoms for them. It is an intensive rather than extensive space, one of distances, not of measures and properties."[51] Vicuña's sites (sand beaches, sea and river, streets, etc.) and works—be it in Chile, Bogota or New York—are "local spaces of pure connection."[52] Her linkages, signals, and orientations change according to temporary vegetation, occupations, and precipitation. The abstract line that she draws is "a line of flight without beginning or end, a line of variable direction that describes no contour and delimits no form."[53]

Yet, Vicuña's two recent outdoor weavings, *Hilo en el cerro* and *12 Hilos en un corral*, seem to enact, respectively, smooth space and striated space and, almost literally, the crossings and passages between both spaces, as though one emanated from the other, "but not without a correlation between the two, a recapitulation of one in the other, a furtherance of one through the other."[54] Her unexpected use of the woven grid in the corral piece visualizes the striation of space as a way to subordinate and measure it within anxiety in the face of all that passes, flows, or varies. As the grid since the Renaissance has been applied on a vertical plane in order to master three-dimensional space in painting, so the grid applied on a horizontal plane in Vicuña's open weaving brings to mind an archaeological method for mapping ancient sites in an "objective" and clear way. Additionally, it is important to mention that among the Quechua of Chinchero (Peru), there are profound conceptual and linguistic links between the processes of working the loom and working the earth. Here the word *pampa* refers both to the agricultural plain and to the large, single-color sections of handwoven textiles. *Khata* is a furrowed field ready for planting as well as the textile warp configuration ready for pattern formation.[55] Since Vicuña's materialization of the grid in this work seems to be projected without vantage point, it may, more importantly, figure the connection in weaving that is protecting. In this sense we can recall two examples of protective clothing: the plain weaving of Penelope's fabric that—because of its possibilities of doing and undoing—kept not only Penelope but also Odysseus alive; and the plain weaving of the poncho, which is made like a blanket with a central slit for the head. Since its structure is part of "an eternal order," as Anni Albers tells us, the open (corral) weaving 'protects' the entering viewer/reader and the land against the multinational grip of North American corporate agro-industry—which eliminates the "inferior" native corn to replace it with its own "rich" corn treated so as not to run to seed, so that the Chilean farmers become completely dependent on those corporations for production.[56]

Moreover, taking up the grid's ambivalent relation to matter and to spirit, Vicuña extends it in her work to imply the overlaying of modernity onto Andean culture, and vice versa. "Flattened, geometrized, ordered, the grid is antinatural, antimimetic, antireal . . . In the flatness that results from its coordinates, the grid is the means of crowding out the dimensions of the real and replacing them with the lateral spread of a single surface. In the overall regularity of its organization, it is the result not of imitation, but of aesthetic decree."[57] According to Rosalind Krauss, "although the grid is certainly not a story, it *is* a structure, and one, moreover, that allows a contradiction between the values of science and those of spiritualism to maintain themselves within the consciousness of modernism, or rather its unconscious, as something repressed." Because of its bivalent structure the grid portends the "centrifugal" or "centripetal" existence of the work of art. Presented as a mere fragment, arbitrarily cropped from an infinitely larger fabric,[58] the grid operates outward, compelling our acknowledgment of a world beyond the frame, this is the centrifugal reading (in relation to the operations of science, paradoxically entailing the dematerialization of the surface). The centripetal one works from the outer limits of the aesthetic object inward. "The grid is, in relation to *this* reading, a *re*-presentation of everything that separates the work of art from the world, from ambient space and from other objects. The grid is an introjection of the boundaries of the world into the interior of the work; it is a mapping of the space inside the frame onto itself" (a reading seemingly issuing from purely symbolist origins, paradoxically opposing "science" and "materialism").[59] Krauss states that, within the whole of modern aesthetic production, "the grid has sustained itself so relentlessly while at the same time being so impervious to change." One of the most modernist aspects of the grid is "its capacity to serve as a paradigm or model for the antidevelopment, the antinarrative, the antihistorical."[60]

Apparently, in Vicuña's spatialized weaving, not only the plain surface of the grid is under consideration but also the subversion of the line. The binary discourse on the grid (nature vs. artifice, signifier vs. real, etc.) is called into question. According to Deleuze and Guattari, "the smooth and the striated are distinguished first of all by an inverse relation between the point and the line (in the case of the striated, the line is between two points, while in the smooth, the point is between two lines); and second, by the nature of the line (smooth-directional, open intervals; dimensional-striated, closed intervals). Finally, there is a third difference, concerning the surface or space. In striated space, one closes off a surface and "allocates" it according to determinate intervals, assigned breaks; in the smooth, one "distributes oneself in an open space, according to frequencies and in the course of one's crossing (logos and nomos)." Textile is a spatial construction realized by negotiating supple and fixed elements. The spatial feature of weaving occurs on several levels, through interpenetrating movements that are both external to a defined surface and at the same time create that surface. Still, there is a difference and a disjunction between the experience of space and the discourse of space, between the hand and the weaving, between the gesture and the work. As Lygia Clarks puts it: "The artisan entered into a dialogue with her/his work, while labor, increasingly automatized and mechanized, had lost every expressiveness in its relation." Thus, Vicuña's weaving opens for the artist the possibility of finding her own gestures filled with new meaning; and it wholly revises the meaning of two values—the variable and the constant, the mobile and the fixed, the supple and the solid—by bringing them simultaneously forward in the service of change. The artist's enduring transpositions are the only constant in her work. With enormous perspicacity she disorganizes and redefines the forms of meaning transmitted to her from her Andean culture and from dominant Western cultures, in order to overturn distinctions between the vernacular and the modern and to shift the international models of language. Her use of multiple fluctuating referents and of ambiguity applies to her visual art as well as to her poetry.

KNOTS IN WOOL AS NOTES

Simultaneously approaching and distancing herself from so-called international movements or institutions, such as body art, land art, and *arte povera*, Vicuña chose a flexible though firm position unassimilable to different cultural programs. Her first spatial work, *Quipu que no recuerda nada*, embraced the aesthetic of silence in an attempt to initiate a critique of the self-reflexive model and its enforced hermeticism by challenging and refusing the quietistic conditions of modernism from within.[61] By the 1950s and the early 1960s, anthologies about twentieth century European modernist thought and art[62] had been translated across the Atlantic, published in Buenos Aires, and found their way to Chile. These books were most important to Vicuña because they strengthened her independent mind and language, and, more importantly, because they demonstrated components of a geometrical abstraction, also attributed to her own Andean and pre-Columbian culture.

It is in one of these art books that she noticed a photograph of Kurt Schwitters' *Merzbau* (1923–36) in Hannover. In 1965, moved by the domestic and precarious aspects of Schwitters's work, Vicuña outlined a bare thread in her own bedroom and entitled the work, significantly: *Quipu que no recuerda nada* (The *Quipu* which

Remembers Nothing). Consisting of woolen cords with knots, the *quipu* is an Inca instrument that registers events, circumstances, and numerals. Ancient documents tell us that these registering artifacts continued to be used during the first period of the *conquista*, to be replaced later by written systems. Nowadays, in certain very traditional communities of the Andean highlands, the use of artifacts similar to the *quipu* still persists.[63] The largest and most complex *quipu*, found within the extensive region of Tawantinsuyu, is on display in the Museo Chileno de Arte Precolombino in Santiago. According to the museum's catalogue it was excavated from an Inca cemetery in Mollepampa, in the valley of the Lluta river, near what is now the city of Arica. Seven white cords without knots, joined to the main cord by a red bow, divide six sets of ten groups of cords each. Near the end of the instrument are nine white, knotless cords and one with only one knot. The *quipu* ends in eleven sets of cords. These sets of cords, each with its knots, are formed by a main cord from which secondary ones derive, some of which produce more cords of a third category. The location of these sets and that of the cords and knots within, the way of twisting each cord, and the colors used are part of a symbolism still not completely deciphered. We know only that the positioning of the knots on the cord makes use of or refers to the decimal system. It seems that the colors encoded nonnumerological information. Recent research suggests that the *quipu* was also used as a mnemonic device for oral poetry and philosophy.

Thus, the entire *quipu* carries meaning: the length, the form, the color, the number of knots. Simultaneously the endless tying and retying of knots allows continuous marking and modification. At the most, on a literal level one could say that in contradistinction to other writing systems the *quipu* provides opportunity for infinite inscription since what is "inscribed" is never fixed. The act of doing and undoing, as in weaving, offers multitudinous possibilities or beginnings, flexibility, and mobility. In this sense Vicuña's

Quipu que no recuerda nada synthezises an attitude toward life, language, memory, and history in a postcolonial country, where the process of transformation generated the foundation for a new socialist collective culture. On the verge of being willing to lose any trace of representation, Cecilia Vicuña oscillates, on the one hand, between the various constructivist strategies of transparency of procedures, self-referentiality of signifying devices, and reflexive spatial organization, and on the other hand, the strategies of differentiation of subjective experience and of historical reflection. Taking into account the experience of colonialism (and even more of neocolonial dependence), with its legacies of oppression and destruction, from which her identity emerged, she holds on to the name: *Quipu*. Taking account of the desire of a new generation to be "absolutely modern," Vicuña wanted to articulate a beginning and to position herself at this beginning, but within the pre-Columbian and colonial history. She perceives "beginning" the way Edward W. Said describes it: "Beginning is making or producing difference; but difference which is the result of combining the already-familiar with the fertile novelty of human work in language."[64]

KNOT IN A HANDKERCHIEF

Perhaps at first the connection seems incongruous. However, I wish to analyze and emphasize the relationship between the work of Cecilia Vicuña and that of Kurt Schwitters in the context of Chilean colonial history. Although her earliest encounter with the German artist's work was no more than the encounter with a photograph, and although it was only much later, in the 1980s, that she learned more about his work, there is an affinity worth exploring. Both artists' oeuvres agree on several issues: nonrepresentational multimedia constructions, a "nonobjective" art, emphasis on connection and interaction—the "directional" rather than the "dimensional"; the use of refuse; the strategies of naming (*Merz* and *Precario*); and also the experimentation with

other art forms, for example poetry. The elements of poetry such as letters, syllables, words, and sentences are permitted to interact and create meaning.[65] Most striking, however, is the similarity in the construction procedure of the *Merzbau*, conceived in Schwitters's house, and Vicuña's *Quipu*, which was realized in her bedroom without knowledge of the former's installation method, and would be the groundwork for all her later spatial weavings. Their thought processes seem to run parallel. As a result of the particular interest in how various materials, including the components of his own works, combine and interact, Schwitters started by tying strings in his studio from one object, picture, or work to another to emphasize or materialize that interaction. Eventually, the strings became wires, then were replaced with wooden structures, which, in turn, were joined with plaster of Paris. The structures grew and merged, and eventually filled several rooms, resembling a huge abstract grotto.[66] (In a way this structure also reminds us of the system of suspended threads that Gaudi used in the Iglesia de la Colonia Güell (1908–14) to research

Figure 15.4. Cecilia Vicuña, *Ceq'e*, New York, 1994. Photograph by César Paternosto.

construction principles and modeling methods, which would later be applied in La Sagrada Familia in Barcelona.[67] During his experiments of forms in tension, Gaudi used loose threads and weavings to visualize the constitution of walls and ceilings.)

Schwitters had called his principle of artistic creation with any material *Merz*. Since a fragment of a scrap of a bank advertisement pasted in a collage happened to show the four casual letters *MERZ*, this became the general term by which he referred to his work. His naming process is clearly based on his appreciation for the accidental, the trivial, the inconsequential. Elsewhere, he wrote that this word *Merz* came from the German *ausmerzen* (to weed out, extirpate), and that ironically it threw light on both the bright side of dadaism and the dark side of expressionism.[68] The *Merz* works are characterized by diverse materials glued and nailed on the picture surface, and by the application of color in limited sections. Schwitters used to say: "The material is as unimportant as myself. Important is only the creation. And because the material is unimportant, I take any material a picture demands. As I let different materials interact, I have an advantage compared to oil painting, as I can create interaction, not only between colour and colour, line and line, form and form, but also between material and material, e.g. wood and sackcloth."[69] A few artists among his contemporaries were also literally choosing this diversity of materials from the urban environment.[70] Later on, after World War II, many artists began to select their materials from the refuse generated by urban life and industrial "progress." Vicuña was also motivated to use discarded objects in defiance of an excluding differentiation. This impartiality (or abstractness) is maintained once the found objects are appropriated as materials. Such nonhierarchical use of materials allows reflections on balance, equality, and freedom, which are emphasized by the fragile state of equilibrium in many of her precarious objects (e.g., *Balancin*, 1981; *Pesa*, 1984; *Espiral de Jezik*, 1990).

In addition to the aesthetic considerations and the formal analogies of Schwitters's and Vicuña's work, it is of interest to compare the recurrences of both the process of naming and the use of waste materials in a specific socioeconomic environment: Schwitters in Germany before World War II and Vicuña in Chile before the dictatorship.[71] While Vicuña elucidated extensively her attention (later to become studiousness) to dadaism and its precedents in her art and poetry practices, she noticed the exaltation of memory and lament in both the pre-Columbian and German romantic poetry. Dissolving identities and shattering the communicative, representative aspect of language in favor of a dynamic conception of art, the avantgarde artists further gave rise to a theory of the subject in process, a subject equally constituted by symbolic and semiotic elements. Considering them rebels in a restraining society, Vicuña embraced the modernist vanguard aesthetic and poetry as a liberating force, contributing in one inward movement to both—on the one hand, to the newly defined social production of culture propagated by the Unidad Popular of the Marxist President Salvador Allende, and on the other hand, to the resistance against colonization and its ramifications in an emerging totalitarian regime.[72]

DESIRE OF THE HAND

If my presumed equation were based on a linear thought that implied notions of filiation and belatedness, instead of on aesthetic and sociopolitical recurrences and convergences in time, it would constitute yet another neocolonial attempt to create predecessors of South American art in Europe. It remains imperative to read Vicuña's work as well, which fuses the knowledge of a colonial Chilean and local Andean culture with the quest for a global avant-garde, in reference to propositions made by her contemporaries in South America. Her determination to break away from the universalist claims of geometric abstraction, without abandoning a nonfigurative, geometric vocabulary and the general social concerns of constructivism, and her desire to take on the complexity of human reality and still remain receptive to her immediate environment, parallel the earlier attitudes of the neoconcrete group in Brazil (Lygia Clark, Hélio Oiticica, Lygia Pape, Amilcar de Castro, Franz Weissmann, Reynaldo Jardim, Theon Spanudis, the poet Ferreira Gullar, and the art critic Mario Pedrosa). These artists affirmed the values of modernity and eschewed "regionalist realism," but restated the problem of subjectivity in a specific Brazilian context. In the *Manifesto neoconcreto*[73] (1959) they attacked the positivism and mechanistic reductionism of the philosophy of Max Bill and the Hochschule für Gestaltung Ulm as ignoring the real conditions of Brazil; it was designed for an advanced capitalist/industrial society. Significantly, the neoconcrete work of Lygia Clark and Hélio Oiticica "gradually lost the technological sheen associated with constructivism and moved (in very different ways) towards the use of common and relatively valueless materials which were 'at hand' in the everyday environment of Rio."[74] Notwithstanding the isolation of these artists and the lack of communication among most countries in South America, it appears that in 1966 in Chile Vicuña was naming her works *arte precario*. That same year in Brazil Clark was describing "*precariousness* as a new idea of existence against all static crystallization within duration; and the very time of the act as a field of experience."[75] As much as Vicuña seems to rejoin the pursuit of Schwitters, Clark and Oiticica seem to reawaken visionary proposals and efforts of prewar artists (such as Duchamp, Mondriaan, and Van Tongerloo, known through the Biennals of Sao Paulo) to resist "the growing realm of the commodity." At the same time, in the 1960s and 1970s, these South American artists positioned themselves in relation to the international claims of the *arte povera*, resolutely stressing their own terminology and its intrinsic differences. In a letter to Clark (10/15/68), Oiticica states:

For European and North American expression, this is the great difference: the so-called Italian *arte povera* is done with the most advanced means: it is the sublimation of poverty, but in an anecdotal, visual way, deliberately poor but actually quite rich: it is the assimilation of the remains of an oppressive civilization and their transformation into consumption, the capitalization of the idea of poverty. To us, it does not seem that the economy of elements is directly connected with the idea of structure, with the nontechnique as discipline, with the freedom of creation as the super-economy, in which the rudimentary element in itself liberates open structures.[76]

According to Guy Brett, "material-linguistic objects like Oiticica's *Bolides* (*bolide* = fireball in Portuguese), his *Parangolés* (capes), *Penetrables*, *Nests* etc., and Clark's individual and collective 'propositions' using plastic, sacking, stones, air, string, sand, water etc., are not 'representations' but cells, nucleuses, or energy-centres. The object itself is secondary, appropriated, incomplete, existing only to initiate dialogue, and to indicate 'environmental and social wholes' (Oiticica). Literally, in many cases, they cannot exist without human support."[77] In her country Vicuña responded to the same cultural necessity and was drawn to the same tendencies of "expanding beyond the concept of the art object, beyond the gallery and the museum, into the environment, mixing media, and inviting the participation of the public."[78] Striking here are the concurrences not only in the use of "precarious" materials (netting, strings, shells), but also in the notions of space/time, of beginning, of bodily action (perception, touch, manipulation, voice, smell; the "eye-body"), of dialogue, even of another basic human creation: architecture. If for Lygia Clark a "living biological architecture" was created by people's gestures, and if Oiticica's sensory and social nucleuses, like his *Nests*, cabins, and *Penetrables*, poetically suggest new ways of constructing and inhabiting the environment—"as a metaphor of communication," then Vicuña's *Weavings* show points of interface within the semiotic/linguistic research of "nest" and "text" (discussed earlier).

LO NUNCA PROJECTADO[79]

However, in all these works it is the action of time and of "spatialization" that is most intelligible. What they mean by spatialization of the work is "the fact that it is *always in the present, always in the process of beginning over*, of beginning the impulse that gave birth to it over again—whose origin and evolution it contains simultaneously" (Neoconcretist Manifesto). In this sense the repetitive texture of crisscrossing straight lines, and eventually the grid, in Vicuña's woven works are formally closer to the accumulative system of joining wire cables in the kinetic *Reticulárea* (*ambientación*) (1968–76) and the *Dibujos sin papel* (Drawings without Paper) by the Venezuelan artist Gego, than to the arbitrary clusters of thread in *La Bruja* (The Broom) by Cildo Meireles (Brazil) at the Biennal of São Paulo,[80] or the earlier installation work by Marcel Duchamp at the exhibition *First Papers of Surrealism* (1942) in New York. The use of thread in these latter installation works is rather dealing with the problems of cultural institutionalization and reception to "openly denounce the validity of the retrospective exhibition and criticize the quasi-religious veneration of the acculturation."[81] At first sight Meireles's work appears as a gratuitous gesture enhancing chaotic dispersal, dust and dirt (at least the critics were heavy), but then one discovers that it is organized by this small domestic cleaning tool. Is sweeping a space not the best way to know it? Is it not about making measurements in the head with the hands?

Basting the space with large, loose stitches, Vicuña recently constructed *Hilumbres/allqa* at the Béguinage Saint-Elizabeth in Kortrijk.[82] To realize a double "weaving in space" she uses industrial black and white cotton spun in Flemish factories out of raw materials mainly imported from the so-called third world (Turkey, Egypt, Peru, etc.):

"I speak to the moment in which the visible becomes invisible and vice versa," said Vicuña, "to the moment when the cognition, the definition, has not yet been formed. Moving through the room people should discover the limits and traps of their own perception, the wandering attention." *Hilumbres*, a word invented by Vicuña, is composed of two words *hilo/lumbre* (thread/light), meaning "the thread catching light" or "the thread of light"; *allqa* is an Aymara word and a textile term that refers to a sharp contrast in the play of light and shadow. In weaving, it applies to the connection or encounter of things that can never be together: black and white. In Andean weaving this union of oppositions generates a degradation—or, as Vicuña formulates it, "a soft stairway," which argues for a model of subjectivity not rooted in binary thought: self/other, love/hate, aggression/identification, rejection/incorporation. Similarly it should be noted that in Andean and Mayan textiles the joints between two woven panels are often the focus of articulation and elaboration. "The seam itself is not rendered unobtrusive as it is in our apparel. Instead it is emphasized by silk or rayon stitching of bold color and emphatic form. This is called the *randa*."[83] Dealing with the past and the other, the crossing of borderlines and the seams of cultural articulation are highlighted in this work.

The words of Lygia Clark about her *Trailing* (1964) express similar thoughts about a continuum, a "matrixial" space: "If I use a Möbius strip for this experiment, it's because it breaks with our spatial habits: right/left; front/back, etc. It forces us to experience a limitless time and a continuous space."[84] The exploration of another possibility of seeing that is not the phallic gaze is at stake in Vicuña's work and in this sense it rejoins the issues in the paintings of Bracha Lichtenberg Ettinger, who developed the psychoanalytical theory of "Matrix and Metamorphosis."[85] Griselda Pollock, who has systematically and profoundly analyzed the painting of Lichtenberg Ettinger, explains that modalities based on the rejection/assimilation paradigm apply to how paintings are viewed as much as to how societies treat immigrants. "What is not us, strange and unknown, be that woman for man, the other for the white European, the painting for the viewer is positioned under this phallic logic as either one of the two terms: to be assimilated and if that is not possible to be cast off as completely other."[86] Lichtenberg Ettinger argues for "a shift of the phallic" by introducing the "matrix." For

if we allow ourselves to introduce into culture another symbolic signifier to stand beside the phallus (signifier of difference and division, absence and loss and orchestrating these either/or models), could we not be on the way to allowing the invisible feminine bodily specificity to enter and realign aspects of our consciousnesses and unconsciousnesses? This will surely extend as do all these metaphors of sexual difference to other others—issues of race, immigration, diaspora, genocide are tangled at the moment around the lack of means to signify other possible relations between different subjects—I and non-I. The matrix as symbol is about that encounter between difference which tries neither to master, nor assimilate, nor reject, nor alienate. It is a symbol of the coexistence in one space of two bodies, two subjectivities whose encounter at this moment is not an either/or.[87]

POETRY IN SPACE

Vicuña's *ouvrage* challenges such questions of recent art as the status of the object, the relation of the artist and the viewer/reader, bodily action, the space/time relation, the environment, inner and outer, the connection of the visual to the other senses, at once moving viewers away from their habit of compartmentalizing artistic production into separate media. At the same time it evokes a polemical attitude toward modernity, investigating a universal artistic development without negating local forms of expression. Her elaboration of popular elements shows links with bricolage and as such involves continual reconstruction

from the same materials (in the sense that it is always previous ends that are called upon to play the part of means).[88] Thus Vicuña reconsiders the changes of the signified into the signifying and vice versa. Vicuña dwells in im/possibility (as did Violeta Parra and Xul Solar). She demands a laying open of the mechanisms that produce meaning: particularly, the formation of a language. Her ideal is a discourse characterized by plurality, the open interplay of elements, and the possibility of infinite recombination.[89] However, Vicuña concludes that "(visual) language speaks of its own process: to name something which can not be named."

Working with and writing about Cecilia Vicuña is a privilege and a pleasure, and I therefore thank her. For their continuous support and for critically reading this essay my warm thanks go to Benjamin Buchloh, and also to Jean Fisher and Sally Stein. Last but not least I am very thankful to my family who allowed me—but luckily not always—to disappear behind my desk.

NOTES

1. Julia Averkieva and Mark A. Sherman, *Kwakiutl String Figures*, Anthropological Papers of the American Museum of Natural History, vol. 71 (New York, 1992).
2. Ibid., xiii.
3. L. A. Dickey (1928), *String Figures from Hawaii*, in B. P. Bishop Museum Bulletin, no. 54 (New York: Kraus Reprint, 1985), 11.
4. Cecilia Vicuña, "Metafísica del textil," in *Revista Tramemos II* (Buenos Aires, 1989).
5. Elizabeth Wayland Barber, *Women's Work: The First 20,000 Years. Women, Cloth, and Society in Early Times* (New York and London: W. W. Norton, 1994), 29–33.
6. Ibid.
7. Cecilia Vicuña creates the new verb *palabrir*, which means "to open words," noting that *abrir* (to open) originally meant *parir* (to give birth).

8. *Huipil* is a rectangular or square shirt, sewn on the sides, with a circular opening for the head, made of cotton or wool, and usually embroidered. Worn in Mesoamerica since pre-Columbian times, it is still used in the south of Mexico and Guatemala, where indigenous women continue to weave *huipiles* both for their own use and for trade.

9. Janet Catherine Berlo, "Beyond Bricolage: Women and Aesthetic Strategies in Latin American Textiles," in *Textile Traditions of Mesoamerica and The Andes: An Anthology*, ed. Margot Blum Schevill (New York: Garland Press, 1991), 437–467.

10. Cecilia Vicuña, *Unravelling Words and the Weaving of Water* (St. Paul, Minn.: Graywolf Press, 1992).

11. Cecilia Vicuña, *La Wik'uña* (Santiago, Chile: Francisco Zegers Editor, 1990).

12. Lucy Lippard, *Overlay* (New York: Pantheon Books, 1983), 106.

13. Henri Michaux, *The Beginnings*, trans. James Wanless; from *Sulfur* no. 34 (Spring 1994), 116.

14. Lygia Clark, "Nostalgia of the Body,' *October 69* (Summer 1994), 85–109.

15. Lippard, *Overlay*, 106.

16. Cecilia Vicuña, *Precario/Precarious*, trans. Anne Twitty (New York: Tanam Press, 1983).

17. Clark, "Nostalgia," 85–109.

18. Cecilia Vicuña quotes that "art" and "order" derive both from the same root, *ar* (to fit together). The word *armus* (upper arm) comes from what the arms did. In this sense the Latin *ars* (art) was "skill," and the Latin *ordo* (order) from *ordiri* (to begin to weave) was "a row of threads in a loom."

19. Jean Fischer, "1:1 Lynn Silverman," exhib. cat. (Angel Row Gallery, Camerawork, and the University of Derby, 1993).

20. Guy Brett, about Roberto Evangelista's *Immersion*, in *America. Bride of the Sun. 500 years Latin America and the Low Countries*, exhib. cat. (Antwerp: Royal Museum of Fine Arts, 1992), 245–246.

21. The *desaparecidos*, or the "disappeared ones," was the name given by the people of the southern cone (Chile, Uruguay, and Argentina) to men and women who were led away by the secret police from their homes or in the streets during the dictatorships of the seventies, because they were never seen again, and the military police denied having taking them in the first place. Only after years of struggle, human rights organizations were able to demonstrate that the people who had been "disappeared" by the thousands not only did exist, but had been effectively tortured to death and/or murdered by the military regimes of the three countries. Only some of the collective or individual burials have been found; sometimes their bodies were exploded by dynamite, sometimes bathed in lime and then covered by soil to render them unrecognizable.

22. Vicuña, *Precario/Precarious*.

23. Averkieva and Sherman, *Kwakiutl String Figures*, 137–150.

24. Kathleen Haddon, *Artists in String* (London: Methuen, 1930), 145; (reprint ed.: New York: AMS Press, 1979).

25. Claude Lévi-Strauss, *Structural Anthropology* (New York: Basic books, 1963), 31–54.

26. Cecilia Vicuña, *Palabrir* (forthcoming; Editorial Sudamericana, Chile).

27. Cecilia Vicuña, *Sabor a mí* (Devon, England: Beau Geste Press, 1973).

28. Barbara and Dennis Tedlock, "Text and Textile: Language and Technology in the Arts of the Quiché Maya," *Journal of Anthropological Research* 41.2 (1985), 121–146.

29. Berlo, "Beyond Bricolage."

30. Lévi-Strauss, *Structural Anthropology*, 21.

31. César Paternosto speaks of "Major Art"; William Conklin of "Textile Age." See César Patermosto, *The Stone and the Thread: Andean Roots of Abstract Art* (Austin: University of Texas Press, 1996).

32. André Leroi-Gourhan, *L'homme et la matière*, Albin Michel, 244.

33. Mary Jane Jacobs, "Anni Albers: A Modern Weaver as Artist," in *The Woven and Graphic Art of Anni Albers* (Washington, D.C.: Smithsonian Institution Press, 1985), 65.

34. Ibid., 22 and plate 1.

35. Ibid., 66.

36. Ibid., 71–72.

37. Cecilia Vicuña says that this dichotomy is not a general rule in the continent. Women shamans in many indigenous societies have used words in their healing practices. Also Maria Sabina among the Mazatecs, the Machi among the Mapuche in Chile and Argentina, and the Quechua women of Ecuador have subverted this dichotomy.

38. Berlo, "Beyond Bricolage."

39. *Mola* is a rectangular piece of cotton cloth, with applique of other cotton pieces sewn in, to make designs and symbols as in patchwork. Originally worn and created by the Cuna indigenous women of Panama, today it is a flourishing form of social commentary, with *molas* carrying political messages, sports, and TV events, together with the ancient symbols, to be worn by the women themselves (as part of their shirt) and to be sold to tourists.

40. Mary W. Helms, *Cuna Molas and Cocle Art Forms*, Working Papers in the Traditional Arts, no. 7 (Philadelphia: Institute for the Study of Human Issues, 1981).

41. Berlo, "Beyond Bricolage."

42. Ruth Bunzel, *Chichicastenango: A Guatemalan Village* (Seattle: University of Washington Press, 1952), 308.

43. Berlo, "Beyond Bricolage."

44. Ibid.

45. A famous example is the "Manifesto" that Oliverio Girondo (1891–1967) wrote for the fourth issue of *Martin Fierro* (1924). "Summoning the avant-garde forces to the task of resuscitating the language, Girondo asserts that fresh life can be brought to Spanish only by finding new models outside literary Spanish: the agitated and frenetic tones of the technologized era of mass communications."

46. Naomi Lindstrom, "Live Language Against Dead: Literary Rebels of Buenos Aires," review in *Latin American Literature and Arts*, no. 31, New York (jan–april 1982).

47. *El mirar cruzado* means: looking at something from (two) different points of view, mixing the sources; in Cecilia Vicuña's unpublished manuscript *Fragmentos de Poeticas*.

48. Gilles Deleuze and Félix Guattari, *A Thousand Plateaus, Capitalism and Schizophrenia*, trans. Brian Massumi (Minneapolis and London: University of Minnesota Press, 1987), 474–500.

49. Deleuze and Guattari, *A Thousand Plateaus*, 475.

50. Deleuze and Guattari say on p. 429 that "'Haptic' is a better word than 'tactile' since it does not establish an opposition between two sense organs but rather invites the assumption that the eye itself may fulfill this nonoptical function."

51. Ibid., 493.

52. Ibid.

53. Ibid., 499.

54. Ibid., 446–447.

55. Berlo, "Beyond Bricolage."

56. In fact this situation is part of an ongoing process of destroying native agriculture since colonial times. At first not only most of the wild wheat was devastated by the *conquistadores*—to be replaced by imported western wheat, which the Indian population had to buy—but also a great number of alpacas and llamas were killed so that these herds had to be replaced by sheep and cows sold at very high prices. See also Cecilia Vicuña, "The Invention of Poverty," in *America. Bride of the Sun*, 514–515.

57. Rosalind E. Krauss, *The Originality of the Avant-Garde and Other Modernist Myths* (Cambridge, Mass.: MIT Press, 1986), 8–22.

58. Cf. Anni Albers, who said: "It is for this reason that we can find certitude in the belief that we are taking part in an eternal order." In Jacobs, *The Woven and Graphic Art of Anni Albers*.

59. Krauss, *Originality of the Avant-Garde.*

60. Ibid.

61. Benjamin H. D. Buchloh, "Refuse and Refuge," in *Gabriel Orozco*, exhib. cat. (Kortrijk: Kanaal Art Foundation, 1993).

62. Examples are: Jean Cassou's *Panorama de las artes contemporaneas*; J. E. Cirlot's *El arte otro*; and Aldo Pellegrini, ed. and trans., *Antologia de la poesía surrealista* (Buenos Aires: Fabril Editora, 1961).

63. *A Noble Andean Art*, exhib. cat. (Santiago de Chile: Museo Chileno de Arte Precolombino), 72–73, no. 0780: *Quipu*, Camelid fibers, Inca, 1470–1532 A.D.: main cord length: 168 cms.

64. Edward W. Said, *Beginnings: Intentions and Method* (New York: Columbia University Press, 1985).

65. Kurt Schwitters said: "I let nonsense interact with sense. I prefer nonsense, but that is a purely personal matter. I feel sorry for nonsense, since, so far, it has rarely been formed artistically. Therefore I love nonsense." See Ernst Schwitters, "Kurt Schwitters—Father of *Merz*—My Father," 141.

66. *Merz = Kurt Schwitters*, Karnizawa, The Museum of Modern Art, Seibu Takanawa, Tokyo, Oct–Nov. 1983; Ernst Schwitters, "Kurt Schwitters—father of *Merz*—My Father," 142.

67. Jean François Pirson, *La structure et l'objet* (Liege: Metaphores, 1984), 29. The Iglesia de la Colonia Güell was commissioned by Eugenio Güell to Gaudi in 1898. It was constructed for a colony of textile workers and became a laboratory for experiences related to the construction of La Sagrada Familia. Gaudi collaborated with the architects, F. Berenguer and J. Canaleta, and with the engineer, E. Goetz.

68. Werner Schmalenbach, *Kurt Schwitters* (Köln, 1967), 93. *Merz* is the second syllable of *Kommerz* (commerce). The name originated from the *Merzbild*, a picture in which the word *Merz* could be read in between abstract forms. Schmalenbach quotes Schwitters as saying "When I first exhibited these pasted and nailed pictures with the Sturm in Berlin, I searched for a collective noun for this new kind of picture, because I could not define them with the older conceptions like Expressionism, Futurism or whatever. So I gave all my pictures the name 'Merz-pictures' after the most characteristic of them and thus made them like a species. Later on I expanded this name '*Merz*' to include my poetry (I had written poetry since 1917), and finally all my relevant activities."

69. Schwitters, "Kurt Schwitters—Father of *Merz*—My Father," 141.

70. Yusuke Nakahara, in *Merz = Kurt Schwitters.*

71. The grandfather of Vicuña, who was the writer and civil rights activist and lawyer Carlos Vicuña Fuentes (Dean of the University of Chile and Deputate to the Chilean Parliament), had received in his home a group of refugees from the Spanish Civil War. Among the refugees were the playwriter José Ricardo Morales and the editors Arturo Soria and Carmelo Soria, who was later murdered by the secret police of Pinochet. These men and their families became part of Cecilia Vicuña's family and education. It should be remembered here that the Nazis were also instrumental in the rise of Franco and the defeat of the Spanish Republic. Carlos Vicuña Fuentes was made an "honorary jew" by the Jewish community in Santiago as a result of his antifascist activities.

72. During the nineteenth and twentieth centuries several presidents carried out an explicit policy of "Germanization" and facilitated German immigration to the South of Chile "in order," so they said, "to bring prosperity to a forsaken land and to improve the Indian race." Thus they were encouraging the "populating" of the provinces south of the Araucania (Valdivia, Osorno, Llanquihue) by taking the land from the Mapuche. During World War II a German

fascist presence in the South of Chile was evident through the existence of support groups for the Nazis (National Socialist Parties) and after the war this presence was enforced by the arrival of exiled and former Nazis, from whom it is now known that they participated in the dictatorship of General Pinochet.

73. Reproduced in Ronaldo Brito, *Neoconcretisimo, Vertice e Ruptura* (Rio de Janeiro: Funarte, 1985), 12–13; reprinted in French translation in *Robho* 4, and in English translation in October 69, (Summer 1994), 91–95.

74. Guy Brett, "Lygia Clark: The Borderline Between Art and Life," *Third Text* 1 (Autumn 1987), 65–94.

75. Clark, "Nostalgia of the Body," 106.

76. "Isso é a grande diferença para a expressão européia e americana do norte: a tal povera arte italiana é feita com os meios mais avançados: é a sublimaçao da pobreza, mas de modo anedótico, visual, propositalmente pobre mas na verdade bem rica: é a assimilação dos restos de uma civilização opressiva e sua transformação em consumo, a capitalização da idéia de pobreza. Para nós, não parece que a economia de elementos está diretamente ligada à idéia de estrutura, à náo-técnica como disciplina, à liberdade de criação como a supra-economia, onde o elemento rudimentar já libera estruturas abertas." In *Lygia Clark e Hélio Oiticica*, Sala especial do 9. Salão Nacional de Artes Plásticas (Rio de Janeiro: Funarte, 1986–87).

77. Brett, "Lygia Clark," 75.

78. Ibid.

79. *Lo nunca projectado* is the title of an album with poems by Alfredo Silva Estrada and illustrations by Gego (1964).

80. *La Brucha* consisted of 2500 km of white cotton thread unrolled in a fortuitous way through every single space all over the three floors of the Biennal Building to end up at a broom placed in a little store-room near the toilets.

81. Benjamin H. D. Buchloh, "The Museum Fictions of Marcel Broodthaers," *Museums by Artists*, ed. A.A. Bronson and Peggy Gale (Toronto: Art Metropole, 1983). "Vintage cobweb? Indeed not!" Duchamp was reported to have said.

82. Exhibition of Cecilia Vicuña in the series "Inside the Visible. Begin the Beguine in Flanders," organized by the Kanaal Art Foundation as Cultural Ambassador of Flandres, (Oct. 1–Dec. 11), 1994.

83. Berlo, "Beyond Bricolage," 453.

84. Clark, "Nostalgia of the Body."

85. Bracha Lichtenberg Ettinger, "Matrix and Metramorphosis," in *Differences: A Journal of Feminist Cultural Studies* 4.3; and 'The Becoming Threshold of Matrixial Borderlines," in *Travellers' Tales* (London: Routledge, 1994).

86. Griselda Pollock, "Oeuvres Autistes," *Versus* 3 (1994): 14–18.

87. Ibid.

88. Claude Lévi-Strauss, *The Savage Mind* (Chicago: University of Chicago Press, 1966), 21.

89. Naomi Lindstrom, "Xul Solar: Star-Spangler of Languages," *Review: Latin American Literature and Arts* 25/26, 121.

16

PIECING AND WRITING

Elaine Showalter

Editor's introduction: The American literary critic Elaine Showalter presented "Piecing and Writing" at the Poetics of Gender colloquium held at Columbia University in the United States in 1985. Showalter is celebrated for her contribution to "gynocritics"—literary criticism from a feminist perspective. Here, she compares the structural similarities of the quilt and the short story, suggesting that American women's writing (and our reading of it) found structural templates in a far more familiar creative construction of the time: quilting. "I would like to suggest that a knowledge of piecing, the technique of assembling fragments into an intricate and ingenious design, can provide the contexts in which we can interpret and understand the forms, meanings, and narrative traditions of American women's writing," she explains. Part of the logic driving Showalter's comparison of structures is based on time. Writing short sections of fiction for installments in magazines and quilting are seen as creative acts capable of surviving multiple interruptions: creativity that can be picked up and put down.

Can you read it? Do you understand?
By squares, by inches, you are drawn in.
Your fingers read it like Braille.
History, their days, the quick deft fingers.
Their lives recorded in cloth.
A universe here, stitched to perfection.
You must be the child-witness,
You are the only survivor.

—Joyce Carol Oates, "Celestial
Timepiece" (1980)

As one of the critics from an English department to have invaded the hitherto French space of the poetics conference, I am faced with some special anxieties. I am going to look at the development of women's writing within a framework that is both historical and American—a critical position that may make me about as authentic in the Maison Française as a Pepperidge Farm croissant. But my purpose is in fact to ask about the difference of American women's writing, and less directly, about the difference of American feminist criticism, through the use of a downhome, downright Yankee historical approach which I hope will fit

Source: Elaine Showalter, "Piecing and Writing," in Nancy K. Miller (ed.), *The Poetics of Gender* (New York: Columbia University Press, 1986) pp. 222–247. Reproduced with permission of Columbia University Press.

Alice Jardine's view of "American contextual feminism" and Susan Suleiman's definition of "thematic reading." If we move away from some of the universal, even global, constructs of psychoanalytic feminist criticism to consider American women's writing, will we find a literature of *our* own, and an American poetics of gender? Do we need to develop new forms of inquiry in order to account for a female tradition which is also multiracial? Does the special configuration of women's culture in the United States, the intimate world of female kinships, friendships, and rituals which has been so brilliantly studied by historians such as Gerda Lerner, Nancy Cott, and Carroll Smith-Rosenberg, suggest a special context for American feminist literary history?

Specifically, I want to ask whether the strongly marked American women's tradition of piecing, patchwork, and quilting has consequences for the structures, genres, themes, and meanings of American women's writing in the nineteenth and twentieth centuries. Here some quick definitions may be in order. "Piecing" means the sewing together of small fragments of fabric cut into geometric shapes, so that they form a pattern. The design unit is called the block or patch; "patchwork" is the joining of these design units into an overall design. The assembled patches are then attached to a heavy backing with either simple or elaborate stitches in the process called quilting. Thus the process of making a patchwork quilt involves three separate stages of artistic composition, with analogies to language use first on the level of the sentence, then in terms of the structure of a story or novel, and finally the images, motifs, or symbols—the "figure in the carpet"—that unify a fictional work.

While piecing, patchwork, and quilting have a long tradition in Europe, they became identified as specifically American feminine art forms in the nineteenth century. Quilting was an economic necessity in a society where readymade bedding could not be easily obtained before the 1890s, and where in the cold New England or prairie winter each family member might need

five quilts. Nineteenth-century American women's autobiographies "frequently begin with a childhood memory of learning patchwork from a mother or grandmother" (Hedges, 295). Moreover, early art, writing, and mathematical exercises taught to little girls emphasized geometric principles of organization, and such lessons were applied practically to the design of quilts: "Obsessive repetition of the same small block pattern comprised the entire quilt, which was in essence a grid system, an emphasis on structure and organization" (Dewhurst et al., 139). Often, a little girl was encouraged to finish a small quilt in time for a fifth birthday, and the event was celebrated by a quilting bee; indeed, the making of textiles occasioned many of "the sanctioned social events of a young girl's life" (Dewhurst et al., 9; Hedges, 295–96). An American girl aspired to have a dozen quilts in her dower chest by the time she was engaged; the thirteenth quilt of the trousseau was the Bridal Quilt, made of the most expensive materials the family could afford, and assembled at a special quilting bee.[1]

Quilting was an art that crossed racial, regional, and class boundaries, produced by slave women in the south as well as by pioneer housewives on the trek west and by New England matrons in their homes. Alice Walker has suggested that the quilt was indeed a major form of creative expression for black women in this country. "In the Smithsonian Institution in Washington, D.C.," she writes,

> there hangs a quilt unlike another in the world. In fanciful, inspired, and yet simple and identifiable figures, it portrays the story of the Crucifixion. . . . Though it follows no known pattern of quiltmaking, and though it is made of bits and pieces of worthless rags, it is obviously the work of a person of powerful imagination and deep spiritual feeling. Below this quilt I saw a note that says it was made by "an anonymous Black woman in Alabama a hundred years ago. (239)

The discourse of American quilting drew upon designs from African and from Native American culture, and from the nonrepresentational Amish and Mennonite traditions. Furthermore, the social institutions of quilting, such as quilting bees, figure in American women's history, as places where women came together to exchange information, learn new skills, and discuss political issues; it was at a church quilting bee in Cleveland, for example, that Susan B. Anthony gave her first speech on women's suffrage.

For at least the past decade, too, metaphors of pen and needle have been pervasive in feminist poetics and in a revived women's culture in the United States. The repertoire of the Victorian lady who could knit, net, knot, and tat, has become that of the feminist critic, in whose theoretical writing metaphors of text and textile, thread and theme, weaver and web, abound. The Spinster who spins stories, Ariadne and her labyrinthine thread, Penelope who weaves and unweaves her theoretical tapestry in the halls of Ithaca or New Haven, are the feminist culture heroines of the critical age. Furthermore, metaphors of the female web of relationship have taken on positive associations with feminist psychology; as Carol Gilligan observes, "Women's place in man's life cycle has been that of nurturer, caretaker, and helpmate, the weaver of those networks of relationships on which she in turn relies" (17).

These theoretical images have material counterparts in the revival of feminine crafts which were despised in the early days of the women's movement but have been brought back into fashion under the auspices of a new women's culture, celebrated by such feminist art events as Judy Chicago's "The Dinner Party." The historical moment of transition, for me, was made vivid in 1980, when, at a scholarly conference in honor of the George Eliot centennial, Germaine Greer made a majestic entrance into the auditorium and withdrew a large roll of knitting from her briefcase. If, with her needles clicking loudly as the men read their papers, she hinted less of Mrs. Ramsay than of Madame Defarge, nonetheless her presence signaled a return of the repressed, a hint perhaps that, when in the early 1960s my Bryn Mawr classmates and I knitted as well as noted in lecture after lecture on the male literary classics, we were protesting against patriarchal culture in a secret women's language we used even if we did not fully understand it.

The patchwork quilt has become one of the most central images in this new feminist lexicon. As the art critic Lucy Lippard explains, "Since the new wave of feminist art began around 1970, the quilt has become the prime visual metaphor for women's lives, for women's culture. In properly prim grids or rebelliously 'crazy' fields, it incorporates Spider Woman's web, political networking, and the collage aesthetic" (32). The history of quilting is closely associated with the recording of American female experience; as one historian notes, women "were stitching together the history of the country making the great American tapestry" (Cooper and Buferd, 18). Feminist poetry of the 1970s also celebrates the quilt as a female art of nurturance and sisterhood. In Marge Piercy's "Looking at Quilts," it is "art without frames," covering "the bed where the body knit/ to self and other and the/ dark wool of dreams" (35–36). In advertising, fashion, and the media, too, the quilt motif has been borrowed as an icon of feminist chic, from the short-lived Broadway musical "The Quilters," which opened and closed in fall 1984, to the designs for Ralph Lauren sweaters and Perry Ellis skirts.

Piecing and patchwork have also been widely discussed as models for a female aesthetic. As Patricia Mainardi explains,

because quiltmaking is so indisputably women's art, many of the issues women artists are attempting to clarify now—questions of feminine sensibility, of originality and tradition, of individuality versus collectivity, of content and values in art—can be illuminated by a study of this art form, its relation to the lives of the artists, and how it has been dealt with in art history. (36)

Among the leading feminist theoreticians of quilting is the Bulgarian artist and quiltmaker Radka Donnell-Vogt, who has written about piecing as a way of rethinking the maternal.[2] Donnell-Vogt views quilting as a primal women's art form, related to touch and texture, to the intimacy of the bed and the home, and to issues of sexuality. She believes that the basic quilt patterns are archetypal representations of the female body. In her own art, Donnell-Vogt explains, quiltmaking

> was essential in giving me a base for exploring my situation as a woman and as an artist . . . quilts became for me a reconfirmation and restatement of women's toils in child-raising, of the physical labor in the cultural shaping and maintenance of persons. . . . Finally, I saw quilts as the bliss and the threat of the womb made visible, spread out as a separate object shaped by the imaginative wealth of women's work and body experience. (49–50)[3]

Insofar as she deals with piecing as jouissance, with quilting as an art expressive of the preverbal semiotic phase of mother-child bonding, with the aesthetic possibilities of the pre-Oedipal phase, and with the cultural significance of *écriture couverture*, Donnell-Vogt can be called the Kristeva of quilting, the Other Bulgarian.

In literary theories of a Female Aesthetic, the metaphor of piecing has been used as a model for the organization of language in the wild zone of the woman's text. According to Rachel Blau DuPlessis, a pure women's writing would be "nonhierarchic . . . breaking hierarchical structures, making an even display of elements over the surface with no climactic place or moment, having the materials organized into many centers." In the "verbal quilt" of the feminist text, there is "no subordination, no ranking" (274).

My approach to the poetics of gender in piecing and writing, however, will be through history, genre, and theme, rather than through a model of a female aesthetic, on the one hand, or a structuralist analysis of textual units, codes, sequences,

and narrative functions, on the other. I would like to suggest that a knowledge of piecing, the technique of assembling fragments into an intricate and ingenious design, can provide the contexts in which we can interpret and understand the forms, meanings, and narrative traditions of American women's writing. But in order to understand the relationship between piecing and American women's writing, we must also deromanticize the art of the quilt, situate it in its historical contexts, and discard many of the sentimental stereotypes of an idealized, sisterly, and nonhierarchic women's culture that cling to it. We must then consider nineteenth-century women's writing with a similar detachment, avoiding a binary system in which we contrast women's art to male "high art" in an alternative vocabulary of anonymity, artlessness, privacy, and collaboration.

Piecing and quilting were not anonymous arts, although the names and identities of quiltmakers have frequently been suppressed by contemporary art history and museum curatorship. As Mainardi has pointed out, "the women who made quilts knew and valued what they were doing: frequently quilts were signed and dated by the maker, listed in her will with specific instructions as to who should inherit them, and treated with all the care that a fine piece of art deserves" (37). In addition, the myth of the quilting bee as the model of "an essentially nonhierarchical organization" (de Bretteville, 117–18) and as the place where women all collaborated on the making of a quilt comes from the cultural belief that women lack individuality, creativity, and initiative. In reality, expert needlewomen were invited to quilting bees to help the designer stitch her original pieced material to a heavy backing. Finally, the substitution of the term "pattern" for "design" in discussions of patchwork obscures the degree of intentionality and innovation possible within the form, and minimizes the autonomy and individuality of the artist. Piecing was not simply a repetitious and unoriginal recombining of design elements, but a creative manipulation of conventions. Even when working with such well-known patterns as the Star, Sun, or Rose, "the quilt artist exploited the design possibilities through her color relationships, value contrasts, and inventive variations on the original pattern" (Dewhurst, 48; Parker and Pollock, 71).

The relationship between piecing and writing has not been static, but has changed from one generation to another, along with changes in American women's culture. In antebellum American women's writing, piecing appears as a marker of female difference from the patriarchal literary tradition. The quilt is a moral artifact, an emblem of the deliberate ordering of women's separate cultural lives as well as fictions, and of the writer's control over her materials. After the Civil War, as women writers had to redefine themselves as artists working within two sexual and cultural traditions, the meaning of the quilt motif changed as well. Allusions to the structure and design of the pieces become more explicitly related to narrative problems and to the decline of a female aesthetic. And in contemporary writing, when quilts have been raised to the level of high art within a commodity market, and when a generation of feminists have returned to the past to reclaim a female heritage and its practices, the quilt stands for a vanished past experience to which we have a troubled and ambivalent cultural relationship.

Yet there are also significant historical continuities between these phases. As a twentieth-century quilter explains, piecing is an art of scarcity, ingenuity, conservation, and order: "You're given just so much to work with in a life and you have to do the best you can with what you got. That's what piecing is. The materials is passed on to you or is all you can afford to buy . . . that's just what's given to you. Your fate. But the way you put them together is your business. You can put them in any order you like. Piecing is orderly" (Cooper and Buferd, 20).

Furthermore, piecing is the art form which best reflects the fragmentation of women's time, the dailiness and repetitiveness of women's work. As Lucy Lippard observes, "the mixing and matching of fragments is the product of the interrupted life. . . . What is popularly seen as 'repetitive,' 'obsessive,' and 'compulsive' in women's art is in fact a necessity for those whose time comes in small squares" (32). I will be arguing that because of the structures and traditions of women's time, the dominant genre of American women's writing has been the short story, the short narrative piece. As the novel became the dominant genre of nineteenth-century American writing, women adapted the techniques of literary piecing to the structural and temporal demands of the new literary mode.

The women's novels which flourished before the Civil War have always been an anomalous form for literary history. Sometimes called sentimental, sometimes called domestic, and most recently named "woman's fiction," they do not seem to fit either the patterns of English women's novels, or the patterns of the American "romance." American women writers in fact did not self-consciously situate themselves in either artistic tradition. As Nina Baym has explained, "they saw themselves not as 'artists' but as professional writers with work to do": "The literary women conceptualized authorship as a profession rather than a calling, as work and not art. Women authors tended not to think of themselves as artists or justify themselves in the language of art until the 1870s. . . . Often the women deliberately and even proudly disavowed membership in an artistic fraternity." Thus in their work, "the dimensions of formal self-consciousness, attachment to or quarrel with a grand tradition, aesthetic seriousness, all are missing" (32). Instead they wrote highly conventionalized novels, which, as Baym points out, all are variations on a single overplot: "the story of a young girl who is deprived of the supports she had . . . depended on to sustain her throughout life and is faced with the necessity of winning her own way in the world." In this system, like quiltmakers, "individual authors are distinguished from one another largely by the plot elements they select from the common repertory and by the varieties of setting and incident with which they embellish the basic tale" (11–12). As in piecing, in the hands of an imaginative writer, women's novels based upon conventional designs could achieve true artistic stature and power.

Before 1850, the standard genre of women's writing was the sketch or piece written for ladies' magazines or albums. While the sustained effort of a novel might be impossible for a woman whose day was shattered by constant interruption, the short narrative piece, quickly imagined and written, and usually based on a single idea, could be more easily completed. When, in the 1850s, the "book became the predominant mode of literary packaging, established authors such as Harriet Beecher Stowe and Fanny Fern first gathered their sketches into volumes with such titles as 'Fern Leaves from Fanny's Portfolio'" (32). During the same period album quilts, the most prized and expensive examples of American quilt art, were a standard genre of female craft. . . . Album quilts are composed of pieced or appliquéd squares "that are entirely different, even if their construction has been carefully planned and orchestrated by a single quilter. The effect is as if each square were a page in a remembrance book" (Pilling, 72).[4] They were made to be presented to young men on their 21st birthdays (known as Liberty quilts), or exchanged among women friends (Medley, Friendship, or Engagement quilts), and were signed square by square. These squares, like the sketches in a literary album, reflected the fragmentation of women's time.

A number of nineteenth-century women's texts discuss the problem of reading a quilt, of deciphering the language of piecing. Most of these women's texts suggest that the language or meaning of the quilt, its special symbolism, resides in the individual piece, the fragment that recalls a costume and a memory. In "The Patchwork Quilt," an anonymous essay by a factory girl printed in the *Lowell Offering* in 1845, the author's quilt is described as "a bound volume of hieroglyphics." But only a certain kind of reader can decipher these female signifiers. To the "uninterested observer," the narrator declares, it looks like a "miscellaneous collection of odd bits and

ends," but to me "it is a precious reliquary of past treasure." The quilt's pieces, taken from the writer's childhood calico gowns, her dancing school dress, her fashionable young ladies' gowns, her mother's mourning dress, her brother's vest, are an album of the female life cycle from birth to death. Its unmarried creator, a self-styled old maid aunt, recalls learning to piece as part of that initiation into pain and blood that is recorded as part of female destiny in texts from Sleeping Beauty to Helene Deutsch: "O what a heroine was I in driving the stitches! What a martyr under the pricks and inflictions of the needle . . . those were my first lessons in heroism and fortitude." There is the record of "patchwork hopes," the piecing done in the expectation of marriage. And there is the era in the "history of my quilt" when it was given instead to the younger but married sister: "Yes, she was to be married and I not spoken for! She was to be taken, and I left. I gave her the patchwork. It seemed like a transference of girlish hopes and aspirations, or rather a finale to them all. Girlhood had gone and I was a woman" (150–54). Finally the quilt serves the sister on her deathbed after childbirth, and is stained by her blood; the woman artist survives to record this history through the hieroglyphics of the quilt.

Nineteenth-century women writers also drew attention to the way in which pieces were put together, as a moral allegory of the inventive and resourceful composition of a life. It was a quilter's truism that no two women would make the same design out of a given set of pieces. As "Aunt Jane of Kentucky," a character in the stories of Eliza Calvert Hall, comments, "How much piecing a quilt is like living a life! You can give the same pieces to two persons, and one will make a 'nine-patch' and one will make a 'wild-goose chase'. . . . And that is jest the way with livin'" (in Dewhurst, 138).

Louisa May Alcott's children's story "Patty's Patchwork" combines a discussion of the emotional significance of the piece with a moralized account of the aesthetics of piecing and writing.[5] Ten-year-old Patty, visiting her Aunt Pen while her mother has a new baby, grows impatient with her patchwork, and flings the pieces into the air, declaring that "something dreadful ought to be done to the woman who invented it." But Aunt Pen has a different point of view. The quilt, she explains, is a "calico diary," a record of a female life composed of "bright and dark bits . . . put together so that the whole is neat, pretty and useful." As a project, Patty sets out to make a "moral bed-quilt" for her aunt to read and decipher, while she herself is learning to become a "nice little comforter," the epitome of female patience, perseverance, good nature, and industry. When the infant sister dies, Patty nonetheless goes on to finish the quilt, which Aunt Pen not only reads and interprets as a journal of her psychological maturity but also inscribes—that is, writes upon—with verses and drawings that become a textual criticism of both the work and the life. Aunt Pen is obviously a figure for Alcott herself, the woman writer, who is not the mother with the dead child, but who instead offers an alternative model of female power and creativity. While the discipline of the pieced quilt itself represents women's confinement within the grid of nineteenth-century feminine domestic morality, it also offers the potential creative freedom of textuality and design.

Like Alcott's, many stories about piecing, patchwork, and quilting use as their central figure a woman who is not a mother or a sister, but a maiden aunt, the creative female figure who is of the mother's generation but is not bound by the laws of reproduction. In the American tradition, it seems to be aunts who have organized the cultural activity of quilting, such as Aunt Dinah and her quilting party in a Stephen Foster song about seeing Nelly home. Aunts are also the organizers and custodians of folklore and stories, and these too are associated with piecing, as we see in the titles of such short story collections as Caroline Hentz's "Aunt Patty's Scrap Bag" (1846), or Louisa May Alcott's "Aunt Jo's Scrap Bag" (1872). Relationships between women in these stories are often represented as those of aunt and niece, rather than the more familiar and intense kinship bonds of

mother and daughter, or the intense friendships of the female world of love and ritual. These stories are also about apprenticeship in an ongoing artistic tradition.

One of the most interesting examples of the relationship between piecing and writing in narrative design can be found in the work of Harriet Beecher Stowe. Stowe's literary career began in the 1840s with a series of sketches or pieces on various topics written for Christmas gift annuals, ladies' albums, and religious periodicals. As Mary Kelley has shown in her important study of the nineteenth-century American domestic novelists, Stowe thought of her writing in terms of temporal blocks; as she wrote an editor, she could not afford to write except by "buying my time." When the "family accounts wouldn't add up," Stowe recalled, "then I used to say to my faithful friend and factotum Anna . . . Now if you will keep the babies and attend to the things in the house for one day I'll write a piece and then we shall be out of the scrape" (169). A "piece" could be written in a day and bring in $2.00 a page. Stowe regarded these short texts as pictorial, visual, grouped together less by plot than by principles of contrasting design. When she began to write *Uncle Tom's Cabin*, serialized in short weekly installments, Stowe continued to think of her writing as the stitching together of scenes. As Bruce Kirkland notes in his study of the manuscripts of *Uncle Tom's Cabin*, the novel was not a break with Stowe's narrative technique but rather developed out of her earlier writing and "was of a piece with it" (77).

Despite the unparalleled success of *Uncle Tom's Cabin*, and its current acclamation by feminist critics, however, Stowe's reputation has generally suffered from assumptions about her failure to live up to dominant standards of literary form. As one nineteenth-century critic complained, *Uncle Tom's Cabin* seemed to lack unity and formal design; "it is a rule of art," he declared, "that a work of fiction should be so joined together that every passage and incident should contribute to bring about an inevitable though unexpected catastrophe" (Holmes, in Ammons, 7–24). Even her feminist defenders have noted such flaws, and have had to explain them. While the book is "defective according to the rules of the modern French romance," George Sand wrote, the "conventional rules of art . . . never have been and never will be absolute. . . . In matters of art there is only one rule: to paint and to move" (in Ammons, 3–6). In our own day, feminist critics have interpreted Stowe's design in terms of male genres; Jane Tompkins, for example, calls it an American jeremiad; Ellen Moers sees it as a female epic structured geographically and metaphorically by the river (in Ammons, 135–38). Yet these redemptive readings, to some degree, cannot be produced without making the novel wrong in some other respect. In Moers's reading of the book as epic, for example, the title seems bizarre, or as she says, "misbegotten," for as Moers observes, "little of importance in the novel happens inside Uncle Tom's Cabin" (in Ammons, 136).

Uncle Tom's cabin, which Stowe first describes in the fourth chapter, is a log cabin whose facade is "covered by a large scarlet begonia and a native multiflora rose, which entwisting and interlacing, left scarcely a vestige of the rough logs to be seen." The title, I would suggest, is what Nancy K. Miller calls the "internal female signature: an icon or emblem within the fiction itself that obliquely figures the symbolic and material difficulties involved in becoming a woman writer."[6] "Uncle Tom's Cabin" is an allusion in the referential system of women's culture to the Log Cabin quilt, which by 1850 was the most popular American pieced quilt pattern. The basic Log Cabin pattern begins with a central square, often in red, which is sewn on to a larger block of fabric. "A narrow strip, or log, is then pieced to the edge of the center square. Subsequent strips are added, each perpendicular to the previous strip, until the center square is entirely bordered by logs" (Bishop et al., 74). The compositional principle of the Log Cabin quilt is the contrast between light and dark fabric. Each block is divided into two triangular sections, one section executed in light colored fabrics, the other in dark. When the blocks are pieced together to make the quilt, dramatic visual effects and variations can be created depending on the placement of the dark sections. We can see this first in the diagram of log cabin blocks, and then in quilts with such named variants as Light and Dark, Barn Raising, Courthouse Steps, and Streak of Lightning. . . .

Radka Donnell-Vogt, moreover, sees the Log Cabin pattern as the most archetypal, profound, and symbolically significant of all quilt designs. It can also be found in the swaddling of infants, the wrapping of corpses, and in the inscriptions on sacred entrances. It can be read as either phallic or vaginal, depending on whether we see it as a projecting pyramid or a depression. "It is a universal convertible bisexual pattern protecting the union of opposites in human beings, and securing safe passage from one world into the other, from day to night, from life to death. Swaddling, doors, quilts, thus mediate in the dichotomy of inside and outside, that is, in the problems of physical, psychological, and social boundaries" (51). In its symbolic relationship to boundaries, the Log Cabin design is particularly apt for Stowe's novel of the borders between the states, the races, and the sexes.

We can understand the composition of the novel in relation to the elements of contrast and repetition in the Log Cabin pattern. As Stowe explained, she organized her text in terms of contrasting pieces of narrative. To the editor of the *National Era*, in which the novel was serialized, she wrote, "I am at present occupied upon a story which will be a much longer one than any I have ever written, embracing a series of sketches which give the lights and shadows of the 'patriarchal institution.' . . . My vocation is simply that of a painter. . . . There is no arguing with *pictures*, and everybody is impressed by them, whether they mean to be or not" (in Kirkland, 66–67). Uncle Tom's cabin becomes the iconographic center upon which narrative blocks are built up. Each block of the novel is similarly centered on a house, and around it Stowe constructs large contrasts of white and slave society. The novel does not obey the rules which dictate a unity of action leading to a denouement, but rather operates through the cumulative effect of blocks of events structured on a parallel design.

Stowe's later New England local color novel, *The Minister's Wooing* (1859), is even more explicit about the structural and narrative correspondence between piecing and writing. The novel begins with a passage of authorial commentary: "When one has a story to tell, one is always puzzled which end of it to begin at. You have a whole corps of people to introduce that *you* know and your reader doesn't; and one thing so presupposes another that whichever way you turn your patchwork, the figures still seem ill-arranged" (527). In this story, Stowe chooses to begin with a particular female character, a widow who possesses the female art of order Stowe terms "faculty," and to build the design around her.

Stowe's purpose in *The Minister's Wooing* was to contrast the arid theology of New England Calvinism with the fertile spirituality of women's culture, and to balance the allegorical art of the Transcendentalists such as Hawthorne with the social art of the feminists. The motif of the pieced quilt recurs throughout the text to remind us of her design, and to emphasize the consequences for narrative of the difference between female realism and male romanticism. "Where theorists and philosophers tread with sublime assurance," Stowe comments in a chapter significantly titled "The Kitchen," "woman often follows with bleeding footsteps; women are always turning from the abstract to the individual, and feeling where the philosopher only thinks." The pieces of her plot are the chapters of the novel, with such titles as "the interview," "the letter," "the doctor," "the party," "the sermon," "the garret-boudoir," "the betrothed," and "the quilting." The artist in the novel, clearly a figure for Stowe herself, is the local dressmaker, Miss Prissy Diamond, another woman with "faculty," a genius at piecing, and a daring creative spirit who "never saw any trimming that she could not make" (p. 791). It

is Miss Prissy who lies awake the night before the betrothal quilting party, thinking about a new way to get the quilt on to the frame, as Stowe is thinking about a new way to frame her text. The quilting bee is at the center of the book, epitomizing the aspirations of female artistic creation. As Stowe explains: "Many a maiden, as she sorted and arranged fluttering bits of green, yellow, red, and blue, felt rising in her breast a passion for somewhat vague and unknown, which came out at length in a new pattern of patchwork" (788). Piecing these fragments together into a beautiful design is an emblem of "that household life which is to be brought to stability and beauty by reverent economy in husbanding and tact in arranging the little . . . morsels of daily existence" (p. 789). Writing out of the security of a historically strong women's culture, Stowe can assert that this faculty is limited to women and alien to those whom she satirically calls, in this self-consciously oppositional novel, "that ignorant and incapable sex which could not quilt" (p. 789).

By the 1880s, the parallels between piecing and women's writing were being more self-consciously, but much less happily, explored by a new generation of American women writers wishing to assert themselves as artists rather than crafters, and looking towards both native and foreign models of narrative design. That the transitional generation of the 1880s and 1890s who have been called the first artistically respectable women writers in America are generally referred to as the Local Colorists perhaps suggests their continuity with the visual design traditions of their precursors. Their stories are much more explicitly about the frustrations of the woman writer struggling to create an appropriate form for her experience within a literary culture increasingly indifferent or even hostile to women's cultural practices. As women's culture began to dissolve under pressures both from the external male society and from a younger female generation demanding education, mobility, and sexual independence, older women artists felt themselves isolated and uprooted. These are stories that represent women's culture as sour and embittering, and that frequently end in tragedy or defeat. Their quilts are crazy quilts, moving away from the comforting design traditions of the past and unsure of their coherence, structure, and form.

We can see the generational contrast in two related stories about the quilting bee, Ann S. Stephens's "The Quilting-Party," written in the 1850s, and Mary Wilkins Freeman's "A Quilting-Party in Our Village," written in 1898.[7] In Stephens's story the "quilting frolic" is an all-day festival of female bonding; a bevy of girls in silk dresses stitch merrily away on a rising-sun pattern while they sing romantic ballads. At night there is a lavish feast, and the gentlemen arrive to dance in a room filled "with a rich fruity smell left by dried apples and frost grapes" (209). In this story, women's culture is at its peak of plenitude, ripeness, and harmony. In Freeman's story, however, the quilting bee takes place on the hottest day of a July heat wave. Wearing their oldest dresses, the quilters set grimly to their task, gossiping among themselves about the bride's age, ugliness, and stinginess. The supper is sickening in its coarse abundance, and when the gentlemen arrive for a sweaty dance, the women nearly come to blows competing for their attention. The rising-sun pattern which they also quilt now seems like a mocking allusion to the setting sun of women's culture, and to the disappearance of its sustaining aesthetic rituals.

Freeman's story, "An Honest Soul," also mocks the conventions of quilting and female solidarity and nurturance. The quiltmaker Martha Patch—the name requires no comment—nearly starves to death in her dogged efforts to complete two pieced quilts for women clients named Mrs. Bennett and Mrs. Bliss, who seem to represent two traditions of quilting and women's writing. The pieces belonging to Bennett (the Austen heritage of the women's novel) and to Bliss (women's culture or literary jouissance) become confused in the mind of the old woman, whose claustrophobic separation from other sources of vision is signified by her windowless house. Rescued by neighbors after days of obsessive sewing and piecing which have brought her close to death, Martha Patch decides that she is "kinder sick of bed-quilts," and will make other things henceforth. A male neighbor cuts a front window in the blank wall of her house, and the story thus suggests that the traditional art of women is obsolete, blinded, claustrophobically and perhaps dangerously isolated from mainstream traditions.

"Elizabeth Stock's One Story," by Kate Chopin, also takes up this issue. It is the tale of an unmarried woman, a maiden aunt, whose desk after her death of consumption at the age of thirty-eight is found to contain "scraps and bits of writing." Out of this "conglomerate mass," the male editor, who may be either her nephew or her longtime suitor, assembles the only pages which seem to resemble a "connected or consecutive narration." They begin, however, with Elizabeth Stock's lament that she cannot write because of her inability to imagine a narrative both in conformity with a patriarchal literary tradition and in creative relation to it: "Since I was a girl I always felt as if I would like to write stories," but "whenever I tried to think of one, it always turned out to be something that some one else had thought about before me." Despairing of her efforts to imitate male traditions of plot that are "original, entertaining, full of action, and goodness knows what all," Elizabeth Stock turns to the female tradition, which seems to offer a more authentic but less orderly plot: "I . . . walked about days in a kind of a dream, twisting and twisting things in my mind just like I often saw old ladies twisting quilt patches to compose a design." But the one story she finally tells turns out to be the ironic account of her own betrayal, loss of employment, and death, as if women's one story were being fatally undermined by the pressure of new aesthetic expectations and competition. The designs of quilt patches are dreams of a past inhabited by old ladies, and finally her scraps and bits of writing, her stock of experience, will be edited, condensed, and preserved according to the consecutive and linear models of the male tradition.

Yet the feminist writers who come at the end of this transitional generation at the point where it begins to join with modernism, turn back to the model of piecing as a vehicle for discussing literary aspiration, and for altering the validity of a female tradition. Dorothy Canfield Fisher's story, "The Bedquilt," published in 1915, is a paradigmatic American women's text about piecing and writing. The story describes the design and creation of a magnificent quilt by an elderly woman, an unmarried dependent in her sister's household. At the age of sixty-eight, Aunt Mehetabel suddenly conceives a great artistic project: a spectacular quilt, pieced according to a dramatically difficult and original design. As Fisher writes,

> She never knew how her great idea came to her. Sometimes she thought she must have dreamed it, sometimes she even wondered reverently, in the phraseology of her weekly prayer-meeting, if it had been "sent" to her. She never admitted to herself that she could have thought of it without other help. It was too great, too ambitious, too lofty a project for her humble mind to have conceived. . . . By some heaven-sent inspiration, she had invented a pattern beyond which no patchwork quilt could go. (36–37)

As Aunt Mehetabel becomes absorbed in the "orderly, complex mosaic beauty" (39) of her pieces, so too her family begins to give her recognition, praise, and a sewing table of her own. She places the thimble on "her knotted, hard finger with the solemnity of a prophetess performing a rite." As the legend of the extraordinary quilt spreads through the region, "Mehetabel's quilt came little by little to become one of the local sights." No visitor to town went away without looking at it, and thus it becomes necessary for the aunt to be better dressed. One of her nieces even makes her a pretty little cap to wear on her thin white hair. At the end of five years the quilt is completed, and Mehetabel, who has never been more than six miles away from her home, is taken to the county fair to see it on display. The trip is the

consummation of her life; at the Fair she can see nothing but her own quilt which has received the first prize; returning home, she can find no words to describe to her relatives what she has seen or felt, but "sat staring into the fire, on her tired old face the supreme content of the artist who has realized his ideal" (35–43).

The story is obviously a parable of the woman writer, and her creative fantasies. Fisher, who had received a Ph.D. in French from Columbia in 1905, and then abandoned academia to become a writer, confessed in an essay her anxieties about the "enormous difficulties of story telling, often too great for my powers to cope with" ("What My Mother Taught Me" 34). The writer's ambition to create an orderly and complex beauty of form, and the insecurities that make her attribute the power of design to a supernatural force rather than to skill, are figured in the image of the ultimate divinely inspired quilt.

Other feminist narratives used piecing as a metaphor for the difference between male and female discourse. This contrast is brilliantly represented in Susan Glaspell's story "A Jury of Her Peers" (1917). Two women, the sheriff's wife, Mrs. Peters, and a neighbor, Mrs. Hale, accompany their husbands to a lonely farmhouse where the local miser has been strangled, and his wife, Minnie, jailed for the crime. Because there is no evidence of a motive for the murder, the men search the house and barn, while the women clean up the strangely disordered kitchen. Gradually they begin to notice domestic details which reveal Minnie Foster's troubled mind and hint of her oppression in a cruel marriage. The most telling clue is her unfinished quilt, which becomes a hieroglyphic or diary for these women who are skilled in its language. The "crazy sewing" of a block pieced all askew speaks powerfully of the anger and anguish of a woman who cannot control her feelings enough to create an orderly art. As Mrs. Hale and Mrs. Peters discover the other missing evidence—the body of a pet canary whose neck had been twisted by the husband—they recognize their own bonds within a cultural system meaningless to men, and their own complicity in the isolation of a woman who has been driven mad. In a moment of silent conspiracy, they resew the pieces and destroy the other evidence, under the very eyes of their husbands who are going over the evidence they can perceive "piece by piece." While the men laugh and tease their wives about whether Minnie Foster was going to knot or quilt her patchwork, the clue is in both the language and the act: it would have been knotted, as she has knotted the rope around her husband's neck, because knotting can be done alone; the solitary Minnie has no sisterhood of friends to join her in quilting (Alkaley-Gut, 8).[8] As Annette Kolodny observes, "Glaspell's narrative not only invites a semiotic analysis, but, indeed, performs that analysis for us. If the absent Minnie Foster is the 'transmitter' or 'sender' in this schema, then only the women are competent 'receivers' or 'readers' of her message, since they alone share not only her context (the supposed insignificance of kitchen things), but, as a result, the conceptual patterns which make up her world" (53).

To continue this analysis through modernist women's writing would take us perhaps to the fiction of Willa Cather, who learned to tell stories by sitting under the quilting frame listening to her mother's friends, and whose first serious novel, *O Pioneers!* (1913), was constructed by piecing together two short stories. We might also look at the modernist pieces of Gertrude Stein, or at the pieced narratives of Eudora Welty.

But a very recent quilt story, Bobbie Ann Mason's "Love Life," which appeared in the October 29, 1984, *New Yorker*, raises some of the most important issues of piecing, writing, and women's culture for literary historians. Mason is from Western Kentucky, a region in which most of her powerful and disturbing fiction is set, and her story alludes to the Kentucky tradition of the burial quilt. The best-known example is Elizabeth Roseberry Mitchell's Kentucky Graveyard Quilt, done in Lewis County in 1839, and now in the collection of the Kentucky Historical Society. . . .

When a member of Mitchell's family died, she would remove a labelled coffin from the border and place it within the graveyard depicted in the center of the quilt.[9]

In Mason's story two women represent two generations of women's culture—Aunt Opal, the retired schoolteacher, the old woman who is the caretaker of tradition; and her niece, Jenny, the New Woman of the 1980s, whose unfinished love affairs and backpack existence suggest the loss of traditions: "She's not in a hurry to get married, she says. She says she is going to buy a house trailer and live in the woods like a hermit. She's full of ideas and she exaggerates." Returning to Kentucky from her wanderings, Jenny pleads with Opal to see the family's celebrated but hidden burial quilt. "Did Jenny come back home just to hunt up that old rag? The thought makes Opal shudder." The burial quilt is made of dark pieced blocks, each with an appliquéd tombstone. Each tombstone has a name and date on it: "The shape is irregular, a rectangle with a clumsy foot sticking out from one corner. The quilt is knotted with yarn, and the edging is open, for more blocks to be added. "According to family legend, a block is added whenever someone dies; the quilt stops when the family name stops, so "the last old maids finish the quilt."

Who will be the last old maid? Ironically, Opal has rejected the cultural roles of the past. To her, the quilts mean only "a lot of desperate old women ruining their eyes." The burial quilt is a burden, "ugly as homemade sin," a depressing reminder of failure and loneliness. Opal plans to take up aerobic dancing, to be modern; meanwhile she spends all her time watching the video quilt of MTV. Jenny will finish the quilt. She will use it to mourn for relationships that never began, to stitch herself back into the past.

Like the Kentucky burial quilt, Mason's story is also composed of blocks of elegy, memory, and flashback, and remains open-ended, an irregular shape, with a clumsy foot of narrative (in this case the description of the video Opal is watching, Michael Jackson's "Thriller") sticking out from one corner. Using the familiar nineteenth-century women's plot of an emotional interaction between aunt and niece, Mason brings us back, through Aunt Opal's Scrap Bag, to a sense of continuity in an American female literary and cultural tradition.

Yet does she really? The story also suggests that these traditions may be burdens rather than treasures of the past, and that there may be something mournful and even self-destructive in our feminist efforts to reclaim them. Is Jenny a feminist critic full of ideas who exaggerates the importance of women's culture? Are we ruining our eyes finishing a female heritage that may have become a museum piece? Is it time to bury the burial quilt rather than to praise it? Mason's story is a useful reminder of the complex relationship of women's culture and women's writing in any era, a warning that in tidily closing off our critical pieces we may miss some of the ragged edges that are a more accurate image of our literary history.

NOTES

This paper is dedicated to the members of the 1984 NEH Summer Seminar on "Women's Writing and Women's Culture": Joanne Braxton, Dorothy Berkson, Mary DeJong, Elizabeth Keyser, Peggy Lant, Joanne Karpinski, Andree Nicola-McLaughlin, Shirley Marchalonis, Ozzie Meyers, Adele McCullom, Sandee Potter, Cheryl Torsney, and Gail Kraldman.

1. See Mainardi (56–57), and Parker and Pollock (76).
2. See Burke, "Rethinking the Maternal," in *The Future of Difference* (107–13).
3. Thanks to Radka Donnell-Vogt for many helpful discussions of the quilt aesthetic, and to Lynn Miller for introducing me to her work. Donnell-Vogt is one of the women featured in the documentary film, "Quilts in Women's Lives."
4. Thanks to Gail Kraldman for this reference.
5. Thanks to Elizabeth Keyser for bringing this story to my attention; my analysis is indebted

to her presentation in our NEH seminar. See also Marsella, *The Promise of Destiny.*
6. Thanks to Nancy K. Miller for this definition from her current work on French women's writing.
7. Thanks to Jeslyn Medoff for research assistance.
8. Log Cabin quilts were usually knotted rather than quilted. See Bishop et al. (74).
9. According to an unpublished letter by Mitchell's grand-daughter, the Graveyard Quilt was originally made as a memorial to two sons who had died in childhood. See Nina Mitchell Biggs, "Old Days, Old Ways," in the collection of the Kentucky Historical Museum.

WORKS CITED

Alcott, Louisa May. "Patty's Patchwork." In *Aunt Jo's Scrap Bag.* Boston: Roberts, 1872. Vol. 1, pp. 193–215.

Alkaley-Gut, Karen. "A Jury of Her Peers: The Importance of Trifles." *Studies in Short Fiction* (Winter 1984), 21:1–10.

Ammons, Elizabeth, ed. *Critical Essays on Harriet Beecher Stowe.* Boston: G. K. Hall, 1980.

"Annette" [Harriet Farley or Rebecca C. Thompson]. "The Patchwork Quilt." In *The Lowell Offering.* Ed. Benita Eisler. New York: Harper, 1977; pp. 150–54.

Baym, Nina. *Woman's Fiction: A Guide to Novels by and about Women in America* 1820–1870. Ithaca: Cornell University Press, 1978.

Bishop, Robert; Secord, William; and Weissman, Judith Reiter. *Quilts, Coverlets, Rugs and Samples.* New York: Knopf, 1982.

Bretteville, Sheila de. "A Re-examination of Some Aspects of the Design Arts from the Perspective of a Woman Designer." *Women and the Arts: Arts in Society* (Spring–Summer 1974), 11:117–18.

Burke, Carolyn. "Rethinking the Maternal." In *The Future of Difference.* Ed. Alice Jardine and Hester Eisenstein. Boston: G. K. Hall, 1982.

Cahill, Susan, ed. *Women and Fiction 2.* New York: New American Library, 1978.

Chopin, Kate. "Elizabeth Stock's One Story." In *"The Awakening" and Selected Stories*. Ed. Sandra M. Gilbert. New York: Penguin, 1984: pp. 274–80.

Cooper, Patricia, and Buferd, Norma Bradley. *The Quilters: Women and Domestic Art*. New York: Doubleday, 1978.

Dewhurst, C. Kurt; MacDowell, Betty; and MacDowell, Marsha. *Artists in Aprons: Folk Art by American Women*. New York: E. P. Dutton, 1979.

Donnell-Vogt, Radka. Memoir in *Lives and Works: Talks with Women Artists*. Ed. Lynn F. Miller and Sally S. Swenson. Metuchen, N.J.: Scarecrow Press, 1981.

DuPlessis, Rachel Blau. "For the Etruscans." In *The New Feminist Criticism*. Ed. Elaine Showalter. New York: Pantheon, 1985.

Fisher, Dorothy Canfield. "What My Mother Taught Me" and "The Bedquilt." In *Women and Fiction 2*. Ed. Susan Cahill. New York: New American Library, 1978.

Freeman, Mary Wilkins. "A Quilting Bee in Our Village." In *The People of Our Neighborhood*. Philadelphia: Curtis, 1898; pp. 113–28.

Gilligan, Carol. *In a Different Voice*. Cambridge: Harvard University Press, 1982.

Hedges, Elaine. "The Nineteenth-Century Diarist and Her Quilts." *Feminist Studies* (Summer 1982), 8:293–99.

Holmes, George F. *The Southern Literary Messenger* (October 1852), vol. 18; repr. in *Critical Essays on Harriet Beecher Stowe*. Ed. Elizabeth Ammons. Boston: G. K. Hall, 1980.

Kelley, Mary. *Private Woman, Public Stage: Literary Domesticity in Nineteenth-Century America*. New York: Oxford University Press, 1984.

Kirkham, Bruce. *The Building of Uncle Tom's Cabin*. Knoxville: University of Tennessee Press, 1977.

Kolodny, Annette. "A Map for Rereading: Gender and the Interpretation of Literary Texts." In *The New Feminist Criticism*. Ed. Elaine Showalter. New York: Pantheon, 1985.

Lippard, Lucy. "Up, Down and Across: A New Frame for New Quilts." *The Artist and the Quilt*. Ed. Charlotte Robinson. New York: Knopf, 1983.

Mainardi, Patricia. "Quilts: The Great American Art.' *Radical America* (1973), 7:36–68.

Marsella, Joy A. *The Promise of Destiny: Children and Women in the Short Stories of Louisa May Alcott*. Westport, Conn.: Greenwood, 1983.

Mason, Bobbie Ann. "Love Life." *New Yorker*, October 29, 1984, pp. 42–50.

Moers, Ellen. "Harriet Beecher Stowe." In *Critical Essays on Harriet Beecher Stowe*. Ed. Elizabeth Ammons. Boston: G. K. Hall, 1980.

Parker, Roszika, and Pollock, Griselda. *Old Mistresses: Women, Art and Ideology*. New York: Pantheon, 1981.

Piercy, Marge. "Looking at Quilts." In *In Her Own Image*. Ed. Elaine Hedges and Ingrid Wendt. New York: Feminist Press, 1980. pp. 35–36.

Pilling, Ron. "Album Quilts of the Mid-1800s." *Art & Antiques* (November–December 1982), pp. 72–79.

Stephens, P. "The Quilting Party." In *Female Prose Writers of America*. Ed. John S. Hart. Philadelphia: E. H. Butler, 1857); pp. 204–10.

Stowe, Harriet Beecher. *The Minister's Wooing*. New York: The Library of America, 1980.

Walker, Alice. *In Search of Our Mother's Gardens*. New York: Harcourt Brace Jovanovich, 1983.

17

TESTING ORTHODOXY: COLLECTING, THE GAZE, KNITTING THE IMPOSSIBLE

Paul Whittaker and Clio Padovani

Editor's introduction: Dr. Paul Whittaker and Clio Padavani suggest that the structure of knitting—the basic loop and, more important, the void at the center of that loop—can be understood as a system for seeing the world. The pair test the psychoanalytic "gaze" and the notion of "collecting" as systems for the analysis of knitting. The knitting they write of is extreme and often unsettling, present in the difficult photographs of the German artist Margi Geerlinks and the complex large-scale installations of the late French artist Louise Bourgeois. Here, the innocuous structure of the loop is used to pull together a range of theoretical thinking. At the heart of the inquiry is the seemingly simple question "What is it to knit?"

Dr. Paul Whittaker is associate dean of the Faculty of Business and Law, and director of education at Winchester School of Art, University of Southampton. Clio Padovani is an artist and lecturer at Birmingham City University. An earlier version of this essay first appeared in *In the Loop: Knitting Now*, published by Black Dog in 2010.

This essay tests the orthodoxy of knitting by proposing an elaboration in our understanding of its taxonomy and aims to establish what might be at stake in an extended classification of the practice of the knotting and looping of thread.

Originally a domestic activity, knitting is now a long-standing practice that encompasses the handmade and industrial manufacture of a complex range of utilitarian products: knitted things that serve a practical and often decorative purpose. For centuries handcrafting techniques and machine technologies have been utilised across the globe to create a diverse range of accessories and items of clothing often differentiated by different cultural and climate requirements. The European aristocracy first wore fine woollen knitted stockings in the thirteenth century. Fair Isle techniques were utilised to produce warm utilitarian sweaters for the peoples of the Scottish Isles in the seventeenth and eighteenth century, and in the twentieth century, machine-knitted fabrics have been utilised to enhance the function and appeal of automotive interiors.

Knitting has, as well as a utilitarian history, a strong social tradition. This can be demonstrated by, but not limited to, a variety of examples where the practice of knitting has contributed to the development and maintenance of a prevailing social

Source: Paul Whittaker and Clio Padovani, "Twists, Knots and Holes, Collecting, the Gaze and Knitting the Impossible." First published in Jessica Hemmings (ed.), *In the Loop: Knitting Now* (London: Black Dog, 2010) pp. 10–17. A revised version of the original essay is published here. Reproduced with permission.

order or ideology. In the pioneering history of America, as wagon trains extended the frontier of civilization, women knitted on the move, in covered wagons, to ensure their family was protected from the elements. Again in America, during the eighteenth-century resistance to British colonial rule, the American Daughters of Liberty supported the dissidents by utilising homespun yarns to produce knitted domestic clothing to compete with and replace the need for fashions made from 'modish bolts and bales from England'[1]. The role of knitting in support of the patriotic fervour of the Bostonian rebellion is amply demonstrated through this extract from a letter posted at the time.

'You may keep your goods . . . Thank God we have a glorious country; we can subsist independent of the whole world . . . A spirit of economy and industry has wonderfully diffused itself thro' this whole province . . . This daughter is constantly employed in spinning; both myself and wife, and all my children, wear clothes of her industry alone, all our stockings and gloves. My girl spins, and my wife assists in knitting . . . I cannot buy a pair of English woven stockings here under 6s[hillings] sterling a pair; & I firmly declare, that 1 pair of mine is worth the whole three.'[2]

Reminiscent of the American Daughters of Liberty, the twentieth-century British knitting circles offer another example of knitting in the service of opposition. During the World Wars the women in the United Kingdom were encouraged by the government to form knitting circles and produce warm clothing for the troops. Due to the short supply of raw materials underused garments were often unpicked and re-knitted to produce socks, balaclavas, sweaters and gloves. The actions of the knitting circles not only fulfilled a very practical need but also instilled in the protagonists a collective sense of contributing to the war effort.

Although the practice of knitting encompasses a complex range of products and a rich, social political history, its diversity is underpinned by a simple orthodoxy, one underlying law: the knotting and looping of a thread.

According to Jacques Lacan, the Law is not judicial legislation but instead a set of fundamental principles. It is the set of universal principles which underpin and govern 'all forms of social exchange, whether gift giving, kinship relations or the formation of pacts.' The Law regulates and prohibits our pleasure and excess and it is 'maintained by way of language, symbols, signs, the different modes of representation through which communication is maintained'.[3] Lacan states;

Law, then, is revealed clearly enough as identical with an order of language. For without kinship nominations, no power is capable of instituting the order of preferences and taboos that bind and weave the yarn of linage through succeeding generations.[4]

For Lacan, the Law is inscribed in the order of the symbolic and, as such, both the Law and the symbolic constitute a radical alterity, an otherness that cannot be assimilated. The symbolic is an all-encompassing complex universe of language, social protocols and authorities through which the individual subject emerges. The Law and symbolic mediate our experience of reality by establishing the principles upon which society is based; the principles that work to maintain the social order: the prevailing ideology. If the Law and symbolic constitute the regulatory control of the subject, the process through which subjects enter into ideology and become subjected to its constraints involves, as Althusser states, 'concrete individuals misrecognizing themselves as subjects by taking up a socially given identity'.[5] In other words, for Althusser, as for Lacan, it is impossible for the subject to access the real conditions of existence due to their reliance on the symbolic; the language, ideals, signs, and representational forms that constitute the Law and which mediate existence. The symbolic, also referred to by Lacan as the big Other, pulls the strings. The subject doesn't so much speak or express itself through its assumed social position. It is instead "spoken" by the symbolic structure with which it identifies.

This is not to say that the subject's assimilation of ideology is complete or whole; or that the scope of available ideological identities is not complex. On the contrary, by necessity all ideologies include a point within their structures that they cannot account for or represent; and, in addition, ideology is never fixed, it is instead constantly in a state of being redefined.

In a way not very much removed from the practices of the Daughters of Liberty who knitted to communicate and practically effect a resistance to the strictures of a colonial ideology, knitting is today a practice or medium of choice for many contemporary artists who seek to explore, comment upon and promote new thinking about society and their understanding of it. By way of illustration, Rosemary Trockel has made pictures from machine-knitted woollen material that depict familiar signs and logos such as the hammer-and-sickle so as to ironically promote a feminist comment; Louise Unger has sculpted representations of body-like forms through the knitting of steel wire that force their audience to reconsider the veracity of the everyday object; Mike Kelly's soiled hand-knitted toys and blankets foraged from thrift stores, confront the values and systems of familial authority through their uncanny qualities and the suggestion of repression and Margi Geerlinks creates emotive photographic portraits that force a reconsideration of maternalism. For example, in *Young Lady One* a girl framed by a homely setting sits knitting in a familiar pose. Despite the context of the scene however, this girl's needles produce not a scarf or mittens but craft, instead, the fragment of a woman's body, a maturing breast. In *Untitled,* a transfixed woman dressed in white stares out from the photograph. In her hands she holds knitting needles from which hang the half finished knitted body of a young girl while a thread of wool snakes down from the knitted body and pools into a ball on the floor. The pictorial alliance of woman, child and the practice of knitting might conventionally suggest a content of motherhood and the familial. In these two images, however, these alliances,

Figure 17.1. Margi Geerlinks, *Untitled*, 1997–1998. Edition of six each, cibachrome, plexiglass, and dibond, 99 x 73.5 cm, 178 x 124.5 cm. Image courtesy of TORCH gallery.

arranged around the partial form of a knitted body, appear not familial but monstrous. The act of creation, rendered inert by the photograph, appears in these images to be more self-driven than a selfless act of life giving: more Dr Frankenstein than a Madonna and child.

These artists and others like them, utilise knitting in a way that might be reasonably understood to contribute to the social history of knitting but in doing so their work exceeds strongly the craft, utilitarian or the social conventions of knitting. If we accept that Geerlinks' photographs are by virtue of content and reference, worthy of classification in the codex of knitting, we also accept that by merging art and craft, concept and function, her works and others by Trockel, Unger etc. challenge the conventions of knitting. These works transform our understanding of knitting by making knitting more than a technique of making that creates desirable objects with practical use value or a practice of knotting and looping of thread that is the expression of a social order: they promote the question, what is it to knit?

Susan Stewart offers a key to how we might consider the challenge that works made by artists such as Geerlinks offer to the definition of knitting, but also provides a stepping-stone to addressing what it means to knit. In *On Longing*, Stewart meditates on how objects collected and stored in museums, whether public or private, mediate experience in time and space. For Stewart, such objects engender interest because 'when [they] are defined in terms of their use value, they serve as extensions of the body into the environment, but when [they] are defined by the collection, such an extension is inverted, so the environment is subsumed into the scenario of the personal.' The implication in Stewart's thinking is that collections are constructions or compositions, and that 'the ultimate term in the series that constitutes a [collection] is the "self," the collector's own "identity"'.[6]

We may hypothesise, if we follow Stewart's lead, that the components that make up Geerlinks composed image of the knitted baby; the photograph, the background, the posed figure, selected attire, knitted form and the spool of wool, offer the possibility that knitting for Geerlinks, supplements more than the composition of an image. What Geerlinks can be construed to have done, according to Stewart's thinking, is collected and composed with parts or signifiers, including a knitted object, so as to communicate her message. Like a three-dimensional textile, she has knitted together, in time and space, personally significant objects, and organised those conceptual, sometimes literal threads necessary to promote her ideas. In doing so, she has proposed an emergent narrative and herself as a significant term in the collection: the maker, or knitter, of monstrous tales. Geerlinks' image, elaborated by way of Stewart's model, proposes that what we

have come to know as the act of knitting might reasonably include the practice of collecting; knitting as the collection and construction of narratives: narratives in which the artist is a primary factor but not always, necessarily, the creator of obscene tales.

If we can rethink and extend the taxonomy of knitting to include the practice of collecting, what might be at stake in an art that knits by way of collecting; art that unconventionally tests the boundaries of knitting's principle orthodoxy, the Law of the knotting and the looping of threads?

Louise Bourgeois is a prolific artist known for her intense psychologically driven sculptures, installations and drawings. Her work draws upon her childhood memories and the complex emotions involved in familial relationships. The Daros Collection of Bourgeois drawings completed between 1994 and 1995, published under the title *The Insomnia Drawings*, offers a number of images that interestingly represent and reference the making of a textile. For example, *Le Cauchemar de Hayter*, an ink on lined paper drawing, does not appear to be a representation of a particular object, but instead, suggests, through its overlapped meandering lines with peaks and troughs, a looped pattern, a knitted doodle.

When considered by way of the writings of Lacan, Bourgeois' unconventional textiles serve the purpose of suggesting the gaze as a pertinent critical tool through which we might identify and explore what is at stake in an art that knits unconventionally. Referring to the work of Catherine Yass, the psychoanalyst Parveen Adams quotes how Lacan describes, in the process of psychoanalysis, 'that which from time makes a stuff of [what is said] is not borrowed from the imaginary, but rather from a textile, where the knots speak of nothing but the holes which are there.'[7] This means that, no matter how much material the patient enunciates there is always something missing in the process of analysis and that what is described there circles around a hole.

All textiles, even knitted doodles, are composed in part of holes or gaps and this allows both Lacan and Adams to identify the textile as a metaphor for the subject's experience during analysis. The hole around which Lacanian analysis circles is the gaze and the gaze stands for the object that can never be attained: the lost object. 'It is a [hole] in the subject's seemingly omnipotent look': a gap that 'marks the spot at which our desire manifests itself in what we see.'[8] The gaze is the cause of desire rather than the object towards which desire tends and as such it is a hole that sets the drives in motion.

Fantasy allows the subject to relate to the unattainable gaze by constructing a scene through which we, as subject, can take up a relation to its impossibility. The form of the fantasy image intercedes between the subject and the gaze or lost object but 'it allows the subject to relate to the lost object as an object that is simply out of reach'.[9] Although the subject may not gain the object in the fantasy, 'the subject can imagine obtaining it as a possibility, even if not for the subject itself'.[10] For psychoanalysts, fantasy is an imaginary scenario that fills in the gaps, holes or lost objects that permeate ideology. Fantasy 'serves as a way for the individual subject to imagine a path out of dissatisfaction produced by the demands of social existence'.[11] By distorting social reality through an imaginative act, fantasy creates both an opening to the impossible object and simultaneously allows the subject to take pleasure in an otherwise unattainable enjoyment.

The film theorist Todd McGowan argues that it is the excess in the fantasy image that marks the hole or gap of the gaze. He argues, by way of reference to the cinematic image, that the excess of the image may be seen in such factors as 'unconventional camera work, obtrusive editing, or in the content of the film, when [for example], the dominant story line is unexpectedly interrupted in a surprising or shocking manner'.[12] A scene near the end of David Lynch's *Blue Velvet* exemplifies McGowan's argument. In the scene, the naked and badly beaten body of Dorothy Vallens (Isabella Rossellini) appears within an idyllic neighbourhood and Jeffrey (played by Kyle McLaughlan) is confronted by the ex-boyfriend of his new girlfriend Sandy. This scene does not, however, turn on the envy driven violent confrontation of the two men, but the appearance, 'as if from thin air', of Dorothy. At first, she is an undecipherable blot that no one—including the spectator—notices, but when her presence is detected it disorientates the scene completely. Her form disturbs the fantasy of the small town mis-en-scène by interrupting the predictable with an excess of embodied desire. The naked body speaks of the normally hidden extremes of sex, violence, fear and loathing and as such, found here at the level of the imaginary, represents an unexpected encounter with the Real.[13]

Although McGowan might identify the cinematic image as especially supporting of fantasy, we might also accept the premise that fantasy is a condition of other art forms. The cinema influences many contemporary artists and common photographic and digital practices utilise much the same means of communication as Hollywood. In the same way that contemporary cinema can be critiqued by way of fantasy stained by the excesses of the gaze, so can, we might argue, contemporary arts that similarly construct a fantasmatic appearance. The compositions of fantasy scenes, whether in film, paint, fabric, knitting or collections, offer an opportunity for narrative interpretation and discussion of the gaze as a concern of making.

Louise Bourgeois' *Red Room (Parents)* and its companion piece, *Red Room (Child)*, both 1994, offer the viewer an installation experience that might very well be described as the fantasy product of a process of knitting through collecting. The works constitute two installations of objects; each arranged in a circular cell-like structure made from old doors. The pieces are experienced in cinematic fashion by navigating apertures in the door-structures. These apertures focus the look of the viewer and facilitate the unfolding narrative of the scene by virtue of the viewer's movement.

Inside the enclosed space of *Red Room (Parents)* we find an arranged display of a bed and furniture. Yet everything in this room is not as it, at first, appears. More pertinently, this room appears conditioned by the double. The bed is double, the chests of drawers are double and a large oval mirror doubles all. In this world of reflections, the bed is made and the pillows are plumped up and ready for use. This is, however, no place of rest. Although orderly, this bed does not lend itself to relaxation. The room is a stage set for the imaginary action of its occupiers: the absent and imagined parents.

Although similarly installed as a hidden space screened from the viewer, the character and suggestive quality of *Red Room (Child)* is very different. Where the room of the parents is cool, orderly and distant by virtue of the reflective doubling, the room of the child is comparatively disordered, immediate and compelling. The collected objects, arranged and displayed around the walls, vary in their material but are compelling by virtue of their colourful unity. Central to the scene is an industrial thread stand that holds several spools of red thread. As Rainer Crone and Petrus Graf Schaesberg write, 'if the smoothed out sheet [of the parent's bed] is concealing chimeras of hidden desire, lust, and sensual pleasure; if its dense weave is imbued with the complexities of an unrestrained, unbridled imagination; if a solid warp and weft of complicity knots together this sheltered world of conventional, traditional, acceptable sentiments; then the thin, breakable thread in the child's room reveals the unfinished process of creative construction, a loosely-structured world of possibilities.'[14]

In these stage sets for the imagination, from where might the lost object marked by an excess of vision, look back at us and prompt our desire to know, interpret and fantasise? If we remember Geerlinks' excessive images, here the monstrously deformed red glass hand and forearm, placed in tender proximity to smaller child-like versions, might promote interpretation through the excesses of the body. There are, however, two other instances of real excess that might properly be considered examples of the gaze; one is formal, the other an unexpected, unexplainable alien interruption to the predominant fantasy scene.[15]

At a formal level, the zoetrope wooden-door structure of both installations offers an excess that stains our vision in two ways. Firstly, the many vertical gaps between each door invite new and different perspectives, although the excess of vantage points reveals only more partial or occluded looking, and do not illuminate previously unseen detail. Secondly, when viewed outside and from a distance, the straining eye of the viewer sees an outside punctuated by many holes; an excess of holes that obscure the external world through the fantasy of the interior.

The alien object that interrupts the interior scene of the installations is the pink rubberised and elongated form which hangs from a hook on the industrial thread stand. This pink form has a matt sheen, smooth surface, occasionally punctured by long pins. Its form alludes to organic matter and the body. It is excessive because of its infinite capacity to suggest interpretation. This is an object that can be many things and simultaneously nothing. It is suggestive of ham, sexual parts, body limbs, even a bladder. For Lacan, that which drives desire (the gaze, object *a*, the Real), is outside language and inassimilable to symbolisation. It is that which resists signification because it is impossible to integrate into the symbolic order and this accounts for its traumatic quality. Based on this definition, Bourgeois' pink rubber intrusion may be thought, through its incomprehensibility, a truly impossible object.

The aim of this essay was to test the orthodoxy of knitting by proposing an elaboration in our understanding of its taxonomy and to establish what might be at stake in an extended classification of the practice of the knotting and looping of thread. Susan Stewart's thinking about language and objects has enabled us to propose that more elaborate thinking about the act of knitting might reasonably include knitting as collecting; the collection or composition of diverse objects selected and arranged to promote a narrative thread: a fantasy of the "self". The metaphor of the hole in textiles allowed us to utilise the theories of Lacan to critique an example of this extended classification of knitting and establish what might be at stake in such modes of making. From the study of Bourgeois' *Red Room* installations we can speculate that what is at stake in these works is potentially an encounter with the gaze. We may therefore conclude that in an extended taxonomy of knitting what may be at stake is not only the perpetuation of a self-fantasy but an encounter with the un-assimilatable: the impossibility of the lost object.

AFTERWORD

As we have seen, the Law and the symbolic mediate our experience and maintain the social order by regulating pleasure and governing how we interact with reality. Despite the prohibitions of the Law however the gaze can, in certain circumstances, stimulate fantasy and in so doing expose an encounter with the lost object. An encounter with the lost object constitutes both an opening to the impossible and an opportunity to take pleasure in that which is unattainable because it is beyond the symbolic. For Lacanian psychoanalysts, the transgression of the regulated pleasure principal of the Law or symbolic has powerful implications for the subject. Firstly, the subject mediated by the symbolic is conditioned to bear only a certain amount of pleasure. Consequently, when the subject goes beyond the limit set by the symbolic, pleasure becomes pain. Lacan calls this "painful pleasure" *jouissance*. Secondly, a traumatic encounter with the gaze may not only constitute an experience of *jouissance*—the pleasure and pain of exceeding the authority that mediates experience. It might according to McGowan entail the potential politicisation of the subject. He writes:

'Ideology constantly works to obscure the traumatic [Real] of the gaze because this [Real] threatens the stability of the social order that ideology protects. This stability depends on the illusion of wholeness and the power to account symbolically for everything. The [gaze] marks a point of failure, not just of the subject's look but also of ideology's explanatory power. That is to say, the [gaze or Real] traumatizes not just the subject that encounters it but also the big Other as well. The hold that symbolic authority has over subjects depends on the avoidance of the traumatic [Real] that exposes the imposture of all authority. When the subject experiences the traumatic [Real], it recognizes symbolic authority's failure to account for everything. This is the key to the political power of the gaze. Though the encounter with the gaze traumatizes the subject, it also provides the basis for the subject's freedom—freedom from the constraints of the big Other.'[16]

If we follow the thoughts of Lacan and McGowan we may proffer an additional speculative and radical afterthought to our conclusions regarding the testing of the orthodoxy of knitting. The social political history of knitting traces many occasions of gentle resistance: handcrafted oppositions to authority. A practice that tests orthodoxy and the Law of the knotting and looping of thread can suggest however, the capacity to not only contribute to a cause or raise political awareness, but the opportunity to not be "spoken" by the symbolic structure. It can effect an occasion of freedom.

NOTES

1. Macdonald, Anne L., *No Idle Hands: The Social History of American Knitting*, Ballantine Books, New York, 1998, p. 28.
2. Ibid, p. 30.
3. Evans, Dylan, *An Introductory Dictionary of Lacanian Psychoanalysis*, Routledge, London, 1996, pp. 98–99.
4. Lacan, Jacques, *Ecrits*, Routledge, 1977, p. 66.
5. McGowan, Todd, *The Real Gaze: Film Theory After Lacan*, State University of New York Press, 2007, p. 2.
6. Stewart, Susan, *On Longing*, Duke University Press, 1993, p. 162.

7. Lacan, Jacques, trans. Parveen Adams, chap 6, *Time and the Image*, Manchester University Press, 2000, p. 61.

8. McGowan, Todd, *The Real Gaze: Film Theory After Lacan*, State University of New York Press, 2007, p. 6.

9. Ibid., p. 24.

10. Ibid., p. 24.

11. Ibid., p. 24.

12. Ibid., p. 28.

13. The Real is the undifferentiated state that exists prior to the subject's insertion into the symbolic. The world of words creates the world of things but in doing so also creates the Real. The Real is the domain outside of the symbolic. The Real is the impossible and beyond capture by the symbolic. For this reason the Real has a traumatic effect on the subject. The gaze and object *a* have a Real effect.

14. Crone, Rainer & Schaesberg, *Louise Bourgeois, The Secret of the Cells*, Prestel, Munich-London-New York, p. 104.

15. We are indebted here to the exegesis of the different properties of the staged fantasy scene, Todd McGowan, *The Real Gaze: Film Theory After Lacan*, State University of New York Press, 2007.

16. McGowan, Todd, *The Real Gaze: Film Theory After Lacan*, State University of New York Press, 2007, p. 16.

18

1440: THE SMOOTH AND THE STRIATED

Gilles Deleuze and Félix Guattari

Editor's introduction: The influence of French philosophers Gilles Deleuze and Félix Guattari can be found throughout the writing collected in this *Reader*. Among their many publications, the pair co-wrote *Capitalism and Schizophrenia: Anti-Oedipus* (1972) and *A Thousand Plateaus* (1980), and Deleuze wrote *The Fold: Leibniz and the Baroque* (1988). In the excerpt printed here, Deleuze and Guattari propose that smooth and striated space are not equal opposites. In their words, the two "fail to coincide entirely." A number of examples are offered—of textile interest is the borrowing of felt and woven cloth to explain their thinking. Other observations reveal an interest in the woven textile as structure, when they state that "space of this kind seems necessarily to have a top and a bottom; even when the warp yarn and woof yarn are exactly the same in nature, number, and density, weaving reconstitutes a bottom by placing the knots on one side." Their writing offers examples of how the textile structure has been adopted to illustrate abstract thought.

Smooth space and striated space—nomad space and sedentary space—the space in which the war machine develops and the space instituted by the State apparatus—are not of the same nature. No sooner do we note a simple opposition between the two kinds of space than we must indicate a much more complex difference by virtue of which the successive terms of the oppositions fail to coincide entirely. And no sooner have we done that than we must remind ourselves that the two spaces in fact exist only in mixture: smooth space is constantly being translated, transversed into a striated space; striated space is constantly being reversed, returned to a smooth space. In the first case, one organizes even the desert; in the second, the desert gains and grows; and the two can happen simultaneously. But the de facto mixes do not preclude a de jure, or abstract, distinction between the two spaces. That there is such a distinction is what accounts for the fact that the two spaces do not communicate with each other in the same way: it is the de jure distinction that determines the forms assumed by a given de facto mix and the direction or meaning of the mix (is a smooth space captured, enveloped by a striated space, or does a striated space dissolve into a smooth space, allow a smooth space to develop?). This raises a number of simultaneous questions:

Source: Gilles Deleuze and Félix Guattari, "1440: The Smooth and Striated," in *A Thousand Plateaus: Capitalism and Schizophrenia*, trans. Brian Massumi (Minneapolis: University of Minnesota Press, 1987) pp. 474–477. Copyright 1987 by the University of Minnesota Press. Originally published as *Mille Plateaux*, volume 2 of *Capitalisme et Schizophrénie* © 1980 by Les Editions de Minuit, Paris. By kind permission of Continuum International Publishing Group.

the simple oppositions between the two spaces; the complex differences; the de facto mixes, and the passages from one to another; the principles of the mixture, which are not at all symmetrical, sometimes causing a passage from the smooth to the striated, sometimes from the striated to the smooth, according to entirely different movements. We must therefore envision a certain number of models, which would be like various aspects of the two spaces and the relations between them.

THE TECHNOLOGICAL MODEL

A fabric presents in principle a certain number of characteristics that permit us to define it as a striated space. First, it is constituted by two kinds of parallel elements; in the simplest case, there are vertical and horizontal elements, and the two intertwine, intersect perpendicularly. Second, the two kinds of elements have different functions; one is fixed, the other mobile, passing above and beneath the fixed. Leroi-Gourhan has analyzed this particular figure of "supple solids" in basketry and weaving: stake and thread, warp and woof.[1] Third, a striated space of this kind is necessarily delimited, closed on at least one side: the fabric can be infinite in length but not in width, which is determined by the frame of the warp; the necessity of a back and forth motion implies a closed space (circular or cylindrical figures are themselves closed). Finally, a space of this kind seems necessarily to have a top and a bottom; even when the warp yarn and woof yarn are exactly the same in nature, number, and density, weaving reconstitutes a bottom by placing the knots on one side. Was it not these characteristics that enabled Plato to use the model of weaving as the paradigm for "royal science," in other words, the art of governing people or operating the State apparatus?

Felt is a supple solid product that proceeds altogether differently, as an anti-fabric. It implies no separation of threads, no intertwining, only an entanglement of fibers obtained by fulling (for example, by rolling the block of fibers back and forth). What becomes entangled are the microscales of the fibers. An aggregate of intrication of this kind is in no way *homogeneous:* it is nevertheless smooth, and contrasts point by point with the space of fabric (it is in principle infinite, open, and unlimited in every direction; it has neither top nor bottom nor center; it does not assign fixed and mobile elements but rather distributes a continuous variation). Even the technologists who express grave doubts about the nomads' powers of innovation at least give them credit for felt: a splendid insulator, an ingenious invention, the raw material for tents, clothes, and armor among the Turco-Mongols. Of course, the nomads of Africa and the Maghreb instead treat wool as a fabric. Although it might entail displacing the opposition, do we not detect two very different conceptions or even practices of weaving, the distinction between which would be something like the distinction between fabric as a whole and felt? For among sedentaries, clothes-fabric and tapestry-fabric tend to annex the body and exterior space, respectively, to the immobile house: fabric integrates the body and the outside into a closed space. On the other hand, the weaving of the nomad indexes clothing and the house itself to the space of the outside, to the open smooth space in which the body moves.

There are many interlacings, mixes between felt and fabric. Can we not displace the opposition yet again? In knitting, for example, the needles produce a striated space; one of them plays the role of the warp, the other of the woof, but by turns. Crochet, on the other hand, draws an open space in all directions, a space that is prolongable in all directions—but still has a center. A more significant distinction would be between embroidery, with its central theme or motif, and patchwork, with its piece-by-piece construction, its infinite, successive additions of fabric. Of course, embroidery's variables and constants, fixed and mobile elements, may be of extraordinary complexity. Patchwork, for its part, may display equivalents to themes, symmetries, and resonance that approximate it to embroidery. But the fact remains that its space is not at all constituted in the same way: there is no center; its basic motif ("block") is composed of a single element; the recurrence of this element frees uniquely rhythmic values distinct from the harmonies of embroidery (in particular, in "crazy" patchwork, which fits together pieces of varying size, shape, and color, and plays on the *texture* of the fabrics). "She had been working on it for fifteen years, carrying about with her a shapeless bag of dingy, threadbare brocade containing odds and ends of colored fabric in all possible shapes. She could never bring herself to trim them to any pattern; so she shifted and fitted and mused and fitted and shifted them like pieces of a patient puzzle-picture, trying to fit them to a pattern or create a pattern out of them without using her scissors, smoothing her colored scraps with flaccid, putty-colored fingers."[2] An amorphous collection of juxtaposed pieces that can be joined together in an infinite number of ways: we see that patchwork is literally a Riemannian space, or vice versa. That is why very special work groups were formed for patchwork fabrication (the importance of the quilting bee in America, and its role from the standpoint of a women's collectivity). The smooth space of patchwork is adequate to demonstrate that "smooth" does not mean homogeneous, quite the contrary: it is an *amorphous*, nonformal space prefiguring op art.

The story of the quilt is particularly interesting in this connection. A quilt comprises two layers of fabric stitched together, often with a filler in between. Thus it is possible for there to be no top or bottom. If we follow the history of the quilt over a short migration sequence (the settlers who left Europe for the New World), we see that there is a shift from a formula dominated by embroidery (so-called "plain" quilts) to a patchwork formula ("appliqué quilts," and above all "pieced quilts"). The first settlers of the

seventeenth century brought with them plain quilts, embroidered and striated spaces of extreme beauty. But toward the end of the century patchwork technique was developed more and more, at first due to the scarcity of textiles (leftover fabric, pieces salvaged from used clothes, remnants taken from the "scrap bag"), and later due to the popularity of Indian chintz. It is as though a smooth space emanated, sprang from a striated space, but not without a correlation between the two, a recapitulation of one in the other, a furtherance of one through the other. Yet the complex difference persists. Patchwork, in conformity with migration, whose degree of affinity with nomadism it shares, is not only named after trajectories, but "represents" trajectories, becomes inseparable from speed or movement in an open space.[3]

NOTES

1. André Leroi-Gourhan, *L'homme et la matière* (Paris: Albin Michel, 1971), pp. 244ff. (and the opposition between fabric and felt).
2. William Faulkner, *Sartoris* (New York: Random House, 1956), p. 151.
3. On the history of the quilt and patchwork in American immigration, see Jonathan Holstein, *American Pieced Quilts* (New York: Viking, 1973) (with reproductions and bibliography). Holstein does not claim that the quilt is the principal source of American art, but he does note the extent to which the "white on white" of plain quilts and patchwork compositions inspired or gave impetus to certain tendencies in American painting: "We can see in many [quilts] such phenomena as 'op' effects, serial images, use of 'color fields,' deep understanding of negative space, mannerisms of formal abstraction and the like," (p. 13).

19

FOLDS, FRAGMENTS, SURFACES: TOWARDS A POETICS OF CLOTH

Pennina Barnett

Editor's introduction: "Folds, Fragments, Surfaces: Towards a Poetics of Cloth" was written by Pennina Barnett for the catalog accompanying the exhibition *Textures of Memory: The Poetics of Cloth*, initiated and curated by Barnett and Pamela Johnson in 1999. The exhibition was first shown at Angel Row Gallery (now closed) in Nottingham, England, followed by a UK tour, and included work by seven artists: Polly Binns, Maxine Bristow, Caroline Broadhead, Alicia Felberbaum, Marianne Ryan, Anne Wilson, and Verdi Yahooda. In her catalog essay, Barnett proposes cloth not only as a poetic language—with its emotive vocabulary of fold, drape, tear, touch—but also as an alternative and organic way of thinking that challenges binary structures and their limiting categories. Drawing on the work of Gilles Deleuze and Michel Serres, she asks, "What if the poetics of cloth were composed of 'soft logics', modes of thought that twist and turn and stretch and fold?" This idea of "textile thinking" is subsequently taken up in a number of pieces of writing in the *Reader* and from varying perspectives. Here, Barnett takes the image of the fold in motion as a metaphor for expansive thinking, potentialities, and "multiple possibilities."

White satin shapes and reshapes
charged like the erotic flower paintings of
       Georgia O'Keefe,
organic forms, intimate recesses,
inner landscapes.

Soft velvet curls in upon itself
vibrating light and shade.
Pigment saturates
strokes
caresses.

A needle pierces.
Harmless
save for an empty eye, a taut posture.
Cotton, white and benign.
Silver silhouettes against black and white and
          black.

Small gestures pass easily by.

Yet this is a space where small gestures slide into dreams; where the familiar turns. A place of quiet intensity. Where the textures of memory

Source: Pennina Barnett, "Folds, Fragments, Surfaces: Towards a Poetics of Cloth," in *Textures of Memory: The Poetics of Cloth* [exhibition catalog] (Nottingham: Angel Row Gallery, in collaboration with Pitshanger Manor and Gallery, London (1999) pp. 25–34). Reproduced with permission.

are smooth and white and velvet and blue and layered with gesso and paint. Where they absorb into linen and cotton and canvas and celluloid; are of mass and material, shadow and ghost; are as fine as hair, as ephemeral as light, as sharp as pins, as random as discarded thread. Where there is the will to repair and disrepair, to reveal and conceal, to caress and embrace. And to imagine and muse, and to invent and create, and to remember and forget, and

to fold and unfold . . .

'Rigid little boxes fit inside a big one, but the reverse isn't true. It is impossible to put the big one . . . in any of the smaller ones . . . Now if there is a logic of boxes, perhaps there is a logic of sacks. A canvas or jute sack . . . is supple enough to be folded up in a sack with all the other folded sacks, even its former container. I believe that there is box-thought, the thought we call rigorous, like rigid, inflexible boxes, and sack-thought, like systems of fabric. Our philosophy lacks a good organum of fabrics.'

'. . . Let us learn to negotiate soft logics. They are only crazy if we do not understand them. Let us finally laugh about those who called rigorous what was precisely their soft discourse. And let us no longer scorn what is soft . . .'[1]

What if the poetics of cloth were composed of 'soft logics', modes of thought that twist and turn and stretch and fold? And in this movement new encounters were made, beyond the constraint of binaries? The binary offers two possibilities, 'either/or'; 'soft logics' offer multiple possibilities. They are the realm of the 'and/and', where anything can happen. Binaries exclude; 'soft logics' are 'to think without excluding'[2]— yet one is not set against the other, (that would miss the point). And if 'soft' suggests an elastic surface, a tensile quality that yields to pressure, this is not a weakness; for 'an object that *gives in*

is actually stronger than one that resists, because it also permits the opportunity to be oneself in a new way'.[3]

the artist, the philosopher and the baker

An artist is watching a philosopher watching a baker. The artist is Yve Lomax; the philosopher, Michel Serres.

The philosopher: 'What does a baker do when he kneads dough? At the beginning there is an amorphous mass, let's say a square. The baker stretches it, spreads it out, then folds it over, then stretches it out and folds it over again. He does not stop folding the mass over on itself—an exemplary gesture . . .'[4]

The artist: 'The baker and the philosopher; and between the two a becoming. When we practice the baker's logic, theory knows no bounds; it becomes soft and flexible. Air enters into the dough; things soon will expand. To get some air in your life, practise the baker's logic'.[5]

. . . to fold and unfold and enfold . . .

. . . this is a space to curl and to clasp, to enclose and to disclose: a space of encounter . . .

'The question always entails living in the world . . . We are discovering new ways of folding, akin to new envelopments . . . what always matters is folding, unfolding, refolding'.[6]

'. . . to unfold is to increase, to grow; whereas to fold is to diminish, to reduce, "to withdraw into the recesses of a world" '.[7]

For philosopher Gilles Deleuze (1925–1995), the fold is an image of conceptual space, a mental landscape: 'the image thought gives itself of what it means to think'.[8] In classical philosophy, thought is related to truth. But for Deleuze, the task of the philosopher is to create new concepts and to alter existent meanings. This is not 'thinking' as something we automatically do, or a knowledge we already have.[9] But 'thinking' as immanent, a form of experimentation: an essentially creative and critical activity, activated when the mind is 'provoked by an encounter with the unknown or the unfamiliar . . .', or when 'something in the world forces us to think'.[10] New concepts unfold in ways we cannot anticipate, and bring into consciousness significant or important events.[11]

The Deleuzian fold is a virtual, even cinematic image—of 'points . . . referrals, spaces';[12] an infinity of folds always in motion, composing and recomposing without inside or outside, beginning or end. And in this movement disparate elements encounter and separate, continuous and discontinuous, a relation of difference with itself. It is a universe more than a world, in which there are also spaces, not so much of rupture, but what we might call 'distribution'. Here, folds double back on themselves like ocean waves, withdraw, and almost cease to generate. Yet within the hollow of the fold, and despite its closure, a leap may still be possible: not a leap 'elsewhere (as if another world would open up) but rather leaping in place . . . and thus distorting or displacing the ground (the foundation, or its unfounding)'.[13]

. . . turning . . . inside out . . .

. . . Folds spill out from canvas into marble and architecture, and into the hurly-burly of the piazza. Inside a dark candle-lit space, the air is heavy with incense. Bernini's *St Teresa* writhes in ecstatic bliss, pleasure suffused with pain. A flaming golden arrow pierces her heart. Folds that cannot be explained by the body, multiply and become autonomous.[14] We are in the Baroque. A period of swathing draperies and billowing clothes. The Baroque, with its fantastic curves—'the fold that goes out to infinity'.[15] An art of dynamic movement, emotional display, swooning saints in spiritual and somatic rapture, all expressed through

the agency of the fold, or folds. 'They convey the intensity of a spiritual force exerted on the body, either to turn it upside down or to stand or raise it up over and again, but in every event to turn it inside out and to mold its inner surfaces'.[16]

. . . The piazza empties. The Baroque fades. Yet something remains . . .

. . . for this is a space of quiet, but not one of silence, where gestures, though small, stir sense and sensation; and senses confuse and cause a vibration; where visual is tactile and tactile is visual, and what is at stake is—not representation but— the composing of folds that take place in slow motion, as intimate moments steal into view . . .

. . . From the Baroque to the white cube: the carnal to the retinal. Yve-Alain Bois writes that the modernist discourses that have come to dominate our approach to the visual deny the space that our bodies occupy. For one of the founding myths of modernism is 'that visual art, especially painting, addresses itself uniquely to the sense of sight'.[17] Even when art history does address the 'tactile', it is through a *visual representation* of tactility, which remains 'purely visual'. Drawing on Freud and Bataille, he argues that the modernist picture is conceived as a vertical section, which has implications for the way in which we experience it. For this presupposes the viewing subject as an erect being (*homo erectus*), distinct from the four-legged creature from which we evolved, a creature parallel with the ground. But this 'civilising' change of axis, he asserts, was only achieved through the sublimation of the body:

'. . . man is proud of being erect, (and of having thus emerged from the animal state, the biological mouth-anus axis of which is horizontal), but this pride is founded on a repression. Vertical, man has no other biological sense than to stare at the sun and thus burn his eyes . . .'[18]

What he forgets, is that his feet are still in the dirt.[19]

Despite the dominance of this myth, there are, of course, many examples of painting, *within* modernism, that challenge the idea of art as an activity that alienates the viewer (and artist) from their bodies. Think of Pollock, his canvasses stretched horizontally out beneath him—they aren't addressed to *homo erectus*; or a Cézanne still life, where objects seem about to roll onto the floor in defiance of gravity.[20]

Yet myths are powerful, and perhaps it is no coincidence that cloth, with its special relationship to the body, has been largely marginalised by these dominant discourses. Always close, it has an immediacy that is part of its etymology, cloth as 'that which clings to the body'.[21] But above all, cloth addresses the most intimate of senses: touch. Limited by the reach of the body, touch marks the juxtaposition of body and world; for while it is possible to see without being seen . . .[22]

'. . . to touch is always to be touched . . .'[23]

And one never emerges *intact* from any encounter, for to be touched involves a capacity to be moved, 'a power to be affected'. And although there are encounters which weaken our power to be affected—making us 'mean-spirited little selves'—there are others that enrich all those involved, encounters where 'subjectivity and affectivity become inseparable, (and) enfold each other'.[24]

And if 'everything round invites a caress',[25] this is true of the baker's art of folding; it requires a caress, rather than a grip. To grip is to seek possession, possession of knowledge and thought; while to caress has the tenderness of an open gesture, open to what is not known and what is to come.[26]

. . . the texture of the intimate . . .

. . . this is an intimate space, a space of close-vision: the curl of a hair, the twist of a thread, the crease of a cloth. A place to lose oneself in the intimacy of the fold, as satin reshapes and velvet vibrates . . .

To set the tactile *against* the visual is to presume the separation of the senses; to forsake soft logics for rigid boxes. The eye, one sense-organ amongst others, does not simply look. It also feels. Its response is both visual *and* tactile. This is the affect of synaesthesia—where senses participate and merge, each enfolded in the other—where we speak of a 'white noise', a 'black mood'. The visual-tactile is a dimension of the haptic where 'there is neither horizon nor background nor perspective nor limit nor outline or form nor centre'.[27] It is what Deleuze and Guattari call a *smooth* or nomadic space,[28] like the consistency of felt. Because it is made by rolling fibres back and forth until they enmesh, felt can potentially extend in all directions, without limit, entangled in a continuous variation—a fabric, at least in principle, without top, bottom or centre. Woven cloth, on the other hand, has a fixed warp which defines its edges and limits; it has a bottom and top—a beginning and an end. This makes it a *striated or* sedentary space of long-distance vision, form and outline.[29] Yet smooth space and striated space are not set in opposition. Although striated space is more optical, the eye is not the only organ to have this capacity; the two spaces exist in mixture and passage, one giving rise to the other.[30]

folds of matter and force . . .

. . . this is a space of surface and texture, material and matter: the physical stuff from which things are made. Of cloth that sags, and linen that wears, and acrylic that washes through warp and through weft. Of gesso that cracks like sun-bleached earth; transformed from ground in days of old, to surface and subject that starts to speak of closeness and distance, and inside and out. . . .

Cloth Folds by Tina Modotti, a platinum palladium print from the late 1920s: fabric caught in motion, creased like the cratered surface of the moon, or the flux and flow of matter. Matter, not conceived of as particles of sand, but as 'a sheet of paper divided into infinite folds'. That's how Deleuze imagines it—matter unfolding its pleats at great length, some smaller, some larger, all endlessly dividing.[31]

And now folds appear everywhere: not just in the draperies of the Baroque, but in the curling fruits and vegetables of its still life paintings; in wind and water; in sound, as it moves through the air; in the layers of sediment that make up the earth. The world becomes a body of infinite folds and surfaces, twisting and weaving through compressed time and space. But what does matter imply? Perrin speaks of 'a particular and very condensed form of energy'.[32] While for Deleuze 'matter that reveals its texture becomes raw material, just as form that reveals folds becomes force',[33] an invisible force that can be *harnessed* through art or music; and for Deleuze this, rather than the reproducing or inventing of forms, is the task of the artist. Thus he writes of Cézanne as a painter who goes beyond sensation, turning it back on itself,

> 'to render visible the force that folds the mountains, the germinative force of the apple, the thermic force of a landscape . . . '[34]

the body of folds . . .

> ' . . . we are "folded" in many entangled, irregular ways, none the same . . . and . . . this "multiplicity" goes beyond what we can predict or be aware of: we are "folded" in body and soul in many ways and many times over, prior to our being as "subjects" . . . but not because we divide into distinct persons or personalities looking for a unity . . . rather that our modes of being are "complicated" and "unfold" in such a way that we can never be sure just what manners our being will yet assume'.[35]

Folded in utero, creased in death, and between, shifting in twists and turns: are we subject to similar forces—experiencing sensations more somatic than cerebral, more felt than remembered; sensations that seem to by-pass the brain and act directly on the nervous system?[36] *Cloth Folds*, unashamedly fleshy and organic. Creased, like skin beneath a microscope. An image that permeates my surfaces, heightens my sense of corporeality. Yet what does it mean—phenomenologically—to become aware of the body?

the fragmented body . . .

My face, my back, the top my head: all elude me. I know my body only in parts. Yet my sense of totality—although an abstraction—is crucial. How else could I exist in the world? According to psychoanalytic theories developed by Freud and Lacan, for perhaps the first six months of our lives, we do not have an awareness of our bodies as fixed and bounded space encased by skin, the surface through which we mediate and encounter the world 'outside'. In Lacan's formulation, the infant—the 'subject-to-be'—is caught up in a shifting field of libidinal forces and chaotic drives which lap across it like waves,[37] as objects and part-objects merge and disappear without differentiation. Its body is experienced as disorganised and fragmented—in bits and pieces—the infant making no distinction between self and other, subject and object, inside and out.[38] An integrated sense of self, as discrete subject, gradually develops through the maternal body which gives form and meaning to the infant's internal and external worlds; and for this, the process through which subjectivity is formed, Lacan uses the metaphor of the mirror, in which the infant finds, in reflection, a unified image of itself.

'matter-materiality-maternity . . .'[39]
the body of material dissolution. . . .

If subjectivity is achieved through the sublimation of the fragmented body, the price is self-alienation: we can only know our(whole)selves, through an *external* image and this turns the subject into an object of its own gaze.[40] To become aware of the body, to 'perceive' with the body, is to trespass the boundary that maintains its closure. It is to enter our own materiality: the soft tissue of organs, the snaking folds of the intestines, the pulse of the heart: a series of body parts, each with its own impulse, one dissolving into the other, undoing the fragile unity that holds us in check. To cross the line—to encounter 'the otherness of the soma',[41] with its chaotic drives and sensations—produces uncanny affect: an otherness felt through 'the irruption of the carnal',[42] with its endless beat; a 'pulsatile effect' through which the whole body is returned to 'part objects'.[43] The mirror, the double, repetition: each are manoeuvres against dissolution, and a materiality so raw, so close, it exceeds and resists representation.[44]

To cross the line might even offer strange comfort: an imaginary fusion with the maternal body, and promise of plenitude. Yet '. . . the mother's gift of life is also the gift of death . . . the embrace of the beloved, also a dissolution of the self'.[45] What is it to become aware of the body? It is to acknowledge that material dissolution is the *presence of death in life*, not as a binary opposite—but enfolded at its very centre.[46]

'the body of sensation . . .'[47]

. . . where sky meets earth and earth meets sky, soft and diffused and without clear line. . . .

The body of sensation', what Deleuze calls 'the body without organs',[48] is the un-organised body, where body and world become one, a 'body-world of non-formed elements and anonymous affective forces',[49] that corresponds to the level of pre-subjective experience. It is a body always in the process of formation and de-formation. Erwin Straus makes a useful distinction between sensation and perception. *Perception* refers to the experience of a rational, verbally mediated-world in which space and time are uniform and atomistic, with subject and object

clearly demarcated; *sensation*, to the experience of a world that is prerational and alingual, where space and time are perspectival and dynamic, the difference between subject and object less clear.[50] This has parallels with aspects of the smooth and striated: sensation as smooth and unbounded, always in movement, experienced close at hand; perception as striated, of surface and form, outline and order, meaning and sign. Yet if sensation is related to a pre-subjective, alingual world, how can it encompass perspective? For perspective orders the world from a central and singular viewpoint, an 'I'/eye that knows its boundaries. 'The body of sensation' is not concerned with such things. Drawing on Straus's work, Deleuze says that when we are moved by a work of art at the level of sensation, the world emerges with us, subject with object:

'. . . it is being-in-the-world, as the phenomenologists say: at the same time I *become* in sensation and something *arrives* through sensation, one through the other, one in the other. And finally it is the same body that gives and receives sensation, that is at the same time object and subject'.[51]

the space of the incomplete . . .

This is a space of fragments, a space of the incomplete. But it is not a lack or a failure. Why tie up loose ends? Penelope knew it well—weaving by day, undoing by night, 'a secret work always begun again',[52] and all the richer for this double action.

White satin shapes and reshapes: and if there are elements here of repetition in the Freudian sense[53]—where what cannot be 'remembered' returns in behaviour, the past relived in the present—it is also true that each repetition has its own inflection distinct from the first, never the same. For as with the baker kneading his dough,

'. . . each folding over changes the ensemble of the beginning into a more complex ensemble.

The same square is conserved, and yet it is not the same square'.[54]

The poetics of cloth are composed of folds, fragments and surfaces of infinite complexity. The fragment bears witness to a broken whole; yet it is also a site of uncertainty from which to start over; it is where the mind extends beyond fragile boundaries, beyond frayed and indeterminate edges, expanding in the fluidity of the smooth. The surface is a liminal space, both inside and out, a space of encounter. To fold is to 'withdraw into the recesses of a world'.[55] Yet it is not a lament or a loss, for the fold is without beginning or end.

The poetics of cloth are a stretching out: an invitation to leap inside the hollow of the fold, to see what happens. And to think *inside the continuity of the fold* is to think in a continuous present. It is to believe in the presence of the moment, of the fold as the power to "begin" again . .'.[56]

Pennina Barnett
June 1999

I gratefully acknowledge the support of Goldsmiths College, University of London, for granting me Leave of Absence during Spring 1999 in order to research and write this essay and to research the exhibition. I would also like to thanks my colleagues Irit Rogoff and Mo Price for their suggestions and comments on this essay.

NOTES

1. Michel Serres, *Rome, The Book of Foundations*, (1983) translated by Felicia McCarren, Stanford University Press, Stanford, California, 1991, p. 236. I was introduced to the work of Michel Serres through reading Yve Lomax, 'Folds in the photograph', *Third Text* 32, Kala Press, London, Autumn 1995, pp. 43–58. I am indebted to Lomax's text for the ideas it suggested to me for various sections of this essay.

2. Michel Serres, cited in Yve Lomax, 'Folds in the photograph', p. 47.

3. Max Kozloff, 'The Poetics of Softness' in *Renderings, critical essays on a century of modern art.* (1961), Studio Vista, London, 1968, p. 233. Kozloff is referring to Oyvind Fahlstrom's writing on Claes Oldenburg.

4. Michel Serres, cited in Lomax, 'Folds in the photograph', p. 51.

5. Yve Lomax, 'Folds in the photograph', p. 52.

6. Gilles Deleuze, *The Fold: Leibniz and the Baroque* (1988), trans Tom Conley, Athlone Press, London, 1993, Chapter 10, 'The New Harmony', p. 137. (See also Tom Conley's introduction 'Translator's Forward: A Plea for Leibniz', in which he explains how Deleuze developed the concept of the fold through reading the work of Leibniz (1646–1714). Deleuze considered him the 'first great philosopher and mathematician of the pleat, of curves and twisting surfaces', and the preeminent philosopher of the Baroque.)

7. Ibid., Chapter 1 'The Pleats of Matter', pp. 8–9. (Deleuze is citing Leibniz here, in a letter to Artauld of 1687.)

8. Gilles Deleuze, What Is Philosophy? (1991), cited in Paul Patton, 'Introduction', in Paul Patton (ed.), *Deleuze: A Critical Reader*, Blackwell, Oxford, UK and Cambridge Mass, 1996, p. 6.

9. Paul Patton, 'Introduction', ibid., p. 9.

10. Gilles Deleuze, *Difference and Repetition*, (1969) cited in Paul Patton, ibid., p. 9.

11. Paul Patton, ibid., pp. 13–14.

12. see Jean-Luc Nancy, 'The Deleuzian Fold of Thought', in Paul Patton, op. cit., p. 108.

13. ibid., p. 109.

14. Gilles Deleuze, *The Fold: Leibniz and the Baroque*, op. cit., Chapter 10, 'The New Harmony', pp. 121–123.

15. ibid., p. 121.

16. ibid., p. 122.

17. Yve-Alain Bois, 'The Use Value of "Formless"', in Yve-Alain Bois, Rosalind E. Krauss,

Formless: a user's guide, Zone Books, New York 1997, see pp. 25–27. (catalogue of an exhibition held at the Centre Georges Pompidou, Paris, 1996).

18. ibid., p. 26.

19. ibid., p. 25.

20. ibid., pp. 27–28.

21. See Ewa Kuryluk, *Veronica and her Cloth: History, Symbolism, and Structure of a "True" Image*, Basil Blackwell, Cambridge, Mass, and Oxford, UK, 1991, p. 179. She writes that the word "cloth" has a Germanic origin, and appears in *Kleid* (dress), *Kleidung* (clothing) and in the Dutch *kleed*. It is thought to come from the root *kli-* 'to stick' or 'to cling to', making "cloth," "that which clings to the body".

22. Denis Hollier, *The Politics of Prose: Essay on Sartre*, [1986], cited in Joan Livingstone and Anne Wilson, 'The Presence of Touch', in *The Presence of Touch*, (exhibition catalogue), Department of Fiber and Material Studies, The School of the Art Institute of Chicago, Chicago 1996, p. 6.

23. Paul Rodaway, *Sensuous Geographies: Body, Sense and Place*, [1994], cited in Joan Livingstone and Anne Wilson ibid., p. 1

24. All citations here are from 'They talk, they write, they make together, Vit Hopley and Yve Lomax on Vit Hopley and Yve Lomax', in *Make* no 75, April–May 1997, p. 15.

25. Gaston Bachelard, *The Poetics of Space*, (1958), Beacon Press, Boston, Mass, 1994, p. 236.

26. Yve Lomax, 'Folds in the photograph', op. cit., p. 32.

27. Gilles Deleuze and Felix Guattari, *A Thousand Plateaus: Capitalism and Schizophrenia* (1980), trans. Brian Massumi, University of Minnesota Press, Minneapolis, 1987. See Section 14, 'The Smooth and The Striated', p. 494.

28. ibid., pp. 492–3. (The authors acknowledge here Alois Riegl's notion of 'close-vision-haptic space'.)

29. ibid., pp. 475–6.

30. ibid., p. 493.

31. Gilles Deleuze, *The Fold: Leibniz and the Baroque*, op. cit., Chapter 1, 'The Pleats of Matter', p.6, and Chapter 10, 'The New Harmony', p. 123, respectively.

32. J. Perrin cited by Jean François Lyotard, *The Inhuman. Reflections on Time*, trans. Geoffrey Bennington and Rachel Bowlby, Polity Press, Cambridge, 1991, p. 43.

33. Gilles Deleuze, *The Fold: Leibniz and the Baroque*, op. cit., Chapter 3. 'What Is Baroque?' p. 35.

34. Gilles Deleuze, *Francis Bacon: The Logic of Sensation* (1981), cited in Ronald Bogue, 'Gilles Deleuze, The Aesthetics of Force', in Paul Patton, op. cit., p. 261.

35. John Rajchman, 'Out of the Fold', in *Architectural Design* Magazine, vol. 63, parts 3–4, March/April 1993, p. 63.

36. Francis Bacon, *The Brutality of Fact: Interviews with David Sylvester*, referred to in Daniel W. Smith, 'Deleuze's Theory of Sensation: Overcoming the Kantian Duality', in Paul Patton, op. cit., p. 32.

37. See Terry E. Eagleton, Literary Theory [1983], Blackwell, Oxford UK and Cambridge USA, 1993 edition, p. 154.

38. See Elizabeth Grosz, 'The Body', in Elizabeth Wright (ed.), *Feminism and Psychoanalysis*, A Critical Dictionary, Blackwell, Oxford, U.K. & Cambridge, Mass. 1992, pp. 36–7.

39. 'the unencompassable body of "matter-materiality-maternity," which indexically figures death', Elizabeth Bronfen cited in Anne Raine, 'Embodied geographies, subjectivity and materiality in the work of Ana Mendleta', in Griselda Pollock (ed.), *Generations and Geographies in the visual arts—Feminist Readings*, Routledge. London and New York, 1996, pp. 244–245.

40. See Madan Sarup, *An Introductory Guide to Post-Structuralism and Postmodernism*, Har-

vester Wheatsheaf, London, 1993, Chapter 1, 'Lacan and Psychoanalysis', p. 22.

41. Anne Raine, 'Embodied geographies', op. cit., p. 246.

42. Yve-Alain Bois, 'The Use Value of Formless', in Yve-Alain Bois & Rosalind E. Krauss, *Formless*, op. cit., p. 31.

43. Rosalind E. Krauss, 'Pulse: "Moteur!"' in Yve-Alain Bois & Rosalind E. Krauss, *Formless*, op. cit., p. 136.

44. Anne Raine, 'Embodied geographies', op. cit., p. 245.

45. Elizabeth Bronfen, 'Death Drive' in Elizabeth Wright (ed.), *Feminism and Psychoanalysis. A Critical Dictionary*, op. cit., p. 56.

46. ibid., p. 53.

47. Gilles Deleuze, *Francis Bacon: The Logic of Sensation* [1981], referred to in Ronald Bogue, 'Gilles Deleuze, The Aesthetics of Force', op. cit., p. 262.

48. see Ronald Bogue, op. cit. p. 262.

49. Ibid., p. 268.

50. Erwin Straus, *The Primary World of Senses: A Vindication of Sensory Experience* [1935], in Ronald Bogue, ibid., p. 258.

51. Gilles Deleuze, *Francis Bacon: The Logic of Sensation* [1981], cited in Ronald Bogue, ibid., p. 260.

52. Michel Serres, Rome, *The Book of Foundations*, op. cit., p. 79.

53. Sigmund Freud, *Beyond the Pleasure Principle* [1920], trans. and edited by James Strachey, Hogarth Press and The Institute of Psycho-Analysis, London 1974.

54. Michel Serres, *Rome, The Book of Foundations*, op. cit., pp. 80–81.

55. Leibniz, cited by Gilles Deleuze, *The Fold: Leibniz and the Baroque*, op. cit., Chapter 1 'The Pleats of Matter', pp. 8–9.

56. Eva Mayer, 'On a matter of Folds', paper presented at Goldsmiths College, University of London, March 1999. To be published in the forthcoming edition of the journal *Parallax*.

20

STATEMENT VI

Judith Clark

Editor's introduction: Judith Clark trained as an architect before turning her attention to fashion curation. She is currently a reader in fashion and museology at the London College of Fashion, University of the Arts, London. Her interest in how we understand the space of the gallery through the human scale of the garment has led to a number of innovative curatorial projects including the exhibition *Spectres: When Fashion Talks Back*, held at the Victoria and Albert Museum in 2005. Organized as thirty-nine numbered observations, the lecture notes reprinted here evoke the spoken voice of Clark's thoughts surrounding the topic of fashion and curation. The appendix that follows is a stream-of-consciousness continuation of Clark's ideas, written over a number of years. In her writing Clark considers exhibitions she has curated, as well as questions about what curation could become in the future, always challenging the suggestion that there might be a static or single solution to our understanding of how the garment may meet the public in a museum or gallery setting. Clark adopts an unconventional attitude toward the purpose of chronology in critical writing, and her eloquent lists are purposeful rather than polished, foregrounding her observation that curators speak through their "use of objects, not of words."

I'll tell you something which is extreme, it is about 'squatting'. It is about inhabiting space. That's what it is for me—don't you think? I have always said that my role in magazines is to squat, which is—where there is free space then that's where I place myself. And then you expand, you adapt, you synthesize and most of all you defend your position, you push against the other material

Anna Piaggi talking to Judith Clark, Milan, September 2005

15. Last year I sent Naomi Filmer a photo of Simonetta Colonna di Cesaro' and the most important part of the photo was her beautiful right forearm. In exhibitions things stand in for other things, objects are suggestive (the exhibition space marks them as evocative, provocative objects). In fact, everything in exhibitions is standing in for something else—to effect, so to speak.

16. Exhibitions are made up of equations: mannequins + dresses = ?. If we could forget about photos and videos standing in for exhibitions of

Source: Unpublished statement available online: http://www.judithclarkcostume.com/publications/essays_05.php. Reproduced with permission.

dress—exhibitions could be free to stand in for other ideas—a broader range of realities. These notes are jump cuts. I think of curating dress as to do with clashes and combinations, hauntings and improvisations; and I want these notes—a work in progress—to reflect this process.

17. Mannequins went out of fashion. They became more and more and more minimal—they lost their hair, then their skin tone, then their heads and then they 'peaked' as officially invisible with the 'Giorgio Armani' exhibition at the Guggenheim in New York in 2000. Not a millimetre showed beyond the dress however thin the shoulder straps. In 2006 the 'Anglo-mania' show at the Metropolitan Museum Costume Institute treated styling instead as a tannoi for the extravagance of the gowns rather than as a distraction from their crafted forms.

18. But what of conceptual dress—when the mannequins are married to an idea, an extension of the dress but also of the space, and a carrier of adjacent meaning? Mannequins have an acknowledged history of their own—they are no longer bound just to the projects of verisimilitude or invisibility.

19. In 2004, for the exhibition 'Malign Muses: When Fashion Turns Back', Linda Loppa, the then Director of ModeMuseum, Antwerp, allowed me to commission Naomi Filmer to create a kind of mannequin prosthetic. Each themed section of the exhibition would have its mannequin 'equivalent'. These prosthetics as we have called them, would explicitly add to the ways the research could be translated into exhibition values.

20. So for the section dedicated to Harlequins—or rather the persistence of the harlequin theme within fashion—she carved a pair of ballet shoes on their points in wood. The ballet shoes were painted on feet in a balletic pose. They simultaneously underlined the importance of harlequins' ballet shoes and also gestured to the presence of Elsa Schiaparelli's Harlequin Jacket from the V&A collection in the section, an allusion to Surrealism—and to fashions (sometimes too easy) relationship to surrealist games.

The mannequins could have been archive mannequins; but the presence of the wooden feet bolted to the ground adjacent to the mounted garment meant we were simultaneously reminded of the harlequin's pose and the surrealist project. It was a project that used objects instead of words. Both could have been represented photographically and through a caption but they would not have engaged in the same way with issues of exhibition-making and its repertoire.

It was a series of speculative conjectures to do with exhibition-making. The prosthetics created an expensive and sporadic reference to the research that overlapped with ideas about mannequins, (or bodies): 19th Century wax figures, Hans Bellmer's perverse and traumatised bodies or the harlequins appeared throughout the trajectory of the exhibition. These were all included within Caroline Evan's look at the dark themes that dominated the late 20th century in fashion that formed the starting point for the exhibition.

21. So when I sent Naomi Filmer the photo of Simonetta, it was to conjure a new body, a new subject, to conjure hauteur with elongated chins, arms, or headdresses, all the areas that are visible beyond the garment and belong intrinsically to the silhouette.

What could stand in for the cult of her elegance and aristocratic beauty? Her eye-liner, pearls, bangles—where does a curator place elements that are extrinsic to the acual dress. My question was at the time, how does one curate eyeliner? It performs a different kind of eloquence.

It is required for the performance, to narrate it more precisely.

An archive mannequin can appear 'natural' until you do something to it.

22. With so much reality and record we fear the reconstruction. Diana Vreeland was fearless. In her autobiography, 'D.V.' she recalls a story that went around about her.: "Apparently I'd wanted a billiard-table green background for a picture. So the photographer went out and took the picture. I didn't like it. He went out and took it again. I didn't like it. Then . . . he went out and took it

again and I *still* didn't like it. "I asked for billiard-table green" I'm supposed to have said; "But this *is* a billiard table, Mrs Vreeland" the photographer replied. "My dear" I apparently said, I meant the *idea* of billiard-table green, not a billiard table".

Exhibitions could for example be based on idea of free association. The curators repertoire of associations meets the spectators associations. The spectator is free to make personal sense of the exhibition. They are free to notice what occurs to them, what crosses their minds as they look. Clearly some exhibitions are more coercive, more dictatorial than others. One question that the curator might ask herself is how free is the spectator to surprise herself?

When objects are placed in the same room, in the same cabinet on the same plinth, the curator is choosing to give objects something in common and something antagonistic—shape vs. colour, period vs. style, reference over chronology; the brief is visually translated and the narrative clarified in a very particular way.

23. Exhibitions can style getting stuck in time, they can stage ideas about 'micro-geography', they can perform 'claustrophobia' or 'aristocracy'. What if the pose says more than the dress?. What if the particular way that Simonetta smoked her cigarette was the memorable thing about her clothes?

24. Maybe themes should be replaced by sequences, sequences of rooms and ideas and the distributions of one within the other? Leaving the gallery I used to run I gained (museum) space, and extra rooms, but maybe lost the clarity of single statements. In museum exhibitions as opposed to those in a gallery where the statement is usually contained in one room, one space, one view, we look at exhibitions of dress through the lens of a predetermined sequence of rooms: the architecture is then invested with the rhythm reflecting the curatorial brief, the exhibition is cut up to fit within a predetermined space.

Architecture dramatises the tyrrany of the space that encloses clothes—or the system that defines them. It can stand in for other metaphorical barriers/institutions as well as its own.

25. I designed an exhibition about fashion and time, and about patterns that emerge when the words historical reference, or re-interpretation are made central to fashion. Each existed as a kind of island within the larger space of the museum—as my first museum exhibition I think I had to divide the exhibition space into smaller statements (each similar in scale to the gallery I had until then run).

I wanted the difference between the sections—each representing a different curatorial narrative strategy—to be its subject—not dress. It was intended to refer to a history of exhibitions that included those of Frederick Kiesler or Ilya and Emilia Kabakov or the utopian repositories of Yuri Avvakumov. Where are the histories of exhibitions about looking at looking?. This question has preoccupied me and made me a misfit.

26. Exhibitions and protagonists from one narrative are quickly and easily absorbed into others sometimes linked only by the re-presentation of one object. The inaugural exhibition at Judith Clark Costume Gallery (Dai Rees, Pampilion) has this year been absorbed into FIT's Gothic Dark Gamour through the swarovski crystal encrusted sheep's pelvis; Hussein Chalayan's remote control dress has toured constantly, last year included in the Skin and Bones: Parallel practices in Fashion and Architecture. They were complete exhibitions that will never be perceived now without the others. The gallery exhibitions have been given multiple futures in an imaginary ever-expanding exhibition genealogy.

27. Fashion: An anthology by Cecil Beaton staged at the V&A in 1971, has in 2009 become Hats: An Anthology by Stephen Jones, one title alludes to another, and is immediately underwritten by it.

28. Museum exhibitions carry with them the anxiety of the idea of completion, of telling the whole, the most accurate story (and if accuracy is the question what is it assumed that the exhibition should correspond to?). When objects are used in such different contexts it becomes immediately clear that their allegiances vary.

At the Victoria and Albert Museum I tried to stick to Anna Piaggi's loyalty to the non-academic (squatting, lists, anecdotal provenance, vivid approximations that become truer than the truth) I became committed to her initials and to those of the hosting institution, and walls that seen drawn in plan created A's and V's or V's and A's determined the route of the exhibition, and so determined its reading.

29. I believe that everything follows from the site of an exhibition—the architecture, or venue. For me there is no such thing as designing hypothetically; even if I am designing a hypothetical exhibition it needs to have a hypothetical venue first. Anna Piaggi: Fashionology squatted in the V&A: its angular walls at odds (from all perspectives) to the institution.

Equivalents are different to similarities—there has been a lot of parallelism coupling fashion and architecture—the curating of fashion should be as much about un-linking, as much about attacking conventional links.

30. Curating is a way of thinking about spatial analogies.

31. Bob Verhelst who designed the inaugural Backstage exhibition at ModeMuseum has recently designed the Maison Martin Margiela 20th Anniversary exhibition.—drawing our attention not to the museum's hand (collecting, conserving and theming) but the anonymous, disorienting, and distorting hand of Martin Margiela himself. The architecture was 'rearranged' to reinforce the design house's subtle games with classic sartorial vocabulary.

Photographs of the side windows were placed at 1:1 scale within the exhibition—replacing the east with southerly views. The building work across the street that was captured by the photos was completed during the exhibition adding further disorientation or rather keeping a record of passing time within the exhibition or game itself. As it was reconstruction—the opposite of decay, just a turning back of the clock—a n unanticipated impossible game that Martin Margiela would undoubtedly enjoy and could easily map onto current ideals of beauty. The allusions go on and on.

32. An exact original experience can never be created. An original experience can never be created exactly.

33. Another example is Viktor and Rolf's Milanese boutique in via sant'andrea designed by Siebe Tettero which is a neoclassical boutique turned upside down. (witty details include herring-bone parquet ceilings, and moulded floors, upturned arches and perfume bottles glued to the shelves—upside-down).

We know—as though we have always known—what neo-classical architecture looks like, though we might not know how to name it or its historical dates. We know about columns, about arches, and we know absolutely when they are upside down. This elementary game is at the heart of Viktor and Rolf's project of disrupting the recognisable codes within the fashion industry, its calendars, and branding rules. The repetition of historical designs, familiar and transformed, means we get it, we get the project; we can be perturbed, or disturbed, or simply intrigued.

I love a quote that I found when reviewing In the House of Viktor and Rolf for the Symposium at the Barbican: Siebe Tettero said something like: If I were to turn minimalist architecture on its head it wouldn't work—i.e. if you turn a simple rectangle on its head it stays the same. If you go for the familiar orders of architecture we understand the game, it is immediate.

34. Captions—Instead of fixing the discipline, they can open it up

For Barthes, words and objects have in common the organised capacity to say something; at the same time, since they are signs, words and objects have the bad faith always to appear natural to their consumer, as if what they say is eternal, true, necessary, instead of arbitrary, made, contingent.

—Edward Said

The captions for the Spectres: When Fashion Turns Back exhibition when it came to the V&A Contemporary Space were removed from the space immediately adjacent to the objects and instead placed on a leaflet/map of the space. The open design of the set made it difficult to find adjacent walls for individual objects. It was only when this 'decision of mine' was criticised did I realize that it was interesting, and how constraining captions are. I am now much more wary of them, suspicious about what they demand from, ask of, the spectator.

35. The installations were already illustrations of Caroline Evans words in her book *Fashion at the Edge*. So the objects were already at the service of the words—what would more words do?—creating a sort of never ending explanation.

Captions focus our attention, tell us what to look at and make sure we do not stray too far. Roland Barthes suggested in a 1967 interview published in *Le Monde* why 'photos in newspapers are always captioned: to reduce the risk engendered by a multiplicity of meanings'.

36. Richard Gray re-described in his Morphoillogical Friday Late at the V&A, what we can, in a sense, already see—he translated decoration into more decoration. He created captions made up of images, of collage, of visual references. He, (like Anna Piaggi explaining current couture through her collaged Doppie Pagine), explained objects from the parmanent collection of the V&A. Here superficiality in a very contemporary way is the point, not the problem; it is where the sophistication of fashion is revealed.

37. Viktor & Rolf brought fragments of gallery exhibitions into the museum, the history of their clothes is also a history of their installation—a huge plane of glass as important as the white dresses resting against it.

We experience, so to speak, the experience of the mannequin. We experience the vertigo of the plinth, the claustrophobia of the crowded cabinet.

"[In the exhibition 'In the House of Viktor and Rolf'] we were given the same information three times. The exhibition used the importance of repetition to narrative, organised curatorially, but also alluded to its Freudian association to trauma. Nightmare and trauma—the trauma of nightmare—never seem very far away from the project. In Viktor and Rolf's vision fashion is itself a both a trauma and an attempted self-cure for a trauma. It opens up alternative readings of the same outfit, which is not described through object and text alone and which often closes down the readings of the garments. . . .

The repositioning of the same object adds to its eloquence and like a chorus, by the end, they are all familiar objects—we learn the tune and get the jokes.

Exhibition design incorporates its own repetitions and histories, as well as those of the garments themselves by association. We think of what circumstances have generated miniature couture and miniature display in the past. . . .

In Viktor & Rolf's exhibition there is a sense of claustrophobia in their demonic sartorial repetition. It is the self referential nature of their design—details over and over again are conceptual in a way that say other designers such as Hussein Chalayan might refer to an abstract concept, the silk route, technology etc. With Viktor and Rolf it is as though you can't escape the dress itself, trapped in a predetermined language, leaving them free only to manipulate size, repetition, colour etc. It draws attention to fashions repertoire with nightmarish insistence. . . .

And through the virtuoso repetitions and manipulation of motifs we learn the rules, we recognise the rituals and regulations as part of the design. We know what oversize bows look like because we have a vocabulary in our minds which incorporates bows—maybe 1950s nostalgic cocktail dresses, for example. They trap you in a dark mis-en-abime of circular arguments, about the inside and outside of the system, about their love and hatred for clothing, about wealth and virtual wealth that is itself expensive (the collectors of expensive doll's houses themselves simulated and stimulated wealth). The allusions cannot rest, and that restlessness is the point. . . .

Along with this there is an acknowledgment of the naivety of 'minimal design'. A route is a chronology, returns are repetitions: spatial metaphors track and trace our understanding of exhibitions and our descriptions of them." (note 1.)

38. There is a move (with the rise of more and more written fashion theory) to make exhibition design more articulate—to incorporate some of the abstract ideas within the experience of the exhibition. What are the drawbacks of this? Does theory inhibit or censure our associations.

Labyrinths have been recently used to symbolise a corrupted or complex curatorial route—intentionally devoid of its progressive inevitability—they are also potent graphic symbols of time folding back on itself. It is not only about the extended route but the proximities that are created in doing so.

39. 'But if, either on the basis of what poets try to tell you, or by biological research, with or without the tools of the psychologist, you attempt to explain a poem, you will probably be getting further and further away from the poem without arriving at any other destination. The attempt to explain the poem by tracing it back to its origins will distract attention from the poem, to direct it on to something else which in the form in which it can be apprehended by the critic and his readers, has no relation to the poem and throws no light upon it.'
T.S.Eliot
END

NOTE

1. Judith Clark: Lecture presented 13th September 2008 on the occasion of the Symposium In the House of Viktor and Rolf, Barbican Gallery, London.

APPENDIX 1

Statement I*

'I dream of immense cosmologies reduced to the dimensions of an epigram . . . I would ike to edit a collection of tales consisting of one sentence only, or even a single line. But so far I haven't found any to match the one by the Guatemalan writer Augusto Monterroso: 'When I looked up, the dinosaur was still there.'

'I would say that the moment an object appears in a narrative, it is charged with a special force and becomes like a pole of a magnetic field, a knot in the framework of invisible relationships. The symbolism of an object may be more or less explicit but it is always there. We might say that in a narrative any object is always magic'

Italo Calvino, *Six Memos for the next Millennium,* from 'Quickness'.

1. Galleries are associated with immediate experience—with impact; like quick-acting barometers, as opposed to the reflective retrospective museum exhibition. When curating for a small place, for one room, it is about ruthless selection and the clarity of connections, or it is conceived as a fragment, a key to a larger story or a clue to a different project.

2. What then is the difference between the small, the complete and the fragment?

3. I have always loved short literary forms: notes, short stories, Borges's potential literature, manifestos and their visual counterparts, sketches, scaled-down models, trailers, the avant-gardes of architecture never built but promised and documented (as alternative urban histories or utopias). These find their most powerful equivalents in fashion in Anna Piaggi's Fashion Algebra, her monthly 'Doppie Pagine' (double pages) for Italian Vogue, which consist of catwalk images juxtaposed with images torn from books and turned into 'superficial' (to use her phrase) themed collages, leaps into the past to illuminate contemporary fashionableness.

4. I feel as though I have been working on potential exhibitions of dress. Historical reference in dress has never been about evolution, continuity. There are other ways of plotting this. In dress, surfaces float free of their histories.

5. Curating is like creating a new grammar, new patterns of time and reference. The readability of objects shifts. I am constantly amazed at the simplicity of the routes taken in exhibitions, their inevitable logic. Unlike language but more like the multiple meanings of a pack of tarots cards, objects can be read back to front and side to side.

6. Anthropomorphic imagination makes clothes magical.

7. Curating is about creating sympathetic allegiances between objects, investing them through association with a lop-sided eloquence.

8. Each piece is then invested with the spatial equivalent of exclamation marks.

9. The first exhibition of dress I curated Satin Cages, 1997, was a hypothetical exhibition of crinolines. The exhibition of scaled-down crinolines (1:50) was housed in a balsa wood model, itself based on a hypothetical project by visionary architects Brodsky and Utkin. The outcome was a three minute film exhibited at the Architecture Foundation in London—supposedly of the exhibition, though of course filmed in miniature, with a leaflet commentary carefully mimicking those from the V&A Museum stating dates, venue, policy and selection. The idea was of designing for a recession. In a way my work is still an extension of that idea.

10. I have spent the last five years within the confines of the small space (four metres by nine metres) of the gallery I set up in London, Judith Clark Costume Gallery: twenty exhibition fragments, displaying as many as fifteen garments and as few as one. Cultural range was privileges over consistency, so equal space was devoted to Hussein Chalayan's Remote control Dress, when the gallery was a children's playground, Naomi Filmer's ice jewellery, when it had to be an ice box, Adelle Lutz's Urban Camouflage, when a building site, or Madeleine Vionnet's precious gowns, when a room in a museum.

11. The idea was to draw attention to the curatorial project itself, to Calvino's invisible network of relationships. Small exhibitions were also then fragments of larger exhibitions.

12. I created a rather ostentatious hardback inaugural catalogue—way beyond the resources of the gallery. The photographs by Mat Collishaw were used decadently in the catalogue and not shown in the exhibition. It was therefore more like a hypothetical catalogue to a museum show. The intention—like recruiting Pentagram later to design the journal, or inviting Harold Koda to introduce Adelle Lutz's exhibition—was a magnifying device, a way of playing with scale.

13. I am interested in the relationship between curating and digression, in the connections made by visitors who stray.

14. What would it be to be the Lawrence Sterne of fashion curators, to be free to lose the thread?

*The statement was commissioned by Linda Loppa and Kaat Debo in 2001 to coincide with their inaugural exhibition at ModeMuseum in Antwerp (opened 21 September 2002). The catalogue 'Backstage', like the installation of the exhibition, aimed to both mark a point in time—mindful of creating a 'first' a new beginning, an opportunity that is rare in museum culture, and to look around them to a moment created by disparate voices—in this case my own, and statements 2, 3, 4 and 5, by Valerie Steele, Claire Wilcox, Thimo te Duits and Sylvie Richoux respectively. We were asked to present a short statement—printed in a sequence that felt like it might have been a conversation.

FURTHER READING: STRUCTURE

Anni Albers, *Selected Writings on Design* (Middletown: Wesleyan University Press, 2000.

Surpik Angelini, Laura Hoptman, and David Levi Strauss, *Cecilia Vicuña: Cloud-Net* (New York: Art In General, 1999).

Roland Barthes, *The Pleasure of the Text*, trans. Richard Miller (New York: Hill and Wang—Farrar, Straus and Giroux, 1975).

Roland Barthes, *S/Z* (Oxford: Blackwell, 1974).

Anne Brennan, "Running Stitch and Running Writing: Thinking about Process," in *Craft and Contemporary Theory*, ed. Sue Rowley (St. Leonards, Australia: Allen & Unwin, 1997) pp. 85–97.

Judith Clark, *Spectres: When Fashion Turns Back* (London: V&A Publications, 2004).

Steven Connor, "Witchknots, Knitwits and Knots Intrinsicate," available at http://www.stevenconnor.com/knots/knots.pdf.

Gilles Deleuze, "The Pleats of Matter," in *The Fold: Leibniz and the Baroque* (Minneapolis: University of Minnesota Press, 1993) pp. 3–13.

Rebecca Houze, "The Textile as Structural Framework: Gottfried Semper's Bekleidungsprinzip and the Case of Vienna 1900," in *Textile: The Journal of Cloth and Culture* 4, no. 3 (2006) pp. 292–311.

Kathryn Sullivan Kruger, *Weaving the Word: The Metaphorics of Weaving and Female Textual Production* (London and Selinsgrove: Associated University Press and Susquehanna University Press, 2001).

Sylvie Krüger, *Textile Architecture* (Berlin: Jovis, 2009).

Matilda McQuaid, "Lace Formation," in *Lace in Translation* (Philadelphia: The Design Centre at Philadelphia University, 2010) pp. 28–31.

Lesley Millar, *Textural Space* (Surrey: The Surrey Institute of Art and Design University College, 2001).

Victoria Mitchell, "Folding and Unfolding the Textile Membrane: Between Bodies and Architectures," in *The Body Politic: The Role of the Body and Contemporary Craft*, ed. Julian Stair (London: Crafts Council, 2000) pp. 176–183.

Bradley Quinn, *The Fashion of Architecture* (Oxford: Berg, 2003).

PART IV

POLITICS

PART INTRODUCTION

The textile occupies a peculiar role in relation to power. On the one hand, many contributors to the *Reader* observe that textiles are underestimated and overlooked; the labor and skill behind the making of textiles are seen by many as misunderstood and dismissed. But in the same breath, textiles command extraordinary influence. Their accessibility makes them an influential tool for communication, and their contribution to the formation of identity makes them of individual as well as cultural value.

Politics here is understood with a lowercase *p*, as it relates to social relations and power. This section's contributors discuss projects that critique or speak against existing regimes of power. This includes hierarchies of perceived value within the arts, and the power, or lack of power, that the textile has been able to command within the broader world of fine art. It also includes the influence of postcolonial thinking on our understanding of textiles today and the values of feminism. Recurring throughout this diverse collection of writing is a shared theme of identity—both group and individual—and how the textile can assist in our understanding, communication, and revision of personal and collective identity.

Arthur C. Danto opens the section with a reminder that the ancient Greeks used the woven structure to explain the responsibilities of citizenship and government. Interestingly, this metaphor is not applied in a restrictive sense. Instead, Danto reminds us how the metaphor was used by Plato to suggest the adaptable nature of decision making in the absence of laws. Following Danto, Elissa Auther writes about fiber art made in America, with attention to the power structures that have contributed to its misunderstood and devalued status. Auther refers to the "extra-aesthetic forces affecting the formation of the fibre movement" and reveals the numerous stakeholders who, intentionally and unintentionally, have contributed to the image of American fiber art. Diana Wood Conroy takes up a similar line of inquiry but in relation to tapestry made in Australia. In her catalog essay, she suggests that psychoanalytic theory can be used to help us understand some of the values in textile work that have previously been underappreciated or misunderstood.

While previous contributors have tackled the undervalued place of the textile in the recent history of visual culture, Gandhi's use of the textile provides us with an example of the enormous impact the textile has also wielded. Susan S. Bean considers the remarkable influence of textiles in Gandhi's nonviolent resistance movement, which contributed to Indian independence. Sarat Maharaj continues this postcolonial theme with his writing on the textile in relation to Britain's waning identity as a colonial power. In his interview with Anthony Downey, the artist Yinka Shonibare discusses the use of batik cloth in his work and his interest in the impossible notion of an "authentic" identity for a textile or a culture. The interview format allows us to hear the artist's intentions with minimal mediation and, in Shonibare's case, reveals the articulate and wide-ranging thinking that underpins his practice. Gayatri Chakravorty Spivak's challenging writing tackles the complex issue of transnational identity as it relates to textile production and labor conditions. Maharaj and Spivak take up different points of emphasis but share a desire to work through the histories of power in a search for suitable models of resistance.

From the dense theoretical writing we then move to poetry. Pamela Johnson takes up ideas of cultural identity and the appropriation of cultural traditions and language in a poem written to work through ideas for a longer future piece of prose. Johnson reminds us that certain garment shapes and terms familiar to us today, such as *pajamas*, are part of Britain's complex colonial past. Johnson's poem captures the many ways Britain's contemporary multicultural identity operates in daily life and offers us another reminder of the impossibility of a single "authentic" identity.

Julia Bryan-Wilson's catalog essay on the work of Lisa Anne Auerbach considers the political commentaries that Auerbach embeds in her knitting. Bryan-Wilson situates this work in a broader understanding of the humble sweater, which Auerbach often uses as the basic format for her work, as well as feminism and performance art. Bryan-Wilson observes, "Auerbach asserts a canny sense of domesticity, and by this I mean that her employment of conventionally female 'homemaking' is knowing, self-aware, and even a bit devious in the era of Homeland Security." In the late Rozsika Parker's new introduction to her influential book *The Subversive Stitch*, she considers the changes that have taken place in textile thinking from the time of the original introduction, written in the mid-1980s, to the release of the second edition in 2010. Parker's observations acknowledge the ground gained by textiles in the powerful textile work of artists such as the late Louise Bourgeois but also the momentum lost, particularly with regards to values such as the feminist movement.

The final writing in this section continues this theme but steps back over a century to Charlotte Perkins Gilman's short story "The Yellow Wallpaper." Gilman uses pattern as the basis for a story about the expectations and demands placed on a women's identity. The story is communicated to us via an unreliable narrator, and we are left wondering whether Gilman's yellow wallpaper is a physical prison or a mental one. Perhaps it is both. Time has moved on, but some may wonder if the doubts Gilman raises have in fact progressed significantly in the 120 years that have passed since the story was first published.

21

WEAVING AS METAPHOR AND MODEL FOR POLITICAL THOUGHT

Arthur C. Danto

Editor's introduction: American art critic Arthur C. Danto's essay "Weaving as Metaphor and Model for Political Thought" appeared in the monograph of the American artist Sheila Hicks's miniature weavings published in 2006. Danto begins with the observation that we often look beyond our local cultures to learn about the meaning of textiles. He writes, "Our culture rests on Greek foundations, and weaving is as much a part of our conceptual scheme today as it was in the time of Homer." The essay goes on to consider the use of weaving by the ancient Greeks as a model and metaphor for public life and observes that textile metaphors were held in "high regard" by Plato and that weaving "serves him as the root metaphor in his mature reflections on the art of ruling." Danto focuses on Plato's *Republic* where the metaphor of weaving stood for the "the ability to make decisions in the absence of rules or of laws," a quality Danto acknowledges that the philosopher Immanuel Kant defined as "genius."

Contemporary writers on the meaning of textiles and of weaving often draw their illustrations from cultures very distant from ours. This is valuable in that it shows what meanings are humanly possible, even if they are not especially our meanings. I instead shall briefly examine the way weaving figures, as model and metaphor, for the Greeks. Our culture rests on Greek foundations, and weaving is as much a part of our conceptual scheme today as it was in the time of Homer.

The complex Western attitude toward the fine arts—that they are simultaneously dangerous and frivolous—was famously articulated in the core writings of Plato two and a half millennia ago.[1] The most familiar of Plato's disenfranchising texts

on the subject is, of course, *The Republic*, where he develops a metaphysics of reality and at the same time a visionary political order, in both of which the arts are marginalized: they are marginal in the universe as a whole, having only the substance of illusions, and they are more than marginal in Plato's ideal state, because the artists are to be driven into exile as inimical to the political well-being of its citizenry. But the deep mistrust stains the entire fabric of Platonic speculation—to compound a metaphor from the crafts of dyeing and especially of weaving, for which Plato had a particularly high regard and which serves him as the root metaphor in his mature reflections on the art of ruling. Since Plato stands at the origin

Source: Arthur C. Danto, "Weaving as Metaphor and Model for Political Thought," in Nina Stritzler-Levine (ed.), *Sheila Hicks: Weaving as Metaphor* (New Haven, CT: Bard Graduate Center for Studies in the Decorative Arts, Design, and Culture/Yale University Press, 2006) pp. 22–36, 384. Reproduced with permission.

of Western reflection on the status of the arts, it is perhaps excusable to attempt to weave into an essay on fabric and fine art a discussion of the metaphorical uses Plato makes of weaving, and to explore some of the ways fabric and its forms figure in Greek literature.

In one of the less frequently consulted dialogues, known as *Statesman*, an anonymous spokesman, identified only as the Stranger, undertakes to instruct a young thinker (identified as the Younger Socrates) in a form of philosophical method, which, if rigorously enough pursued, will yield up a definition of whatever we seek to understand. The task at hand is to define the statesman or ruler, and as the dialogue evolves, it turns out that ruling is itself a kind of art, in the sense that the ruler must make decisions often in the absence of laws. There cannot, after all, be laws for everything, and the ruler must be able to act wisely in their abeyance. What kind of art is the art of statesmanship? In the course of an exhaustive review of possibilities, Plato, predictably enough, disparages the fine arts, which the Stranger identifies as "every art which produces artistic representations whether in the visual arts or for the ear in poetry and music."[2] These "are wrought simply to give pleasure," the spokesman states without opposition. "None of them has a serious purpose; all are performed for sheer amusement." This is the "arts are frivolous" part of the Platonic indictment, which he had taken up in those dismissive passages of *The Republic* and of *Ion*, where he is bent on denying that artists have knowledge and on asserting that works of art are at best forms of illusion. Still, the investigation is governed by the thought that ruling itself is some kind of art, whatever the form of government, and the question remains: if not one of the fine arts, what sort of art can it be? Interestingly enough, in view of the invidious contrast sometimes drawn between craft and the so-called fine arts today, Plato's spokesman locates his paradigm in the art of weaving:

What example is there on a really small scale which we can take and set beside kingship, and which, because it comprises an activity common to it and to kingship, can be of real help to us in finding what we are looking for? By heaven, Socrates, I believe I know one. Do you agree that, if there is no other example ready to hand, it would be quite in order for us to select the art of weaving for the purpose?[3]

After considerable further analysis, in which the Stranger and his interlocutor identify the various "arts" necessary to the state—legislation, judging, and the like—they go on to the view that "there is an art which controls all these arts. It is concerned with the laws and with all that belongs to the art of the life of the community. It weaves all into its unified fabric with perfect skill."[4] And to make certain that more than a useful metaphor is involved in this claim, the Stranger immediately says:

We must describe the kingly weaving process. What is it like? How is it done? What is the fabric that results from its labors?

It is not necessary perhaps to press further into the details of the discussion here, but it is interesting to note a certain analogy between this way of thinking about "the kingly art of weaving" and what one might call the art of justice, as discussed by Plato in *The Republic*. There the aim was to find what kind of virtue justice was, in a list consisting of bravery, temperance, and wisdom; and the conclusion was that justice itself is not another item on the list, but a way of harmonizing the other virtues in the interest of producing a unity. And it must be clear that had the image of weaving occurred to him in this earlier discussion, Plato would certainly have used the art of weaving as the illuminating analogy he finds it to be in *Statesman*. Injustice, after all, is disunity or disharmony in *The Republic*, and this means a failure in the weave of the state or, since "the state is man writ large," in the fabric of the human soul. In any case, the dialogue ends with a rather exalted speech on the Stranger's part:

Now we have reached the appointed end of the weaving of the web of the state. It is fashioned by the statesman's weaving: the strands run true, and these strands are the gentle and the brave. Here these strands are woven into a unified character. For this unity is won where the kingly art draws the life or both types into a true fellowship by mutual concord and by ties of friendship. It is the finest and best of all fabrics.[5]

It is at times thought remarkable that Plato should have drawn so exalted a metaphorical use of what some today might dismiss as a mere craft, and one, moreover, that was associated with women in ancient Greece. Weaving is almost always an attribute of female characters in Greek literature, much as armor or weaponry is the attribute of males. When we first encounter the radiant Helen in *The Iliad*, she is "weaving a growing web, a dark red folding robe, / working into the weft the endless bloody struggles / stallion-breaking Trojans and Argives armed in bronze / had suffered all for her at the god of battle's hands."[6] Helen's red web symbolically reproduces the web of violence her beauty has unleashed upon the world, and in general, like arms, weaving is not a simple emblem of domestic order and harmony: it can even be a weapon in its own right, through which women are able to achieve their ends. Weaving—and unweaving—famously emblematizes the means through which faithful Penelope, the crafty and exemplary wife, keeps her suitors at bay while her husband makes his zigzag way home. But the tapestries Clytemnestra and her maids wove for the homecoming of Agamemnon were a trap: Agamemnon, urged by his treacherous wife to walk on purple cloths, is entangled and tethered, and, rendered helpless by what was presented in a ceremony of welcome, he is slain. Andromache weaves a warm cloak for her noble husband, Hektor, but Medea weaves a poisoned garment through which she kills the princess her unfaithful husband has fallen in love with. The woven object is at once a symbol of protection and of betrayal. But Plato is anxious to play down female superiority in such domestic

accomplishments as weaving in order to argue that there is no "feminine mystique" that would bar women from the role of administration in the state: "Must we make a long story of it by alleging weaving and the watching of pancakes and the boiling pot, whereon the sex plumes itself?"[7] So a state can be just as well ordered if men were to do the weaving and women the ruling as the other way round—the only serious damage is done when someone capable of ruling is wasted in other tasks, whatever their gender. However reactionary we find Plato on the subject of the fine arts, he was singularly enlightened in his readiness to admit women to the highest functional rank of the ideal society.

Weaving remains a powerful metaphor for certain integrative activities—we weave stories, for example, and poets, speaking in a metaphysical voice, have spoken of the way Will "has woven with an absent heed / since life first was; and ever so will weave."[8] But the industrialization of the weaving process has set between most of us and the reality of weaving a cognitive barrier opaque enough that it must come as a surprise that Plato should have found common to the arts of weaving and of statesmanship a quality of mind that is very central to the practice of an art, namely a certain kind of creative judgment—the ability to make decisions in the absence of rules or of laws—that Kant, in his great work on aesthetic judgment, should have identified as genius. The concept of genius has created great mischief for the distinction between art and craft in post-Romantic times, and it is worth highlighting Kant's way of thinking about it, inasmuch as it corresponds exactly to the way Plato thought of ruling and, by analogy, of weaving.

Kant defines genius as follows: "(1) Genius is a *talent* for producing that for which no definite rule can be given; it is not a mere aptitude for what can be learned by rule. Hence *originality* must be its first property. (2) But since it can also produce original nonsense, its products must be models, i.e., *exemplary,* and . . . must serve as a standard or rule for others."[9] Plato thinks of weaving as exercising a certain kind of judgment, which cannot be formulated nor, in consequence, applied mechanically. It is a judgment that guards against exceeding the due measure or falling short of it. It is precisely by "this effort they make to maintain the due measure that they achieve effectiveness and beauty in all that they produce."[10] Some pages further on, Plato speaks of "the kingly weaving process" in which different and even opposed human materials are combined and interwoven.[11]

This perhaps helps to explain why weaving should have struck Plato as so natural a metaphor for statecraft, and why the fine arts, as he understood them, are of no use in thinking about politics at all. It is because Plato held to the theory that the fine arts are mimetic, or imitative, and hence involve nothing he would recognize as originality, since they involve merely copying an external reality. The artists are as passive in this respect as the camera would be. (Aristotle knew the principle of the *camera obscura*, but Plato uses the mirror as his paradigm of the sheer passivity he ascribes to such arts as painting and sculpture.) Imitation, of course, played a central role in the educational programs of his ideal state, but the problem for him would be one of finding the right models to imitate rather than the problem of imitating itself, which he must have regarded as relatively natural. The beauty of the weaving metaphor is that each move made by the weaver has the whole fabric in view, and although we know that this would be something of concern to painters, concerned as they were to make, as nineteenth-century terminology has it, *tableaux* rather than *morceaux*—works rather than fragments—none of this seems to have struck Plato in his discussions of mimesis, though it is the primary consideration in regard to constructing the state. The aim of state making is justice, which means, in effect, weaving together the various social virtues without allowing one more than the other to dominate. And it is that which makes weaving so apt a metaphor for statesmanship. The task is "to make the city as a whole as

happy as possible . . . not modeling our ideal of happiness with reference to any one class."[12]

I want to stress that Plato's appropriation of the weaving metaphor is enough more than casual that we can see how natural it would be in the discourse of a business executive today. Plato saw two basic and often opposed kinds of human materials needed to fabricate an enduring society: "Those to whom courage predominates will be treated by the statesman as having the firm warlike character as one might call it. The other will be used by him for what we may likewise call the woof-like strands of the web. He then sets about his task of combining and weaving together these two groups exhibiting their mutually opposed characters."[13]

Plato thought of human beings as having very different natural endowments. As he put it in his last great treatment of these matters, *The Laws*:

> Now just as in the case of a web or other piece of woven work, woof and warp cannot be fashioned of the same threads, but the material of the warp must be of a superior quality—it must be tough, you know, and have a certain tenacity of character, whereas the woof may be softer and display a proper pliancy. Well, the distinction shows that there must be some similar distinction made between citizens. . . . For you must know that there are two things which go to the making of a constitution. The conferring of office on individuals is one; the other is the providing of a code of laws.[14]

Plato had a very vivid sense that various irreducibly different kinds of skill are required if there is to be what we today would call a "sustainable" political order. We need philosophers, guardians, and producers, all of them necessary and none of them dominant. And weaving naturally suggests itself as a metaphor to him because of the way in which these disparate but necessary elements can he held together in a whole that offers shelter, protection, and fulfillment.

Figure 21.1. Sheila Hicks, *Advancing, Beginning to End*, 1970. Photographer: Bastiaan van den Berg.

NOTES

1. This piece was originally written as part of an essay on philosophy and the concept of fabric that was commissioned by the Fabric Workshop in Philadelphia. Its title was "The Tapestry and the Loincloth." A very large section of the essay was published in the celebratory volume that marked the twenty-fifth anniversary of the Fabric Workshop. I hope and expect that one day the entire essay will appear as an integral whole. Meanwhile, it gives me pleasure to have the section on weaving appear in a volume dedicated to the work of the artist Sheila Hicks.

2. Plato, *The Statesman* (288c), translated by J.B. Skemp, in *Plato: The Collected Dialogues, including the Letters*, edited by Edith Hamilton and Huntington Cairns (Princeton: Princeton University Press, 1989).

3. *Statesman* 279a–b.

4. *Statesman* 305e.

5. *Statesman* 311e.

6. Homer, *Iliad*, translated by Richmond Lattimore (Chicago: University of Chicago Press, 1951): III.125–28.

7. Plato, *The Republic* (V.455c), translated by Paul Shorey, in Hamilton and Cairns, eds., *Plato: The Collected Dialogues* (1989).

8. Thomas Hardy, *The Dynasts, a drama of the Napoleonic wars, in three parts, nineteen acts, & one hundred and thirty scenes, the time covered by the action being about ten years*, part I, *Fore-Scene* (London: Macmillan, 1925).

9. Immanuel Kant, "Beautiful Art is the Art of Genius," *Critique of Judgment*, translated by J.H. Bernard (New York: Hafner, 1951): 150–51.

10. *Statesman* 284a.

11. *Statesman* 309b.

12. *Republic* V.466a.

13. *Statesman* 309 b.

14. Plato, *The Laws* V.734e–735, translated by A.E. Taylor, in Hamilton and Cairns, eds., *Plato: The Collected Dialogues*.

22

FIBER ART AND THE HIERARCHY OF ART AND CRAFT, 1960–80

Elissa Auther

Editor's introduction: In this article, published in the first issue of the *Journal of Modern Craft*, Elissa Auther lays out many of the ideas that are explored in her book-length project *String, Felt, Thread and the Hierarchy of Art and Craft in American Art*, published in 2009. The use of textile materials and techniques in American art of the 1960s and 1970s and the efforts of Mildred Constantine and Jack Lenor Larsen to "elevate" this work are addressed. Auther's research strategy pays considerable attention to factors that are seemingly peripheral to the actual objects under discussion. Through the adoption of this broader view, the curators, galleries, collectors, and social networks that have had a significant impact on the reception and definition of work as sculpture (made from fiber) or fiber art (struggling for validation) are brought to light. Auther shows that the value systems that are used to legitimate much of our visual art often involve considerations and loyalties that go well beyond the physical object in question.

Alan Saret's *Untitled* (1968) . . . , a work of rope and wire and Alice Adams's *Construction* (1966) . . . , of rope and steel cable, share significant formal similarities. Both works are floor based, of similar size and shape, and both utilize materials associated with "craft," hand labor or industry. Indeed, one could conclude that the same artist made both works. But this is not the case, and the two artists were associated with very different artistic circles in the 1960s: Saret was an anti-form sculptor, whereas Adams was associated with what came to be known as the fiber art movement. Moreover, the works were exhibited and received very differently. Comparing the varied reception of these two similar objects reveals not only fiber's arrival as a new medium of "high art" but also how this elevation of fiber issued from multiple sites or positions, each with a distinct location within the complex network of power relations governed by the application of the term "craft" in the United States in the 1960s and 1970s.

In 1972, Mildred Constantine—a former curator of architecture and design at the Museum of Modern Art (MoMA), New York—reproduced Adams's *Construction* in *Beyond Craft*, the first in-depth study of the emerging fiber art movement.[1] This important text, co-authored with textile designer Jack Lenor Larsen, chronicled the movement's evolution, defined its aesthetic priorities

Source: Elissa Auther, "Fiber Art and the Hierarchy of Art and Craft, 1960–80," *Journal of Modern Craft* 1, no. 1 (2008) pp. 13–34. Reproduced with permission.

and defended work made of fiber as "fine art." In 1963, Adams's unorthodox woven works had been included in New York's Museum of Contemporary Crafts' exhibition *Woven Forms . . .* , a show that Constantine and Larsen's study singled out as groundbreaking.[2]

Significantly, critic Lucy Lippard also exhibited Adams's *Construction* in her eclectic, "postminimalist" show *Eccentric Abstraction*, at the Fischbach Gallery in New York in 1966. . . . Unlike *Beyond Craft*, *Eccentric Abstraction* situated Adams's *Construction* among avant-garde work by such emerging artists as Eva Hesse, Bruce Nauman and Keith Sonnier. The show's works utilized a variety of non-traditional, flexible media, including wire mesh, vinyl, cloth and rope.

Saret exhibited *Untitled* in 1970 in New York's Sidney Janis Gallery's January group show *String and Rope . . .* , alongside works by Christo, Fred Sandback, Bruce Nauman and Robert Morris. *Arts Magazine*, one of the era's major fine-art periodicals, reproduced Saret's piece and a critic writing for the *Christian Science Monitor* noted the use of fiber as an autonomous abstract element. The "artists included," he wrote, "use string or rope (or thread), not as line, but as falling, tangling, stretching, or coiling matter" (Andreae 1970: 58).[3]

Studies like *Beyond Craft* (1972), exhibitions such as *Woven Forms* (1963), *Eccentric Abstraction* (1966) and *String and Rope* (1969), and works in fiber like Saret's and Adams's are representative of a number of projects in the 1960s and 1970s that signaled fiber's potential as a fine-art medium and illustrate different relations to the art world's center of power. In each case, fiber, that is, craft—typically dismissed or even invisible as a force shaping the art world in this period—was in actuality central to its constitution. *Beyond Craft* and *Woven Forms* attempted to elevate fiber from the realm of "craft" to that of "art" and were undertaken by individuals and institutions dedicated to legitimating new work in materials traditional to craft. The goal of legitimating so-called fiber art as "Art" sets these projects apart from exhibitions

such as *Eccentric Abstraction* and *String and Rope*, which attempted to capture sculpture's latest vanguard. Here craft functioned as a conceptual limit, essential to the elevation of art—in the words of Glenn Adamson, as "a border that can never be reached, but is nonetheless intrinsic to any sense of position" (Adamson 2007: 2). *Eccentric Abstraction* and *String and Rope* were both produced by members of the art world whose authority in itself legitimated the work in question, a privilege not fully extended to Constantine and Larsen. Rather than focusing on whether Saret's *Untitled* was a work of art, these exhibitions theorized the artistic use of fiber and fiber-like materials in relation to previous examples of nontraditional media in sculpture and to other conditions, such as craft, that oppose the definition of art.

Despite these differences in the projects' orientations and goals, they all probed fiber's symbolic power, paradoxically generated by its subordination in the history of art through deep-rooted associations with utility or craft, a phenomenon Saret's and Adams's works also illuminate. In challenging the subordination of fiber as a medium of craft or of primarily utilitarian value, Adams's and Saret's works additionally illustrate the role fiber played in testing the art world's aesthetic boundaries in the 1960s and 1970s. Yet, with the exception of Adams's *Construction*, which circulated widely, the status of "high art" remained elusive for the objects that Constantine and Larsen featured in *Beyond Craft*. In fact, fiber art in this period was typically viewed as neither art nor craft, but as between the two categories, thwarting the works' potential to undermine the hierarchy of media responsible for fiber's low aesthetic status.

This article examines the efforts of Mildred Constantine—the movement's principal architect and supporter—and her collaborator Jack Lenor Larsen to eliminate this ambiguity, securing fiber's identity as a medium of high art. Their strategy was defined by the goal of assimilating fiber-based work to the fine arts and did not address the fact that the boundary separating art from craft is constructed rather than natural. Although this strategy led to an unfortunate collusion with the very hierarchy of media they sought to transform and in hindsight might seem obviously flawed, my analysis suggests that the options available to them as defenders of fiber art were tremendously constrained by the period's artistic discourse defining the work of art, particularly its autonomy from social contexts and practices outside the art world with which fiber was intimately connected. The reasons surrounding the art world's resistance to fiber art were complex and varied, involving the cultural connotations of fiber, popular trends in fiber crafts and gender bias deriving from fiber's association with women and the domestic realm; with such factors working against their project, perhaps no curatorial strategy Constantine and Larsen could have adopted at the time would have fared better.

THE AESTHETIC STATUS OF FIBER IN THE 1960S AND 1970S

In 1961, with Lenore Tawney's solo exhibition at the Staten Island Museum, fiber art as it would be recognized in the following two decades made its public debut in a fine-art context. The show consisted of forty works produced between 1955 and 1961 in a technique now referred to as open-warp weave: a structure in which large parts of the warp are left unwoven. The reception of this and subsequent work demonstrates that from the start fiber artists experienced considerable resistance from the realms of both craft and fine art for the way their work violated conventions of both practices. Tawney recalled that her early "open-warp weaves . . . caused quite a controversy [amongst weavers]. No one had done this kind of weaving . . . It's against the rules and those people who go by the rules were against it" (Tawney 1978: n.p.).

However, posing a challenge to the definition of weaving in the 1960s did not automatically confer the status of "art" on Tawney's work; in the "high" art world too, her work's identity was unstable. For instance, the small catalog for Tawney's

1961 exhibition reveals that on the one hand the show was sponsored by the "Section of Handcrafts" but elsewhere attempts to position Tawney as a "fine artist." In particular, the appreciation written by Tawney's close friend, painter Agnes Martin, defends her artistic identity, praising the work's "originality" and its relation to larger art-world trends toward exploring new media.

Before Tawney's Staten Island Museum show was even mounted, the artist had started using her open-warp method to combine different weave structures in a single work by dividing and redividing the warp as the weave was in progress. The resulting works, which she called "woven forms" . . . , were monumental in scale, departed from the rectilinear shape of loom-woven fabrics and were not even remotely utilitarian. Given their size, which ranged from 11 to 27 feet (3.3 to 8.1 m) in height, their abstraction (like some of her earlier open-warp weaves, the "woven forms" have no pictorial content) and Tawney's method of hanging them from the ceiling, her work sharply departed from the conventions of the "decorative wall hanging," the category in which weaves without everyday utility were normally classified in the 1960s.

Yet this work too fell between accepted divisions between art and craft. For instance, Tawney's 1962 solo exhibition at the Art Institute of Chicago was installed in the Textiles Department and *Woven Forms*, the 1963 group show at the Museum of Contemporary Crafts that included her work, also institutionally situated her weaving as craft. Even so, a reviewer for the *New York Times* remarked that Tawney "is more than just a weaver—she is also an artist. Unfortunately, craft work has for many years implied to the general public work done by amateurs . . . with little merit . . . Miss Tawney's craft is in marked contrast to this mistaken concept and her woven forms are considered by experts to be works of fine art" (O'Brien 1963).

This reviewer's willingness to embrace Tawney's work as "fine art" against prevailing sentiment that connected craft media to the amateur or hobbyist, however, was more the exception than the rule. Subsequent reviews continued to question her work's artistic status. As late as 1990, on the occasion of Tawney's retrospective at the American Craft Museum, Roberta Smith drew a negative conclusion in her review for the *New York Times*, leaving the impression that the intervening years had done little to resolve questions about the works' status and identity within the art world: "Mrs. Tawney's work exists in a limbo that is endemic to much contemporary craft: it has departed from craft and function without quite arriving at art . . . Handsome and impressive as her best efforts often are . . . [m]ost of them sustain comparison neither to such achievements in weaving as Navajo blankets, nor to contemporary painting and sculpture" (Smith 1990).

Smith's evaluation presents another facet of the picture that often consigned Tawney's work to an art world "limbo," the artist's refusal of the utilitarian associations of craft. Instead of exploring this aspect of her work, however, Smith uses Tawney's departure from utility or function to reassert the differences between craft (Navajo weaving) and art (painting and sculpture) that the woven forms actually complicated.

These equivocations over the value of Tawney's woven work indicate the institutional obstacles artists, critics and curators of fiber art faced in trying to legitimate their work or the genre of fiber art. Examining Constantine and Larsen's efforts to consecrate fiber art provides an opportunity to look more systematically at the questions of artistic legitimacy that Tawney's work provoked.

WALL HANGINGS

The first major American exhibition of the new genre of fiber art was MoMA's *Wall Hangings* . . . , co-curated by Constantine and, at her invitation, Larsen. With this exhibition, the two established themselves as the fiber movement's leading experts and also set the canon of vanguard fiber art (or "Art Fabric," as they called it). *Wall Hangings* presented to the American museum-going public the first international survey of primarily large-scale, abstract woven and off-loom work in fiber. Planned by Constantine since 1966, the exhibition toured eleven cities in 1968, returning in early 1969 to MoMA, where it was installed, at Constantine's insistence, in the museum's first-floor special exhibition galleries, rather than in the Department of Architecture and Design. To the American fiber world's leading triumvirate of Lenore Tawney, Sheila Hicks . . . and Claire Zeisler, Constantine and Larsen added Kay Sekimachi . . . , Walter Nottingham and Ed Rossbach, among others. Some of the exhibition's most advanced work came from abroad, including that of the Swiss Françoise Grossen, Yugoslavian (Croatian) Jagoda Buic, and Poles Magdalena Abakanowicz and Wojcieh Sadley, whose woven forms radically departed from the conventions of tapestry as practiced in Europe at the time.

Regrettably, given the exhibition's importance in the history of the American fiber movement, the only national art-world press *Wall Hangings* received was a review that *Craft Horizons* commissioned from sculptor Louise Bourgeois.[4] Bourgeois's response to the show contrasts strikingly with the curatorial statement written by Constantine and Larsen for the exhibition catalog. Whereas they asserted: "During the last ten years, developments in weaving have caused us to revise our concepts of this craft and to view the work within the context of twentieth-century art" (1969: n.p.), Bourgeois concluded:

> The pieces in the show rarely liberate themselves from decoration . . . A painting or a sculpture makes great demand on the onlooker at the same time that it is independent of him. These weaves, delightful as they are, seem more engaging and less demanding. If they must be classified, they would fall somewhere between fine and applied art. (Bourgeois 1969: 33f)

These opposing evaluations speak to the period's symbolic boundaries between art and non-art and such boundaries' centrality to maintaining a hierarchy of media separating fine art from craft. They also point to a set of real and conceptual obstacles heavily borne by fiber artists and their supporters, who sought to transcend the aesthetic boundaries structuring the art world in the 1960s and 1970s. It is clear that although Bourgeois disagreed with Constantine and Larsen about the works' value, the question of their identity preoccupied them all. This preoccupation continued to burden Constantine and Larsen and subsequent scholars of fiber art, who took up issues of category over the nature of the work itself. Bourgeois also exhibits concern about categories of art, which she strategically upheld in this review by using fiber art to explain what painting and sculpture were not.

Bourgeois's evaluation of the works in *Wall Hangings* as "decoration" traded upon the distinction between art and craft, reasserting the aesthetic boundaries fiber artists and their supporters sought to overcome.[5] In her words, the objects were "delightful" and "engaging." In the writing of modernist critics such as Clement Greenberg, to be either was to succumb to the decorative by making "immediately pleasing" what true artists achieved through rigorous intellectual struggle and risk-taking (Greenberg 1945; 1986: 41). Bourgeois reasserts the high-art status of painting and sculpture by claiming that these genres place a "demand" upon the viewer absent in fiber art. The opposition she reinforces—that between the merely attractive object and that which requires sustained attention—is central to the hierarchy of art and craft, which associates art with the cognitive realm, craft with mere surface effect.

In an interview, Constantine related her reaction to Bourgeois's review of *Wall Hangings*: "I was furious," she reported. "It represented exactly the attitude we were trying to work against" (conversation with the author 1999). Despite their awareness of the negative art-world attitudes concerning media traditionally associated with craft, Constantine and her co-curator attempted to assert fiber's art status by introducing the new genre into the fine art world on the terms set by that

world. This strategy required that they adhere to the dominant philosophy of art voiced by Bourgeois and that they collude in maintaining the hierarchy of media responsible for fiber's general exclusion from "high art."

Two factors in particular made this strategy meaningful to Constantine and Larsen, factors that were themselves effects of the hierarchy of art and craft and indicate its self-perpetuating nature. The most important such factor was that contesting the hierarchy of art and craft rather than assimilating select objects (those without utility, for instance) into the category of "high art" would have been to destabilize the very artistic status they claimed for fiber artists. The identity of fiber artists, because they worked in a medium traditional to craft, required authorization different from that bestowed upon artists working securely within the "high art" world. The necessity of establishing one's art *as art* was a handicap that belonged only to the artist working in craft media. An excellent example of the nearly automatic security afforded the artist with a position within the "high art" world is demonstrated by the critic Hilton Kramer's review of Lucy Lippard's 1966 exhibition *Eccentric Abstraction* for the *New York Times*. About the show, which featured work that radically flouted sculptural conventions of the time, Kramer wrote: "[although the] work is neither painting nor exactly sculpture . . . art—of some sort—it is" (1966). The lack of legitimacy afforded an exhibition such as *Wall Hangings* illustrates that this basic security was not extended to fiber artists in the 1960s and 1970s.

A second factor informing Constantine and Larsen's approach was the fact that overtly challenging the hierarchy of art and craft might also undermine their authority as curators, with negative consequences for fiber art's legitimation. Constantine, like others of her generation at MoMA (she joined the staff in 1948), was committed to the museum's mission of identifying and collecting modern works of the highest achievement in art and design, a goal that included examples of applied art or craft to the extent such objects conformed to modernist norms of innovation and abstraction. Anni Albers's solo exhibition in 1949, MoMA's first exhibition of weaving, exemplifies this approach to craft and design. Albers's association with the Bauhaus, her commitment to experimentation and her adaptation of non-objective form to weaving all reflected the museum's vision of the modern in art.

In the 1960s, exemplary objects of craft and design were still subject to this form of evaluation, which helped to shape Constantine's curatorial vision for *Wall Hangings*. An anecdote of Constantine's about her experience as a curator while MoMA was directed by René d'Harnoncourt is revealing in this regard. Sometime in the mid-1960s a hand-thrown vessel by the celebrated Japanese potter Kitaoji Rosanjin was under consideration for acquisition. In Constantine's account, d'Harnoncourt put this rhetorical question to his curators at the acquisitions meeting: "Do you know when a pot is no longer a pot but a work of art?" (in conversation with the author).[6] To Constantine, such a question affirmed that the distinction to be found between art and craft resided *in* the object rather than being culturally projected onto it. Such an assumption underscores Constantine and Larsen's confidence regarding the art status they asserted for the objects exhibited in *Wall Hangings*.

The story also foregrounds the authority that rested in the curator (in the capacity of his or her "eye") to discern quality in objects of cultural significance—that is, to distinguish between good and bad, "high" and "low," "fine art" and mere "craft."[7] A theory of boundary maintenance in the arts that pointed to the role of extra-aesthetic factors such as gender, different contexts of production, or cultural presumptions about craft in the production of distinctions of value had the potential to undermine this curatorial and ultimately institutional form of power in the 1960s. To the extent that the authorization of an object as art is only as good (that is, as convincing) as the authority of the authorizer, undercutting the myth of the "good eye," could result in the

forfeiture of institutional validation required by a new genre or movement.

A straightforward way of approaching the conception of value that Constantine and Larsen used—a conception of value as intrinsic to an object—is to consider it alongside the recontextualization of non-Western objects from ethnographic specimens to works of art, a taxonomic shift to which Constantine and Larsen's conception is related. Recent anthropological and art historical considerations of shifts in classifying objects previously recognized for their ethnographic value demonstrate that museum strategies of acquisition and display that elide issues of context, technique and utility in favor of disinterested contemplation of an object according to a modernist theory of art are premised upon art's autonomy from the social realm.[8] As Mary Anne Staniszewski has shown in her study of the history of exhibitions at MoMA, the type of installation now considered standard in fine-art museums—in which works are spotlit, arranged at eye level on a neutral-colored wall and widely spaced—emerged in the US in the 1930s.[9] This type of installation, which "facilitated appreciation of the singular artwork," was also applied to the exhibition of ethnic "artifacts" in museums in the 1930s and 1940s, reflecting a growing aesthetic appreciation of non-Western objects. In general, the aestheticized display of ethnographic objects suppressed issues of utility and highlighted form, creating an atemporal, formalist viewing experience unencumbered by the social formations that gave rise to the work. As scholars of exhibition history have pointed out, this reconceptualization confirms the aesthetic categories and assumptions of the West's "high art," leaving intact the hierarchy of the arts and stripping those aspects of non-Western objects in conflict with that hierarchy's values.

Constantine, who assisted d'Harnoncourt in a major exhibition that employed this strategy—1954's *Ancient Art of the Andes*—was familiar with such a curatorial strategy and it undoubtedly influenced the conception of *Wall Hangings* and subsequent fiber-art projects. As installation photographs of the show suggest . . . , Constantine and Larsen hung the work according to a method of displaying painting and sculpture calculated to enhance the objects' visual impact and autonomy. Although such installation was by then typical at MoMA for painting and sculpture, its adoption in *Wall Hangings* can be seen as strategic given fiber's lack of autonomy—that is, its extensive use in cultural and practical contexts outside the art world. The exhibition displayed works in relative isolation within the austere, white-walled special exhibition galleries. This strategy was carried over to the catalog, which lacked detailed information about technique and enhanced the works' formal qualities by using photographs in which each object was suspended in space against a dark ground, a classic mid-century method of photographing ethnic objects that privileged form over implied utility.[10]

Constantine and Larsen's approach to the consecration of fiber art has a logic rooted in a belief in formalism as a democratic, legitimating discourse capable of transforming any work into an object of pure, aesthetic contemplation. As the negative reception of *Wall Hangings* suggests, however, applying a formalist exhibition strategy did not resolve the hierarchy of art and craft Constantine and Larsen sought to transcend. An important factor at play here is the way fiber's "low" aesthetic status derived in part from its extensive use in cultural and practical contexts outside the art world. Briefly examining these contexts illuminates the larger challenge that Constantine and Larsen faced in attempting to elevate fiber as a medium of "high art."

UTILITY AND AMATEURISM

Outside the "high" art world, fiber gained a new visibility in the United States in the 1960s and 1970s with revivals of the traditional crafts of hand weaving, quilting, embroidery, dyeing, knotting and basketry. The social and artistic contexts and practices surrounding these revivals

included the back-to-the-land and hippie movements, the renewed interest in folk art around the American Bicentennial, trends in the personalization of clothing like the adoption of African dress by African Americans, the feminist recuperation of women's history, the revival of traditional arts of minority communities in the South and Southwest, and the popular craze of macramé. Increased funding from the National Endowment for the Arts to support regional arts and a burgeoning commercial market for craft and folk art bolstered interest in such work.[11] These contexts and practices demonstrate both the richness of what ought to be defined as a major craft revival in the United States in the 1960s and 1970s and the difficulty, for fiber artists, of distinguishing their work from this nebulous conglomeration.

The frequent connection made between fiber art and macramé—an association encouraged by fiber artists' extensive use of off-loom techniques such as knotting, looping, linking and plaiting—shows why fiber artists strove to distinguish their work from popular craft. The term macramé, which denotes a form of lateral knotting probably Arabic in origin, referred in the late 1960s and 1970s to a genre of useful objects (jewelry, belts, handbags, lampshades, plant holders and hammocks, for instance) produced using "decorative" knotting techniques. Macramé's enormous popularity is attested to by the fact that fiber artist and macramé specialist Mary Walker Phillip's best-selling book *Step-by-Step Macramé* (1970) had sold more than a million copies by 1976. In 1971, macramé's mass cultural appeal even led the Museum of American Folk Art in New York to organize a major exhibition on the subject as part of its NEA-funded series, *Rediscovery of Grass Roots America*.[12] Unusually, this exhibition placed contemporary macramé within the larger history of knotted-fabric construction, bringing together, among other examples, seventeenth- and eighteenth-century European lace, knotted fabrics and jewelry of North American Indians, the decorative knotted work of sailors from the nineteenth and twentieth centuries, and the large-scale knotted work of fiber artist Françoise Grössen, which emphasized the fiber art-macramé connection.

The macramé hobby craze was problematic for the fiber movement because it reinforced assumptions about fiber as a woman's medium or of "low" art status. In her 1979 interview for *Arts Magazine*, Claire Zeisler . . . took advantage of a question about technique to distinguish her knotting (often in macramé) from the "decorative" knots used by "macramé artists," suggesting the sensitivity of the topic for artists working in fiber.

J. PATRICE MARANDEL: In your own mind, do techniques such as knotting or cutting . . . set you apart from other fiber artists?

CLAIRE ZEISLER: When I first started knotting, it was not a trend . . . You certainly have heard the word *macramé*. Some people referred to my work as Claire Zeisler's macramé. That's when I hit the ceiling . . . I do mind the word macramé because macramé today means a decorative knot and I use my knotting technique as structure . . . The knot becomes the base for the piece, like the canvas is the base for a painting. (*Arts Magazine* 1979: 151f)

Zeisler's insistence on distinguishing between her work and popular craft underscores the degree to which macramé had become a cultural phenomenon that impinged upon the fiber movement's bid for status as art. It is likely that Zeisler's discussion of technique in the pages of *Arts Magazine*—then a leading periodical of contemporary art that rarely dedicated copy to work in traditional craft media—was a deliberate attempt to persuade readers that work in fiber shared important features with art rather than the popular hobby of macramé. Her reference to knotting as integral to the "structure" of her pieces emphasizes her art's formalist nature, as does her explicit parallel between her work and painting. The latter comparison places her work firmly in the category of

"high art" by invoking its pre-eminent medium to highlight not craft-oriented technique but art-oriented practice. Zeisler's rhetorical strategy was similar to that adopted by numerous fiber artists and their supporters who were working to change the place of fiber in the art world's traditional hierarchy, dismissing its connections to activities classified as "non-art."

This effort was actually initiated some years earlier by Anni Albers, who in 1940 entered into a debate over the function and value of hand weaving with Mary Atwater, America's leading spokesperson for the non-professional weaver, in the pages of *The Weaver*, a nationally distributed quarterly for the American hand-weaving community. Atwater and Albers's conflict over the meaning and role of textiles not only helps to demonstrate how deep the association of amateurism with fiber runs, but also points to another serious hurdle fiber artists (working on or off the loom) faced in defining their work as art in the 1960s and 1970s—fiber's gendered associations.

Atwater, perhaps best known as the founder of the Shuttle Craft Guild and its correspondence course in weaving in 1920, advocated a view of weaving as a leisure-time or therapeutic activity. She also researched nineteenth-century weaving traditions, publishing her findings alone or in publications for hand weavers. Her research was instrumental to the survival of these historical and regional practices, but her practical how-to approach ran counter to the idea of weaving as an art form. As Ed Rossbach put it, "She told Americans what to weave, how to weave, [and] what to do with their weavings" (Rossbach 1983: 22).[13]

Unlike Atwater, Albers regarded herself as an artist and was particularly outspoken regarding hand weaving's potential to move beyond a leisure pursuit with utilitarian imperatives. She encapsulated her views in a statement from 1959 that implored, "let threads be articulate . . . and find a form for themselves to no other end than their own orchestration, not to be sat on, walked on, only to be looked at" (Albers 1959: 5).

Albers's article for *The Weaver* commented upon the state of contemporary hand weaving in the United States and illustrated textiles produced by her students at Black Mountain College in North Carolina.[14] The publication coincided with the height of the Appalachian craft revival, in which weaving played a major role, providing the immediate context for her sharp critique of "recipes" and "traditional formulas, which once proved successful" (Albers 1940: 3). Albers argued that "such work is often no more than a romantic attempt to recall a *temps perdu*" and that it reflected the state of "isolation" and "degeneration" of US hand weaving in the period (Albers 1940: 3). Albers called for a return to "fundamentals" and free experimentation on and off the loom to foster innovation and she suggested that the resulting development of new forms in fiber could be art.

Atwater, who had no interest in the imperatives of industry, modern design, or art, responded to Albers with the predictably titled piece "It's Pretty—But is it Art?" which she published in her advice column for *The Weaver*.[15] Not surprisingly, Atwater took offense at Albers's criticisms of faithfulness to tradition and reproduction of historical patterns (or "recipes," as Atwater called them). Atwater found the idea that a textile might lack utility or be considered art preposterous and she asserted that fiber and weaving were essentially useful and of value primarily as an "escape from the distresses or the hum-drum detail of our daily lives" (Atwater 1941: 13). Atwater responded to Albers's emphasis upon experimentation, imagination and the creation of new forms (key elements of modernism in the arts) with similar disdain, defending the right of her readers (mostly women isolated at home with little access to artistic training) to draw aesthetic pleasure from weaving regardless of their level of expertise or whether they relied upon a pattern. Atwater's acceptance, even promotion, of her audience's amateurism raises the issue of fiber's connections to femininity and domesticity, associations that plagued fiber artists in the 1960s and 1970s.

FEMININITY AND DOMESTICITY

As Rozsika Parker and Griselda Pollock asserted over twenty-five years ago in their groundbreaking study *Old Mistresses: Women, Art and Ideology*, "the sex of the artist matters. It conditions the way art is seen and discussed" (Parker and Pollock 1981: 50). This is nowhere more evident in the late twentieth century than in the history of the fiber movement, whose status and reception was affected by weaving's near-universal association with women and the domestic realm.

At its worst, the effort to challenge the gendering of fiber as "women's work" actually reinforced its association with femininity and its low place in the art-world hierarchy. In the late 1960s, when off-loom techniques rose to prominence, the work of fiber artists adopting these techniques was interpreted as free from the craft tradition's conventional values by virtue of their rejection of the loom. Critics such as Rose Slivka posited an antithesis between loom and off-loom construction techniques, praising the latter's superior artistic quality. In the provocatively titled piece "Hard String," her review of the 1972 group exhibition *Sculpture in Fiber* for *Craft Horizons*, Slivka characterized the loom as an impotent instrument, a gendering of technology that had the unintended effect (as did the title of the show) of associating off-loom fiber art with the perceived masculine virility of modern art.[16]

Not surprisingly, given this context, the housewife is a key figure in critical considerations of fiber art, where she signifies amateurism and lack of creativity. In criticism about fiber art, this set of associations often had to be overcome before the writer could consider a work of fiber art worthy of discursive attention. Fiber's problematic association with the domestic accounts for the distinctly confessional tone or hedging found in fiber-art criticism that invokes the figure of the housewife. Katherine Kuh's article about the work of Lenore Tawney and Claire Zeisler for *Saturday Review* in 1968, "Sculpture: Woven and Knotted," is typical. Despite her eventual enthusiasm, Kuh opens the article by admitting her own negative assumptions about weaving, shared, presumably, by her readers: "Until recently, I always considered weaving a ladylike pursuit for frustrated housewives, but I am drastically changing my mind. The best weavers are, to be sure, still women, but some of them are also first-rate artists" (Kuh 1968: 36). The use of the qualification "also," as in "also first-rate artists," echoes George O'Brien's language in his review of Tawney's work in the 1963 exhibition *Woven Forms* cited earlier. In that piece, Tawney is "more than a weaver—she is also an artist," a qualification that O'Brien used later in the review to question craft's amateur associations. In Kuh's assessment, the amateur associations of craft are now inflected by gender, yet another barrier to participation in the art world in this period faced by fiber artists—a problem shared by female artists generally, in fact. Critic Gregory Battcock's review of Claire Zeisler's show at the Richard Feigen gallery in 1969 provides another example of how the image of the housewife was used to great effect in backhanded compliments during the 1960s:

Mops, floppiness and house-wifey dumpiness might distract the viewer, but only momentarily. The colors are certainly more arresting than the Sheriff in Darien Conn. and the general tone is more elegant than The Hilton Inn. Zeisler's sculptures emphasize texture at the expense of form and since texture is emphasized in just the right way, it's O.K. (Battcock 1969: 65)

For Kuh the housewife is capable but frustrated, while for Battcock she is dumpy—differences that might have to do with the differing gender of the two critics or the audience for whom they were writing. In any case, Battcock's idea of the housewife and the comparison of Zeisler's work to mops remove fiber from even the sphere of craft, downgrading it to drudgery. Ultimately, Kuh's and Battcock's language permits notice of Zeisler's work only to the extent that their own

critical authority regarding the evaluation of art is assured.

This brief examination of fiber's extra-aesthetic associations sheds additional light on Constantine and Larsen's approach to elevating fiber in a manner that completely elided its history as a craft and its presence in numerous contemporary non-art contexts. Alternate approaches proved no more successful and further demonstrate the severity of the constraints they faced in championing a material historically categorized and marginalized as craft.

For instance, hybrid categories that could bridge the divide between "art" and "craft," presumably better accommodating fiber art, also faced serious resistance in the art world. Two such categories were "soft art" and "soft sculpture." Both functioned as organizing rubrics for several shows in the late 1960s and 1970s such as the New Jersey State Museum's *Soft Art* (1969), curated by Ralph Pomeroy; Lucy Lippard's traveling exhibition for the American Federation of the Arts, *Soft and Apparently Soft Sculpture* (1968–9); and the New York Cultural Center's traveling exhibition, *Softness as Art* (1973). *Soft Art* included work by Tawney as well as Richard Tuttle, Robert Morris, Eva Hesse and Claes Oldenburg. *Softness as Art* included one work by Françoise Grössen, amongst that of Jackie Ferrara, Harmony Hammond, Richard Serra, Robert Morris and Hannah Wilke. Fiber artists recognized the potential of the categories "soft art" or "soft sculpture" to bridge the divide separating art from craft. In a 1970 article for *Craft Horizons*, "When Will Weaving Be an Art Form?" Virginia Hoffman observed that "soft sculpture"

could logically include any three-dimensional form made by flexible joinings, fibrous materials, modules with no fixed beginning or end, soft materials made hard and vice versa . . . One thinks of . . . works by Eva Hesse, Alan Saret, Robert Morris, [and] Alice Adams. (Hoffman 1970: 18)[17]

However, art critics were not as enthusiastic about the soft art phenomenon. Some went to great lengths to reassert boundaries between genres and materials that the rubric blurred. In his *Artforum* review of the New York Cultural Center's exhibition, *Soft as Art*, James Collins asserted, "one of the things artists shouldn't do today is to make art with anything soft" (Collins 1973: 89). Most problematic for him was the category itself, which "denies criticism the luxury of a single critical framework" (Collins 1973: 89). His response to this dilemma was to divide the work in the show into four categories: "process," "revamped painting," "craft/fetish," and "novelty art." In his review these categories redrew boundaries distinguishing "art" from "craft" through a separation of works in fiber into either the "process" category or the "craft/fetish" category. In the "process" category, Collins singled out a felt work by Robert Morris (along with a work by Richard Serra) as worthy of attention for its "theoretical underpinnings" (Collins 1973: 89). The rest of the work in the exhibition was "neither experientially nor theoretically interesting" (Collins 1973: 90). In the "craft/fetish" category, Collins placed the work of Françoise Grössen, Jackie Ferrara and Brenda Miller, all of whom exhibited work in fiber.

Anticipating readers' objections to his application of the term craft to the work of three female artists working in rope and other forms of fiber, Collins asserted that "labeling a work as craft orientated isn't an attack on women" (Collins 1973: 90). He continued:

[it] is only to say they give the impression of manual over mental dexterity and people who are manually dextrous aren't necessarily interesting artists . . . Both Jackie Ferrara with her *Four Balls II* made of cotton bailing, rope and chains and Brenda Miller's *Abscissa*, consisting of a numbering system dictating the structure of a twine wall piece just by the use and association of their materials suggest a "grass skirt" reference—a gender neutral one. (Collins 1973: 90)

That the term "grass skirt" in this context is not gender neutral hardly requires elucidation. By rejecting the hybrid category "soft art" and reinforcing fiber's association to femininity and primitiveness, Collins neatly maintains the boundary between art and craft. Given the degree to which fiber's associations to craft overwhelm Collins's response to Ferrara and Miller's work, one can imagine how easily the hybrid character of work by fiber artists such as Grossen, Sheila Hicks, or Ed Rossbach could be dismissed as illegitimate.

Thanks to such challenging associations, Constantine and Larsen's goal of elevating fiber art, in *Wall Hangings* and subsequent projects, was difficult if not impossible to accomplish in the 1960s and 1970s. In addition, their acceptance of the division between "high" and "low" art—and, one might argue, their refusal to engage with the very non-art connotations of fiber that were so problematic for their goals—left art-world prejudices intact. Despite Constantine and Larsen's efforts, the work of Alan Saret—a male artist who had worked previously in other media and was part of the "high" art world—was critically received as art, while Alice Adams's remarkably similar work—emerging from her previous practice as a weaver—was viewed with skepticism.

Despite these setbacks, however, evidence suggests that Constantine and Larsen's work did make an impact, albeit one that did not come to fruition until fairly recently. In 1993 the well-known independent curator Mary Jane Jacob wrote about the influence of Constantine upon her own innovative, unorthodox, curatorial mission, which has been instrumental in promoting an open use of non-traditional materials without regard to the art world's hierarchical distinctions:

Unbeknownst to me, I began following [Constantine's] work as a young visitor to The Museum of Modern Art on frequent occasions from 1965 to 1969. Reading and just looking at the images in *Beyond Craft* sent my own curatorial work in another direction. Most of all, her avantgarde philosophy of inclusionism remains compelling and her career—battling to bring into the mainstream art and artists from the outside—is a model of independent vision and courage. (Jacob 1993: 9)

Dramatic change in the use and reception of fiber in the art world *has* occurred since the 1970s, thanks in part to curators such as Jacob, as well as artists of the first-wave feminist art movement, who set as one of their goals the analysis of the hierarchy of art and craft and women's low position within it through the incorporation of fiber into their work. For feminists, fiber craft played a role in the construction of an alternate history of art making. A shared marginality between the female traditional artist and the contemporary feminist artist helped the latter negotiate the paradoxical goal of seeking recognition in the mainstream art world, while at the same time attempting to critique it. In this context, the once negative associations of fiber or craft with femininity and the home were recast as distinctive and culturally valuable features of an artistic heritage specific to women.

While I'm not convinced that the use of fiber by artists today demonstrates the complete effacement of the hierarchy of art and craft, the medium's ubiquitous use in contemporary art no doubt represents an important stage in a decades-long process of art-world assimilation of the medium. The evolution of Louise Bourgeois's attitude toward fiber—from one of dismissal in the 1960s to full embrace with her latest soft sculptures made from her personal collection of linens and fabric remnants—is only one example of the medium's new currency. The limitations of their strategy aside, the work of Constantine and Larsen in the 1960s and 1970s to legitimate fiber as a medium of art represents a historically important moment in this process.

NOTES

1. Constantine, Mildred and Larsen, Jack Lenor. 1972. *Beyond Craft: The Art Fabric*. New York: Van Nostrand. For an assessment of Constantine's career see Sorkin, Jenni. 2003. Way Beyond Craft: Thinking Through the Work of Mildred Constantine. *Textile* 1(1): 30–47.

2. *Woven Forms*. 1963. New York: Museum of Contemporary Craft.

3. See also Atirnomus, "String and Rope at Janis." *Arts Magazine*. February 1970: 58.

4. Bourgeois, Louis. 1969. "The Fabric of Construction." *Craft Horizons* 29 (March): 31–35.

5. On the subject, see my 2004 essay "The Decorative, Abstraction and the Hierarchy of Art and Craft in the Art Criticism of Clement Greenberg," in *Oxford Art Journal* 27(3): 339–64.

6. Constantine also recounts this experience in *The Art Fabric: Mainstream* (New York: Van Nostrand Reinhold, 1981, p. 8).

7. Thanks to Judith Bettelheim, Constantine's daughter, for helping me clarify this point.

8. On the subject, see Marcus, George E. and Myers, Fred R. (eds). 1995. *Traffic in Culture: Refiguring Art and Anthropology*. Berkeley: University of California Press.

9. Staniszewski, Mary Anne. 1998. *The Power of Display: A History of Exhibition Installations at the Museum of Modern Art*. Cambridge, MA: MIT Press, chapter two, passim.

10. See Price, Sally. 1989. *Primitive Art in Civilized Places*. Chicago: University of Chicago Press; and Staniszewski (1998).

11. See National Endowment for the Arts. 1977. *To Survey American Crafts: A Planning Study*; and McLean, John. (ed.). 1981. *National Crafts Planning Project*. National Endowment for the Arts.

12. See *Macramé*. 1971. New York: Museum of American Folk Art. See also Mary Walker Phillips's review of the exhibition for *Craft Horizons* (December 1971): 62.

13. Rossbach also reported that "[Atwater's] writings were consulted (often a bit sheepishly) by many who deplored her approach to textiles, who did not believe that weavers should be provided with 'recipes,' as she called them, for works that ought to have been creative and individual. I remember the small regard I once felt for Atwater and her coverlet weaves, even

though my first weaving experience consisted of following a pattern carefully selected from her book" (1983: 22).

14. Albers, Anni. 1940. Hand Weaving Today: Textile Work at Black Mountain College. *The Weaver* 6(1): 3–7.

15. Atwater, Mary. 1941. It's Pretty, But is it Art? *The Weaver* 6(3): 13–14 and 26.

16. Slivka, Rose. 1972. Hard String. *Craft Horizons* (April): 16–17.

17. See also Meilach, Dona Z. 1974. *Soft Sculpture and Other Soft Art Forms with Stuffed Fabrics, Fibers and Plastics.* New York: Crown Publishers.

REFERENCES

Adamson, Glenn. 2007. *Thinking Through Craft.* Oxford and New York: Berg.

Albers, Anni. 1940. Hand Weaving Today: Textile Work at Black Mountain College. *The Weaver* 6(1): 3–7.

Albers, Anni. 1959. *Pictorial Weaves.* Cambridge, MA: MIT Press.

Andreae, Christopher. 1970. String and Rope. *The Christian Science Monitor*, January 23.

Atwater, Mary. 1941. It's Pretty, But is it Art? *The Weaver* 6(3): 13–14, 26.

Battcock, Gregory. 1969. Claire Zeisler. *Arts Magazine*, 43(6): 65.

Bourgeois, Louise. 1969. The Fabric of Construction. *Craft Horizons* 29: 31–5.

Collins, James. 1973. Review. *Artforum* 11(10): 89–93.

Constantine, Mildred. 1999. Personal interview with the author, February 23.

Constantine, Mildred and Larsen, Jack Lenor. 1969. *Wall Hangings.* New York: Museum of Modern Art.

Constantine, Mildred and Larsen, Jack Lenor. 1972. *Beyond Craft: The Art Fabric.* New York: Van Nostrand.

Greenberg, Clement. "Review of Exhibitions . . . " 17 November 1945. *The Nation.* Reprinted in John O'Brian, ed. 1986. *Clement Greenberg, The Collected Essays and Criticism.* Vol. 2, *Arrogant Purpose, 1945–1949*: 39–42.

Hoffman, Virginia. 1970. When Will Weaving Be an Art Form? *Craft Horizons* 30: 18.

Jacob, Mary Jane. 1993. Beyond Craft: Curating for Change. *Small Works in Fiber: The Mildred Constantine Collection.* Cleveland, OH: The Cleveland Museum of Art, pp. 1–9.

Kramer, Hilton. 1966. And Now "Eccentric Abstraction": It's Art But Does It Matter? *New York Times* September 25: 27.

Kuh, Katherine. 1968. Sculpture: Woven and Knotted. *Saturday Review.* July 27: 36–7.

Lenore Tawney: A Personal World. 1978. Brookfield, CT: Brookfield Craft Center.

Lippard, Lucy. 1966. *Eccentric Abstraction.* New York: Fischbach Gallery. Reprinted in *The New Sculpture 1965–1975: Between Geometry and Gesture.* 1990. New York: Whitney Museum of American Art, pp. 54–8.

Marandel, J. Patrice. 1979. An Interview with Claire Zeisler. *Arts Magazine* 54(1): 150–152.

O'Brien, George. 1963. Many Materials Used in Unusual Technique. *New York Times.* April 29

Parker, Rozsika and Pollock, Griselda. 1981. *Old Mistresses: Women, Art and Ideology.* New York: Pantheon Books.

Phillips, Mary Walker. 1970. *Step-by-Step Macramé: A Complete Introduction to the Craft of Creative Knotting.* New York: Golden Press.

Rossbach, Ed. 1983. Mary Atwater and the Revival of American Traditional Weaving. *American Craft* 43(2): 22–26.

Smith, Paul. 1963. *Woven Forms.* New York: Museum of Contemporary Craft.

Smith, Roberta. 1990. Lenore Tawney's Work in Fiber and Beyond. *New York Times.* May 18.

String and Rope. December 1969/January 1970. New York: Sidney Janis Gallery.

23

TAPESTRY AND IDENTITY IN AUSTRALIA

Diana Wood Conroy

Editor's introduction: Diana Wood Conroy trained as an archaeologist and is an honorary professional fellow in the Faculty of Creative Arts at the University of Wollongong, Australia. "Texts from the Edge: Tapestry and Identity in Australia" was written in 1994 to accompany the exhibition of the same name. Wood Conroy compares the vitality of tapestry in Australia from the late 1960s onward to the fiber art movement (tackled by Elissa Auther, who uses American examples, in this section) and observes that, much like the majority of Australia's population today, "tapestry is an immigrant." The essay begins with a detailed list of artists who have contributed to the development of tapestry in Australia from the 1960s on. Tapestry is then compared to fiber art with tapestry's permanence (on the textile scale) and historical ties with painting cited as differentiating factors. While critics of the time derogatively referred to fiber art as a "period of the 'hairy monstrosities'" Wood Conroy uses the theoretical insights of psychoanalytic/poststructural thought to reconsider these negative connotations; she positions tapestry in a way similar to Roszika Parker's influential work with Victorian embroidery: as a discipline simultaneously defined by rigid gender and power paradigms but equally available to artists as a medium that can challenge these limiting options.

Not only do we not see the Sirens but we can't even make out the heavens any more. And yet we can still draw that tattered cloth around us, still immerse ourselves in the mutilated stories of the gods. And in the world as in our minds, the same cloth is still being woven.[1]

The persistence of myth in unexpected forms, the Sirens who continue singing against reason, implicate the artists of *Texts from the edge* in an ongoing necessity to weave images in the ordered precision of tapestry. The slow and meditative construction of the woven fabric itself, that tantalising but anachronistic medium, offsets experiences that may well have been tattered, mutilating and fragmenting.

Texts from the edge draws attention to particular areas of current tapestry practice which concern the formation of the individual through the forces of language, gender, migration, place and displacement. These concerns may also be found in the 'cutting edge' of the artworld, but the

Source: Diana Wood Conroy, "Tapestry and Identity in Australia," in *Texts from the Edge: Tapestry and Identity in Australia* [exhibition catalog] (Adelaide, South Australia: Jam Factory, Craft and Design Centre, 1994) pp. 1–6. Reproduced with permission.

edginess of tapestry, and its close relationship to text and narrative (textum, Latin means 'woven fabric') is usually far removed from mainstream exhibition. This edge bounds both art and craft, with allegiances to both areas.

The emergence of artist weavers who individually design and make their own tapestries outside of a workshop is the distinctive focus of this exhibition.

CURATING TEXTS FROM THE EDGE

How did such a collection of work come together? This rare exhibition in a public space of twelve artist weavers from South Australia, Victoria, New South Wales and Tasmania evolved through debates and conferences that have developed since the Melbourne International Tapestry Symposium of 1988. The impetus to broaden and extend the tapestry practice of individual artists was given momentum by the assistance of the Australia Council to allow Marie Cook, Valerie Kirk, Kay Lawrence and Diana Wood Conroy to travel to Lodz in Poland in June 1992 and present papers to the international tapestry conference *Distant lives/Shared voices*.[2] These four artists, with Sara Lindsay and Liz Nettleton, became the 'core' group in discussions with the Jam Factory in November 1992 for a substantial exhibition of tapestry.

At first, the key aim for such an exhibition of tapestry was conceived as historical by the 'core' group. Originally, the scheme was to include many significant tapestry weavers from the 1960s and 1970s in New South Wales and from the highly trained weavers who developed through the Victorian Tapestry Workshop in Melbourne in the 1970s and 1980s.

Ambitious plans at first considered representing New South Wales tapestry weavers working before the establishment of the Victorian Tapestry Workshop in 1976. For example, Margaret Grafton made the earliest commissioned tapestry in Australia for the architect Philip Cox in 1963[3] and Mona Messing made a vast flat woven

tapestry for the John Clancy Auditorium at the University of New South Wales in 1971.[4] Ian Arcus, Tom Moore, Mary and Larry Beeston were all active in fulfilling tapestry commissions in the late 1970s and early 1980s[5] and Lise Cruickshank in the late 1980s.[6] In New South Wales 'tapestry' at this time was often deeply imbued with the structural principles of the burgeoning fibre arts movement, and associated with it.

In Victoria the establishment of the Victorian Tapestry Workshop in 1976 led to the training and employment of many notable weavers who not only interpreted the designs of other artists but also designed and wove their own pieces.

Cresside Collette, Meryl Dumbrell, Joy Smith, Cheryl Thornton and Kate Derum have all contributed to the rich field of tapestry practice in Victoria. Younger artists, such as Catherine Hoffmann have trained with Marie Cook through the influential tapestry course at Warrnambool. Because of the pervasive authority of the Victorian Tapestry Workshop artists in Victoria developed a crisp and intricate 'style' of flatwoven tapestry and a dialogue between the woven and drawn image that is quite different from the New South Wales emphasis on the materiality of medium as content.[7]

South Australia, like Victoria, had also developed a distinguishing emphasis on community tapestries, with tapestry weavers such as Elaine Gardner working collaboratively and as coordinators of community groups.[8] As well, individual bodies of work have come from Pru La Motte (previously Medlin), Gary Benson, Margie Patrick and Sue Rosenthal, artists who have achieved remarkable pieces in tapestry, working both with large commissions in public spaces, and in the private domain.[9] Other tapestry practitioners such as Lucia Pichler are developing a heightened private expression, and working as community artists in the tapestry medium.

The unwieldy nature of a comprehensive survey which would try to give equal balance to all these elements in the different regions soon became evident to the curating group. Such an exhibition of the vibrant diversity of tapestry in Australia must be left for the future, for a larger gallery space and a different curatorial direction.

THE IMAGES: PUBLIC AND PRIVATE

Rather than trying to offer a wide survey of tapestry, *Texts from the edge* centres around issues of contemporary practice, addressing the relationship between tapestry and the painted and drawn image. An intense meditation on personal issues includes tapestries investigating the borders of gender and the innuendos of text, of family histories, of journeys and loss, and perceptions of environment.

Such themes can also seem suddenly to represent with vitality and urgency the public sphere, the artworld search for national identities. For example, Kay Lawrence's *Gender* tapestry, a prior version of the tapestry exhibited here, was shown in the exhibition *Identities: Art from Australia* at the Taipei Fine Arts Museum, Taiwan, earlier in 1994.[10] The bi-sexual image intrigued, and also shocked Taiwanese viewers, who perceived the construction of gender, and the understanding of maternity in their own cultural terms. Kay Lawrence's obsessively personal image took on an 'Australian' quality of forthright directness. The artists in *Texts from the edge* can therefore be seen to explore that edge between private and public, where the symbols of the private imagination come to stand for the wider sphere of national identity.

Tapestry is not only at the art/craft edge, it is also about edges. The way the edge is woven between vertical elements of the image can open up a whole history—dovetailing, sewing, interlocking all have their own adherents in the diverse tapestry traditions of, for example, France, Eastern Europe, Scandinavia, the United Kingdom and the United States of America.

The guidelines of curating *Texts from the edge* required exhibitors to conceive and weave their own pieces with a highly informed intent in both concept and medium, and to have been working and exhibiting consistently in tapestry for a substantial period of time. 'Tapestry' in the curatorial guidelines was defined quite strictly as the traditional Gobelin flat woven technique that is woven in discontinuing wefts that build up blocks of the design between the selvedges of the weaving.

HISTORY AND TRAINING

The lives of several artists in *Texts from the edge* have spanned the short history of tapestry in Australia, and through them we can trace its development. Like so many significant Australian weavers of European origin, tapestry itself is an immigrant, corning from elsewhere to find new life in Australia. Of the artists here, Sara Lindsay, Valerie Kirk and Tass Mavrogordato are from the United Kingdom, and Catherine K is from France. In trying to address the issue of training craftspeople the Crafts Council of Australia in the 1970s[11] did bring out well known weavers from Europe, America and Japan who gave important workshops to cater to the growing interest in tapestry and sculptural weaving.

Lengthy apprenticeships in the skills of tapestry, however, only became available in Australia with the establishment of the Victorian Tapestry Workshop in Melbourne in 1976. Before this time, weavers learnt tapestry overseas. Belinda Ramson studied in Edinburgh with Archie Brennan in 1973, Kay Lawrence also trained there with Maureen Hodge in 1977 and I too learnt tapestry in London in 1969 from Ruth Hurle. Valerie Kirk and Tass Mavrogordato graduated from tapestry courses in United Kingdom art schools before coming to Australia to be teachers themselves. Catherine K studied weaving in the Gobelin Workshops in Paris as recently as 1989, and Robyn Daw also studied in France in 1992.

There are mingled interrelationships between the artists here, who have in many cases been teachers and students together. Before studying her true vocation of tapestry at Edinburgh, Belinda Ramson learnt fabric weaving from Solvig Baas Becking in Canberra in the early 1960s, who had

Figure 23.1. Sara Lindsay, *Throw Away Your Dahlias*, 1993. Woven tapesty, cotton, silk, wool, rayon, 130 × 220 cm. Courtesy of Sara Lindsay.

come to live in Australia from Holland with professional Bauhaus weaving skills. Solvig's husband Dick Baas Becking had made tapestry designs in the French style of Jean Lurcat, who had initiated the great resurgence of tapestry in post-war France. As the first weaving consultant at the Victorian Tapestry Workshop from 1976–1978, Belinda Ramson's teaching has been fundamental to many of the artists in Texts from the Edge, such as Marie Cook, Sara Lindsay, Kay Lawrence and Catherine K. Meryn Jones, Robyn Daw and Leonie Besant have worked closely with Marie Cook and Sara Lindsay at the Victorian Tapestry Workshop, with which Liz Nettleton has also been associated.

The main influence in the Australian tapestry presented here has certainly been the witty and controlled use of the medium made famous by Archie Brennan and the Edinburgh School of Art, and disseminated also through the Victorian

Tapestry Workshop.[12] Yet other influences are apparent—Sara Lindsay's immersion in Japanese textiles is manifested in her discriminating formality and use of non-traditional rag wefts. The authority of early Coptic tapestries from the ancient Mediterranean and the eastern European emphasis on the inherent structure of tapestry as content—using slits, 'eccentric' wefts and rough materials—can be seen in Catherine K's pieces and in my own work.

'SEMIOTIC' TEXTILES AND 'SYMBOLIC' TAPESTRY

A particular issue in Australia has been the 'aura' of tapestry as historically defined and static.[13] This comes from the long practice of referring to European tapestry by aristocratic patrons of the art, through the tradition and reputation of workshops such as those of Gobelin or Aubusson, and to the reputation of the artist, usually male, who designs the tapestry. In discussion of such official workshops the weavers' gender is not specified, but their expertise in producing tapestries over generations is emphasised. The role of tapestries as transmitters of power is evident in this European history, where tapestries represent the classical mythology that then confers distinction on the owner and upholds the renown of the state. Unlike the history of textiles, the prestige of tapestry is not prejudiced by any hint of the daily domestic sphere.[14]

Precious hangings in public spaces, such as those tapestries commissioned from the Victorian Tapestry Workshop can justify and enhance the display of power as discussed by the anthropologists Annette Wiener and Jane Schneider:

Once cloth attains a degree of permanence, absorbing value from the passage of time, political elites attempt to hoard and store it . . . as treasure to be saved in the face of all exigencies that force its dissipation. More than an economic resource or an affirmation of political status, treasure facilitates claim to the past—its names, legends and events—that justify the transactions and extend the power of living actors. . . . . .[15]

Tapestry, so tightly woven and firmly beaten, is one of the most permanent textiles, and can be handed on from generation to generation as tangible evidence of time and history. Tapestry practitioners who desire to retain a pure Gobelin form of tapestry see themselves as fundamentally different to the aims of the 'fibrearts' movement, though the two are often aligned together under the heading of 'textiles'.

Although, of course, tapestry is a textile, is formed by interwoven threads, and much of its unconscious force as a visual sign derives from its 'textility', this textility is hidden by the force of a traditional connection to painting. It is intriguing to link the eventual establishment of the 'official' tapestry workshop, supported by the Victorian State Government, to the social and political circumstances of Australia at this time. At a moment when air travel made international exhibitions and contacts accessible, we affirm our ties with our language roots in Europe, and with an idea of power and credibility being linked within a medium, tapestry. Tapestry can function as a ritual object in an increasingly de-ritualised artworld, where radical art practice was assumed to be anti-establishment. By translating the work of noted Australian artists through the new interpretative skills of an ancient tradition freshly invigorated in Australia, contemporary painting could be made accessible to the public buildings and the burgeoning architectural restructuring of our major cities. I suspect that the main impulse in establishing a tapestry workshop is essentially conservative at a period of rapid change: to incorporate eminent traditions in a land with few ceremonious artefacts. The archaic technique gives resonance and solidity to the vigorous and questioning image makers of Australia and substantiates a 'claim to the past'.

Let me contrast this institutional and historical ambience of tapestry with the fibre movement that was so dominant in the emerging crafts of the 1970s in Australia. Beginning in the mid 1960s in eastern Europe and in the United States the textile revolution made its way to Australia and by the early 1970s was a dominating force in the emerging craft world. 'Tapestry' was perceived as part of the vocabulary of textile techniques by fibre artists. The 1970s sensual involvement with exuberant texture and a three-dimensional surface indicated large scale possibilities for this new medium.

Traditions from many cultures were raided and transformed into a new kind of textile that could be exhibited in major galleries and command serious critical attention, even from the avantegarde artworld.[16] In contrast to the tenets of the newly established Victorian Tapestry Workshop, the emphasis was on producing pieces that had little reference to European traditions, that mirrored ideas of instinctive expression, of intuitive responses to tactility.[17] In the 1990s this period of the 'hairy monstrosities' is often referred to derogatively, and even with abhorrence.

Because these fibre works still bring forth strong responses, often expressions of intense dislike and embarrassment, psychoanalytic/post-structural areas of theory are very relevant. The innate physicality of fibre art of the 1970s constantly referred to a world of tactility and structure bound up with 'nature' and reflected in the 'instinct' of the artists. There seems to me to be alluring convergences in playing off contemporary ideas of the formation of the subject, of pre-linguistic modes of being, against the very materialistic, and very feeling world of this exceptional moment in fibre in 1970s. I think the theories do offer an intriguing model for placing textiles, and tapestry, within the wider social realm.

Contemporary French thought has suggested a layering in the levels of language which reflect the layering of society. The 'symbolic' mode, in Jacques Lacan and Julia Kristeva's writing, is acquired with language, with the naming and perception of the world as outside of the subject. Below all conscious thought, according to Jacques Lacan[18], is a primary level of sensation which precedes the acquisition of language in the child. Over this inchoate mass, called the 'semiotic' by Kristeva, is imposed language which forms a 'symbolic' order.

According to Kristeva, separation from the 'semiotic' maternal ambience brings the child into the realm of the 'father', the world of language which structures and gives institutional system and law to the unformed, unconscious signs and traces of the state before language.[19]

Here I would like to compare the position of textiles to that of the prelinguistic area of pure sensory experience, which occasionally overflows the 'symbolic' and allows periods of wild artistic liberty, such as that seen in this textile uprising of the 1970s. If textiles can be aligned to a 'semiotic' area of the subject, tapestry, to play with this paradigm further, can be called a 'symbolic' order of experience. Such a psychoanalytic model for looking at the phenomena of textiles and tapestry is advantageous because it pinpoints the unconscious roots of actions and offers a useful comparative model for explaining the contradictions and underlying relationships within the textile/tapestry field.

The role of the whole area of textiles/tapestry has been constituted as 'feminine' in relation to the dominant 'masculine' artforms that hold most prestige: painting and sculpture. In this modernist understanding, deeply rooted in the demarcations of western art history since the sixteenth century, the craft area can be perceived as art's 'other'[20]. In the complexities of relationship within the textile/tapestry arena, tapestry plays a 'paternal' role, identified with public institutions and symbols that carry the power of the state, while textiles are allied to more bodily and sensual processes that refer to 'intuitive' maternal domains.

TAPESTRY AND GENDER IN THE 1990S

It is clear that historical tapestry in the last three hundred years in Europe has had a 'male' status, connected to the institutions of power and organised by men. In *Texts from the edge* we find a group of women using this traditional vehicle for the interpretation of 'great art' in an idiosyncratic way. The historical emanations of the tapestry medium itself are juxtaposed with seeming subversions of this history with often disturbing autobiographical images and journeys and a private realm of domestic interiors and intimately observed landscapes.

Yet because of the past history of tapestry as 'symbolic' of systems of power and claims to the past, such developments in content in tapestry take on a political and social perspective, and do not merely evoke personal positions.

Much of the work in this exhibition has its roots in an investigation of subjectivity, the 'who am I' which lays claim to an identity. Subjectivity is itself defined by political structures, by the relative positioning of male/female, black/white, middle class/working class. (It was apparent to tapestry artists travelling in Poland in 1992 that subjectivity took a very different form in the radically different circumstances of Polish art and society.) Autobiography is an expanding artform in the late twentieth century, which sees a multipicity of forms of describing the elusive self. As Sidonie Smith comments about women's writing, 'on the eve of the twenty first century we find autobiographical subjects all around us, and they are stretching textual forms . . . to fit their excessive negotiations of subjectivity, identity and the body . . .'[21]

How can women see themselves as 'artists' when the idea of 'self' has traditionally been constituted as male, unhindered by a body dedicated to nurturing? Women have been excluded from innovative roles in western tapestry history, except as 'imitators' and interpreters of male styles. There is no mirror of the past in which to reflect a clear role for women artists in this medium, except the antique Greek myth/history cited here. For women (and men) born in the 1950s, as Marie Cook observed to me, the issues of feminism underpin thinking, issues which are not resolved, and require a continuing balancing between the requirements of nurturing and the will to have power in one's chosen field.

The re-inscribing of the body and its complex positionings into this previously male domain of tapestry is obvious in the work displayed. Elizabeth Grosz suggests this approach to art practice in her discussion of French feminist theory:

Instead of seeking the inherently artistic properties of a work, to see the mark inscribed within it, and which it, in turn, re-inscribes on its producers and audience. The erasure of this process within patriarchy is an attempt to remove all traces of the body, its corporeal residues and limits, for any account of art. This closure functions to evade the questions of sexual positions inscribed through the processes of artistic production and reception.[22]

Stretching ideas of subjectivity does not lead to strident positionings of the female in opposition to a dominantly male history here, but 'corporeal residues' are evident. Sharp lines between male and female are blurred in images of ambivalent gender boundaries explored with wit and irony—Kay Lawrence's phallic mother, Tass Mavrogordato's androgynous heroine, Liz Nettleton's Lesbian policewomen, or Marie Cook's angels. In Meryn Jones' installation matriarchy is clearly evoked, and the fertile and desiring female body fully re-instated.

Such content is a departure from old models of tapestry where the producing and receiving eye was constituted as only male. The order and logic, the historic force of the medium is delicately subverted by confrontations with 'peripheral' worlds of women's imagination. A serious woman's voice is involved in Catherine K's playful texts, which contemplates the symbolic language of patriarchy through a speaking, weaving feminine stance. The piquancy comes in noting that the much loved medium itself is not in any sense 'male', though in the last two hundred years it may have come to speak for a dominant 'symbolic' position.

In *Texts from the edge* the 'semiotic' area of the haptic, maternal and the corporeal are subtly asserted both in the content of these pieces and through the tactility of the woven medium. This tactility/textility is enhanced through attention to non conventional materials such as rags and paper, to tiny gaps, slits and ruptures in the fabric of tapestry.

Yet the 'symbolic' aura of tapestry, with its weight of power and history is acknowledged as fundamental by these contemporary tapestry weavers. This is why it is *essential* that these weavers retain the framework of traditional techniques. This tapestry 'language' is used in conjunction with provocative and confronting images—the unpredictable images work *because of* the contrast with the disciplined and historic language.

The 'historic aura' of the medium holds in check any tendency for such 'semiotic' forces to overflow, and the tension between the two, as between conscious and unconscious, illuminates the work.

PLACE AND DISPLACEMENT

The Australian environment has been at the end of the long journey for Europeans, as for the tapestry medium itself. Our brief history of settlement and colonisation overlaid, and laid waste, the much greater antiquity of the indigenous inhabitants. Through an archaeological gridding of the surface of the ground my work tries to bring together these oppositional elements in the sadness of this history. The voyages of migration are also imbued with loss, held in the flower icons transported to the Antipodes, and exquisitely expressed through the use of gingham rag in Sara Lindsay's tapestry.

The sheer beauty of a remote edge of New South Wales coast, saturated with light, permeates Belinda Ramson's triptych. The land is like a textile, patterned and marked with the intricate signs of culture in Valerie Kirk's patchwork tapestry. Here signs of identity referring to early textiles are layered over the surface of the land.

Grids hold the image in the work of these four artists, both in the larger forms of the work, and in the microscopic gridding of the tapestry itself. Perceptions of land are observed through a feminine eye, a self-reflexive eye which would question stereotypes of national identity through re appraisal of history.

Leonie Besant also questions the cliches of 'Australianness' and 'femaleness' in her representation of still life and landscape images, which engage with unconscious assumptions about such images in the formation of subjectivity. Robyn Daw interrogates the subjugated role of ornament in history, and selects minimal abstract motifs and devices from medieval iconography to comment on contemporary ways of seeing.

TRANSLATION AND TEMPORALITY

Zeus chose the copy, he wanted that minimal difference which is enough to overturn order and generate the new, generate meaning [23]

A common criticism of tapestry comes from the perception that it 'imitates' or 'copies' the drawn and painted image, usually followed by a comment on the labour intensive process. This perception implies integrity is located only in the 'original', and to follow such an argument consistently any translations from one medium to another could be seen as lesser versions of an 'original' inviolable concept. A drawing should not be made into an etching or lithograph, a novel should not be translated into another language, a photograph into a painting, or a play into a film. Yet from an older or non-western viewpoint, the drawn image achieves significance only when it is interpreted into textile, and is validated by the woven structure.[24] In such societies the 'copy' from one material into another does lead to other meanings specific to that medium.

Within tapestry, mimicry of other mediums from the photographic dot matrix, to the computer screen, the infinite variations of the drawn line, or representation of other textiles such as lace or velvet is one of the great pleasures which change perceptions of visual reality. Our current technological visual world is far more imbued with copies than with 'originals'. The woven fabric contrasts with this flickering transient world of media images, and implies relationships, interconnectedness through its very structure, and as we have seen, a 'claim to the past' through transmission of myth and history in a way specific to tapestry.

Both Valerie Kirk and Belinda Ramson have observed that this notion of the 'copy' as derogatory may be due, not only to the dogmas of modernism, but also to a lack of knowledge and familiarity with the characteristics of tapestry and its relatively recent status in Australia. The Victorian Tapestry Workshop's program of interpreting paintings into tapestry, with a division between the weaver and the artist, is the most familiar model of tapestry in Australia. The viewing of the works in *Texts from the edge*, where the same hand has conceived and woven the work may help to change the rigidity of that model.

Wait, although you are pressing for marriage with me, until this cloth I have finished . . . this funeral cloth for the hero Laertes, which is for whenever deadly fate shall bring him down in death[25]

Tapestries are pondered, not made quickly, an essential difference from other media. The highly patterned tapestry woven by Penelope was a funerary cloth, the shroud of Laertes, which incorporated the appropriate myths for the passing of a hero. The edge between life and death is an area mitigated by the use of textiles, and particularly tapestry. The time factor is a constant motif in Greek myth/history—the slowness became itself a ritual element giving significance to the final object, and a rhythm to the days of privileged women.

In our own era, when the technological super highway cuts visual and textual communication across continents to a fraction of a second, time indeed becomes a fascinating dichotomy in the making of tapestry. Contrasts of time are implicit in the representation in tapestry of a transient television screen or newspaper photograph. Yet tapestry weavers engage without hesitation in computer technology, familiar in its innate structure to weaving, and the momentum of the international tapestry community over the last few years takes place through E-mail and fax. If indeed, as Carolyn Barnes states 'the work of art is an index to spatial and temporal constructs, exemplifying the ideas of time and space to general social, economic and political conditions'[26] such contrasts of time within the art production of the late twentieth century may indicate a necessity to insist on 'very slow' as well as 'very rapid'. A different meaning is engendered, an underside of this speeding precipitate time of ours is revealed.

Texts from the edge allows us to see that the cloth is still being woven which brings to light other levels of perception and stories of new deities. In the developing and vibrant pattern of tapestry in Australia we may yet glimpse the mythical forms of the Sirens.

NOTES

1. Robert Calasso, *The marriage of Cadmus and Harmony*, translated from the Italian by Tim Parkes, Vintage, London, 1994, p.280.

2. Each artist received $7000 to travel in Europe and attend the conference. Reports by Diana Wood Conroy on *Distant lives/Shared Voices*: 'Distant lives/Shared Voices: a report', *International Tapestry Newsletter* (published in USA) Fall Issue 1992, vol 3 no 3, p.3–10; 'Tapestry: Signs and Histories', *Object*, Spring, 1992, p.24–28; 'Re: Distant Lives/Shared Voices, Lodz, Poland, June 21–28, 1992', *Textile Fibreforum*, vol.11, no.35, 1992, pp.20–21.

3. In 1963 Margaret Grafton was commissioned by Philip Cox to make a 1.83 x 4.88 tapestry for the Tocal Agricultural College near Maitland, NSW, see Grace Cochrane, *The Crafts movement in Australia,: a history*, New South Wales University Press, 1992, p.171. Margaret Grafton is still an active weaver, and theorist.

4. Mona Hessing's work is well documented in Grace Cochrane, *The Crafts movement in Australia,: a history*, New South Wales University Press, 1992, p.172. Diana Wood Conroy's early commissions included: Macquarie University, 3 metres square, 1973, NSW State Planning Authority, .75 m x 2.4 m, 1973 University of Sydney Union, 1.5 metres square, St. Andrew's House, Sydney Square, 3.3m x 4.8.m., 1976, Aldo Moratelli, Architects, North Sydney, 1976.

5. see Diana Wood Conroy, 'Tapestries: Ian Arcus', *The Australian Hand Weaver and Spinner*, vol. XXXII, no. 1, 1979, pp.2–4, and entries on Ian Arcus, Tom Moore, Mary and Larry Beeston in Grace Cochrane, *The Crafts Movement in Australia: a history*, New South Wales University Press, 1992, pp.171, 218–219.

6. see catalogue *World Tapestry Today*, touring exhibition to Australia, U.S, Germany and France, American Tapestry Alliance, featured event of the International Tapestry Symposium, Australian Bicentennary, 1988; for more

recent international shows with Australian artists see *ITNET Exhibit 1* International Tapestry Network and Anchorage Museum of History and Art, U.S.A. 1990; *ITNET Exhibit 2*, International Tapestry Network and Anchorage Museum of History and Art, U.S.A. 1992.

7. Sue Walker, 'The Victorian Tapestry Workshop', *Craft Australia*, 1978/3, p.28–33. and *Australian Tapestry*, catalogue of the Victorian Tapestry Workshop, October, 1980, at Crafts Council of New South Wales Gallery at the Rocks, Sydney.

8. *2000 Bobbins, an exhibition of community tapestry weavings 1981–1988*, presented by the Adelaide Centre Festival Trust, researched and organised by Elaine Gardner, preface by Kay Lawrence, Melbourne, 1988.

9. for a discussion of this time, Grace Cochrane, *The Crafts Movement in Australia: a history*, New South Wales University Press, Sydney, 1992, pp.215–219.

10. catalogue *Identities: Art from Australia*, Taipei Fine Arts Museum, Taiwan, December 1993–February 1994. Catalogue entry, 'Kay Lawrence', by Diana Wood Conroy, pp.97–99.

11. e.g. Mary Leland from U.S visited Australia in 1974, Professor Vurbanov from Bulgaria in 1975, Magdalena Abakanowicz from Poland in 1976, Jun Tomita from Japan in 1977.

12. More recently, Marie Cook's successful and innovative correspondence course in tapestry through the South West University of Victoria at Warrnambool has opened up the medium to a wide variety of students, as have tapestry courses in major art schools. Canberra School of Art, and Monash University in Melbourne, the South Australian School of Art offer specific tapestry tuition.

13. Anna Burch, 'Tapestry: Safely removed from Creative Struggles?' *Craft Australia* 1988/4 p.12.

14. In my doctoral thesis for the University of Wollongong I investigated the positioning of tapestry in such early articles as:

P.R MacMahon, Mrs,(ed.)'Tapestry Curtains for the Sydney Opera House', *The Australian Hand Weaver and Spinner*, vol. XXV, November, 1972, pp.11–12; *Hommage a Jean Lurcat*, touring exhibition Australia, June 1973–November 1974, foreword by Erik Langker, President of the Board of Trustees of the Art Gallery of NSW, 1973; Alice Filson, 'An unchanging tradition . . . ' *The Australian Handweaver and Spinner*, November 1973, pp.4–6; Sylvia Burkitt (ed.) 'A visitor from Bulgaria' *The Australian Handweaver and Spinner*, November 1975, pp.4–5; Sylvia Burkitt (ed.) 'Marin Vurbanov—Looking back on a four month course' *The Australian Handweaver and Spinner*, February 1976, pp.25–28: Ross Griffith, 'Tapestry Weaving' *The Australian Handweaver and Spinner*, November 1975, pp.6–8 and Jean Eldridge, 'Studying Gobelins tapestry at Venasque', *The Australian Handweaver and Spinner*, November 1973, pp20–21. Belinda Ramson, 'The year at Dovecot', *Craft Australia*, vol 4/1 September, 1974, p.25.

15. Annette B. Wiener and Jane Schneider, *Cloth and Human Experience* Smithsonian Institution Press, Washington and London, 1989, p.5 and 6.

16. In Sydney in the 1970s 'tapestries' were shown in the best galleries. Mona Hessing's work filled the Bonython gallery in 1971, where Olga de Amaral also showed in 1977. Magdalena Abakanowicz showed in the Art Gallery of N.S.W. in jute and sisal sculptures of great theatrical presence and prehistoric resonance. Ritzi and Peter Jacobi had their large sculpture *Transylvania* on display at the Coventry Gallery in 1981, constructed from paper and wrapped fibre elements. Other Australian weavers who used tapestry within a textile/sculptural idiom were Bruce Arthur, Solvig Baas Becking, Robert Bell, Rinske Car, Deanna Conti, John Corbett, Jutta

Feddersen, Ann Greenwood, Kate Hodgkinson and Prue Medlin to mention only some.

17. My doctoral thesis looks closely at evidence for these different modes of relating to textiles through an analysis of many articles written in *Craft Australia* and *Hand Weaver and Spinner*, 1975–1984, and the monograph *The Artist Craftsman in Australia: Aspects of sensibility*, Jack Pollard Pty. Ltd., Crows Nest, Australia, 1972.

18. Jacques Lacan, *Ecrits: A selecton*, Tavistock Publications, London, 1977. See also discussion in Elizabeth Wright, *Psychoanalytic Criticism: Theory in practice*, Routledge, London and New York, 1984, reprinted 1989, chapter 7, 'Structural psychoanalysis: psyche as text', pp.133–150.

19. Elizabeth Grosz, *Jacques Lacan: A feminist introduction*. Sydney, Allen and Unwin 1990, pp.152–153.

20. Sue Rowley explored this issue in 'Mind over Matter?: Reading the Art/Craft Debate' *West*, vol.1, no.1, 1989, p.6. The issue is extensively debated in Norris Ioannou (editor) *Craft in Society: an anthology of perspectives*, Fremantle Arts Centre Press, Fremantle, 1992.

21. Sidonie Smith, *Subjectivity, identity and the body: Women's auto biographical practices in the twentieth century*, Indiana University Press, 1993, p.188.

22. Elizabeth Grosz, 'Feminist theory and the politics of art', in *Dissonance*, edited by Catriona Moore, Allen and Unwin in association with Artspace, Sydney, 1994, p.152.

23. Robert Calasso, *The marriage of Cadmus and Harmony*, translated from the Italian by Tim Parkes, Vintage, London, 1994, p.24.

24. E.J.W. Barber, *Prehistoric Textiles: The development of cloth in the Neolithic and Bronze ages*, Prineton University Press, Princeton, New Jersey, 1991. See chapter 17, 'And Penelope?' pp.358–382.

25. *Odyssey*. 2. 94–110, quoted by E.J.W. Barber, *Prehistoric Textiles: The development of cloth in the Neolithic and Bronze ages*, Prineton University Press, Princeton, New Jersey, 1991.p.358.

26. Carolyn Barnes, 'Specific Objects: the second time around, two installations by Peter Cripps, *Binocular*, Moet and Chandon, Sydney, 1992, p.97.

24

GANDHI AND *KHADI*, THE FABRIC OF INDIAN INDEPENDENCE

Susan S. Bean

Editor's introduction: The textile is shown, throughout this *Reader*, to be powerful in many different ways. One of the most notable examples of this, in terms of sheer scale, can be found in Mahatma Gandhi's use of the textile as a protest tool in the ultimately successful Indian independence movement. The essay reprinted here, by anthropologist, art historian, and curator Susan Bean, first appeared in the often-cited collection of essays titled *Cloth and Human Experience*, edited by Annette B. Weiner and Jane Schneider. Bean outlines Gandhi's use of the textile, noting that "from 1908 on, these two elements—the economics of cloth and the semiotics of cloth—united in Gandhi's thought." The essay charts Gandhi's own experience of dress as a tool for expressing identity and status and the evolution of these ideas into the use of the textile as a method for nonviolent resistance. Creating and wearing *khadi* became a powerful instrument of resistance as, Bean explains, "English cloth had become the most potent symbol of English political domination and economic exploitation." Bean reminds us that Gandhi's choice of dress to communicate his political values was of crucial importance to a nation with multiple languages and high illiteracy rates, which made visual (rather than written or spoken) communication all the more vital.

Susan Bean is curator of South Asian and Korean art at the Peabody Essex Museum in the United States.

Cloth was central to the Indian struggle for national self-government—cloth as an economic product and cloth as a medium of communication. Cloth was officially incorporated into the nationalist program in 1921 when the Indian National Congress resolved to campaign for the boycott of foreign cloth, to require its officers and workers to spin cotton yarn and wear hand-spun, hand-woven cloth (*khadi*), and to adopt a flag with the spinning wheel in the center. Mahatma Gandhi was the force behind the adoption of these resolutions, but they were successful because Gandhi had achieved an understanding of the role of cloth in Indian life, the culmination of decades of experimentation with cloth as a medium of communication and means of livelihood.

Gandhi's changing sociopolitical identity can be traced through his costume changes as well

Source: Susan S. Bean, "Gandhi and *Khadi*, the Fabric of Indian Independence," in Annette B. Weiner and Jane Schneider (eds), *Cloth and Human Experience* (Washington, DC: The Smithsonian Institution Press, 1989) pp. 355–376. Copied with permission of Smithsonian Books. Copyright 1989.

as through his speeches, writings, and activities. As he came to appreciate the semiotic properties of cloth, he learned to use it to communicate his most important messages to followers and opponents and to manipulate social events. Once he had appreciated the economic importance of cloth in India, he made it the centerpiece of his program for independence and self-government. The development of Gandhi's thought and practice, which is explored in the following pages, is illuminated by the historical and cultural context provided in Cohn (this volume) and Bayly (1986). Cohn analyzes the use of costume in the reorganization and management of hierarchical relations during the British Raj. Bayly provides valuable insights into the role of cloth in Indian culture, emphasizing its moral nature—its capacity to embody and transmit social value—a characteristic of cloth which Gandhi appreciated.

LESSONS IN THE SOCIAL MEANING OF COSTUME

When Mohandas K. Gandhi disembarked at Southampton in 1888, he was wearing white flannels given to him by a friend and saved especially for the occasion, because he "thought that white clothes would suit [him] better when [he] stepped ashore" (Gandhi 1957:43). On his arrival at Southampton he realized that white flannels were not worn in late September. Later he replaced his Bombay-style clothing, which he thought "unsuitable for English society" (Gandhi 1957:50), with an evening suit from Bond Street, patent leather shoes with spats, and a high silk hat, "clothes regarded as the very acme of fashion" (Fischer 1982:37). Gandhi was sensitive to the connection between costume and social status, and perceived that changes in social position required changes in costume. His sensitivity became self-consciousness because Gandhi, the student from India, was so ignorant of how Gandhi, the London barrister, should appear.

In 1891 when Gandhi returned home to Rajkot, a barrister, he promoted the westernization

of his household, begun for him by his brother, by adding items of European dress (Gandhi 1957:92). Gandhi believed his success was dependent on westernization. Later, in the harsher, more repressive, and openly racist South Africa where he went to work as a barrister in 1893, he confronted his indelible Indianness.

On this third day in South Africa, he visited the Durban court. It was explained to him that Hindus had to remove their turbans in court, though Muslim Indians were permitted to keep their turbans on. Turbans were not like hats: In this context, removal was not deferential, it was demeaning (see Cohn, this volume). Gandhi thought he could solve the problem by wearing an English hat, but his employer warned him that he would be undermining efforts for recognition of the Indian meaning of the turban and for permission to keep it on in court. His employer added, in appreciation of Indian dress: "An Indian turban sits well on your head." Besides, he said, "If you wear an English hat you will pass for a waiter" (Gandhi 1957:108). (Most waiters in South Africa were Indian converts to Christianity who wore English dress.)

Gandhi kept his turban and began to appreciate the limits of his Englishness—limits imposed by the colonial regime and by his pride as an Indian and a Hindu. But still he thought he could make his Indianness compatible with Englishness. He wore a fashionable frock coat, pressed trousers, and shining shoes with his turban (Fischer 1982:57). After he was thrown off the train to Pretoria for traveling first class, he reapplied for a first-class ticket, presenting himself to the station master "in faultless English dress" (Gandhi 1957:116). He succeeded. The station master said, "I can see you are a gentleman" (Gandhi 1957:117).

Gandhi later also succeeded in persuading the railway authorities to issue first- and second-class tickets to Indians "who were properly dressed" (Gandhi 1957:128). He sought to demonstrate that Indians could be as civilized as Englishmen and therefore were entitled to the same rights and privileges as citizens of the British Empire. This belief seemed to be supported by the Empress Victoria herself, who stated that there was a distinction between "aliens and subjects of Her Majesty [and] between the most ignorant and the most enlightened of the natives of India. Among the latter class there are to be found gentlemen whose position and attainments fully qualify them for all the duties and privileges of citizenship" (Queen Victoria, quoted in Erikson 1969:172–3).

When Gandhi brought his family to South Africa in 1896 he believed "that in order to look civilized, our dress and manners had as far as possible to approximate to the European standard. Because, I thought, only thus could we have some influence, and without influence it would not be possible to serve the community. I therefore determined the style of dress for my wife and children. How could I like them to be known as Kathiawad Banias? The Parsis used then to be regarded as the most civilized people amongst Indians, and so, when the complete European style seemed to be unsuited, we adopted the Parsi style. Accordingly my wife wore the Parsi sari, and the boys the Parsi coat and trousers. Of course no one could be without shoes and stockings. It was long before my wife and children could get used to them. The shoes cramped their feet and the stockings stank with perspiration" (Gandhi 1957:186).

Soon the prospect began to fade that one could be an Indian and a full citizen of the British empire by wearing Indian headgear with an English suit. For one thing, it had become clear that the color of one's skin was as much a part of one's costume as a frock coat, and this fundamental Indianness Gandhi would not have changed even if he could. He began to admire Indian dress. In 1901, back in India for a visit, he met some rulers of Indian states at the India Club in Calcutta. Gandhi recalls, "In the Club I always found them wearing fine Bengalee *dhotis* [Hindu garments of seamless cloth, wrapped and folded around the lower body] and shirts and scarves. On the darbar day [Viceroy's audience] they put on trousers befitting *khansamas* [waiters] and shining boots. I was

pained and inquired of one of them the reason for the change. "We alone know our unfortunate condition [began the reply]. We alone know the insults we have to put up with, in order that we may possess our wealth and titles. . . .' 'But what about these *khansama* turbans and these shining boots?' I asked. 'Do you see any difference between *khansamas* and us?' he replied, and added, 'They are our *khansamas*, we are Lord Curzon's *khansamas*. If I were to absent myself from the levee, I should have to suffer the consequences. If I were to attend it in my usual dress, it would be an offence'" (Gandhi 1957:230). As in the Durban court, the sartorial dictates of the Empire were demeaning for its Indian citizens (see Cohn, this volume). During the same visit he remarked on his mentor, Gokhale: "In the Congress I had seen him in a coat and trousers, but I was glad to find him wearing a Bengal *dhoti* and shirt [at home]. I liked his simple mode of dress though I myself then wore a Parsi coat and trousers" (Gandhi 1957:234). Gandhi began to experiment with his own costume. Soon he embarked on a tour of India to learn about its people; he traveled third class. For clothing he took a long woolen coat, a *dhoti*, and a shirt. But on his return to Bombay in 1902 he resumed the life of the well-dressed, well-housed barrister riding first class on the trains.

Gandhi's responses to the costumes of others and his experiments with his own attire indicate a growing awareness of the meaning of clothes— their importance as indicators of status, group identity, social stratification, and political beliefs. He had begun to doubt the possibility of being both a dignified Indian and an English gentleman. The sartorial requirements of the Empire forced Indians to humiliate themselves, and revealed the true relationship—of master and slave—between the English and the Indians. Gandhi's experiments with simple, inexpensive Indian garments expressed his growing disdain for possessions and his growing identification with the poor.

By 1908 he had come to believe that Indians could not be Englishmen and that India should be ruled for the benefit of India by Indians. He set forth these views in *Hind Swaraj* (*Indian Home Rule*) (1908), where he also said: "If people of a certain country, who have hitherto not been in the habit of wearing much clothing, boots, etc., adopt European clothing, they are supposed to have become civilized out of savagery" (Gandhi 1922:32). He himself had believed this when in 1893 he appealed to the railroad authorities to allow Indians in European dress to ride first class, and in 1896 when he brought his family to South Africa and insisted on the further westernization of their dress. By 1908, he no longer believed that European garments were an index of civilization and Indian ones of its lack.

In *Hind Swaraj*, Gandhi first articulated the importance for India of the economics of cloth. For fifty years, an economic nationalism (whose roots were in fact much older) had been evolving in India. British rule had not benefited India, as the British maintained. On the contrary, British rule had destroyed the economy of India by taking its wealth back to England, by overtaxing its farmers, and by destroying Indian industries that might compete with English ones, thus causing poverty, famine, and disease. Cloth manufacture had been the premier industry of India and its decline was a chief cause of Indian poverty. These views were set out in detail in R.C. Dutt's two-volume *Economic History of India* (Dutt 1901 & 1903). Gandhi commented in *Hind Swaraj*: "When I read Mr. Dutt's *Economic History of India* I wept; and, as I think of it, again my heart sickens. . . . It is difficult to measure the harm that Manchester [the seat of the English mechanized textile industry] has done to us. It is due to Manchester that Indian handicraft has all but disappeared" (Gandhi 1922:105).

From 1908 on, these two elements—the economics of cloth and the semiotics of cloth—united in Gandhi's thought. By 1921, *khadi* (homespun cloth) had become central to his politics. The intervening years were full of experiments with costume and with the production of handmade cloth.

CLOTH IN ECONOMIC NATIONALISM

Gandhi's campaign for *khadi* was a product of economic nationalism. Gandhi's views on cloth and clothing were unique, but the elements of which they were composed were not. According to the economic nationalists, India's decline was due largely to British destruction of Indian manufactures beginning in the late eighteenth century. Cotton textiles had been India's premier industry. Weavers and dyers so excelled in producing both coarse, inexpensive textiles and fine, exquisitely dyed, luxury textiles that Indian cloth was prized in Rome, China, Egypt, and Southeast Asia.

> As early as 200 B.C. the Romans used a Sanskrit word for cotton (Latin, *carbasina*, from Sanskrit *karpasa*). In Nero's reign, delicately translucent Indian muslins were fashionable in Rome under such names as *nebula* and *venti* textiles (woven winds) the latter exactly translating the technical name of a special type of muslin woven in Bengal up to the modern period. . . . The quality of Indian dyeing, too, was proverbial in the Roman world, as we know from a reference in St. Jerome's fourth century Latin translation of the Bible, Job being made to say that wisdom is even more enduring than the "dyed colors of India" (Irwin 1962).

In the fifth century A.D. an Indonesian diplomatic mission carried textiles from India and Gandhara to China. In the eleventh century, "500 Jewish families on their way to settle in the Northern Sung capital of China, bought cotton goods in India to take as gifts" (Gittinger 1982:13). Fifteenth-century fragments of Indian cloth found at Fostat, near Cairo, show that the trade was not exclusively in fine textiles. The fragments are "often lacking in care or precision [in dye craftsmanship] and only occasionally showing exceptional skill. Inescapable is the sense that these were made for a modest clientele and do not represent elements of a 'luxury' trade" (Gittinger 1982:33).

Until the sixteenth century, Indian and Arab merchants dominated the trade in Indian cottons. From the late sixteenth century, Europeans gained increasing control of the world trade in Indian cottons (Chaudhuri 1978). At first European traders were interested in Indian cottons as trade goods which could be exchanged in Southeast Asia for spices. By the middle of the seventeenth century, the traders had discovered that if they supervised the design of the textiles made in India, these could be sold at a reasonable profit in London. At the end of the seventeenth century, the demand for Indian painted cottons had become so great that France banned chintz imports to protect its own silk industry (Irwin and Brett 1970:3,4). England followed suit a few years later. So popular were these fabrics that the prohibitions were ignored. In 1720 "a second prohibition was introduced . . . to forbid 'the Use and Wearing in Apparel' of imported chintz, and also its 'use or wear in or about any Bed, Chair, Cushion, or other Household furniture'" (Irwin and Brett 1970:5).

The great popularity of Indian cottons was due both to the cheapness and to the superiority of Indian products. Indian hand-spun yarns were superior to those produced in England and were imported for the weaving of fine cloth. Indian dyers were expert in the technology of mordant dyeing, which produced washable cottons in vibrant colors (Chaudhuri 1978:237ff). While the competition from Indian cloth could be fought with duties and prohibitions, the technological superiority remained unchallenged until the industrial revolution.

From the late eighteenth century, with the development and growth of machine spinning and weaving and the adoption and modification of Indian cotton-dyeing technology (Gittinger 1982:19), England began to produce quantities of inexpensive cotton textiles. English political control of India permitted adjustments in tariffs (and import prohibitions) to assure the advantage of Lancashire cottons in trade. English cotton-spinning mills secured supplies of raw cotton from India, and British traders succeeded in competing in India with the local hand-loom industry, thus opening a vast new market for the products of the Lancashire mills. The hand-spinning of cotton yarns had virtually died out in India by 1825. Only the highest counts of cotton yarns could not be reproduced by machinery. Even Indian hand-loom weavers used the cotton yarns produced in Lancashire. During the nineteenth century, exports fell drastically and the world's greatest exporter of cottons became a major importer of cotton yarns and piece goods. "In the first four years of the nineteenth century, in spite of all prohibitions and restrictive duties, six to fifteen thousand bales [of cotton piece-goods] were annually shipped from Calcutta to the United Kingdom. . . . After 1820 the manufacture of cotton piece-goods declined steadily, never to rise again" (Dutt 1906:296). Between 1849 and 1889, the value of British cotton cloth exports to India increased from just over 2 million pounds a year to just less than 27 million pounds a year (Chandra 1968:55). At the end of the nineteenth century, the development in Europe of inexpensive, easier-to-apply chemical dyes dealt the final blow to Indian technological superiority in textile production.

The interpretation of these changes has long been a subject of heated debate among historians and economists. Did British cloth destroy the demand for Indian hand-looms or supplement it? Did indigenous production really decline or was it simply consumed in the domestic market? Did British policy destroy Indian manufactures or was the demise of Indian industry the inevitable result of the competition between artisans and machines? Did India fail to industrialize because British policy prevented it or because Indian society was infertile soil for industrialization?

During the late nineteenth century, an interpretation of England's economic relations with India evolved that became the economic basis of Indian nationalism. In this economic nationalism, the history of cotton production and trade was central. Especially significant was the transformation of India from the world's most advanced producer of cotton textiles to an exporter of raw cotton and an importer of cloth.

Dadabhai Naoroji was the recognized leader of this movement and codified the theory of economic nationalism. In his view, "the continuous impoverishment and exhaustion of the country" (Naoroji 1887) was unquestionably the result of British rule. Wealth was taken from India to pay the Englishmen in London who ruled India and to pay large salaries and pensions to English civil servants, who spent much of this wealth in England. Grinding poverty and severe famines resulted from the enormous tax burden on the cultivators. British protection of English industries, through trade advantages in the structure of tariffs, destroyed indigenous artisanry and prevented the development of machine industry.

Naoroji and other early nationalists (e.g., Ranade, Tilak, Gokhale) believed that the low tariffs on British yarns and cloth coming into India and the high tariffs on Indian textiles taken out of India caused the decline of the textile industry, forced more people onto the land, and created an unbalanced economy that exacerbated the poverty of India. Furthermore, they believed that the tariff structure on cotton goods revealed the true nature of British rule:

> Be that as it may, as regards this question of the cotton duties, the mask has now fallen off the foreign English administration of India. The highest officials in the country, nay the entire official body and the leading newspapers in England, have had to make the humiliating confession—The boast in which we have been so long indulging, the boast that we govern India in the interest and for the welfare of the Indians, is perfectly unfounded; India is held and governed in the interests of the English merchants (*The Bangabasi*, 17 March 1894, quoted in Chandra 1966:235).

The national leadership united or and on the importance of protectio artisans and nascent industries. More..., the first time they united in action, around the issue of cotton tariffs. In 1896 they urged the boycott of foreign goods (Chandra 1966:250). The tactic of appealing to the English government of India to practice what it preached—just government—had begun to give way to active opposition. The seeds of opposition, the idea of *swadeshi* (the promotion of indigenous products), had already been planted:

> In 1872 Justice Ranade delivered a series of public lectures at Poona on economic topics, in which he popularized "the idea of *swadeshi*, of preferring the goods produced in one's own country even though they may prove to be dearer or less satisfactory than finer foreign products." These celebrated lectures so inspired the listeners that several of them including Ganesh Vasudeo Joshi . . . and Vasudeo Phadke . . . enthusiastically "vowed to wear and use only swadeshi articles." Joshi used to spin yarn daily for his own *dhoti*, shirt and turban; he started shops at several places to popularise and propagate *swadeshi* goods, and, at the Delhi Durbar of 1877 and in the midst of pageantry and flamboyancy, he represented the Sarvajanik Sabha dressed in pure self-spun khadi (Chandra 1966:122–3).

Indians could fight the destructive power of the English government by using Indian products in preference to foreign ones. The ideology and practice of *swadeshi* grew among nationalists and then, when the English government of India imposed excise duties on Indian cloth, *swadeshi* promoters turned to their most powerful weapon, boycott. In 1896, many people in Dacca resolved to boycott Manchester cloth and to patronize Indian mills (Chandra 1966:126). The center of activity was the Bombay Presidency, home of the nascent textile industry (the first mill opened only in the

1850s). Indians showed their opposition to English clothing by refusing to buy it or wear it, and by burning it. "According to the *Nyaya Sindu* of 2 March 1896 huge bundles of English clothing were thrown into the Holi fire that year" (Chandra 1966:130,n.167). A *Times* correspondent reported that "It was impossible for a respectable citizen to go with a new English piece of cloth without being asked a hundred perplexing questions" (Chandra 1966:130). Even though agitation subsided in subsequent years, *swadeshi*, the promotion of indigenous products, with cloth as its main platform, became a permanent feature of the nationalist movement.

English cloth had become the most potent symbol of English political domination and economic exploitation. As cloth is used mainly in clothing, the results of English exploitation—the demise of indigenous industry—were constantly there for all to see, on the backs of Indians who wore Manchester cloth made into British-style garments, and on Indians who used Manchester cloth for turbans, *kurtas* (shirts), *saris*, and other Indian garments. *Swadeshi*, an attempt to revive and promote Indian industry, required that each person be counted as a patriot-nationalist or a supporter of English domination and exploitation. An individual's political views, encoded in his or her costume, were exposed to public view.

Indeed, part of the reason for the decline of the *swadeshi* movement was the difficulty in procuring, and resistance to wearing, *swadeshi* costume. In the late nineteenth century, the Indian mills and handloom weavers together did not have the capability to clothe the nation. More significantly, most nationalist leaders, including Gokhale and Naoroji (but not the more militant Tilak), continued to wear English costumes with Indian headgear in public. They still believed that the way to gain a just administration of India was to show the English rulers the errors of their ways, so that English fair play and justice would prevail, Indians would be given a greater voice in the government of their land, and artisanry and industry would be revived. Like Gandhi when he appealed

to the railway authorities in South Africa in 1893, they seemed to believe that they had to show their English rulers that they were like the English, that they were English gentlemen, and were entitled to all that the English government would give to its own people.

Thus a fascinating paradox was generated from the semiotic and economic characteristics of cloth. These early nationalists wanted to revive and modernize Indian manufactures, especially the textile industry. But their political beliefs stood in the way of utilizing its products. Cloth is made to be worn and to express the social identity of its wearer. They expressed their belief in English values and their right to English justice by comporting themselves as English gentlemen in English dress (albeit with a special hat or turban to signify a slight cultural distinctiveness). Because they were still committed to this Englishness of dress, they were incapable of carrying out their own program of *swadeshi*.

Gandhi, following the lead of Tilak, Joshi and others, came to the more radical position that to promote Indian industry, foreign notions of civilization and gentlemanliness would have to be discarded. Economic Indianization was intrinsically connected to sociocultural Indianization. One could not promote the Indian textile industry without wearing its products and one could not wear its products and remain a proper Englishman. And if one gave up frock coats and morning suits, one would no longer be an English gentleman entitled to treatment as such. A new strategy would be required to achieve the nationalists' goals for India, a strategy based more on confrontation and opposition than on persuasion and cooperation.

THE MAHATMA AS SEMIOTICIAN

Gandhi began his conscious experimentation with costume on his trip to India in 1901. He had begun to question the political efficacy of gentlemanly dress. The experiments intensified during the *satyagraha* (truth force) campaign of militant non-violence in South Africa, from the 1906 opposition to the Black Act until his departure in 1914. In 1909, when Gandhi settled at Tolstoy Farm, he is said to have put on "laborer's dress"— workman's trousers and shirt in the European style, which were adapted from prison uniform (Nanda 1958:109). There is a photograph of him during the *satyagraha* campaign wearing *lungi* (South Indian wrapped lower garment), *kurta* and coat. His head and feet are bare; he carries a staff and a bag slung across his shoulders. This costume was similar to the one he wore on his third-class pilgrimage through India in 1901. The transformation was so radical and unfamiliar that the Reverend Andrews, who arrived to join the movement in 1913, did not recognize the "man in a *lungi* and *kurta* with close cropped head and a staff in hand," reported Prabhudas Gandhi who added "probably he took him for a *sadhu* (ascetic holy man)" (Gandhi, P. 1957:176).

That same year, after being released from jail, he attended a meeting in Durban in a *dhoti* (perhaps a *lungi*). His feet were bare and he had shaved his moustache. He was in mourning for the dead coal strikers (Ashe 1968:124). However, when he sailed for England in 1914 he was dressed as an Englishman (Fischer 1982:151), and when he landed in India the following year he was dressed as a Kathiawari (Gujarat) peasant, in *dhoti*, *angarkha* (robe), upper cloth, and turban, the most thoroughly Indian of his costumes. His *satyagrahi* garb was his own design, and expressed simplicity, asceticism, and identity with the masses. His Kathiawari dress was more formal. It identified his region of origin and presented him as a totally Indian gentleman. In his autobiography he comments on this costume "with my Kathiawadi cloak, turban and *dhoti*, I looked somewhat more civilized than I do today" (1982:374). The costume was an attempt to provide an Indian resolution for the contradiction between being civilized and being Indian.

His colleagues were not sure what to make of him. He "was an eccentric figure, with his huge white turban and white clothing, among the western attired delegates" (Gold 1983:63). By appearing in this eccentric fashion he forced his colleagues to notice and accommodate his view of a truly Indian nationalism. He deliberately used costume not only to express his sociopolitical identity, but to manipulate social occasions to elicit acceptance of, if not agreement with, his position.

Despite the thoroughgoing Indianness of his Kathiawari costume (actually because of it) it was inadequate for Gandhi's purposes because it indicated region, class, and religion. Gandhi's program called for the unity of all Indians throughout the subcontinent, rich and poor, Hindu, Sikh, and Muslim. He needed a costume that transcended these distinctions. His experiments continued. He arrived in Madras in 1915 traveling third class and wearing a loose shirt and pair of trousers (Erikson 1969:279). He was photographed in Karachi in 1916 wearing a dark-colored hat similar in shape to what has become known as a "Gandhi cap" (Gold 1983:59). Again during the Kheda *satyagraha* in 1918 he was photographed in his Kathiawari turban. At the 1919 Amritsar Congress he first wore the white homespun "Gandhi cap." Some believe it was derived from South African prison garb (Ashe 1968:199). The cap also resembles some worn by Muslims and it may be important that Gandhi began to wear it during the campaign to support the Caliph of Turkey, a campaign important to Gandhi for its promotion of Hindu-Muslim unity. The cap, which Gandhi discarded two years later, was to become part of the uniform of Indian nationalists (see Cohn, this volume).

Gandhi's final costume change took place in 1921 when he began his national program for the revival of handmade cloth. *Khadi* (homespun) was scarce and expensive, so he urged his followers to wear as little cloth as possible:

> I know that many will find it difficult to replace their foreign cloth all at once. . . . Let them be satisfied with a mere loin cloth. . . . India has never insisted on full covering of the body for the males as a test of culture. . . . In order, therefore, to set the example, I propose to discard at

least up to the 31st of October my *topi* (cap) and vest, and to content myself with only a loin cloth, and a *chaddar* (shawl) whenever found necessary for the protection of the body. I adopt the change, because I have always hesitated to advise anything I may not myself be prepared to follow. . . . I consider the renunciation to be also necessary for me as a sign of mourning, and a bare head and bare body is such a sign in my part of the country. . . . I do not expect coworkers to renounce the use of the vest and the *topi* unless they find it necessary. . . . (29 September 1921, quoted in Jaju 1951:98).

Later recalling the same event, Gandhi added he "divest[ed] [him] self of every inch of clothing [he] decently could and thus to a still greater extent [brought himself] in line with the ill-clad masses . . . in so far as the loin cloth also spells simplicity let it represent Indian civilization" (quoted in Jaju 1951:99). Gandhi had completely rejected the English gentleman and replaced him with the Indian ascetic, the renouncer, the holy man. When he visited the Viceroy in 1921 (and still later, when he attended the Round Table Conference in London in 1931 and visited King George and Queen Mary at Buckingham Palace) wearing his *mahatma* garb, nothing could match the communicative power of a photograph of Gandhi in loincloth and *chadar* sitting among the formally attired Englishmen. He communicated his disdain for civilization as it is understood in the West, his disdain for material possessions, his pride in Indian civilization, as well as his power—an ordinary man would not have been granted entry. By dealing openly with a man in *mahatma* garb, the British accepted his political position and revealed their loss of power.

The communicative power of Gandhi's costume was, however, uniquely Indian. Paradoxically, as his popularity grew, the messages he brought to the Indian public in his speeches and writings had increasingly limited range. Gatherings were huge, running to a hundred thousand or more. Only in the cities were public address systems available to him. Most people who went

to see him could not hear him. Even if they could hear him the Gujarati or Hindustani or English in which he spoke could not be understood by many, sometimes most, of his audience. In a nation about three-quarters illiterate, his writings were available to still fewer.

Gandhi needed another medium through which to communicate with the people of India. He used his appearance to communicate his most important messages in a form comprehensible to all Indians. Engaged in the simple labor of spinning, dressed as one of the poor in loincloth and *chadar*, this important and powerful man communicated the dignity of poverty, the dignity of labor, the equality of all Indians, and the greatness of Indian civilization, as well as his own saintliness. The communicative power of costume transcended the limitations of language in multilingual and illiterate India. The image transcended cultural boundaries as well. His impact on the West was enhanced by his resemblance, in his simplicity of dress and his saintly manner, to Christ on the Cross.

In India, visual communication has a unique force. The sight of the eminent or holy blesses and purifies the viewer; the experience is called *darshan*. People came, literally, to *see* Gandhi. Through *darshan*, the power of Gandhi's appearance surpassed his message in words. "For the next quarter of a century, it was not only for his message that people came to him, but for the merit of seeing him. The sacred sight of the *Mahatma*, his *darshan*, was almost equivalent to a pilgrimage to holy Banaras" (Nanda 1958:213).

During this same period, Gandhi was experimenting with the economics of cloth production. Gandhi recalled: "It was in London in 1908 that I discovered the wheel. . . . I saw in a flash that without the spinning wheel there was no *Swaraj* [self-government]. But I did not then know the distinction between the loom and the wheel, and in *Hind Swaraj* used the word loom to mean the wheel" (quoted in Jaju 1951:1). "I do not remember to have seen a handloom or a spinning wheel when in 1908 I described it in *Hind Swaraj* as the panacea for the growing pauperism of India. In that book I took it as understood that anything that helped India to get rid of the grinding poverty of her masses would in the same process also establish *Swaraj*. Even in 1915 when I returned to India from South Africa, I had not actually seen a spinning wheel" (Gandhi 1957:489). By the time Gandhi returned to India in 1915, cloth production had become central to his program.

Like most leaders of the nationalist movement, Gandhi thought the reindustrialization of India to be of paramount importance, but unlike most of them he was opposed to mechanized industry, which he viewed as a sin perpetrated on the world by the West. He wanted to revive artisanry. From the establishment of Phoenix farm in 1904, Gandhi had committed himself to the simple life of labor. Machines were labor-saving devices that put thousands of laborers out of work, unthinkable in India where the masses were underemployed. Factory production facilitated the concentration of wealth in the hands of a few big capitalists, and transformed workers into "utter slaves."

Gandhi selected Ahmedabad, the Manchester of India, as the site for his settlement because this "great textile center was best suited for experiments in hand-spinning and weaving which appeared to him the only practicable supplementary occupations for the underworked and underfed masses in the villages of India" (Nanda 1958:134), and ". . . as Ahmedabad was [also] an ancient centre of hand-loom weaving, it was likely to be the most favourable field for the revival of the cottage industry of hand-spinning" (Gandhi 1957:395). Erikson, who has written so brilliantly on the early years in Ahmedabad, observes that "Gandhi blamed the disruption of native crafts [not only for the poverty of India, but also] for the deterioration of Indian identity. He was soon to elevate the spinning wheel to significance as an economic necessity, a religious ritual and a national symbol . . . Gandhi wanted to settle down where both tradition and available materials would permit him and his followers to build a community around the cultivation of spinning and weaving" (Erikson 1969:260).

By the time he settled at Ahmedabad his goal for India was the achievement, through *satyagraha*, of the reduction of poverty, disease, and immorality, and the restoration of dignity. Spinning offered solutions to all these problems. The English had destroyed the greatest cotton producer in the world in order to protect their own industries from competition, to create a source of raw materials not available in the British isles, and to make a ready market for their finished products. Gandhi sought to restore India's lost supremacy, to revive this "second lung" of India (the first was agriculture). His reasoning was simple: If Indians returned to the production of their own cloth there would be work for millions of unemployed, Indian wealth would not be taken to England and Japan, and Indians would again be their own masters (See Jaju 1915:8). "*Swadeshi* is the soul of *Swaraj*, *Khadi* is the essence of *Swadeshi*" (Gandhi quoted in Jaju 1951:12).

Until its demise in the 1820s, spinning had been a supplementary occupation of women all over the country. Weaving, by contrast, had always been a caste occupation. Though at first Gandhi concentrated on reviving spinning among women, he soon broadened his program. Spinning would become the leisure pursuit of all. The wealthy would spin as service; the poor to supplement their incomes. Through spinning, India would be able to clothe itself, and thereby free itself from foreign exploitation and domination. Through spinning, all Indians, rich and poor, educated and illiterate, would be laborers, equal and united through their labor (see Bean 1988):

Originally there was one specific objective: to give work and clothing to the half-starved women of India. To this was related from the beginning the larger objective of khadi—the cloth itself as a means of economic self-sufficiency (swadeshi) which in turn must inevitably produce self-government (swaraj). This progression, *Khadi = swadeshi = swaraj*, was Gandhi's incessant preachment for the rest of his life. . . . His genius had found a tremendous symbol which was at the same time a practical weapon . . . for the liberation of India. . . . The symbol he had found, the wheel itself, assumed enormous importance with the passage of time: it related itself to the whole of life, to God, to the pilgrimage of the spirit. . . (Sheean 1949:154,157,158, see also Bayly 1986).

Gandhi had returned from South Africa determined to wear handmade cloth. He brought a weaver to the ashram, but there was no hand-spun yarn available for the loom, so Gandhi began looking for a spinner. It was not until 1917 that his associate Gangabehn located spinners who would produce yarn to be woven at the ashram—if slivers, carded cotton for spinning, could be supplied to them. Until then, Gandhi had relied on machine-spun yarn from Ahmedabad mills for his looms, but he still had to get the slivers for hand-spinning from the mills. Gandhi's *khadi* had to be entirely handmade, so he asked Gangabehn to find carders who could provide the slivers. Gandhi "begged for [the raw] cotton in Bombay" (Gandhi 1957:492). Finally the entire process of making cloth could be done by hand.

At this time, Gandhi's *dhoti* was still of Indian mill cloth. The *khadi* manufactured at the ashram was only 30 inches wide. Gandhi "gave notice to Gangabehn that, unless she provided . . . a *khadi dhoti* of 45 inches width within a month, [he] would do with coarse, short *khadi dhoti*. . . . well within the month she sent [him] a pair of *khadi dhotis* of 45 inches width, and thus relieved [him] from what would then have been a difficult situation. . . ." (Gandhi 1957:493). Perhaps Gandhi was looking for an opportunity to change to a loincloth, a change he accomplished two years later. From 1919 on, he was clothed entirely in *khadi*, and instead of the turban, he began wearing the white *khadi* "Gandhi cap." *Khadi* was much too coarse for wrapping as a Gujarati turban.

In 1920 as part of the Non-cooperation Movement, the leaders of the Indian National Congress endorsed hand spinning and weaving, to supply cloth to replace boycotted foreign cloth and to engage the masses in the nationalist cause. In this

they followed Gandhi, but they were by no means in full agreement with him. "Tagore argued that trying to liberate three hundred million people by making them all spinners was like urging them to drown the English by all spitting together: it was 'too simple for human beings.' Complaints came in against *khadi* as a material in the conditions of modern living. It wouldn't stand up to the wear and tear of a factory. It was too heavy. It was hard to launder and therefore unsuitable for children. Gandhi's answer was that with more skill there would be better *khadi*" (Ashe 1968:249).

Most nationalists disagreed with Gandhi's opposition to mechanized industry. Many, including Jawaharlal Nehru, believed industrialization crucial for India's economic well-being. Few felt Gandhi's love for the purity and simplicity of coarse white *khadi*. Jawaharlal Nehru's sister Vijayalakshmi Pandit thought *khadi* rough and drab. She felt deprived to have to wear a wedding sari of *khadi*, though it had been spun and woven by Kasturbai Gandhi and dyed the traditional Kashmiri pink. Their father Motilal Nehru, at the meeting of the Congress Working Committee in Delhi during November 1921, burst out laughing when he heard Gandhi say that a person must know hand-spinning in order to participate in civil disobedience (Nanda 1958:235). In a letter to his son, the elder Nehru spoke of the *khadi* movement as one of Gandhi's hobbies.

Despite their disagreement, the Nehrus and other nationalist leaders supported hand-spinning and *khadi* because they recognized its symbolic and economic importance in the programs of *swadeshi*, boycott, and noncooperation. Mrs. Pandit noted the effects of wearing *khadi* "Gandhi caps," *kurtas*, and *dhotis*: She could no longer detect the social class of the visitors to her family's home. The uniform was a leveler, all Congressmen were the same (Pandit 1979:82). Accommodations were made for intranational variation: *dhotis* for Hindus, *pyjamas* (trousers) for Muslims, turbans distinctive for Sikhs or southern Brahmins. *Khadi*, the fabric of nationalism, transcended and encompassed these distinctions. Gandhi had taught his followers that costume can transform social and political identities. When Gandhi, clothed in loincloth and *chadar*, was received by the Viceroy Lord Reading in 1921, his followers (and his opponents) also saw that costume can be used to dominate and structure a social event. The most important result of those meetings was that Gandhi, wearing his opposition to English values and representing the people of India, was accepted to negotiate as an equal with the representatives of the British Empire in India. Gandhi forced the Empire to compromise its standards and thus demonstrated the power of the freedom movement he led.

By 1921, all Congressmen were dressed in *khadi*. The Governor of Bombay Presidency, C.R. Das, made *khadi* the uniform of civic employees. From July 1922, no member of Congress was allowed to wear imported cloth, and dues were to be paid in hand-spun yarn instead of cash. Hand-spinning and *khadi* had become a fixture in the freedom movement. Economic revitalization and self-government would be accomplished through mass organization, carried on by *khadi*-clad Congress workers promoting indigenous industries and mass action by teaching spinning to everyone, spreading the boycott of foreign products to the most remote villages, and preparing the way for mass civil disobedience.

Khadi had become, in Nehru's words, "the livery of freedom."

REFERENCES CITED

Ashe, Geoffrey
1968   Gandhi. New York: Stein and Day.
Bayly, C.A.
1986   The Origins of Swadeshi (Home Industry): Cloth and Indian Society, 1700–1930. *In* The Social Life of Things. Arjun Appadurai, ed. Cambridge: Cambridge University Press.
Bean, Susan S.
1988   Spinning Independence. *In* Making Things in South Asia: Proceedings of the South Asia Regional Studies Seminar. Michael Meiter, ed. Philadelphia: University of Pennsylvania.
Chandra, Bipin
1965   Indian Nationalists and the Drain, 1880–1905. Indian Economic and Social History Review 2(2):103–44.
1966   The Rise and Growth of Economic Nationalism in India. New Delhi.
1968   Reinterpretations of Nineteenth Century Indian Economic History. Indian Economic and Social History Review 5:35–75.
Chatterji, Basudev
1980   The Abolition of the Cotton Excise, 1925: A Study in Imperial Priorities. Indian Economic and Social History Review 17(4):355–80.
1981   Business and Politics in the 1930s: Lancashire and the Making of the Indo-British Trade Agreement. Modern Asian Studies 15:527–74.
Chaudhuri, K.N.
1968   India's International Economy in the 19th Century. Modern Asian Studies 2:31–50.
1978   The Trading World of Asia and the English East India Company 1660–1760. Cambridge: Cambridge University Press.
Cohn, Bernard
1988   Cloth, Clothes, and Colonialism: India in the Nineteenth Century. (This volume).
Dewey, Clive
1978   The Eclipse of the Lancashire Lobby and the Concession of Fiscal Autonomy to India. *In* C. Dewey and A.G. Hopkins, eds. The Imperial Impact. London: Althone Press.
Dutt, Romesh Chunder
1968   Romesh Chunder Dutt. Delhi: Government of India, Ministry of Information and Broadcasting.

1901, 1903   The Economic History of India, 2 vols. London.

1906   India Under Early British Rule. London: Kegan Paul

Erikson, Erik
1969   Gandi's Truth. New York: W.W. Norton.

Fischer, Louis
1982(1951)   The Life of Mahatma Gandhi. London: Granada.

Gadgil, D.R.
1942   The Industrial Evolution of India in Recent Times. Calcutta.

Gandhi. M.K.
1922(1908)   Indian Home Rule. Madras: Ganesh & Co.

1941   Economics of Khadi. Ahmedabad: Navajivan Press.

1957(1927–29)   An Autobiography: the Story of My Experiments with Truth. Boston: Beacon Press.

Gandhi, Prabudas
1957   My Childhood with Gandhiji. Ahmedabad: Navajivan Press.

Ganguli, B.N.
1965   Dadabhai Naoroji and the Mechanism of External Drain. Indian Economic and Social History Review 2(2):85–102.

Gittinger, Mattiebelle
1982   Master Dyers to the World. Washington, D.C.: Textile Museum.

Gold, Gerald
1983   Gandhi: A Pictorial Biography. New York: New Market Press.

Irwin, John
1962   Indian Textiles in Historical Perspective. Marg XV(4).

Irwin, John and K. Brett
1970   The Origins of Chintz. London: Victoria and Albert Museum.

Jaju, Shrikrishnadas
1951   The Ideology of Charka. Tirupur.

Masani, Rustom Pestonji
1939   Dadabhai Naoroji: The Grand Old Man of India. London: Allen & Unwin.

Mehta, Ved
1977   Mahatma Gandhi and His Apostles. New York: Penguin Books.

Nanda, B.R.
1958   Mahatma Gandhi. Boston: Beacon Press.

Naoroji, Dadabhai
1887   Essays, Speeches and Writings. C.L. Parekh, ed. Bombay.

Pandit, Vijayalakshmi
1979   The Scope of Happiness. New York: Crown.

Pradhan, G.P. and A.K. Bhagwat
1958   Lokamanya Tilak. Bombay.

Sarkar, Sumit
1973   The Swadeshi Movement in Bengal, 1903–1908. Calcutta.

Sharma, Jagadish
1955,1968   Mahatma Gandhi: A Descriptive Bibliography.

Sheean, Vincent
1949   Lead Kindly Light. New York: Random House.

Sitaramayya, Pattabhi
1969   History of the Indian National Congress, vol. 1 (1885–1935). Delhi: S. Chand.

Wolpert, Stanley
1962   Tilak and Gokhale. Berkeley: University of California Press.

25

ARACHNE'S GENRE: TOWARDS INTER-CULTURAL STUDIES IN TEXTILES

Sarat Maharaj

Editor's introduction: Sarat Maharaj is professor of visual art and knowledge systems at Lund University and the Malmo Art Academies, Sweden. In his often-cited essay reprinted here, Maharaj begins by revisiting the Greek myth of Athena and Arachne and discovering two models of textile production and knowledge: the ordered, polite, and conformist (Athena) versus the challenging, questioning, and inescapably messy (Arachne). Maharaj observes differing ways of seeing the world (via the textile) that reveal the problematic Europe-versus-"other," rational-versus-exotic thinking tackled by postcolonial theory. The essay then moves its attention to the British trade journal *Textilia*, published between 1918 and 1920 and directed at colonial textile buyers to improve morale after World War I. Here, Maharaj finds another power struggle, this time organized in terms of gender (the trader versus consumer of textiles), and also between the past and the near future that will bring with it the decline of the British colonial power and textile trade. Turning to Gandhi's writings, which Maharaj suggests stand for the modern version of the Indian epic the Mahabharata, a " 'de-feminizing' of the textiles-making terrain" is observed as a move to situate textile production as a "sexually indifferent practice." The essay concludes with the "ethnic look" that took to the catwalk in the late 1980s and finds the textile to be a discipline that takes joy in remaking and escaping the categories set for it.

ARACHNE VERSUS ATHENA

'Do' and 'Do not' says the law of genre. (Derrida)

Arachne or Athena? Who ends up the more wronged, the more shabbily-treated in the fateful contest to decide who is the better textile-maker of the two, 'the champion'? The question is not easily shaken off—something of it unsettles even the most clipped, zero-degree renderings of the Arachne story. The more we feel for Arachne the more we seem to stop short of taking her side altogether: at the same time, we become less and less sure about Athena's wisdom.

It is this ebbing double movement which Ruskin strives to counteract in telling the Arachne story, part of his Address on prize-giving day, 13 December 1870, to the Woolwich section of the Art and Science Department.[1] He does not simply run through the story start to finish. He cuts into his own narration just before the climax

Source: Sarat Maharaj, "Arachne's Genre: Towards Inter-Cultural Studies in Textiles," *Journal of Design History* 4, no. 2 (1991) pp. 75–96. Reproduced with permission.

to make a special plea for Athena and to caution his audience: they should not be taken in by the fact that everything appears to end quite disgracefully, demeaningly for the goddess. To set things in her favour he paces his audience through a reading of the fable.

Why the desperate need to shore up Athena's reputation? What clues does it give about how we have come to think of textiles and textiles-making and the world of idea and imagination associated with it? To explore this we might perhaps recall the bare bones of the myth.

Arachne, a Lydian woman renowned for her needlework, sewing, and stitchery, challenges Athena, goddess of the crafts, to a contest of textile skills. Athena, disguised as an old woman, tries to dissuade her. But Arachne persists with her challenge. The test begins, Arachne's hands fly across the taut loom-netting with the shuttle as swiftly, as ably as Athena's. Athena inspects the completed piece, finds it faultless, as lovely as her own. The dénouement is best left in Ruskin's words: 'She loses her temper; tears her rival's tapestry to pieces, strikes her four times across the forehead with her boxwood shuttle. Arachne, mad with anger, hangs herself; Athena changes her into a venomous spider.'

Ruskin's staging of the myth projects a norm for textiles-making and womanhood, for 'proper' textile work, and 'proper' sexual identity. 'Athena' serves as the device through which this feminine/textiles norm is constructed and dramatized. He justifies her wrath by presenting her as a corrective, sobering force exercised in the name of the law, the norm. How she enforces it—the matter of her aggressive jealousy, her violent fury, the all-too-final punishment meted out to Arachne, is side-stepped.

Athena, figure of the notion of 'proper' genre and gender? Arachne, at the opposite pole, sign of everything improper, deviant? The opposition is summed up in their embroidery. Through the 'trim-leaved olive of peace' motif the former signalled a sense of poise, control, restraint. The latter's imagery of ivy leaves, as Ruskin puts it, 'in

their wanton running about everywhere' spoke of wild abandon, of Bacchus—disruptive forces of a topsy-turvy world of tabooed desires, unchecked longings, feelings quite outside 'the law'.

Athena had embroidered the council of the gods—a serious, weighty theme. It celebrated order, reasoned exchange, measured discourse. The composition touched on the sense of civic manners, virtues, morals, on the civilizing force, the laws of men. What Arachne had pictured might be called 'the unmentionable'. Ruskin describes it as 'base and abominable'. It demystified the lives of the gods—exposing their trickery, the devious means to which they stooped to get their way. Arachne had driven home the point by depicting the 'Rape of Europa' and twenty other episodes involving the gods' abduction and violation of women.[2]

For Ruskin, Athena's idiom and imagery are at one with the established order of sensibility—bringing together ideas of 'needlework within the bounds of good taste' with those of 'the decent, respectable woman'. How he constructs the 'textiles/feminine' is underscored by the fact that the goddess had sprung fully-created from Zeus's head—something of a male-centred projection of the feminine? At odds with this order, Arachne's work seems unbecoming, lewd, in poor taste. It smacked of the shameful and licentious. Athena was 'legitimately' provoked into curbing, as Ruskin puts it, 'her fault of a poisonous and degrading kind, sensual, insolent, foul'.

His address seems fine-tuned for the women in his audience, at times as if for their ears alone. A confessional mood is evoked. Do young girls still sew samplers he asks in an aside? Let's hope they have not let such sound, Athena-work lapse. It would amount to courting Arachne's fate. The intense terms in which he describes her transformation into the 'meanest and most loathsomely venomous of creatures' impresses, repels, instructs. With allusions to Penelope, faithful at her loom, and to 'the Queen of our own William the conqueror, maker of Bayeux tapestry', his model of 'proper needlework/womanhood' is rounded off and heightened—against any temptation to stray onto the reckless path Arachne had taken.

What Ruskin subsumes under the term 'textiles' seems surprisingly all-embracing 'good stout clothes to knit and weave but also to make pictures on them'. It seems to take in the spectrum of textiles genres, cutting across all its modes and effects—everything from production of cloth, through commodities and goods, to textiles as art practice, as something which may be read as fine art statement or object. Should we take this, in the spirit of Barthes' 'endless garment',[3] as a seamless, unending textile text worthy of attention at any of its countless points?

Ruskin, however, privileges and validates simply one site of this vast textile text—Athena's genre. He sees its force as essentially institutionalizing—at the four corners of her tapestry she had embroidered 'admonitory panels' depicting the dreadful fate of those who dare question the established order. He favours its capacity to replay received imagery and iconography, to cite and re-cite an approved, accepted system of attitudes and values—a logic encapsulated by the notion of 'sewing sampler'.

He excludes Arachne's space, subordinates it—sensing in it a swirling stream-of-consciousness energy, the destabilizing force of tinkering at will with elements of received representations, for playing them off and turning them against themselves. What he is denouncing is its potential for prising open a gap through which other versions and voices, other inflections and differences may appear. It is on the drive towards such an exploring, experimenting sensibility—on a questioning, independent creativity—that he comes down heavily towards the end of his address.

The genre of Athena as repetition; that of Arachne as resistance? The former as sheer production, as prescribed representation, as saying the same thing again, as 'naked repetition'; the latter as expressive, self-reflexive practice, saying it again with a difference no matter how apparently small, as 'clothed repetition'?[4]

These may serve as signposts in mapping textiles today. We may see Arachne's space as a metaphor for avant-garde textiles practice—in which handed-down notions of art practice/genre/gender come to be cited and overturned, displaced and played out. A space on the other side of Athena's male-order decencies—one shot through with a sense of the obscene, orgasmic?

ARACHNE—EXOTIC EMBROIDERESS?

To the blonde goddess's eyes, Arachne's tapestry border of ivy leaves was 'faultless': she tore it to shreds. To Ruskin's eyes it is 'exquisite': he condemns it as signifying everything 'wanton, foul, abominable'. It suggests something not unlike that split in the gaze which constructs the exotic object—between irresistible attraction to the thing and a sense of revulsion for what it is taken to mean—the split of the Eurocentric gaze.

Arachne is a Lydian needlewoman, 'a poor little Lydian girl' for Ruskin. Lydia, in Asia Minor, stands as part 'the Greek world'. But it is also too much at its edge, at that dangerous point where 'the Attic' must meet and tussle with whatever it constructs as other than itself, as different. The word 'Lydian' connotes a sense of the voluptuous as against 'Attic' restraint, self-control. As a musical mode, against the latter's manly, robust clarity, its strains are orientalizing, effeminate. It serves as a metaphor for the exotic, the Oriental Other—impossibly necessary and unacceptable in one go.

The Athena/Arachne poles, in various guises, have tended to underpin modern versions of the Eurocentric gaze in art and design history and theory. 'When the Attic migrates eastwards', Winckelmann, founder of the discipline's modern career, observes, it risks 'lapsing into Asiatic luxury, becoming voluptuous, wanton'.[5] The artistic norm, the idea of the beautiful in 'the Greek' he counterposes to the wayward extra-ordinariness of 'the Eastern other'—grotesque, non-manly, excessive.[6] For Hegel, too, 'the bizarre extra-ordinary' signals the exotic other; he situates it in

Indian art, which he constructs with formidable consistency as the split sign—at once shamelessly sensual and sublime.[7]

Ruskin's split view of the Lydian as the exquisite or foul is not separate from this tradition of looking. It is tied to his own distinction between the Greek ideal, 'Daedalus work', and what he sees as Indian art's excess and moral inferiority.[8] Indian textiles, design and craftwork count as exquisite in his scheme only because he hives *it* off from the distasteful content he finds in Indian art.

The pattern persists even where we would have expected change. Fry attempts in the 1930s, under the impact of modernism and primitivism, to dethrone the Attic norm. He ends up constructing Indian art in terms of exotic excess, as a sign riven by lush lifelikeness and pornographic content—summed up in what he sees as its 'provocative dehancement of the female figure'.[9]

For inter-cultural studies the concern is not only with how the Eurocentric gaze constructs itself historically. It is with the fact that it is the inescapable factor in analysis.[10] Athena's piercing eyes dart across the Lydian's embroidery—scanning, scrutinizing—till she lashes out. How do we go beyond the relations of power and domination of the Eurocentric gaze which constructs the 'otherness' of non-European cultures—beyond the violation following on Athena's gaze?

But could she have made sense of Arachne's embroidery as a Lydian might have? The possibility of an epistemic barrier needs to be admitted. To speak of cultural orders whose ways of patterning and picturing experience are 'radically at odds with ours' is to face up to incommensurable elements of systems which cannot be decoded one to another. There is no 'common idiom' in which to do so, hence their 'radical difference'.[11] Foucault highlights this by reference to the 'bafflingly fantastic way' in which animals are classified in Borges' Chinese encyclopaedia:

(a) belonging to the Emperor, (b) embalmed, (c) tamed, (d) sucking pigs, (e) sirens, (f) fabulous, (g) stray dogs, (h) included in the present classification (i) frenzied, (j) innumerable, (k) drawn with a very fine camelhair brush, (l) et cetera, (m) having just broken the water pitcher, (n) that from a long way off look like flies.[12]

Its impact on 'our own' logic of representation is to show it up as only one of many ways of arranging things. It makes us rethink the view of inter-cultural studies as simply stepping out of 'our' ways of knowing and feeling into those of another culture. It is more likely we are thrown into tussling with 'radical difference', with an epistemic barrier we might never quite pass. The more we strive to get under the skin of another system the more we find ourselves glancing over our shoulders to see how 'our system' is reshuffled. By the inter-cultural stance we would need to understand something like this anxious, two way, self-searching process—scene of never-ending exchange?

The view seems not unrelated to post-war economic and cultural developments.[13] It is not easy to see how we could continue to speak of cultures as discrete entities, separate worlds of life and living closed in on themselves. As Clifford notes, the forces of post-war communications and internationalization, of global economics, cultural centralization, of 'entry into modernity', have produced what may be spoken of as a world-system. The exotic, once tantalizing far-away, is now increasingly part of our local, everyday; at the same time, we stumble over the familiar in the most unexpected, 'exotic' of places.

It suggests a breaking down of differences between cultures, a levelling out of those distinctions, oppositions, contrasts, on which received ideas about culture were based. At least, of notions of clear-cut, essential forms of difference centred on stabilities and continuities such as tradition, roots, clothing and custom, language. The breakdown of the 'old orders of difference' might be understood as a process of loss, of homogenization. Or as an opening for creating new, critical statements of difference and identity. Neither seems to tell the whole story. Each undermines the other and slips out of the privileged grasp of a totalizing account.

In this setting we might think of culture less in terms of a final, enclosing identity, more as an unceasing activity of unmaking and remaking. It stages itself as a stalling, a perpetual putting off the point of arrival. We might see it as play of inflections of difference, images of self rubbed out even as they are written up. By the idea of post-imperial identity we thus grasp something not unlike 'a fable of our Caribbean selves'—metaphor for a sense of self as a process of up-rooting, grafting, copying.[14] It makes itself up as it goes along out of the dizzying mix of elements of the late modern world.

But it remains arguable whether this breath-taking spectacle of diversities amounts to a realm of expressive liberties or to one of repressive tol-erance. It is not unlikely that what we gain on a micro-level in terms of expressing difference through dress, fashion, clothing, style, we lose on a macro-level to a tighter, intensified standardiza-tion and corporate uniformity.

It suggests an interplay of liberating and im-prisoning forces—or even perhaps their stale-mate. What sense should we thus give the claim that the Eurocentric gaze has been met and scat-tered?[15] Does it persist through this scene in the guise of fashion-textiles up-to-dateness, the 'Eth-nic Look', or is the latter a travestying of Athena's gaze, turning it against itself?

TEXTILES' PRIMAL SCENES

The Arachne Story or *The Tapestry Weavers*—is Velasquez's *Las Hilanderas* on a mythological or historical theme? For all the hard evidence now in the former's favour the verdict remains open because so much in the picture does not fit the case made out by either side. Ortega suggests that Velasquez turns myth 'inside out': he does not let it run away with representation into make-believe, he draws it into the real world, he histori-cizes myth. 'He finds the root of every myth in its logarithm of reality.'[16]

The view echoes the long-standing counterpos-ing of the mythic to the historical—the former as representation on an imaginary, timeless plane; the latter as in specific time and place. The one an order wrought out of idea and concept, the other out of sticking to the empirical facts. Myth as run-ning on the spot, replay—as 'naked repetition'—how textiles tend to be written about. History as cutting through myth in steady advance towards progressive enlightenment, a chronicle of bursts of originality and creative leaps—the way fine art practice is written.

It loses its force as we grasp the complex ways in which myth intertwines with enlightenment, metaphor with unembellished historical fact.[17] Historical writing may thus be seen as a 'white, colourless light' spun *out of* the colour spectrum that is epic and myth, rather than as something entirely separate from it.[18] The force of metaphor in historical writing, in what stages itself as a me-ticulous representation of 'things as they actually happened' seems inescapable. We rarely, though, see anything of the machinery, the figures and tropes, with which it pulls off the effect.

Such metaphors are not unlike worn-out im-ages on coins, defigured through use and ren-dered 'invisible'. Drained of their lifeblood, a 'white mythology' they figure forth representa-tion which has the look of a flat, factual, 'histori-cal' account of things, of 'literal meaning'.[19] We would have to think of textiles in the spirit of this interleaving, beyond the 'reassuring opposition of metaphor and proper meaning', myth and his-tory. It would be to alert ourselves to metaphor's and myth's force in language—how it shapes the social, political, institutional discourses in which textiles are imagined and made.

The myth of the primal scene serves as a device for imagining that 'origin' through which the tex-tiles world comes to be decisively carved out. At the same time the idea of an 'originary moment' is cancelled, for we reach back to more than one scene, more than a single 'origin'—to the high modernist avant-garde, to ancient Greece and India, to the *Odyssey* and the *Mahabharata*—to

Penelope in the former and Draupadi in the latter—epics in which textiles function as pre-eminent signifiers.

For much of the epic we have a portrait of Penelope, drawn by a male-order placing of the feminine, as patient, prudent, adamant. We witness her highly-praised loyalty to Odysseus who has not returned from the Trojan war. She waits faithfully at her loom as the years pass, managing to keep at bay the suitors who lodge themselves in her home and who refuse to leave till she has chosen to marry one of them.

It is at odds with how she is portrayed in the final book, the Hades section of the epic. There the suitors, recounting the events leading to their slaughter by Odysseus on his return, see her as deceiving, double-dealing. They complain of the calculated way in which she misled them into waiting. She had promised to make up her mind about whom to marry when she had finished weaving her husband's shroud. But she had only pretended to be doing this. All day she would weave at the loom. By night she would sneak out to undo her day's work.[20] She had devised a delay tactic, a way of stalling for time.

The ruse stamps something of the motif of the guileful, weaving woman, the notion of feminine craftiness across the textiles scene. Penelope herself seems to come through largely unscathed in literary, artistic representations. As we have seen, Ruskin invokes her image as the 'good needle-woman' and endorses it. But the point is not that we rarely, if ever, see Penelope herself cast as the cunning 'bad needlewoman'. It is that 'good or bad needlewoman', they amount to two sides of the same male-order coin of feminine images.

In the *Mahabharata*, Yudistra stakes himself, his brothers, even Draupadi, their collective wife, in a game of dice he loses to his greedy cousins. She is dragged by her hair, out of the seclusion due to her at the time of menstruation, into the assembly hall, as the Sabha Parva section of the epic notes, 'trembling like a plantain in the storm'.[21] The victors try to disrobe her in public.

The final humiliation they wish on her, however, does not quite come off.

For every yard of her sari her tormentor manages to pull off another seems to add itself on. He ends up in a tangle of cloth. Draupadi asks, 'has the house of the Kurus sunk so low that women are not respected?' Draupadi's violation mirrors the even more ancient figure of feminine hurt, Amba, whose name means 'the womb' and who haunts the epic's events. Both voices counterpoint through the epic a complaint which is never silenced against male-order and its power.

Penelope's suitors, Draupadi's husbands; Penelope's unending shroud, Draupadi's endless sari; a weaving and a denuding which never reaches finality, a stalling tactic, a perpetual deferring which encapsulates something of their 'recalcitrance', the sense of feminine resistance. The motifs come to be echoed and inflected in the avant-garde, in the Bachelors' attempt at disrobing the Bride which is part of the turbulent narrative of desire in Duchamp's *Large Glass* or *The Bride Stripped Bare by her Bachelors, Even* (1915–23; Philadelphia Museum of Art).

In the *Large Glass* drama the Bride's 'intense desire for orgasm' leads her to take charge of her own undressing. That is, even when the Bachelor machine—'9 malic moulds, a cemetery of uniforms and liveries', as Duchamp describes his cross-section of the hierarchy of male stereotypes—assumes the initiative in her stripping, in which she aids and abets. But she backs off and rejects his brusque offer. Frustrated, the bachelor turns to auto-eroticism, 'grinds his own chocolate', culminating in its own spectacular splash.[22]

Against this Duchamp sketches the Bride's struggle to go it alone, to work out and achieve climax under her own steam. Her desire springs from a voluntary stripping imagined by herself. Duchamp pictures her effort in terms of a motor car climbing a slope in low gear. 'The car wants more and more to reach the top while slowly accelerating. As if exhausted by hope, the motor of the car turns faster and faster until it roars triumphantly.'[23] It dramatizes something of a sense of independent feminine desire, activity and achievement.

It is not without significance that *The Large Glass* is subtitled 'A Delay in Glass'. We might understand it as a holding back in a double sense—in terms of the work's theme and its genre. The encounter between the Bride and the Bachelors is fraught, incomplete. It puts off the idea of some final coming together, a moment of total erotic fulfillment—metaphor for the notion of the inundating, full presence of meaning? The search for such a moment is left open-ended.

But *The Large Glass* as 'delay' also refers to holding back from identifying with any particular genre. Duchamp conceived the piece as a resisting of the 'painterly visual', of its mindless excess, in favour of the conceptual. His notes on how to render the orgasmic cloud—Milky Way imagery in the topmost part of the work—recoils from a full, grandiose fine art treatment of pigment. A lush, expansive painterliness, smeary impasto flourish and facture is cited but held at bay by more reserved, laconic, 'taste-neutralizing' forms of marking and imprinting based on varnish, dust-breeding techniques, on lead-wire thread and threading.[24]

The work stops short of the genres of fine art statement, holding them up for long as possible. The painterly institution of the canvas as window on the world, its perspective conventions are played *ad absurdum*. Our sight passes from the glass surface, through and beyond it into the extra-pictorial. The piece is not a 'painting on the wall'; if it is a freestanding object it is not quite so in a 'sculptural sense'. It has a craft dimension to it, a sense of meticulously-calculated design set off against ready-made, manufactured elements. The myths of a painterly genre, the sense of free expressivity and its flourish are detoured and side-tracked.

A genre which cuts across genres—which seems both less than painting, the ready-made, sculpture, the craft-design object, visual and conceptual statement, and yet more than them. A genre which keeps itself at play between them, eluding

them, not unlike the Bride's 'going it alone'. With this configuration of genre and the sexual identity do we begin to approach Arachne's space?

The historical moment of Duchamp's *Large Glass*—from 1915 to 1923—saw the opening of two discourses grappling with 'the cloth famine' from opposite ends of the world system of textiles: in England, a discourse centred on the new journal *Textilia* (1918–20)—trade and corporate interests searched for the way forward after the Great War, to recover imperial normality 'without delay'.[25] In India, Gandhi's views and debates on textiles addressed to Indians struggling to shake off British rule 'without delay', centred on the paper *Young India*, collected and reprinted in the thick of the independence movement as *Wheel of Fortune* (1918–22).[26]

TEXTILIA: 1919–20

Never was a time more inauspicious than the present, it would seem, for the publication of a new journal—when all the great nations are engaged in the greatest war ever waged, when industry and commerce are plunged in difficulties hitherto never dreamed of and new anxieties appear on the darkened horizon almost every moment.[27]

Textilia was launched with these words in July 1918—a monthly journal but published quarterly because of wartime economies. It embraced some fairly long-standing journals and bulletins acting as the mouthpiece of the spectrum of established textiles trades.[28] They grouped under the *Textilia* umbrella to speak with one voice, a common front in the face of an important element of the wartime crisis—buyers at home and abroad felt that the trade was taking unfair advantage of war shortages to push up prices; there were allegations and suspicions of outright profiteering.[29]

It was a prime factor in *Textilia*'s original reasons for appearing at what seemed an inauspicious time. It saw its purpose as 'created by the exigencies of the present and writ large on its pages': 'to tell in the language of truth the real position of the Textilian and allied industries of Great Britain and Ireland at the present time, their struggles to maintain output in the face of the gravest difficulties which have ever beset the trade, and their loyal services to their country in its hour of peril.' It set out to reveal the facts behind 'abnormal prices, the vital details of which are perhaps not fully grasped or understood'.[30]

'Vital details'—a sustained commentary on them. That is how we might look on *Textilia*, a 'fair-minded' defence of the trade's views on the rising textiles prices, an issue which dogged it to its final number in 1920. With an eye on the big South American market, it resorted to quoting a Brazilian minister on the trade's bona fides: he vouched for the fact that Britain's name was synonymous with 'reliability, sound workmanship and good faith, punctuality and straightforwardness'.[31] The testimonial unwittingly spotlights the very problems which made for the textiles crisis!

The journal sought to dispel worries about inordinate rises in prices, the future of the trade given the cloth famine and bleak world-wide shortages. It aimed at boosting morale—at encouraging colonial buyers who were fighting shy of placing firm orders in the hope that prices might come down. Against crashes, breakdowns, distortions in the wake of the government's diverting of massive textiles resources for the war effort, it sought to inspire confidence in the trade, in a return to something like pre-war normalities.[32]

To restore trust, to reaffirm old alliances and contacts—*Textilia* embarked on a robust publicity drive on the trade's will to weather the crisis. Its advertising campaign promised 'business as usual' after the war. For 'textilian entrepreneurs and tradespeople' it was not unlike a pep talk, a barometer of market fluctuations. For the British public, colonial buyers, new consumers—it saw itself as an exercise in persuasion and propaganda to stave off growing competition.

'Vital details'—the issue of rising yarn and cloth prices—which *Textilia* tried to account for so tirelessly so 'that nothing might besmirch that fair character attaching to British production' thus comes to signal two conflicting desires. The wish to go back to 'familiar prices', stabilities and normalities of the pre-war imperial textile system at odds with the awareness that there was no going back, that 'abnormal prices' had come to stay. The desire to restore the old order plays off against the desire to move forward, the pull of the traditional against that of modernity and change.

Textilia's discourse structures itself in this double movement. On one plane a narrative of past enterprise, achievement and success which runs as a series of tales on specific sectors of the trade: each becomes a mythic, heroic saga of determination, skill, triumph.[33] Against this, on another narrative plane, run reports on the actual, contemporary condition of the trade—glimpses of hardship, loss, adaptation, grappling with modernity.

In this sense, it structures itself as 'representation of representation'. The textiles narrative it constructs is through other narratives on the subject. We have a heightened sense of the mode with the 'Great Trade Novelists' series.[34] The textiles world is depicted through citing other depictions. Literary/historical, fictive/documentary, statistical/imaginary—the lines between them blur in the journal's representation of the trade.

The visual representation of textiles it constructs is, in not dissimilar mode, through representations of art works related to textiles-making. Pieces by the great masters build up into the sense of an unbroken, grand tradition.[35] What is evoked is a textiles culture at one with fine art masterpieces and the world of high culture—sign of traditional order, wholeness, stability of value.

That the journal should have been subtitled 'Argosy of Informative Textilian Commerce and Industry' takes on some significance in this context. It seems to connote little more than a formal, literary convention as we might understand in a 'treasury' of stories and reports. But against the background of crisis, the desire for 'the homecoming' to stable values and prices, the framing power of the Odysseus myth is not far away—ideas of survival against all odds, sacrifice and ordeal, of adventure and exploration, even conquest and colonization. Audley Gunston's cover design pictures a safely berthed, textile-laden argosy to dramatize the point—an inspiring image for the trade striving to make it through the stormy times.

As if to stress the homecoming theme, the April 1919 issue featured, at a dark hour of the crisis, Bernardino Pintoricchio's *Scenes from the Odyssey*. It entitled it *The Return of Penelope to Ulysses* which, though not inaccurate, tends to inflect our reading in a more positive, affirmative register. We see Penelope at her loom and Ulysses (though it is more likely Telemachus) as striking figures in their prime—not, as the epic text might have led us to imagine, somewhat aged and ravaged by testing years of separation and exile.

Through the window we catch a glimpse of the 'argosy' safely in harbour (though it is more likely a snapshot of the tormenting Sirens episode). In the journal's context, the picture comes to be projected as an idealized sign of reunion—at any rate, a shorthand image of homecoming as a sense of total completeness and reprise which mirrors the journal's narrative of the trade weathering the crisis back to the productive fullness of its imperial heyday.

As Renaissance art work, the Pintoricchio itself stands as a sign of 'the standard of value' as opposed to its breakdown in the contemporary avant-garde. *Textilia*'s projection of this version of the myth may be contrasted to two other avant-garde uses of it around the time. In Joyce's *Ulysses* (1915–23), the heroic myth is at every turn punctured by the mundane, the contemporary everyday. Bloom's return is to a 'cold, cuckolded bed': Molly is modelled on the tradition of the 'disloyal' Penelope who was said to have chosen to sleep with her suitors rather than to have saved herself for her husband. Joyce holds back on the notion of a grand reunion—everything is left open-ended, in flux.

His language would not permit otherwise. Meanings slide across other meanings, a perpetual staving off safe arrival at some enclosing finality of meaning. It is not unlike the Vorticist language of William Roberts' *Return of Ulysses* (1913); angular, jagged forms keep at bay the sense of organic totality. They discourage and interrupt build up of sentiment and feeling associated with the reunion theme. Swerving, dissonant juxtaposings of planes and perspectives, a terse, speeded-up idiom break up the received regularities of our ways seeing and picturing things.

Textilia's inaugural number signalled the idea of 'the homecoming' both as a return to the prewar imperial order of textiles and as a reclaiming of the 'essence of British identity'. The trade's resilience, its capacity to fight and win back its pre-eminence is tied to grit and determination, 'the characteristic of the British race'. Its capacity to prove its strength and resolution against all odds, in the darkest hour of crisis, is presented as 'an axiom' of the national identity. The tenacity which brought its military captains such success is linked with the spirit of its industrial and commercial adventurers who managed by 'their indomitability in penetrating to the uttermost parts of the earth'.[36]

The journal noted a year later that the portrait it had penned had not been unjustified. It sprang from 'the sure record of our national history, where there is no instance to be found of our defeat, when to the world it seemed inevitable'.[37] But, from the October 1918 issue onwards, there was growing awareness that it had become less easy to speak of Britishness in terms of the received grand myth: other voices, of textiles workers and the public of consumers, now cut across it. If the lead article, 'Renascens Britanniae', continued to couch Britishness in rather grandiose figures of the fifteenth-century revival, the imagery was also deployed to dramatize the possibility of regress, of lapse 'into decadence and decline'.

The concern was that despite the forging of a new sense of Britishness—'pulsating with new aims, new hopes, new visions of the future'—injustices, vices, evils of the industrial past[38] would linger on. The inflection it was adding sought to appeal to both ruling and subordinate elements of society. The search was for an identity built on a spirit of co-operation and togetherness. In a rather laboured tapestry metaphor the lead article, 'Dawn', was to speak of the 'Great Design that now had to be woven', of 'New units in a harmonious whole', of unity through interdependence.[39]

The corporatist overtones of this vision of Britishness, centred on an organic unity of 'head/hand, brain/brawn, capital/labour',[40] were not uncoloured by the period's new order political ideologies. It reflected its classic oppositions: keenness to thrust into the industrializing future set off against the wish to reaffirm what was seen as the human, personal quality in pre-industrial work relationships. As its scan of Britain's historical development reveals, *Textilia* favoured an idealized model of close, individual contacts, family-community bonds of workers associated with the era of artisanal labour.[41]

If the age of machinery had created great manufacturing concerns, workmen's combinations, and federations, it had also unleashed bureaucratizing forces—'a maze in which the individual is lost', a wounding division between 'soulless corporations called employers and soulless combinations called employees'. The journal held out little hope for schemes of betterment for workers until the 'old relationship could be restored without being attended by the old evils'; a restorative and transformative desire in one go—not the first time we see this pattern in its discourse.

The 'Britishness' *Textilia* pondered was understood as forged within the network of Britain's relationships with the colonies—national identity as something defined through 'other worlds' and against them. 'Lancashire', textilian symbol for Britain, was seen as both tied to and set off against India, sign of the colonial world. The latter's purchasing behaviour came in for anxious scrutiny—sustained speculation about whether Indian dealers would follow up price inquiries with commitments to buy. If Lancashire was to be baled out of the slump this was crucial. What is unwittingly conveyed is that India—portrayed

as Lancashire's special dependent, steady and subordinate client—is really its prop and lifeblood, its *raison d'être*!

The anxiety was over the colonial other's 'bewildering' behaviour which did not appear as legible as in the past. If it provoked a feeling of the loss of grip over 'the other' it also had something of an unnerving impact on the sense of self. There was fear that the 'fat days of Lancashire were over'.[42] It was expressed in tetchy, exasperated remarks about the colonial market: 'Frankly India so far has been disappointing.'[43] It was suggested that she might have 'burnt her fingers'[44] in holding back with firm orders: 'Calcutta was a particularly bad sinner in this respect. Bombay was not very much behind, with Karachi a good third'.[45] There was worry that this meant 'competition, menace, a threat' from the 'greatest of outlets for Lancashire' which would 'put in jeopardy its supremacy'.

In this respect, *Textilia* saw matters almost exclusively in terms of a return to the pre-war, imperial pattern of trade. It was keenly aware that 'upcountry India had been swept clean of cloth and starved of yarn'.[46] Why the delay in placing orders? It marked the limits of its response. Many factors were involved in the tardiness of Indian buyers—whether colonial British or native—which are not at issue here. The striking thing is that throughout the journal there is no hint of the swelling resistance in India to dependency on Britain—a movement which, ironically, was making Lancashire cloth and yarn the very issue of struggle.

Notions of Britishness touched on in *Textilia* were mainly in the 'masculine mode'. Audley Gunston's cover design dramatizes this. An argosy laden with materials and garments stands safely at anchor. From it a man carries forward fabrics and offers them, ritual fashion, to 'woman'—pictured as an ideal, classical nude with attendants. The two activities involved seem to be centred in the masculine, or at any rate initiated from its standpoint: the seafarer's business of gathering and bringing back exotic cloth and the issue of constructing the 'feminine' by dressing it up, fashioning it, condense into one.

The image seems to capture the journal's overriding concern with the sphere of trade and trading: textiles and the feminine become signs of a male-centred exchange and turnover of commodities. By depicting the business of obtaining textiles and its usage as very much in the hands of men the image suggests a linking of sexual place, position and power. The division it implies seems to be between 'masculine' obtaining of materials through trade, putting them to 'manly' use as necessities, at the service of 'woman': this is set off against the 'feminine' receiving of textiles, displaying them as part of the spectacle object.

It is a scene of relationships carried through in no small measure in other pictures on the theme of 'textile goods and exchange' reproduced in the journal. The Gunston cover design shares much the same ground of ideas and attitudes as Lord Leighton's *Phoenicians Bartering with the Ancient Britons*.[47] The field encompasses the dramatic Derry and Toms' advertising image on the subject. The journal notes: 'The scene represents the Port of London, where are gathered together merchants from four quarters of the globe, laden with the choicest fabrics, the most costly furs and exquisite textiles that their countries produce for the adorning of women and beautifying of the home.'[48] Across the spectrum of representation—fine art to advertising images—the turnover of textiles commodities seem to be depicted in and through the image of woman, the consumer-spectacle.

With the journal's emphasis on the sphere of textiles exchange and consumption the Viyella advertisement it almost regularly featured as its back cover may seem unusual in showing women in the act of textile production. But it is also phrased to evoke a sense of the glamorous, exotic spectacle object—women exhibiting cloth and themselves 'as if only to themselves'. Beyond this double-edged image, *Textilia* reveals little about the sexual division of labour and its coding in the sphere of production.

In *Textilia*'s pronouncements on taste and its orders—through which it signalled notions of difference of culture, class, nation and ethnic provenance—we see a condensed version of those oppositions which characterize its wider reflections on Britishness. 'Each nation's taste is different, each demands a different line of design—Africa, on the Gold Coast requires more brilliance than the sea-girt islands of Japan.' The view, however, was not so much part of an open pluralism of taste as a fixed stereotyping of difference based on market demands.[49]

It marked out something like a universal ground of fine taste—'educated taste'. This centred on a rather rough and ready distinction between garish, brilliant colour as sign of 'less educated, provincial, crude taste', and 'softer, muted colour as that of fine taste'. It is not unlikely the view reflected, in broad terms, dominant norms of colour and taste of Britain of the day. It was evoked in the face of workers 'tasteless', high spending on costly silks. If the aim was to give guidance on good taste it was no less to regulate buying, to steer it out of the 'elysium of luxury goods' towards more sober, mainstream textiles on the market.[50]

In these respects, *Textilia* seemed to conform to the old orders of taste. But it was not completely sealed off from the new, as may be noted in its reaction to the Mayor of Brighton's criticism of the English as 'the most inartistic nation on the face of the earth'. 'In our homes, our furniture, decorations, pictures and ornaments are all hideously ugly. All middle class and working class homes throughout the country want refurbishing.'[51] The journal seemed to demur before the sweeping, almost Vorticist ring of his views. But it called for a positive response to the simpler, cleaner line of the modernist style coming into vogue—away from the 'old stodgy standard of Victorian taste'.

The switches of focus from traditional to modernist orders of taste are part of the overall double movement of the journal's discourse. It also depended on the particular area of textiles on which it was commenting. At one end, a conservatism of taste: matter of fact acceptance that little could be changed with straw hats, 'the boater design',[52] or the desire to catch up with Parisian *haute couture*, sign of established fine taste. At the other, an incipient modernist taste: rejection of muted colours associated with the old world in favour of colour suggestive of the 'brass band with more stridency than tune', a taste for the vibrant, easy-going, dissonant, for experiment, futurism and modernity.[53]

One item captured the sense of these switches: government promises to put aside cloth for something like mass-produced, reasonably-priced suits. From the outset the project appeared to get bogged down by delays, diversions of promised material, high prices. *Textilia's* last issue comments on the innovative scheme's failure; the trade and its customers are urged to report unfair prices to the Committee on Profiteering.[54]

The idea of constructing a textiles world based on 'standardization and concentration'—mass-produced goods and special items, ready-made and one-off, made-to-measure clothes—appeared to have to come to grief. The standardized suit, recalling Penelope's incomplete shroud, turns up as a pre-eminent signifier of the unfinished product of modernity—'new order Britishness'.

GANDHI'S *WHEEL OF FORTUNE*: 1918–22

Who has denuded India? The question reverberates through the Gandhi texts centred, not unlike *Textilia*, on the desire to remake the world of textile-making. The latter serves as both practical instrument and metaphor for 'Swaraj'—the remaking of India, of something like an Indian identity quite independent of British rule and outside the network of colonial subordination.[55]

The stripping of Draupadi replays itself in the actions of the modern denuders of India who strip her of wealth and assets. Gandhi identifies them as representatives of the colonizing power, Messrs Bosworth Smith & Co. and

the O'Briens and native agents, the Shree Rams and the Maliks. He links them with the insolent power of men who 'lift women's veils with their walking sticks', to peer at them as if they were commodities—disrespect and violation no less than that suffered by Draupadi.[56]

The tone seems unusually sharp—he is responding to the British shooting of unarmed Indians at Amritsar in April 1919. The backdrop is the jittery reaction of the colonial authorities to the Russian Revolution's impact on agitation for home rule. The moment is the aftermath of the Great War. The 'Mahabharata', a figurative expression in many Indian languages, had come to mean literally the 'Great Conflict'.[57] In this sense, we might say, the Gandhi texts speak to 'the time of the modern Mahabharata'.

His focus is on the unequal relations of the imperial system. It has brought poverty, 'a famine of cloth in India'.[58] At one end, prosperity in 'Lancashire' developed with protective laws: at the other, pauperism with the indigenous textiles industry run down and reduced to consumer, client status. Indians had themselves come to believe that cloth could not be manufactured in India, that they were at the mercy of imports. They had been 'amputated in a figurative sense'—crippled, rendered into state of dependency.[59] Gandhi's allusion is to the trauma of East India Company rule, of control over textile production sometimes enforced by mutilating workers, by chopping off their fingers.

How do the colonized break the bonds of dependency? Gandhi saw only part of the answer in 'Swadeshi'—the boycott of British cloth. To give up foreign clothes is 'to decline to wear the badge of slavery'.[60] But could this be anything more than an aggressive desire to punish 'the English'— a sign of weakness?[61]

For Gandhi the post-colonial self could not be forged in a clear-cut instant by simply negating the colonizing other: independence, self-determination were not so much ready-made states of being and mind as a self-creating process on the part of the colonized—a struggle to awaken new capabilities and qualities in themselves no less than in the colonizer. A mutually transforming, binding project, a 'sacrificial quest'—they redefine themselves and the colonizer without feeling the latter could be simply bypassed.

Gandhi grounds the search in homespun—the 'rudimentary' mode of textile-making, but something not out of people's reach, even the poor. They, above all, would need to experience through spinning and weaving a sense of what it might mean to do things for themselves, to stand on their own feet. Gandhi put great store on it as a practical-symbolic mode for shaking off the sense of dependency, for grasping the idea that deliverance from colonial subjugation lay in their own hands. He is thus wary of mill-loom, machine-made cloth not because of a backward-looking glorifying of artisanal modes. It is because he assesses it, in the circumstances, as the less effective instrument for undoing the structures of colonial power.

He codes the homespun/mill-made divide thus: the former, has a potential for activating the mass of people into making of cloth—drawing them into the arena of reforging themselves and their energies, of rethinking identities and subjectivities. Mill-made cloth, on the other hand, no matter how 'native' in origin, remained a product churned out over their heads: it tended to leave relationships of subordination and dependency largely intact.

Gandhi is also aware that to opt totally for mill-cloth would be to hand over to the colonizers the lever of a 'machinery blockade' of native mills. It would mean stepping out of the old order of dependency on foreign cloth only to step into the new one of dependency on imported technology and machinery.

Homespun/mill-made—signs of counterposed economic systems and politics? 'Capitalists do not need popular encouragement', Gandhi notes drily, in associating mill-cloth with a rising class of native industrialists, entrepreneurs, and merchants.[62] Their aspirations, however movingly expressed 'in the name of the nation and independence', amount to stepping into the colonizing power's shoes.

Homespun, at the other pole, he links to the making of a people, their coming to awareness in personal ways of fresh connections and contacts which cut across caste and class in new co-operative communities.[63] In this sense it serves as a critical gloss on the prevailing system of textiles production. Where mill-made cloth signals a consolidating of corporate forces, hand-spun, based 'anarchically' in individual desire and demand, comes to signify resistance.

But is it 'manly' activity?[64] The question is put by Swadeshis not at ease with the spinning and weaving regime Gandhi recommends for men and women alike. It seemed radically at odds with accepted ways of being men and women, with received ideas about 'virile labour' and 'women's activity', productive work time and leisure time.

Gandhi suggests a kind of 'de-feminizing' of the textiles-making terrain, displacing its traditional axis of sexual position and power. He seeks to shift it into a space where it might be seen more as a sexually indifferent practice, where it might become 'as graceful for either sex as music'[65]—something like an unmotivated sign system, an abstractive notation all the more flexible for that for constructing sexual identities in fresh ways.

A sexually indifferent 'gracefulness', the sense of stepping out of the state of dependency towards co-operative living—Gandhi pictures the post-colonial self as a site of transformation where the orders of taste come to be turned inside out. People would have to consider revising their sense of fashion and feeling for cloth textures. It would involve training themselves to revalue the lowly, subordinate product of homespun, to see 'art and beauty in its spotless whiteness', to appreciate its soft unevenness.[66] It would mean cultivating a different textiles sensibility altogether—an aesthetic more responsive to elements of the raw, native, vernacular.

'Will the nation revise its taste for Japanese silks, Manchester calico or French lace and find all its decoration out of hand-spun, hand-woven cloth, that is, Khaddar?'[67] Gandhi is responding to reports sent in by women's groups on debates and discussion over tastes, fabric textures, a new textiles sensorium.

The activist Sarladevi writes from a Swadeshi meeting at Sialkot attended by 1,000 women: they are sorry she has given up costly fine silks for a heavy, coarse, homespun white sari. She answers that it is easier to bear than the weight of helpless dependence on foreign manufactures however apparently fine and light.[68] Her sari impresses more than her speech: as with Draupadi, it stands out as the signifier pre-eminent.

ARACHNE—'GENRE DÉBORDÉ'?

Athena or Arachne? In one of his *Irish Tracts*, Swift sides with the latter in the name of 'colonized Ireland'. In another, no matter its doubtful and suppositious status in the Swift canon, he sides with the former in the name of 'colonizing England'. Each stance comes to overrun its own borders into the other. An 'undecided' space opens up.

Swift recounts the Arachne story in *A Proposal for the Universal Use of Irish Manufacture in Cloaths and Furniture of Houses etc. Utterly Rejecting and Renouncing Every Thing Wearable that comes from England* (1720).[69] 'From a Boy, I always pitied poor Arachne', he confesses. 'I could never heartily love the Goddess, on account of so cruel and unjust a sentence'. He likens it to the even more painful sentence of English exploitation of Ireland: 'for the greater Part of our Bowels and Vitals is extracted, without allowing us the Liberty of spinning and weaving them.'

Swift speculates on a boycott of materials and yarns not grown in Ireland or made there. Would that all 'silks, velvets, calicoes and the whole lexicon of female fopperies' were excluded in favour of Irish stuffs. He suggests a 'firm resolution by Male and Female, never to appear with one single shred that comes from England'. Would Ireland then stand on her own feet, this land where 'the

faces of the Natives, their manner and dwellings' spoke of 'universal oppression'?

His counter-tract *A Defence of English Commodities Being an Answer to the Proposal for the Universal Use of Irish manufactures . . . etc.* (1720),[70] portrays Arachne as ungrateful, guilty of presumption and pride. Her sentence is seen as fair, as a warning against the ill-consequences of her putting her trust in herself, of contending with superiors. The stress is on the old woman's advice to Arachne: to accept her subordinate position, to obey so that the blessings given to her might not be revoked. Swift's arguments on her behalf are seen as misleading—a topsy-turvy interpretation in which he makes 'Madness pass for Wisdom and Wisdom for folly'.

It calls into question his account of the downtrodden, 'native Irish'. 'They have been chastised by England with great severity; if they shared Arachne's fate it was for the same crime— Madness, Pride, Presumption.' But it claims the punishment had its creative, transforming side, eliciting from them skills and sensibilities for a new world. 'They have been metamorphosed not into spiders but Men—transformed from savages into reasonable creatures, delivered from a state of nature and barbarism, and endowed with Civility and Humanity'.

If we have a striking picture of the violent, wounding induction of the colonized to modernity it is a double-edged one. Fiercely corroding as this force is, it is paradoxically creative: it brings into being conditions in which the colonized come to reforge themselves as identities in a modern world.

The Swift tracts tend to leave us less sure about imagining power as a dominating force radiating outwards from a focal, colonizing source. We are alerted to the possibility of its being something like a two way, destructive/creative process— even when 'the one' seems to be calling all the shots. The idea of stepping out of the 'state of dependency' would not be easily grasped without taking this field of interconnectedness into account.

Swift's eye for elements of this intertwined relationship of demand/response is keen: 'biass among our people', he notes, 'is in favour of things, persons and wares of all kinds that come from England.' They admire English things and are attached to them, desire for foreign textiles not easily shed off—an issue not unfamiliar to Gandhi in the Indian setting. To interpret such desire simply in terms of abject dependency and collusion, as artificial and false needs, seems limiting, brittle, not least belittling. It is better to see here a field of needs and wants in interplay: they mutually define, mould and elaborate one another, often taking on a momentum of their own.

The discourses of both *Textilia* and Gandhi are not unaware of this and have to reckon with it. Their constructions of 'Britishness' or 'Swaraj' come face to face with a world-system of inter-linking needs and wants, symbolized by the Lancashire/India connection, and, wittingly or not, are conceived in its terms.

In the post-war setting of avant-garde textile practice, by 'Arachne's space' would be signalled something less than the absolutely separate and totally autonomous and something more than it. At any rate, not simply a self-enclosed space with clear-cut, fixed boundaries demarcated in straight opposition to that of Athena's. We would have to imagine it as approaching a condition not unlike that 'state of débordement' with which Derrida rethinks genre:[71] a marking out of borders with their spoiling, a spilling out and beyond them, a taking into itself 'its outside and other'—Athena's space.

Judy Chicago's *Mother India* is a principal landmark in this textiles field. It situates itself squarely in Arachne's space—terrain on the 'other side of male-order' from where it launches its powerful critique of the actual subordination of women, the devaluing of the female body and childbirth in institutions of Indian life and living. But in drawing Athena's gaze into itself can we say it manages to turn it inside out and displace it—to make it speak about, even against, itself? Or does it simply replicate its way of seeing?

A Eurocentric gaze at the heart of a feminist critique and at odds with it—deadlock of insight and blindness?

The Chicago piece stages itself through Katherine Mayo's *Mother India* (1927)[72]—a controversial report, at a high point of the Swaraj movement, on the condition of women in India, on Gandhian action for change. The Mayo work does battle with the Mother India of tradition and 'obscurantism'. The myth had been remobilized in the 'Bande Mataram'—Hail Mother India!—movement against colonial rule. She sought to combat the forms it took in native practices attending women's health care and childbirth, to cut through the latter's 'superstitious world' in the name of progress, humane medical knowledge.

The female 'child-fabric'—how it is rent and ripped by the force of the Indian male-order—is the focus of Mayo's moving account of Indian women.[73] Her story is devised through figures and imagery which share not a little with Orientalist narratives of the colonized other. She documents shocking, unspeakable conditions. But the more harrowing the data the more everything tips over into an Orientalist fable of exotic brutalities and horrors.

Through vivid anecdotes and vignettes, a spellbinding tale of bizarre habits, practices, and morals emerges which is no less 'factual' for that. In querying Mayo's sources, Wyndham Lewis was to draw attention to this phenomenon. It makes his critique of *Mother India* significant for our review of Athena's gaze if in other ways it simply expresses the imperial male's embarrassed defence of the 'great Indian people' against the 'suffragette outsider'.[74]

If Mayo's insights were crucial they were also not easy to dissociate from a sense of the Western, medical gaze as invasive, punitive. We see something of a collision between a traditional symbolic ordering of divisions between pure/polluted and a modern, 'literal', clean/dirty hygienic code. As systems of representation they seem utterly closed off to each other, incommensurate: we reach something like an epistemic barrier.

Chicago's own focus on the 'hygienic body' tends to replicate this framework. As such it seems at one with the period's forceful assertion of this stance, with Naipaul's troubling double-edged, sanitizing scan of the Indian body.[75] She notes that the hospital system for childbirth might be a questionable blessing for modern Indian women.[76] For a moment it seems she is leading up to opening a gap for a critical review of the gaze; the moment seems to slip by.

Chicago voices far more explicitly and strikingly the politics of 'stepping out of dependency' than Mayo. But her desire to take 'an enlightened, compassionate' view of the 'Indian other's world' suggests less of that self-reflexive element with which the latter accounted for her forthright, plain-speaking and brisk 'truth-telling'. Mayo was putting together 'living facts of India today'—however problematical such an enterprise might be. Its equivalent, a sense of the 'living facts' of the post-colonial contemporary condition of women in India, appears to be the missing—at least unnegotiated—dimension of the Chicago world.

Hence the work's repetition of an array of received, 'sensationalized' scenes: arranged and child marriages, infanticide, sati, purdah and the like. Mayo speaks of midwives inserting balls of hollyhocks roots into the uteruses of women in labour.[77] The Chicago piece pictures them in the 'Birth Scene' probing the woman's body with a whole hollyhock stem—a raising of the horror stakes, a heightening turn not out of keeping with the Orientalist mode. The decorative elements add not a little to this sense of stereotyping.

A sense of the static, unchanging 'other' comes to be reaffirmed. The tendency is for the grand received text of the Eastern world of 'self-inflicted sorrows' to re-install itself. Perhaps even quite against its intentions, the piece veers towards depicting the other unremittingly as victim. It is as though everything is seen through Athena's gaze—as a world waiting to be uplifted and in which the 'other' cannot speak and must be spoken for.

Against this force, to make room for this voice, Chicago tries to allude to 'stepping out of dependency' by means of strips of mirror-worked Gandhian homespun. The device is perhaps too muted to mark itself off as critical, counterpointing inflection against the rest of the representation. In staging a tableau on the suffering of Indian women the Chicago piece gets inexorably caught up in an eyeball to eyeball encounter with the 'Athena vision': the showdown tends to leave it somewhat transfixed by it, even captive to it.

Mayo had confronted the grand mythologies of feminine power, 'Mother India' goddesses, with the desperate condition of women in India of the day. The Chicago piece, ironically, tends to take up her diagnosis and to institute it as a negative, fixed mythology. We sense little of the condition of women in the India of Chicago's day.[78]

It is as if a half-century of the story of Indian women—signposted by the popular post-independence film *Mother India*, which had such an impact across the decolonizing world, picturing a woman's and a people's struggle 'to step out of dependency'—should go missing. Its upshot is to vacate the field for the unintercepted sway of Athena's gaze, blunting the vigorous sense of exposé which inspired the piece.

'Ethnic, ethnic everywhere', observes Katherine Hamnett, commenting on the late 1980s fashion textiles craze for the 'Ethnic Look'.[79] Its lexicon is derived from elements of 'tribal raffia work and dress', references to colonial clothing, 'ethnic design, motifs and decoration', pop synthetic sari fabrics, 'folk-kitsch' materials, 'native embroidery, bead and sequin work and stitchery'. These collage into some topsy-turvy statement about 'self as the other'—at least, some blurring of the received demarcating lines between them. But does the Eurocentric gaze gain a further lease of life in this masquerade, in the guise of the 'Ethnic Look'?

Does the latter simply mime and endorse the former, as a straightforward mirroring and celebrating of Eurocentric textile-fashion-costume constructions of otherness? The heightened manner in which it stages its borrowed and lifted elements suggests otherwise. In parading them in a larger than life register it tends to open up a self-reflexive gap between 'source and cited version', 'original and copied item'.

Hence the air that everything has been 'expressed to the second power'—whether they are quite placed in quotation marks or not. In uneven ways the elements come to be rendered in an ironic mood. Each item—fabric, texture, threading, stitching, pleating, motif, design, imagery—is mimicked in a version which sets it all askew enough for new inflections and tones to be marked. Is it in the 'Ethnic Look' that Athena's gaze is met, splintered, deflected—its codes brusquely scrambled?

Arachne's genre, where everything surges beyond its borders and overruns it in an endless referring to something other than itself may be contrasted to the self-referring character of the modernist conception of genre. At least, to the version which came to post-war pre-eminence with Greenberg.[80] For him the modernist genre, *par excellence*, involved a reductive, involuting process—a paring down by each art of its medium to its essential qualities.

The stress is on each art alluding back to the logic of its own idiom and shadowing it, divesting itself of every element of the 'extra-pictorial'. It amounts to a sense of the strict autonomy of each art practice—an underlining of firm boundaries and borders between them. Everything in this view of genre is driven by a self-enclosing force: to use Greenberg's words 'the arts, then, have been hunted back to their mediums, and there they have been isolated, concentrated and defined'.

Amongst the many reasons for this purist conception of genre, we need mention only one: 'the threat' to fine art's autonomy posed by both 'art in the service of politics' and the spectacular growth of mass culture forms. Strictly defined, genre was part of a holding operation against this dynamic of dissolution. It aimed at staunching the outward flow of representation, out of its received generic confines, at curbing tendencies towards the flattening out of differences between artistic practices.

Greenberg recalled not only Lessing's Enlightenment project of defining the classic, clear-cut spheres of each of the arts against what was seen as the medieval confusion of the arts, their undifferentiated mix.[81] He echoed Babbitt's rearguard project which had appeared with high modernism. Babbitt was against the 'effeminate' mixing and blending of the arts into one another in a 'mélange des genres'. Against their 'restless striving away from their own centres toward that doubtful periphery where they pass over into something else' he sought to assert a more strict, 'manly' division of the arts, 'genre tranché'.[82]

The 'uneven undecidedness' of Arachne's genre might be seen as placed both between the world of 'genre tranché' and that of a 'mélange des genres'—and beyond them. Between the former's manly power, its strict demarcations and steely divisions and the latter's 'effeminate' force, its yielding, submissive lines—and beyond them in something like a sexually indifferent terrain? Avant-garde textiles practice thus begins to map out an inside/outside space. An 'edginess'—it cites established genres and their edges even as it cuts across and beyond them.

We would perhaps have to remind ourselves that it is not, therefore, so much a matter of elevating it from its 'subordinate' place in the hierarchy of art practices, of legitimating and adding it to the official list of genres. This would be to see things simply in terms of extending the list—as if the idea were to equal or top the breathtaking range of art genres recognized in the *Kama Sutra* and *Sukraniti*.[83]

It is rather that it throws out of joint the list itself, its ordering of the arts. As a genre of 'boundaried boundarilessness' it marks that protracted exit out of the modernist landscape of genres into the post-modern scene of art practices. This uneven passage might be signposted by Magdalena Abakanowicz's invention of the 'Abakan genre' which spans the years 1964–75. Hanging forms, genre between wall and floor, a 'débordement' in which all genres are played and deferred the series is perhaps best summed up by the piece *Abakan—Situation Variable*.[84]

The two orders of genre sketched by Derrida are centred on the issue of borders.[85] They might be related to the 'edgy matter' Ruskin made of the borders embroidered by the Goddess and the Lydian needlewoman. A law of genre based on purity—clear demarcations of a practice's edges and boundaries. We might liken this to Athena's trim-leaved olive of peace border: measured interval, decisive, crisp outlining. It suggests a manly territorializing force constantly staking its ground, hemming in things, patrolling its frontiers to find out what belongs inside and what outside. A regulating, self-enclosing drive keen to ensure, to use Chicago's words, that 'borders should not be wonky'.[86] Against this, is Derrida's counter-law of genre based on contamination and impurity in which everything belongs by not belonging, scene of the undecided, unsteady. We might liken this to Arachne's border of ivy leaves, with its 'wanton running about everywhere', hither and thither—a dispersing, incontinent force, 'genre débordé', to use Derrida's words, a 'fabric of traces'.[87]

SARAT MAHARAJ
Goldsmiths' College, University of London

NOTES

My special thanks to Tag Gronberg for help with this research. One version took the form of an address to the Arts Council of Great Britain in September 1989, another a paper to the 'Textiles Today Symposium' held at Bradford University in April 1990. Thanks also to Ian Paggett, Central-St. Martins, the London Institute, for photos of students' work.

1. J. Ruskin, *Complete Works*, George Allen, 1905, vol. XX, pp. 371–80.
2. Ovid, *Metamorphoses*, Harvard University Press, 1977, vol. 1, lines 1–145, pp. 289–99.
3. R. Barthes, *The Fashion System*, Hill & Wang, 1984, p. 42.
4. G. Deleuze, *Difference et repetition*, Presses Universitaires de France, 1968, pp. 36–7.
5. J.J. Winckelmann, *Reflections on Painting and Sculpture of the Greeks* (1756), Scolar Press, 1968, pp. 160–1.
6. J.J. Winckelmann, *History of Ancient Art* (1764), Low, Marston, 1881, vol. 1, p. 162 (17) & (18).
7. G.W.F. Hegel, *Aesthetic* (1835), Clarendon Press, 1975, pp. 322–47.
8. Ruskin, op. cit., p. 347.
9. R. Fry, *Last Lectures* (1933–4), Cambridge University Press, 1939, pp. 150–69.
10. E. Said, *Orientalism*, Penguin, 1987, pp. 1–28.
11. J.L. Lyotard, *The Postmodern Condition*, Manchester University Press, 1984, pp. 15–27.
12. M. Foucault, *The Order of Things*, Tavistock Publications, 1970, p. xv.
13. F. Jameson & S. Hall, *Marxism Today*, September 1990, pp. 28–31.
14. J. Clifford, *The Predicament of Culture*, Harvard University Press, 1988, p. 182.
15. Ibid., p. 256.
16. Ortega y Gasset, *Velasquez, Goya and the Dehumanization of Art*, Studio Vista, 1972, pp. 101–2.
17. T.W. Adorno, *Dialectic of Enlightenment*, Verso, 1979, pp. 43–80.
18. W. Benjamin, *Illuminations*, Fontana, 1970, p. 95.
19. J. Derrida, *Margins of Philosophy*, Harvester Press, 1982, pp. 209–29.
20. *Odyssey*, Clarendon Press, 1932, Book XXIV, lines 114–50, pp. 496–7.
21. *Mahabharata*, Indian Press, 1915, Sabha Parva.
22. M. Duchamp, *The Green Box*, 1915. M. Sanouillet & E. Peterson, *The Essential Writings of Marcel Duchamp/Marchand du Sel*, Thames & Hudson, 1973, pp. 62–8.
23. Ibid., p. 43.
24. Ibid., p. 36.

25. *Textilia* (An Informative Journal of Textilian Industry and Commerce), London, 1918–20.

26. M. K. Gandhi, *The Wheel of Fortune*, Ganesh, 1922.

27. *Textilia*, no. 1, vol. 1, July 1918, p. 2.

28. *Textilia* (Woollens, Cottons, Silks etc.): *Linen* (Organ of the Linen Trade); *British Lace* (Journal of British Lace, Embroidery & Curtain Trade); *Hosiery and Underwear*; *British Clothier*; *British Glovemaker*; *British Hatter*. With the April 1919 issue *Textilia* took under its wing *The British Spinner* and *the Carpet Maker*.

29. No. 4, vol. 1, April 1919, p. 232.

30. No. 1, vol. 1, July 1918, p. 2.

31. No. 1, vol. 1, July 1918, p. 2.

32. No. 1, vol. 1, July 1918, pp. 2–5.

33. 'Story of the Sailor Suit', no. 1, vol. 1, July 1918, pp. 33–92; 'Story of Hosiery', no. 1, vol. 1, July 1918, p. 93; 'History of Hats', no. 1, vol. 1, July 1918, p. 98; 'History of Lace', no. 3, vol. 1, Jan. 1919, p. 127; no. 4, vol. 1, April 1919, p. 257; 'History of Gloves', no. 3, vol. 1, Jan. 1919, p. 146.

34. The first featured Mrs Henry Wood, 'Novelist of the Glove Trade', with reference to her novel *Mrs Halliburton's Troubles*, no. 1, vol. 1, Jan. 1919, pp. 143–6; the second Mrs Gaskell, 'Novelist of the Cotton Trade', in a discussion of *Mary Barton*, no. 4, vol. 1, April 1919, p. 185.

35. Vermeer's *The Lace Maker*, no. 2, vol. 1, Oct. 1918, p. 76; Rembrandt's *The Syndics*, no. 1, vol. 1, July 1918, p. 7; Hals' *Man with Glove*, no. 1, vol. 1, Oct. 1918, p. 86; Velasquez's *Las Hilanderas* and *Lady with Fan and Gloves*, no. 1, vol. 4, April 1919, p. 209; no. 2, vol. 1, Oct. 1918, p. 85; Van Dyck's *The Embroidery Age*, no. 3, vol. 1, Jan. 1919, p. 135; Titian's *Man with Glove*, no. 3, vol. 1, Jan. 1919, p. 144; Lord Leighton's *Phoenicians Bartering with the Ancient Britons*, no. 4, vol. 1, April 1919, p. 214; Moore's *Blossoms*, no. 2, vol. 2, Oct. 1919, p. 155. Only the Irish linen industry

engravings and Spenser-Pryse's *The Workers' Way*, no. 3, vol. 2, Feb. 1920, p. 207, go against the grain of the myth thus woven.

36. No. 1, vol. 1, July 1918, p. 2.

37. No. 4, vol. 1, April 1919, p. 50.

38. No. 4, vol. 1, April 1919, p. 51.

39. No. 3, vol. 1, Jan. 1919, p. 127.

40. No. 4, vol. 1, April 1919, p. 3.

41. No. 1, vol. 2, July 1919, p. 3

42. No. 4, vol. 1, April 1919, p. 233.

43. No. 1, vol. 2, July 1919, p. 12.

44. No. 3, vol. 2, Feb. 1920, p. 241.

45. No. 2, vol. 2, Oct. 1919, p. 135.

46. No. 3, vol. 1, Jan. 1919, p. 162.

47. No. 4, vol. 1, April 1919, p. 214.

48. No. 1, vol. 2, July 1919, p. 90.

49. No. 2, vol. 2, Oct. 1919, p. 137.

50. No. 1, vol. 1, July 1918, p. 55.

51. No. 1, vol. 2, July 1919, p. 34.

52. No. 4, vol. 1, April 1919, p. 289.

53. No. 3, vol. 2, Feb. 1920.

54. No. 1, vol. 1, July 1918, p. 17; no. 2, vol. 2, Oct. 1919, pp. 222–3; no. 3, vol. 3, Feb. 1920, p. 313.

55. M.K. Gandhi, *Wheel of Fortune*, 1922, pp. 8–14.

56. *Young India*, 7 July 1920, p. 29.

57. The Spenglerian grand cycles of conflict and decline in which D. Tagore places Western civilization and the Great War in his introduction to the Gandhi texts adds to the sense of a modern Mahabharata (pp. i–xii). See also A. Besant, *The Great War*, Theosophical Publishers, 1899. Gandhi explicitly tied the wheel (chakra) to the symbolism of the Gita section of the Mahabharata (*Young India*, 20 Oct. 1921), pp. 93–6.

58. Ghandi, op. cit., p. 11.

59. Ibid., pp. 24–5.

60. Ibid., p. 45 (*Young India*, 6 July 1921).

61. Ibid., pp. 2–5.

62. Ibid., p. 20 (*Young India*, 18 August 1920).

63. Ibid., p. 54 (*Young India*, 6 July 1921).

64. Ibid., p. 78 (*Young India*, 10 Nov. 1921).

65. Ibid., p. 12.

66. Ibid., p. 8.

67. Ibid., p. 6.

68. Ibid., p. 27 (*Young India*, 7 July 1920).

69. J. Swift, *Irish Tracts* (1720–3), Basil Blackwell, 1948, vol. IX, pp. 15–22.

70. Ibid., pp. 269–77.

71. J. Derrida, 'Living On Borderlines', *Deconstruction and Criticism*, RKP, 1979, pp. 75–176 and 'The Law of Genre', *Glyph*, 7, 1980, pp. 202–32.

72. K. Mayo, *Mother India*, Jonathan Cape, 1935, pp. 76–98.

73. Ibid., p. 51.

74. W. Lewis, *Paleface*, Chatto & Windus, 1929, pp. 289–300.

75. V. S. Naipaul, *India—A Wounded Civilisation*, Deutsch, 1977.

76. J. Chicago, *Birth Project*, Doubleday, 1985, p. 180.

77. K. Mayo, *Mother India*, 1935, pp. 80–3.

78. Even though she mentions three works on post-war India (1985, p. 231).

79. L. White, 'The Empire Strikes Back', *Vogue*, no. 6, whole no. 2305, vol. 153, June 1989, p. 168. Also see *L'Image*, no. 2, Summer 1989, pp. 42–3.

80. C. Greenberg, *Towards a Newer Laocoon,* the *Collected Essays and Criticism*, vol. 1, 1939–44, University of Chicago Press, 1988, p. 88.

81. G. Lessing, *Laocoon* (1766), Bobbs-Merrill Publishing, 1977.

82. I. Babbitt, *The New Laocoon*, Riverside Press, 1910, pp. viii, 159.

83. Vatsyayana, *Kama Sutra*, Taraporevala, 1961, pp. 75–80; Sukracharya, *Sukraniti*, Manoharlal Publishers, 1975, pp. 156–60.

84. *Magdalena Abakanowicz*, Museum of Contemporary Art, Chicago, 1983, pp. 46–50.

85. Derrida, op. cit., pp. 201–10.

86. Chicago, op. cit., p. 133.

87. Derrida, op. cit., 1979, p. 82.

26

SETTING THE STAGE: YINKA SHONIBARE MBE IN CONVERSATION WITH ANTHONY DOWNEY

Anthony Downey

Editor's introduction: London-born Nigerian artist Yinka Shonibare is well known for his use of batik cloth in installations that often question the possibility of an "authentic" identity. In this interview with Anthony Downey (program director of the MA in contemporary art at Sotheby's Institute of Art, London), Shonibare explains the thinking behind his use of batik cloth, Victorian ideals, and the art historical references he plays with in his work. Batik textiles have a complex history and are claimed by a number of cultures with differing associations and meanings. Shonibare has described himself as a "postcolonial hybrid," and in this conversation about his work he reveals the range of theoretical intentions that inform his ongoing practice.

ANTHONY DOWNEY *I have always been particularly interested in* The Victorian Philanthropist's Parlour *(1996–97), the most notable aspect of which is that everything is covered with Dutch wax fabric. Can you elaborate upon why you chose that specific material?*

YINKA SHONIBARE The fabrics are signifiers, if you like, of 'Africaness' insofar as when people first view the fabric they think of Africa. When I was at college in London my work was very political. I was making work about the emergence of *perestroika* [restructuring] in the then Soviet Union and I was also quite intrigued by the idea of the Cold War coming to an end. However, my tutor, upon seeing this work, said to me: 'You are African aren't you; why don't you make authentic Africa art?' I was

quite taken aback by this but it was through the process of thinking about authenticity that I started to wonder about what the signifiers of such 'authentic' Africaness would look like. The fabrics, in this context, happen to be the one obvious thing that people think of when they think about Africa, so I went to Brixton Market where the fabrics are sold. I started to speak to people who sold them and they told me that they were influenced by Indonesian batiks that the Dutch had later mass-produced. The intention was to sell these mass-produced batiks back to the Indonesians but, for largely political and cultural reasons, the Indonesians wanted to promote their own locally produced and better quality batiks. So the industrially produced versions were largely sold in West Africa in the nineteenth century where they subsequently became very popular and today they are seen as a signifier of Africa. It was with this in mind that I started to explore precisely what was meant by authentic in the context of Africa.

AD *The other notable aspect of* The Victorian Philanthropist's Parlour *is that it references the Victorian period (c.1830–1890), as does a significant amount of-your work. Why is the Victorian period such an important point of reference for your work?*

YS Let me begin to answer that question by noting that I am an African speaking English to you. The reason for that is because of the colonial period, empire-building, and the British encounter with Africa. The Victorian era in Africa coincided with the height of the British Empire so there are historical reasons for my interest in the period and its legacy in Africa. There are also more immediate reasons: in the 1980s the then Prime Minister Margaret Thatcher started to talk about Victorian values. My first instinct upon hearing these comments was to flee or run from this idea of Victoriana because it seemed so repressed and so far away from me. But then, on the other hand, I thought it would be ironic to play with precisely that notion of Victorian 'values'. There was a way of subverting that idea of the historical authority of the Victorian period by appropriating it or being complicit with it. As for the idea behind *The Victorian Philanthropist's Parlour*, it is relatively simple: the philanthropist wants to help the less fortunate; however, in this opulent environment of the parlour, where he has decorated his walls with images of black footballers, there will always be a relationship of patronage; or, if you like, a relationship between the 'haves', the colonial philanthropist, and the so-called 'have-nots', the poor colonials. Philanthropy is more about dominance in the colonial context that it is about altruism; it is more of a condescending idea where the power relationship is never equal.

AD *This is interesting insofar as your work would appear to not only deconstruct notions of so-called authentic African signifiers but also the notion of Victorian values and the legacy of the Victorian period in contemporary politics and culture.*

YS Yes, I agree. I am very interested in that legacy and being a Londoner moving around the city of London, you quickly begin to realise that the buildings you see—from the Tate gallery to the National Gallery to Lloyds Insurance offices, not to mention the entire banking system of this country—were based firstly on the trade in slaves and thereafter on forms of inequitable trading practices. And, of course, there has always been a relationship between Europe and Africa; and the maintenance of a so-called developed and civilised Europe through these various institutions is underpinned by an uneven relationship with the less fortunate—not unlike the practice of Victorian philanthropy.

AD *In the context of trade or exchange, there is also a cultural dimension that you draw upon: the trade in ideas, for example. And as much as your work looks at colonial history, the legacy of slavery and the aftermath of imperialism, it also looks at western art history for its sources. I am thinking here of works such as* The Swing (after Fragonard) *(2001) which is now actually part of the Tate's collection in London. What attracted you to Fragonard?*

YS I was drawn to Fragonard because—like the Victorian period—it is one of the references you would least expect. Although I cannot recall my first actual encounter with Fragonard, it seems to have been there forever, it was an iconic art historical image. More specifically, I like the frivolity of the image and the wild abandon of the lady on the swing. I wanted to reference frivolity over profundity, but in choosing frivolity I wanted to make a comment on profundity itself. This reply might need a more immediate historical reference inasmuch as the generation working before me, the so-called Black Art Movement which included Eddie Chambers and Keith Piper, was dealing with a lot of really important political issues but in a largely serious way that some people have described as being didactic. I wanted to come to things from a different angle and look at the notion of frivolity and playfulness; however, my playfulness has an inverted form of politics underlining it. Being a black artist looking at frivolity and playfulness is the least expected thing you would expect me to do— and that has a political resonance in light of the history of black artists working in Britain. I think this is why I accepted an MBE [Member of the British Empire] when it was offered: it was the last thing you would have expected of me and it also sets up a series of expectation of behalf of others about who I am and what I do—expectations which, I hope, are being constantly put into question by my work.

AD *This point references further issues. Firstly, Fragonard is widely viewed as part of the Rococo movement which critics then viewed in derogative terms as both frivolous and merely fashionable. And there has always been a dichotomy in art history between frivolity, fashionability, decoration and the apparent profundity of high art. It seems to me that you play with this in a way that disarms the viewer.*

YS Looking back to art history for images is central to my work insofar as it often yields unexpected images and resonances. If we look at another of my works, *Reverend on Ice* (2005), which is after Henry Raeburn's *Reverend Robert Walker Skating on Duddingston Loch* (c.1795), you get some sense of both this frivolity and seriousness. In the original painting, the reverend is both a 'man of the cloth', a reverend, and a 'man of the book'. He is a serious chap and to be respected. And yet this painting has caught him in a moment of frivolity and playfulness; a moment when he thinks no-one else is looking

at him and he can be a bit naughty. It is the last thing we would expect from him, this joyousness and our catching him in the act of being joyful. I also like the play on words in the title, *Reverend on Ice*, which gives a sense of the reverend being frozen in time and space; or being 'kept on ice' for this one surprising outing.

AD *It is almost as if we too have come across him unexpectedly, and this is the last thing we are expecting from him, this most frivolous of gestures.*

YS Yes, he is indeed a very irreverent reverend!

AD *Let's further explore this notion of irreverence here as it seems important in your work.*

YS It was certainly the twin poles of irreverence and reverence that drew me to the original painting and with a lot of the references that I use there is a degree of both reverence and irreverence on my part. If I work with a Thomas Gainsborough painting such as *Mr and Mrs Andrews* (c.1750), then that painting historically stands for something and in using it my work, *Mr and Mrs Andrews Without Their Heads* (1998), I am appropriating a degree of its power whilst at the same time offering up a critique of it. In the contemporary world, Gainsborough's painting is an anachronism of sorts insofar as a man stands next to his belongings, in this case his wife, dog and gun—in no particular order—and displays the extent of his land ownership in the background. The view of his estate in the background indicates a society where reverence, if not deference, is absolute. This painting is first and foremost a celebration of deference and I want to deflate that somehow. I think I achieve that by beheading them which is an allusion to the French Revolution and the beheading of the French landed gentry and aristocracy. It amused me to explore the possibility of bringing back the guillotine in the late 1990s, not for use on people of course— my figures are mannequins—but for use on the historical icons of power and deference.

AD *In adopting that iconic image of Gainsborough's* Mr and Mrs Andrews *there would appear to be a form of complicity with the power of the image but also a very irreverential take on that image too, which brings us back to your practice as an artist of adopting the iconography of power to deconstruct power itself. In a recent show in 2007 you were invited to display your work in the hallowed halls of the National Gallery in London—becoming in turn one of the few living artists to have been extended such an honour. Could you talk a little bit more about how you felt about being invited into such a venerable establishment, which houses, amongst other works, Gainsborough's* Mr and Mrs Andrews.

YS That was an interesting experience for sure. I later heard that when my show opened some of the board members refused to come to the opening because they felt very strongly that the National Gallery is not a place for contemporary art. As for my work being placed in that context, the curators looked for works within their collection that had a relationship to the slave trade—bearing in mind that 2007 was the bicentenary anniversary of the abolition of the slave trade—and asked me to engage with them. They found two portraits, one of Colonel Tarleton and the other of Mrs Oswald, both of whom had had connections to the slave trade. These works were removed and I put my work, *Colonel Tarleton and Mrs Oswald Shooting* (2007), in their place. Both are life-size mannequins, dressed in Georgian outfits made of Dutch wax fabric, and both have just blown apart an unfortunate pheasant—an activity that relates to their social status and the leisured classes. The part of the gallery where the work was placed is a very busy part. It acts as a centre point, so I decided to do an installation that would happen above people's heads where it could be seen by all. The fact that they are shooting a pheasant that has exploded 'blood' on people's heads also gives it a comic

element, which would have no doubt further displeased some of the National Gallery board who had objected to it in the first place.

AD *It would seem that quite a number of your chosen subjects are actively engaged, so to speak, in leisure pursuits. I am also thinking here of* Leisure Lady (with ocelots) *(2001) and* Hound *(2000).*

YS Yes, that is obviously intentional. To be in a position to engage in leisure pursuits, you need a few bob. You cannot be a peasant and be off shooting for a day because you would have had work to do. You need spare time and money buys you spare time. Whilst the leisure pursuit might look frivolous—we are back to that word again—my depiction of it is a way of engaging with that power. It is actually an expression of something much more profoundly serious insofar as the accumulation of wealth and power that is personified in leisure was no doubt a product of exploiting other people.

AD *It also appears that leisure may lead to a degree of ennui if not the breakdown of social order on behalf of the so-called leisured classes; a degree of dysfunctionality that results in the scenario represented in* How to Blow Up Two Heads at Once (Ladies) *(2006), in which two individuals literally blow each other's head off.*

YS *How to Blow Up Two Heads at Once* is the perfect duel with a 100 per cent result because these two Victorians simultaneously shoot each other's head off and guarantee a form of Mutually Assured Destruction [MAD]. The work was in part a reaction to the world we live in today. We are living in a post-9/11 environment that has recently seen war in Afghanistan and subsequently Iraq and what it has came down to in popular cultural and political terms is the pitching on one side of the Americans and on the other side militant Muslims. This seems reductive to me and this work may initially appear humorous and perhaps frivolous, but it is examining the pointlessness of conflict in general. It is not just about the Iraq war but an opportunity to think about what happens when conflict turns to violence: you literally blow each other's heads off because no-one actually comes out of a war a winner, not even the victor.

AD *One of the things that strikes me about all of these works is their sheer unabashed theatricality and their frieze-like appearance. Each has a centralised narrative that appears to be suspended in time. I am thinking here of* Scramble for Africa *(2003), which draws upon the* mise en scène *of colonial history and visualises it as if on a stage of sorts.*

YS Theatricality is certainly a device in my work, it is a way of setting the stage; it is also a fiction—a hyper-real, theatrical device that enables you to re-imagine events from history. There is no obligation to truth in such a setting so you have the leeway to create fiction or to dream. *Scramble for Africa* examines how history repeats itself and when I was making it I was really thinking about American imperialism and the need in the West for resources such as oil and how this pre-empts the annexation of different parts of the world. This is what happened in the 1880s with Africa, which was carved up arbitrarily by European powers. I thought about a historical equivalent for what is happening today and that historical equivalent was the so-called 'Scramble for Africa' whereby a conference in Berlin (1884–85), attended by the then European superpowers, decided which Europeans could trade in Africa and who would get which territory. *Scramble for Africa* is about people having a conference about a continent that was not theirs and deciding how they are going to divide it up without any form of consultation with those who would be most affected—the Africans.

AD *The strangeness of the image also appeals to me—fourteen headless men sitting around a table with a contested map of Africa on it. I first*

saw *this piece in a room at Stephen Friedman Gallery in London and it was not easily forgotten. I found this strangeness in another of your works,* Gallantry and Criminal Conversation *(2002), when I first saw it in* Documenta 11. *I was initially intrigued by the impossibility of it all, which you have mentioned in previous conversations: the impossibility of headless people having sex, for example, or the impossibility of eighteenth-century costumes made of African fabric.*

YS I enjoy presenting 'impossibility' but the reality of *Gallantry and Criminal Conversation* is more concerned with power relationships and how the exploitation of Africa had a counterpart of sorts in the Grand Tour—the latter being an original form of tourism that was popular from the mid-seventeenth century onwards and which mostly involved the upper classes travelling to Venice and Rome for reasons of 'improvement'. The Grand Tour was also a form of sex tourism that belied the cultural tone of its apparent purpose. This is also about power and you could relate it to the present-day relationship between the so-called First World and the Third World. I am thinking here about people making trips to Thailand and elsewhere for the purpose of having sex; that is a power relationship that finds expression in sexuality. Although I read books such as *Ladies of the Grand Tour* (2001), I made up the title myself: criminal conversation is what people used to be accused of if they committed adultery in the eighteenth century.

AD *I was also thinking here of the sheer excessiveness of the work—there is a lot of it and it is very theatrical in its excess. There is for one, a full-sized carriage floating over the scene.*

YS Excess generates its own reactions and forms of critique that are not immediately apparent. When you think about Africa and about being an African artist, people most likely think about poverty and political struggle; they also think about independence and civil rights. None of those things actually sit well with the ideas of frivolity or excess, and so this returns us to notions of the unexpected. It is saying, 'Look, I'm not going to be where you expect me to be, I'm not going to play victim, and I'm not going to play nature to your culture'—the last phrase is a reference to Barbara Kruger's work, *We Won't Play Nature to Your Culture* (1983) and the possibility of adopting a stance that questions not only the status quo but your own assumptions about that status quo.

AD *And this brings us back to the sense of unexpectedness in your work, both in terms of its sources, the way it is presented, and the positions you take in relation to historical and contemporary events. One of the other unexpected angles to your work is the fact that you started out as a painter and periodically return to that form.*

YS Yes, I did start off as a painter and it is something I still do. There is the tactile aspect to it and the use of materials. There are also the two opposing forces of decoration and abstraction which reflect the history of modernism and Greenbergian notions of what painting was supposed to be. I try to marry those two things in the kind of paintings I have chosen to do, which are neither just decorative nor just abstract—they are both. They also play with the idea of the Minimalist grid, so that the rigid structure is played within a manner that is very much post-Minimalist.

AD *You have also referenced people like Rothko and that motif of the heroic white male—to what extent is a painting such as* Deep Blue *(1997) engaging with that legacy?*

YS In a purely physical way, and bearing in mind I have a disability, it is much easier for me to paint things that are broken down into smaller pieces. And so rather than actually trying to make some heroic large painting what I

do is fragment that heroism by reducing it to smaller manageable chunks.

AD *Which is, in certain ways, a complicity with art history, an adoption of certain codes and the authority associated with those codes in order to disrupt them—not unlike your use of Gainsborough's* Mr and Mrs Andrews.

YS Yes, you could put it that way.

AD *I am also interested here in the way you have adopted and adapted the code of the dandy in your work, a figure that returns us to both the Victorian period but also—in its soi-disant demeanour and display of wit—a somewhat excessive and unexpected figure. I am thinking here of* Diary of a Victorian Dandy *(1993) and* Dorian Gray *(2001).*

YS Historically, the dandy is usually an outsider whose only way in is through his wit and his style. Coming from a middle-class background the dandy aspired to aristocratic standing so as to distinguish himself from both the lower and middle classes. In this sense, his frivolous lifestyle is a political gesture of sorts, containing within it a form of social mobility. Needless to say, Oscar Wilde is a good example of the dandy and he played that role well; he used his wit and his style to progress within English society and was brutally penalised in the end for his apparent frivolity. His apparent lack of seriousness of course belied an absolute seriousness and that attracts me to the dandy as a figure of mobility who upsets the social order of things. As a black man living in the UK, I find myself in a position where I am not so-called 'upper class'; however, in Nigeria I would be considered 'upper class'. And this got me thinking about social and class mobility in the context of the dandy. The dandy can remake himself again and again; he can do that through the image, he can remake his own image and thereafter re-create and remake himself.

AD *I was reminded of two quotes here, one from Oscar Wilde, who you just mentioned, and his notion that 'One should either be a work of Art, or wear a work of Art', and one from Charles Baudelaire who wrote that 'The dandy is one who elevates aesthetics into a living religion'. Again, just as the figure of the dandy alluded to a politics of sorts, aesthetics always has a political context; the adoption of clothing, for example, being the means to go beyond one's allotted class in a time where such mobility was rigorously policed. To identify with such a figure would suggest an inclination towards role-playing for political purposes and an intention to disrupt certain accepted ways of seeing things—would you agree with that?*

YS All identity construction is a form of re-enactment. You are playing a role and to do so you have to construct that role. The dandy is a figure who not only lives out this fact but he is also both an insider and an outsider who disrupts such distinctions. When *Diary of a Victorian Dandy* was first shown it was in the London Underground and the audience for that was in excess of 3 million people. Again, the sheer unexpectedness of this image had a huge impact. The organisation that commissioned the piece, InIVA [Institute of International Visual Arts], did a survey where they asked people who they thought the character in the photographs was. And some people either imagined that he was a real Victorian character who existed and some people thought that they were posters for a film. I enjoyed that open-endedness and the disruptiveness in the display of the image insofar as it already depicted a figure, the dandy, who is a sign of disruption.

AD *These images could be seen in terms of visual disruption, an unexpected image, but could they also be seen as a moment of historical revisionism—a moment of going back in time and pointing out that Victorian society was not as mono-cultural as we think it was.*

YS I would not necessarily go with that reading because I do not really go for that kind of revisionism; for me, that would come across as merely illustrative and it is more about disruption and unexpectedness. It is not about expressing something that once existed but people did not know about. The images in *Diary of a Victorian Dandy* are fakes—it is pure theatre and it is Yinka Shonibare in that picture, not some obscure historical character. It is a contemporary person doing this and it is playing with this idea of making people look twice and re-engage in what they are looking at.

AD *Let's take this notion of fakery further. I was reminded just now of a quote from an interview of yours from a few years back in which you said, 'To be an artist, you have to be a good liar'.*

YS I think that sometimes people have a problem distinguishing artifice from so-called reality. Artifice is not reality; they are two different things and I think that once that is understood you can perhaps read into the work of the artist a bit better. For me it is about providing people with alternative possibilities and that sometimes requires the device of the lie.

AD *Which brings us to another aspect of your work, your use of film—often seen in terms of artifice and alternative realities—in works such as* Un Ballo in Maschera (A Masked Ball) *(2004) and* Odile and Odette *(2005). What has film enabled you to do that you cannot do in, say, painting and sculpture?*

YS In the most basic sense, it has allowed me to explore movement. There is an aesthetic quality with movement and the resonance of the image that you cannot get when it is presented as a still image. There is also the sense of repetition and, in *Un Ballo in Maschera* for example, I did not want to make a film with a beginning, middle and end; instead, I wanted to explore the reflexivity of the film and how it reflects back on itself.

AD *Which recalls the films of the French New Wave period.*

YS Yes, very much so, and I am thinking here of Jean-Luc Godard's works and in particular Alan Resnais' *Last Year in Marienbad* (1961), which is a film that had a great influence on me because of the way it consistently draws the viewer back to the filmic moment and refers to the fact that it is a film and not a reality in itself. It also does this with its repetitive, almost incomprehensible, structure and plot and the blurring of the distinction between truth and fiction, artifice and fact. It is a very Modernist approach, I guess, and in *Un Ballo in Maschera* I use devices such as repetition to draw attention to the filmic nature of what we are seeing.

AD *Could you describe that a little bit more, because the film examines a relatively obscure event: that is the assassination at a masked ball of the Swedish King Gustav III in 1792.*

YS In the 1780s and '90s, Gustav III was attempting to expand Sweden's borders into Russia. These attempts were not only costly and divisive but drew attention away from poverty at home and his own extravagances. One of Gustav III's major preoccupations was going to the ball, another frivolity I guess, and I thought of this as a metaphor for the kind of imperialist figure who, like in Rome before, is 'fiddling' whilst the seat of empire is burning. However, things are of course more complicated than that inasmuch as he was also a great patron of the arts. In the film, and this returns us to the formal devices mentioned above in relation to the French New Wave, I use repetition and open-ended narratives to suggest alternative readings. In one, he dies as a result of the assassination; in the other he lives. And the narrative repeats itself so it is not closed by any means; rather, it is open-ended and the outcome depends on where the audience wants to stop viewing it or indeed how they want to view it. If you stop viewing after his assassina-

tion you do not see him rise up again and the whole thing starts over again.

AD *This notion of repetition, in part, brings us to your second film to date,* Odile and Odette, *which is taken from Tchaikovsky's* Swan Lake *(1875–76). Could you describe what attracted you to* Swan Lake *and, in particular, what attracted you to the relationship between Odile and Odette?*

YS This film is more about doubling than repetition. In the original story Odile is von Rothbart the magician's daughter and Odette is the beautiful swan that Prince Siegfried has promised to marry. Siegfried and Odette have an agreement between them that they would stay faithful but von Rothbart dresses his daughter Odile—who bears an uncanny resemblance to Odette—to trick Siegfried into kissing her at a ball at the palace. Odette sees this and their union is broken forever. There are a number of endings, one involving Siegfried throwing himself from the castle ramparts when he realises his mistake, whereas another has Odette do the same thing after she has seen Siegfried kiss Odile. What interested me most here is that when the ballet is performed it is usual that the two roles of Odette and Odile are danced by the one performer. Odile is usually in black, signifying a certain malign intent, whilst Odette is traditionally in white. In my version of the ballet I have used two dancers, one black and one white, and composed them so they appear to be mirror reflections of one another. They synchronise each other's movements in a framed 'mirror' to give the impression that it is a mirror we are looking at. The idea is that one woman is the reflection of the other woman, so that although you are seeing two different ballerinas essentially you are seeing one person.

AD *It seems that* Odile and Odette *personifies precisely what you said earlier in relation to the medium of film giving you the ability to look at movement and the ambiguities of narrative and time with the context of film itself.*

YS Yes, very much so; it is difficult to fully portray that in painting and sculpture.

AD *Your most recent work went back further than the Victorian age to a time broadly commensurate with the Enlightenment period and the high water-mark of European reason and rationality. In* The Sleep of Reason Produces Monsters *(2008), you have produced a series of photographs after Goya's series of etchings* Los Caprichos, *which he produced in the 1790s, but there is also a broader reference to the figure of Caliban who figures prominently in Shakespeare's* The Tempest *(c.1610–11).*

YS The Enlightenment period is a time of being liberated from the Dark Ages, from the shackles of tradition into the empirical methods of science and rationality. Our traditional notions of democracy were refined in this period and emerged in the Age of Enlightenment alongside the ideals of liberalism. However, it is precisely the arrogance of liberal democracy that has been used as a justification for a number of wars and, most recently, the war in Iraq. The appeal to a transcendentalist notion of democracy has effectively presaged an unjust war. The arguments are familiar from a colonial period: they, the other, are an 'uncivilised' people and we, enlightened Europeans that we apparently are, will endeavour to enlighten them. However, like Caliban in *The Tempest*, they refuse to be enlightened so we will force democracy upon them by the gun. This act is irrational in itself: the arrogance of liberal democracy has led to the most irrational acts of genocide. In *The Sleep of Reason Produces Monsters*, I have taken the text from Goya's original aquatint prints and their formal composition. I have turned the original statement, reproduced on the desk where a figure sleeps, and put a question mark after it so that it reads in French, 'The

sleep of reason produces monsters in America?' The original statement becomes rhetorical and I used French in particular here as it was the French who gave America its Statue of Liberty. There are five images in all, representing five continents. In Africa, it is an image of an old white man, rather than an African, asleep at the desk. In Asia, the figure is a black man. In the most basic terms I am suggesting that irrational aggression, born out of a form of Enlightenment rational reasoning, towards a race that you do not understand produces a sleep of 'reason' out of which comes monsters—and the term 'monsters' could be substituted here with any amount of atrocity. Your enlightened intentions, in sum, do not necessarily produce enlightened results.

AD *When this work was first shown in 2008 in New York, it was under the collective title* Prospero's Monsters—*what is the reference to Caliban, the figure in the play that you just mentioned?*

YS There were no images in that show depicting Caliban, or Prospero for that matter, but I felt it was a good title to frame the exhibition with because in a broader context I am talking about the relationship between the other and the master. I was attracted to the play because in it Caliban refuses to be civilised, he fights back and is not as passive as is often portrayed; he not only fights back but refuses to learn Prospero's language and the codifications that go with it. When he does learn the language he learns only the swear words which is very irreverent of him. And that, I thought, was a form of empowerment.

AD *In that show you also had a series of figures more closely associated with the Enlightenment, including Adam Smith, often seen as the father of modern economics, and the eighteenth-century physicist and philosopher Jean le Rond d'Alembert. In each case, these figures, of which there are five in all, have been given disabilities—why was this?*

YS I'm doing two things there, one is an autobiographical device. I have my own physical disability but also the Enlightenment scientists and philosophers had their own human frailties too; however, it is the human, the sense of frailty that is too irrational and disorganised, that is often factored out of discussions about reason and rationalism. Because it is unpredictable, disability does not lie well with the essence of Enlightenment certainty—bearing in mind the overarching empiricism associated with the time. In giving Adam Smith and Jean le Rond d'Alembert disabilities, alongside the figures of Antoine Lavoisier, Gabrielle Emile Le Tonnelier de Breteuil, and Immanuel Kant, I wanted to also use it as a device for showing how these figures, who were partly responsible for defining otherness in the context of the Enlightenment, could be also 'othered' in the context of disability.

AD *It seems that these works question the empiricist underpinnings of the Enlightenment period and invert its processes of thinking about otherness and how we look at other cultures.*

YS That is very much part of what I am doing there.

AD *Finally, can I ask you what you are working on presently?*

YS At present I am re-reading Jonathan Swift's *Gulliver's Travels* (1726), which interests me on a number of levels. I am particularly interested in the question of Gulliver's empathy with the different cultures he encounters. He sees that they are different and they see that he is different, and they are trying to learn from his culture and he is trying to learn from their culture. He rarely seems to come down in favour of one group over the other before he has had a chance to listen to both sides of the story. I am at a relatively preliminary stage in my thinking about this and re-reading a book I first read as a child, but it holds a number of points of interest for me at this moment in time—and will no doubt provoke some thoughts on my behalf. Gulliver's voyages also see him becoming involved in internal power struggles in the lands he visits but he himself is also, at various stages, both powerful and powerless depending on the context. Which brings us back to the question of power and its contexts and how we assume and in some cases are beholden to power itself.

27

CULTURE

Gayatri Chakravorty Spivak

Editor's introduction: Gayatri Chakravorty Spivak is an Indian literary critic. In 1988 she wrote, "Can the Subaltern Speak," an influential text for postcolonial theory. Spivak's notoriously dense writing style has been criticized for its lack of accessibility. Nonetheless, her contribution to postcolonial thinking has been considerable. The excerpt printed here comes towards the end of her study *A Critique of Postcolonial Reason: Toward a History of the Vanishing Present*, published in 1999. It is notable for its personal tone and, in keeping with this *Reader*, her use of the textile to work through some of her thinking about multiculturalism and globalism. Midway through the essay, Spivak uses herself, dressed in a jacket, sari, and cotton top for a winter museum opening in New York City, as a physical example not only of a transnational identity but also of transnational textile production. In the final pages, she asks that we make "human rights a trade-related investment issue."

Re-enter the web of textile in conclusion.

First, the briefest glimpse of the cultural self-representation of Britain in textile in colonialism; next, a look at contemporary Northern "social dumping," with the female child worker, specifically in the garment industry, being made to support the new global hyperreal. This bit is written without scholarly research, with the fieldwork contacts developed by an embarrassingly part-time activist.[1] It is also New York that brings me an awareness that some of us must continue to place the South in the history of its own present, instead of treating it as a locus of nostalgia and/or human interest.

Doubletake: a coda of how I can temporize my own critical path during the writing of this book. But textility escapes the loom into the dynamics of world trade.

First, then, colonial discourse; a reminder of *Jane Eyre* in the making. If I had wanted simple cases of rampant neo-colonialism in the fashion world, I could have chosen more blatant examples such as the renewed inscription of an unrecognizable "India" and "Africa" into fashion after the films and videos of the Raj and in the legacy of *Out of Africa*. I am, however, predictably more interested in the implicit working of the axiomatics of imperialism in the vocabulary of radical critique.

Source: Reprinted by permission of the publisher from "Culture" in *A Critique of Postcolonial Reason: Toward a History of the Vanishing Present* by Gayatri Chakravorty Spivak, pp. 409–21, Cambridge, Mass.: Harvard University Press, Copyright © 1999 by the President and Fellows of Harvard College.

I have, therefore, chosen a subtler example. In order to narrativize the constitution of the self-consolidating other by way of a discourse of fashion freely assuming a radical aesthetic vocabulary into those axiomatics, I will step back a couple of centuries and refer more elaborately to a text I have cited in an earlier chapter: Rudolf Ackerman's *Repository of Arts, Literature, Commerce, Manufacture, Fashion and Politics*, published from 1809 to 1829 (see page 119).

Each issue of this compendium magazine contained (along with market reports, bankruptcy lists, and detailed lists for a convincing life-style for the aspiring British bourgeoisie) sketches of the season's fashions, of course, but also what was called "Allegorical Presentations containing examples of British Manufactures."

Typically, each design is filled in by drawings of British Palladian architectural themes, whose general connotation, with vague invocations of Rome, is Empire. They "mark deeper, more enduring claims upon a national present as part of a past."[2] Holding up the design are, generally two, sometimes three, massive and decent Graeco-Roman figures, genitalless if male, draped if female. The design itself is two, three, or four pieces of actual textile material, manufactured presumably in nineteenth-century Britain. It is eerie to handle these actual pieces of cloth or silk, more mutely empirical than human bones, nearly two hundred years old, less overtly legitimized than the genuine antique in a museum, so precariously fixed on these brittle pages. It seems curious that no explanation or key is ever given for the "allegories," although they are specifically called that, in issue after issue. Short descriptions of the textile material are all that is provided, with brief hints for their proper use. The stuff is often coarse imitations of Chinese or Indian material, although they are never called that, of course. What significance might we assign to this specific denomination—"allegory"—if the figure so designated is not going to be interpreted? Is an allegory, in the sense accessible to Rudolph Ackerman, not precisely an at least second-level semiotic code that exists to be decoded?

We can, of course, assume that these "allegories" simply allude to the presence of a vast organization of signification, under the authority of the Empire, which charges the female British class subject's everyday self-representation with a lexical burden far beyond her own grasp; a reminder, as it were, of the responsibility simply of being such a subject in the geopolitical context. (One can imagine Jameson's pedagogic project of "cognitive mapping" for the male U.S. class subject to be a good countermeasure to corresponding ideological formations in operation today.)[3]

There can also be another indexical reading of this ostentatious foregrounding of the "allegorical" status of these representative designs. They dissimulate another narrative—the text of the *production* of these collages (in the strictest sense—these are "stick-on" affairs) in an unwitting allegory of the fixing of the imperial textile trade as a special place of signification, a referentially privileged discursive field.[4] The entire design marks something like "management," covering over the exploitative and violating aspects of colonialism by ostentatiously pointing at some other rusing thing. This "thing" is the representational material, at least five times "historically" inscribed (Greek to Roman to Christian through English to Imperial), which foregrounds itself but is not decoded. The "real" bits of cloth, in the English simply "stuff" or "material," insert themselves into the acknowledged realm of representations, empire of signs, and are coded carefully. There are no named subjects (Van Gogh, Warhol, Portman, Perelman in Jameson's essay) celebrating the coding, and no sign of a euphoric utopia. This "metaphoric" utopia is part of the "concept" of imperialist commerce, the manipulation of the consumer for the cloth trade. In my fancy, the allegorical material signals mutely to the indefinite possibility of the thickening or complicating of the signifying potential of the bits of material as such, themselves literal metonyms—one might mark the oxymoron—of a *text fabricated* out of *raw* material and then staged in a theater of exploitation that provided "the individual (female) subject" a model to imitate. Fashion is not the normative narrative of aesthetic styles in the cultural dominant isomorphically lockstepped to a narrative of modes of production. This is rather the story of the production of the dominant self-representation of the clamorous "individual subject," the *source* of cultural explanations. Jameson's or Baudelaire's stunning intuitions about "our world" as well as the trendy self-assured patter of the New York radical can be serialized with this. Today's "social dumping," by contrast, silences the new subaltern.

Increasingly and metaleptically, transnationality, a new buzzword for cultural studies, is becoming a synonym for the movement of people. To recode a change in the determination of capital as a cultural change is a scary symptom of cultural studies, especially feminist cultural studies. Everything is being made "cultural." I hope the reader will notice the difference and alliance between this statement and Jameson's (page 315).

As the United Nations Library on Transnational Corporations tells us, a transnational corporation is an enterprise that owns value-added activities in two or more countries.[5]

The word "value" stands for me here as a mockery of both Marx and academic marxism, which apparently gave the Marxist notion of "value" a decent burial by showing that it was not theoretically viable (just as, in terms of another kind of theory, Hindess and Hirst laid "mode of production" to rest).[6] Yet because "value" or "worth" (German *Wert*) (for Marx the "simple contentless form" that allows any kind of measurement) is as slippery a word as "supplement," it now measures the difference between the "cheapness" of *their* labor and the expenses of *our* enterprise: value-added—in a hyperreal electronic simulation of mercantile capitalism.

The relations of production in a TNC is FDI—foreign direct investment—which is finessed as the occasion for the transfer of a package of resources—technology or management skills—over national boundaries and, thus, once

again provides support for the global hyperreal; via, sometimes, the silenced subaltern's relocated great-granddaughter. I should like to use a humble anecdotal example to prove this obvious point.

Before I do so, let me explain why, whenever I speak of transnationality and alternative development, I move to Bangladesh. As long as the work was focused on colonial/postcolonial discourse, general knowledge of Hindi (the national Indian language), basic knowledge of Sanskrit (the Hindu classical language), bilinguality in Bengali (mother tongue) and English, and the politico/cultural mulch of a conscientized diasporic allowed me to plough along, as long as I did not profess South Asian expertise. As interest developed in the history of the transnational present, two things came clear: First, that the real front against globalization was in the countless local theaters of the globe-girdling movements. Bangladesh, a small subcolonial country that came into being when transnational electronic exploitation was beginning to take hold, offered a much more active terrain of resistance; although India certainly had its share of large, well-publicized movements. I also realized that if one wanted to intervene—rather than stop at exchanging ideas with the activist leaders—and learn from those seemingly "local" initiatives, one had to know the language well enough to move with dialectal shifts, and that for me was Bengali, the national language of Bangladesh.

The difference between India and Bangladesh in terms of transnationality was rather important. Indian independence was the first large-scale negotiated decolonization. The 1947–1949 constitution was written at the inception of neo-colonialism, when one could imagine that the nascent Bretton Woods organizations would dispense global social justice. That constitution provided for an economic structure somewhat protected from the depredations of international exploitation. And the situation of West Bengal, my native state, where Bengali is the local language, was doubly different because its government had been Left Front for more than two decades. Thus neither India (with its protected economy), nor, and especially, West Bengal (with its Left Front government) was a fertile field for foreign direct investment. (The situation is of course rapidly changing under post-Soviet economic restructuring.)

To place the export-based garment industry in transnationality, then, allow me to use a bland everyday happening that I put in a frame for a seminar on feminist cultural studies, to explain that transnationality did not primarily mean people moving from place to place, although labor export was certainly an important object of investigation.

The example is Gayatri Spivak on a winter's day at an opening in New York's New Museum. I was wearing a jacket over a sari, and, to layer myself into warmth I was wearing, under the jacket, a full-sleeved cotton top, rather an unattractive duncolored cheap thing, "made in Bangladesh" for The French Connection. By contrast, the sari I was wearing, also made in Bangladesh, was an exquisite woven cloth produced by the Prabartana Weavers' collective under the coordination of Farida Akhter and Farhad Mazhar. Until I saw these weavers at work, I had had no idea how the *jāmdānis* that I had so admired in my childhood and youth were fabricated. It is complicated teamweaving and simultaneous embroidery at speed, hard to believe if you haven't actually seen it, certainly as delicate and difficult as lacemaking. As a result of the foreign direct investment related to the international garment industry, the long tradition of Bangladeshi handloom is dying. Prabartana not only subsidizes and "develops" the weavers' collective, but it also attempts to undo the epistemic violation suffered by the weavers by recognizing them as artists. This is not merely a reversal, but also a displacement of Ackerman's *Compendium*; there is no allegory-referenced transcoding here. Thus I was standing in the museum wearing the contradiction of transnationalization upon my body, an exhibit, though no one knew it. No persons or groups had moved much to make this possible. There *can* be labor

migrancy associated with transnationalization, but in fact it is not necessary—with postfordism and export processing zones. The demographic determining factors for labor migrancy lie elsewhere, and are beyond the scope of these concluding pages.

What I am about to write is not a commentary on the traffic in children in general. It is not even about child labor everywhere, the eradication of which would be an unquestionable good. It is about making human rights a trade-related investment issue. It is about the easy goodwill of boycott politics. It is about the lazy cruelty of moral imperialism. It is about doing deals with local entrepreneurs, themselves bound by their own greed and the greed of global trade resulting in no labor laws. It is about finding in this a justification for a permanent involvement in a country's affairs through foreign aid. Once again, the writer's plea is for the recognition of the agency of the local resistance, as it is connected with the peoples' movements that girdle the globe.

With the comparative opening of the markets after the signing of the General Agreement on Tariffs and Trade in 1994, it seemed as if Northern markets would be swamped with garments manufactured in the South. This was the reason why, after the closure of GATT in 1995, and the establishment of the World Trade Organization as independent and permanent watchdog, what is now called "social dumping" began to be enforced on specifically the export-based *garment* industry: boycott their products because they employ child labor. Nationalism and racism were deployed to unify Northern labor behind management in this regard. The infamous Harkin Bill passed by the U.S. Senate in 1993 ("Child Labor Deterrent Act of 1993") was based on a report compiled by the AFL-CIO, which often works in conjunction with the American Asian African Free Labor Institute (AAAFLI) to undermine labor demands in the South. Between the first and final versions of the act, an NBC television report revealed to the public that 52 percent of FDI-related cloth-ing manufactured in Bangladesh (not my sari, in other words, but my French Connection top— the sari is yet another textile text, in history and economics) came to U.S. markets; next *The Wall Street Journal* reported that Wal-Mart, the big-gest retail sale outlet in the United States, had lost $0.75 per share as a result of importing clothing manufactured by child labor.[7]

At a gender studies meeting at my own univer-sity, an explanation of this interested use of "child labor" as a way of blocking export from develop-ing countries was summarily dismissed in an ab-surd cultural relativist way by a U.S.-nationalist (domestic) welfare sociologist: as if child labor was just a part of Bangladeshi culture and we should not interfere! It is beyond the scope of this book to develop further the social textuality of this one impatient gesture. Suffice it to say that precisely as colonialism made and makes interested use of patriarchy, transnational capital makes use of rac-ism and thus divides a trades union movement already focused on little more than job security in the rank-and-file and management-collaboration at the top (incidentally inhabited by the U.S. aca-demic, willy-nilly, thanks to the Yeshiva decision of the U.S. Supreme Court in 1980). The sorry story of the Second International is played out again with a global focus.

Complicity with patriarchy puts the blame for the exhaustion of the world's resources between the legs of the poorest women of the South, lead-ing to pharmaceutical dumping of dangerous co-ercive long-term contraception, an unexamined population control rigorously to be distinguished from family planning. The transnationally illit-erate benevolent feminist of the North supports this wholeheartedly, with "ignorant goodwill."[8] Any critique is put down to a culturally conserva-tive position *against* family planning.

Similarly, complicity with racism allows the benevolent transnationally illiterate liberal to stop at supporting sanctions against Southern garment factories that use child labor. (It will occur to people of goodwill that the point may be to make the labor less "cheap"—raise the cost of variable capital—by implementing fairer labor laws, but that is, in the "hot peace," a pipe dream; the World Bank is a force against unionization. I am no longer sure of this, given Rorty's easy dup-ing [see note 59]. The real project is, clearly, that "[a]dult workers in the United States and other developed countries should not have their jobs imperiled by imports produced by child labor in developing countries" ["Child Labor Deterrent Act of 1993," clause 9]. The U.S. government is not duped.) Human interest videos are already in place, such as the one that lyrically films the backbreaking day of the Pakistani girl who makes bricks, with an "empowering" voiceover relaying her Urdu; and the one about the carpet-weav-ing boys. Their viewers are neither willing nor able to read or hear the countless dispassionate factual brief testimonies given by the so-called child workers to labor activists in the field.[9] The children certainly do not present their working conditions favorably. But, in the absence of any redress or infrastructural support, they find the remote American decision to take their jobs away altogether confusing.[10]

What happens to the innocent restricted en-thusiasts who cannot see beyond an easy moral-ism and hear how the child is made to "unspeak" herself? For reasons already given, I can only dis-cuss the Bangladeshi case. Any theoretical con-clusions must be made mutatis mutandis. The case of Bangladesh will not fit the entire South. It is easier to speak of postnationalism when one participates in a single-state civil society in the metropolis. Economic descriptions of develop-ing countries depend on the history of the nation upon the geopolitical map. A ready cosmopoli-tanism can be an alibi for geopolitics.

In a chapter going back at least to Rudolph Ackerman, we must consider the text of capital as it manipulates textile. The garment industry did not establish itself upon uninscribed earh to inaugurate "development" for women. It is cer-tainly true that women who would otherwise have been homebound went to work in factories and thus entered the world. But to enter a world without infrastructural support is not an unquestioned good; that is where the caring reader must reintroduce the singularity of ethics. In this respect, the encouragement of women's microenterprise—credit-baiting with no infrastructure—is a comparable phenomenon in the arena of finance capital.

When the boycott began, the factories sometimes employed children with their ages altered. When the children did lose their jobs, they became twenty-four-hour domestic workers for little or no pay, or perhaps prostitutes—perhaps they starved. Sometimes the girl children had come to work with their older female relatives. This is, of course, last-ditch "child care." But with no infrastructural followup, the loss of this was pretty crucial for the child worker, silenced subaltern. And the words of the Harkin Bill: "The employment of children under the age of 15, often at pitifully low wages, undermines the stability of families" (clause 8) seemed an incomprehensible mockery to her.

Early in 1995, the Bangladesh Garment Manufacturers and Exporters Association entered into an agreement with various indigenous NGOs, with a statement of support from the International Labor Organization and the U.S. Ambassador to Bangladesh, that the parents of the children in question would be financially compensated and the children given primary education. Not big money—about $7.50 a month at the current rate of exchange; and, for education, "[t]he unit cost is approximately U.S. $36 per child per year."[11]

Let us first note that the "education" to be provided is materially useless, because it is in no way continuous with the national education system. Admission into the schools has been made contingent upon showing the keypunch machine IDs that had gone with their jobs. Since two or more years often pass before the former child worker even sees one of these schools, the card is not always available. Fifteen parents in the Pyarabag shantytown in Dhaka said that they were ready to give up their monthly allowance if the children were admitted without those useless attendance cards (not photo IDs), but they were refused. The recalcitrant and reduced payment of compensation requires constant agitation by the fieldworkers. The numbers reported on television from time to time bear little relation to reality. Understandably, there is extreme reluctance to part with information. The righteous anger of a Harkin Bill or the benevolence of a long-distance benefactor lose all plausibility when confronted with the actual indifference and deception that follow the dismissal of these children. My own direct involvement is with the nature, quality, effectiveness, and relevance of the teaching in ground-level schools. I can say with conviction that those questions cannot be raised in the hapless situation that follows the so-called restoration of the sanctity of childhood at the direct foreign investment garment factories.[12]

I promised my informant Seema Das, who did the actual footwork, that I would mainstream this information in the mainest of streams, so that the video campaign of pathos, sensationalism, and human interest would not make the girl unspeak herself. (Both she and I have an unjustified confidence in the power of yet another academic book outside the field.) When I spoke, with some hesitation (and upon request), to a small group of writers, journalists, university students and intellectuals in Dhaka about deconstruction, Seema left the group quietly after the first ten minutes. Intellectual, activist, and entrepreneur are not necessarily united there, as they are not here. And in that three-point division, I place this trivial book.

In this chapter I have tried to examine the interplay between multiculturalism and globality. Is postmodernism the cultural logic of late capitalism? Wading through this debate, I have worked up through the textural stream of textile to let myself be encountered by that other book that I have had to keep pushing away while I have revised this one. I could perhaps re-state Jameson's thoughtful title this way: the casualties of economic post-modernization are not culturalists; they teach us to keep our glance fixed at the crossed-out capital logic of postmodernity. The point may not be to think well and ill of capitalism at the same time. Please decide rather, as the web of text and textile roll out asymptotically, if one can stitch together Kant's *Third Critique* and documents like *Chinta* (see notes 133 and 136) without the everyday or corrupt version of the switch from determinant to reflexive judgment—primary/secondary, data/research, fieldwork/ethnography, native-informant/master discourse—that we perform in our studies and classrooms; and the other way around.[13] Marx could hold *The Science of Logic* and the Blue Books together; but that was still only Europe; and in the doing it came undone.

NOTES

1. "Fieldwork" for me has come to mean something else, working in the field to learn how not to formalize too quickly, for one's own benefit in learning to resonate with responsibility-based mind-sets; rather than a generally hasty preparation for academic and semi-academic transcoding.

2. I have turned Charles W. J. Withers's statement around ("Place, Memory, Monument: Memorializing the Past in Contemporary Highland Scotland," *Ecumene* 3.3 [July 1996]: 327), because, in colonialism, the colonizing impulse appropriates and reterritorializes a "past" to temporize itself more grandly. Marx notes this in "Eighteenth Brumaire" in terms of the bourgeois revolution's reterritorializing of postfeudal Europe.

3. Anne McClintock, *Imperial Leather* (New York: Routledge, 1996) elaborates this.

4. "To dissimilate is to feign not to have what one has" (Baudrillard, *Simulations*, p. 5). Baudrillard is writing of disease. Shall we speak of colonial greed as a disease, as Marshall McLuhan will speak of "too many people and too little food" as a "cancer [that] enhances cell reproduction . . . and transforms itself into self-consumption"? Cotton, that labor-intensive industry that was the motor of the large slave acquisitions in the American South, is part of the same disease.

5. "Transnational corporations are enterprises which own or control value-added activities in two or more countries. The usual mode of ownership and control is by foreign direct investment (FDI), but TNCs may also engage in foreign production by means of corporative alliances with foreign firms" ("Introduction: The Nature of Transnational Corporations and Their Activities," in John H. Dunning, ed., *The Theory of Transnational Corporations* [New York: Routledge, 1993], p. 1). I am grateful to Sonali Perera for bringing this to me when I wanted "the simplest possible definition."

6. I have discussed the question of value at greater length in Spivak, "Scattered Speculations on the Question of Value," in *In Other Worlds*.

7. Cited in Seema Das Seemu, "Garment Shilper Shishu Sromik: 31 Octoberer par kee hobey?" *Chinta* 4.15 (30 Oct. 1995). In the same issue, Shahid Hossain Shamim brings up the important question of the discursive constitution of the "child," much debated in metropolitan feminist theory in connection with the ideology of motherhood. Here one risks censorship for fear of instant dismissal as "a supporter of child labor"!

8. So that I am not accused of abuse, I hasten to add that this phrase is taken from Yeats, "Easter 1916," *Collected Works* (New York: Macmillan, 1963), p. 203.

9. These videos ("Rights and Wrongs: Child Labor," nos. 305 and 414, International Center for Global Communications Foundation) are basically about bonded labor, whereby, in "repayment" of a debt, adults and children are supposed to work under slavery conditions, at such savage rates of interest that the labor sometimes continues over generations.

They are excellent videos, and the U.S. public should certainly be educated. Their message to the citizen as consumer is boycott goods produced by child labor, although checking labor conditions in production is next to impossible. Children are shown producing bricks and carpets. Oriental rugs are a luxury item. And, although Pakistan is singled out, India certainly, and China, Turkey, Iran, Tibet, Nepal and the like, probably, use child labor. It is highly unlikely that the conspicuous consumer will suddenly boycott carpets, or that a fall in the carpet trade is going to bring about the infrastructure for children's education. Iqbal Masih, a ten-year-old boy who attempted to break through into resistance, was separated from local resistance groups and transmogrified into a glorified native informant. He was brought to Boston, given a Human Rights award, picked up by U.S. national television ("I want to be like Abraham Lincoln"), and then simply sent home. Thus thrust into unprotected visibility, he was killed by a bullet. Although it has not been proved that this was a trade-related killing, his death can serve as an allegory of how the question of the children themselves is separate from the spectacle of U.S. benevolence. Both videos are frames for documentaries produced by the Swedish videographer Magnus Bergmar. The documentaries do point at local resistance, although the women's speech is inadequately translated, sometimes drowned out by voiceover. (Sweden is an enlightened donor country.) The frame material, spoken by an African-American woman, really focuses only on the garment industry, which is rather different from bonded labor ("traditional" in some South Asian countries), since the work is performed for foreign direct investment under sweatshop conditions. (My text deals with the micrology of "social dumping," specifically in the garment industry, in Bangladesh.) The tone is consistently U.S. nationalistic—even the language is not politically correct—using "underdeveloped" where approved usage dictates "developing." It reaches a high when the talk-show hostess Kathie Lee Gifford weeps on camera, beginning her conversion to child-labor-activist-cum-watchdog-for-boycott-support from purveyor-of-child-labor-produced-garments-under-her-label speech with the words, "I was born in a wonderful country." By contrast *The Small Hands of Slavery* (New York: Human Rights Watch, 1996), produced by two anonymous interviewers, remains focused on bonded labor in India and never mentions the garment industry. Many of the sources are concerned academics. (The first footnote reference, Tanika Sarkar, both of whose parents were my teachers, went to the same school and college in India as I did.) The ignored "critical voice of the South"—local nongovernmental organizations—is often recorded and correctly assigned the task of helping and policing the state. The bulk of the pamphlet, also quite correctly, faults the Indian government for criminal negligence of laws and constitutional guarantees that are in the books, the oldest for seventy-six years! Nothing can condone this, of course. However, when this excellent book cites the role of the World Bank, once or twice, as part of the local NGOs' analyses, it never integrates it into the general problematic of the bank's economically restructuring imperatives for the State, which severely hamper redistributive activities. And, when this book is cited under "bonded labor" on the Internet (Alta Vista has 1,246,120 matches to the phrase), the only imperative— "What You Can Do in India"—is boycotts and sanctions. Under "Activism," for bonded labor, a representative entry is "Ethical Considerations in Corporate Takeovers," which turns out to be an account of a church-based seminar attended by plenty of CEOs, think tanks, and banks, among them the World Bank and Chase Manhattan. No Human Rights Watch will ever comment on the followup record of these financial institutions. Capitalism *is* better than bond-slavery. But is exploitation the only way out? *Small Hands* records one single instance of "community-based savings and credit program" that "will strike a significant blow against bonded child labor" (p. 147). This, alas, is the door through which credit-baiting without infrastructural reform enters under globalization, for the sake of the complete financialization of the globe; or, it provides justification for the opening of the world's poor to the commercial sector, when the officers of such sponsors of micro-enterprise are asked to offer examples of social involvement. We have already taken note of Salman Rushdie's dismissal of Indian-language literatures. And Chapter 2 has already pointed at Mahasweta Devi's analysis of the postcolonial polity in "Pterodactyl." Here I will cite a passage from "Douloti the Bountiful": "There are people for passing laws, there are people to ride jeeps, but no one to light the fire" (Devi, "Douloti," in *Imaginary Maps* [New York: Routledge, 1995], p. 88). Rushdie would dismiss this as "parochial." It should still be pointed out that, by contrast to the triumphalist U.S. moral imperialism, the represented agent of judgment, the character who speaks the quoted words, is Bono Nagesia, a resistant Aboriginal and, as the last instance of the judgment of the criminal state there is the laboring body of the Aboriginal woman, which passes judgment on independent India: "Filling the entire Indian peninsula from the oceans to the Himalayas, here lies bonded labor spread-eagled, kamiya-whore Douloti Nagesia's tormented corpse, putrefied with venereal disease, having vomited up all the blood in its desiccated lungs. Today, on the fifteenth of August, Douloti has left no room at all in the India of people like Mohan for planting the standard of the Independence flag. . . . Douloti is all over India" (p. 93).

10. Most of these accounts are to be found in handwritten field reports. I have heard some of these first-hand. For a small but representative sampling (in Bengali), see the detailed report published in *Chinta* 5.16–17 (15 May 1996).

11. "Proposal for the Provision of Primary Education for Displaced Under-Age Workers," mimeograph, Gonoshajja Sangstha. Apr. 1995, p. 10.

12. Unpublished documentation available upon request.

13. It must be acknowledged that Derrida attempted such a stitching in *Glas*, in the interest of a critique of phallogocentrism. But that, too, is only European-focus. His attempts at intervening in globality (*Specters*) or at speaking for (from?) Algeria or as Franco-Maghrebian must remain on another register.

28

100% COTTON

Pamela Johnson

Editor's introduction: Pamela Johnson, novelist and poet, is associate tutor in creative writing at Goldsmiths, University of London, and edits the website *Words Unlimited* (http://www.wordsunlimited.typepad.com/).

In "100% Cotton," Johnson explores Britain's postcolonial identity. Shifting between the perspectives of a father and daughter, the poem appropriates textile terms and garment shapes to show how culturally specific details are adopted, often with little recognition of the past. Following antagonism between neighbors, the poem opens out to give a glimpse of the wider community. The textiles Johnson evokes throughout the poem carry cultural identities and unavoidable—if unspoken—politics.

I'll defend my own land, Frank shouts across
the privet at the man, in shalwar
and t-shirt, who's moved in next door.

It's only a hedge. Isn't 'land' a bit grand
for your handkie-sized plot? Blood on the boil,
I fought for this country, Frank cries as he falls.

His gashed head lies wrapped in soft lint,
morphine eases the rage from his brow.
Not knowing how to care for a bully,

she brings new pyjamas, finest white cotton,
blue piping, remembering that day when
her mum bought him two-for-the-price-of-one,

polyester, 'seconds' from the market, a fiver,
and his temper sent static crackling
between them that went on for a week.

Did he think he was bettering himself
drawing in the cord, tied tight,
an Englishman, one-hundred-percent cotton?

Source: Pamela Johnson, "100% Cotton," unpublished (2011). Reproduced with permission.

A buddleia grows where smoke
once belched as thousands swarmed
to the sound of the hooter, three shifts
   a day,

and alongside the crumbling chimney
a minaret rises and men, loose-trousered,
fill the close-packed streets

drawn by the call of the muezzin, hugging
woollen coats against an Oldham winter
while she, at his bedside, waits to offer
   nightwear

adopted, adapted from an ancient design
of tailors in the markets of Kharachi,
not sure if he knows *payejama* is an Urdu word.

Pamela Johnson, March, 2011

29

LISA ANNE AUERBACH'S CANNY DOMESTICITY

Julia Bryan-Wilson

Editor's introduction: American Julia Bryan-Wilson is associate professor of art history at the University of California, Berkeley in the United States. She has written and lectured extensively about contemporary craft practice related to North America. Her first book, *Art Workers: Radical Practice in the Vietnam War Era*, was published in 2009, and she is currently researching *Crafting Dissent: Handmade Art and Activism since 1970*. The text reprinted here comes from the catalog for the exhibition *Lisa Anne Auerbach*, curated by Jacob Proctor and held at the University of Michigan Museum of Art in 2009. The American artist Lisa Anne Auerbach is known for her use of knitting to pass challenging commentaries on the state of American politics. Bryan-Wilson situates Auerbach's knitting, and her use of sweaters in particular, within the broader movements of performance and feminist art from the 1970s on, as well as the current popularity of "craftivism" sweeping through North America.

In 2006, Bolivian president Evo Morales wore a sweater while on an international diplomatic tour, igniting a burst of interest in his distinctive sartorial choice. The striped pullover's horizontal bands of alternating red, white, blue, and gray were identifiably indigenous. Morales's sweater became something of a signature look, and the newly inaugurated leader was repeatedly photographed greeting various world leaders while sporting it. Immediately termed the "Evo" sweater, its native Bolivian design was seen as perfectly in keeping with Morales's Aymara heritage and his larger populist message: the garment spoke volumes without the president saying a word. The sweater, traditionally made by hand of local alpaca wool, became a symbol of Morales's investment in domestic production and his resistance to global trade and exploitative labor policies.[1] Ironically, inexpensive mass-produced copies of the Evo were quickly churned out to sell in street markets and online, a reminder that ideological affinities are signaled through style, and that such solidarities are constantly complicated, marketed, and transformed.

As Morales's example demonstrates, wearing a sweater can be both a fashion statement and a political one. It is precisely this intersection that Los Angeles–based artist Lisa Anne Auerbach explores. She probes the possibilities of craft and advocates for a leftist reclamation of homemaking. In her ongoing series of knitted items, Auerbach integrates texts and images—such as historical quotations, forceful polemics, witty catchphrases, and sly references—on sweaters, skirts, banners, caps, ponchos, and flags. One sweater declares "Keep Abortion Legal," and a pair of mittens details the body count of U.S. soldiers killed in Iraq. By inserting text into her clothes, Auerbach turns the implicit politics of Morales's sweater up a notch, for to put on one of her outfits is, as the artist has stated, to use the "body as a billboard."[2] But Auerbach's work is also geared toward provoking local, face-to-face interactions. The sweaters do not simply declare an opinion or state a viewpoint—though they do that, too—since

Figure 29.1. Lisa Anne Auerbach, *Sharrow Sweater (Ghost)*, 2009. Wool. Courtesy of Lisa Anne Auerbach.

their tactile, handmade nature also elicits more intimate exchanges. Auerbach asserts a canny sense of domesticity, and by this I mean that her employment of conventionally female "homemaking" is knowing, self-aware, and even a bit devious in the era of Homeland Security.

Much of Auerbach's practice has been calibrated to the specificity of its current moment. Her *Warm Sweaters for the New Cold War*, an ongoing series begun in 2004, explicitly reference the war in Iraq and the overheated rhetoric of the Bush administration. In the summer of 2006, she conducted an informal poll in which she asked the question, "What's your favorite thing about the War on Terror?" Using the answers she received from friends, she knit five versions of the sweater that posited the question on the front, and a variation of the answer on the back. Some of the answers were irreverent; others more sober. "Gives me an excuse not to go to the Frieze art fair," states the back of one iteration, with a graphic of bomber-like planes fitted head-to-tail under the text. Another confesses: "Getting patted down by women in public in the airport. I like that it's OK to be touched by another woman in public. That and I've become a foot exhibitionist." This answer turns a climate of heightened fear into a moment of illicit and unexpected queer pleasure. Auerbach's sweaters consistently weave together timely political references with teasing tongue-in-cheek comments to generate conversations about serious topics.

The knitted pieces fit into Auerbach's wider practice, in which she utilizes photography, text-based collaborative projects, and installation. Though trained primarily as a photographer at the Rochester Institute of Technology and the Art Center College of Design, in Pasadena, Auerbach has long been fascinated with the so-called women's work of domestic crafts. She founded a 'zine, *American Homebody*, an eclectic publication in print between 1998 and 2001, aimed at fostering support for a dispersed network of radical hermits. Stemming from her investments in feminism and community building, *American*

Homebody sought to provide alternative visions of homemaking and domestic arts that were not limited to the walls of one's own house, but extended out to the street and the community. The 'zine included everything from recipes to gardening tips to an "American Homebody Covergirl"—Auerbach as a campy or outlandish fetishized stereotype of the sexy housewife gracing the cover of each issue. Working with other photographers such as Sharon Lockhart, Daniel Marlos, and Charlie White—much of Auerbach's practice is collaborative—she produced a covergirl calendar, featuring men in drag and the artist-as-sex doll impersonating "perfect" housewives.

Auerbach's desire to provide an outlet for feedback among activist, grassroots homebodies is an extension of feminist reevaluations about what Pat Mainardi called, in 1969, "the politics of housework."[3] Scholars like Alice Kessler-Harris have demonstrated that the realm of the "home" bleeds into the public sphere, as the entire capitalist economy rests upon women's unpaid domestic labor.[4] Auerbach's addressing of the feminization of labor builds on pioneer Faith Wilding's understanding that "contemporary artists who seek to address gendered work and the domestic . . . need to take into account recent economic, cultural, and sociological developments, as well as considering how technological innovations are profoundly altering both public and private work and life globally."[5] It is feminism, of course, that furnishes the most potent method for thinking through the relation between the personal and the political. In the industrial West, knitting sweaters was once a chore of necessity, but as mass-produced methods of production took hold, undertaking such a task became a hobby, or a labor marked by leisure and enjoyment. In addition to their basis in domestic crafts, Auerbach's sweaters draw on the legacy of text-based conceptual art. Her cunning use of words—as in the sweater series *Everything I Touch Turns to $old*—harks back to the slogans of Barbara Kruger that likewise critique commodity culture.

What is more, because they are meant to be worn in public, and this wearing constitutes a sort

Figure 29.2. Lisa Anne Auerbach, *Everything I Touch Turns to $old*, 2006/2009. Wool. Courtesy of Lisa Anne Auerbach.

of performance, they are in dialogue with 1970s feminist body art like that of Linda Montano and Adrian Piper, whose performances often revolved around special clothing choices—think of Montano in her "chicken dance" outfit, or Piper walking the streets in a shirt dripping with wet paint. Auerbach's debts to feminism are multiple, for it was also the women's liberation movement of the 1970s that rekindled interest in crafts such as quilting, crocheting, weaving, and knitting as legitimate modes of artistic production.[6] In feminist works such as Faith Ringgold's story quilts, the Feminist Art Program's *Womanhouse* (1971–72), and Judy Chicago's *The Dinner Party* (1974–79), the divisions between functional craft, decorative objects, and fine art were eradicated, opening up new channels for utilizing conventionally overlooked—or denigrated as "low" and female—methods of handmaking within artistic work.[7]

Along with feminist concerns, other sweaters in Auerbach's series take on the issue of public memory and the incessant use, and abuse, of September 11, 2001 as an overdetermined reference. On the front of one sweater, a series of cartoon voice-bubbles spell out the following exchange: "Knock-knock." "Who's there?" "9-11." "9-11 who?" The back completes the joke: "9-11 WHO?? I thought you said you'd NEVER FORGET." Rendered in a font that looks like a digitized hand-drawn scrawl, the use of the speech bubbles puts the joke at a distance, as if it is articulated by disembodied voices and is not necessarily the expression of the wearer herself. (Auerbach uses a stylus and drawing tablet attached to her computerized knitting machine in order to convert her individual script into a pixilated version that is legible when rendered in yarn.) Winkingly patriotic red, white, and blue trim around the wrists and lower edge of the sweater add color to its palette of light and dark grey. Auerbach has paired this, as she often does, with a short, flared knit skirt—creating an aesthetically unified outfit allows her room to expand the visual range of the sweater—and embedded in its wide patterned hem is an abstracted, yet unmistakable, image of planes flying in the direction of two blocky towers.

The 9-11 sweater and skirt walk a knife's edge between humor, offensiveness, and outrage. Marx's well-known adage about history repeating itself first as tragedy and then as farce yields here to a different dynamic: the joke draws its punch from the fact that in the years after 2001, any admission of collective exhaustion with mention of the attacks on the World Trade Center was hysterically countered by the Bush administration's unceasing recourse to it in order to justify its wartime policies.

Originally inspired by the wordy pullovers worn by Rick Nielsen, lead guitarist of the 1970s rock band Cheap Trick,[8] Auerbach's sweaters, in both form and content, at times flirt with the notion of "bad taste." In this, she acknowledges how sweaters have a dense public life within American popular culture with regards to taste, class, and social identity. They are caricatured as squarely occupying the realm of the tacky—holiday themed

sweaters featuring snowflakes or reindeers are used as condescending shorthand for middlebrow fashion. To cite a well-known example, critical race theorists have argued that Bill Cosby's multicolored, chunkily textured sweaters from *The Cosby Show* (1984–92) served to visually emphasize that his character was a non-threatening black man. The notion that white viewers responded positively to the class codes on offer in *The Cosby Show*, including those represented by clothing, has become a standard reading.[9] With his body blanketed in a comforting, "safe" wardrobe, Cliff Huxtable was firmly secured as respectably upper-middle-class. However, many of Cosby's sweaters were not mass-produced department store purchases, but, in fact, custom-made by Dutch designer Koos van den Akker—and thus more aspirational than is often acknowledged.[10]

As somewhat mobile signifiers, sweaters have also come to connote economy and sacrifice. In 1977, President Jimmy Carter urged Americans to conserve energy by turning down their thermostats and donning sweaters. Auerbach picks up on these multiple meanings—from a rocker's brash self-promotion to canonic sitcom attire to an environmentalist's good deed—but her *Warm Sweaters for the New Cold War* also activate the idea of a sweater as a kind of armor, worn as a shield in the midst of hostile political climate. She writes:

A sweater comes in handy whenever you feel that chill in the air. Sometimes the chill is due to the winds, a sudden gust, a draft, or a blizzard. Other times, the room goes cold when you speak your mind, and suddenly everyone else is clutching their drink a little tighter, clenching their teeth a bit more strongly, and reaching quickly for sweaters and shawls. Continue the conversation with a sweater that talks back.[11]

In particular, Auerbach approaches the paradoxes of Homeland Security by injecting her own feminist brand of domestic homemaking to make knitwear that functions as an alternative security blanket, one that counters the official regime.

A commemorative sweater and skirt set produced on the occasion of the fifth anniversary of the Iraq war stated the number U.S. casualties—3,992 dead and 29,295 wounded as of March 19, 2008. These stark numbers (not widely publicized) are set next to a variety of images, including a spurting oil well and pointing machine guns. A childlike line of men and women holding hands rings the bottom of the army-green colored sweater. An orange inset at the shoulder and along the skirt's hemline that cites the Bush war strategy "shock and awe" completes the design. Far from stereotypes of sweaters as everyday or banal, this is a "sweater that talks back" about that which is most horrifying in the service of publicizing and memorializing.

Over the past five years, her knits have evolved, transitioning from straightforward campaign logos rendered on squares that are sewn together to produce simple skirts and boxy sweaters, to more aesthetically complex responses to issues like reproductive rights and the politics of bicycling. The first hand-knit, text-based garment Auerbach made was a cardigan emblazoned with a large Star of David on the back, created in 1996 after a trip to Germany. When visiting sites of Holocaust tourism, the artist was prompted to consider what it meant to mark one's body through clothing. Historically there have been ramifications in making identity visible, either by force or by choice, and for Auerbach, wearing the Star of David was an act of reclamation. Made from vibrant Dodger-blue yarn, and with the Los Angeles Dodger logo on its front (the logo echoes the artist's own initials), the cardigan was also a tribute to Sandy Koufax, the Jewish baseball player who refused to pitch on the Sabbath.

Though there are many precedents for broadcasting political views through clothing, Auerbach's handcrafted sweaters, ponchos, and gloves arguably function slightly differently than mass-produced T-shirts or buttons. For one thing, they are less disposable than a button or campaign shirt; sweaters and other knit items are more durable and made to last. Furthermore, a recent resurgence of

Figure 29.3. Lisa Anne Auerbach, *Thank God I'm an Atheist (Ghost)*, 2009. Wool. Courtesy of Lisa Anne Auerbach.

popular and critical interest in the do-it-yourself movement asserts that there is something inherently political about a handcrafted object in our era of sweatshop labor.[12] According to these arguments, a handknit sweater—even one without slogans—is an object that registers as a kind of protest against the brutal conditions of labor that manufacture most of the goods we use.[13]

Even if claims for the subversive or revolutionary nature of what has been termed "craftivism" have been overstated, there remains a tangible distinction between an Auerbach knit woolen sweater and a thin cotton T-shirt, not least because of the endurance of knit material and the sturdiness of her construction. Sweaters are also unlikely locations for inflammatory messages; in a time when passengers wearing political T-shirts are being forced off of airplanes, Auerbach has breezed through security even when wearing a sweater that reads "When There's Nothing Left to Burn/You Have to Set Yourself on Fire," and depicts a row of dynamite circling around her midsection.

Long before Tom Wolfe coined the dismissive phrase "radical chic," clothing had been understood as a form of self-fashioning, a performance that invokes complex status (and gender) norms.[14] To return to the body-based nature of Auerbach's works, it is crucial that she designs them *to be worn*, which demands that she takes into considerations how they look in motion. A somewhat crude poncho stating "Kerry/Edwards 04" was the first garment she made on the knitting machine, and it inaugurated further experiments. (Though many knitting machines are completely hand-operated, Auerbach uses a low-tech computer-controlled device that translates the binary notation of knitting patterns into panels of fabric that are then joined together by hand.) Some of these experiments were admitted failures, leading her to refine her process and carefully consider questions of placement, legibility, and intention. For instance, in 2004 Auerbach made a knit hat that read "Ban Bush," laying out the phrase so that each word sits on either side of the head. Because only one word at a time was visible, she realized that, depending on which direction the wearer was facing, the hat could be read as an endorsement of Bush rather than a condemnation. Now Auerbach strives to make statements that are coherent regardless of partial viewing and crafts her work intentionally to provoke the viewer into trying to see both sides, to glimpse front and back of a sweater or hat, or both right and left glove (a metaphor, perhaps, for political dualities). She considers both the body of the viewer and the body of the wearer as they negotiate shared space.

In addition, Auerbach's sweaters are displayed within art contexts, raising questions about the institutionalization of fashion and the displacement of "functional" crafts into fine art spaces.

Other contemporary artists whose work traffics between everyday design and art-world exhibition include German artist Rosemarie Trockel, whose knitted work takes up questions of sexuality and production, and Los Angeles–based Andrea Zittel, whose pared-down uniforms investigate the aesthetic and social possibilities of daily living through sustainable design. Auerbach's insistently two-sided garments raise challenges when displayed, for like sculpture they must be seen in the round. Since they are designed primarily for her own body, putting them on "standard issue" dress forms distorts their shapes. For exhibition purposes, Auerbach worked with a Californian mannequin company to make a mannequin torso that reflects her own proportions. The headless and legless dress forms are suspended from the ceiling, and the sweaters and skirts hover eerily in the gallery like a disembodied crowd that is ready to be mobilized.

Auerbach's outfits interrogate what happens when a person broadcasts sometimes provocative views (such as "Smash Monogamy"), one of a trio of sweaters ambiguously based on the proclamations of the radical Weather Underground group, or states information that is not widely addressed (such as war casualty statistics). Her clothing is often created in response to immediate political circumstances to be worn—by herself or others—when attending specific rallies or meetings. The sweaters activate a different sense of security, here denoting a kind of indestructibility, as well as a cloak or shield of protection. One of her earliest articles of clothing, a skirt stating "Bush is a Turkey" on one side and "Knitters for Kerry" on the other, was made for a friend going to the Republican National Convention in 2004. Multiple levels of meaning are woven together in Auerbach's sweaters, as she integrates evocative patterns and motifs that subtly reinforce her message and refer to the stated text. For instance, this skirt utilizes a visual pun on the word "turkey," as it features a graphic motif that resembled weeds growing up from the hem that she took from a book of Turkish sock patterns.

Her hand-knit *Body Count Mittens*, a series begun in 2005, use the act of knitting as a private way to mark time, as well as a method of visibly registering the growing number of U.S. casualties in the war in Iraq. As she begins each mitten, she inscribes it with the official body count on that day. During the time it takes her to finish one hand, the number of dead inevitably increases, and so she notes the new body count as she moves on to the other hand. Auerbach has posted the pattern for the mittens on her website, and she encourages handknitters to use the pattern to make them in public in hopes of advertising the grim statistic as well as spawning questions and debate. There are shades of Freudian repetition-compulsion in her constant return to chronicling the war dead, as if she is reworking the trauma, and indeed it is a cliché that the act of

Figure 29.5. Lisa Anne Auerbach, *Body Count Mittens*, 2005. Wool. Courtesy of Lisa Anne Auerbach.

Figure 29.4. Lisa Anne Auerbach, *Body Count Mittens*, 2007. Wool. Courtesy of Lisa Anne Auerbach.

handknitting can be therapeutic, a way to harness and redirect obsessive tendencies.

There are other reasons Auerbach has turned to knitting during a time of war. As chronicled in Anna MacDonald's book *No Idle Hands: The Social History of American Knitting*, knitting has historically been encouraged during times of U.S. national conflict as a way for women to keep themselves busy and create necessary items for the troupes such as socks, gloves, and hats.[15] Knitting, because it is transportable "lapwork," can also be done in groups; as such, it forges a social space, and in previous wars this social aspect was also valued as women whose husbands were on the front lines were urged to come together and channel their grief and worry into the wartime activity of group handmaking.

Numerous recent art and activism projects have looked back to this historical connection between female labor, knitting, and war economies, including the British craft advocacy group Cast-Off's *Knit for Peace* demonstrations on the London Underground (2004), Cat Mazza's *Stitch For Senate* balaclava–making undertaking, in which volunteers knit helmet liners and sent them to their senators as an anti-war gesture (2007), and Sabrina Gschwandtner's *War-Time Knitting Circle*, an interactive installation at the Museum of Art & Design's exhibition *Radical Lace and Subversive Knitting* (2007). In *War-Time Knitting Circle*, the artist set up round tables and provided yarn, knitting needles, and instructions for various projects (including Auerbach's *Body Count Mittens*) that members of the public could knit while talking about the war. Gschwandtner's space was demarcated by large machine-knit banners—"photo blankets"—featuring images of previous wartime knitting activities. Other related works include Liz Collins's public knitting event *Knitting Nation*, a part of Allison Smith's public art project *The Muster*, from 2005, which involved a squadron of female knitters on hand-cranked knitting machines turning out a giant abstracted U.S. flag that unspooled impudently onto the ground.[16] Nina Rosenberg solicits participants through her website, redsweaters.org, to knit action-figure-scaled blood-red sweaters, each one representing a U.S. soldier killed in Iraq, which are then strung together and hung in trees. These diverse projects attest to the potency and resonance of knitting during wartime for current feminist artists, though Auerbach's mittens and sweaters—made for herself and for friends as an assertion of both personal style and political conviction—are among the most individualized responses.

Auerbach's focus on the individual and the local is in response to an economy subtended by outsourcing, inequality, consumerism, and gender imbalance. In her photography, she documents that which is eccentric, neglected, and overlooked within the increasingly homogenized commercial landscape. The series "Small Business" from 2007, for instance, chronicles endangered businesses like florists and BBQ restaurants that exist in shacks, garages, and other seemingly too-small spaces that she encounters in her travels throughout the country. Much of her photographic work focuses on mobility and location—she is especially committed to biking and has created a series of "portraits" of unicycles. As such work illustrates, she is keenly interested in the absurd. In collaboration with Alexandra Mir, she journeyed to Naples to "repair" plaster casts of broken Roman statuary with marzipan, fusing the idea of reparation and mending with a surrealist transformation of objects using an unlikely material (*Marzamara*, 2008). In 2008, she was commissioned by the V-Day organization to create a "vagina" for its 10th anniversary, and in response she constructed a large (10 feet in diameter) pink and red yurt, entitled *V-Day Yurt*, that viewers were invited to crawl into. This installation was reminiscent of Wilding's seminal *Womb Room (Crocheted Environment)* created for *Womanhouse*, yet was openly textual, with euphemistic phrases (contributed by V-Day founder Eve Ensler), such as "Welcome to the wetlands" inscribed on the knitted outside of the structure. Such a work underscores how Auerbach is drawn to making new kinds of environments and "homes," however defamiliarized.

While the term *canniness* most usually refers to cleverness, it can also mean frugal or thrifty. In addition, a "canny space" connotes a snug or cozy environment. Thus canny domesticity could sound like a redundant formulation—a homelike home—but it is just this friction that propels Auerbach's work. In a well-known essay, Freud defines the uncanny as that which is "secretly familiar . . . which has undergone repression and returned from it," and discusses the intimate relationship between the *heimisch* (homelike) and the *umheimlich* (uncanny).[17] (Think back to the vaginal yurt—for Freud, female genitals are the ultimate uncanny: the homey place that is also made strange.) From sculptures made whole with marzipan to bleak war statistics juxtaposed onto handmade sweaters that hang like ghosts in the museum, Auerbach's crafty conjoinings are sometimes surprising, sometimes uncomfortable, and always canny.

NOTES

1. Some accounts claim that Morales's famous sweater was made from cheap acrylic rather than wool; nevertheless, it was certainly Bolivian-produced. In 2007, Morales enacted several policies that attempt to preserve and foster the Bolivian textiles industries, including a ban on the sale of used clothing from the United States, as these secondhand cast-offs flood the market and undercut more expensive local goods. See "Morales to ban used clothing in Bolivia," *USA Today* (July 17, 2007).

2. Lisa Anne Auerbach, *Charted Patterns for Sweaters that Talk Back* (New York, 2008), p. 34.

3. Pat Mainardi, "The Politics of Housework," first published in *Redstockings* (Fall 1969); reprinted in *Dear Sisters: Dispatches from the Women's Liberation Movement*, ed. Rosalyn Baxandall and Linda Gordon (New York, 2001), pp. 255–56.

4. Alice Kessler-Harris, *Women Have Always Worked: An Historical Overview* (New York, 1981).

5. Faith Wilding, "Monstrous Domesticity," *M/E/A/N/I/N/G* 18 (November 1995), pp. 3–16.

6. There is a wealth of significant literature on the historical gendering of craft and on the importance of traditionally domestic handmaking in feminist art. For a few influential examples, see Rozsika Parker and Griselda Pollock, "Crafty Women and the Hierarchy of the Arts," in *Old Mistresses: Women, Art, and Ideology* (New York, 1981), pp. 50–81; Lydia Yee, *Division of Labor: "Women's Work" in Contemporary Art* (New York, 1995); and Amelia Jones, ed., *Sexual Politics: Judy Chicago's Dinner Party in Feminist Art History* (Los Angeles, 1996).

7. Glenn Adamson offers an incisive take on the importance of handmaking within a broad range of contemporary art in his *Thinking Through Craft* (London, 2007).

8. Interview with Lisa Anne Auerbach, January 18, 2009.

9. See Sut Jhally and Justin Lewis, *Enlightened Racism: The Cosby Show, Audiences, and the Myth of the American Dream* (Boulder, 1992).

10. Television historian Victoria E. Johnson has pointed out to me that Cosby alternated sweaters with college sweatshirts—many of which promoted historically black colleges and universities—as an extension of the upward mobility explicitly thematized in the show.

11. Auerbach 2008, p. 34.

12. For more on the rise of current crafting in relationship to politics, see Faythe Levine and Cortney Heimerl, *Handmade Nation: The Rise of DIY, Art, Craft, and Design* (New York, 2008); Betsy Greer, *Knitting for Good!: A Guide to Creating Personal, Social, and Political Change Stitch by Stitch* (New York, 2008); and Betty Christiansen, *Knitting for Peace: Making the World a Better Place One Stitch at a Time*, (New York, 2006).

13. Sabrina Gschwandtner has written a cogent argument that troubles the sweeping assertions about crafting as inherently radical; Gschwandtner, "Let 'em Eat Cake," *American Craft* 68, 4 (August/September 2008), p. 62.

14. Wolfe's phrase does not refer specifically to clothing, but to the trendy adoption of political causes; *Radical Chic and Mau-Mauing the Flak Catchers* (New York, 1970). One important examination into earlier links between art, craft, and fashion is found in Nancy J. Troy, *Couture Culture: A Study in Modern Art and Fashion* (Cambridge, MA, 2002).

15. Anna MacDonald, *No Idle Hands: The Social History of American Knitting* (New York, 1990).

16. For more on Collins's *Knitting Nation* and Smith's event, see Anne Wehr, ed., *Allison Smith: The Muster* (New York, 2005).

17. Sigmund Freud, *The Uncanny* (1919), trans. David McLintock (New York, 2003).

30

THE SUBVERSIVE STITCH: EMBROIDERY AND THE MAKING OF THE FEMININE

Rozsika Parker

Editor's introduction: In *The Subversive Stitch*, the late Rozsika Parker observed the "dual face of embroidery . . . [which] provided both a weapon of resistance for women and functioned as a source of constraint." She wrote the new introduction to her influential study, reprinted here, before her death in 2010. In it, Parker laments the lack of progress feminism and embroidery have made since the book's publication in 1984. The work of Tracey Emin is compared to the values of 1970s feminists, and the late Louise Bourgeois's use of textiles, made after the first edition of *The Subversive Stitch* was published, is noted for its importance to textile practice. Taking a longer view, Parker provides a sage reminder that our current economic crisis and the tensions that exist between art and craft are cyclical, rather than unique, events. She places the challenges that face textile practice today in this broader perspective and concludes, "I wish I could end with an unqualified celebration of the recent history of embroidery. Change, however, is slow and uneven."

INTRODUCTION

At first sight embroidery practice is much as it was when *The Subversive Stitch* was first published, twenty-five years ago. There continues to be a huge diversity of practice under the heading of embroidery. Men and women stitch as craft, as art, as professionals and as gifted amateurs. Moreover, 1984 and 2010 have something in common: financial recession. Then I observed a revival of enthusiasm for embroidery as a 'homecraft' with the call for the homemade, the hand-made and the natural. Now the same holds true. The London College of Fashion in August 2009 reported that bookings for sewing classes had increased by almost a third in twelve months.

Yet there are detectable changes in embroidery practice. For a start, the context of the book has altered significantly. Today there is no longer a thriving political movement of women. I wrote the book under the impetus of Second Wave feminism. By righting the neglect of women artists and questioning the downgrading of art forms associated with women—like embroidery—feminist art and craft historians revisioned many of the premises underlying the writing of Art History. Theory and history came alive for us and gathered new meanings. Passion and vibrancy

Source: Rozsika Parker, "Introduction," in *The Subversive Stitch: Embroidery and the Making of the Feminine* (London: I. B. Tauris, 2010) pp. xi–xxii. Reproduced with permission. With the permission of the publisher, some minor corrections or edits have been made in the version of the text published here.

characterised the work of both artists and academics. I feel fortunate to have been part of those times.

Shortly after the publication of *The Subversive Stitch*, a backlash against feminism set in. The political and psychological losses that accrued have been compellingly documented by, for example, Sheila Rowbotham, Susan Faludi and Naomi Wolf.[1] Headlines blared 'When Feminism Failed' and 'The Awful Truth About Women's Lib'. Typically, anti-feminism focussed on the bodies and beings of feminists. It was trumpeted that the fight for equality led to hair loss, worry lines, cellulite and above all infertility. A magazine feature was typically titled 'The Quiet Pain of Infertility; for the success oriented it's a bitter pill' while an ad for face cream inquired 'Is your face paying the price for success?' Of course, nineteen-seventies feminists had no desire for 'success' under the contemporary social and political structures. Far from wishing to climb 'the ladder' we wanted to kick it away. Where embroidery was concerned, feminists of the time were described as rejecting and spurning women's traditional crafts and skills. The ambivalence we experienced in relation to embroidery—our understanding of the medium as both an instrument of oppression and an important source of creative satisfaction—was repeatedly misrepresented as blanket condemnation. Apparently we 'dumped' women's domestic art skills. The Feminist was represented as stitch-hating, sad, ugly and drastically devoid of humour.

Feminism survived—in part by foregrounding a humorous face. Today a feminist magazine on the internet is, for example, satirically titled *The F-Word*, while exhibitions containing embroidery with feminist connotations are titled, for example, 'Not Your Grandmother's Doily'.

But what of other issues raised in the book? I identified the historical hierarchical division of the arts into fine arts and craft as a major force in the marginalisation of women's work. The movement to break down boundaries between different forms of creative expression, which gathered pace in the nineteen-seventies, has undoubtedly intensified. Some working in the crafts today refer to themselves as 'craftists'. *Craft* magazine declared in 2008, 'We now take for granted the cross-pollination of arts and crafts.'[2] And, in recent years, a number of exhibitions have displayed work by artists employing stitchery. The Museum of Arts and Design in New York mounted 'Radical Lace and Subversive Knitting' in 2006, followed by 'Pricked: Extreme Embroidery' in 2007. The latter included 48 artists who, in the words of the *New York Times* reviewer, 'make another case for needlecraft without the "craft"'.[3] In Britain there was 'Cloth and Culture NOW', in which 35 artists from six countries used textile history to investigate the importance of cultural identity and transcultural influences in their work. In 2008 Banners of Persuasion (a visual arts commissioning organisation started by Christopher and Suzanne Sharpe) organised 'Demons, Yarns and Tales', in which 17 artists were invited to explore a textile medium they didn't normally work in. Also in 2008 'The Fabric of Myth' was organised at Compton Verney. The exhibition explored the symbolic function of textiles in classical mythology and their thematic influence on historic and contemporary art. It included the sculptor Louise Bourgeois, whose work I discuss below.

Karen Rosenberg, reviewing 'Pricked: Extreme Embroidery', wrote 'In the 70s artists who swapped their paint brushes for a needle and thread were making a feminist statement. Today, as both men and women fill galleries with crocheted sculpture and stitched canvas, the gesture isn't quite so specific.'[4] Many pieces exhibited were primarily concerned with the formal possibilities of embroidery and new materials, but there were, nevertheless, powerful feminist pieces, for example Christa Maiwald's party dresses for little girls embroidered with images of male world leaders.

The exhibition also showed the work of a number of men, suggesting that embroidery practice seems to have become significantly less gender specific. I use the word 'seems' because it could be that the Internet is revealing previously hidden male embroiderers. Jamie Chalmers, for example, runs a website which functions as a resource for contemporary embroidery, featuring international textile artists, many of whom are men. He says, 'It's not always easy being a Manbroiderer, people sometimes can't get their head around the fact that I'm six feet tall and yet I like stitching. But I'm not too fazed. I know how much I enjoy it and I just want to help other people share that experience.'⁵ Thanks to the Women's Liberation Movement, there is a greater flexibility in what is considered natural or normal behaviour for men and women, yet the associations of embroidery with femininity, triviality and domesticity still need to be warded off by the term 'manbroiderer'— and by the build of the stitcher.

There are real differences between work employing embroidery to comment on the condition of women in the seventies and work produced in later decades influenced by Second Wave feminism. A comparison of the work of the earlier feminist artists described in *The Subversive Stitch* to Tracey Emin's more recent sewn work is telling.

Seventies artists employed embroidery as a medium with a heritage in women's hands, and thus as more appropriate than male-associated paint for making feminist statements. Kate Walker comments (see page 211), 'Embroidery was one technique among many which could be combined in new ways to create forms of art truer to our skills and experience.' Taking the format of the sampler, the sayings she stitched were deliberately defiant, not compliant: 'Wife is a Four Letter Word' (*Illustration no 102*). She said of her sampler, 'I have never worried that embroidery's association with femininity, sweetness, passivity and obedience may subvert my work's feminist intention. Femininity and sweetness are part of women's strength . . . Quiet strength need not be mistaken for useless vulnerability.'

Catherine Riley, who trained as a textile artist, parodied the emotions associated with needlework—purity and chastity—and revealed the limitations they imposed. In an exhibition of her art in 1980 all the pieces were worked in shades of white, conjuring up and cutting across the way whitework embroidery creates the image of women as pure, sexless, spiritual and sensitive. *Illustration No. 106 . . . In a Tin* displays the word 'Sex' spelled out in bone-silk and flowers, and contained in a white sardine tin, beautifully mounted and framed in pure white.

Other feminist artists explored the relationship between embroidery and class. Margaret Harrison assembled examples of traditional needlecraft and contemporary doilies 'made in the factory by working-class women and sold back to them', highlighting the process of de-skilling working-class women since the industrial revolution.

For those who saw themselves as feminist artists, embroidery was the perfect medium to give form to consciousness-raising. The Women's Liberation Movement employed the slogan 'The personal is the political'. Steeped in the personal, yet shaped by the political, embroidery displayed the power of the political on personal life, as well as the political implications of personal relationships. Tensions between traditional expectations of feminine reticence and lived female sexuality were stitched on samplers—for example, Kate Walker's 'Wife is a Four Letter word', described above. The constraints of feminine 'purity and chastity', associated with the construction of femininity, were challenged but not with the aim of achieving masculinity. Nineteen-seventies feminists categorically did not wish to exchange the frying pan of the feminine stereotype for the fire of the masculine stereotype. Embroidering the personal as political was, above all, intended to challenge the subordination and oppression of women.

Feminist artists were part of a thriving political movement, whereas today's embroiderers, most notably Tracey Emin, are working in a very different time. I'd like to be able to claim Emin as the daughter of seventies feminism—the daughter we would have wanted. But it's not that simple. She is the complex product of the confluence of her personal history with celebrity culture, and of the evolution of art practice under the impact of nineteen-seventies feminism.

There are two major ways in which her work differs from her 'foremothers'. Nineteen-seventies feminists eschewed celebrity and leadership in favour of collectivity, whereas Tracey Emin is undoubtedly a celebrity. The number of features that have been written about her is quite extraordinary. But, perhaps more importantly, while nineteen-seventies feminists and Tracey Emin equally use the fact that embroidery, during the twentieth century, had become increasingly categorised as the 'art of personal life', Tracey Emin employs embroidery as the prime medium of personal life not to proclaim that the personal is the *political*, but that the personal is the *universal*. 'Tracey Emin reveals intimate details from her personal life to engage the viewer with her expressions of universal emotion,' reads the commentary on her work in the Saatchi Gallery.

Tracey Emin has nevertheless been described as 'reviving an approach that was previously practised by feminists in the '70s'.[6] Like nineteen-seventies feminists, Emin employs traditional sampler technique with the incorporation of words. Her most famous stitched work was the embroidered tent, 'Everyone I Have Ever Slept With 1963–1995', in which she sewed onto the tent walls all the people's names, including her grandmother and her teddy bear. Peering into the tent was a powerful experience. Sadly, it was destroyed in the Momart warehouse fire. Her other embroidered work includes 'When I Think About Sex', appliquéd with the words 'Drunk' and 'super Bitch'. In another piece the words 'There is no fucking peace' are spelt out against floral rectangles which re-inforce the tension between the message and the medium.

On her website Emin describes herself as producing 'autobiographical art' with the following statement: 'Her confessional subjects include abortion, rape, self-neglect, and promiscuity expressed with the help of gloriously old-fashioned looking, hand-sewn appliqué letters. Her dad quite likes sewing, because it reminds him of his mum.'

Embroidery as 'gloriously old-fashioned' highlights the harsh and painful nature of the contemporary subject matter. The sewing dad saves stitchery from the triviality associated with femininity. That it reminds him of his mum reminds us that Emin is displaying a 'cosy' domestic art in a professional setting, breaking the boundary between the private, the personal and the public—both psychologically and formally.

Second Wave feminists wanted an end to the inhibition and shame that limited women's lives—exemplified by the bowed head of the embroiderer. We wanted women to be free to express a broad spectrum of affects and ways of being without the fear of being shamed. While nineteen-seventies feminists asserted the power of female sexuality, Tracey Emin exhibited it. She achieved a glorious shamelessness with her taboo-breaking embroidery. But the conventions of sexual difference are not so easily overcome. Her work is received not as evidence of the diversity of women's work, extending what is accepted and expected of women. Tellingly it is praised as 'feminine and ballsy'.

Nineteen-seventies feminists wanted women artists and women's traditional media to receive the recognition they richly deserved. With Tracey Emin—thanks in part to the machinery of the new celebrity culture—the aim appears to be achieved. Yet so often in the past we have seen the phenomenon of the Token Woman, raised, praised and soon forgotten—leaving the status of women unchanged. It remains to be seen whether Tracey Emin's success will have an impact on the position of women in the arts.

Believing that only the transformation of the structures of art practice itself would truly improve things for women, nineteen-seventies feminists invented new ways of making and showing art. In Chapter 8 I describe 'Feministo': during 1975, women began exchanging art works through the post, setting up a visual dialogue about their lives as housewives and mothers. They utilised whatever materials they had to hand and whichever domestic skills they possessed, including embroidery. They wanted an end to competitive individualism fostered in the institutions associated with the fine arts, while avoiding idealisation of the domestic sphere. 'We both celebrated the area of domestic creativity and "women's world" and exposed it for its paucity,' commented participant Phil Goodall.

In the same year a group of six women artists took over a house in Lambeth, London and created the installation 'Housework', exposing 'the hidden side of the domestic dream'. The ground-floor rooms dealt with the emotional expectations bound up with marriage. A bride in traditional white gown, standing in an all-white environment with chocolate-box landscapes and collages of Princess Anne's wedding decorating the walls, stretched out her arms to welcome an unseen groom.

In 2007, following in the footsteps of seventies feminists, a group of 12 people calling themselves 'Leftovers' took over a condemned house in London's Hampstead. Their declared intention was not to challenge the constraints, nor to highlight the creative possibilities of the domestic sphere, but to 'democratise creativity'. Whereas seventies feminist alternative exhibition spaces had been women-only, 'Leftovers' involved men and women. Anyone could exhibit anything in the house. A spirit of anarchy informed the project. The desecration of the domestic provided a creative energy. Yet there were echoes of the nineteen-seventies: Lydia Samuels exhibited sewn pictures on the staircase, depicting people enjoying their food. In the medium associated with reticence and restraint, she stitched people eating with unselfconscious relish, refusing the self-denial of the diet. . . . Twentieth-century feminists challenged the constraints on female desire. Twenty-first century feminists depict desire in action.

The historical association between embroidery, collectivity and political protest is evident in the recent world-wide movement of Craftivism. The term was coined in 2003 by Betsy Greer to designate work that combines craft and activism. She comments, 'I make international anti-war cross stitch . . . juxtaposing the masculine "war" with the feminine "craft"'.[7] The London Craftivist Collective was formed by Sarah Corbett in 2009. Craftivist protest banners, exhibited in public spaces, display stitched slogans challenging, for example, capitalism, global poverty and injustice. In 2010 the Arnolfini Gallery in Bristol mounted 'Craftism', an exhibition of 14 projects intended 'to question, disrupt or replace the dominant models of mass culture and consumerism'.

Perhaps the artist whose work has done most to restore fabric and stitching to their place within 'high art' is Louise Bourgeois. Had she frequently employed embroidery and fabric prior to 1984, I would have allocated a large section of the last chapter of the book to her work. Here I can do little more than signal her importance.

Born in France in 1911, she has spent most of her working life in the USA. During the

Figure 30.1. Louise Bourgeois, *Untitled*, 2002. Tapestry and aluminum, 17 x 12 x 12 in., 43.1 x 30.4 x 30.4 cm. Photo: Christopher Burke, © Louise Bourgeois Trust.

mid-1990s, having established herself as a successful sculptor employing conventional materials—marble, bronze and wood—she began increasingly to work with fabric.

Whereas Tracey Emin's use of embroidery and fabric highlights the disjuncture between imposed femininity and lived female sexuality, Louise Bourgeois' work brings out the deeper meanings of textiles' evocation of women. In her work fabric is associated directly with female sexuality, the unconscious and the body. Familiar with psychoanalysis, she explores the infantile roots of female sexuality in the family through her own history, which was closely tied to textiles, as her parents ran a tapestry restoration business.

Occasionally Louise Bourgeois utilises the traditional employment of embroidered words: an installation of 1997 which involved hanging garments, included a white coat embroidered on the back with the words *The Cold of Anxiety is very real.* The strength of her work lies in her ability to use fabric to convey psychological processes. The stitches themselves convey meaning. Linda Nochlin has commented on the ferocity of the bad sewing, with large, awkward stitching, far from the tradition of professional tapestry making.[8] Often employing tactile fabrics like terry towelling to create stuffed, sewn figures, she explores relationships, with couples having sex, women giving birth and figures conveying pain and vulnerability.

Louise Bourgeois says of herself, 'My feminism expresses itself in an intense interest in what women do. But I'm a complete loner. It doesn't help me to associate with people, it really doesn't help me. What helps me is to realize my own disabilities and express them.'[9]

Scrutinising her own experiences led to works with an obvious feminist content. Take, for example, 'Femme Maison' of 2005, an image she had earlier explored in various materials. A stuffed, headless female torso lies on its back covered with a patchwork quilt. Emerging from the torso is a house. The piece evokes women's isolation and incarceration in the home as well as suggesting the significance of women as the foundation of the home, while the inclusion of patchwork celebrates, though ambivalently, women's traditional media.

Particularly powerful are her recent fabric heads. Taking the template of the portrait bust in stone or bronze, Louise Bourgeois reworks the form in patched-together fabric: tapestry, towelling, ticking or pink bandages. The medium of personal life well conveys internal conflict, age, pain and doubt.

The psychoanalyst Melanie Klein (whose work Louise Bourgeois knew) considered creativity to be driven by the unconscious desire to make reparation—specifically to the mother for destructive attacks motivated by infantile ambivalence. We can speculate on the unconscious processes that may have led Louise Bourgeois to turn to stitching in her old age. She wrote, 'When I was growing up, all the women in my house were using needles. I have always had a fascination with the needle, the magic power of the needle. The needle is used to repair damage. It's a claim to forgiveness. It is never aggressive, it's not a pin.'[10]

Her work, to my mind, associates stitching not only with reparation but also with aggression and destruction. A theme that recurs in The *Subversive Stitch* is the dual face of embroidery. Historically, through the centuries, it has provided both a weapon of resistance for women and functioned as a source of constraint. It has promoted submission to the norms of feminine obedience and offered both psychological and practical means to independence. Colette describes observing the latter process in her daughter. She writes, '. . . she is silent when she sews, silent for hours on end . . . she is silent, and she—why not write it down the word that frightens me—she is thinking.'[11]

Psychoanalytic theory provides a way of understanding how creativity fosters thought. The psychoanalytic theorist W.R.Bion described the process of 'containment' occurring between parent and child, and between analyst and patient. The parent and clinician take in the formless fears and raw experience of the child and patient, make sense of them and return them in a form that can be thought about. Psychoanalyst Margot Waddell has related Bion's theory of 'containment' to the experience of the artist and the art work. She writes that 'the art object promotes and expands mental capacities by offering a shape and containing structure for the transformation of emotional experience into recognizable form'.[12]

The processes of creativity—the finding of form for thought—have a transformative impact on the sense of self. The embroiderer holds in her hands a coherent object which exists both outside in the world and inside her head. W.R. Winnicott's theory of mirroring helps us understand how the experience of embroidering and the embroidery affirms the self as a being with agency, acceptability and potency. Winnicott developed his theory of mirroring in the context of the mother–child relationship. The child sees in the mother's face a reflection of him or herself, mediated by the mother's feelings of love and acceptance. The embroiderer sees a positive reflection of herself in her work and, importantly, in the reception of her work by others.

The containing and mirroring function of embroidery, with the associated capacity for thought and self-esteem, is evident in the work produced under the aegis of Fine Cell Work, a charity established in 1997. Following a tradition begun by the eighteenth-century prison reformer Elizabeth Fry, the charity provides skills and embroidery materials for men and women in prisons throughout the United Kingdom. Volunteers deliver material to prisoners, who carry out the work in their cells. The embroidered cushions, bags, cases, quilts and wall hangings are then sold, with money going to the prisoners.

Sam, who embroiders in Wandsworth, writes,

I am learning a new skill which I did not think possible, I also know that people do care about me and what I do because otherwise why would people take an interest in my fine cell work. I now believe what others think about me makes a real difference to how I conduct myself.[13]

Embroidery promotes and reflects a richer, more meaningful internal world, which is in turn substantiated by the reception of the work in the outside world.

Sam found that the reception of his work changed both his relationship to himself and others. Dee describes how the processes of embroidering promoted the capacity to think, as well as confirming her sense of agency and the ability to love and feel loved. She writes,

I put many hours of love and concentration into the commission. As I saw it grow I became more and more excited. It was never far from my mind at all times. I puzzled, imagined different colours, stitches. All in all I am proud of this piece. The appreciation I got from everyone is the value of this hard work for me.[14]

The parallel between women historically stitching in the home and those stitching in captivity is obvious. But there is a significant difference. Both prisoners and domestic embroiderers find psychological growth and release in creativity, both benefit from the power of positive mirroring provided by the work, but the prisoners are paid for their work. Paul in Wandsworth describes how the money will enable him at Christmas to 'send out postal orders to my daughters so they will know I still think about them'.[15] James in Wynot says, 'I bought myself a nice pair of shoes with some of the money I made and I'm keeping as much as I can by for getting out.'[16] However, Ron in Wandsworth highlights the aspect of embroidery that has, so to speak, kept women and prisoners sitting still and in place over the centuries: 'I find the quality work soothing,' he says, adding, 'I am saving for my release.'[17]

I wish I could end with an unqualified celebration of the recent history of embroidery. Change, however, is slow and uneven. Consider the fact that many of the beliefs that fired feminist embroiderers in the late twentieth century were also central tenets of the Arts and Crafts Movement that began in the late nineteenth century. They too wanted an end to the divide between fine and decorative arts. They too believed in the transformative power of the arts not only on society but also on the lives of the practitioners. Art was to be more like work and work more like art, while William Morris concluded that the transformation of art practice was finally dependent upon social revolution. Similarly, Second Wave feminism, with its condemnation of the denial of female desire and critique of domestic relationships, repeated the insights of the earlier suffrage movement. Yet while similar issues are re-visited—as I hope I have indicated in this brief introduction—both feminism and embroidery continue to evolve, although tracing a pattern of progress which is less suggestive of a straight line than a spiral.

Rozsika Parker

NOTES

1. Sheila Rowbotham, *A Century of Women: The History of Women in Britain and the United States*, London: Viking, 1997. Susan Faludi, *Backlash: The Undeclared War Against Women*, New York: Crown, 1991. Naomi Wolf, *The Beauty Myth: How Images of Beauty are Used Against Women*, New York: Bantham, Doubleday, Dell, 1990.

2. Craft, 214, Sept./Oct. 2008.

3. Karen Rosenberg, 'Needling More Than Feminist Consciousness', *New York Times*, December 2009.

4. Ibid.

5. *Fine Cell Work*, Newsletter, 2009.

6. *Craft*, 214, Sept./Oct. 2008.

7. Kate Mikhail 'Off the Wall: Mosaics with a Message' *Observer Magazine*, 7 February 2010.

8. Linda Nochlin, 'Old-Age Style: Late Louise Bourgeois', in *Louise Bourgeois*, New York: Rizzoli, 2007.

9. Interview with Donaly Kuspit, 1988, in Charles Hanson and Paul Wood, *Louise Bourgeois*, Malden MA: Blackwell Publishing, 2003.

10. J. Gorovoy and P. Tabatabai, *Louise Bourgeois Blue Days and Pink Days*, exhibition catalogue, Fondazione Prada: Milan, 1997.

11. Colette, *Earthly Paradise*, London: Secker and Warburg, 1966 p.205.

12. Margot Wadell, 'The Containing Function of Art', unpublished paper, 2009.

13. Fine Cell Work archives. Names have been changed.

14. Ibid.

15. Ibid.

16. Ibid.

17. Ibid.

31

THE YELLOW WALLPAPER

Charlotte Perkins Gilman

Editor's introduction: The American writer Charlotte Perkins Gilman lived between 1860 and 1935. She wrote poetry, short stories, and nonfiction and is considered by many to be an early feminist role model at a time when such thinking was scarce. Gilman's early life was difficult. Her first marriage to Charles Walter Stetson in 1884 ended in divorce. During her marriage Gilman suffered, after the birth of her daughter, from what we today know as post-partum depression. Treatment in a Philadelphia sanatorium involved the eradication of all activity—both mental and physical. The experience likely contributed to the content of her short story "The Yellow Wallpaper," published in 1892, in which she explores the state of mind of a woman trapped—physically and mentally—by the repressive values of her society. The wallpaper adorning her "rest" prison (depending on your reading) provides Gilman's "un-reliable" narrator with an alternating source of comfort and torment. Her ever-shifting vision of the wallpaper's pattern leaves the final message of this short story open to the reader's interpretation.

It is very seldom that mere ordinary people like John and myself secure ancestral halls for the summer.

A colonial mansion, a hereditary estate, I would say a haunted house, and reach the height of romantic felicity—but that would be asking too much of fate!

Still I will proudly declare that there is something queer about it.

Else, why should it be let so cheaply? And why have stood so long untenanted?

John laughs at me, of course, but one expects that in marriage.

John is practical in the extreme. He has no patience with faith, an intense horror of superstition, and he scoffs openly at any talk of things not to be felt and seen and put down in figures.

John is a physician, and *perhaps*—(I would not say it to a living soul, of course, but this is dead paper and a great relief to my mind)—*perhaps* that is one reason I do not get well faster.

You see he does not believe I am sick!

And what can one do?

If a physician of high standing, and one's own husband, assures friends and relatives that there is really nothing the matter with one but

Source: Charlotte Perkins Gilman, "The Yellow Wallpaper" (1892).

temporary nervous depression—a slight hysterical tendency—what is one to do?

My brother is also a physician, and also of high standing, and he says the same thing.

So I take phosphates or phosphites—whichever it is, and tonics, and journeys, and air, and exercise, and am absolutely forbidden to 'work' until I am well again.

Personally, I disagree with their ideas.

Personally, I believe that congenial work, with excitement and change, would do me good.

But what is one to do?

I did write for a while in spite of them; but it *does* exhaust me a good deal—having to be so sly about it, or else meet with heavy opposition.

I sometimes fancy that in my condition if I had less opposition and more society and stimulus—but John says the very worst thing I can do is to think about my condition, and I confess it always makes me feel bad.

So I will let it alone and talk about the house.

The most beautiful place! It is quite alone, standing well back from the road, quite three miles from the village. It makes me think of English places that you read about, for there are hedges and walls and gates that lock, and lots of separate little houses for the gardeners and people.

There is a *delicious* garden! I never saw such a garden—large and shady, full of box-bordered paths, and lined with long grape-covered arbors with seats under them.

There were greenhouses, too, but they are all broken now.

There was some legal trouble, I believe, something about the heirs and coheirs; anyhow, the place has been empty for years.

That spoils my ghostliness, I am afraid, but I don't care—there is something strange about the house—I can feel it.

I even said so to John one moonlight evening, but he said what I felt was a *draught*, and shut the window.

I get unreasonably angry with John sometimes. I'm sure I never used to be so sensitive. I think it is due to this nervous condition.

But John says if I feel so, I shall neglect proper self-control; so I take pains to control myself—before him, at least, and that makes me very tired.

I don't like our room a bit. I wanted one downstairs that opened on the piazza and had roses all over the window, and such pretty old-fashioned chintz hangings! but John would not hear of it.

He said there was only one window and not room for two beds, and no near room for him if he took another.

He is very careful and loving, and hardly lets me stir without special direction.

I have a schedule prescription for each hour in the day; he takes all care from me, and so I feel basely ungrateful not to value it more.

He said we came here solely on my account, that I was to have perfect rest and all the air I could get. 'Your exercise depends on your strength, my dear,' said he, 'and your food somewhat on your appetite; but air you can absorb all the time.' So we took the nursery at the top of the house.

It is a big, airy room, the whole floor nearly, with windows that look all ways, and air and sunshine galore. It was a nursery first and then playroom and gymnasium, I should judge; for the windows are barred for little children, and there are rings and things in the walls.

The paint and paper look as if a boys' school had used it. It is stripped off—the paper—in great patches all around the head of my bed, about as far as I can reach, and in a great place on the other side of the room low down. I never saw a worse paper in my life.

One of those sprawling flamboyant patterns committing every artistic sin.

It is dull enough to confuse the eye in following, pronounced enough to constantly irritate and provoke study, and when you follow the lame uncertain curves for a little distance they suddenly commit suicide—plunge off at outrageous angles, destroy themselves in unheard of contradictions.

The color is repellent, almost revolting; a smouldering unclean yellow, strangely faded by the slow-turning sunlight.

It is a dull yet lurid orange in some places, a sickly sulphur tint in others.

No wonder the children hated it! I should hate it myself if I had to live in this room long.

There comes John, and I must put this away,— he hates to have me write a word.

We have been here two weeks, and I haven't felt like writing before, since that first day.

I am sitting by the window now, up in this atrocious nursery, and there is nothing to hinder my writing as much as I please, save lack of strength.

John is away all day, and even some nights when his cases are serious.

I am glad my case is not serious!

But these nervous troubles are dreadfully depressing.

John does not know how much I really suffer. He knows there is no *reason* to suffer, and that satisfies him.

Of course it is only nervousness. It does weigh on me so not to do my duty in any way!

I meant to be such a help to John, such a real rest and comfort, and here I am a comparative burden already!

Nobody would believe what an effort it is to do what little I am able,—to dress and entertain, and order things.

It is fortunate Mary is so good with the baby. Such a dear baby!

And yet I *cannot* be with him, it makes me so nervous.

I suppose John never was nervous in his life. He laughs at me so about this wall-paper!

At first he meant to repaper the room, but afterwards he said that I was letting it get the better of me, and that nothing was worse for a nervous patient than to give way to such fancies.

He said that after the wall-paper was changed it would be the heavy bedstead, and then the barred windows, and then that gate at the head of the stairs, and so on.

'You know the place is doing you good,' he said, 'and really, dear, I don't care to renovate the house just for a three months' rental.'

'Then do let us go downstairs,' I said, 'there are such pretty rooms there.'

Then he took me in his arms and called me a blessed little goose, and said he would go down to the cellar, if I wished, and have it whitewashed into the bargain.

But he is right enough about the beds and windows and things.

It is an airy and comfortable room as any one need wish, and, of course, I would not be so silly as to make him uncomfortable just for a whim.

I'm really getting quite fond of the big room, all but that horrid paper.

Out of one window I can see the garden, those mysterious deepshaded arbors, the riotous old-fashioned flowers, and bushes and gnarly trees.

Out of another I get a lovely view of the bay and a little private wharf belonging to the estate. There is a beautiful shaded lane that runs down there from the house. I always fancy I see people walking in these numerous paths and arbors, but John has cautioned me not to give way to fancy in the least. He says that with my imaginative power and habit of story-making, a nervous weakness like mine is sure to lead to all manner of excited fancies, and that I ought to use my will and good sense to check the tendency. So I try.

I think sometimes that if I were only well enough to write a little it would relieve the press of ideas and rest me.

But I find I get pretty tired when I try.

It is so discouraging not to have any advice and companionship about my work. When I get really well, John says we will ask Cousin Henry and Julia down for a long visit; but he says he would as soon put fireworks in my pillow-case as to let me have those stimulating people about now.

I wish I could get well faster.

But I must not think about that. This paper looks to me as if it *knew* what a vicious influence it had!

There is a recurrent spot where the pattern lolls like a broken neck and two bulbous eyes stare at you upside down.

I get positively angry with the impertinence of it and the everlastingness. Up and down and sideways they crawl, and those absurd, unblinking eyes are everywhere. There is one place where two breaths didn't match, and the eyes go all up and down the line, one a little higher than the other.

I never saw so much expression in an inanimate thing before, and we all know how much expression they have! I used to lie awake as a child and get more entertainment and terror out of blank walls and plain furniture than most children could find in a toy-store.

I remember what a kindly wink the knobs of our big, old bureau used to have, and there was one chair that always seemed like a strong friend.

I used to feel that if any of the other things looked too fierce I could always hop into that chair and be safe.

The furniture in this room is no worse than inharmonious, however, for we had to bring it all from downstairs. I suppose when this was used as a playroom they had to take the nursery things out, and no wonder! I never saw such ravages as the children have made here.

The wall-paper, as I said before, is torn off in spots, and it sticketh closer than a brother—they must have had perseverance as well as hatred.

Then the floor is scratched and gouged and splintered, the plaster itself is dug out here and there, and this great heavy bed which is all we found in the room, looks as if it had been through the wars.

But I don't mind it a bit—only the paper.

There comes John's sister. Such a dear girl as she is, and so careful of me! I must not let her find me writing.

She is a perfect and enthusiastic housekeeper, and hopes for no better profession. I verily believe she thinks it is the writing which made me sick!

But I can write when she is out, and see her a long way off from these windows.

There is one that commands the road, a lovely shaded winding road, and one that just looks off over the country. A lovely country, too, full of great elms and velvet meadows.

This wall-paper has a kind of sub-pattern in a different shade, a particularly irritating one, for you can only see it in certain lights, and not clearly then.

But in the places where it isn't faded and where the sun is just so—I can see a strange, provoking, formless sort of figure, that seems to skulk about behind that silly and conspicuous front design.

There's sister on the stairs!

Well, the Fourth of July is over! The people are all gone and I am tired out. John thought it might do me good to see a little company, so we just had mother and Nellie and the children down for a week.

Of course I didn't do a thing. Jennie sees to everything now.

But it tired me all the same.

John says if I don't pick up faster he shall send me to Weir Mitchell in the fall.

But I don't want to go there at all. I had a friend who was in his hands once, and she says he is just like John and my brother, only more so!

Besides, it is such an undertaking to go so far.

I don't feel as if it was worth while to turn my hand over for anything, and I'm getting dreadfully fretful and querulous.

I cry at nothing, and cry most of the time.

Of course I don't when John is here, or anybody else, but when I am alone.

And I am alone a good deal just now. John is kept in town very often by serious cases, and Jennie is good and lets me alone when I want her to.

So I walk a little in the garden or down that lovely lane, sit on the porch under the roses, and lie down up here a good deal.

I'm getting really fond of the room in spite of the wall-paper. Perhaps *because* of the wall-paper.

It dwells in my mind so!

I lie here on this great immovable bed—it is nailed down, I believe—and follow that pattern about by the hour. It is as good as gymnastics, I assure you. I start, we'll say, at the bottom, down in the corner over there where it has not been touched, and I determine for the thousandth time that I *will* follow that pointless pattern to some sort of a conclusion.

I know a little of the principle of design, and I know this thing was not arranged on any laws of radiation, or alternation, or repetition, or symmetry, or anything else that I ever heard of.

It is repeated, of course, by the breadths, but not otherwise.

Looked at in one way each breadth stands alone, the bloated curves and flourishes—a kind of 'debased Romanesque' with *delirium tremens*—go waddling up and down in isolated columns of fatuity.

But, on the other hand, they connect diagonally, and the sprawling outlines run off in great slanting waves of optic horror, like a lot of wallowing seaweeds in full chase.

The whole thing goes horizontally, too, at least it seems so, and I exhaust myself in trying to distinguish the order of its going in that direction.

They have used a horizontal breadth for a frieze, and that adds wonderfully to the confusion.

There is one end of the room where it is almost intact, and there, when the crosslights fade and the low sun shines directly upon it, I can almost fancy radiation after all,—the interminable grotesques seem to form around a common centre and rush off in headlong plunges of equal distraction.

It makes me tired to follow it. I will take a nap I guess.

I don't know why I should write this.

I don't want to.

I don't feel able.

And I know John would think it absurd. But I *must* say what I feel and think in some way—it is such a relief!

But the effort is getting to be greater than the relief.

Half the time now I am awfully lazy, and lie down ever so much.

John says I mustn't lose my strength, and has me take cod liver oil and lots of tonics and things, to say nothing of ale and wine and rare meat.

Dear John! He loves me very dearly, and hates to have me sick. I tried to have a real earnest reasonable talk with him the other day, and tell him how I wish he would let me go and make a visit to Cousin Henry and Julia.

But he said I wasn't able to go, nor able to stand it after I got there; and I did not make out a very good case for myself, for I was crying before I had finished.

It is getting to be a great effort for me to think straight. Just this nervous weakness I suppose.

And dear John gathered me up in his arms, and just carried me upstairs and laid me on the bed, and sat by me and read to me till it tired my head.

He said I was his darling and his comfort and all he had, and that I must take care of myself for his sake, and keep well.

He says no one but myself can help me out of it, that I must use my will and self-control and not let any silly fancies run away with me.

There's one comfort, the baby is well and happy, and does not have to occupy this nursery with the horrid wall-paper.

If we had not used it, that blessed child would have! What a fortunate escape! Why, I wouldn't have a child of mine, an impressionable little thing, live in such a room for worlds.

I never thought of it before, but it is lucky that John kept me here after all, I can stand it so much easier than a baby, you see.

Of course I never mention it to them any more—I am too wise,—but I keep watch of it all the same.

There are things in that paper that nobody knows but me, or ever will.

Behind that outside pattern the dim shapes get clearer every day.

It is always the same shape, only very numerous.

And it is like a woman stooping down and creeping about behind that pattern. I don't like it a bit. I wonder—I begin to think—I wish John would take me away from here!

It is so hard to talk with John about my case, because he is so wise, and because he loves me so.

But I tried it last night.

It was moonlight. The moon shines in all around just as the sun does.

I hate to see it sometimes, it creeps so slowly, and always comes in by one window or another.

John was asleep and I hated to waken him, so I kept still and watched the moonlight on that undulating wall-paper till I felt creepy.

The faint figure behind seemed to shake the pattern, just as if she wanted to get out.

I got up softly and went to feel and see if the paper *did* move, and when I came back John was awake.

'What is it, little girl?' he said. 'Don't go walking about like that—you'll get cold.'

I thought it was a good time to talk, so I told him that I really was not gaining here, and that I wished he would take me away.

'Why darling!' said he, 'our lease will be up in three weeks, and I can't see how to leave before.

'The repairs are not done at home, and I cannot possibly leave town just now. Of course if you were in any danger, I could and would, but you really are better, dear, whether you can see it or not. I am a doctor, dear, and I know. You are gaining flesh and color, your appetite is better, I feel really much easier about you.'

'I don't weigh a bit more,' said I, 'nor as much; and my appetite may be better in the evening when you are here, but it is worse in the morning when you are away!'

'Bless her little heart!' said he with a big hug, 'she shall be as sick as she pleases! But now let's improve the shining hours by going to sleep, and talk about it in the morning!'

'And you won't go away?' I asked gloomily.

'Why, how can I, dear? It is only three weeks more and then we will take a nice little trip of a few days while Jennie is getting the house ready. Really dear you are better!'

'Better in body perhaps—' I began, and stopped short, for he sat up straight and looked at me with such a stern, reproachful look that I could not say another word.

'My darling,' said he, 'I beg of you, for my sake and for our child's sake, as well as for your own, that you will never for one instant let that idea enter your mind! There is nothing so dangerous, so fascinating, to a temperament like yours. It is a false and foolish fancy. Can you not trust me as a physician when I tell you so?'

So of course I said no more on that score, and we went to sleep before long. He thought I was asleep first, but I wasn't, and lay there for hours trying to decide whether that front pattern and the back pattern really did move together or separately.

On a pattern like this, by daylight, there is a lack of sequence, a defiance of law, that is a constant irritant to a normal mind.

The color is hideous enough, and unreliable enough, and infuriating enough, but the pattern is torturing.

You think you have mastered it, but just as you get well underway in following, it turns a back-somersault and there you are. It slaps you in the face, knocks you down, and tramples upon you. It is like a bad dream.

The outside pattern is a florid arabesque, reminding one of a fungus. If you can imagine a toadstool in joints, an interminable string of toadstools, budding and sprouting in endless convolutions—why, that is something like it.

That is, sometimes!

There is one marked peculiarity about this paper, a thing nobody seems to notice but myself, and that is that it changes as the light changes.

When the sun shoots in through the east window—I always watch for that first long, straight ray—it changes so quickly that I never can quite believe it.

That is why I watch it always.

By moonlight—the moon shines in all night when there is a moon—I wouldn't know it was the same paper.

At night in any kind of light, in twilight, candle light, lamplight, and worst of all by moonlight, it becomes bars! The outside pattern I mean, and the woman behind it is as plain as can be.

I didn't realize for a long time what the thing was that showed behind, that dim sub-pattern, but now I am quite sure it is a woman.

By daylight she is subdued, quiet. I fancy it is the pattern that keeps her so still. It is so puzzling. It keeps me quiet by the hour.

I lie down ever so much now. John says it is good for me, and to sleep all I can.

Indeed he started the habit by making me lie down for an hour after each meal.

It is a very bad habit I am convinced, for you see I don't sleep.

And that cultivates deceit, for I don't tell them I'm awake—O no!

The fact is I am getting a little afraid of John.

He seems very queer sometimes, and even Jennie has an inexplicable look.

It strikes me occasionally, just as a scientific hypothesis,—that perhaps it is the paper!

I have watched John when he did not know I was looking, and come into the room suddenly on the most innocent excuses, and I've caught him several times *looking at the paper*! And Jennie too. I caught Jennie with her hand on it once.

She didn't know I was in the room, and when I asked her in a quiet, a very quiet voice, with the most restrained manner possible, what she was doing with the paper—she turned around as if she had been caught stealing, and looked quite angry—asked me why I should frighten her so!

Then she said that the paper stained everything it touched, that she had found yellow smooches on all my clothes and John's, and she wished we would be more careful!

Did not that sound innocent? But I know she was studying that pattern, and I am determined that nobody shall find it out but myself!

Life is very much more exciting now than it used to be. You see I have something more to expect, to look forward to, to watch. I really do eat better, and am more quiet than I was.

John is so pleased to see me improve! He laughed a little the other day, and said I seemed to be flourishing in spite of my wall-paper.

I turned it off with a laugh. I had no intention of telling him it was *because* of the wall-paper—he would make fun of me. He might even want to take me away.

I don't want to leave now until I have found it out. There is a week more, and I think that will be enough.

I'm feeling ever so much better! I don't sleep much at night, for it is so interesting to watch developments; but I sleep a good deal in the daytime.

In the daytime it is tiresome and perplexing.

There are always new shoots on the fungus, and new shades of yellow all over it. I cannot keep count of them, though I have tried conscientiously.

It is the strangest yellow, that wall-paper! It makes me think of all the yellow things I ever saw—not beautiful ones like buttercups, but old foul, bad yellow things.

But there is something else about that paper—the smell! I noticed it the moment we came into the room, but with so much air and sun it was not bad. Now we have had a week of fog and rain, and whether the windows are open or not, the smell is here.

It creeps all over the house.

I find it hovering in the dining-room, skulking in the parlor, hiding in the hall, lying in wait for me on the stairs.

It gets into my hair.

Even when I go to ride, if I turn my head suddenly and surprise it—there is that smell!

Such a peculiar odor, too! I have spent hours in trying to analyze it, to find what it smelled like.

It is not bad—at first, and very gentle, but quite the subtlest, most enduring odor I ever met.

In this damp weather it is awful, I wake up in the night and find it hanging over me.

It used to disturb me at first. I thought seriously of burning the house—to reach the smell.

But now I am used to it. The only thing I can think of that it is like is the *color* of the paper! A yellow smell.

There is a very funny mark on this wall, low down, near the mopboard. A streak that runs round the room. It goes behind every piece of furniture, except the bed, a long, straight, even *smooch*, as if it had been rubbed over and over.

I wonder how it was done and who did it, and what they did it for. Round and round and round—round and round and round—it makes me dizzy!

I really have discovered something at last.

Through watching so much at night, when it changes so, I have finally found out.

The front pattern *does* move—and no wonder! The woman behind shakes it!

Sometimes I think there are a great many women behind, and sometimes only one, and she crawls around fast, and her crawling shakes it all over.

Then in the very bright spots she keeps still, and in the very shady spots she just takes hold of the bars and shakes them hard.

And she is all the time trying to climb through. But nobody could climb through that pattern—it strangles so; I think that is why it has so many heads.

They get through, and then the pattern strangles them off and turns them upside down, and makes their eyes white!

If those heads were covered or taken off it would not be half so bad.

I think that woman gets out in the daytime!

And I'll tell you why—privately—I've seen her!

I can see her out of every one of my windows!

It is the same woman, I know, for she is always creeping, and most women do not creep by daylight.

I see her on that long road under the trees, creeping along, and when a carriage comes she hides under the blackberry vines.

I don't blame her a bit. It must be very humiliating to be caught creeping by daylight!

I always lock the door when I creep by daylight. I can't do it at night, for I know John would suspect something at once.

And John is so queer now, that I don't want to irritate him. I wish he would take another room! Besides, I don't want anybody to get that woman out at night but myself.

I often wonder if I could see her out of all the windows at once.

But, turn as fast as I can, I can only see out of one at one time.

And though I always see her, she *may* be able to creep faster than I can turn!

I have watched her sometimes away off in the open country, creeping as fast as a cloud shadow in a high wind.

If only that top pattern could be gotten off from the under one! I mean to try it, little by little.

I have found out another funny thing, but I shan't tell it this time! It does not do to trust people too much.

There are only two more days to get this paper off, and I believe John is beginning to notice. I don't like the look in his eyes.

And I heard him ask Jennie a lot of professional questions about me. She had a very good report to give.

She said I slept a good deal in the daytime.

John knows I don't sleep very well at night, for all I'm so quiet!

He asked me all sorts of questions, too, and pretended to be very loving and kind.

As if I couldn't see through him!

Still, I don't wonder he acts so, sleeping under this paper for three months.

It only interests me, but I feel sure John and Jennie are secretly affected by it.

Hurrah! This is the last day, but it is enough. John is to stay in town over night, and won't be out until this evening.

Jennie wanted to sleep with me—the sly thing! but I told her I should undoubtedly rest better for a night all alone.

That was clever, for really I wasn't alone a bit! As soon as it was moonlight and that poor thing began to crawl and shake the pattern, I got up and ran to help her.

I pulled and she shook, I shook and she pulled, and before morning we had peeled off yards of that paper.

A strip about as high as my head and half around the room.

And then when the sun came and that awful pattern began to laugh at me, I declared I would finish it to-day!

We go away to-morrow, and they are moving all my furniture down again to leave things as they were before.

Jennie looked at the wall in amazement, but I told her merrily that I did it out of pure spite at the vicious thing.

She laughed and said she wouldn't mind doing it herself, but I must not get tired.

How she betrayed herself that time!

But I am here, and no person touches this paper but me,—not *alive*!

She tried to get me out of the room—it was too patent! But I said it was so quiet and empty and clean now that I believed I would lie down again and sleep all I could; and not to wake me even for dinner—I would call when I woke.

So now she is gone, and the servants are gone, and the things are gone, and there is nothing left but that great bedstead nailed down, with the canvas mattress we found on it.

We shall sleep downstairs to-night, and take the boat home to-morrow.

I quite enjoy the room, now it is bare again.

How those children did tear about here!

This bedstead is fairly gnawed!

But I must get to work.

I have locked the door and thrown the key down into the front path.

I don't want to go out, and I don't want to have anybody come in, till John comes.

I want to astonish him.

I've got a rope up here that even Jennie did not find. If that woman does get out, and tries to get away, I can tie her!

But I forgot I could not reach far without anything to stand on!

This bed will *not* move!

I tried to lift and push it until I was lame, and then I got so angry I bit off a little piece at one corner—but it hurt my teeth.

Then I peeled off all the paper I could reach standing on the floor. It sticks horribly and the pattern just enjoys it! All those strangled heads and bulbous eyes and waddling fungus growths just shriek with derision!

I am getting angry enough to do something desperate. To jump out of the window would be admirable exercise, but the bars are too strong even to try.

Besides I wouldn't do it. Of course not. I know well enough that a step like that is improper and might be misconstrued.

I don't like to *look* out of the windows even— there are so many of those creeping women, and they creep so fast.

I wonder if they all come out of that wallpaper as I did?

But I am securely fastened now by my well-hidden rope—you don't get *me* out in the road there!

I suppose I shall have to get back behind the pattern when it comes night, and that is hard!

It is so pleasant to be out in this great room and creep around as I please!

I don't want to go outside. I won't, even if Jennie asks me to.

For outside you have to creep on the ground, and everything is green instead of yellow.

But here I can creep smoothly on the floor, and my shoulder just fits in that long smooch around the wall, so I cannot lose my way.

Why there's John at the door!

It is no use, young man, you can't open it!

How he does call and pound!

Now he's crying for an axe.

It would be a shame to break down that beautiful door!

'John dear!' said I in the gentlest voice, 'the key is down by the front steps, under a plantain leaf!'

That silenced him for a few moments.

Then he said—very quietly indeed, 'Open the door, my darling!'

'I can't,' said I. 'The key is down by the front door under a plantain leaf!'

And then I said it again, several times, very gently and slowly, and said it so often that he had to go and see, and he got it of course, and came in. He stopped short by the door.

'What is the matter?' he cried. 'For God's sake, what are you doing!'

I kept on creeping just the same, but I looked at him over my shoulder.

'I've got out at last,' said I, 'in spite of you and Jane. And I've pulled off most of the paper, so you can't put me back!'

Now why should that man have fainted? But he did, and right across my path by the wall, so that I had to creep over him every time!

FURTHER READING: POLITICS

Glenn Adamson, "The Fiber Game," *Textile: The Journal of Cloth and Culture* 5, no. 2 (2007) pp. 154–177.

Elissa Auther, *String, Felt, Thread: The Hierarchy of Art and Craft in American Art* (London: University of Minnesota Press, 2010).

Ingrid Bachmann and Ruth Scheuing (eds.), *Material Matters: The Art and Culture of Contemporary Textiles* (Toronto: YYZ Books, 2002).

Pennina Barnett, "Afterthoughts on Curating 'The Subversive Stitch,'" in *New Feminist Criticism: Critical Strategies*, ed. Katy Deepwell (Manchester and New York: Manchester University Press, 1995) pp. 76–86.

Pennina Barnett, "Rugs R Us (And Them)," *Third Text*, no. 30 (Spring 1995) pp. 13–28.

Mildred Constantine and Jack Lenor Larsen, *The Art Fabric: Mainstream* (London: Van Nostrand Reinhold).

Mildred Constantine and Laurel Reuter, *Whole Cloth* (New York: Monacelli Press, 1997).

Katy Deepwell (ed.), "Textiles" section in *New Feminist Art Criticism: Critical Strategies* (Manchester and New York: Manchester University Press, 1995) pp. 164–195.

Janis Jefferies, "Text and Textiles: Weaving across the Borderlines," in *New Feminist Criticism: Critical Strategies*, ed. Katy Deepwell (Manchester and New York: Manchester University Press, 1995) pp. 164–173.

Janis Jefferies, "What Can She Know?" in *Feminist Visual Culture*, ed. Fiona Carson and Claire Pajaczkowska (New York: Routledge, 2001) pp. 189–205.

Patricia Kleindienst, "The Voice of the Shuttle Is Ours", *Stanford Literature Review* 1 (1984).

Melissa Leventon, *Artwear: Fashion and Anti-fashion* (New York: Thames and Hudson and Fine Art Museums of San Francisco, 2005).

Sarat Maharaj, "Textile Art: Who Are You?" in *Reinventing Textiles*, Vol. 2, *Gender and Identity*, ed. Janis Jefferies (Winchestee, England: Telos, 2001) pp. 7–10.

Lesley Millar (ed.), "Cloth and Culture Now" (Surrey, England: University College for the Creative Arts at Canterbury, Epsom, Farnham, Maidstone and Rochester, 2007).

Nancy K. Miller, "Arachnologies: The Woman, The Text, and the Critic," in *The Poetics of Gender*, ed. Nancy K. Miller (New York: Columbia University Press, 1986) pp. 270–295.

Nandine Monem (ed.), *Contemporary Textiles: The Fabric of Fine Art* (London: Black Dog, 2008).

Elaine Reichek, "Spider's Stratagem" *Art in America* (September 2008).

Lacey Jane Roberts, "Put Your Thing Down, Flip It, and Reverse It: Reimagining Craft Identities Using Tactics of Queer Theory," in *Extra/Ordinary: Craft and Contemporary Art*, ed. Maria Elena Buszek (Durham, NC, and London: Duke University Press, 2011) pp. 243–259.

Kirsty Robertson, "Threads of Hope: The Living Healing Quilt Project," *English Studies in Canada* (Aboriginal Redress and Repatriation) 35, no. 1 (March 2009) pp. 85–108.

Paul Sharrad and Anne Collett (eds.), *Reinventing Textiles: Postcolonialism and Creativity*, vol. 3 (Bristol: Telos Art Publishing).

Carol Tulloch (ed.), *Black Style* (London: V&A Publications, 2004).

PART V

PRODUCTION

PART INTRODUCTION

The production of textiles has undergone enormous change over the past century. This section focuses on the making—both by hand and by machine—of the textile. Progress does not reveal itself to be as obvious as may commonly be assumed. Production speed has increased, but a number of contributors reflect on the loss of textile knowledge that has gone hand in hand with the mechanization and then digitization of textile production. The alarming environmental damage, for example, that we now know the textile industry contributes to is an area of increasing concern. So, too, are moments where the transition from mechanical to digital has meant a loss of opportunities (from the loss of employment to the loss of creative options within the design process) for designers. Where change in textile production is proposed, it is often radical—such as the BioCouture's experiments—and could eventually lead to an entirely new system of textile production.

Historian Elizabeth Wayland Barber begins this section with a brief suggestion of why women may have, throughout time, been linked to the production of textiles. Barber's pragmatic suggestion that historians have observed that the production of textiles poses no threat to the care of children offers us an alternative reason for the connection of women to textiles, which has often been couched in negative rather than positive terms. Sadie Plant's writing about Ada Lovelace and the shared history of weaving and computing attempts to carve a place for this overlooked historical figure. While evoking Lovelace and her deserved place in the history of computing, Plant makes use of a writing style that is as experimental and fragmented as the history she works to reintroduce.

Ele Carpenter's lecture about the curatorial project that resulted in the creation of the Open Source Embroidery project (illustrated on the cover of the *Reader*) shows another route through textile and computing thinking, this time engaged with the community-centered production present in open source software and quilting. Kirsty Robertson shares Carpenter's interest in the social and public nature of textile production and writes about increasingly complex issues in copyright law as it affects textile and craft production in North America. She uses Carpenter's project as one of the many examples she discusses. Melanie Miller's catalog essay about the schiffli embroidery project in Manchester, England, provides a focused example of the shift from mechanical to digital, and local to overseas, production. The schiffli project was based at the Manchester School of Art in 2007 and involved the responses of fifteen artists to the last working schiffli embroidery machine in Britain. The project shows us an often-overlooked perspective—the production potential that is lost in the race toward a digital textile future.

Anna Von Mertens produces her work by hand, and her artist's statement addresses the theoretical references, such as Walter Benjamin's writing on mechanical production, that informed her recent "Portraits" series. Von Mertens admits to "an element of the ridiculous" in her mining of Benjamin's theoretical writing alongside her research into the somewhat-dubious field of aura photography. Her statement shows how it is possible to strike a balance between the "seriousness" of theory and the eccentric and eclectic jumping-off points that are equal contributors to the content of her handmade quilts. A conference transcript from the symposium "Upcycling Textiles: Adding Value through Design," led by Rebecca Earley and held in 2008, captures the ongoing debate around the topic of sustainability. The dialogue from the event reveals that the subject area is rife with contradictions and challenges, largely because of the complexity and variety of textile production and consumption that precedes efforts to limit and reuse waste. What can be agreed is that the consumer is as powerful, if not more powerful than, the designer in changing current patterns of consumption.

Many of the contributors in this section look to the future. Anni Albers, writing nearly seventy years ago, reminds us that while textile production witnessed enormous change in the twentieth century, a Peruvian weaver might be dismayed by the lack of technical progress applied to the woven structure. She writes, "He would marvel, we can imagine, at the speed of mass production, at the uniformity of threads, the accuracy of the weaving and the low price. . . . But strangely enough, he may find that neither one would serve him in his specific interest: the intricate interlocking of two sets of threads at right angles—weaving." Albers provides us with a needed reminder that time does not always equal progress and that, in the case of textiles, knowledge is not always moving forward. This section then ends on a positive note with an excerpt from Suzanne Lee's blog of her BioCouture project. Lee's research questions just what our textiles of the future might be through an exploration of alternative sources and production methods for material. Albers's Peruvian weaver may still be hard to impress, but neither would he have known of the crisis in global ecology we are facing today. BioCouture tackles issues of sustainability and proposes a significant alternative for textile production methods of the future.

32

A TRADITION WITH A REASON

Elizabeth Wayland Barber

Editor's introduction: In this excerpt from Elizabeth Wayland Barber's opening chapter to her book-length study *Women's Work: The First 20,000 Years: Women, Cloth, and Society in Early Times,* Barber provides us with an explanation by the historian Judith Brown for the gendered nature of textile production that is so simple it is hard to believe how often it is overlooked. Textiles and women have been linked for less than positive reasons: idle work for idle hands and, worse yet, mindless work to be undertaken by a gender incapable of anything more. While these old associations have today become an irritant, even a joke, it does not change the reality that textile courses around the world are filled with female students and that even the genders represented by the authors in this *Reader* is strikingly uneven. Barber shares in practical terms the historical reasons why women and textiles may have been connected: Women raise children, and the work they undertake must be compatible with this responsibility. Taken from this perspective, the stereotype of textiles as a female occupation is not changed, but it is put in a different light that explains some of the practical concerns that may have led to this division of labor and, eventually, knowledge.

For millennia women have sat together spinning, weaving, and sewing. Why should textiles have become *their* craft par excellence, rather than the work of men? Was it always thus, and if so, why?

Twenty years ago Judith Brown wrote a little five-page "Note on the Division of Labor by Sex" that holds a simple key to these questions. She was interested in how much women contributed to obtaining the food for a preindustrial community. But in answering that question, she came upon a model of much wider applicability. She found that the issue of whether or not the community *relies* upon women as the chief providers of a given type of labor depends upon "the compatibility of this pursuit with the demands of child care." If only because of the exigencies of breast feeding (which until recently was typically continued for two or three years per child), "nowhere in the world is the rearing of children primarily the responsibility of men. . . . " Thus, if the productive labor of women is not to be lost to the society during the childbearing years, the jobs regularly assigned to women must be carefully chosen to be "compatible with simultaneous child watching." From empirical observation Brown gleans that "such activities have the following characteristics: they do not require rapt concentration and are relatively dull and repetitive; they are easily interruptable [I see a rueful smile on every care giver's face!] and easily resumed once interrupted; they do not place the child in potential danger; and they do not require the participant to range very far from home."[1]

Just such are the crafts of spinning, weaving, and sewing: repetitive, easy to pick up at any point, reasonably child-safe, and easily done at home. (Contrast the idea of swinging a pick in a dark, cramped, and dusty mine shaft with a baby on one's back or being interrupted by a child's crisis while trying to pour molten metal into a set of molds.) The only other occupation that fits the criteria even half so well is that of preparing the daily food. Food and clothing: These are what societies worldwide have come to see as the core of women's work (although other tasks may be added to the load, depending upon the circumstances of the particular society).

Readers of this book live in a different world. The Industrial Revolution has moved basic textile work out of the home and into large (inherently dangerous) factories; we buy our clothing ready-made. It is a rare person in our cities who has ever spun thread or woven cloth, although a quick look into a fabric store will show that many women still sew. As a result, most of us are unaware of how time-consuming the task of making the cloth for a family used to be.

In Denmark fifty years ago young women bought their yarns ready-made but still expected to weave the basic cloth for their households. If they went to a weaving school rather than being taught at home, they began with a dozen plain cotton dish towels. My mother, being a foreigner not in need of a trousseau, and with less than a year at her disposal to study Danish weaving, consented to weave half of *one* towel to get started. The next assignment was to weave three waffle-weave bath mats. (Indeed, the three were nicely gauged to last a lifetime. The second wore out when I was in college, and we still have the third.) Next came

the weaving of woolen scarves and blankets, linen tablecloths, and so forth. Most complicated were the elaborate aprons for Sunday best.

Thirty years ago in rural Greece, much had changed but not all. People wore store-bought, factory-made clothing of cotton for daily wear, at least in summer. But traditional festive outfits and all the household woolens were still made from scratch. It takes several hours to spin with a hand spindle the amount of yarn one can weave up in an hour, so women spun as they watched the children, girls spun as they watched the sheep, both spun as they trudged or rode muleback from one village to another on errands. . . . The tools and materials were light and portable, and the double use of the time made both the spinning and the trudging or watching more interesting. In fact, if we reckon up the cleaning, spinning, dyeing, weaving, and embroidering of the wool, the villagers appeared to spend at least as many labor hours on making cloth as on producing the food to be eaten—and these people bought half their clothing ready-made!

Records show that, before the invention of the steam engine and the great factory machines that it could run, this sort of distribution of time and labor was quite normal. Most of the hours of the woman's day, and occasionally of the man's, were spent on textile-related activities. (In Europe men typically helped tend and shear the sheep, plant and harvest the flax, and market any extra textiles available for cash income.)

"So why is it, if women were so enslaved by textile work for all those centuries, that the spinning jenny and power loom were invented by a man and not a woman?" A young woman accosted me with this question after a lecture recently.

"Th[e] reason," to quote George Foster, writing about problems in pottery making, "lies in the nature of the productive process itself which places a premium on strict adherence to tried and proven ways as a means of avoiding economic catastrophe." Put another way, women of all but the top social and economic classes were so busy just trying to get through what had to be done each day that they didn't have excess time or materials to experiment with new ways of doing things. (My husband bought and learned to use a new word-processing program two years before I began to use it, for exactly these reasons. I was in the middle of writing a book using the old system and couldn't afford to take the time out both to learn the new one and to convert everything. I was already too deep into "production.") Elise Boulding elaborates: "[T]he general situation of little margin for error leading to conservatism might apply to the whole range of activities carried out by women. Because they had so much to do, slight variations in care of farm or dairy products or pottery could lead to food spoilage, production failure, and a consequent increase in already heavy burdens." The rich women, on the other hand, didn't have the incentive to invent laborsaving machinery since the work was done for them.

And so for millennia women devoted their lives to making the cloth and clothing while they tended the children and the cooking pot. Or at least that was the case in the broad zone of temperate climates, where cloth was spun and woven (rather than made of skins, as in the Arctic) and where the weather was too cold for part or all of the year to go without a warming wrap (as one could in the tropics). Consequently it was in the temperate zone that the Industrial Revolution eventually began.

The Industrial Revolution was a time of steam engines. Along with the locomotive to solve transportation problems, the first major applications of the new engines were mechanizations of the making of cloth: the power loom, the spinning jenny, the cotton gin. The consequences of yanking women and children out of the home to tend these huge, dangerous, and implacable machines in the mills caused the devastating social problems which writers like Charles Dickens, Charlotte Brontë, and Elizabeth Gaskell (all of whom knew each other) portrayed so vividly. Such a factory is the antithesis of being "compatible with child rearing" on every point in Judith Brown's list.

Western industrial society has evolved so far that most of us don't recognize Dickens's picture now (although it still does exist in some parts of the world). We are looking forward into a new age, when women who so desire can rear their children quietly at home while they pursue a career on their child-safe, relatively interruptable-and-resumable home computers, linked to the world not by muleback or the steam locomotive, or even a car, but by telephone and the modem. For their part, the handloom, the needle, and the other fiber crafts can still form satisfying hobbies, as they, too, remain compatible with child watching.

NOTE

1. Notice Brown's stipulation that this particular division of labor revolves around *reliance*, not around *ability* (other than the ability to breastfeed), within a community in which specialization is desirable. Thus females are quite able to hunt, and often do (as she points out); males are quite able to cook and sew, and often do, among the cultures of the world. The question is whether the society can afford to *rely* on the women as a group for all of the hunting or all of the sewing. The answer to "hunting" (and smithing, and deep-sea fishing) is no. The answer to "sewing" (and cooking, and weaving) is yes.

33

ZEROES + ONES: DIGITAL WOMEN AND THE NEW TECHNOCULTURE

Sadie Plant

Editor's introduction: Sadie Plant's book *Zeroes + Ones* establishes the shared histories of computing and the Jacquard loom via the life of Ada Lovelace. Plant's experimental writing suggests a map of the networks her research charts. Fragments of William Gibson's fiction and Lovelace's diary entries are set side by side in an intentionally fragmented style that is effective in revealing the shared interests of seemingly diverse sources. The excerpt printed here provides a glimpse of Plant's experimental assembly of information, from her likening of written text to a physical network of knowledge, to Sigmund Freud's thoughts on why women weave, to the shifting production methods of the textile industry. At the heart of Plant's exploration is the idea that "textiles themselves are very literally the software linings of all technology."

MATRICES

Distinctions between the main bodies of texts and all their peripheral detail—indices, headings, prefaces, dedications, appendices, illustrations, references, notes, and diagrams—have long been integral to orthodox conceptions of nonfiction books and articles. Authored, authorized, and authoritative, a piece of writing is its own mainstream. Its asides are backwaters which might have been—and often are—compiled by anonymous editors, secretaries, copyists, and clerks, and while they may well be providing crucial support for a text which they also connect to other sources, resources, and leads, they are also sidelined and downplayed.

When Ada wrote her footnotes to Menabrea's text, her work was implicitly supposed to be reinforcing these hierarchical divisions between centers and margins, authors and scribes. Menabrea's memoir was the leading article; Ada's work was merely a compilation of supporting detail, secondary commentary, material intended to back the author up. But her notes made enormous leaps of both quantity and quality beyond a text which turned out merely to be providing the occasion for her work.

Only when digital networks arranged themselves in threads and links did footnotes begin to walk all over what had once been the bodies of organized texts. Hypertext programs and the Net are webs of footnotes without central points, organizing principles, hierarchies. Such networks are unprecedented in terms of their scope, complexity,

Source: Sadie Plant, *Zeroes + Ones: Digital Women the New Technoculture* (New York: Doubleday, 1997). Reproduced with permission.

and the pragmatic possibilities of their use. And yet they are also—and have always been—immanent to all and every piece of written work. "The frontiers of a book,"[1] wrote Michel Foucault long before these modes of writing hypertext or retrieving data from the Net emerged, "are never clear-cut: beyond the title, the first lines, and the last full stop, beyond its internal configuration and its autonomous form, it is caught up in a system of references to other books, other texts, other sentences: it is a node within network."

Such complex patterns of cross-referencing have become increasingly possible, and also crucial to dealing with the floods of data which have burst the banks of traditional modes of arranging and retrieving information and are now leaking through the covers of articles and books, seeping past the boundaries of the old disciplines, overflowing all the classifications and orders of libraries, schools, and universities. And the sheer weight of data with which the late twentieth century finds itself awash is only the beginning of the pressures under which traditional media are buckling. If the "treatment of an irregular and complex topic *cannot be forced in any single direction* without curtailing the potential for transfer,"[2] it has suddenly become obvious that no topic is as regular and simple as was once assumed. Reality does not run along the neat straight lines of the printed page. Only by "criss-crossing the complex topical landscape" can the "twin goals of highlighting multifacetedness and establishing multiple connections" even begin to be attained. Hypertext makes it possible for "single (or even small numbers of) connecting threads" to be assembled into a "'woven' interconnectedness" in which "strength of connection derives from the partial overlapping of many different strands of connectedness across cases rather than from any single strand running through large numbers of cases . . ."

"It must be evident how multifarious and how mutually complicated are the considerations,"[3] wrote Ada in her own footnotes. "There are frequently several distinct sets of effects going on simultaneously; all in a manner independent of each other, and yet to a greater or less degree exercising a mutual influence. To adjust each to every other, and indeed even to perceive and trace them out with perfect correctness and success, entails difficulties whose nature partakes to a certain extent of those involved in every question where *conditions* are very numerous and inter-complicated; such as for instance the estimation of the mutual relations amongst statistical phenomena, and of those involved in many other classes of facts."

She added, "All, and everything is naturally related and interconnected. A volume I could write on this subject."

TENSIONS

Just as individuated texts have become filaments of infinitely tangled webs, so the digital machines of the late twentieth century weave new networks from what were once isolated words, numbers, music, shapes, smells, tactile textures, architectures, and countless channels as yet unnamed. Media become interactive and hyperactive, the multiplicitous components of an immersive zone which "does *not* begin with writing; it is directly related rather to the weaving of elaborate figured silks."[4] The yarn is neither metaphorical nor literal, but quite simply material, a gathering of threads which twist and turn through the history of computing, technology, the sciences and arts. In and out of the punched holes of automated looms, up and down through the ages of spinning and weaving, back and forth through the fabrication of fabrics, shuttles and looms, cotton and silk, canvas and paper, brushes and pens, typewriters, carriages, telephone wires, synthetic fibers, electrical filaments, silicon strands, fiber-optic cables, pixeled screens, telecom lines, the World Wide Web, the Net, and matrices to come.

"Before you run out the door, consider two things: The future is already set, only the past can be changed, and If it was worth forgetting it's not worth remembering."

Pat Cadigan, *Fools*

When the first of the cyberpunk novels, William Gibson's *Neuromancer* was published in 1984, the cyberspace it described was neither an actually existing plane, nor a zone plucked out of the thin airs of myth and fantasy. It was a virtual reality which was itself increasingly real. Personal computers were becoming as ubiquitous as telephones, military simulation technologies and telecommunications networks were known to be highly sophisticated, and arcade games were addictive and increasingly immersive. *Neuromancer* was a fiction, and also another piece of the jigsaw which allowed these components to converge. In the course of the next decade, computers lost their significance as isolated calculators and word processors to become nodes of the vast global network called the Net. Video, still images, sounds, voices, and texts fused into the interactive multimedia which now seemed destined to converge with virtual reality helmets and data suits, sensory feedback mechanisms and neural connections, immersive digital realities continuous with reality itself. Whatever that was now supposed to be.

At the time, it was widely assumed that machines ran on more or less straightforward lines. Fictions might be speculative and inspire particular developments, but they were not supposed to have such immediate effects. Like all varieties of cultural change, technological development was supposed to proceed step after step and one at a time. It was only logical, after all. But cyberspace changed all this. It suddenly seemed as if all the components and tendencies which were now feeding into this virtual zone had been made for it before it had even been named; as though all the ostensible reasons and motivations underlying their development had merely provided occasions for the emergence of a matrix which Gibson's novel was nudging into place; as though the present was being reeled into a future which had always been guiding the past, washing back over precedents completely unaware of its influence.

Neuromancer was neither the first nor the last of such confusions between fiction and fact, future and past. When Gibson described "bright lattices of logic unfolding across that colorless void,"[5] his cyberspace was already implementing earlier—or later—works of nonfiction: Alan Turing's universal machine had drawn the devices of his day—calculators and typewriters—into a virtual system which brought itself on-line in the Second World War; Ada's Analytical Engine, which backed the punched-card processes of the automated weaving machine; and Jacquard's loom, which gathered itself on the gathering threads of weavers who in turn were picking up on the threads of the spiders and moths and webs of bacterial activity.

ON THE CARDS

Until the early eighteenth century, when mechanisms which allowed looms to automatically select their own threads were introduced, it could take a weaver "two or three weeks to set up a drawloom for a particular pattern."[6] The new devices used punched-paper rolls, and then punched cards which, when they were strung together in the early nineteenth century, made the loom into the first piece of automated machinery. It was Joseph Marie Jacquard, a French engineer, who made this final move. "Jacquard devised the plans of connecting each group of threads that were to act together, with a distinct lever belonging exclusively to that group. All these levers terminate in rods"[7] and a "rectangular sheet of pasteboard" moves "with it all the rods of the bundle, and consequently the threads that are connected with each of them." And if this board, "instead of being plain, were pierced with holes corresponding to the extremities of the levers which meet it, then, since each of the levers would pass through the pasteboard during the motion of the latter, they would all remain in their places. We thus see that it is easy so to determine the position of the holes in the pasteboard, that, at any given moment, there shall be a certain number of levers, and consequently parcels of threads, raised, while the rest remain where they were. Supposing this process is successively repeated according to a law indicated by the pattern to be executed, we perceive that this pattern may be reproduced on the stuff."

As a weaving system which "effectively withdrew control of the weaving process from human workers and transferred it to the hardware of the machine,"[8] the Jacquard loom was "bitterly opposed by workers who saw in this migration of control a piece of their bodies literally being transferred to the machine." The new frames were famously broken by Luddite rioters to whom, in his maiden speech in the House of Lords in 1812, Lord Byron offered his support. "By the adoption of one species of frame in particular,"[9] he said, "one man performed the work of many, and the superfluous laborers were thrown out of employment. Yet it is to be observed that the work thus executed was inferior in quality; not marketable at home, and merely hurried over with a view to exportation. It was called, in the cant of the trade, by the name of 'Spider-work.'"

Byron was concerned that his peers in the Lords would think him "too lenient towards these men, & *half a framebreaker* myself." But, unfortunately for both his argument and the hand-loom weavers who were thrown out of work, the fabrics woven on the new looms soon surpassed both the quantity and quality of those which had been made by hand. And the Spider-work did not stop here. These automated processes were only hints as to the new species Byron's daughter had in store.

"I do *not* believe that my father was (or ever could have been)
such a *Poet* as I shall be an *Analyst*."

Ada Lovelace, July 1843

Babbage had a long-standing interest in the effects of automated machines on traditional forms of manufacture, publishing his research on the fate of cottage industries in the Midlands and North of England, *The Economy of Manufactures and Machinery*, in 1832. The pin factory with which Adam Smith had illustrated his descriptions of the division of labor had made a great impression on him and, like his near contemporary Marx, he could see the extent to which specialization, standardization, and systematization had made both factories and economies into enormous automated machines themselves. Babbage was later to look back on the early factories as prototype "thinking machines," and he compared the two main functions of the Analytical Engine— storage and calculation—to the basic components of a textiles plant. "The Analytical Engine consists of two parts,"[10] wrote Babbage. "1st. The store in which all the variables to be operated upon, as well as all those quantities which have arisen from the result of other operations, are placed," and "2nd. The mill into which the quantities about to be operated upon are always brought." Like the computers which were later to run, and still do, the Engine had a store and mill, memory and processing power.

It was the Jacquard loom which really excited and inspired this work. Babbage owned a portrait of Jacquard, woven on one of his looms at about 1,000 threads to the inch and its production had demanded the use of some 24,000 punched cards, each one capable of carrying over 1,000 punch-holes, and Babbage was fascinated by the fine-grained complexity of both the cloth and the machine which had woven it. "It is a known fact,"[11] he wrote, "that the Jacquard loom is capable of weaving any design which the imagination of man may conceive." The portrait was a five-feet-square "sheet of woven silk, framed and glazed, but looking so perfectly like an engraving, that it had been mistaken for such by two members of the Royal Academy."[12]

[. . .]

"Unbuttoning the coat, he thrust his hands into the trouser-pockets, the better to display the waistcoat, which was woven in a dizzy mosaic of tiny blue-and-white squares. Ada Chequers, the tailors called them, the Lady having created the pattern by programming a Jacquard loom to weave pure algebra."

William Gibson and Bruce Sterling,
The Difference Engine

ANNA 1

In 1933, Sigmund Freud made his final attempt to solve the riddle of femininity: "to those of you who are women,"[13] he wrote, "this will not apply—you are yourselves the problem." Having dealt with its wants and deficiencies and analyzed its lapses and absences, he had only a few more points to make. "It seems," he wrote, "that women have made few contributions to the inventions and discoveries of the history of civilization." They lacked both the capacity and the desire to change the world. They weren't logical, they couldn't think straight, they flitted around and couldn't concentrate.

Distracted by the rhythmic beat of a machine, Freud looked up to see his daughter at her loom. She had wandered off, she was miles away, lost in her daydreams and the shuttle's flight. But the sight of her gave him second thoughts. When he took up the thread, he had changed his mind: "There is, however, one technique which they may have invented—that of plaiting and weaving.

"If that is so, we should be tempted to guess the unconscious motive for the achievement," he writes. "Nature herself would seem to have given the model which this achievement imitates by causing the growth at maturity of the pubic hair that conceals the genitals. The step that remained to be taken lay in making the threads adhere to one another, while on the body they stick into the skin and are only matted together." Since she has only a hole where the male has his source of creativity, the folding and interlacing of threads cannot be a question of a thrusting male desire. Unless she was hiding something else, the processes which so engrossed her must, of course, be a matter of concealing the shameful "deficiency" of the female sex.

Take Anna: a weaver and a spinster too, working to cover her wounded pride, her missing sense of self, the holes in her life and the gaps in her mind. She simply doesn't have what it takes to make a difference to the civilized world. Her work is a natural compensation for a natural flaw. All she can discover is her own incompletion; all she can invent are ways and means to process and conceal her sense of shame.

If weaving was to count as an achievement, it was not even one of women's own. Their work is not original or creative: both the women and their cloths are simply copying the matted tangles of pubic hair. Should they have pretensions to authority, they would only be faking this as well. Women "can, it seems, (only) imitate nature. Duplicate what nature offers and produces. In a kind of technical assistance and substitution." Weaving is an automatic imitation of some bodily function already beyond the weaver's control. She is bound to weave a costume for the masquerade: she is an actress, a mimic, an impersonator, with no authenticity underneath it all. She has nothing to reveal, no soul to bare, not even a sex or a self to please. He pulls aside the veils, the webs of lies, the shrouds of mystery, and the layers of deception and duplicity, and finds no comfort, no there there. Only "the horror of nothing to be seen." Good of her to cover it up for him.

This tale of absence, castration, deficiency, negativity, substitution was composed by one whom Gilles Deleuze and Félix Guattari describe as "an overconscious idiot who has no understanding of multiplicities."[14] From Freud's point of view, there is one and its other, which is simply what one sees of it. And what one sees is nothing at all. "Because the path it traces is invisible and becomes visible only in reverse, to the extent that it is travelled over and covered by the phenomena it induces within the system, it has no place other than that from which it is 'missing,' no identity other than that which it lacks."[15]

Anna Freud's biographer describes her as a woman who "specialized in reversals, in making the absent present, the lost found, the past current . . . she could also make the undone done, or—even more valuable—doable. When she was tired and faced with a stack of letters to answer, for example, she would simply set her pen down on a blank page and scurry it along, making quick mountain ranges of scribble. Then she would sign her name under the rows of scribble in her characteristic way, as one flourishing word: ANNAFREUD."[16]

After that, it was downhill all the way. "Having thus written a letter in fantasy with complete ease, she wrote a real letter helped by the sense that the task was accomplished anyway." It's easy to complete a job already done. "Her lectures were composed in the same way. First she lectured in her imagination, enjoying the thunderous applause, and then she made an outline of what she had said, adjusting it if she needed to for greater simplicity and coherence. Later, with her outline in hand, she would give the lecture extempore. The method—if it can be called that—also supplemented her pleasure in sprints of thought. Intellectually she was . . . a quick sketcher."

No doubt Freud despaired at such unorthodox approaches to her work. It seemed she did everything in reverse, backward, upside down, contrary to any rational approach. But if Anna's techniques appeared to be the random tactics of a scattered brain, knowing something backward and inside out is far in advance of any straightforward procedure. And she was hardly alone in her topsy-turvy ways. This ability to win "victories *in advance,* as if acquired on credit"[17] may not figure in the history of discoveries and inventions familiar to Freud, but this is only because it underlies the entire account. According to Marshall McLuhan, "the technique of

beginning at the end of any operation whatever, and of working backwards from that point to the beginning"[18] was not merely an invention or discovery to be added to the list: it was "the invention of invention" itself.

This is hysteresis, the lagging of effects behind their causes. Reverse engineering: the way hackers hack and pirates conspire to lure the future to their side. Starting at the end, and then engaging in a process which simultaneously assembles and dismantles the route back to the start, the end, the future, the past: who's counting now? As Ada said, she "did everything topsy-turvy, & certainly ought to have come into the world *feet downwards.*"[19] Mere discoveries were not enough for her: "I intend to incorporate with one department of my labours a complete reduction to a system, of the principles and methods of *discovery.*"[20]

The prevalence of these backward moves is not the least of the reasons why histories of technology—and indeed histories of anything at all—are always riddled with delicious gaps, mysteries, and riddles just like those perplexing Freud. No straightforward account can ever hope to deal with the tactical advantages gained by such disorderings of linear time. The names and dates and great achievements of the Read Only Memory called history may enjoy their fifteen kilobytes of digital fame on the latest encyclopedic compact disc, but what announce themselves to be founding fathers, points of origin, and defining moments only ever serve as distractions from the ongoing processes, the shifting differences that count. These are subtle and fine grained, often incognito, undercover, in disguise as mere and minor details. If, that is, they show themselves at all.

"Ada's method, as will appear, was to weave daydreams into seemingly authentic calculations."

Doris Langley Moore, *Ada, Countess of Lovelace*

[. . .]

SHUTTLE SYSTEMS

There is always a point at which, as Freud admits, "our material—for some incomprehensible reason—becomes far more obscure and full of gaps."[21] And, as it happens, Freud's weaving women had made rather more than a small and debatable contribution to his great narrative of inventions and discoveries. Far more than a big and certain one as well. It is their microprocesses which underlie it all: the spindle and the wheel used in spinning yarn are the basis of all later axles, wheels, and rotations; the interlaced threads of the loom compose the most abstract processes of fabrication. Textiles themselves are very literally the softwares linings of all technology.

String, which has been dated to 20,000 B.C., is thought to be the earliest manufactured thread and crucial to "taking the world to human will and ingenuity,"[22] not least because it is such multipurpose material. It can be used for carrying, holding, tying, and trapping, and has even been described as "the unseen weapon that allowed the human race to conquer the earth." Textiles underlie the great canvases of Western art, and even the materials of writing. Paper now tends to be made from wood, but it too was woven in its early form, produced from the dense interlacing of natural fibers. The Chinese, with whom the production of paper is thought to have begun some 2,000 years ago, used bamboo, rags, and old fishing nets as their basic materials; papyrus, from which the word paper is itself derived, was used in ancient Egypt, and later Arab cultures used the same flax from which linen is produced. Wood pulp gradually took over from the rags which Europe used until the nineteenth century, and most paper is now produced from fibers which are pulped and bleached, washed and dried, and then filtered onto a mesh and compressed into a fine felt.

Evidence of sophisticated textile production dates to 6,000 B.C. in the southeast regions of Europe, and in Hungary there is evidence that warp-weighted looms were producing designs of extraordinary extravagance from at least 5,000 B.C. Archaeological investigations suggest that from at least the fourth millennium B.C. Egyptian women were weaving linen on horizontal looms, sometimes with some two hundred threads per inch, and capable of producing cloths as wide as nine feet and seventy-five feet long. Circular warps, facilitating the production of seamless tubes for clothing, and tapestry looms, able to weave the dense complications of images visible in weft threads so closely woven as to completely conceal the warps, were also in use in ancient Egypt where, long before individual artisans stamped their work with their own signatures, trademarks and logos were woven in to indicate the workshop in which cloths had been produced. Cloths were used as early currency, and fine linens were as valuable as precious metals and stones. In China, where the spinning wheel is thought to have first turned, sophisticated drawlooms had woven designs which used thousands of different warps at least two and a half thousand years before such machines were developed in the West.

It may be a bare necessity of life, but textiles work always goes far beyond the clothing and shelter of the family. In terms of quality, sophistication, and sheer quantity, the production of textiles always seems to put some kind of surplus in play. The production of "homespun" yarn and cloth was one of the first cottage industries, pin money was women's earliest source of independent cash, and women were selling surplus yarn and cloth and working as small-scale entrepreneurs long before the emergence of factories, organized patterns of trade, and any of the mechanisms which now define the textiles industry. Even when cloths and clothes can be bought off the rack, women continue to absorb themselves in fibrous fabrications.

There is an obsessive, addictive quality to the spinning of yarn and the weaving of cloth; a temptation to get fixated and locked in to processes which run away with themselves and those drawn into them. Even in cultures assumed to be subsistence economies, women who did only as much cooking, cleaning, and childcare as was necessary tended to go into overdrive when it came to spinning and weaving cloth, producing far more than was required to clothe and furnish the family home. With time and raw materials on their hands, even "Neolithic women were investing large amounts of extra time into their textile work, far beyond pure utility,"[23] suggesting that not everything was hand to mouth. These prehistoric weavers seem to have produced cloths of extraordinary complexity, woven with ornate designs far in excess of the brute demand for simple cloth. And wherever this tendency to elaboration emerged, it fed into a continual exploration of new techniques of dyeing, color combination, combing, spinning, and all the complications of weaving itself.

Even in Europe there had been several early and sophisticated innovations. Drawlooms had been developed in the Middle Ages, and while many of Leonardo da Vinci's "machines for spinning, weaving, twisting hemp, trimming felt, and making needles"[24] were never made, he certainly introduced the flyer and bobbin which brought tension control to the spinning wheel. Unlike "the spinster using the older wheel," she now "slackened her hold on the yarn to allow it to be wound on to the bobbin as it was being twisted."

It is often said that Leonardo's sixteenth-century work anticipated the industrial revolution "in the sense that his 'machines' (including tools, musical instruments, and weapons) all aspired toward systemic automation."[25] But it was his intuition that textiles machines were "more useful, profitable, and perfect than the printing press" which really placed him ahead of his time. If printing had spread across the modern world, textiles led the frantic industrialization of the late eighteenth and early nineteenth centuries. "Like the most humble cultural assets, textiles incessantly moved about, took root in new regions . . ."[26] The first

manufactory was a silk mill on an island in the Derwent near Derby built early in a century which also saw the introduction of the spinning jenny, the water frame, the spinning mule, the flying shuttle, the witches' loom, and the power loom. A spiral of "inventions in both spinning and weaving (interacting and mutually stimulating) had attracted capital, concentrated labour, increased output and swollen imports and exports."[27] This was cloth capitalism, a runaway process which quite literally changed the world. In the 1850s, it was said that "if Providence had never planted the cotton shrub those majestic masses of men which stretch, like a living zone, through our central districts, would have felt no existence; and the magic impulse which has been felt . . . in every department of national energy, our literature, our laws, our social condition, our political institutions, making us almost a new people, would never have been communicated." Textiles had not merely changed the world: they seemed to have mutated its occupants as well. *"Almost a new people . . ."* "I was surprised at the place but more so at the people,"[28] wrote one commentator of Birmingham, the site of the first cotton-spinning mill. "They were a species I had never seen."

While the industrial revolution is supposed to have made the break between handheld tools and supervised machines, the handmade and the mass-produced, the introduction of technology to more primitive textiles techniques is both a break with the old ways and a continuation of the lines on which the women were already at work. Even before its mechanization, the loom was described as the "most complex human engine of them all,"[29] not least because of the extent to which it "reduced everything to simple actions: the alternate movement of the feet worked the pedals, raising half the threads of the warp and then the other, while the hands threw the shuttle carrying the thread of the woof." When John Heathcote, who patented a lace-making machine just after Jacquard built his loom, first saw "a woman working on a pillow, with so many bobbins that it seemed altogether a maze,"[30] his impression was that lace was a "heap of chaotic material." In an attempt to unravel the mystery, he "drew a thread, which happened to draw for an inch or two longitudinally straight, then started off diagonally. The next drew out straight. Then others drew out in various directions. Out of four threads concurring to make a mesh, two passed one way, the third another and the fourth another still. But at length I found they were in fact used in an orderly manner . . ." It was then a matter of producing "a fabric which was an exact imitation of the thread movements of handmade lace."[31] This is both the ordering of chaos, and also how its networks replicate themselves.

There were other spin-offs from textiles too. The weaving of complex designs demands far more than one pair of hands, and textiles production tends to be communal, sociable work allowing plenty of occasion for gossip and chat. Weaving was already multimedia: singing, chanting, telling stories, dancing, and playing games as they work, spinsters, weavers, and needleworkers were literally networkers as well. It seems that "the women of prehistoric Europe gathered at one another's houses to spin, sew, weave, and have fellowship."[32] Spinning yarns, fabricating fictions, fashioning fashions . . . : the textures of woven cloth functioned as means of communication and information storage long before anything was written down. "How do we know this? From the cloth itself." This is not only because, like writing and other visual arts, weaving is often "used to mark or announce information"[33] and "a mnemonic device to record events and other data." Textiles do communicate in terms of the images which appear on the right side of the cloth, but this is only the most superficial sense in which they process and store data. Because there is no difference between the process of weaving and the woven design, cloths persist as records of

the processes which fed into their production: how many women worked on them, the techniques they used, the skills they employed. The visible pattern is integral to the process which produced it; the program and the pattern are continuous.

Information can be stored in cloth by means of the meaningful messages and images which are later produced by the pen and the paintbrush, but data can also be woven in far more pragmatic and immediate ways. A piece of work so absorbing as a cloth is saturated with the thoughts of the people who produced it, each of whom can flash straight back to whatever they were thinking as they worked. Like Proust's madeleines, it carries memories of an intensity which completely escapes the written word. Cloths were also woven "to 'invoke magic'—to protect, to secure fertility and riches, to divine the future, perhaps even to curse," and in this sense the weaving of spells is far more than a metaphorical device. "The weaver chose warp threads of red wool for her work, 24 spun one direction, 24 spun the other way. She divided the bunch spun one way into 3 sets of 8, and the other bunch into 4 sets of 6, and alternated them. All this is perhaps perfectly innocent, but . . ."[34]

If the weaving of such magical spells gives priority to the process over the completion of a task, this tendency is implicit in the production of all textiles. Stripes and checks are among the most basic of colored and textured designs which can be woven in. Both are implicit in the grids of the woven cloth itself. Slightly more complex, but equally integral to the basic web, are the lozenges, or diamonds, still common in weaves across the world. These open diamonds are said to indicate fertility and tend to decorate the aprons, skirts, and belts which are themselves supposed to be the earliest forms of clothing. "These lozenges, usually with little curly hooks around the edge, rather graphically, if schematically, represent a woman's vulva."[35] These images are quite unlike those which are later painted on the canvas or written on the page. The lozenge is emergent from the cloth, diagonal lines implicit in the grids of the weave. And even the most ornate and complex of woven designs retains this connection to the warps and wefts. When images are later painted, or written in the form of words on a page, patterns are imposed on the passive backdrop provided by the canvas or the page. But textile images are never imposed on the surface of the cloth: their patterns are always emergent from an active matrix, implicit in a web which makes them immanent to the processes from which they emerge.

As the frantic activities of generations of spinsters and weaving women makes abundantly clear, nothing stops when a particular piece of work has been finished off. Even when magical connections are not explicitly invoked, the finished cloth, unlike the finished painting or the text, is almost incidental in relation to the processes of its production. The only incentive to cast off seems to be the chance completion provides to start again, throw another shuttle, cast another spell.

As writing and other visual arts became the privileged bearers of memory and messages, weaving withdrew into its own screens. Both canvases and paper reduce the complexities of weaving to raw materials on which images and signs are imposed: the cloths from which woven patterns once emerged now become backcloths, passive matrices on which images are imposed and interpreted as if from on high. Images are no longer carried in the weave, but imprinted on its surface by the pens and brushes with which shuttles become superficial carriers of threads. Guided by the hand–eye coordinations of what are now their male creators, patterns become as individuated and unique as their artists and authors. And whereas the weave was once both the process and the product, the woven stuff, images are now separated out from matrices to which they had been immanent. The artist sees only the surface of a web which is covered as he works; the paper on which authors now look down has no say in the writing it supports.

The processes themselves become dematerialized as myths, legends, and metaphors. Ariadne's thread, and the famous contest in which the divine Athena tore mortal Arachne's weaving into shreds, are among the many mythical associations between women and webs, spinsters and spiders, spinning yarns and storylines. For the Greeks, the Fates, the Moirai, were three spinsters—Klotho, Lachesis, and Atropos—who produced, allotted, and broke the delicate contingency of the thread of life. In the folktales of Europe, spindles become magic wands, Fates become fairies, and women are abandoned or rescued from impossible spinning and weaving tasks by supernatural entities, godmothers and crones who transform piles of flax into fine linen by means more magical than weaving itself, as in "Rumpelstiltskin," "The Three Spinsters," and "The Sleeping Beauty." "European folktales are full of references to the making of magical garments, especially girdles, in which the magic seems to be inherent in the weaving, not merely in special decoration."

As for the fabrics which persist: evaluated in these visual terms, their checks and diagonals, diamonds and stripes become insignificant matters of repeating detail. This is why Freud had gazed at work which was so literally imperceptible to him. Struggling only to interpret the surface effects of Anna's work as though he was looking at a painting or a text, the process of weaving eluded him: out of sight, out of mind, out of his world.

This was a process of disarmament which automation should have made complete. But if textiles appear to lose touch with their weaving spells and spans of time, they also continue to fabricate the very screens with which they are concealed. And because these are processes, they keep processing. "Behind the screen of representation," weaving wends its way through even the media which supplant it. While paper has lost its associations with the woven fabrics with which it began, there are remnants of weaving in all writing: yarns continue to be spun, texts are still abbreviated textiles, and even grammar—glamor—and spelling retain an occult connectivity. Silkscreens, printing presses, stencils, photographic processes, and typewriters: by the end of the nineteenth century images, texts, and patterns of all kinds were being processed by machines which still used matrices as means to their ends, but also repeated the repeating patterns downgraded by the one-off work of art. And while all these modes of printing were taking technologies of representation to new heights, they were also moving on to the matrices of times in which these imprinting procedures would reconnect with the tactile depth of woven cloth.

NOTES

MATRICES

1. Michel Foucault, *The Archaeology of Knowledge*, p. 23.
2. George Landow, *Hypertext*, p. 123.
3. Ada Lovelace, Notes to *Sketch of the Analytical Engine invented by Charles Babbage Esq. By L. F. Menabrea, of Turin, Officer of the Military Engineers*, Note D.

TENSIONS

4. Philip and Emily Morrison, eds. *Charles Babbage and his Calculating Engines: Selected Writings by Charles Babbage and others*, p. xxxiii.
5. *Neuromancer*, p. 5.

ON THE CARDS

6. Philip and Emily Morrison, eds. *Charles Babbage and his Calculating Engines: Selected Writings by Charles Babbage and others*, p. xxxiv.
7. ibid., p. 233.
8. Manuel de Landa, *War in the Age of Intelligent Machines*, p. 168.
9. Humphrey Jennings, *Pandemonium The Coming of the Machine as Seen by Contemporary Observers*, p. 132.
10. Charles Babbage, *Passages from the Life of a Philosopher*, p. 89.
11. ibid., p. 88.
12. ibid., p. 127.

ANNA 1

13. Sigmund Freud, "Femininity," in Sigmund Freud, *New Introductory Lectures on Psychoanalysis*, pp. 145–69.
14. Gilles Deleuze and Félix Guattari, *A Thousand Plateaus*, p. 32.
15. Gilles Deleuze, *Difference and Repetition*, pp. 119–20.
16. Elisabeth Young-Bruehl, *Anna Freud*, p. 382.
17. Guy Debord, *Comments on the Society of the Spectacle*, p. 86.
18. Marshall McLuhan, *The Gutenberg Galaxy*, p. 276.
19. Ada Lovelace, September 1843 quoted in Betty A. Toole, *Ada, The Enchantress of Numbers*, pp. 264–65.
20. Ada Lovelace, July 1843, quoted in Dorothy Stein, *Ada, A Life and a Legacy*, p. 129.

SHUTTLE SYSTEMS

21. Sigmund Freud, *On Sexuality*, p. 320.
22. Elizabeth Wayland Barber, *Women's Work*, p. 45
23. ibid., p. 90.
24. W. English, *The Textile Industry*, p. 6.
25. Serge Bramly, *Leonardo, the Artist and the Man*, p. 272.
26. Fernand Braudel, *Capitalism and Material Life*, p. 237.

27. Asa Briggs, *The Age of Invention,* pp. 21–22.

28. Francis D. Klingender, *Art and the Industrial Revolution,* p. 12.

29. Fernand Braudel, *Capitalism and Material Life,* p. 247.

30. W. English, *The Textile Industry,* p. 130.

31. ibid., p. 132.

32. Elizabeth Wayland Barber, *Women's Work,* p. 86.

33. ibid., p. 149.

34. ibid., pp. 159–60.

35. ibid., p. 62.

OPEN SOURCE EMBROIDERY: CURATORIAL FACILITATION OF MATERIAL NETWORKS

Ele Carpenter

Editor's introduction: Ele Carpenter is an artist and curator based in England. She is currently a lecturer on the MFA in curating course at Goldsmiths, University of London, and was formerly a research fellow at HUMlab in partnership with BildMuseet at the University of Umeå in Sweden, 2008–2010. She completed her PhD on politicized socially engaged art and new media art in 2008 with the Curatorial Resource for Upstart Media Bliss (CRUMB) at the University of Sunderland, England. Since 2005 she has developed the Open Source Embroidery project (illustrated on the cover of the *Reader*) to investigate the relationship between craft and code. The text reprinted here is a talk Carpenter gave at the Centre de Cultura Contemporània de Barcelona on May 27, 2010, and introduces the Open Source Embroidery project and open source software. In it, Carpenter considers the history of open source software and the misunderstandings that have arisen around the term, before turning to the Open Source Embroidery project, which, she explains, "evolved to investigate the material and collaborative nature of computing, code and textiles through workshops, artworks and exhibitions." The lecture reproduced here contains additional notes on immaterial labor, materiality, and the amateur.

INTRODUCTION

The starting point for this paper is an interest in the shared language between socially engaged (relational) practices and new media art, which has led me to develop the Open Source Embroidery (OSE) project. Informed by the free and open source software movement and socially engaged arts practice, Open Source Embroidery has been developed through three key concepts:

- Investigation of (im)materiality, with a focus on the digital as material
- Facilitating amateur – professional relationships across craft + code
- Making the tension between object and process visible
- Creating an exhibition as a process, with a balance between spectator and participant

These are huge topics, and can't all be discussed in depth here. So this paper will introduce

Source: Ele Carpenter, "Open Source Embroidery: Curatorial Facilitation of Material Networks," presented at The Present and Future of the Exhibition Format, "Exhibiting the Lab," organized by I+C+i, Centre de Cultura Contemporània de Barcelona (CCCB), Barcelona (May 27, 2010). Reproduced with permission.

the thinking behind the project, focusing on open source, moving on to issues of materiality and the role of the amateur. But, firstly, I shall describe the curatorial landscape in which the Open Source Embroidery project is situated.

Over the last ten years the connective and collaborative characteristics of digital media have re-introduced the language of participatory production-and-distribution into the cultural sphere. New media art has contributed to the rehabilitation of discourse on the nature of the commons, materiality and open methodologies. Although these ideas are informed by new media systems they have older histories in collectives, community organisation, folk and craft culture. Digital art and socially engaged art, along with craft, are historically on the margins of the modern 'fine' art world, also functioning within spheres of popular and folk culture.

While digital and socially engaged art has always embraced a performative and conceptual approach to immateriality, it is only recently that craft has exploded into a fashionable participatory culture. Leaving behind some of the preciousness of the hard-won fine-craft, and embracing public and activist forms of making (craftivism), the coolness of knitting is now being commodified as 'knitted cakes'. (Carpenter, 2010)

The vast amount of contemporary craft online is a perfect example of a specialist community of interest networking itself through the web. But perhaps this is only remarkable because craft, like art, has previously been thought of as an isolated if not autonomous practice.

We are now in the age of ubiquitous computing (almost). But like all art forms, net art, digital art, media art, networked and distributed creativity all have their roots in the relationship between the form and content of the medium: the live connectivity of the network, ability to upload and download, and the compatibility of digital formats across platforms.

Digital art often uses generative code and algorithmic scripts to create live interactions; exploring an aesthetic or literary understanding of code, in relation to its networked functions and user input and visual outcomes. Here the artist deconstructs her/his tools to investigate the values of the media, and its relationship to the world. The website www.sketchpatch.net is a good example, where users are encouraged to patch, copy and modify processing code to create new animated sketches. Sketchpatch works well in a workshop scenario, or accessed privately at home, but is harder to present in a gallery exhibition. (Footnote: In OSE an every-day desk table was used for the Sketchpatch computer, the desktop was also projected onto the gallery wall above to create a public as well as a private viewing space for the work. The table also included Lisa Wallbank's 'Telnit Zero' Crochet computer cover.)

This is true of many online or digital works which often don't sit well within a museum exhibition. The artwork exists within the space of the computer, and the artist often forgets to think of the work in a physical space; sensitivities of light, colour balance, height, proportion, framing, seating, and contextual information are neglected in favour of the interiority of the computer screen. Formally, the work fails in sculptural terms, it is an unintentional presentation of equipment which at best distracts or, worse, hides the actual work of art. However, hiding technical equipment to create a streamlined exhibition space is equally problematic. These problems of 'display' are apparent in several of the works in the current DeCode exhibition at the Victoria and Albert (V&A) museum in London, where exhibition designers have resolved the spatial requirements and created a coherent linear visitor experience flowing between works as if they were pictures inset into a wall. Interestingly the DeCode exhibition at the V&A is on show at the same time as a large quilt exhibition, but there is no curated relationship between the two exhibitions. Both exhibitions are based on the material or medium characteristics of the work as separate and distinct art forms. This is a stark reminder of early media art exhibitions which suffered from a medium-specific focus, trying to create visibility for the work, but also accused of ghetto-ising practice.

Within my curatorial practice I wanted to find a line of critical enquiry based on ideas, rather than medium, which investigated the relationship between the social functions of digital media and art practice. I was finding it hard to talk about new media art without a computer in front of me, or without being online. This was frustrating as many of the concepts I was trying to explain, such as network topologies or open source, were around long before computers and the internet. So I started to learn html, and as I typed I embroidered the code on my T-shirt making it visible and talking about it. I didn't want to instrumentalise either media. I didn't want the digital to 'document' the material, or the material to 'illustrate' the digital. So, I started stitching shared language scarves, delighted by the distinct contrast of cloth to plastic, enjoying the physicality of stitches rather than typing. Glad not to be staring at a screen.

So the OSE project developed in response to the need for a material investigation of the digital and quickly found its form through both conceptual and folk culture. At one point, it could have included other forms of open collective production informed by open source ideas. However, there is such a strong historical, material and metaphorical connection between computing and textiles (Plant, 1997; Essinger, 2004) that I decided to focus on this interdisciplinary approach.

The OSE project evolved to investigate the material and collaborative nature of computing, code and textiles through workshops, artworks and exhibitions. The workshops have taken place in media labs, conferences, exhibitions and seminars. The exhibition has been presented at the Museum of Craft and Folk Art in San Francisco, the Bildmuseet in Umea, Sweden, and in the UK at Furtherfields' HTTP Gallery in London and Access Space in Sheffield.

The exhibition presented contemporary artwork by over 30 artists and collectives that explores how the open source software development model has been incorporated into the language of cultural participation, involving interdisciplinary approaches to skill-share and collaboration. It included material and digital works that make visible the physical characteristics of technology and social communications networks.

The project investigates the relationship between physical and virtual space, not as two opposing architectures, but as symbiotic spaces reflecting, informing and supporting the other. However, this does not mean that they lose their distinct properties, but that the boundary between virtual and real is more fluid and shifting than we might think, as we move between different modes of communication.

People create culture for social and intellectual, as well as creative, reasons. Through my experience of commissioning and facilitating socially engaged art I realise there is no such thing as the 'general public', this abstract body of people is comprised of communities of interest who have very specific social networks across amateur and professional spheres both on and offline. These groups can be mapped as network topologies through their communication patterns. In 1964, Paul Baran illustrated the potential of a distributed communications system which we now know as the internet (Baran, 1964). The distributed network offers the potential for everyone to be connected through a net or web of interconnections. A more familiar topology is the clustering of decentralised groups, in which we recognise our professional, family, and social networks. The OSE project is a distributed project which forms a decentralised international network.

OPEN SOURCE EMBROIDERY AND OPENNESS

In many ways there is no such thing as perfect 'openness'. Open organisational methods simply invite participants to set the parameters within which they agree to work, rather than being imposed from a hierarchy or an institution. But what is open source? And what do we mean by open methodologies in relation to software? To answer these questions it is important to understand the basic principles of free and open source software, which I will outline here.

The history of free software explores software as a form of political action, referencing the Diggers and Luddites and the tensions between utopian and dystopian views of technology in early computing. The story of 'Free Libertarian Open Source Software' (FLOSS) includes both radical (Stallman, 1985, 2007) and libertarian (Raymond, 1999) arguments for free and open source software.

The term 'open source' is used within the title Open Source Embroidery because it best describes how the open source development methodology can be used to rethink practices of participation, collaboration, socio-political functions of tools and the relationship between the value of process and a never-finished product. (Footnote: The term 'Free Embroidery' would refer to financially free work which is not the case, or free-style stitching which would be appropriate.) But there are important differences between open source and free software, which are also reflected in the political complexities behind the intentions of social engagement and digital arts.

The Free Software Foundation (FSF) was established by Richard Stallman early in 1985. The definition of open source wasn't coined by Eric Raymond until 1998, when it became known as a development methodology for popularising FLOSS within a wider social and economic context. As described on the FSF website:

"The fundamental difference between the two movements is in their values, their ways of looking at the world. For the open source movement, the issue of whether software should be open source is a practical question, not an ethical one. As one person put it, 'Open source is a development methodology; free software is a social movement.' For the Open Source movement, non-free software is a suboptimal solution. For the Free Software movement, non-free software is a social problem and free software is the solution." (Stallman, 2005)

The Open Source Initiative (Coar, 2006) defines open source software as licensed under the General Public License (GPL) of Free Software, and freely distributed, although not always financially free. The source code is viewable and modifiable and gives credit to everyone who has contributed to it. Derived works must be distributed under the same licensing terms as the original software. Open source also has clauses to respect the 'integrity of the author's source code'. In stark contrast to proprietary software, open source must not be 'specific to a product' or 'restrict other software' and it must be technology neutral.

The FSF define their concept of freedom:

" 'Free software' is a matter of liberty, not price. To understand the concept, you should think of 'free' as in 'free speech,' not as in 'free beer'." (Stallman, 2007b)

This much quoted and misquoted phrase emphasises the flexibility of freedom to make choices and to have your voice heard and does not advocate a financially free process of product outside of the capital economy. To remind us of the notion of 'freedom' being used here, the FSF declare:

"Free software is a matter of the users' freedom to run, copy, distribute, study, change and improve the software." (Stallman, 2007b)

Raymond argues that the term 'free' is misleading in several ways (Raymond, 1999, p122). Firstly, that purchase of proprietary software is only worthwhile if the technical support is provided. This highlights the fact that the actual programs themselves are cheap and easily reproducible, whilst the investment in learning, maintenance (Raymond, 1999, p120) and support is where the real value lies. So the software is not 'free' but investment is directed into maintenance rather than product. This correlates to socially engaged arts practice where development and maintenance are the core focus of the social process of the work.

Of course, there are problems with the production and distribution of open source software (Brown, 2005; King, 2006), mainly due to the problems of compatibility with proprietary software and operating systems. But its emphasis on communication between producer and user has re-invigorated the debate about who owns, produces and uses culture; asking the question: *Is culture something you buy or something you do?*

The main success story of open source is Linus Torvald's development of the Linux operating system. Raymond discusses the development model of the Linux kernel:

"Linus's cleverest and most consequential hack was not the construction of the Linux kernel itself, but rather his invention of the Linux development model." (Raymond, 1999, p27)

Torvald's model consisted of himself as the co-ordinating software developer at the centre of a core group that released their work to vast numbers of individual independent programmers who highlighted problems, fixed bugs and sent their work back to the core group. If we use Baran's centralized diagram to describe this network it's hard to describe this group as a community because they don't necessarily know or communicate with each other. As Raymond describes, their point of connection is through the centre, keeping simplicity to prevent forking or repetition of work (Raymond, 1999, p30).

So let's consider the analogy between the FLOSS debates and socially engaged art practices: Art can be both a utopian activity outside the traditional labour relations and ideas of what constitutes 'work', its symbolic value the perfect idea of immaterial labour. Or it can be seen as a more efficient way of making high-quality products for a select market, creating the aura of art. Socially engaged art can be seen as working towards

reclaiming culture as something that everyone has, and not simply a 'culture industry'. More negatively, it can be viewed as a poor substitute for social services. Digital art can be understood as empowering people to create their own cultural content collapsing distance between communities of interest. But it can also be a form of control, creating distance between people and forcing us to travel further and further to maintain working patterns. Alex Galloway, in his book *Protocol*, examines the internet protocols that regulate the internet, not as a completely open system, but one which is heavily controlled and managed (Galloway, 2004). FLOSS attempts to keep freedom within the system so that people can develop their own tools and networks, rather than them being owned by a small handful of global corporations (Mansoux & de Valk, 2008).

So to clarify: OSE is not an 'open-exhibition' in the sense of an 'open-submission' where anyone can submit work to be shown. Instead the project is based on three distinct communities of interest: artists, crafters and programmers who are invited to come together to discuss their practice and make new work. Topics of discussion have included: creating a perfect work as a demonstration of skill and ability; translating metaphor; use of English as the universal programming language; gendered materials; history of computing; open source software tools; utopian and dystopian approaches to open systems; attitudes to collective ownership; the cathartic nature of making; systematic creativity; software patches and fabric patches; men's embroidery; hexadecimal codes and the differences between CMYK and RGB colour sequences . . . the list goes on.

Many of the artworks in the Open Source Embroidery exhibition were produced through these workshops (Knitted Flat Screen Cover, Embroidered Digital Commons, GYRMBC Tent etc). The exhibition also presented a range of models for open production, through collectively made artworks such as: *Knitted Blog, Sampler Collective, Knitted Bench, Html Patchwork, Stitching Together* and the *Embroidered Digital Commons*. All of the works can be found on www.open-source-embroidery.org.uk and the curatorial research process is blogged on www.eleweekend.blogspot.com

MATERIALITY, TACTICS AND THE AMATEUR

Emerging from the discussion of open source and distributed networks is an understanding of new ways of working made possible by the internet, which have enabled new economic models. Work is no longer simply manufacturing goods, but includes the more intangible production of knowledge, ideas and services, and, crucially, the maintenance of networks. But Lazzarato's concept of 'immaterial labour' (discussed by Vishmidt, 2006; Terranova, 2006), while helpful in describing the merging of work and life through information networks and computing, can also be a confusing distraction from the material conditions of production.

This confusion can also be found in the visual arts where we often argue for the immateriality of both digital and socially engaged practices as a shift from commodifiable object to social or relational process. At the same time we recognise that an object is also a material network of relations, and that objects can be actors in the wider notion of the social network (Latour, 2005).

So, I intentionally use the word 'material' in several ways. Firstly, to acknowledge that artworks are embedded within their own material network in terms of their physical production, consumption of resources and relationship to the environment. This includes the heavy metals used in microprocessors, and the fuel for my flight to Barcelona. Secondly, 'material' is used to describe the way in which the histories of fabric and computing intertwine. From the beginning of computer history the digital is material—and it is social (Plant, 1997). Computing, far from being an ephemeral and invisible process, is produced through electronics and written instructions called code. Writers such as Alex Galloway, Matthew Fuller (2003), Josephine Berry Slater,

and Tiziana Terranova have investigated the materiality of computer code.

Within OSE I use the phrase 'material network' to describe collectively made embroidery, weaving and patchwork which forms a fabric embodiment of a network of people. Fabric-metaphors are often used to describe communication networks such as weaving a web, spinning a yarn, and the thread of a story.

In the OSE exhibition, many of the works are forms of what Joseph Beuys called "social sculpture" (Beuys, 1992). Not simply that "everyone can be an artist" but in a sculptural sense, the social network can be embedded in or represented by an object. The concept lies in the action, the performativity of the work, whose primary audience is the people who participate in its production. The tension lies in how the object is viewed and mediated in a gallery exhibition, which can sometimes be experienced as an after-effect of intense engagement.

The collectively stitched *Html Patchwork* plays with these multiple senses of materiality (see http://www.open-source-embroidery.org.uk/patchwork.htm for details). The work was created by artists, craftspeople, computer programmers, and html users, all contributing their work for free. But rather than simply 'immaterial labour' there are a number of different exchanges at play: skill-share, gift, individual and institutional networking, publicity, learning and social fun. We should also include the pleasure of making something by hand. But what are the material and immaterial values of this work?

Tiziana Terranova (2006) and Marina Vishmidt (2006) each investigate the concept of immaterial labour in relation to art and curating. Terranova describes how "the concept of immaterial labour challenges not only the modern emphasis on art as an autonomous sphere of existence, but also work as the only domain of economic relations and political struggle" (p27). It is in this in between space of everyday creative making, art, craft and tactics that the OSE project sits.

As Terranova describes:

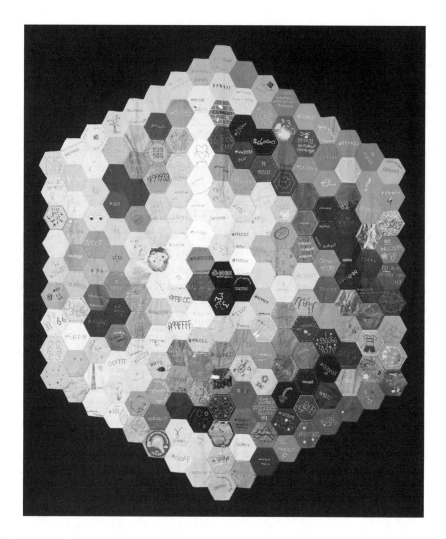

Figure 34.1. *Html Patchwork*, facilitated by Ele Carpenter, 2007–2009. Mixed fabrics, 240 x 250 cm. Supported by Access Space and Arts Council England. http://www.open-source-embroidery.org.uk/patchwork.htm. The *Html Patchwork* was stitched in workshops at Access Space, Sheffield; Isis Arts and Glue Gallery, Newcastle upon Tyne; and Banff New Media Institute, Alberta, Canada; and by individuals across the United Kingdom and internationally from Australia, New Zealand, and Ireland. Pau Ros (see front cover credit).

"Immaterial labour is a Marxist concept that aims at a redefinition of labour in the age of the general intellect—the age where the production of value is dependent on socialized labour power organized in assemblages of humans and machines exceeding the spaces and times designated as 'work'." (Terranova, 2006, p28)

I am certainly an amateur Marxist—but the notion of the 'general intellect', or the level of knowledge in society, is evident in user generated content online and the basis of socially engaged practices which invite people to share their skills and knowledge.

Vishmidt situates dematerialised art and curating as 'immaterial labour' within the realm of the knowledge economy as an abstract form in itself. But she takes care to argue that:

". . . the position of labour in capital remains unchanged. Just so, with 'immateriality' signaling

Figure 34.2. *Html Patchwork* (detail, facilitated by Ele Carpenter, 2007–2009. Mixed fabrics. 240 × 250 cm (see front cover credit).

an epochal displacement of value from object to process and symbolic analysis in art production, the position of the artist in the market remains unchanged. It is only the site of value production that shifts, not the conditions of production. Or, rather, we could contend that the sites of value production have expanded rather than shifted—the dematerialisation of the art object has not deterred the appearance of new art objects, but it has added new types of object, immaterial ones." (Vishmidt, 2006, p40)

OSE is certainly an investigation into the material aspects of immateriality, where informal groups work in their leisure time to create artworks which may or may not gain them cultural capital. These new objects have a precarious status somewhere between art and craft, material and process, professional and amateur.

The role of the Amateur is a significant figure in the discourse of social media and online culture, as well being the main participant of socially engaged art.

The OSE project explores the possibility of cultural value outside of economic exchange relations. Models such as the 'Gift Economy' are more commonly played out in non-professional spheres of life such as the domestic, unemployed, and un-recuperated labour such as craft. All of these roles are amateur, where the sharing of experience and transaction of knowledge is through enthusiast, hobbyist and opportunistic actions.

Lovink & Garcia's definition of *Tactical Media* (1992) situates the amateur as operating tactically within the everyday and outside long-term institutional developmental strategies. These tactical modes of behaviour lie outside the paradigm of Walter Benjamin's producer/consumer, providing a framework for rethinking the value of creativity. De *Certeau's The Practice of Everyday Life* (1984) and his definition of tactical subversive acts 'making do' within the everyday (p29–44), along with Hakim Bey's 'Temporary Autonomous Zones' (1985) provide other frameworks for understanding creativity outside the Marxist production and distribution model.

However, the relationship between amateur and expert is hugely crucial, as highlighted by Critical Art Ensemble (CAE), who value the role of the amateur as a radical interventionist, respecting the relationship between amateur and expert:

"The amateur's relationship to the expert is a necessary one in many ways. For the sake of efficiency, to limit mistakes, to teach fundamental processes and protocols and to reinforce good ideas, dialogues with experts remain a key part of the amateurs' process." (CAE, 2005)

This two-way learning process is an example of strategic value of tactical knowledge, where the institution or expert can support amateur and

Figure 34.3. *Html Patchwork* (reverse detail), facilitated by Ele Carpenter, 2007–2009. Mixed fabrics. 240 × 250 cm. (see front cover credit).

spontaneous practices which test out ideas and (inadvertently) can contribute to institutional development, albeit incredibly slowly.

Vishmidt also introduces the amateur as a character who might circumvent the commodification of their production, but whose "parasitic" role can shift and evolve as they please (Vishmidt, 2006, p52–56). Vishmidt describes a "conservative" and "emancipatory" reading of the amateur. On the one hand the figure of a hobbyist consumer or entrepreneur, on the other hand:

"The emancipatory aspect, however, may come to the fore whenever the amateur positions his/ her production as a challenge to the impoverishment of experience bought about by specialization, and eschews such commodification of abilities in favour of a non-specific production

structured by goals other than economic, whether these be social, political or artistic." (Vishmidt, 2006, p52–3)

Vishmidt also draws a correlation between the unremunerated open source programmer, the amateur and the notion of the commons (2006, p53–4). She proposes that the implications of open source include "renewed attention to questions of organization, hierarchy, economies, economics and ownership and creativity" which are inherent in the amateur, "the unremunerated enthusiast, obscure or feted, that prefigures an existence beyond capital, while expressing all the contradictions that a life within capital dictates" (p54). So we can start to think of the amateur, not as a social figure, but an aspect of all of our knowledge. The expert brain surgeon may be an amateur gardener, the curator an amateur philosopher etc.

In relation to 'work' many artists may more accurately describe themselves as 'amateurs' rather than 'entrepreneurs' as they are mostly unsuccessful at levering the 'capital' value from their practice. Most craft practice is certainly amateur, and intends to stay that way. Curating is also a practice of being an amateur in many subjects. But this position is slowly changing due to the increase in academic-research-based curatorial and artistic practices where there is increasing demand for expert knowledge and analysis.

WHAT IS THE IMPACT OF THE NOTION OF THE AMATEURS ON CURATING CONTEMPORARY ART?

As we have seen, amateur modes of operation are complex and shifting. When they become political they become tactical, manoeuvring to create spaces for spontaneity and improvisation. Everyone is an expert in something and an amateur in other things. Embracing amateurism enables flexibility, different kinds of knowledge and storytelling, and is a prerequisite for any collaborative or interdisciplinary attitude.

Perhaps the biggest issue for the future of exhibitions is how to prevent them from becoming strategically absorbed into cultural tourism by a conglomeration of major institutions. We need to keep spaces for tactical experimentation within a range of labour relations, valuing tactical and amateur approaches to expert fields of knowledge. The mistake with the 'amateur' is to assume that the lowest common denominator will appeal to all. As we know, amateurs are specialists too.

Exhibitions need to be understood as complex poetic experience and open-ended lines of enquiry. Navigating the problems of proprietary social media, and creating spaces for rigorous approaches to amateur–professional collaboration.

Feminist writer Germaine Greer reflects on the complex nature of storytelling. Rather than focusing on the meaning and interpretation of the tale, she argues that:

"If the child's imagination is to work, the story must not be explained away, nor should the child intuit what the grown-up's reason for telling such a tale might be." (Germaine Greer, 2010. p3)

Curatorial work includes the delicate art of storytelling without 'explaining away' the work, despite the driving forces of the tourism industry to create easily marketable exhibitions. Curators work with artists to communicate and disseminate their work, while identifying the complexity and intelligence of audiences who are amateurs in many things, but not necessarily experts in navigating the culture industry.

It is important that we understand the rhetoric of participation as enabling a new role for curators and artists where both individual expertise and collaborative working can co-exist within self-organised networks and horizontal teams. Here, both expert and amateur knowledge can inform each other.

REFERENCES

Baran, Paul (1964). RAND memorandum, On Distributed Communications: 1. Introduction to Distributed Communications Network. (August 1964).

Brown, Andrew (2005). If this suite's a success, why is it so buggy. In: *The Guardian Newspaper*. Thursday December 8, 2005. Available at: http://technology.guardian.co.uk/weekly/story/0,16376,1660763,00.html [Accessed 24.11.07]

Beuys, J. (1992). Joseph Beuys (1921–1986) I am Searching for Field Character, 1973. In: Harrison & Wood, *Art in Theory 1900–1990: An Anthology of Changing Ideas.* Oxford & Malden: Blackwell, p 903.

Bey, Hakim (1985, 1991). T.A.Z.: The Temporary Autonomous Zones. *Autonomedia.* Available at: http://www.t0.or.at/hakimbey/taz/taz.htm [Accessed 24.02.07]

Carpenter, Ele (2010). "Activist Tendencies in Craft." In: *Concept Store #3 Art, Activism and Recuperation.* Eds Geoff Cox, Nav Haq, Tom Trevor. Arnolfini: Bristol. May 2010. ISBN 9780 907738 97 8.

Coar, Ken (2006). *The Open Source Definition, Annotated.* Mon, 2006-07-24 19:04. Available at: http://www.opensource.org/docs/definition.php [Accessed 4.01.08]

Critical Art Ensemble (2005). The Amateur. In: Nato Thompson, *The Interventionists: User's Manual for the Creative Disruption of Everyday Life.* Massachusetts: Mass MoCA, p 147.

Essinger, James (2004). *Jacquard's Web: How a hand loom led to the birth of the information age.* Oxford University Press.

Fuller, Matthew (2003). *Beyond the Blip: Essays on the Culture of Software.* Autonomedia: New York, USA.

Galloway, Alexander R. (2004). *Protocol: how control exists after decentralisation.* Massachusetts: Massachusetts Institute of Technology.

Greer, Germaine (2010) Grandmother's Footsteps. In: Saturday *Guardian,* 15.05.2010. [newspaper] p2–4. Available at: http://www.guardian.co.uk/books/2010/may/15/germaine-greer-old-wives-tales

King, Jamie (2006). The Packet Gang. In: Marina Vishmidt. *Media Mutandis: a Node.London Reader: Surveying art, technologies and politics.* London: Node.London, p. 157–170.

Latour, B. (2005). *Reassembling The Social: An Introduction to Actor Network Theory.* Oxford: Oxford University Press.

Mansoux, Aymeric,. & Marloes de Valk (2008). *FLOSS+Art.* London: Goto10 and Open Mute.

Raymond, Eric S. (1999). *The Cathedral and the Bazaar: Musings on Linux and Open Source by an Accidental Revolutionary.* O'Reilly. Available at: www.oreilly.com

Plant, Sadie (1997). *Zeros and Ones: Digital Women and the New Technoculture.* London: Fourth Estate.

Stallman, Richard (1985). *The Free Software Foundation (FSF).* Available at: http://www.fsf.org/ [Accessed 10.12.07]

Stallman, Richard (2005). *Why Free Software is better than Open Source.* Available at: http://www.fsf.org/licensing/essays/free-software-for-freedom.html [Accessed: 04.01.08]

Stallman, Richard (2007). *Why 'Open Source' misses the point of Free Software.* Available at: http://www.gnu.org/philosophy/open-source-misses-the-point.html [Accessed: 24.12.07]

Stallman, Richard (2007b). *The Free Software Definition.* Available at: http://www.fsf.org/licensing/essays/free-sw.html [Accessed 2.12.07]

Terranova, Tiziana 2006. Of Sense and Sensibility: Immaterial Labour in Open Systems. In: *Curating Immateriality: The work of the curator in the age of network systems.* Edited by Joasia Krysa (2006). Databrowser03. p 27–38.

Vishmidt, Marina (2006). Twilight of the Widgets. In: *Curating Immateriality: The work of the curator in the age of network systems.* Edited by Joasia Krysa (2006). Databrowser03. p 39–62.

35

EMBROIDERY PIRATES AND FASHION VICTIMS: TEXTILES, CRAFT AND COPYRIGHT

Kirsty Robertson

Editor's introduction: Kirsty Robertson is assistant professor of museum studies and contemporary art in the Department of Visual Arts, University of Western Ontario, Canada. She received her PhD from Queen's University in Kingston, Ontario. Her recent research concentrates on craft, wearable technology, and new economies. Here, she writes about the boom of Internet-based trade sites that have been a beneficial platform to those selling crafts but have also opened up growing concerns over the application of intellectual property (IP) protection. America's litigious culture has brought an unfortunate influence to bear on the role of copyright in the craft sector. Robertson observes that it is rumors, far more than facts and legal precedent, that influence the making and selling of craft today. Fears are driven by varied factors including a xenophobic attitude to the impact of Chinese textile trade in the post–Multifiber Arrangement (MFA) era and a long-standing lack of economic value granted to the labor of women.

If you copy or scan a copyrighted pattern and share it with anyone, by posting the pattern on-line, sending it by email or instant message, or even giving a paper copy to someone else, you are engaging in criminal behavior: THEFT! You are stealing money from the designer who made the pattern, the publisher who published the pattern, the shop that sells the pattern and everyone who worked hard to create the pattern for you to enjoy. You may think you are being generous by sharing a copied pattern with someone who perhaps can't afford to buy it, but you are really sharing someone else's property that you don't have the right to share. It would be like you taking money from a bank and handing it out to others—you may feel generous and others may praise you for your kindness, but you are giving them what you don't own and you have stolen it to give to others. Just as every movie has a warning that copying it is a punishable criminal federal offence, copyright theft of craft patterns shares the same punishment! You could end up in court, paying damages and stiff fines and even spend time in jail.—Think about it—Is it really worth it for you to break the law and risk the possible consequences? (Leck 1999)

"Craft designs 4 u," the website where the above quote was published, encourages crafters to: 1. Understand the law, 2. Obey the law and

Source: Kirsty Robertson, "Embroidery Pirates and Fashion Victims: Textiles, Craft and Copyright," *Textile* 8, no. 1 (2010) pp. 86–111. Reproduced with permission.

3. 8 . . . vord. "If you choose to steal, you are c . . . .g to hurt yourself and many other people," the website concludes (Leck 1999).

The hyperbole of the above statement might seem somewhat out of context when taking into account its subjects—US American amateur cross-stitchers—but it is in fact just one of hundreds of such websites that have appeared over the last several years, exhorting and occasionally threatening crafters to get in line with "international copyright law." Such statements are coming neither out of case law nor out of any national or international intellectual property (IP) laws aimed directly at crafters. Rather, they appear to be much more organic, coming from makers themselves. Debates over copyright within crafting communities are particularly thorny, jumping as they do from notions of a common shared history that should be open and welcoming to all, passing through the idea that as a gendered pastime crafting is regularly devalued—something its practitioners should work against—and concluding with more recent arguments that there are lucrative opportunities for professional crafters and designers that need to be protected through the copyrighting, patenting and trademarking of designs and processes.

In this article I analyze the appearance and spread of an intimidating lexicon of copyright protection in the (online) craft world. I argue that the rising interest in copyright and craft needs to be seen not only in the light of growing visibility and marketability for crafting practice online, but also in terms of the positioning of IP as an increasingly important economic strategy for Global North nations. So too, a transition from an ethos of community-based practice to one of individual property rights can be read as a part of ongoing debates over copyrighting (or lack thereof) for fashion designers, regulations concerning craft and textiles as protected national property in indigenous, developing and transitional economies, the changing global textile industry and further debates over open source software and anti-copyright activism. My purpose here is not to lay out how intellectual property rights (IPRs) should be understood by crafters and it is certainly not to define the legal rights and extents of infringement for craft workers. Rather, I am much more interested in how a reiteration of (often incorrect or unsupported) norms is creating a strong atmosphere of policing and protection that contrasts with more traditional understandings of crafting.[1] I ask: is this the transition of a gendered economy formerly on the outskirts to a competitive one very much at the center of the "new economy" and the creative industries? Or is this the loss of a traditional economy based on sharing that offered important ways of rethinking, contesting and undermining the weaknesses of capitalism and the current IP system?

THE RIGHT TO CRAFT

The online crafting world is an amorphous one, loosely connected through traditional knitting and crafting circles, craft fairs and bazaars and more recently through a resurgence of youthful knitters and a burgeoning number of crafting instructional websites, photo blogs, marketplaces such as Etsy.com, pattern resources and personal craft-oriented diary-like blogs. Poised between the new and trendy and the traditional, contemporary amateur crafting maintains popularity across lines of age, income and political affiliation (though gender divisions remain).[2] It is also international, although many of the most popular sites are American-dominated. The US American-centrism of many of these sites perhaps explains why, although copyright protection is nationally defined, on most crafting sites (American or otherwise) it is nonetheless a US American model of infringement and protection that is distributed.

As I explore in the second half of this section, understandings of copyright have become increasingly calcified and rights-driven within this community. Though IP protection has arguably been a concern for crafters, quilters and pattern makers for some time, it is really only over the past two to three years that the emphasis of online discussion has changed from how to protect the community ethos of crafting to how to avoid IP infringement and protect oneself from possible theft.[3] Blogger Idaho Beauty notes this sea change, writing:

> Copyright is not a big part of quilting's tradition. Quilter's are better known for sharing, copying another's work partly out of admiration, freely using the wealth of block patterns and applique [sic] motifs passed through many generations of quilters, being inspired by someone else's idea and racing home to run with it. It was all so innocuous until big money and careers were suddenly at stake. This is not to say that I deny all claims of copyright a modern quilter may make. I only state this to show how the culture of quilting has changed [over] the last 20 or so years and to note how it has cast a certain pall and uneasiness over a number of quilters. There are still those quilters oblivious to copyright issues, but there are many more that now fear that anything they do might infringe if it ends up as a raffle quilt or gets entered into a show with cash prizes. We no longer can show our admiration of a pattern or a teacher through emulation without wondering if we are crossing a line that will get us sued. Many of us are genuinely confused and some of the joy has been taken out of our craft. (Idaho Beauty 2007)

Idaho Beauty's wistful comments speak to a belief that an integral element of quilting is tied up in its community ethos—something that is threatened by the seemingly inevitable implementation of copyright regimes and the consequent fear of being "caught" copying. Notably, the blog entry was written in 2007, by which time major websites such as Etsy.com and Craftster.org had created a significant marketplace for handmade goods and, in so doing, had also become important sources for information on copyright and the protection of IP.

Etsy.com is a particularly interesting example. Launched in 2005, Etsy is essentially an online marketplace for handmade goods and independent sellers, now boasting hundreds of thousands of sales per month and profits in the hundreds of millions of dollars. In some ways Etsy mobilizes the DiY zeitgeist that was such an important part of the punk, riot grrrl and anti-globalization movements. But, in other ways it provides the perfect pathway for such movements to become commoditized. Etsy.com, for example, displays a sort of micro-capitalism that fits immensely well with the cultural turn of capitalism in the 1990s and into the twenty-first century.[4] And in turn, IPRs have played an essential role in developing and maintaining what has become known as "cultural capitalism" (Rifkin 2000). At the time of writing, Etsy.com, for example, had more that 850 active discussion threads concerning copyright (and only three concerning alternative models such as Creative Commons) (Etsy.com, 2009). On these discussion boards and other sites, explanations of copyright tend to group around a few "accepted" rules drawn from sources such as the US Digital Millennium Act and rulings on illegally downloaded music. With regard to craft, it should be noted, these interpretations are often incorrect, overstated or are not supported by case law.

Common statements about copyright or IP include the following. First, it is noted, "[c]opyright protects 'original works of authorship' that are fixed in a tangible form of expression" (Purple Kitty 2009). Patterns, step-by-step instructions, charts and accompanying photographs are protected. This is often supplemented by a warning that the publisher or designer maintains ownership of the IP of the copyrighted design and thus the rights owner must grant permission before any pattern can be copied. In addition, permission must be granted before any finished project made from the copyrighted pattern can be sold. Commercial sale often becomes the bugbear while personal use is allowed (even garments made from free patterns, crafters are repeatedly told, cannot be sold without permission).[5] Nevertheless, crafters are informed that some autonomy remains—ideas or techniques are not covered by copyright law (although techniques can be patented) and "as long as you do not copy another designer's work, you may use a similar idea or the same techniques to create something new and unique" (Purple Kitty 2009). And finally, public domain, it is repeated, is open to all. Confusion often arises over what constitutes public domain (as the seventy-year rule is not necessarily clear with regard to certain designs and does not apply in all countries). Crafters are assured that it is illegal to copy a sweater seen in a department store or to sell goods made with fabric that has a trademark on it (in fact, precedent shows that neither of these is the case) (Steiner 2003). One cannot copy a quilt viewed at a county fair, to the point that many fairs and displays actually forbid the taking of photographs without express permission (Rolfe n.d.). Stories are regularly circulated about quilting groups forced to pay up after using a pattern without paying its designer and about knitting designers coming down hard on eBay sellers advertising sweaters made from their patterns (Girl from Auntie 2005). In almost all cases, owner rights are privileged over user rights.

According to Laura Murray and Samuel Trosow (2007: 1–2) this is fairly typical of responses to IP. They write, "Most people . . . see copyright law . . . as static: some things are illegal, some things are legal and the judge will tell us which is which." And yet, this is not necessarily the case. Murray and Trosow argue that the law is, in fact, not at all static, but continuously developing and changing. In terms of the craft world, they suggest: "In practical terms, hobbyists probably have little to fear in terms of litigation. Even if a rights holder did object to the use of a design, there would be little hope for gain and a large chance of bad publicity in pursuing a lawsuit. When it falls to the individual to decide how to act in situations of dispute, the decision would probably be based as much on ethical considerations and community norms as on legal precedent" (Murray and Trosow 2007: 107). But it is precisely those community norms that are currently in flux. On

Etsy and Craftster.org can be found numerous discussions generally steering makers away from using trademarked or copyrighted goods (for example, images from the Twilight movie or Disney characters) and just as many accounts of crafters looking for support when faced with others (individuals and businesses) copying their designs. The latter is in fact a significant problem—and one that might have been brought into being by sites such as Etsy and Craftster.

Nevertheless, what are arguably three of the most publicized cases concerning crafting and copyright are all, in contrast to calls for greater protection, centered on defending a community ethos. The response to the restriction on use of Amy Butler's fabrics and the trademarking of the term "Stitch and Bitch" by the company Sew Fast/Sew Easy (SFSE) clearly demonstrate a vocal and well-organized counter-narrative to strict IP regulation (even if, in the first case, misunderstandings of how copyright works might ultimately have been counterproductive). The third case, that of the "embroidery pirates" and the Embroidery Software Protection Coalition, can also be seen as an example of how copyright protection is seen to infringe upon the rights of makers. Each of these cases also presents the complexity of IP—none (except for possibly the SFSE case) are a straightforward instance where either wholesale protection or sharing could have avoided the controversy.

In the first case, designer Amy Butler's fabrics, which are extremely popular amongst crafters and independent creators, were sold with a warning that products made from the fabrics could not be used for resale. Such a warning is fairly typical and can often be found stamped on fabrics. For crafters who had been widely using Butler's fabrics in quilts, bags, stuffed animals, clothing and upholstery . . . the warning was greeted with a great deal of resentment, an effort to boycott Butler's fabrics and a vocal debate around the quashing of creativity implicit in such announcements (Dudnikov 2009; Kight 2006). Butler quickly assured readers that her warning was only for fabrics bought wholesale and that she was in support of work done by independent crafters. Nevertheless, the backlash against Butler grew so quickly that a message on her website now states in capital letters that YES her fabrics can be used in the manufacture of finished goods for sale and that "We tried to keep the designs exclusive for the small and independent retailers and manufacturers but it caused more confusion than help. We are opening the line usage to everyone. So large manufacturers and small can now use the fabrics whether or not they buy it wholesale or retail" (Butler n.d.). Thus, what appears to be a victory for independent workers is, in fact, because of the confusion surrounding Butler's position, a victory for larger companies.[6] Butler's history of selling only to small independent retailers and of refusing to sell to discount chains, is thus contradictorily interpreted on the one hand as encouraging the craft community, but on the other as a sort of elitism exemplified by the protection of her IP in her pattern designs, her apparent discouragement of the resale of her patterns and fabrics on eBay and her trademarking of her name (so that, for example, a teddy bear made from Amy Butler fabric cannot be advertised as an "Amy Butler" teddy bear). Interestingly, however, though Butler allowing the use of her fabric for resale was seen as a victory for crafters she has recently again come under attack—this time for using vintage public domain patterns as inspiration without changing them enough to constitute originality in the minds of some bloggers (Dorie 2006). Interesting too is the fact that the trajectory of these controversies—from not being open enough to not being original enough—traces also the incursion of narrower definitions of copyright into the online crafting world.

A second case includes a boycott of the company Sew Fast/Sew Easy (SFSE), whose targeting of Café Press accounts and Yahoo discussion groups using a variant of the trademarked term "Stitch & Bitch Café" provoked a great deal of ire and a well-organized protest campaign.[7] In 2000, SFSE filed a service mark application for the term "Stitch & Bitch Café," which was registered in 2002.[8] It was not until June of 2005, however, that SFSE filed a trademark application for "Stitch and Bitch," pertaining to certain sewing supplies, patterns and goods.[9] Slightly earlier, in May 2004, Debbie Stoller, author of the extremely popular line of *Stitch 'n Bitch* books . . . , filed four trademark applications for specific goods (such as a potential television show, knitting kits and books) using the term "Stitch 'n Bitch." Inspired by the *Stitch 'n Bitch* publications, the title quickly became a popular designation for a social network of knitters who met in various cities to chat and craft and maintained links across the Internet (Krementz 2006). This online usage drew the attention of SFSE: "Once they start walking on trademarks and brands, you have to do something," Elissa Meyrich, founder and owner of SFSE, is quoted in *The Telegraph* in 2006 (Elsworth 2006). In 2005, Café Press websites using the name "Stitch 'n Bitch" in their titles began to receive cease-and-desist letters from the webhost asking them to remove the potentially actionable material (by changing group names, for example).

Shortly thereafter www.freetostitchfreetobitch.com was formed to "make sure that the word stitch and the word bitch are free to be used by all, in any way they wish, without harassment" (Elsworth 2006). The site called for a boycott of SFSE and expressed interest in gathering examples of the use of the term "Stitch and Bitch" (or Stitch 'n Bitch) prior to 1997. Freetostitchfreetobitch.com also protested the alleged editing of user remarks (particularly negative ones) on SFSE discussion boards and forums (Veverka 2005). In July 2005, Stoller's trademark applications were refused, citing potential confusion with the "Stitch and Bitch Café" application. Shortly thereafter, Stoller filed a Petition to Cancel SFSE's trademark, arguing that the term café was widely used to describe online chat rooms and that the term "Stitch and Bitch" had been in use long before 1998. The petition and protest were successful in that in 2008 SFSE settled with Debbie Stoller—the trademark applications for "Stitch 'n Bitch" as it pertains to knitting were accepted and SFSE stopped urging Yahoo and Café Press to send cease-and-desist letters to knitting groups sporting the contested title.

A third and final case that I will mention here involves the so-called "embroidery pirates" found in the title of this article.[10] In this case the Embroidery Software Protection Coalition (ESPC)—supposedly a coalition representing business interests selling embroidery software and patterns for specialized sewing machines—began sending cease-and-desist letters to thousands of Ebay bidders who had allegedly bought counterfeit embroidery software and patterns.[11] Most of those targeted were embroiderers without significant knowledge of IP law and the actions of the ESPC led to a great deal of fear and anxiety. Targeted embroiderers posting on online discussion boards were assured that unknowingly purchasing pattern CDs that infringed copyright was not illegal (although this claim was contested by a number of posters).[12] Even as those discussions were gaining steam, the ESPC began sending out letters contending that infringers might face costs of "$30,000.00 per design, not per CD. Additionally, the Court has discretion to increase the amount of statutory damages to $150,000.00 for each Copyright violated if the infringement was willful" (Foster 2006).[13] Upon phoning the number on the letter for the ESPC legal department, embroiders were told that they could "pay a nominal monetary sum to the ESPC for your past wrongful conduct." That sum was $300. Though a number of designers also posted on the same discussion boards, claiming that counterfeiting ate their profits, most of those posting felt that they had unknowingly bought the CDs and therefore should not be held culpable. Wrote one poster, "They were all about the same

price, How was I to know they were pirated? I never would have purchased if I had known" (patnnancy 2006).

As the ESPC's campaign heated up, those who had been targeted continued posting in online forums. In June 2006, the ESPC sent a subpoena to Yahoo Inc. (which hosted one of the forums), demanding the identities of posters be revealed so as to consider suing them for defamation (Searcey 2006: A1). Dionne Searcey (2006: A1), writing in the *Wall Street Journal* noted, "In its legal filings, [the ESPC] likened some of the stitchers' online screeds to 'terrorist activities' and accuses them of posting slanderous statements 'that marched across the Internet bulletin boards and chat groups similar to Hitler's march across Europe.'" In the same article, Gary Gardner, head of the ESPC argues, "Although they're a grandma, they're not a nice grandma . . . Some of them are outright vicious, even when we point out to them what they're doing is illegal" (Searcey 2006: A1). Eventually, the Electronic Frontier Foundation intervened on behalf of the Yahoo posters and the suit was dropped (McSherry 2006). The ESPC continues to send cease-and-desist letters to eBay bidders who have bought (possibly) counterfeit designs.

Though some of the information around this case might make it seem like a joke or a scam, it was not. In spite of the tactics of the ESPC and the idea that "they are targeting the Grandmothers of America!!!!!!" (patnnancy 2006), news coverage tended to divide between those who felt sympathy for the "grannies" and those who advocated for the ESPC's "no mercy" stance on piracy. Coverage in *Forbes Magazine* sympathizes with Gary Gardner (who also owns Great Notions Embroidery, one of the main businesses behind the ESPC). In the article, the claim is made that Great Notion's profits dropped by half when their patterns were illegally posted online by an Alberta-based company (Schoenberger 2000). Suing is described as the only practical way of halting such rampant counterfeiting practices.

The three cases described above raise questions not only about community norms in the online crafting world, but also about issues of class, age and political affiliation. Although no empirical research exists, an initial survey of posters on these three events reveals both differences and similarities in response. Both Amy Butler and *Stitch 'n Bitch* tend to be associated with a new generation of crafters who often embrace third-wave feminism and who successfully organized protests against what were seen as incursions by big business into the crafting world. By contrast, in the ESPC case, where the targets tended to self-describe as older and further removed from "craftivist" practices associated with the aforementioned venues, there are few attempts to organize a strategic response and an overwhelming wish to perceive ESPC as a scam and therefore as illegitimate. The "vicious grannies" described by Gardner are, more accurately, those hoping to demonstrate that the law is on their side. There was very little questioning IP law itself—something that characterized all three cases. Those behind the freetostitchfreetobitch website, for example, were careful to state that they were not against IP protection *per se*, only in the specific case where a seemingly generic term was removed from the community. In situations where IP protections are contested (or when the fluidity of the law is used to the advantage of "copyright trollers," or those *looking* for possible infringement) the answer has been largely to advocate for tighter and clearer restrictions. The Butler case demonstrates that there is not necessarily agreement in all situations, but given that the *vast* majority of posts on Etsy.com and Craftster.org advocate a "why do something that could get you in trouble" kind of mentality, the likelihood of other non-IP protection models coming out of such sites seems slim to none.

The gendering of craft make these arguments even more difficult, as there is also (particularly in pre-2006 cases) an underlying assumption that those making handmade goods (often women), should not expect to make money from their craftwork, so that fighting to receive payment for IP is somehow tainted, belligerent and beyond the bounds of acceptable practice. Such was the case for Amy Butler. When this transfers to industry, the same arguments do not work. In coverage sympathetic to the ESPC copyright is written about as if it is an inalienable right. And in turn, in coverage sympathetic to the perpetrators, that is, the embroidery pirates, they are described as "victims" rather than activists and their political efficacy is almost always undermined through further stereotyping and ageism. These are "sweet little old ladies," grandmothers and stay-at-home-moms, described as cloistered handworkers whose peace has been invaded by the nasty world of copyright. The fact that the patterns involved in the majority of cases are created for computer-operated, technologically sophisticated sewing machines is generally overlooked in favor of highlighting the fact that these women made a mistake (rather than a conscious decision). This is not a political position—it is not a position from which to advocate for alternative practices. Though portrayed as transparent, these are a complicated politics.

Nevertheless, all of these issues, alongside the three cases mentioned above have broadly changed the crafting scene. Marked with a contradictory Martha-Stewartesque-style cocooning often associated with conservative family values and a massive resurgence into "cool" crafting (that is crafting by a generally young, trend-oriented, often feminist and politically left-wing audience), questions have arisen over the relationship of crafting with interpersonal re-engagement in a technologically saturated world. In the loose network of crafters on the Internet, questions have also arisen over contemporary understandings of ownership, individuality and, indeed, private property that underlie systems of capitalist accumulation. Though semantically separate, community and individual ownership actually come together quite well in the crafting world where innovation is met in equal measure with both a system of reproduction central to crafting and also with a sort of jealousy of ownership and a burgeoning star system that vacillates between the a corporate and community ethos.

There are two things here that are of interest to me. The first is that many of the arguments spring up at the juncture of the handmade with the technological—the point where software-created patterns meet with hand-embroidery, or where handmade goods meet Etsy sales. The second is the timeline and the recent rapid increase in interest in IPRs at this particular moment in time. In the second half of this article I attempt to unravel these two interwoven points—what is it about this current moment that has brought copyright to the crafting world with such force?

CRAFTING (IP) RIGHTS

Online crafting tends to be described as if it exists in something of a theoretical vacuum and as if the actions of crafters are in no way connected to Internet communications, other debates over IPRs, or the global industries that provide the supplies with which to craft. Nevertheless, the attempt to lay down boundaries for "safe" copying to my mind cannot be separated from wider justifications for the implementation of harsh copyright legislation. The three cases noted above suggest that at least initially, codified rights protection is seen as a negative addition to crafting. The most obvious reaction is one of shock—shock that their work could be seen as infringement, shock that anyone would want to protect their fabrics from resale, shock that a corporation would try to trademark the term "Stitch 'n Bitch." And yet, in many cases that have come out since (including the ESPC) and that pepper discussion boards there is an assumption that those doing the accusing are correct, that those doing the making *need* to be protected, a combination that comes with the consequent result that crafters pay up or back off. In the online crafting world protecting one's creations has come to be solely equated

with obtaining copyright protection and in turn with supporting disciplinary strategies for "outing" copiers, counterfeiters and pirates.

Copyright is not, however, the only direction that protection in the online craft world could have taken. As Murray and Trosow (2007: 186) note, copyright is not the only tool that protects creators' and users' rights. Crafters could have followed the model of fashion design, where, at least in the USA,[14] "fashion designs fall into intellectual property's 'negative space' and derive virtually zero benefit from current legal protections" (Hedrick 2008: 216–17).[15] With very few exceptions (for example the design of printed fabric can be copyrighted) (Bronstad 2006), in the USA, fashion design can be copied because clothing is seen as a "useful article," and useful articles cannot be copyrighted (Hedrick 2008: 228).[16] While there have been numerous calls for copyright protection in the US American industry, it is just as often noted that in this sector innovation is encouraged through imitation (Hedrick 2008: 217–18).

Crafters might also have followed the open source movement, using collaboration, recirculation and sharing to create a "copyleft" practice. In such practices, which are often grouped beneath Creative Commons licenses (used by many pattern makers) the designer "retains the right to be recognized for their contributions, but do not hold exclusive economic rights and cannot block reuse of the work" (Murray and Trosow 2007: 191). While a number of crafters do make use of such systems and occasionally refuse IP protection altogether, such strategies take research, whereas the fallback position seems to be increased protection via copyright. Interestingly enough, this does work the other way—open source projects are often compared to quilting bees, while one popular Java software development tool is called "Quilt," through which software is built as a series of "patches." The anarchist poet Hakim Bey chose to use the quilting bee as an example of a "temporary autonomous zone"—a zone of communal activity outside of the disciplinary strategies of capitalism (Bey 1993).

Finally, crafters might also have tapped into movements coming primarily from developing and indigenous nations, where craft is positioned as national property or traditional knowledge and therefore outside of the norms of current IP regulation. In these cases questions of protection collide with questions of rights, royalties and limitations based on customary law (Franklin 2008: 27).[17] Though this final model is the most complex, it also could potentially capture the needs of traditional crafting communities that have changed rapidly due to Internet communications. Alternatively, crafters might have developed their own model made up of a hybrid of the three understandings I've outlined above and drawing on a strong history of collaboration prevalent in earlier associations such as the Arts and Crafts movement or the Bauhaus. However, in this case the path of least resistance appears to have been instead an unquestioning following of the example set by the music and entertainment industries, which seems actually to be the most uncomfortable fit.

At the end of this article I look very briefly at some artists and activists who have countered the language of copyright with specific anti-copyright or open source projects, but first I try to answer the question of how copyright policing entered the crafting world by outlining the background of international IP regulation that underlies many of the arguments made by the ESPC, on Etsy.com and elsewhere. Is it possible that the trend is even wider, that what is happening in the cases I have described is a watered-down side-effect of a massive effort to secure profits for the Global North via a repositioning of global trade to privilege the policing of IP? The protection of IP has for some time been a central goal for Global North powers (most notably the USA and the European Union (EU)). Piracy, counterfeiting and other forms of IP infringement have been labeled as anti-democratic behavior and in turn, the policing of counterfeiting has become an essential component of the extension of foreign investment and goodwill. Though the implications stretch much

further (and are fairly obviously tied up with the monolithic American entertainment and pharmaceutical industries), I draw out these ideas through recent changes in the textile industry, arguing that transformations made in this sector in conjunction with the construction of IP protection as a patriotic duty have vastly changed the shifting terrain of crafting practice (both online and otherwise). The global textile industry does not register in the online crafting world, but in fact, what is happening in the textile and clothing sector actually acts as a vast undercurrent to the rhetoric around homemade and crafted goods. Thus, the following comments are necessarily circumscribed but are offered as a way of opening up the conversation of what might happen to crafting practice should it fall in line with IP protection trends found in the entertainment and pharmaceutical industries.

CRAFTING INTERNATIONAL TRADE NEGOTIATIONS

In 1993, at the Uruguay round of talks that established the World Trade Organization (WTO), negotiations to set up a transnational body for economic consultation faltered over the trade in textiles. At that time, trade in textiles and clothing was largely governed by the unwieldy set of thousands of bilateral quota agreements grouped under the Multifibre Arrangement (MFA) (MacDonald 2006: 21, 24).[18] The original MFA (which came into being in 1974, though it had roots long before that) had essentially been instituted to protect textile industries in developed countries from developing country exporters, who could produce textiles and apparel at cheaper costs (MacDonald 2006: 21). In order for the WTO to come into being (something the USA and the EU very much wanted) some concessions had to be made and phasing out the MFA to allow for greater market access for developing and transitional nations was a crucial concession. Quotas, it was felt, slowed down development. The USA and EU conceded, but in exchange for looser investment requirements and, importantly, new international rules protecting IP (McGarvey 2004: 15). The quota system was changed over a ten-year process and at the end of 2004, the WTO's Agreement on Textiles and Clothing (ATC) superseded the MFA, removing all quantitative trade restrictions on textiles and clothing for all WTO members (Audet 2007: 267). The ATC was meant to both protect some sections of US and EU textile and clothing production while also creating textile sectors in emergent economies. What was not foreseen in 1993, however, was the developing economic prowess of China, China's acceptance into the WTO in 2001 and particularly the strength of the Chinese textile sector, which was built up partly in anticipation of the end of the MFA (Ross 2005: 50; Rushford 2004: 32).[19]

Between 2004 and 2006, Chinese textile exports to the USA increased as much as 118% (Susman and Schneider 2008: 492).[20] In 2005 alone, textile imports from China grew at the extraordinary rate of 97% (Jackson 2007: 587). The speed with which China (and India, although India is less often a scapegoat) have monopolized the post-MFA textile sector has created a great deal of anxiety, often filtered through xenophobic narratives that pit China's recent economic performance as dependent upon the decline of the USA. Contrasting Americans toasting in the New Year with Chinese workers lined up outside 3,000 new textile factories set to open at midnight on December 31, 2004, Ayelish McGarvey (2004: 15) argued that:

> once quotas are lifted, China will take over $220 billion in world garment trade—one of the biggest short term transfers of wealth ever. If China captures its anticipated new market share—including an estimated 50 per cent of the U.S. market—30 million textile- and apparel-manufacturing jobs will disappear worldwide, including an estimated 650,000 in the USA.

McGarvey continues, in his notably incendiary article, pointing out that such a transfer of wealth

could result not only in a loss of jobs in the USA, but (in his opinion) in global destabilization. He (2004: 16) argues:

> China's monopolizing of the world market in record speed will effectively yank the textile industry out of Turkey, explains AMTAC Director Augustine Tantille. "Pull those 4 million jobs out of Turkey and the huge export earnings as well. The Turkish economy destabilizes and the nation experiences political unrest . . . What in the world are we thinking?" he nearly shouts into the phone during an interview. "Are we going to willingly create a breeding ground for terrorists who prey on hopelessness and unrest?"

Though potential destabilization is linked here with nascent terrorism, the more obvious response has been a desperate attempt to sign trade agreements with the USA, putting export agreements in place and eliminating tariffs on textiles and garments before the 2004 deadline. "For us, [a free-trade pact with the USA] is a question of life or death," said Jesus Canahuati, president of the Honduran Maquiladora Assn., an industry group representing clothing manufacturers (Magnusson et al. 2003: 54). Preferential treatment and yarn-forward regulations (meaning that clothing sewn elsewhere can be imported to the USA duty-free so long as the fabric was woven in the USA) have been important parts of trade deals with Jordan, Singapore, Chile, Morocco, Australia and other African and Caribbean partners. Each has the purpose, according to Rushford (2004: 33), of creating a disadvantage for Asian textile manufacturers.

However, the strength of Chinese textile and clothing manufacture suggests that such responses are temporary at best. In the wake of the MFA, there are not many trade weapons left in the arsenal. After all, the USA and the EU spearheaded the formation of the WTO and agreed to the phasing out of the MFA. In fact, both used the MFA as a bargaining chip to better position their own nations, economies and multinational corporations (who, it should be noted, have largely benefited from a post-MFA situation) (Jackson 2007: 587). It has been noted that prices on goods no longer covered by quotas have fallen by 30% and that buyers from major multinationals such as Nike and the Gap "have been flocking to China in anticipation of the end of the quota regime" in a process that further forces down prices and labor standards (Magnusson *et al.* 2003). These too are a complicated politics. As Andrew Ross notes, any US American threats of a trade war (in order to be seen to be dealing with the link between the "China threat" and job losses) are largely bluster. He writes, "Allowing China to enter the WTO had been sold at home as the best way to get American-made goods into the China market, thereby boosting domestic manufacturing jobs. But it had become clear that the real agenda was to boost the returns of corporate investments in China itself through access to the China market for their own China-made products" (Ross 2006: 86–7).[21] Out of the trade situation created by the end of the MFA have emerged two strategic discourses that I argue feature prominently in the rhetoric that has filtered back to the crafting world—piracy and cheap (meaning badly made and occasionally dangerous) products. In turn, suggested solutions have been IP protection and locally- or handmade goods.

Not just in the USA and the EU, but globally, copyright has been called in to protect national industries, often national textile industries. Implementing anti-piracy legislation also has the added incentive of placing developing and transitional countries onside with EU and US strategies for future economic growth through profits derived from the protection of IPRs. Countries hoping to sign bilateral trade agreements with the USA and the EU (the same agreements that might save domestic textile and garment industries) have had to come in line with international copyright legislation as laid out by the WTO Agreement on Trade-Related Aspects of IP Rights (TRIPs). In fact, James Surowiecki (2007: 52), writing in *The*

New Yorker, argues (referring to national copyright legislation) that increasingly, "countries use free-trade agreements to rewrite the laws of their trading partners."

To all intents and purposes, given that the vast majority of protected IP is produced in Global North countries, such legislation can be seen as giving the Global North economic advantages that were threatened by the flight of manufacturing South and East. For example, in the early 1990s (notably before the end of the MFA), under pressure, Indonesia allowed greater access for the American film industry in exchange for a 35% increase in US quotas for Indonesian textile exports. The result was a brief interlude of extra exports followed by the demise of the Indonesian film industry and, eventually, the move of textile production to other, cheaper markets (Nostbakken and Morrow 1993: 82–3; Smiers 2003: 104–5). In November 2006, Russian trade officials agreed to "significantly upgrade" their IP protections in exchange for membership in the WTO (Dames 2007: 16). Meanwhile, Australia, Korea, the East African Community, Nigeria, Thailand and Indonesia are just some of the many countries and communities that have recently attempted to tackle counterfeiting and piracy.

Increasingly, counterfeiting and copying are described in the mainstream press as if they are *only* harmful to local economies (although access to generic medications, for example, would show this not to be the case). The influx of counterfeit products had, according to Nigerian Senator Jubril in 2008, led to the closure of 150 Nigerian companies with the result that "the textiles industry in the country had reduced from 175 to 20 [companies], . . . it has also dropped from a staff strength of 250,000 to 24,000 and it cannot cope because our products are copied in China and sold back to us" (*This Day* 2008). In Thailand in May 2009 as I was writing this article, pirated products were violently removed from the Patpong night market in Thailand. "We need to . . . eradicate pirating. These items are destroying many industries—textiles, fashion, shoes and entertainment—causing a loss of tens of billions of baht," Alongkorn Ponlaboot (Deputy Minister of Commerce) said (*The Nation* 2009).

Luke Eric Peterson, a senior member of the Canadian-based International Institute of Sustainable Development notes that bilateral agreements tend to "do a great job of protecting investment (property rights, contracts, IP) but do not provide protection for other human rights nor do they place countervailing responsibilities on foreign investors" (Senser 2007: 13). In such agreements patent and copyright holders are granted stronger protection for longer periods of time, which can affect national health care plans, the protection of national culture, reduced access to new technologies and so on and so forth. The idea is that protection encourages innovation—if drugs, for example, could be copied immediately there would be no incentive to invest in research and development (Surowiecki 2007: 52). Arguably, such protections also do the opposite, keeping costs extremely high, undermining competition, limiting innovations that build one on the other, "it also encourages companies to use patents as tools to keep competitors from entering new markets" (Surowiecki 2007: 52). And, in the case of local textile production—anti-piracy initiatives have been shown to be largely ineffective (Rabine 2002).

Nevertheless, the liberalization of trade, coupled with anti-piracy and anti-counterfeiting initiatives have come to be coupled with economic patriotism in the USA. A recent IP Rights Enforcement Act, introduced by Senator Evan Bayh of Indiana argues that tighter IP legislation would "safeguard the economic health of the U.S. and the health and safety of U.S. citizens" (*US Fed News Service* 2007). Text from the proposed legislation suggests that, "The greatest economic assets of the USA are its innovators, entrepreneurs and workers." If this is the case, then such assets need to be protected, particularly if Senator Bayh is correct in stating that counterfeiting and piracy cost US businesses and creative workers billions

of dollars a year, result in hundreds of thousands of lost jobs and "Terrorist groups have used the sale of counterfeit goods to finance their activities" (*US Fed News Service* 2007). Such rhetoric is supported by the United States Department of Justice which notes on its website that,

> Intellectual property ("IP") is critical to the vitality of today's economy. IP is an engine of growth, accounting for an increasing share of jobs and trade. In 2002, the core copyright industries alone were estimated to account for 6% or more of U.S. GDP and in 2005 the overall value of 'intellectual capital' of U.S. businesses—including copyrights, trademarks, patents and related information assets—was estimated to account for a third of the value of U.S. companies, or about $5 trillion. (United States Department of Justice 2009)

This kind of thinking has its roots in the recent Republican government's pursuit of trade liberalization, made possible through the 2001 granting to President Bush of Trade Promotion Authority (TPA), legislating him to "fast track" international economic negotiations (for example being able to speed trade agreements through Congress without possible amendments or committee hearings). If this seems disconnected from craft and copyright, the argument might become clearer when Ian Jackson notes that TPA legislation was passed against a backdrop of the 2001 attacks in Washington and London. Jackson (2007: 575) argues that the Bush government "linked the expansion of international trade with winning the war on terror."[22] The attack on the World Trade Center was painted as "a symbolic attack on American economic values," and economic expansion assumed a moral dimension (Jackson 2007: 575). "Trade, moreover, would be summoned to promote American values and interests across the global system" (Zoellick 2001; Jackson 2007: 576). In turn, copyright protection, which is actually far removed from liberalized, barrier-free trade or *laissez-faire* economics and that actually promotes a great deal of government intervention, has come to be seen as acceptable as an essential component of such economic nationalism. A lack of protection is now seen to leave makers completely open to piracy (on small and large scale) and crafters are repeatedly encouraged to both protect themselves and avoid anything that might hint at unlawful copying.

In turn, accusations of unfair competition practice are regularly leveled against Chinese manufacturers. The regulation of the yuan to the US dollar, the strict regulation of foreign imports to China, subsidized production of textiles and nationally owned textile factories (for example, electricity is often paid), start-up loans that are actually subsidies, low labor cost and the occasional substitution of high-grade for low-grade materials are all cited as instances where Chinese textile manufacturers are seen to have unfair advantage (McGarvey 2004: 16). For example, in 2005, shortly after the ATC had been implemented, the European Parliament held a session on unfair competition and "mainland China's perceived failure to comply with social and environmental standards and infringements of Intellectual Property Rights (IPRs)" (European Parliament 2005). Environmental and social standards of production are repeatedly used to explain the strength of Chinese textile manufacturing, while further attempts are also made to impose minimum standards (thus raising costs). It is difficult to say whether this is about raising labor or environmental standards, or about maintaining current markets for Global North products.

To bring this back to online crafting, copyright is discussed in parallel to scandals over the use of lead paint on children's toys made in Chinese factories and the discovery of melamine in children's milk in China—both scandals that received a great deal of coverage on Etsy.com and other crafting sites. There are also numerous threads discussing the change in exports, that is, the vast number of crafting products (fabrics, buttons, needles, scrapbooking supplies and so on) coming from Asia. Often such actions are translated into encouragement to buy locally and to buy handmade.[23] So too, since the "Global economic crisis" of 2008–9, crafters have encouraged a return to the homemade as a thrifty response to economic downturn. Though the economic crisis had deep roots in the ballooning American deficit under the Bush regime, uncontrolled consumer spending and spiraling consumer debt, dependence on foreign oil imports and an unsustainable trade deficit (Jackson 2007: 573), there is a sense that the economy can be saved through handmade goods and thriftiness. And in turn, the ability to make money off handmade goods and to stimulate the economy brings with it the necessity of IP protection.

In the final section of this article, I look at several craft projects that have dealt with IP from different perspectives. First, however, what I hope I have made clear is how the debates over copyright in online craft forums have roots that stretch far outside of the craft world itself, reflecting current economic policy and occasionally xenophobic understandings of the growing economic prowess of China. I link this also to the centrality of IP within recent trade negotiations.[24] While the community organization and debate that grew around the use of Amy Butler fabrics for resale and attempts to quash the use of the term "Stitch 'n Bitch" both suggested efforts to keep the craft world open to sharing and borrowing, gradually a much more rights-oriented discourse has emerged. Often the two coexist in interpretations of craft as a traditional activity whose practitioners require protection in a contemporary world. My argument is that, as IPRs have gained publicity through the music industry and other sources, and as the global trade in IP has grown, such rhetoric has come to be seen as more comfortably related to craft production than it might otherwise have been. Perhaps it should not be surprising then, that projects that do specifically and critically consider IP and craft often do so by returning to the more traditional interpretations of craft as a gendered pastime reliant on sharing and interchange.

EPILOG

To conclude this article, I tie the elements of this argument together with a brief discussion of a few "craftivist" projects that have specifically dealt with issues of IP. Though none of them engage far beyond the idea that craft has a history of sharing, all of them do intervene (inadvertently or not) in the situation that I have described above. Groups such as Knitta—the knitting graffiti artists—and Microrevolt, who knit corporate logos to draw attention to sweatshop labor, have kept far away from anything to do with copyright in the crafting world, but they do focus their ire on the well-known branded logos of massive multinational corporations. Both use open source software—Microrevolt with their knitpro tool that converts images to knitting or cross-stitch patterns and Knitta with their shared patterns for parking meters . . . and door cozies. The sharing of patterns is, in fact, an important component of many radical knitting groups, among them the Canadian Revolutionary Knitting Circle, with its freely circulated patterns for peace socks, armbands and banners. Nowhere, however, on any of these sites is copyright in particular questioned.

This is not the case with Ele Carpenter's *Open Source Embroidery Project*. Begun in 2005, the project examines the relationship between textile arts such as embroidery, knitting and weaving and open source computer programming. All, for example, rely fundamentally on binary codes and, as Carpenter writes, have at their base "gendered obsessive attention to detail; shared social process of development; and a transparency of process and product" (Carpenter 2005). Carpenter describes the project as follows:

> Embroidery is constructed (mostly by women) in hundreds of tiny stitches which are visible on the front of the fabric. The system of the stitches is revealed on the back of the material. Some embroiderers seal the back of the fabric, preventing others from seeing the underlying structure of the pattern. Others leave the back open for those who want to take a peek. A few integrate the backend process into the front of the fabric. The patterns are shared amongst friends in knitting and embroidery "circles." Software is constructed (mostly by men) in hundreds of tiny pieces of code, which form the hidden structure of the programme or interface. Open Source software allows you to look at the back of the fabric and understand the structure of your software, modify it and distribute it. The code is shared amongst friends through online networks. However the stitches or code only make sense to those who are familiar with the language or patterns. The same arguments about Open Source vs Free Software can be applied to embroidery. The needlework crafts also have to negotiate the principles of "freedom" to create, modify and distribute, within the cultural and economic constraints of capitalism. The Open Source Embroidery project simply attempts to provide a social and practical way of discussing the issues and trying out the practice. Free Software, Open Source, amateur and professional embroiderers and programmers are welcome to contribute to the project.

The project developed into the HTML patchwork, which, . . . was "comprise[d] of 216 fabric patches individually embroidered with their websafe colour codes and stitched into a collective patchwork quilt" (Carpenter 2005). In an interview at furtherfield.org, Carpenter notes,

> . . . the project has many aspects: It is a collaboration . . .; a facilitated social network; and a skill-share experience based on sharing rather than "training." It's also a way for me to make things that are useful in articulating my research valuing objects as social processes, whether this is embroidery or software. I think the shift from purchasing a "finished product" to investing in an ongoing developmental process is really valuable to how we rethink

patterns of consumption, production and distribution. We need to find ways of connecting programming back into a craft culture. (Laccetti 2006)

Carpenter's project takes what Idaho Beauty felt was being lost from the crafting community—collaboration and sharing—and turns it into a project that celebrates the sharing inherent in another field more often thought about through strict anti-piracy commitments. The thrust of Carpenter's project seems so different from that of the "craft designs 4 u" statement quoted at the opening of this article. Yet ultimately, the combination of the two can be seen as a cross-section of a community that is itself a patchwork of differences and contrasts, made up of numerous constituencies all adapting in their own ways to the possibilities offered by the Internet. In many ways, crafting provides an excellent example of a network of entrepreneurs very much in keeping with definitions of the "flexible personality" so beloved of twenty-first-century creative entrepreneurialism (Holmes 2002). Craftworkers are innovative entrepreneurs, adapting to new possibilities and searching for ways to protect themselves within those opportunities. And yet, as hinted at by Carpenter's project, there is a significant history here of disavowal and denigration that leads me to read the incursion of copyright as just that—an incursion and an expropriation of traditional, community-based practice into a model that offers not protection but entry into the marketplace at a high price. My goal here is not to argue for a return to a (never-existing) utopian past, nor to suggest that crafters deserve no protection, but to draw attention to the fact that the current system has numerous flaws for the often precarious female workers who use craft to supplement or to make a living.

Thus, to conclude, I bring up a point that has not yet been discussed, but that should not go unnoted. The argument that I have made relating the global textile industry to the growing prevalence of discussion of copyright in crafting circles has an important corollary for those knitters, sewers and embroiderers who would describe themselves as (third-wave) feminists. Given the vast global system of trade that I see underlying and seeping into community crafting, one must ask whether protection for Global North crafters selling their wares on sites such as Etsy.com relies fundamentally on the strategic disempowerment of primarily pink-collar workers laboring in the factories that represent a post-MFA move of textile and garment production East, even as that move has aided in the replication of stricter IP negotiation. What is the role of "protection" for the many women involved at each level of this community (who is making the fabric and embroidery thread used by those subscribing to "craft designs 4 u")? To my mind, the importance of sites such as Etsy.com and of a crafting revival needs to be seen in light of such relationships, so as to create lasting change. Otherwise the result is not a greater presence of the handmade, or a renewal of feminine/feminist modes of making, but rather an extension of dubious forms of "protection" that will actually do very little to protect makers and very much to erase the particularities that make the craft scene such an interesting one to analyze.

NOTES

1. This is likely the point where I should say "I'm not a lawyer." However, part of my goal is to show how important community norms are to the way IPRs are defined within a given field. Having said that, nothing written here should be construed as legal advice.
2. Interestingly, for "craftivists" such as Betsy Greer, the ability to make links across trenchant political separations (for example, Republicans and Democrats in the USA) was a profoundly important goal of activist knitting. However, though sites such as Etsy.com cater to both the rigidly conservative and the anarchist radical, lines of political separation are maintained

through discussion boards, forums, group affiliations and purchasing choices.

3. See Lara Kriegel's article (2004) for a wonderful example of a similar copyright debate, only this time taking place in the eighteenth and nineteenth centuries.

4. Average sales on Etsy are around US$15 to $20. "95% of Etsy sellers are women (average age, 33), mostly stay-at-home moms and college students looking to supplement their income rather than make a full-time living" (Miller 2007).

5. One site notes "There is much controversy over the fact that a finished product that you make is copyrighted. It is the law, nonetheless, since it is the author's expression that you have reproduced and the fact that you have reproduced a copyrighted pattern does not eliminate the copyright protection" (Purple Kitty 2009).

6. In turn, this has led to the widespread use of Butler's fabrics and a secondary debate on whether they are now in fact overused—are Butler's fabrics classic or clichéd (Decorology 2008)?

7. For a full and detailed timeline, see www.free-tostitchfreetobitch.com.

8. The service mark covered "sewing instruction and manuals distributed in connection therewith," and "providing on-line chat rooms for the transmission of messages among computer users concerning sewing via a global computer network" (www.freetostitchfreeto-bitch.com).

9. It has also been pointed out that SFSE did use the term Stitch & Bitch Café prior to 2005 for their online discussion site, but the application was filed for Stitch and Bitch—a discrepancy that was noted and in 2006 SFSE re-filed a new drawing that included the ampersand (and therefore supported their claim that the mark had been used earlier) (Girl from Auntie 2006).

10. The case of the ESPC is a fascinating one and deserving of more attention than it has been given here. Thousands of posts online document the fear of those targeted, their unwillingness to comply with what appears to be a scam and their suggestions for addressing the situation (contacting Oprah and Bill O'Reilly, contacting major sewing and crafting corporations to express their dismay and conspiracy theories are just some of the tactics mentioned on an eBay discussion thread) (Ggsgirl 2006).

11. An earlier settlement with eBay through their vEro program allowed the ESPC access to information on the buyers. Often, when companies are caught selling pirated designs they hand over the names of buyers as part of the settlement (Searcey 2006: A1).

12. Buying the CD was not actionable, but installing it was considered a reproduction and hence was considered to be in violation—but only if the embroidery patterns were considered to be software rather than patterns. Because the specific issue had not been addressed in court, in fact, any interpretation was largely guesswork.

13. See http://www.embroideryprotection.org/faqs.html (accessed September 10, 2009) for the ESPC's interpretation.

14. This is in the USA only. A Community Design system in the EU protects designers for a minimum of three years. Similar systems exist in Japan and elsewhere. In Canada fashion design can be copyrighted so long as less than fifty items are produced (Murray and Trosow 2007: 107).

15. See, for example, Hemphill and Suk (2009) and Scafidi (n.d.).

16. Although technically clothing designs could be patented, it is generally agreed that the process to obtain a patent is longer than the shelf life of any given garment.

17. See also UNESCO/WIPO Regional Consultation on the Protection of Expressions of Folklore for Countries of Asia and the Pacific (Boateng 2008).

18. Countries that signed bilateral trade agreements with the USA before the phasing out of the MFA were often granted preferential textile export quotas. To a certain extent this has continued in the wake of the MFA although these agreements are more often geared towards protecting local and domestic textile industries from being overwhelmed by Chinese exports. Some of these agreements include NAFTA, the Caribbean Basin Initiative, the Andean Trade Preference Act, the African Growth and Opportunity Act (particularly to Kenya and Lesotho). There is also the so-far unsuccessful Free Trade Area of the Americas and the proposed Middle Eastern Free Trade Area (MEFTA) by 2013 (Jackson 2007: 578).

19. And indeed, as the ATC has come into existence, "free trade" has decimated textile industries in nations where quota systems allowed for the development of garment manufacturing industries, but where now wages cannot be set low enough to compete with labor and transport costs in places where there are both domestic textile and garment industries (Audet 2007: 269; Rushford 2004: 36).

20. There are slightly different statistics depending on which source is read. Ross (2005: 49) cites an 86% change for apparel post-MFA.

21. Ross continues, noting that this situation is made even more unbalanced by the fact that China has essentially been servicing the USA's deficit: "China's massive investment in U.S. government securities was directly financing America's current-account deficit. By purchasing Treasury bonds to the tune of hundreds of billions of dollars a year, Beijing was keeping down interest rates and funding a domestic economic recovery that was allowing Americans to go on consuming products made in China" (Ross 2006: 87).

22. The legislation passed by the narrowest of margins—215 votes to 214.

23. On Etsy.com there is a clear distinction made between the "Chinese people" and "Chinese products." Economic nationalism is seen as entirely disconnected from xenophobia and Americans are often blamed as the catalysts of overconsumption resulting in cheap goods from China.

24. IPRs are about to become of even greater importance. Set to conclude in 2010, secret negotiations are already underway for the Anti-Counterfeiting Trade Agreement (ACTA) between Canada, Australia, the EU and its member countries, Japan, Korea, Mexico, Morocco, New Zealand, Singapore, Switzerland and the USA. According to its critics, under the guise of being an anti-counterfeiting treaty, ACTA will further criminalize copyright infringement, often to the advantage of already developed countries and to the detriment of practices of sharing.

REFERENCES

Audet, Dennis. 2007. "Smooth as Silk? A First Look at the Post-MFA Textiles and Clothing Landscape." *Journal of International Economic Law* 10: 267–84.

Bey, Hakim. 1993. *The Criminal Bee* (a performance). San Francisco. http://www.evolutionzone.com/kulturezone/bey/bey.criminal.bee.html (accessed July 18, 2009.)

Boateng, B. 2008. "Local and Global Sites of Power in the Circulation of Ghanaian Adinkra." In P. Chakravartty and Y. Zhao (eds) *Global Communications: Toward a Transcultural Political Economy*, pp. 163–88. Lanham, MD: Rowman & Littlefield.

Bronstad, Amanda. 2006. "A Pattern of Suing over Patterns." *National Law Journal* March 27.

Butler, Amy. n.d. "Frequently Asked Questions." *Amy Butler Designs*. http://www.amybutlerdesign.com/faqs/ (accessed December 8, 2009).

Carpenter, Ele. 2005. "Introduction." *Open Source Embroidery*. http://www.opensource-embroidery.org.uk/osembroidery.htm (accessed December 8, 2009).

Dames, K. Matthew. 2007. "Trade Agreements as the New Copyright Law." *Online* 31: 16–20.

Decorology. 2008. "Amy Butler: Always a Classic or Already Cliché?" *Decorology: Interior Design and Decorating* August. http://decorology.blogspot.com/2008/08/amy-butler-always-classic-or-already.html (accessed December 8, 2009).

Dorie. 2006. "Belle Chrysanthemum." *Tumbling Blocks* August 10. http://tumblingblocks.blogspot.com/2006/08/belle-chrysanthemum.html (accessed December 8, 2009).

Dudnikov, Karen. 2009. "Tabberone's Trademark & Copyright Abusers' Hall of Shame." *Tabberone*. http://www.tabberone.com/Trademarks/trademarks.html (accessed December 8, 2009).

Elsworth, Catherine. 2006. "It's Getting Bitchy in Knitting Circles." *The Daily Telegraph* February 11. http://www.telegraph.co.uk/news/worldnews/northamerica/usa/1510240/Its-getting-bitchy-in-knitting-circles.html (accessed December 8, 2009).

HKTDC: Industry News. 2005. "European Parliament Pushes for Fair Trade in Textiles Sector." *HKTDC: Industry News* October 21. http://info.hktdc.com/alert/eu0521a.htm (accessed September 10, 2009).

Foster, Ed. 2006. "Embroidering on a Copyright Shakedown Theme." *The Gripelog* September 11. http://www.gripe2ed.com/scoop/story/2006/9/11/82110/2869 (accessed July 15, 2009).

Franklin, Jonathan. 2008. "Protecting Traditional Cultural Expressions." *Information Outlook* 12: 27–31.

Geist, Michael. November 3, 2009. "The ACTA Internet Chapter: Putting the Pieces Together." *Michael Geist.* http://www.michaelgeist.ca/content/view/4510/125/ (accessed December 9, 2009).

Ggsgirl. 2006. "Embroidery Software." January 3. http://forums.ebay.com/db2/topic/Hobbies-Crafts/Embroidery-Software/2000065715&start=30 (accessed July 15, 2009).

Hedrick, Lisa J. 2008. "Tearing Fashion Design Protection Apart at the Seams." *Washington and Lee Law Review* 65: 215–73.

Hemphill, C. Scott and Suk, Jeannie. 2009. "The Law, Culture and Economics of Fashion." *Stanford Law Review* 61: 1147–99.

Holmes, Brian. 2002. "The Flexible Personality: For a New Cultural Critique." *International Seminar of Class Composition in Cognitive Capitalism.* Paris: The Sorbonne. http://www.geocities.com/Cognitive-Capitalism/holmes1.html (accessed July 15, 2009).

Idaho Beauty. 2007. "Copyright, Derivative Work, Influences." *Idaho Beauty's Creative Journey.* October 13. http://idahobeautyquilts.blogspot.com/2007/10/copyright-derivative-work-influences.html (accessed July 16, 2009).

Jackson, Ian. 2007. "The Geopolitics of President George W. Bush's Foreign Economic Policy." *International Politics* 44: 572–95.

Kight, Kim. 2006. "More on Fabric and the Man." *True Up.* http://www.trueup.net/?p=22 (accessed December 8, 2009).

Krementz, Cheryl. 2006. "Stitch & Bitch Slap." *Knit 1* (Summer). http://freetostitchfreetobitch.org/pdfs/knit1.gif (accessed December 8, 2009).

Kriegel, Lara. April 2004. "Culture and the Copy: Calico, Capitalism and Design Copyright in Early Victorian Britain." *Journal of British Studies* 43(2): 233–66.

Laccetti, Jess. 2006. "Open Source Embroidery: Jess Laccetti Inquires about Ele Carpenter's Latest Work." *Furtherfield.* http://www.furtherfield.org/displayreview.php?review_id=229 (accessed December 8, 2009).

Leck, Cherie Marie. 1999. "PLEASE STOP and Consider . . . Copyright Theft HURTS!" *Craft Designs 4 You.* http://www.craftdesigns4you.com/stop2.htm (accessed December 8, 2009).

MacDonald, Stephen. 2006. "The World Bids Farewell to the Multifiber Arrangement." *Amber Waves* 4: 20–6.

McGarvey, Ayelish. 2004. "Clothes Call." *The American Prospect* 15: 15–16.

McSherry, Corynne. 2006. "Anonymity Preserved for Online Embroidery Fans." *Electronic Frontier Foundation* September 14. http://www.eff.org/press/archives/2006/09/14 (accessed July 15, 2009).

Magnusson, Paul, Balfour, Frederik and Shari, Michael. 2003. "Where Free Trade Hurts: Thirty million Jobs Could Disappear with the End of Apparel Quotas." *Business Week* December 15. http://www.businessweek.com/magazine/content/03_50/b3862007.htm (accessed September 15, 2009).

Miller, Kerry. 2007. "Etsy: A Site for Artisans Takes Off." *Business Week* June 12. http://www.businessweek.com/smallbiz/content/jun2007/sb20070611_488723.htm (accessed July 15, 2009).

Murray, Laura and Trosow, Samuel. 2007. *Canadian Copyright: A Citizen's Guide*. Toronto: Between the Lines.

Nostbakken, David and Morrow, Charles. 1993. *Cultural Expression in the Global Village*. Penang: Southbound.

patnnancy. 2006. "Embroidery Software." *Embroidery Software: eBay Discussion Forum*, posted January 6, 2006. http://forums.ebay.com/db2/topic/Hobbies-Crafts/Embroidery-Software/2000065715&start=0 (accessed July 15, 2009).

Purple Kitty. 2009. "Crochet Patterns, Knitting Patterns and Copyright Law." *Purple Kitty*. http://www.purplekittyyarns.com/info/copyright.html (accessed December 8, 2009).

Rabine, Leslie. 2002. *Global Circulation of African Fashion*. New York and London: Palgrave MacMillan.

Rifkin, Jeremy. 2000. *The Age of Access: How the Shift from Ownership to Access is Transforming Capitalism*. London: Penguin.

Rolfe, Margaret. n.d. "Copyright FAQ." http://www.quilt.com/FAQS/CopyrightFAQ.html (accessed December 8, 2009).

Ross, Adam. 2005. "Bursting at the Seams." *The China Business Review* September 1: 49.

Ross, Andrew. 2006. *Fast Boat to China: High Tech Outsourcing and the Consequences of Free Trade—Lessons from Shanghai*. New York: Vintage Books.

Rushford, Greg. 2004. "America's Dirty War on Chinese Clothing." *Far Eastern Economic Review* 168: 31–6.

Scafidi, Susan. n.d. *Counterfeit Chic*. http://www.counterfeitchic.com/ (accessed December 8, 2009).

Schoenberger, Chana R. 2000. "So Sew Me Quilting." *Forbes* December 25. http://www.forbes.com/forbes/2000/1225/6616090a.html (accessed July 15, 2009).

Searcey, Dionne. 2006. "Sewing and Suing Aren't a Happy Mix For Embroiderers." *Wall Street Journal* September 14: A1.

Senser, Robert A. 2007. "The W.T.O. in Crisis." *America* 196: 10–14.

Smiers, Joost. 2003. *Arts Under Pressure: Promoting Cultural Diversity in the Age of Globalisation*. New York: Zed Books.

Steiner, Ina. 2003. "David versus Goliath: eBay Seller Take on Corporate America." *Auction Bytes: The Independent Trade Publication for Online Merchants* August. http://www.auctionbytes.com/cab/abn/y03/m08/i05/s02 (accessed December 8, 2009).

Surowiecki, James. 2007. "Exporting IP." *New Yorker* May 14. http://www.newyorker.com/talk/financial/2007/05/14/070514ta_talk_surowiecki (accessed June 16, 2009).

Susman, Paul and Schneider, Geoffrey. 2008. "Institutional Challenges in the Development of the World's First Worker-owned Free Trade Zone." *Journal of Economic Issues* XLII: 489–99.

The Girl from Auntie. 2005. "The Alice Chronicles, Part One." *The Girl From Auntie Journals*. http://www.girlfromauntie.com/journal/index.php/2002/the-alice-chronicles-part-one/ (accessed December 8, 2009).

The Girl from Auntie. 2006. ". . . And New York Answers." *The Girl From Auntie Journals*. http://www.girlfromauntie.com/journal/index.php/category/themes/stitch-v-bitch/ (accessed December 8, 2009).

The Nation. 2009. "Piracy Crackdown to Continue Despite Violence." *The Nation*. www.nationmultimedia.com/worldhotnews/30102247/Piracy-crackdown-to-continue-despite-violence:-Alongkorn (accessed November 23, 2009).

This Day. 2008 "Nigeria, Senate Considers Sanctions against Fake Products." *Africa News* November 5: n.p.

United States Department of Justice. 2009. "Computer Crime & Intellectual Property Section." *Cybercrime*. http://www.cybercrime.gov/ipmanual/01ipma.html (accessed December 8, 2009).

US Fed News Service. 2007. "Sen. Bayh Introduces Intellectual Property Rights Enforcement Act." *US Fed News Service* February 21: n.p. http://www.encyclopedia.com/doc/1P3-1219861291.html (accessed December 8, 2009).

Veverka, Becky. 2005. "Timeline." *Free to Stitch Free to Bitch*. http://freetostitchfreetobitch.org/info.htm (accessed December 8, 2009).

Zoellick, Robert. 2001. "Countering Terror with Trade." *Washington Post* September 20: A35. http://www.peacenowar.net/Corporation-1.htm (accessed December 8, 2009).

36

THE ROMANCE OF MODERN MANUFACTURE[1]— A BRIEF HISTORY OF EMBROIDERED EMBELLISHMENT

Melanie Miller

Editor's introduction: "Mechanical Drawing: the schiffli project" was an ambitious attempt to save Britain's last surviving schiffli embroidery machine housed at the Manchester School of Art, Manchester Metropolitan University, in England. In the final months of its use, invited artists used the schiffli to create work that explored the technical potential of a machine designed to stitch in close repeat. The accompanying exhibition catalog, edited by Melanie Miller and June Hill, documents this work and the historical significance of the machine to Macclesfield's embroidery industry. In her catalog essay, Melanie Miller, a senior lecturer at Manchester Metropolitan University, outlines the historical significance of the machine and speaks about some of the strengths that mechanical production continues to enjoy in the face of growing competition from the digital world. The text reprinted here is a revised version of the original catalog essay.

THE LAST SCHIFFLI

In order to understand the significance of the schiffli machine it is necessary to have an appreciation of the history of the commercial mass-production of embroidery. It is a surprisingly complex area. A vast range of different specialist machines have been utilised over the last 180 years to create embroidered embellishment on clothing and household textiles. These machines have ranged from individually controlled machines that stitch only one item at a time, such as the Cornely and the Irish, to the machines that employ a multitude of needles to literally mass-produce embroidery. The hand embroidery machine, the schiffli machine, and the multi-head machine fall into this category.

Embroidered decoration has been a feature of clothing since early times—the first known examples are of Egyptian embroidery from the 6th century AD. Whilst embroidery was traditionally done by hand, a machine to replicate hand stitching was invented as early as 1828, pre-dating the lockstitch sewing machine by some 20 or so years. It is intriguing that the first machine capable of embroidering a piece of cloth was invented *before* a satisfactory method of machine stitching two fabrics together was resolved. The hand embroidery machine[2]—so-called since it replicated the way hand embroidery was done—was invented

Source: Melanie Miller, "The Romance of Modern Manufacture—A Brief History of Embroidered Embellishment," in Melanie Miller and June Hill, *Mechanical Drawing—The Schiffli Project* [exhibition catalog] (Manchester: Righton Press/Manchester Metropolitan University) pp. 18–25. Reproduced with permission.

Figure 36.1. Melanie Miller, *The Last Schiffli*, 2007. Embroidery on the Manchester Metropolitan University schiffli machine. Courtesy of Melanie Miller.

in 1828 by Josué Heilmann of Mulhouse, France. Heilmann "resolved to make something new and startling, yet at the same time useful. I thought men have woven and printed textiles by machinery but no one has ever embroidered by machinery. The very words 'machine embroidery' are never encountered in books on textiles—all the more reason for my endeavour".[3] It seems probable that Heilmann's mission was also fuelled by the fashion for 'flowered muslin', gossamer-fine webs of cloth embroidered by hand, white on white, a key component of the long flowing empire line gowns fashionable for women at the beginning of the 19th century.

The principle on which the hand embroidery machine operated differed from that of hand embroidery: rather than moving the needles across a piece of fabric, the piece of fabric moved to create the required pattern. The fabric was held vertically in a frame, its movement controlled by a pantograph, and a long row of double pointed needles, with an eye in the middle for the thread, stitched the design into the fabric. The needles passed right through the fabric, being held by two sets of pincers, one on each side of the fabric. The design to be stitched was enlarged by a factor of six. The machine was controlled by a single operative, who had to co-ordinate all of his/her limbs in a complex and precise operation. A wheel was turned forwards and backwards with the right hand to move the pincer bars containing the needles towards and away from the fabric. The feet operated mechanisms that opened and closed the pincers, thus releasing/grasping the needles. The left hand traced the enlarged design and thus moved the frame holding the fabric. And all the time, with each stitch, the length of thread left in the needle got shorter and shorter, so the distance the right hand travelled became marginally less and less.[4]

It might be imagined that the quality of work produced on such a machine would be crude, but in fact the work created was exquisite. The extensive output of the hand embroidery machines is not always acknowledged—since the method of production resulted in work that looked identical to hand embroidery some confusion can arise over the attribution of production method. Outputs included fine *broderie anglais* whitework and complex guipure fabrics, metallic threads on sheer chiffons, textured wools that mimicked woven structures, anything that was done by hand was replicated by machine.[5] Specialist embroidery designers understood perfectly the technology of production, and could thus exploit the creative potential available.

The hand embroidery machine was in widespread use throughout Europe from the 1830s–1950s, especially in Switzerland. Appropriately, given that Manchester is the location of the last schiffli embroidery machine in the UK, the first hand embroidery machines in the UK were located in Manchester, Henry Houldsworth purchasing two machines in 1829.

After the development of the lockstitch sewing machine in the 1840s it was inevitable that the same principle—of using two continuous threads to create a line of stitching—would be applied to embroidery. The schiffli machine was invented in Switzerland in 1863 by Isaac Groebli, and in widespread use throughout Europe and America by the 1870s. It combined the basic principles of the hand embroidery machine: long rows of needles stitching into fabric stretched over a vertical frame—with the principle of the lockstitch sewing machine, utilising a row of bobbins, or shuttle threads. The largest machines are 19 metres long, and contain 1,416 needles. Within embroidery manufacture the development of a new production method does not immediately make a previous method obsolete—use of the hand embroidery machine continued alongside the schiffli

Figure 36.2. Melanie Miller, *Costume Nation* (detail), 2006. Schiffli embroidery, 112 x 57 cm. Courtesy of Melanie Miller.

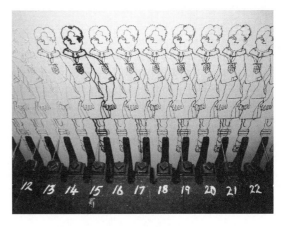

Figure 36.3. Melanie Miller, *11-11-3*. Detail of work in progress on the schiffli machine, 2006. Courtesy of Melanie Miller.

machine—many factories utilised both production methods.

Figure 36.4. Melanie Miller, *Costume Nation* (detail), 2006. Schiffli embroidery, 112 x 57 cm. Courtesy of Melanie Miller.

Initially a pantograph controlled the schiffli machine, the same pattern control method as used on the hand embroidery machine. In the first decade of the 20th century, however, a punchcard system was developed so that designs could be replicated automatically, without the need for a pantograph operator. It was costly to adapt machines to this new operating system, so many schiffli machines continued to be operated by pantograph.[6]

THE UK SCHIFFLI INDUSTRY

Used extensively in the 19th and 20th centuries in the UK for the manufacture of decorative embroidery, with a strong base in Nottingham and Macclesfield, the schiffli industry is no longer indigenous to the UK. As recently as the 1990s there were still a significant number of schiffli manufacturing companies operating in the UK. However, as with so many aspects of clothing and textile production, cheaper manufacturing costs in the Far East led to the closure of all the UK schiffli companies who were unable to compete economically with offshore production. The machine at MMU is therefore the sole remnant of what was once an important industry in the UK: it is the last working schiffli machine in the UK.

Taking up a not inconsiderable amount of workshop space, some concern has been raised in recent years as to how appropriate it is to maintain a supposedly "obsolete" machine within an

Figure 36.5. Alice Kettle, *Nepenthe*, 2007. Omnistitch, free machine stretch, schiffli embroidery, 2.5 x 2 m. Photographer: Stephen Yates, Visual Resources Centre, Manchester Metropolitan University. Courtesy of Jo Loe.

art school. The Schiffli Project was developed to highlight the significance of this unique machine both within and outside MMU, and question contemporary approaches to technology, innovation and obsolescence. Using 'mechanical drawing' as the theme, since the machine can be seen as a huge drawing machine, demonstrations and workshops were offered to staff within the faculty of Art and Design. The project grew; interesting work was being produced—it should be exhibited. As the long-term future of the machine remained uncertain, it also seemed appropriate to document work as it was produced on the machine, thus recording the schiffli process for posterity. Thanks to the dedication of support staff within MMU, the users of the machine unwittingly secured starring roles in the DVD 'Mechanical Drawing'.

Whilst the Art and Design staff came from a variety of disciplines, it also seemed appropriate to open up the use of the machine to artists from outside MMU. With the support of an Arts Council grant this became possible.[7]

THE MMU SCHIFFLI

The schiffli machine at MMU is approximately one hundred years old. It is a Plauen machine, built by Vogtlandisher Maschinenfabrik in Plauen, Germany. As schiffli machines go, it is relatively small, with "only" 86 needles, and a stitching area two metres wide. It was purchased in the mid 1970s from Hewetson, a large embroidery manufacturing company in Macclesfield, where it was used as a sample machine.

Augustus Hewetson established the Hewetson company in Macclesfield in 1898 with four hand embroidery machines. Over the next few years it was gradually expanded, with the purchase of further hand embroidery machines, and schiffli machines in 1905. In 1927 'automatic machines were installed and the firm claimed to be "the largest manufacturer of all types of embroidery in the world".'[8]

During the two world wars Hewetson was a major supplier of badges for the Allied armed forces, embroidering fifty million badges during the Second World War. By 1958 there were about 1,000 employees on several different sites. During all this time (1898–1958) the company was tightly controlled by one family, the Hewetsons. There was a change in ownership in 1982 when it joined the Berisford group. Following re-structuring of the company in 1993 Hewetson ceased to operate as a schiffli manufacturing company.

While contemporary schiffli machines are now computerised and able to offer faster production within an art school environment the pantograph schiffli machine provides a unique opportunity to be physically involved in the creation of the embroidered image. Images are created by moving a pantograph by hand. The design has to be drawn up six times larger than the finished embroidery, the operator traces around the design, pressing a trigger to make the needles shoot forwards to create the stitches. The slightest movement by the operator is mimicked, in miniature, by the thread on the cloth.

It is a very seductive process, there is something magical seeing an image simultaneously repeated twenty, thirty or forty times or more across a piece of cloth; and the rhythmic squeak as the machine progresses is quite hypnotic, if a little noisy. The machine looks intimidating—but is surprisingly easy to operate. It is an amazing, beautifully balanced piece of engineering: a huge mechanical drawing machine.

Although the potential canvas for the artists in this exhibition is relatively large—fabric two metres wide and up to two and a half metres long can be stretched into the frame—the artists have to work within certain parameters. The needles are set a fixed distance apart, and the area visible to embroider at any one time is limited to a height of about 40 centimetres. The maximum width of an image or pattern is about 13 centimetres. Colour change can only be achieved by re-threading needles, a time-consuming, backbreaking operation. The artists represented in 'Mechanical Drawing' have each approached the machine in a very individual way, bringing something of their own practice to the machine and challenging the usual pre-conceptions of commercial embroidery.

Dr Melanie Miller
Senior Lecturer
School of Design
Manchester Metropolitan University

NOTES

1. Title taken from 'The Romance of Modern Manufacture: a popular account of the marvels of manufacturing' by Charles R. Gibson, published in London, 1910. This book includes a

chapter on embroidery mass production, 'Embroidery done by steam-power', that succinctly describes the mechanisms of both the hand embroidery machine and the schiffli machine. It is interesting to note that the book is almost exactly contemporaneous with the MMU schiffli machine, and thus provides an interesting contemporary account of the automation of manual labour.

2. Also known in the US as the 'handloom', and in contemporaneous sources as the 'put-through' or 'nipper'.

3. Josué Heilmann, quoted by Patricia Wardle in 'Machine Embroidery' by Christine Risley, 1961.

4. The Appenzeller Folkskunde Museum in Stein, Eastern Switzerland, has a hand embroidery machine on which mesmerising demonstrations are periodically given.

5. The Textile Museum in St Gallen, Switzerland, has an unparalleled collection of pattern books from Swiss embroidery companies, showing the vast range of effects possible.

6. In the 1970s the punchcard system was computerised. However some schiffli manufacturers even in the 1990s were still utilising pantograph pattern control.

7. Fifteen artists took part in 'Mechanical Drawing—the schiffli project': Rowena Ardern, Jill Boyes, Nigel Cheney, Isabel Dibden Wright, Stephen Dixon, Nina Edge, Kate Egan, Roxanne Hawksley, Alice Kettle, Jane McKeating, Melanie Miller, Sally Morfill, Susan Platt, Lynn Setterington, Alison Welsh.

8. Collins L. and Stevenson M. 'Silk, Sarsenets, Satin, Steels and Stripes', The Macclesfield Museums Trust, 1994

37

ARTIST'S STATEMENT

Anna Von Mertens

Editor's introduction: Over the past decade, American artist Anna Von Mertens has used the quilt to investigate a range of statistical and historical facts. All of her work is developed as a series and is hand-stitched, hand-dyed, and large in scale. Working on such an ambitious scale for hand-stitching confirms Von Mertens's unwavering commitment to the self-imposed restrictions common to her early investigations. The *Via* series from 2001 finds color references in sources as varied as video games, Martha Stewart color charts, and the sky at specific times of the day. *As the Stars Go By* from 2006 is based on the pattern of stars in the night sky at violent moments in American history where, Von Mertens explains, "what came before seems separate from what follows." Von Mertens's articulate statement for the *Portraits* series, reprinted here, reveals a genuine integration of critical and creative thinking that informs her dedicated making.

Von Mertens graduated from Brown University in 1995 with a BA and was awarded an MFA from the California College of Arts and Crafts in 2000 in the United States.

Playing off Walter Benjamin's question of the aura in the age of mechanical reproduction, in *Portraits* I take iconic portraits from art history and interpret an actual aura for each painting. My process involves researching the relationship between sitter and painter, the character and personality of both, and the historical context of the painting. I then paint dye onto fabric to create an aura in the same proportions as the original painting. Superimposed is a layer of hand-stitching that includes the silhouette from the source painting and the subject's chakra pattern. The result is a defined figure with an aura-like emanation.

If Benjamin's "aura" is the sense of awe felt in the presence of a unique work of art, my works acknowledge the myth built around each painting as it becomes more a story of the artwork than the actual artwork itself. I remember traveling to Italy and being surprised by what some of the real paintings looked like versus what they looked like projected in my art history class. These works are so well-known the real painting and the idea of that painting become two different things. Flipping Benjamin's definition of the aura, my auras reference what is layered over the unique work of art.

Figure 37.1. Anna Von Mertens, *Kurt Cobain's Aura (Zoe's), after Elizabeth Peyton*, 2009. Hand-dyed, hand-stitched cotton, 13.75 x 11 in. Courtesy of Anna Von Mertens.

And yet my auras simultaneously uphold the opposite: they return to the original intention of a portraitist working to capture the essence of their subject. While I admit to an element of the ridiculous—painting auras of dead people—these works are sincere portraits. As I researched how to read the prescribed distinctions of the tones and placement of colors in an aura photograph, I found myself getting seduced by belief. I found that in building a narrative of the subject's life through color, an emotional presence surfaced. Allowing myself to believe seemed part of the process.

The tension of belief informs this work. The strange bed fellows of technology and New Age beliefs are brought together in the aura photograph, a process involving hand sensors that translate the electromagnetic field of an individual into a Polaroid print. Rather than question the authenticity of the aura photograph, I chose to respect the desire to investigate our existence more fully. We hold our beliefs in diverse—and precarious—ways.

As I began this series, I considered aura photographs as pure abstraction. I realized creating interpretative auras would allow me to explore abstract painting how I might not otherwise allow myself. I like that at the heart of this exploration, amid the questions of belief and representation, is a search for beauty.

38

UPCYCLING TEXTILES: ADDING VALUE THROUGH DESIGN

Rebecca Earley

Editor's introduction: In 2008 the Textiles, Environment, Design (TED) research hub based at the Chelsea College of Art and Design, London, hosted a symposium titled Upcycling Textiles: Adding Value Through Design; this was part of the Arts Humanities Research Council-funded project "Worn Again: Rethinking Recycled Textiles" (2005–2009). An excerpt from the final session of the day, led by Dr. Jo Heeley, a senior research fellow at the University of the Arts London, is transcribed here. Speakers include academics, designers, and industry representatives. What becomes clear through the course of the conversation is both the enthusiasm and commitment many have for sustainable design and also the complexity of what sustainable design is, and may be in the future. Many inspirational examples exist in the work of independent designers and small-scale businesses. While these models are useful, their impact is limited by scale. Throughout the event, Becky Earley, a reader in textiles, environment, and design based at Chelsea, called on participants to consider how to upscale "upcycling" (a term coined by William McDonough and Michael Braungart in their influential 2002 book *Cradle to Cradle: Remaking the Way We Make Things*). As this text emphasizes, dialogue is a crucial component of the challenging future of sustainable practice.

SESSION 4—DESIGNER/INDUSTRY INTERFACE—DR JO HEELEY

Jo Heeley: I thought it would be quite useful to try to draw together the strands of today because it's been a very jam packed, exciting rollercoaster set of thoughts and ideas. I feel a bit of a metamorphosis, I feel that I need a butterfly net to catch all these wonderful ideas and things that have been going on. Does anybody else feel like that? [. . .] if we want to go back and start to apply some of these ideas and these notions of upcycling. How could we take these ideas forward and upscale them? How can we make it more mainstream so more people can do it?

Orsola De Castro: I can say that, as the curator of Estethica I am seeing a huge surge in precisely these types of solutions for the future of sustainable design. As I said, I feel very much that using organic and Fair Trade is a decision, it's a boardroom decision, while recycling is a design solution to a problem. What we are seeing is a great surge of creativity precisely within upcycling and recycling in the new labels that are coming out.

Personally, having been doing it for a long time I will take home the knowledge that, yes, I've been doing the right thing and perhaps, many times that I thought I should have compromised and I didn't, it's okay. I can also bring back the message that this is a street that people are following and are following it creatively, intelligently, funnily to a certain extent, and there's a lot more street to go. At the same time there are quite a lot of people walking it.

Emmeline Child: Certainly on a practical level for you out there that actually want to go and tangibly start something, research is the key but there's a lot more networks out there now to support it and assist. I'm sure when you first started it was you, by yourself and perhaps a couple of other people. Since I've been in it myself, just year by year there are more and more networks out there to support people. That's going to help increase awareness and help spread the word about the possibilities with environmental issues, and recycling and upcycling in particular.

Marie O'Mahony: Things are changing and I see a big difference with what we've seen and heard here today, compared to conversations or similar events even 5 and certainly 10 years ago. I'm not directly involved in manufacturing, so maybe some of our manufacturers would like to come in on this, but from where I am, what I see is very similar to what was happening in the technical textile industry back in the early 90's when I first got involved with it. When I first went to Tech-Textil in Frankfurt I was about the only female and found myself talking to people there about design and trying to use these carbon fibres, glass fibres for product design. The actual design was an emergency housing shelter and I was working with ARUP on it but the technical textile manufacturers regarded that as design, in those days. They couldn't figure out how their product would fit in with what I was trying to do. I had a real struggle, it was a real Tower of Babel thing, trying to talk to advanced textile companies about that.

Now, 15 years on, going to TechTextil in Frankfurt, there are probably at least 50%, maybe 60%,

what I would call creatives between product design, fashion, architecture, right across the board. It's really changed. You walk up to any stand, even first time stands and you can talk about design. That dialogue has happened not overnight but it has happened. To me, that's where we are with this. We are seeing people going out to China or Devon or wherever and talking about small production runs and discussing it, starting that dialogue going. From these small beginnings snowballs start to happen and things will eventually move up in scale. For instance, in about five years time we can all be sitting here and it will be, instead of three or four large company manufacturers that are out there, they're going to be down here and it's going to be a very different feel to it and a very interesting evolution and development. It takes time, it's not easy. Nobody's going to open the door and say 'Here's the resource, here's everything'. It's hard work but it's also a very exciting time and the doors are opening and the dialogues are starting, so it's good.

Jo Heeley: I'm going to open it up to the floor now. Has anybody got any burning questions they'd like to put to our panel or to any of the speakers they've heard today? When you ask your question, will you stand up and say who you are and where you're from, please.

Kay Politowicz: It's Kay Politowicz, I'm from Chelsea. I think it's a pity that Cindy Rhoades isn't here now only because I wanted to raise the issue of where Cindy appears to be, to an audience member anyway, to my mind, which looks like another stage on from the beautifully formed businesses I'm looking at now. She seems to represent a move into a bigger production. How do you all relate to that? Is it the sort of thing you might aspire to or would that kind of pattern only work for certain approaches and yours needs to stay small? It's the link to bigger things that I'm really interested in.

Rebecca Earley: Cindy's product was a product that was introduced to an existing company that had networks set up already. Terra Plana has factories that work with its shoe design, so in one sense it was easier to explore those routes, to go to China and to invest and they went to the factory that was already making their shoes. I think for me, that's the problem, it's bridging the gap between being an individual designer or a very small company, and then getting a larger factory to take on your production and having the orders to fulfil them. I think it's a good model for how these things can move forward. To work with the bigger companies that have the set up there and then to innovative within an existing set up. She's gone a stage further and said 'Okay, that works but I'm not happy with that, I want to make it more sustainable. I want to build it around local models in different continents.' She's rolling the idea out now from there. The thing about Cindy's trainers, they're £65, it's incredible really. I went to buy a pair and I expected to pay £120 but they're making them for £65 which is really quite amazing to put themselves in the market at that level. One of the real reasons behind putting today on, for me, was to start those discussions to see if we could start talking about those models. Unfortunately, all the big companies have left.

Orsola De Castro: I've been twice in my 10 year career making very big numbers and working with very big productions. The first time it was a decision of mine not to continue. We did a collection for an Italian sportswear company, they do millions. We did cocktail dresses out of their football and shirting t-shirts. The idea was you could have this thing scrunched up and bring it down and it was perfectly ironed, jump in the pool, come out. We didn't take that into bigger numbers because of their wanting to operate with us. They were happy not to do it within the recycling but maybe scrunch a little recycled bit on to it but the possibility was there and the product could have held that production.

We produced in Poland up until a few years ago, quite large runs for a small company like ours, particularly for a recycling company. People always assume that you can't repeat with recycling but we were repeating things. We can make up to 500 pieces of one particular design and, for

instance, with something like this skirt the difference would be fairly minimal. The reality is that, in an odd sort of way, since this whole eco thing our numbers have gone down. The eco has created a market which is very specific. It follows a certain customer and it has a certain price tag. For us, who have been quite happily selling alongside the same designers whose fabrics we use, very high end, the minute the whole eco thing came along, we became pigeon-holed into something that frankly we are not. It's been a question of recuperating.

The way that I see it and this is again, our story, that our type of recycling is absolutely reproducible, I'm not saying mass producible but it could even get to mass production the amount of waste that this is at pre-consumer level which by the way is unaccounted for. There are statistics as to how much the consumer consumes. There are no statistics as to how much the actual factories and manufacturers are getting rid of. I can tell you it's a lot more than what the consumers are going through because there's all the stuff that they get wrong. They get it wrong all the time, runs and runs of wrong things. There is the material there and the knowledge and the know-how to make big runs.

Jo Heeley: Can I follow on that question. If there is all this waste in the manufacturing chain which we know there is, how can we get more companies to get involved and accept that, okay, we create this waste, let's make something valuable out of it?

Orsola De Castro: We now operate with six or seven specific Italian manufacturers. Italy has lost an enormous amount of industry to the Far East so it's quite a dilapidated scene. You arrive at these wonderful factories that have been family run and were in the 1980's the top of modern technology. They've invested so much money in these incredible machines and now they struggle and they close. Every year a couple of them close. We've been doing this since approximately 2002 and I am the in-house recycler for a couple of these people. They collect the waste, very much like we would collect our household waste, according to our method, dividing it by thick and thin. The problem is really what they need is the patience to store, the place to store and the patience to store. It's a full-time job. This is why it should be run in collaboration with colleges, with other institutions to recuperate it because it is an enormous amount. We can just about deal with the hundreds of kilograms of bales we rescue but we're tiny. It is an issue that the companies themselves should address on a regular basis. I think progressively if more designers were to embrace pre-consumer and show that out of rubbish can come a profit, then I think that companies are very quickly going to turn around and start looking in their own rubbish bin themselves.

Amy Twigger Holroyd: Might it be a problem that the retailers don't own the factories so it's not their waste, like high street shops that manufacture in the Far East?

Orsola De Castro: If I haven't done it in 10 years, obviously my thoughts haven't been successful. The fashion industry is one of these industries where you have to have an enormous amount of patience because the longer you're seen there somehow the more you are believable. I'm just waiting, I'm very patient. In the meantime, I'm doing whatever it is I can in order to make an environment whereby, because I can sometimes be quite persuasive, I'm given a chance to speak, like today. Estethica at London Fashion Week is definitely one of them. I am a believer. I don't know whether you can run a business and be an idealist at the same time but I'm trying. I believe that we have consumed so much for so long that we've already got everything on this planet to reuse in order to continue consuming. This message is going to be coming along over the next few years. More and more I see things coming out of colleges which are so mind-bogglingly inspiring in terms of creativity and solutions about how to transform one thing from another, it's almost molecular. I just sit and wait and hopefully it will happen within a few years.

Rebecca Earley: I wanted to bring all those comments together a bit because it's about teaching, it's about education, today's about design and the comments about the consumers not being ready, not wanting recycled fashion or paying a bit more. When my students hand in a dissertation and they've written 8,000 words around one of these subjects to do with sustainable fashion, and their conclusion is that it's the consumers' fault and that they're not ready to buy it. They behave really badly, they buy fast fashion, they go shopping on a Saturday afternoon and then they thrown stuff away. When the conclusion is, it's the consumers' fault; I get a big red pen out because frankly it's not good enough. It's not good enough as a designer to have that as the answer because this is about offering enough choice.

All of this started through the lack of good quality design out there, using recycled materials. We are so much further on than we were five years ago and it's so joyful to be able to draw together this group of people and have a look at this work. This goes from us making stuff as designers into us being tutors and disseminating this and working with students, improving the quality of design, education and sustainability issues. It is going on and rolling out from that point, offering good design ideas and good design approaches and offering a better range of products and the consumer will follow. It takes time, your point about time and waiting, yes, in the meantime we'll carry on doing what we do.

Can I just say one more thing and then you can carry on. The seventh strategy for TED which we are going to publish next year is the designer as activist, the designer not just designing products but being an entrepreneur that thinks about their business in a different way. About a curator that brings together other people and makes a change happen in the London fashion industry, about educating, holding workshops. It's about the designer taking on these other roles. Our job today and our message to take away as designers is to be involved in more ways than just making a product. Actually network and disseminate, set up websites, make links and be activists, maybe be political as well.

Marie O'Mahony: Following on from all of those discussions we've still got a bit of an image problem. There is still a sense of 'buy this because it's good for you', 'buy this because it's the right thing to do'. You've got the oatcake and you've got the chocolate cake. Even though the oatcake might be very nice and the chocolate cake is actually a disgusting readymade thing or something, you will still go for the one that is being a bit naughty. You're out shopping, you want to do something that is good design and you don't want to feel like 'Oh, I should buy this.' It's the wrong attitude to buy something with. You don't want to have something like that. It's ok if you've got your food trolley and you think 'I'll buy some Fair Trade, but I can also get this other thing.' You don't have that really with larger products, clothing, furniture or whatever. The design is good, what we've seen here today is fabulous stuff; it's good it doesn't need this extra tag. It should be inherent in it. The same as fit for purpose is inherent in products that we buy.

Participant: It's not really a question, it's following on from what Marie said and what Becky said about choice. Surely a solution is—and it came about during a discussion I had at Central Saint Martins on the Textiles Futures Course—what if we take away that choice? A consumer is very savvy. A consumer by no means is stupid or unintelligent. We do follow trends, as pointed out with the advertising and all the rest of it, but what if we take away those bad choices? All we are left with is good choices but we don't know that they're there as in this eco label, that's all we can buy, that's all we can purchase. Surely that's what we should aim for?

Rebecca Earley: That's good design then isn't it?

Emmeline Child: I think that's the perfect idea and we'd all like to see that happen. Unfortunately, what we've got today in our consumer society is the fact that we've got large companies who are in control of the government. They're the ones that are keeping the economy of the country going. Unfortunately, they're able to call the shots more and they're money-making companies so they're wanting their high turnover. The idea behind that is lovely. I think the reality of taking away all manufacturing from China or wherever, is going to be a lot harder because effectively the world does run on money.

Kate Goldsworthy: We're in a really interesting phase at the moment as well, in terms of material values, I think things are shifting. If you look at oil prices, the cost of these virgin materials is just going to keep going up. I can't imagine a time when it's going to drop back to what it was. Perhaps some of these economic levels will shift anyway as recycled fibres just become more economic. Talking to technology companies at Avantex last year, already I'd say there was a 50/50 split. There were still companies, these are technical textile non-woven polyester companies, saying that recycling still wasn't economic but on the other hand, there were people, mainly who had invested in more of the technology, saying that it was becoming cost efficient and beneficial to their processes.

Dilys Williams (in the audience): I'm Dilys Williams, I run the Centre for Sustainable Fashion at London College of Fashion. A few things that have been said by Orsola, Becky, various people, posing a question really. Do we have to become big in order to be able to be commercial, to take on big companies, talking about having to become bigger? If we're lots of connected small [companies], can we not actually offer the public an amazing plethora of all these different design companies? It's really getting it out there. It's accessibility to customers, isn't it? How can all the little amazing different things be connected to make it a very different offer rather than trying to homogenise it into a bigger offer.

Orsola De Castro: I totally see your point. If you think about it, historically speaking the great mass consumption in fashion is relatively new. We are talking franchising. We're talking luxury as being available to everybody. We're talking the end of the 1980s. This is really relatively new and we've been taught to want differently. When I was younger, [for the] older generation, it wasn't about, you have a fiver in your pocket and you match it to a pair of jeans. You have a fiver in your pocket, you wait until you have a tenner and then you get yourself the type you really want. It's our attitudes that have been completely discombobulated. I reckon that it's going to take enough time to go back to a different way of desiring and that's where we're going.

I have to say, going back to what we were saying before, I agree with Becky about better design but at the same time I really have been seeing design coming along. I disagree about ethical fashion or sustainable fashion being less qualitatively outstanding than mainstream. When was the last time one of you went into a trade fashion fair and left thinking everything I've seen was inspirational, it just doesn't happen. There is bad taste and good taste in all of the fashion industry. It just so happens that there are so many fewer people doing sustainable fashion. Sustainable fashion generates quite logically from a type of consumer that was interested in a certain type of design. It is again, up to the educators and up to the businesses to say 'Yes, okay, I'm taking that on board but I'm creating a new type of design'. There is no higher amount of bad design in ethical fashion than there is in normal fashion.

Rebecca Earley: Can I jump back to Dilys' question because it's a really good comment and it's been on my mind because on the one hand, I'd like to reinvent thousands of Marks & Spencer's shirts using my techniques and my ideas. On the other hand I've been reading books like *The Long Tail* and *The Beauty of Small Businesses*, this American economic theory about small giants. About how these small companies perform so much better and they make a conscious decision to stay small. Inspired by those ideas I saw straight away that's what we've got really. We've got hundreds of recyclers and actually we could offer a great range of choice. It's about availability; it's about offering a sleeker marketed package. But what I can

imagine is, through using the internet and setting up groups and systems, designers becoming much more connected with each other.

Kate showed a great slide of the plastic bottle, one person who's taking waste already can't use all of the bottle. Kate's found people for the middle part and the top part and finally the bottle top. So you've got four people, haven't you? Last time you spoke somebody said to you, so, have you put them in touch with each other? That's the next stage maybe. That's a lovely model because that's the way the small people could network and work together. The internet offers a great potential for that to happen and lots of this activity can only be done on a small scale. That's what makes some of these products special. There certainly is a really strong argument for us working on models to keep small people connected. Then there's this other question as well of improving the level of design and improving the level of the recycled product in the larger stores too. Offering the consumer who just wants to go down Oxford Street on a Saturday afternoon, offering them something that they really want to buy too. That's not there yet.

Amy Twigger Holroyd: We should interconnect the small people but not ignore how enormous the huge people are. These large high street retailers are moloiths, but they pretend they're all these different shops. They should be broken up and they should be sent to different parts of the country.

Orsola De Castro: In a way sustainable designers are, in terms of business, an oxymoron. Here we are saying we want to slow down the industry, when all of those guys are saying 'No, we want to speed it up'. So inevitably, there's going to be a communication problem, which there is.

Participant: We've had a lot of contact with the supply chain. On Wednesday I was talking to farming groups from West Africa, talking about their Fair Trade crop and talking about how we can set up the supply chain. So many people within the supply chain all want to do the same thing. As big as my company is [a major

UK retailer] and as evil as people might think we actually are, we are trying to achieve something that the consumer actually does want to know of. The research is saying consumers want the sustainable products, they want ethical products and we're trying to deliver those things.

Amy Twigger Holroyd: What I feel, from the meetings I've been at, is that the people from the really big companies are maybe not having the opportunity to dream up the next really lovely, beautiful concept because they're feeling very defensive from everyone going 'Yes, the big companies and the sweatshops' and this and all that.

Participant: I can give you a good example of that. We [major UK retailer] produced nearly a quarter of a million recycled polyester fleeces in our menswear group last year. We got numerous phone calls from customers saying 'I really don't like the idea of recycled polyester because I'm not sure if it's clean or whether it's hygienic'. When you've got 11, 12 million customers coming through the front door every day, you get lots of different messages coming back. We're trying to do the right thing, what the right thing is by sustainable fashion, and we're getting our customers asking these things. I take on board what you say. We can't just sit back and blame it all on the consumer but when you deliver these things that they've asked for and they don't buy them it clogs up your whole supply chain.

What can we do with all of this waste? We're trying to find a way of using that waste. If someone from this group here said to us 'Look, you've got all this waste fabric and we can find a home for it and we'll pay discount prices for it', that would be a solution to resolving one of the problems we have. But it's about linking all of those things up together and linking what is actually a global market, a global industry where you've got manufacturing units in China, India, Sri Lanka, back to the UK, and how do you actually put all those together? That's one of the difficult things as well. It's not just scale, it's not just about the consumer, it's about linking all these aspects of the supply chain up and actually delivering what the consumer wants and what the consumer's willing to pay for.

Rebecca Earley: It's really funny that they phone up saying 'Is it dirty?'. You guys have got great poster campaigns going on at the moment and everybody is going to you and looking at the clothing and reading about Fair Trade and the dyes that you're using. You're one of the pioneering stores that are actually doing that. Stick a poster up and say 'Our polyester's not dirty, in fact it saves 72% of energy'. Stick a poster up, you're good at that.

Participant: Really I was just following on from what Becky was saying. To me it's about marketing and communication. You have got millions at your disposal for marketing and communications.

Participant: I'm trying to find those millions of pounds.

Participant: Right, okay, you have a very tiny marketing budget. But if you put that at your disposal for this particular sector of your retail sales as you have done with food. Your answers in your food marketing are very clear and people are able pick up on the fact that you use free range eggs or Fair Trade this or that, and that message has got through. You could borrow from yourself, from your own expertise.

Katarina Gronmyr (in audience): My name is Katarina and I'm from a small company in Norway, a small project in Norway called Fretex. We do post-consumer recycling. The company that I work with is a subsidiary of the Salvation Army in Norway, and we have started a project where we're trying to produce new design from used materials that we've been given. I wanted to comment on the design question and the market. What we did quite early on was we made a really slick look for the design because one of the agents told us that it's very good that it's redesigned, and it's even better when you can't tell. We are actually selling okay of the expensive things because it doesn't look like it's redesigned.

The other thing that we've done, we have developed more or less two types of products; one that we can produce easily that we're now looking to try to get produced somewhere and find out how we're going to deal with all the details. We're selling that to the company market as company gifts and that gives it a much better ratio between cost and income. It means that a lot of companies are very interested because they see this as part of a bigger marketing package and it makes it possible for them to say 'This is what we're doing'. Christmas gifts are given every year anyway, so there's a big market there for that.

Participant: Yes, but you know that Christmas gifts usually end up in landfill.

Participant: I can't remember who said it: 'All we can ever do is transform it'.

Orsola De Castro: You cannot destroy matter.

Participant: I was a bit concerned when I hear about all this pre-consumer waste. Surely that is a design problem at that stage. Why is there so much pre-consumer waste? If the designers at that stage were doing their job properly they would be much more economical with the fabrics they had and wouldn't be producing so much pre-consumer waste.

Emmeline Child: From my perspective because I'm a small company I can cut a dress, for example, out of a piece of fabric and then I can use the left over to make tote bags, and then scale it down even further to make little accessories, and then down further to make badges. So I'm using my waste but that's very labour intensive and very time consuming. When you're going through the normal CMT [cut, make and trim] process where you're laying up 50 sheets of fabric and then just cutting it out with an industrial knife, it's too labour intensive to start collecting all those excess pieces up unfortunately, well for the big companies it certainly is. To then start designing things that are going to fit in within the waste supply.

Orsola De Castro: The real issue is not really offcuts, the real issue is damaged [products]. What happens is that at production level an enormous amount of stuff is damaged. Designers are not, although they are finding solutions, they're not capable of working with something that just didn't turn out the way that they were expecting

it. Some of the bigger Italian fashion houses, if something shows up which is maybe 0.5 centimetre longer than the original pattern, that's considered waste. But because they have to protect their image they cannot resell it, either in charity shops or give it away because that would be against their image and they're protecting their quite strict quality control.

The other one is, particularly in terms of textile mills, again one of the biggest wastes is damaged fabrics. For instance, 90% of the jerseys we use are damaged. What do you do with a big ladder? We pretend that we have a fantastic laddering machine because basically we cut the panel bang in the middle and use the ladder as a decoration for that panel. Another enormous waste, and here we go, is colour charts. Every textile company has to produce, twice every year, vast amounts of fabrics to tell all of their clients, this is what I'm doing now, all of that is land filled and chucked. That's where the consumer waste comes from. Off cut is a relatively precious material which we are very, very lucky to get hold of but it's not the bulk of what is pre-consumer.

Jo Heeley: Can I raise a point about fast fashion and slow fashion? When I was doing research into the major high street retailers, you've got your seasons and then you've got your phases, then you've got more phases. Is that still increasing or are you starting to see a slowdown of the phases because as you've got more phases and this is where we're speeding up and getting much more disposable fashion. What is the sense in the industry? Where are we at?

Participant: I guess it's been speeding up from what we see.

Jo Heeley: How long does a phase last?

Participant: With some fast fashion retailers you're talking about four or six weeks and then they get the next products in. From a business point of view, we [major UK retailer] have to compete with these people. We have to find ways of doing that. We could go down the track of saying we'll do the same thing and do four week turnarounds or we could talk about trying to do sustainable. One of the reasons I talked about the consumers in my first question was, how do we actually link consumers with all this fast fashion? How do we get the fashion designers working to try and drive some sustainability into fashion retail? I don't know what the answer to that is and that's part of the reason why I'm here today is to just try and understand it.

Amy Twigger Holroyd: To try and make the fast fashion actually fast, all the way through the process and not just fast in the time that you wear it and then throw it away. It still takes the same amount of time to make it and it still sits in landfill for the same amount of time.

Rebecca Earley: So you can still have fast fashion but it has to be light.

Orsola De Castro: Fast fashion ought to be biodegradable. That really ought to be the answer. You want to make enormous profits on fast fashion, lose some of your margin but use biodegradable fabrics. For the stuff you want to last longer use fabrics that aren't biodegradable.

Jo Heeley: Can I bring in Emma's points because I thought there were some really striking images in there? So the billboard image was really pertinent but the City just said, right, we're not doing any more advertising and that's it. In a few months time or a few years time there will be that type of backlash and how would the high street deal with that?

Amy Twigger Holroyd: Do you mean anti-advertisement or do you mean anti-fast with that backlash?

Jo Heeley: Anti-advertising. I mean that's really strong. It's happened so far just in Sao Paulo and Paris in the last two years. People held protests like Becky was saying, more activism.

Participant: I think we are seeing a shift, definitely. I go round a lot of schools and recycling is in the school syllabus now in the design technology part of their GCSE and everything. You see these children coming up through further education and they're very clued up about recycling and about the whole process. Unfortunately in my generation I've always been used to high

street stores and being able to get that product and not really understanding where it's coming from.

Jo Heeley: That's teenage though. They hit teenage, they forget all the primary school education and then they go out shopping. But can I just say I don't think people want to go to M&S for fast fashion. I think they go to Zara and Primark. I think people want things to last still, which is how things were. But I think if M&S went down the route of, not anti-fast fashion, but actually really pushing the idea that their clothes could be mended, looked after, exchanged, classics well made, really good quality and actually took—I suppose it sounds so political when I say take a stand against fast fashion. It's just that you don't go to M&S for a quick fashion fix. I know they're competing in that way at the moment and their advertising campaign tries to do that. But I still think people just go to Top Shop for the stuff that they want to throw away.

Participant: I saw recently a high street fashion retailer in Denmark or Sweden has opened up a secondhand shop that only sells their secondhand clothes to show how long they last and how classically they've been designed. So that shop existing is a statement about what you can expect.

Jo Heeley: Yes, there's a really good piece of research in the TED resource done by an undergraduate where they looked at Vivien Westwood's and Katherine Hamnett's stuff selling on Ebay, saying actually which is the most sustainable design. Vivien Westwood doesn't go out there to try to be eco and she was looking then for pieces of Hamnett that were eco and were they reselling. Of course, everything there is Westwood. It's lasting, it's being collected, it's actually been designed to last. The Hamnett stuff was down there.

Participant: Just on that point about fast and slow fashion. I think fashion is inevitably going to slow down, that whole life cycle thing will slow down as the Chinese economy develops. It won't be cheap to produce in China and we'll never see that scale of cheap production, there isn't anywhere else that it can go. The other thing is the oil and the economy is beginning to slow down. So I think those two things are with us.

Participant: Sorry, I disagree with that because I think it will move from China. It will move to India, it will move to Africa.

Participant: The thing is China can't keep speeding up forever, it can't get any faster. It will start to slow. We're already seeing people bringing some production back to Europe. We've now lost our machinery. Half of the machinery has been sold to Asia. We've now got a situation where certain products are no longer economical to ship. With the oil price going up they're becoming less and less economical. We've got now in parts of Europe really already beginning to really regret the loss of the industry and looking at solutions to bring that back. In Italy, in France, in Spain, that's happening already.

Participant: Yes, but in Italy you're also getting crazy things. You're actually getting people being shipped over from China to do the work at Chinese labour rates.

Orsola De Castro: Absolutely and one of the biggest sweatshops in Italy, they're Chinese.

Participant: That's because the skills are all in China now, the skills have died out [elsewhere].

Participant: No, it's the economics because they're paying them below European rates, they're paying them the Chinese rates.

Participant: Until I retired last year, I ran the Salvation Army recycling unit in the UK. It's a plea really to the designers. I'm actually gobsmacked of the sheer beauty of the things I've seen today. However, last year we completed a report for DEFRA, working with Leeds University. We buy two million tons of clothes every year. We recycle or we collect for recycling and reuse 300,000 tons. The charity shops use 50,000 tons. You get people who use 100 tons together perhaps, maybe, it doesn't really matter. But we throw 1.2 million tons into the waste bin, there is the real problem, not the 100 tons. What you do serves to lift awareness.

So I think my plea to you as designers, and you were saying about networking, about thinking about cradle to cradle, secondary and tertiary and more uses. Don't just think about turning these fibres, because that's what they are, into clothes, there are many, many other uses. The report on the website that I happened to know of DEFRA has got recorded there six new areas: air conditioning, automotive, hydroponics, plastic composites instead of glass fibre, insulation. I could go on and on and on. If we are going to think resource management, if we are going to manage our resource more effectively we can't just think about how beautiful it looks. We've got to look about the chemical and physical properties of the fibre so it can have a cradle to cradle use.

Rebecca Earley: That's really good, thank you for that. We wanted it to be beautiful but I think to start the discussion and celebrate 10 years it needed to be beautiful. We were looking around for those people that are working at recycling and using the fibre reclamation in different ways, and wanting to actually hook up with them to see whether we can work with the products and actually improve the products too. The fastest growing waste stream out of that 1.2 is fast fashion, they've identified in DEFRA as well, haven't they? The group that are actually actively dumping it in landfill are the 15-25 year olds.

Participant: No.

Rebecca Earley: Fast fashion, no?

Participant: No, the fast fashion. It's not 25 year olds that are using fast fashion. It used to be those that were trying to eke out their budget. It's now those that go on holiday and buy seven sets of this so they don't have to bring them back, etc, etc. It's now instead of buying one handbag at £100, goes in and buys five or six because they're all in different colours. The composition of the market and their audience has changed significantly in the last five years.

Participant: Can I just come in on what you were saying about those other markets? I think probably why we're not seeing more of these people here is that it takes a lot longer to get something like that out there into the market, simply because you've got a lot more long-term health and safety issues and testing that needs to be done. Whereas with fashion, with accessories, this kind of area, it's relatively quick to take something in, do something with it and get it out there.

Participant: I couldn't agree more. It's essential to work together, it's a team effort. It's not me, it's us.

Jo Heeley: I think that's a really good point too.

Thank you very much for your questions everybody. Thank you to the panel.

39

CONSTRUCTING TEXTILES

Anni Albers

Editor's introduction: The German textile designer Anni Albers was also a teacher and writer. When Albers became a student at the acclaimed Bauhaus in Weimar, Germany, in 1922, textiles were considered the suitable media for women to work in. The school is credited with the original prototype of workshop learning that underpins art and design education around the world today. Perhaps less deserving of celebration were the gender divisions applied to certain subjects at the Bauhaus. Albers, an aspiring painter, was sent to weave. The change of direction may not have been by choice, but her talent was well matched for the discipline, and she went on to design some of the most iconic woven textiles of the century. Albers's beguilingly simple weavings often made use of uncommon material combinations. In this piece of writing, penned nearly seventy years ago, she notes that while materials have changed over time (and mechanization has impacted production), the actual structure of woven cloth has seen a curious lack of technological advancement. Albers's observations offer a useful counterpoint indicating that not all forms of knowledge are on a fast track aided by technology.

Retrospection, though suspected of being the preoccupation of conservators, can also serve as an active agent. As an antidote for an elated sense of progress that seizes us from time to time, it shows our achievements in proper proportion and makes it possible to observe where we have advanced, where not, and where, perhaps, we have even retrogressed. It thus can suggest new areas for experimentation.

When we examine recent progress in cloth-making, we come to the curious realization that the momentous development we find is limited to a closely defined area . . . the creation of new fibres and finishes. While the process of weaving has remained virtually unchanged for uncounted centuries, textile chemistry has brought about far-reaching changes, greater changes perhaps than even those brought about through the fast advance in the mechanics of textile production during the last century. We find the core of textile work, the technique of weaving, hardly touched by our modern age, while swift progress in the wider area has acutely affected the quality as much as the quantity of our fabrics. In fact, while a development around the center has taken place, methods of weaving have not only been

Source: Anni Albers, "Constructing Textiles," pp. 29–33 from *Anni Albers: Selected Writings on Design* (Middletown, CT: Wesleyan University Press, 2000). © 2000 by the Josef and Anni Albers Foundation.

neglected, but some have even been forgotten in the course of time.

It is easy to visualize how intrigued, as much as mystified, a weaver of ancient Peru would be in looking over the textiles of our day. Having been exposed to the greatest culture in the history of textiles and having been himself a contributor to it, he can be considered a fair judge of our achievements. He would marvel, we can imagine, at the speed of mass production, at the uniformity of threads, the accuracy of the weaving and the low price. He would enjoy the new yarns used . . . rayon, nylon, aralac, dacron, orlon, dynel, and Fibreglas, to name some of the most important ones. He would admire the materials that are glazed or water-repellant, crease-resistant, permanent pleated, or flame-retarding, mothproof or shrinkage-controlled and those made fluorescent . . . all results of our new finishes. Even our traditionally used fabrics take on new properties when treated with them. He would learn with amazement of the physical as well as of the chemical methods of treating fabrics, which give them their tensile strength or their reaction to alkalis or acids, etc. Though our Peruvian critic is accustomed to a large scale of colors, he may be surprised to see new nuances and often a brilliance hitherto unknown to him, as well as a quantitative use of color surpassing anything he had imagined.

The wonder of this new world of textiles may make our ancient expert feel very humble and may even induce him to consider changing his craft and taking up chemistry or mechanical engineering. These are the two major influences in this great development, the one affecting the quality of the working material, and the other the technique of production. But strangely enough, he may find that neither one would serve him in his specific interest: the intricate interlocking of two sets of threads at right angles—weaving.

Concentrating his attention now on this particular phase of textile work, he would have a good chance of regaining his self-confidence. A strange monotony would strike him and puzzle him, we imagine, as he looked at millions of yards of fabric woven in the simplest technique. In most cases, he would recognize at one glance the principle of construction, and he would even find most of the more complex weaves familiar to him. In his search for inventiveness in weaving techniques, he would find few, if any, examples to fascinate him. He himself would feel that he had many suggestions to offer.

An impartial critic of our present civilization would attribute this barrenness in today's weaving to a number of factors. He would point out that an age of machines, substituting more and more mechanisms for handwork, limits in the same measure the versatility of work. He would explain that the process of forming has been disturbed by divorcing the planning from the making, since a product today is in the hands of many, no longer in the hands of one. Each member of the production line adds mechanically his share to its formation according to a plan beyond his control. Thus the spontaneous shaping of a material has been lost, and the blueprint has taken over. A design on paper, however, cannot take into account the fine surprises of a material and make imaginative use of them. Our critic would point out that this age promotes quantitative standards of value. Durability of materials, consequently, no longer constitutes a value per se and elaborate workmanship is no longer an immediate source of pleasure. Our critic would show that a division between art and craft, or between fine art and manufacture, has taken place under mechanical forms of production; the one carrying almost entirely spiritual and emotional values, the other predominantly practical ones. It is therefore logical that the new development should clarify the role of usefulness in the making of useful objects, paralleling the development of art, which in its process of clarification has divested itself of a literary by-content and has become abstract.

Though the weight of attention is now given to practical forms purged of elements belonging to other modes of thought, aesthetic qualities nevertheless are present naturally and inconspicuously. Avoiding decorative additions, our fabrics today are often beautiful, so we believe, through the clear use of the raw material, bringing out its inherent qualities. Since even solid colors might be seen as an aesthetic appendage, hiding the characteristics of a material, we often prefer fabrics in natural, undyed tones.

Our new synthetic fibres, derived from such different sources as coal, casein, soybeans, seaweed or lime have multiplied many times the number of our traditionally used fibres. Our materials therefore, even when woven in the simplest techniques, are widely varied in quality, and the number of variations are still increased through the effects of the new finishes. Yards and yards of plain and useful material, therefore, do not bore us. Rather they give us a unique satisfaction. To a member of an earlier civilization, such as our Peruvian, these materials would be lacking in those qualities that would make them meaningful to him or beautiful.

Though we have succeeded in achieving a great variety of fabrics without much variation of weaving technique, the vast field of weaving itself is open today for experimentation. At present, our industry has no laboratories for such work. (Today, 1959, the situation is changing.) The test tube and the slide rule have, so far, taken good care of our progress. Nevertheless, the art of building a fabric out of threads is still a primary concern to some weavers, and thus experimenting has continued. Though not in general admitted to the officialdom of industrial production, some hand-weavers have been trying to draw attention to weaving itself as an integral part of textile work.

At their looms, free from the dictates of a blueprint, these weavers are bringing back the qualities that result from an immediate relation of the working material and the work process. Their fresh and discerning attempts to use surface qualities of weaves are resulting in a new school of textile design. It is largely due to their work that textures are again becoming an element of interest. Texture effects belong to the very structure of the material and are not superimposed decorative patterns, which at present have lost our love. Surface treatment of weaving, however, can become as much an ornamental addition as any pattern by an overuse of the qualities that are organically part of the fabric structure.

Though it is through the stimulating influence of hand-weaving that the industry is becoming aware of some new textile possibilities, not all hand-weaving today has contributed to it. To have positive results, a work that leads away from the general trend of a period has to overcome certain perplexities. There is a danger of isolationism . . . hand-weavers withdrawing from contemporary problems and burying themselves in weaving recipe books of the past; there is a resentment of an industrial present, which due to a superior technique of manufacture, by-passes them; there is a romantic overestimation of handwork in contrast to machine work and a belief in artificial preservation of a market that is no longer of vital importance.

Crafts have a place today beyond that of a backwoods subsidy or as a therapeutic means. Any craft is potentially art, and as such not under discussion here. Crafts become problematic when they are hybrids of art and usefulness (once a natural union), not quite reaching the level of art and not quite that of clearly defined usefulness. An example is our present day ash tray art . . . trash.

Modern industry is the new form of the old crafts, and both industry and the crafts should remember their genealogical relation. Instead of a feud, they should have a family reunion. Since the craft of weaving is making, in an unauthorized manner, its contribution to the new development and is beginning to draw attention to itself, we can look forward to the time when it will be accepted as a vital part of the industrial process.

The influence that hand-weaving has had thus far has been mainly in the treatment of the appearance, the epidermis, of fabrics. The engineering work of fabric construction, which affects the fundamental characteristics of a material, has barely been considered. It is probably again the task of hand-weavers to work in this direction. For just as silk, a soft material by nature, can become stiff in the form of taffeta, through a certain thread construction, and linen, a comparatively stiff material, can be made soft in another, so an endless number of constructional effects can produce new fabrics. The increasing number of new fibres incorporating new qualities creates a special challenge to try the effects of construction on them. Just as chemical treatment has produced fluorescence, so structural treatment can produce, for example, sound-absorption. Our ancient Peruvian colleague might lose his puzzled expression, seeing us thus set for adventures with threads, adventures that we suspect had been his passion.

Industry should take time off for these experiments in textile construction and, as the easiest practicable solution, incorporate hand-weavers as laboratory workers in its scheme. By including the weaver's imaginative and constructive inventiveness, as well as his hand-loom with its wide operational scope, progress in textile work may grow from progress in part to a really balanced progress.

1946

40

BIOCOUTURE OR HOW TO GROW A FROCK . . .

Suzanne Lee

Editor's introduction: Suzanne Lee is a senior research fellow at Central Saint Martins College of Art and Design, London. Her ongoing BioCouture project questions our assumptions about the way we make and consume fashion. In the portion of her blog reprinted here, Lee uses the platform to muse on recent experiments, celebrate the project's deserved recognition within the broader community of creative thinking, and point readers toward notable research that shares a similar desire to challenge the way we build and use the materials of our designed environment. The time-sensitive nature of blogging provides us with an incisive snapshot of a dynamic period in the progress of Lee's long-term research project. In experimental research such as this, the very nature of what a textile might be is questioned. The proposed solutions tell us much about our own, often unarticulated, expectations of the textile as a material.

FEBRUARY 8, 2011

Cellulose Composites

BioCouture has been investigating the use of microbial cellulose as a textile. One question is 'Is it possible to extend the range of material qualities by introducing different substrates?'. These are some experiments exploring the addition of various substrates to grow cellulose. There are two main techniques shown, during the growth process and after. Firstly, I tried taking a wet, grown cellulose sheet and placing it on different textile substrates so that as the water evaporated the fibres from the cellulose 'pick up' those of the substrate. [. . .]

Initially all the samples worked to some extent, the substrates all appeared to have penetrated the cellulose. However with force applied, either by manipulating the cloth or trying to pull layers apart, some performed better than others. The smaller cotton mesh stayed completed trapped unlike the larger, more open hemp net which looked embedded but was relatively easy to separate. The lace sample could be teased apart quite easily but left its embossed pattern behind on the cellulose while the wool mohair was probably the least integrated and happily came away leaving behind a few longer fibres. The conclusion was that this method was really only suitable for the open, small holed cotton mesh. In creating a cellulose/cotton mesh composite that

Source: Suzanne Lee, *Biocouture–Or How to Grow a Frock*. Available online: http://biocouture.posterous.com. Reproduced with permission.

cellulose dictates the dominant material quality, it retains its strength and removes the stretch from the mesh which is now trapped with no expansion. This led to thinking about non-stretch nets, both cellulose and nylon and embedding them during the growth process.

JANUARY 27, 2011

New work for ModeMuseum Belgium

This piece has just shipped to the ModeMusuem in Hasselt, Belgium to go in their 'Alter Nature: The Future That Never Was' exhibition. It explores visions of the future from the past, and the possible future of tomorrow (see my book). Featured are the influential Space Age couturiers of the 60s; Paco Rabanne, André Courreges, Pierre Cardin and Rudi Gernreich alongside contemporary designers working with innovative materials, processes and new social environment concerns.

I've wanted to make a piece for some time that played with how home grown microbial-cellulose looks uncannily like human skin. When wet it can be formed over 3D shapes so this bodice was constructed by applying a pattern of dried beans to a wooden body form and allowing the wet cellulose material to dry down onto it. It took about a week before it could be lifted off, I then sewed a conventional zip fastening (as yet there is no biodegradable alternative). The scarification pattern was inspired by various African tribal markings. The bean shape is similar to the (microscopic) bacteria which produce the cellulose so there's a

Figure 40.1. Suzanne Lee, *Scarbodice* microbial cellulose (2010). Image Courtesy of Suzanne Lee.

resonance that appeals to me, ghosts of the nano-fibril factories that spun the cloth.

. . .

JANUARY 10, 2011

TEO Fellowship 2011!

Can't think of a better way to start 2011 than with the announcement that I've been made a TED Fellow. TED is a nonprofit organisation that promotes the sharing of ideas through its conferences, events and free to view online talks. It's a great opportunity to see some of the world's greatest thinkers in action; previous speakers have included Al Gore, Stephen Hawking, James Cameron, Steve Jobs, Richard Branson, Annie Lennox and Michelle Obama. The theme of TED2011 is The Rediscovery of Wonder so I look forward to sharing some of the wonder of BioCouture with a wider audience and meeting all the inspirational 2011 Fellows.

. . .

NOVEMBER 16, 2010

BioCouture in Time's Top 50 2010

BioCouture has been included in Time Magazine's annual roundup of 'The Top 50 Best Inventions of 2010'. Although the BioCouture project has been around for a few years it seems to have caught the imagination this year. Similarly Fabrican's spray on fabric, is also included in Time's fashion section. I wrote about it in my book back in 2005/7 but for some reason this year it has come to the fore. Well done to Manel Torres Fabrican's designer cum chemist.

The other two products in the fashion section are Martin Margiela's plastic tag fur coat and Heleen Klopper's Woolfiller. So clothing grown from bacteria, created with biodegradable spray-on polymers, recycled plastic and a new darning technique. Anyone see a theme here? Sustainability

seems to be a determining factor in Time's choices and not in a token way since all these inventions deal with some aspect of environmental and sustainable concern for fashion's future.

Apart from purely covetable items like the iPad, my other favorite inventions are the beef-powered Amtrak train, using waste fat as biodiesel, China's straddling bus that drives over the top of other traffic (Wacky Races for real), the almost waterless washing machine, let's face it, it's this end of the garment's life that is most environmentally damaging and of course Craig Venter's first synthetic cell (see Synbio elsewhere on the blog). Oh and Sugru, for the accident-prone among us.

. . .

NOVEMBER 8, 2010

What is Synthetic Biology?

I've been meaning to post about this for a while and now seems the perfect opportunity. This week I'm teaching a project brief on 'Fabricating Life—Synthetic and Systems Biology and Design' to 1st year MA Textile Futures and MA Industrial Design at Central Saint Martins.

BioCouture, which started as a project to design clothing produced from a microbial material has evolved into a biological investigation looking at the design of an organism to produce clothing (and other things). So far we have been applying a top down approach; grow material and fashion it into garments. This is ok but it doesn't really allow us to address some of the material issues that arise such as hydrophilicity and biodegradation. Bacterial-cellulose is extremely absorbent and with no additional treatment is subject to environmental degradation. We have certain variables we can play with to do with recipes, production processes etc. But we can't fundamentally change these material qualities using our existing approach.

But what if we could re-design the actual cellulose-producing organism? What if we could make the bacteria produce cellulose more efficiently, more abundantly, what if we could engineer in some hydrophobicity, what if we could make it biodegrade when we want, what if we could get it to adhere to a 3D form so it grows into a finished product? All these questions lead us into a world of Synthetic Biology where we can design and build such biological functions/systems.

. . .

OCTOBER 25, 2010

The BioCouture project sprang from research I conducted for my book "Fashioning The Future: tomorrow's wardrobe" published by Thames and Hudson. In fact Chapter 3, 'The Growable Suit' features a short interview with Dr. David Hepworth about using bacterial-cellulose to grow fabric and with whom I undertook the early BioCouture investigation.

. . .

Here's to a future generation of visionary designers!

FURTHER READING: PRODUCTION

Walter Benjamin, "The Work of Art in the Age of Mechanical Reproduction," in *Illuminations* (New York: Schocken Books, 1968; English translation) pp. 217–251.

Sandy Black, *Eco-Chic: The Fashion Paradox* (London: Black Dog, 2008).

Jane Collins, *Threads: Gender, Labor and Power in the Global Apparel Industry* (Chicago: University of Chicago Press, 2003).

Martin Davis and Virginia Davis, "Mistaken Ancestry: The Jacquard and the Computer," in *Textile: The Journal of Cloth and Culture* 3, no. 1 (2005) pp. 76–87.

Janet Hethorn and Connie Ulasewicz, *Sustainable Fashion: Why Now?* (New York: Fairchild Books, 2008).

Janis Jefferies, *Selvedges: Writings and Artworks since 1980*, ed. Victoria Mitchell (Norwich: Norwich Gallery, 2000).

Naomi Klein, *No Logo* (London: Harper Perennial, 2000).

Suzanne Lee, *Fashioning the Future: Tomorrow's Wardrobe* (London: Thames & Hudson, 2005).

Joan Livingstone and John Ploof (eds.), *The Object of Labor: Art, Cloth, and Cultural Production* (Chicago: School of Art Institute of Chicago Press; Cambridge and London: MIT Press, 2007).

Alexander Mackendrick (director), *The Man in the White Suit* (London: Ealing Comedy, 1951).

Margaret Maynard, "Clothing: Is There a Responsible Choice?" in *Dress and Globalisation* (Manchester: Manchester University Press, 2004) 134–152.

William McDonough and Michael Braungart, *Cradle to Cradle: Remaking the Way We Make Things* (New York: North Point Press, 2003).

Richard Sennett, *The Craftsman* (London: Penguin Books, 2008).

Susan Snodgrass (ed.), *Anne Wilson: Wind/Rewind/Weave* (Knoxville, TN: Knoxville Museum of Art & WhiteWalls, 2011).

PART VI

USE

PART INTRODUCTION

Textiles function. This unremarkable statement is of wildly varying degrees of interest to those who engage with textile thinking and textile making. For some it is *everything*. Performance textiles, for example, are useless if they do not perform as required. But for others the textile's capacity for function is a distraction. Textiles created for their ceremonial and symbolic value, for example, are done a disservice in the eyes of some when misunderstood as mere objects of function. Thus the usefulness of the textile can be found in a mundane object, such as an umbrella. But it is also present in the less overt ways a textile communicates or contributes information to society. The content of this final section of *the Reader* is in many ways the most eclectic of the book. Throughout attention is paid to the varied ways in which textiles are used.

Matilda McQuaid writes about high-performance textiles—materials with sophisticated functional qualities. Here, use is both physical and extreme. McQuaid observes that "technical textiles represent, in volume, the smallest segment of the enormous textile industry, yet they are some of the most innovative and purest examples of design today." What is interesting to note about performance textiles is their ability to be known for what they do, rather than what they are. Using the categories of stronger, faster, lighter, safer, and smarter, McQuaid reminds us that textiles are functioning in more aspects of our constructed world than we necessarily acknowledge, or even see. From McQuaid's example of high-performance textiles we move to Sabrina Gschwandtner, who writes about how the act of knitting has provided her with a template for her diverse practice. Knitting informs not only what she makes as an artist but also how she thinks as a critic and what she orchestrates as a curator. "The model for my career as an artist, curator, writer, editor and publisher is knitting," offers Gschwandtner. Her use of knitting extends far beyond the production of cloth to suggest that knitting can provide a model of thinking that guides a vast range of creative actions.

The aspirations of fashion may seem useless. But trends are in fact at the heart of what drives the complex fashion industry. Lou Taylor looks back through history and provides us with a list of attributes that have allowed textiles in fashion to meet the illusive criteria of "being fashionable." Taylor posits, "Twelve cultural characteristics are identified, which have to be conjoined fortuitously together before the desired 'discrete elite' position is reached." Taylor offers us logic in an area of knowledge that is often dismissed as illogical or fickle. In doing so she offers a calculation for the usefulness (in fashion terms) of the textile used in fashion. From the fashionable we then move to an opposite: the stigmatized. Nathaniel Hawthorne's story *The Scarlet Letter*, published in 1850, tells a harrowing account of a woman made to embroider and wear a scarlet-colored letter *A* as the punishment for what her community assumes to be the actions of an adulteress. Here, the use of the textile is to identify and mark out an individual for unishment. The larger issue of the textile as an indicator of a particular identity is an important aspect of its use within cultures around the world today. Hawthorne's example shows us—via fiction—that this is not always a positive or even well-meaning undertaking.

Finally, Alice Walker concludes this section, and the book, with a short story set in America that pokes fun at a superficial interest in craft and handwork. Walker creates two strikingly different sisters who hold starkly different reasons for valuing their modest material inheritance. The narrative questions a fleeting connection to textile making and use, and in doing so challenges one of the sister's motivations for gathering heirlooms. In this short story Walker allows the textile to be cherished, not as a decorative flourish, but through its potential for use.

41

STRONGER, FASTER, LIGHTER, SAFER, AND SMARTER

Matilda McQuaid

Editor's introduction: Matilda McQuaid is deputy curatorial director and head of the textiles department at the Smithsonian Institution's Cooper-Hewitt, National Design Museum in New York City. In 2005 McQuaid curated *Extreme Textiles: Designing for High Performance*, held at the Cooper-Hewitt. The exhibition and accompanying book focus on high-performance textiles found across diverse industries from medicine and sports to transportation and architecture. In her introduction, "Stronger, Faster, Lighter, Safer, and Smarter," McQuaid observes the coincidental beauty to be found in technical textiles that are designed for performance above all else. The five attributes of the title are drawn from the performance standards of the technical textiles industry and remind us that textiles are of value to different industries for vastly different reasons. But even in their most extreme forms, they always surround us. As McQuaid observes, textiles are "in every part of our physical environment."

What can be stronger than steel, faster than a world's record, lighter than air, safer than chain mail, and smarter than a doctor? Hint: it is in every part of our physical environment—lying under roadbeds, reinforcing concrete columns, or implanted into humans. A riddle with one answer and many parts, it is also the subject of the exhibition and accompanying book *Extreme Textiles: Designing for High Performance*. Textiles are the answer, and the world of technical textiles—high-performance, purely functional, and precisely engineered fabrics—is the vital component.

Technical textiles represent, in volume, the smallest segment of the enormous textile industry, yet they are some of the most innovative and purest examples of design today. Aesthetic and decorative qualities are not requirements for a technical textile, and if one finds such a textile visually arresting, it is by pure coincidence. Some of these materials and their applications represented here are unique, others are experimental, many are collaborations across a variety of disciplines, and all represent extraordinary amounts of research and dedication by artists, designers, scientists, engineers, and visionaries.

The journey to find these often peculiar but essential cultural artifacts of our day has been a long one. For me, it started fifteen years ago at the Museum of Modern Art (MoMA), when I was reading a catalogue for the 1956 exhibition *Textiles*

Source: From *Extreme Textiles: Designing for High Performance* by Matilda McQuaid (London: Thames & Hudson, 2005) pp. 11–30. © 2005. Reprinted by kind permission of Thames & Hudson Ltd., London. With the permission of the author, some minor corrections or edits have been made in the version of the text published here.

USA. The catalogue featured a special category of industrial fabrics (with swatches within the pages), which included materials for convertible car tops, tires, and radar deflection. Arthur Drexler, one of the curators of the exhibition, wrote about these fabrics:

> Many industrial fabrics inadvertently heighten properties familiar to us in other materials. The blond opulence of loosely plaited tire cord, though it is always hidden within layers of rubber, rivals fabrics used for formal gowns. . . . Industrial fabrics rarely if ever are designed for aesthetic effect, yet they seem beautiful largely because they share the precision, delicacy, pronounced texture, and exact repetition of detail characteristic of twentieth-century machine art.

These beautiful and engineered accomplishments, sometimes mundane and at other times monumental, were on par with the core of MoMA's design collection—the machine art as exemplified by the exalted ball bearing and propeller blade. I wondered how technical textiles had evolved nearly fifty years later.

The textiles and applications presented in *Extreme Textiles* are certainly examples of twentieth- and twenty-first-century machine art, but they are also studies in ingenuity, creativity, and perseverance. The objects in the show do not represent the most common uses of technical textiles; instead, the selection is based on objects for extreme applications, such as the textile integral to the first controlled flight by man, future apparel for explorers visiting Mars, and the garment that can monitor the vital signs of and provide live communication with a soldier on the battlefield. They might be unfamiliar to us now, but they have already had repercussions in areas such as aeronautics and the medical industry.

These textiles are causing a quiet revolution. Quiet because the innovations that have occurred over the last forty to fifty years, with the development of high-performance fibers such as aramids and carbon fibers, have been largely contained within the small markets of aerospace and the military. Not until the 1980s did the rest of the world become more familiar with the existence and potential uses of these fibers and textiles, which resulted in exceptional growth in the field. While more mature commercial development occurred in the 1990s, the new millennium has been, and will continue to be, marked by the global networking of these technologies and the further expansion of the markets and applications for these textiles.

There is not an area of our world unaffected by the advances in technical textiles. Architecture, transportation, industry, medicine, agriculture, civil engineering, sports, and apparel have all benefited from the tremendous progress and the unique collaborations that have taken place in the field. Principles of textile science and technology merge with other specialties such as engineering, chemistry, biotechnology, material/polymer science, and information science to develop solutions unimaginable a century ago. Who would have thought that we would have the technology to design and some day build a forty-story tower out of carbon-fiber composite, or walk on a planet that is fifty-one million miles away, or have clothing that can automatically react and adapt to the surrounding environment? These are achievements that rely on an interface between many disciplines, and require a willingness to experiment time and time again.

Because these objects are extreme and their ultimate success is determined by how they perform under very specific conditions, the organization of the exhibition and book has followed the lead of the technical-textile industry. These performance standards will be the barometers and categories in which to assess the textiles and applications: stronger, faster, lighter, safer, and smarter. Some objects fit neatly into one classification, others into several depending upon their ultimate function. Choices for placement usually respond to the primary motivation for the objects' creation. The essays included in this book elucidate significant events across the major areas of technical textiles, examine the different technologies that have made some of these extraordinary inventions possible, and demystify material and technique in order for us to understand how and why textiles play such a significant role in our lives.

STRONGER

Incredible strength is one advantage of many of the new textile fibers, which have the capability to reinforce as well as lift hundreds of tons. Susan Brown explains through specific case studies the innovative fibers and the extraordinary structures and techniques that have made it possible to achieve such exceptional strength. Basic textile techniques have been around for centuries—weaving, braiding, knitting, and embroidery—but with new fibers, coupled with new types of machinery, or even old looms that have been retooled to accommodate these fibers, the results and final applications are astonishingly different.

An example of a very simple woven structure is tire-cord fabric, which has been used to reinforce tires for over 115 years. Pneumatic tires were originally patented in 1845 in England by R. W. Thompson, but they were first applied to a bicycle in 1888 by John Boyd Dunlop, a Scottish veterinarian, who fitted a rubber hose to his son's tricycle and filled this tire with compressed air. Dunlop patented the pneumatic tire the same year and began limited production; within a decade it had been adopted by the automobile industry. Simultaneously, Dunlop was the first to use a canvas fabric to reinforce the rubber. Over time the canvas was replaced with nylon and rayon, and today primarily steel cord and polyester are used—except when aramids are needed, in specialty vehicles and racing cars. KoSa (now Invista), a leading producer of polyester resin, fiber, and polymer products, has developed a reinforcement fabric made of high-modulus, low-shrinkage polyester industrial filament yarns that is principally used in radial passenger and light-truck tires. Loosely

woven and heat-stabilized, it is hidden under layers of rubber, but its significant structural function contributes to successful performance, road handling, and tire durability. . . .

Large, flexible bulk containers, which on first impression seem relatively low-tech and not much more than an oversized tote bag, provide more than reinforcement. These custom-designed containers, such as Super Sack® by B.A.G. Corp.®, are capable of lifting up to twelve tons of liquid or solid. Made of woven recyclable polypropylene, they have been engineered to achieve maximum container capacity while compacting to a fraction of their size when empty. . . .

An even larger container, designed to transport fresh water to the southern and eastern coasts of the Mediterranean, the Gulf states, and southern California, is the Very Large Flexible Barge (VLFB), currently being designed by Buro Happold. The concept of towable bags was developed several decades ago, but the bags were used only in small sizes, as larger sizes were unreliable.[1] The new VLFB will have the capacity to transport 250,000 cubic meters of water (over 66,000,000 gallons)—a two-day supply of water for a population of approximately one million people. Its dimensions are 1,148 feet (length) by 236 feet (width) by 46 feet (depth), and, although the material is proprietary, it will likely be made of a polyurethane-coated nylon. . . .

FASTER

Faster implies a high-performance edge in various types of sporting equipment—cars, sailboats, racing sculls, and bicycles—which have all benefited from the combination of strength, rigidity, and lightness attained in carbon-fiber composites. The WilliamsF1 BMW FW26, the Formula One (F1) car designed and raced in 2004, can reach sixty miles per hour within two and a half seconds, and achieve top engine speed of over two hundred miles per hour. Sailboats are attempting to reach record-breaking times of fifty knots powered only by the wind, and downhill skiers achieve speeds of more than 140 miles per hour. These exceptional performances are due to a combination of physical and mental stamina and material and technological development, and advanced composites provide the successful link to make these events possible.

Advanced composites have been available only since the 1960s, and they were primarily used in aerospace and the military until the early 1980s. All areas of the sports industry realized their enormous potential, with carbon fiber providing the highest stiffness, aramids absorbing the greatest amounts of energy, and both having the ability to replace heavier metal with lighter components. Because lightness ultimately affects speed, textile-reinforced composites are providing major new areas of opportunity for the technical-textile market.

The WilliamsF1 featured here is a blend of endurance and performance, and has achieved these goals through a combination of research in materials and electronics. . . . Although there are many components of the F1 that are either reinforced or made exclusively out of high-performance fibers—for example, brake discs and tires—the largest is the chassis. The car is made of advanced composite materials, such as a carbon-fiber reinforcement within a polymer matrix—mostly taking the form of epoxy resin. Components are molded by laminating layers of the carbon/epoxy material onto a shaped mold (tool) and then curing the resin under heat and pressure. The form of raw materials is the same as that employed in the aerospace industry, i.e., carbon fiber preimpregnated with epoxy in a "staged" condition (partly cured, not wet, and therefore stable to handle) or what is commonly called "prepreg." Woven carbon fiber is primarily used because it can be draped and tailored into complex shapes, although unidirectional fiber is also employed. Plies of the prepreg are stacked onto the mold and sealed in a vacuum bag, which has the effect of compacting the laminate prior to curing. This assembly is then put into an autoclave, or a pressurized oven, where nitrogen is applied at around

seven bar (seven atmospheres, or one hundred pounds per square inch) to properly consolidate the laminate through the bag. At the same time the temperature in the vessel is raised to approximately 175°C (350°F) in order to cure it. After ninety minutes the part is cooled and is then ejected from the mold as a solid piece.[2]

This same technology, at smaller and larger scales, is used to make everything from high-performance speed-skiing helmets to racing sailboats, as revealed in an interview with master boat builder Eric Goetz. Over the years it has been the elite athlete—whether a race-car driver, skier, or sailor—who has played an important role in the design process. User becomes designer more and more, as racing experience is invaluable in understanding the practical and performance issues of the equipment.

Beat Engel, a downhill racer, started making speed-skiing helmets for himself in the mid-1980s. Over the years he has made helmets for world champions such as Tracie Max Sachs, the 2004 International Ski Federation (FIS) World Cup champion. . . . Clocking speeds greater than 140 miles per hour, Sachs's performance relies on the highest level of aerodynamics to permit the least resistance as she plummets down the track. Her Speed-monster helmet completely envelops her head and neck so that legs, torso, and head become like one compact bullet. . . . The helmet is a double-shell system with a thin outer layer, used primarily to enhance performance, that breaks away if she should fall, leaving behind an inner helmet for protection. Both shells are made out of woven Kevlar® compressed between two layers of woven and nonwoven glass fiber and applied with polyester resin. It is durable, fast, and light.

LIGHTER

The quality of lightness is always a focus of design for space and aeronautics, as we continue to be fascinated with the ongoing dream of human flight. This dream has inspired some of the most dramatic and curious inventions across all ages.

Beginning with the most rudimentary hand-crafted wings made from a variety of materials of their time, humans have attempted to mimic birds to achieve self-powered flight. A group of flying enthusiasts called birdmen have come closest to attaining this vision. Since the 1930s, these men have donned wing suits in order to decelerate free fall and prolong their time aloft for aerial stunts. Most of these early birdmen used a single layer of canvas, stretched from hand to foot like a bat's wing, which allowed little control and virtually no horizontal movement (glide). The breakthrough came in the early 1990s when Patrick de Gayardon invented a wing suit that was neither flat nor rigid, and had wings between his arms and body as well as his legs, with an upper and lower surface that provided an inlet for air—much like a modern parachute. Since then a number of suits have expanded the idea of skydiving into sky flying, such as Alban Geissler's Skyray, an attachable wing system with a rigid composite made of Kevlar and carbon fiber. . . . Daniel Preston and Tom Parker of Atair Aerospace have developed their own wing suit, which consists of a jumpsuit and attached wings made of nonwoven polyethylene laminate and Spectra® fiber. . . . The experience of flying in this suit is different from skydiving, as the wings fill with air as soon as the birdman spreads his limbs. The fabric has no porosity, so the wings remain rigid in flight. The shape of the wing is determined by its three-dimensional inflatable sewn structure and the disposition of the arms and shoulders of the person in the suit.

The birdman still relies on the parachute to land safely on the ground. Parachutes were first used to jump from an airplane in 1912. Atair Aerospace, founded in 2000 by Daniel Preston, grew out of their European counterpart, Atair Aerodynamics, established by Stane Krajnc in 1992. Atair is dedicated to creating state-of-the-art parachute designs as well as flight-navigation systems for all varieties of clients, from the military to major corporations. Their composite parafoil improves upon the most basic building block of parachutes by replacing ripstop nylon, whose construction

had remained unchanged for more than fifty years, with a flexible nonwoven composite material. This advanced fabric is made by sandwiching an engineered pattern of high-strength fibers, such as ultra-high molecular weight polyethylene (Spectra/Dyneema®) or aramids, between layers of thin polymer foil, and then fusing them under extreme heat. . . . The resulting parafoils have proven to be 300% stronger, 600% less stretchable, and 68% lighter than those constructed in nylon. As the canopy size grows, the strength of this composite material will increase exponentially, and the weight will decrease. This will become an enabling technology for parachutes to be used with extremely heavy cargo weights, where nylon has proven to be a limiting factor.

Orville and Wilbur Wright may not have intentionally mimicked birds, like the birdmen, when the brothers achieved the first fully controlled flight in an aircraft in 1902. . . . Although this was one year before the landmark day in December when, under power, they sustained heavier-than-air flight, this earlier flight marked the invention of the airplane and officially inaugurated the aerial age.[3]

The textile that they used for covering the wings of the 1902 glider was a type of cotton muslin called "Pride of the West," typically used for ladies' slips. They purchased it off-the-shelf from Rike-Kumler Company, a department store in their hometown of Dayton, Ohio. The brothers used the muslin in its natural state and applied it on the bias. This formed a very tight surface that would distribute landing (or crashing) loads across the wing.[4] They needed a fabric that was flexible and durable in order to achieve their groundbreaking idea for controlling the aircraft, referred to as wing warping, which entails twisting the wing tips of the craft in opposite directions.

ILC Dover's Unmanned Aerial Vehicle (UAV) is another example of innovation in wing technology. . . . This inflatable wing, made out of a Vectran® restraint, or outer and structural layer, and a polyurethane bladder, can be packed down to a bundle ten times smaller than its deployed wing span of seventy-five inches. It has the potential to fly into any area or situation that would endanger human life—firefighting, military, search and rescue missions—as well as when conditions need to be assessed for risk, such as avalanche/volcanic activity, iceberg patrol, and forest fire survey. Although inflatable wings have been around for several decades, what has evolved during this time are smart materials like electronic textiles for adding functions to the wing. Such electronic textiles are integrated into the UAV, providing a means of controlling direction, communicated remotely. Control can be obtained simply through deformation of the wing geometry.[5] The UAV project has benefited from using technology that ILC Dover implemented in spacesuits and the airbags for the Mars Lander, including the use of high-strength fibers. Fabrics with high strength-to-weight ratios, such as Kevlar and Vectran, have improved the packing efficiency in inflatable wing designs.[6]

There are also more earthbound examples of lightness, which Philip Beesley and Sean Hanna discuss in their essay on textiles and architecture. Exploring areas outside of traditional tensile and membrane structures, Beesley and Hanna find that advanced composites are being used more and more, and on a much larger scale, in architecture. From future projects like Michael Maltzan's house on Leona Drive to Peter Testa's forty-story tower, textile foundations are often at the core of building structures and materials.

SAFER

Certainly world events have broadened the role of protective applications in recent years, and unique combinations of high-performance fibers and structures are making textiles resistant to cuts, abrasions, bullets, or punctures, and providing protection against extreme cold and heat, chemical or biological hazards, radiation, or high voltages. NASA and the military are playing essential roles in the research and development of

textiles in this area, and they are also turning to small, cutting-edge companies such as adventure-gear makers to supply their astronauts and elite soldiers.

Some of these textiles are now very familiar to us—Gore-Tex®, Mylar®, and Kevlar—as they have been integrated into apparel and accessories that may be in our closet today. Cara McCarty discusses and cites examples of this phenomenon, referred to as transfer technology, and acknowledges the important role NASA has played in finding and developing materials that are tested for extreme environments like space, but eventually have great potential on Earth.

Perhaps the ultimate in protective clothing is the spacesuit, a multi-layered body armor and life-support system designed to protect against known and unknown hazards in space. Amanda Young, the official keeper of spacesuits at the Smithsonian Institution's National Air and Space Museum in Washington, D.C., discusses the evolution of the spacesuit, from the first prototypes to the most current developments. Consistent with the process used today, NASA employed the most advanced materials in their prototypes, which led to the white spacesuit that is so familiar to us now. For example, silica Beta cloth, produced by Owens Corning under contract to NASA during the Apollo program, is a nonflammable, Teflon®-coated glass fiber that was used in spacesuits and inside the command module. . . . This was replaced in the mid-1970s with multifibrous Ortho fabric—a combination of Nomex®, Kevlar, and Gore-Tex fibers, and the material of choice for spacesuits throughout assembly of the International Space Station.[7] Chromel-R®, a metallic-fiber fabric, was developed for resistance to abrasions and cuts. The fibers were made of chromium-nickel alloy, which exhibited, at the time, relatively high tensile and tear strength. Although never used in the overall suit (except in an early prototype), it was applied to gloves and boots in the Apollo program.

The gloves that accompany the spacesuit are elaborately customized for each astronaut. Besides fitting properly, they have to be flexible and light-weight while protecting against heat and cold, and must not impede movement or dexterity. Other types of protective gloves may not be customized so much for the specific user as they are for the particular function. SuperFabric® is a new fabric that was first developed for cut and puncture resistance in the medical profession. It has since been adapted for industrial, military, recreational, and household applications. For instance, FingerArmor™ protects two of the most vulnerable and valuable digits for professional butchers. . . . Miniscule circular guard plates cover all sides and are bound to the nylon base fabric. The base fabric can vary depending upon the use, but it is the guard plates that provide the ultimate protection against cuts. In the Razor-wire gloves, the guard plates are only on the palm side and spaced more widely apart than the FingerArmor. . . . These plates also vary in terms of density, surface texture, and coating, and can fulfill additional performance requirements such as enhanced grip or higher flexibility.

A counterpoint to the SuperFabric gloves is currently being used by the Army for handling razor wire—a hand-cut and sewn suede glove that is covered on the palm side with evenly spaced industrial staples. . . . The "teeth" of the staple face inward, and the interior of the glove has been lined with flannel to protect the hand from being punctured. The positioning of staples takes into account the barbs of the razor wire and performs like chain mail. Although the Army is currently testing SuperFabric to replace the staple-issued gloves, this medieval masterpiece exemplifies the ingenuity that results from necessity and an acute awareness of performance qualities in existing materials.

Motorcycle racing requires unique glove technology that, like the astronaut's glove, provides flexibility, comfort, grip, and resistance to abrasion and moisture. Held, a German company that specializes in gloves, uses kangaroo hide in its Krypton glove along with palm and side hand protection of Kevlar brand fiber ceramic and a lining of Suprotect® shock-absorbing foam. . . . Other areas of the glove are reinforced with these materials to enhance shock resistance and provide the lightest and most protective glove possible.

SMARTER

Textiles are the natural choice for seamlessly integrating computing and telecommunications technologies to create a more personal and intimate environment. Although clothing has historically been passive, garments of the twenty-first century will become more active participants in our lives, automatically responding to our surroundings or quickly reacting to information that the body is transmitting. These extraordinary examples and uses of electronic textiles are discussed by Patricia Wilson, whose interest in historical metallic embroidery has provided inspiration and guidance in her profession as a material scientist and engineer. She discusses some of the most radical and innovative work being done in this burgeoning field of electronic textiles and, from personal experience, recounts the important collaborations that have taken place between artists, designers, scientists, and engineers.

One of the main incubators for such interdisciplinary study and thought is the MIT Media Lab, which has produced many remarkable designers. Three graduates recently formed Squid:Labs, a consulting and research group focused on developing breakthrough technologies in the fields of robotics, materials, and manufacturing. One area they have been investigating is the incorporation of metallic fibers into ropes. . . . Those metallic fibers can be used to transmit information and act as antennas for wireless communication, and, potentially more interesting, they can be used as sensors. Squid:Labs has developed an electronic rope made by braiding traditional yarns, such as nylon or polyester, with metallic yarns. There are many variables in the braiding process, including the total number and diameter of yarns, ratio of metallic yarns to polyester/nylon, and the arrangement of metallic yarns. For instance, these yarns could be entirely contained within the rope, but if testing for abrasion, then every few feet, a metallic yarn could migrate to the outside and then back inside the rope. This way, if conductivity is lost in a certain segment of the rope, it is assumed that abrasion has taken place on the external metallic yarn.

There are numerous applications for these intelligent ropes. Mountain climbers could rely on sensors to estimate critical strain in order to know when to retire overly stressed ropes; construction sites could reduce on-site inspection with these sensors, which would indicate when ropes have been compromised because of abrasion; and high-tension power lines, oceanic communication lines, and other electric cables could be enhanced dramatically by adding a thin, intelligent rope around the outside of the cable. All of these examples employ different types of structures that have been used for centuries, but have been transformed into flexible machines or computers that can transmit vital signs of their internal parts.

The variety of applications and design techniques in *Extreme Textiles* attests to the fact that textiles can be anything. They offer the versatility to be hard or soft, stiff or flexible, small or large, structured or arbitrary. They are collectors of energy, vehicles of communication and transport, barriers against physical hazards, and carriers of life-saving cures. They have been created by teams of professionals whose disciplines are diverse, yet who have joined forces with conviction and dedication to chart a course that is reinventing textiles. The future of design lies with these examples of disruptive innovation as textiles continue to push boundaries, eliminate borders between the sciences, and remain a foundation of our physical world.

NOTES

1. Ian Lidell, "Very Large Flexible Barges," in *Patterns 14* (newsletter, Buro Happold Consulting Engineers for Aquamarine Transportation, forthcoming).
2. Brian P. O'Rourke (chief composites engineer, Williams Grand Prix Engineering, Ltd.), in correspondence with the author, June 2004.
3. For a complete history of the Wright brothers, see Tom D. Crouch and Peter L. Jakab, *The Wright Brothers and the Invention of the Aerial Age* (Washington, D.C.: Smithsonian National Air and Space Museum, 2003).
4. Rick Young, in discussion with the author, June 2004.
5. David Cadogan, Tim Smith, Ryan Lee, Stephen Scarborough, David Graziosi, "Inflatable and Rigidizable Wings for Unmanned Aerial Vehicles" (paper, 44th AIAA/ASME/ASCE/AHS Structures, Structural Dynamics, and Materials Conference, April 7–10, 2003), (American Institute of Aeronautics and Astronautics, 2003), 6.
6. Ibid., 1.
7. Evelyne Orndoff, "Fine Gems: The Rare Fabrics of NASA," *Industrial Fabric Products Review* (July 2001): 61.

42

KNITTING IS . . .

Sabrina Gschwandtner

Editor's introduction: Sabrina Gschwandtner is an artist, curator, and writer. From 2002 to 2007 she edited and published the 'zine *KnitKnit*, now held in the permanent collection of the Museum of Modern Art, New York. Her book *KnitKnit: Profiles and Projects from Knitting's New Wave* was released in 2007. Gschwandtner's practice crosses the disciplines of textiles, video, and film—often through work that observes no disciplinary boundaries between the three. The text reprinted here was written for the first issue of the *Journal of Modern Craft*, published in 2008. Using knitting as her focal point, she considers the varied ways in which the technique has provided her with an entry point into making, thinking, collaboration and conversation. Knitting is treated as a template for interdisciplinary practice, finding a far-reaching application that moves beyond the functional use of discrete knitted objects to instead offer a way of acting and commenting on the world around us.

When I'm asked what I do I often reply that I'm an artist who works with film, video and textiles. To me the link between the three is instinctive and implicit—media is a textile—and my work expresses why and how I find that to be true. The model for my career as an artist, curator, writer, editor and publisher is knitting.

I started knitting in my final semester of college as an art/semiotics student at Brown University. Two of my roommates were textile students at the Rhode Island School of Design and when they came home late at night, still full of energy, they'd climb onto the yellow stools in our kitchen and chatter and spool yarn toward their needles like addicts. They showed me the basics of knitting and crochet (my mother had taught me when I was eight but I had mostly forgotten) and I was charmed. I started to knit during breaks from the dense theory I was reading for school; stitching, I was completely concentrated on the rhythm of my hands and my frenetic mind would go empty. Within a few months, although I had been rigorously devoted to experimental and avant-garde film during all four years of college, handcraft had become my guiding creative format.

I'd knit or crochet something, leave it, come back, rip it up, fix it, wear it, add some other material, hang it up, leave it, project film onto it, record that, edit it, show it, give it away and start over. Even when I'm not working with knitting as my actual medium or technique I'm still working with it as a single thread out of which emerges a

Source: Sabrina Gschwandtner, "Knitting Is . . . ," *Journal of Modern Craft* 1, no. 2 (2008) pp. 271–278. Reproduced with permission.

Figure 42.1. Sabrina Gschwandtner, *A History of String*, 2007. Hand-embroidered cotton floss on cotton fabric, one wooden standing embroidery hoop, zoetrope, and video (color, sound, RT = loop). Image courtesy of Sabrina Gschwandtner and the Museum of Arts and Design, New York.

surface, a fabric, a narrative, an outfit, a pattern, a text, a recording, and even, despite my seemingly erratic way of working, a form that encompasses all of these things.

KNITTING IS SCULPTURE

Stitching was how I first conceived of working with film as a sculptural material. For an early project, I sewed onto 35 mm slides that had come back from the lab blurry and unusable as the documentation I'd intended. I found that when the sewn slides were projected, the pattern of the thread and the holes left by the sewing needle became the foreground imagery, instead of the photographic image on the slide. The fan of the slide projector blew the loose threads in all directions, which also caused an unusual kind of animation. The slide projector's automatic focus mechanism struggled to focus on the three-dimensional thread hanging in front of and behind the slides and it sometimes gave up, leaving the viewer to inspect a blurry field in between thread and image. I selected a group of eighty slides, put them into the carousel and let them project for ten seconds each in a continual loop. This was the piece; all the ways in which the slide projector abstracted and activated a non-narrative about space. In conceiving of an approach to filmmaking that was in part defined by the craft ethos of mending and recycling but still devoted to the history of avant-garde cinema, I was able to expand on the potential for the

Figure 42.2. Sabrina Gschwandtner, *Phototactic Behavior in Sewn Slides*, 2007. Cotton thread, 35 mm slides, and Kodak Ektapro 9020 slide projector. Image courtesy of Sabrina Gschwandtner.

projected image, but place it within the context of handcraft.

KNITTING IS PARTICIPATION

The more I worked with handcraft materials, the more I came to think about the social spaces they implied. I swung from making quiet, sculptural spaces to creating sites of conversation. I realized that knitting had potential to reach out to a different audience and that collective crafting and dialogue could be part of the art experience: it could catalyze a different kind of exchange, outside of traditional art audience boundaries. This reflected a new interest in the public sphere and in creating artwork with social and political components.

I started thinking about handcraft as a site of resistance—to an oppressively commodity-based art market and to an omnipresent, excessive, and high-speed communicative landscape—but also as a site of empowerment and activism. Knitting has, after all, become popular during every major American war.[1] During wartime, knitters have used their craft for civic participation, protest, therapeutic distraction, and even direct attack.[2]

For my piece *Wartime Knitting Circle*, an interactive installation created for the Museum of Arts & Design's 2007 exhibition "Radical Lace and Subversive Knitting," I wanted to exploit these different uses of wartime knitting in order to incite political conversation between different kinds of people. Knitters represent a diverse audience group in terms of age, race, politics and economics (for every knitter using qiviut, spun copper, or other high-priced yarns there is a knitter making clothes out of economic necessity).

Figure 42.3. Artist Sabrina Gschwandtner at Rachael Matthews's house in London (with Rachael's bunny Rfid), 2007. Photo: Jason Spingarn-Koff.

The installation consisted of nine machine-knitted photo blankets—which in 2005 became a popular way for families to honor their relatives who had been deployed to Iraq and Afghanistan—depicting images culled from newspapers, historical societies and library archives that all showed different ways knitting has been and is being used during war. The installation provided a space and materials for knitters to work on wartime knitting projects; it was also a place for them to consider the role their handcraft could play in the Iraq war. Knitters were allowed to bring in their own projects, or they could choose to work on one of four wartime knitting patterns that were provided. The patterns included Lisa Anne Auerbach's Body Count Mittens,[3] which memorialize the number of US soldiers killed at the time the mittens are made; a simple square to be used for blankets, which were either mailed to Afghans for Afghans[4] or to US soldiers recovering in military hospitals; balaclavas to be sent either to troops in Iraq and Afghanistan or to Stitch for Senate, microRevolt.org's war protest project;[5] and *USS Cole* Slippers, sent to troops on ships. Many of these items were knit by several different people; one knitter would cast on, add a few stitches or rows, then put the project down and later another knitter would advance the piece.

I witnessed several heated arguments at the knitting table and I participated in one of them.

Figure 42.4. Sabrina Gschwandtner, *Wartime Knitting Circle*, 2007. Machine-knit cotton, cotton tablecloth, wooden table and chairs, wool yarn, knitting needles, tape measure, scissors, stitch markers, and other knitting notions. Phyllis Rodriguez, sitting with Sabrina, is also pictured in one of the photo blankets on view as part of the installation. Image courtesy of Sabrina Gschwandtner and the Museum of Arts and Design, New York. Photo: Alan Klein.

A visitor comment book included in the installation recorded some of what happened when I wasn't there:

Political associations made for a more interesting group knitting experience. *Devon Thein*

Added a bit to the helmetliner—Kay worked a square, of course. *Ann Shayne*

Knitting in public is a radical act. *Bonnie Gray*

My earliest memories are the clack of knitting needles (on the therapeutic theme)—my grandmother knitted continuously as we sat in the air-raid shelters in Scotland 1942–45. *S. Holton*

KNITTING IS COMMUNITY

When I started KnitKnit in 2002 it was a very personal format for my thinking through the connections between handcraft and fine art. I had been making one-of-a-kind knit and crochet clothes by hand and selling them to boutiques in Manhattan for about two years when I decided that I wanted to return to art making. I interviewed two friends who had come to handcraft, like me, after studying fine art in college and I put that text into a very rough, photocopied and stapled booklet with spray-painted stencils. *KnitKnit* became a biannual 'zine that took different formats each time and included contributions by all kinds of artists, designers, writers and makers: producing

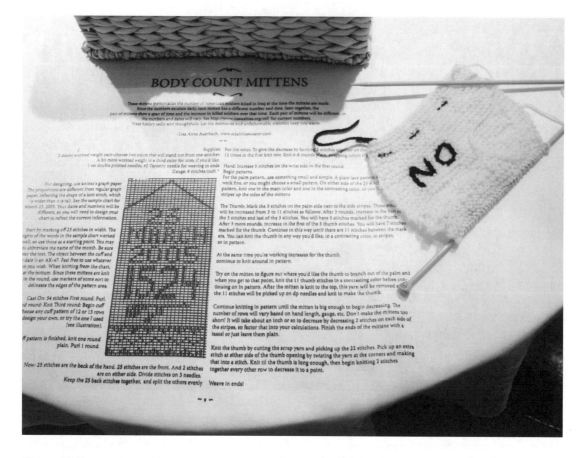

Figure 42.5. Sabrina Gschwandtner, *Wartime Knitting Circle* (detail), 2007. Image courtesy of Sabrina Gschwandtner and the Museum of Arts & Design, New York. Photo: Sabrina Gschwandtner.

KnitKnit, distributing it, and organizing KnitKnit launch events and art exhibitions were ways to create a far-flung community of people interested in displacing the boundaries between art and craft.

When I initiated a KnitKnit book in 2006, I purposely situated it as a craft *and* an art endeavor, working with a craft book editor at Abrams, a publishing house that also makes and distributes art books. With the publisher committed to sending the book to major chains, art bookstores and yarn shops, I chose to profile a mix of knitters making clothing, sculpture, graffiti, therapy, protest and performance, juxtaposing political and conceptual gestures with functional and technical achievements.

KNITTING IS WRITING

This is why so many knitters blog; they're dauntingly aware that making a sweater is, in a way, writing history. As Jim Drain told me when I was interviewing him for my book, ". . . knitting is a living tradition—it's physical knowledge of a culture. Knowledge of language dies so quickly. It's awesome to find a sweater and look at the language of it—to see how it's made, what yarn was

Figure 42.6. Sabrina Gschwandtner, *Wartime Knitting Circle* (detail), 2007. Image courtesy of Sabrina Gschwandtner and the Museum of Arts & Design, New York. Photo: Sabrina Gschwandtner.

used, and how problems were solved. A sweater is a form of consciousness."[6]

My 2007 video, *A History of String*, includes a chapter on quipus, which are recording devices from the Inca Empire. Quipus are beautiful bundles of twisted and knotted colored threads that were continuously tied and retied and presumably read by touch and sight. Each part of the quipu—length, color of string, number of knots, and type of knots—is thought to contain meaning. Because the Spanish destroyed as many quipus as they could find during

their colonial conquest, only about 600 pre-Columbian examples survive, preserved in private and museum collections. Although quipus are generally believed to contain numerical information, some anthropologists are working to translate them into language, reading them as three-dimensional binary code (similar to the way computers translate eight-bit ASCII into letters and words).[7]

One has to wonder how future generations might read our sweaters if written and photographic records of them are lost.

KNITTING IS GIFT

I co-curated (with Sundown Salon founder Fritz Haeg and producer Sara Grady) a salon called the KnitKnit Sundown Salon in 2004. The daylong event included a meeting of the Church of Craft, an exhibition of art and craft works, a film/video screening, a performance and several impromptu fashion shows, among other happenings. It wasn't just the quality of the work inside the geodesic dome where the event was held, nor the abundant activities there that made the salon so memorable; it was the complete reciprocity with which the work was given and received. For eight hours on a cold February day in Los Angeles, the KnitKnit Sundown Salon existed as a utopian, three-tiered marvel of handmade wonders and a communal undertaking that gave me hope for the rise of a new social order.[8]

KNITTING IS PLEASURE

As my mentor Leslie Thornton wrote to me by email:

> I know I've told you this, many women my age must tell you the same thing, but making things, sewing, designing all of my own clothes,

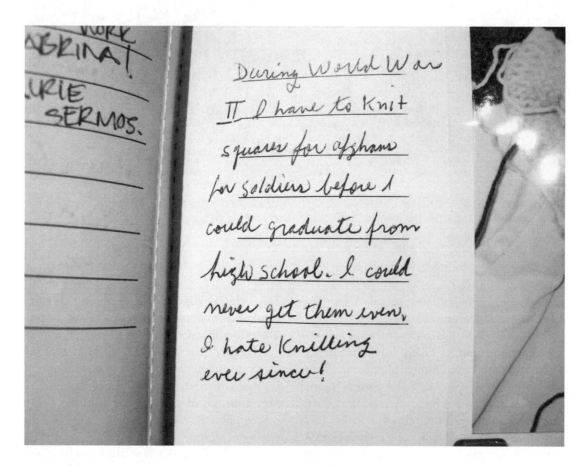

Figure 42.7. Sabrina Gschwandtner, *Wartime Knitting Circle* (detail), 2007. Image courtesy of Sabrina Gschwandtner and the Museum of Arts and Design, New York. Photo: Sabrina Gschwandtner.

knitting, even making beads, but that was much later, when the train to Providence was driving me crazy, so anyway, I was saying, in this very long sentence, possibly the longest I've ever written in my life, I made things nearly constantly when I wasn't in school, studying, going to rock concerts or sleeping, playing kickball, or riding my bike or picking flowers in our huge beautiful yard or catching frogs, from the age of three on.

KNITTING IS HOME

Through my friend Alysa Nahmias, who had at the time just started her architecture degree at Princeton, I learned of Gottfried Semper, the nineteenth-century architect and theorist who asserted that woven and knitted materials effectively separated inner and outer life to create what we know as "home." After a trip to a library, where I read more of his writings, I ended up reprinting one of his texts in *KnitKnit's* third issue. Brian Sholis, an art critic, wrote an introduction to the issue that included the following lines: "Semper not only rehabilitates arts and crafts, integrating them more fully with our understanding of architecture and other fine arts; he also smudges the line between 'advanced' and 'barbaric' contributions to culture, reincorporating the contributions

Figure 42.8. Sabrina Gschwandtner, *Wartime Knitting Circle* (detail), 2007. Image courtesy of Sabrina Gschwandtner and the Museum of Arts and Design, New York. Photo: Sabrina Gschwandtner.

of minority citizens to the achievements of ancient Greece, Egypt, and beyond."[9]

At a "Stitch In" at the Jersey City Art Museum in October 2007 I gave a short talk about war and handcraft. It concluded with a recollection of someone telling me that she thought women did housekeeping/homemaking activities with a kind of irony these days. I asked how the audience felt about that. It really got people going—everyone has an opinion about their home. One by one people spoke up and their responses ranged from detailed explanations of 1970s fiber art to Martha Stewart's design influence on the marketplace to the agony of making a decision about whether to hire a housekeeper to ideas about post 9/11 nesting.

Swedish critic Love Jönsson put this forward during a recent lecture: avant-garde art proposes an access to the everyday that craft, through its traditional link to utility and material culture, already has. Young artists working with handcraft do not need an art world seal of approval, he said, and in reevaluating the craft tradition they have emphasized that:

• making things by hand is joyful; and
• "the functional object is the most interesting one."[10]

Whether knitting is high architecture, hip Home Ec, functional art, or a reaction to terrorism, it is helping us think through our notions of domesticity.

KNITTING IS MEDIA

It's true that people pick up crochet hooks as an escape from the computer. In the face of everything fast and glinting, they want something real—a reinjection of the artisanal or some sense of the integrity of labor. But handcraft will usually send them to the web, which is a contemporary Whole Earth Catalog if you know where to look. When crafters go online searching for instruction they usually end up commenting on other crafters' blogs or posting to myriad threads on craft community boards. In contrast to the lifestyle associated with the professional craftsperson of the late twentieth century (which is still the academic craft model), DIY crafters fluidly use technology to market and sell their work and participate in their communities. As artist and knitwear designer Liz Collins has remarked, "putting together a MySpace page is not that different from collaging or quilting. You're using different materials, to different ends, but along the way you're starting with matter and transforming it into something else, using your hands and your brain."[11]

Knitting is a site, and it can and should be used as a form of broadcasting, just like the Internet, television, or any other public media.

NOTES

1. Allison Smith, *The Muster* (New York: Public Art Fund, 2007).
2. Anne MacDonald, *No Idle Hands: the Social History of American Knitting* (New York: Ballantine Books, 1990).
3. See www.stealthissweater.com/patterns/mittenpattern.pdf.
4. See www.afghansforafghans.org.
5. See www.stitchforsenate.us.
6. Sabrina Gschwandtner, *KnitKnit: Profiles and Projects from Knitting's New Wave* (New York: Stewart, Tabori and Chang, 2007), p. 52.
7. Sabrina Gschwandtner, "A Brief History of String," *Cabinet* 23 (Winter 2006): 38–41.
8. Fritz Haeg (ed.), *Sundown Salon 2001–06 In Words and Pictures* (New York: Evil Twin Productions, 2008).
9. Brian Sholis, "Writings of Nineteenth Century Architect Gottfried Semper," in Sabrina Gschwandtner (ed.) *KnitKnit* 3 (January 2004): 1.
10. Urban FIELD symposium, University College for the Creative Arts, Farnham, England. November 14, 2007.
11. Julia Bryan-Wilson (ed.), "The Politics of Craft," *Modern Painters* (February/March 2008): 78–83.

43

DE-CODING THE HIERARCHY OF FASHION TEXTILES

Lou Taylor

Editor's introduction: Lou Taylor is a dress historian and professor at the University of Brighton, England. In this essay, she writes about the textiles used in fashion. The essay begins by working through the various fabrics used to make clothing, noting their historical value as well as the (often changed) status they command in contemporary fashion. Taylor then proposes twelve qualities that contribute to the status of cloth in the seemingly fickle world of fashion over the past two centuries. While fashion can seem illusive to define, Taylor's systematic approach provides a solid example of how textiles can be analyzed through a variety of value systems. A number of considerations are proposed such as rarity of material, technique of construction or embellishment, price, and the power of a designer or company's brand to confer value on the cloth they use. Even when attempting to define something as slippery as being "in fashion," Taylor finds space to apply a systematic value system that is useful, in large part because of the comprehensive considerations that go beyond taste and timing.

The fabrics of fashion (the term in this context signifies the cloth from which fashionable dress for women is made) remain an under valued social and cultural history research source. Bourdieu's analysis of 'the correspondence between goods production and taste production' of 1979[1] provides, however, a valuable framework around which a useful methodological approach to their study can be constructed. 'Cultural objects', he wrote, 'with their subtle hierarchy, are pre-disposed to mark the stages and degrees of the initiatory progress which defines the enterprise of culture'.[2] Le Wita, citing Balzac, emphasises,

additionally, that an important key to cultural analysis is 'to pay attention to the 'little details,'[3] and indeed the 'little details' which define the status of the fabrics of clothing are an invaluable means of identifying and interpreting complex issues within the 'enterprise of culture'.

We need to remember, though space here precludes debate, that women and men of every culture and every strata of society adorn themselves with some cloth or covering and as Eicher and Barnes point out, the element of fashion is 'often mistakenly considered characteristic only of societies with complex technology'.[4]

Source: Lou Taylor, "De-coding the Hierarchy of Fashion Textiles," in Mary Schoeser and Christine Boydell (eds), *Disentangling Textiles: Techniques for the Study of Designed Objects* (London: Middlesex University Press, 2002) pp. 67–80. Reproduced with permission. With the permission of the author, some minor corrections or edits have been made in the version of the text published here.

Assessed here is one aspect of women's clothing—the forces which add 'distinction' and 'fashionability' to fashion textiles worn within the European and North American fashion tradition, from the eighteenth century onwards and which rank them within a 'hierarchy of fashion textiles'. Twelve cultural characteristics are identified, which have to be conjoined fortuitously together before the desired 'discrete elite'[5] position is reached. When some of these characteristics are missing or reversed, the fabrics acquire increasingly negative status both in cultural and social terms. This notion of positive or negative impact applies to every fashion fabric and had (and has) deep influence on levels of manufacture and consumption.

THE SHIFTING STATUS OF FABRICS

In Europe by the late seventeenth and early eighteenth centuries, the social usage of fashion fabrics was no longer so controlled by sumptuary laws of court and church but had become subject to new forces—those of market economies, which created a whole new set of economic and cultural pressures. The difficulty when trying to examine this development is the problem of identifying each fabric's specific hierarchical status within its own period. Their life span has never been a constant. One major commercial problem for manufacturers has always been this instability because every fashion textile has its own specific cultural biography which can only be generalized here. Further, there is no room here to discuss yarn mixes, although their role too is both important and interesting.

Wool has remained at a constantly stable hierarchical position, with wide consumer demand at every social level. In price terms, over the centuries, the product itself has been subject to vast design and production changes, but has stabilized in the middle and upper market range, where it still remains today. Rothstein points out that Barbara Johnson, moving on the fringes of court society in the mid to late eighteenth century purchased

one really expensive fabric above all the 121 samples she kept in her scrapbook—even more expensive than silk. Given by her brother in May 1760, it cost 20/- a yard. It was a good quality 'Pompadour broadcloth' for making a riding habit, doubtless a long lasting one. In comparison, her best silk, a plain 'garnet colour paduasoy' for Christmas, 1762 cost 10/- a yard.[6] This same hierarchical ranking survived throughout the twentieth century. In 1908, the Paris department store, La Samaritaine, was selling fashion wools in the range of 1.45 francs a meter up to 3.25 for a grey drap *anglais* for tailored costumes. Silks ranged from the cheapest, imported Japanese pongées also at 1.45 francs a meter, up to 8.75 for a Pekin satin voile. Prices for even their best fancy cottons were far below either of these ranges, running from 0.65 for a floral percale up to 1.25 for a tartan zephir.[7]

Silk until the last fifteen or so years, was always the unchallenged queen of fashion fabrics. Silk workshops were established to provide the exclusive, luxury cloths of power. The political and economic strength of great empires and kingdoms was mirrored by the cultural development of court silk weaving workshops—in China, in Ottoman Turkey and in the various rival kingdoms of Renaissance Italy, for example. Silk's position at the top of the hierarchy of fabrics has since remained constant—albeit that it has now to take the form of specific 'designer' lengths to retain this high ranking. As a fibre it now faces the challenge of high status experimental synthetics and suffers from a severe degradation of reputation because of the world-wide flood of cheap, lightweight, exported Chinese silks.

The hierarchical position of **cotton**, by contrast, has been less stable and far more chaotic over the last 250 years. After a weak start in the 1640s when imported Indian designs were seen as too 'bizarre', the product was adapted successfully to Western European fashion taste and chintz became a rage in the highest royal courts.[8] In the mid eighteenth century when Mulhouse, in Alsace, started its printing industry 'the idea of success, of easy winnings, led to a kind of contagious fever in Mulhouse. All sorts of people from chemists to bakers abandoned their professions and took up chintz printing.'[9] This state of distinction lasted through to the early nineteenth century. After that printed cotton lost for ever this supreme 'hot' place in the fashion fabric hierarchy as the 1908 La Samaritaine prices confirm. However, different forms of cotton, notably denim, have steadily climbed the cultural ladder since the 1960s. Now, in the shape of 'designer' jeans, denim has reached the summit of elite status, (also interestingly, whilst retaining mass and sub-cultural success too). 'Denim . . . . is a lucrative market which rakes in money for a design house', explained *Fashion Weekly* in May, 1995. 'Todd Oldham, Romeo Gigli and Dolce and Gabbana are the latest designers to capitalise on the sector.'[10]

The place of **linen** at the top end of the status hierarchy is relatively novel and new because it was seen as a merely practical summer fabric throughout the nineteenth and most of the twentieth century. Despite various efforts to promote the fabric in the 1950s, it remained low in the hierarchy because of its crumple tendencies. 'Sybil Connolly uses pale blue, finely pleated Irish linen for this exquisite ball gown', urged an advertisement in April, *Vogue* of 1956. 'Crush it in a suitcase and it will emerge pleat perfect.' Consumers remained unconvinced. Creases had for too long indicated slovenliness and poverty. It was not until the 1980s, when the Italian notion of crushed, *froissé* linen caught on as a major fashion trend, that linen finally reach a high status positioning for the first time.

Man-made fabrics have seen their fashion ranking rise steadily since a weak start, caused by severe quality problems. In the USA in 1920, consumption of textiles showed only 0.3% rayon, (less even than elitist silk consumption at 0.9%,) with wool at 9.9%, whilst cotton overshadowed both at 88.9%. By 1928, the Silk and Rayon Editor of *Women's Wear* judged the fabric to be 'cheap-looking,' with rayon crepes still seen as 'coarse

and shiny for general dressmaking purposes.'[11] By 1936, with some of these properties technically overcome, 85% of all dresses bought in the USA were made of rayon, with the fabric produced in every price range.[12] Colcombet of Lyons, working with Schiaparelli in the mid 1930s, achieved top success for a very limited range of experimental synthetics,[13] but it was really not until the 1980's, with patronage from top designers such as Issey Miyake, that rayon's hierarchical ranking finally climbed.[14] 1995 reaction to the already demodé nature of ecologically-correct, lumpy, fabrics of early 1990s, was wet and metallic-look nylon or any other hard-edged shiny, crinkled synthetic textiles now at the absolute top of the hierarchy of fashion textiles.

'MARKS OF DISTINCTION'

This movable 'fashionability' of fabrics is dependent upon a set of overlapping 'marks of distinction'. Bourdieu notes that 'the dynamics of the field in which (luxury) goods are produced and reproduce and circulate . . . . lies in the strategies which give rise to their variety and to belief in their value.'[15] These strategic marks of distinction, as they impact on fashion textiles, can be identified basically as follows:

1. Rarity of fibre or cloth type adds exclusivity and high cost and, with those in place, notions of luxury and high positive hierarchical status. A list of such fabric titaniums would include many specific types of complex brocaded and embroidered silk. Silk manufacturers in eighteenth century Lyons developed a deliberate, commercial, hierarchy of fashion silks. Miller has identified these fabric types, prices and their corresponding hierarchical place. *Dorures* silks, some woven with real gold and silver yarns, were clearly at the top.[16] In June, 1957, English *Vogue* was promoting Lyon brocades such as one 'woven in a tiny flower design of 'gold' thread, 'reminiscent of a Bergère print' and selling expensively at £7.19s 6d at Dickens and Jones. This elitist Lyonnais product is still termed today 'Haute Nouveauté'.

A group of rare wools such as cashmere and vicuna were also (and indeed remain) very high on the hierarchical ladder. Kashmir shawls cost a fortune at the height of their success. In 1818 original imported Kashmir shawls sold in Britain from £70 to £100 whilst more bourgeois-oriented Paisleys cost £12.[17] However, once the vogue for shawls finally ended in the early 1870s, Kashmirs fell so rapidly down the hierarchical scale of fashionability that weavers in Kashmir, with hands 'so refined that they were useless at any other occupation, simply died of starvation'.[18]

As Bourdieu explains: 'At each level of the distribution, what is rare and constitutes an inaccessible luxury or an absurd fantasy for those at an earlier or lower level, becomes banal and common and is relegated to the order of the taken-for-granted by the appearance of new, rarer and more distinctive goods'.[19] The easy availability inherent in 'second class' products is the death knell to fashion fabrics. Out of season, unsold, they were and are the stuff of sales. In the days of the British Empire, they were shipped off to the colonies. Australia was a useful dumping ground in the nineteenth century.[20]

2. Novelty: Rarity becomes 'fashionable novelty' once the middle and mass manufacturers get hold of it, yet still has a crucial function within the hierarchical system. James Thomson, a distinguished calico printer, summed it up well in the mid nineteenth century: 'Novelty, the hand maid of fashion and sometimes the enemy of Taste, enjoys but a short and fleeting existence. It is, of its very essence, quick to fade and pass away.'[21]

A new distinction-giving novelty today is the element of shock in fabric design, especially when this involves games play over images of gender and femininity. Red or Dead an avant garde London fashion company, seem to have upset the reporter from *Draper's Record* who felt that their 1994 'mandarin and lemon-yellow Lycra tops, emblazoned with risqué phrases, were more for those who wished to resemble the oriental prostitutes from which they took their inspiration.'[22]

3. Use at an elitist social-ritual function: Cultural distinction is added to fashion fabrics when they are produced for specific, public rites of passage, even more so if these are royal. To give just two examples: William Andrews, working for the Coventry silk ribbon industry at the time of the International Exhibition in London noted in his diary 'I am drafting a ribbon with Prince's Feathers on it for the International exhibition,'[23] whilst the Silver Studio created fifteen 'May silks' designed with blossoms for the wedding of Princess May of Teck to the Duke of York in 1893.[24]

4. Elitist status of wearers: Manufacturers have long used the distinction-enhancing publicity technique of getting their fabrics on to the backs of famous women: royalty, actresses, famous courtesans, movie stars—any woman in the public eye will be of service. Empress Eugenie had to be persuaded to wear heavy silk state dresses, due to industrial unrest in Lyon. She called them her 'political dresses'. She may have been less than delighted therefore to receive as a gift from the Chamber of Commerce of Lyons, thirty-nine 'magnificent' robes, which were first displayed to the public at the Palais Saint Pierre.[25] In July 1995, the actress Liz Hurley, caught up in the publicity avalanche centering on her partner actor Hugh Grant's legal 'difficulties' in Los Angeles, was filmed and photographed massively in her Versace lady bird print dress. This was the company's seasonal theme for spring/summer 1995 and the publicity will have done their sales figures no harm at all.

If such direct royal-media association is not possible, then to give a fabric the name of a famous or royal personage, or to use a related pattern, or colour, is the next best thing. The calico printers Hargreaves of Broad Oak, Accrington, produced a printed tartan cashmere in the early 1840s and called it Glenlyons 'in commemoration of the Queen's visit to the Highlands.'[26] Queen Victoria's famously public version of widowhood added such 'distinction' to mourning that her very public example helped escalate the production and consumption of mourning cloth.

More than sixty different types of mourning fabric were on sale in Britain by the second half of the nineteenth century. The cheaper the cloth type, the more grandiose became the name: Albert Crape, Queen's Crape Cloth, Crepe Imperial. The cheapest of all imitation silk crapes was a crimped cotton version named Victoria Crepe.[27]

5. Country of Origin: From the late seventeenth century France rose to a position of domination of the design of fashion fabrics at an international level and the British textile industry was obliged to copy French style. James Thomson complained in the mid nineteenth century that even the first class calico companies in Britain produced designs 'far below the French.'[28] This strength was still undented in the 1950s when Henri Gowns advertised a dress and jacket in the April, 1956 edition of *Vogue* 'in a wild silk . . . printed in Lyons exclusively for us.' Now Italy and Japan are the latest sources of hot fashion status.

The negative side of country of origin is the lack of status given, for example, to printed rayons now exported in huge tonnage from India. In East and Central Europe the poor, post-war design quality of fabrics ensured that even in times of real shortages in the late 1980s, the unwanted, state-produced cloth gathered dust in the state stores, whilst second hand, western clothes were eagerly snapped up in street markets.[29]

6. Known elitist designer's and/or manufacturer's name: Unlike the designers of fashionable garments for women, textile designers have been, with the exception of a top few internationally known names, largely anonymous.[30] However, on occasion, in France and in the UK, usually when the textile industries were in crisis, the notion of calling up the names of famous 'artist-designers' to boost status and sales was a regular technique. In 1811 'French textile manufacturers wrote to Napoleon's Minister of the Interior asking him to encourage distinguished contemporary artists (such as Isabey) to prepare cone designs (for the French shawl industry) more in keeping with French taste.'[31] The same idea was repeated in post World War One Lyons, when shortages of raw silk and increased international competition caused economic panic. Bianchini-Férier continued commissioning the artist Raoul Dufy whilst la Societé Veuve Berger used Marie Laurencin.[32]

By the 1990s designs were sold to manufacturing companies so freely all around the world by specialist agents, that it is harder than ever to name the designer. However, within the international industry today, top designers would include Makiko Minagawa and Hiroshi Natsushita for Miyake and in Britain, for example, Nigel Atkinson and Bernard Nevill, who is now having a success with bold chintz design, for Unitika/Selmer in Japan.[33]

6a. Known elitist manufacturing names: With few exceptions, these too are often as fleeting as the fabrics they made. A few great names survive from la Grande Fabrique in eighteenth century Lyons, such as Revel and LaSalle though Lesley Miller found a further four hundred, largely unknown designer/manufacturer names of the same period.[34] James Thomson was described in 1850 as the 'Duke of Wellington of calico printers',[35] though Victorian fashion consumers would barely have been aware of his name. Courtaulds, starting their new rayon manufacture at the bottom end of the hierarchical ladder in 1906, and aware that neither their rayon products nor their own company name carried any level of distinction, worked with the London couture house Reville in 1930, in an effort to upmarket the fashion status of rayon.[36] Reville produced a couture collection made in rayon and cotton mixes. One garment was ordered by Princess Helena Victoria. In 1995, the company is still publicly linking its name to elite designers for the same reasons. It held a conference: 'Design in Courtaulds Textiles in the 1990's', with the designer Paul Costelloe as an invited speaker.[37] A London fashion retailer notes in 1995 that: 'People are willing to pay an extra £30 for a designer name' (on a pair of denim jeans). . . . 'It is all down to the label at the back.'[38]

7. High level of aesthetic quality: Here debate enters the complex realms of taste cultures. Bourdieu explains: 'Choosing according to one's tastes is a matter of identifying goods that are objectively attuned to one's position and which 'go together' because they are situated in roughly equivalent positions in their respective spaces.'[39] Thus the range of taste cultures, as Herbert Gans has explained, incorporates every level of social community.[40] In consequence, most design historians reject concepts of 'good' or 'bad' taste.

Taste is what 'brings together things and people that go together'[41] states Bourdieu, but it is also the essence of what separates them. What may seem 'common' to the elite, will be novelty to the poorer client. James Thomson described the two branches of the mid nineteenth century calico trade in just such terms: 'the first, high in character, fewest in numbers and foremost in the race of competition' . . . identifiable by . . . 'the general merit and good taste of their designs. The second class is a numerous, motley . . . mass of dissimilar and discordant elements . . . associated with vulgar ignorance.'[42] Bourdieu calls this a kind of cultural terrorism 'symbolic violence through which the dominant groups endeavour to impose their own life-style . . . flashes of self interested lucidity sparked off by class hatred and contempt.'[43]

We have seen how shock has become an aesthetic device within the avant-garde's challenge to conventional dominant taste. Red or Dead's collection of October, 1994 astonished many in the trade with its 'floral shirts with images taken from garden catalogues and glittering majorette-style lurex mini-skirts'.[44]

Such specific aesthetic judgments are central to elitist fashion fabric design—subtleties of colour, intellectual play with imagery, cleverness of repeats, and elegance of the drawn line in print images are all well understood, especially in top and middle levels of the trade. To give just one example, the *Journal of Design*, dedicated by Henry Cole to the 'improvement' of 'Industrial Art', is littered with his personal, and many might say, dogmatic, aesthetic judgments. In 1850, the journal even went as far as including one calico sample . . . in order to insult its design as follows: 'It is a random blot—a daub, more formless than the first essay of a child, instead of the heightened and refined selection of the matured artist.'[45]

8. Unusual or costly manufacturing technique: Status was and is conferred by complexity of manufacture. Weaving and rich embroidery were for centuries seen as more status-giving than printing. Couturiers demanded, and got, unique one-off fabrics, especially in the inter-war period. Vionnet once asked François Ducharne . . . to produce a special 'woven crepe brocaded with metallic yarns, with one large image in the centre of the fabric—a knot with floating trails. . . . It needed a special loom . . . and the weaver had to make a hole in his ceiling up into his bedroom' to get it into his studio.[46]

Style-related hand embroideries, if beaded and laced with time-consuming detail, still remain status giving today—witness the success of the House of Lacroix in Paris, famous for this type of inventive, luxury fabric.[47] English *Vogue* in October, 1990 featured a tiny mini-dress by Krizia, simple and strapless, but decorated with 13 fringes of large, unusual dangling grey metallic bugle beads—for £2350.

9. High price: Clearly the more costly, the greater the level of distinction-status is achieved through a quite simple and obvious display of 'conspicuous consumption'. Miller has identified the hierarchal range of prices for Lyon's silks in 1751, which shows 'dorures' to be two hundred times more expensive than plain silk.[48] Ducharne's haute nouveauté silks cost 1295 francs a meter in 1925, whilst the bourgeois-oriented Paris department store, Au Printemps, was selling its own 'soieries nouveautés in the same season, for 9.90 to 39 francs.[49] Marion Hume, at the summer couture shows of 1995 in Paris, reported that the 'starting price for clothes is now £10,000 running up to £35,000 for a cocktail frock.'[50]

Yet the gift to Barbara Johnson in 1760 of expensive 'Pompadour broadcloth', owes its high price not to fashionability at all, but to durability, excellence of quality and value for money. The riding habit, a non-fashion garment, was intended to last through many hunting seasons. However, if durability is combined with cheapness, negative status sets in. As John Irwin wrote, 'one of the factors contributing to the abandonment (of the use of shawl) 'in upper class circles, was undoubtedly its increasing popularity amongst the lower classes. By 1870, a Jacquard-woven Paisley could be bought for as little as £1.'[51]

10. Newness of pattern and colour were and are central to considerations of distinction. Fashion fabrics were strongly subject to status-enhancing, bi-annual fashion cycles of image and colour from the early eighteenth century onwards, if not before. A Paisley shawl manufacturer, described the sequence of shawl fashion colours over a seven year period: yellow in 1817, replaced by dark green with crimson and orange, followed by crimson grounds figured in black, blue and greeny-white. When George IV visited Edinburgh in 1822 patriotic Scottish blue styles with white grounds came 'in' with great éclat.[52] Chintz patterns were subject to faster changes. To cite just one manufacturer's turn-over: the *Journal of Design* of March 1850, received samples of 100 cambrics, 200 calicoes and 'sundry specimens of half-mourning . . . adapted to the coming season' from W. Benecke of Manchester. . . .

Methods of diffusing information are an essential feature in the seasonal style race. The first French textiles forecasting journal was published, monthly, in 1838: the *Journal des Manufactures d'Etoffes Nouvelles et de Négociants en Nouveautés*.[53] The silk industry in Lyons was producing its own *Carte de Nuances* by the 1920s.[54] The launching of autumn and spring colours was still strong in UK, retail window displays right through to the 1980s. This has since largely been exploded by the commercial need of manufacturers to sell collections at least every three months. The *Draper's Record* reported the Italian Designer collections on October 15, 1994. Versace showed 'pistachio, aqua, primrose, pink and cappuccino', whilst Missoni used 'delicate aquatic colours'. By the spring of 1995, high street rails were hung with soft pastels. There was no hope for the shopper who wanted fiery red in summer 1995.

11. Tactile qualities of delicacy, vulnerability, exceptional softness etc: Delicacy is the heaven of fashion fabrics whilst durability is the graveyard. Fabrics such as cotton muslin and silk chiffon, do not even have to be costly, as long as they are delicate, used in profusion and clearly require a lot of time consuming care. All of that counteracts the negativity of cheap price, as evidenced in the highly fashionable, befrilled, trained, bustle-back, pale muslin, evening dresses in Tissot's famous 1873 painting 'Too Early'.[55]

In direct contrast, mass produced rayon or nylon versions of silk chiffon and organza, always carried the most negative hierarchical status. Briefly successful marketing promotions were launched in the mid-1950s, aimed at a mid stream market, with garments made up by companies such as Eastex.

English *Vogue* of April, 1956 featured 'rose printed, sheer nylon organza' . . . made into . . . 'enchanting dresses by the talented New York designer Anne Fogarty.' . . . The fabrics could be heat set into pleats, washed well, barely needed ironing but draped badly, were extremely hot to wear and unfortunately never wore out. This added up to that least desirable of all qualities, durability.

12. Elitist-oriented marketing: The use of marketing (including retailing through exclusive outlets), clearly also plays a significant status-raising role. Miller's recent research shows that the success of the famous eighteenth century Lyonnais silk fabricant, Jean Revel, who sold his silks to European royalty from Madrid to St. Petersburg, owed his triumph not at all to any personal design skills but rather 'his talent lay in marrying fine art with lucrative business practice'.[56] The business world of fashion has long recognized the commercial importance of such distinction-enhancing marketing. Henry Mayhew, taken to the mourning fabric department at Jay's by his aunt in the 1850s, remembered the 'unshoppy'[57] appearance of the grandiose store, with no vulgar images of commerce or trade to be seen. In 1928, the fabricant François Ducharne developed the chic marketing ruse of

publishing a limited edition folio of his firm's
Michel Dubost designs, with an introduction by
Colette. She duly wrote: 'Everything is magnificent . . . look at this gigantic gloxinia . . . like a
little whirlwind in the corner of a silk shawl. It is
as miraculous as a rainbow and as beautiful as the
eye of an octopus.'[58]

Whereas it might be genuinely easy to eulo-
gize about the successful marriage of complex
weaving-printing techniques and refined aesthetics found in these masterly *haute nouveauté*
designs, efforts to use marketing to upgrade the
fashion status of mass produced fabrics are more
problematic. Rayon (and later nylon, polyester etc,) producers launched distinction-seeking
advertising campaigns from the late 1920s, to
imbue their fabrics with what Bourdieu calls an
image of 'would be' luxury: 'The new petite bourgeoisie distinguishes itself by particular frequent
choice of the adjectives (and one can add here 'invented names') which most declare the intention
of distinction.'[59] This myriad of names included
Courtaulds 'Witchcraft,' a viscose lace of 1929
and even 'Courgette,' an imitation georgette.[60]
The Sunsilk Weaving Company chose 'Syl-de-
Chine—a most delightful fabric. Colours will not
fade'.[61] Pontings, in a 1933 mail order catalogue,
optimistically featured 'Glorichene.'[62]

Aggressive marketing has ensured that cotton, in the shape of denim, is once again high
up in the hierarchy of fabrics. Levi's sales figures
in Japan alone in 1994 were £3 billion. Their
USA 1995 launch used an Inuit model, Irina
Pantaeva from Siberia, who, according to Marion Flume, was tipped as the first Asian super
model.[63]

Negative marketing appproaches include the
use of any term such as durable, long-lasting, economical,[64] good value for money because all of
these are anathemas to the concept of 'fashion'.
These terms were only used for products aimed at
the poorest consumers, such as rayons described
as 'inexpensive . . . quality not having been sacrificed for price' . . . giving . . . 'hard wear on all
occasions'.[65]

CONCLUSION

Fashion textiles are born out of the professional
design and commercial activities of generations
of designers, merchants and manufacturers and
out of the taste cultures of consumers. They deserve specific, detailed examination in their own
right, whether costly or lowly, whether rare or
commonplace.

Each and every fabric has its own ranking
within a constantly shifting hierarchy of fashion textiles dependent upon the twelve strategic 'marks of distinction' identified here, which
can be used to de-code the intricate web of social
and cultural 'meanings' hidden within the folds
of fashion fabrics. It is only when all or most
of these twelve marks of distinction come together
that a fashion fabric acquires 'high' style. It is then
that mere warps and wefts acquire what Bourdieu
identifies as 'the mysteries of culture' . . . with
a . . . 'discrete elite character' which lifts them well
beyond the 'common'. When all or many of these
twelve are missing, the 'relationship of distinction' is lost and the fabric is no longer a desired
elitist product. Le Wita describes these elements
(which could just as easily be applied to the whole
field of fashionable dress as well as textiles) which
make up the complex of personal taste and behaviour, as a form of 'trivia' but trivia with 'a particular function, namely to create distinction'.[66] This
system is built upon a knowing collaboration between elite designers, producers and consumers,
who all play their role 'in the game'.[67]

One example seen through the 'eyes' of its period will serve as a conclusion: Seker's, an elitist British fashion textile company, produced a
'special' fabric in 1953: a limited production,
evening dress silk, jacquard-brocaded in royal
colours of white and gold, in scrolled motifs. It
was designed by the famous stage designer Oli-
ver Messel and was used for a ball dress, with
many yards of costly fabric in its full and slightly
trained skirt. This one-off dress was designed by
the avant garde young London couturier, John
Cavanagh and worn by Messel's sister Anne,

Countess of Rosse, to the Coronation ball of 1953. All of this has given this fabrics a lasting prestige, such that it was carefully kept by its original owner for nearly thirty years, and was given a place of public honour—on display in the Fashion Gallery at Brighton Museum. This fabric scores excellently on distinction-giving marks, as follows: 1- rarity; 3—use at elitist functions; 4—status of wearer; 7—aesthetic quality; 8—costly technique and probably on 9—high price (though this is currently not known). However, it is weaker on: 2—fashionability and 10—fashionable newness, because it was not a conventional, fashion-related textile design, though this is somewhat counterbalanced by the seasonal correctness of the design of the dress itself. There are also weakish scores at the most elite fashion status levels. Despite the internationally known reputations of both Sekers and Cavanagh, the absence of the names of a top Lyons fabricant or Paris couturier, mitigate against high scores for marks 5 and 6.

Thus analysis of the nature of both 'distinction' and its reverse, 'commonness' as they impact on the processes of designing, making, selling and consuming the fabrics of fashion, provides a useful research route because every fabric of fashion is 'imbued with the values and cultural schemata' of its specific social setting.[68]

NOTES

1. Bourdieu, P. *Distinction: A Social Critique of the Judgement of Taste* [1979], Routledge & Kegan Paul, London, 1984, p.231.
2. Ibid. p.229.
3. Le Wita, B. *French Bourgeois Culture*, Cambridge University Press, 1994, p.58. The complete quote reads: 'What a delight it is', in connection to debate about the democratization of fashion in the 1840's: 'to read the pages of Balzac's 'Autres études des femmes' in which the author describes with quite extraordinary meticulousness how it was still possible between 1839 and 1840, to tell a female aristocrat and a woman of the bourgeoisie apart, the key being to pay attention 'to the little details.'
4. Barnes, R. and Eicher, J.B. *Dress and Gender—Making and Meaning, Berg*, Oxford 1993, p.23. For further studies in this vein see: Cordwell, J.M. and Schwarz, R.A. *The Fabrics of Culture—The Anthropology of Clothing and Adornment*, Mouton, The Hague, 1979.
5. Bourdieu, p.229.
6. Rothstein, N. (ed.) *Barbara Johnson's Album of Fashions and Fabrics*, Thames & Hudson, London, 1987, p.29.
7. *Nouveautés- Eté, Grand Magazine de la Samaritaine, Rue de Rivoli, Paris*, 1908, mail order catalogue; author's collection.
8. see Irwin, J. and Brett, K. *The Origins of Chintz*, HMSO, London, 1970, for a detailed account of this development.
9. Tuchscherer, Jean-Michel, 'Les Debuts de l' Impression sur Etoffes à Mulhouse', *Bulletin Trimestriel de la Sociéte Industrielle de Mulhouse*, no.761, 4/1975, p.18.
10. Rhys, G. 'Designers' Denim Dependency', *Fashion Weekly*, 18 May 1995, p.8.
11. Mullany, A, 'The Fashion Significance of Rayon', *Handbook: Rayon and Synthetic Yarns*, Dept. of Industrial Art, Brooklyn Museum, New York, 1936–37, p.25.
12. Ibid. pp.26–27.
13. English *Vogue*, May–June, 1947, with Colcombet listed in the Groupement de la Haute Nouveauté, St. Etienne, p.63.
14. See the pleated design on plate 120 of Tsurumolo, S.(ed.) Issey Miyake Bodyworks, Shogakukan, Tokyo, 1983.
15. Bourdieu, p.250.
16. Miller, L.E. 'Jean Revel: Silk Designer, Fine Artist or Entrepreneur', *Journal of Design History*, vol.8(2), 1995, pp.85–86.
17. Irwin, J. *The Kashmir Shawl*, HMSO, London, 1973, p.25 quoting *The Weaver's Magazine*, 20 October 1818.
18. Irwin, J. 'The Kashmir Shawl', *Marg*, vol. VI(1), 1952, p.43.

19. Bourdieu, p.247.

20. Willis, G. and Midgeley, D. *Fashion Marketing*, Allen & Unwin, London, 1973, p.42, quoting Bigg, H. *The Evils of Fashion*, London, 1883.

21. 'Memoirs of the late James Thomson Esq. FRS of Clitheroe', *Journal of Design*, vol.111, 19 September 1850, p.71.

22. 'London Report', *The Draper's Record*, 15 October 1994, pp.20–21.

23. Andrews, W. *Master and Artisan in Victorian England: Documents of Social History*, Evelyn, Adams & Mackay, London, 1965; see also Chancellor, V.(ed.) *The Diary of William Andrews*, Augustus M. Kelley, New York, 1969.

24. Bury, H. *A Choice of Design, 1850–1980: Fabrics by Warner & Sons Limited* [catalogue, Warner & Sons Ltd], London, 1981, p.27.

25. Vanier, H. *La Mode et ses Métiers: Frivolités et luttes des classes, 1830–1870*, Armand Colin, Paris, 1960, p.163, quoting *Le Journal du Marechal Castellane*, 8 December 1853.

26. Journal of Design, March 1850, vol.111, p.47.

27. Taylor, L. *Mourning Dress: A Costume and Social History*, Allen & Unwin, London, 1983, Appendix 3 and p.301, quoting Cunnington, C.W. *English Women's Clothing in the Nineteenth Century*, Faber, London, p.436.

28. 'Memoirs . . .', p.71.

29. The author saw this in Warsaw's Centrum Store in the 1985–1990 period.

30. See Jacqué, B. 'Le Dessin Pour l'Impression sur Etoffe dans les Collections du Musée', *Bulletin Trimestriel de la Sociéte Industrielle de Mulhouse*, no.761, 4/1975, p.63.

31. *op cit*, note 18.

32. Taylor, L. 'Dufy, the Lyons Silk Industry and the Role of Artists', *Textile Society Newsletter*, no.2, Summer 1984, quoting Luc-Benoist in *Les Tissus, La Tapisserie, Les Tapis*, in the series 'L'Art Français Depuis Vingt Ans', F. Reider, Paris, 1926, p.93.

33. English *Vogue*, May 1995, p.117.

34. Miller, L.E., 'Designers in the Lyon Silk Industry, 1712–1787', unpublished PhD (CNAA) thesis, Brighton Polytechnic, 1988; see the biographical listing of all these names in Appendix 2, pp.1–168.

35. 'Memoirs . . .', p.68

36. Hogan, K. 'Courtaulds Rayon, Advertising Publicity 1920–50', unpublished BA dissertation, Brighton Polytechnic, 1985, Chapter 3, ref.12, quoting Hemming, D. 'British Fashions in British Fabrics', *Silk and Rayon World*, 1930, p.53. Reville produced a couture collection made in rayon and cotton mixes; one garment was ordered by Princess Helena Victoria.

37. 'Courtaulds Increases Design Element', *Fashion Weekly*, 18 May 1995, p.3.

38. Rhys, p.8.

39. Bourdieu, p.232.

40. see Gans, H. *Popular Culture and High Culture: An Analysis and Evaluation of Taste*, Basic Books, New York, 1974.

41. Bourdieu, p.243.

42. *Journal of Design*, vol.111, 19 September 1850, p.68.

43. Bourdieu, p.511.

44. *The Draper's Record*, (note 22), pp.20–21.

45. 'Counsel to Practical Designers for Woven Fabrics', *Journal of Design*, vol.111(16), June 1850, p.148.

46. *Les Folles Anées de la Soie*, Musée Historique des Tissus, Lyon, exhibition catalogue, September 1975; see Ducharne, F. *Souvenirs-en ce temps là*, p.34.

47. See illustrations in Lacroix, C. *Pieces of a Pattern: Lacroix by Lacrois*, Thames & Hudson, London, 1992.

48. Miller, 'Designers . . .', vol.1, p.83, Table 2.1 based on Godart, *L'Ouvrier en Soie* [1899], Geneva, 1976, p.390, which uses the 1751 'Memorial to de Gournay'.

49. *Au Printemps*, mail order catalogue, Paris, Hiver 1924–25, author's collection. The most expensive fabrics, at 39 francs a metre, were

an embroidered crepe marocain in wool and silk and a velvet chiffon.

50. Hume, M. 'Less is more . . . er, well more or less', *The Independent*, Section Two, London, 18 July 1995, p.12.

51. Irwin, *The Kashmir Shawl*, p.25.

52. Cross, W. 'Changes in the Style of Paisley Shawls', lecture given at the Museum, Paisley, in 1872. Library of the Royal National Museum of Scotland, Edinburgh, no.21054.

53. O'Neil, M. 'Fashion in Printed Textiles: 1810–50', *Bulletin Trimestriel de la Société Industrielle de Mulhouse*, no.761, 4/1875, pp.83–4.

54. The Musée Historique des Tissus in Lyon owns several of these.

55. In the collection of the Guildhall Art Gallery, London.

56. Miller, 'Jean Revel . . .', p.91.

57. Adburgham, A. *Shops and Shopping*, Allen & Unwin, London 1967, p.66, quoting Mayhew, H. *The Shops and Companies of London*, 1865.

58. Taylor, 'Dufy . . .', p.8, quoting Colette, G. *Le Voyage Egoiste: Soieries*, Paris, 1928.

59. Bourdieu, p.579.

60. Hogan, Chapter One, Table of Rayon Types.

61. *The Sunsilk Weaving Company Ltd.*, Hanksford Bridge Mills, Tyldesley, Lancashire, undated advertising booklet (c.1929): with thanks to my colleague, Dr. Suzette Worden, for giving me her copy of this.

62. Author's collection.

63. Hume, M. 'All in the Jeans', *The Independent on Sunday*, 23 July 1995, pp.48–9.

64. Taylor, L. *Mourning Dress, a Costume and Social History*, p.195. Peter Robinson's sold a lin of mourning cloth in 1887 called Borada Crape Cloth, described as economical.

65. *The Sunsilk Weaving Company*, mail order catalogue: Introduction.

66. Le Wita, p.141.

67. Ibid. p.226, p.229 and p.256.

68. Ibid. p.141.

44

THE SCARLET LETTER

Nathaniel Hawthorne

Editor's introduction: Nathaniel Hawthorne is one of America's celebrated nineteenth-century novelists. His novel *The Scarlet Letter* (1850) is a criticism of the punishing religious morals that governed parts of New England in the seventeenth Century. Hester Prynne, Hawthorne's main character, is forced to the margins of her community and required to create and wear an embroidered scarlet-colored letter *A* after giving birth to a daughter who is assumed to be the result of adultery. The letter is never explicitly defined as referring to adultery, and at times during the story the reference transfers to other possible—even positive—meanings. Hawthorne's tale is a brutal example of textile being used to quite literally mark out an individual's identity. But its meaning and purpose are far from simple. We learn, for example, that Hester stitches the most exquisite letter despite the punishment it is intended to be, and while she and her daughter are essentially banished to the very edges of the judgmental community, her skills as an embroiderer are in demand to stitch religious clothing worn by men with far more dubious morals than her own character.

When the young woman—the mother of this child—stood fully revealed before the crowd, it seemed to be her first impulse to clasp the infant closely to her bosom; not so much by an impulse of motherly affection, as that she might thereby conceal a certain token, which was wrought or fastened into her dress. In a moment, however, wisely judging that one token of her shame would but poorly serve to hide another, she took the baby on her arm, and, with a burning blush, and yet a haughty smile, and a glance that would not be abashed, looked around at her townspeople and neighbors. On the breast of her gown, in fine red cloth surrounded with an elaborate embroidery and fantastic flourishes of gold thread, appeared the letter "A." It was so artistically done, and with so much fertility and gorgeous luxuriance of fancy, that it had all the effect of a last and fitting decoration to the apparel which she wore; and which was of a splendor in accordance with the taste of the age, but greatly beyond what was allowed by the sumptuary regulations of the colony.

The young woman was tall, with a figure of perfect elegance on a large scale. She had dark and abundant hair, so glossy that it threw off the sunshine with a gleam, and a face which, besides being beautiful from regularity of feature and richness of complexion, had the impressiveness belonging to a marked brow and deep black

Source: Nathaniel Hawthorne, *The Scarlet Letter* (London: Penguin Books, 1850).

eyes. She was ladylike, too, after the manner of the feminine gentility of those days; characterized by a certain state and dignity, rather than by the delicate, evanescent, and indescribable grace, which is now recognized as its indication. And never had Hester Prynne appeared more ladylike, in the antique interpretation of the term, than as she issued from the prison. Those who had before known her and had expected to behold her dimmed and obscured by a disastrous cloud, were astonished, and even startled, to perceive how her beauty shone out and made a halo of the misfortune and ignominy in which she was enveloped. It may be true that, to a sensitive observer, there was something exquisitely painful in it. Her attire, which, indeed, she had wrought for the occasion, in prison, and had modelled much after her own fancy, seemed to express the attitude of her spirit, the desperate recklessness of her mood, by its wild and picturesque peculiarity. But the point which drew all eyes and, as it were, transfigured the wearer—so that both men and women, who had been familiarly acquainted with Hester Prynne, were now impressed as if they beheld her for the first time—was that *Scarlet Letter*, so fantastically embroidered and illuminated upon her bosom. It had the effect of a spell, taking her out of the ordinary relations with humanity and enclosing her in a sphere by herself.

"She hath good skill at her needle, that's certain," remarked one of her female spectators; "but did ever a woman, before this brazen hussy, contrive such a way of showing it! Why, gossips, what is it but to laugh in the faces of our godly magistrates, and make a pride out of what they, worthy gentlemen, meant for a punishment?"

"It were well," muttered the most iron-visaged of the old dames, "if we stripped Madam Hester's rich gown off her dainty shoulders; and as for the red letter, which she hath stitched so curiously, I'll bestow a rag of mine own rheumatic flannel, to make a fitter one!"

"O, peace, neighbors, peace!" whispered their youngest companion; "do not let her hear you! Not a stitch in that embroidered letter, but she has felt it in her heart."

The grim beadle now made a gesture with his staff.

"Make way, good people, make way, in the King's name!" cried he. "Open a passage; and, I promise ye, Mistress Prynne shall be set where man, woman and child may have a fair sight of her brave apparel, from this time till an hour past meridian. A blessing on the righteous Colony of the Massachusetts, where iniquity is dragged out into the sunshine! Come along, Madam Hester, and show your scarlet letter in the market place!" . . .

Lonely as was Hester's situation, and without a friend on earth who dared to show himself, she, however, incurred even no risk of want. She possessed an art that sufficed, even in a land that afforded comparatively little scope for its exercise, to supply food for her thriving infant and herself. It was the art—then, as now, almost the only one within a woman's grasp—of needlework. She bore on her breast, in the curiously embroidered letter, a specimen of her delicate and imaginative skill of which the dames of a court might gladly have availed themselves, to add the richer and more spiritual adornment of human ingenuity to their fabrics of silk and gold. Here, indeed, in the sable simplicity that generally characterized the Puritanic modes of dress, there might be an infrequent call for the finer productions of her handiwork. Yet the taste of the age, demanding whatever was elaborate in compositions of this kind, did not fail to extend its influence over our stern progenitors, who had cast behind them so many fashions which it might seem harder to dispense with. Public ceremonies, such as ordinations, the installation of magistrates, and all that could give majesty to the forms in which a new government manifested itself to the people, were, as a matter of policy, marked by a stately and well-conducted ceremonial and a sombre, but yet a studied magnificence. Deep ruffs, painfully wrought bands and gorgeously embroidered gloves were all deemed necessary to the official state of men assuming the reins of power; and were readily allowed to individuals dignified by rank or wealth, even while sumptuary laws forbade these and similar extravagances to the plebeian order. In the array of funerals, too—whether for the apparel of the dead body, or to typify, by manifold emblematic devices of sable cloth and snowy lawn, the sorrow of the survivors—there was a frequent and characteristic demand for such labor as Hester Prynne could supply. Baby linen—for babies then wore robes of state—afforded still another possibility of toil and emolument.

By degrees, nor very slowly, her handiwork became what would now be termed the fashion. Whether from commiseration for a woman of so miserable a destiny; or from the morbid curiosity that gives a fictitious value even to common or worthless things; or by whatever other intangible circumstance was then, as now, sufficient to bestow on some persons what others might seek in vain; or because Hester really filled a gap which must otherwise have remained vacant; it is certain that she had ready and fairly requited employment for as many hours as she saw fit to occupy with her needle. Vanity, it may be, chose to mortify itself by putting on, for ceremonials of pomp and state, the garments that had been wrought by her sinful hands. Her needlework was seen on the ruff of the Governor; military men wore it on their scarfs, and the minister on his band; it decked the baby's little cap; it was shut up, to be mildewed and moulder away, in the coffins of the dead. But it is not recorded that, in a single instance, her skill was called in aid to embroider the white veil which was to cover the pure blushes of a bride. The exception indicated the ever relentless vigor with which society frowned upon her sin.

Hester sought not to acquire anything beyond a subsistence, of the plainest and most ascetic description, for herself, and a simple abundance for her child. Her own dress was of the coarsest materials and the most sombre hue; with only that one ornament—the scarlet letter—which it was her doom to wear. The child's attire, on the other hand, was distinguished by a fanciful, or, we might rather say, a fantastic ingenuity, which served, indeed, to heighten the airy charm that early began to develop itself in the little girl, but which appeared to have also a deeper meaning. We may speak further of it hereafter. Except for that small expenditure in the decoration of her infant, Hester bestowed all her superfluous means in charity, on wretches less miserable than herself, and who not unfrequently insulted the hand that fed them. Much of the time which she might readily have applied to the better efforts of her art, she employed in making coarse garments for the poor. It is probable that there was an idea of penance in this mode of occupation, and that she offered up a real sacrifice of enjoyment in devoting so many hours to such rude handiwork. She had in her nature a rich, voluptuous, Oriental characteristic—a taste for the gorgeously beautiful, which, save in the exquisite productions of her needle, found nothing else in all the possibilities of her life to exercise itself upon. Women derive a pleasure, incomprehensible to the other sex, from the delicate toil of the needle. To Hester Prynne it might have been a mode of expressing, and therefore soothing, the passion of her life. Like all other joys, she rejected it as a sin. This morbid meddling of conscience with an immaterial matter betokened, it is to be feared, no genuine and steadfast penitence, but something doubtful, something that might be deeply wrong, beneath.

In this manner, Hester Prynne came to have a part to perform in the world. With her native energy of character and rare capacity, it could not entirely cast her off, although it had set a mark upon her more intolerable to a woman's heart than that which branded the brow of Cain. In all her intercourse with society, however, there was nothing that made her feel as if she belonged to it. Every gesture, every word, and even the silence of those with whom she came in contact, implied, and often expressed, that she was banished, and as much alone as if she inhabited another sphere, or communicated with the common nature by other organs and senses than the rest of humankind. She stood apart from moral interests, yet close beside them, like a ghost that revisits the familiar fireside and can no longer make itself seen or felt, no more smile with the household joy, nor mourn with the kindred sorrow; or, should it succeed in manifesting its forbidden sympathy, awakening only terror and horrible repugnance. These emotions, in fact, and its bitterest scorn besides, seemed to be the sole portion that she retained in the universal heart. It was not an age of delicacy; and her position, although she understood it well and was in little danger of forgetting it, was often brought before her vivid self-perception, like a new anguish, by the rudest touch upon the tenderest spot. The poor, as we have already said, whom she sought out to be the objects of her bounty, often reviled the hand that was stretched forth to succor them. Dames of elevated rank, likewise, whose doors she entered in the way of her occupation, were accustomed to distil drops of bitterness into her heart, sometimes through that alchemy of quiet malice, by which women can concoct a subtile poison from ordinary trifles, and sometimes, also, by a coarser expression, that fell upon the sufferer's defenceless breast like a rough blow upon air ulcerated wound. Hester had schooled herself long and well; she never responded to these attacks, save by a flush of crimson that rose irrepressibly over the pale cheek, and again subsided into the depths of her bosom. She was patient—a martyr, indeed—but she forebore to pray for her enemies, lest, in spite of her forgiving aspirations, the words of the blessing should stubbornly twist themselves into a curse.

Continually, and in a thousand other ways, did she feel the innumerable throbs of anguish that had been so cunningly contrived for her by the undying, the everactive sentence of the Puritan tribunal. Clergymen paused in the street to address words of exhortation that brought a crowd, with its mingled grin and frown, around the poor, sinful woman. If she entered a church, trusting to share the Sabbath smile of the Universal Father, it was often her mishap to find herself the text of the discourse. She grew to have a dread of children; for they had imbibed from their parents a vague idea of something horrible in this dreary woman, gliding silently through the town, with never any companion but one only child. Therefore, first allowing her to pass, they pursued her at a distance with shrill cries, and the utterance of a word that had no distinct purport to their own minds, but was none the less terrible to her, as proceeding from lips that babbled it unconsciously. It seemed to argue so wide a diffusion of her shame that all nature knew of it; it could have caused her no deeper pang had the leaves of the trees whispered the dark story among themselves, had the summer breeze murmured about it—had the wintry blast shrieked it aloud! Another peculiar torture was felt in the gaze of a new eye. When strangers looked curiously at the scarlet letter—and none ever failed to do so—they branded it afresh into Hester's soul; so that oftentimes, she could scarcely refrain, yet always did refrain, from covering the symbol with her hand. But then, again, an accustomed eye had likewise its own anguish to inflict. Its cool stare of familiarity was intolerable. From first to last, in short, Hester Prynne had always this dreadful agony in feeling a human eye upon the token; the spot never grew callous; it seemed, on the contrary, to grow more sensitive with daily torture.

But sometimes, once in many days, or perchance in many months, she felt an eye—a human eye—upon the ignominious brand, that seemed to give a momentary relief, as if half of her agony were shared. The next instant, back it all rushed again, with still a deeper throb of pain; for, in that brief interval, she had sinned anew. Had Hester sinned alone?

Her imagination was somehow affected, and, had she been of a softer moral and intellectual fibre, would have been still more so, by the strange and solitary anguish of her life. Walking to and fro with those lonely footsteps in the little world with which she was outwardly connected, it now and then appeared to Hester—if altogether fancy, it was nevertheless too potent to be resisted—she felt or fancied, then, that the scarlet letter had endowed her with a new sense. She shuddered to believe, yet could not help believing, that it gave her a sympathetic knowledge of the hidden sin in other hearts. She was terror-stricken by the revelations that were thus made. What were they? Could they be other than the insidious whispers of the bad angel, who would fain have persuaded the struggling woman, as yet only half his victim, that the outward guise of purity was but a lie, and that, if truth were everywhere to be shown, a scarlet letter would blaze forth on many a bosom besides Hester Prynne's? Or, must she receive those intimations—so obscure, yet so distinct—as truth? In all her miserable experience, there was nothing else so awful and so loathsome as this sense. It perplexed as well as shocked her by the irreverent inopportuneness of the occasions that brought it into vivid action. Sometimes the red infamy upon her breast would give a sympathetic throb, as she passed near a venerable minister or magistrate, the model of piety and justice, to whom that age of antique reverence looked up as to a mortal man in fellowship with angels. "What evil thing is at hand?" would Hester say to herself. Lifting her reluctant eyes, there would be nothing human within the scope of view, save the form of this earthly saint! Again, a mystic sisterhood would contumaciously assert itself as she met the sanctified frown of some matron, who, according to the rumor of all tongues, had kept cold snow within her bosom throughout life. That unsunned snow in the matron's bosom, and the burning shame on Hester Prynne's—what had the two in common? Or, once more, the electric thrill would give her warning—"Behold, Hester, here is a companion!"—and, looking up, she would detect the eyes of a young maiden glancing at the scarlet letter, shyly and aside, and quickly averted, with a faint, chill crimson in her cheeks as if her purity were somewhat sullied by that momentary glance. O Fiend, whose talisman was that fatal symbol, wouldst thou leave nothing, whether in youth or age, for this poor sinner to revere?—such loss of faith is ever one of the saddest results of sin. Be it accepted as a proof that all was not corrupt in this poor victim of her own frailty, and man's hard law, that Hester Prynne yet struggled to believe that no fellow-mortal was guilty like herself.

The vulgar, who, in those dreary old times, were always contributing a grotesque horror to what interested their imaginations, had a story about the scarlet letter which we might readily work up into a terrific legend. They averred that the symbol was not mere scarlet cloth tinged in an earthly dyepot, but was redhot with infernal fire, and could be seen glowing all alight whenever Hester Prynne walked abroad in the nighttime. And we must needs say it seared Hester's bosom so deeply, that perhaps there was more truth in the rumor than our modern incredulity may be inclined to admit. . . .

It was perceived, too, that while Hester never put forward even the humblest title to share in the world's privileges—further than to breathe the common air, and earn daily bread for little Pearl and herself by the faithful labor of her hands—she was quick to acknowledge her sisterhood with the race of man, whenever benefits were to be conferred. None so ready as she to give of her little substance to every demand of poverty; even though the bitter-hearted pauper threw back a gibe in requital of the food brought regularly to his door, or the garments wrought for him by the fingers that could have embroidered a monarch's robe. None so self-devoted as Hester, when pestilence stalked through the town. In all seasons of calamity, indeed, whether general or of individuals, the outcast of society at once found her place. She came, not as a guest, but as a rightful inmate, into the household that was darkened by trouble, as if its gloomy twilight were a medium in which she was entitled to hold intercourse with her fellow-creatures. There glimmered the embroidered letter, with comfort in its unearthly ray. Elsewhere the token of sin, it was the taper of the sick-chamber. It had even thrown its gleam, in the sufferer's hard extremity, across the verge of time. It had shown him where to set his foot, while the light of earth was fast becoming dim, and ere the light of futurity could reach him. In such emergencies, Hester's nature showed itself warm and rich; a wellspring of human tenderness, unfailing to every real demand, and inexhaustible by the largest. Her breast, with its badge of shame, was but the softer pillow for the head that needed one. She was self-ordained a Sister of Mercy; or, we may rather say, the world's heavy hand had so ordained her, when neither the world nor she looked forward to this result. The letter was the symbol of her calling. Such helpfulness was found in her—so much power to do and power to sympathize—that many people refused to interpret the scarlet "A" by its original signification. They said that it meant "Able"; so strong was Hester Prynne, with a woman's strength.

45

EVERYDAY USE

Alice Walker

Editor's introduction: The author and poet Alice Walker won the Pulitzer Prize for her acclaimed novel *The Color Purple* in 1983. Walker wrote the short story "Everyday Use" in her thirties—first published in 1967 as one of thirteen stories about women in a collection of her writing titled *In Love and Trouble*. In it, Walker creates the characters Maggie and Dee—two sisters with vastly different regard for the material culture of their childhood. Narrated by the sisters' mother, the story pokes gentle fun at Dee's "back to Africa" values and interest in reappropriating craft objects—made out of necessity—as souvenirs. The family's hand-stitched quilts are the point of greatest tension, cherished by both sisters but for extremely different reasons. Dee despairs of her sister (who ironically is the one who has learned how to quilt), "She'd probably be backward enough to put them to everyday use." Walker's story highlights two conflicting value systems that the textile is often torn between.

I will wait for her in the yard that Maggie and I made so clean and wavy yesterday afternoon. A yard like this is more comfortable than most people know. It is not just a yard. It is like an extended living room. When the hard clay is swept clean as a floor and the fine sand around the edges lined with tiny, irregular grooves, anyone can come and sit and look up into the elm tree and wait for the breezes that never come inside the house.

Maggie will be nervous until after her sister goes: she will stand hopelessly in corners, homely and ashamed of the burn scars down her arms and legs, eying her sister with a mixture of envy and awe. She thinks her sister has held life always in the palm of one hand, that "no" is a word the world never learned to say to her.

You've no doubt seen those TV shows where the child who has "made it" is confronted, as a surprise, by her own mother and father, tottering in weakly from backstage. (A pleasant surprise, of course: What would they do if parent and child came on the show only to curse out and insult each other?) On TV mother and child embrace and smile into each other's faces. Sometimes the mother and father weep, the child wraps them in her arms and leans across the table to tell how she would not have made it without their help. I have seen these programs.

Sometimes I dream a dream in which Dee and I are suddenly brought together on a TV program of this sort. Out of a dark and soft-seated limousine I am ushered into a bright room filled with many people. There I meet a smiling, gray, sporty man like Johnny Carson who shakes my hand and tells me what a fine girl I have. Then we are on the stage and Dee is embracing me with tears in her eyes. She pins on my dress a large orchid, even though she has told me once that she thinks orchids are tacky flowers.

In real life I am a large, big-boned woman with rough, man-working hands. In the winter I wear flannel nightgowns to bed and overalls during the day. I can kill and clean a hog as mercilessly as a man. My fat keeps me hot in zero weather. I can work outside all day, breaking ice to get water for washing; I can eat pork liver cooked over the open fire minutes after it comes steaming from the hog. One winter I knocked a bull calf straight in the brain between the eyes with a sledge hammer and had the meat hung up to chill before nightfall. But of course all this does not show on television. I am the way my daughter would want me to be: a hundred pounds lighter, my skin like an uncooked barley pancake. My hair glistens in the hot bright lights. Johnny Carson has much to do to keep up with my quick and witty tongue.

But that is a mistake. I know even before I wake up. Who ever knew a Johnson with a quick tongue? Who can even imagine me looking a strange white man in the eye? It seems to me I have talked to them always with one foot raised in flight, with my head turned in whichever way is farthest from them. Dee, though. She would always look anyone in the eye. Hesitation was no part of her nature.

"How do I look, Mama?" Maggie says, showing just enough of her thin body enveloped in pink skirt and red blouse for me to know she's there, almost hidden by the door.

"Come out into the yard," I say.

Have you ever seen a lame animal, perhaps a dog run over by some careless person rich enough to own a car, sidle up to someone who is ignorant enough to be kind to him? That is the way my Maggie walks. She has been like this, chin on chest, eyes on ground, feet in shuffle, ever since the fire that burned the other house to the ground.

Dee is lighter than Maggie, with nicer hair and a fuller figure. She's a woman now, though sometimes I forget. How long ago was it that the other house burned? Ten, twelve years? Sometimes I can still hear the flames and feel Maggie's arms sticking to me, her hair smoking and her dress falling off her in little black papery flakes. Her eyes seemed stretched open, blazed open by the flames reflected in them. And Dee. I see her standing off under the sweet gum tree she used to dig gum out of; a look of concentration on her face as she watched the last dingy gray board of the house fall in toward the red-hot brick chimney. Why don't you do a dance around the ashes? I'd wanted to ask her. She had hated the house that much.

I used to think she hated Maggie, too. But that was before we raised the money, the church and me, to send her to Augusta to school. She used to read to us without pity; forcing words, lies, other folks' habits, whole lives upon us two, sitting trapped and ignorant underneath her voice. She washed us in a river of make-believe, burned us with a lot of knowledge we didn't necessarily need to know. Pressed us to her with the serious way she read, to shove us away at just the moment, like dimwits, we seemed about to understand.

Dee wanted nice things. A yellow organdy dress to wear to her graduation from high school; black pumps to match a green suit she'd made from an old suit somebody gave me. She was determined to stare down any disaster in her efforts. Her eyelids would not flicker for minutes at a time. Often I fought off the temptation to shake her. At sixteen she had a style of her own: and knew what style was.

I never had an education myself. After second grade the school was closed down. Don't ask my why: in 1927 colored asked fewer questions than they do now. Sometimes Maggie reads to me. She stumbles along good-naturedly but can't see well. She knows she is not bright. Like good looks and money, quickness passed her by. She will marry John Thomas (who has mossy teeth in an earnest face) and then I'll be free to sit here and I guess just sing church songs to myself. Although I never was a good singer. Never could carry a tune. I was always better at a man's job. I used to love to milk till I was hooked in the side in '49. Cows are soothing and slow and don't bother you, unless you try to milk them the wrong way.

I have deliberately turned my back on the house. It is three rooms, just like the one that burned, except the roof is tin; they don't make shingle roofs any more. There are no real windows, just some holes cut in the sides, like the portholes in a ship, but not round and not square, with rawhide holding the shutters up on the outside. This house is in a pasture, too, like the other one. No doubt when Dee sees it she will want to tear it down. She wrote me once that no matter where we "choose" to live, she will manage to come see us. But she will never bring her friends. Maggie and I thought about this and Maggie asked me, "Mama, when did Dee ever *have* any friends?"

She had a few. Furtive boys in pink shirts hanging about on washday after school. Nervous girls who never laughed. Impressed with her they worshiped the well-turned phrase, the cute shape, the scalding humor that erupted like bubbles in lye. She read to them.

When she was courting Jimmy T she didn't have much time to pay to us, but turned all her faultfinding power on him. He *flew* to marry a cheap city girl from a family of ignorant flashy people. She hardly had time to recompose herself.

When she comes I will meet—but there they are!

Maggie attempts to make a dash for the house, in her shuffling way, but I stay her with my hand. "Come back here," I say. And she stops and tries to dig a well in the sand with her toe.

It is hard to see them clearly through the strong sun. But even the first glimpse of leg out of the car tells me it is Dee. Her feet were always neat-looking, as if God himself had shaped them with a certain style. From the other side of the car comes a short, stocky man. Hair is all over his head a foot long and hanging from his chin like a kinky mule tail. I hear Maggie suck in her breath. "Uhnnnh," is what it sounds like. Like when you see the wriggling end of a snake just in front of your foot on the road. "Uhnnnh."

Dee next. A dress down to the ground, in this hot weather. A dress so loud it hurts my eyes. There are yellows and oranges enough to throw back the light of the sun. I feel my whole face warming from the heat waves it throws out. Earrings gold, too, and hanging down to her shoulders. Bracelets dangling and making noises when she moves her arm up to shake the folds of the dress out of her armpits. The dress is loose and flows, and as she walks closer, I like it. I hear Maggie go "Uhnnnh" again. It is her sister's hair. It stands straight up like the wool on a sheep. It is black as night and around the edges are two long pigtails that rope about like small lizards disappearing behind her ears.

"Wa-su-zo-Tean-o!" she says, coming on in that gliding way the dress makes her move. The short stocky fellow with the hair to his navel is all grinning and he follows up with "Asalamalakim, my mother and sister!" He moves to hug Maggie but she falls back, right up against the back of my chair. I feel her trembling there and when I look up I see the perspiration falling off her chin.

"Don't get up," says Dee. Since I am stout it takes something of a push. You can see me trying to move a second or two before I make it. She turns, showing white heels through her sandals, and goes back to the car. Out she peeks next with a Polaroid. She stoops down quickly and lines up picture after picture of me sitting there in front of the house with Maggie cowering behind me. She never takes a shot without making sure the house is included. When a cow comes nibbling around the edge of the yard she snaps it and me and Maggie *and* the house. Then she puts the Polaroid in the back seat of the car, and comes up and kisses me on the forehead.

Meanwhile Asalamalakim is going through motions with Maggie's hand. Maggie's hand is as limp as a fish, and probably as cold, despite the sweat, and she keeps trying to pull it back. It looks like Asalamalakim wants to shake hands but wants to do it fancy. Or maybe he don't know how people shake hands. Anyhow, he soon gives up on Maggie.

"Well," I say. "Dee."

"No, Mama," she says. "Not 'Dee,' Wangero Leewanika Kemanjo!"

"What happened to 'Dee'?" I wanted to know.

"She's dead," Wangero said. "I couldn't bear it any longer, being named after the people who oppress me."

"You know as well as me you was named after your aunt Dicie," I said. Dicie is my sister. She named Dee. We called her "Big Dee" after Dee was born.

"But who was *she* named after?" asked Wangero. "I guess after Grandma Dee," I said.

"And who was she named after?" asked Wangero. "Her mother," I said, and saw Wangero was getting tired. "That's about as far back as I can trace it," I said. Though, in fact, I probably could have carried it back beyond the Civil War through the branches.

"Well," said Asalamalakim, "there you are."

"Uhnnnh," I heard Maggie say.

"There I was not," I said, "before 'Dicie' cropped up in our family, so why should I try to trace it that far back?"

He just stood there grinning, looking down on me like somebody inspecting a Model A car. Every once in a while he and Wangero sent eye signals over my head.

"How do you pronounce this name?" I asked.

"You don't have to call me by it if you don't want to," said Wangero.

"Why shouldn't I?" I asked. "If that's what you want us to call you, we'll call you."

"I know it might sound awkward at first," said Wangero.

"I'll get used to it," I said. "Ream it out again."

Well, soon we got the name out of the way. Asalamalakim had a name twice as long and three times as hard. After I tripped over it two or three times he told me to just call him Hakim-a-barber. I wanted to ask him was he a barber, but I didn't really think he was, so I didn't ask.

"You must belong to those beef-cattle peoples down the road," I said. They said "Asalamalakim" when they met you, too, but they didn't shake hands. Always too busy: feeding the cattle, fixing the fences, putting up salt-lick shelters, throwing down hay. When the white folks poisoned some of the herd the men stayed up all night with rifles in their hands. I walked a mile and a half just to see the sight.

Hakim-a-barber said, "I accept some of their doctrines, but farming and raising cattle is not my style." (They didn't tell me, and I didn't ask, whether Wangero (Dee) had really gone and married him.)

We sat down to eat and right away he said he didn't eat collards and pork was unclean. Wangero, though, went on through the chitlins and corn bread, the greens and everything else. She talked a blue streak over the sweet potatoes. Everything delighted her. Even the fact that we still used the benches her daddy made for the table when we couldn't afford to buy chairs.

"Oh, Mama!" she cried. Then turned to Hakim-a-barber. "I never knew how lovely these benches are. You can feel the rump prints," she said, running her hands underneath her and along the bench. Then she gave a sigh and her hand closed over Grandma Dee's butter dish. "That's it!" she said. "I knew there was something I wanted to ask you if I could have." She jumped up from the table and went over in the corner where the churn stood, the milk in it clabber by now. She looked at the churn and looked at it.

"This churn top is what I need," she said. "Didn't Uncle Buddy whittle it out of a tree you all used to have?"

"Yes," I said.

"Uh huh," she said happily. "And I want the dasher, too."

"Uncle Buddy whittle that, too?" asked the barber.

Dee (Wangero) looked up at me.

"Aunt Dee's first husband whittled the dash," said Maggie so low you almost couldn't hear her. "His name was Henry, but they called him Stash."

"Maggie's brain is like an elephant's," Wangero said, laughing. "I can use the churn top as a centerpiece for the alcove table," she said, sliding a plate over the churn, "and I'll think of something artistic to do with the dasher."

When she finished wrapping the dasher the handle stuck out. I took it for a moment in my hands. You didn't even have to look close to see where hands pushing the dasher up and down to make butter had left a kind of sink in the wood. In fact, there were a lot of small sinks; you could see where thumbs and fingers had sunk into the wood. It was beautiful light yellow wood, from a tree that grew in the yard where Big Dee and Stash had lived.

After dinner Dee (Wangero) went to the trunk at the foot of my bed and started rifling through it. Maggie hung back in the kitchen over the dishpan. Out came Wangero with two quilts. They had been pieced by Grandma Dee and then Big Dee and me had hung them on the quilt frames on the front porch and quilted them. One was in the Lone Star pattern. The other was Walk Around the Mountain. In both of them were scraps of dresses Grandma Dee had worn fifty and more years ago. Bits and pieces of Grandpa Jarrell's Paisley shirts. And one teeny faded blue piece, about the size of a penny matchbox, that was from Great Grandpa Ezra's uniform that he wore in the Civil War.

"Mama," Wangero said sweet as a bird. "Can I have these old quilts?"

I heard something fall in the kitchen, and a minute later the kitchen door slammed.

"Why don't you take one or two of the others?" I asked. "These old things was just done by me and Big Dee from some tops your grandma pieced before she died."

"No," said Wangero. "I don't want those. They are stitched around the borders by machine."

"That'll make them last better," I said.

"That's not the point," said Wangero. "These are all pieces of dresses Grandma used to wear. She did all this stitching by hand. Imagine!" She held the quilts securely in her arms, stroking them.

"Some of the pieces, like those lavender ones, come from old clothes her mother handed down to her," I said, moving up to touch the quilts. Dee (Wangero) moved back just enough so that I couldn't reach the quilts They already belonged to her.

"Imagine!" she breathed again, clutching them closely to her bosom.

"The truth is," I said, "I promised to give them quilts to Maggie, for when she marries John Thomas." She gasped like a bee had stung her.

"Maggie can't appreciate these quilts!" she said. "She'd probably be backward enough to put them to everyday use."

"I reckon she would," I said. "God knows I been saving 'em for long enough with nobody using 'em. I hope she will!" I didn't want to bring up how I had offered Dee (Wangero) a quilt when she went away to college. Then she had told me they were old-fashioned, out of style.

"But they're *priceless!*" she was saying now, furiously; for she has a temper. "Maggie would put them on the bed and in five years they'd be in rags. Less than that!"

"She can always make some more," I said. "Maggie knows how to quilt."

Dee (Wangero) looked at me with hatred. "You just will not understand. The point is these quilts, *these* quilts!"

"Well," I said, stumped. "What would *you* do with them?"

"Hang them," she said. As if that was the only thing you *could* do with quilts.

Maggie by now was standing in the door. I could almost hear the sound her feet made as they scraped over each other.

"She can have them, Mama," she said, like somebody used to never winning anything, or having anything reserved for her. "I can 'member Grandma Dee without the quilts."

I looked at her hard. She had filled her bottom lip with checkerberry snuff and it gave her face a kind of dopey, hangdog look. It was Grandma Dee and Big Dee who taught her how to quilt herself. She stood there with her scarred hands hidden in the folds of her skirt. She looked at her sister with something like fear but she wasn't mad at her. This was Maggie's portion. This was the way she knew God to work.

When I looked at her like that something hit me in the top of my head and ran down to the soles of my feet. Just like when I'm in church and the spirit of God touches me and I get happy and shout.

I did something I never had done before: hugged Maggie to me, then dragged her on into the room, snatched the quilts out of Miss Wangero's hands and dumped them into Maggie's lap. Maggie just sat there on my bed with her mouth open.

"Take one or two of the others," I said to Dee.

But she turned without a word and went out to Hakim-a-barber.

"You just don't understand," she said, as Maggie and I came out to the car.

"What don't I understand?" I wanted to know.

"Your heritage," she said. And then she turned to Maggie, kissed her, and said, "You ought to try to make something of yourself, too, Maggie. It's really a new day for us. But from the way you and Mama still live you'd never know it."

She put on some sunglasses that hid everything above the tip of her nose and her chin.

Maggie smiled; maybe at the sunglasses. But a real smile, not scared. After we watched the car dust settle I asked Maggie to bring me a dip of snuff. And then the two of us sat there just enjoying, until it was time to go in the house and go to bed.

FURTHER READING: USE

Sarah E. Braddock and Marie O'Mahony, *Techno Textiles: Revolutionary Fabrics for Fashion and Design* (London: Thames and Hudson, 1998).

Sarah E. Braddock and Marie O'Mahony, *Techno Textiles 2* (London: Thames and Hudson, 2005).

Andrew Dent and George M. Beylerian, *Ultra Materials: How Materials Innovation Is Changing the World* (London: Thames and Hudson: 1997).

Trevor Keeble, "Fabricating the Domestic Surface: A Very Brief History of an Old Problem," in *Lost Narratives: The Work of Catherine Bertola* ed. Jon Bewley (Sunderland, England: Art Editions North, 2005) pp. 84–97.

Jamaica Kincaid, "Girl," in *At the Bottom of the River* (London: Pan Books, 1984) pp. 3–5.

Faythe Levine and Cortney Heimerl, *Handmade Nation: Rise of DIY, Art, Craft, and Design* (New York: Princeton Architectural Press, 2008).

Rohinton Mistry, *A Fine Balance* (London: Faber and Faber, 1995).

Michel Pastoureau. *The Devil's Cloth: A History of Stripes* trans. Jody Gladding (London: Washing Square Press and Columbia University Press, 2001).

Sue Rowley (ed.), *Reinventing Textiles: Tradition and Innovation*, vol. 1 (Winchester: Telos Art Publishing, 1999).

John Styles, *Threads of Feeling: The London Foundling Hospital's Textile Tokens 1740–1770* (London: Paul Holberton, 2010).

INDEX